REVOLUTIONARY AND DISSIDENT MOVEMENTS

KEESING'S PUBLICATIONS

Other Keesing's Reference Publications (KRP) titles (all published by Longman Group UK Limited) include the following:—

The Radical Right: A World Directory, compiled by Ciarán Ó Maoláin (1987)

Border and Territorial Disputes (2nd edition), edited by Alan J. Day (1987)

Trade Unions of the World, edited and compiled by F. John Harper (1987)

The World Financial System, compiled and written by Robert Fraser (1987)

Communist and Marxist Parties of the World, compiled by Charles Hobday (1986)

OPEC, Its Member States and the World Energy Market, compiled by John Evans (1986)

Treaties and Alliances of the World (4th edition), compiled by Henry W. Degenhardt (1986)

Peace Movements of the World: An International Directory, edited by Alan J. Day (1986)

State Economic Agencies of the World, edited by Alan J. Day (1985)

Maritime Affairs: A World Handbook, compiled by Henry W. Degenhardt (1985)

Latin American Political Movements, compiled by Ciarán Ó Maoláin (1985)

Political Parties of the World (2nd edition), edited by Alan J. Day & Henry W. Degenhardt (1984)

The following titles are currently available in the Keesing's International Studies series (all published by Longman Group UK Limited):—

Conflict in Central America, by Helen Schooley (1987)

From the Six to the Twelve, by Frances Nicholson and Roger East (1987)

China and the Soviet Union 1949–84, compiled by Peter Jones and Siân Kevill (1985)

Keesing's Record of World Events (formerly *Keesing's Contemporary Archives*), the monthly worldwide news reference service with an unrivalled reputation for accuracy and impartiality, has appeared continuously since 1931. Published by Longman Group UK Limited on annual subscription; back volumes are also available.

REVOLUTIONARY AND DISSIDENT MOVEMENTS

An International Guide

A KEESING'S REFERENCE PUBLICATION

Edited by
HENRY W. DEGENHARDT

REVOLUTIONARY AND DISSIDENT MOVEMENTS
An International Guide

First published as Political Dissent 1983
2nd Edition (revised and updated) 1988

Published by Longman Group UK Limited, Longman House, Burnt Mill, Harlow, Essex CM20 2JE, United Kingdom

Distributed exclusively in the United States and Canada by Gale Research Company, Book Tower, Detroit, Michigan, 48226, United States of America

ISBN 0-582-00986-3 (Longman)
ISBN 0-8103-2056-8 (Gale)

British Library Cataloguing in Publication Data
Revolutionary and dissident movements: An
International Guide.——2nd ed.——(A Keesing's reference publication).
1. political parties
I. Degenhardt, Henry W. II. Degenhardt, Henry W. Political dissent III. Series
320 JC328.3

ISBN 0-582-00986-3

Library of Congress Cataloguing-in-Publication Data
Degenhardt, Henry W.
Revolutionary and dissident movements.
(A Keesing's reference publication)
1. Government, Resistance to——Societies, etc.——Handbooks, manuals, etc. I. Title. II. Series.
JC328.3.D433 1987 322.4'2'06 87–29718

Typesetting by Tradeset, Welwyn, Herts.
Printed in the United Kingdom by The Eastern Press, London and Reading

CONTENTS

Introduction ... ix

Afghanistan ... 1
Albania ... 4
Algeria ... 6
Angola ... 8
Antigua and Barbuda ... 12
Argentina ... 13
Australia ... 17
Austria ... 18
The Bahamas ... 19
Bahrain ... 19
Bangladesh ... 20
Barbados ... 21
Belgium ... 22
Belize ... 23
Benin ... 24
Bhutan ... 25
Bolivia ... 25
Bophuthatswana ... 26
Botswana ... 26
Brazil ... 27
Brunei ... 27
Bulgaria ... 28
Burkina Faso ... 29
Burma ... 30
Burundi ... 37
Cameroon ... 37
Canada ... 39
Cape Verde ... 40
Central African Republic ... 41
Chad ... 44
Chile ... 45
China ... 55
Ciskei ... 58
Colombia ... 58
Comoros ... 64
Congo ... 65
Costa Rica ... 66
Côte d'Ivoire ... 66
Cuba ... 67
Cyprus ... 70
Czechoslovakia ... 70
Denmark ... 79
Djibouti ... 80
Dominica ... 80
Dominican Republic ... 81
Ecuador ... 82
Egypt ... 84
El Salvador ... 88
Equatorial Guinea ... 97
Ethiopia ... 99
Fiji ... 106
Finland ... 106
France ... 107
Gabon ... 121
The Gambia ... 122
German Democratic Republic ... 123
Federal Republic of Germany ... 124
Ghana ... 134
Greece ... 136
Grenada ... 137
Guatemala ... 138
Guinea ... 143
Guinea-Bissau ... 143
Guyana ... 144
Haiti ... 145
Honduras ... 146
Hungary ... 149
Iceland ... 151
India ... 151
Indonesia ... 160
Iran ... 163
Iraq ... 171
Ireland ... 175
Israel ... 176
Italy ... 178
Jamaica ... 187
Japan ... 188
Jordan ... 191
Kampuchea ... 193
Kenya ... 200
Kiribati ... 202
Democratic People's Republic of Korea (North Korea) ... 203
Republic of Korea (South Korea) ... 203
Kuwait ... 206
Laos ... 207
Lebanon ... 209
Lesotho ... 222
Liberia ... 223
Libya ... 225
Luxembourg ... 227
Madagascar ... 227
Malawi ... 228
Malaysia ... 230
Maldives ... 232
Mali ... 232
Malta ... 233
Mauritania ... 233
Mauritius ... 235
Mexico ... 235
Mongolia ... 237
Morocco ... 237

Mozambique 240
Namibia 243
Nauru 247
Nepal 247
Netherlands 250
New Zealand 251
Nicaragua 251
Niger 255
Nigeria 256
Norway 257
Oman 257
Pakistan 258
Palestinian Movements 266
Panama 285
Papua New Guinea 286
Paraguay 286
Peru 290
Philippines 293
Poland 299
Portugal 310
Qatar 312
Romania 312
Rwanda 314
St Christopher-Nevis 314
St Lucia 315
St Vincent and the Grenadines 315
São Tomé and Príncipe 316
Saudi Arabia 317
Senegal 318
Seychelles 319
Sierra Leone 321
Singapore... 322
Solomon Islands 323
Somalia 323
South Africa 326
Spain 337
Sri Lanka... 348
Sudan 351
Suriname 354
Swaziland... 356
Sweden 356
Switzerland 357
Syria 358
Taiwan 361
Tanzania 364
Thailand 364
Togo 371
Trinidad and Tobago 372
Tunisia 372
Turkey 375
Uganda 385
Union of Soviet Socialist Republics ... 387
United Arab Emirates 394
United Kingdom 395
United States of America 404
Uruguay 408
Vanuatu 408
Venezuela 409
Vietnam 410
Western Samoa 413
Yemen Arab Republic 413
Yemen People's Democratic Republic 414
Yugoslavia 415
Zaïre... 421
Zambia 424
Zimbabwe 424
International Revolutionary Groupings 425

Select Bibliography 427
Index 433

INTRODUCTION

The information contained in this book, like that provided in its predecessor, *Political Dissent – An International Guide to Dissident, Extra-Parliamentary, Guerrilla and Illegal Political Movements* (published in 1983), is based on the resources of *Keesing's Record of World Events*, formerly known as *Keesing's Contemporary Archives*.

As indicated by its title, this book is concerned with the activities of movements and not with those of individual dissidents. It does not cover legal political parties, which are described in another volume of the Keesing's Reference Publications series, *Political Parties of the World*. A directory of peace movements was published in 1986 (in the same series) as *Peace Movements of the World*. Neither does this book deal with pressure groups which do not constitute an actual or potential threat to the stability of the state. Revolutionary or liberation movements which have come to power have also been excluded from this book.

Most of the movements listed in this book have used violence to further their ends. Their activities have ranged from bank robberies with the aim of raising funds for revolutionary purposes, the taking of hostages in order to extort ransom and/or political concessions, and the hijacking of aircraft (or ships) for similar purposes, to bombing attacks and eventual open warfare with the object of overthrowing the existing regime or of setting up a separate state.

However, also listed in this book are organizations which have adopted non-violent policies, among them the Charter 77 group in Czechoslovakia and the Solidarity free trade union movement in Poland, as well as illegal political parties, parties in exile, and groups representing religious dissent and coming into conflict with the authority of the state.

By 1984 the problem of international terrorism had become one of the major preoccupations of the Western nations. At its 53rd annual general assembly held in Luxembourg in that year, the International Criminal Police Organization (Interpol) revised its objects in order to enable it to combat international terrorism more effectively. Until then Interpol had under its constitution been prevented from undertaking "any intervention or activities of a political, military, religious or racial character". The assembly agreed that Interpol would be free to become involved in cases where the criminal element of any violent act such as murder, serious injury, kidnapping or bomb attack outweighed the political aspect.

According to US State Department figures issued in March 1987 there was a slight decline in international terrorist incidents from 785 in 1985 to 737 in 1986, and a sharp decline in such incidents in Western Europe from 218 in 1985 to 150 in 1986, this being attributed in part to the expulsion of Libyans from European states.

In a survey published in *The Times* (of London) on Jan. 1, 1987, it was pointed out that there were then 25 major armed conflicts in the world. Only one of these—the war between Iran and Iraq—was an international conflict, while 15 were classed as civil wars, in Afghanistan, Angola, Chad, Colombia, El Salvador, Indonesia (East Timor), Kampuchea, Lebanon, Mozambique, Nicaragua, Peru, the Philippines, Sudan, Suriname and Uganda; another four were classed as secessionist wars, in Ethiopia, Sri Lanka, Turkey (Kurdish rebels) and Western Sahara. The five conflicts which remained unclassified were those in France (autonomists in Corsica), Spain (ETA in the Basque region), the United Kingdom (Northern Ireland), Namibia (attacks by SWAPO) and South Africa (activities of the African National Congress, ANC). The review made no mention of the Arab–Israeli conflict.

If revolutionary movements are to be classified according to the degree of their success it will be found that most of them have failed to achieve their ultimate objective. This applies in particular to the extreme left-wing movements in Western Europe and Latin America (where Cuba and Nicaragua have been the exceptions). The movements which have had an impact upon the regimes against which they have fought include SWAPO in Namibia (where a wing of the movement has been allowed to operate legally), the ANC in South Africa (whose economy has been severely affected by the conflict), the Basque ETA movement in Spain (where regional autonomy has been promoted) and in Sri Lanka (where Indian mediation has led to an agreement between the government and Tamil separatists). On the other hand no concessions have been made to movements such as the Kurdish separatists in Iraq and Turkey, the revolutionary Armenians of Turkey, the Eritrean and Tigrean separatists in Ethiopia, the (South) Sudan People's Liberation Army, the Polisario Front of Western Sahara (which is involved in armed conflict with Morocco), the Provisional Irish Republican Army, and generally the Palestine Liberation Organization (although Israel has on occasion agreed to exchanges of prisoners with Palestinian groups).

Various views have been expressed on what constitutes terrorism. The editor of the *Annual Register* for the year 1985 has concluded that terrorism is "not confined to revolutionary fanatics" but "may be committed by governments, military forces, police, embattled workers, ruthless employers [and] sectional interests", and that it is "a permanent feature of organized society which inevitably has enemies within, for whom some of the organs of society are themselves perceived as enemies", and it is "commonly a feature of efforts at destabilizing a disliked regime". On the other hand Walter Laqueur, in his second edition of *The Age of Terrorism,* is concerned only with "the gunman or bomb-thrower who acts in opposition, and with the use of covert violence by a small group for political ends, usually directed against a government".

In his book *The Financing of Terror* (published in 1986) James Adams has come to the conclusion that the idea of state-sponsored terrorism has only limited validity. He asserts that attempts by the West to arm underground movements in the communist world have failed (although it is known that the West has supplied weapons to rebels in Afghanistan); that Communist states have given no direct aid to the Palestine Liberation Organization (PLO) and other revolutionary movements (although arms of communist origin have been sold to them); that Libya, which at first had given indiscriminate aid to all terrorists (out of its oil revenue), had ceased to support the PLO in 1982; and that in fact Saudi Arabia had supplied more money to the PLO than any other country (without the West condemning Saudi Arabia as a promoter of terrorism). He also states that the PLO no longer depends on donations from Arab countries, and that by 1986 the PLO had an annual income of US$600,000,000, with more than $500,000,000 coming from investments, and that all groups under the PLO umbrella had assets around $5,000 million and a total annual income of $1,250 million.

In Colombia the two principal left-wing guerrilla organizations are said to have provided "protection" to drug growers and thus to have obtained their main income from dealers in illegal drugs and to have been enabled to increase the numbers of their followers by over 10,000 each in recent years.

What of the future? It is not unnatural that in the contemporary world of growing internationalism, expressed in the creation of more and more international organizations and in the power of multinational corporations, there should exist revolutionary autonomist or secessionist movements inspired by extreme nationalism. They have fought to preserve their ethnic identity in a more or less independent state, but these groups, which include extremist Armenians, Basques, Corsicans, Palestinians, Kurds (in Iran, Iraq and Turkey), Sikhs in India, the Polisario Front (in Western Sahara), Tamils (in Sri Lanka) and ethnic minorities in Burma, in most cases represent only sections of their respective ethnic communities. Even when they appear to have little prospect of achieving their ultimate objective, most of them show no signs of willingness to abandon their struggle.

September 1987 *HWD*

Contributors to the compilation of this book, in addition to the editor, were: Kate Devereux, Martin Greensill, F. John Harper, Heather Jackson, Cathy Jenkins, Steve Lewis, Susan Mushin, Cornelia Rulf, Darren Sagar, Helen Schooley and Martin Wright.

The indexer was Alison Cowan.

Note

Events recorded in this book do not extend beyond mid-1987.

The population figures given for each country are with few exceptions based on UN estimates as at mid-1985.

Abbreviations used in this book are the following:

ch. = chairman
gen. sec. = general secretary
l. = leader
pres. = president
sec.-gen. = secretary-general
sec. = secretary

Afghanistan

Capital: Kabul Pop. 14,000,000

The Democratic Republic of Afghanistan was set up on April 27, 1978, by a Revolutionary Council which established a Government dominated by the (communist) People's Democratic Party of Afghanistan (PDPA) which effectively became the country's sole legal political party. Afghanistan has no parliament. Following massive Soviet intervention from December 1979 onwards, a provisional Constitution (known as the Basic Principles of the Democratic Republic of Afghanistan) was ratified by the PDPA on April 13, 1980, and by the Revolutionary Council on the following day. It laid down inter alia that Afghanistan would proceed "from backwardness to social, economic and cultural progress under the leadership of the PDPA"; that "the sacred and true religion of Islam" would be protected, and that the "traditional friendship and co-operation with the USSR" would be strengthened and broadened. It also provided that a Grand National Assembly or Supreme Council (*Loya Jirga*) would be the highest organ of state power but that pending its election by free and direct vote the Revolutionary Council would hold supreme power.

The National Front (NF), a broad alliance of political parties, mass organizations and tribal bodies, is the umbrella organization for all authorized political activity in Afghanistan. It was formed as the National Fatherland Front at a congress on June 15, 1981, with the object of promoting national unity, and was to be under the guidance of the PDPA. Its national congress was scheduled to meet at least once every five years but the second NF congress was postponed until Jan. 14-15, 1987, because of party infighting which followed the appointment of Maj.-Gen. Mohammad Najibollah—later known simply as Dr Najib—as PDPA general secretary on May 4, 1986.

Reports of rebel activities have generally referred to *mujaheddin* guerrillas without specifying their allegiance to any of the groups or alliances listed below. Among rebel leaders, Ahmad Shah Masood has repeatedly been mentioned as being the commander of *mujaheddin* groups active in the Panjshir valley (north of Kabul) in 1982-84 and in areas bordering on Pakistan in later years.

The volume and value of external support for rebels opposed to the rule of the PDPA, and particularly to the Soviet intervention in Afghanistan, has been considerable (the most important factions of the *mujaheddin*, or the holy warriors, are detailed below). The United States has been supplying arms to the *mujaheddin* since 1979 and a *Washington Post* report of Jan. 15, 1985, showed that aid to the rebels by the Central Intelligence Agency (CIA) had risen to $250,000,000 for fiscal year 1984-85, amounting to over 80 per cent of the agency's annual budget for covert action. The British MI6 has also reportedly been collaborating with the CIA since 1985 to supply the *mujaheddin* with surface-to-air Blowpipe missile launchers and these and US "Stinger" missiles have been recently used to appreciable effect. Pakistan, Israel and Egypt have been involved in the training of the rebels, while Saudi Arabia has provided substantial financial support.

Greater Soviet firepower and the factionalism within the 200,000-strong *mujaheddin* has for some years done much to limit their successes to ambushes, the disruption of supply routes and rocket attacks on government-held cities and bases. However, by mid-1987 government troops were under severe pressure in several areas and in July 1987 the Soviet press acknowledged the extent of military losses.

There have been an estimated 100,000 *mujaheddin* and civilian deaths since 1979, while in October 1986 the US State Department estimated the number of Soviet casualties to be around 10,000 dead and 20,000 wounded. The protracted conflict has also led to the exodus of over 3,000,000 refugees, mostly to Pakistan.

In a new initiative announced on Dec. 30, 1986, Dr Najib declared a ceasefire of all Afghan government and Soviet forces from Jan. 15, 1987. He also announced an amnesty for the *mujaheddin* rebels and called upon all "oppositionists" to join in a government of national unity. Dr Najib reiterated his plan for national reconciliation at the second NF congress on Jan. 15 and announced that the Afghan government had reached an accord paving the way for the complete withdrawal of Soviet troops from Afghanistan.

The ceasefire call was immediately rejected by *mujaheddin* leaders, and at a rally on Jan. 17 of the seven Pakistan-based rebel groups comprising the Islamic Unity of the Mujaheddin of Afghanistan, a statement was issued rejecting the ceasefire and the proposal for a government of national reconciliation.

Islamic Unity, however, was divided over the suggestion by Dr Najib on June 14, 1987, that Afghanistan's exiled former King Mohammad Zahir Shah, who ruled the country from 1933 to 1973, should return to head an interim government in Kabul once the Soviet Union had agreed to a troop withdrawal. The former King turned down the offer, saying he could not accept "sharing power" with Dr Najib. Dr Najib further announced on July 14, 1987, that his government would be prepared to share power with three "moderate" leaders of the *mujaheddin* alliance, Sayed Ahmed Gailani, Seghbatullah Mujjaddedi, and Maulavi Nabi Mohammadi, and stated that the portfolios of at least 13 Cabinet posts would be available to rebels and others interested in "national reconciliation". This offer, which was seen as reflecting Soviet pressure arising from the failure to find a military solution to the conflict, was subsequently rejected in early August at a conference inside Afghanistan attended by 1,200 guerrilla commanders, when it was resolved to establish a "supreme holy-war council".

Mujaheddin Alliances

Afghan Islamic Coalition

According to the Iranian news agency INRA this body was formed on June 18, 1987, its member organizations being named as the Afghan Nasr Organization, the Guardians of Islamic Jihad of Afghanistan, United Islamic Front of Afghanistan, the Islamic Force of Afghanistan, the Da'wa Party of Islamic Unity of Afghanistan, the Islamic Movement of Afghanistan, and Islamic Struggle for Afghanistan. The coalition denounced all negotiations or power-sharing proposals, including the return of the King and stated that its purpose was to defend the "revolutionary Islamic" values of the *mujaheddin* and to prevent any deviation from the policy of "neither East, nor West".

Islamic Alliance for the Liberation of Afghanistan (IALA)

Leadership. Prof Ghulam Abdur Rasoul Sayaf

This Alliance (also known as the National Alliance) was formed on Jan. 27, 1980, at an extraordinary meeting of the Foreign Ministers of the Organization of the Islamic Conference in Islamabad (Pakistan) by representatives of the Afghan rebel organizations—the Afghan Islamic Association (*Jamaat-i-Islami Afghanistan*), the Movement for the Islamic Revolution (*Harkat-i-Inkalab-i-Islami*), the Afghan National Liberation Front, the Afghan Islamic and Nationalist Revolutionary Council, the faction of the Islamic Party (*Hizb-i-Islami*) led by Gulbuddin Hekmatyar, and the other faction of this party led by Maulavi Mohammad Yunus Khales; the former faction, however, withdrew from the IALA in March 1980 because of disagreement over representation on a proposed Supreme Revolutionary Council (see separate entry).

At the 11th session of the Foreign Ministers of the Organization of the Islamic Conference held in Islamabad on May 17-22, 1980, Prof Rasoul Sayaf presented a list of demands calling inter alia for (i) the severance of diplomatic relations with the Soviet Union and Afghanistan and (ii) the recognition of the insurgent organizations as the sole legitimate representatives of Afghanistan and their acceptance as a member of the Organization of the Islamic Conference. The meeting, however, adopted a resolution providing for the establishment of a three-member committee to seek "ways and means for a comprehensive solution of the crisis with respect to Afghanistan". (The Islamic Conference Organization had suspended Afghanistan's membership in January 1980 and a number of its member states had provided funds, among them Saudi Arabia, "to assist Afghan insurgents and refugees".)

Talks between the three-member Islamic Conference committee and an IALA delegation, led by Prof Rasoul Sayaf, in Switzerland on June 20-21, 1980, ended inconclusively. The committee assured the IALA of the moral and political support of the Islamic nations and restated its aim of seeking a peaceful solution to the conflict on the basis of "immediate, total and unconditional withdrawal of Soviet troops from Afghanistan" in order to restore to that country political independence, sovereignty, non-alignment, an Islamic identity and freedom to choose its own form of government as well as political social and economic system. The IALA delegation, on the other hand, restated their refusal to negotiate with Kabul or Moscow, called for the withdrawal of Soviet troops, demanded the recognition of the *mujaheddin* as the sole legitimate representatives of the Afghan people and their own participation in the committee in this capacity, and pledged that under their leadership Afghanistan would pursue a policy of "active non-alignment" and would decide on its own future freely and without super-power interference. The delegation also called (i) for special UN and Islamic meetings to be held on Afghanistan, (ii) for the Islamic nations to re-examine their relations with the Soviet Union and (iii) for the opening of a special Afghan resistance fund financed partly by members of the Organization of Petroleum Exporting Countries (OPEC).

The IALA was by this time, however, deeply divided. The Hekmatyar faction of the Islamic Party had left the IALA in March 1980. A moderate faction consisted of the Afghan National Liberation Front, the Movement for the Islamic Revolution and the Afghan Islamic and Nationalist Revolutionary Council (also known as National Islamic Front of Afghanistan). Another faction embraced two Moslem fundamentalist groups—the Afghan Islamic Association and the faction of the Islamic Party led by Maulavi Mohammad Yunus Khales.

Prof Rasoul Sayaf on July 17, 1987, rejected the coalition initiatives of the Kabul government and stated that only a *mujaheddin* government would be acceptable.

Islamic Unity of the Mujaheddin of Afghanistan

This organization was finally constituted in May 1983 with seven rebel groups and 20,000 members. It embraced the two factions of *Hizb-i-Islami*, two factions of the Islamic Afghan Association, two factions of the Movement for the Islamic Revolution, and the Afghan National Liberation Front.

Islamic Unity, based in Pakistan, issued a joint statement at a rally on Jan. 17, 1987, firmly rejecting the Afghan government's ceasefire and its proposals for a government of national reconciliation.

It was reported in April 1987 that the seven groups

constituting the alliance had failed to reach agreement on the structure of a government-in-exile.

Supreme Revolutionary Council

Leadership. Mohammad Babrak Zai (1.)

This Council was formed in May 1980 at a special tribal meeting (*loya jirga*) in Peshawar (northern Pakistan), attended by delegates from all areas of Afghanistan. The meeting passed a number of "fundamental resolutions" designed to form the basis of a future Constitution for Afghanistan, and it is also decided that all treaties signed after April 1978, notably the Soviet-Afghan treaty of friendship under which Soviet troops had entered the country, would be considered void.

Mujaheddin Organizations

Afghan Islamic Association (*Jamaat-i-Islami Afghanistan*)

Leadership. Prof Ustad Burhanuddin Rabbani (1.)

This movement has been supported by the *Jamaat-i-Islami* of Pakistan, a component of the Pakistan National Alliance, members of which have held posts in the Government of President Zia ul-Haq. On Jan. 27, 1980, it took part in the formation of the Islamic Alliance for the Liberation of Afghanistan, of which Prof Ghulam Abdur Rasoul Sayaf (the deputy leader of the *Jamaat-i-Islami Afghanistan*, who had spent six years in prison) became leader on March 19, 1980—see separate entry.

On June 16, 1986, President Reagan had a meeting in Washington with Prof Rabbani who urged the President to sever diplomatic relations with the Afghan government and extend full diplomatic recognition to the *mujaheddin*. Prof Rabbani also met with the French Prime Minister, Jacques Chirac, on June 23.

The Association's offices in Peshawar (Pakistan) were bombed on Feb. 19, 1987, when at least 14 persons were killed.

Prof Rabbani has opposed the Soviet-backed offer to restore the King, stating that the monarchy had been responsible for the present condition of Afghanistan. Rabbani has stated a willingness to negotiate directly with the Soviet Union, but not with the regime in Kabul, and has said that no other power would be allowed to establish bases in Afghanistan after a Soviet withdrawal.

The movement was said to have 20,000 men in the field as of mid-1987.

Afghan National Liberation Front (*Nejat-e Melli Afghanistan*)

Leadership. Imam Seghbatullah Mujjaddedi (1.)

On March 12, 1979, this Front—which also embraced a faction of the Islamic Party (*Hizb-i-Islami*)—called for a *jihad* (holy war) against the Kabul regime. On Jan. 27, 1980, it took part in the formation of the Islamic Alliance for the Liberation of Afghanistan. On June 1, 1981, however, it formed—together with the National Islamic Front of Afghanistan led by Sayed Ahmed Gailani and the Movement for the Islamic Revolution led by Maulavi Mohammadi—the Islamic Unity of the Mujaheddin of Afghanistan (see separate entry).

Islamic Movement Organization of Afghanistian (*Harekat Islami Afghanistan*)

Leadership. Sheik Mohammed Assef Mohseni (1.)

This Movement seeks the establishment of an Islamic Republic of Afghanistan on the model of that of Iran.

Islamic Party (*Hizb-i-Islami*)

Leadership. The party has two factions led respectively by (i) Gulbuddin Hekmatyar and (ii) Maulavi Mohammad Yunus Khales

The party announced in Islamabad (Pakistan) on July 30, 1978, that it had launched guerrilla attacks against the (communist) government of President Nur Mohammad Taraki and was the following year reported to be seeking the restoration of the monarchy in Afghanistan. On Aug. 11, 1979, the Yunus Khales faction of the party joined the Afghan National Liberation Front (see separate entry). Both factions of the party joined the Islamic Alliance for the Liberation of Afghanistan formed on Jan. 27, 1980 (see separate entry). A strike by shopkeepers in Kabul, later joined by civil servants and office workers, on Feb. 21-27, 1980, was instigated by the Hekmatyar faction of this party, and led to the imposition of martial law and a curfew in the capital on Feb. 22 and to demonstrations on the same day, when at least 300 civilians and an unknown number of Soviet and Afghan troops were reported killed, and many thousands arrested. Parallel strikes took place in several regional towns.

The Hekmatyar faction withdrew from the Islamic Alliance for the Liberation of Afghanistan in March 1980 because of disagreements over representations on a proposed Supreme Revolutionary Council (see separate entry). In mid-1981 this faction was reported to have begun, in May of that year, to co-operate in guerrilla activities with a local resistance group based near Kabul and known as SAMA, and also to have reached a new agreement with five other Pakistan based groups on the merging of weapons, funds and manpower.

The Islamic Party was in 1982 thought to be the largest of the *mujaheddin* groups but also to have made demands for a disproportionate degree of influence in various unions of different guerrilla groups. A new such union, reported in mid-March 1982, was said to embrace the two *Hizb-i-Islami* factions, two factions of the Afghan Islamic Association, two factions of the Movement for the Islamic Revolution, and the Afghan National Liberation Front—with the chairman of the new union to be appointed on a rotating basis from among the leaders of the seven groups, and its deputy chairman being Gulbuddin Hekmatyar of the *Hizb-i-Islami*.

On March 21, 1982, *Hizb-i-Islami* spokesmen claimed in Quetta (Pakistan) that the *mujaheddin* were facing opposition from groups of Baluchi guerrillas in Afghanistan (who had fled there because they rejected the 1947 incorporation of much of Baluchistan into the Republic of Pakistan).

Hizb-i-Islami rebels claimed on June 3, 1984, to have destroyed more than 35 Soviet helicopters and MiG fighters and to have killed or wounded a number of Soviet troops. In August 1985, the group claimed to have shot down a Soviet military transport plane taking off from Kandahar.

Abdul Haq, a leader of *Hizb-i-Islami*, met with the UK Prime Minister, Mrs Margaret Thatcher, in London on March 11, 1986.

Mohammad Ishaq (also known as Lala Malang), another of the group's leaders, taken prisoner near Kandahar in 1984, was exchanged on Feb. 24, 1986, for a captured Soviet soldier.

Hizb-i-Islami is regarded as the most fundamentalist and uncompromising of the major *mujaheddin* groups, and Gulbuddin Hekmatyar has rejected any role for the former king. On April 22, 1987, he claimed that 90 per cent of Afghanistan was in *mujaheddin* hands, and that the Soviet forces had sustained 91,000 casualties, including 29,000 killed.

Yunus Khales stated in February 1987 that once Soviet troops withdrew, "those people we know to be committed communists will be killed", while "those who are prepared to return to Islam will be spared".

Movement for the Islamic Revolution (*Harkat-i-Inkalab-i-Islami*)

Leadership. Maulavi Mohammad Nabi Mohammadi (1.)

On Jan. 27, 1980, this Movement joined the Islamic Alliance for the Liberation of Afghanistan, and on June 1, 1981, it formed—together with the Afghan National Liberation Front led by Imam Seghbatullah Mujjaddedi and the National Islamic Front of Afghanistan led by Sayed Ahmed Gailani—the Islamic Unity of the Mujaheddin of Afghanistan (see separate entry).

National Islamic Front of Afghanistan (*Surrah-e Melli Inkalab-i-Islami*)

Leadership. Sayed Ahmed Gailani (1.)

This Front was originally known as the Afghan Islamic and National Revolutionary Council, which took part in the formation of the Islamic Alliance for the Liberation of Afghanistan in January 1980 (see separate entry). Later in 1980 it adopted a new title and on June 1, 1981, it formed (together with the Afghan National Liberation Front led by the Imam Seghbatullah Mujjaddedi and the Movement of the Islamic Revolution led by Maulavi Mohammadi) the Islamic Unity of the Mujaheddin of Afghanistan (see separate entry). A spokesman for the organization was on July 5, 1982, quoted as saying that the Soviet military forces in Afghanistan were turning the country into a forward military base for possible moves into South-West Asia (i) by developing a major air base at Shindand (western Afghanistan), (ii) by building a bridge across the Amu Darya river (on Afghanistan's frontier with the Soviet Union) and starting a railway line from the frontier to Kabul, and (iii) by annexing (in 1981) the Wakhan corridor (in north-east Afghanistan, bordering on Pakistan, China and the Soviet Union). (This annexation would deprive Afghanistan of its frontier with China and would give the Soviet Union a common frontier with Pakistan.)

It was reported in May 1987 that Gailani was willing to accept a role for the former King in a transitional government, but on July 18 he rejected Dr Najib's offer of a power-sharing role (see introductory section).

Albania

Capital: Tirana Pop. 2,960,000

The Socialist People's Republic of Albania is, under its Constitution adopted by the People's Assembly in December 1976, "the state of the dictatorship of the proletariat" exercised in effect by the Albanian Party of Labour, which is "the sole directing political power in state and society". The single-chamber People's Assembly of 250 members (the supreme legislative body) is elected every four years on a single list of candidates nominated by the Democratic Front mass organization controlled by the party. The Albanian regime claims to be the sole guardian of true Marxism-Leninism and is opposed to all other forms of communism, notably those of the Soviet bloc, China, Yugoslavia and the Euro-communist parties.

In elections to the People's Assembly held between Feb. 1 and 20, 1987, the 250 candidates of the Democratic Front were elected unopposed.

There has been no reliable evidence of the existence of internal opposition groups, and there appears to have been little resistance by religious believers to the complete suppression of all religion since 1967—apart from occasional reports of imprisonment, ill-treatment or execution of priests and other believers, and the survival of a number of Moslem customs (Islam having been the religion of the majority of Albania's inhabitants). Under Albania's criminal code the death penalty is provided for anti-state activities as well as for the dissemination of religious propaganda.

Outside Albania, however, émigré groups opposed to the Tirana regime have continued to be sporadically active, notably those associated with the aspiration to bring about a restoration of the Albanian monarchy.

From the death in unclear circumstances of a long-time Prime Minister, Mehmet Shehu, in December 1981 (officially attributed to suicide) it appeared that a power struggle had taken place within the regime. On Nov. 10, 1982, Enver Hoxha (the first secretary of the ruling Albanian Party of Labour) alleged that M. Shehu had been a traitor and a long-standing agent of Yugoslavia which, he claimed, had plotted to assassinate him (Enver Hoxha) and other Albanian leaders. In a book entitled *The Titoists,* published in December 1982, Enver Hoxha elaborated his accusations against M. Shehu, alleging that the latter had, at various stages since World War II, worked for the US, British, German, Italian, Soviet and Yugoslav intelligence services as an instrument of plots to undermine Enver Hoxha's policies. Hekuran Isai, who had been appointed Minister of Internal Affairs in January 1982, claimed on June 29, 1982, that M. Shehu had intended to overthrow the regime of the Albanian Party of Labour and to set up a "bourgeois political system" in Albania.

In September 1983 it was reported that a number of former ministers and other officers had been convicted of espionage for the United States, the Soviet Union and Yugoslavia and had been executed; they included Feçor Shehu (ex-Minister of Internal Affairs), Kadri Hazbiu (ex-Minister of People's Defence) and Llambi Ziçisti (ex-Minister of Health); severe prison sentences were said to have been imposed on others, among them M. Shehu's widow and two sons as well as Nesti Nase (former Foreign Minister).

Under a bill approved on June 29, 1983, control of the General Investigator's Office was transferred from the Ministry of Internal Affairs to the People's Assembly (Parliament) so as to make the Office independent of the state administration.

Amnesty International claimed in a report of Dec. 12, 1984, that it had the names of 400 political prisoners held in Albania over the last 14 years; that the death sentence could be imposed for 34 offences, of which 12 were considered political; that attempts to leave the country illegally could lead to imprisonment for 25 years; that suspects in political trials were denied defence lawyers; and that there was extensive mistreatment of political prisoners.

Under an amnesty declared by the President of the People's Assembly with effect from Jan. 13, 1986, a pardon was granted to certain categories of convicted persons, in particular (i) all persons sentenced to up to six years' deprivation of liberty for agitation and propaganda against the state or for treason to the homeland in the form of escape outside the state (except those with previous conviction for crimes against the state); (ii) all women sentenced to deprivation of liberty for 20 years or less; and (iii) all persons under the age of 18 years.

Monarchist Movement

Leadership. Mbret Shquiparvet Leka ("King Leka I of the Albanians")

Mbret Shquiparvet Leka is the son of ex-King Zog (who fled from Albania in 1939, was deposed in absentia in 1946 and died in 1961) and styles himself "King Leka I of the Albanians". In March 1977 he was reported to have told a press conference in New York that he was training guerrilla forces to harass the Albanian government and that a number of guerrillas had already entered the country. Arms were found in his possession when he was in Thailand in April 1977 and again when he was in Madrid in January 1979, when he was quoted as having said that he was pledged "to fight hard to help my country escape from communist dictatorship". Expelled from Spain in February 1979, he lived for a period in Rhodesia (Zimbabwe) and eventually settled in South Africa with his Australian-born wife Susan after an interim stay in Egypt.

In a statement made in Paris on Sept. 29, 1982, "King" Leka said that an attempted armed invasion of Albania a few days earlier had been carried out by a "National Liberation Army" of his supporters but added that he had personally refused to be associated with the operation because of its "suicidal" nature. According to the Albanian authorities, the abortive invasion had occurred on the night of Sept. 25-26, when "a gang of criminal Albanian émigrés" had made an armed landing on the Albanian coast (the precise location being unspecified); the group had been discovered at daybreak and within five hours had been "totally liquidated" by the Albanian Army. No details were given as to the strength of the group, but the Albanian authorities claimed (i) that the infiltrators had been equipped with automatic rifles, pistols, binoculars, a radio transmitter, disguises and quantities of foreign and local currency, and (ii) that they had been led by "the bandit Xhevdet Mustafa", who was subsequently described as a "well-known criminal" active in émigré circles (although his name was unfamiliar to Western experts).

In the absence of further clarification or confirmation, some Western observers suggested that the alleged invasion was a device used by the Albanian government to explain the elimination of an internal opposition group (see Introduction above).

Algeria

Capital: Algiers (El Djezaïr) Pop. 21,720,000

The Democratic and Popular Republic of Algeria is, under its 1976 Constitution, a one-party state in which the ruling party is the National Liberation Front (FLN). There are an executive President (nominated by the FLN and elected, and re-eligible, for a five-year term by universal adult suffrage), a Cabinet headed by a Prime Minister, and a 295-member National People's Assembly elected by universal adult suffrage, also for five years, from among FLN candidates. In elections held on Feb. 26, 1987, three candidates were chosen by local FLN committees to stand for each seat. Less than half the sitting deputies stood for re-election. The turnout was officially stated to have reached 87.29 per cent.

A revised National Charter was endorsed by a national referendum on Jan. 16, 1986. It laid greater emphasis on the role of Islam in state affairs, called for the application of "pragmatic socialism" and stressed the importance of social justice.

According to a report by two members of the International Federation of Human Rights who visited Algeria in April 1985, a total of 145 prisoners were held in that country for political reasons—100 Moslem fundamentalists, 30 supporters of ex-President Ahmed Ben Bella and 15 members of the (Trotskyist) *Organisation socialiste des travailleurs*.

Between Nov. 8 and Nov. 10, 1986 unrest which had begun in a student hostel in Zouaghi near the eastern Algerian town of Constantine spread across the town. The students were protesting against low standards of living conditions. They were joined by school pupils demonstrating against a further rumoured Arabization of the education system. President Chadli Bendjedid accused "enemies of the revolution" of causing the riots. Subsequently, 186 demonstrators were sentenced to between two and eight years' imprisonment but were released on April 22, 1987.

Berber Organizations

Berber Cultural Movement

The Berbers, as the oldest inhabitants of Algeria, make up almost a quarter of the country's population, with a distinct language (Kabyle) and culture. Militant Berber students, protesting against the alleged repression of Berber culture, took strike action in March-April 1980 at Algiers University. Their action spread to other centres and culminated in a general strike on April 16. In counter-action taken by security forces against students at the Tizi-Ouzou University on April 20 and ensuing riots, up to 200 people were injured and 32 killed. The government subsequently announced measures designed to appease the militant Berbers, promising in particular to create a chair of Kabyle studies at Tizi-Ouzou University and to restore such a chair which had previously been abolished at Algiers University.

Although continuing with its Arabization programme—designed to replace the hitherto French-oriented Algerian Society but in effect giving advantages, especially in employment, to Arab speakers rather than speakers of other languages such as Kabyle—the government announced in September 1981 that special courses on the Kabyle language and popular Algerian Arabic would be instituted at four universities, but not at Tizi-Ouzou.

On Oct. 28, 1981, one-year prison sentences were imposed on three members of the Berber cultural movement, arrested on May 23 and charged with rioting, while 19 others were given shorter sentences or were released.

Front of Socialist Forces (*Front des Forces Socialistes*, FFS)

Leadership. Dr Hocine Aït Ahmed (l.)

Dr Aït Ahmed was a leading Berber figure in the Algerian war of independence (1954-62) but later instigated an unsuccessful revolt in Kabyle against President Ben Bella in September 1963. In February 1964 the newly-formed FFS announced that it was resuming the armed struggle against President Ben Bella's "dictatorship". However, in this attempt it also failed. Dr Aït Ahmed was arrested on Oct. 17, 1964, and was on April 10, 1965, condemned to death, this sentence being commuted to life imprisonment. However, on May 1, 1966, he escaped from prison and he subsequently reached France, from where he repeatedly called for a "democratization" of Algeria's institutions.

In 1980 the Algerian state-controlled media asserted that the current Berber agitation against the government's Arabization measures had been organized by "external influences", France and French-based organizations, in particular the FFS.

In December 1985 Dr Aït Ahmed agreed to create a united front with ex-President Ben Bella, the leader of the Movement for Democracy in Algeria (see separate entry).

Ali Mecili, a member of the FFS who had lived in France since 1966 and had worked for the unification of the Algerian opposition in Europe, was murdered on April 7, 1987. Dr Aït Ahmed stated afterwards that the Algerian secret service was to blame for the murder.

Sons of the Martyrs of the Revolution

This organization was set up to defend the rights of the Berbers and supported Dr Hocine Aït Ahmed, the leader of the Front of Socialist Forces (see separate entry). Twelve members of the organization, arrested on July 5, 1985, were in December of that year convicted of illegal association and sentenced to prison terms ranging from six months to three years. Demonstrations were held at Tizi-Ouzou in October 1985 in support of demands for the release of political activists, including a popular singer (Ait Menguellet, sentenced to three years in prison for possessing arms), and led to prison sentences of from six months to two years for 29 of the demonstrators.

Moslem Fundamentalist Movements

Moslem Fundamentalists

Towards the end of 1982 it emerged that Moslem fundamentalists (or "integrationists") enjoyed a measure of support among students in Algiers. In a clash between some of these students and others, mainly "progressive" secularists and Berbers, a young man (though not a Moslem fundamentalist) was killed on Nov. 2, and 29 people were thereupon arrested, most of them being Moslem fundamentalists. To protest against these arrests some 5,000 people rallied in the centre of Algiers on Nov. 12. In mid-December 23 Moslem fundamentalists were arrested and charged with subversion by distributing pamphlets deemed to be "against the national interest" and forming an organization aimed at destabilizing the state. On Dec. 19-20 some 30 people were arrested when they were found in possession of stolen explosives, bombs, firearms and false documents and administrative seals; in the government newspaper *El-Moudjahid* it was stated on Dec. 21 that these people had armed themselves to "fight progress by fire and blood" and that they had sought to "restore a medieval era and stop our people's march towards progress and prosperity".

Following disturbances at the Ben Akoun University in 1982, five out of 19 Moslem fundamentalists accused of involvement were sentenced to between five and eight years in prison on Sept. 1, 1984.

In 1982 Moslem fundamentalists promoted an "Islamic Charter", and about 175 of them were detained in that year and in early 1983 on suspicion of involvement in the planting of bombs. In April 1985 about 75 of them were convicted on various charges, with about 40 of them being released after receiving sentences of less than two years in prison, and the remainder being sentenced to between three and 12 years in prison.

Islamic Jihad of Sheikh Sadiq al Moundiri

This organization was made up of a group of Moslem fundamentalists who claimed responsibility for an attack on a police training barracks in Souma, near Blida, about 50 km south of Algiers on Aug. 29, 1985, when one policeman was killed and arms were seized. The organization also claimed responsibility for a bomb attack outside the Algerian embassy in Beirut (Lebanon) Sept. 4, 1985, and for a previously unreported attack on a police station in Oran, during which six policemen were killed. The group was apparently also responsible for an attack in Larba (to the north-east of Blida) in which five policemen were killed on Oct. 21, 1985. In a gun attack in Bir Touta (near Blida) Nov. 2, 1985, two of the group were killed and three others "neutralized". The group was said to have local sympathy in the area in which they operated.

The organization's leader, Mostafa Bouyali, was killed with six of his supporters in a shoot-out with Algerian security forces on Jan. 3, 1987, near Larba. He had previously been sentenced in absentia to life imprisonment in April 1985 with a group of about 135 Moslem fundamentalists (see separate entry for "Moslem Fundamentalists"). On June 15, 1987, the trial of 202 Moslem fundamentalists opened in Medea, 100 km south of Algiers. Twenty of the accused were charged with criminal association, sabotage against the state, robbery and murder in connection with the campaign waged by Bouyali's followers from late 1985 onwards. On July 10, four of the accused were sentenced to death, others were sentenced to prison terms, and 15 were acquitted.

Human Rights and Other Movements

Algerian League of Human Rights (*Ligue algérienne des droits de l'homme,* LADH)

Leadership. Abdelnour Ali Yahia (ch.)

Founded. June 30, 1985

At its foundation the League stated that it would protest against the "considerable shortcomings in the defence of human rights in Algeria". A. A. Yahia, a lawyer and defence counsel at trials of various groups of Moslem fundamentalists, had been detained from October 1983 until May 13, 1984, when he was released under an amnesty of May 8 involving the release of 92 prisoners. He was again detained from July 9, 1985, to June 10, 1986.

The League was affiliated to the International Federation of Human Rights in early December 1986, following which A. A. Yahia and other officials to the League were again detained.

An alternative government-approved Algerian League For The Defence of the Rights of Man (*Ligue algérienne pour la défense des droits de l'homme*) was formed in April 1987 under the leadership of Miloud Brahimi.

Movement for Democracy in Algeria (*Mouvement pour la démocratie en Algérie,* MDA)

Leadership. Ahmed Ben Bella (l.)

Founded. May 1984

Ahmed Ben Bella, the founder of the MDA, had been President of Algeria from 1963 until he was deposed in a coup in June 1965. After his release from prison and subsequent house arrest, he moved to Europe and lived in Switzerland. He announced on May 20, 1984, that he was in the process of forming a new political party whose "minimum objective" was "the creation of a democratic framework in which to discuss the future of the country". He claimed that a "democratic collective body" had been set up by Algerians and Frenchmen which had been successful in pressurizing the Algerian government to release "several militants who had been unjustly detained". He added that one of the priorities of the new party would be to persuade Algerians to return home.

Subsequently Ahmed Ben Bella appeared at a press conference with the Berber cultural activist Dr Hocine Aït Ahmed in London on Dec. 11, 1985, to announce the formation of a united front consisting of a joint programme. The two men called for pluralist elections to a constituent assembly which would draw up a Constitution separating the powers and guaranteeing political and ideological freedoms. Ahmed Ben Bella said inter alia: "We hope our approach will be peaceful, but we do not condemn acts of despair".

On Dec. 25, 1985, 18 alleged supporters of Ben Bella were imprisoned for between one and 13 years on charges of threatening internal security. Abdelwahab Benchenouf, described as being a Ben Bella supporter, was arrested in France in early April 1986. He faced charges of possessing illegal weapons and leaflets calling for revolution in Algeria.

On June 7, 1987, 12 Ben Bella supporters were sentenced to between two and 10 years for plotting against the state (by a court in Medea, 100 km south of Algiers, which acquitted 10 other defendants).

El Badil, the monthly newspaper of Ben Bella supporters, was ordered to cease publication in France as from Dec. 31, 1986.

Socialist Organization of Workers (*Organisation socialiste des travailleurs*)

The International Federation of Human Rights (a non-governmental organization affiliated to the United Nations) reported on April 29, 1984, that 15 members of this (broadly Trotskyist) Organization were among 145 political prisoners being held in Algeria at the time.

Socialist Vanguard Party (*Parti de l'avant-garde socialiste,* PAGS)

This party has replaced the Algerian Communist Party (banned since the country achieved independence in 1962). It has given qualified support to the government since 1971, and from early 1979 onwards the government tolerated its existence, but dual membership of the PAGS and the ruling National Liberation Front was not permitted. In September 1981 the PAGS proclaimed a 10-point programme which included the "defence of the state sector" of the economy, the ending of "anti-democratic measures", the strengthening of co-operation with socialist states and an end to attempts to buy weapons from "imperialist countries". However, in April 1982 the ruling National Liberation Front (FLN) accused members and supporters of the PAGS of having infiltrated the National Union of Algerian Youth (*Union nationale de la jeunesse algérienne,* UNJA), a congress of which, held on March 15, 1982, had been followed by demonstrations in Oran by students protesting against examination procedures.

The PAGS is recognized by the Soviet-bloc communist parties.

Angola

Capital: Luanda Pop. 8,750,000

The People's Democratic Republic of Angola is a one-party state, its sole legal party being the (Marxist-Leninist) Popular Movement for the Liberation of Angola—Party of Labour (MPLA-PT). This party is responsible for the political, economic and social leadership of the nation, and its president is also President of the Republic. The supreme state body is a National People's Assembly of 282 members elected every three years (first in 1980) by colleges composed of representatives chosen by all "loyal" citizens over 18 years old. There is a government presided over by the head of state.

The end of Portuguese colonial rule in 1975 was followed by a fierce struggle for power in Angola between the three principal liberation movements, from which the MPLA (as it was then known) emerged victorious, mainly due to military backing from Cuban "volunteers" and Soviet advisers. Nevertheless, the government of President José Eduardo dos Santos (who succeeded Antônio Agostinho Neto in 1979) continued to face a continuing security threat from the two movements in question, notably from the National Union for the Total Independence of Angola (UNITA) operating in southern Angola with the backing of South African forces based in based in Namibia. Moreover, in the north separatist forces continued to be sporadically active in the enclave of Cabinda, regarded by the government as an integral part of Angola.

National Front for the Liberation of Angola (*Frente Nacional de Libertaçãõ de Angola,* FNLA)

The FNLA was formed in April 1962 by the merger of an Angolan People's Union (*União das Populações de Angola,* UPA) led by Holden Roberto and a Democratic Party of Angola, and on April 5 of that year Roberto announced in Léopoldville (later Kinshasa, Zaire) the formation of a Revolutionary Angolan Government-in-Exile (*Govêrno Revolucionario de Angola no Exilio,* GRAE) with himself as "Prime Minister". The UPA had in March 1961 begun a rebellion against Portuguese rule in Angola, causing thousands of casualties and widespread destruction in northern Angola, but by January 1963 the Portuguese authorities claimed to have regained control of the situation.

The GRAE was formally endorsed by a Foreign Ministers' conference of the Organization of African Unity (OAU) in February 1964; but in November 1964 the OAU also decided to give aid to the MPLA, which was supported by the Soviet Union and its allies. In December of that year the People's Republic of China decided to support the FNLA and to cease its aid to the MPLA. In June 1965 dissidents within the GRAE raided the organization's offices in Léopoldville and destroyed its records, accusing Roberto of having embezzled funds and of failing properly to organize the fight against the Portuguese. GRAE forces had in fact been in conflict with units of the MPLA, but on Oct. 15, 1966, the two organizations agreed to cease all hostile propaganda against each other. Although GRAE forces continued guerrilla warfare during the next few years, the OAU withdrew its recognition of the FNLA and the MPLA as "freedom fighter" movements.

In 1972 the FNLA and the MPLA attempted a reconciliation, and under an agreement signed in Kinshasa on Dec. 13 the two organizations were to merge in a "Supreme Council for the Liberation of Angola" (CSLA). However, after the overthrow of the Caetano regime in Portugal in April 1974 the FNLA and the MPLA signed separate ceasefire agreements with Portugal on Oct. 11 and 21 respectively.

On Jan. 9, 1975, the FNLA was recognized by the OAU liberation committee as one of Angola's three official liberation movements, together with the MPLA and Dr Jonas Savimbi's National Union for the Total Independence of Angola (UNITA—see separate entry). But although all three movements took part in the formation of a transitional government in Angola on Jan. 31, 1975, fighting continued between MPLA and FNLA forces, leading to considerable loss of life. Even after the signing of a truce agreement providing for the integration of MPLA, FNLA and UNITA troops into a combined force on March 28 (as laid down in the independence agreement), fighting continued between units of the three movements and in particular the MPLA and the FNLA, with the result that virtual martial law was declared on May 15, 1975. Nevertheless, the three movements decided, under an agreement signed in Nakuru (Kenya) on June 21, 1975, to renounce the use of force, to carry out elections to a constituent assembly and to guarantee each other the right to free political activity in all parts of the country.

The agreement, however, soon broke down and new hostilities began on June 23, 1975. On July 12 the FNLA headquarters in Luanda were destroyed by MPLA units; and by Aug. 10-11 all remaining FNLA (and UNITA) forces were withdrawn from Luanda. While the MPLA proclaimed the independence of the People's Republic of Angola in Luanda on Nov. 11, 1975, Holden Roberto declared in Ambriz (north of Luanda) on the same day that the country would be known as the Democratic People's Republic of Angola. After the MPLA had formed a government in Luanda on Nov. 14, the FNLA and UNITA established, on Nov. 23, 1975, a separate coalition government with two Prime Ministers (one from each organization) and with Roberto and Dr Savimbi as joint military chiefs of staff.

Early in 1976 the FNLA forces were driven northwards towards the Zaïre border by Soviet-equipped MPLA forces, and also southwards (together with UNITA forces), with the result that on Feb. 24, 1976 the FNLA announced that it would resort to guerrilla warfare. The MPLA government was thereupon recognized by numerous African and European governments, and it became a member of the OAU on Feb. 23, 1976.

Also in February 1976, following the Clark amendment, Congress barred military aid to movements opposed to the MPLA.

The South African government claimed in an official statement of Feb. 3, 1977, that it had during 1975 acted in an advisory capacity to the FNLA but that Holden Roberto had scorned South African advice and had engaged in unsuccessful attacks, with "disastrous" results for the FNLA. During 1975 the FNLA, which had a training camp in Zaïre, had already lost the support of President Mobutu of Zaïre (Holden Roberto's brother-in-law), and under an agreement concluded between the governments of Angola and Zaïre in Brazzaville on Feb. 28, 1976, each side undertook not to allow on its territory any military activity against the other; on May 5 Zaïre closed the FNLA headquarters in Kinshasa. Holden Roberto, however, did not leave Zaïre finally until Nov. 12, 1979 (after a non-aggression pact had been concluded between Angola, Zaïre and Zambia on Oct. 12, 1979).

Daniel Chipenda (a former leader of a dissident MPLA faction and later secretary-general of the FNLA) claimed on Nov. 11, 1977, that the FNLA's 18,000 men controlled large areas of northern Angola and also said that the FNLA was "ready to ask South Africa" for military help against "a common enemy" and that, if victory became imminent, the FNLA would join forces with UNITA. However, on March 7, 1980, Holden Roberto was reported to have sought political asylum in France.

In August 1980 FNLA commanders led by Paola Tuba established the Military Council of Angolan Resistance (Comira) as a breakaway faction opposed to the leadership of Holden Roberto. Since the early

1980s, however, there has been almost no significant military activity carried out in the name of Comira or the FNLA.

Luanda radio on June 15, 1987, broadcast an interview with Pedro Afamando, who called himself the "chief of operations and general commander" of the FNLA and said that he had returned to Angola of his own free will after listening to a speech by President dos Santos. According to government reports in late June 1987 more than 300 persons formerly belonging to the FNLA had surrendered to the authorities in Uíge province (northern Angola) and had been granted clemency.

National Union for the Total Independence of Angola (*União Nacional para a Independência Total de Angola,* UNITA)

Leadership. Dr Jonas Savimbi (pres.); Jeremiah Chitunda (vice-pres.)

This organization, established in 1966 and based mainly on the Ovimbundu and Chokwe tribes of central and southern Angola (constituting about 40 per cent of Angola's population), was one of the three original Angolan liberation movements (with the MPLA and the National Front for the Liberation of Angola, FNLA). UNITA's president (Dr Jonas Savimbi) had been "Foreign Minister" in the Revolutionary Angolan Government-in-Exile (GRAE) formed in 1962 by the FNLA, but he resigned this post on July 18, 1964, stating that the Portuguese had eliminated all significant groups of Angolan nationalist guerrillas and that there could be no successful offensive by "freedom fighters" until all political groups (then said to number about 17) had formed a common front. He subsequently established UNITA, at first with headquarters in Lusaka (Zambia) and later in Cairo. By 1970 his guerrillas were active in south-eastern Angola, and in 1973 he was said to be the only guerrilla leader actually inside Angola.

After the overthrow of the Caetano regime in Portugal in April 1974, UNITA signed a separate ceasefire agreement with Portugal on June 17 of that year. On Jan. 9, 1975, UNITA was recognized by the liberation committee of the Organization of African Unity (OAU) as one of Angola's three official liberation movements (together with the MPLA and the FNLA). UNITA also agreed to take part, with the two other movements, in independence negotiations with Portugal (which regarded the FNLA as right-wing, UNITA as centrist and the MPLA as "progressive" or left-wing), and the Angolan independence agreement was thereupon signed on Jan. 15, 1975, by the leaders of the three movements together with Portuguese ministers. On Jan. 31 of that year UNITA also took part in the formation of a transitional government of Angola by the three movements.

UNITA initially stood apart from the fighting which nevertheless continued between the MPLA and the FNLA, until in August 1975 it began to operate jointly with the FNLA in the southern half of Angola. During the weeks leading up to the achievement of Angola's independence (on Nov. 11, 1975) each of the three liberation movements intensified its efforts to consolidate its military position. In November 1975 the South African government admitted that its troops and military advisers were actively supporting the FNLA-UNITA forces in southern Angola. The South Africans officially stated on Feb. 3, 1977, that they had acted on an appeal by UNITA and the FNLA; that in October-December 1975 South African battle groups had captured numerous Angolan towns (including Sá da Bandeira, Moçamedes, Benguela, Lobito and Novo Redondo); and that the 2,000 South African troops involved could have captured the whole of Angola had not Dr Savimbi insisted that he was interested only in controlling the traditional UNITA area because he wanted "to reach a settlement with the MPLA to the advantage of the whole of Angola". South African troops were therefore withdrawn early in 1976.

At the achievement of independence UNITA had held six of the provincial capitals in southern Angola, and it held a separate independence celebration on Nov. 11, 1975, in Huambo (formerly Nova Lisboa, south of Luanda), where a "Joint National Council for the Revolution" was formed by UNITA and the FNLA. Early in 1976, however, UNITA's forces were driven southwards by the Cuban-supported MPLA. The UNITA headquarters were moved from Huambo to Bié (Silva Porto, 100 miles east of Huambo) and on Jan. 19 UNITA leaders appealed for military help from "any country willing to provide such assistance". By February 1976 UNITA had been forced to move its headquarters again, to Serpa Pinto (over 200 miles south of Bié); and later that month UNITA was forced to evacuate the last of its positions and to resort to guerrilla warfare in the bush.

Despite its military defeat UNITA issued on May 10, 1976, a manifesto drawn up at a congress at Cuanza (central Angola), calling for an intensification of the armed struggle "against the regime imposed by the Cubans and Russians", and stating there would be no dialogue with the MPLA as long as it was supported by foreign troops. It threatened to attack the Benguela railway (running from Lobito to Zaïre via the border town of Dilolo) and to sabotage all other forms of communication; it also proposed to reorganize its own military and political structure and create an armed people's militia.

Subsequent clashes between MPLA and UNITA forces in southern and eastern Angola led to widespread losses and chaotic conditions, especially in the south. In November 1976 Dr Savimbi claimed to have 6,000 men at his disposal and gave the number of Cubans in Angola as 15,000, plus 4,000 administrative personnel carrying out local defence duties. On Dec. 28, 1976, it was reported in Lusaka that UNITA had been prohibited from using Zambian territory as a base for military activities against the MPLA government and that its officials had been expelled from Zambia (which formally recognized the MPLA government on Jan. 6, 1977).

A UNITA congress held at Mavinga (south-eastern Angola) at the end of July 1982 issued a "Mavinga Declaration" stating inter alia (i) that UNITA was now willing to negotiate with the MPLA without any prior conditions (such as the withdrawal of Cuban troops from Angola) as a first step towards the formation of a government of national union—although the latter would not be possible until all foreign troops were withdrawn; (ii) that any ceasefire in Namibia would be valid only if it involved the departures of Cuban forces from Angola (without their replacement by other foreign troops); and (iii) that all foreigners should leave the country, of whose 16 provinces 10 had been declared zones of war.

In a South African government newspaper, Dr Savimbi described himself (on Aug. 27, 1982) as having ties with South Africa; he also pointed out that a takeover of Namibia by the South West Africa People's Organization (SWAPO) would expose UNITA to attack on two fronts, in the north by the MPLA and in the south by SWAPO. (In the light of the Angolan government's backing for SWAPO, South African forces carried out several major military incursions into southern Angola in the late 1970s and early 1980s.)

In the ensuing months UNITA claimed to have inflicted heavy losses on government forces. Col. Juan Bock, head of UNITA logistics, stated on Sept. 21, 1982, that during the previous 12 months UNITA had killed about 1,500 Cubans and 3,000 MPLA soldiers. Allegations by the Angolan news agency that UNITA had massacred about 150 villagers (as reported on Oct. 6) and another 300 and 150 respectively on two other occasions (reported on Oct. 11) were denied by UNITA on Oct. 19.

From 1982 onwards UNITA guerrilla attacks were increasingly directed against economic targets. In addition to succeeding in keeping the Benguela railway unworkable, UNITA forces abducted a considerable number of foreign specialists (with their families). Most of these were taken to UNITA base camps and were later released via South Africa, with the help of the International Committee of the Red Cross, but several of the abducted persons lost their lives.

By 1982 it had become clear that UNITA was receiving considerable material and moral support from abroad, in particular from South Africa and the United States.

The Angolan government claimed on Aug. 28, 1982, that since July 16 of that year two motorized South African brigades (totalling 5,500 men) had been operating alongside UNITA guerrillas.

In an unwritten Lusaka accord concluded on Feb. 16, 1984, between Angola and South Africa (with Dr Chester Crocker, US Assistant Secretary of State for African Affairs as mediator with a view to ending South African military intervention in Angola) South Africa undertook inter alia to cease logistical and other support for UNITA from Namibia. Talks between Dr Savimbi, "Pik" Botha (the South African Foreign Minister) and Dr Crocker thereupon took place in Cape Town on April 27, 1984.

In the United States the Senate voted on June 11, 1985, and the House of Representatives on July 10, 1985, to repeal the Clark Amendment of 1976 which had prohibited military and financial support for UNITA (after the US Central Intelligence Agency had been providing covert military aid to UNITA).

Gen. Magnus Malan, the South African Minister of Defence, admitted publicly on Sept. 20, 1985, that South Africa had provided material, humanitarian and moral help to UNITA for a number of years and added that such aid would not be suspended until all foreign forces had been withdrawn from Angola. He said that this support was intended to arrest foreign intervention in Angola by Cuban and other communist powers and to halt "Marxist infiltration and expansionism".

The Angolan government stated early in October 1985 that South African Air Force raids had taken place during a government offensive against UNITA (launched in July 1985 along the Benguela railway but halted some 24 km west of Mavinga). Dr Savimbi, however, denied any South African involvement but admitted that South African doctors were treating his wounded; he claimed that he had received "more sophisticated equipment from South Africa, Arab states and indirectly from Europe than in the previous 10 years".

Further South African incursions, ostensibly directed against SWAPO bases, occurred through 1986 and into 1987. The USA and the UK on June 18, 1986, vetoed a draft resolution in the UN Security Council condemning South Africa for any alleged attack on the southern port of Namibe launched on June 5, and for its continued occupation of parts of southern Angola.

During a 10-day visit to the United States Dr Savimbi met President Reagan on Jan. 30, 1986. It was afterwards reported that the United States would allocate $15,000,000 for covert aid to UNITA.

It appeared later that the government of Zaïre had also undertaken to provide aid for UNITA. At a meeting held on Oct. 19, 1986, at Kabasa Bay (northern Zambia) the Presidents of Angola, Mozambique and Zambia attempted to dissuade President Mobutu of Zaïre from providing such aid.

At a conference held at Jamba on June 1-2, 1985, under the auspices of a "Citizens for America" private group led by Lewis Lehrman (who claimed to have President Reagan's support) and attended by representatives of anti-Soviet guerrilla organizations from Afghanistan, Laos and Nicaragua as well as UNITA, it was decided to form a "Democratic International" with the aim of achieving "independence from Soviet colonialism".

By November 1986 reports suggested that UNITA has succeeded in opening a northern front in the guerrilla war, which had hitherto been confined largely to the east and south of the country. It was widely believed that UNITA forces operating in the northern Angolan provinces of Zaïre and Uíge obtained supplies including US military equipment via Zaïre. Government forces had, however, mounted an offensive in southern areas in mid-1986, making use of chemical weapons, according to UNITA, and in a further government offensive (apparently aimed at blocking the movement of UNITA men and material to the northern provinces) 274 UNITA troops were reported killed in Huambo and Bié provinces (central Angola) in June 1987. UNITA again claimed in June 1987 that combined Soviet, Cuban and government forces had again used chemical weapons. Government strategy had been to attempt to confine the UNITA forces to the south-east (i.e. where the UNITA "provisional capital", Jamba, is located). UNITA forces were estimated at about 65,000 regular and guerrilla troops.

The USA in mid-1987 estimated that there were 35,000 Cuban troops in Angola and nearly 1,000 Soviet advisers. It was reported that Cuban troops were increasingly deployed with Angolan troops in operational areas. *The New York Times* reported in February 1987 that 55,000 Angolans had fled into Zaïre to escape the civil war in the previous 18 months.

Dr Savimbi in a statement released on March 26, 1987, said that UNITA would permit the re-opening of the Benguela railway, which had largely been closed since 1976, in order to assist neighbouring African states and to promote reconciliation with the government in Luanda; the offer was made on condition that the line was not used for military purposes and that UNITA could inspect railway carriages (the latter condition being rejected by the Angolan government). On April 16 Angola, Mozambique, Zambia and Zaïre agreed to rehabilitate the railway. Government and UNITA representatives met in Washington on June 18, 1987, although there was no indication of any immediate move to a negotiated settlement of the conflict. The Angolan government had in the past repeatedly rejected appeals from UNITA for direct talks leading to the formation of a coalition government.

On June 11, 1987, it was reported that the US administration had decided to continue to provide military aid to UNITA, and that such aid would include the supply of Stinger anti-aircraft missiles and of anti-tank missiles. (US State Department officials had claimed that the Angolan government had recently received Soviet arms worth $1,000 million.)

Cabinda Separatists

Front for the Liberation of the Enclave of Cabinda
(*Frente de Libertação do Enclave de Cabinda,* FLEC)

Leadership. Francisco Xauter Lubota (commander of operations)

FLEC was set up in 1963 as a separate national liberation movement of the enclave of Cabinda (bordering on the Congo and Zaïre, but with no common border with Angola). In a statement broadcast by Brazzaville (Congo) radio on Jan. 12, 1975, FLEC rejected any attempt to intergrate Cabinda with Angola.

In 1975-77 FLEC was divided into four factions, two of which claimed to have set up independent governments in Cabinda. One of these two, that headed by Luis de Ganzaga Ranque Franque as "president" and F. X. Lubota as "prime minister", claimed in Brussels in June 1979 that it held 30 per cent of the territory of Cabinda and that some 150,000 Cabindans had fled to Zaïre, but admitted that it had to face 8,000 Cubans and 2,000 Angolan soldiers. FLEC forces continued armed activities in later years. In May 1981 six men were condemned to death in Angola for carrying out bomb attacks. FLEC itself claimed that its saboteurs had exploded bombs at Cabinda's only airport on Dec. 31, 1981, and had totally destroyed the state oil installation in the enclave. On May 13, 1982, three persons were sentenced to death for planting bombs and 18 others to imprisonment for up to four years for FLEC activities.

By early 1987 Cuban troops continued to guard Cabinda in support of Angolan government forces.

Antigua and Barbuda

Capital: St John's Pop. 80,000

Antigua and Barbuda, consisting of the Caribbean islands of Antigua, Barbuda and Redondo (the last-named being uninhabited) became an independent state within the Commonwealth on Nov. 1, 1981, with the British monarch as head of state, represented by a Governor-General. It has a bicameral Parliament consisting of (i) a House of Representatives (currently of 17 members) elected for five years by universal adult suffrage and (ii) a Senate to which 11 members are appointed on the advice of the Prime Minister, four on the advice of the Leader of the Opposition, one on the advice of the Barbuda Council and one at the Governor-General's discretion. The Prime Minister and the Cabinet are collectively responsible to Parliament.

In general elections held on April 17, 1984, the ruling Antigua Labour Party gained an overwhelming victory, winning all 16 Antiguan seats in the House of Representatives. The remaining seat representing Barbuda was retained without contest by an independent. The Progressive Labour Movement lost the three seats it gained in the 1980 elections. The United People's Movement (UPM) formed in 1982, gained none.

The election was called one year early after opposition allegations of corruption and maladministration which first appeared in the ("new left") Antigua Caribbean Liberation Movement's newspaper *Outlet,* but this movement did not contest the elections.

In April 1986 the United National Democratic Party was formed by the merger of the UPM and the National Democratic Party (formed in 1985). In March 1985, the Organization for National

Reconstruction (ONR), a Barbuda-based party advocating co-operation with the ALP government, won a majority on the Barbuda Council in local elections.

As regards political dissent, the new state had been faced in particular with agitation for a separatist state of Barbuda, but there have been no reports of disturbances in recent years.

Argentina

Capital: Buenos Aires

Pop. 30,600,000

Following seven years of rule by successive military juntas Argentina returned to civilian and democratic government in December 1983. The legislature consists of a Chamber of Deputies of 254 members elected directly for six-year terms, with half of the seats renewable every three years, and a 46-member Senate nominated by the legislatures of each of the 23 provinces for nine-year terms with one one-third of the seats renewable every three years. Executive power is vested in the President who, with the Vice-President, is elected for a six-year term by an electoral college of 600 directly elected members. The President governs with the assistance of an appointed Cabinet.

In the presidential election of Oct. 30, 1983, Dr Raúl Alfonsín of the Radical Civic Union (*Unión Cívica Radical*, UCR) won 51.8 per cent of the vote and 317 of the 600 seats in the electoral college.

In the Chamber of Deputies the UCR gained 129 seats, the Justicialist National (Peronist) Movement 111, the Intransigent Party three, the Union of the Democratic Centre two, the Christian Democratic Party one and regional parties eight.

An anti-terrorist law passed by the government on Sept. 23, 1983, was to "give the nation an adequate legal instrument for deterring, controlling and punishing subversive or terrorist activities and for protecting the rights guaranteed to the people by a democratic regime".

Human Rights Issues

The question of the violation of human rights during the military regimes from 1976 to 1983 centred on the fate of thousands of persons who had disappeared after being arrested in the so-called "dirty war" against alleged subversive and terrorist activities. According to a report submitted to the President on Sept. 20, 1984, by a National Commission on the Disappearance of Persons, at least 8,960 persons (who were named) had gone missing after the 1976 military coup. The report also described in detail the torture, abduction and murder of men, women and children on the basis of testimony from relatives and others, and also the way in which repression was systematically organized by the military authorities.

The new civilian government undertook to punish those guilty of violations of human rights and also passed a law against torture, which came into force on Oct. 26, 1984. The government's measures were, however, resisted by large sections of the armed forces, and in December 1986 the Senate and Chamber of Deputies passed a "Full Stop Bill" imposing deadlines for bringing new cases of alleged human rights violations to court. Sentences passed in such cases included life imprisonment imposed on Dec. 9, 1985, on Gen. Jorge Rafael Videla (a former President) and Adml. Eduardo Emilio Massera, and 25 and 14 years in prison for two former Buenos Aires police chiefs in December 1986.

The Supreme Court on June 23, 1987, upheld by four votes to one a "due-obedience" law signed on June 8, which exempted most military officers from prosecution for human rights violations, on the ground that they were acting under orders.

Mothers of the Plaza de Mayo (*Madres de la Plaza de Mayo*)

Leadership. Hebe de Bonafini (pres.); María del Rosario de Cerruti (sec.)

This grouping, founded in April 1977, consists principally of the mothers of persons who disappeared under the military juntas of 1976-83. The organization takes its name from the square in Buenos Aires in front of the presidential palace where every Thursday silent demonstrations are held to demand the return alive, or an official admission of the death, of those who have disappeared. In 1982 these vigils developed into more pronounced anti-government demonstrations.

Despite moves by the civilian government to address the human rights situation the Mothers have, since 1984, maintained that progress has been both too limited and too slow. Demanding the trial and conviction of all those guilty of human rights crimes they have deplored the government's "political solution" of limiting state prosecution of human rights violators to the military commanders and former junta members and, subsequently, of excluding cases in which "due obedience" was being exercised by subordinate officers. More recently, the Mothers have reportedly refused to collaborate with official investigation procedures.

Left-wing Movements

Authentic Peronist Party (*Partido Peronista Auténtico,* PPA)

Leadership. Óscar Bidegaín, Ricardo Obregón Cano

The PPA was formed on March 12, 1975, with Dr Bidegaín (a former Governor of Mendoza province) as its president, to "fight monopolies, promote worker participation in the planning and control of the national economy, and denounce the compromise [of the government] with imperialism to the detriment of the people". On April 4, 1975, some of the founders of the PPA, including its president, were expelled from the mainstream Peronist movement, the Justicialist Liberation Front (Frejuli), and on Sept. 21 the PPA created its own national council. On Dec. 24, 1975, the PPA was officially banned, together with its newspaper *El Auténtico*, after arms and ammunition had been found at two ranches belonging to Dr Bidegaín, who subsequently left the country.

In 1977 the PPA merged with the Peronist Montonero guerrilla Movement (*Movimiento Peronista Montonero*, MPM—see separate entry), creating a Supreme Council of Peronist Montoneros (*Consejo Supremo de Montoneros Peronistas*).

After the country had reverted to civilian rule Dr Bidegaín returned from exile on Dec. 20, 1983, in order to regain political and legal status for the PPA (while declaring that the MPM had been formally dissolved).

R. Obregón, who had also returned from abroad, was immediately arrested and was, on Aug. 27, 1985, sentenced to 10 years' imprisonment for illegal association.

October 17 Montoneros (*Montoneros 17 de Octubre*)

Leadership. Miguel Bossano (1.)

This group was formed in April 1980 as a dissident faction of the Peronist Montonero Movement (*Movimiento Peronista Montonero,* MPM—see separate entry) and was named after the date of the mass mobilization which started the Peronist movement in 1945. The group has described itself as "completely committed to insurrection".

Peronist Montonero Movement (*Movimiento Peronista Montonero,* MPM)

The discovery of a nationwide network of alleged pro-Castro "terrorists" was first announced in July 1964 by the counter-espionage service of the (anti-Peronist) government of President Arturo Illia. One of the "terrorists", however, alleged that many of the terrorist acts committed were part of a plan of the (Peronist) General Confederation of Labour (CGT) designed to create chaotic conditions in which ex-President J. D. Perón, then in exile in Spain, might be received as the only possible "pacifier".

As an openly left-wing Peronist urban guerrilla group, under the leadership of Mario Eduardo Firmenich, the MPM, named after irregular cavalry forces of the 19th century, began guerrilla activities in 1970. The first major action carried out by the Movement was the abduction of Lt.-Gen. Pedro Eugenio Aramburú (who had been President of Argentina in 1955-58) on May 29, 1970, and his "execution" on June 1 by a "revolutionary court" on the grounds (i) that he had ordered the execution, on June 9, 1956, of Peronist leaders, including Gen. Juan José Valle, who had unsuccessfully tried to restore Gen. Perón to power, and (ii) that he had been guilty of "271 crimes" during his presidency.

In a message found on June 11, 1970, the MPM called on the people of Argentina to resist the government and to support the return of Gen. Perón. The government, however, had reacted on June 2 by the introduction of the death penalty (which had not existed in Argentina since 1886) for persons who murdered or seriously injured victims of kidnapping or who used a service uniform while committing a crime (as two of the kidnappers had done) and of the provision of prison sentences for kidnapping.

After the election of the (Peronist) President H. J. Cámpora in April 1973, the MPM and the (Peronist) Revolutionary Armed Forces (*Fuerzas Armadas Revolucionarias*, FAR), led by Roberto Quieto, declared that they would respect the new government even though only a battle had been won and the "war" was "not finished". On June 28, 1973, it was reported that the *Montoneros* had decided to lay down their arms and to support President Cámpora. At a mass rally organized near Ezeiza international airport for the reception of Gen. Perón on his return from exile in Spain on June 20, 1973, armed clashes took place between *Montoneros* and members of the FAR on the one hand and traditionalist Peronists on the other, with at least 34 people being killed and 342 injured. Declaring their support for Gen. Perón, who was inaugurated as President on Oct. 12, the MPM and the FAR announced their amalgamation on Oct. 13.

The strength of support for the MPM among Peronists in 1974 became evident at a May Day rally addressed by President J. D. Perón, who strongly condemned left-wing extremists, calling them "stupid, treacherous and mercenary", with the result that some 30,000 MPM supporters, or about half his audience, left the rally in protest.

In the circumstances the period of peaceful coexistence with the government was shortlived. On Sept. 6, 1974, the MPM declared that, due to "aggression by police and para-police groups against the people's forces", it was returning underground to fight "a popular war" against the government, and that they would use arson, assassination, sabotage and bombings. This decision was not approved by other left-wing Peronists, however, and on Sept. 10 over 60 orthodox Peronist organizations published a declaration stating that the MPM had been unmasked as "a band of delinquents . . . damaging the process of reconstruction and liberation which Gen. Perón had left as an essential mandate".

Among the first major actions of the MPM after its decision to resume warfare was the kidnapping of Jorge and Juan Born (two brothers) of the firm Bunge y Born (one of Argentina's largest grain dealers) on Sept. 19, 1974. The brothers were released on June 20, 1975, on payment of US$60,000,000 in ransom and after distribution of $1,000,000 worth of food and clothing to the poor "as a punishment for shortages inflicted on the people" by the company, and also the publication of a lengthy MPM statement in two international newspapers, in which the guerrillas undertook to continue "without truce the resistance to the present government, laying bare its antipopular, repressive and pro-imperialist essence . . . until we achieve its annihilation".

Later in 1975 the MPM launched the largest guerrilla operations ever undertaken in Argentina (i) by blowing up a Navy missile-launching frigate near La Plata in August that year; (ii) by planting a bomb in the path of an Air Force transport aircraft carrying 114 soldiers (for anti-guerrilla operations) at Tucumán on Aug. 25, causing four deaths and injury to 25 people; and (iii) by seizing the airport at Formosa (near the border with Paraguay) on Oct. 5, and hijacking an airliner which took about 20 guerrillas to Rafaele (Santa Fé province) from where they escaped by road. At least 30 soldiers and guerrillas were killed in the last-named operation, and about 30 of the guerrillas were captured by the armed forces on Oct. 7, 1975.

Targets of *Montoneros'* other actions in 1975-76 included kidnappings and assassinations of foreign business executives in Argentina and an attack on a police academy in La Plata on Feb. 1, 1976, in which numerous MPM guerrillas lost their lives. Later in 1976 the MPM was responsible for a number of other attacks on military targets or police premises. On Sept. 29, 1976, five MPM leaders were killed in Buenos Aires and M. E. Firmenich narrowly escaped arrest. Norma Arrostito, a founder-member of the Movement involved in the kidnapping of ex-President Aramburú in May 1970, was killed by security forces on Dec. 3, 1976; in reprisal MPM guerrillas killed 14 people and injured 20 by exploding a bomb in a Defence Ministry lecture hall on Dec. 15.

On April 20, 1977, it was officially confirmed that a group of Argentinian financiers headed by David Graiver had been financing the MPM by investing about $17,000,000 and securing interest for it of about $130,000 a month. D. Graiver was alleged to have been killed in an aircrash in Mexico in August 1976 (although there were rumours to the contrary). On Dec. 9, 1977, a military court imposed prison sentences of 15 years each on David Graiver's father, brother and widow, and of five years on his mother, for having "knowingly aligned themselves with the ranks of the self-proclaimed *Montoneros*, whom the nation has decided to annihilate in order to save its traditions and way of life based on freedom and human diginity".

Also in April 1977 Jacobo Timerman, editor of the daily *La Opinión*, was detained in Buenos Aires on suspicion of being connected with MPM guerrillas; in December 1977 he was deprived of his political rights and his property was confiscated; on April 17, 1978, he was placed under house arrest, from which he was released on Sept. 25, 1979, when he was deprived of his Argentine nationality and expelled from the country (whereupon he joined his family in Israel). The Supreme Court had ruled twice—in July 1978 and again on Sept. 20, 1979—that he should be freed as there was no basis for his continued house arrest.

M. E. Firmenich announced in Rome on April 20, 1977, that the MPM and the Authentic Peronist Party (*Partido Auténtico Peronista* PPA—see separate entry) had merged and established a Supreme Council of the Peronist *Montoneros* (*Consejo Supremo de Montoneros Peronistas*). He also announced an eight-point pacification and liberation programme which, he said, was "not a surrender or a truce but an appeal to the common sense of all national forces" and did not mean the abandonment of the armed struggle. The programme called inter alia for a new economic policy favouring national and popular interest, the restoration of constitutional rights and guarantees, the rehabilitation of all political parties, the liberation of all political prisoners and the closure of "concentration camps", the institution of proceedings against those responsible for torture, kidnappings and murder, the rehabilitation of trade unions and the holding of general elections.

The MPM suffered heavy losses in the ensuing years and by 1980 it was thought to have been reduced to some 350 active members. It was virtually inactive during 1980-82 and in early 1983 military sources asserted that it had been completely defeated. However, in May of that year security forces in Córdoba were reported to have found a cache of grenades, revolvers and terrorist manuals and to have killed a leading member of the movement, Raúl Clemente Yaguer, during a gun battle. According to Arab sources at the time, a small number of *Montonero* guerrillas were being trained in guerrilla warfare camps of the Palestine Liberation Organization in Syria and Lebanon.

On Oct. 19, 1983, a Montonero leader, Carlos Dante Gullo, was among 242 detainees whose release had been authorized following the implementation of a Law of National Pacification. He had been imprisoned for eight years and had frequently been tortured.

The MPM's then secretary-general, Mario Eduardo Firmenich, fled to Brazil in 1983, and after being arrested there, he was extradited to Argentina on Oct. 21, 1984, and sentenced to life imprisonment on May 19, 1987—the Radical administration reportedly being keen to sentence him as a demonstration of fairness to the military. From prison Firmenich continued to influence the small Peronist Revolutionary Movement (*Movimiento Revolucionario Peronista*), a breakaway splinter group which claimed to represent authentic Peronism and whose members have been expelled from the mainstream Peronist movement.

Revolutionary Communist Party (*Partido Comunista Revolucionario*, PCR)

This offshoot of the Communist Party of Argentina (*Partido Comunista de Argentina*, PCA—legalized in 1983) adopted a pro-Chinese line on its formation in

1968 and has experienced particular opposition from right-wing paramilitary movements such as the Argentine Anti-communist Alliance (*Alianza Anticomunista Argentina*, AAA—see separate entry).

Revolutionary Workers' Party—People's Revolutionary Army (*Partido Revolucionario de Trabajadores—Ejército Revolucionario del Pueblo,* PRT-ERP)

Leadership. Luis Mattini (1.)

The ERP was formed in July 1970 as the armed wing of the (nominally Trotskyist) Workers' Revolutionary Party (*Partido Revolucionario de los Trabajadores*, PRT). It had affiliations with the *Tupamaro* guerrillas in Uruguay. Its first major operation was the abduction, on March 21, 1972, of Dr Oberdán Sallustro, director-general of the Fiat Concord company, and his assassination on April 10 after he had, according to an ERP statement, been tried by a "people's court". His kidnappers had put forward demands, inter alia, for gift parcels of food, clothing and classroom equipment worth US$1,000,000 to be distributed among children in nearly 800 schools, the release of prisoners, the reinstatement of dismissed workers and payment of an indemnity to the ERP. The government, however, ordered Fiat not to take any action which could be construed as assisting the guerrillas.

Also on April 10, 1972, the ERP, in co-operation with the (Peronist) Revolutionary Armed Forces (*Fuerzas Armadas Revolucionarias*, FAR—see separate entry for Peronist Montonero Movement, MPM), killed Gen. Juan Carlos Sánchez, commander of the Second Army in Rosario. The general had previously claimed to have "smashed" 85 per cent of the urban guerrillas in Rosario.

On Aug. 15, 1972, a group of 29 detained members of the ERP, the FAR and the MPM overpowered their guards at Rawson (Patagonia), killing one of them. The ex-detainees thereupon occupied the nearby naval air base at Trelew, where 10 of them (including Roberto Mario Santucho, the founder of the ERP) forced the crew of an airliner to take them to Chile, where they were accepted as "political refugees" on Aug. 24 but from where they left for Cuba on Aug. 25. Of the other 19 ex-detainees, who had meanwhile surrendered to Argentinian troops, 16 were killed by security forces on Aug. 22 (allegedly while trying to escape).

The ERP subsequently abducted and/or killed numerous businessmen as well as officers of the armed forces and newspaper publishers, and was also responsible for the hijacking of an Argentinian airliner on July 4, 1973, and its diversion to Havana (Cuba), from where the aircraft with its passengers and crew was returned to Argentina on July 6 after the hijackers' extradition had been unsuccessfully demanded by Argentina.

Following the 1973 election victories of the (Peronist) Justicialist Liberation Front (*Frejuli*)—leading to the election of Dr Hector José Cámpora as President on April 26—the ERP stated on May 27, 1973, that it would not attack the government unless the latter attacked the people or repressed the guerrillas, but that it would pursue "the hostilities against foreign and national enterprises and against the counter-revolutionary armed forces". It demanded the nationalization of all foreign enterprises and land reform and on May 30 it declared that Dr Cámpora's government could not, and would not, "by its methods and its composition, effectively pursue the revolutionary struggle".

After the assassination on Sept. 25, 1973, of José Ignaci Rucci, secretary-general of the (Peronist) General Confederation of Labour (CGT), the ERP was on the same day declared unlawful. The ERP claimed on Sept. 27 that it was in no way responsible for J. I. Rucci's death and the ban did not diminish its violent activities, which continued with further kidnappings of foreign business executives and attacks on military targets. The ERP was in particular held responsible for the murder of Dr Arturo Mor Roig, a former Minister of the Interior, on July 15, 1974.

During 1974 the ERP was particularly active in Catamarca and Tucumán provinces (north-western Argentina), where late in September it accused the armed forces of having summarily executed 16 guerrillas who had surrendered; the ERP thereupon decided to "execute" a similar number of members of the armed forces in retaliation, and in fact two officers (one of them being the commander of a division of the Third Army) were killed on Sept. 25 and another on Oct. 7 in Buenos Aires. On the other hand the police discovered, on Sept. 7, 1974, the printing press of the ERP near Buenos Aires, where the ERP's organ, *Estrella Roja* (Red Star), had been produced.

On Oct. 8, 1974, the ERP notified the government that it was "disposed to an armistice" on condition that all political prisoners were freed, repressive legislation was repealed and the decree outlawing the ERP was revoked. The government, however, ignored this initiative, and in the following years it became obvious that the security forces had gained the upper hand over the ERP.

In an ERP attack on police headquarters in Córdoba on Aug. 20, 1975, seven people were killed and at least 20 injured. However, a major co-ordinated ERP attack on military targets in the Buenos Aires area on Dec. 23-24, 1975, was decisively defeated by the armed forces, using heavy artillery and helicopter gunships, with over 160 people being killed. A further ERP attack on an army communications base at La Plata was similarly repulsed on Dec. 27, 1975.

On July 19, 1976, the ERP leader, Roberto Mario Santucho, and several other members of the group were killed near Buenos Aires. By 1977 the ERP's activities in rural Tucumán were repressed, but arrests and trials of alleged ERP supporters continued in later years. The Paraguayan police alleged that ERP members were involved in the assassination in Asunción on Sept. 17, 1980, of the exiled Nicaraguan dictator, Anastasio Somoza Debayle.

Although originally Trotskyist, the PRT-ERP broke off all relations with the Fourth (Trotskyist) International in 1973, as the latter had not approved the ERP's guerrilla strategy. In February 1974 the ERP set up a Revolutionary Co-ordinating Board (*Junta Coordinadora Revolucionaria*, JCR), linking it with the Bolivian National Liberation Army (*Ejército de Liberación Nacional*, ELN), the Chilean Movement of the Revolutionary Left (*Movimiento de Izquierda Revolucionaria*, MIR—see separate entry) and the Uruguayan National Liberation Movement (*Movimiento de Liberación Nacional*).

The ERP was not in evidence for several years. However, a powerful explosive device was defused on May 19, 1987, at the home of the intelligence chief of the Second Army Corps in Rosario; a slogan painted on a wall opposite his house proclaimed: "Death to those guilty of genocide! People's Revolutionary Army".

Right-wing Organizations

Argentine Nationalist Commando (*Commando Nacionalista Argentino*)

The existence of this right-wing paramilitary group formed in memory of Gen. Jorge Cáceres Monié, one of the first military officers killed by leftist guerrillas in the years before the 1976 coup, was reported in October 1984. The tactics of the commando group were described as similar to those used by the Argentinian Anti-Communist Alliance (see separate entry).

The group was reported to have vowed to kill Ernesto Sábato, head of the National Commission on the Disappearance of Persons (CONADEP), as well as Oscar Alende, president of the socialist Intransigent Party (*Partido Intransigente*, a faction of the UCR which, in 1980, refused to take part in talks with the military regime on the normalization of political activities), Vicente Leónidas Saadi, then the president of the Justicialist Party (*Partido Justicialista*) and Mario Firmenich, the former leader of the Peronist Montonero Movement (see separate entry).

Argentinian Anti-Communist Alliance (*Alianza Anticomunista Argentina*, AAA)

Leadership. Aníbal Gordon (l.)

Established in 1973, this organization aimed to eliminate known or suspected communists and other politicians whom it regarded as leftists. On Nov. 21, 1973, a senator of the (opposition) *Unión Cívica Radical* (UCR) was injured by a car bomb said to have been placed by AAA members. On July 31, 1974, an extreme left-wing deputy and co-editor of the Peronist journal *Militancia* was assassinated by AAA members; at his funeral on Aug. 2 the police arrested some 350 left-wing demonstrators.

Following the death of President Juan Perón on July 1, 1974, the AAA began, in September 1974, to publish lists of persons whom it intended to kill, with the result that a number of those listed, notably left-wing academics, left the country. Further murders attributed to the AAA occurred nevertheless, the victims being known left-wingers prominent in public life.

On June 1, 1975, the AAA announced that in response to an appeal by the Minister of the Interior it would observe a 90-day truce. It had earlier been alleged by some Peronists that the "intellectual author and instigator" of the AAA had been José López Rega, who had for many years been a close adviser to Gen. Perón and his wife, Isabel, and who left Argentina in July 1975. (During Isabel Perón's government there were 535 victims of paramilitary action, including workers, students, lawyers, doctors and teachers.) J. López Rega had also incurred growing hostility within the armed forces. On April 2, 1975, opposition leaders in the Chamber of Deputies had asked (i) why security forces had neglected to investigate murders by right-wing extremists and (ii) why no official investigation had been carried out into the AAA.

Later in 1975 the AAA resumed its killings, and in November of that year it claimed to have killed some 30 left-wing personalities during the previous three months. Early in February 1976, the AAA issued a warning of the imminent assassination of leaders of the (pro-Soviet) Communist Party, the (Maoist) Revolutionary Communist Party, the Authentic Peronist Party, Marxist-Leninist guerrillas and the Radical Revolutionary Youth (a left-wing branch of the UCR) and also of "progressive" priests.

The introduction of military rule in March 1976 brought about a reduction in AAA activities as their role was taken over by semi-autonomous "task forces" operated by different branches of the armed forces under the overall direction of the ruling junta. However, the organization resumed its activities following the return to civilian rule in 1983. On Aug. 24, 1983, Guillermo Patricio Kelly, a prominent independent politician and human rights activist, was kidnapped in Buenos Aires. Although he was set free on the following day, the AAA leader, Aníbal Gordon, was at the end of 1986 sentenced to 16 years in prison, and his son Marcelo to eight years, for this abduction.

Australia

Capital: Canberra (ACT) Pop. 15,000,000

The Commonwealth of Australia (a member of the Commonwealth) is a parliamentary democracy with the British monarch as head of state represented by a Governor-General. It comprises six states as well as the Australian Capital Territory (ACT) and the Northern Territory. Legislative power is vested in a (federal) Parliament consisting of the British monarch, a 76-member Senate whose members serve six-year terms and a 148-member House of Representatives elected for three years by universal adult suffrage. There is a Cabinet headed by a Prime Minister, responsible to Parliament. Five of the constituent states have their own bicameral legislatures, while Queensland and the Northern Territory each have a Legislative Assembly.

As a result of elections held on Dec. 1, 1984, seats in the federal House of Representatives were distributed as follows: Australian Labor Party 82, Liberal Party 45, National Party 21. Among Australia's other political parties, the Australian Democratic Party holds seven seats in the Senate and the Nuclear Disarmament Party one. Federally-unrepresented parties include the Australia Party, the Australian Democratic Labor Party, the Communist Party of Australia, the Communist Party of Australia (Marxist-Leninist), the Independent Labor Party, the Progress Party, the Nuclear-Free Australia Party, the Socialist Party of Australia, the Socialist Workers' Party and the North Queensland Party.

Political violence in Australia has been largely confined to acts by foreigners, in particular by Croation and Armenian nationalists, in pursuit of their specific political objectives; there are also some political organizations of the extreme right.

Extreme Right-wing Groups

Australian League of Rights

This group has tried to infiltrate so-called "opinion-moulders" into various Australian institutions, including the Liberal Party.

Australian National Front

This front has been described as a Nazi organization and is a counter-part to the National Front in Great Britain.

Austria

Capital: Vienna Pop. 7,560,000

Under the Austrian State Treaty of May 15, 1955, the Republic of Austria is a "sovereign, independent and democratic state" with a government "based on elections by secret ballot" and by "free, equal and universal suffrage". There is a bicameral Parliament consisting of a 183-member *Nationalrat* (Lower House) and a 58-member *Bundesrat* (Upper House), the latter being elected by the legislatures of the country's nine federal provinces (*Länder*).

As a result of elections held on Nov. 23, 1986, seats in the *Nationalrat* were distributed as follows: Austrian Socialist Party 80, Austrian People's Party 77, Austrian Freedom Party 18, Green Alternative 8.

Among a number of smaller parties without parliamentary representation is the National Democratic Party, whose leader has led a Munich-based South Tirol liberation group; members of this group have been convicted in Italy of terrorist activities, and its followers were still engaged in acts of violence in the Alto Adige-Trentino region of Italy during 1982.

Neo-Nazi Groups

Neo-Nazi groups in Austria, estimated to have between 15,000 and 20,000 sympathizers, include the following:

(i) *Nationale Front*, the founding meeting of which was banned in November 1984 on the grounds that the group's founding document stated that Hitler had been right to annex Austria and Czechoslovakia in 1938 and 1939 and that the 1955 Austrian State Treaty should be revoked;

(ii) *Neue Aktion Rechte*, the youth wing of the NDP, and said to be the most militant of the neo-Nazi groups; and

(iii) the "Stop the Foreigners" group, which had obtained 0.3 per cent of the vote in the 1983 general elections.

At the trial of alleged neo-Nazis Ekkehard Weil (a West German previously sentenced in West Germany in 1970 and pardoned in 1975) was on April 12, 1984, found guilty of bomb attacks on property owned by

Jews in Vienna in 1981-82 and was sentenced to five years in prison, while three others involved were given prison sentences from three months to three years, and another four were put on probation. (The leader of the NDP denounced E. Weil as an East European spy who had infiltrated the Austrian extreme right in order to discredit it.)

Bahamas

Capital: Nassau (on New Providence Island) Pop. 231,000

The Commonwealth of the Bahamas, a member of the Commonwealth, with the British monarch as head of state represented by a Governor-General, has a bicameral Parliament consisting of (i) a 49-member House of Assembly elected for five years by universal adult suffrage and (ii) a 16-member Senate to which nine members are appointed on the advice of the Prime Minister, four on that of the Leader of the Opposition and three at the Governor-General's discretion. The Prime Minister and his Cabinet are collectively responsible to Parliament.

In elections to the House of Assembly held on June 19, 1987, the ruling Progressive Liberal Party gained 31 seats, the Free National Movement 15, and independents 2 (with one seat remaining undecided).

There have been no reports of activities by extra-parliamentary opposition groups.

Bahrain

Capital: Manama Pop. 420,000

The Amirate of Bahrain, which has no Parliament and no political parties, is ruled by the Al-Khalifah dynasty, who are Sunni Moslems, whereas the majority of the population are Shi'ite Moslems.

Following the establishment of the (Shi'ite) Islamic Republic of Iran in 1979, Shi'ites in Bahrain were called upon to demonstrate against their government by Shi'ites in Iran, some of whom claimed that Iran held sovereignty over Bahrain. The authorities of Bahrain thereupon deported a number of leading Shi'ites who supported the Islamic revolution in Iran, the influence of which is regarded by the government as the principal current threat to Bahrain's internal security.

There have been several reports of attempted coups in Bahrain in recent years. In May 1985 Tehran Radio broadcast reports which were strongly denied by Bahrain that Bahraini security services had foiled a coup mounted by an underground organization under the direction of Iraqi diplomats.

In June 1985 eight Arab men (six Bahrainis, one Saudi Arabian and one Kuwaiti) said to have been planning the overthrow of the government were arrested by British police. Two of the eight were deported and the others were asked to leave.

According to the Arab Human Rights Organization which issued a report in August 1986 Bahrain has 3,000 political detainees.

Committee for the Defence of Human Rights in Bahrain

This committee reported that 22 Bahrainis, including two teachers and four students, were arrested for political reasons during July and August 1986.

Islamic Front for the Liberation of Bahrain (IFLB)
(*Al-Jabihah al-Islamiyah Litahrir al-Bahrain*)

In a statement issued in Beirut and broadcast from Tehran on Jan. 15, 1980, the Tehran-based IFLB affirmed the independence of Bahrain as an Islamic state but denounced the Al-Khalifah government for having had close ties with the former regime of the Shah and for having adopted an antagonistic position towards the Islamic revolution in Iran and its leader. The statement listed a number of measures alleged to have been taken by the Bahraini authorities against supporters of the Islamic revolution and Iranian interests; it accused these authorities of allowing the United States to use Bahrain's civil airport as a base for US military aircraft; and it called "on all Moslems to support the Moslem Bahraini masses in their struggle against the US and Zionist oppressors".

Between Dec. 13 and 19, 1981, the Bahraini authorities announced that 60 members of the IFLB had been arrested (comprising Bahraini citizens and other Gulf nationals) who had come to Bahrain after receiving military training in Iran and in order to carry out sabotage and create anarchy. On Dec. 30 it was reported that this sabotage plan had been masterminded by Hojatoleslam Hadi al-Mudarasi, who had earlier been deported from Bahrain and had thereafter been appointed director of a "Gulf affairs section" of the Iranian government. The trial of 73 people charged with involvement in the plot (60 Bahrainis, 11 Saudi Arabians, one Kuwaiti and one Omani) subsequently opened on March 13, 1982, and concluded on May 23 with the conviction of all the defendants, three of whom were sentenced to life imprisonment and the remainder to terms of between seven and 15 years.

There have been no recent reports of activities carried out by members of a group of this name.

National Liberation Front of Bahrain

This organization is recognized by the Soviet bloc and is based in Damascus, Syria. It is not known to have any significant strength.

Bangladesh

Capital: Dhaka (formerly Dacca) Pop. 98,657,000

The People's Republic of Bangladesh, an independent state within the Commonwealth which was from March 1982 until November 1986 placed under martial law, is a democratic republic with a president elected by universal suffrage for five years. It has a Council of Ministers appointed from a 330-member Parliament (*Jatiya Sangsad*), 300 members of which are directly elected by universal suffrage and 30 of which are women appointed by other members.

President Hossain Mohammed Ershad, who assumed power as Army Chief of Staff in March 1982, lifted martial law on Nov. 10, 1986, and restored the Constitution following the holding of parliamentary and presidential elections in 1986. Fundamental rights suspended under martial law were officially restored and a bill was passed which ratified all actions, reforms and laws passed by the government since 1982. At the same time, opposition parties (which had been banned from political activities up until Jan. 1, 1986) were warned to control political agitation.

The postponed parliamentary elections held on May 7, 1986, after demonstrations and demands for a boycott, proceeded amidst allegations of violence and intimidation of voters, with polling suspended in 284 centres and official reports of 12 people killed. Three British observers brought in by the People's Commission for Free Elections reported that the principal offenders were supporters of the *Jatiya* Party (formed at the beginning of 1986 and comprising Cabinet members); that returning officers were physically intimidated, and that polling booths closed early. The elections were boycotted by the opposition Bangladesh National Party (BNP), which demanded the lifting of martial law prior to elections.

Official results showed the seats in the *Jatiya Sangsad* to be divided as follows: Jatiya Party 183 (including the 30 women appointed), Awami League 76, *Jamaati-i-Islami* (the Moslem fundamentalist group) 10, Bangladesh Communist Party five, National Awami Party (*Bhashani*) five, Bangladesh Moslem League four, *Jatiya Samajtantrik Dal-Rob* four, *Jatiya Samajtantrik Dal* (*Shahjahan Siraj*) three, other parties eight, independents 32. The inaugural session of parliament was boycotted by 119 opposition members. As a result of by-elections held on Aug. 26, 1986, and party realignments since May 1986, the *Jatiya* Party eventually held 208 seats.

Allegations of pre-marked ballots and the forging of voting registers followed the presidential elections (also postponed) held on Oct. 15, 1986, in which official results gave President Ershad 83.6 per cent of the votes. (President Ershad had resigned as Chief of Army Staff to facilitate his nomination as *Jatiya*'s presidential candidate.) The elections were boycotted by the BNP and the Awami League, who claimed that only three per cent of those eligible voted. Prior to the elections, full martial law (which had been in part rescinded) was reinstated, anti-election rallies were banned, 2,000 political agitators were arrested, and the leaders of the BNP (Begum Zia) and of the Awami League (Sheikh Hasina) were placed under house arrest until after the elections.

Widespread agitation demanding President Ershad's resignation has continued since the lifting of martial law. In March 1987 seven people were killed in university riots, and in July 1987 a 32-hour general strike was called against the passage of a bill giving the military the right to sit in civilian administration.

Chittagong Autonomists (*Shanti Bahini*)

Autonomist aspirations had already been expressed at the time of the East Pakistan government (overthrown in 1971) by (mainly Buddhist, Christian or Hindu) tribal people of the Chittagong Hill Tracts. In this area the population had traditionally lived on a "slash and burn" basis (cultivating burnt forest land until it is exhausted, which forces the inhabitants to move elsewhere). Since 1947 the government had encouraged the tribal people to take up settled farming and had moved in (mainly Moslem) Bengalis, and this process was speeded up in 1978-79 with the result that the proportion of Bengalis in the area rose from 11.6 per cent in 1974 to 39 per cent in 1981.

Guerrilla warfare by Chittagong Hill Tracts tribes began in 1975 under the leadership of Manabendra Larma (a former independent member of the *Jatiya Sangsad*) after appeals for regional autonomy had met with no response from the government.

Since 1975, there have been widespread atrocities committed by guerrillas on Bengali settlers, thousands of arrests, and counter-claims of reprisal "massacres" carried out by the Bangladesh army on tribal people. In December 1980 the government adopted a Disturbed Areas Bill (with implied reference to the Chittagong Hill Tracts situation), giving police officers and army NCOs unlimited authority to fire upon a person or to make arrests without a warrant. Government figures in December 1986 put the number of people killed in tribal warfare since 1975 at 1,000.

In October 1983 the government offered a general amnesty, a cash reward, free rations and a plot of land to all guerrillas who surrendered by Feb. 25, 1984 (extended to April 26), but only 200-300 of an estimated 3,000 active members were reported to have given themselves up.

On April 30, 1985, 233 rebels were reported to have surrendered on the basis of an agreement signed by the zone martial law administrator, tribal leaders and *Shanti Bahini* leaders: those who surrendered said that they renounced violence and agreed with government plans for development of the hill region.

Despite a Dhaka Radio claim on Feb. 19, 1985, that the *Shanti Bahini* group was "practically non-existent", fighting continued through 1985, and in May 1986 some 20,000 troops were placed on alert in south-east Bangladesh after an incident in which 15 people died in raids on Bangladesh army camps and four Bengali Moslem villages, followed by claims of army reprisals in which 53 (Bhuddist) Chakma tribesmen were killed. In a 1986 "Christmas Day massacre", 18 mainly ethnic Bengali Moslems were killed.

In July 1986 representatives of the Chakma tribe reported to a United Nations human rights subcommission working group that Buddhist tribespeople faced virtual genocide unless they converted to Islam. The (London-based) Anti-Slavery Society reported to the working group 325 attacks on individual tribespeople by security forces.

A mass exodus of refugees to the neighbouring Indian states of Tripura and Mizoram numbered 24,000 between April 1986 and January 1987 alone. Reports of alleged army brutality against fleeing refugees included one of up to 200 people shot and killed after being lured into a narrow defile.

Barbados

Capital: Bridgetown Pop. 253,000

Barbados, a member of the Commonwealth with the British monarch as head of state being represented by a Governor-General, has a 27-member House of Assembly elected for five years by universal adult suffrage and a 21-member Senate appointed by the Governor-General (12 senators on the advice of the Prime Minister, two on that of the Leader of the Opposition and seven at the Governor-General's discretion). The Prime Minister and his Cabinet are collectively responsible to Parliament.

In general elections held on May 28, 1986, the Democratic Labour Party won 24 seats in the House of Assembly, defeating the ruling Barbados Labour Party which took the remaining three. Violent clashes were reported between supporters of the rival parties.

There have been no signs of internal political opposition outside existing legal parties or pressure groups such as the People's Pressure Movement, formed in 1979, or the Workers' Party of Barbados, a small left-wing organization formed in 1985.

Belgium

Capital: Brussels Pop. 9,910,000

The Kingdom of Belgium is a constitutional monarchy with a multi-party parliamentary democracy. It has a bicameral Parliament consisting of (i) a 212-member Chamber of Representatives elected for a four-year term by a system of proportional representation and (ii) a 181-member senate (to which 106 senators are elected directly).

As a result of elections held on Oct. 13, 1985, seats in the Chamber was distributed as follows: Christian People's Party (Flemish) 49, Socialist Party (Walloon) 35, Socialist Party (Flemish) 32, Liberal Reformist Party (Walloon) 24, Party for Freedom and Progress (Flemish Liberal) 22, Christian Social Party (Walloon) 20, People's Union (*Volksunie*) 16, Ecologist Party (Ecolo) 5, *Anders gaan leven* (Agalev, ecologist) 4, *Front démocratique des francophones* 3, *Vlaamse Blok* 1, *Respect voor Arbeid en Democratie-Union démocratique pour le respect du travail* (RDT/DRT) 1. Parties which contested the elections without gaining any seats were the Communist Party of Belgium, the Labour Party of Belgium, the Socialist Workers' Party, the *Solidarité et participation* (a group of the Walloon Christian labour movement) and the Walloon Party.

Devolution plans providing for Belgium to have, in addition to its central government, separate governments for Brussels, Flanders and Wallonia have been debated for some years but are not yet fully implemented. There have been violent incidents between French- and Flemish-speaking Belgians from time to time, arising out of disputes over the boundaries of the respective language areas. Moreover, several extreme left-wing groups claimed responsibility for acts of violence committed in Belgium between 1979 and 1987.

Extreme Right-wing Groups

Flemish Militant Order (*Vlaamse Militanten Orde*, VMO)

The VMO, formed in 1950, has been involved in militant action against French-speaking groups in various disputes over linguistic areas, in particular in the district of Voeren (Fourons), which was in 1962 transferred from the (Walloon) province of Liège to the (Flemish) province of Limburg. This transfer was opposed by militant Walloon groups, including a "Back to Liège" movement led by J. Happart. Following armed confrontations in the district in August and October 1979, a 1934 law banning the maintenance of uniformed private armies was invoked against the VMO.

An appeal court in Ghent confirmed on May 26, 1983, that the VMO was illegal under the 1934 law. The court also confirmed 33 prison sentences passed on May 4, 1981, when a total of 105 persons had been given prison terms ranging from five days to one year. The sentences confirmed included a one-year prison term imposed upon the group's leader, Bert Erikson, who was later reported to have announced that he would disband the VMO. (The government had, however, confirmed on June 5, 1981, that Voeren would remain part of Flemish territory.)

The VMO was a more extreme nationalist organization than the two Flemish nationalist political parties—the People's Union (*Volksunie*) and the more radical Flemish Bloc (*Vlaamse Blok*).

Were Di

This Flemish neo-Nazi group has called for an amnesty for wartime collaborators with the Nazis.

Westland New Post (WNP)

Leadership. Paul Latinus ("marshal")

Two members of this clandestine neo-Nazi group, Marcel Barbier and Eric Lammers, went on trial on murder charges in Belgium in May 1987.

Youth Front (*Front de la jeunesse*)

This group was declared illegal by a Brussels court on May 4, 1981, when suspended sentences and fines were imposed on 14 defendants for setting fire to the offices of an organization for aid to Vietnamese refugees in Belgium.

Extreme Left-wing Groups

Direct Action (*Action directe*)

This Belgian offshoot of the French Direct Action movement (see entry under France) claimed responsibility for a bomb explosion at a synagogue in Antwerp on Oct. 20, 1981, causing the death of two persons and injury to 98 others. The Belgian authorities, however, attributed this action to a Palestinian splinter group (the Palestine Liberation Organization having condemned it).

Fighting Communist Cells (*Cellules combattantes communistes*, CCC)

The CCC first emerged in October 1984 with a spate of bomb attacks directed against the Brussels offices of US and West German multinational concerns supplying NATO and against centre-right party offices in Brussels and Ghent. These attacks were followed by the bombing of two military communications masts near Liège on Nov. 26, 1984, and the explosion of six bombs damaging NATO's fuel pipeline on Dec. 11, and of a car bomb near a NATO building in Brussels. After announcing that its "armed struggle against the imperialist bourgeoisie" was to be directed not against the people but against the enemies of the people, the CCC declared after Jan. 15 that in a new campaign human life would not be respected. Thereafter an explosion in Brussels on May 1, 1985, killed two firemen and injured 13 other people.

There followed further numerous bomb attacks by the CCC from October 1985 onwards, mainly on banks, NATO installations and premises of firms supplying NATO. In a letter sent to the media in November 1985, the CCC described its aim as the destruction of the Belgian state and the establishment of a Marxist-Leninist dictatorship of the proletariat.

On Dec. 9, 1985, the CCC indicated that an unspecified "international communist group in France" had assisted in a bomb attack on NATO's Central European Operating Agency in Versailles, for which the CCC had claimed responsibility.

CCC activities subsided in 1986 following a series of arrests by Belgian police in December 1985-January 1986 of suspected CCC activists.

Peace Conquerors

A group using this name claimed responsibility for a bomb attack at Frankfurt airport (in West Germany) on June 19, 1985, when three persons were killed and 42 injured (several other left-wing and Arab groups also claiming responsibility for this incident), and on the Belgian headquarters of the West German chemical concern Bayer AG in Brussels on June 22 of that year. The group said that the latter bomb had been planted as a protest over the dumping of chemical waste in the North Sea by Bayer and the seizure of a ship of the environmental protest organization Greenpeace.

Revolutionary Front of Proletarian Action (*Front révolutionnaire d'action prolétarienne,* FRAP)

This group emerged on April 20-21, 1985, claiming responsibility for bomb explosions at the parliamentary secretariat of the North Atlantic Assembly and the premises of a West German company in Brussels.

Belize

Capital: Belmopan

Pop. 170,000

Belize became, on Sept. 21, 1981, a "sovereign democratic state" and an independent member of the Commonwealth as a constitutional monarchy with the British monarch being head of state and represented by a Governor-General, who acts on the advice of a Cabinet headed by a Prime Minister. There is a bicameral National Assembly consisting of (i) a House of Representatives of up to 29 members, elected by universal adult suffrage, and (ii) a Senate of eight members (five appointed by the Governor-General on the advice of the Prime Minister, two on the advice of the Leader of the Opposition and one on that of a Belize Advisory Council). Cabinet ministers are appointed similarly from among the members of the National Assembly.

In elections to the House of Representatives held on Dec. 14, 1984, the (centre-right) United Democratic Party (UDP) gained 21 of 28 seats, overturning 30 years' of rule by the People's United Party (PUP) which took the remaining seven. The UDP had opposed the terms under which Belize was granted independence. Other parties which unsuccessfully contested the elections were the Christian Democratic Party, formed in 1983, the small Progressive Party (which is generally considered to be pro-Guatemalan) and two independent candidates.

In 1985, the Belize Popular Party was formed by two former members of the PUP, Louis Sylvestre and Fred Hunter, who resigned from the PUP claiming that elements within the party were involved in a communist plot to take over Belize.

Benin

Capital: Porto Novo Pop. 3,600,000

The People's Republic of Benin (formerly Dahomey) is ruled by a (military) National Council of the Revolution which takes decisions in conformity with those of the central committee of the left-wing Benin People's Revolutionary Party (*Parti de la révolution populaire du Bénin,* PRPB), the country's sole legal political organization. There is a National Revolutionary Assembly of 196 People's Commissioners elected for five years by direct universal suffrage on June 10, 1984, on a list of PRPB candidates. The Assembly elects the President of the Republic, who is head of state and of the National Executive Council (Cabinet).

Three former members of the Presidential Council overthrown in 1972, who had been placed under house arrest—ex-President Justin Ahomadegbe, Sourou Migan Apithy and Hubert Maga, were in later April 1981 reported to have been allowed to leave the country.

Dahomeyan Communist Party (*Parti communiste dahoméen,* PCD)

Five former members of this banned pro-Albanian party, who had been temporarily imprisoned after student demonstrations in 1979, were in 1985 members of an elected student bureau at the National University of Benin, which demanded greater freedom of expression and the release of detainees. On April 27, 1985, the government announced that the student bureau would be disbanded, and on May 3 the above five members were expelled from the university for "attempting to destabilize the government". (Following further student demonstrations all educational establishments were closed from May 6 to June 3, 1985, and the university's rector, vice-rector and secretary-general as well as the director of the College of Education were dismissed from their posts on June 11, 1985.)

Dahomey Liberation and Rehabilitation Front (*Front de libération et de réhabilitation du Dahomey,* FLRD)

This illegal organization was established in France after the military takeover on Oct. 26, 1972, bringing to power the left-wing military regime which has been in office since then. The object of the FLRD has been the return to a democratic government in Benin. Among the personalities joining it was Gratien Pognon, who until August 1975 was Dahomey's ambassador in Belgium and at the European Communities.

Several unsuccessful attempts to overthrow the regime in Benin have not been expressly attributed to the FLRD. Following the discovery of one such plot in February 1973, another was foiled on Jan. 21, 1975, and resulted in death sentences being passed on March 17 by a "national revolutionary tribunal" on seven men alleged to have been involved. These included Dr Emile Derlin Zinsou (President of Dahomey in 1968-69 and resident in France since 1970), who was sentenced in absentia, while life sentences were passed on five army officers and 15-year prison sentences on two civilians. The uncovering of a further plot was announced on Oct. 18, 1975, and attributed to Dr Zinsou, who denied its existence; 11 persons accused of involvement in it were on Feb. 3, 1976, condemned to death by the National Council of the Revolution (sitting as a special court), three others to life imprisonment and one to 20 years' hard labour; those sentenced to death included a former Minister of Information under Dr Zinsou.

On the other hand, an invasion by some 100 armed men (about 40 of them White)—who arrived at Cotonou airport in a DC8 aircraft on Jan. 15, 1977, but were repulsed with losses—was on Jan. 24, specifically attributed to the FLRD, and in particular to Dr Zinsou and 11 other persons. A UN Security Council mission sent to Benin in February 1977 to investigate the attempted coup stated in its report (submitted to the UN Secretary-General on March 8, 1977) that the operation had been staged by a French colonel engaged by the FLRD. Allegations made in this report of involvement by France, Gabon, the Ivory Coast, Morocco and Senegal were rejected by the governments of all these countries as being untrue.

On May 25, 1979, it was officially announced that the National Council of the Revolution, constituted as a revolutionary court, had condemned to death in absentia a total of 100 persons alleged to have been involved in the invasion, with three other defendants being given prison sentences ranging from five to 10 years. Those sentenced to death included 11 Benin citizens described as "traitors", among them Dr Zinsou and Gratien Pognon, as well as 62 European mercenaries; the latter group included the French colonel referred to by the UN mission, who was identified as Col. Bob Denard (who had led various other mercenary operations in Africa).

An amnesty for political prisoners, announced on Aug. 1, 1984, applied to Lt.-Col. Alphonse Alley (who had been President in 1967-68), sentenced to 20 years in prison in May 1973 for his part in the attempted coup of that year, two majors also involved in that attempt, and several persons sentenced to death for their part in the 1975 attempt, among them Dr Zinsou. The amnesty, however, did not cover those involved in the attempted coup of January 1977.

Bhutan

Capital: Thimphu

Pop. 1,420,000

The Kingdom of Bhutan has a National Assembly (*Tsogdu*), to which 101 members are elected for a three-year term by direct universal adult suffrage while 12 seats are reserved for Buddhist bodies and the remaining 34 for ministers, officials and the nine members of a Royal Advisory Council. There is also a five-member Council of Ministers. There are no political parties and there has been no evidence of active political opposition.

Bolivia

Capital: La Paz

Pop. 6,429,000

The Republic of Bolivia has an executive President elected for a four-year term by universal adult suffrage and a 157-member Congress consisting of a 130-member House of Representatives and a 27-member Senate similarly elected for four years.

In elections held on July 14, 1985, in which an estimated 72 per cent of an electorate of 2,000,000 voted, parties gained aggregate seats in Congress as follows: National Revolutionary Movement—Historic Faction (MNR-H) 59, National Democratic Action (ADN) 51, Movement of the Revolutionary Left (MIR) 16, Leftist Revolutionary Nationalist Movement (MNRI) eight, Vanguard Nationalist Revolutionary Movement six, Socialist Party-One (PS-1) five, United People's Front (FPU) four, Bolivian Socialist Falange (FSB) three, Christian Democratic Party (PDC) three, Tupaj Katari Revolutionary Liberation Movement (MRTK-L) two.

Following presidential elections held on the same day in which none of the 18 candidates won an absolute majority, the new President, Dr Paz Estenssoro, was elected by a vote of Congress and sworn in on Aug. 6, 1985. In contrast to frequent government changes caused by military intervention which have characterized Bolivian politics, the transfer was the first peaceful change of power between two democratically elected heads of state in Bolivia since Dr Estenssoro (President three times before) first succeeded the defeated President, Dr Hernán Siles Zuazo, 25 years previously.

In recent years, unrest amongst trade unionists, workers and peasants in Bolivia has been caused by the government's severe economic measures, which resulted in August 1986 in a 90-day state of siege enforced on the grounds that left-wing extremists had conspired to overthrow the administration. Opposition politicians and trade unionists were detained or sent into internal exile, and radio stations whose broadcasts allegedly criticized the government's policies were temporarily closed.

"Fiancés of Death" (*Los Novios de la Muerte*)

This neo-Nazi organization was alleged to have instigated a coup plot in June 1984 on the instructions of Klaus Barbie, extradited from Bolivia to France in 1983 to face charges relating to war crimes. Apparently in preparation for the coup, the then President, Dr Hernán Siles Zuazo, was kidnapped for 10 hours on June 30, 1984, by members of the security forces, but the coup was foiled by the military command.

On Sept. 10, 1984, the government agreed to extradite to Italy an alleged member of the organization, Emilio Carbone Bacigalupo, wanted in connexion with bombings at Bologna railway station, Italy, in 1980.

Shining Path (*Sendero Luminoso*)

This Peruvian-based "Marxist-Leninist-Maoist" party which wages a "people's war" from the countryside of Peru (see separate entry) was accused in a report of Nov. 14, 1983, by police in La Paz of five bombings of civilian targets which took place in a period of general unrest.

In April 1987 Shining Path members were rumoured to be behind guerrilla activities which had started up in the country. The Bolivian Interior Minister, Juan Carlos Durán, stated that the reports were being investigated, although there was no clear indication that Shining Path was involved. Security forces in Bolivia fear the group's activities will spread to Bolivia.

Bophuthatswana

Capital: Mmabatho Pop. 1,500,000

The Republic of Bophuthatswana, whose independence is recognized only by the governments of South Africa, Ciskei, Transkei and Venda, has an executive President who is appointed by the country's Legislative Assembly and acts on the advice of an Executive Council (cabinet) appointed and headed by him. Of the Legislative Assembly of 105 members, 72 are elected by citizens over the age of 18 years (including those resident outside Bophuthatswana), 30 are nominated by regional authorities and three are nominated by the President.

Under Bophuthatswana's Constitution strikes are illegal, and under an industrial conciliation act of March 1984, South African-based trade unions were banned from operating in Bophuthatswana.

In elections held on Oct. 19, 1982, the ruling Bophuthatswana Democratic Party gained an overwhelming majority of seats.

A constitutional amendment act passed on Dec. 3, 1985, empowered the President to administer any government department if he considered it necessary, to close educational institutions and to restrict the enrolment of certain students. Under an internal security amendment act of the same date he was given powers to control the movement of persons and to prohibit the holding of meetings.

Botswana

Capital: Gaborone Pop. 1,090,000

The Republic of Botswana, a member of the Commonwealth, has an executive President responsible to a 38-member National Assembly, of which 34 members are elected for a five-year term by universal adult suffrage, four are nominated by the President and two are ex-officio members. There is also an advisory 15-member House of Chiefs. In general elections held on Sept. 8, 1984 (and a by-election on Dec. 1), parties gained elective seats in the House of Assembly as follows: Botswana Democratic Party 28, Botswana National Front 5, Botswana People's Party 1. The (left-wing) Botswana Independence Party and the Botswana Progressive Union gained no seats. There has been no evidence of extra-parliamentary opposition in Botswana.

Botswana's internal security has to some extent been jeopardized by the presence of large numbers of political refugees both from South Africa and from Zimbabwe. The official policy of the Botswana government has been not to grant political asylum to such refugees unless they undertook not to engage in activities directed against the government of their country of origin.

On Jan. 31, 1984, the South African Minister of Foreign Affairs stated that there had been a marked increase in the number of ANC (African National Congress) fighters entering South Africa from Botswana via (the nominally independent) Bophuthatswana (whose President announced on Feb. 4 of that year that unless this passage ceased his forces would invade Botswana). The South African government had, by then, on several occasions sent agents or members of its security forces into Botswana to attack alleged ANC centres. The Botswana Foreign Minister, however, said on May 30, 1984, that his government would never sign a non-aggression pact with South Africa (such as had been concluded between South Africa and Mozambique, with both sides agreeing not to allow "subversive elements" to operate from their territories).

In December 1984 the South African Foreign and Defence Ministers both again stated that Botswana was used as an infiltration route by ANC fighters, and the Foreign Minister added that the South African Defence Force would if necessary "strike back" over a wider front and not necessarily limit its actions to attacks on "terrorist" targets. There followed, on June 14, 1985, an attack by South African security forces on buildings in Gaborone, where at least 12 people were killed and six injured in a search for ANC members. A car bomb killed three persons in Gaborone on April 9, 1987, a few hours after a warning from the South African Foreign Minister that South Africa would "take whatever steps are necessary to retaliate and to protect our borders" against ANC incursions.

In Zimbabwe it had been alleged on March 10, 1983, that the Dukwe refugee camp (in northern Botswana), containing an increasing number of Matabele refugees from Zimbabwe, was a "dissident training camp".

Brazil

Capital: Brasília

Pop. 135,564,000

The Federative Republic of Brazil consists of 23 states, one Federal District, and three territories. Legislative power is exercised by a bicameral National Congress consisting of (i) a Chamber of Deputies of 487 members elected for four years by universal adult suffrage and (ii) a Senate of 72 seats elected for eight-year terms, one-third of its members being elected after four years and the other two-thirds after another four years; one-third of the Senate is elected indirectly. Executive power is exercised by the President, aided by ministers of state. Hitherto the President has been elected for six years by an electoral college consisting of all members of the National Congress and delegates appointed by state legislatures, with a Vice-President appointed at the same time: a constitutional amendment of May 1985 provides that a future President will be elected directly by universal adult suffrage.

In 1985 Brazil returned to civilian rule after 21 years of military rule. The transition was marked by the swearing-in of a civilian President, José Sarney, on April 22, 1985. (President Sarney had served as Acting President for Tancredo Neves, who was the first civilian to be elected President for 21 years, but who died before his inauguration.)

In May 1985 a constitutional amendment restored the free formation of political parties, following a reform bill of 1979 which had laid down initial rules for the introduction of a multi-party system. On Nov. 15, 1986, in the second multi-party contest since 1962, elections were held for a new National Congress which was to act from Feb. 1, 1987, as a Constitutional Assembly to determine the length of the current presidency and to rewrite the Constitution.

Of a 62,000,000-strong electorate, 85 per cent voted for 487 Deputies and 49 Senators in the election in which the (centre-left) Party of the Brazilian Democratic Movement (PMDB) secured an overall majority in both Chambers. The distribution of seats in the Chamber of Deputies was as follows: PMDB 259, the (right-wing) Liberal Front Party (PFL) 115, Social Democratic Party 36, Democratic Labour Party 24, Workers' Party 19, Brazilian Labour Party 19, Liberal Party seven, Christian Democratic Party three, Brazilian Communist Party two, Communist Party of Brazil two, Brazilian Socialist Party one.

The political situation in Brazil has been dominated recently by frequently violent demonstrations staged by critics of the government's harsh economic policies who have demanded immediate direct presidential elections. Progressive elements within the PMDB demanded that President Sarney should serve only four years of his six-year term. On May 18, 1987, President Sarney announced his own decision to serve five years of his term.

At the end of military rule in 1985 several previously illegal right- and left-wing organizations were officially recognized and took part in subsequent municipal elections and the 1986 congressional elections. Activities by ultra right-wing groups were reported up to the early 1980s, but there have been no recent incidents attributed to any specific movement.

Brunei

Capital: Bandar Seri Begawan

Pop. 220,000

The Sultanate of Brunei (*Negara Brunei Darussalam*), which had been a British protectorate since 1888, became a fully independent sovereign state within the Commonwealth on Jan. 1, 1984. The Sultan of Brunei is head of state and also Prime Minister of an 11-member Cabinet. There is also a Legislative Council of 20 members nominated by the Sultan.

Under a state of emergency which was imposed in 1962 all political parties had been banned and the government was empowered to detain people without trial. No elections have been held since 1962, and on the achievement of independence on Jan. 1, 1984, the Sultan declared that there would not be any move towards democracy. However, a Brunei National Democratic Party (BNDP), a moderate party with principles based on Islam and liberal nationalism and committed to achieving a system of parliamentary democracy, was formally launched in September 1985, having been registered by the government in May 1985. Members of the Chinese community (20 per cent of the population) and government employees (40 per cent of the workforce) were prohibited by the government from joining the BNDP. An offshoot of the BNDP, the pro-government Brunei National United Party, a 21-strong group, open to all Malay ethnic groups, was registered by the government in February 1986.

People's Party of Brunei (PRB) (*Party Ra'ayet*)

Established in 1959, the PRB won all elective seats in the Legislative Council in August 1962, but on Dec. 8 of that year a "North Borneo Liberation Army" linked with the PRB carried out a revolt with the object of preventing Brunei's entry into the then proposed Federation of Malaysia. By Dec. 17 the revolt was suppressed with the help of a British task force. A state of emergency had been declared on Dec. 8, the PRB was banned and hundreds of its members were arrested. The Constitution was suspended on Dec. 20, and the Legislative Council was dissolved. Thereafter the Sultan (who eventually declined in July 1963 to join Malaysia) ruled by decree.

The PRB subsequently operated from exile in Malaysia, with the use of facilities in Sarawak (East Malaysia). In 1976 there were still 37 political detainees in Brunei, most of them PRB members arrested in 1962. At the United Nations the PRB has been one of several petitioners for the granting of "the inalienable right of the people of Brunei to self-determination and independence". In a resolution initiated by Malaysia and adopted by the UN General Assembly on Nov. 28, 1977 (with Britain not participating in the vote), the British government was called upon "to facilitate expeditiously the holding of free and democratic elections in Brunei and the lifting of the ban on all political parties and . . . the return of all political exiles to Brunei".

Three members of the PRB imprisoned since 1962 were released on Independence Day, Jan. 1, 1984. In March 1985 Amnesty International reported the names of seven members of the PRB who had been detained without trial since 1966 and one who had been detained since 1970.

Bulgaria

Capital: Sofia Pop. 9,000,000

In the People's Republic of Bulgaria the Communist Party plays, in terms of the 1971 Constitution, the leading role in the state, holding 272 seats in the 400-member single-chamber National Assembly. Of the remaining seats in the Assembly, 100 are held by the Bulgarian Agrarian People's Union (the country's only other legal party). All candidates for elections, however, are nominated by the Fatherland Front mass organization, which is controlled by the Communist Party. The ruling party has closely followed the political line of the Communist Party of the Soviet Union.

There has been little evidence of activities by political opposition or human rights groups inside Bulgaria, whereas externally exiled opponents of the Sofia regime are grouped within a number of organizations.

In the West the Bulgarian security services were widely believed to be responsible for attacks on Bulgarian exiles, the object being to eliminate émigré opponents to the regime as well as their influence (in particular in the case of Georgi Markov, who had worked in the Bulgarian section of the BBC World Service and for Radio Free Europe and who was killed in London in September 1978).

In Bulgaria a number of "terrorist actions", including bomb explosions which took place in August 1984 and March 1985, were officially (by the Bulgarian Attorney General on May 16, 1985) attributed to "hostile elements and criminals" who were "mainly directed by various international centres". No specific organizations were named as being responsible for these actions, but Western diplomats thought that the bombings had been carried out by members of the Turkish minority.

Social Democratic Party of Bulgaria

Leadership. Stefan Tabakov (ch.)

The Social Democratic Party of Bulgaria was founded in 1891 and became a left-wing member of the pre-1914 Second International. The breakaway of the revolutionary wing in 1919 to form the Bulgarian Communist Party left the Social Democrats in a weakened position, but they nevertheless played a prominent role in the anti-Nazi resistance during World War II, for most of which Bulgaria was allied to Germany. With the Communists, left-wing Agrarians and other groups, the party participated in the Fatherland Front which seized power in September 1944 with the backing of the Red Army. Pressure for a merger with the Communist Party then developed, but its formal accomplishment in October 1947 was preceded by the departure into exile of those surviving

Social Democrats who wished to preserve the party's non-communist identity.

The exiled party currently has its headquarters in Vienna and is a consultative member of the Socialist International as well as a constituent party of the Socialist Union of Central and Eastern Europe (SUCEE). The party chairman is also vice-chairman of a Bulgarian National Committee in exile.

Turkish Minority Protests

In January 1985 reports were received of disturbances in parts of Bulgaria where there was a significant Turkish population. The incidents were said to be due to official efforts to make members of the Turkish minority change their names to Bulgarian forms.

All reports of clashes were, however, denied by the Bulgarian authorities. The official line, as expressed by the Bulgarian President (Todor Zhivkov, quoted on Feb. 16, 1985), was that the Bulgarian Turks were not part of the Turkish nation and were not being coerced to change their names.

However, according to a Yugoslav report of March 5, 1985, plans had been discovered towards the end of 1984 among Bulgarian Turks "to create a special republic and its secession, as in Cyprus", and several thousand Turks had been arrested.

A secretary of the central committee of the Bulgarian Communist Party (BCP) stated in a speech on March 9, 1985, that the Bulgarization of "Turko-Arabic names" was a voluntary campaign which had developed within three months from the end of 1984, and that there would be no emigration of Bulgarian citizens to Turkey (the Turkish Prime Minister having stated on Feb. 27, that his country was ready to welcome 500,000 refugees or more).

(Mass emigration of Turks from Bulgaria to Turkey had taken place in 1950-52 and in 1968-78, whereafter such emigration had been suspended. The Turkish population in Bulgaria was variously estimated at 500,000, which was the official figure, and 700,000-1,000,000, as suggested by the Turkish government.)

While the Bulgarian government continued to maintain that the name changes had been voluntary, a senior BCP official was, in July 1985, quoted as having admitted that some ethnic Turks had not yet matured sufficiently to accept new names and that there had been "sporadic instances of anti-social meetings".

In a census held in Bulgaria on Dec. 4-12, 1985, no opportunity was given to register nationality or religion. A number of Bulgarians sought political asylum in Turkey or Greece during 1985-86. Relations between Bulgaria and Turkey deteriorated markedly as a result of these developments.

The Parliamentary Assembly of the Council of Europe adopted, on Sept. 26, 1985, a draft resolution denouncing the non-observance of the rights of ethnic minorities in Bulgaria.

In a report published on April 2, 1986, Amnesty International claimed to have the names of more than 100 ethnic Turks killed by the Bulgarian security forces during the Bulgarization campaign and of more than 250 people detained for refusing new identity cards bearing Slavic names, including people detained or killed after the campaign was officially described as "safely completed" at the end of March 1985. In Bulgaria this report was officially described as "malevolent and absolutely groundless".

Burkina Faso

Capital: Ouagadougou

Pop. 7,919,895

The Republic of Burkina Faso, known as Upper Volta until Aug. 4, 1984, is ruled by a National Revolutionary Council (*Conseil national de la révolution,* CNR) which is headed by Capt. Thomas Sankara and which came to power on Aug. 4, 1983, by overthrowing the previous military regime headed by Maj. Jean-Baptiste Ouedraogo. The regime was pro-Libyan and its installation was welcomed by Col. Moamer al Gadaffi, the Libyan leader, on Aug. 6, 1983. Its Council of Ministers is presided over by Capt. Sankara as chairman of the CNR.

There is no Parliament, but committees for the defence of the revolution (*comités de défense de la révolution,* CDRs) were, as announced on Oct. 24, 1983, to be established at all places of work and in representative offices overseas. Late in August 1985 it was announced that these committees would discuss with councils at each ministry all proposals prior to submission for approval by the President. Following a visit to Burkina Faso by Col. Gadaffi on Dec. 9-11, 1985, Capt. Sankara announced the creation of a Burkina Faso *Jamahiriya* (i.e. the Libyan system of government under which authority is seen as vested in the masses through institutions such as the people's committees).

A night-time curfew imposed in August 1983 was not lifted until Aug. 4, 1985, when amnesties and partial amnesties were announced for 40 persons. These included Maj. Jean-Baptiste Ouedraogo, who was transferred from prison to house arrest.

On June 10, 1984, the government confirmed that an attempted coup planned for May 27, 1984, had been foiled by the arrest of seven officers and five non-commissioned officers. A military tribunal subsequently sentenced seven alleged conspirators to death and five to terms of hard labour; the death sentences were carried out on June 12, 1984.

Patriotic League for Development (*Ligue patriotique pour le développement,* Lipad)

Leadership. Dr Hamilton Coulibaly

The members of this Marxist movement included several cabinet ministers, among them Ibrahima Koné, who was dismissed on May 21, 1984. It was suggested that his dismissal indicated a measure of dissent within the government. In a cabinet reorganization carried out on Aug. 31, 1984, two ministers who were members of the Lipad were not reappointed.

Affiliated to the Lipad was a Burkinabe Confederation of Trade Unions (*Confédération syndicale burkinabe,* CSB), whose secretary-general, Soumane Touré, was arrested in January 1985 for stating that members of the CNR were guilty of embezzlement of funds. Touré was released on Oct. 3, 1986, but re-arrested on May 31, 1987, as a "counter-revolutionary" and "notorious recidivist".

Voltaic Progressive Front (*Front progressiste voltaïque,* FPV)

Leadership. Prof. Joseph Ki-Zerbo

This socialist party was suspended after a military coup of 1980, with Prof. Ki-Zerbo being placed in internal exile. In June 1984 the authorities accused him of having been behind the conspiracy which had planned a coup for May 27, 1984. It was also alleged that the French Socialist Party had supported him and that the plotters had been promised French and Israeli aid.

Burma

Capital: Rangoon Pop. 37,150,000

The Socialist Republic of the Union of Burma is, under its Constitution approved in a referendum in December 1973, a one-party socialist state with a People's Assembly whose 489 members have been approved by the ruling Burma Socialist Programme Party (BSPP, Lanzin Party). The country has a President (who is chairman of the State Council) and a Cabinet (Council of Ministers) elected by the People's Assembly and headed by a Prime Minister. Gen. Ne Win, the chairman of the BSSP and formerly Burma's President, has been the effective national leader since 1962.

Of Burma's population about 65 per cent are Burman. The principal ethnic minorities are the Karen (the most numerous of the non-Buddhist indigenous people) in southern and eastern Burma, the Shans (Theravada Buddhists like the Burmans and the ethnic kinfolk of the Thai and Lao people) on the eastern plateau; and the Chins, Kachins, Mons and Arakanese in the north and north-east. There are also some 350,000 Chinese and over 100,000 Indians and Pakistanis, mainly in the urban areas. Official government figures for the campaign against communist and tribal rebels for the year ending March 21, 1987, state that 2,538 insurgents were killed and 781 surrendered during 3,160 encounters with the Burmese forces, who in turn lost 651 men and had 1,887 injured.

An alleged conspiracy by young officers of the armed forces to kill the country's leading personalities and to "destroy the economy", uncovered on July 2, 1976, led to the trial of six officers (including Gen. Tin U, who had resigned in March 1976 as Minister of Defence and Chief of Staff), who were sentenced on Jan. 11, 1977, one of them to death and the others to imprisonment ranging from five years to life. Their plot was said to have been planned in the name of "joint venture capital" with the aim of restoring Burma's socialist economy to private enterprise.

On May 28, 1980, the government decreed an amnesty for political detainees and insurgents who surrendered within 90 days; prison sentences were reduced and persons under sentence of death were reprieved. It was officially claimed that 2,198 persons had accepted the amnesty, among them U Nu (who had been Prime Minister in 1948-62, had left Burma after his overthrow, had been associated with Burmese living in Thailand and been held responsible for a number of bomb attacks in Rangoon, and who had later lived in India) as well as Bo Thet Tun, a member of the central committee of the Burmese Communist Party.

Arakan Liberation Party (ALP)

Leadership. Maj. Khaing Ye Khaing (ch. of ALP and Chief of Staff of ALA)

This party advocates the secession from Burma of the region of Arakan (bordering on southern Bangladesh), which is largely inhabited by Moslems, whereas the majority of Burma's inhabitants are Buddhists. It superseded a Moslem Mujahid movement which had conducted guerrilla operations in 1952-54 but by 1961 had been reduced to insignificance. The party's armed wing (the Arakan Liberation Army, ALA) was established in 1974 and was subsequently trained by the Karen National Union (KNU—see separate entry).

The party itself agreed in May 1975 to join other national minority movements in the federal National Democratic Front (see separate entry). In 1977 ALP forces (in conjunction with forces of the Arakan Independence Organization) made an unsuccessful attempt to cross Burma from the eastern states, where they were operating with Karen and Kachin forces, to Arakan in order to establish new bases. Both organizations were ambushed by government forces in the Chin state and lost large numbers of supporters; among those killed was the ALP leader, Khaing Mo Lin.

On Feb. 23, 1976, four men charged with involvement in an attempt to establish a separate independent state of Arakan (two of whom were said to have been in contact with the Bangladeshi military attaché in Rangoon) were condemned to death and two others to life imprisonment and 10 years in prison respectively; the death sentences were carried out shortly afterwards.

The Burmese government stated on April 29, 1978, that in a census operation begun in 1977 it had been found that there had been massive illegal immigration into Burma, particularly from Bangladesh into Arakan; the following month it was claimed that over 100,000 people had left the towns of Buthidaung and Maungdaw in Arakan to "escape an immigration check", most crossing the border into Bangladesh and others going into hiding in the jungle.

The government of Bangladesh had earlier claimed that thousands of Moslems had been expelled from Burma and on June 6, 1978, gave the number of Moslem refugees from Burma in Bangladesh as 167,000. After this situation had caused serious strains in relations between the two countries, an agreement providing for the repatriation of the refugees to Burma was eventually reached on July 9, 1979.

Current strength is put at no more than a few dozen men, in KNU bases along the Thai border.

Burmese Communist Party (BCP)—("White Flag" Party)

Leadership. Thakin Ba Thein Tin (ch. of central committee); Tin Yee (also known as Ne Win—chief of staff of the "people's army")

Having been established in August 1939, the Communist Party in 1946 divided into (i) the Stalinist "White Flag" Communists led by Thakin Than Tun and (ii) the Trotskyist "Red Flag" Communists (see separate entry). The "White Flag" BCP became a powerful force partly owing to its alliance with militant Kachins and Shans and partly because of the overt support which it received from China following its gravitation to a pro-Chinese orientation. Having previously operated mainly in the Arakan and Pegu mountains and in the Irrawaddy delta, the BCP transferred its headquarters to the Chinese border area in 1968. There was heavy fighting throughout 1970 in Shan state (bordering on China, Laos and Thailand); after the establishment of friendly relations between Burma and China in 1971 there were few reports of insurgent activities but in 1973 hostilities revived in Shan state. (For Shan secessionist movements, see separate entries below.)

Of the 22 members of the BCP's central committee elected in 1962, only two were still at large in Burma in 1975. The former chairman, Thakin Than Tun, was assassinated in 1968 by one of his followers. Four central committee members were murdered in a purge in 1967-68; seven were killed in action; one had died of natural causes; one had been captured; two had surrendered, and four were outside the country. Of the later office bearers, Thakin Zin and Thakin Chit, respectively chairman and general secretary, were killed in a clash with troops in the Pegu Yoma mountains (north of Rangoon) on March 15, 1975. On May 17, 1975, the central committee announced that Thakin Ba Thein Tin, the head of the party's delegation in Peking, had been elected chairman.

An army spokesman claimed on March 20, 1975, that the communist rebellion in central Burma had been crushed and that during the previous two years 172 communists had been killed, 146 had been captured and 500 had surrendered (the Army's casualties being given as 135 killed and 143 wounded). The communist rebels, however, remained active in Shan state, near the Chinese border, where, according to an army communiqué of June 28, 1975, a total of 120 communists and 32 soldiers were killed within a week.

During a visit to China in November 1975 by Gen. Ne Win, then Chairman of Burma's State Council, it was agreed that neither side would engage in any aggressive move against the other. Nevertheless the Chinese Communist Party continued to give support to the BCP and its forces in rebellion against the government of Burma. Burmese official announcements on the fighting were made on Jan. 7, 1976 (to the effect that in four major battles and more than 40 skirmishes in November-December 1975 in eastern Burma, 216 communist rebels and Shan tribesmen had been killed and 43 rebels had surrendered or been captured), and on March 26, 1976 (stating that on March 16-21 a total of 1,200 communists and 300 other rebels had been repulsed at Mong Yang, 20 miles from the Chinese border). On April 11, 1976, the government announced that in clashes in eastern Burma on March 22-26 its troops had killed 96 communist rebels and wounded 150, with 35 soldiers being killed and 62 injured in these engagements. In Rangoon, 47 party members were arrested in August-September 1976, for distributing anti-government publications.

The BCP's radio station, the "Voice of the People of Burma" (VOPB), repeatedly made claims of successful communist military operations, and on Dec. 10, 1980, it summed up its findings for the period from November 1979 to December 1980, stating that 772 battles during that period in northern and north-eastern regions and in central Shan state had resulted in the death of 1,908 soldiers, injury to 3,341 others and the capture by communists of 320 men.

Following the expiry of an amnesty offered on May 28, 1980, to insurgents who surrendered within 90 days, the government proposed to Thakin Ba Thein Tin that talks should be held to "end the internal strife"; that a ceasefire should be effected by both sides; and that negotiations should be started but be kept secret for the time being. The BCP refused to effect a ceasefire but agreed to secret talks, at which the BCP proposed that the BCP and its armed wing should be allowed to exist and the BCP should also be allowed to use the border area (where it was located) as its base area. (The BCP had earlier warned the Burmese government against "the threat of Soviet social-imperialism and its invasion of Afghanistan" and also against the "hegemonist" aspirations of Vietnam in South-East Asia.) The Burmese government in turn proposed that BCP members could join the ruling Burma Socialist Programme Party and take part in elections at various levels to the people's councils; that BCP soldiers could join the government security and police forces; and that BCP members could help to solve the country's internal problems.

The BCP subsequently proposed in draft form (i) that, as the party had never wanted Burma to be divided, the "liberated" areas should be recognized as an autonomous region under a single government; that the BCP's People's Army should be recognized as a military unit controlled by a state defence council under the single government with one or two representatives from either the BCP or its army sitting on that council; and (ii) that the BCP should be permitted to continue to exist. However, Gen. Ne Win, disclosing the talks on May 14, 1981, declared that the demands of the BCP should not be honoured and would not be met, and that the government had therefore decided to stop the negotiations completely. Thakin Ba Thein Tin thereupon denounced the government (in a statement broadcast by the VOPB on Jun. 14, 1981) as being responsible for unilaterally breaking off the negotiations, and as "obstructors of democratic rights" and "destroyers of national unity".

On Nov. 22, 1981, a VOPB report on nine months of fighting claimed that up to Sept. 30, 1981, the People's Army of the BCP had fought 30 battles against government forces in central Shan state, killing 40 soldiers and injuring 57, while in battles fought elsewhere another 10 soldiers were killed and six wounded. In February and March 1982 the VOPB reported various People's Army guerrilla attacks from the Kengtung area (eastern Shan state) and other parts of Shan state.

Government announcements claimed that 67 BCP guerrillas had surrended in April-May 1982 and that clashes had occurred later that year in June and July. The government also claimed that 83 rebels and 27 Burmese troops had been killed in an offensive on April 6, 1983, against a BCP camp at Panglong in the north-east. By mid-1983 BCP forces had reportedly penetrated into their former stronghold in the Pegu Yoma mountain range, north of Rangoon, from which the government had driven them out in 1974. Reports indicated clashes between BCP and government forces near the towns of Hsi-seng and Pyinmana as the insurgents attempted to establish supply routes from the BCP headquarters at Panghsai (sometimes referred to as Kyukok) on the Chinese border, 300 miles to the north-east.

The BCP's military and financial support from the Chinese Communist Party was reduced in the 1980s as the Chinese government sought better relations with the Burmese government. In response to declining Chinese aid the BCP reportedly turned to opium and narcotics trafficking. At the party's third national congress held on Sept. 9-Oct. 2, 1985, "in a liberated area of Burma", the leadership reportedly acknowledged the reduction in Chinese support for the BCP, but the BCP retained its pro-China identity. Changes made at the third congress included the appointment of Khin Maung Gyi as secretary of the central committee and of Tin Yee (also called Ne Win) as chief of staff of the BCP's "People's Army".

In March 1986 a meeting was held at the BCP headquarters in Panghsai between the leadership of the BCP and representatives of the National Democratic Front (NDF—see separate entry for prior NDF meeting in December 1985-January 1986 at which it was agreed to open a dialogue with the BCP and also for the agreements reached at the March 1986 meeting).

Fighting between BCP guerrillas and government forces in north-east Burma, near the border with the Chinese province of Yunnan, started in November 1986 and culminated in early January 1987 in the Burmese Army capturing the BCP headquarters at Panghsai. According to government figures the hostilities resulted in the death of 591 insurgents and 175 government troops. As a result of the fighting approximately 6,000 civilians from Panghsai and Mong Paw crossed into the Chinese border town of Wanting where they were reportedly cared for by the Chinese authorities (BCP guerrillas were not officially allowed to enter China).

In early 1987 the BCP was thought to have 12,000 regular members and an 8,000 strong militia. It controlled some 20,000 square kilometres in north-eastern Shan state and along the Chinese border in Kachin state and had approximately 400,000 people living under its control. Its forces also moved freely in areas ("guerrilla zones") controlled by BCP allies (i.e. the Shan State Nationalities Liberation Organization—SSNLO—see separate entry), the Kayan New Land Council and the Ka La La Ta (a Karenni organization).

Committee for the Restoration of Democracy in Burma (CRDB)

Leadership. Kyaw Win

This US-based exile group is led by Kyaw Win, once associated with former Prime Minister U Nu (who accepted amnesty in 1980). It is reported to have some links with individual members of the National Democratic Front (NDF—see separate entry).

Communist Party of Arakan

Leadership. Maung Hun (chairman)

This party consisted originally of defectors from the now-defunct "Red Flag" Communist Party of Burma (see separate entry). It has consistently demanded the establishment of a "Republic of Arakan with the right to secede from the Union of Burma" and as such is alone amongst Burmese rebels in being a separatist communist party. Its strength is very limited.

Peace talks with Gen. Ne Win's Revolutionary Council (which came to power in 1962) were broken off in November 1963 because the Council did not accede to the Party's demands. In 1979 government forces launched a successful attack on the Party's bases at Kyauktaw and Myebon. None the less, guerrilla units, under the control of Saw Tun Oo, continue to operate near the border with India and Bangladesh.

In 1985 the Communist Party of Arakan reportedly formed a joint committee with the Arakan Liberation Party (ALP—see separate entry) and the Arakan Independence Organization; reports indicated that the Arakan National Liberation Party (a small organization led by Maung Sein Nyunt) would at some stage join the committee.

Communist Party of Burma—"Red Flag" Party

This Trotskyist party was formed in 1946 as a result of a split in the (then Stalinist) Burmese Communist Party (see entry above). It conducted its own guerrilla operations but ceased to function in the 1970s.

Kachin Independence Organization (KIO)

Leadership. Brang Seng (pres.); Brig.-Gen. Zau Mai (military leader)

The KIO, which was founded in 1961, is widely recognized as the most radical, effective and best organized of the non-communist insurgent forces and derives financial strength from its control of the Kachin state jade trade. Its military wing, the Kachin Independence Army (KIA), has probably maintained a constant strength of some 5,000 soldiers since it began conducting guerrilla operations in 1958 and the KIO/KIA control substantial territory in Kachin state and parts of northern Shan state. The KIO was a member of the National Democratic United Front in the 1960s and is currently considered to be the leading member of the Front's successor, the coalition National Democratic Front (NDF—see separate entry), which it joined in September 1983. The KIO leader Brang Seng advocates regional autonomy rather than separation.

Negotiations between Gen. Ne Win's Revolutionary Council (which came to power in 1962) and the KIO broke down in November 1963, because no agreement could be reached on a ceasefire. In late 1967 a KIO delegation visited China and met with that country's leaders and the leadership of the Burmese Communist Party (BCP—see separate entry). During the visit, in early January 1968, BCP forces entered Kachin-controlled territory in Burma and the ensuing fighting and animosity between the two groups did not come to an end until 1976. The KIO held several rounds of talks with the Burmese government, in Rangoon and in Kachin state, between August 1980 and May 1981. At the talks the KIO insisted that it was willing to accept Burma's one-party system of government, but would never compromise on its demand for autonomy. The talks broke down after the government offered the KIO no political concessions, only the opportunity for "rehabilitation".

KIA guerrillas attacked the town of Hkamti in the north-eastern district of Sagaing on Feb. 28, 1984, killing up to 30 police officers and soldiers, releasing over 120 prisoners and obtaining large supplies of arms and ammunition. On March 1, Kachin rebels destroyed a main railway line at Mogaung, thereby temporarily isolating the Kachin state capital Myitkyina from the rest of Burma. Government troops operating against Kachin guerrillas in the hill districts of Kachin state (much of which was under Kachin control, to the extent that many schools in the area were KIO-funded and operated) were joined on June 1, 1984, by a further 11 Burmese battalions. As a result many KIA rebels abandoned their bases and retreated into areas from where they might operate a guerrilla war against the Burmese forces.

Brig.-Gen. L. Khun Phan, an ethnic Kachin, was assassinated in Myitkyina on Oct. 16, 1985, by Kachin rebels; he was a member of the central committee of the Burma Socialist Programme Party (BSSP—the sole party allowed under the 1974 Constitution) and had been elected to the People's Assembly during elections held on Oct. 6-20, 1985.

Notwithstanding its support for a tactical alliance between the NDF and the BCP, the KIO is close to right-wing circles in the US, Taiwan and South Korea and has sponsored a chapter of the "World Anti-Communist League". There is a strong Christian influence.

The Burmese army mounted a major offensive against the KIA in May-June 1987, capturing several of its bases.

Karen National Union (KNU)

Leadership. Gen. Bo Mya (pres. and chief of staff)

Established in 1948, the KNU has a long history of guerrilla warfare against the Burmese government through its armed wing, the Karen National Liberation Army (KNLA) in pursuit of its aim of setting up a separate Karen state. Among the various ethnic guerrilla organizations the KNU has been the strongest and leads the Federal National Democratic Front formed in 1975 (see separate entry). In 1971 the KNU's then president claimed that his organization's armed forces consisted of 16,000 men, including 4,000 regulars, and by 1974 they were said to control considerable areas in south-east Burma. The KNU was financing its activities by levying a 5 per cent tax on goods brought into the area under its control from Thailand by smugglers supplying the black market in Rangoon.

On June 20, 1975, the Army was reported to have launched a major offensive against the KNLA but this did not end the latter's activities. On April 26, 1976,

Karen rebels attacked a ferry off Burma's southern coast, killing 45 and injuring 75 people.

On March 24, 1980, it was reported than an assault by Burmese troops had driven over 2,000 Karen refugees across the border into the Mae Sor district in Thailand. The Burmese government announced on March 25 that two KNU camps on the Thai border had been destroyed. Further fighting was reported in March and on April 15, when another 1,500 Karens were said to have crossed the border into north-eastern Thailand. In response to the amnesty offered on May 28, 1980, to insurgents who surrendered within 90 days, several KNU leaders returned to Burma from Thailand. On Sept. 22-27, 1980, another 1,000 Karen civilians were reported to have escaped to Thailand after Burmese troops had launched another major offensive against the KNLA at Kawkareik (east of Moulmein and about 20 miles from the Thai border). On Nov. 23, 1981, some 1,000 Karen rebels ambushed about 500 Burmese troops near the Thai border north-east of Rangoon and killed or wounded at least 100 of these troops. KNU guerrillas were also responsible for blowing up a passenger train between Rangoon and Moulmein, killing three persons and injuring 19, in February 1982. In late-1982 the active strength of the KNU was estimated at between 5,000 and 8,000 men.

In late September 1982 a five-man group of heavily-armed KNU insurgents mounted what was thought to be the first Karen attack on Rangoon. After the group had been intercepted by security forces two were killed (including the leader, Mahn Ngwe Aung) and three captured.

KNU guerrillas gained renewed international attention in late 1983 following the kidnapping of a French couple on Oct. 18 from Myaing Galay near the Karen state capital of Pa'an. The guerrillas reportedly demanded the cessation of French aid to the Burmese government as a condition for releasing the captured couple (who were released unharmed in late November).

In January 1984 Burmese forces of the 44th and 66th light infantry divisions began a major offensive against KNLA forces (estimated to number between 4,000 and 5,000) based in the Dawna mountain range bordering Thailand east of Rangoon. In this offensive government forces captured a KNLA camp at Mae Tha Waw, but in 1985 this camp reverted to KNLA control. Further fighting took place throughout Karen state in 1985-86, and early in 1987 an offensive by government troops remained largely unsuccessful.

At a meeting of the National Democratic Front (NDF—see separate entry) in August 1986 the KNLA leaders denounced the NDF's alliance with the Burmese Communist Party (BCP), arguing that the BCP, to which the KNU was traditionally opposed, supported a one-party system of government and was involved in the production and distribution of narcotics.

Karenni National Progressive Party (KNPP)

Leadership. Saw Maw Reh Bya Reh (chairman); Gen. Bee Htoo (military leader)

The KNPP is a member of the National Democratic Front (NDF—see separate entry) and was a member of the Front's predecessor, the National Democratic United Front. On April 13, 1986, following a nine-day battle, Burmese forces captured the headquarters of the KNPP's military wing, the Karenni Revolutionary Army (KRA), at Hwe Pon Long in Kayah state. Saw Maw Reh the then KNPP chairman (and now leader of the National Democratic Front—see separate entry), was among 250 Karenni insurgents who fled into neighbouring Thailand as a result of the action of the Burmese forces. Strength is estimated at about 400 men.

Karenni People's Liberation Organization

Leadership. Nya Maung Mae (l.)

Small pro-BCP splinter group based in Kayah state.

Kawthoolei Moslem Liberation Force (KMLF)

Leadership. Mohammad Zaid

This organization was established on Aug. 31, 1983, in response to anti-Moslem riots in areas of the Irrawaddy delta in June and July 1983. It claims to represent Burma's minority Moslem population and seeks freedom of worship and the introduction of guarantees against religious persecution, rather than the establishment of a separate Moslem state. The KMLF is thought to have absorbed other Moslem groups including the Ommat Liberation Front (established in Mandalay in 1976) and the Rohingya Patriotic Front (previously active in Arakan). Its forces are reportedly linked with the Karen National Union (KNU—see separate entry).

Kayan Newland Council

Leadership. Shwe Aye (l., also known as Naing Lu Hta)

This is a small pro-BCP group of less than 100 men active in the hill country of south-western Shan state.

National Democratic Front (NDF)

Leadership. Saw Maw Reh (pres.)

This Front was formed on May 27, 1975, by five insurgent organizations of national minorities with the object of overthrowing "Ne Win's one-party military dictatorship" (which had come to power in 1962) and establishing in Burma a federal union based on national self-determination. By May 1976 the NDF was said to have been joined by four other organizations, since when numerous changes in the membership of the NDF have been reported. As at mid-1987 the NDF comprised nine organizations, as follows: the Karen National Union (KNU), the Karenni National Progressive Party (KNPP), the Kachin Independence Organization (KIO), the Shan State Progress Party (SSPP), the Palaung State Liberation Organization (PSLO), the Pa-O National Organization (PNO), the New Mon State Party (NMSP), the Wa National Organization (WNO) and the Arakan Liberation Party (ALP) (see separate entries).

The Front superseded an earlier National Democratic United Front (NDUF), led by Mahn Ba Zan, which had been deserted by many Karens in 1968 because their allies in the Front, the ("White Flag") Burmese Communists, were allegedly fanatically emulating the "Cultural Revolution" of China.

In mid-1982 the Front reportedly held what it described as its first congress at a secret camp in Burma. The congress agreed to establish a common fighting force, a process which was to begin with token contingents joining the KNU's armed wing from the various other member organizations. It was reported in February 1984 that a common NDF force comprising Arakanese, Mon, Pa-O and Karen members had recently been formed.

A conference attended by representatives of the NDF was held at the Kachin Independence Organization headquarters in north-east Burma close to the border with China, from Dec. 16, 1985, to Jan. 20, 1986. It was agreed to open a dialogue with the Burmese Communist Party (BCP—see separate entry) which had previously been regarded by most NDF members as subordinate to Chinese interests. It was also agreed to divide the military wings of the NDF into three regional command areas. It was reported in July 1986 that one of the command groupings (northern command, comprising Kachin, Shan and Palaung guerrillas and code-named battalion 861) had, that month, launched a successful assault on a Shan United Army (SUA—see separate entry) base at Mong Ket in Shan state.

At a meeting held on March 17-24, 1986, at the BCP headquarters in Panghsai between the NDF and BCP leadership both sides agreed to allow safe passage through their individual areas of control and to waive their collection of taxes on goods passing through these areas. However, at an emergency NDF meeting in August 1986 the KNU denounced the alliance with the BCP. The NDF held its second congress at the KNU headquarters near the Thai border in June 1987 and chose Saw Maw Reh, a former chairman of the Karenni National Progressive Party, as its leader in succession to Bo Mya of the KNU, apparently thereby rejecting the KNU's position on alliance with the BCP.

National Liberation Front (NLF)

The NLF was active in the 1970s but there have been no reports of activity in recent years.

New Mon State Party (NMSP)

Leadership. Nai Nol Lar (pres. of NMSP and chief of staff of MNLA)

Based on the Mon ethnic minority of northern Burma, the NMSP joined with other secessionist organizations to form the National Democratic Front (NDF—see separate entry) in May 1975. An earlier movement of Mon insurgents was said to have been "practically eliminated" by 1961, when only about 40 were left. The surrender of a leader of the NMSP at Moulmein was officially announced on June 6, 1980. The Bangkok-based *Nation* newspaper reported on Nov. 22, 1986, that Nai Tala Mon, NMSP general secretary and leader of the party's armed wing, the Mon National Liberation Army (MNLA), had died on Sept. 24 of that year.

According to an official announcement, 20 people were killed on March 12, 1987, when Mon ethnic rebels bombed a pagoda festival at a village in Ye township, Mon state. Estimated strength is a few hundred.

Palaung State Liberation Organization (PSLO)

Leadership. Khrus Sangai (PSLO); Maj. Ai Mong (military wing)

The PSLO and its military wing the Palaung State Liberation Army operate north-east of Namshan in Shan State. The PSLO is a member of the National Democratic Front (see separate entry).

Pa-O National Organization (PNO)

Leadership. Aung Kham Hti (chairman); Col. Htoon Yi (chief of staff of military wing)

The PNO, and its military wing the Pa-O National Army (PNA), has a few hundred men in the hill country of southern Shan state. It is a member of the National Democratic Front (see separate entry).

People's Patriotic Party (PPP)

Leading figures in the PPP accepted amnesty in 1980, and there have been no reports of the PPP's continued existence.

Revolutionary National Party

This Arakan-based organization was formed in November 1985, and its members included people of the Kami, Chin and Mro hill-tribes.

Shan State Progress Party (SSPP)

Leadership. Col. Sai Lek (gen. sec.); Col. Gaw Lin Da (chief of staff of SSA)

This party's armed wing, the Shan State Army (SSA), was formed in 1964 out of the Shan State Independence Army which had arisen at the time of the Shan rebellion of 1958, when a 10-year period of Shan participation in the Union of Burma had expired and the central government had moved to curtail the traditional autonomy of the Shan tribes-people on the eastern Burmese plateau. By the early 1970s the SSA was reported to consist of some 4,000 guerrillas, many of whom were armed with Chinese weapons. Apart from fighting government troops, the SSA has been engaged in a struggle for supremacy in the Shan region with the Shan United Revolutionary Army (SURA—see separate entry). Based in strongholds on the western side of the Shan plateau, the SSA has had considerable support among the Palaung and Wa tribes further north. It does not control any large homogeneous base area however.

In May 1976 the SSPP participated with other ethnic minorities in the formation of the National Democratic Front (NDF—see separate entry).

Since the mid-1960s the SSA enjoyed close relations with the Burmese Communist Party (BCP—see separate entry) and with Kachin rebels. However, in 1977 the SSA broke off all relations with the BCP, charging that communist rebels had begun to exert too much influence on Shan affairs. Sao Hso Noom, the SSA commander and SSPP president, was instrumental in restoring links with the BCP in June 1982.

In early 1983 the SSPP and the SSA reportedly divided into two factions, one supporting the BCP and the other an anti-BCP faction led by former SSPP president U Sao Hso Lane, who subsequently surrendered to the government on June 21, 1983. On Nov. 14, 1983, Sao Hso Noom died and was reportedly succeeded by Kaw Lin Da (SSPP political commissar) and Hpang Hpa (SSA commander).

In early 1985 remnants from the SSA and from SURA joined with the forces of the Shan United Army (SUA—see separate entry under Thailand) to form the Thai Revolutionary Council.

Shan United Revolutionary Army (SURA)

Leadership. Moh Heng (ch.); Chau Nor Fah (sec.-gen.)

The SURA was formed in January 1969 by Shan insurgents opposed to the communist-backed Shan State Army (SSA—see separate entry), its original nucleus being the forces of the veteran rebel Chau Noi (who later abandoned his role in the insurgency). The SURA chairman, Moh Heng, fought the Japanese during World War II and joined the Burmese Communist Party (BCP) in 1952, but left in 1956 in disagreement with its land policy and communization of Shan village life; in the early 1960s he lost his left arm while leading an attack on a Burmese Army garrison.

Strongly anti-communist and equipped with US-made weapons, the SURA became engaged in open conflict with the SSA from 1972 and was on the defensive until 1975. Later it appeared to have consolidated its influence in the southern-central region of Shan state and during 1982 it claimed to have received a growing number of high-ranking defectors from both the BCP and the SSA. Its active strength was then estimated at between 2,000 and 3,000 guerrillas in the field, with a further 8,000 trained reservists being available when needed. In its struggle with communist elements, the SURA has received backing from the remnants of the Kuomintang Third Army led by Gen. Li Wen-han, whose forces settled in Burmese border areas after fleeing from China in 1949.

Basing its strategy on a combination of political propaganda and guerrilla warfare, the SURA seeks to appeal to both the nationalistic and the religious sentiments of the Shan people. Its constitution advances the principles of federalism among tribal groups, parliamentary democracy and preservation of the tribal religious and cultural heritage. The SURA's Shan soldiers are required to observe Buddhist precepts and practices (although many of its Kachin recruits are Christians, and are allowed to practise their faith).

Like other insurgent armies in Burma, the SURA derived most of its income from taxes on households in its area of control and from levies on cross-border trade, notably the substantial traffic in precious stones such as jade. The movement was strongly opposed to the growing of opium poppies (a traditional source of income for the Shan people) and disclaimed any involvement in the narcotics trade; at the same time, it recognized that, given the depressed state of the Shan region (which it attributes to government neglect), many inhabitants had few alternative means of livelihood in the short term.

In April 1983 government forces reportedly attacked a network of SURA-controlled opium refineries, situated near the Thai border. This and other reports suggested that the SURA had surrendered many of its genuine secessionist aspirations for increased involvement in narcotic production and trafficking.

Shan State Nationalities Liberation Organization (SSNLO or "Red Pa-O")

Leadership. Tha Kalei (ch.)

The Voice of the People of Burma (VOPB) radio station of the Burmese Communist Party (BCP) reported on Nov. 22, 1981, that the SSNLO was undertaking combined guerrilla operations with units of the People's Army of the BCP and also of the Kayah New Land Revolutionary Council (a local organization in Kayah state, north-east of Rangoon). This combined force was said to have fought, in the first nine months of 1981, a total of 49 battles in southern Shan state, killing 131 soldiers and wounding 98.

As of early 1987 the SSNLO controlled a small "guerrilla zone" north of Loikaw and west of the Salween river in Shan state within which BCP forces could operate freely. Estimated strength is a few hundred.

Wa National Organization/Army (WNO/WNA)

Leadership. Ai Chau Hseu (chief of staff)

The armed wing of this small Shan state-based organization, the Wa National Army, has some 300 members. It joined the National Democratic Front (NDF—see separate entry) in December 1983 and its members are thought to operate within the NDF's central command along with Pa-O and Karenni forces.

Burundi

Capital: Bujumbura

Pop. 4,740,000

The Republic of Burundi has an executive President elected by universal adult suffrage for a five-year term, the sole candidate for this office being the president of the *Union pour le progrès national* (Uprona, the country's only legal political organization) and a 65-member National Assembly, to which 52 members are elected for a five-year term by universal adult suffrage and 13 are nominated by the President. In parliamentary elections held in October 1982 each elective seat was contested by two Uprona candidates.

Although no organized opposition groups appear to exist in Burundi, in the period since independence the government has been faced with a major internal security problem in the shape of serious ethnic tensions between the minority Tutsi tribe (forming about 15 per cent of the population) and the majority Hutu (about 84 per cent). These tensions developed into an open conflict in 1972 resulting in substantial loss of life, in the light of which the regime of President Bagaza (who came to power in 1976) has officially proscribed any reference to Tutsi or Hutu and declared all inhabitants to be Burundi, i.e. one nation of Burundi. On another plane, the Bagaza regime has experienced conflict with the country's Roman Catholic Church, which the President in 1979 described as forming "a hierarchy parallel to that of the state and the party". Following the expulsion of hundreds of missionaries and the arrest of several priests it was officially announced on April 22, 1987, that Catholic parish councils would be abolished and lay-preaching prohibited.

Cameroon

Capital: Yaoundé

Pop. 10,100,000

The Republic of Cameroon has an executive President elected for a five-year term by universal adult suffrage (and re-eligible) and a Cabinet headed by the President and consisting of ministers who are not members of Parliament. The country's 120-member National Assembly is elected also by universal adult suffrage and for a five-year term from a list submitted by the Cameroon People's Democratic Movement (*Rassemblement démocratique du peuple camerounais,* RDPC) as the country's sole legal party, which has succeeded the *Union nationale camerounaise* (UNC) since the latter's fourth congress held on March 21-24, 1984, and also from independent candidates who must, however, demonstrate nationwide support.

In a broadcast made on Aug. 22, 1983, President Paul Biya announced emergency measures to deal with a plot against the state, including the arrest of persons who were alleged to intend an attack on the security of the Republic and to have made a complete confession. They included a former security chief under President Ahmadou Ahidjo (President Biya's predecessor) and a former presidential bodyguard. President Ahidjo had resigned in November 1982 and had since left the country for Geneva, where he criticized his successor and accused him of creating "a police state" and "a regime of terror". On Feb. 28, 1984, a military tribunal passed death sentences for subversion and conspiracy to assassinate President Biya on the above two former aides of ex-President Ahidjo and also on the latter (tried in absentia) for having ordered the proposed assassination. On March 16, 1984, however, it was reported that President Biya had commuted the death sentences to detention.

On April 6-9, 1984, an attempted coup by elements of the Republican Guard was put down by forces loyal to President Biya, with some 70 persons being killed (according to official estimates). On April 12 it was officially stated that 1,053 insurgents had been captured and that 265 gendarmes were reported missing. The rebels were said to be all Moslems from the north of Cameroon and to have been encouraged by ex-President Ahidjo (which the latter denied). On May 16, it was announced that 617 of those captured had been released, that 46 had been sentenced to death (three of them in absentia), two to life imprisonment and 183 to prison terms of from two to 20 years. There followed further trials, and by early August 1984 a total of 120 persons were believed to have been executed. Additional trials took place later in 1984, and by December 1984 a total of 51 defendants were said to have been sentenced to death and 205 to imprisonment for from two years to life, whereas 203 persons had been released. On Sept. 26, 1985, it was announced that 13 death sentences passed on April 10, 1985, were to be commuted to life imprisonment.

Opposition Groups Abroad

Cameroonian Organization Fighting for Democracy (*Organisation camerounaise de lutte pour la démocratie,* OCLD)

The French authorities refused this Paris-based organization (on Feb. 8, 1986) permission to hold a conference (following an official visit to France by President Biya).

National Union of Cameroon Students (*Union nationale des étudiants de Kamerun,* UNEK)

Leadership. Albert Moutoudou (ch. of executive committee)

This Union has held annual congresses in Paris. On Dec. 28, 1976, a "group of militants" of the UNEK issued a document alleging that since July 1976 "hundreds of young people—pupils, students and workers"—were being "detained in Yaoundé without being tried" and that many of them had been tortured; the document listed some 30 political detainees.

Albert Moutoudou stated in January 1977 that, although the UNEK was "not a movement in opposition to the Yaoundé regime", its demands were not separable from "the global struggle of the people of Cameroon for independence, peace and social well-being". He also supplied a list of 118 political detainees held in Cameroon.

Union of Cameroonian Peoples (*Union des populations camerounaises,* UPC)

Leadership. M. Woungly-Massaga (l.)

This clandestine party based in Paris was banned in Cameroon in 1955, when it was regarded as communist-led and responsible for riots which had occurred in Douala in May of that year. The party took no part in elections held on Dec. 23, 1956, for a 70-member Legislative Assembly for the then French Cameroons. The UPC was thereafter divided into a Marxist wing led by Dr Félix Moumié (then in Cairo) and a nationalist wing led by Ruben Um Nyobé, who led a rebellion inside Cameroon but was killed by security forces in September 1958. Many members of this wing thereupon surrendered, and in April 1959 a UPC leader was elected to the Legislative Assembly as a member of the "legal opposition".

Dr Moumié, however, announced in June 1959 that the "revolution" would continue, and guerrilla warfare followed. On Aug. 18, 1959, he and André-Marie M'Bida (a former Premier of the Cameroonian government) issued a warning that "revolutionary action" would continue until the French government agreed to abolish the existing institutions in Cameroon, to annul the decree banning the UPC, and to convene a round-table conference to be followed by general elections as essential prerequisites for real independence. While UPC guerrilla activities continued, Dr Moumié died in Geneva on Nov. 3, 1960, after he had alleged that he had been poisoned by the "Red Hand", a French organization engaged in counter-terrorist activities against the Algerian nationalists.

In post-independence Cameroon the UPC was held responsible for protracted unrest until 1970, when its leader, Ernest Ouandié, was captured by security forces. He was later tried for "attempted revolution" and other crimes, together with the Roman Catholic bishop (Albert Ndongmo) and 25 other defendants; on Jan. 5, 1971, he and two other accused were sentenced to death and the bishop to life imprisonment (after he had admitted that he had sometimes given material aid to the UPC), while 13 other defendants were given prison sentences of from five to 20 years. However, at a second trial on charges of having plotted the assassination of President Ahmadou Ahidjo of Cameroon, the bishop and two other defendants were sentenced to death on Jan. 6, 1971, when prison sentences ranging from five years to life were imposed on 58 further defendants. Ouandié and two others were executed on Jan. 15, but the sentence on the bishop was commuted to life imprisonment; he was subsequently allowed to leave the country, and was officially reprieved on May 17, 1975. Early in August 1985, President Biya authorized the bishop's return to Cameroon.

According to a statement made in April 1975 by Ouandié's successor as leader of the UPC, Woungly-Massaga, the widow of Ouandié was, after being extradited from Equatorial Guinea, being held in Cameroon in detention without trial.

On March 6, 1984, the UPC demonstrated in Paris against the trial procedures in Cameroon and called for the democratization of Cameroon's laws. On Jan. 8, 1986, the UPC claimed that there was growing repression of the anglophone minority in Cameroon, that between 200 and 300 arrests had been made since October 1985 and that cases of torture had occurred.

Yaoundé radio on Aug. 26, 1986, announced the release of 14 detainees described as former members of the UPC. The detainees had returned from exile in France after President Biya had stated that members of the UPC were free to return to Cameroon, but they were later accused of showing allegiance to banned organizations and distributing subversive literature, and were imprisoned for 14 months.

Canada

Capital: Ottawa

Pop. 25,327,900

The Dominion of Canada, a member of the Commonwealth with the British monarch as head of state (represented by a Governor-General), has a Parliament consisting of a 104-member Senate appointed by the Governor-General and a 282-member House of Commons (*Chambre de Communes*) elected by universal adult suffrage for a five-year term. There is a federal Cabinet presided over by a Prime Minister. Of the country's 10 provinces each has its own legislature and government, while the North-west Territories and the Yukon Territory each have elected Legislative Councils. As a result of general elections held on Sept. 4, 1984, seats in the House of Commons were distributed as follows: Progressive Conservative Party 211, Liberal Party 40, New Democratic Party 30, independent 1.

Parties represented in provincial legislatures are the *Parti québécois* (in Quebec) and the Social Credit Party (in British Columbia). Parties without parliamentary representation include the Communist Party of Canada, the Communist Party of Canada (Marxist-Leninist) and the Green Party of Canada.

Left-wing Groups

Direct Action

On May 31, 1982, this group claimed responsibility for a bomb attack on an electric power station under construction on Vancouver Island (British Columbia). On Oct. 20, 1982, the group addressed a nine-page letter to the Toronto left-wing weekly *The Clarion,* claiming responsibility for a bomb explosion on Oct. 14 at a factory of Litton Systems Canada (outside Toronto) engaged in the production of guidance systems for the (US nuclear-armed) cruise missiles. In the letter, in which the group outlined its aims, it expressed its opposition to nuclear weapons but claimed to have no connexion with any of the peace movement organizations which had previously been involved in anti-nuclear demonstrations.

Trotskyist League

Orientation. This group is, unlike other left-wing groups, opposed to co-operation with the New Democratic Party and not unwilling to use violence.

Publication. Spartacus Canada (monthly)

International Affiliations. International Spartacist Tendency

Separatist Movements

Democratic Movement for Independence (*Rassemblement démocratique pour l'indépendance*)

Founded. March 4, 1985

Object. This movement was established by Camille Laurin, not as a political party but as a pressure group within the *Parti québécois,* to obtain independence for Quebec.

National Indian Brotherhood

Leadership. David Ahenakew (pres.); Wallace Labillois (ch. of council of elders)

The council of elders of this Brotherhood claims to represent 300,000 pure-bred Indians in 50 tribes in Canada. It has worked in co-operation with other associations which claim to represent 1,500,000 "original Canadians", including also Inuit (or Eskimo) and Métis (i.e. half-caste) people.

Wallace Labillois did not accept the official British view that all responsibility for the aboriginal people of Canada was formally handed on by Britain on the attainment of independence by the Canadian government in 1931 under the Statute of Westminster; in common with other Canadian Indian leaders he maintained the view that the British Crown continued to have the obligation of safeguarding Indian rights. The National Indian Brotherhood in particular claimed in 1981 that the Canadian colonial authorities had a record of broken pledges on aboriginal rights. The Indian demand was for a guarantee of autonomous enclaves in a legally independent Canada, mainly in the area of Prince Rupert Land, around Hudson Bay.

The leader of an Indian delegation, Chief Solomon Sanderson (president of the Federation of Saskatchewan Indians), said in London on Nov. 3, 1981, that the Canadian Indians would fight for their political independence.

Chief Ahenakew, who was also head of the Assembly of First Nations (of status Indians, who live in the reserve), has said that he does not acknowledge the supremacy of the Parliament of Canada, and Chief Max Gros-Louis, leader of the Huron Indians, stated in February 1983 that his group (like the Provincial government of Quebec) did not recognize the Constitution of Canada. Indians have also claimed that "existing aboriginal rights" as referred to in the Canadian Constitution's Charter of Rights should cover not only the right to "hunting, fishing and gathering" but also ownership of land and its resources.

Quebec Liberation Front (*Front de libération du Québec*, FLQ)

Leadership. Mathieu Hébert (Pierre Vallières)

The FLQ, founded in 1963, has operated under various names to further its aims of the complete separation of the province of Quebec from the rest of Canada, an end to English-language "colonialist" domination of Quebec and transition to a socialist economy. By 1970 it was held responsible for various terrorist and subversive activities, involving seven deaths, bomb explosions and other acts of sabotage, armed robberies, thefts of weapons and plots to kidnap diplomats or politicians. Within seven years 135 persons had been arrested in Quebec for subversive activities.

On Oct. 5 and 10, 1970, respectively, FLQ members kidnapped the British trade commissioner in Montreal (James Richard Cross) and the Quebec Minister of Labour and Immigration (Pierre Laporte). Demands made by the kidnappers in return for the release of their victims were inter alia for payment of Can. $500,000 to the FLQ, the release of 23 "political prisoners" to be given a safe passage to Algeria or Cuba, the publication of an FLQ manifesto and a ban on any police action against the kidnappers. On Oct. 8, the Canadian Broadcasting Corporation broadcast an FLQ manifesto which praised Dr Fidel Castro, the Cuban leader, and strongly denounced a large number of Canadian politicians and business leaders. Following unsuccessful attempts to achieve negotiations between the government and the kidnappers, the Federal government invoked, on Oct. 16, at the request of the Quebec government, the 1914 War Measures Act providing for emergency powers; on the same day police supported by troops arrested 250 political suspects in 170 separate raids. However, almost all of those arrested were released within weeks.

P. Laporte was found murdered on Oct. 18, 1970, but J. R. Cross was released on Dec. 3 after his kidnappers had accepted a government offer of a safe passage to Cuba. Two alleged murderers of P. Laporte—Paul Rose and Francis Simard—were sentenced to life imprisonment on March 13 and May 20, 1971, respectively. In connexion with the abduction of J. R. Cross, prison sentences were imposed in August and November 1979 on three former FLQ members who had returned to Canada after many years in exile, and a further defendant said to be involved in the Cross case was given a four-year sentence in June 1980. A further former FLQ member involved in the Cross case (Yves Langlois) obtained political asylum in France but returned to Canada on June 9, 1982, to face trial.

Since the *Parti québécois* came to power in 1976 committed to the achievement of political sovereignty for Quebec in an economic association with Canada, there has been an abatement of extremist separatist activity.

Mathieu Hébert is editor of the socialist theoretical journal *Révolution Québécoise*.

Other Organization

Sons of Freedom

This group, reported as having a few hundred adherents, is a faction of a religious sect, the Doukhobors, which migrated to Canada from Tsarist Russia. The Sons of Freedom have refused to accept Canadian laws and customs. Three elderly women adherents staged a protracted hunger strike in late 1985 in protest at their imprisonment for arson, and one of the three, Mrs Marey Astaforoff, 71, died in consequence.

Cape Verde

Capital: Praia Pop. 390,000

The Republic of Cape Verde is, under its Constitution approved on Sept. 7, 1980, a "sovereign, democratic, unitary, anti-colonialist and anti-imperialist republic". It has a National People's Assembly, an executive President and a Cabinet headed by a Prime Minister. The President is also the secretary-general of the country's sole legal political party, the African Party for the Independence of Cape Verde (PAICV), established on Jan. 20, 1981, as the successor to the Cape Verde branch of the African Party for the Independence of Guinea-Bissau and Cape Verde (PAIGC), whose government in Guinea-Bissau was overthrown on Nov. 14, 1980.

Elections to the 83-member National Assembly were held on Dec. 7, 1985, on a single list of candidates proposed by the PAICV to be accepted or rejected by the voters. In a turnout of 69 per cent of registered voters only 5.1 per cent voted against the list. There are said to be no political prisoners in the Cape Verde Islands. Three members of the government who resigned during 1979 were expelled from the PAIGC as "Trotskyites".

Independent Democratic Union of Cape Verde (UCID)

This clandestine opposition movement was opposed to the ruling PAIGC's policy of eventual union between Cape Verde and Guinea-Bissau, on the grounds that such a union would extend Soviet influence in the region. Since the successor party to the PAIGC, the PAICV, has declared itself in favour of an independent state of Cape Verde, the UCID's influence has declined. It has admitted that its organization exists only among emigrant Cape Verdian communities overseas, who are opposed to a governmental land reform involving the expropriation of land owned by absentee landlords.

In June 1982 prison sentences were imposed by a military court on 16 defendants alleged to be linked to the UCID and charged with attempting to alter the Constitution of Cape Verde by violence; in particular, they were said to have incited rebellion on San Antão island against the implementation of the land reform during August 1981, when at least one person was killed in riots which were quelled by the security forces.

Central African Republic

Capital: Bangui

Pop. 2,610,000

The Central African Republic has been under military rule since Sept. 1, 1981, when President David Dacko was deposed and the Constitution and the country's political parties were suspended. Legislative and executive powers were assumed by a new Military Committee for National Recovery (CMRN) whose chairman, Gen. André Kolingba (Army Chief of Staff), became Chief of the General Staff of the Armed Forces, head of government and Minister of Defence.

The political parties legalized under the Constitution promulgated on Feb. 6, 1981, but subsequently banned or suspended (finally in September 1981) as well as a newly-formed party in exile are described below.

In a referendum held on Nov. 21, 1986, over 90 per cent of the voters were officially stated to have approved a new Constitution providing for the establishment of a one-party state and for the continuation in office of Gen. Kolingba as President for a further six years, for which he was sworn in on Nov. 29. The party envisaged under the Constitution was established on Feb. 7, 1987, as the *Rassemblement démocratique centrafricain* with President Kolingba as chairman.

The new Constitution also provided for the election of a legislative body.

Jean-Bédel Bokassa, who ruled the country from 1966 to 1979 (from 1976 as Emperor of the Central African Empire), was on June 12, 1987, sentenced to death for mass murder, embezzlement and other charges. He had returned voluntarily to the Central African Republic in 1986.

Central African Democratic Union (*Union démocratique centrafricaine,* UDC)

Leadership. David Dacko (l.)

The UDC was established in March 1980 by President Dacko as the country's sole legal party to serve as his power base until elections were held. Dacko had first become head of the Central African government in 1959 and head of state on independence in 1960; although overthrown in 1966 by President Bokassa (who later became Emperor), he was appointed as the latter's personal adviser in September 1976; three years later he overthrew the Emperor's regime and restored, with French help, the Central African Republic. In the presidential elections of March 15, 1981, Dacko was officially stated to have received 50.23 per cent of the valid votes cast in a 77 per cent poll (but this result was contested by the opposition parties which considered the elections to have been fraudulent).

Central African Movement for National Liberation (*Mouvement centrafricain de libération nationale,* MCLN)

Leadership. Alphonse Mbaikoua; François Bozize

The MCLN was founded as a pro-Libyan party in August 1980 by Rodolphe Idi Lala after he had been excluded from the Oubangian Patriotic Front (led by Dr Abel Goumba) for which he had been spokesman.

In a statement issued from Nigeria on July 16, 1981, the MCLN claimed responsibility for a bomb explosion at a cinema in Bangui on July 14, when three persons were killed and 32 others injured. Lala later threatened to commit further acts of violence unless President Dacko formed a unity government comprising all political parties and also arranged for the repatriation of the French troops stationed in the Central African Republic. The MCLN was officially banned on July 18, 1981.

On June 6, 1983, a special tribunal passed sentences of imprisonment for life on five members of the MCLN's political bureau (among them Idi Lala, who was tried in absentia) and 10-year prison sentences (with an additional 10 years to be served in an open prison) on 16 other defendants for their part in the July 1981 bomb explosion.

On Dec. 10, 1984, A. Mbaikoua joined the provisional government of national salvation formed by the Movement for the Liberation of the Central African People (MLPC). He had earlier been accused of leading armed rebels in southern Chad and of collaborating with anti-government forces in Chad in a cross-border attack on Nov. 9, 1984, on the town of Markounda (in the Central African Republic). (This incident was followed by allegations that the Libyan people's bureau in Bangui was a place of contact for Central African and Chadian dissidents.)

Central African People's Rally (*Rassemblement du peuple centrafricain*)

Leadership. Gen. Sylvestre Bangui (l.)

Gen. Bangui had been ambassador of the Central African Empire in France until May 22, 1979, when he resigned in protest at a massacre of school children (committed with Emperor Bokassa's participation) and founded a Oubangian Liberation Front; on Sept. 11, 1979, he announced (in Paris) the formation of a provisional government-in-exile of the "Republic of Oubangui" with the aim of overthrowing the Emperor, drafting a new constitution and holding elections to a new National Assembly within 18 months. After the overthrow of the Emperor on Sept. 21, 1979, he returned to Bangui and subsequently was Deputy Prime Minister with responsibility for Foreign Affairs until Nov. 12, 1980, when this post was abolished. The following month he announced the formation of the *Rassemblement du peuple centrafricain.*

He was a minister of state from Feb. 10, 1983, until January 1984. On Dec. 10, 1984, he took part in the formation of the provisional government of national salvation by the leaders of the Central African Movement for National Liberation (MCLN).

Central African Revolutionary Party (*Parti révolutionnaire centrafricain,* PRC)

This party was formed at a secret meeting held on Aug. 5, 1983, by representatives of the major opposition groups—the Oubanguian Patriotic Front—Party of Labour (FPO-PT), the Central African Movement for National Liberation (MCLN) and the Movement for the Liberation of the Central African People (MLPC).

Central African Socialist Party (*Parti socialiste centrafricain,* PSC)

Leadership. Jean Tandalet Ozi Okito (l.)

This party's leader stated on Feb. 21, 1981, that the presidential elections scheduled for March 15 were premature, that proper electoral lists needed to be prepared and that he was withdrawing his candidature.

The party's leader was imprisoned in April 1984 but was subsequently released under an amnesty of Dec. 31 of that year.

Independent Grouping of Reflection and Action (*Groupement indépendant de réflexion et d'action,* GIRA)

Leadership. François Pehoua (l.)

Standing as an independent in the presidential elections of March 15, 1981, François Pehoua, a banker and former minister, advocated democracy and a liberal economic policy leading to self-sufficiency in food production; however, he obtained only 5.33 per cent of the valid votes cast (according to the official results). The GIRA was one of the four parties which formed a "provisional political council" seeking (according to a statement issued in Paris on July 25, 1981) the resignation of President Dacko and the establishment of a national council charged with setting up a "provisional government of national unity"; the four parties also reaffirmed their determination to work for peace and "true democracy" in the Central African Republic.

Movement for Democracy and Independence (*Mouvement pour la démocratie et l'indépendance,* MDI)

Leadership. François Guéret (l.)

François Guéret was a member of the Cabinet under President Dacko from September 1979 until March 1980, when he was dismissed after having prepared, as Minister of Justice, a report on crimes of the Emperor Bokassa's regime; in this report he had incriminated various members of President Dacko's regime (in particular Henri Maidou, who had been Prime Minister under the Emperor and later was Vice-President under President Dacko). Guéret established the MDI in 1981.

On April 21, 1983, he was appointed High Commissioner of State, and on Jan. 23, 1984, he was entrusted with the department of State Enterprises and Joint Ventures. However, on Feb. 13, 1985, he was arrested on unspecified charges and dismissed from his post. On Aug. 13, 1985, a special court sentenced him to 10 years in prison for threatening the security of the state and planning to overthrow the government with the help of mercenaries. However, he was released, together with 63 other detainees described as "political prisoners", under an amnesty declared on Nov. 29, 1986.

Movement for the Liberation of the Central African People (*Mouvement de libération du peuple centrafricain,* MLPC)

Leadership. Francis-Albert Ouakanga (sec.-gen.); Raphaël Nambele (sec. for external relations)

History. This movement was founded by Ange Patasse, who was Prime Minister from September 1976 to July 1978 (when he was replaced by Henri Maidou, later the leader of the Republican Progress Party). After he had left the country he stated in Paris on June 7, 1979, that a "committee of national union" was being formed to speed up the liberation of the country from the Emperor, whom he accused inter alia of being responsible for numerous summary executions and of trying to poison him (Patasse). While in exile he set up the MLPC, which rejected the government of President Dacko established in September 1979; Patasse was nevertheless allowed to return to Bangui in October of that year. On Nov. 3, 1979, however, he was arrested for "fomenting unrest", and he was not released until Nov. 24, 1980. By that time the MLPC had obtained widespread support in the country, and in the presidential elections of March 15, 1981. A. Patasse came second with 38.11 per cent of the valid votes (according to the official results).

The MLPC was suspended on July 18, 1981, but was on Aug. 10 of that year allowed to resume its activities. It was one of the four parties which formed a "provisional political council" and which (in a statement issued in Paris on July 25, 1981) called for the resignation of President Dacko and the establishment of a national council charged with setting up a "provisional government of national unity".

However, on March 6, 1982, the MLPC was banned after a number of its members and several army officers had been arrested in connexion with an unsuccessful attempt to overthrow the military government on March 3. Ange Patasse took refuge in the French embassy in Bangui on March 6, and on April 13 he was flown to Togo (where he was granted political asylum).

On Dec. 10, 1984, the MLPC formed a provisional government of national salvation headed by Alphonse Mbaikoua and François Bozize (the leaders of the Central African Movement for National Liberation, MCLN) and joined by Rodolphe Idi Lala (also of the MCLN), Joseph Potolot (a former minister under the Emperor Bokassa in 1978) and Lt.-Gen. Sylvestre Bangui (leader of the *Rassemblement du peuple centrafricain* and a minister of state until January 1984).

Orientation. The MLPC is a democratic socialist movement and has called upon Gen. Kolingba to start the process of democratization and to meet the opposition parties.

Oubangian Patriotic Front—Party of Labour (*Front patriotique oubangais—Parti du travail*, FPO-PT)

Leadership. Dr Abel Goumba (1.); Patrice Endijimongou (sec.-gen. for external relations)

Dr Goumba had been an opponent of David Dacko (then president) since 1959. He was leader of a *Mouvement d'évolution démocratique d'Afrique Centrale,* which was officially accused of being based on tribalism and which was dissolved in February 1961, when Dr Goumba and other leaders of the movement were placed under house arrest. He was later allowed to leave the country and became an official of the World Health Organization. From the Congo he set up an Oubangian Patriotic Front, which in a statement issued in January 1980 rejected the government of President Dacko, and called for the departure of French troops from the country and for a general election to bring about the restoration of free democracy.

After 17 years in exile Dr Goumba returned to Bangui in February 1981 and stood as a candidate for the FPO-PT in the presidential elections of March 15, 1981, but obtained only 1.42 per cent of the valid votes (as officially stated). The FPO-PT was banned on July 18, 1981, but was allowed to resume its activities on Aug. 10, of that year. However, after the coup of Sept. 1, 1981, it was suspended with all other political parties.

The FPO-PT had been one of the four parties which formed a "provisional political council" and which (in a statement issued in Paris on July 25, 1981) called for the resignation of President Dacko and the establishment of a national council charged with setting up a "provisional government of national unity".

However, on Aug. 30, 1982, the authorities of the Central African Republic announced that "subversive documents" had been found three days earlier in the possession of the banned party's secretary-general for external affairs at Bangui airport, and that both he and Dr Goumba, who had supplied the documents, had been arrested. The authorities also claimed to have formal evidence of the existence of close ties between Dr Goumba and the leader of an unnamed foreign political party (believed to be the French Socialist Party). On April 22, 1983, they were both sentenced to five years' imprisonment and 10 years' deprivation of civil rights for trying to set up a "clandestine revolutionary organization".

However, both were released under an amnesty announced on Aug. 31, 1983. Dr Goumba was nevertheless rearrested on Jan. 27, 1984, when Henri Maidou (president of the Republican Progress Party) and Simon Narcisse Bozanga (a former Prime Minister under President Dacko) were also arrested, all three being sent into temporary internal exile for alleged contacts with striking students. They were subsequently released under another amnesty, announced on Dec. 31, 1984, and covering 53 alleged political offenders, among them P. Endijimooungou, who had been sent into internal exile in August 1984.

Republican Progress Party (*Parti républicain du progrès,* PRP)

Leadership. Henri Maidou (l.)

Although Henri Maidou had been Prime Minister under the Emperor Bokassa, he served as Vice-President under President Dacko from September 1979 to Aug. 23, 1980, when he was dismissed and placed under house arrest for a month, having been incriminated (in a report of Jan. 19, 1980, by François Guéret, then Minister of Justice) of involvement in the imprisonment of school children and misappropriation of public funds under the Emperor. In the presidential elections of March 15, 1981, he obtained only 3.23 per cent of the valid votes as the candidate of the newly-formed PRP, which called for representative democracy and free debate.

The PRP was one of the four parties which formed a "provisional political council" and which (in a statement issued in Paris on July 25, 1981) called for the resignation of President Dacko and the establishment of a national council which would be charged with setting up a "provisional government of national unity".

Chad

Capital: N'Djaména Pop. 5,020,000

Chad, which achieved independence from France in 1960, has been in a condition of intermittent civil war since the 1960s. The capital and the southern half of Chad has been controlled by the government of President Hissène Habré since 1982. Goukouni Oueddei, who held power in N'Djaména with Libyan support from October 1980 to June 1982 and had previously been the leading figure with Habré in the *Front de libération national du Tchad* (Frolinat), continued the civil war in the north of the country with Libyan backing, and in January 1984 France (which supported Habré) declared Chad south of the 16th parallel to be an exclusion zone, effectively dividing the country into two with the south, including N'Djaména, held by Habré and the Libyan-backed rebels (calling themselves the Transitional Government of National Unity, GUNT) holding the north. In late 1986 significant elements of the GUNT forces defected to Habré and in a major offensive in the early months of 1987 forces supporting Habré, with French backing, succeeded in driving the Libyans out of the country (other than the Aouzou Strip, claimed by Libya, on the northern border).

Idriss Miskine Group

This anti-Habré Group claimed responsibility for two bomb explosions at N'Djaména airport on March 10, 1984, when a French airliner was severely damaged. The Group took its name from the former Foreign Minister who died on Jan. 7, 1984; the Group accused President Habré of having killed him.

Transitional Government of National Unity (*Gouvernement d'union nationale de transition,* GUNT)

The GUNT was formed in 1979 uniting forces loyal to Habré and Goukouni but was opposed by Libya; it quickly disintegrated into opposing factions with Goukouni (backed by Libya) driving Habré's forces from N'Djaména in October 1980. After Habré regained power in 1982 the GUNT united anti-Habré forces and enjoyed substantial Libyan military support gaining effective control in the northern half of the country. In the latter months of 1986, however, the GUNT was seriously affected by internal divisions, with several factions defecting to the Habré government, and the *Forces armées populaires* (FAP), which had formed the core of its fighting strength and supported Goukouni, engaged in clashes with Libyan troops. At a meeting of several GUNT factions in Cotonou (Benin) on Nov. 14-18, Goukouni was declared "expelled" and Acheikh Ibn Oumar, the leader of the *Conseil démocratique révolutionnaire* faction, was chosen as GUNT president.

A Cabinet announced by the Ibn Oumar group on Dec. 28 included Maj. Nadjita Yombal Leonard as vice-president and Dr. Facho Balaam as "foreign minister". Ibn Oumar on March 14, 1987, stated that the GUNT "is not a fiction as some people think", reaffirmed that the "assistance that we are receiving from our Libyan friends is a real fact", and called for a negotiated settlement with the N'Djaména government under the auspices of the Organization of African Unity (OAU).

Goukouni, who was reportedly under guard in Tripoli (Libya), stated on Feb. 1, 1987, that Libya was "our haven and our natural ally", that confrontation between FAP and Libyan forces had been the result of a "misunderstanding", and denied reports that he was in detention. He arrived in Algiers on Feb. 8 and subsequently engaged in talks with the Habré government (announcing in April his belief that the war was over and his willingness on certain conditions to recognize Habré's authority), while stating his hopes for an eventual amelioration of relations between Chad and Libya. There were parallel reports of secret peace talks between Libya and Chad reflecting the major Libyan military reverses.

Chile

Capital: Santiago Pop. 12,070,000

The Republic of Chile has since the overthrow of its parliamentary government on Sept. 11, 1973, been ruled (under emergency provisions) by a four-member junta of the commanders of the armed services and the para-military police, who dissolved the National Congress, banned the country's Marxist parties, placed all other parties into "indefinite recess" and prohibited all political activities. All remaining political parties were also banned on March 12, 1977. On June 26, 1974, Gen. Augusto Pinochet Ugarte was designated Supreme Chief of State, and in December, President of the Republic (although he did not formally assume that title until March 1981). The junta proclaimed various "constitutional acts" in 1976 purporting to establish an "authoritarian democracy", and in 1981 a "fundamental law", separating the presidency from the junta, provided for a bicameral legislature which would not, however, be elected until 1989. In the latter year the junta would nominate a single presidential candidate who, if confirmed by plebiscite, would remain in power until 1997, when free presidential elections would take place; if the candidate was rejected President Pinochet would remain in office for another year but would call for such elections within that year. The new Constitution, which entered into force on March 11, 1981, had been approved in a national plebiscite on Sept. 11, 1980, by 67.01 per cent of the votes cast, with 30.14 per cent against it.

Following the 1973 coup many left-wing and centrist activists were killed, arrested, tortured, exiled or "disappeared", but most parties continued to operate in exile and more or less clandestinely inside Chile forming a number of alliances and coalitions to press for a rapid return to democracy; some on the left adopted a strategy of armed resistance to the junta, especially after 1983. The continued existence of parties was acknowledged by members of the regime from 1981. In December 1982 the government showed some willingness to open up political life in a process referred to as the *abertura*, with the announcement that certain political exiles (variously estimated at between 11,000 and 200,000) would be allowed to return to Chile. On Sept. 16, 1983, a decree was issued establishing regulations for the holding of public meetings provided at least 48 hours' notice was given and, in 1984, the regime announced that parties would be allowed to function under certain conditions, notably that they accepted the 1981 Constitution. On July 21, 1986, the President denied reports that he intended to extend his term of office beyond 1989.

On Dec. 31, 1986, President Pinochet announced that the state of siege, which had been in force since 1973, would not be renewed when it expired on Jan. 6, 1987, and that the banishment order against "anyone who deserves to return to the country" was to be lifted within 90 days. On Jan. 29, 1987, it was disclosed that the registration of Chile's 7,500,000 voters was to begin on Feb. 25. However, a draft law restoring the right to form political parties, approved by the military junta on Jan. 15 and signed by the President on March 11, was immediately rejected by the opposition as "undemocratic" because of the numerous restrictions which it contained. ("Marxist" parties were to remain banned.)

From 1983 to the end of 1986 some 7,034 exiles had reportedly been given permission to return to Chile although only 1,656 had apparently done so. Moreover, of that number, only 908 had stayed, citing various social, economic and political limitations imposed upon them by the regime. The President promised, on Dec. 31, 1986, to put an end to the practice of exile and during the following three months authorized the return of 2,027 exiles. However, as at March 31, 1987, only 28 of those granted permission to return had actually done so and a further 1,400 Chileans remained barred from the country.

In addition to the political movements which existed until Sept. 11, 1973, numerous new organizations have opposed the Pinochet regime. They have included new political parties and alliances, human rights pressure groups, the Roman Catholic Church and various trade unions. Terrorist activities against left-wing organizations and supporters have been carried out by small groups of extreme right-wingers.

Traditional Parties and Movements

Christian Democratic Party (*Partido Democrático Cristiano*, PDC)

Leadership. Gabriel Valdés Subercaseaux (pres.); Eugenio Ortega (sec.-gen.)

The PDC (often known as the *Democracia Cristiana*, DC) was created in 1957 as the successor to a National Falange founded in 1934; as a democratic reform party, it advocated a new social doctrine based on Christian humanism to overcome Chile's poverty and economic underdevelopment. The PDC's leader, Dr Eduardo Frei Montalva, was President of the Republic from 1964 to 1970, when he was succeeded by the Socialist, Dr Salvador Allende Gossens, whose regime was strongly opposed by the PDC. The party at first gave tacit support to the military junta which had seized power in 1973 but by 1974 many PDC leaders increasingly opposed the regime. In effect, the PDC became divided, as members of its right wing began to co-operate with the junta whereas what appeared to be the party's main body opposed it and took part in meetings and initiatives outside Chile organized by the Popular Unity alliance of left-wing parties (see separate entry).

At a secret congress held in March 1975 the PDC issued a declaration describing the ruling military junta as a "right-wing dictatorship with fascist manifestations" and their policies as "erroneous, unjust and incompatible with our principles regarding human rights, economic orientation and the situation of the workers". On the other hand, the congress rejected any liaison with "clandestine organizations".

Dr Frei Montalva declined to become a member of a consultative Council of State established on Dec. 31, 1975, on the grounds that the Council had no juridical basis and that the government would in no way be bound by its advice. On the other hand, the authorities allowed "as an exception", on Jan. 23, 1976, the publication of a booklet by Dr Frei, criticizing various aspects of the military junta and pleading for a "democratic alternative" to its totalitarian rule.

On March 12, 1977, the Santiago press published the plans of two Christian Democrats—Andrés Zaldívar Larraín and Tomás Reyes—calling for the co-operation of all political forces in order to achieve a peaceful gradual transition to democracy. The Secretary-General to the Cabinet said that such plans would be "called subversive in any country", and on the same day the junta issued a decree banning all the remaining parties, i.e. the Christian Democrats, the National Party, the Radical Democrats and the Radical Left, on the ground that there was a Christian Democratic plot to overthrow the government.

In a document released in Venezuela on Oct. 17, 1977, the PDC proposed that a "national movement of democratic restoration" should be created to replace Chile's military government and demanded the convocation of a directly elected constituent assembly leading to an eventual full return to parliamentary democracy with an elected President; as an immediate step it proposed the lifting of the state of siege in force since September 1973 and renewed from time to time.

On Dec. 27, 1977, the PDC issued a statement urging the electorate to vote "no" in a plebiscite called for by President Pinochet (for Jan. 4, 1978) to endorse a declaration of support for the President and for the "legitimacy" of the government. The PDC condemned the holding of the plebiscite while the country was still under a state of siege, stating that the result would have no validity.

On Jan. 14, 1978, a military court ordered the indefinite exiling to remote villages in the northern Andes of 12 leading Christian Democrats (including Tomás Reyes, the party's vice-president) arrested with several others on Jan. 13 for indulging in political activity by holding a meeting. On Jan. 17, 1978, the PDC claimed that 60 of its members had been arrested, mistreated or banished. On Jan. 30 the federal court of appeals decided that the authorities could not deprive persons of their liberty unless they were convicted of a crime, and that the 12 persons exiled on Jan. 14 would have to be transferred to a hotel in Arica (a port near the border with Peru)—exile from one province to another being permitted. The 12 were, however, allowed to return to Santiago on March 2, 1978.

Ex-President Frei, addressing an authorized meeting on Aug. 28, 1979, called for the formation of a civilian-military transitional government to restore full democracy within the next two to three years. The meeting, however, turned into an opposition demonstration which was broken up by police. Other such demonstrations took place that year.

On Oct. 16, 1980, the junta announced that A. Zaldívar Larraín, then PDC president touring Europe, would not be allowed to re-enter Chile unless he signed a document accepting the results of the plebiscite of Sept. 11, 1980, approving the new Constitution and the authority of the government and the Constitution. The PDC presidency was subsequently assumed by Gabriel Valdés.

Ex-President Frei died in Santiago on Jan. 22, 1982, when President Pinochet declared three days of official mourning; the government service on Jan. 25 was boycotted by the family who held an alternative service attended by thousands and addressed by Cardinal Raúl Silva Henríquez (Archbishop of Santiago and Primate of Chile).

Four exiled Christian Democrats who were not allowed to enter Chile for ex-President Frei's funeral included Jaime Castillo Velasco, president of the Chilean Human Rights Commission, who had been expelled in August 1981 with three other prominent opposition figures after they had been accused of violating the ban on political activity and showing a "defiant attitude". In his capacity as a lawyer, Jaime Castillo Velasco had been acting for the family of Orlando Letelier, the former Chilean ambassador in Washington and minister in the Allende government, who had been murdered in the US capital in 1976 by Chilean secret agents.

The arrest, on July 9, 1983, of G. Valdés, of José de Gregorio (then the PDC secretary-general) and of Jorge Lavandero (the leader of the Project for National Development—see separate entry), on charges of organizing demonstrations against the regime caused widespread unrest in which two people were killed, dozens injured and 570 arrested. The three men were set free on July 14. In August 1983, A. Zaldívar Larraín was granted permission to return to Chile.

Under Valdés the PDC has advocated co-operation among a wide range of democratic parties (but not the Communist Party of Chile, PCCh—see separate entry) to secure an end to military rule. It was a founder member of the Multi-party Alliance and has given complete support to the Democratic Alliance (*Alianza Democrática*, AD) formed respectively on March 14 and Aug. 6, 1983 (see separate entries). On Aug. 25, 1985 it was party to the "National Accord for Peaceful Evolution towards Complete and Genuine Democracy" (see entry for Democratic Alliance).

In 1986 the PDC refused to support a 48-hour strike called for Sept. 4-5 by the Popular Democratic Movement (MDP—see separate entry), apparently to avoid association with what it considered the violent tactics of the far left. The PDC argued that violence played into the hands of Gen. Pinochet, and advocated instead peaceful action and the search for dialogue with members of the government other than the President. In a press conference on Sept. 26, 1986, Valdés announced his party's acceptance of the current Constitution as a political "fact" and reiterated both his preparedness to negotiate with the armed forces and his criticism of the PCCh for refusing to denounce the use of violence and the guerrilla tactics of the Manuel Rodríguez Patriotic Front (FPMR—see separate entry) in the struggle against the military regime.

On Nov. 21, 1986, the PDC became a founding member of the National Democratic Accord (ANDE, see separate entry), Eugenio Ortega having been among three opposition politicians to take part in the first-ever formal contacts between members of the ruling military junta and the opposition in mid-November.

The PDC is directed by a political commission elected by a national congress. It has a youth wing, the Christian Democratic Youth (*Juventud de la Democracia Cristiana*, JDC).

The PDC is a member of the Christian Democratic International and of the Christian Democratic Organization of America.

Christian Left (*Izquierda Cristiana*, IC)

Leadership. Luis Maira (l.)

This small Christian Left formation was formed by elements of the Christian Democratic Party (PDC—see separate entry) which, influenced by liberation theology, supported the candidacy of the Socialist leader, Dr Salvador Allende Gossens, in the November 1970 presidential elections. As part of the Popular Unity alliance (see separate entry), the Christian Left was banned by the military junta which seized power in September 1973. Since then it has participated in anti-junta activities and has in particular acted as a bridge between the Popular Unity parties and the left-wing section of the PDC itself. It is a member of the Democratic Alliance, of the Chilean Socialist Bloc and of the Popular Democratic Movement, all formed in 1983 (see separate entries), and its leadership has given guarded welcome to the 1985 proposal for a "national accord" on the restoration of democracy (see entry for Democratic Alliance). On Nov. 21, 1986, the IC became a founding member of the National Democratic Accord (ANDE—see separate entry), whose aim was to campaign for free and open elections in 1989.

Communist Party of Chile (*Partido Comunista Chileno*, PCCh)

Leadership. Luis Corvalán Lepe (sec.-gen. in exile)

A Socialist Workers' Party (*Partido Socialista de los Trabajadores*, PST) founded in 1912 decided at its fourth congress held in Rancagua in January 1922, to affiliate with the Third International and to change its name to Communist Party of Chile. By 1970 the PCCh was the third largest among pro-Moscow Communist parties (after those of France and Italy) outside the Communist-ruled countries. In congressional elections held on March 2, 1969, the PCCh gained 22 out of the 150 seats in the Chamber of Deputies; in the presidential elections of Nov. 4, 1970, it was part of the Popular Unity alliance, whose candidate, the Socialist Dr Salvador Allende Gossens, was elected President with 36.3 per cent of the votes cast. In the Popular Unity Cabinet formed subsequently, the PCCh was given ministerial posts.

Following the banning of the PCCh by the junta which took power on Sept. 11, 1973, the party went underground, carrying out secret activities despite serious losses resulting from the arrest or death of many of its members. The party claimed at the end of October 1973 that "a communal struggle" was being prepared "for the overthrow of the military regime". Thereafter the party co-ordinated its anti-junta activities in exile within the framework of the Popular Unity alliance (see separate entry).

On Dec. 18, 1976, Luis Corvalán Lepe (former secretary-general of the PCCh, held in detention in Chile since September 1973) was exchanged at Zurich airport against Vladimir Bukovsky (the Soviet dissident imprisoned in the Soviet Union since 1972). L. Corvalán Lepe was taken to the Soviet Union, where he made several statements on the policy of the PCCh, notably one on Dec. 30, 1976, when he alleged that there were 3,300 political prisoners in Chile and that another 2,000 persons had disappeared. (On June 19, 1977, Jorge Montes—a PCCh leader detained in Chile since July 1974—was released in exchange for the release of 11 German political prisoners held in the German Democrate Republic.)

On Jan. 4, 1977, L. Corvalán Lepe called (in Moscow) for the formation of a united front of all democratic forces, including the Chilean Christian Democrats, against the "military dictatorship" in Chile; at the same time he declared that the PCCh firmly adhered to the principles of "proletarian internationalism" and of the "dictatorship of the proletariat", claiming that the latter concept was more democratic than "any bourgeois form of government", although in Chile its implementation was a problem to be solved at a later stage.

In October 1983, Gen. Fernando Matthei, the commander of the air force and a member of the ruling military junta, stated his willingness to negotiate with the PCCh because "the Marxists are a reality in this country and I prefer to face reality".

In recent years the party has pursued a mainly political campaign although it has not rejected the use of military tactics, and the left-wing guerrilla group, the Manuel Rodríguez Patriotic Front (FPMR) formed in 1984 (see separate entry), is regarded by the regime as the military wing of the Party. The PCCh is a member of the socialist Popular Democratic Movement (MDP) formed on Sept. 3, 1983, but not of the Democratic Alliance (AD, see separate entries).

In August 1985 the PCCh indicated its opposition to the proposed terms of the "national accord" for the transition to democracy as announced by the AD on Aug. 26, and, in a communiqué issued on Oct. 12, 1986, it deplored the fact that "Christian Democracy and the Democratic Alliance have rejected dialogue with the popular forces, seeking instead to talk with the dictatorial regime"; the PCCh, it said, was "willing to hold dialogue with the armed forces to negotiate a transition to democracy, but without Pinochet". Such a dialogue "should be based on the total unity, without exception, of all political forces" and assisted by the struggle of the people manifested in social mobilization.

In early December 1986 the PCCh, along with the Christian Left (IC—see separate entry) and the Almeyda faction of the Socialist Party of Chile (PSCh—see separate entry), issued a document condemning terrorism and rejecting both "military defeat and negotiating within the system" as a means to a democratic solution to Chile's problems, emphasizing instead their support for a "democratic struggle of the masses" and an agreement reached by all of the opposition forces.

A Socialist conclave held in Santiago by the various socialist and other leftist parties, including the PCCh, issued on Dec. 17 a communiqué rejecting any political solution in Chile from which its participants were excluded, and contending that a military approach without the participation of the masses was not the proper way to oust the regime. The conclave (the first such gathering inside Chile since 1973) asserted that it was essential to deploy a national civil disobedience campaign in order to make the country ungovernable.

The PCCh is recognized by the communist parties of the Soviet Union and its allies.

Movement of the Revolutionary Left (*Movimiento de la Izquierda Revolucionaria*, MIR)

Leadership. Andrés Pascal Allende (sec.-gen.)

Under the Christian Democratic government headed by President Eduardo Frei Montalva (in 1964-70) the MIR, established in 1965 as an extreme left-wing group committed to guerrilla activities, was illegal. It gave conditional support to President Allende after the latter's election in 1970, but repeatedly called for much more radical revolutionary procedures than those of the government. On Nov. 1, 1971, its secretary-general at the time (Miguel Enríquez) demanded the abolition of Parliament, its replacement by a "people's assembly" and the takeover of farms and factories without compensation.

After the assumption of power by the military junta the MIR was in open conflict with the regime. An offer of a truce, said to have been made by the Armed Forces Intelligence Service, was publicly refused by the MIR on Sept. 10, 1974. On Oct. 5, 1974, M. Enríquez was killed in a gun battle with troops in Santiago. On Jan. 8, 1975, a group of 12 army officers were given prison sentences of up to 15 years for collaboration with the MIR. On Nov. 10, 1975, the government announced that it had arrested 15 MIR members in connexion with an "operation red boomerang" designed to infiltrate 1,200 extremists into southern Chile from Argentina in collaboration with the Argentinian People's Revolutionary Army (ERP); the organizers of this operation were said to include A. P. Allende.

In January 1976 safe-conducts out of Chile were issued for four leading MIR members who had been involved in a gunfight with police on Oct. 15, 1975, when another MIR leader had been killed; the four men included A. P. Allende, who arrived in Costa Rica on Feb. 2, 1976.

From 1976 onwards MIR guerrillas were involved in numerous actions. During 1980 alone they claimed to have carried out more than 100 armed attacks, and in clashes with security forces casualties were caused on both sides. MIR members were, in particular, accused of involvement in the killing of a former intelligence chief in 1980 and of a military commander in 1983.

In late 1984 the MIR announced the establishment of a new guerrilla arm, the Popular Resistance Armed Forces (FARP—see separate entry).

The MIR has described as its ultimate objective the creation of a single revolutionary party (*Partido Unico de la Revolución*) embracing all existing left-wing and popular parties and movements. In mid-January 1981 the MIR leadership stated that it had joined with exiled leaders of the Popular Unity formations in signing a declaration providing for joint opposition to the Pinochet regime. During a clandestine press conference held in Santiago on Aug. 5, 1986, A. P. Allende, who had secretly returned from exile, announced that the MIR would accept the formation of "an emergency government" but not the idea of a "social pact to guarantee a democratic future".

The MIR is a member of the Popular Democratic Movement (see separate entry) but has opposed the terms of the "national accord" for a transition to democracy proposed in August 1985 (see entry for Democratic Alliance).

On May 7, 1987, however, it emerged that the MIR was split into (i) a MIR National Secretariat supporting A. P. Allende's policy of conducting clandestine guerrilla warfare and (ii) the central committee in Chile, which sought to maintain an "open relationship with the popular social sectors".

National Party (*Partido Nacional*)

Leadership. Carmen Sáenz de Phillips (l.); Fernando Ochagavia (vice-pres.)

The National Party, a traditional right-wing party, remained active in Chile during the 1980s despite having been banned on March 12, 1977, together with all other parties. It lost most of its support to the anti-military Republican Party which was formed in 1984 (see separate entry).

The party was involved in the August 1985 discussions leading to the formulation of a "national accord" on a return to democracy (see entry for Democratic Alliance). It has nevertheless been associated with attempts to form a more restricted coalition with right-wing parties, and in particular with the National Democratic Party (see separate entry), joining with a section of that party in October 1984 to publish a call for a "democratic consensus" and a liberalization of the regime.

In mid-November 1986 the National Party (represented by Pedro Correa) took part in the first ever formal contacts between members of the ruling military junta and the opposition, becoming later that same month a founding member of the National Democratic Accord (ANDE—see separate entry).

Popular Unity (*Unidad Popular*)

Leadership. Dr. Clodomiro Almeyda Medina (first sec. of executive committee)

Set up in 1969 as an electoral alliance of left-wing parties, which led to the election of the Socialist Dr

Salvador Allende Gossens as President on Nov. 4, 1970, the Popular Unity was deprived of all power through the military coup of Sept. 11, 1973 (on which day President Allende was killed or committed suicide). A secretariat of the Popular Unity was thereupon set up in Rome (Italy) by the Communist ex-Senator Volodia Teitelboim on Sept. 18, 1973. The secretariat later disseminated news of persecution and repression of President Allende's supporters in Chile.

A meeting of leaders of the Popular Unity parties and the left wing of the Christian Democratic Party was held in July 1975 in Caracas (Venezuela), where they decided to work together for the restoration of "a just and socialist democracy in Chile"; at a further meeting in East Berlin in August 1975 they published a joint programme aimed at resisting the military regime and restoring democratic freedoms; and in October they met in London to discuss the establishment of unified headquarters. A further meeting of Popular Unity parties' leaders and left-wing Christian Democrats was held in New York in September 1976, whereafter Dr Almeyda Medina (who had been expelled from Chile on Jan. 11, 1975) declared again that the aim of the Popular Unity was to establish an "anti-fascist" front with the participation of the Christian Democrats.

In a communiqué issued to the press in Santiago in mid-January 1981 it was announced that the parties constituting the Popular Unity alliance—the Communist Party of Chile, the Radical Party, the Christian Left, two wings of the Chilean Socialist Party, the Unified Popular Action Movement and the latter's Worker and Peasant offshoot (see separate entries)—had joined with the Movement of the Revolutionary Left (see separate entry) to sign a declaration of unity providing for joint opposition to the Pinochet regime.

The alliance has largely been superseded by new coalitions such as the Multi-party Alliance, the Democratic Alliance and the Popular Democratic Movement (see separate entries).

Radical Party (*Partido Radical*)

Leadership. Enrique Silva Cimma (pres.); Anselmo Sule (vice-pres.); Ricardo Navarrette (sec.-gen.)

The Radical Party, founded in 1863, became Chile's main progressive formation in the early 20th century and held the presidency in 1938-52. Strongly anti-communist in the 1940s and 1950s, it later gravitated to the left and in 1969 joined the Popular Unity (see separate entry) which secured the election of the Socialist leader, Dr Salvador Allende Gossens, to the presidency in November 1970. Radicals held ministerial posts in successive Popular Unity administrations, although the party was weakened by the breakaway of elements opposed to its espousal of Marxism in 1971. Within Chile the Radical Party has its main strength among white-collar workers and public officials.

As part of the Popular Unity, the party was banned by the military regime which seized power in 1973, and was forced to operate clandestinely or from exile. Thereafter it has aimed at the formation of broad fronts, both among Chilean parties and internationally, in opposition to the junta. Since 1980 the party has experienced divisions between the exiled leadership (in Mexico), which favoured armed struggle and closer relations with Marxist-Leninist groups, and the internal leadership, which presented social democratic policies. This led in 1983 to the replacement of Anselmo Sule as internal leader by Enrique Silva, a former president of the constitutional tribunal. The party then initiated a reunification process with the elements which left in the early 1970s, with the aim of building a strong social democratic presence on the Chilean left. There are still marked right- and left-wing tendencies in the party.

In 1983 the party joined the Multi-party opposition alliance and, subsequently, the Democratic Alliance (see separate entries). As part of its effort to strengthen the non-Marxist left, the party joined the Democratic Socialist Federation (see separate entry) in April 1984. In November 1986 the Radical Party was a founding member of the National Democratic Accord (see separate entry).

The party is the Chilean member of the Socialist International.

Socialist Party of Chile (*Partido Socialista de Chile*, PSCh)

The PSCh was one of the constituent parts of the Popular Unity (*Unidad Popular*, UP) alliance (see separate entry). After the party was banned with all other UP members on Sept. 11, 1973, its leaders went into exile. Early in 1980 it was divided into two factions—one led by Dr Clodomiro Almeyda Medina (former Foreign Minister and Vice-President under President Allende) and a second led by party sec.-gen. Carlos Altamirano who had formed his own breakaway socialist party. On April 30, 1984, C. Altamirano was replaced as secretary-general of the majority group by Prof Carlos Briones. The majority group joined the Multi-party Alliance formed on March 14, 1983 (see separate entry) and, in September 1983, it was the main founder of the Chilean Socialist Bloc (BSCh—see separate entry). At its congress on April 30, 1984, the Briones faction of the PSCh reaffirmed its membership of the Democratic Alliance (AD, also formed in 1983), and later it welcomed, although with certain reservations, the "national accord" for a transition to democracy as proposed in August 1985 by 11 democratic parties (see entry for Democratic Alliance). Within the AD itself it has proposed the creation of a Civic Front (*Frente Cívico*) which would include the AD parties, non-AD democratic parties and other "social organisations", largely as a means of associating communists with the AD platform without the formal integration of the PCCh into the Alliance. During 1986 Briones was succeeded as sec.-gen. by Ricardo Núñez Muñoz (also coordinator of the BSCh).

In contrast to the majority faction of the PSCh, the PSCh (Almeyda) faction has close links with the PCCh, with which it is allied in the Popular Democratic Movement (MDP); it advocates increased co-operation among the parties of the left, while agreeing with the majority leadership that there should be collaboration with non-socialist democratic parties; it therefore joined the Multi-party Alliance but was not party to the AD and has refused to endorse the 1985 proposal for a "national accord" on a transition to democracy.

In early December 1986 the Almeyda faction of the PSCh was reported to have signed a document with the PCCh and the Christian Left (IC—see separate entry), condemning terrorism and rejecting both "military defeat and negotiating within the system" as a means to a democratic solution to Chile's problems, emphasizing instead their support for a "democratic struggle of the masses" and an agreement reached by all of the opposition forces.

Further factions of the PSCh, whose existence emerged in 1985-86, included the PSCh (*Unitario*), the PSCh (*Mandujano*), the PSCh (*Núñez*), the PSCh (*Auténtico*), the PSCh (*Dirección Colectiva*) and the PSCh (*Histórico*).

It was reported on July 2, 1987, that Dr Almeyda had been convicted under the anti-terrorism law as a "promoter of terrorism".

Unified Popular Action Movement (*Movimiento de Acción Popular Unida*, MAPU)

Leadership. Oscar Garretón (l. in exile); Víctor Barrueto (sec.-gen.)

The MAPU was one of the members of the Popular Unity alliance in power under President Allende in 1970-73. It was banned after the 1973 military coup and subsequently engaged in underground activities, as did its small Worker and Peasant offshoot (MAPU-OC—see separate entry).

The MAPU was a member of the Popular Democratic Movement formed in 1983, and also a member of the Chilean Socialist Bloc and, as such, associated with the Democratic Alliance (also formed in 1983—see separate entries). In November 1986 the MAPU was a founding member of the National Democratic Accord (ANDE—see separate entry).

Worker and Peasant United Popular Action Movement (*Movimiento de Acción Popular Unitaria —Obrero Campesino*, MAPU-OC)

Leadership. Sr Gazmuri (l. in exile); Marcelo Contreras (sec.-gen. in Chile)

This faction of the United Popular Action Movement (see separate entry) has also operated clandestinely since the 1973 coup. Its then leader, Jaime Anselmo Cuevas Hormazábal, was arrested in April 1980.

As a member of the Chilean Socialist Bloc, the MAPU-OC was also associated with the Democratic Alliance (see separate entries) and, in November 1986, it became a founding member of the National Democratic Accord (ANDE—see separate entry).

New Opposition Organizations

Ad Mapu

Leadership. José Santos Millao (pres.); Rosamel Millamán (sec.-gen.)

This group, formed by indigenous Mapuche communities in southern Chile, was suppressed by the security forces, and its leaders were sent into internal exile in the Atacama desert in April 1984. A leader of the group had been assassinated by the Chilean Anti-Communist Alliance (Acha—see separate entry) in January of that year.

Ad Mapu is linked with the South American Indian Council (*Consejo Indio Sud-americano*, CISA), of which R. Millamán was treasurer in 1984.

Chilean Socialist Bloc (*Bloque Socialista Chileno*, BSCh)

Leadership. Ricardo Núñez Muñoz (co-ordinator)

Preceded by a Socialist Convergence (*Socialista Convergencia*), this alliance was created on Sept. 17, 1983, by parties which had belonged to the Popular Unity coalition (see separate entry), namely the majority sections of the Chilean Socialist Party (PSCh, the major participant), the Christian Left (IC), the United Popular Action Movement (MAPU) and its Worker and Peasant faction (MAPU-OC)—see separate entries. The BSCh has supported the days of protest against the Pinochet regime, held irregularly since 1983. On Nov. 7, 1984, raids on the organization's headquarters led to the arrest of several leading members of the group.

Together with other parties the Bloc has been active in the broader-based Democratic Alliance (AD—see separate entry) also formed in 1983 but from which it withdrew its support on Dec. 24, 1986. In November 1986 the BSCh was a founding member of the National Democratic Accord (ANDE—see separate entry).

Democratic Alliance (*Aliánza Democrática*, AD)

Leadership. René Abeliuk Manasevich (pres.); Eduardo Cerda (sec.-gen.)

The AD was formed on Aug. 6, 1983, by the same non-communist progressive formations which had formed the Multi-party Alliance earlier in the year (see separate entry) to work for the restoration of democracy and stability. The AD called for far-reaching reforms in state and society, and at the same time rejected any form of one-party government which exercised control of the means of communication and used violence against its political opponents.

Following mass anti-government demonstrations early in August 1983, the group called for the resignation of the Pinochet regime and the holding of elections to a constituent assembly which would reform the Constitution and act as a legislature during a transitional period.

In October the AD formed an executive committee comprising Gabriel Valdés Subercaseaux, president of the Christian Democratic Party (PDC—the largest party within the alliance), Enrique Silva Cimma of the Radical Party, Marcial Mora and Ricardo Lagos of the Chilean Socialist Party and Armando Jaramillo of the Republican Party. On Nov. 21, it was reported that Valdés had refused a request by the PSCh that the Chilean Communist Party (PCCh—see separate entry) should be included in the AD. Valdés was formally declared president of the AD on March 2, 1984.

During demonstrations held on Oct. 27, 1983, G. Silva called on every Chilean to "take an active part in the resistance" to the government and join in the protests. In clashes between demonstrators and police one student was killed, seven were wounded by bullets and 50 were detained. On Nov. 18, 1983, the AD held a rally (the first to receive the government's authorization) which it estimated was attended by 1,000,000 people although official spokesmen put the attendance at 95,000.

A proposed draft law to legalize political parties, to regulate their internal organization and to prepare for elections was on March 8, 1984, denounced by the AD as one of the government's "vain attempts to prolong an exhausted regime". The AD stated that its members could not accept the law because to do so would require them to recognize the 1980 Constitution. Despite the introduction of a state of emergency on March 23, 1984, the AD proceeded with a planned day of national protest on March 27. According to police sources 269 people were arrested on the eve of the protest for violation of the curfew and in the ensuing clashes (which lasted until March 29) six people were killed, 20 wounded and up to 400 detained, 15 of whom were sent into internal exile.

On April 13, 1984, Valdés called for a grand national accord, which would bring together the opposition political groups and supporters of the government to work out a system to establish laws on political activity and the electoral process, while maintaining the AD's demand for the holding of elections by the end of 1985.

During two days of national protest organized by the AD for Sept. 4-5, 1984, 11 people died, over 100 were wounded and as many as 1,000 were believed to have been arrested. Several AD leaders were temporarily detained in early October but on Oct. 10, President Pinochet ordered the withdrawal of charges "for the sake of national unity".

At the initiative of the Archbishop of Santiago, Cardinal Juan Francisco Fresno, leaders of the AD constituent parties met leaders of the National Party (PN), the National Union Movement (MUN) and other parties on Aug. 25, 1985. The following day the parties issued a joint statement on a "national accord for the peaceful evolution towards complete and genuine democracy" (*Acuerdo Nacional para la Evolución Pacífica hacia la Democracia Plena y Auténtica,* AN) calling for the lifting of the state of emergency, the restoration of civil liberties and the introduction of new electoral legislation subject to approval in a referendum. The document, which did not call for the immediate resignation of the President and which included an undertaking that there would be no prosecutions for violations of human rights committed by servants of the military regime, was described by the AD president, Valdés (whose leadership had been confirmed at an AD congress earlier in the year) as a historic political act, the most important of the past 12 years, involving a precise agreement among all democratic groups on the criteria for a return to democracy.

Among national figures who added their endorsement to the proposal was Gen. Gustavo Leigh, one of the orginal members of the four-man junta installed in 1973.

In a speech on Sept. 11 President Pinochet reaffirmed his intention of staying on in power until 1989 and rejected the AN, saying that Chile would achieve "true democracy" only by adhering to the terms of the 1980 Constitution. He also argued that the AN lacked coherence because it had been drawn up by groups ranging from the conservative right to socialists, and described it as a "political manoeuvre" which could be taken advantage of by the agents of "totalitarian communism".

The largest public demonstration of opposition to the government since Nov. 18, 1983, was held on Nov. 21, 1985, when an estimated 500,000 people participated in a rally organized by the AD and supported by all parties of the AN and the Popular Democratic Movement. The demonstration, only the second to receive the government's authorization, was called under the theme "Chile Demands Democracy" and no incidents of violence were reported until police used tear-gas grenades to disperse youths attempting to erect barricades at the end of the demonstration. Speaking at the rally Valdés demanded a rapid return to democracy and reaffirmed that the AN provided the basis for negotiations in the transition to democratic rule.

Democratic Socialist Federation (*Federación Socialista Democrática*)

This alliance was founded in April 1984 at the initiative of the Radical Party as part of its efforts to strengthen the social democratic presence on the Chilean left. The founding members of the Federation were the Radical Party, the Social Democratic Party and the People's Socialist Union (see separate entries).

Liberal Movement (*Movimiento Liberal*)

Leadership. Gastón Ureta (pres.)

This small, right-wing democratic party (also known as the *Partido Liberal*) was in August 1985 one of 11 to sign the proposal for a "national accord" on the return to democracy (see entry for Democratic Alliance).

Manuel Rodríguez Patriotic Front (*Frente Patriótico Manuel Rodríguez*, FPMR)

Leadership. Daniel Huerta (cdr.)

This movement, named after a guerrilla leader of the independence era and also known as the Rodríguez Militia (*Milicias Rodríguistas*), is thought to be linked to the Communist Party of Chile (PCCh—see separate entry). It made itself known when six members occupied a radio station on March 7-8, 1984, to broadcast an anti-government statement. Thereafter the organization carried out numerous bomb attacks, in particular at power stations (causing widespread blackouts), on railway lines and at premises of US-based multinational companies, such attacks being continued throughout 1985 and during the first half of 1986.

In a manifesto issued in December 1984 the FPMR had offered its support to the demands of political parties for a return to democracy, and to those of trade union organizations for economic reforms, but it had also called for widespread actions of sabotage and "armed propaganda" in order to hasten the fall of the Pinochet regime.

In August 1986 the Chilean security forces claimed that they had uncovered the largest clandestine arsenal ever found in Latin America, comprising over 70 tonnes of munitions valued at over $10,000,000 and including weapons from the Soviet Union and Cuba for use by the FPMR.

On Sept. 12, 1986, the FPMR confirmed that an attempt to assassinate President Pinochet on Sept. 7, when he escaped with only slight hand injuries (but which left five of the President's guard dead and 11 injured), had been carried out by its "September 4 Commando", all of whom had returned safely to their bases. Although this attempt was followed by the imposition of a state of siege and a number of suspects were arrested, the FPMR maintained late in October that all the attackers remained free.

Twelve members of the FPMR were killed by the security police in Santiago on June 16, 1987.

Multi-party Alliance (*Multipartidaria*)

This broad democratic opposition coalition was launched on March 14, 1983, with the publication of a "democratic manifesto" signed on behalf of the Christian Democratic Party (by Gabriel Valdés), the Radical Party (by Enrique Silva and Luis Fernando Luengo), the Republican Party (by Hugo Zepeda and Julio Subercaseaux), the Social Democratic Party (by Luis Bossay), and the main factions of the Socialist Party of Chile (by Hernán Vodavonic, Julio Stuardo and Ramón Silva). The Communist Party remained outside the new alliance, principally because of opposition to its inclusion by the Christian Democrats.

The Alliance presented proposals for constitutional reforms to the Pinochet regime calling for a return to democratic government, the lifting of restrictions on political and trade union activities, and other political reforms. As a political force it was superseded by the Democratic Alliance (see separate entry).

A Project for National Development (see separate entry) was constituted as the information and publicity wing of the *Multipartidaria*.

National Assembly of Civil Society (*NACS*)

Leadership. Dr Juan Luis González

The NACS, Chile's largest opposition coalition, formed at the end of April 1986, grouped together professional associations, community groups, academics, students, teachers, lorry drivers, shopkeepers and two multiple union confederations. In April some 600 representatives of the above groups had issued a 50-point statement entitled "The Demand of Chile" which called for a democratically approved Constitution, a complete revision of social and economic policies, an end to military intervention in the running of universities (which had led to a student strike on April 15-16), and full compensation for victims of human rights abuses. The Assembly warned that its members would apply "generalized and peaceful pressure" if by May 31 the government of President Pinochet had not responded positively to its demands. Members of all political tendencies were present, although the parties themselves were not directly represented.

At the beginning of June 1986 the Assembly called for a month-long campaign of civil disobedience, culminating in a two-day general strike on July 2-3 to demand a return to democracy. Gen. Pinochet described the protest, which resulted in eight deaths, 50 wounded and over 1,000 arrests, as an attempt to depose his military government by "revolution and anarchy", although witnesses and local priests blamed the "excessive methods" of troops and paramilitary police for most of the violent incidents. On July 3 warrants were issued for the arrest, on charges of violating state security laws, of 17 of the 22-member NACS directorate, all of whom had gone into hiding. The Assembly immediately replaced its leadership with a 10-member council headed by the president of the teachers' confederation, Osvaldo Verdugo, and announced plans for further anti-government rallies. Fifteen of the protest leaders had given themselves up voluntarily by July 11; 12 were released on bail on Aug. 19.

National Democratic Accord (*Acuerdo Nacional Democrático*, ANDE)

The ANDE was formed on Nov. 21, 1986, by 13 political parties ranging from the political right to the moderate Marxist left, who, on Sept. 8, had signed an 87-point political pact outlining their proposals for a return to democracy. In mid-November 1986 the proposals, which included changes to the 1980 Constitution to allow for free elections in 1989 (rather than a plebiscite on a single candidate nominated by the military junta) and elaboration of proposals already contained in the "national accord" for the transition to democracy (see entry for Democratic Alliance), were presented by Eugenio Ortega of the Christian Democratic Party, Jorge Molina of the Chilean Socialist Party and Pedro Correa of the National Party, to two members of the military junta, Gen. Rodolfo Stange Oelckers and Adml. José Toribio Merino Castro, commanders of the police and the navy respectively. The meetings represented the first-ever formal contacts between members of the ruling military junta and the opposition.

Apart from the above-mentioned parties other signatories to the accord were the National Democratic Party, the United Popular Action Movement and its Worker and Peasant faction MAPU-OC, the Republican Party, the Radical Party, the Social Democratic Party, the People's Socialist Union and the Christian Left (see separate entries).

National Democratic Party (*Partido Democrático Nacional*, Padena)

Leadership. Luis Minchell (l.)

In late 1985 this party was divided into two tendencies, one of which was very close politically to the National Party (see separate entry). On Nov. 21, 1986, Padena became a founding member of the National Democratic Accord (ANDE, see separate entry), whose aim was to campaign for free and open elections in 1989.

National Union Movement (*Movimiento Unión Nacional*, MUN)

Leadership. Andrés Allamand Zavala (l.)

The centre-right MUN was one of the original signatories of the "national accord" proposal of August 1985 (see entry for Democratic Alliance). With approval by the military junta on Jan. 15, 1987, of a draft law restoring the right to form political parties, the MUN merged with the Independent Democratic Movement (*Unión Democrática Independiente*, UDI) and the National Workers' Front (*Frente Nacional de Trabajadores*, FNT) to form the National Renewal Party (*Partido de Renovación Nacional*).

People's Socialist Union (*Unión Popular Socialista*, UPS)

Leadership. Ramón Silva Ulloa (l.)

In April 1984, together with two other social democratic groups, the UPS formed the Democratic Socialist Federation (see separate entry). In August 1985 it was one of 11 parties to call for a transition to democracy (see entry for Democratic Alliance) and on Nov. 21, 1986, became a founding member of the National Democratic Accord (ANDE—see separate entry), whose aim was to campaign for free and open elections in 1989.

Popular Democratic Movement (*Movimiento Democrático Popular*, MDP)

Leadership. Germán Correa (1.)

The MDP, combining the Communist Party, the Almeyda faction of the Socialist Party, the Movement of the Revolutionary Left (MIR), the Christian Left and the Movement for United Popular Action (MAPU), was formed on Sept. 3, 1983. It has called for the immediate restoration of representative democracy and of civil liberties and also for the formulation of a new economic strategy designed in particular to relieve unemployment. It has been involved in the organization of a number of protests against the regime's economic policies, some of which were held even after the imposition of a state of siege on March 23, 1984. Following such a protest, held on March 27 with the participation of the Democratic Alliance (see separate entry), Jaime Isunza (then secretary-general of the MDP and leader of the Communist Party) was expelled from Chile to Brazil for alleged "communist activities".

Two further days of national protest called for by the MDP and beginning on Oct. 29, designed to coincide with a general strike organized by the National Workers' Command for Oct. 30, resulted in nine deaths, over 40 injuries and some 200 arrests while at least 19 bombs exploded in Santiago and other cities on the night of Oct. 29. Some 140 detainees were subsequently sent to remote detention camps.

On Feb. 1, 1985, the MDP was declared illegal. The Movement nevertheless continued to support days of protest and anti-government demonstrations and endorsed its principle that "mass self-defence" was a legitimate response to repression, a principle which was not supported by two of its member parties—the MAPU and the IC, which were also members of the Democratic Alliance (see separate entry). On March 12, 1987, the MDP explicitly warned that those who believed that pressures and circumstances which did not involve a popular mobilization could "thwart the government's will" were following the wrong path.

It was reported on June 26, 1987, that the United Left Coalition (see separate entry) had been formed in succession to the MDP, although the MDP would continue to function for some time.

Popular Resistance Armed Forces (*Fuerzas Armadas de la Resistência Popular*, FARP)

The formation of the FARP was announced by the Movement of the Revolutionary Left (MIR—see separate entry) following the killing of four policemen in an attack in central Valparaíso on Nov. 2, 1984.

Project for National Development (*Projecto para el Desarrollo Nacional*, Proden)

Leadership. Jorge Lavanderos (1.)

The Proden was formed in 1982 by a group of centrist and right-wing politicians and trade union leaders as the information and publicity arm of the Multiparty Alliance (see separate entry). On Feb. 24, 1983, it called for the transfer of power from Pinochet to the four-man military junta "as a preliminary step to democracy". On July 9, 1983, Lavandero (along with two leaders of the Christian Democratic Party—see separate entry) was arrested and charged with organizing demonstrations against the regime. He was released on July 14 after widespread unrest. A rally organized by the Proden on Oct. 11, 1983, attracted some 40,000 people. In March 1984 it was reported that Lavandero had been attacked and beaten up by a small right-wing group, the Chilean Anti-Communist Alliance (Acha—see separate entry).

Republican Party (*Partido Republicano*)

Leadership. Armando Jaramillo Lyon (pres.); René León Echaiz (sec.-gen.)

This centre-right party was established in 1983 by a majority faction of the National Party (see separate entry) and is itself divided into factions. It has called for an end to military rule and a rapid return to constitutional government.

The Republican Party, a founding member of both the Multi-party Alliance and of the Democratic Alliance (on March 14 and Aug. 6, 1983, respectively), became a founding member of the National Democratic Accord on Nov. 21, 1986 (see separate entries).

Social Christian Movement (*Movimiento Social Cristiano*)

Leadership. Juan de Dios Carmona (pres.); Manuel Rodríguez (sec.-gen.)

This group, which drew its support from the right wing of the Christian Democratic Party, was founded in 1984.

Social Democratic Party (*Partido Social Demócrata*)

Leadership. Mario Sharpe (pres.); René Abeliuk Manasevich (vice-pres.)

This small, centre-left group was a founding member of both the Multi-party Alliance and subsequently of the Democratic Alliance, both formed in 1983 (see separate entries) and, in August 1985, it was a signatory of the "national accord" on the restoration of democracy. In April 1984 it joined the Democratic Socialist Federation (see separate entry) and, in November 1986, was a founding member of the National Democratic Accord (ANDE—see separate entry), whose aim was to campaign for free and open elections in 1989.

United Left Coalition (*Coalición Izquierda Unida*)

The formation of this grouping was announced on June 26, 1987, under the leadership of former Foreign Minister Clodomiro Almeyda (of the Socialist Party of Chile—see separate entry) and comprising the Christian Left (IC), the United Popular Action Movement (MAPU), the Movement of the Revolutionary Left (MIR), the Chilean Communist Party (PCCh), the Radical Party, the Socialist Party of Chile (PSCh) and the Socialist Party of Chile—Historic Faction (see separate entries). It was announced that Luis Fernando Luengo, the president of the Radical Party, would be acting president, and that the new coalition would ultimately replace the Popular Democratic Movement (MDP—see separate entry).

Church Opposition

On March 27, 1977, the Permanent Committee of the (Roman Catholic) Episcopal Conference published a document in which it described the existing government as unrepresentative and declared that a suitable political system could only emerge as the result of "a free national consensus, expressed in a legitimate manner". The document requested President Pinochet to investigate the cases of those persons who had disappeared since September 1973 and criticized the lack of freedom of expression. It also stated: "We do not believe that human rights will be guaranteed until the country has a Constitution and as long as laws are dictated by those who are not the legitimate representatives of the people and all organs of state are not subject to the Constitution and the law". The Church leaders were thereupon strongly criticized by the Minister of Justice who, however, resigned on April 21, 1977.

On Nov. 16, 1977, police broke up a meeting held in a Dominican convent; in reply to a complaint by Cardinal Raúl Silva Henríquez (then the Archbishop of Santiago and Primate of Chile), President Pinochet maintained that the meeting had been a clandestine political gathering and part of a plot to create social agitation with those attending having included the president and the vice-president of the Christian Democratic Party and two trade union leaders.

Relations between the military government and the Roman Catholic Church continued to deteriorate during the 1980s as the Church became increasingly vociferous in its denunciations of human rights abuses and in its call for a rapid return to democracy.

In August 1985 the Archbishop of Santiago, Cardinal Juan Francisco Fresno, sponsored talks between 11 opposition groups, which resulted in the drafting of a "national accord for peaceful evolution towards complete and genuine democracy" (see separate entry for Democratic Alliance), but, on Sept. 18, radio stations were prohibited from broadcasting live an Independence Day sermon by Cardinal Fresno in which he urged the government and the opposition to settle their differences.

A pastoral letter issued by the Permanent Committee of the Episcopal Conference on Nov. 13 accused the government of carrying out state terrorism; it distinguished between "terrorism which comes from the state through its security organizations" and "terrorism which comes from those who resort to terrorist methods as an expression of frustration and discontent". In a further statement reported on March 9, 1986, the Episcopal Conference called for a "serious revision" of the 1980 Constitution and strongly criticized the courts for failing to deal with cases of political violence. For the first time the Church directly referred to the need for changes in the Constitution. In a subsequent document on the causes of violence, issued on July 13, the bishops condemned the "militarization of civilian life" and suggested that General Pinochet's government was as much to blame as any other factor for the rise in political violence in Chile.

Extreme Right-wing Movements

Anti-Marxist Group (*Grupo Antimarxista*, GRAPA)

This ultra-right paramilitary group carried out attacks in 1984.

April 5 People's Detachment (*Destacamento del Pueblo 5 de Abril*)

This group claimed responsibility for a bomb attack on the office of United Press International in Santiago, in August 1986.

Chilean Anti-Communist Alliance (*Alianza Chilena Anticomunista*, Acha)

This ultra-right-wing death squad claimed responsibility for a number of attacks on centrist and left-wing activists in 1984, including the killing in January of a leader of Ad Mapu (see separate entry) and an assault in March on Jorge Lavandero of the Project for National Development (see separate entry).

Movement against the Cancer of Marxism (*Movimiento Contra el Cáncer Marxista*, MCCM)

This ultra-right-wing paramilitary group was active in 1984.

September 11 Commando (*Comando 11 de Septiembre*)

This group claimed responsibility for the murder of four members of the Chilean left, three of whom were found dead on Sept. 8, 1986, after having been taken from their homes during curfew hours the previous day by unidentified armed men. A spokesman for the group described it as "the antithesis" of the Manuel Rodríguez Patriotic Front (FPMR—see separate entry) and said that one member of the left would be killed for every guard who had died in the Sept. 7, 1986, assassination attempt against the President.

China

Capital: Beijing (Peking)

Pop. 1,059,520,000

The People's Republic of China is, under its Constitution of 138 articles adopted by the Chinese National People's Congress on Dec. 4, 1982, "a socialist state under the people's democratic dictatorship led by the working class and based on the alliance of workers and peasants" in which "all power belongs to the people" and "the organs through which the people exercise state power are the National People's Congress (NPC) and the local people's congresses at different levels". The NPC consists of deputies elected for a five-year term "by the provinces, autonomous regions and municipalities directly under the central government and by the armed forces".

All Chinese citizens above the age of 18 years have the right to elect and to be elected (except persons mentally ill or deprived of their political rights). The NPC and its permanent body, the Standing Committee, "exercise the legislative power of the state". The Standing Committee inter alia supervises the work of the State Council, i.e. "the central people's government" and "the executive body of the highest organ of state power".

Contrary to the 1978 Constitution, the 1982 Constitution contained no references to the Chinese Communist Party (CCP), to Marxism-Leninism or to Mao Zedong Thought in any of its articles, although in its preamble there were several references to "the Chinese people of all nationalities under the leadership of the CCP and the guidance of Marxism-Leninism and Mao Zedong Thought". The preamble also referred to the existence of "a broad patriotic united front" under the leadership of the CCP and "composed of democratic parties and people's organizations" and embracing "all socialist working people, all patriots who support socialism and all patriots who stand for reunification of the motherland" (i.e. for the incorporation of Taiwan in the Republic of China). Eight existing minor political parties date back to before the proclamation of the People's Republic on Oct. 1, 1949, and are composed mainly of intellectuals.

In elections to the NPC held between March 17 and the end of April 1983 only 700 of the 3,500 members of the NPC elected in 1978 were re-elected; the number of army personnel was reduced from 508 to 267; the number of representatives of national minorities was increased; and 13 deputies were elected for Taiwan from among candidates nominated by citizens of Taiwan origin.

Regulations on state secrets adopted in 1951 were reissued on April 10, 1980, when such secrets were defined as secret information on virtually all aspects of military, political and economic affairs, and punishment as a counter-revolutionary was provided for anyone who sold or divulged such information to "enemies at home or abroad" or to "domestic and foreign profiteers".

The power struggle within the CCP which followed the death of Chairman Mao in September 1976 was accompanied by various manifestations of opposition to the government, although organized groups were largely confined to those seeking full observance of human rights in China. The conviction in January 1981 of the so-called "gang of four" radicals and six former associates of the late Marshal Lin Biao demonstrated the victory in the party power struggle of the "reformist" faction led by Deng Xiaoping, which was further consolidated at the 12th CCP congress held in September 1982. However, while vigorously denouncing the "leftist deviation" of the "gang of four" and their followers, those controlling the country also took steps to clamp down on other forms of opposition which were seen as challenging the leading role of the CCP.

An anti-crime campaign launched in 1983 provided draconian punishments for those found guilty of criminal acts; and a "spiritual pollution" campaign initiated later in the same year sought to limit the "corrupting effects" of Western influences within China by providing for the stricter censorship of artistic and literary work and the closure of several journals which were deemed to have been critical of the leadership of the CCP.

Although the latter campaign was curtailed in early 1984 amidst fears that it might develop into a second Cultural Revolution, a widespread series of student demonstrations in late 1986 and early 1987 was the catalyst for a renewed drive against advocates of Western "bourgeois liberalization", with a concomitant increase in state censorship.

The communist regime in Beijing is faced with no serious external threat from opposition groups, even though two potential centres for such opposition exist close to China's borders, namely the British colony of Hong Kong and the island of Taiwan. As regards Hong Kong, anti-communist sentiments within elements of its predominantly Chinese population (substantial numbers of whom are refugees from communist China) have been moderated by the colony's close economic ties with the mainland and by the agreement signed with Britain in 1984 which provided for the restoration of full Chinese sovereignty over the area in 1997. The Kuomintang regime in Taiwan, although continuing to claim that it is the legitimate government of the whole of China, has generally confined concrete expressions of this claim to the receiving of individual defectors from the People's Republic.

Internal Opposition Groups

New regulations announced on July 15, 1980, required all publications to be registered with the local authorities, forbade printing works to do business without the local authorities' consent, and banned the supply of paper and other printing material to unlicensed printing works. These measures led to the virtual disappearance of the human rights organizations which had emerged in the late 1970s (see below). On Aug. 31, 1980, the editors of four unofficial publications were arrested in Canton, and an unofficial periodical appearing in Beijing (a non-political literary magazine called *Today*) was suspended by police in September 1980.

Under an amendment to the 1978 Constitution, adopted by the NPC in September 1980 and incorporated into the 1982 Constitution, the rights of citizens "to speak out freely, air their views fully, hold great debates and write big-character posters" was deleted, although this did not affect the guarantees in the same article of freedom of speech, correspondence, the press, assembly, association, procession and demonstration, and the freedom to strike. The display of posters had been severely restricted by the Beijing municipal authorities on Dec. 6, 1979, and authors were not only required to register their names, addresses and places of work, but were also to be held responsible for the contents of posters.

Student demonstrations, which had been an infrequent occurrence in China since the end of the Cultural Revolution in 1976, were held throughout the country in late 1986 and early 1987. The protests, which begin in Hefei and Wuhan in early December, were linked initially to specific grievances. Throughout the month they spread rapidly to Kunming, Shenzhen, Tianjin, Jinan, Xian, Suzhou and Nanjing, however, and broadened in the scope of their demands to include general calls for greater democracy and press freedom. Although the demonstrations lacked any national organizational co-ordination, it was believed that foreign radio broadcasts played an important role in keeping the participants abreast of events in cities elsewhere in China.

Several days of protests began in Shanghai on Dec. 19, 1986, which involved up to 70,000 students demanding the right to put up wall posters and to engage openly in debate, greater freedom for the press and an assurance that no reprisals would be undertaken against those participating in the protests. Although new regulations were issued by the city's authorities on Dec. 22, which prohibited unauthorized demonstrations, the protests continued with the police displaying considerable tolerance towards the demonstrators. Protests in Beijing began on Dec. 23 and, despite the issuing of similar regulations as those in Shanghai on Dec. 26, continued into early January 1987. The police policy of tolerance towards the demonstrators was maintained and there were few arrests, even though police cordons erected in the path of the demonstrators were repeatedly breached.

The protests were the catalyst for the initiation of a campaign against "bourgeois liberalization" which involved expulsion from the CCP or dismissal from official posts for those alleged to be the advocates of corrupting Western values. Hu Yaobang, the general secretary of the CCP, was dismissed from his post, as were several party officials and academics, and on Jan. 22 it was announced that a new Media and Publications Office had been established under the direction of the State Council in order to increase the state's censorship of published material with a view to eliminating trends towards bourgeois liberalization. In February the editor of a small literary magazine was sentenced to seven years' imprisonment for "counter-revolutionary" statements; and a well-known author and magazine editor, Liu Xinwu, was suspended from his post for publishing extracts from a novel which was considered to be obscene.

In March 1987, however, both Deng Xiaoping and Premier Zhao Ziyang indicated that the campaign against bourgeois liberalization would not be allowed to develop into a full-scale assault upon the structural reforms which had been implemented in China since the death of Mao Zedong.

April 5 Group

This human rights group was formed in March 1979 and named after the date on which riots broke out in 1976 in Tien An Men Square in Beijing directed against the radical wing of the Communist Party leadership and in support of Deng Xiaoping; it published an unofficial organ, the *April 5 Tribune,* until April 1980. On July 30, 1980, Liu Qing, as editor of the *April 5 Tribune,* who had been arrested for selling a transcript of the trial of Wei Jingsheng, the editor of

Exploration was sentenced to three years of "re-education through labour". Two former editors of the *April 5 Tribune* were arrested on April 10, 1981 (with four other dissidents associated with unofficial publications being also arrested in the same month).

Association for the Study of Scientific and Democratic Socialism

This Association convened a meeting in Tien An Men Square (Beijing) on Sept. 13, 1979 (attended by about 1,000 people), when speakers protested against the plight of peasants and others who had staged demonstrations seeking redress for their grievances, and also against the privileges of party officials.

Chinese Democratic Movement

A Chinese student announced in New York on Nov. 17, 1982, that a journal called *China Spring* was to be established as the organ of the Chinese Democratic Movement. Its activities were to be confined to publishing material critical of the communist regime as selected by an editorial board, half of whom were said to be resident in China.

Human Rights Alliance

Leadership. Ren Wanding (founder)

This Alliance was responsible for the publication on Jan. 5, 1979, of a manifesto containing 19 demands, including the removal of Chairman Mao's body from its mausoleum, the re-establishment of friendly relations with the Soviet Union, the release of all political prisoners, a constitutionally-guaranteed right to criticize state and party leaders, representation of non-communist parties in the National People's Congress, open sessions of the Congress and freedom to change one's work and to travel abroad. Although the Alliance's founder Ren Wanding was arrested on April 4, 1979, the movement's manifesto was again displayed on a poster on Sept. 23, 1979. There was no reported activity by the Alliance after this date, however, and Ren Wanding was eventually released from prison on Dec. 30, 1983.

Xinjiang Dissidents

On Oct. 9, 1980, a secretary of the Communist Party of the Uighur autonomous region (Xinjiang, previously Sinkiang) confirmed that there had been "events harmful to unity between nationalities and between the Army and the people". According to earlier unofficial reports there had been armed clashes between (Moslem) Uighurs and Chinese officials and soldiers in April 1980, apparently caused by Uighur resentment against mass immigration of Chinese into the region. In the Hong Kong newspaper *Zheng Ming* it was alleged in September 1981 that a conspiracy by dissident Uighurs for a rising against Chinese rule had been discovered by the authorities.

On Jan. 14, 1983, serious rioting occurred in the city of Kashgar in north-western Xinjiang, after a Chinese student was reported to have murdered a Uighur peasant. Although the authorities quelled the disturbance, sporadic unrest was believed to have occurred in the region throughout the remainder of the year. The Chinese policy of conducting nuclear tests in Xinjiang was also the cause of protests. In December 1986 student demonstrations were held in Urumqi, the region's capital, and in Beijing, to protest over the nuclear issue and to demand greater local autonomy and increased opportunity for those of Uighur birth.

External Opposition

Nationalist Party of China (*Chung-kuo Kuomin-tang* or Kuomintang, KMT)

This party, now the ruling party of Taiwan, was originally founded in November 1894 as the *Hsing Chung Hui* by Dr Sun Yat-sen. It played a major role in the overthrow of the Manchu regime in 1911 and was renamed the Kuomintang in October 1919. Under President Chiang Kai-shek it united most of China by 1927, when it was purged of Communists. During part of the war with Japan which began in 1931 the KMT co-operated with the Communists, but civil war which broke out between the KMT and the Communists after the end of World War II ended with victory for the latter in 1949, when the KMT leadership withdrew to Taiwan.

Parts of the KMT's armed forces, however, fled into Thailand and Burma. These included the KMT Third Army, led by Gen. Li Wen-han, which gave support to the (nationalist and anti-communist) Shan United Revolutionary Army (see separate entry under Burma) by assigning to this movement three brigades to assist it in its struggle against pro-communist Shans. However, by 1982 these two brigades had been reduced to about 200 men, while the whole of the remaining KMT Third Army numbered no more than 3,000.

In recent years the Taiwan government has consistently rejected overtures from Beijing for negotiations on peaceful reunification, detailed proposals for which have been put forward from time to time by Chinese government spokesmen. In June 1982 it was officially announced in communist China that the last batch of soldiers and officials of the former Kuomintang regime (numbering 4,237) had been released after 33 years in prison.

The Chinese Premier, Zhao Ziyang, emphasized on Sept. 30, 1984, that China was ready to open consultations with Taiwan with a view to reunifying the island with the Chinese mainland in accordance with the "one country, two systems" strategy which had formed the basis of the agreement reached with the United Kingdom regarding the restoration of Chinese sovereignty over the territory of Hong Kong. The Taiwanese President, Chiang Ching-kuo, dismissed the Hong Kong agreement as "nothing but a fraud", on Oct. 10, and reiterated the view that "the Chinese Communists have no right to represent the Chinese people and any accord bearing their signature is invalid". The defection to China of a Taiwanese civil airline pilot on May 3, 1986, however, led to the first official contact between the two countries since 1949, as representatives of the two state-run airlines met in Hong Kong to negotiate the return of the aircraft and its remaining crew members. An agreement to this effect was concluded on May 20, after four days of talks, although the Taiwanese authorities stressed that it was the product of humanitarian concerns and did not alter Taiwan's attitude towards the legitimacy of the communist government.

Ciskei

Capital: Bisho Pop. 2,100,000 (of whom only 700,000 are permanent residents)

The Republic of Ciskei, which is recognized as independent only by the governments of South Africa, Bophuthatswana and Venda (but not Transkei) has an executive President elected for a five-year term by a National Assembly consisting of 50 elected members and 37 hereditary chiefs. Elections to the National Assembly are held every five years with all citizens over 18 years (including those living outside Ciskei) being entitled to vote. To be officially recognized, political parties must have at least 10,000 members. The President of the Republic is responsible for appointing a Vice-President and a Cabinet.

Maj.-Gen. Charles Sebe, former commander of Ciskei's armed forces and brother of President Lennox Sebe, was, on June 15, 1984, sentenced to 12 years' imprisonment for incitement to public violence (but was found not guilty of a charge of attempting to overthrow the government). However, on Sept. 25, 1986, Maj.-Gen. Sebe was released from prison by unidentified white armed men, while another group seized two senior officers of Ciskei's security forces, one of them being Maj.-Gen. Kwane Sebe (a son of the President) and demands were made for the release of two of the President's nephews who had also been imprisoned.

Colombia

Capital: Bogotá Pop. 28,620,000

The Republic of Colombia has an executive President elected by direct popular vote for a four-year term and a bicameral Congress consisting of a 114-member Senate and a 199-member House of Representatives, both elected for four-year terms by universal adult suffrage.

In elections held on March 9, 1986, seats were gained in the House of Representatives (in a 45 per cent poll) as follows: Liberals 100, Conservatives 82, Patriotic Union (UP) 10, New Liberalism seven. In presidential elections held on May 25, 1986, the Liberal Party candidate, Virgilio Barco Vargas, was elected with 58.2 per cent of the votes cast.

The UP had been founded in May 1985 as the political wing of the guerrilla movement *Fuerzas Armadas Revolucionarias Colombianas* (FARC), but in November 1986 the elected UP members withdrew from Congress following the deaths (allegedly at the hands of right-wing death squads) of 18 party members within five months.

Political violence has a long tradition in Colombia. During the period of Colombia's history between 1946 and 1953, known as "La Violencia", about 180,000 Colombians were killed in acts of violence due to banditry as well as to civil war. Since then, violence by left-wing guerrilla groups and right-wing "death squads" has dominated Colombian politics. According to military statistics cited by the US-based human rights group Americas Watch, left-wing guerrillas were responsibile for 186 civilian assassinations and 27 kidnappings in the first six months of 1986, whilst right-wing groups carried out the assassination of 300 criminals and guerrillas in and around the city of Cali. In a report of Jan. 4, 1986, Americas Watch stated that although killings were carried out by left-wing rebels, the armed forces were responsible for "the great majority of violent abuses of human rights". Amnesty

International stated in a report of July 18, 1986, that 600 people had been killed in the first six months of 1986 by security forces or gunmen working on their behalf.

Various peace initiatives have been launched in Colombia since President Turbay Ayala on June 20, 1982, lifted a state of siege which had been in force almost continually for 34 years. An amnesty law passed by Congress in May 1985 under the presidency of Dr Belisario Betancur Cuartas allowed for the reintegration into civilian life of guerrillas accused of political offences other than kidnapping, extortion and murder outside armed combat. A peace commission was set up in 1981, but ceasefire agreements with various guerrilla groups have yet to prove conclusive. In 1987 President Barco announced a programme for rehabilitation, normalization and reconciliation in which he recognized the need to address the social and economic roots of urban and rural unrest, from which the guerrilla movements draw their support.

The Colombian authorities also face a massive drugs-trafficking problem, with drug rings being variously linked to right-wing paramilitary groups, and drug barons implicated in the assassination of critics of the drug trade.

Right-wing Groups

Death Squads (*Escuadrones de la Muerte*)

These right-wing terror groups have been held responsible for numerous killings of alleged left-wing activists. In a report on *The Central-Americanization of Colombia* published on Jan. 4, 1986, the US-based human rights organization Americas Watch said that paramilitary death squads operating freely in areas under military control were responsible for 1,455 assassinations between early 1982 and August 1985, with some 540 people listed as "disappeared". The victims of the death squads included students, teachers, Indian community leaders, trade unionists, lawyers who defended political prisoners, human rights activists and supporters of left-wing opposition parties.

Death to Kidnappers (*Muerte a los Secuestradores*, MAS)

This group emerged in 1982 in the city of Medellín, its avowed aim being to act against guerrilla groups which carried out abductions to finance their operations. Its victims included suspected guerrillas, trade unionists and peasants. The deaths in 1982 of the M-19 leader Camilo Restrepo Valencia (see separate entry), shortly after his release from prison, and of Henry Castro, the amnestied leader of the National Liberation Army (ELN—see separate entry) were attributed to the MAS. It was held responsible for the death of the only Roman Catholic Indian priest in Colombia and campaigner for peasant rights, Fr Alvaro Orcue, on Nov. 11, 1984, and for the killing of seven peasants found decapitated in the northern Magdalena river on July 28, 1985.

Left-wing guerrillas have constantly maintained that the MAS has close links with the armed forces, and evidence of this emerged in a trial in 1983. Following an inquiry ordered by President Betancur, a list was published in February 1983 containing the names of 163 people allegedly involved with the MAS. Of those, 59 were serving members of the armed forces, the most senior being Col. Hernando Darío Velandia Hurtado and Col. Emilio Gil Bermúdez, but no convictions were reported.

The MAS is thought to have been linked from its formation to the drug trade and to have received financial backing from drug dealers.

Left-wing Movements

America Battalion (*Batallón América*)

This group of rebels is said to be made up of members of the M-19, Quintin Lame Commando, the Peruvian Tupac Amarú Revolutionary Movement (*Movimiento Revolucionario Tupac Amarú*) and the Ecuadorean *Alfaro Vive, Carajo!* group (see separate entries). Early in 1986 Ecuadorean troops were reported to have cut off 100 guerrillas attempting to cross into southern Colombia to join up with the Battalion.

The group was reportedly founded by Carlos Pizarro Léon Gómez, who became leader of the M-19 in 1986.

April 19 Movement (*Movimiento 19 de Abril*, M-19)

Leadership. Carlos Pizarro León Gómez

Formed in 1974, the M-19 took its name from the date on which ex-President (Gen.) Gustavo Rojas Pinilla, the leader of the National Popular Alliance (*Alianza Nacional Popular*, ANAPO), had been defeated in presidential elections in 1970. The M-19 claimed to be the armed wing of ANAPO, although the latter rejected this claim. The M-19 came by the end of the 1970s to be regarded as left-wing and Marxist, and its leaders declared as its aim the achievement of a democratic and ultimately socialist state by political means.

The first operation of the M-19 was the theft from a museum outside Bogotá of the sword and spurs of Simon Bolívar (the liberator of Spanish America) in January 1974. On Feb. 15, 1976, the president of the Colombian Confederation of Workers (CTC), José Raquel Mercado, whom the M-19 accused of being a traitor to the working class, was kidnapped and later killed.

On Aug. 28, 1978, the M-19 was reported to have "declared war" on the (right-wing Liberal) government of President Julio César Turbay Ayala.

Major M-19 operations in 1980 included the temporary occupation of the embassy of the Dominican Republic in Bogotá from Feb. 27 to April 27, 1980, when M-19 guerrillas led by Rosemberg Pabón Pabón (a former university professor) seized 57 hostages including the ambassadors of 14 countries—among them those of Israel, Mexico and the United States—as well as the papal nuncio. On April 27, the guerrillas left for Havana (Cuba), taking with them 12 hostages who had not yet been released, having been assured that trials of 219 M-19 members then in progress would be monitored by the Inter-American Human Rights Commission. The remaining hostages were freed in Cuba.

By September 1980 the M-19 was officially regarded as the second strongest guerrilla organization with 531 active members.

The abduction of a US citizen (Chester Allen Bitterman), accused of being a "spy" of the (US) Central Intelligence Agency (CIA), on Jan. 19, 1981 and his later killing, were attributed to a radical faction of the M-19 (see below). After an attack on March 11 by M-19 guerrillas on the town of Mocoa (southern Colombia) the army launched major anti-guerrilla operations in southern Colombia. Among 50 who fled to Ecuador (but were arrested in that country and handed over to the Colombian authorities) were Dr Toledo Plata and Rosemberg Pabón Pabón.

President Turbay Ayala announced on March 23, 1981, that his government was severing its diplomatic relations with Cuba on the grounds that the latter was arming and aiding the M-19; but Cuba denied the accusation.

When President Turbay Ayala proposed an amnesty bill, which was finally approved by the Senate on March 4 and signed by the President on March 13, 1981, the M-19 was already divided into two factions, the major one of which (led by Jaime Bateman Cayón, Dr C. Toledo Plata and Iván Marino Ospina) favoured a legal political role, as was offered in the President's amnesty bill to all guerrillas who laid down their arms within four months. The smaller faction constituted itself as the *Coordinadora Nacional de Bases* (CNB), which rejected peaceful negotiations.

On the expiry of the amnesty on July 23, 1981, the M-19 reiterated its earlier peace proposals for a general amnesty without exclusions and for the abrogation of the 1978 security legislation. At the same time it intensified its guerrilla operations, partly in collaboration with the Colombian Revolutionary Armed Forces.

On the recommendation of a peace commission set up by President Turbay Ayala in October 1981, the government announced, on Feb. 19, 1982, a second amnesty for all those who had committed "rebellion against the state" (but again not those who had carried out murders and kidnappings). However, the amnesty was rejected by most guerrillas.

A further presidential amnesty offer came into effect in November 1982, with the major crimes to which it would not be applicable being limited to "premeditated murder and murders which take advantage of the inferior strength of the victim"; this amnesty therefore also covered acts of sedition, rebellion and conspiracy. As a result the seven-member political command of the M-19 had talks with the Minister of the Interior with a view to obtaining a guarantee of "social justice" before the M-19 laid down its arms. J. Bateman Cayón was quoted as saying that a six-month armistice would be needed to ensure the success of the amnesty. In October 1982 he had described the M-19 as being a "nationalist, ideologically pluralist and 80 per cent Catholic" movement.

Following a truce declared by the M-19 in November 1982, Dr Toledo, Pabón and 23 other M-19 leaders were released from prison. The truce ended in April 1983 after accusations that the President had succumbed to pressure from the army and reactionary elements, as acts of violence had continued during the truce period. On April 28, 1983, Bateman was reported to have died in an aircrash. Amnesty talks continued during 1983 with an October meeting between President Betancur, Iván Marino Ospina (then leader of the M-19) and his deputy, Alvaro Fayad. In November 1983 the M-19 reached an agreement for a political alliance with the Colombian Revolutionary Armed Forces (FARC) and the National Liberation Army (ELN)—see separate entries.

Peace talks were jeopardized in 1984 when 200 M-19 members launched an attack on Florencia prison (Caqueta) on March 14, releasing 158 prisoners after fighting in which 140 hostages were taken and 26 guerrillas, four civilians and one prison guard were killed. A state of siege was announced in the region, and the attack was denounced by Ospina and Fayad, who expelled its leaders from the movement. On April 4, the M-19 carried out a further attack in conjunction with the FARC on Corinto (Cauca), in which 30 guerrillas, two soldiers and one policeman died.

On Aug. 10, 1984, Dr Toledo was assassinated; on Aug. 11, a retaliatory attack on the town of Yumbo by 200 M-19 and FARC guerrillas led by Pabón resulted in the deaths of three policemen, two civilians and 12 guerrillas, while 18 prisoners were freed. M-19 leaders said that a truce would not be signed until the safety of former guerrillas was guaranteed.

A one-year ceasefire agreement was, however, signed on Aug. 24, 1984, although five guerrillas were wounded in clashes with police on the way to the ceremony; an M-19 leader, Carlos Pizarro Léon Gómez, stated that the M-19 had to continue its fight to broaden the people's participation in Colombian democracy before becoming a political party. The arrest of three M-19 leaders on charges of possessing arms led to the temporary withdrawal of the M-19 from the peace commission talks, but the acquittal of the three in November 1984 prevented a total breakdown of negotiations. However, major clashes with the armed forces occurred in the Corinto region in December 1984-January 1985.

In February 1985 Fayad was elected the M-19 leader at the group's congress, replacing Ospina who remained in the five-person command but who admitted his mistake in calling for M-19 members to murder US diplomats in reprisal for the extradition of Colombians linked to the drug trade.

Popular support for the M-19 grew at this time, especially in cities such as Cali, where the M-19 had set up 21 urban encampments in shanty town areas since the 1984 agreement.

In May 1985 the M-19 withdrew from the peace commission following death squad attempts to assassinate members of the M-19 command. Armed activities resumed in June with an attack on June 28 by 200 guerrillas on the central town of Génova in which 19 people died, and the occupation on July 11 of Ríofrío, south-west of Bogotá. On August 14, the military high command declared a total war on the M-19, and on Aug. 28 Ospina was killed in a clash with armed forces.

In October 1985 sixty deaths were reported in fighting in the Cauca valley, and on Oct. 23, the M-19 attempted unsuccessfully to assassinate the C.-in-C. of the Colombian army, Gen. Rafael Samudio Molina.

On Nov. 6, 1985, guerrillas entered the Palace of Justice in Bogotá, taking 400 people hostage and demanding inter alia the publication of all documents relating to the peace settlement to show that the army had been responsible for the breakdown of the ceasefire. The guerrillas were offered a safe passage and fair trial by President Betancur, but he refused to negotiate with them, and on Nov. 7 security forces stormed the building. Three hundred hostages were freed, but 106 people died in the attack and the resultant fire, including the president of the Supreme Court, Alfonso Reyes Echanelía, and all 41 guerrillas. (Unconfirmed reports later said that 55 guerrillas took part and some escaped.)

In March 1986 tanks and aircraft were used to support troops in a battle against some 300 M-19 fighters trying to take control of a residential area of Cali; in July 1986 the then Interior Minister, Jaime Castro, survived an assassination attempt in a revenge attack for the storming of the Palace of Justice.

In March 1986 leadership of the M-19 was assumed by Carlos Pizarro Léon Gómez (who also founded the American Batallion—see separate entry) after Fayad was killed by police; his leadership was reported in October 1986 to have produced a crisis within the movement, with his policy of waging open struggle leading to heavy losses.

The M-19 leadership had stated in September 1985 that the movement had links with revolutionary movements in Equador, El Salvador, Panama and Venezuela, but not with the Shining Path (*Sendero Luminoso*) movement in Peru. In November 1985 it was disclosed that Pabón had stated that some 100 Palestine Liberation Organization fighters had been brought in to aid guerrillas in Colombia.

(For M-19 co-operation with other guerrilla organizations see separate entry for National Guerrilla Coordinating Board.)

Colombian Revolutionary Armed Forces (*Fuerzas Armadas Revolucionarias Colombianas,* FARC)

Among several independent republics set up during the period of "La Violencia" (1946-53) was that of Gaitania (later called Marquetalia, in the department of Tolima). It was founded in 1949 by Fermín Charry Rincón (a member of the central committee of the Communist Party and also known as Jacobo Frias Alape), who was killed in January 1960 and was succeeded by Manuel Marulanda Vélez (also called Pedro Antonio Marín or Tiro Fijo—"Sure Shot"). Marquetalia was occupied by the Colombian army in May 1964, but its guerrillas decided to continue their struggle and set up, in April 1966, the FARC under the leadership of M. Marulanda Vélez and other members of the Communist Party's central committee. On Sept. 14, 1970, M. Marulanda Vélez was reported to have died.

Between 1976 and 1980 FARC members were involved in a number of armed attacks and in clashes with army units. An amnesty offer made by President Turbay Ayala was rejected by the FARC on June 17, 1980. However, although it continued its attacks, the FARC showed interest in an amnesty offer of President Betancur, which came into force in November 1982, and early in 1983 FARC delegates had talks with a presidential armistice commission.

Nevertheless the FARC commenced insurgency activities together with the April 19 Movement (M-19—see separate entry) in June 1983, and in November 1983 it reached agreement on forming a political alliance with the M-19 and the (pro-Castro) National Liberation Army (ELN—see separate entry).

In October 1983 the FARC proposed a ceasefire to become effective on Jan. 20, 1984, and a truce from Jan. 20, 1985 (which would give it time to demobilize its forces and to form a political party). Agreement was reached with the peace commission on March 28, 1984, for a ceasefire to take effect on May 28 of that year, on terms including the demilitarization of rural areas. The ceasefire was to run until Dec. 1, 1984, but on a FARC request of Sept. 9, it was (on Nov. 28) extended until Dec. 31, 1985.

A process of reintegrating guerrillas into civilian life began on Dec. 1, 1984, and on May 28, 1985, the FARC founded a political party (the *Unión Patríotica*, UP). It also agreed to hand over to the authorities a list of those who had deserted after the truce to a splinter group (the Ricardo Franco Front—see separate entry). In September 1985 the FARC requested that the ceasefire be extended until September 1986, and it agreed not to engage in armed campaigning during the forthcoming elections in which the UP was taking part.

Progress towards a final peace settlement, which the FARC had supported since 1982, appeared to falter shortly after the new Liberal administration took over in 1986. On Sept. 19, 1986, the FARC presented a list of violations of the truce to the new government, and claimed that 300 FARC members had died in the 30 months of the ceasefire. In January 1987 speculation that extreme right-wing groups were trying to provoke the FARC into giving up the ceasefire followed claims that a total of 342 members of the UP had been killed over a period of 10 months.

In June 1987 some 2,000 Colombian soldiers were despatched to "exterminate communist guerrillas" after a 200-strong force of suspected FARC guerrillas had ambushed and killed 27 soldiers, wounding 42 others, in the south-eastern jungles of Caqueta. On June 24 the President announced that the ceasefire would effectively end in those areas where the FARC operated, if evidence of the group's involvement was substantiated.

Estimates of the FARC's active membership have been put at 10,000-12,000 in 1987, with up to 33 fronts in operation.

Free Homeland (*Patria Libre*)

This group joined with other guerrilla organizations in forming the National Guerrilla Co-ordinating Board (see separate entry) in December 1985, when it was reported to have temporarily held a town in northern Colombia.

National Guerrilla Co-ordinating Board (*Coordinadora Nacional Guerrillera*, CNG)

The proposed formation of this unified command of the M-19, the National Liberation Army (ELN), the People's Liberation Army (EPL), the Workers' Revolutionary Party, Free Homeland (*Patria Libre*) and the Quintin Lame Commando (see separate entries) was announced on Nov. 21, 1985. The CNG claimed responsibility for an ambush carried out in Bogotá on Dec. 6, 1985, when two soldiers were killed in retaliation for the killing on Nov. 26 of Oscar William Calvo, the EPL representative at talks with the government's peace commission. Fighting involving between 400 and 1,000 CNG guerrillas took place in January 1986. Further clashes with police and soldiers in February and March 1986 led to the death of at least 60 CNG guerrillas. After some 250 CNG guerrillas had temporarily occupied Belacazar (Cauca) on Aug. 6, 1986, the government ruled out any further peace talks with the M-19 on Aug. 9.

On March 17, 1987, eight CNG members (and seven policemen) were reported to have been killed in an attack on San Pablo (Santander).

National Liberation Army (*Ejército de Liberación Nacional*, ELN)

Leadership. Nicolas Rodríguez Bautista

Established in January 1965, the ELN at first operated in the department of Santander (north-eastern Colombia) under the leadership of Fabio Vásquez Castaño and with the support of a (pro-Chinese) Workers' Students' and Peasants' Movement (MOEC). It repudiated the pro-Soviet Communist Party on Aug. 1, 1967, after that party had condemned guerrilla warfare as "an erroneous form of revolution". Earlier, on Jan. 7, 1966, Fr Camilo Torres Restrepo, a former Dominican priest who had advocated a "Christian revolution" to overthrow the existing social order, disclosed that he had joined the ELN, explaining that as all lawful means of obtaining redress were barred to the people he would pursue the armed struggle in the country until the people had gained power; however, on Feb. 15, 1966, he was killed in a clash between guerrillas and an army unit.

In June 1975 ELN guerrillas were reported to be active in several departments, and a major military operation was launched against them in the northern Bolívar department.

In September 1976 the ELN confirmed that Fabio Vásquez Castaño had been replaced as leader of the ELN by Nicolas Rodríguez Bautista.

By September 1980 the ELN was officially stated to have been reduced to less than 40 active members. However, notwithstanding President Turbay Ayala's amnesty offer of March 1981, the ELN intensified its guerrilla activities near the Venezuelan border in mid-1981.

In response to the November 1982 amnesty, an ELN leader, Diego Uribe Escabor, said that the group would not accept the "sham" amnesty, but would continue to fight "exploitation and oppression". However, 25 ELN guerrillas did surrender and others followed, despite the assassination of the ELN's amnestied leader, Henry Castro, in 1982 (see separate entry for Death to Kidnappers, MAS).

In September 1983 the armed forces claimed that the ELN had a pact with the *Bandera Rojo* group of Venezuela, the *Sendero Luminoso* of Peru and the *Farabundo Martí* National Liberation Front of El Salvador.

On Nov. 22, 1983, ELN members kidnapped the brother of President Betancur, Dr Jaime Betancur Cuartas, and made several demands including an increase in the minimum monthly wage, a price freeze on consumer goods, a reduction in public service prices, the release of political prisoners, the arrest of MAS suspects and the demilitarization of rural areas. After the kidnapping had been denounced by the Colombian Revolutionary Armed Forces (FARC—see separate entry) and had received no support from Cuba, Dr Betancur was released.

In August 1984 the ELN refused to enter into a ceasefire agreement (together with other guerrilla groups).

During 1986 the ELN was reported to have carried out attacks in several departments, including Antioquia, Atlántico, César, Córdoba and Santander, and it claimed responsibility for attacks on the Caño Limón-Coveñas oil pipeline owned by the Colombian Petroleum Enterprise.

(For ELN co-operation with other guerrilla organizations see separate entry for National Guerrilla Co-ordinating Board.)

New People's Revolutionary Front (*Nuevo Frente Revolucionario del Pueblo*)

According to reports of November 1986 this group was a dissident faction of the M-19 (see separate entry) which had emerged in the rural areas of the central Cundinamarca department.

Non-conformist Youth of Colombia (*Juventudes Inconformes de Colombia*, JIC)

This group, founded in 1984, announced in late December of that year that it had carried out two bombings in Cali and that it proposed to eliminate all drugs dealers, kidnappers and thieves.

Oscar William Calvo

A column of guerrillas carrying the name of the former leader of the People's Liberation Army (EPL—see separate entry) killed in 1985 was reported in November 1986 to have been created in western Colombia by the (legal) *Partido Comunista de Colombia—Marxista-Leninista*.

Pedro León Abroleda Brigade (PLA)

This Marxist guerrilla group is thought to be an offshoot of the People's Liberation Army (see separate entry) and has claimed responsibility for a number of acts of violence, in particular for two bomb attacks on Feb. 18, 1987, on the Bogotá Chamber of Commerce and a police station.

People's Liberation Army (*Ejército Popular de Liberación,* EPL)

Leadership. Francisco Caraballo

The formation of the EPL was announced in January 1968 by the (pro-Chinese) *Partido Comunista de Colombia—Marxista-Leninista* which had broken away from the (pro-Soviet) *Partido Comunista de Colombia* (PCC) in July 1965. The EPL went into action in the department of Córdoba but it survived severe setbacks inflicted by the army.

The EPL was still active in 1980, and on March 17 of that year a total of 14 EPL members were sentenced to altogether 400 years in prison. By September 1980 the EPL was officially stated to consist of only 60 active guerrillas.

However, by 1983 it was estimated to be the third largest guerrilla group in Colombia, numbering 250 members. It claimed responsibility for an attack in the northern El Crucero region which killed two policemen in March 1984 and for an attack on police in Bogotá on July 24, in which five people died.

During 1984 it held ceasefire talks with the government and concluded a one-year ceasefire effective from Sept. 1. The truce broke down in 1985 and the EPL undertook further violent attacks; security forces claimed that it had redoubled its efforts along with other guerrilla groups in the Valle del Cauca region.

On Nov. 20, 1985, the EPL leader Oscar William Calvo, the group's representative at the peace commission, was killed and the EPL withdrew from the commission.

On Feb. 16, 1987, Francisco Caraballo was named as the new EPL leader after the death of Jairo de Jesús Calvo in clashes with security forces. Caraballo had been a leader of the (legal) *Partido Comunista de Colombia—Marxista-Leninista*, the political wing of the EPL. Shortly before the death of Jairo Calvo (who had also been known as Ernesto Rojas) the EPL had published its intention to restart peace talks with the government.

(For EPL co-operation with other guerrilla organizations see separate entry for National Guerrilla Co-ordinating Board.)

Quintin Lame Commando (*Comando Quintin Lame*)

This group, founded in 1984, takes its name from the indigenous leader Manuel Quintin Lame (who died in October 1967) and consists mainly of Paez Indians from the south of Colombia around Cauca. Its first action was a reprisal raid on factory premises for the eviction of 150 indigenous families from the company's land. On Jan. 4, 1985, it attacked Santander de Quilichao (Cauca) together with members of the Ricardo Franco Front (see separate entry.) In April 1985 it briefly occupied Caloto (Cauca), and on June 30, 1985, it attacked the south-western town of Mondomo. On Jan. 21, 1987, it was reported that 10 of its members had been killed in the San Andrés de Pensilvania municipality.

(For this group's co-operation with other guerrilla organizations see separate entry for National Guerrilla Co-ordinating Board.)

Ricard Franco Front (*Frente Ricardo Franco,* FRF)

Leadership. Javier Delgado

This splinter group broke away from the Colombian Revolutionary Armed Forces (FARC—see separate entry) in 1984 in order to continue armed struggle, claiming that the army had broken the 1984 ceasefire concluded with the FARC. It claimed responsibility for nine bombs which killed two people in Bogotá on May 22, 1984. In early 1985, the FARC offered to the government a list of members who had deserted after the ceasefire, and in May it declared war on the Front, following which Delgado offered ceasefire negotiations. The group remained active and on June 4, 1985, attempted unsuccessfully to assassinate Hernando Hurtado, a leader of the (legal pro-Soviet) *Partido Comunista de Colombia* (PCC).

In December 1985, a total of 113 bodies were found in 30 mass graves in the Andean region around Tacueye (Cauca), and on Jan. 11, 1986, Delgado claimed responsibility and said that he was proud of having ordered the assassination of a total of 164 people who had allegedly infiltrated the group in order to spy for the army. On April 3, 1986, the bodies of 30 mutilated guerrillas who had reportedly died in an FRF internal struggle were found in the Cauca department.

Student Revolutionary Movement (*Movimiento Revolucionario Estudiantil*)

This group claimed responsibility for the death of an official of the Colombian state-owned oil company, Ecopetrol, at the end of June 1985.

Workers' Revolutionary Party (*Partido Revolucionario de los Trabajadores,* PRT)

Leadership. Valentín González

This Marxist group claims to have operated clandestinely for a number of years, organizing strikes, peasant land rights struggles and student protests. In July 1984 a PRT group reportedly led by Adriana Garces and Carlos Mario García kidnapped an industrialist and secured a substantial ransom.

The group announced its existence and objectives with the issue of a periodical, *El Combatiente,* in June 1985. It did not adhere to the 1984 ceasefire agreement.

(For PRT co-operation with other guerrilla organizations see separate entry for National Guerrilla Co-ordinating Board.)

Workers' Self-Defence Movement (*Movimiento de Autodefensa Obrera,* MAO)

Leadership. Adelaida Abadia Rey

This Trotskyist group was responsible for the killing of the Minister of the Interior, Dr Rafael Pardo, on Sept. 12, 1978, for which eight members were given lengthy prison sentences in November 1980.

In 1980 the group was estimated to have only 20 members, but it continued to be active in rural areas. It rejected the amnesty offer of November 1982, but as from Sept. 1, 1984, it had a ceasefire agreement with the government.

Comoros

Capital: Moroni (on Njazidja or Grand Comoro) Pop. 370,000 (excluding Mayotte)

The Federal and Islamic Republic of the Comoros has, under its Constitution approved in a referendum on Oct. 1, 1981, a President elected for a six-year term by universal adult suffrage and a 39-member Federal Assembly elected similarly for a five-year term. There is a Cabinet appointed by the President. In elections to the General Assembly held on March 22, 1987, all seats were won by the ruling Comorian Union for Progress (*Union comorienne pour le progrès*), formed in January 1979 as the country's sole political organization (for 12 years). This official result was, however, disputed by the opposition which claimed that the poll had been rigged.

Within what it regards as its own borders, the government of President Ahmed Abdallah has no authority over the island of Mayotte, whose population has opted by a substantial majority to remain under the sovereignty of France (the former colonial power in the Comoro Islands). Apart from Mayotte separatism, organized opposition to the government has consisted mainly of groups based abroad, in particular in France. Internally, more than 40 people arrested on the island of Grand Comoro (known as Njazidja since 1980) in mid-February 1981 were accused of planning to overthrow the government after some of them had been found in possession of arms originating from the armoury of the presidential guard.

On May 13, 1983, President Abdallah announced an amnesty for political prisoners (and for all common criminals serving less than 10 years) as well as substantial reductions of life sentences.

In Perth (Western Australia) John Pilgrim, one of three men charged with recruiting mercenaries to overthrow the government of the Comoros, was in April 1984 found guilty and sentenced to two years in prison, having allegedly planned to recruit 50 mercenaries.

Ten persons arrested in November 1984 were charged with plotting to assassinate President Abdallah. They were alleged to include members of the Mapindouzi militia of the late Ali Soilih (whose left-wing regime was overthrown in 1978).

Democratic Front (*Front démocratique,* FD)

Leadership. Mustapha Said Cheikh (sec.-gen.)

This group was technically banned but it was tolerated within the islands. When on March 8, 1985, elements of the Presidential Guard attempted to stage a coup, President Ahmed Abdallah blamed "a local Marxist-Leninist movement" for the attempt. This was generally regarded as a reference to the FD, which in the government's view was a front for communist activities. An FD representative in Paris stated on April 18 that between 400 and 600 of his movement's supporters had been arrested (among them its secretary-general), but a government spokesman said on May 19 that only 60 persons had been arrested. Of 68 people tried in November for alleged involvement in the attempt 17 (including the FD's secretary-general) were given forced labour sentences for life, 50 were given prison sentences of up to eight years, and one was acquitted. (According to Amnesty International the defendants were refused the right to designate a defence lawyer of their choice.)

An amnesty announced by the President on Dec. 31, 1985, covered 58 prisoners, 26 of them being political detainees, including 17 FD members. (None of those serving life sentences was believed to have been released.)

National Committee of Public Salvation (*Comité national du salut public*)

Leadership. Saïd Ali Kemal (founder)

The formation of this Committee was announced in Paris on Oct. 14, 1980, by Saïd Ali Kemal, a former ambassador of the Comoros to France, who had in July 1980 declined to accept a post in the Cabinet under President Ahmed Abdallah; at the same time he had resigned as ambassador, accusing the President of corruption and calling for his resignation, the establishment of a government of national unity, a general amnesty, land reform and a just distribution of wealth, and in foreign affairs a policy of non-alignment and a rapprochement with Madagascar. He also contended that the President had sought to pass on to him responsibility for dealing with embarrassing problems concerning political prisoners in the Comoros. (In January 1981 a Paris advocate, who had acted as defence counsel for former army officers found guilty of crimes committed under the left-wing regime of President Ali Soilih—overthrown in May 1978—stated that there were about 100 former supporters of that regime in detention; however, on Jan. 27, 1982, it was reported that 14 political prisoners had been released.)

Union for a Democratic Republic of the Comoros (*Union pour une république démocratique des Comoros,* URDC)

Leadership. Mouzaoir Abdallah (founder)

The creation of this Union was announced early in August 1981 by Mouzaoir Abdallah, who had been

Foreign Minister under the left-wing regime of President Ali Soilih in 1976-78; thereafter he had been under house arrest for nearly three years, had fled the country in June 1981 but had returned after declaring that he had been in contact with a number of friendly and neighbouring states including France, Madagascar, Seychelles and Tanzania. On Nov. 7, 1981, he was arrested and accused of being engaged in subversive activities in the company of Yves Lebret, a former roving ambassador. On May 19, 1982, he was given a suspended two-year prison sentence but on May 28 he was pardoned.

Several hundred supporters of the URDC were imprisoned at the time of the March 1987 elections, in which Mouzaoir Abdallah was not permitted to stand.

United National Front of the Comoros (*Front national uni des Komores,* FNUK)

Leadership. Abubakar Ahmed Burdin (l.)

Based in Dar-es-Salaam, this Front of supporters of the former left-wing regime of President Ali Soilih issued, in June 1980, an open letter to President Ahmed Abdallah, accusing him of "tyranny, and "despotism", especially in his treatment of political prisoners and of the press through censorship, and also in gaining profits for politicians. By 1982 the FNUK was allied, under the leadership of Abubakar Ahmed Burdin, with the Association of Comorian Trainees and Students (*Association des stagiaires et des étudiants comoriens*) in an organization referred to as FNUK-UNIKOM.

Congo

Capital: Brazzaville Pop. 1,913,000

The People's Republic of the Congo has been ruled by a military Committee of the Congolese Party of Labour (*Parti congolais du travail*, PCT) since the assassination of President Marien Ngouabi on March 18, 1977, whereafter the Constitution was suspended and the National Assembly dissolved. Under a new Constitution approved in a referendum on July 8, 1979, provision was made for a popularly elected National People's Assembly consisting of members nominated by the PCT. The congress of the PCT appoints the country's President, who presides over a Council of Ministers headed by a Prime Minister.

Claude-Ernest N'dalla, a co-founder of the PCT and former Education Minister, was sentenced to death by the Revolutionary Court of Justice in August 1986 on charges of involvement in bombings in 1982.

Patriotic Armed Group of the Congo (*Groupe armé patriotique du Congo*)

This Group surfaced in March 1982 when a telephone caller in Paris identified himself as a member and reportedly stated that an earlier explosion in a Brazzaville cinema was due to a terrorist action which had killed 15 persons (and not five, as officially reported). He stated that his Group wanted clarification of the murder of President Ngouabi and also of the imprisonment of President (Col.) Joachim Yhombi Opango in 1979 after he had relinquished power to Col. Sassou-Ngouesso. It had been announced that Col. Yhombi Opango would be tried for treason for allegedly trying to establish a "rightist faction" within the ruling PCT. However, on Nov. 10, 1984, President Sassou-Ngouesso announced that the colonel had been released "in the interest of national unity and peace".

Costa Rica

Capital: San José Pop. 2,490,000

The Republic of Costa Rica is a democratic multi-party state with an executive President elected for four years by universal adult suffrage. He appoints, and presides over, a Cabinet. Legislative power is held by a Legislative Assembly similarly elected by universal adult suffrage.

As a result of elections held on Feb. 2, 1986, the ruling National Liberation Party (PLN) retained power but its majority in the Assembly was reduced from 33 seats to 29; of the remaining seats 25 were won by the Social Christian Unity Party (PUSC), one each by the two left-wing coalitions, People United (PU) and Popular Alliance, and one by an independent candidate. The Popular Alliance was formed in 1985 to contest the elections after a series of divisions among left-wing parties, and in particular the pro-Soviet communist Popular Vanguard Party (PVP), which was excluded from the PU in February 1985. The simultaneous presidential election of February 1986 was won by Oscar Arias Sánchez of the PLN, who was inaugurated on May 8, 1986.

Under its 1949 Constitution, Costa Rica has no Army, and successive governments have reiterated the country's commitment to neutrality. This commitment has been strained in relations with Nicaragua, which has accused Costa Rica of aiding "contra" rebels based in the border region in their attacks on Nicaraguan targets. Although the Costa Rican Civil Guard dismantled contra camps in 1983 and the authorities have expelled a number of contra leaders, the government apparently came under greater pressure from the United States during the presidency of Luis Alberto Monge Alvarez (1982-86) to take a firmer stance against the Nicaraguan government.

Costa Rican People's Army (*Ejército del Pueblo Costarricense,* EPC)

The EPC is a right-wing guerrilla group which was formed in 1984.

Free Costa Rica (*Costa Rica Libre*)

This neo-fascist movement emerged in 1985 and included among its founder members the then Minister of Public Security, Benjamín Piza. In 1985 its members had reportedly been involved in stone-throwing incidents at the Nicaraguan embassy in San José, and in December had attacked a group of people travelling across Central America on an International March for Peace.

Homeland and Truth (*Patria y Verdad*)

This right-wing guerrilla group emerged in 1985 and was believed to have been responsible for the bombing of a power line near the Nicaraguan border on June 11, 1985.

Côte d'Ivoire

Capital: Yamoussoukro Pop. 9,810,000

The Republic of Côte d'Ivoire has an executive President elected for a five-year term, and re-eligible, by universal adult suffrage. He appoints, and presides over, a Cabinet, while legislative power is held by a 175-member National Assembly also elected for five years by universal adult suffrage from a list submitted by the *Parti démocratique de la Côte d'Ivoire* (PDCI), the country's sole political party. In elections to the National Assembly held on Nov. 10, 1985, the 175 seats were contested by 546 PDCI candidates, of whom 114 were elected to the Assembly for the first time.

No organized opposition movements have emerged in Côte d'Ivoire, which has been one of the most prosperous, stable states of sub-Saharan Africa. Nevertheless, attempts to overthrow the government of President Félix Houphouët-Boigny have been made by groups of individual conspirators, notably one in 1973 by 12 former army officers.

A number of strikes among students and professional people, which began in late 1980, culminated in one which lasted from April 18 to May 3, 1983, when it was ended by presidential decree. President Houphouët-Boigny suggested on April 24, 1983, that an unnamed foreign power (i.e. Libya) was intent upon destabilizing the country, and on April 29 he announced the introduction of conscription by which personnel in specified professions would be compelled to continue their work under pain of prison sentences or fines.

On June 21, 1981, it had been officially announced that there were no political prisoners in Côte d'Ivoire, but it was later disclosed that a number of journalists had been conscripted to military service.

A strike among staff in the national public enterprises begun on June 5, 1985, led to the dismissal of numbers of strikers by June 8 on the ground that the strike was "against the national interest".

A general amnesty declared on Dec. 6, 1985, affected some 9,500 prisoners (but not those convicted of murder or armed robbery). President Houphouët-Boigny declared on this occasion that there were no political prisoners in Côte d'Ivoire.

Cuba

Capital: Havana Pop. 10,090,000

The Republic of Cuba has a government which since December 1961 has been designated as communist. Under a Constitution approved in a referendum in February 1976 the Republic was defined as "a socialist state of workpeople and other manual and intellectual workers"; the leading role of the Communist Party of Cuba was recognized; and the "fraternal friendship, aid and co-operation of the Soviet Union and other socialist countries" were acknowledged. Under this Constitution a 510-member National Assembly is elected indirectly for a five-year term by delegates elected to municipal assemblies (the basic organs of "people's power") by universal suffrage of citizens above the age of 16 years. Most of the candidates are Communist Party members; they need to obtain an overall majority in a first ballot, failing which a second (run-off) ballot is held. The head of state and government (currently Dr Fidel Castro Ruz, First Secretary of the Cuban Communist Party) is elected by the National Assembly as President of the Council of State, which is the country's highest representative body and which, in addition to its President, five Vice-Presidents and its secretary, has another 23 members. There is also a Council of Ministers headed by an Executive Committee, of which Dr Castro is Chairman.

In secret ballots held on Oct. 19 and 26, 1986, a total of 13,257 delegates were elected to the country's 169 municipal assemblies in a 97 per cent poll. These delegates subsequently elected the National Assembly which was inaugurated on Dec. 27 of that year.

Political opposition to the Castro regime has found most of its support among Cuban refugees, of which several hundred thousand have settled in the United States. Following the abortive "Bay of Pigs" invasion attempt in April 1961 (planned by the US Central Intelligence Agency and approved by President Kennedy), various other landings by small groups of Cuban exiles have been reported from time to time, as have plots to assassinate Dr Castro. The Inter-American Human Rights Commission of the Organization of American States (from which Cuba has been excluded since 1962) claimed in a report released in Washington in March 1980, and based largely on evidence of former prisoners, that Cuba ill-treated political prisoners, of whom there were still about 1,000 (some held without trial); the report added that treatment was worst for those prisoners who refused to conform to socialist principles.

Refugee Activities

According to a report by a US Senate intelligence committee, issued on Nov. 20, 1976, Cuban exiles had been involved in plans to assassinate Dr Castro conceived by officials of the (US) Central Intelligence Agency (CIA) between 1960 and 1965, most of these plans being made without the knowledge of the US government. Between December 1965 and April 1973, a total of 260,737 Cubans entered the United States, most of them by means of airlifts agreed between the two countries. Dr Castro said on Sept. 28, 1968, that "counter-revolutionaries" were active in Cuba; two men accused of sabotage were executed on Oct. 7, 1968.

Of a group of Cuban exiles who landed near the US base of Guantánamo on May 7, 1969, three were killed, three others were sentenced to 20 years' imprisonment by a military court, and four were shot dead at Santiago de Cuba on Dec. 7, 1969. Of a further group which landed in eastern Cuba in September 1970, and were captured shortly afterwards, five were sentenced to death and two to 30 years in prison in March 1971.

Cuban exiles were also held responsible for a machine-gun attack on two Cuban fishing boats off Florida on April 6, 1976; the bombing of the Cuban embassy in Lisbon on April 22, when two persons were killed; the bombing of the Cuban mission at the United Nations on July 5; an explosion at an airline office representing the Cuban airline in Barbados on July 10; the kidnapping of two Cuban embassy officials in Argentina on Aug. 9; and the bombing of the Cuban airline office in Panama on Aug. 18.

A new influx of Cubans into the United States began in 1978, when it was disclosed that the Cuban government had unilaterally agreed to release several hundred Cuban political prisoners to allow them and others freed earlier to leave for the United States. The first group of 66 such Cubans arrived in Miami (Florida) on Oct. 21. Dr Castro announced on Nov. 22, 1978 (after talks with Cuban exiles invited to Havana), that he intended to release some 3,000 political prisoners at a rate of at least 400 a month, provided the United States agreed to accept those who wished to go there. He said that of a total of 4,263 (i.e. 3,238 political prisoners, 600 who had tried to leave Cuba illegally and 425 regarded as war criminals of the pre-1959 Batista era), about 80 per cent would be freed and the remainder would be considered later.

On Dec. 8-9, 1978, President Castro added that an agreement had been signed for the release of 3,000 political prisoners (with 400 of them to be freed immediately); that 12,000 former prisoners and their families would be allowed to leave Cuba for a place of their choice; and that Cubans living abroad would be allowed to visit Cuba as tourists. On June 5, 1979, it was officially announced in Havana that until then 1,900 prisoners had been released, and further releases were announced of 500 on July 24 and of another 400 on Aug. 24 (the latter included Rolando Cubelas, sentenced in 1966 to 25 years in prison for conspiring to kill Dr Castro).

A group of other released political prisoners flown to Costa Rica with their families on Oct. 21, 1979, included Maj. Huber Matos, who had played a leading part in the overthrow of the Batista regime in 1958-59 but had thereafter protested against the rising influence of communism in Cuba and had, at the instigation of Dr Castro, been sentenced late in 1959 to 20 years in prison for treason; during his imprisonment he had refused "political re-education" and therefore had to forgo certain privileges. Maj. Matos stated in Costa Rica on Oct. 23 that he had suffered permanent physical damage from his treatment in prison but that he still believed in the ideals of the Cuban revolution to which, he said, Dr Castro was the real traitor.

Following the release of another 400 political prisoners on Nov. 14, 1979, the Cuban government claimed that all prisoners (numbered at 3,600) whom it had undertaken to release had by then been freed. However, a new exodus of Cubans to the United States between April and June 1980 resulted in the arrival by boat of 114,475 Cubans in Florida where they joined another 500,000 who had settled there in earlier years. After more than 10,000 Cubans wishing to leave their country had sought refuge in the Peruvian embassy in Havana early in April 1980, Dr Castro let it be understood that Cuban exiles in the United States would be permitted to pick up by boat anyone who wished to leave Cuba. At a meeting of Foreign Ministers of the Andean Pact member states (Bolivia, Colombia, Ecuador, Peru, and Venezuela) on April 9, 1980, it was agreed that several countries would accept certain quotas of these Cuban refugees at the Peruvian embassy, and these were later announced as United States 3,500, Peru 1,000, Venezuela 500, Spain 500, Canada 300, Costa Rica 300, Ecuador 200 and Belgium 150.

On June 3 it was reported that an estimated 100,000 Cubans were still wanting to leave their country, including 5,000 former political prisoners who had registered at the US interest section of the Swiss Embassy in Havana (the United States having broken off diplomatic relations with Cuba in 1961). Political prisoners still detained in Cuba included Armando Fernando Valladares, sentenced in 1961 to 30 years in prison for offences against the state but now in poor physical condition; a campaign for his release was being co-ordinated in Europe by Maj. Matos, who announced in Paris on June 19, 1980, that he was forming an anti-Castro organization.

On Sept. 26, 1980, the Cuban government ended the exodus of refugees (whose total since April 21, 1980, it gave as 123,000). On Oct. 27 the Cuban government released all 33 US citizens serving prison sentences in Cuba and allowed 30 of them to fly to the United States (with the remaining three having chosen to stay in Cuba). According to a statement made in December 1980 by the US interests section at the Swiss embassy in Havana, about 100,000 Cubans were still waiting for permission to leave the island. Over the following two years extensive illegal immigration of Cubans into the United States took place, usually by means of small boats.

In October 1980 a conference of anti-Castro elements held in Caracas under the chairmanship of Maj. Matos approved a plan to create the necessary conditions for a rising of the Cuban people against the government of President Castro.

In the United States it was reported in January 1982 that anti-Castro refugees from Cuba were, in Florida, undergoing clandestine training in guerrilla warfare and use of sophisticated weapons, although under US law they were not allowed to use weapons other than semi-automatic ones.

In October 1984, a dozen Cubans who had been in the Peruvian embassy in Havana since 1980—but had not taken part in the subsequent mass exodus by sea to the United States—came out under an "amnesty with full guarantees".

In December 1984 Maj. Matos was reported to be organizing a Cuban émigré detachment to fight alongside the Nicaraguan "contra" forces, partly out of solidarity with their cause and partly in order to obtain practical experience of modern guerrilla warfare.

In an agreement signed in December 1984 between Cuba and the United States, Dr Castro agreed to the repatriation of 2,746 "excludable aliens" from the United States—who had been among the 123,000 people who had entered the USA by boat in 1980 and most of whom were held in US prisons or mental institutions or were on parole. In exchange, the United States agreed to the resumption of emigration from Cuba to the USA to take 3,000 political prisoners, whom Dr Castro agreed to release, and to take up to 20,000 regular Cuban immigrants per annum. From Feb. 21 to 23, the "excludable aliens" were flown back to Cuba while early on May 20, 1985, the first group of 28 political prisoners and relatives arrived in Miami. The immigration agreement was abrogated by Castro on May 20, 1985, following the commencement of broadcasts to Cuba by the Florida-based anti-Cuban propagandist Radio Martí. Castro subsequently stopped all visits to Cuba by Cuban-Americans except on humanitarian grounds.

During 1986 the remaining prisoners serving sentences for their involvement in the 1961 "Bay of Pigs" invasion were released, and another 69 prisoners were also set free, all being allowed to leave the country for the United States. Eloy Gutierrez Menoyo was released on Dec. 21, 1986, and allowed to return to Spain after serving 21 years of his prison sentence.

In the United States it was claimed in March 1987 that Cuba was currently detaining more than 15,000 political prisoners. Dr Castro, however, denied on March 19 that any Cuban was in prison for his political beliefs and added that there were approximately 100 convicted criminals serving sentences for hostile acts against the Cuban state.

Exiled Groups

Alpha-66 Group

Leadership. Andrés Nazario Sargen (sec.-gen.); Humberto Pérez Alvarado (chief of military operations)

This Group, set up by 66 Cuban refugees in Miami in 1962 with the aim of overthrowing the Castro regime, was involved in several attempted landings in Cuba. On April 17, 1970, a group of 13 members of the group, led by Col. Vicente Méndez, landed in eastern Cuba, but four of the group were killed and the remainder taken prisoner by Cuban troops (who themselves lost five soldiers killed while one was wounded). Dr Castro refused on May 13, 1970, to exchange those captured against 11 Cuban fishermen held by Alpha-66 members who had sunk two Cuban fishing boats during the previous week.

In 1981 the Group attempted a landing in Matanzas province (east of Havana) with the object of killing Dr Castro and sabotaging industrial installations, but Havana radio announced on July 11 that five "counter-revolutionaries" involved in the attempt had been arrested.

Cuban Nationalist Movement (*Movimiento Nacionalista Cubano,* MNC)

Three members of this US-based Movement—Alvin Ross Díaz, Guillermo Novo Sampol and Ignacio Novo Sampol—were sentenced in Washington on March 23, 1979 (the first two to life imprisonment and the last-named to eight years in prison), for complicity in the murder (on Sept. 21, 1976) of Orlando Letelier (a former Chilean ambassador and former minister under President Allende of Chile) and a passenger in his car. Two other Cuban exiles accused of involvement in the murders were believed to be in Nicaragua.

Cubans United (*Cubanos Unidos*)

Leadership. Wilfredo Navarra (sec.-gen.)

This exile group based in the United States sent several boats to the US base of Guantánamo on Cuba during the second half of August 1981 to set up a government-in-exile; however, their attempts were frustrated by a tropical storm as a result of which 60 members of the expedition were shipwrecked while about 16 others were rescued by US Coastguards.

Omega 7

Leadership. Eduardo Arocena

This terrorist group of Cuban exiles in the United States opposed any negotiations with the Castro regime by Cuban exiles. It was responsible for a bomb explosion in front of the Cuban mission at the United Nations in New York on Sept. 9, 1978, and for bombing the offices of a moderate Cuban exiles' newspaper in New York on Oct. 21 of that year. On March 25, 1979, Omega 7 carried out bomb attacks on Cuban-linked premises in New Jersey and at Kennedy Airport (New York).

Other Omega 7 attacks in 1979 were directed against a member of the "Committee of 75", and on April 28 it killed (in Puerto Rico) a Cuban travel agent who organized exiles' tours to Cuba.

On Sept. 11, 1980, a Cuban diplomat at the UN mission in New York was murdered by an Omega 7 member. Orlando Bosch, believed to be linked to Omega 7, was one of four men acquitted by a Venezuelan court in September 1980 after being accused of having placed a bomb on a Cuban airliner over Barbados on Oct. 6, 1976, when 73 people were killed for which an *El Condor* group claimed responsibility.

Following the assumption of office by President Reagan in the United States in January 1981, Omega 7 announced a "truce" in its activities, but on Sept. 21, 1981, it announced that it had ended the truce, and it proceeded to bomb Mexican consular premises in Miami and New York in protest against Mexico's friendly relations with the Castro regime.

On Nov. 9, 1984, Arocena was sentenced to life imprisonment for the murder of the Cuban diplomat and various other bombing and shooting attacks; he was also sentenced in Miami in May 1985 to 20 years' imprisonment after having been convicted of most of the bombings of diplomatic premises (against Nicaraguan, Mexican, Venezuelan and Soviet consulates in Miami and New York between 1979 and 1983).

Cyprus

Capital: Nicosia Pop. 657,000

Since February 1975 the Republic of Cyprus (a member of the Commonwealth) has been de facto divided into two states—the (Greek-Cypriot) Republic of Cyprus and a not internationally recognized Turkish state, created after the occupation by Turkish troops of about 40 per cent of the island's area in July 1974. Both are multi-party states and have an executive President presiding over a Cabinet, as well as unicameral Parliaments elected by universal adult suffrage.

The Cypriot House of Representatives has 56 seats for Greek Cypriots and 24 seats allocated for Turkish Cypriots (not taken up since the creation of a separate Turkish state in Cyprus). As a result of elections held on Dec. 8, 1985, to the 56 Greek Cypriot seats on the basis of proportional representation in multi-member constituencies these seats were distributed as follows: Democratic Rally (DISY) 19, Democratic Party (DIKO) 16, (pro-communist) Progressive Party of the Working People (AKEL) 15, Socialist Party (EDEK) six. No other parties took part in the elections, and two independent candidates were unsuccessful.

In the Turkish state, until then known as the Turkish Federated State of Cyprus, the Legislative Assembly unanimously adopted, on Nov. 15, 1983, a declaration of an independent "Turkish Republic of Northern Cyprus"—but this new state received no international recognition except from Turkey, while the United Nations Security Council deemed the declaration to be "legally invalid". On Dec. 2, 1983, the Legislative Assembly adopted legislation creating a 70-member Constituent Assembly comprising the 40 members of the existing Assembly and 30 nominated members. A new draft Constitution was approved by the Constituent Assembly on March 12-13, and also in a referendum held on May 5, 1985 (by 49,447 votes to 21,012).

Under the new Constitution a 50-member Legislative Assembly was elected on June 23, 1985, seats being distributed as follows: National Unity Party 24, (Marxist) Republican Turkish Party (which had campaigned for a "no" vote in the referendum) 12, Communal Liberation Party (TKP) 10, New Dawn (or "Renaissance" or "New Birth") Party four. Parties which obtained no seats included the Democratic People's Party, the Communal Leap Party, the Social Democratic Party, the Cyprus Democracy Party and the New Turkish Unity Party (an offshoot of the New Dawn).

There has been little evidence of extra-parliamentary opposition to the two governments in Cyprus in recent years. However, the former director of the Cyprus Central prison was killed by a car bomb in Nicosia on June 7, 1987, the motive not being known. Cyprus has been affected by the activities of Middle Eastern groups, including an attack on British military staff quarters, in which no one was killed, on Aug. 3, 1986, which was claimed by a previously unknown group calling itself the Unified Nasserite Organization—Cairo, and the ambush of a British army land rover on April 20, 1987, in which two people died, in connection with which two Libyans were subsequently arrested.

Turgut Ozal, the Turkish Prime Minister, alleged on July 23, 1986 that the Greek Cypriot government was involved in the supply of arms to Kurdish separatist groups operating within Turkey.

Czechoslovakia

Capital: Prague Pop. 15,500,000

The Czechoslovak Socialist Republic has since Jan. 1, 1969, been a federal socialist republic comprising the Czech Socialist Republic and the Slovak Socialist Republic, each of them with its own government and National Council (unicameral Parliament, with 200 deputies in the Czech Council and 150 in the Slovak Council). There is a federal government and a bicameral Federal Assembly consisting of a directly elected House of the People and a House of Nations elected by the Czech and the Slovak National Councils. Direct elections consist of the endorsement of a list of candidates nominated by the National Front, a mass organization embracing the Communist Party and also the Czechoslovak People's Party, the Czechoslovak Socialist Party, the Slovak Freedom Party, the Slovak Reconstruction Party, trade unions and youth organizations.

Since 1948 the Czechoslovak Communist Party has been the leading political force in the country, although with varying political programmes. Early in 1968 a new Central Committee with Alexander Dubcek as First Secretary embarked on a liberalization programme (also known as the "Prague Spring" and designed to bring about "socialism with a human face"). However, in the view of the Communist Party leaders of the Soviet Union (and also those of Bulgaria, the German Democratic Republic, Hungary and Poland) this programme was liable to lead to the detachment of Czechoslovakia from the "socialist community". The subsequent intervention by forces of these five Warsaw Pact member countries in August 1968 entailed the abandonment of the liberalization programme and the progressive removal of Dubcek from all positions of power in 1969-70. Since April 1969 the party has, under the leadership of Dr Gustáv Husák, been guided by the need to maintain "friendly relations with the Soviet Union and other socialist countries", without whose aid in August 1968 (as stated by Dr Husák on May 25, 1972) "the power of the working class of the country would have been overthrown".

1968 Reform Programme

"Prague Spring" Action Programme

The 1968 reform programme of the "Prague Spring" was set out in a 24,000-word "action programme" published by the Czechoslovak Communist Party on April 9, 1968. The main aim, it was stated, was to "reform the whole political system so as to permit . . . the combination of a broad democracy with a scientific, highly qualified management, the strengthening of the social order, the stabilization of socialist relations, and the maintenance of social discipline". At the same time the basic structure of the political system "must provide firm guarantees against a return to the old methods of subjectivism and highhandedness from a position of power".

The Communist Party of Czechoslovakia would "use every means to develop such forms of political life as will ensure the expression of the direct will of the working class and all working people in political decision-making in our country". The National Front as a whole, and its components, "must have independent rights and their own responsibility for the management of our country and society. . . ."

In a long section on the role of the Communist Party it was stated inter alia that the party should be based on the voluntary support of the people; it did not fulfil its function by ruling over society but by "serving faithfully the free and progressive development of society". After emphasizing that the party's authority must be renewed, not by orders but by the deeds and work of its members, the programme stated: "The leading role of the party was too often understood in the past as a monopolistic concentration of power in the hands of the party organs. . . . This weakened the initiative and responsibilities of the state and of economic and social institutions, damaged the authority of the party, and made it impossible for the party to fulfil its basic tasks. The party must fight . . . for the voluntary support of a majority within the framework of the democratic rules of a socialist state. . . ."

In the constitutional sphere, assurances were given that freedom of assembly would be implemented "this year"; that censorship before publication would be eliminated; that the rehabilitation of people who had been the victims of judicial injustice in the past would be accelerated; that freedom of minority interests and opinions, as well as other freedoms, would be guaranteed more exactly; and that the "constitutional freedom of movement, in particular travel by our citizens abroad, must be guaranteed by law". In the latter connexion it was stated that Czechoslovak citizens should have "the legal right to long-term or permanent sojourn abroad", although in the interests of the state it would be necessary by law to prevent a "brain drain" of certain categories of specialists. Freedom of assembly and association must also be "legally guaranteed and applied to various religious denominations".

Another section of the programme said that the security police would limit their activities solely to matters involving the security of the state. "Every citizen not guilty in this respect," it was stated, "must feel sure that his political convictions and opinions do not become the subject of attention by the state security. Its organs may not be used to solve questions of internal policy."

On relations between the Czechs and the Slovaks, the programme said "Our Republic, as a joint state of two equal nations—Czechs and Slovaks—must ensure that the constitutional arrangement of relations between our fraternal nations and the status of all other nationalities of Czechoslovakia develops as demanded by the strengthening of the unity of the state, the development of the nations and nationalities themselves, and in keeping with the needs of socialism." To this end a constitutional law would be passed which would "embody the principle of a symmetrical arrangement" and which would, "on the basis of full equality, solve the status of Slovak national bodies in the nearest future". A statute would also be worked out for the other nationalities in Czechoslovakia—Hungarians, Poles, Ukrainians, and Germans—which would "guarantee the possibilities of their national life and the development of their national individuality".

The "basic orientation of Czechoslovak foreign policy", it was stated, was "alliance and co-operation with the Soviet Union and other socialist countries . . . on the basis of mutual respect, sovereignty and equality, and international solidarity".

After saying that Czechoslovak society had entered a new stage of development since the end of the 1950s, the document stated that the present stage of development was marked by the following characteristics:

(1) Antagonistic classes no longer existed, and the main feature of internal development was becoming "the process of rapprochement of all social groups of our society".

(2) Existing methods of management and the orientation of the national economy had become outdated, and urgent changes were required having intensive economic growth as their objective.

(3) It was necessary to "prepare the country's link-

up with the process of the scientific technical revolution in the world", a task which would require "especially intensive co-operation between workers and peasants and the intelligentsia and which will lay great demands on people's knowledge and qualifications. . . ."

(4) An "open exchange of views and the democratization of the whole social and political system is becoming literally a condition of the dynamics of socialist society. . . ."

Suppression of Reform Movement

The Soviet-led invasion of Czechoslovakia in August 1968 forced the abandonment of the reform programme, while the replacement of Dubcek as party leader by Dr Husák in April 1969 marked the beginning of concerted action by the authorities to remove all traces of the "Prague Spring" in terms both of its supporters and of the liberalization measures introduced during Dubcek's brief ascendancy.

As a protest against the Soviet intervention, Jan Palach (a 21-year-old student) burned himself to death in Prague on Jan. 17, 1969, after writing down that he had been a member of a group which demanded the immediate abolition of censorship and the prohibition of the distribution of *Zpravy* (a Soviet-sponsored propaganda publication). His death was followed by mass demonstrations and demands for the restoration of democratic liberties.

Anti-Soviet demonstrations took place in several localities in Czechoslovakia on March 28-29, 1969 (following the defeat of a Soviet ice hockey team by a Czechoslovak one), the resultant disorders being condemned by the government and the Communist Party in a statement issued on April 2, 1969, saying that a "psychosis nourished by anti-Soviet and anti-socialist forces for political ends" had been "fanned by irresponsible articles and transmissions in the press and on radio and television"; that there had been "more or less open invectives against the Soviet Union" and against the Communist Party and its leaders through both the written and the spoken word; and that this had created "an atmosphere in contradiction with the government's efforts to achieve a normalization of life in Czechoslovakia". Further disturbances occurred on Aug. 19-20, 1969 (the first anniversary of the 1968 Soviet-led invasion), when five persons were killed and (in Prague alone) 1,377 were arrested.

After his removal from all political posts in the period 1969-70, Dubcek repeatedly defended his own position. In a letter published in Italy on March 13, 1974, he wrote inter alia that Czechoslovakia was "ruled by a system of personal power from the top to the bottom"; that the government had lost "what counts most in the work of a Leninist-type party—the confidence of the masses in the party"; and that he was still unable to understand how false reports about his liberalization plans could have been accepted as true in Moscow. He concluded: "We [i.e. his wife and he himself] have no rancour towards the party, its movement and its ideas. They are stronger than the obstacles along the path which will nevertheless still lead onward. We have not let ourselves be discouraged."

In a letter written to the Czechoslovak Federal Assembly on Oct. 28, 1974 (according to the Stockholm *Dagens Nyheter* of April 13, 1975), Dubcek claimed that in the party there was no democracy; that no attempt was made to gain a majority by discussion; that the courts were "totally dependent" on the Ministry of the Interior; and that it was "impossible to speak of legality when the judiciary can express no opposition". He also claimed that the "compromise policy" adopted in November 1968 might have succeeded had it not been for the "sectarian opportunism" adopted by Dr Husák (his successor as First Secretary of the party) with his "dogmatic and divisive tactics under the pretext of struggling against counter-revolution". He added that during the entire invasion period not a single counter-revolutionary had been arrested, but "hundreds of thousands of loyal Communists, many of them veterans of the wartime resistance . . . were branded as anti-Soviet and punished". He dismissed as nonsense the allegation that the "Prague Spring" was a return to capitalism. Claiming that the working class in Czechoslovakia knew that it was "being manipulated", he wrote: "It is necessary consciously to overcome this system, to thwart it through legal means and to prevent its perpetuation and existence", and he condemned the misuse of power and the violation of socialist principles as "a violation of human rights".

Dr Husák, however, called this letter "a falsification of history" in which Dubcek had slandered "the state, the party and parliamentary bodies" and had worked his way to "the position of a traitor". On Aug. 17, 1975, Dubcek was reported to have been expelled from his trade union because of his letter of October 1974.

At the first congress of the Czech Writers' Union (founded in 1971), held in Prague on May 31, 1972, the newly-elected chairman stated that writers who had been "the organizers of the revisionists' anti-socialist actions" (during 1968) could not become members of the union. Moreover, the eighth congress of the Central Council of the Czechoslovak Revolutionary Trade Union Movement, which opened in Prague on July 12, 1972, annulled all documents and resolutions of the previous congress (held in March 1969, shortly before the fall of Dubcek), including the right of workers to strike. The Council's chairman, Karel Hoffmann, denounced "right-wing deviationist opportunism" and declared that the March 1969 congress had given "anti-socialist forces" a last opportunity for "an open political manifestation".

Legislation to empower the government to restrict more effectively the influence of Dubcek's followers and other dissenters was passed in 1973-74. In amendments to the penal code approved by the Federal Assembly on April 25, 1973, the existing maximum prison sentence of 15 years was increased to 25 years for "capital" crimes, including "anti-socialist" activities; the existing law against spreading false information abroad was expanded to cover also "untrue reports" about Czechoslovakia's international status and foreign policy; and any person found guilty of such charges would not only be imprisoned for up to three years but would also lose his property by confiscation. The amendment also introduced "protective surveillance" which could be ordered by a court and involved the control, through the security services, of the movement of persons who had served prison sentences.

Under a bill which came into force on July 1, 1974, the police were empowered to "infringe the rights and freedom of citizens if required for the protection of the social system and the socialist state, for public order or for the safety of persons or property".

The writer Václav Havel, who had supported the 1968 reforms and who later became a leading member of the Charter 77 movement (see below), wrote in an open letter handed to Western correspondents in Prague in mid-April 1975 that there was "an ever-deepening crisis in our society" based on "fear, corruption and apathy". He continued: "Our present rulers actually offer bribes to those whom they want to win over to their side. . . .The prerequisite to any advancement, or even retention of one's current position, is an assent to lie to oneself, to betray one's friends and to deceive one's employers." He held Dr Husák personally responsible for the "paralysis of our cultural activity" and "the drastic suppression of our history", as well as for "ceaselessly degrading human dignity, for the puny sake of protecting your own power".

In a 90-page dossier presented in Vienna on May 24, 1976, by Jirí Starek (a former cultural attaché at the Czechoslovak embassy in Austria) it was asserted that, since November 1970, 7,000 army officers had been expelled from the Czechoslovak Communist Party and had lost their posts; that 2,000 others dismissed had been regarded as "right-wing deviationists"; that 2,000 journalists had been "purged" and several thousand academics had been prevented from continuing their work; and that entry to the country's only theological seminary had been restricted, at first to 16 young people a year and from 1974 onwards to 26.

Repression of political dissenters has ranged from surveillance and house arrest to detention and trials resulting in prison sentences. In a report published on Aug. 13, 1985, Amnesty International claimed that a law of "protective surveillance" originally designed to protect society from antisocial actions of mentally sick persons and common criminals had since 1981 been abused by police and applied in political cases.

Charter 77

Leadership. Charter 77 has no official leaders, but three spokespersons have been appointed on an annual basis. Its founding spokesmen (from January 1977) were Prof. Jirí Hajek, Dr Václav Havel and Prof. Jan Patocka (who died in March 1977). Later spokespersons included Prof. Ladislav Hejdanek, Marta Kubisova, Prof. Václav Benda, Zdena Tominova, Jirí Dienstbier and Prof. Jaroslav Sabata. The spokespersons for 1986 were Anna Sabatova, Jan Stern and Dr Martin Palous.

Manifesto. The official publication in Czechoslovakia on Oct. 13, 1976, of the UN Covenants on Civil and Political Rights and on Economic, Social and Cultural Rights (which after their ratification by Czechoslovakia in December 1975 had entered into force on March 23, 1976) gave rise to the drafting of a manifesto by a new movement calling itself "Charter 77". While the manifesto, dated Jan. 1, 1977, was not published in Czechoslovakia, copies of it were sent to the government and to its initial 242 signatories (who increased to about 800 by mid-1977 and later to over 1,000), and it was printed in West German newspapers (in translation) on Jan. 6-7, 1977, whereupon police action was taken against a number of its signatories.

After welcoming the fact that Czechoslovakia had acceded to the covenants, the manifesto continued as follows:

"At the same time their publication urgently reminds us that in our country many fundamental civil rights—regrettably—exist only on paper. The right of free expression of opinion, as guaranteed by Article 19 of the first covenant, for instance, is quite illusory. Tens of thousands of citizens are prevented from working in their professions merely because they hold views at variance with the official ones. Moreover, they often become the targets of all kinds of discrimination and chicanery by the authorities and social organizations; being deprived of any possibility of defending themselves, they become in effect victims of apartheid. Hundreds of thousands of other citizens are deprived of 'freedom from fear' (see the preamble of the first covenant) because they are forced to live in constant danger of losing their jobs or other facilities should they express their opinion.

The Right to Education. "Contrary to Article 13 of the second covenant which guarantees the right to education for everybody, innumerable young people are refused admission to higher education merely because of their views or even the views of their parents. Countless citizens have to live in fear that, if they express themselves in accordance with their convictions, they themselves or their children may be deprived of the right to education.

"Insistence on the right 'to seek, receive and impart information and ideas of all kinds, regardless of frontiers, either orally, in writing or in print [or] in the form of art' (Paragraph 2, Article 19 of the first covenant) is persecuted not only outside the courts but also by the courts themselves, often under the pretext of criminal indictment (as evidenced, inter alia, by the trials of young musicians).

Freedom of Expression of Opinion and Freedom of Conscience. "The freedom of public expression of opinions is suppressed as a result of the central administration of all media and of the publishing and cultural institutions. Neither any political, philosophical or scientific view nor any artistic expression can be published if it deviates in the slightest degree from the narrow framework of official ideology or aesthetics; public criticism of manifestations of social crises is made impossible; it is out of the question to conduct a public defence against untrue and defamatory assertions in official propaganda organs (there is in practice no legal protection against 'attacks on honour and reputation' as explicitly guaranteed in Article 17 of the first covenant); false accusations cannot be refuted, and any attempt to obtain a remedy or rectification from the courts is futile; and in the field of intellectual or cultural work no open discussion is possible. Many who are active in academic and cultural affairs, and other citizens, are being discriminated against merely because years ago they published or openly expressed views which are condemned by the existing political power.

"Freedom of conscience, expressly guaranteed in Article 18 of the first covenant, is systematically limited by arbitrary acts of those in power—by curtailing the activities of the clergy who are constantly threatened by withdrawal or loss of the state's permission enabling them to exercise their functions; by reprisals affecting, in respect of their livelihood or otherwise, persons who express their religious convictions in word or deed; and by the suppression of religious instruction, etc.

Absolute Power of Authorities. "The limitation, and often the complete suppression, of a series of civil rights is effected by a system of de facto subordination of all institutions and organizations in the state to the political directives of the ruling party's apparatus and the decisions of despotically influential individuals. The Constitution of Czechoslovakia, other laws and legal norms regulate neither the contents, the form nor the application of such decisions; they are mainly taken behind closed doors, often merely verbally; they are unknown to citizens in general and cannot be checked by them; their authors are responsible to no one except themselves and their own hierarchy; but they exert a decisive influence on the activities of legislative and executive organs in the administration of the state, the courts, trade unions, professional and all other social organizations, other political parties, enterprises, works, institutions, authorities, schools and other establishments—their orders taking precedence even before the law.

"If, in the interpretation of their rights and duties, organizations or citizens come into conflict with the directives they cannot appeal to any impartial arbitrator because there is none. All these facts seriously limit the rights resulting from Articles 21 and 22 of the first covenant (on freedom of assembly and the prohibition of any restriction of exercising this freedom), as well as from Article 25 (equality of the right to take part in the conduct of public affairs) and from Article 26 (equality before the law). This state of affairs prevents workers and other employees from establishing trade unions and other organizations and freely to apply the right to strike (Paragraph 1, Article 8 of the second covenant) in order to protect their economic and social interests without any restriction.

"Further civil rights, including the express prohibition of 'arbitrary interference with privacy, family, home or correspondence' (Article 17 of the first covenant), are also gravely violated by the fact that the Ministry of the Interior controls the lives of citizens in various ways, e.g. by telephone tapping, observation of homes, control of mail, personal surveillance, searches of homes, and the establishment of a network of informers from among the population (often recruited by means of unlawful threats or by promises), etc. In such cases the Ministry often interferes with employers' decisions, inspires discriminatory acts by authorities and organizations, exerts influence on the organs of justice and also directs propaganda campaigns through the media. These activities are not regulated by laws, they are secret and the citizen has no defence against them.

"In cases of politically motivated prosecutions the investigative and court organs violate the rights of the defendants and their defence, as guaranteed by Article 14 of the first covenant and also by Czechoslovak laws. In our prisons persons thus convicted are treated in a manner which violates their human dignity, endangers their health and aims at breaking them morally.

"Generally violations are also carried out in respect of Paragraph 2, Article 12, of the first covenant, which guarantees a citizen's right freely to leave his country; under the pretext of 'protecting national security' (Paragraph 3) this right is tied to various unlawful conditions. There is arbitrary procedure also in the granting of entry visas to nationals of foreign states, many of whom cannot visit Czechoslovakia because, for instance, they have had professional or friendly contacts with persons discriminated against in our country.

"Many citizens draw attention—either privately, at their place of work, or in public (which in practice is possible only in foreign media)—to the systematic violation of human rights and democratic freedoms and demand remedies in concrete cases; in most instances, however, their voice finds no echo or they become targets of official investigations.

The Object of Charter 77. "The responsibility for maintaining civil rights in the country lies, of course, above all with the political power and the state—but not exclusively. Every person has his share of responsibility for the general conditions and thus for the observance of the codified covenants, which is obligatory not only for governments but also for all citizens. The feeling of such co-responsibility, the belief in the meaningfulness of civil commitments and the will to carry them out, as well as the general need to find new and more effective expression for them, has given us the idea of forming Charter 77, the establishment of which is announced today.

"Charter 77 is a free, informal and open community of persons of varying convictions, religions and professions, joined together by the will to work individually and collectively for respect for civil and human rights in our country and in the world—those rights which are granted to man by the two codified international covenants, by the Final Act of the Helsinki conference [i.e. the 1975 Conference on Security and Co-operation in Europe (CSCE)], by numerous other documents opposing war, the use of force and social and intellectual oppression, and which have been expressed succinctly in the UN Universal Declaration of Human Rights.

"Charter 77 is based on the solidarity and friendship of people who are motivated by a common concern for the fate of the ideals to which they have attached, and are still attaching, their lives and their work.

"Charter 77 is no organization, and has no statutes, no permanent organs and no organized membership. Everyone belongs to it who agrees with its idea, takes part in its work and supports it.

"Charter 77 is no base for oppositional political activity. It wishes to serve the common interest, as do many similar civic initiatives in various countries of the West and the East. It therefore does not intend to draw up its own programmes for political or social reforms or changes but wants to conduct, within its sphere of activity, a constructive dialogue with the political and state authorities, in particular by drawing attention to various concrete cases in which human and civil rights are infringed, by preparing their documentation, proposing solutions, submitting various general suggestions aimed at strengthening these rights and their guarantees, and acting as a mediator in situations of conflict which may be caused by unlawful measures.

"Charter 77 emphasizes, by its symbolic name, that it is created at the beginning of the year which has been declared the year of the rights of political prisoners, and in the course of which the Belgrade conference is to review the fulfilment of the Helsinki obligations.

"As signatories of this manifesto we entrust Prof. Jirí Hajek, Dr Václav Havel and Prof. Jan Patocka with the task of acting as spokesmen for Charter 77. These spokesmen are empowered to represent Charter 77 before state and other organizations, before the public in our country and in the world, and by their signature they guarantee the authenticity of Charter 77 documents. They will find in us, and in other citizens who will join us, collaborators who, together with them, will support the necessary actions, undertake specific tasks and share all responsibility with them.

"We believe that Charter 77 will contribute to enabling all citizens of Czechoslovakia to work and live as free human beings."

Further developments. Prof. Hajek (a former Foreign Minister) said on Jan. 7, 1977, that the purpose of the manifesto was to put the international covenants on human rights into practice and claimed that the initiative was "fully within the framework of the Czechoslovak Constitution" and was not meant to be "a political action or a basis for opposition activity". Late in January 1977 it was reported that Prof. Hajek and Prof. Patocka had asked the government in an open letter to declare whether the organs of the state were bound by the Covenant on Civil and Political Rights and, if so, why "the defenders of civil rights" were "subjected to repression and discrimination, and publicly insulted and defamed".

Dr Zdenek Mlynar (a former Communist Party secretary) declared on Jan. 17, 1977 (in an open letter addressed to leaders of Communist and Socialist parties in the West), inter alia: "I am a Communist , and I am convinced that socialism must give people more political and civil rights than capitalism. I thus share the conviction which many European Communist parties represent today, behaving accordingly. For this I am publicly branded as a traitor to socialism and an agent of imperialism." Prof. Hajek stated in a television interview broadcast in Vienna on Feb. 7 that the signatories of the manifesto, who regarded themselves as Marxists, felt that respect for the civil rights covenant would mean, on the one hand, "a deepening of the Czechoslovak socialist system towards democracy, humanism and greater efficiency" and, on the other hand, "a contribution to progress of détente in Europe".

However, the public prosecutor in Prague told Prof. Hajek on Jan. 31, 1977, that his movement contravened Article 4 of the Czechoslovak Constitution, under which the Communist Party was established as the "leading force" in society and the state. Prof. Hajek said later that he did not deny this role and that the manifesto was "a lawful expression of the right of citizens to petition the government".

Charter 77 was strongly attacked by *Rudé Právo,* the Communist Party's organ, which inter alia stated on Feb. 5, 1977, that the signatories of the manifesto were "objectively playing a sorry role in the actions of rabid anti-communism" and that their objectives were "to disrupt the peaceful climate in the country, to divert attention from the problems of the capitalist countries beset by unemployment, inflation and an economic, social and moral bankruptcy, to inculcate in the people of the West the fear of socialism, and to obstruct international détente". Despite such attacks, Charter 77 expanded its activities and subsequently issued a number of documents describing alleged violations of human rights in Czechoslovakia.

A statement said to have been written by Prof. Patocka on March 8, 1977 (shortly before his death), contained inter alia the following passages: "The legal character of the Charter, the fact that its aim is to foster an unconditional and publicly accountable legality, the obvious refusal of the authorities to accept this principle of the equality of the citizen before the law, their refusal to conduct a dialogue about the issues involved, has given us a considerable political advantage and forced our adversary to seek new methods in his struggle against us. . . . We are convinced that there is no one in the world who does not know that the Helsinki accords *must* be accepted if we are to escape a future of major wars and minor conflicts. But it is only now that we have come to realize just how terribly long a road it is going to be, and we know it thanks to the Charter."

Shortly after a meeting on March 1, 1977, with the then Dutch Foreign Minister, Max Van der Stoel, during a visit by the latter to Prague, Prof. Patocka had been interrogated by police for more than 10 hours and was thereafter taken to hospital, where he died on March 13, two days after suffering a cerebral haemorrhage. In his memory Charter 77 supporters subsequently established the "Jan Patocka Alternative University" to promote teaching and learning independent of the government-controlled system. Inspired principally by Dr Julius Tomin and Prof. Radim Palous (both philosophers), the Alternative University developed close contacts with Western academics, several of whom assisted in its seminars. However, by mid-1980 the enterprise appeared to have been effectively suppressed amid constant harassment by the authorities of its members and also of visiting academics from the West.

A number of signatories of the "Charter 77" manifesto were given prison sentences in 1979-81, while others were allowed to leave the country, many of the latter being subsequently deprived of their Czechoslovak citizenship. Such developments and other forms of harassment by the Czechoslovak authorities reduced the scope of the movement's activities, although it continued in being and celebrated its fifth anniversary in January 1982. In two appeals issued in the course of 1982 to coincide with sessions of the Madrid follow-up meeting of the CSCE, the Charter 77 spokesmen (i) urged the Czechoslovak government in March to adopt a document guaranteeing freedom of religion, and (ii) called in October for the release of all political prisoners in the country.

In subsequent years Charter 77 continued to issue statements on various occasions.

On Jan. 8, 1982, it publicly criticized the declaration of martial law in Poland.

Charter 77 was not admitted to an official "World Assembly for Peace and Life, against Nuclear War", held in Prague on June 21-26, 1983. The movement issued, on June 15, a declaration stating inter alia: "Any government which lives in a permanent state of tension with its society is in a state of permanent mobilization that . . . is not conducive to hopes that it will be a reliable partner in efforts to secure a real and lasting peace in the world. . . . What is understood by the term 'human rights' and by the term 'peace' are but mutually dependent aspects . . . of a truly human life; . . . any attempt to rescue one at the expense of the other (to gain peace at the expense of freedom) will in the end fail to achieve either."

On June 23, 1983 (i.e. during the Assembly), representatives of Charter 77, the British Campaign for Nuclear Disarmament (CND), Dutch peace groups and the West German Green Party signed a joint declaration linking peace with respect for human rights. (Their meeting was broken up by plain-clothes police who seized journalists' tapes and film which they later returned erased.)

A "Prague Appeal" issued by Charter 77 on March 11, 1985, called for the unification of Europe which would be a first step towards the dissolution of military blocs and involve the reunification of Germany.

Prison sentences were imposed on several Charter 77 signatories in 1982-84. Among them, Petr Pospichal, sentenced to 11 months in prison in 1978, was given a 1½-year sentence in May 1982; Ladislav Lis was on July 21, 1983, sentenced to 14 months in prison and three years' house arrest for "incitement to rebellion" (after he had claimed that his children had been threatened); and Jirí Gruntorad, who had been sentenced to four years in prison in July 1981, was on June 4, 1984, sentenced to a further 14 months for "perjury".

Other dissidents sentenced to imprisonment in 1982-83 included four young people sentenced on Dec. 17, 1982, to from one to four years for distributing leaflets supporting the banned Solidarity movement in Poland; Dr Jaromir Savrda (a writer), sentenced to 25 months in prison on March 3, 1983, for "subversive activity" (having previously served a 2½-year sentence); Antonin Dobner (an engineer), sentenced on Oct. 5, 1983, to two years in prison for misinformation in letters sent abroad; and Jirí Wolf, sentenced in December 1983 to six years in prison for passing information on prison conditions in Czechoslovakia to the Austrian embassy in Prague.

Charter 77 activists were temporarily detained on various occasions, among them J. Dienstbier and Ladislav Lis (on Aug. 9-11, 1985). Prof. Jirí Hajek was on April 9, 1985, requested to leave Prague for 48 hours, apparently to prevent him from meeting Sir Geoffrey Howe (the British Foreign and Commonwealth Secretary), then due to visit Prague. (The latter, however, did have a meeting with five representatives of Charter 77 and the Committee for the Defence of Persons Unjustly Persecuted, VONS.)

In a statement of Aug. 20, 1985 (the 17th anniversary of the Warsaw Pact powers' intervention in Czechoslovakia), Charter 77 pointed out that the Czechoslovak regime was out of step with policies which were being advocated elsewhere in Eastern Europe, where reformist efforts were being made in neighbouring countries with similar political systems. The statement continued: "Even the leaders of countries which suppressed the revival process of 1968 openly proclaim measures aimed at making the economic and political system more flexible." In the statement it was claimed that speeches by the Soviet leadership condemning corruption and advocating economic and administrative reform were being censored in Czechoslovakia.

Early in 1986, however, Anna Sabatova was reported to have said that police measures against Charter 77 activists had been relaxed, that telephones had been restored in the homes of some Charter 77 signatories and that confiscated typewriters had been returned.

On Jan. 6, 1987 (the tenth anniversary of its creation) Charter 77 held a press conference at which a statement was issued expressing hope for political change in Czechoslovakia and calling on the people to seize the opportunity to create greater democracy. In particular the statement demanded an end to the privileges of Communist Party officials and appealed for religious freedom. Security forces temporarily detained six Charter 77 members and prevented at least eight others (among them Prof. Hajek and Václav Havel) from leaving their homes to attend the conference.

In April 1987 four former office bearers under Alexander Dubcek (including Prof. Jirí Hajek) signed a letter addressed to Mikhail Gorbachev, the General Secretary of the Central Committee of the Communist Party of the Soviet Union, who was then about to pay an official visit to Czechoslovakia. The letter was handed in at the Soviet embassy in Prague on April 4, 1987, and contained the following passages:

"We have been following with great sympathy and interest the new revolutionary developments—the reconstruction of Soviet society—inaugurated under your leadership. This development has revived in us the hope that the time for renewal has come for our society as well. . . . Mankind needs to be given back its self-reliance, faith in its strength, space to breathe freely and air to breathe—that is, to us, socialist democracy. You point out that there is no need to fear democracy. Whoever is afraid of it is afraid of the people—and there is no need to fear the people, they need to be understood. . . . The traditional friendship between our two nations . . . was compromised by the manner in which the Soviet leadership . . . reacted to the process of revival of 1968. We are ready to play an active part in the reconstruction of our society . . . and would be happy if your visit could help open the way towards such activity. We are convinced that this would result in strengthening trust." Claiming that "hundreds of thousands of people hitherto excluded from public activity" might be included in the reconstruction effort, the letter concluded: "People in Czechoslovakia want to overcome all the obstacles which hold back the creative forces of the country."

Committee for the Defence of Persons Unjustly Persecuted (VONS)

Leadership. Rudolf Battek, Dr Václav Havel, Dr Gertruda Sekaninova-Carterova

This Committee was formed in May 1978 as an offshoot of the Charter 77 movement (see separate entry) with the specific purpose of mobilizing support for Charter signatories and others whose activities had brought them into direct conflict with the Czechoslovak authorities. VONS is affiliated to the International Federation of Human Rights.

Members of VONS were co-signatories (with Prof. Ladislav Hejdanek and Marta Kubisova, then spokesmen for Charter 77) of an open letter addressed on Nov. 6, 1978, to the heads of states who had signed the 1975 Helsinki Final Act and also to Dr Kurt Waldheim (then UN Secretary-General) stating that Charter supporters were being "subjected to the most diverse provocations, accused of acts which they have not committed, arrested . . . and detained for months contrary to legal provisions in force". The letter asserted that "an atmosphere of fear" reigned in Czechoslovakia and that "most people dare not express their true opinions", and called on the addressees to put pressure on the Prague regime to "fulfil their human rights obligations under the Helsinki agreement".

Prison sentences were subsequently imposed on VONS members for subversive activities (in some cases allegedly in collaboration with foreign agents) as follows: on Dr Havel (4½ years), Petr Uhl (five years), Prof. Václav Benda, Otta Bednarova and Jirí Dienstbier (three years each), all on Oct. 23, 1979 (all sentences being confirmed on appeal on Dec. 20, 1980); on Albert Cerny (3½ years) on Nov. 28, 1979 (confirmed on appeal on March 28, 1980); on Rudolf Battek (7½ years, reduced on appeal to 5½ years, with an additional three years of official "surveillance"); and on Jan Litomisky (three years) on Oct. 26, 1981. Mrs Bednarova was released because of ill-health on Sept. 26, 1980.

On Feb. 17, 1986, the VONS called on six Western nations to hand over convicted Eastern bloc spies in exchange for six detainees held in Czechoslovakia, among them two Charter 77 signatories (Jirí Wolf and Walter Kania).

Jazz Section

Leadership. Karl Srp (ch.); Vladimir Kouril (sec.)

This group was formed in 1971 as a branch of the Czechoslovak Musicians' Union and has about 7,000 members. Its activities broadened to include extensive publishing of literature regarded with disfavour by the authorities, and the sponsorship of "decadent" cultural activities, and the government sought to close the Section down by dissolving the Musicians' Union in 1984. The Jazz Section continued to function, however, its leaders maintaining that it enjoyed a separate identity as a member of the International Jazz Federation (IJF).

The chairman and secretary received prison sentences of 16 months and 10 months, respectively (three other leaders being given suspended sentences) on March 11, 1987, following conviction for "illegal commercial activities". The group's leaders emphasized that its purposes were "humanitarian and cultural" and that it had not opposed the Czechoslovak constitution.

Preparatory Committee for Free Trade Unions

This committee, first heard of in 1981, claimed to be active in the industrial centres of Plzen, Ostrava and Kladno.

On Dec. 18, 1983, it was disclosed that the committee had sent a letter to the official Revolutionary Trade Union Movement (ROH), urging that movement to "launch a firm protest against the installation of [Soviet nuclear] missiles on Czechoslovak territory", arguing that most workers felt equally threatened by Soviet and US missiles, criticizing the cost of the weapons to both the economy and the environment and claiming that people were being asked to support measures threatening their living standards and even their survival. The committee was also said to have organized a petition calling for a referendum in each country where US or Soviet missiles were to be deployed, and to propose the setting-up of clandestine "informal cells" among the workers to unite "critical opinion . . . on questions basic to our life, and first of all war and peace". (Petitions against the deployment of Soviet missiles were reported to have been signed in Prague and at Hradec Kralove during March 1983.)

External Movements

Committee for the Defence of Liberties in Czechoslovakia

Leadership. Artur London

This Paris-based organization of exiled dissidents and their supporters campaigns specifically for the release of political prisoners in Czechoslovakia and for the ending of official persecution of Charter 77 activists. In November 1982 the Committee organized a protest petition for presentation to the Czechoslovak embassy in Paris to mark the 30th anniversary of the 1952 show trial of Rudolf Slansky and 13 other former Communist Party leaders accused of being "Trotskyist - Titoist - Zionist - bourgeois - nationalist traitors and enemies of the Czechoslovak people".

Artur London (a former Deputy Foreign Minister) had been a defendant in the 1952 trial and was one of three sentenced to life imprisonment (the other 11 being sentenced to death and executed). Following Nikita Khrushchev's denunciation of Stalin at the 20th congress of the Soviet Communist Party in February 1956, London was released from prison and rehabilitated in April of that year (most of those executed in 1952 being posthumously rehabilitated in 1963).

Czechoslovak People's Party

This party has continued to exist in exile since the advent of communist rule in Czechoslovakia and is a member of the Christian Democratic World Union.

Czechoslovak Social Democratic Party

Leadership. Vilem Bernard (ch.)

Having disputed the leadership of the workers' movement with the Communists in the inter-war period, the Czechoslovak Social Democrats participated in the communist-dominated National Bloc of Working People formed in 1945 and thereafter came under intense pressure to accept a merger with the Soviet-backed Communists as the latter gradually established full control of the state apparatus. A campaign of violence and intimidation against Social Democrats in 1946-47 led to the formal merger of the party with the Communists on April 1, 1948, but those Social Democrats who escaped into exile have always maintained that the "unification" was carried out against the wishes of most party members. In exile the Czech Social Democratic Party has consistently stood for the re-establishment of full party pluralism in Czechoslovakia, where it claims to have retained extensive underground support. During the 1968 "Prague Spring" a proposal that a Social Democratic Party should be reconstituted was rejected by the Communist Party then led by Alexander Dubcek.

The exiled Social Democratic Party is a consultative member of the Socialist International as well as a constituent party of the Socialist Union of Central and Eastern Europe (SUCEE).

The Issue of the Hungarian Minority

Among members of the Hungarian minority in Slovakia, Miklos Duray was arrested in November 1982 after issuing material alleging that Hungarians in Slovakia were suffering discrimination. His trial on charges of subversive activities opened in Bratislava on Jan. 31, 1983, but he was released on Feb. 24 of that year. Rearrested on May 10, 1984, he was eventually released under an amnesty on May 10, 1985.

Dissent within the Church

Relations between the Roman Catholic Church and the state in Czechoslovakia have been strained for many years.

A pro-government clerical organization, *Pacem in Terris,* was officially stated to comprise at least half of the country's 3,200 priests, whereas the Vatican (which forbids priests from being members of political organizations) estimated the figure at 500 in June 1983. Following a meeting with the Pope on March 11, 1982, the Primate of Czechoslovakia (Cardinal Frantisek Tomasek, Archbishop of Prague) had called on priests who were members of *Pacem in Terris* to resign from the organization.

A number of priests were, in 1982-83, given prison sentences for illegal religious activities (such as the clandestine taking of vows, illegal circulation of religious publications, private religious instruction and the celebrating of mass by priests who had lost their licence to practise). Thus Father Frantisek Lizna, who had already served four prison terms, was on Jan. 21, 1982, sentenced to seven months in prison for attempting to supply information on public trials of believers to the West; after his release in June 1983 he served as a medical orderly but was said to have attracted a large following among the young; he was also a signatory of Charter 77. Jana Micianova, a Slovak Roman Catholic, was dismissed from her teaching post in 1983 on the grounds that she had attempted to influence the inhabitants of her home town towards religion and that her religious conviction was not compatible with the behaviour of a socialist teacher (expected to propagate Marxism-Leninism).

(Members of other denominations arrested and tried included Pentecostalists and Jehovah's Witnesses.)

Vatican Radio reported on April 18, 1983, that some of about 17,000 people who had signed a petition requesting the Pope to visit Czechoslovakia had been interrogated by the police.

On Feb. 8, 1984, it was reported that seven Czechoslovak bishops had issued a pastoral letter condemning the production and deployment of nuclear weapons as a crime against humanity.

By 1985 the authorities had refused to license priests in sufficient numbers to meet the needs of the Catholic community. In March 1985 it was disclosed that the central committee of the Communist Party of Czechoslovakia had sent out a circular containing a warning against "manifestations of clericism directed against Czechoslovakia and other socialist countries".

In response to an article in the September 1985 issue of the journal *Problems of Peace and Socialism* accusing the Vatican of attempting to harness the Catholic Church in Czechoslovakia for "actions which weaken and destabilize socialism" Cardinal Tomasek stated (in a letter issued in November 1985) inter alia: "The Church here is not the centre of political opposition. All it wishes to do is carry on its pastoral and missionary work." He went on to criticize state interference in Church affairs and in the activities of believers, and with reference to official peace propaganda he commented: "Talk of peace and disarmament would only become relevant when justice and respect for human rights prevail."

Denmark

Capital: Copenhagen Pop. 5,150,000

The Kingdom of Denmark, a democratic multi-party state, has a monarch who exercises power through a Cabinet headed by a Prime Minister, while legislative power lies jointly with the monarch and the Diet (*Folketing*), a unicameral Parliament elected for a four-year term by universal adult suffrage and consisting of 179 members (including two each for the Faroe Islands and Greenland).

As a result of elections held on Jan. 10, 1984, the 175 metropolitan seats in the *Folketing* were distributed as follows: Social Democrats 56, Conservative People's Party 42, *Venstre* Liberals 22, Socialist People's Party 2, Radical Liberals 10, Centre Democrats 8, Progress Party 6, Christian People's Party 5, Left Socialists 5. Of the two Faroes representatives one was a member of the *Venstre* Liberal Group and the other co-operated with the Conservative People's Party; the two Greenland representatives co-operated with the *Venstre* Liberals and the Social Democrats respectively.

In the Faroe Islands elections to the 32-member *Loegting* or *Lagting* (Parliament) held on Nov. 8, 1984, resulted in the following distribution of seats: Social Democratic Party 8, People's Party 7, Union Party 7, Republican Party 6, Home Rule Party 2, Progress and Fishing Industry Party 2.

In Greenland elections to the *Landsting* held on March 10, 1984, resulted as follows: *Attasut* (Unity Party) 11, *Siumut* (Forward Party) 11, *Inuit Ataqatigiit* (Eskimo Movement) 3.

In 1985 unrest was caused in Denmark by protesters against the immigration of foreigners and also by Islamic militants.

In July 1985 some 500 anti-immigration protesters raided a hotel where Iranian refugees were accommodated. On Oct. 2 of that year a group known as the Green Jackets caused anti-Turkish riots, and on Oct. 19 a taxi driver was found dead in his car after threats to taxi drivers made by a person calling for the expulsion of all immigrants.

Changes to the Aliens Act made in October 1986 provided that asylum seekers without valid visas for Denmark could be refused entry unless they were travelling directly from countries where they were exposed to persecution or their lives were at risk. The changes (which were to have effect for an initial period of one year) were expected principally to affect asylum seekers from Third World countries entering Denmark from West Germany.

Anti-Israel and anti-American bomb attacks occurred in Copenhagen on July 22, responsibility being claimed both by the militant Moslem *Al Jihad al-Islami* and by an unknown "Front 219 AF".

In earlier years there had been some evidence of the existence in Denmark of both right-wing and left-wing extremist groups.

Danish National Socialist Alliance

This Nazi organization was in 1980 reported to have links with other similar extreme right-wing groups in Europe, Australia, Canada and Latin America. A commando which daubed the walls of the Copenhagen offices of El Al (the Israeli airline) with swastikas on Jan. 19, 1981, was also held responsible for attacking and seriously injuring the head of these offices. The organization has attracted only minimal support on the extreme right-wing fringe.

"Revolutionary Army" Group

The police announced in Copenhagen on Nov. 13, 1980, that 16 members of this Group had been arrested after being found in possession of drugs (worth the equivalent of £1,400,000), the sale of which was intended to finance its plans to assassinate the Danish royal family and leading politicians and to overthrow Parliament. The police had also found machine guns which had been used against drug dealers who had not paid the Group.

Djibouti

Capital: Djibouti Pop. 430,000

The Republic of Djibouti has a President (elected for a six-year term by universal adult suffrage), a Prime Minister who heads a Cabinet, and a 65-member Chamber of Deputies (also elected by universal adult suffrage). In elections held on April 24, 1987, all 65 candidates were elected to the Chamber on a list of the ruling *Rassemblement pour le progrès* (RPP) by 87 per cent of the electorate. The list contained the names of several former leaders of the (opposition) *Parti populaire djiboutien,* the formation of which had been nullified by the adoption by the Chamber on Oct. 19, 1981, of a law providing for the introduction of a one-party system, which was implemented under a further law according the RPP the status of the country's sole legal party.

In March 1986, 1,009 people were detained in two "security sweeps" that followed the murder of a prominent businessman. Approximately one-third of these were subsequently deported to their countries of origin, while most of the remainder were released. Responsibility for a bomb explosion in a café in Djibouti-Ville in March 1987 (when 11 persons were killed and over 40 injured) was claimed by a Tunisian citizen who said that he was protesting against the French military presence in Djibouti. According to a government spokesman, he had been recruited in Damascus (Syria) by a hitherto-unknown group, the "Troops of Revolutionaries and Resistance Fighters".

National Movement for the Establishment of Democracy in Djibouti (*Mouvement national djiboutien pour l'instauration de la démocratie*)

Leadership. Aden Robleh Awale (founder)

This exiled opposition movement was set up by Robleh Awale in France, where he had sought asylum after being expelled from the *Rassemblement pour le progrès* in May 1986. Robleh had served in the Djiboutien Cabinet until March 1983, after which he had become leader of an unofficial dissident RPP faction and a frequent critic of the government. On Sept. 7, 1986, he and two others were sentenced in absentia to life imprisonment after being convicted of "attempting to destabilize the government and to murder senior officials". The principal specific charge against him had been that he had acted as a "sleeping partner" in a bomb attack on the RPP headquarters in January 1986.

Dominica

Capital: Roseau Pop. 83,266

The Commonwealth of Dominica has been an independent republic within the Commonwealth since Nov. 3, 1978. It has a President elected by the House of Assembly, a government headed by a Prime Minister, and a unicameral House of Assembly with 21 members elected by universal adult suffrage, with 11 senators being elected or appointed to it in addition.

In elections to the House of Assembly held on July 1, 1985, the ruling conservative Dominica Freedom Party took 15 seats, the Labour Party of Dominica (LPD) (formed from the Dominica Labour Party, DLP, and United Dominica Labour Party) five, and a candidate not officially endorsed by the LPD one. In a by-election held in May, 1986, the DFP gained a further seat whilst the LPD still held five. The Dominica Liberation Movement Alliance did not contest the elections, but claimed the support of two of the successful Labour candidates.

The former DLP Prime Minister Patrick R. John returned to the House as an LPD candidate whilst on bail awaiting retrial along with two other men accused of having conspired to overthrow the government of Miss Eugenia Charles in 1981. The LPD election manifesto said it would seek to reinstate the Dominica Defence Force (DDF), disbanded in 1981 by the Charles government after insurrectionist activities (the DDF was composed almost exclusively of DLP supporters). In August 1986 the former commander of the DDF was hanged for the murder of a policeman in an assault on police headquarters in 1981 to secure the release of P. R. John before his trial. In October 1985 P. R. John received a 12-year prison sentence.

The government of Miss Charles has accused Libya of offering scholarships to young Dominicans and training them "in the methods and in the philosophy of overthrowing governments".

The Rastafarians

Leadership. Desmond Trotter (spiritual l.)

The Rastafarians, known as "Dreads" in Dominica, originated in Kingston (Jamaica) as a cult of Blacks advocating the return of the Blacks in the Americas to Africa, the use of natural food, the cultivation and smoking of marijuana (cannabis or "pot") and the playing of music. Adherents have made the former Emperor of Ethiopia, Haile Selassie (whose original name was Ras Tafari), the object of a cult and compare the "heaven" of Ethiopia with the "hell" of places such as Jamaica and Dominica.

As some Rastafarians in Dominica had been involved in acts of violence, the Dominican Labour Party government (of Patrick R. John) passed in 1974 a "Dread Act" under which Rastafarians could be shot on sight. D. Trotter was condemned to death in 1976 but after riots he was released in 1979 (following the removal of P. R. John from office).

Details of the conspiracy to overthrow the Charles government in 1981 which emerged in trials in the United States included evidence of a meeting held in the "Dread" stronghold in the Dominican mountains, where agreement on the execution of the plot was reached (and was said to have been finally signed by P. R. John, who was to be restored to the premiership which he had lost in 1979).

The US proceedings included the sentencing in New Orleans on July 22, 1981, of two men linked with the Ku Klux Klan, who were given three-year sentences for violating the (US) Neutrality Act and five years suspended for conspiracy. Five other men were given three-year sentences on July 1; they included Michael E. Perdue, said to be the ringleader of the intended invasion of Dominica. In a further ramification of the conspiracy (Miss) Marian McGuire, a Canadian citizen said to have connexions with the Irish Republican Army and reportedly sent to Dominica by a "grand wizard" of the Ku Klux Klan in Canada to act as a spy for M. E. Perdue, was sentenced to three years in prison in Dominica on Sept. 17, 1981.

Clashes between "Dreads" and police had led to the declaration of a state of emergency in Dominica on Feb. 13, 1981. A state of emergency was again in force from Dec. 19, 1981, to March 31, 1982, and was extended in January 1983 for a further 12 months. However, it was reported in July 1983 that the drugs-related Rastafarian problem appeared to have subsided.

Dominican Republic

Capital: Santo Domingo Pop. 6,416,000

The Dominican Republic has an executive President elected by universal adult suffrage for a four-year term and a Congress consisting of a 120-member Chamber of Deputies and a 27-member Senate, both similarly elected at the same time as the President. The latter appoints and presides over a Cabinet. In congressional elections held on May 16, 1986, the Social Christian Reformist Party (PRSC) won 56 seats in the House of Representatives; the Dominican Revolutionary Party (PRD) gained 48 and the Dominican Liberation Party (PLD) 16 seats. The leader of the PRSC, Dr Joaquín Balaguer, narrowly won the presidential elections held at the same time and was on Aug. 15 inaugurated as President for the fifth time in 26 years. The PRSC also controls 21 of the seats in the Senate.

Since 1983, there has been mounting opposition to the government's austere economic policies. The main forces behind the protest movement in 1984 were the Dominican Left Front (FID) and the Popular Struggles Committees (two umbrella groups organized by left-wing parties), who organized strikes and demonstrations in 1984 and 1985, during which there were violent clashes between demonstrators and the police. At least 55 people were killed in rioting in April 1984. There were widespread arrests of left-wing activists and trade unionists in 1984 and 1985, who were held without trial. General strikes were called in January, February and June 1985 in protest over the government's economic policy and its refusal to increase the minimum wage and carry out land reform.

Left-wing Groups

Dominican Left Front (*Frente de Izquierda Dominicana,* FID)

Leadership. Damian Jiménez

This umbrella group of 10 left-wing parties and 43 other organizations was the main force behind the strikes and demonstrations held in 1984-85 to protest against the government's austerity programme and its failure to control inflation. Many of its activists, including Jiménez, were among the groups of socialist politicians arrested in late 1984 and early 1985. It planned demonstrations in April 1985 to mark the 20th anniversary of the US intervention, giving rise to accusations by the government that it was involved in efforts to destabilize the country.

The Front has called for the breaking-off of negotiations with the International Monetary Fund, the declaration of a moratorium on foreign debt payments until a renegotiation adjusts the terms in the Republic's favour, general wage increases, the nationalization of the financial sector, import and exchange controls and other radical economic measures.

Dominican Popular Movement (*Movimiento Popular Dominicano*, MPD)

Leadership. Julio de Peña Valdés

The founders of the Maoist MPD included many former members of the Communist Party. Although it was refused legal status because of alleged involvement in political violence, the MPD was one of the parties which constituted a 1974 opposition electoral alliance. In November 1985 at least 17 members of the Movement were arrested and said to be involved in a plot to assassinate prominent conservatives.

Popular Struggles Committees (*Comités de Lucha Popular*)

This network of autonomous local groups, mostly organized by active members of left-wing parties, was created in 1984, in order to co-ordinate the protest movement against the government's economic policies. It was responsible for the organization of strikes and demonstrations held in 1984 and 1985, including a particularly successful general strike on Feb. 11, 1985.

Social Christian Action Movement (*Movimiento de Acción Social Cristiana,* ASC)

This group was reportedly active in the early 1980s.

Right-wing Group

National Salvation Movement (*Movimiento Nacional de Salvación,* MNS)

Leadership. Luis Julián Pérez

Pérez had been a close associate of Dr Balaguer, leader of the Reformist Party and current President of the Republic. However, shortly after the formation of the MNS, the general secretary of the Reformist Party, said that government officials who sympathized with the new party would be dismissed as "traitors" on suspicion of seeking to oust President Balaguer.

Ecuador

Capital: Quito Pop. 9,380,000

The Republic of Ecuador has an executive President elected for a four-year term by universal adult suffrage. There is a 71-member unicameral Congress to which 59 members are elected on a provincial basis every two years, and 12 are elected on a national basis for four years. The President is not eligible for re-election.

On Aug. 10, 1984, President León Febres Cordero of the right-wing Social Christian Party (PSC) took office after winning 52.2 per cent of the vote in a poorly supported second-round presidential ballot held on May 6 which followed an inconclusive first ballot.

In mid-term elections to the Congress held on June 1, 1986, for the 59 provincial seats, the President lost his congressional majority. The pro-government parties retained only 27 of the total 71 seats which, including the 12 members elected nationally in 1984, were distributed as follows: Democratic Left (ID) 17, PSC 15, People's Democracy (DP) eight, Socialist Party (PSE) six, Ecuadorean Roldosista Party (PRE) five, Democratic Popular Movement (MDP) four, Concentration of Popular Forces (CFP) four, Broad Left Front (FADI) three, Alfarista Radical Front (FRA) three, Radical Liberal Party (PLR) three, Conservative Party (PC) one, Democratic Party (PD) one, Popular

Roldosista Party for People, Change and Democracy (PCD-PRD) one. (The combined parties of the centre-right alliance, the National Reconstruction Front (FRN), of which the PSC is the principal component, won only 17 provincial seats.)

Following the elections, opposition parties announced that they would restore the Progressive Democratic Front first formed in 1984 by the ID, the PD, the PSE, the FADI, the DP, the MDP and the PRE.

On Jan. 16, 1987, President Febres, together with 40 aides, was held hostage for 12 hours by air force commandos who demanded an amnesty for the dismissed Chief of Staff of the Armed Forces and Commander of the Air Force, General Frank Vargas Pazzos, who in March 1986 took over an air base and demanded the ousting of President Febres and the formation of a new military-civilian government. (Gen. Vargas, who had alleged that major corruption scandals had been covered up, and who demanded the resignation of the Defence Minister and the army Commander, was arrested along with 400 military and civilian supporters.) President Febres granted the amnesty under duress and also undertook not to take action against those involved. However, on July 21, 1987, a total of 58 commandos were sentenced by a court martial to between six months' and 16 years' imprisonment.

Harsh economic measures imposed by the government and consequential unrest led to the declaration of a temporary state of emergency in March 1984, and further strike action by trade unions took place in 1987.

In May 1986 Amnesty International stated that the improvement in Ecuador's human rights record since the restoration of democratic rule in 1979 appeared to have been reversed, with evidence of torture against suspected criminals and students suspected of collaborating with the *Alfaro Vive, Carajo!* group (see below).

Eloy Alfaro Popular Armed Forces (*Fuerzas Armadas Populares Eloy* or *Alfaro Vive, Carajo!*)

This organization derives its name from Eloy Alfaro, a liberal leader who died in 1912 after leading a rebellion against a Conservative government. It originated in the 1970s, attracting former student sympathizers of the Ecuadorean Communist Party, and began armed activities in 1984.

During the campaign for the second round of the 1984 presidential elections members of the group called for votes to be cast for the candidate of the Democratic Left.

The group's leader, arrested in Costa Rica in August 1984 and taken to Ecuador on Aug. 29, revealed upon interrogation (as announced by the government on Sept. 3) that a "wide-ranging subversive plan" involving urban and rural guerrillas was being prepared. On Nov. 2, 1984, about 50 members attacked the premises of a major newspaper in Quito and forced it to publish a proclamation. On March 13, 1985, a group of 26 guerrillas stole about 400 firearms from the Quito police arsenal. On June 5, 1985, guerrillas seized a radio station in Quito and forced it to issue an anti-goverment broadcast.

On Aug. 7, 1985, a leading banker, Nahim Isaías Barquet, was kidnapped by five group members who demanded a US$5,000,000 ransom (reduced to US$1,000,000), an aircraft to fly them to an area in Colombia controlled by the M-19 group (which was also reported to be involved in the kidnapping), and the release of 50 Ecuadorean prisoners. However, one guerrilla was shot dead by security forces on Sept. 1, whilst the others were killed on the following day in a raid in which the hostage also died.

On Jan. 4, 1986, the group's second-in-command, Fausto Basantes Borja, was killed in a clash with police, and on Oct. 1, 1986, three guerrillas were reported to have died in a battle at a guerrilla safe house. On Oct. 27, 1986, it was announced that the alleged leader of the group, Ricardo Arturo Jarrín, had been killed resisting arrest. Members of the group, which in 1985 numbered an estimated 3,000, are also reported to belong to a rebel Colombian group called the America Battalion *(Batallón América)* which allegedly includes members of the M-19 and the Quintin Lame Commando of Colombia, and the Tupac Amaru Revolutionary Movement of Peru. In 1986 Ecuadorean soldiers were reported to have intercepted a group of about 100 guerrillas who were attempting to cross into southern Colombia to join the Battalion.

Free Homeland Montoneros (*Montoneros Patria Libre*, MLP)

According to a communiqué of Jan. 22, 1986, this organization called for the "consolidation of an opposition front which will halt authoritarianism". In May 1986 members of the group kidnapped Enrique Echeverría, a member of the Court of Constitutional Guarantees, and demanded that the President be indicted for "constitutional violation". The hostage was released after five days on May 25, the guerrillas having accepted the promise of a fair trial.

Egypt

Capital: Cairo Pop. 48,500,000

Under its 1971 Constitution as subsequently amended, the Arab Republic of Egypt is "a democratic and socialist state" with a limited system of party pluralism. Elections to the 448 elective seats of the People's Assembly (*Shura*) held on April 6, 1987, resulted in the following distribution of these seats: National Democratic Party (NDP) 346, Alliance of Socialist Labour Party and Liberal Socialist Party (including Moslem Brotherhood candidates) 60, New *Wafd* 35, independents 7. A further 10 NDP members were subsequently nominated by the President. No seats were gained by the National Progressive Unionist Party or the *Umma* Party. The franchise was restricted under a set of principles approved in a referendum in May 1978, providing that the right to belong to political parties and engage in political activities did not apply to those who had "participated in the corruption of political life" before the 1952 revolution or to those convicted of political offences or proved to have "carried out actions tending to corrupt political life or to subject the national unity or social peace to danger".

Under a code of ethics ("law of shame") approved by the People's Assembly on April 29, 1980, newly defined punishable offences included the inciting of opposition to the state's economic, political and social system and the dissemination of "false" or "extremist" statements deemed to have endangered national unity or social peace. Penalties proposed were imprisonment, fines, house arrest, suspension from political activity, dismissal from employment in the service of the state and restrictions on overseas travel.

Among groups opposing the Egyptian regime, the Moslem Brotherhood has been the most powerful, and its Islamic fundamentalism has been supported also by many small militant groups intent upon the violent removal of the state's leadership, one of them being held responsible for the assassination of President Sadat in October 1981. Communist and other left-wing groups have also been involved in acts of violence, particularly in protest against the government's post-1977 policy of rapprochement with Israel. In addition, the government has been faced with hostility by groups of former politicians and military men calling for the abandonment of Egypt's pro-Western policies and a return to closer relations with the Soviet Union and radical Arab states, and to more pronounced support for the Palestinian cause.

Moslem Fundamentalist Groups

Moslem Brotherhood (*Ikhwani*)

Leadership. Omar Telmessani ("supreme guide")

Founded in Ismailia in 1928 by Shaikh Hassan Al-Banna as a society of religious resurgence, the Moslem Brotherhood claimed, in the early 1950s, a membership of 2,000,000 throughout the Arab world. At that time it was said to have a terrorist wing known as the Secret Organ. In Egypt the Brotherhood was suppressed in 1948 by the then Prime Minister, Nokrashy Pasha, who was subsequently assassinated by one of its members. Shaikh Al-Banna was himself murdered in 1949, allegedly by agents of King Farouk of Egypt.

The Brotherhood was legalized by the Wafdist government in 1951. In the following year it welcomed the officer's coup which overthrew the monarchy but it later adopted an increasingly hostile attitude to the Neguib government. On Jan. 13, 1954, the government ordered the dissolution of the Brotherhood and temporarily arrested some 450 of its members, among them Dr Hassan el-Hodeiby, its supreme guide, after clashes between Brotherhood supporters and pro-government demonstrators. The Brotherhood's dissolution was, however, revoked on July 8, 1954.

Following an unsuccessful attempt to assassinate Gamal Abdel Nasser on Oct. 26, 1954, the Brotherhood was again dissolved on Oct. 29 and death sentences were passed on Dec. 4 of that year on seven of its leading members, among them Dr el-Hodeiby (whose sentence was commuted to life imprisonment), and six other members of the Brotherhood's executive were given life sentences. On Dec. 12, 1954, four more members were condemned to death for complicity in the plot to overthrow the government and in terrorist activities, and another 26 were given hard-labour sentences ranging from 10 years to life (the death sentences being later commuted to life imprisonment). Meanwhile, President Neguib had been deposed by Nasser on Nov. 14, 1954, after it had been alleged that he had been involved in a conspiracy by the Moslem Brotherhood. Between Dec. 14, 1954, and Jan. 19, 1955, another 15 members of the Brotherhood were condemned to death and over 300 to imprisonment for from five years to life—but all the death sentences were commuted to life imprisonment. At the same time thousands of its supporters were said to have been imprisoned or interned without trial.

In 1964, however, an amnesty was declared and Brotherhood adherents (as well as communists) were released. In order to counteract the influence of communists, a number of Brotherhood members were appointed to official posts, and some of these played a leading role in anti-government plots uncovered in 1965 and followed by a new wave of trials and wholesale arrests between July 1965 and January 1966. The trials, one of them on charges of plotting to assassinate President Nasser, resulted in numerous sentences of death or imprisonment but only three of the death sentences were eventually carried out.

In the wake of Egypt's defeat by Israel in 1967, the Moslem Brotherhood was revived in Egypt, and President Sadat (who succeeded President Nasser in 1970) gradually came to regard it as a natural ally against the Nasserite socialists and the communists. After the 1973 war, however, President Sadat reorientated his policies, adopted the "open door" approach to Western investors and a policy of political alignment with the United States, leading eventually to the signature of a peace treaty with Israel in 1979. These changes provoked renewed opposition by all Islamic fundamentalist organizations, among which the Moslem Brotherhood in particular published increasingly harsh criticism of the President's policies and offered a detailed political alternative based on Islamic law.

The Moslem Brotherhood was able to rally considerable support, particularly in the universities, and openly called for the creation of an Islamic government. Its influence was further strengthened by the social disruption caused by the increasing Westernization of Arab countries, the growing strength of the Arabs through oil wealth and later the Islamic revolution in Iran. The Brotherhood also infiltrated the Egyptian Army, where its strength was, however, estimated not to exceed 1 per cent of the forces. No Moslem Brotherhood candidates were allowed to take part in the People's Assembly elections of October-November 1976 or in those of June 1979.

After the assassination of President Sadat in October 1981 and the arrest of many hundreds of Islamic fundamentalists, suspected Brotherhood sympathizers were purged from the armed forces, 30 officers and 104 conscripts being transferred to civilian posts (as announced on Oct. 19, 1981). Thereafter security clamp-downs on Islamic fundamentalists tended to be concentrated on an array of smaller groupings rather than on the Brotherhood as such, and from mid-1982 there were indications that the government had adopted a policy of encouraging the Brotherhood as a moderate alternative to the more extreme fundamentalist groups.

Banned from electioneering in their own right, the Brotherhood aligned itself with the New *Wafd* for the purposes of the May 1984 elections to the People's Assembly, in which approximately eight of the 58 New *Wafd* candidates elected were reported to have close links to the Brotherhood.

Over the next two years, the Brotherhood continued to be officially tolerated, although its supporters periodically came into conflict with the authorities over a number of issues, including demands for the implementation of sharia (Islamic law), relations with the Coptic Church, and various questions of social policy. In this area, fundamentalist activists scored a significant success when the Constitutional Court in May 1985 declared invalid a series of legislative amendments which had introduced limited divorce rights for women (although these provisions were effectively reintroduced under new amendments passed by Parliament in July).

The Brotherhood was still technically banned from fielding its own candidates in the April 1987 elections. It was, however, informally aligned with the Socialist Labour/Liberal Socialist Party alliance, and of the 61 seats won by this group, at least half were expected to be taken up by Brotherhood supporters. During the run-up to the election, the Brotherhood had campaigned openly under the slogan "God is our aim; the Prophet is our leader; the Koran is our constitution". Several hundred Brotherhood supporters were reportedly arrested before the polls.

Atonement and Holy Flight from Sin (*Al Takfir Wal Hijira*)

Leadership. Shukri Ahmed Mustapha (founder)

This movement was established in 1971 after breaking away from a clandestine Islamic Liberation Party active in several Arab countries. Following an attack on the Egyptian Military Academy in Heliopolis in 1974, *Al Takfir Wal Hijira* was accused of having organized an attempted coup to overthrow the government of President Sadat. In 1975 a number of its members were arrested after burning Moslem shrines in the Nile delta. In August 1976, when it was estimated to have 500 members, the movement was said to have been dismantled by the police. However, it was thought to have participated in the food riots of January 1977—the most serious disturbances since 1953, causing at least 79 deaths—which were in part directed against luxury establishments disapproved of by strict Moslems.

On July 3, 1977, the movement claimed responsibility for the assassination of Dr Mohammed el-Dahabi (a former Minister of Islamic Affairs), and several of its members were subsequently hanged, while its founder was given a six-month prison sentence. It was also held responsible for planting bombs at Dr Dahabi's funeral on July 6 and at Mansura (in the Nile delta) on July 14-15, 1977. The Egyptian government claimed on July 20, 1977, that the movement had received money and arms from Libya for the abduction and murder of prominent persons and members of President Sadat's government, but this was officially denied in Libya.

Those arrested in connexion with the assassination of President Sadat on Oct. 6, 1981, were said to be members of a group (*Al Jihad* or "Holy War"—see separate entry) loosely associated with *Al Takfir Wal Hijira*, 230 suspected members of which were subsequently detained for planning assassinations and other acts of violence, including an uprising in Asyut on Oct. 8-11, when 50 people were reported killed and some 100 injured. Further arrests of members of the movement were announced by the government in mid-1982, it being officially stated on June 13 that the security forces had broken up over 30 fundamentalist groups over the previous few months.

Holy War (*Al Jihad*)

Leadership. Mohammed Abdel-Salam Faraq (l.)

This extremist Moslem fundamentalist group was loosely associated with the *Al Takfir Wal Hijira* movement, and its earlier leader, Ali Mustafa al-Mughrabi, died in hospital on Jan. 22, 1980. On Aug. 28, 1977, some 80 members of the group were reported to have been arrested. In November 1981, its leader and 23 other members of the group were charged with involvement in the assassination of President Sadat on

Oct. 6, and also with attempting to overthrow the government by force and with other offences.

Sheikh Omar Abdel Rahman, a blind mufti from Asyut University who was described as the group's ideologue and was said to have been named as temporary leader of a regime which would replace the government, was reported to have issued a religious decree giving permission to the fundamentalist conspirators to kill all officials taking part in the funeral of the late President Sadat on Oct. 10, 1981, and on Oct. 26 he was reported to have been arrested.

At the trial of 24 defendants said to have been involved in the assassination of the President, the four men charged with murder pleaded "not guilty" but their leader, Lt. Khalid Hassan Sharfiq Islambouli, told the court on Nov. 30, 1981, that he had killed the President and was proud of it. One of the defence counsels said on the same day that the case did not concern "premeditated murder" but "an ideological process" in which no accusation should be made against the defendants; he pointed out that one of the defendants (presumed to be Sheikh Omar Abdel Rahman) had called for a "holy war" against "a deprived and apostate society".

The trial concluded on March 6, 1982, with the conviction of 22 of the 24 defendants—Mohammed Abdel-Salam Faraq, Lt. Islambouli and his three associates being sentenced to death (and executed the following month) and the other 17 to prison terms ranging from five years to life. Sheikh Omar Abdel Rahman and another theologian from Asyut University, Ismail Salamuni, were acquitted but were quickly rearrested and charged with membership of *Al Jihad*.

In December 1982, the trial opened of 300 people, most of whom were reportedly *Al Jihad* supporters, who were accused of attempting to overthrow the regime in the wake of Sadat's assassination. The charges related in particular to disorders in the town of Asyut. At the end of proceedings, in February 1984, 174 of the accused were acquitted; 107 were convicted, of whom 16 were sentenced to imprisonment with hard labour for life, 89 to imprisonment with hard labour for periods of between three and 15 years, and two to simple prison terms of two years. A further 19 remained at large. Given the serious nature of the charges, the sentences, which were not passed until September, were widely regarded as lenient, leading observers to speculate that the government was anxious to avoid inflaming fundamentalist anger. A Supreme Court report, published in the semi-official *Al-Ahram* newspaper, said that it had been "established beyond doubt" that some of the accused had been tortured while in detention. According to the report, these included Prof. Rahman, who had been acquitted at the end of the trial, and about whom the report stated that "it has been proven to the court that his will was not free and that his statements were affected by torture".

In October 1984, the Supreme Court ordered the indefinite postponement, on the request of the prosecution, of the trial of a further 176 people, including 64 alleged *Al Jihad* members, who had been facing charges relating to events surrounding Sadat's assassination. All of the accused were released.

Prof. Rahman was rearrested in July 1985 on charges of plotting to overthrow the regime and attempting to reconstitute *Al Jihad*. Although subsequently found innocent by a military court, he remained in detention under emergency provisions until the Supreme Court ordered his release, together with that of 55 other detained fundamentalists, in May 1986.

Al Jihad supporters were linked to the riots involving central security force conscripts which broke out in February 1986, and they were believed to be associated to a greater or lesser extent with a number of other disturbances involving fundamentalists, including confrontations with Coptic Christians. In June 1986, *Al Jihad* claimed responsibility for a bomb explosion in a southern suburb of Cairo. Charges of membership of *Al Jihad* were preferred against 33 people, including four army officers, in December 1986. The charges also referred to the possession of weapons and subversive documents.

Islamic Groupings (*Al Gamaa al-Islamiya*)

This group, closely associated with the Moslem Brotherhood and said to have received funds from Saudi Arabia, was particularly strong at the universities of Cairo and of Asyut. It was held responsible for attacks on Christians early in 1978 and for involvement in a protest by some 5,000 demonstrators at Asyut on March 30, 1980, against the arrival in Egypt of the former Shah of Iran. The aim of the group is to replace the existing secular regime in Egypt by one based on strict Islamic doctrine as well as morality and respectability in public and private life. The group continued to be active during the early and mid-1980s.

On May 7, 1987, the group was reported to have claimed responsibility for attempting to murder Hassan Abu Basha, a former Minister of the Interior.

Islamic Guidance Society

Leadership. Sheikh Hafez Salama (l.)

This group emerged to prominence when it began to agitate openly for the implementation of sharia (Islamic holy law) in early 1985. Sheikh Salama warned in an address in a Cairo mosque in late May that he would lead a "Green March" of Moslems on the presidential palace if the government failed to implement sharia by June 14 (corresponding to the 26th day of Ramadan, which in Islamic tradition was the anniversary of the day when God began to reveal the Koran to the Prophet Mohammed). The march was postponed by Sheikh Salama after it had been banned by the Interior Ministry. Sheikh Salama and 12 of his associates were arrested in July and charged with inciting the people against the government. The Sheikh was released the following month after a Cairo tribunal ruled that his detention was illegal.

Islamic Liberal Party (ILP)

According to the Egyptian state prosecutor, the Islamic Liberal Party was founded in Jordan in 1948, and first established in Egypt in 1955. After the arrest of 25 alleged ILP members in July 1983, the semi-official daily *Al-Ahram* claimed that the party was "aimed at overthrowing the system of government by force, changing the basic structure of the state, and setting up an Islamic regime". A further 35 ILP supporters were detained later the same month. Egyptian security forces had claimed to have uncovered a branch of the ILP in September 1980, on which occasion the government had also alleged that the ILP had been responsible for an attack on the Heliopolis military academy carried out in 1974.

Society of Repudiation and Renunciation

The semi-official daily *Al-Ahram* reported in November 1983 that 35 members of this Society were currently being interrogated by security officers after being accused of planning to overthrow the government. According to the report, the Society, whose members believed in seclusion and purification of the soul, denounced all forms of government as heretical.

Left-wing Movements

Arab Socialist Nasserite Party

Leadership. Farid Abdel Karim (l.)

This Party was established by Farid Abdel Karim, a former member of President Nasser's Arab Socialist Union, in late 1985. Karim stated that he intended to apply for legal recognition.

Egyptian Communist Party (ECP)

Leadership. Farid Muhajid (gen. sec.)

This illegal party has maintained close relations with other pro-Soviet Communist parties and has posed a security threat to Egyptian governments in periods when the latter have pursued a Western-aligned foreign policy. On Oct. 31, 1957, 13 of its members were sentenced to prison terms of from one to seven years for conspiring to overthrow the government by force, and all property belonging to organizations of the ECP was ordered to be confiscated. Following President Nasser's adoption of a pro-Soviet stance, it was announced on April 25, 1965, that the proscribed ECP had dissolved itself and had merged with the Arab Socialist Union (then the country's sole legal political organization).

After President Sadat had broken with the Soviet Union in the earlier 1970s, an underground ECP became active again, and on Jan. 26, 1977, the Prosecutor-General claimed that it had been "smashed"; in July of that year prison sentences were imposed on a number of persons accused of having taken part in the creation of the ECP with the object of overthrowing the regime. However, between Aug. 16 and the end of September 1979 some 60 alleged activists of the ECP were temporarily detained.

Gen. Mohammed Nabawi Ismail (then Deputy Prime Minister and Minister of the Interior and Services) stated on Sept. 29, 1980, that "leaders and cadres" of a subversive communist organization "working with the Soviet Union" had been arrested during the past two days, but it was not clear whether he referred to the ECP. On March 1, 1981, President Sadat stated that no known communist would be permitted to hold a post in the country's press and information organizations.

At its 1980 congress (the first to be held on Egyptian territory) the ECP adopted a programme focusing on "the liberation of the whole Arab homeland from imperialism and Zionism". The ECP was estimated to have some 500 members (in 1985).

Six suspected ECP leaders were arrested in November 1984. Prior to the April 1987 People's Assembly elections, 10 members of the (legal) National Progressive Unionist Party (NPUP) were detained on the grounds that they formed part of a "communist ring" which was using the NPUP as a "legal façade" for the distribution of propaganda urging people to support the ECP. All but one of the accused were later released.

Egyptian Communist Workers' Party (ECWP)

This party was founded as an offshoot of the Egyptian Communist Party (ECP). It was said to have links with the ruling National Liberation Front (later the Yemen Socialist Party) of South Yemen and with the Palestinian "Rejectionist Front" led by Dr Georges Habash's Popular Front for the Liberation of Palestine. On Jan. 26, 1977, the Egyptian Prosecutor-General claimed that the ECWP had been "smashed", and in July of that year a number of ECWP members were sent to prison for taking part in the creation of the ECWP with the aim of overthrowing the Egyptian regime; the court also declared that its verdict dissolved the secret ECWP and provided for the "confiscation of all seized books, leaflets and publications".

Nevertheless, arrests and trials were periodically reported in the late 1970s and early 1980s of alleged activists of the ECWP, often in conjunction with members of the (legal) National Progressive Unionist Party.

Socialist Arab Nasserist Party

On Oct. 9, 1981, it was reported from Baghdad that this Party had issued a call on all factions of the Egyptian nationalist movement to draw up a joint working plan to continue the struggle which had led to the assassination of President Sadat.

Other Secular Organizations

Egyptian Liberation Organization

This previously-unknown body claimed responsibility in letters to Kuwaiti newspapers for the November 1985 hijacking of an Egyptian airliner to Malta (see entry under "Egypt's Revolution").

Egypt's Revolution

This group was first reported in June 1984 and claimed responsibility for the assassination of an administrative attaché at the Israeli embassy in Cairo in August 1985. It also claimed the hijacking to Malta of an Egyptian airliner on a flight from Athens to Cairo in November 1985. The hijack ended bloodily, with over 60 people dying in a bungled rescue attempt by Egyptian commandos. The sole survivor of the five hijackers was a Lebanese-born Palestinian, and some observers suggested that the name "Egypt's Revolution" had been employed as a cover by the militant Palestinian Abu Nidal Group. The incident was condemned by the Palestine Liberation Organization.

Egypt's Revolution said that its supporters were responsible for a shooting incident outside the Israeli pavilion at the Cairo trade fair in March 1986, in which one Israeli was killed, and for an attempt on the life of a US diplomat in Cairo on May 26, 1987 (the first such since the re-establishment of diplomatic relations with the USA in 1974).

The People's Movement

The trial of 16 alleged members of this organization, which, the government claimed, advocated violent revolution, opened in February 1984. Defence lawyers claimed that the government had staged the arrests of the accused in October 1983 by way of providing justification for the recent renewal of the state of emergency, and they argued that confessions signed by the 16 were inadmissible as they had been obtained by torture.

Religious Bodies

Bahai Community

A number of members of the Bahai community were reportedly arrested in early 1985 on accusations of belonging to a heretical organization, their faith having been proscribed in Egypt since 1960, and 48 were subsequently sentenced to prison terms for "heresy" and "immorality". (For details of the Bahai faith, see entry under Iran.)

The Coptic Orthodox Church

Leadership. Pope Shenouda III

This Church, with 6,000,000 members in Egypt and 16,000 elsewhere, is the largest Christian Church in Egypt. Hostility between Moslems and Copts has led to numerous clashes resulting in casualties. On Sept. 28, 1978, a Coptic priest was reported to have been killed at Samalout (about 200 km south of Cairo) by extremist Moslems, and during Christian-Moslem clashes in March 1979 two churches in Asyut and one in Cairo were destroyed by fire.

On May 14, 1980, President Sadat accused Pope Shenouda III and other Coptic clergy of seeking to partition Egypt and to set up a Christian state with Asyut as its capital, but this charge was strongly denied by the Coptic leaders. Following further sectarian clashes between Moslems and Christians in June 1981 (when at least 10 persons died) and a bomb attack on a Coptic church in Cairo on Aug. 3 (when three people were killed and over 50 injured), security measures led to the arrest of 1,536 people by Sept. 7, 1981. Pope Shenouda himself was placed under restriction in a desert monastery and his temporal powers were transferred to a five-member committee appointed by the government (although he remained spiritual leader of the Copts).

The Pope was allowed to resume his duties in January 1985, when he officiated at a mass which was attended by President Mubarak and other senior (Moslem) government officials. In his sermon on this occasion, Pope Shenouda called for reconciliation between the Moslem and Coptic communities. His release from confinement was criticized by Sheikh Omar Abdel Rahman, a Moslem fundamentalist leader (see entry under *Al Jihad*), who claimed that the government was demonstrating bias against fundamentalists, and demanded that Moslem clerics should be allowed to preach freely.

Confrontations between Copts and radical Moslems continued during 1985-86, including a number of violent incidents in which churches and mosques were attacked.

El Salvador

Capital: San Salvador Pop. 4,820,000

The Republic of El Salvador is governed by an elected executive President and a unicameral legislature. The two-round presidential election of 1984 was won by José Napoleón Duarte of the Christian Democratic Party (PDC), who succeeded Alvaro Magaña, chosen by the Assembly as an interim President in April 1983. The PDC unexpectedly gained a majority of seats in the Assembly in the March 1985 legislative elections, with 33 seats as against 13 for the National Republican Alliance (Arena), 12 for the National Conciliation Party (PCN) and one each for Democratic Action (AD) and the Salvadorean Authentic Institutional Party (PAISA). The sole left-wing party to participate, the Renewal Action Party (PAR), had no success. In the Constituent Assembly elected in March 1982 the right-wing parties had held a majority of 33 seats.

El Salvador, a densely populated country with the highest population growth rate (of 3.5 per cent per annum) in Central America, was for a long time under military rule following the suppression of a peasant rebellion in 1932 (at a cost of 30,000 lives including that of Farabundo Martí, the rebel peasants' leader). After elections held in 1972 and 1977 the opposition (and in particular the PDC) accused the PCN of massive electoral fraud, and many opposition candidates sought asylum abroad. Following the overthrow of President Carlos Humberto Romero in October 1979, El Salvador's various left-wing groups became increasingly critical of the alleged right-wing tendencies of the new ruling junta and from 1980 mounted a concerted military and diplomatic campaign to overthrow the government.

Anti-regime guerrilla forces, operating mainly in the northern border region, are grouped within the Farabundo Martí Front for National Liberation (FMLN), the political arm of which, the Revolutionary Democratic Front (FDR), acts as the main umbrella organization of a complex array of left-wing opposition parties and other bodies. The FMLN-FDR boycotted the March 1982 elections and has repeatedly called on the San Salvador government to enter into a dialogue with a view to a restoration of "genuine democracy"; at the same time they have rejected the government's demand that the guerrilla war should be halted as a prelude for negotiations. In October 1984 President Duarte proposed talks (without preconditions) with FMLN-FDR representatives at La Palma, and a second round of talks was held at Ayagulo a month later, but no substantial progress was made. Attempts by both sides and church leaders to renew the talks in 1985 and 1986 all foundered because of the government's insistence on a prior ceasefire on the one hand and on the FMLN-FDR's refusal to recognize the Duarte regime as a legitimate government on the other. According to reports the war in El Salvador in 1986 (to Dec. 23) claimed 1,725 victims, including 59 people killed by mines, 1,031 killed in insurgency actions, 42 killed by death squads and 425 Army dead.

Main Left-wing Alliances

Farabundo Martí Front for National Liberation (*Frente Farabundo Martí para la Liberación Nacional*, FMLN)

Leadership. Roberto Roca, Jorge Schafik Handal, Fermán Cienfuegos, Joaquín Villalobos, Leonel González

The FMLN (named after a peasant leader killed in a 1932 rising) is headed by a unifying revolutionary directorate (DRU) formed in May 1980 with the object of launching a "final offensive" against the government on the (Marxist-Leninist) theoretical basis of a strategy of "prolonged popular war" or "war of attrition". The stated aim of the FMLN was to create a "proletarian unity party" which would form the basis of a "people's state" after a guerrilla victory. The FMLN's main components are (i) the Communist Party; (ii) the Farabundo Martí Popular Liberation Forces (FPL), themselves the armed wing of the Popular Revolutionary Bloc (BPR); (iii) the Armed Forces of National Resistance (FARN), the armed wing of the Unified Popular Action Front (FAPU); and (iv) the People's Revolutionary Army (ERP), the armed wing of the February 28 Popular Leagues (LP-28).

The FARN leader, Fermán Cienfuegos, stated in December 1980 that the guerrilla offensive should lead to "an irreversible political and military situation in El Salvador" before the assumption of office by President Ronald Reagan in the United States on Jan. 20, 1981; he added that the FMLN and its political wing, the Revolutionary Democratic Front (FDR—see separate entry), would both form part of the future "democratic revolutionary government".

The planned "general offensive for a final onslaught" was started on Jan. 10-11, 1981, with heavy fighting breaking out in many parts of the country. The FMLN took over a radio station and issued a call to arms, whereupon the government declared martial law and imposed a curfew on Jan. 12; it also linked up all radio stations in order to block guerrilla broadcasts, which were nevertheless continued from two transmitters under the name "Radio Venceremos". On Jan. 12 the guerrillas claimed to have taken four cities but the Army stated that the offensive had already been crushed, and by Jan. 19 the armed forces and the government claimed to have the country under complete military control, with the Minister of Defence (Col. José Guillermo García) stating that 980 guerrillas and 142 soldiers had been killed (whereas the Red Cross stated that most of those killed had been civilians). Fighting continued, however, between guerrillas and the Army, especially north of San Salvador.

At the end of May 1981 the FMLN claimed to be in control of four provinces and was launching attacks against police and army positions in the capital. By the end of the year it was thought to have about 5,000 active guerrillas (and claimed to have 30,000 reservists) and had begun to consolidate its positions in the north and north-east of the country.

In a memorandum made public by the US government on Feb. 19-20, 1981, it was asserted that on the basis of documents captured from guerrillas it was clear that the insurgency in El Salvador had been "progressively transformed into a textbook case of indirect armed aggression by communist power through Cuba". An FDR spokesman had earlier asserted in London that neither the Soviet Union nor Cuba were major suppliers of arms to Salvadorean guerrillas, whose more important suppliers were Algeria, Libya, the Palestine Liberation Organization, Iraq and the US black market; FDR leaders in Mexico pointed out on Feb. 23 that three of the five member-groups of the FMLN were "strongly anti-Soviet". (The Reagan Administration announced on March 2, 1981, that an extra US$25,000,000 in military aid had been allocated to the government of El Salvador for the year up to Sept. 30, 1981—bringing the total for that year to US$35,400,000—and that the number of US military advisers would be increased from 34 to 54.) The Cuban government strongly denied on Sept. 3 that it was sending advisers or Soviet weapons to the guerrillas in El Salvador, as had been alleged by the US authorities.

The FMLN announced in December 1981 that fighting would continue before, during and after the Constituent Assembly elections of March 1982, but that its leadership was prepared to enter into a dialogue with the government at any time. In an open letter to President Reagan of the United States (published on Jan. 29, 1982) the leaders of the FMLN's component groups accused the United States of prolonging the civil war in El Salvador and of "sustaining at the peak of power the most repressive elements of the Salvadorean Army", but proposed negotiations without preconditions at any time.

Particularly heavy fighting took place in the Morazán department between December 1981 and February 1982. On Jan. 27 FMLN guerrillas attacked the Ilopango airbase near San Salvador and claimed to have destroyed 28 military aircraft (for the replacement of which the USA allocated US$55,000,000 in emergency military aid, as announced on Feb. 1).

After the US government had repeated its earlier assertion that Nicaragua was supplying the FMLN guerrillas with weapons, President López Portillo of Mexico, on Feb. 21, 1982, proposed a three-point plan to end the war in El Salvador and to settle US differences with Cuba and Nicaragua. The FMLN-FDR accepted the Mexican President's offer of mediation on March 3. In the United States the House of Representatives had on Feb. 3 (by 396 votes to three) urged President Reagan to press for "unconditional discussions among the major political factions in El Salvador in order to guarantee a safe and stable environment for free and open democratic elections".

In February-April 1982 FMLN attacks were reported from numerous towns in northern and central parts of the country. In June fierce fighting took place in Morazán, where the FMLN was temporarily in control of the town of Perquín (a town which has been repeatedly captured, lost and recaptured by the guerrillas).

After an apparent lull in FMLN operations in the latter part of 1982, the government's rejection of a new offer of a dialogue issued by the FDR-FMLN on Oct. 5, 1982, was followed by a renewed guerrilla offensive in northern El Salvador in early 1983, named the "January Revolutionary Heroes" campaign. Several towns were seized, including Berlín in Usultán with a population of 35,000, which the FMLN held for three days before being driven out by aerial bombardment.

The next major offensives were launched in September 1983, May 1984 (after the presidential elections) and October 1985, and were all followed by large-scale army sweep operations, establishing the pattern of repeated advance and retreat by both sides. Because of the heavy losses sustained in its military actions, from early 1985 the FMLN concentrated more on its sabotage against economic and infrastructure targets. This change of policy caused division between the ERP, which favoured the change, and the FPL, which did not, although the FMLN announced plans in August 1985 to unite its fighting groups into a single force. These plans were not put into action, and likewise a declaration made in September 1985 that a single Marxist-Leninist party would be formed within the FMLN (thereby alienating more moderate members of the FDR) did not take effect.

In the areas which the FMLN controlled (and termed "liberated zones") it had since mid-1981 set up structures of local popular power (*Poder Popular Local,* PPL), with each PPL having, for about 1,000 persons, an elected junta responsible for administration, social services, education, production and defence. The fighting forces of the FMLN in these areas consisted of frontline fighters with special training and improved weapons, guerrillas operating almost exclusively in the controlled areas and along main roads, and militia for defence measures. By 1984 the guerrillas claimed to control about one fifth of the country, which contained some 250,000 inhabitants.

However, during 1986 the Army increasingly extended its operations towards eastern Chalatenango and to the north of the Torola River in Morazán, the areas considered the strategic rearguard of the FMLN. These operations included the removal of the civilian population from areas under guerrilla control and an attempt to prevent food and other supplies from reaching the guerrillas. While FMLN numbers had been reduced to some 6,000 by 1986 (from 11,000 in the early 1980s), the number of government troops had increased fourfold to some 56,000 and these were better trained and equipped than previously. US aid to the military peaked at nearly US$200,000,000 in 1984, and stood at about US$130,000,000 in 1985 and 1986.

A renewed intensification of FMLN activity was reported in the early months of 1987, this typically involving small units. The campaign included the kidnapping of small town mayors, the laying of "people's mines" designed to maim, interruption of traffic, and sabotage of electricity lines and utilities. Such activities were also reported in the western provinces which had hitherto been little affected, and in the capital San Salvador, which had apparently been re-infiltrated by FMLN-FDR guerrillas in the confusion following an earthquake in October 1986.

Revolutionary Democratic Front (*Frente Democrático Revolucionario,* FDR)

Leadership. Guillermo Manuel Ungo (ch.)

This Front was set up as the political arm of the Farabundo Martí Front for National Liberation (FMLN—see separate entry), and had Enrique Alvarez Córdova as its first secretary-general. It comprised (i) a Democratic Salvadorean Front (*Frente Salvadoreño Democrático,* FSD) set up earlier in April 1980 and including the National Revolutionary Movement (MNR), the Christian Social Popular Movement (MPSC) then led by E. Alvarez Córdova, and several trade union, student and professional organizations, and also (ii) the Popular Revolutionary Bloc (BPR), the Unified Popular Action Front (FAPU), the February 28 Popular Leagues (LP-28), the People's Liberation Movement (MPL) and the (communist) National Democratic Union (UDN).

A general strike organized by the FDR for Aug. 13-15, 1980, was intended to be "the commencement of a co-ordinated left-wing effort to ignite a popular insurrection" but it was not widely followed and in clashes with troops at least 40 people were reported to have been killed; the FDR, however, claimed that its "neighbourhood defence organizations" had proved that they could not be neutralized by the military.

On Nov. 28, 1980, six FDR members—including E. Alvarez Córdova and Juan Chacón, leader of the MPL—were found murdered after they had been kidnapped on the previous day; responsibility was claimed by the Maximiliano Hernández Martínez Anti-Communist Alliance (see separate entry). On Jan. 5, 1981, Guillermo Manuel Ungo (the MNR leader, who had briefly been a member of the ruling junta following the overthrow of President Romero in October 1979) was elected as the new leader of the FDR. In support of a military offensive launched on Jan. 10, 1981, by the FMLN the FDR called a general strike for Jan. 13, but it had only limited effect.

On Jan. 14, 1981, the FDR formally announced in Mexico City that it had formed a seven-member diplomatic-political commission which would seek to establish a "democratic revolutionary government". The commission consisted of leading members of the MNR, the MPL, the People's Revolutionary Army (ERP), the FAPU, the Farabundo Martí Popular Liberation Forces (FPL), the UDN and the MPSC. On the same day the FDR called for direct negotiations (leading to a political settlement) between the guerrillas and the United States (which the FDR accused of having "contributed to the radicalization and polarization" of the situation in El Salvador). Although the FDR renewed this call on Feb. 23, it was rejected by the US Administration on Feb. 26, with the advice to turn to the government of El Salvador. International attempts to mediate between the warring parties, made during 1981 in particular by members of the Socialist International, were all rejected by the government of El Salvador, and the idea of negotiating a settlement with the guerrillas was also rejected on July 16 by Thomas O. Enders, US Assistant Secretary of State for Inter-American Affairs.

On the other hand, the Foreign Ministers of France and Mexico, in a joint statement issued in Mexico City on Aug. 28, 1981, recognized the FMLN-FDR alliance as "a representative political force" which was "ready to assume its obligations and exercise the rights deriving from it" and therefore to help establish the framework for a political settlement of the crisis. The declaration was, however, condemned on Sept. 2, 1981, by the Foreign Ministers of nine Latin American countries—Argentina, Bolivia, Chile, Colombia, the Dominican Republic, Guatemala, Honduras, Paraguay and Venezuela; within the region only Cuba, Panama and Nicaragua expressed support for the Franco-Mexican declaration, with Panama offering on Sept. 30 to help solve the conflict.

In October 1981 the FDR proposed that a dialogue should immediately begin and lead to negotiations between all the forces in the conflict with international mediation, and that no prior conditions should be laid down by any of the parties. Having boycotted the March 1982 elections, FDR leaders in exile repeatedly called for a dialogue with the new government in San Salvador, while making it clear that the guerrilla war would continue until a satisfactory agreement for a return to full democracy had been achieved.

In 1983 FDR leaders agreed to meet Richard Stone, the US Special Envoy to Central America, but rejected US offers of mediation on the grounds that the United States was an involved party in the conflict. In January 1984 the FMLN-FDR called for the establishment of a broad-based provisional government, and the FDR refused either to participate in, or to recognize the validity of, the presidential elections. The FMLN-FDR did, however, agree to meet President Duarte in October at the town of La Palma, after the President dropped his previous condition of a prior ceasefire. After a second round of talks at Ayagulo in November the initiative collapsed, and an attempt to renew talks at Sesori in September 1986 failed when the government refused the guerrillas' demands for a demilitarized area around Sesori.

In late 1983 the FDR had announced its decision to close its office in Managua (Nicaragua) and to move to Mexico because of what it considered to be the "constantly growing danger" of a US invasion of Nicaragua.

Guerrilla Movements

Armed Forces of National Resistance (*Fuerzas Armadas de Resistencia Nacional,* FARN)

Leadership. Fermán Cienfuegos (l.)

The FARN group was formed in 1975 as an offshoot of the People's Revolutionary Army (ERP) and became the armed wing of the Unified Popular Action Front (see separate entry). From 1978 onwards the FARN group was responsible for the kidnapping of a number of foreign businessmen in support of demands for ransom as well as for the release of alleged detainees and the publication of FARN statements.

Those kidnapped included a Japanese businessman (abducted on May 17, 1978, and found murdered on Oct. 13); the Swedish manager in El Salvador of the Ericsson telephone company (kidnapped on Aug. 24, 1978, and subsequently released after his company had paid for the publication of a FARN manifesto in Swedish and Japanese newspapers and had also paid a ransom); the local manager of the (Dutch) Philips electronics firm (abducted on Nov. 24, 1978, and released on Dec. 30, after payment by Philips for publication of a FARN manifesto in newspapers throughout the world, as well as of a ransom); two British executives of the Bank of London and South America (abducted on Nov. 30, 1978, and released on July 2, 1979, on payment of an undisclosed ransom); and the (Salvadorean) honorary consul for Israel (kidnapped on Jan. 17, 1979, and found murdered on March 22, although the government had released 22 political prisoners on the previous day). These kidnappings caused a general exodus of foreigners from El Salvador.

In July 1980 some 300 FARN members temporarily occupied San Miguel (El Salvador's third largest town) until they were driven out by troops. The FARN leader Ernesto Jovel was killed in September 1980. By mid-1980 FARN's guerrilla forces were estimated at 800 men and were operating as part of the

Farabundo Martí Front for National Liberation (see separate entry).

Clara Elizabeth Ramírez Front (*Frente Clara Elizabeth Ramírez*)

This Marxist guerrilla group was formed in November 1983 as an offshoot of the Popular Liberation Forces (FPL) specifically to wage an urban guerrilla campaign. Its activities in 1984 included the assassination of two right wing deputies of the Legislative Assembly, and it claimed responsibility for the killing on March 7, 1985, of the director of the Armed Forces Press Committee.

Farabundo Martí Popular Liberation Forces (*Fuerzas Populares de Liberación Farabundo Martí,* FPL)

Leadership. Leonel González (commander-in-chief); Dimas Rodríguez (alternate commander)

This group—the armed wing of the Popular Revolutionary Bloc (see separate entry)—was formed in 1970 by a radical faction of the (pro-Soviet) Salvadorean Communist Party (PCS) led by Salvador Cayetano Carpio. Its first major action was taken in 1977, when its guerrillas kidnapped the then Foreign Minister (Mauricio Borgonovo Pohl) on April 19 and demanded, in return for his release, that 37 named political prisoners should be set free. The then President (Arturo Armando Molina) declared on April 20 that the government would not negotiate with the guerrillas and that anyway only three of the 37 named were in fact in detention; and on May 11 the Minister was found shot dead. The FPL stated that its operation was "part of the prolonged war which the FPL is continuing until it achieves an ultimate popular revolution towards socialism".

In 1978 the FPL called for a boycott of general and municipal elections (which were held on March 12 with an estimated participation of between 40 and 50 per cent of the registered voters); during the election campaign the FPL committed several bomb attacks.

The FPL also claimed responsibility for the murder of the Minister of Education (Dr Carlos Herrera Rebollo) on May 23, 1979. The FPL was further held responsible for the murder of President Romero's brother on Sept. 6, 1979, whereafter clashes between teenagers and security forces led to the death of 14 people on Sept. 8-9; a demonstration of some 1,000 people was fired on by snipers on Sept. 14, when six people were killed and 21 wounded; and 10 other persons were killed in clashes between FPL members and police as well as National Guards.

The FPL was also responsible for the kidnapping of the South African ambassador (Archibald Gardner Dunn) on Nov. 28, 1979, this action being coupled with demands for the severance of diplomatic relations with Chile, the freeing of political prisoners, the trial of ex-Presidents Romero and Molina. (The government had broken off its relations with South Africa before the seizure of the latter's ambassador.) On Oct. 9, 1980, however, the FPL announced that the ambassador had been killed because its demands had not been met.

On Jan. 8, 1980, the FPL was joined by Salvador Samayoa, who had six days earlier resigned as Minister of Education. From May 1980 FPL forces conducted operations as part of the Farabundo Martí Front for National Liberation (see separate entry).

Divisions within the FPL came to a head in April 1983 with the murder of its second-in-command, Ana Melida Montes, by another member, Rogelio Bazzaglio Recino, who opposed the integration of the FPL into the FMLN. Salvador Cayetano Carpio (also known as Comandante Marcial), who was later reported to have instigated this murder, committed suicide on April 12.

Pedro Pablo Castillo Front (*Frente Pedro Pablo Castillo*)

This guerrilla group, named after a hero of the independence movement, was formed in July 1985, and claimed to represent left-wing political prisoners, although it was disowned by the FMLN-FDR. It claimed responsibility for the kidnapping of President Duarte's daughter in September 1985, and released her in October in return for the freeing of several left-wing prisoners.

People's Revolutionary Armed Forces (*Fuerzas Revolucionarias Armadas del Pueblo,* FRAP)

The relatively small FRAP group was formed in 1975 as an offshoot of the People's Revolutionary Army (see separate entry); it later became the armed wing of a Workers' Revolutionary Organization (*Organización Revolucionaria de Trabajadores,* ORT) which has been active since 1979.

People's Revolutionary Army (*Ejército Revolucionario del Pueblo,* ERP)

Leadership. Joaquín Villalobos (l.); Ana Guadalupe Martínez

Established in 1972, this extreme left-wing guerrilla group—the armed wing of the February 28 Popular Leagues (LP-28—see separate entry)—was responsible for kidnappings, including that of an industrialist on Jan. 27, 1977, for whose release the ERP collected a ransom of US$1,000,000 but of whom it disclosed on Jan. 29 that he had died of gunshot wounds. Bombs planted by the ERP early in February 1979 (in retaliation for the killing of a priest and four youths by security forces on Jan. 20) resulted in the death of 14 National Guards and two civilians and injury to 20 other persons.

The ERP also frequently used bombs, especially against army units, and after the overthrow of President Romero on Oct. 15, 1979, it incited (together with the LP-28) three townships near San Salvador to rise against the new government; however, this attempt was foiled by the Army.

The ERP was also responsible for the kidnapping on Oct. 31, 1979, of Jaime Hill (a member of one of El Salvador's most powerful "14 families"), who was released on March 15, 1980 after his family had paid for the publication of anti-government statements in foreign newspapers. The ERP claimed responsibility for an attack on the US embassy on Sept. 16, 1980, and in the week ended on Oct. 15 a large-scale military offensive was reported to have been mounted against ERP strongholds in eastern parts of El Salvador.

Although in May 1980 it became a member of the Farabundo Martí Front for National Liberation (see separate entry), the ERP has retained its own strategy aimed at mass insurrection, for which it has propagated armed self-defence by its militants, especially in urban areas, who were in mid-1980 estimated to number 800 men.

Popular Liberation Army (*Ejército Popular de Liberación,* EPL)

This small group was established in November 1979 as an offshoot of the Farabundo Martí Popular Liberation Forces (see separate entry). Its leader, Humberto Mendoza, was killed in November 1980.

Revolutionary Party of Central American Workers (*Partido Revolucionario de Trabajadores Centroamericanos,* PRTC)

Leadership. Roberto Roca (l.)

The PRTC was formed in 1979 and is also known as the Mardoqueo Cruz Urban Guerrillas and as the Liberation Leagues (*Ligas de Liberación,* LL). It is the military wing of the People's Liberation Movement (see separate entry). On Sept. 21, 1979, it claimed responsibility for the kidnapping of two businessmen, both of whom were released unharmed on Nov. 7 after their US employers had paid for the publication of a lengthy PRTC manifesto in US, Central American and European newspapers. It also claimed responsibility for the bombing of a San Salvador café in June 1985 in which four US marines and nine bystanders were killed. It has links with similarly named parties in Guatemala and Honduras.

Roberto Sibrián People's Revolutionary Movement (*Movimiento Popular Revolucionario Roberto Sibrián*)

This Marxist-Leninist guerrilla group was formed on Oct. 29, 1984, and as it took its name from a deceased member of the leadership of the Popular Liberation Forces (FPL) it was assumed to be a splinter group of the FPL. The Movement announced that it had joined the "revolutionary struggle in El Salvador, advocating a strategy with a Central American perspective".

Salvador Cayetano Carpio Workers' Revolutionary Movement (*Movimiento Obrero Revolucionario Salvador Cayetano Carpio,* MOR)

This left-wing group was formed in November 1983 by a faction of the Popular Liberation Forces (FPL), and was named after that organization's founder. It was condemned by the FPL on the grounds that it "maintained the sectarian, anti-unity positions of the past as upheld by Carpio, denying the FMLN's role as vanguard of the revolution and proclaiming itself the sole representative of the working class".

Salvadorean Suicide Commandos (*Comandos Suicidas Salvadoreños,* CSS)

This guerrilla group was formed on Oct. 18, 1984, and threatened action against extreme right-wing politicians and to kill the commander of the death squads. It also demanded the withdrawal of US diplomats and military advisers from the country. Although ostensibly a left-wing group, it may have been formed by right-wing elements to create confusion.

Unified Popular Action Front (*Frente de Acción Popular Unificada,* FAPU)

This direct action group of activists who broke away from the (pro-Soviet) Salvadorean Communist Party (PCS) in 1974 drew its strength from among industrial workers and the lower middle-class; it has remained Marxist, tending towards Leninism, and has had links with the Armed Forces of National Resistance (FARN) and with similar groups elsewhere in Latin America. It is a member of the Democratic Revolutionary Front (see separate entry).

From 1979 onwards it was responsible for a number of violent acts. On Jan. 16 of that year some 60 FAPU members occupied the Mexican embassy and the office of the Organization of American States in San Salvador, taking more than 150 hostages, in support of a demand for the release of all political prisoners. President Romero of El Salvador, however, declared that there were no political prisoners in the country and that persons who were alleged to have disappeared had in fact gone underground or left the country. As a result of negotiations between FAPU and the government, all the hostages were freed on Jan. 18 and the FAPU members concerned were flown to Mexico, where they were granted political asylum.

Other Left-wing Movements

February 28 Popular Leagues (*Ligas Populares de 28 de Febrero,* LP-28)

The LP-28 took their name from the date of disturbances after the 1977 general elections, which were widely regarded as fraudulent. They are supported by urban and rural workers, and most of their leaders and activists are former members of the National Opposition Union defeated in the 1977 elections. Their armed wing is the People's Revolutionary Army (ERP—see separate entry in previous section).

LP-28 members were said to be involved in bomb attacks at the presidential palace and elsewhere on Sept. 25, 1979, when seven people were reported as having been killed. On Sept. 21-27 of that year LP-28 members occupied the Ministry of Labour in support of their demand for the release of imprisoned leaders of their organization.

Four days after the overthrow of President Romero on Oct. 15, 1979, the LP-28 announced that they had decided to suspend violent activities while continuing to "organize the masses". Nevertheless, the LP-28 continued to be involved in violent clashes with the security forces and in early 1980 they followed other left-wing groups in reverting to a policy of outright opposition to the regime. In April 1980 the LP-28 became a member of the Revolutionary Democratic Front (see separate entry), while the ERP thereafter became part of the Farabundo Martí Front for National Liberation (see separate entry).

The LP-28 were also engaged in actions against several foreign embassies in San Salvador in January-February 1980. (As a result of these incidents, a number of countries withdrew their diplomats from El Salvador—Britain at the end of January, West Germany on Feb. 7 and Israel on Feb. 19.)

Christian Social Popular Movement (*Movimiento Popular Socialcristiano,* MPSC)

Leadership. Roberto Lara Velado; Rubén Zamora; Jorge Villacorta

The MPSC was formed in 1980 as an offshoot of the Christian Democratic Party, and it opposed the participation in 1980 of that party's leader, José Napoleón Duarte, in the junta which took power in October 1979. The MPSC has been joined by other Christian groups and stands for social justice, respect for human life and an equitable distribution of wealth. It is not recognized by the Christian Democratic Organization of America (ODCA).

It is a member of the Democratic Revolutionary Front (see separate entry).

National Revolutionary Movement (*Movimiento Nacional Revolucionario,* MNR)

Leadership. Guillermo Manuel Ungo; Francisco Marroquín; Héctor Oqueli

The MNR is a social democratic party with a programme for the development of a modernized capitalism and radical reformism. All its leaders are in exile in Costa Rica, Mexico, Venezuela or the United States. The MNR is a member of the Socialist International and is recognized by the Democratic Action Party of Venezuela and the National Liberation Party of Costa Rica. The MNR leader, Guillermo Manuel Ungo, became a member of the civilian-military junta formed after the overthrow of President Romero in October 1979 but resigned in early January 1980 in protest against the new regime's alleged "swing to the right". He subsequently became chairman of the Revolutionary Democratic Front (see separate entry) of opposition parties formed in April 1980 as the political arm of the Farabundo Martí Front for National Liberation (see separate entry). In this capacity Guillermo Manuel Ungo has acted as the principal political spokesman of the various forces seeking to overthrow the present regime.

Nationalist Democratic Union (*Unión Democrática Nacionalista,* UDN)

Leadership. Mario Aguiñada Carranza (l.)

The UDN is a socialist and popular democratic party standing for the modernization of capitalism and national democratization. It is supported by workers, trade union leaders, teachers, students and peasants. It has been in alliance with the Salvadorean Communist Party. In January 1981 its leader went underground after he had been the target of an attempt on his life.

In 1980 the UDN became one of the members of the Revolutionary Democratic Front and also of the Revolutionary Co-ordination of the Masses (see separate entries).

People's Liberation Movement (*Movimiento de Liberación del Pueblo,* MLP)

Leadership. Fabio Castillo (l.)

This small militant group was active in 1980 and became a member of the Revolutionary Democratic Front (see separate entry). Its leader was a former rector of the National University of El Salvador. It is linked to the Revolutionary Party of Central American Workers (PRTC—see separate entry).

Popular Revolutionary Bloc (*Bloque Popular Revolucionario,* BPR)

Leadership. Leonel González; Dimas Rodríguez

Based on a majority of the country's teachers, as well as members of the revolutionary lower middle class, radical workers, students and rural workers, the BPR is a Marxist-Leninist formation standing for a revolutionary socialist society independent of Soviet influence. Formed in 1975, the BPR has proclaimed its thesis of a prolonged people's war; it has rejected any alliance with non-proletarian parties and has attracted other sectors taking the same line; and it has become the strongest of the rural guerrilla movements through its armed wing, the Farabundo Martí Popular Liberation Forces (see separate entry).

Although founded as a mainly non-violent movement, the BPR engaged in acts of violence from November 1977, when demonstrators led by BPR members occupied the Ministry of Labour in San Salvador and seized at least 86 hostages. Members of the BPR on April 11-13, 1978, peacefully entered the embassies in San Salvador of Costa Rica, Panama, Switzerland and Venezuela and also occupied the cathedral in San Salvador, requesting embassy officials to intercede with the government "to stop the repression of the people and immediately to withdraw the Army, the police and the paramilitary groups from the occupied zone and to allow the peasants who were forced to flee to return to their homes"; they claimed that the military had committed "genocide" and demanded the release of 75 detained peasants. However, on April 19 the BPR members withdrew after mediation by ambassadors, the Red Cross and local representatives of the Church.

During May 1979 the BPR took a number of new violent actions against the Venezuelan, Costa Rican and French embassies in San Salvador in support of a demand for the release of five BPR leaders believed to have been arrested recently.

Another group of BPR members occupied the cathedral in San Salvador on May 4, 1979; when some 100 people out of a crowd of 500 tried on May 8 to join those inside the cathedral, police opened fire, whereupon 23 persons were reported killed and 70 of them wounded. On May 10 some 10,000 people took part in the funeral procession, and Archbishop Romero of San Salvador called on the people "to unite in the face of military repression". On May 11 the government ordered the release of two imprisoned BPR leaders—Facundo Guardado (secretary-general) and José Ricardo Mena—but denied holding the three others whose release had been demanded. A state of siege was proclaimed throughout the country on May 23; the occupation of the cathedral and other churches by BPR militants ended on May 25; and the nine BPR members were evacuated to Panama with the 16 from the French embassy—all of them being subsequently granted asylum in Cuba.

By the middle of 1979 the BPR embraced the following major groups: the Salvadorean Christian Peasants' Federation, the Agricultural Workers' Union, the National Association of Salvadorean Teachers (ANDES), the University Revolutionary Front (FUR-30) based at the University of Central America, the Revolutionary University Students (UR-19) based at the University of El Salvador, the Slum Dwellers Union (UPT) and the Trade Union Co-ordinating Committee (CCS).

After the overthrow of President Romero on Oct. 15, 1979, the BPR declared that it would not accept any truce with the new "counter-revolutionary" government, and BPR members proceeded to occupy the cathedral in San Salvador on Oct. 22. After similarly occupying the Ministries of Labour and of the Economy on Oct. 24, the BPR demanded a 100 per cent wage increase, freedom for all political prisoners, the dissolution of the security forces, the lowering of basic food prices and compensation for the families of victims of political violence. After four BPR members were shot dead outside the Ministry of Labour, the government offered negotiations on a peaceful solution, and on Oct. 29 the BPR released most of the hostages held by it but retained some, including the two ministers. After further negotiations the occupation of the ministries ended on Nov. 6, when the government agreed to some of the BPR's demands, in particular to lower certain food prices, to end two labour conflicts in progress since mid-October and to dissolve the extreme right-wing National Democratic Organization (Orden).

From April 1980 the BPR formed part of the Revolutionary Democratic Front (see separate entry) set up by left-wing opposition parties as the political arm of the Farabundo Martí Front for National Liberation (see separate entry).

Revolutionary Co-ordination of the Masses (*Coordinación Revolucionaria de las Masas,* CRM)

This organization was set up on Jan. 10, 1980, as a "revolutionary alliance" of three major left-wing organizations: (i) the Popular Revolutionary Bloc (BPR) with the Farabundo Martí Popular Liberation Forces (FPL) as its armed wing; (ii) the February 28 Popular Leagues (LP-28) with the People's Revolutionary Army (ERP) as their armed wing; and (iii) the Unified Popular Action Front (FAPU) with the Armed Forces of National Resistance (FARN) as its armed wing; other participants were the Salvadorean Communist Party and the Nationalist Democratic Union (UDN).

At the end of February 1980 the new alliance announced its aims as the overthrow of the current government; the installation of a "democratic revolutionary government"; the nationalization of the means of production, the banking and financial system and foreign trade; the creation of a new army; and the investigation of cases of missing persons dating back to 1972. A march held on Jan. 22, 1980, to mark the formation of the new alliance led to an armed conflict in which at least 22 persons were killed and 135 wounded.

Despite a far-reaching land reform programme (announced by the government between February and April 1980), which would cover 90 per cent of the country and from which 1,250,000 people (80-90 per cent of the rural population) were expected to benefit, the CRM called during March 1980 for a general strike as a sign of opposition to the government and especially to action taken against peasants by the security forces.

A partly successful general strike was organized by the CRM for June 24-25, 1980, in protest against the imposition of a state of siege in March 1980 and its monthly extension since then. During a meeting of the CRM at the University of El Salvador on June 26, 1980, at least 50 people were killed and many others injured by troops.

Revolutionary Movement of Salvadorean Students (*Movimiento de Estudiantes Revolucionarios Salvadoreños,* MERS)

Members of this Movement (a component of the Popular Revolutionary Bloc—see separate entry) occupied the Ministry of Education on Feb. 5, 1980, seizing about 400 hostages in support of various educational demands; the occupation ended peacefully on Feb. 12 with agreements being signed with the ministry.

Salvadorean Christian Peasants' Federation/Agricultural Workers' Union (*Federación de Campesinos Cristianos Salvadoreños/Unión de Trabajadores Campesinos,* Feccas/UTC)

Feccas was formed in 1965 by the Christian Democratic party and in 1975 combined with the UTC, which had been established the previous year. After joining in demonstrations for the release of political prisoners on May 1, 1977, when 10 persons were shot dead by security forces, it was declared illegal on the grounds that it had "communist links" (which it denied). In March 1978 peasant unrest in various parts of the country resulted in the death of 29 people and injury to 50 others, and the government claimed that Feccas/UTC had attempted to gain control of some areas with the support of "religious organizations", had used violence to try to recruit people into their organizations, and had killed members of the paramilitary pro-government National Democratic Organization (Orden).

Feccas/UTC in turn declared that they were campaigning for "fair wages, the right to organize and the radical transformation of our society to construct a new society where there is no misery, hunger, repression or exploitation of one group by another"; they accused vigilantes belonging to Orden to have murdered peasants and evicted villagers from their homes. The peasants' stand was supported by Archbishop Romero of San Salvador, who denied that the Church had been behind the incidents of March 1978 but also issued a warning that, if wages were not raised and land rents lowered, and if force continued to be used against the peasants, violence would spread in the country.

In a demonstration in San Salvador on March 17, 1978, for which Feccas and the UTC were officially held responsible, and which was dispersed by troops, nine people were said to have been killed and 25 injured. On Jan. 20, 1980, Feccas supporters occupied 25 plantations in the country's northern part in support of a 50 per cent pay increase. In the late 1970s and early 1980s Feccas formed part of broader alliances of left-wing opposition forces, notably the Popular Revolutionary Bloc and the Revolutionary Democratic Front (see separate entries).

Salvadorean Communist Party (*Partido Comunista Salvadoreño,* PCS)

Leadership. Jorge Schafik Handal (l.); Américo Mauro Araujo (dep. l.)

This party has been illegal for most of the time since its formation in 1930. Although it was not legalized at the time, one of its members briefly was Minister of Labour and Social Welfare in the Cabinet formed on Oct. 22, 1979 (a week after the overthrow of President Romero). However, in January 1980 the PCS joined (see separate entry) the Revolutionary Co-ordination of the Masses and subsequently became an influential force in the broader Revolutionary Democratic Front formed in April 1980 (see separate entry). Its armed wing is the Armed Forces of Liberation (FAL), and the PCS-FAL belongs to the main left-wing guerrilla organization, the Farabundo Martí Front for National Liberation (see separate entry).

The PCS is officially recognized by the Communist parties of the Soviet-bloc countries.

University Revolutionary Front (*Frente Universitario Revolucionario,* FUR-30)

This group, a student branch of the Popular Revolutionary Bloc (BPR—see separate entry), has been active since 1980, as a component of the BPR. On Feb. 15, 1980, members of the group stormed the (Jesuit) University of Central America in San Salvador and seized 60 hostages, including the chancellor (a Spanish Jesuit)—but all were released on Feb. 18. A right-wing death squad killed 14 members of the FUR-30 on Jan. 19, 1984.

Extreme Right-wing Groups

Activities of right-wing death squads declined following the election of President Duarte in 1984, but increased in the early months of 1987 in response to intensified FMLN activity.

Anti-Communist Political Front (*Frente Político Anticomunista,* FPA)

Established in May 1979, this militia has, like others, been active in attacks on alleged left-wing leaders.

Eastern Anti-Guerrilla Bloc (*Bloque Anti-guerrillero del Oriente,* BAGO)

Established in 1980, this group has been responsible for a number of killings and bomb attacks, in particular for the death of 14 alleged left-wing guerrillas on Sept. 24, 1980.

Maximiliano Hernández Martínez Anti-Communist Alliance (*Alianza Anticomunista Maximiliano Hernández Martínez*)

This group was named after President Martínez who was in power in 1931-44 and under whose regime the 1932 peasant rebellion was suppressed. It was thought to have been responsible for the assassination of Archbishop Oscar Romero in March 1980, and claimed responsibility for the murder of six leaders of the (left-wing) Revolutionary Democratic Front (see separate entry) in November 1980. This group was also reported to have delivered to a San Salvador radio station (in March 1982) a "death list" of 34 (mainly foreign) journalists alleged to have contacts with left-wing guerrillas. In June 1987 it threatened to kill 14 left-wing university students.

National Democratic Organization (*Organización Democrática Nacional,* Orden)

Founded in 1968 by Gen. José Medrano this mainly rural anti-guerrilla militia was officially disbanded after the October 1979 coup (in which President Romero was overthrown) but members of it have continued their activities since then. Many leading military figures trained within Orden, including Maj. Roberto D'Aubuisson (the runner-up in the 1984 presidential elections who was reputed to be responsible for the assassination of Archbishop Oscar Romero in March 1980), Gen. Carlos Eugenio Vides Casanova (Minister of Defence since April 1983) and Capt. Eduardo Avila (who was believed to have ordered the murder in 1981 of the president of the Agrarian Reform Institute and of his two US assistants). Gen. Medrano was killed by unidentified assailants in March 1985.

National Liberation Party—Anti-Communist Secret Army (*Partido de Liberación Nacional—Ejército Secreto Anticomunista,* PLN-ESA)

Leadership. Aquiles Baires (sec.-gen. of PLN and commander-in-chief of ESA)

In 1980 the ESA was held responsible for numerous acts of persecution directed notably against teachers, priests, monks and nuns, and on June 29, 1980, it was reported to have bombed the print shop of the University of El Salvador. The PLN announced its formation in December 1983 as an extreme right-wing political movement, for which the ESA acts as a death squad.

New Death Squad (*Escuadrón de la Muerte Nuevo,* EMN)

This anti-communist execution squad has claimed a membership of 3,000 and has been involved in bombings and killings since September 1980.

Organization for Liberation from Communism (*Organización para la Liberación del Comunismo,* OLC)

This paramilitary group has been active since early 1980. It killed four Popular Revolutionary Bloc (BPR) members on Jan. 29, 1980, and it was reported to have planted bombs which had, on Feb. 18, 1980, destroyed the transmitter of the radio station belonging to the archbishopric of El Salvador and also publishing offices at the (Jesuit) University of Central America.

White Warriors' Union (*Unión de Guerreros Blancos,* UGB)

This terrorist organization was responsible for numerous actions against alleged left-wing activists and in particular against Jesuit priests said to be involved in subversive peasant organizations. In revenge for the killing of an industrialist by members of the Farabundo Martí Popular Liberation Forces (FPL) in April 1977, the UGB killed a Jesuit priest and in June of that year it threatened to kill the 47 Jesuits still remaining in the country if they had not left by July 20. The government, however, subsequently placed these priests under guard. The UGB was also held responsible for the murder of further priests in late June and on Aug. 4, 1979, and for that of 16 garage mechanics in San Salvador on Aug. 16 of that year.

Equatorial Guinea

Capital: Malabo Pop. 383,000

The Republic of Equatorial Guinea is ruled by a Supreme Military Council headed by Lt.-Col. Teodoro Obiang Nguema Mbasago and in power since Aug. 3, 1979, when it overthrew the dictatorial regime of President Francisco Macias Nguema. There is no Parliament nor are there any legal political parties. A new Constitution approved by 95 per cent of the voters in a referendum on Aug. 15, 1982, provided for Lt.-Col. Obiang Nguema to remain head of state for a further seven years, after which there would be presidential elections by direct popular vote. The Constitution also provided for elections to a National Assembly with a five-year term and for the formation of a Council of State. The first elections to the National Assembly were held on Aug. 23, 1983, when voters approved 41 representatives (one per constituency) selected by the President to serve for a five-year term. There were no political parties, and the President retained control over the Assembly.

Opposition to the regime has been directed by groups in exile. An attempt to overthrow the government was reported to have been made on April 10, 1981, and between 60 and 180 persons were estimated to have been arrested in this connexion, among them two former ministers of the Macias Nguema regime. On June 13 of that year a court-martial sentenced one soldier to death and seven others and four officials to 30 years in prison each inter alia for acting against the process of "national reconstruction".

A further attempt to overthrow the government was made in May 1983 by junior army officers and non-commissioned officers but was suppressed with some 100 alleged conspirators being arrested. At a trial which opened in Malabo on July 1 it was stated by one of the defendants that the aim of the attempt had been to instal in power two former members of the Supreme Military Council (who had been dismissed respectively in December 1981 and June 1982). On July 5 the tribunal passed death sentences on three of the accused. Two of them, including a former member of the Supreme Military Council, were executed on July 7, while the third had his sentence commuted.

On July 19, 1986, it was reported that the government had foiled another attempt to remove President Obiang from power. (According to later reports the attempt was a pretext for the arrest of certain government members and opposition figures.) Some 30 persons were said to have been arrested, among them Lt.-Col. Fructuoso Mba Oñana Nchama (Deputy Prime Minister), Marcos Mba Ondo (Minister of Planning) and Damian Ondo Mena (Director of the Central Bank). The leader of the attempt was named as Eugenio Abesu Ondo (former military attaché in Madrid). In a trial held on Aug. 14-18, 1986, Abesu Ondo was sentenced to death (being executed on Aug. 18); his brother received a 20-year sentence; five army officers were sentenced to 18 years in prison each; and Lt.-Col. Mba Oñana, Mba Ondo and Ondo Mena to two years and four months each. It was widely believed that the plotters had opposed the President's policy of rapprochement with France and had favoured a continued close relationship with Spain (as did opposition groups based in Spain—see below).

April 1 Bubi Nationalist Group

Leadership. Bwelalele Bokoko Itogi (sec.-gen.)

Founded. April 7, 1983

This group was established in Valencia (Spain) by the Fernando Póo Liberation Front, the Bubi Union, the Real Union of Bubi People of Eri and other Bubi independence groups with the object of achieving independence for Fernando Póo (renamed Bioko in 1979), where the Bubi population outnumbered the Fang (the predominant ethnic group in the rest of the country) by 60,000 to 40,000. The group also rejected the proposal that Equatorial Guinea should become a member of the Franc Zone (which it did in 1985) and stressed the importance of retaining links with Spain (the former colonial power) for reasons of "historical and common interest". On Nov. 1, 1983, the group denounced alleged violations of the human rights of the Bubis and declared its intention to raise its flag on the island of Bioko in the cause of independence from Equatorial Guinea.

Co-ordinating Board of Opposition Forces (*Junta Coordinadora de las Fuerzas de Oposición de Guinea Ecuatorial*)

Leadership. Teodoro Mackuandji Bondjale Oko (ch.); Alejo Ecube (sec.-gen.)

Founded. April 3, 1983

This organization was established at a meeting in Zaragoza (Spain) by representatives of several opposition movements—the National Alliance for the Restoration of Democracy (ANRD), the Movement for the Liberty and Future of Equatorial Guinea (Molifuge), the Liberation Front for Equatorial Guinea (Frelige), the Democratic Reform Party, the Progress Party and a number of smaller opposition groups—but it did not include the Bubi groups (see above). At a meeting held in Zaragoza on Oct. 29-30, 1983, A. Ecube proposed that talks should be held with the governments of Cameroon, France, Gabon, Morocco, Nigeria and Spain to persuade them to impose a diplomatic, political and economic embargo on Equatorial Guinea to force its government to negotiate with the opposition.

On Aug. 12, 1984, representatives of the ANRD announced in Barcelona that their organization had left the Co-ordinating Board because there was doubt as to whether it was representative of the opposition and whether some of the parties which supported it really existed.

In October 1984 the Board denounced Equatorial Guinea's entry into the Franc Zone and the Customs and Economic Union of Central Africa (UDEAC), as these steps had "practically frozen" co-operation between Spain and Equatorial Guinea.

Following the attempted coup of July 19, 1986, the Board denounced the government of Equatorial Guinea for having brought the country to a state of "permanent instability" by failing to create the necessary infrastructure. T. Mackuandji Bondjale said in particular that President Obiang had been forced to lean on traditional structures such as his clan but that through the suppression of the attempted coup he had lost the support of his (Mongomo) clan, and other coups would follow.

Democratic Movement for the Liberation of Equatorial Guinea (RDLGE)

Leadership. Manuel Rubén Ndongo (l.)

Founded. 1981

This movement expressed doubts about the authenticity of the official result of the referendum of Aug. 15, 1982, approving the new Constitution, but it later accepted this Constitution. On March 2, 1983, the RDLGE announced that it would form a 12-member provisional government-in-exile, to be known as the Executive Council for Reorganization. In September 1982 Lt.-Col. Obiang Nguema had proposed a reconciliation between his government and the RDLGE, but the latter had come to the conclusion that its demands for guarantees had not been met by the government, and in April 1983 M. Rubén Ndongo declared that the newly-formed Executive Council intended to bring about the collapse of the existing regime by persuading other countries and international organizations to carry out an economic boycott of Equatorial Guinea.

Guinean Liberal Party (*Partido Liberal Guineano*)

Leadership. Francisco Jones Ivina (ch.)

On Feb. 24, 1986, the chairman of this party, in a statement made in Madrid, criticized the Spanish government for collaborating with the regime of President Obiang and for refusing to respond to representations made by representatives of the opposition.

National Alliance for the Restoration of Democracy (*Alianza Nacional de Restauración Democrática*, ANRD)

Leadership. Martin Nsomo Okomo (sec.-gen.)

Founded. 1974

In August 1979 the ANRD claimed that Lt.-Col. Obiang Nguema Mbasago, who had overthrown the regime of President Macias Nguema on Aug. 3, had been responsible for the killing of several of his military colleagues before the coup.

The change of regime was, in the view of the ANRD, merely a palace revolution unless all political prisoners were released; all exiles were allowed to return; national independence and integrity were safeguarded; a date was set for an end to military government; slavery, forced labour, deportations, arbitrary arrests and other outrages against the population were ended; the repressive bodies of the former regime were dissolved; and all those responsible for atrocities under the former regime were brought to trial. The ANRD also protested against the introduction of the new Constitution approved in August 1982, which it regarded as merely a manoeuvre to attract foreign aid and capital to Equatorial Guinea.

In April 1983 the ANRD joined the newly formed Co-ordination Board of Opposition Forces (see separate entry) but it left this organization in August 1984.

Progress Party of Equatorial Guinea (*Partido del Progreso de Guinea Ecuatorial*)

Leadership. Severo Moto Nsa (sec.-gen.)

Founded. February 1983

This party's orientation is Christian democratic, and it is a member of the Co-ordinating Board of Opposition Forces created in April 1983 (see separate entry). On Aug. 2, 1985, S. Moto Nsa issued, in Madrid, a proposal which was to be sent to President Obiang for "national reconciliation and democratic normalization" in Equatorial Guinea, including a full amnesty for political prisoners, the legalization of political parties and the establishment of a government consisting of civilians. On Feb. 24, 1986, he defined the aims of the opposition of Equatorial Guinea as the restoration of human rights in that country and the resumption of Spanish aid.

Sole Bloc of Guinean Democratic Forces (*Bloque Unico de las Fuerzas Democráticas Guineas*)

This organization was set up in Paris in September 1981 by Daniel Oyono, a nephew and protégé of the late President Nguema (executed on Sept. 29, 1979). The announcement of its foundation was followed by the arrest in Equatorial Guinea on Sept. 16 of 20 persons, of whom 19 were released on the following day, but not Luis Ngeuma Oyono, a brother of Daniel Oyono.

Ethiopia

Capital: Addis Ababa Pop. 43,300,000

The People's Democratic Republic of Ethiopia, established on Dec. 12, 1986, on the basis of a new Constitution published on June 7, 1986, was to be "a unitary state consisting of administrative regions and autonomous regions based on worker-peasant co-operation". The Workers' Party of Ethiopia was to be "the leading force of the state and society". A National Assembly was to be elected on the basis of proportional representation (but with reserved representation for various nationalities) as the highest state body. The Assembly was to elect the President of the Republic. The country's economy was to be centrally planned and based on socialist principles. The Constitution containing these provisions was approved in a referendum held on Feb. 1, 1987.

According to a report of Sept. 23, 1982, by the (London) International Institute for Strategic Studies the Ethiopian Army had 250,000 men and 113 combat aircraft (and was thus the second largest army in Africa, after that of South Africa) and was supported by 13,000 Cuban, 1,450 Soviet and 250 East German personnel.

On a number of occasions the Ethiopian government declared amnesties involving the release of political prisoners.

Under the first amnesty since 1974 over 1,000 prisoners were released in September 1981, among them 55 former officials of the previous regime and a number of Ethiopian Orthodox Church leaders. Under a further amnesty the government released, on Sept. 11, 1982, a total of 716 prisoners, some of them held since 1974, including Ketema Yifru (former Foreign Minister) and two other ministers of the late Emperor's administration, as well as several members of the royal family and three bishops of the Orthodox Church. On Sept. 8, 1983, the government announced the release of 1,163 prisoners (including 117 political prisoners). An amnesty of Sept. 11, 1985, covered 88 political and some 700 other prisoners, and a further amnesty of May 31, 1986, applied to 775 prisoners and also provided for the reduction of a number of life sentences to 25 years in prison.

Among a number of high-ranking officials who have defected from the government, Lt.-Col. Goshu Wolde (until then Foreign Minister) announced on Oct. 27, 1986, that his government was causing widespread "misery and destruction".

The most serious threats to the continued unity of the Ethiopian state have been the separatist movements in Eritrea and the Western Somali Liberation Front (supported by the government of Somalia). The regime has also faced opposition from political movements opposed to its pro-Soviet policies and from sections of the Protestant Church in Ethiopia. In the face of such challenges, however, the regime has shown no indication of being prepared to make concessions and has in particular deployed massive military forces against the separatists.

According to an Amnesty International report of June 1986 there were in Ethiopia some 1,600 political prisoners. They included the daughter of the late Emperor Haile Selassie, her two daughters and five other members of his extended family, all held without trial since 1974. The bulk of these prisoners, however, were regarded as members of the Eritrean People's Liberation Front (EPLF), the Eritrean Liberation Front—Popular Liberation Forces (ELF-PLF), the Tigre People's Liberation Front (TPLF) and the Oromo Liberation Front. Many prisoners were said to have disappeared, some had died as a result of torture and others had been executed without trial.

Eritrean Separatists

Now Ethiopia's most northerly province, Eritrea had been an Italian colony until World War II and was in 1952 placed by the United Nations under Ethiopian sovereignty with a federal arrangement whereby the province retained its own government, administration and flag. However, under Ethiopia's Constitution of 1955 the country became a unitary state, and by 1956 the Ethiopian authorities had established de facto control of Eritrea's administration. In 1962 Eritrea became de jure one of Ethiopia's 13 provinces. Of its inhabitants rather more than half are Moslems (with certain ties to Moslems in Arab countries) and most of the remainder are Christians.

The first Eritrean liberation front was founded in 1956, initially with the object of achieving some measure of autonomy and later increasingly calling for complete independence for Eritrea. New liberation movements were formed subsequently, some of them being Marxist rather than traditionalist pro-Arab. Efforts to forge a unitary liberation movement were not successful, however. After the secessionists had gained control of most of Eritrea's countryside through their warfare against Ethiopian forces, the latter gradually gained the upper hand from 1975 onwards, largely as a result of massive military aid from the Soviet Union and Cuba.

Among the four Eritrean anti-government organizations the Eritrean People's Liberation Front (EPLF) had been by far the strongest and has been operating without outside aid. Of the three other groups, only the Ethiopian Liberation Front—Revolutionary Council (ELF-RC) was recognized by the EPLF, which regarded the two remaining groups, the Ethiopian Liberation Front—Popular Liberation Forces (ELF-PLF) and the Popular Liberation Front—Revolutionary Committee (PLF-RC), merely as splinter groups of the EPLF. The last-named three groups received assistance from Arab states, notably Iraq, Saudi Arabia and Syria, but this aid declined from 1980 onwards because of a treaty of friendship and co-operation concluded by Syria with the Soviet Union (which has close ties with the Ethiopian government) in October 1980 and the outbreak of the Iran-Iraq war. In addition Saudi Arabia threatened to cease all aid to these groups unless they reached agreement on a common front. When the three groups agreed, in January 1983, to form within six months a single Eritrean Liberation Front, this decision was, at the end of January 1983, condemned by Issaias Afewerki (the founder of the EPLF) as "a conspiracy designed to thwart the struggle for the unity of the people of Eritrea". He demanded that, as a precondition for a union between the EPLF and the ELF-RC, the latter's military wing would have to be absorbed in the EPLF command structure. It was later reported that an action and unity agreement had been reached by representatives of the EPLF and the ELF-RC at a meeting held on March 8-11, 1984.

Lt.-Col. Mengistu Haile Mariam, the head of the Ethiopian government, declared on Nov. 16, 1984, that there was no possibility of a truce with the rebel movements as they consisted of "terrorists and mercenaries" with whom his government would not negotiate.

Nevertheless it was disclosed in June 1985 that secret indirect preparatory talks had been held between the government and the EPLF, which had, however, continued to demand a government commitment to independence for Eritrea prior to serious negotiations. These talks appear to have been discontinued.

Eritrean Liberation Front—Popular Liberation Forces (ELF-PLF)

Leadership. Omar Mohamed al-Burj (ch.)

An Eritrean Liberation Front (ELF) was set up in 1958 in Cairo and was, from 1961 onwards, increasingly active in preparing for armed struggle inside Eritrea with weapons brought in from the Sudan (although the government of that country officially did not allow Eritrean refugees to engage in subversive activities against Ethiopia). In 1969 and 1971 ELF members committed a number of acts of sabotage and hijacking of Ethiopian airliners. The ELF also undertook guerrilla warfare inside Eritrea, with the result that a partial curfew was imposed by the Ethiopian army in 1969 and a state of emergency was declared in the greater part of the province on Dec. 16, 1970, by which time the ELF forces were estimated at between 1,500 and 2,000 men equipped with small-arms from Libya. However, claims of spectacular ELF successes, made by Osman Saleh Sabbe (then the ELF leader) in Damascus, were categorically denied by the Ethiopian authorities, which claimed to have the situation under control.

In the following years ELF guerrilla activities increased greatly; by 1974, when the ELF claimed to be in control of certain areas in Eritrea, its forces were estimated at between 5,000 and 10,000 men. Nevertheless, after the deposition of Emperor Haile Selassie by Ethiopia's armed forces in September 1974, the ELF reduced its military activities and indicated its willingness to negotiate a peaceful settlement with Ethiopia's military rulers provided they recognized the ELF as the sole legitimate representative of the Eritrean people.

A Popular Liberation Front (PLF) had earlier been set up as a more radical liberation movement than the ELF. At a conference held in Rome early in July 1974 the PLF claimed that in the 10-year "liberation war" against the Ethiopian "occupation" of Eritrea 20,000 Eritreans had died and 70,000 had fled to the Sudan. The PLF asserted that Ethiopia and Eritrea were two separate countries, different at every level—historically, ethnically and culturally. It also expressed readiness to negotiate with the Ethiopian government provided the latter recognized the PLF as the sole legitimate representative of the Eritrean people and also their right to self-determination and independence (i.e. not a return to federal status, which was out of the question).

In the latter part of 1974 both the ELF and the PLF intensified their military activities and greatly increased their influence in the countryside, holding two mass meetings near Asmara (the Eritrean capital), the second of which (on Oct. 13) was said to have been attended by between 20,000 and 30,000 people. Tentative talks between government representatives and ELF and PLF leaders, however, remained inconclusive. Early the following year (1975) the ELF and PLF reached agreement (at a conference in Coazien) on the formation of a common front, and thereafter the two organizations gradually coalesced into a unitary movement based on non-Marxist principles.

On Jan. 28, 1975, the military government declared that it had "come to the end of its patience" with the Eritrean rebels and would launch an all-out offensive against them. The Army thereupon cleared Asmara on Feb. 2 of guerrillas who had infiltrated it; the ELF appealed to "the conscience of the world" to "stop the bombardment of residential parts of Asmara" and the "war of extermination". On Feb. 4 the ELF appealed to "all other liberation movements in Ethiopia" to co-operate with it, and it claimed to have received "generous assistance" from Arab states, including arms supplies from Libya worth $5,000,000.

In view of continued heavy fighting, during which ELF units freed about 1,000 prisoners held in and near Asmara, the state of emergency was on Feb. 15, 1975, extended to the whole of Eritrea. By that time casualties caused in the Asmara area were given as over 2,000 secessionists, at least 1,500 government troops and up to 2,000 civilians killed. However, between March and June 1975 the Ethiopian Army regained full control over Eritrea's three main cities of Asmara, Keren and Massawa while secessionist forces largely retained control over the countryside. During the period, joint ELF-PLF operations were carried out against US citizens in Ethiopia in retaliation for the supply of American arms to Ethiopia's armed forces.

An offer of "immediate autonomy" for the people of Eritrea and the lifting of the state of emergency was made on May 16, 1976, by the then head of government (Brig.-Gen. Teferi Benti) but was rejected by O. S. Sabbe. The latter was on July 8 reported to have said in Baghdad that his organization maintained "our right to full national independence" and to have claimed that the "Eritrean revolution" would now set up "a provisional government on more than 80 per cent of Eritrea's land". A "Voice of the Eritrean Revolution", a Baghdad radio station claiming to be the organ of the ELF-PLF, was first heard in August 1976.

A proposal for a ceasefire made by the rival (Marxist) Eritrean People's Liberation Front (EPLF) on Nov. 24, 1980, was opposed by the ELF-PLF, on whose behalf O. S. Sabbe recommended a united EPLF and ELF-PLF approach to negotiations with the Ethiopian government. However, no such rapprochement took place and by August 1981 the EPLF claimed to have demolished the ELF-PLF, with the latter's remaining guerrillas having been forced to retreat across the border into the Sudan.

Owing to a rapprochement between the governments of Ethiopia and the Sudan in 1980, the latter's government in August 1981 extended its restriction on the movement of Eritrean refugees (estimated at 450,000) to control the movement of Eritrean guerrillas along the border and inside the Sudan. On Aug. 25 the ELF-PLF stated that its offices in Khartoum and other Sudanese cities had been closed. Other sources indicated that ELF-PLF arsenals near the border had been confiscated, that guerrillas had been disarmed and that some had been arrested.

In May 1980 the ELF-PLF had split into two factions when a group led by Osman Agyp (who was based in Iraq) broke away in opposition to the leadership of O. S. Sabbe (who was based in Egypt and Dubai). Osman Agyp was, however, assassinated in Khartoum on Nov. 15, 1980, by an unknown assailant. Shortly after the murder, the Sudanese government expelled the Cuban chargé d'affaires in Khartoum.

At a party congress held in May 1984 (the first for seven years) the ELF-PLF endorsed recent Arab-inspired moves to achieve unity among the Eritrean movements. Saudi Arabia had advocated such unity in order to force Lt.-Col. Mengistu Haile Mariam to accept a negotiated settlement and to abandon his alliance with the Soviet Union.

By 1986 the ELF-PLF appeared to be split into two separate organizations—the ELF-Unified Organization, of whose executive committee Osman Saleh Sabbe was chairman, and the ELF-National Council. The latter announced in Kuwait of Nov. 2, 1986, that its 43 members had elected Abdallah Idris Mohammad as chairman of the Council's executive committee and Abd al-Wahab Mahmud Jam as chairman of the National Council, and also 10 other members of its executive committee.

Osman Saleh Sabbe said in Doha (Qatar) on Nov. 25, 1986, that his organization was ready to hold direct negotiations with Ethiopia without any preconditions and in the presence of a third party to reach a just and peaceful solution granting the Eritreans their right to self-determination. He also said that the Eritrean revolution had managed to liberate about 75 per cent of Eritrean territories and that what remained to be done now was for the Arab, Moslem and friendly states to launch an initiative to present the Eritrean question to the United Nations.

On Jan. 5, 1987, he said in Kuwait that some 70,000 young Eritreans had fled their country in the past five years to evade being conscripted in the Ethiopian Army. He also called for the resumption of Arab aid to his organization (which had been severely reduced or even halted). He added that direct negotiations with the Ethiopian government had become impossible as the Ethiopian regime was isolated at home, was fighting seven armed opposition movements and had suffered the defection to the United States of about 80 senior officials.

O. S. Sabbe died in Cairo on April 3, 1987, and was succeeded as leader by Omar Mohamed al-Burj, who had been his close ally.

The strength of the ELF-PLF has largely been among the Moslem lowlander population. Its administration is based at Kassala in Sudan.

Eritrean Liberation Front—Revolutionary Council (ELF-RC)

Leadership. Ahmed Muhammad Nasser (ch).

This organization was set up at a national council meeting called in December 1971 by a "General Command" which had itself been formed in August 1969 as a breakaway group from the Eritrean Liberation Front (ELF). The ELF-RC was to have its own People's Liberation Army organized on a socialist basis. In 1972 the ELF-RC was in open conflict with the Popular Liberation Forces (which later joined the ELF), but in September 1975 it was reported from Beirut that the ELF-RC and the ELF had, at a meeting in Khartoum (Sudan), agreed in principle on forming "a unified national democratic front with one liberation army". On Oct. 20, 1975, an agreement was signed between the ELF-RC and the Eritrean People's Liberation Front (EPLF) to set up joint co-ordination committees.

At the end of April 1978 the ELF-RC claimed that there were 115,000 Ethiopian troops ready for an offensive against the Eritrean liberation movements. Lt.-Col. Mengistu Haile Mariam (the Ethiopian head of state) said on June 7, 1978, that until then 13,000 soldiers and between 30,000 and 50,000 civilians had lost their lives in 13 years of fighting in Eritrea, and that 200,000 people had fled the country; after stating that mediation efforts by both socialist and Arab states had failed, he declared that the "socialist, democratic and progressive forces" had "the revolutionary duty of siding with us in the struggle to safeguard the unity and revolution of Ethiopia". However, an offer made by him to grant both an amnesty and a measure of internal autonomy was rejected by the EPLF and the ELF-RC, who declared that the autonomy stage had long since passed and the struggle was now for independence.

An attempt by Ahmed Muhammad Nasser to dissuade the Soviet Union (which he was said to have visited in the second week of June 1978) from intervening in Eritrea appeared to have failed. In fact Soviet pressure on Iraq, Libya and Syria was said to have resulted in the cessation of aid to the Eritrean movements by these countries.

After suffering some severe military setbacks in mid-1978, the ELF-RC agreed in the following year on the establishment of a joint command with the EPLF; both organizations remained committed to a demand for recognition as the sole legitimate representatives of the Eritrean people and acceptance of Eritrea's right to self-determination. Later, however, the ELF-RC was in conflict with the EPLF, and it suffered a decline; it rejected a ceasefire proposal made by the EPLF on Nov. 24, 1980 (and ignored by the Ethiopian government).

In the course of 1981 the ELF-RC was reported to have been obliged to surrender territory to the forces of the EPLF. It was also reported to have suffered a depletion of its fighters as a result of desertion to the EPLF or to the Ethiopian army.

The ELF-RC was reported in March 1987 to be engaged in negotiations with the EPLF in Khartoum. Its links have been primarily with the Soviet Union and Iraq.

Eritrean People's Liberation Front (EPLF)

Leadership. Issaias Afewerki (sec.-gen.)

This Front was established in 1970 as a breakaway organization from the Eritrean Liberation Front (ELF) by Issaias Afewerki, who defined its object as "a national democratic revolution without ethnic or religious discrimination", a "state at the service of the people" and "an independent nation" which would be "nobody's satellite". At a congress held in January 1977 the EPLF elected a 43-member central committee and a 13-member political committee (comprising six Moslems and seven Christians).

A movement well organized on Marxist-Leninist lines, the EPLF regarded the Eritrean Liberation Front—Popular Liberation Forces (ELF-PLF) of Osman Saleh Sabbe as reactionary and anti-Marxist, and it broke all links with this organization on March 22, 1976. By May 1977 the EPLF, which was active mainly in the areas bordering the Red Sea, had some 12,000 fighters and was in control of most of Sahel province, having taken Nakfa, its chief town, on March 24.

The EPLF claimed further military successes in 1977, capturing numerous towns, among them Keren in July 1977; by December 1977 Ethiopian forces in Eritrea were left in control only of Asmara, Barentu, Massawa and Assab. The EPLF had set up its own administration and also claimed to hold between 4,000 and 5,000 Ethiopian prisoners (although this was denied by the Ethiopian government). However, from 1978 onwards the Soviet Union was giving massive support to the Ethiopian forces (on the grounds that the secessionists were "objectively helping the realization of imperialist designs" to weaken Ethiopia and deprive it of its outlets to the Red Sea).

On April 25, 1978, it was reported from Agordat (northern Eritrea) that the EPLF and the ELF—Revolutionary Council (of Ahmed Muhammad Nasser), also regarded as Marxist, had agreed to join forces and to merge their various committees administering large parts of Eritrea, in order eventually to set up an independent state.

From July 1978 onwards, however, a government offensive succeeded in retaking some 30 towns from secessionist movements—although Keren, where the EPLF had established its headquarters after capturing it in 1977, did not fall to the superior Ethiopian forces until Nov. 27, 1978. According to EPLF sources, the town's inhabitants had previously been evacuated; an estimated 100,000 people had withdrawn towards the northern mountains and the Sudanese border; and 13,000 civilians had been killed in the fighting in the area. I. Afewerki, by then EPLF deputy secretary-general, said in mid-December 1978; "We are no longer fighting the *Derg* [i.e. the Ethiopian military government]; now it is the Soviet Union."

While the earlier agreements between the EPLF and the ELF-RC had largely remained ineffective, the two organizations concluded a new agreement in Khartoum on Jan. 27, 1979, providing for the setting up of a unified delegation with common political programmes for any future negotiations and for a joint military headquarters and a unified command; the formation of this command was announced in Paris on April 10 and that of a joint political command in Kuwait on May 19.

During 1979 the EPLF still held Nakfa (whose 40,000 inhabitants had been evacuated in February) and maintained its links with the Sudan through the border town of Karora. An EPLF radio station, "The Voice of the Broad Masses of Eritrea", broadcasting from "liberated areas of Eritrea", was first heard on Aug. 11, 1980.

An EPLF proposal for a ceasefire made on Nov. 24, 1980—and to be followed by a referendum offering a choice between independence, a return to Eritrea's federal status or regional autonomy within the Ethiopian state—was ignored by the Ethiopian government.

By February 1981 the latter's forces were firmly in command of all major towns in Eritrea except Nakfa, which was still held by the EPLF (by then the strongest of the Eritrean liberation movements). Towards the end of November 1981 the EPLF claimed to have extended the area under its control by repelling an Ethiopian force near Afabet (not far from the Red Sea) and also taking territory from ELF-RC units (some of which had deserted to the EPLF and others to the Ethiopian Army). The EPLF also claimed to have repulsed a further Ethiopian offensive on Dec. 16, 1981.

Between August 1981 and January 1982 the EPLF made several attacks on Ethiopian forces. Having claimed to have taken as many as 8,000 Ethiopian prisoners since 1976 the EPLF announced on Nov. 30, 1981, that it had decided to release 3,000 Ethiopian Army prisoners. Owing to the rapprochement between the governments of Ethiopia and the Sudan in 1980, the office of the EPLF in Khartoum was closed between August and November 1981; it was reopened thereafter.

In February 1983 the EPLF claimed to have set up, in the areas under its control, over 100 secondary schools, seven hospitals with 22 doctors as well as nurses and midwives, and the production of medicaments, and also to have built 800 kilometres of paved roads.

The EPLF had its own food relief organization—the Eritrean Relief Association based in Khartoum—which in November 1984 appealed for more emergency aid for an estimated 1,500,000 people in Eritrea where the government had allegedly "hampered food supplies". The EPLF also regarded the food distribution to peasant associations as a bribe in return for conscription into the Ethiopian Army (the conscription of peasants having contributed to the decline in food production).

While the EPLF remained in firm control of Nakfa, it attempted to seize other towns in Eritrea but was only temporarily successful. It captured Tessenei (near the Sudanese border) on Jan. 15, 1984, and in March it defeated government forces north of Nakfa, where the EPLF claimed to have killed 4,000 government troops and taken 2,500 prisoners, while hundreds were said to have fled to the Sudan. In subsequent months the EPLF inflicted further casualties on government troops in other areas. On July 7, 1985, the EPLF claimed to have seized the town of Barentu while defeating two Ethiopian Army divisions and a mechanized brigade; however, on Aug. 25 government forces retook Barentu after having earlier also recovered Tessenei.

On Aug. 27, 1986, the EPLF announced that forces of the EPLF and also of the Eritrean Liberation Front—Popular Liberation Forces had been successful in various localities, including the outskirts of Barentu, in inflicting heavy losses on government troops and in capturing large quantities of weapons, among them machine-guns, rocket launchers, ammunition and bombs. Other EPLF attacks in late August were directed against Umm Hagar (near the Sudanese border) and on Asmara airport. Further claims of successful operations against government forces were made by the EPLF in September and October 1986.

On Nov. 22, 1986, the EPLF merged with a small faction of the ELF known as the Central Leadership of the Eritrean Liberation Front, led by Giorgis Tekle Mikael as chairman. Following a unity congress held on March 12-19, 1987, Issaias Afewerki declared at a press conference on March 20 that the EPLF, which was "stronger and more organized than ever before" and continued to be ready for a peaceful solution of the Eritrean problem, had decided to create a broad national democratic front among nationalist forces in Eritrea. The congress adopted a number of resolutions in which it called, inter alia, on the United States and the Soviet Union "to accord the legal, just and human right of self-determination to the Eritrean people" and to "halt their political, military and economic assistance to Ethiopia". It also called on the Organization of African Unity and all African states to support "the just cause of the Eritrean people". The positions taken by the congress represented a distancing of the EPLF from the Soviet Union and a formal end to denunciations of the United States.

According to a report of Dec. 14, 1986, some 10,000 Ethiopian soldiers had been held as prisoners of the EPLF for up to 10 years. They ran their own camps, produced sufficient food for themselves and helped to build roads for the EPLF.

On March 25, 1987, it was reported that (according to EPLF sources) secret meetings had taken place in a European capital between representatives of the EPLF and the Ethiopian government and that the latter had rejected an EPLF plan for the holding of a referendum on the question of self-determination—i.e. a choice between total independence, self-rule or a federal government structure. The principal base of the EPLF has been in the Christian highlander population.

The EPLF receives support from Kuwait, United Arab Emirates and Syria; South Yemen and Libya are hostile, while Saudi Arabia is said to have promoted rifts within the EPLF. In general, support from Arab countries has tended to decline over the past decade.

Eritrean Unified National Council (EUNC)

Founded. Jan. 25, 1985

The EUNC was formed in Khartoum (Sudan) after lengthy negotiations between the Eritrean Liberation Front—Popular Liberation Forces (ELF-PLF), the Eritrean Liberation Front—Revolutionary Council (ELF-RC) and the Popular Liberation Front—Revolutionary Committee (PLF-RC). The new organization's aim was reported to be independence for Eritrea, although elements of the new grouping had advocated a federal solution.

Popular Liberation Front—Revolutionary Committee (PLF-RC)

Leadership. Abu Bakr Gimma (1.)

This organization was regarded as a splinter group

by the Eritrean People's Liberation Front (EPLF). In 1982 it was involved in negotiations with the Eritrean Liberation Front—Popular Liberation Forces (ELF-PLF) and the Eritrean Liberation Front—Revolutionary Council (ELF-RC) which led to a meeting in Jeddah (Saudi Arabia) on Jan. 6-10, 1983, after which it was announced that the three groups had signed an agreement to unite within six months to form a single Eritrean Liberation Front.

Other Separatist Movements

Oromo Liberation Front (OLF)

This Front, set up among the Oromo (Galla) people in the southern provinces of Shoa, Hararghe, Bale and Sidamo, was trained by the Eritrean People's Liberation Front (EPLF). Although in June 1976 separatists were said to control much of the countryside in Bale province, the OLF did not appear to play an important role. It set up an office in Mogadishu (Somalia) in January 1980, which enabled it to co-operate more closely with the Western Somali Liberation Front (WSLF). On April 27, 1981, the OLF alleged that between 2,000 and 3,000 people had been killed or wounded in the first Ethiopian air raids in the Oromo tribal area on March 19-21 of that year.

In 1986 the OLF began to resist the central government's policy of resettlement and villagization of the Oromo communities. Its military activity has been on a small scale, however.

Tigre People's Liberation Front (TPLF)

The TPLF was set up in 1976 under the auspices of the Eritrean People's Liberation Front to further separatist aspirations among the people of Tigre province (south-west of Eritrea). Its forces were involved in fighting against peasants mobilized by the military regime for supporting the country's regular forces in a march into Eritrea in 1976.

In 1979 the government announced that the forces of the TPLF had been destroyed in a four-month campaign in the western and central parts of Tigre province. The TPLF, however, claimed to have launched a successful counter-offensive in July-August 1979, capturing the Amba-Alagi pass on the road from Addis Ababa to Asmara (the capital of Eritrea); in September 1979 the TPLF claimed to have taken the airport at Axum (northern Tigre). During 1980 the TPLF extended its guerrilla operations, capturing a number of towns between January and August and claiming control of most of the countryside in Tigre province. The TPLF made numerous further guerrilla attacks in September-October 1980, and a spokesman for the Front stated in Khartoum on Sept. 29 that Ethiopian troops had displaced 80,000 people and destroyed churches, schools and mosques in retaliation for guerrilla attacks. On March 2, 1981, the spokesman claimed that the TPLF had killed about 420 Ethiopian soldiers and trapped 4,000 others involved in a new offensive.

Between August 1981 and May 1982 the TPLF claimed to have carried out numerous further actions against Ethiopian forces, to have taken several towns and to have carried the struggle into Wollo province. The TPLF also claimed to control 90 per cent of the countryside in Tigre province and to have received the surrender of hundreds of "government agents". In the Western press the TPLF's success was attributed to failure of the government to extend its political re-education programme to the rural areas of Tigre, demoralization of Ethiopian ground forces and massive support from the EPLF.

Later in 1982 and during 1983 the TPLF operated in Tigre, Eritrea and Wollo provinces and claimed to have killed and wounded hundreds of government troops. The first major government offensive against the TPLF was launched in February 1983 and involved between 40,000 and 50,000 troops. It succeeded in dislodging guerrilla bases in western Tigre and cutting the TPLF's links with the EPLF. The TPLF, however, claimed in May to have killed 4,000 Ethiopian soldiers within two months. A new offensive was launched against the TPLF by the government in September 1983 but failed to defeat the movement's forces. Early in 1984 the TPLF claimed to have inflicted about 5,000 casualties on government troops and to have taken nearly 1,000 prisoners. On Jan. 21, 1984, TPLF guerrillas ambushed a train near Diredawa (230 miles east of Addis Ababa), and on April 14, 1984, it was reported to have signed a co-operation agreement with the Western Somali Liberation Front (WSLF—see separate entry).

During that year the Ethiopian government was receiving massive food aid from overseas to relieve the famine affecting millions of people. The TPLF alleged that the government was refusing to send famine relief food consignments to guerrilla-held areas. On Nov. 4, 1984, TPLF forces took and held for 48 hours the town of Korem, disrupting food distribution to 100,000 people from that town (the largest famine relief centre in Ethiopia). The TPLF also tried to disrupt the government's resettlement programme which it regarded as an attempt to force people to leave their traditional homes and thus to deprive the TPLF of civilian support. Moreover, some 80,000 refugees from Tigre had (according to the office of the UN High Commissioner for Refugees) entered the Sudan in October-December 1984 and 1,500 were continuing to cross the border every day.

In February-May 1985 government forces conducted a new offensive against TPLF-held areas and made substantial gains. The EPLF gave no assistance to the TPLF; it had earlier rejected TPLF approaches towards the establishment of political and military unity among the anti-government organizations.

Western Somali Liberation Front (WSLF)

Leadership. Abdi-Nasir Sheikh Abdullahi (sec.-gen.)

The first congress of the WSLF was held by some 500 participants in 1975 at Badhiweyne (on the Somali side of the border between Ethiopia and Somalia), the Front's aim being to implement self-determination for the Somalis living in Ethiopia. In Somalia's 1960 Constitution it was stated that the Somali Republic would "provide, by all legal and peaceful means, the union of all Somali territory"(which in the official Somali view included the Ogaden region of Ethiopia). In the 1969 Revolutionary Charter of Somalia it was proclaimed as one of the objects of the revolution to "fight for the unity of the Somali nation".

A member of the WSLF's central committee stated on Aug. 25, 1977, that it would be for the people of the Ogaden region (called Western Somalia by the Front) to decide whether the region should become part of Somalia. The WSLF's secretary-general (and military commander) said on Sept. 4, 1977, that the WSLF claimed all territory east of the line running from Moyale (on Ethiopia's border with Kenya) through Awash (about 100 miles east of Addis Ababa) to El Adde (on the border with Djibouti); he claimed that this area of 240,000 square miles (625,000 sq. km.) was "inhabited by 10,000,000 ethnic Somalis". By August 1977 the WSLF claimed to have captured about 85 per cent of the provinces of Bale and Sidamo, killing or taking prisoner at least 23,000 Ethiopian troops. While the government of Somalia consistently denied any involvement of regular Somali forces in the fighting, the Ethiopian government produced some evidence of such involvement.

In the second half of August 1977 the Somali advance was halted by Ethiopian forces east of Diredawa and Harar. The WSLF nevertheless rejected, late in September, any ceasefire unless the Ethiopian government recognized "the people's right to self-determination", and it reaffirmed its determination to "liberate" Diredawa and Harar and to advance as far as Awash (about halfway between Diredawa and Addis Ababa). In October and November 1977 the WSLF first reported the presence of Cuban advisers and troops supporting the Ethiopian forces (and on Nov. 13 of that year the Somali government decided, as a result of Soviet and Cuban aid given to Ethiopia, to abrogate its existing treaty of friendship with the Soviet Union and demanded the withdrawal of all Soviet personnel then stationed in Somalia).

Notwithstanding the withdrawal of Somali forces from Ethiopia before a joint Cuban and Ethiopian offensive in March 1978, WSLF guerrillas continued their activities. On May 29, 1978, the WSLF and the Somali Abo Liberation Front (SALF) were reported to have concluded an agreement with the Eritrean Liberation Movement—Popular Liberation Forces (ELF-PLF) to join forces against the intervention of the Soviet Union, Cuba and other socialist states in the Horn of Africa.

With the WSLF reportedly in control of 90 per cent of the Ogaden area, heavy fighting continued during 1979-80.

In the second half of 1980 the WSLF suffered severe reverses as it was inferior in manpower and equipment to the Ethiopian army supported by heavy artillery and (Soviet-built) MiG-21 and MiG-23 fighters and Mi-24 helicopters. By the end of 1980 Ethiopian forces had reoccupied almost all territory of the Ogaden area up to the border with Somalia.

In view of this situation, the WSLF held a congress in February 1981 (according to its own claim "somewhere in the liberated area" but in fact inside Somalia some 30 kilometres, or 18 miles, from Mogadishu), when it elected a new and younger central committee and declared that it was fighting for the creation of an independent state in the Ogaden area (and not for the transfer of the area to a "greater Somalia"). Nevertheless, Somalia remained, together with Egypt, Iraq and Pakistan, the principal supplier of arms to the WSLF.

The WSLF later still carried on guerrilla activities. On Oct. 3, 1982, and again on Sept. 14, 1983, it accused the Ethiopian government of having massacred hundreds of civilians in retaliation for WSLF actions.

Other Opposition to the Regime

Ethiopian People's Democratic Union

This union included among its leadership a number of former members of the (illegal radical) Ethiopian People's Revolutionary Party and of the (right-wing) Ethiopian Democratic Union. In 1983 it was reported to be acting in concert with the Tigre People's Liberation Front (TPLF). Its stated object was to fight for "the democratic rights of the people of Ethiopia".

On Feb. 4, 1984, it was announced that 17 alleged members of the union had been arrested while distributing leaflets in Addis Ababa; they were accused of "imperialist-supported" anti-state activities, including spying and rumour-mongering.

Ethiopian People's Revolutionary Party (EPRP)

In 1976 the EPRP described itself as Marxist and denounced the military regime as "fascist", whereupon the government, describing the EPRP as "anarchist", began to conduct an intensive campaign against its members. In November 1976 the EPRP's military branch, the "Revolutionary People's Army", was said to be fighting in several provinces.

Early in 1977 the EPRP, as a party which rejected the government's thesis that a people's revolution would emanate from a military takeover, was involved in mutual mass killings between supporters and opponents of the regime. The EPRP was held responsible for the killing of a number of high-ranking officials late in 1977 and early in 1978. The EPRP itself claimed in Khartoum on Jan. 30, 1978, that during the previous three years the military government had "assassinated 3,500 persons" and that in Addis Ababa alone about 8,000 had been arrested and deported to the countryside. In the Western press it was reported that the "red terror" of the EPRP had been countered by the "white terror" of the Ethiopian military regime. Further arrests of EPRP members were announced in May and on Sept. 27, 1979, and the execution of Berhane Meskel Reda Wolde (one of its leaders captured in March 1979) was confirmed on July 12, 1979. By that time the EPRP appeared to have been effectively liquidated by the regime.

However, late in 1986 and early in 1987 units of the EPRP's Ethiopian People's Revolutionary Army appeared to have resumed guerrilla warfare. It claimed responsibility for an attack on an Italian assistance project in the Gojjam region on Dec. 27, 1986, when some 40 Ethiopians were killed and two Italians and a number of Ethiopian soldiers were captured. Following Sudanese mediation the two Italians and also seven Ethiopians were released on Feb. 7, 1987. On Feb. 9 it was reported that six of the Ethiopians had refused to return home and expressed their intention to travel to Italy. In another attack, reported on Feb. 26, the EPRP had, on Feb. 19, killed 32 Ethiopian soldiers and seized another two Italians as well as 37 Ethiopians.

Protestant Church Opposition

In September 1986 it was reported that, although a number of religious leaders had been released from detention, there had been a new wave of arrests of church leaders. While some churches previously closed had been reopened, others had been closed, and those which remained open were kept under heavy censorship.

Fiji

Capital: Suva Pop. 660,000

Fiji is an independent state within the Commonwealth, with the British monarch as head of state being represented by a Governor-General.

It has a bicameral Parliament consisting of a 22-member Senate and a 52-member House of Representatives. While the senators are appointed for a six-year term, the House of Representatives is elected for five years by universal adult suffrage under a complex system embracing 12 Fijian communal seats, 12 Indian communal seats, three general communal seats, 10 Fijian national seats, 10 Indian national seats and five general national seats.

In a general election on April 12, 1987, an opposition alliance under Dr Timoci Bavadra (and with its base in the Indian population, comprising 49 per cent of the total) defeated the Alliance Party, which had been in power since independence in 1970, and which drew its support mainly from the native Melanesians, who accounted for about 47 per cent of the population. The new Bavadra government was removed from power on May 14, however, by a military coup led by Lt.-Col. Sitiveni Rabuka, the third in command of the 2,600-strong Fijian Armed Forces (over 95 per cent of whom were Melanesian). An attempt was made to resolve the resulting constitutional crisis.

Finland

Capital: Helsinki Pop. 4,910,000

The Republic of Finland, a democratic multi-party state, has a President elected for a six-year term by a college of 301 electors chosen by universal adult suffrage. He holds supreme executive power and appoints a Cabinet under a Prime Minister which must enjoy the confidence of the 200-member unicameral Parliament (*Eduskunta*) elected for a four-year term by universal adult suffrage. In elections held on March 15-16, 1987, seats in Parliament were gained as follows: Social Democrats 56, Conservatives (National Coalition Party) 53, Centre Party 40, Finnish People's Democratic League (led by the Communist Party) 16, Swedish People's Party 12, Rural Party 9, Finnish Christian Union 5, Democratic Alternative 4, Greens 4, delegate from the Aaland Islands 1. (The Democratic Alternative consisted of "Stalinists" expelled from the Finnish People's Democratic League in June 1986.) Parties which contested the elections without gaining any seats included the Pensioners' Party and the Liberal People's Party.

Under a law approved by the *Eduskunta* on July 12, 1985, and effective from Jan. 1, 1987, conscientious objectors were allowed to make a written declaration that they had the conviction required by the law (instead of having to prove it before an investigating panel); they would have to perform civilian service of 16 months (compared with eight months' military service); and this was to include some civil defence training. In peacetime Jehovah's Witnesses were totally exempt from military service.

Under the 1947 peace treaty with the Soviet Union the Finnish government was obliged to dissolve all political, military and paramilitary "fascist" organizations and all organizations engaged in propaganda against the Soviet Union and other friendly nations, and also not to tolerate the existence of such organizations in the future (Article 8). Moreover, it was forbidden to give any military, naval or air instruction to persons other than members of the Finnish Army, Navy or Air Force (Article 15).

In November 1977 the government prohibited the activities of four unregistered extreme right-wing organizations (with a total membership of not more than 100).

Patriotic People's Front

Leadership. Pekka Siitoin (l.)

Pekka Siitoin, the alleged leader of this organization (one of the four prohibited by the government in November 1977), was on Nov. 14, 1979, reported to have been sentenced to five years in prison for involvement in an attempt to set fire to the printing works of two communist newspapers a year earlier, and also for founding and directing an illegal political organization. Five other persons sentenced to imprisonment at the same time included the "secretary-general" of the proscribed organization, who was given a 3½-year prison sentence.

France

Capital: Paris Pop. 54,000,000

The French Republic has an executive President elected for a seven-year term by universal adult suffrage, a government headed by a Prime Minister and a bicameral Parliament consisting of (i) a 319-member indirectly-elected Senate and (ii) a 577-member National Assembly elected for a five-year term by universal adult suffrage under a system of proportional representation allowing for one deputy per 108,000 inhabitants. In general elections held on March 16 and 23, 1986, parties obtained seats in the National Assembly as follows: Socialists 207, Union for French Democracy–Rally for the Republic (UDF-RPR) 147, RPR 77, UDF 53, Communists 35, National Front 35, Left Radical Movement 2, various right-wing groups 14, various left-wing groups 7. There is a multiplicity of other "orthodox" political parties without parliamentary representation, including several on both the extreme left and the extreme right.

Partly in consequence of France's traditional status as a haven for political refugees from other countries, numerous non-French extremist groups have pursued their aims while operating on French soil, notably in the capital, and have posed a major threat to internal security in recent years. Such groups (which are dealt with under appropriate country headings elsewhere in this volume) include Armenian nationalists committed to violent action against Turkish targets, militant Palestinian splinter groups seeking to extend their struggle against Israel and Zionism beyond the Middle East, and various other Arab groups pursuing assorted inter-Arab rivalries. At the same time, numerous specifically French extremist groups are committed to aims and methods which pose a threat to the existing order, those active in recent years encompassing both ends of the political spectrum. The French polity has also been under challenge from various separatist or autonomist movements (notably in Corsica) and from a number of pro-independence groups active in the overseas departments and territories.

In view of what it regarded as a deterioration in the internal security situation, the French government on Aug. 17, 1982, introduced new anti-terrorist measures, including a strengthening of the security forces, tighter controls on illegal border entries and arms trafficking and the installation of more computer capacity in anti-terrorist information units. The government made it clear that its main aim was to curb the current wave of "international" terrorism in France, but also indicated that the new measures reflected its concern over the intensification of anti-Jewish attacks attributed to French extreme right-wing groups.

Under new laws approved by the Council of Ministers on May 28, 1986, and adopted by Parliament in July and August 1986, cases involving terrorism were to be tried by special central courts in Paris with juries made up of judges (and no longer of ordinary citizens); some 17 crimes were specified as falling within the "terrorism" category; and victims of past and future terrorism were to be compensated. The law relating to terrorism was promulgated on Sept. 9, 1986, with subsequent modifications being adopted on Dec. 20 by both Houses of Parliament allowing for offences committed before these dates to be tried by the special courts.

Among security measures taken to combat a wave of bomb attacks in Paris (attributed widely to the Committee of Solidarity with Arab and Middle Eastern Political Prisoners [CSPPA—see below], but also claimed by various organizations of Arab origin) the Prime Minister announced on Sept. 14, 1986, the introduction (for the next six months) of visa requirements for foreigners except citizens of the European Community member countries and Switzerland entering France. In February 1987 these requirements were extended to apply until further notice.

Extreme Right-wing Movements

Charles Martel Club

Named after the 8th-century Carolingian king who stemmed the Moslem Arab penetration of Europe at Poitiers in AD 732, this group had its origins in the forces which opposed the granting of independence to Algeria in 1962. Its first violent action was a bomb attack on the Algerian consulate in Marseilles in December 1973, when four people were killed. Among its further actions was a bomb attack on the Algerian consulate in Aubervilliers (Paris) on May 11, 1980.

The club was one of four groups which claimed responsibility for planting a bomb at a Marseilles trade fair on Sept. 30, 1983, when one person was killed and 26 were injured. It also claimed responsibility for an attack on the Paris office of the weekly *Jeune Afrique* in March 1986.

Civic Action Service (*Service d'action civique,* SAC)

Leadership. Pierre Debizet (sec.-gen.)

The SAC was established in 1958 on the return to power of Gen. De Gaulle to act as the unofficial security arm of the Gaullist movement and as a focus for Gaullist sympathizers outside the orthodox party political framework. It subsequently gained a reputation for using violent methods in pursuit of its aims and for having links with the French underworld.

The organization came into sharp public focus in July 1981 in connexion with the murder in Marseilles of Jacques Massie (a police inspector and former local SAC chief) together with five members of his family. Of about a dozen SAC members subsequently arrested by the police, four reportedly confessed to having participated in the killings, apparently because Massie had refused to surrender documents in his possession which incriminated the SAC.

After a parliamentary investigation committee had recommended the dissolution of the SAC on the grounds of its clandestine criminal activities, the French Cabinet on July 28, 1982, announced the official banning of the organization. A government statement said that "the action of this organization is founded on violence and on practices bordering on banditry, as evidenced by the numerous judicial cases in which certain of its members and leaders have been implicated".

Commandos in France against the Maghrebian Invasion

This extreme right-wing group, opposed to immigration from Algeria, Morocco and Tunisia, claimed responsibility for bomb attacks against immigrant targets in Marseilles, Nice and Toulon in May 1986.

Peiper Vengeance Group

This clandestine group, named after a former German SS officer, has claimed responsibility for numerous bombings and other assaults on Jewish and Moslem premises in France.

The group also claimed responsibility for a bomb attack on a Paris cinema to disrupt a Jewish film festival on March 29, 1985.

Secret Builler-Roussarie Army

This anti-ETA group threatened in August 1983 to carry out anti-terrorist attacks in order to "cleanse the French Basque region of the ETA gangrene".

Extreme Left-wing Movements

Bakunin-Gdansk-Paris-Guatemala-Salvador Group (*Groupe Bakounine-Gdansk-Paris-Guatemala-Salvador,* GBGPGS)

This grouping of militant anarchist activists emerged in the early 1980s when it claimed responsibility for a series of attacks on US-owned multinational companies in France and also on the premises of firms trading with Eastern Europe and Latin America. The title assumed by the movement is believed to indicate the broad international concerns of its members.

The GBGPGS has also mounted attacks on East European trading organizations with offices in Paris, notably those of Poland and the Soviet Union, as well as on South African business premises in the French capital. The Group has expressed particular opposition to the policy of the Socialist-led government which came to power in mid-1981 of maintaining trading links with South Africa and of continuing to sell armaments to "repressive" third-world regimes.

The Group subsequently claimed responsibility for 16 bomb attacks carried out mainly in the Paris area between December 1981 and February 1983.

Black War (*Guerre noire*)

This extreme left-wing group has claimed responsibility for attacks on the Paris offices of *Défense légitime* (a right-wing self-defence group) in December 1985 and of the (right-wing) European Workers' Party in April 1986.

Committee of Solidarity with Arab and Middle Eastern Political Prisoners (*Comité de solidarité avec les prisonniers politiques arabes et du Proche-Orient,* CSPPA)

The CSPPA first emerged in early 1986 when it exploded bombs in and around Paris in pursuit of its demand for the release of three prisoners held in France: these were Georges Ibrahim Abdallah, a pro-Syrian Christian Maronite from Lebanon and the suspected leader of the Lebanese Armed Revolutionary Faction (FARL), who had been arrested in Lyon in October 1984; Anis Naccache, serving a life sentence for the attempted assassination of the former Iranian Prime Minister Shapur Bakhtiar in Paris in July 1980; and Varadjian Garbidjian, a member of the Armenian Secret Army for the Liberation of Armenia (ASALA), who was serving a term of life imprisonment for an attack at Orly airport in July 1983 in which eight people were killed.

A further wave of bomb attacks began in Paris on Sept. 8, 1986, when a post office employee was killed in an explosion at the Paris city hall, and reached a climax on Sept. 17 when seven people were killed by a bomb thrown into a crowd of shoppers in Montparnasse. Responsibility for these incidents was also claimed by various organizations of Arab origin, including from Beirut by the Partisans of Justice and Freedom (PDL), but they were generally accepted as being the work of the CSPPA. The exact origin and character of the CSPPA was uncertain, however, and it was suggested as being a front for the FARL enjoying tactical support from the ASALA and possibly also from the French group Direct Action (AD—see separate entry). French police were reported to believe that the CSPPA had close ties with other Lebanese factions, including the Shia fundamentalists of the *Al-Jihad al-Islami*.

In response to these attacks, which provoked intense public anxiety in Paris, the French government on Sept. 14 announced strict controls on entry into France (see above). Street posters issued by the Ministry of the Interior identified G. Abdallah's four brothers as among the prime suspects. G. Abdallah, who had been sentenced to four years' imprisonment in July 1986 for using false documents, possession of arms and explosives, and criminal association, was further sentenced by a special non-jury court on Feb. 28, 1987, to life imprisonment for complicity in the murder of the US military attaché in Paris, Lt.-Col. Charles Ray, in January 1982, and an Israeli diplomat, Yacov Barsimantov, in April 1982. The sentences were seen as emphasizing the independence of the judiciary from political control, the government chief prosecutor having called for a sentence of not more than 10 years on the grounds that to apply the maximum penalty would only "turn the accused into a martyr and France into a hostage". It was reported that a cessation of the attacks had been negotiated by the French authorities through the intercession of Syria and Algeria.

After a period of silence following the September bombings, the CSPPA on May 25, 1987, threatened a "very warm" summer in France unless G. Abdallah, A. Naccache, and V. Garbidjian were released.

Direct Action (*Action directe,* AD)

Leadership. Jean-Marc Rouillan

AD emerged in 1979 as a new revolutionary movement embracing elements of the anarchist *Groupe d'Action révolutionnaire internationaliste* (GARI) and a Maoist formation known as the *Noyaux armés pour l'autonomité populaire* (NAPAP). In the course of 1980 it claimed responsibility for a series of attacks on government buildings and other targets, including a machine-gun assault on the Ministry of Co-operation in Paris on March 18, 1980. After this incident the French security authorities on March 27-28, 1980, carried out a major anti-terrorist sweep in the capital, seizing quantities of arms and explosives and arresting about 30 suspected AD activists, of whom 19 were later charged with various offences. The Paris raids were co-ordinated with similar police operations in Toulon and Nice in southern France, in which four Italians suspected of being members of the Red Brigades were arrested.

In addition to having contacts with the Italian Red Brigades, AD was also believed to have established a relationship with the militant leftist wing of the Basque separatist movement ETA as well as with militant Palestinian or pro-Palestinian groups operating in France. From late 1980 AD activists were thought to include a substantial contingent of Turkish political refugees who had left their own country following the military takeover of September 1980.

Although the police believed that the AD network had been largely dismantled by the March 1980 operations, the movement subsequently claimed responsibility for a bomb explosion and two rocket attacks on the Transport Ministry in Paris on April 15, 1980; moreover, a series of acts of sabotage on computer equipment in Toulouse in early April 1980 was also attributed to AD or to an apparently connected "Committee to Liquidate or Neutralize Computers" (CLODO).

On Sept. 13, 1980, the presumed leader of AD, Jean-Marc Rouillan (who in the early 1970s had founded the GARI) was arrested in Paris together with his female companion Nathalie Ménignon. A few days later, on Sept. 19, AD claimed responsibility for a machine-gun attack on the Military School in Paris, following which the police on Sept. 23 raided a farmhouse in Ardèche (southern France), arrested three people thought to be connected with AD and seized a substantial quantity of explosives. At this stage the French authorities were again convinced that AD had been effectively neutralized.

In May 1981, however, 16 AD activists then in custody, including Rouillan but not Ménignon, benefited from a general amnesty for political prisoners declared by the incoming President Mitterrand (Ménignon being released some months later after staging a hunger strike), and by the end of the year the movement was again claiming responsibility for bomb attacks on "capitalist" targets in Paris. In early 1982, moreover, AD elaborated its theoretical stance, notably in two documents entitled *Pour un projet communiste* and *Sur l'impérialisme américain* published in March and April 1982 respectively. At the same time members of the movement followed the anarchist tradition of robbing banks—termed "expropriations"—to finance the organization's activities.

Renewed arrests of suspected AD members and seizures of arms from AD hideouts in April and May 1982 were accompanied by further bomb attacks in Paris and elsewhere for which the movement claimed responsibility. Several were perpetrated against US targets, while from early August 1982 the movement carried out several attacks on "Zionist" (i.e. Jewish) persons and property. This latter change of emphasis was thought to reflect the existence of links between AD and an extremist group calling itself the Lebanese Armed Revolutionary Factions, which had earlier claimed responsibility for the killings of a US diplomat in January 1982 and of an Israeli diplomat in April 1982—both in Paris. AD itself claimed responsibility for a bomb explosion outside an Israeli trading company's premises in Paris on Aug. 11, 1982.

On Aug. 18, 1982, the French government announced the formal banning of AD, adherence to which in itself thereby became a criminal offence. This announcement followed the publication in the left-wing newspaper *Libération* of a claim by Jean-Marc Rouillan that AD had been responsible in recent weeks for three attacks on "Zionist targets". Two days before the banning decision the French police had arrested the presumed press spokesman for AD, Helyette Besse. On the day after the banning a bomb attack on the Paris offices of the right-wing journal *Minute* was claimed as the work of AD.

Further arrests of suspected AD activists took place in the latter months of 1982, including those of Michel Camilleri (said to be leader of a hard-line faction within the movement) on Sept. 17 and of Frédéric Oriach (a former NAPAP leader) on Oct. 12. Following the arrest of the latter the French authorities claimed to have firm evidence of links between AD and militant anti-Zionist/pro-Palestinian organizations with a presence in France. Bomb attacks attributed to AD continued to occur in late 1982 and early 1983, by which time AD was thought to have split into several separate factions, each with its own distinct theoretical position.

AD was responsible for further attacks in 1984 on government buildings and premises connected with arms manufactures, as well as on the European Space Agency building in Paris (on Aug. 2).

On Jan. 15, 1985, an "internationalist" faction of the group, led by Rouillan and Ménignon, and the West German Red Army Faction (RAF) announced the establishment of a united urban-based politico-military front in Western Europe to act against "the multinational structures of NATO, its bases and strategies, its plans and propaganda" and to oppose the deployment of nuclear missiles in Europe, the revival of the Western European Union, the creation of a French "rapid action force" and the allegedly proposed participation of West Germany in the French nuclear force and integration of that force in NATO.

On Jan. 25, 1985, AD shot dead Gen. René Audran (who was responsible for French arms sales) in Paris, with the Elisabeth van Dyck Commando being responsible. In a joint statement issued on Jan. 31, 1985, AD and the RAF declared that the general had been killed because "his economic and military role put him at the head of NATO's strategic project of imperialism to homogenize European states under its control". On July 2, 1985, AD announced in a communiqué signed by an Antonio lo Muscio Commando (named after an Italian Red Brigade member killed in 1977) that it had made an abortive attack on the Controller-General of the French Armed Forces but that it would continue its campaign against NATO and "imperialism".

Numerous incidents linked to the AD were recorded during 1985 and 1986, including an unsuccessful attempt on the life of the deputy president of the employers' federation, the CNPF, and attacks on offices of industrial companies, Interpol, the OECD, police buildings and other targets. On Nov. 17, 1986, Georges Besse, managing director of the Renault group, was shot dead by two women AD members.

However, on Feb. 21, 1987, the four leading members of AD— Jean-Marie Rouillan, Nathalie Ménigon, Georges Cipriani and Joëlle Aubron—were arrested at a remote farmhouse near Orleans, where arms and explosives were also found. On March 5 Ménignon and Aubron were charged with the murder of G. Besse and Cipriani and Rouillan with complicity.

On June 13, 1987, Régis Schleicher, a leading member of AD captured on March 15, 1984, was sentenced to life imprisonment for being an accessory to the murder of two policemen on May 31, 1983, and for the attempted murder of two other persons. The trial was held before a special non-jury tribunal of seven judges; this was the second time that the newly constituted court had been used (the first occasion being in the trial of Georges Abdallah—see entry for Committee of Solidarity with Arab and Middle Eastern Political Prisoners) and followed the abandonment of a trial before a jury in 1986 when Schleicher threatened the jury with "the rigours of proletarian justice".

M-10

This group claimed responsibility for placing a bomb in the car of Alain Peyrefitte, editor of *Le Figaro* and a former Minister of Justice, which exploded on Dec. 15, 1986, killing the chauffeur as he drove away alone.

Section squarely against Le Pen (*Section carrément contre Le Pen,* SCALP)

This group, which had vowed to "dig up the hatchet" against Jean-Marie Le Pen, the leader of the legal *Front national* (FN), was engaged in demonstrations against the FN in Toulouse on June 4-6, 1984, when two bombs exploded and 14 persons were injured in clashes with police.

Regional Movements

BASQUE REGION

In that the separatist organization called Basque Nation and Liberty (*Euzkadi ta Azkatasuna,* ETA) seeks the establishment of an independent Basque state comprising Basque-populated areas on both the Spanish and the French sides of the Pyrenees, its aspirations pose an implicit threat to the territorial integrity of France. Both the ETA and the associated Enbata Movement have been banned by the French government—in October 1972 and January 1974 respectively—and their subsequent clandestine activities in French territory have been directed at giving support to Basque activists operating in Spain. (For details of the ETA and other Basque movements within Spain, see pages 342–346.)

Enbata Movement

The Enbata Movement and publication of the same title were founded in April 1963, the name being taken from a storm-bearing seawind prevalent in the Basque region. Closely linked to the ETA, Enbata presented candidates in the 1967 and 1968 French general elections, but with no success; thereafter it concentrated on journalistic and propaganda activities and also on providing support and shelter for ETA activists from Spain.

As a result of the assassination of the Spanish Prime Minister by Basque guerrillas in December 1973, the French authorities increased their surveillance of Basque activists operating in France, and on Jan. 30, 1974, the government announced the official banning of Enbata. In its statement justifying the banning decision the government asserted that Enbata "supports the use of violence" and that its declarations "give the appearance of a joint association with the commandos operating in Spanish territory".

Those of the North (*Iparretarak*)

This French Basque separatist group, founded in 1973, is held responsible by French police for more than 60 attacks on public buildings and for three killings of police officers (in 1982-85) in the French Basque region.

One member of the group was killed by a bomb of his own construction on June 22, 1987. The presumed leader is Philippe Bidart, a former seminary student, and the group describes itself as close to ETA (see Spain—Basque Nation and Liberty).

CORSICA

Over recent years Corsica's internal stability has been seriously threatened by a campaign of violence waged against "French colonial" targets by separatist elements mainly grouped within the Corsican National Liberation Front (FLNC). These elements seek independence for the island (possibly in association with France) and the rehabilitation of the Corsican language and culture, which they regard as having been steadily eroded since the island was purchased for the French crown from Genoa in 1769. Such aspirations have, however, found little support among the 240,000 inhabitants of the island, the political representation of which remains largely in the hands of Corsican sections of the mainland parties favouring the maintenance of Corsica's status as an integral part of France.

The main legal nationalist party is the Union of the Corsican People (UPC) led by Dr Edmond Siméoni, which advocates autonomy for the island within the French Republic. In 1975-76 leaders of the UPC's predecessor, the Association of Corsican Patriots (APC), were involved in a number of violent actions; but since the APC was reconstituted as the UPC in July 1977 the party has repeatedly condemned the use of violence in pursuit of Corsican aims. In contrast, the smaller *Consulta di i Cumitati Nationalisti* (CCN), formed in 1980 as a legal pro-independence movement, has consistently refused to condemn the use of violence, although it stresses that it is committed to "means and objectives significantly different from those of the FLNC".

As part of its major decentralization plan for the whole of France, the left-wing government which came to power in Paris in mid-1981 enacted legislation in January 1982 elevating Corsica from regional status to that of a "territorial collectivity" (*collectivité territoriale*), with a directly-elected Assembly and significantly increased administrative and economic powers. In the first elections to the new 61-seat Assembly held on Aug. 8, 1982, Corsican offshoots of the left-wing metropolitan parties returned 23 members (including 12 Left Radicals), while the right-wing formations secured 29 seats. The balance of power thus went to the UPC with seven seats (and 10.6 per cent of the popular vote) and the small nationalist *Partitu Populare Corsu* (PPC) with one seat—the remaining elected member being independent. Divisions within the right subsequently enabled Prosper Alfonsi (Left Radical president of the outgoing regional council) to secure election on Aug. 20 to the presidency of the new Assembly and to form a left-wing administration.

Whereas the UPC declared its intention to participate in Corsica's new political structure as a stage towards its goal of eventual autonomy, both the FLNC and the CCN called for a boycott of the elections (in which the acutal abstention rate was 31.5 per cent). Shortly after the elections the FLNC officially declared the truce which it had observed in principle since April 1981 (but which had effectively broken down early in 1982) to be at an end, following which there occurred a sharp escalation of bomb attacks and other violent incidents. In the face of a deteriorating situation the government announced the banning of the FLNC on Jan. 5, 1983, and took steps to strengthen security arrangements for the island.

The extensive use of political violence by Corsican nationalist elements has led to the emergence of extremist pro-French movements which have themselves been prepared to resort to violent methods: 284 bombing incidents were recorded in Corsica from the beginning of 1987 to June 10, compared with 100 in the same period in 1986. Other significant features of the Corsican situation include (i) widespread hostility among the native Corsican population of all persuasions to the presence on the island of French "settlers", including some 17,000 "*pieds-noirs*" from the former French territories of North Africa; and (ii) periodic tensions, often leading to violent incidents, between the local population and immigrant Arab workers. In the latter context, the FLNC has consistently condemned attacks on Arab workers.

Elections to the Corsican Assembly held on Aug. 12, 1984, were contested by 10 parties. The turnout was 68.57 per cent of the electorate, and the seats were distributed among the parties as follows: the (right-wing) *Opposition nationale pour la Corse* consisting of the *Rassemblement pour la république* (RPR), the *Union pour la démocratie française* (UDF) and the Bonapartists 19, the Left Radical Movement 9, an alliance of the Socialist Party and the

Left Radical Movement of *Corse du Sud* 9, the Communist Party 7, the National Front 6, an alliance of the *Centre national des indépendants et paysans* (CNIP) and RPR dissidents 5, the *Mouvement corse pour l'autodétermination* 3 and the autonomist *Unione di u populu corsu* 3.

Confederation of Nationalist Committees (*Confédération des comités nationalistes,* CCN)

This organization, consisting of 12 nationalist committees, was officially regarded as the political wing of the illegal *Front de libération nationale de la Corse* (FLNC). It was itself banned on Sept. 27, 1983, whereafter CCN militants formed, on Oct. 2, 1983, the Corsican Movement for Self-Determination (*Mouvement corse pour l'autodétermination,* MCA—see separate entry).

Corsican Guerrillas and Partisans (*Francs-tireurs et partisans corses,* FTPC)

The FTPC was reported to have been founded in March 1981 by former members of a National Front of Corsica (an early precursor of the Corsican National Liberation Front—see separate entry) to carry on the tradition of Pasquali Paoli (1725-1807), the founder of Corsican nationalism and the head of a Corsican Republic in 1755-69. The FTPC was held responsible for several acts of violence in mainland France, including a fire at a Total oil depot in Châteauroux on March 14, 1981. However, it denied any responsibility for a bomb explosion at Ajaccio airport on April 16, 1981 (shortly after the arrival of President Giscard d'Estaing on an election campaign visit), and it affirmed that its military objective would "always be to attack targets associated with the economy, the French state, the force of repression and the despoilers of the Corsican people".

Corsican Movement for Self-Determination (*Mouvement corse pour l'autodétermination,* MCA)

The MCA was founded as a legal party on Oct. 2, 1983, by former militants of the Confederation of Nationalist Committees (CCN, banned on Sept. 27, 1983). It described itself as being "at odds with capitalism" and advocated "public struggles, including electoral ones, to contribute to the cleansing of political life in Corsica"; it also called for "the recognition of the Corsican people and their national rights". In elections to the Corsican Assembly held on Aug. 12, 1984, the MCA gained three seats. However, on Jan. 27, 1987, the MCA was banned on the grounds that it represented a reconstitution of a criminal organization, i.e. the Corsican National Liberation Front (FNLC).

The banning followed the arrest, on Jan. 12, of Alain Orsoni, an MCA regional councillor and brother of Guy Orsoni (for whose death see entry for the FNLC), in whose bar police found documents setting out "a politico-military programme" for the FNLC in 1987 and the complete restructuring of the organization. A. Orsoni was taken to Paris for trial by a new centralized court specializing in terrorist cases.

MCA militants decided later on Jan. 21, 1987, to form a new movement of the same political orientation. Moves to unity with the UPC party were halted by the latter on April 12, 1987.

Corsican National Liberation Army (*Armée corse de libération nationale*)

This group, which was possibly under the previous leadership of the *Front de libération nationale de la Corse* (FLNC), claimed responsibility for a number of violent incidents in June-July 1983.

Corsican National Liberation Front (*Front de libération nationale de la Corse,* FLNC)

Leadership. Yves Stella ("political commissar")

The FLNC was formed in May 1976 by former members of an earlier *Front paysan corse de libération* (FPLC) and the *Ghjustizia Paolina*. The FPLC had been responsible for a series of bomb attacks between September 1973 and January 1974, at the end of which month it was officially banned by the French government; it nevertheless continued its violent activities until being subsumed by the broader FLNC.

The FLNC's programme issued in May 1976 listed as its aims the "recognition of Corsica's national rights, the destruction of all instruments of French colonialism, the setting-up of a people's democracy, the confiscation of all large colonial properties and tourist trusts, the implementation of land reform and the right to self-determination". At a secret press conference on May 5, 1977, the FLNC members present described their movement as being both military and political; claimed that tourism was "ravaging" Corsica; denounced as "treason" the reformist policy of the legal autonomist Association of Corsican Patriots—which was in July 1977 reconstituted as the Union of the Corsican People (UPC); blamed France for having "erased our history in order to impose its own"; and declared their determination to continue military actions, carrying their struggle into French territory. At a further press conference held on Aug. 15-16, 1977, the FLNC declared that it would fight to "disorganize the police apparatus in order to bring about conditions for political negotiations". The FLNC has propagated its views in a clandestine tabloid entitled *U Ribellu* ("The Rebel"), first produced in December 1977.

On May 5, 1976, the FLNC announced that it was responsible for causing 16 explosions in Corsica during the previous night, and also for attacks on the Palace of Justice in Marseilles and an electric relay station in Nice (damage being estimated at the equivalent of more than US$1,000,000). It carried out further attacks on the house of a divisional army commandor in Corsica (on July 23-24); on the car of a Secretary of State at the Ministry of Agriculture (on Aug. 14); on an Air France Boeing 707 at Ajaccio airport (on Sept. 7); and on the home of the Foreign Legion commander and an ammunition dump—in support of a call for the withdrawal of the Legion from Corsica (on Sept. 26).

During 1977 the FLNC was said to have carried out

63 attacks against property of "colonialists" (i.e. non-Corsican settlers, mainly from Algeria); it was also responsible for explosions at government offices, a railway station, police stations, a tourist camp and a television relay transmitter near Bastia (on Aug. 13, 1977); and on Jan. 14, 1978, it partly destroyed a French Air Force radar station.

In 1979 it was held responsible for 287 bomb explosions, 32 of them in Paris and Corsica on March 9-10, one at the French Foreign Minister's villa in Corsica on March 18, another at the Palace of Justice in Paris on April 25 and a further 30 explosions in Corsica on May 6-7, and also for 22 bombs placed in Paris on May 30-31. Other bombs were planted by the FLNC in Lyons on Sept. 12-13, 1979, and military fuel tanks were blown up north of Paris on Oct. 25, 1979.

In 1980 there were 378 bomb explosions caused by the FLNC in Corsica. It also claimed responsibility for an attack on security forces guarding the Iranian embassy in Paris on May 14, 1980, when four gendarmes were injured. On April 2, 1981, the FLNC announced that it would halt its bombing campaign until after the presidential elections were completed by May 10 (while it called on Corsicans to abstain from voting in these elections).

Meanwhile, a number of FLNC members had been tried by the State Security Court in Paris. On July 11, 1979, the court sentenced 17 members to imprisonment for from five to 13 years for 36 bomb attacks on public buildings in Corsica and Paris in the previous two years; seven of them were in addition sentenced to concurrent prison terms of from five to 10 years for treason committed on March 25-26, 1977, by blowing up a military communications station in Corsica.

Yves Stella, reported to be the FLNC's "political commissar", who had been arrested in June 1978, was on Sept 29, 1980, given a 15-year sentence for participating in bombings in 1977-78; he was said to have continued to direct FLNC bombing operations from prison for several months after his arrest. On July 9, 1980, another FLNC member was given a 13-year sentence, and two others were sentenced to five years each (with 2½ years suspended) for travelling to Lebanon in March 1978 to obtain arms and training from Palestinian guerrillas.

The FLNC maintained its truce after the election of a left-wing government in Paris in mid-1981; a number of imprisoned Corsican activists were released under a political amnesty granted by President Mitterrand; and the new Socialist Interior Minister, Gaston Defferre, stated his willingness to enter into a dialogue with the Front and other Corsican nationalist groups with reference to the detailed application in Corsica of the government's decentralization plans for the French regions. However, although the new political structure for Corsica (which as eventually enacted in January 1982 provided inter alia for the island to become a "territorial collectivity" with a directly-elected Assembly) was given a qualified welcome by the UPC, it was rejected by the FLNC on the grounds that it maintained the island's "colonial" status in all essentials.

Dissension appeared within the FLNC's ranks when on Sept. 19, 1981, militant members publicly denounced the truce being observed by the Front as a "strategic error"; this development was accompanied by a recurrence of bomb attacks in Corsica for which FLNC dissidents claimed responsibility. Following the enactment of the new Corsican political structure in January 1982, the FLNC demonstrated its opposition by carrying out a "blue night" of violence of Feb. 11-12, during which a Foreign Legionnaire was killed and two injured in an attack on a military camp in Corsica, while some 25 bomb explosions caused severe damage to various official buildings as well as to secondary homes.

In claiming responsibility for the new spate of attacks (which continued over the next few days and included some 20 bombings in Paris on Feb. 16), the FLNC said that they were intended as a warning to the French government that its new measures for Corsica were insufficient. In a communiqué issued on Feb. 12 the Front said inter alia:"Concrete political acts wiping out the symbols of colonialism should have been announced, with their implementation well under way. There has been nothing of the sort. The Front could wait no longer. The new government must rapidly acknowledge the rights of the Corsican people." The communiqué repeated the FLNC's demands for the immediate withdrawal of the Foreign Legion from Corsica, the departure of all French "settlers", the rehabilitation of the Corsican language and culture, and the dismantling of the "clan" system permeating the public life of the island.

Although the FLNC maintained at this stage that the truce remained technically in effect, the February 1982 violence marked its effective end in Corsica (although there was a further lull in attacks on the mainland). Arrests of suspected FLNC activists over the following months were accompanied by a steady escalation of violent incidents, culminating in a major FLNC offensive before and after the August 1982 elections to the new Corsican Assembly in support of the Front's call for a boycott. After 100 bomb explosions marking the election of the Assembly's president on Aug. 20, the FLNC announced at a clandestine press conference during the night of Aug. 24-25 the official "resumption of the armed struggle", which would involve attacks on "continental interests" to bring about "decolonization"and to demonstrate that "the Corsican people and the French colony can no longer cohabit". At the same time, however, the Front declared its intention to maintain the truce on the mainland.

Thereafter the security situation in Corsica rapidly deteriorated, to the extent that by the end of 1982 official statistics gave the number of bomb attacks and other violent incidents for that year at over 800, approaching double the level during 1981; of the 1982 incidents, nearly 50 per cent had been officially claimed by the FLNC. At the end of December 1982 the Front officially confirmed that it was seeking to exact a "revolutionary levy" from residents of mainland origin—several of whom were the subject of attacks after refusing to pay the levy. In the light of this latter development in particular, the French government on Jan. 5, 1983, announced the official banning of the FLNC (which at that time was officially thought to have only about 30 activists and about 200 supporters).

As well as banning the FLNC the French government also reinforced the security forces in Corsica and appointed a new police chief with special powers to combat terrorism; the Front responded with further bombings, but by the end of March 1983 the arrest of more than 100 suspect extremists had contributed to a significant reduction in the level of violent incidents attributed to the FLNC. During this period the French authorities were believed to have accumulated evidence of links between the FLNC and other extremist groups such as the Irish Republican Army (IRA) and the mainland Direct Action movement, and also with an international terrorist group led by Ilich Ramirez Sánchez ("Carlos Martinez"), the Venezuelan revolutionary held responsible for numerous acts of terrorism in various countries during the 1970s.

On the political level the FLNC appeared to moderate its demands when at the end of January 1983 it declared itself ready to accept an "association" between an independent Corsica and the French Republic; at the same time, however, the Front warned that lack of immediate progress towards Corsican self-rule would force it to end the mainland truce. After the security offensive of the next three months, this threat was carried out at the end of April, when some 15 bomb explosions in Paris and its environs on April 29 were officially claimed by the FLNC. Immediately after the Paris bombings the French police announced on May 1 the arrest of a cell of Corsican extremists operating in the capital and the seizure of quantities of explosives.

The FLNC continued its bombing campaign in 1983-84 both in Corsica and on the mainland. It also claimed responsibility for the killing, on Sept. 13, 1983, of the secretary-general of the conseil général of Haute-Corse for his alleged involvement in the abduction and probable murder of Guy Orsoni, a prominent nationalist, in June 1983. Of seven persons arrested in connexion with the Orsoni affair, two were killed on June 7, 1984, by an FLNC commando which broke into the Ajaccio prison. For these two murders, three members of the commando were sentenced, on July 16, 1986, to eight years' imprisonment.

Of more than 600 bomb attacks carried out in Corsica during 1984, the majority were attributed to the FLNC. Persons killed during 1985 included the leader of an Association for a French Republican Corsica (the largest anti-FLNC group), shot dead in Ajaccio on Jan. 31, 1985.

Despite a truce observed by the FLNC between July 1985 and May 1986, a total of 353 bomb attacks were carried out by the FLNC in 1985, and for the year 1986 the FLNC claimed responsibility for 497 "terrorist" attacks in Corsica and 25 actions on the French mainland.

An anonymous caller claiming to represent the FLNC claimed responsibility for the assassination of Dr Jean-Paul Lafay, president of the Association of Aid for Victims of Terrorism in Corsica and a leading opponent of the Corsican separatists, on June 17, 1987; an FLNC spokesman subsequently denied responsibility, however, but police were said to believe the FLNC to be responsible.

The FLNC has staged a sustained campaign of intimidation and bombings against teachers from "the continent", with the objective of forcing them to leave the island, leading to a teachers' strike on May 15, 1987.

French Overseas Departments and Territories

During the 1980s extremist pro-independence movements have become increasingly active in several of the French overseas departments and territories (DOM and TOM), notably in the two Antilles departments of Guadeloupe and Martinique (in the Caribbean), in the department of French Guiana (on the South American mainland) and in the overseas territory of New Caledonia (in the Pacific). Majority political representation remains largely in the hands of local sections of the metropolitan parties which support the maintenance of French status; but the various pro-independence movements appear to be mounting a growing challenge to the longer-established autonomist parties in favour of a gradual loosening of the French connexion.

Economic grievances have figured prominently in the campaigns of both the autonomist and the pro-independence movements in the DOM and TOM. In French Guiana, Guadeloupe and Martinique particular criticism has been directed not only at the high level of local unemployment but also at the increasing emigration of local workers to metropolitan France. A further source of tension in these three departments is the growing influx of White French "settlers", who tend to dominate the local tourist industries as well as other important economic sectors.

In a move to cater for legitimate political aspirations in the overseas departments, the left-wing government which came to power in Paris in mid-1981 eventually secured the enactment in December 1982 of major decentralization measures under which French Guiana, Guadeloupe, Martinique and Réunion (in the Indian Ocean) were each endowed with an Assembly to be elected directly on the basis of proportional representation.

Overseas Departments

FRENCH GUIANA

Increasing unrest in this, the largest overseas French possession (although with a population of only about 60,000), has been mainly associated with the activities of the extremist pro-independence movement described below. By mid-1980 the principal vehicle for non-violent pro-independence opinion in French Guiana was the (Marxist) *Unité Guyanaise* led by Albert Lecante, a former member of the department's Socialist Party (PSG) who had been imprisoned in 1974 for illegal political activities. The PSG responded by radicalizing its traditional autonomist stance into a demand for autonomy as a "necessary and preparatory state" towards the establishment of an independent state.

In the first elections to the new departmental Assembly on Feb. 20, 1983, the PSG-led list secured 14 of the 31 seats, a centre-right list 13, an extreme left-wing list of the (independent) *Union des travailleurs de Guyane* 3 and an independent associated with the PSG 1.

Boni Liberation Front—see under Guiana National Liberation Front

Guiana National Liberation Front (*Front national de libération guyanais*, FNLG)

Leadership. Raymond Charlotte (co-ordinator)

The FNLG leader, Raymond Charlotte, was one of eight French Guiana separatists who were, in December 1974, charged with plotting "to substitute an illegal authority for that of the French state" and were taken to Paris; however, the State Security Court decided on March 12, 1975, to cancel all charges against them, stating inter alia that the authorities in French Guiana had exceeded their powers.

Following bomb attacks at the Kourou space station on April 20, 1980, and a former police building in Cayenne (the capital of French Guiana) on April 22, four suspected FNLG members were on July 15, 1980, flown to Paris to face charges in connexion with these explosions. They included Charlotte and Antoine Aouegui ("Lamoraille"), who had in 1976 helped to form a Boni Liberation Movement to promote nationalist ideas among the Boni people in the Suriname border region. By April 1981 two further pro-independence militants had been arrested and taken to Paris.

Charlotte was released in July 1981 under the terms of a political amnesty granted by the new Socialist President, François Mitterrand, as were the other FLNG detainees in the same period.

GUADELOUPE

A campaign of violence associated with some of the pro-independence movements described below was condemned not only by Guadeloupe's ruling centre-right formations but also by the island's pro-autonomy Communist Party (PCG). In the first elections to the new departmental Assembly on Feb. 20, 1983, the centre-right list won 21 on the 41 seats, the PCG-led list 11 and the local Socialists 9.

Armed Liberation Group (*Groupe de libération armée*, GLA)

This extremist pro-independence group was widely believed to be the armed-action wing of the Popular Union for the Liberation of Guadeloupe (UPLG—see separate entry). It was responsible for 11 acts of violence carried out in Guadeloupe between March and December 1980. It warned all French residents (in March 1980) that those of them who did not leave the island by the end of 1980 would be considered "enemies of the Guadeloupe people" and would be treated as such. The victims of GLA attacks included an army sergeant-major killed while he was trying to defuse a bomb on Sept. 17, 1980.

Claiming responsibility for all attacks carried out in 1980, the GLA announced on Jan. 8, 1981, that it would continue its campaign against "French capitalism and colonialism" both on the island and in metropolitan France. After further acts of violence five suspected GLA members were arrested in March and April 1981 and flown in Paris for trial by the State Security Court. On March 21-22 some 5,000 demonstrators protested in Pointe-à-Pitre (the capital of Guadeloupe) against the transfer to Paris of four of the suspects.

All of the detained GLA activists were released by early July 1981 under a political amnesty granted by the new Socialist President, François Mitterrand. In a "warning" to the left-wing government in Paris the GLA subsequently noted that certain of its members were still due to appear before "colonial tribunals" and continued: "The GLA will oppose any plan supposedly 'specific' to Guadeloupe . . . which seeks to reinforce the economic and political departmentalization of Guadeloupe, [which is] the cause of the ruin and degeneration of our country. Only the national independence of Guadeloupe, with a socialist content, will permit recovery of our country's economy, through the taking of control of the affairs of the country by the Guadeloupians themselves." The statement concluded: "For our part, no compromise, no truce should or can be envisaged—our objective, irrespective of the colour of successive governments in France, being the unconditional accession of our country to national independence."

One of the principal GLA leaders was Luc Reinette, a younger son of a prominent Guadeloupe family, who was one of those detained in Paris in 1981. The following year he announced the formation of his own party, called the Popular Movement for Independent Guadeloupe (see separate entry).

Camus

This clandestine pro-independence cell has claimed responsibility for several violent acts, including the ransacking of government offices in Pointe-à-Pitre.

Committee against Genocide of Blacks by Substitution (*Comité contre le génocide des noirs par substitution*)

This previously unknown group claimed responsibility for starting a fire in the carpark of Pointe-à-Pitre airport during the night of July 30-31, 1982. The group was believed to be demonstrating its opposition to the extent of the French "settler" presence in Guadeloupe. The Committee's name is taken from a slogan used by Aimé Césaire, leader of the Progressive Party of Martinique.

Metro Clandestine Committee of Resisters (*Comité clandestin des résistants métro,* CCRM)

This little-known extremist group favouring the maintenance of Guadeloupe's French status has mounted "punitive" attacks on persons identified with the pro-independence movement.

Movement for the Unification of National Liberation Forces of Guadeloupe (*Mouvement pour l'unification des forces de libération de la Guadeloupe,* MUFLNG)

Leadership. Rosan Mounien (l.)

The MUFLNG was formed in January 1982 as an alliance of pro-independence organizations, notably the Popular Union for the Liberation of Guadeloupe (UPLG—see separate entry), with the aim of "mobilizing the people in joint action to eliminate French colonial domination in Guadeloupe and to attain national independence".

The other components of the Movement are the *Union générale des travailleurs de la Guadeloupe* (UGTG), the *Union des paysans pauvres de la Guadeloupe* (UPPG), the *Syndicat général de l'éducation en Guadeloupe* (SGEG), the *Syndicat des instituteurs, professeurs et agents de la Guadeloupe* (SIPAG), the *Association générale des étudiants Guadeloupéens* (AGEG), the *Union nationale des élèves et étudiants de la Guadeloupe* (UNEEG) and *Chrétiens pour la libération du peuple guadeloupéen* (CLPG).

During the night of Feb. 14-15, 1982, the owner of Guadeloupe's largest banana plantation, Max Martin, was assassinated at his residence at Capesterre on the eastern coast of Basse-Terre. One of the UGTG's affiliated unions, the *Union des travailleurs agricoles* (UTA), was at the time involved in a bitter industrial dispute with Martin.

National Liberation Army (*Armée de libération nationale,* ALN)

The previously unknown ALN claimed responsibility for starting a fire at the premises of the Peugeot concessionaire in Pointe-à-Pitre on April 7, 1982.

Popular Movement for Independent Guadeloupe (*Mouvement populaire pour la Guadeloupe indépendante,* MPGI)

Leadership. Luc Reinette (founder and l.)

This militant pro-independence Movement was launched in June 1982, its founder having earlier been a prominent activist within the Armed Liberation Group (GLA—see separate entry). Two members of the Movement, including Max Safrano (a founding member and prominent trade unionist), were arrested immediately after four bombs had exploded during the night of Aug. 26-27, 1982, causing serious damage to government buildings and other premises.

Popular Union for the Liberation of Guadeloupe (*Union populaire pour la libération de la Guadeloupe,* UPLG)

Leadership. Théodore François (founder)

Established in 1978, this semi-clandestine pro-independence organization succeeded an earlier *Groupe d'organisation nationale guadeloupéene* (GONG), which had been founded in 1958 by students from Guadeloupe in Paris and established on the island in 1964. Together with the Communist Party of Guadeloupe, the GONG had formed a short-lived *Front guadeloupéen pour l'autonomie* (which was divided when the Communists supported François Mitterrand in the presidential elections of December 1965, whereas the GONG called for abstention). The GONG was officially dissolved after disturbances in May 1967.

Théodore François carried on clandestine political activities in the 1970s, and in 1973 he founded the *Union générale des travailleurs de la Guadeloupe* (UGTG) as a rival to the (Communist-led) *Centrale générale des travailleurs guadeloupéens* (CGTG), which, however, remained the island's principal trade union federation. It was initially believed that the Armed Liberation Group (GLA—see separate entry) was the armed wing of the UPLG, but the latter dissociated itself publicly, during 1980, from the GLA's violent actions and claimed that the attacks attributed to the GLA were in fact "police provocations" designed to discredit the independence movement.

In January 1982 the UPLG became a founding component of the broader Movement for the unification of National Liberation Forces (MUFLNG—see separate entry).

Revolutionary Caribbean Alliance (*Alliance révolutionnaire caraïbe,* ARC)

Leadership. Luc Reinette (l.)

This group claimed responsibility for 16 bomb explosions on May 28-29, 1983, in French Guiana (where a man thought to have planted one of the bombs was killed), in Guadeloupe and in Martinique, as well as in Paris. In a communiqué issued afterwards the ARC proclaimed that until "total independence" had been achieved for "our countries" it would "not cease to harass and to strike at our common enemy, French colonialism and its local collaborators wherever they are found". The ARC also stated that its object was "the ejection of the French presence from Guadeloupe, Guiana and Martinique" and the creation of "a new society cleansed of exploitation". It was widely believed that the French Guiana cell of the ARC had been formed by activists of the Guiana National Liberation Front (FNLG).

The ARC was officially dissolved in April 1984, and its leader (who had earlier founded the *Mouvement populaire pour la Guadeloupe indépendante)* was arrested but escaped from prison in June 1985. On Jan. 19, 1987, he launched an appeal for "civil and patriotic resistance". This appeal was accompanied by a message from Prof. Henry Bernard, who had also gone underground and had been charged with attempts and plotting against the security and integrity of the state.

MARTINIQUE

Pro-independence feeling has increased in Martinique in recent years, notably on the left wing of the Progressive Party (PPM) led by Aimé Césaire (one of the department's three deputies in the French National Assembly, where he sits with the Socialist Group). The PPM majority has nevertheless remained committed to the achievement of greater autonomy rather than outright independence as advocated by the groups described below.

In the first elections to the new departmental Assembly on Feb. 20, 1983, the left-wing pro-autonomy formations won a narrow aggregate majority of 21 of the 41 seats (PPM 12, Socialists 5 and Communists 4) against 20 for a list comprising local sections of the centre-right metropolitan parties.

Armed Liberation Group of Martinique (*Groupe de libération armée de la Martinique,* GLA-Martinique)

This Group, said to be an offshoot of the GLA of Guadeloupe, claimed responsibility for attacks carried out in December 1980, including one on the headquarters of French television in Martinique.

Martinique Independence Movement (*Mouvement indépendantiste martiniquais,* MIM, or *La parole au peuple)*

Leadership. Prof. Alfred Marie-Jeanne (l.)

The leader of the Movement, who is Mayor of the town of Rivière-Pilote, declared in March 1980: "It is not through elections that we will take power, but we shall use the *conseil général* and the mayors' offices to help our struggle for revolutionary unity in the Caribbean. We do receive help from other countries (including Cuba and the Soviet Union). . . . Our revolution embraces all solutions, including armed struggle."

The MIM called for abstention in the June 1981 National Assembly elections, regarding the pro-autonomy parties as "using the same language as the departmentalists" and directing particular criticism at Aimé Césaire of the PPM for being the "incorrigible valet of the French state". In the latter part of 1981 there were signs of dissension within the MIM, some members of which resigned in protest against Prof. Marie-Jeanne's personalized style of leadership.

REUNION

Although pro-independence sentiment exists in Réunion, the main political debate in recent years has been over the degree of local autonomy which is appropriate for the island. In this debate the local sections of the metropolitan left-wing parties have argued for more local self-rule in the context of continued French status, whereas the Réunion centre-right formations have resisted changes in that direction and have in particular opposed the new left-wing metropolitan government's December 1982 measures creating a departmental Assembly directly elected by proportional representation.

In the first elections to the new Assembly on Feb. 20, 1983, the combined centre-right list obtained 18 of the 45 seats, the Réunion Communists 16, the Socialists 6 and "various right" candidates 5.

Militant Departmentalist Front (*Front militant départmentaliste,* FMD)

Leadership. Jean Fontaine (founder and l.)

This Front emerged in December 1981 with the aim of preserving Réunion's departmental status as it then existed and of rallying "all the anti-Marxist family" in this cause. The Front's founder and leader is Mayor of Saint-Louis and an unattached deputy in the French National Assembly.

Movement for the Independence of Réunion (*Mouvement pour l'indépendance de la Réunion,* MIR)

This Marxist pro-independence grouping was formed in November 1981 as the successor to the *Mouvement pour la libération de la Réunion* (MPLR), which itself had sprung from the *Organisation communiste marxiste-léniniste de la Réunion* (OCMLR). At its foundation the MIR stated that "the people of Réunion cannot achieve responsibility unless it is . . . totally sovereign" and expressed the view that the government in Paris "can only perpetuate, with the active complicity of the parties of the presidential majority [i.e. of President Mitterrand], the existing colonial situation".

ST PIERRE AND MIQUELON

Unlike the four overseas departments dealt with above, the population of St Pierre and Miquelon (in the north-west Atlantic) is predominantly of French stock and overwhelmingly in favour of retaining the islands' French status. Nevertheless, the elevation of the islands from overseas territorial to overseas departmental status in 1976 has been opposed by substantial sections of the local population, notably the trade unions, which have demanded the application of a "special status" under which St Pierre and Miquelon would enjoy fiscal and customs arrangements suited to its geographical situation while remaining an integral part of the French Republic. Such demands have been pursued through local sections of the metropolitan political formations.

Overseas Territories

FRENCH POLYNESIA

Elections to the territorial Assembly of French Polynesia in May 1977 resulted in the United Front for Internal Autonomy (FUAI) retaining its aggregate majority, following which increased internal autonomy was granted under a bill enacted by the French parliament later in the year and accepted by both government and opposition parties in the archipelago. However, the question of the territory's status was effectively reopened in late 1978 when John Téariki (leader of the *Pupu Here Aia* party, the strongest component of the FUAI) declared his support for an orderly transition to eventual independence, whereas the then political head of the government council, Francis Sanford, stated on behalf of his United Front Party (*Te Eaa Pi*, the other major component of the FUAI) that the future should not be risked with "ill considered decisions".

In further elections to the territorial Assembly in May 1982 the pro-autonomy formations lost their overall majority to the local section of the metropolitan Rally for the Republic (RPR, Gaullist), which opposes any further loosening of the link with Paris. In the May 1982 elections the left-wing *Ta Mana Te Nunaa* formation obtained three of the 30 seats on a platform of seeking independence by way of "class struggle" against "colonialist capitalism"; it has, however, not associated itself with the extremist pro-independence groupings described below.

In early 1985 the independence movement in French Polynesia increased its activities in response to the developments in New Caledonia. A rally held on March 16 by the *Front de libération de la Polynésie* (FLP), a legal party succeeding an earlier *Tavini huiratiraa*, attended by over 1,000 persons, was addressed by two leaders of the New Caledonian *Front de libération nationale kanak et socialiste*, although the territorial government had asked the French authorities to expel them. A monarchist pro-independence movement, the *Pomare parti*, was on several occasions prohibited from holding a march.

The Ancestors' Blood (*Te Toto Tupana*)

This organization was described as an anti-French terrorist group with which the (legal) pro-independence *Te Taata Tahiti Tiama* party led by Charlie Ching was suspected of having co-operated in 1978-79.

Maohi Republic Provisional Government (*Gouvernement provisoire de la République Maohi*)

Leadership. Tetua Mai ("president of the provisional government")

This small pro-independence movement came to prominence when its leader, Tetua Mai, and 40 of his followers were arrested on Aug. 15, 1982, after two local policemen had been briefly held and ill-treated by members of the group. The latter abductions had been carried out after police had the previous day stopped a uniformed group of the movement's members and confiscated their banners. On Aug. 17 Tetua Mai and 16 others were charged with premeditated violence against representatives of public order and other offences.

A section of the Maohi Republic movement, known as the *Pupu tiama Maohi,* took part in the demonstration in favour of the New Caledonian *Front de libération nationale kanak et socialiste* on March 3, 1985.

MAYOTTE

Mayotte, one of the four main islands of the Comoros in the Indian Ocean, has a special status virtually equivalent to that of a French overseas department, with a view to the possible attainment of overseas departmental status if its population so decides in a referendum. Mayotte's population had opted to remain within the French Republic following the July 1975 unilateral declaration of independence by the other three Comoro Islands (whose government has since then claimed sovereignty over the island).

The island's dominant political formation is the *Mouvement populaire mahorais* (MPM) whose leader, Younoussa Bamana, in August 1982 launched an attack on what he described as "pro-Comoros intellectuals" resident in metropolitan France for having distributed a tract blaming the French presence for the island's economic and social difficulties. The tract appeared during a general strike called by the *Union des travailleurs de Mayotte* (UTM).

NEW CALEDONIA

In elections to the New Caledonian Territorial Assembly held in July 1979 the (pre-dominantly Melanesian, or Kanak) pro-independence parties allied within the *Front indépendantiste* (FI) retained 14 of the 36 seats, whereas the (Gaulist) Popular Caledonian Rally for the Republic (RPCR) secured 15 and the (autonomist) Federation for a New Caledonia (FNSC) 7. In that consultation, parties favouring the maintenance of the territory's French status (with varying degrees of internal autonomy) obtained 65.6 per cent of the vote and the pro-independence formation 34.4 per cent, although the support of the latter among the Melanesian population amounted to about 60 per cent of voters. (New Caledonia's population of about 135,000 then comprised some 60,000 Melanesians, 50,000 Europeans and 25,000 Polynesians and others.)

The metropolitan government took the view that on the basis of the July 1979 election result New Caledonia had the opportunity to enjoy political stability and economic progress and made it clear that any violent attempt to challenge the existing status of the territory would be firmly resisted by the authorities. However, speaking in Paris on Oct. 29, 1979, the FI leader, Roch Pidjot, denounced "French colonialism and imperialism in the Pacific" and declared that "by its obstinate refusal to grant the Kanak people sovereignty in their own country" the French government bore full responsibility for the "inevitable" confrontation to come.

In opposition the FI and its constituent formations adopted an increasingly radical approach to the independence issue, including the drawing up of plans for the occupation of European-owned plantations by Front supporters with the aim of gaining control of enough territory in which to make an early declaration of independence. Moreover, the most militant of the pro-independence movements, the Kanak Liberation Party (Palika), has been associated with various acts of violence, including disturbances during a demonstration on July 13, 1980, for which three Palika members were sentenced to imprisonment.

The conflict between those favouring independence (mainly Melanesians) and those opposing it (mainly Europeans and other population groups) was greatly intensified by the assassination on Sept. 19, 1981, of Pierre Declercq, a French Roman Catholic school teacher and secretary-general of the Caledonian Union (UC), the principal party within the FI. A young European was arrested as the suspected murderer but denied any involvement and was later released on bail pending further inquiries. Acts of violence during the ensuing months included an attack on a hotel on the east coast of the main island by some 50 Melanesians on Oct. 10-11, 1981, when three police officers were injured, and incidents in Nouméa (the capital) on Nov. 6-7, involved attacks on Whites, damage to property and looting, with six policemen being injured and 88 people arrested.

On the other hand, Europeans staged demonstrations against a pro-independence administration installed in June 1982 after the FNSC had broken with the RPCR and entered a coalition with the FI under the leadership of Jean-Marie Tjibaou (UC). Europeans also protested against proposed reforms which would give imposed economic and social rights to Melanesians and enable officials to expropriate White-owned land for the benefit of the traditional tribal owners. From such a demonstration some 250 Europeans broke away on July 27, 1982, invaded the Assembly and fought with politicians; police intervened and arrested 10 people, while 19 policemen were injured; 17 persons were later charged with possessing arms and other dangerous objects and with using violence against the police force.

In further violence early in 1983, two policemen were killed and four injured when Melanesian tribesmen ambushed a convoy carrying equipment for a timber plant in the La Foa area 60 miles north of Nouméa. On Jan. 13 a total of 18 Melanesians were charged with involvement in the ambush, which was seen as reflecting local concern over environmental damage allegedly being caused by the plant to which the convoy had been proceeding.

In widespread political disturbances between Nov. 13 and Dec. 31, 1984, a total of 107 road blocks were erected, 15 bombs exploded, 96 cars or buildings were burnt, 41 buildings were ransacked and 12 Kanaks died in act of violence.

The French high commissioner proclaimed a state of emergency and imposed a curfew on Jan. 12, 1985. On Feb. 13 the French government notified the Council of Europe that it had temporarily suspended the relevant clause of the European Convention on Human Rights in respect of New Caledonia. After the curfew had been relaxed on two occasions, it was lifted on May 3, but it was reimposed on May 8 following 10 hours of rioting on that day. It was eventually lifted on June 14, and the state of emergency was ended on June 30, 1985.

In 1984-85 the French government made various proposals for the future constitutional development in New Caledonia.

A new statute for the territory, approved by the French National Assembly on July 31, 1984, provided for changes in the local legislature for a period up to a referendum to be held in 1989 on the options of independence or continued association with France. The FI, however, sought independence by 1986 at the latest. Some elements of the RPCR regarded certain sections of the proposed statute as discriminating in favour of the Melanesians (Kanaks) who accounted for 43 per cent of the total population (then 145,000). The FI decided by a majority vote at an extraordinary convention held on July 28 to apply an "active boycott" to elections scheduled for later in 1984, and to withdraw progressively from participating in territorial and metropolitan institutions. (The minority faction of the FI thereupon decided to form the *Front de libération nationale kanak et socialiste*, FLNKS, which demanded inter alia that the franchise for the proposed referendum should be restricted to Kanaks, or at least to all those who had lived in New Caledonia for a considerable time.)

The proposed elections to the Territorial Assembly were held on Nov. 18, 1984, when there was a turnout of 39,296 out of the 78,271 registered voters and the RPCR gained 34 of the 42 seats.

A "Pisani plan" announced on Jan. 7, 1985, provided for the maintenance of the Territorial Assembly for the near future and the holding of a referendum in July 1985; if the result favoured independence there would be a form of associated statehood by 1986 and gradual progress to fuller independence; all land would revert to Kanak ownership, with very long-term leases for French settlers of long standing; and Nouméa would have a special status. The plan was rejected outright by the RPCR, while the FLNKS gave it a guarded welcome but added that, if the referendum rejected the plan, the FLNKS would continue to demand independence.

A new "Fabius plan", announced by the French government on April 25, 1985, provided for the creation of four regional councils (of which the FLNKS could expect to control at least two) and the postponement of the referendum until "before the end of 1987". The plan was well received by the FLNKS and the (centre left) *Libération kanake socialiste* (LKS) party, but on May 30 it was rejected by the Territorial Assembly by 30 votes to one.

A revised form of the Fabius plan was adopted by the French National Assembly on Aug. 20, 1985, and elections for the four new regional councils were held on Sept. 29 of that year, the principal contestants being the FLNKS and the RPCR. The result was that the FLNKS obtained a majority of seats in the northern and central regions and in the Loyauté Islands, but that the overall majority of seats was obtained by the RPCR (which in the southern region gained 17 of the 21 seats). Over 80 per cent of the Kanak voters had voted for the pro-independence parties, but 60 per cent of the total votes had been cast for parties opposed to independence.

The 46 elected representatives of the regional councils formed the new Territorial Congress which was controlled by the RPCR.

A bill proposing an amnesty for crimes against property committed before Sept. 29, 1985, was passed by the French National Assembly on Dec. 2 and became effective on Jan. 1, 1986.

Outbreaks of violence, however, continued during the six months following the elections. On Nov. 15, 1986, a 14-year-old boy was killed and 12 persons were injured in a clash between RPCR and FLNKS supporters in Thio.

Caledonian Front (*Front calédonien*, FC)

Leadership. Claude Sarran (pres.)

Founded. 1981

The leader of this ultra-right group was given a three-month prison sentence for an attack on the Territorial Assembly in mid-1982. In the 1984 elections the FC campaigned for the National Front list. On Feb. 21, 1985, the French high commissioner ordered the expulsion from New Caledonia of C. Sarran and four FC supporters, but they were able to evade being expelled.

The FC claimed to have 300 members, most of whom were thought to be metropolitan or ex-Algerian French.

Crisis Committee (*Comité de crise*)

This secret committee was formed in January 1985 by a group of Frenchmen resettled in New Caledonia from Algeria (known as *pieds-noirs*). Some members of the Committee were arrested between June 7 and 10, 1985, and several of these were charged in connexion with bombings carried out in Nouméa on May 13, and others with running an extortion racket.

Movement for Order and Peace (*Mouvement pour l'ordre et la paix*, MOP)

This Movement was founded in 1979 by Europeans in opposition to extremist Melanesian pro-independence elements. Early in January 1980 an off-duty police inspector (who according to pro-independence sources was an MOP member) shot and killed a Melanesian youth—which led to increased unrest among the pro-independence Melanesians.

National and Socialist Kanak Liberation Front (*Front de libération nationale kanak et socialiste*, FLNKS)

Leadership. Jean-Marie Tjibaou (l.); Yéweiné Yéweiné (sec.-gen.)

The FLNKS was formed in July 1984 by a minority faction of the *Front indépendantiste* (FI) led by the *Libération kanake socialiste* (LKS) and containing elements of the *Union calédonienne* (UC) and the *Front uni de libération kanake* (FULK), all of whom withdrew from the FI. The FLNKS was also joined by the *Union progressiste mélanesienne* (UPM), the *Parti socialiste calédonien* and the *Parti de libération kanake* (Palika), as well as trade unions, protestant church leaders, cultural movements, women's groups and other favouring rapid progress towards independence. The constituent congress of the FLNKS held on Sept. 22-24, 1984, called for the establishment of local committees which would designate delegates to an assembly which was to meet on Nov. 24-25; this assembly was to elect 32 deputies who would choose from their number an eight-member provisional government to be formally constituted on Dec. 1 and to proclaim, by Sept. 24, 1985, at the latest, the independence of New Caledonia as "a centralized, democratic and socialist republic" to be known as Kanaky.

On Dec. 1, 1984, the FLNKS raised the (red, green and blue) Kanak flag some five miles from Nouméa and held a ceremony to swear in the provisional government of Kanaky with Jean-Marie Tjibaou as "Prime Minister". On the following day FLNKS militants seized a large number of weapons from Europeans and Wallisians in the Thio area, and burnt down the house of Dick Ukeiwé (the President of the territorial government and RPR member of the French Senate), whereas the house of J.-M. Tjibaou was bombed by anti-independence activists.

Following serious disturbances and the imposition of a state of emergency on Jan. 12, 1985, a confrontation took place between FLNKS supporters and police at La Foa, where Eloi Machoro, until then secretary-general of the FLNKS, and his deputy were shot dead by sharpshooters. Further acts of violence followed. On Jan. 21 sabotage at the Thio nickel mine caused damage estimated at US$3,000,000; the FLNKS denied responsibility but stated that the mine would not be reopened until 87 "political prisoners" had been released. In connexion with another attack on a mine at Kouaoua on Jan. 22, six FLNKS members were arrested on Jan. 28.

Late in January 1985 the FLNKS confirmed that 17 of its members, including E. Machoro, had visited Libya, but it denied reports that it had received material support from foreign powers and declared that it could not and would not mount a full-scale military campaign against the French government. (The FLNKS received moral support from the governments of Australia and New Zealand as well as of Papua New Guinea, the Solomon Islands and Vanuatu, from the ruling National Liberation Front of Algeria and from the Greens in the Federal Republic of Germany and in the European Parliament.)

At a congress held on Feb. 9-10, 1985, the FLNKS decided on a dual strategy of dialogue with the government and "actions of destabilization" by its 32 committees of resistance and self-defence. However, a call made by the FLNKS on Feb. 28, 1985, for a boycott of the government schools and for the establishment of Kanak schools was unsuccessful.

Despite a ban on all demonstrations, both the FLNKS and the (anti-independence) RPCR held rallies which often led to clashes. In 10 hours of rioting on May 8, 1985, a Kanak student was killed and 103 people were injured in Nouméa.

At a congress held on May 25-26, 1985, the FLNKS voted in favour of taking part in regional elections but reaffirmed its goal of independence and decided to maintain its "provisional government" until at least Dec. 31, 1985, although J.-M. Tjibaou had, in an action brought by the territorial government, been sentenced by a Paris court on May 14 to one year in prison suspended and a fine for "conspiracy against the integrity of the national territory".

Socialist Kanak Liberation (*Libération kanake socialiste*, LKS)

Leadership. Nidoish Naisseline (l.)

The leader of this movement, one of the most extremist advocates of independence for New Caledonia, declared after the assassination of the secretary-general of the Caledonian Union in September 1981 that his group would continue the struggle for independence, so far waged by the murdered leader, until final victory; he alleged that "fascist groups" were threatening the lives of elected pro-independence representatives. On Nov. 10, 1981, the LKS put demands to the French high commissioner for initiating the process of decolonization, the dissolution of extreme right-wing movements and the requisition of all weapons.

The LKS was a member of the Independence Front (FI) but in 1984 it became the leader of the minority group of the FI which broke away to form the *Front de libération nationale kanak et socialiste* (FLNKS). In the regional elections of Sept. 29, 1985, however, the LKS gained only one seat (in the Loyauté Islands).

WALLIS AND FUTUNA ISLANDS

There have been no reports of active pro-independence movements in the Wallis and Futuna Islands (a French overseas territory situated in the Pacific north of Fiji and west of Samoa). In the June 1981 French National Assembly elections the one Wallis and Futuna seat was retained by a representative of the local section of the (Gaullist) Rally for the Republic (RPR), which kept this seat in the 1986 elections.

Gabon

Capital: Libreville

Pop. 1,150,000

The Gabonese Republic has an executive President who is elected for a seven-year term by universal adult suffrage and who is head of state and of the government, presiding over a Cabinet under a Prime Minister. There is a 120-member National Assembly, also elected for a seven-year term. On March 3, 1985, voters approved (by universal adult suffrage) a list of 111 candidates selected on Feb. 17 by officials of the Gabonese Democratic Party (*Parti démocratique gabonais,* PGD, the country's sole legal party) from a list of 268 candidates (all being members of the PDG). Another nine members were nominated to the Assembly by President Omar Bongo who was, on Nov. 9, 1986, re-elected with over 99 per cent of the votes cast (as officially announced).

Movement for National Renewal (*Mouvement de redressement national,* Morena)

Leadership. Max Anicet Koumba Mbadinga (president)

This Movement was named as the leading opponent of the regime among students at the Omar Bongo National University in Libreville, which was closed from Dec. 14, 1981, to Jan. 11, 1982, because of a student strike begun on Dec. 5. Morena had claimed that the regime was corrupt and and failed to promote the country's development. During the disturbances caused by the student strike leaflets were distributed calling for the creation of a second political party (in addition to the ruling Gabonese Democratic Party). Among persons arrested at the time was the rector of the university, who was dismissed from his post. President Bongo said on Feb. 20, 1982, that the Constitution did not allow for a multi-party system and that the only way in which Morena could come to power was through a coup d'état.

Charges made against those arrested included (i) participating in the creation of a movement aiming to change the constitutional regime; (ii) participating in actions and manoeuvres aimed at jeopardizing the security of the state: (iii) acting in a manner likely to disturb the implementation of state laws and regulations and (iv) abusing the head of state. In a trial which ended on Nov. 26, 1982, a total of 29 defendants were given sentences ranging from 18 months in prison to 20 years' hard labour (the latter being given to the former rector of the university and a former Minister of Education arrested in early 1982). Following an appeal by Amnesty International for the release of the 29 convicted persons, the President announced on March 11, 1983, that the sentences would be reduced by five years; this meant that seven prisoners were released immediately. Six of those convicted in Nov. 1982, described as the last political prisoners being held in Gabon, were released by President Bongo in August 1985 as part of an amnesty to mark the country's 25th anniversary of independence.

The formation of a "government in exile", composed largely of Morena members and with M. A. K. Mbadinga (then Morena secretary-general) as "Prime Minister", was announced in Paris in August 1985. An extraordinary Morena Congress in Paris in March 1987 resulted in M. A. K. Mbadinga being elected president in succession to Paul Mba-Adessole, who had previously sought to dismiss Mbadinga from the organization.

The Gambia

Capital: Banjul Pop. 670,000

The Republic of The Gambia, a member of the Commonwealth, has a President who is elected by direct universal adult suffrage and is head of state as well as of government. There is a House of Representatives with 36 elective seats and eight other seats filled by four nominated members and four head chiefs (elected by the country's Chiefs in Assembly). Both the President and the House of Representatives are elected for five-year terms.

As a result of elections held on May 11, 1987, the elective seats in the House of Representatives were distributed as follows: Progressive People's Party (PPP) 31, National Convention Party 5. Parties which contested the elections without gaining any seats were the Gambian People's Party and the People's Democratic Organization for Independence and Socialism.

On Feb. 1, 1982, The Gambia joined the Republic of Senegal in a Confederation of Senegambia, in which both states retained their independence and sovereignty, but agreed on the integration of their armed forces and security forces, economic and monetary union, and co-ordination in the fields of external relations, communications and other fields in which the confederal state might agree to exercise joint jurisdiction. The Confederation has a President (the President of Senegal), a Vice-President (the President of The Gambia), a Council of Ministers and a Confederal Assembly (one-third of its members to be chosen by the Gambian House of Representatives and two-thirds by Senegal's National Assembly).

Prior to the establishment of the Confederation, Senegalese forces had in July 1981 played a key role in overcoming an attempted coup in The Gambia by left-wing elements opposed to the government of President Sir Dawda Jawara.

Gambian Socialist Revolutionary Party (GSRP)

Leadership. Pingon Georges (l.)

The GSRP was banned on Nov. 1, 1980 as a "terrorist organization".

Movement for Justice in Africa (Moja-Gambia)

Established in 1979, this Movement took its name from a Liberian formation then in opposition to the government of President William Tolbert. The government banned the Movement on Nov. 1, 1980, and later that month the President described it as a "terrorist organization" which was under investigation in connexion with the burning of boats in Gambian ports.

The founder of this Movement, Koro Sallah, was killed in the attempted coup of July 1981.

National Liberation Party

This small left-wing opposition party was formed in October 1975 and was an unsuccessful contender in the 1977 general elections. Its leader, Cheyassin Papa Secka, was one of five people sentenced to death on June 18, 1982, after being found quilty of participating in the unsuccessful coup attempt of July 1981 led by the Socialist and Revolutionary Labour Party (see separate entry).

Socialist and Revolutionary Labour Party (SRLP)

Leadership. Kukli Samba Sanyang (l.)

This party's leader had unsuccessfully contested the 1977 general elections as a candidate of the (opposition) National Convention Party before he became a Marxist-Leninist and founded the SRLP in 1978 as a vehicle for revolutionary change. In the absence of President Sir Dawda Jawara in London (for the wedding of Prince Charles) the SRLP, supported by elements of the paramilitary Field Force, staged a coup on July 29-30, 1981, and formed a National Revolutionary Council (NRC) consisting of nine SRLP members and three Field Force officers. On July 30 the NRC announced the suspension of the Constitution; accused the President's government of "corruption, tribalism, social oppression and creating a bourgeois class"; and added that there was to be a "dictatorship of the proletariat" led by a "Marxist-Leninist party".

The rebels also freed and armed prisoners from the prison in Banjul, and this action was followed by looting (especially of shops owned by Lebanese and Indian traders) and indiscriminate killing, whereby the rebels lost much of the initial support they had gained in Banjul. On July 30 the President invoked a mutual defence agreement with Senegal, and a Senegalese task force, eventually 2,700 men strong, subdued the rebellion within a week and released hostages taken by the rebels, who fled. A state of emergency having been declared on Aug. 2, a total of 814 persons, including some opposition politicians, were arrested. In trials held later in 1981 and the first half of 1982, a total of 27 Gambians were sentenced to death for high treason (by participating in the attempted coup); they included three members of the NRC. Kukli Samba Sanyang and nine of his supporters, who had fled to Guinea-Bissau, were later expelled from that country (as announced by the President of Guinea-Bissau on April 6, 1982), but it was not stated which country had received them.

In July 1982 nine more officers and civilians were sentenced to death; another death sentence was passed in December 1983; and there followed two more on Jan. 31, 1984, and another 24 on April 24, 1984. It was subsequently reported that a number of death sentences had been commuted to life imprisonment by the President, and that no executions had taken place.

German Democratic Republic

Capital: East Berlin

Pop. 16,660,000

Under a Constitution adopted in 1968 the "supreme organ of state power" in the German Democratic Republic (GDR) is the unicameral Parliament (People's Chamber or *Volkskammer*) of 500 seats filled by members of the (communist) Socialist Unity Party (SED), as well as by members of four other parties and of mass organizations. The *Volkskammer* elects a council of State (whose Chairman is in effect the head of state) and a Council of Ministers (Cabinet). Real power, however, is held by the Politburo of the Central Committee of the SED.

There has been no organized internal opposition in recent years, but criticism of the regime has been expressed occasionally by small groups and by some dissident intellectuals. There has been freedom of worship for the Protestant Churches (of some 8,000,000 members), the Roman Catholic Church (with about 1,300,000) and other Churches. The Protestant Churches in particular have accepted the existing social and political order as "ordained by God" and have increasingly co-operated with the authorities since 1978, though not without criticizing the introduction of compulsory military education in schools as from Sept. 1, 1978.

In 48 amendments to the GDR penal code, passed by the *Volkskammer* on June 28, 1979, and in force from Aug. 1 of that year, increased prison sentences were provided for internal security offences, and new offences were introduced for the collection and communication of "treasonable" secret or non-secret information and "possessing illegal connexions" with a view to communicating critical material to the foreign press and to publishing abroad books or manuscripts not registered with the GDR authorities.

New laws on military service and on the state border, passed by the *Volkskammer* on March 25, 1982, contained inter alia an order (previously part of military secret orders) for border guards to shoot citizens trying to escape to West Berlin or West Germany if a warning shout or shot was ignored. (Since 1961 some 180 would-be escapers were thought to have been killed.)

In a report completed on July 31, 1986, by the GDR Committee for Human Rights it was stated inter alia: "The mass media in the GDR are public property. Therefore the contradiction between the right to freedom of opinion and freedom of information and the rule of private press corporations over the mass media and 'free' information flow does not exist in this country. . . . As far as the content of the right to freedom of opinion is concerned, it is significant that the Constitution of the GDR explicitly stipulates that this right has to be exercised in accordance with the spirit and aims of the Constitution. In this country the working class and its alliance partners have eradicated capitalism by revolutionary means and they will not allow it to be restored."

A West Berlin Working Group for Human Rights stated in 1979 that since 1949 there had been some 100,000 political trials in the GDR, with 167 persons having been condemned to death and 590 to life imprisonment. A West German working party claimed on June 14, 1984, that there were some 9,500 political prisoners in the GDR (against 5,000 in 1982). About 2,000 of them were alleged to be conscientious objectors and 70 per cent persons convicted of trying to escape to the West (as stated in the *New York Times* on July 27, 1984). Prison sentences were, however, said to be generally only half as long as previously. During 1984 some 40,000 East Germans were permitted to leave the GDR as legal émigrés. In addition 2,121 prisoners were allowed to leave against payments by the West German government. In 1985 some 25,000 East Germans were said to have been resettled in West Germany. According to unofficial reports there had been between 600 and 750 successful escapes per annum in the latter part of the 1970s but only 190 in 1984. According to the West Berlin Working Party 2,341 political prisoners were released to the West in 1984, and 2,497 in 1985.

On Oct. 22, 1982, the SED politburo member responsible for science and culture had stated in a speech that East German authors who had been granted exit visas and continued to visit the GDR but still criticized this country would lose their GDR citizenship. However, on March 7, 1985, the GDR government announced that émigrés who wished to return to the GDR because of their disillusionment with the West would be allowed to come home.

Major clashes were reported in East Berlin on June 6-8, 1987, when police attempted to break up groups of youths assembled near the Berlin wall to listen to open air rock concerts in West Berlin. The crowd, chanted "The wall must go", and "Gorbachev!, Gorbachev!" (i.e. in reference to the *glasnost* policies of Mr Gorbachev in the Soviet Union, which had not been reflected in East Germany).

On July 17, 1987, the East German authorities announced an amnesty (effective in October) for all prisoners except Nazi war criminals, spies, murderers and people convicted of crimes against humanity, and the abolition of the death penalty (effective immediately). The West German sources suggested that the amnesty would apply to an estimated 2,000 persons imprisoned for political offences.

Dissent within the Churches

The leaders of the Protestant Churches in the GDR were greatly disturbed by the suicide of two of their pastors in 1976 and 1978 respectively.

The Rev. Oskar Brüsewitz set himself on fire at Zeitz (south of Leipzig) on Aug. 18, 1976, and died four days later; he was said to have acted in protest against "the suppression of youth" by communism. A Church spokesman declared on Aug. 22 that the impediments and restrictions imposed on young Christians and on church life had repeatedly been discussed with the state authorities and that a government which had signed the Helsinki Final Act could expect to be asked to what extent it was ready to observe freedom of religion and of conscience.

The Rev. Rolf Guenther burnt himself to death in his church at Falkenstein (near Plauen) on Sept. 17, 1978, allegedly in apparent despair at the lack of Christian piety in his community; it was also alleged that he had wished to protest against compulsory military education in the (state-controlled) schools of the GDR.

In a petition to the government the Roman Catholic Bishops' Conference had on June 12, 1978, objected to the measure as "education for hatred", and on Sept. 24 of that year the Protestant Churches also protested against the "idealization of military life and the minimization of the consequences of war" resulting from the introduction of such military education.

In 1981 protests against the "growing militarization" of the East German society were supported by some church groups which called for (i) a "social peace service" to be made available for conscientious objectors and (ii) an end to pre-military training for 15-16-year-old school children. (Conscientious objection for religious reasons had been admitted in 1964 but objectors still had to serve in "construction brigades" which were part of the army.)

A "Berlin Appeal" calling for the withdrawal of both Soviet and Western Allied troops from Germany, with both sides guaranteeing non-intervention in the two German states, was launched on Jan. 25, 1982, by an East Berlin pastor, Rainer Eppelmann; it was said to have obtained some 700 signatures.

An emblem containing the words "Swords into ploughshares" worn by peace supporters was officially banned in 1982 on the ground that it had been "misused to express a way of thinking hostile to the state and to participation in an illegal movement"; young people wearing the emblem face expulsion from school or loss of their apprenticeship. A number of members of peace groups were arrested and sentenced to imprisonment, among them those of a Jena peace circle who had organized a silent march on Dec. 24, 1982. In January 1983 Roman Catholic bishops published a pastoral letter outlining their attitude towards peace issues, criticizing the military education in schools and maintaining that conscientious objectors should not be disadvantaged for their beliefs.

In 1984, 40,000 dissidents, including many Lutheran priests, and other peace group supporters, were allowed or persuaded to leave East Germany. By late 1984 the members of unofficial peace groups were estimated at no more than 2,000.

In November 1984 members of the peace movement issued a joint statement with the Charter 77 group in Czechoslovakia protesting against the deployment of Soviet intermediate-range nuclear missiles in the GDR and Czechoslovakia.

By December 1986 the residual unofficial peace movement reportedly comprised about 27 groups with about a dozen members each.

Federal Republic of Germany

Capital: Bonn Pop. 61,020,000

The Federal Republic of Germany is, under its Basic Law (Constitution) of 1949, "a democratic and social federal state" whose organs are (i) the federal Diet (*Bundestag*) elected by universal adult suffrage for a four-year term; (ii) the federal Council (*Bundesrat*) consisting of 45 members of the governments of the Republic's 10 *Länder* (constituent states) and of West Berlin; (iii) the federal President elected for a five-year term by the Federal Assembly (*Bundesversammlung*) consisting of the members of the *Bundestag* and an equal number of delegates nominated by the *Länder* parliaments; and (iv) the federal government consisting of the federal Chancellor elected by the *Bundestag* on the proposal of the federal President and of ministers appointed by the President upon the proposal of the Chancellor.

Of the *Bundestag*'s 518 members, 248 are elected by simple majority vote in single-member constituencies; another 248 by proportional representation from party lists for each *Land*; and 22 nominated by the House of Representatives of West Berlin (but having no voting rights in the *Bundestag*). To qualify for representation in the *Bundestag* a party must gain at least 5 per cent of the total national votes cast or secure the election of at least three of its candidates by votes in the constituencies. Parties are legally defined as being a constitutionally necessary element of a free democratic order and as contributing to the formation of the national political will, inter alia by influencing public opinion, by encouraging public participation in political life and by training citizens for the assumption of public office.

As a result of elections to the *Bundestag* held on Jan. 25, 1987, parties gained seats as follows: Social Democratic Party 186, Christian Democratic Union 174, Christian Social Union 49, Free Democratic Party 46, and *Die Grünen* (the Greens—ecologists opposed to nuclear weapons) 42. Parties which contested the elections without gaining any seats were the Bavaria Party (*Bayernpartei*), Citizens of Voting Age (*Mündige Bürger*), Patriots for Germany (*Patrioten für Deutschland*), German Centre Party (*Deutsche Zentrumspartei*), Marxist-Leninist Party of Germany, Christian Bavarian People's Party—Movement of Bavarian Patriots, All Socially Insured People and Pensioners and Free German Labour Party. Parties not taking part in the elections were the Republicans and the (pro-Soviet) German Communist Party (the latter having called on its supporters to vote for the Social Democrats or the Greens).

On Jan. 27, 1972, the federal government issued guidelines for checking political affiliations of job applicants, making provision for a so-called *Berufsverbot* barring from public service employment (including teaching and working in local government services) anyone who was engaged in "activities against the Constitution" or who was a member of (right- or left-wing) organizations regarded as hostile to the Constitution. A committee campaigning against the *Berufsverbot* stated in 1985 that since 1972 about 6,500,000 job applicants had been checked and that proceedings had been taken or bans on employment imposed in about 7,000 cases. (In Saarland the *Land* government revoked the *Berufsverbot* on June 25, 1985, and on the following day two courts ruled that the *Berufsverbot* did not apply to members of the (legal) German Communist Party.)

On Dec. 5, 1986, the *Bundestag* passed a bill designed to increase the effectiveness of existing measures to curb extremist attacks, including a wider definition of terrorist action and the introduction, for a limited period, of the practice of using "state evidence" whereby criminals could expect milder sentences for agreeing to give "supergrass" testimony against their accomplices in cases of terrorist crimes. (The bill was criticized by the opposition which claimed that the use of "supergrasses" had not proved successful in Italy and the United Kingdom.)

Extreme Right-wing Groups

The federal Ministry of the Interior stated in December 1983 that "right-wing extremist action [could] no longer be passively accepted". It was said that 52 violent attacks had been committed by neo-Nazis in 1983 alone, and that of the 1,400 neo-Nazis known to the authorities 300 were considered to be militants.

In a federal government statement of May 9, 1985, it was reported that the number of neo-Nazis organizations had risen from 16 in 1983 to 34 in 1984. The (opposition) Social Democratic Party, however, had claimed in September 1984 that it had details of 158 neo-Nazi and other extreme right-wing organizations. According to the (federal) Ministry of the Interior the neo-Nazi organizations had 22,000 members and had been responsible for 74 violent incidents in 1984.

Charges were brought on Feb. 1, 1987, against 104 individuals who had allegedly gathered in West Berlin the previous day to form a neo-Nazi Free German Workers' Party (*Freiheitliche Deutsche Arbeiterpartei*); the existence of such groups in Berlin was forbidden by the Allied forces.

Action Front of National Socialists/National Action (*Aktionsfront Nationaler Sozialisten/Nationale Aktion* ANS/NA)

Following police raids on the homes of 70 neo-Nazis from whom membership cards, right-wing literature and emblems were seized, this organization was banned on Dec. 7, 1983. On Jan. 7-8, 1984, Michael Kühnen and 11 other persons were arrested for attempting to found a similar organization. On Jan. 25, 1985, Kühnen was sentenced to three years and four months in prison while Arnd Heinz Marx (already serving a 27-month sentence for assault) was given a 2½-year sentence, both for spreading anti-constitutional propaganda; they were also banned from voting and taking public office for five and three years respectively.

On Dec. 17, 1986, a West Berlin court imposed prison sentences ranging from six to 18 months on three activists who had tried to set up a branch of the organization in West Berlin (with one of them having committed offences against the Allied presence in West Berlin).

Conservative Action (*Konservative Aktion*)

Leadership. Ludek Pachmann (l.)

Founded. 1981

This organization, said to have 45,000 members, held a meeting in Hamburg on Nov. 30, 1985, to demand the release from Spandau prison of Rudolf Hess, Hitler's former deputy, serving a life sentence. Some 2,000 people demonstrated against the holding of the meeting and clashed with police.

German Action Groups (*Deutsche Aktionsgruppen*)

This organization claimed responsibility for an attack on Feb. 22, 1980, on an exhibition on the Auschwitz concentration camp—condemning the exhibition as "anti-German agitation". The organization was also suspected of having been involved in an attack on a hostel in Hamburg housing 211 Vietnamese refugees in August 1980, when one of the refugees was killed and another died later of burns. (Several other bomb attacks obviously also directed against foreigners took place in various localities during 1980.)

Michael Kühnen, described as an organizer of these groups, was sentenced to imprisonment on Jan. 25, 1985 (see entry for Action Front of National Socialists).

Hoffmann Defence Sport Group (*Wehrsportgruppe Hoffmann*)

Leadership. Karl-Heinz Hoffmann (l.)

Following the establishment of this organization in 1974, Karl-Heinz Hoffmann was in 1977 given a suspended prison sentence for involvement in an attack on left-wing students at Tübingen University; in November 1979 he was convicted of wearing Nazi insignia and an illegal uniform in public. After the organization was said to have conducted paramilitary manoeuvres near Nuremberg as "an element in the formation of an illegal military unit", the Group was banned by the federal Ministry of the Interior on Jan. 30, 1980. On that day police raided a number of premises in Baden-Württemberg, Bavaria and Hesse and confiscated an armoured vehicle, an anti-aircraft gun and large quantities of firearms, ammunition and other military equipment assembled by the Group.

Members of the Group were suspected of having caused a bomb explosion in Munich on Sept. 26, 1980, when 13 persons were killed and over 200 injured (one of those killed being a member of the Group). On June 23, 1981, it was reported that the Group had planned a kidnapping with the object of enforcing the release from Spandau prison of Rudolf Hess (the former Nazi leader serving a life sentence for war crimes).

K.-H. Hoffmann was known to have paid several visits to the Middle East for the purpose of buying military-type vehicles. Two other members of the Group—Franz Joachim Bojarsky and Klaus Hubel—were arrested by Italian police on Jan. 18, 1982, at Avellano (Abruzzi), where arms and ammunition were found; the two arrested men were said to have recently returned from Lebanon.

Those members of the Group who returned from Lebanon did not reconstitute the Group but their influence was said to have continued in the German Action Groups and the People's Socialist Movement of Germany—Party of Labour (see separate entries).

On Jan. 19, 1983, K.-H. Hoffmann was charged with involvement in the murder of Shlomo Levin, a Jewish publisher, and his woman companion in Erlangen on Dec. 19, 1980. The alleged perpetrator of the murders, Uwe Behrend, was reported to have committed suicide in Lebanon in the latter half of 1981. On June 30, 1986, K.-H. Hoffmann was sentenced to 9½ years in prison for grievous bodily harm caused to members of his Group, illegal possession of arms, forging currency, and the kidnapping of a member of his Group. For lack of evidence he was acquitted of the murder of Shlomo Levin.

On Jan. 23, 1987, three former members of the Group were sentenced to imprisonment for from 27 months and 4½ years for forging money, the causing of bodily harm, deprivation of liberty and intimidation.

The Group was estimated to have had some 80 active members and 400 sympathizers and to have aimed at destroying the existing social order in Germany and replacing it by an authoritarian ("*Führer*") state.

Liberal German Workers' Party (*Freiheitliche Deutsche Arbeiterpartei*)

Supporters of this neo-Nazi group clashed with anti-Nazi demonstrators in Stuttgart on June 7-8, 1986.

On Jan. 31, 1987, a total of 104 persons were arrested at a meeting held in West Berlin allegedly called to form this party in West Berlin (where such meetings were banned by the Allied powers and the existence of extremist right-wing parties was prohibited by these powers).

People's Socialist Movement of Germany—Party of Labour (*Volkssozialistische Bewegung Deutschlands—Partei der Arbeit,* VSBD-PdA)

Leadership. Friedhelm Busse (ch.)

The organization was founded in 1971 as the Party of Labour (as an offshoot of the National Democratic Party of Germany, NPD) and adopted its extended name in 1975. It has a youth group known as *Junge Front.* In 1981 Friedhelm Busse was reported to have secretly visited France to meet members of the *Fédération d'action nationale européenne* (FANE) with a view to creating a European Nazi umbrella organization for the various neo-Nazi movements in France, Belgium, Austria, Britain and Switzerland as well as West Germany. On Oct. 21, 1981, two alleged members of the party were killed and three others, including its chairman, were arrested while attempting to carry out a bank raid near Munich; four other party members were arrested by police in Belgium on Oct. 23 and were subsequently extradited to West Germany.

The VSBD-PdA was officially banned on Jan. 27, 1982.

After the police had found a large quantity of arms and explosives, F. Busse was on April 9, 1982, sentenced to six months in prison for disseminating racist propaganda, and on June 23, 1982, he was charged with running a terrorist organization, conspiracy, weapons offences and extortion.

Young National Democrats (*Junge Nationaldemokraten*)

Members of this offshoot of the (legal) *Nationaldemokratische Partei* were involved in armed robbery and arms offences, for which Joachim Gröning was sentenced to 6½ years in prison and Walter-Franz Kohnert to 2½ years on July 17, 1981.

RAF and Related Groups of the Extreme Left

Extreme left-wing groups engaged in acts of violence have (especially in the 1970s) had an effect on public life in the Federal Republic of Germany (FRG) quite out of proportion to the numerical strength of their membership. Although they have not succeeded in creating a revolutionary mass party and their sympathizers have never constituted more than a small minority of the population (more particularly among left-wing students), their acts of terrorism have necessitated a considerable law enforcement effort on the part of the state. By early 1983 it appeared that the majority of known left-wing terrorists had been imprisoned or were dead (some of them as a result of suicide) or had abandoned their cause, and by 1987 it was widely assumed that the threat to public order constituted by these groups had been finally eliminated.

The principal organization of these left-wing guerrillas styled itself the Red Army Faction and was generally known as the Baader-Meinhof Group or Gang. Some of this organization's members formed separate commandos to carry out specific acts of violence and others formed entirely independent groups.

These acts included the assassinations of leading personalities, in particular Günter von Drenkmann (president of the West Berlin Supreme Court) on Nov. 10, 1972; Dr Siegfried Buback (Chief Federal Prosecutor) on April 7, 1977; Dr Jürgen Ponto (chief executive of the Dresdner Bank) on July 30, 1977; and Dr Hanns-Martin Schleyer (president of the Federal Union of German Industry and the Federation of German Employers' Associations) on Oct. 18, 1977.

Red Army Faction (*Rote Armee Fraktion,* RAF)

Leadership (original). Andreas Baader, Ulrike Meinhof

Established in 1968, the RAF (also known as the Baader-Meinhof Group or Gang) took its name from the Japanese Red Army [for which see under Japan]. The history of the RAF can be traced back to a *Sozialistischer Deutscher Studentenbund* (SDS), which had originally been formed in 1946 and enjoyed the support of the Social Democratic Party (SPD) until 1961, when a section of the SDS remained loyal to the SPD and formed a new organization, whereas the SDS became a revolutionary group of some 1,600 members (out of a total student population of some 300,000) and formed the core of the so-called "extra-parliamentary opposition" hostile to the "establishment" and in particular to the "grand coalition" government formed in 1966 by the SPD and the Christian Democrats.

The SDS's aim was a radical reform of West German society and the setting-up of a communist society, although not in the forms represented in the Soviet Union and the German Democratic Republic. Its ideological mentors were not only Marx, Engels and Lenin but also the dissenting Marxists Rosa Luxemburg, Mao Tse-tung (Mao Zedong) and Prof Herbert Marcuse; its "heroes" included Ho Chi Minh (the Vietnamese communist leader), Fidel Castro and Che Guevara. In 1967 the federal Ministry of the Interior named as the most influential person in the SDS Rudi Dutschke, who described himself as "a professional revolutionary and a Marxist", whose aims were the overthrow of the "corrupt establishment" represented by capitalism in the West and Stalinism in the East, which he hoped to achieve by protest demonstrations and "discussion" rather than violence.

During a riotous demonstration by left-wing students against a visit to West Berlin by the Shah of Iran on June 2-3, 1967, a 26-year-old student, Benno Ohnesorg, was shot dead by a police detective (while 44 persons, including 20 police officers, were injured). On Dec. 17, 1967, the federal Ministry of the Interior declared the SDS a "danger to the Constitution" because of its stated aim to overthrow the constitutional order and parliamentary democracy. R. Dutschke was severely injured by a right-wing attacker on April 11, 1968, and this attack was followed by violent demonstrations by SDS followers on April 11-15 in West Berlin and many other cities, in particular against premises of the Springer concern which controlled between 30 and 40 per cent of West Germany's total newspaper circulation, and 65-70 per cent of that in West Berlin. The demonstrations led to the deaths of a press photographer and a student in Munich.

The SDS decided on March 21, 1970, to dissolve itself because of dissension among its numerous sections, one of which was the RAF. This group was responsible for arson at a Frankfurt department store on April 2, 1968, for which Andreas Baader was, on May 14, 1968, sentenced to three years' hard labour; he had described his action as an act of "extra-parliamentary opposition to the policy and social order of the Federal Republic". On May 14, 1970, however, he was freed by three RAF members—Ulrike Meinhof, Ingrid Schubert and Irene Görgens—while he was, under escort, visiting an institute in West Berlin to consult some books.

In connexion with this action I. Schubert and I. Görgens were on March 21, 1971, sentenced to six years' imprisonment and four years' juvenile detention respectively (for attempted murder and illegal possession of arms). Horst Mahler, a lawyer and member of a "socialist lawyers' collective" (closely linked with the "extra-parliamentary opposition") was at the same time acquitted on similar charges; however, on Feb. 23, 1973, H. Mahler was sentenced in West Berlin to 12 years in prison on charges of having founded the RAF, of having acted as its ringleader until arrested on Oct. 8, 1970, and of having taken part in three bank raids in West Berlin.

In connexion with bank robberies, car thefts and other crimes committed by alleged members of the Baader-Meinhof group, several of them were killed in clashes with police—notably Petra Schelm in Hamburg on July 12, 1971, Georg von Rauch (who had escaped from detention) in Berlin on Dec. 4, 1971, and Thomas Weisbecker (sought for inflicting grievous bodily harm and committing arson) in Augsburg on March 2, 1972.

Among alleged RAF members tried, Karl-Heinz Ruhland (arrested on Dec. 20, 1970) was sentenced in Düsseldorf on March 15, 1972, to 4½ years in prison for participating in a bank robbery in West Berlin and in two acts of burglary (to obtain documents and rubber stamps for forging identity cards); during his trial he made a detailed confession and named a number of sympathizers.

Bomb attacks attributed to the Baader-Meinhof group took place during May 1972 at the headquarters of the US Army Fifth Corps in Frankfurt (killing an officer and injuring 13 other people) on May 11; at the city police headquarters in Augsburg and at the Bavarian criminal police office in Munich on May 12; on the car of a judge investigating the group in Karlsruhe on May 15; at the headquarters of the Springer publishing group in Hamburg on May 19; and at the US army's European Command headquarters in Heidelberg on May 24 (when three US servicemen were killed and five other persons injured).

In June 1972 the police arrested several prominent members of the group. A. Baader, Holger Meins and Jan-Carl Raspe were arrested in Frankfurt on June 1; as was Dorothea Ridder the following day near the Bavarian-Austrian border. Gudrun Ensslin was arrested in Hamburg on June 7 (having in October 1968 been sentenced to three years in prison for jointly committing arson with A. Baader in Frankfurt but having disappeared after being provisionally released pending the hearing of her appeal). Also arrested were U. Meinhof near Hanover on June 16 (when she was found in possession of several pistols, a sub-machine-gun, two home-made hand grenades and a bomb); Gerhard Müller (at the same time and place); Siegfried Hausner in Stuttgart on June 19 (being suspected of being the group's bomb specialist); Klaus Jünschke (thought to have taken over the group's leadership after the arrest of A. Baader and U. Meinhof); and Irmgard Möller in Offenbach on July 8.

A police raid carried out in Hamburg in February 1973 resulted in the seizure of sub-machine-guns, sawn-off shotguns, pistols, explosives and hand grenades of a type used by NATO forces; another raid in Frankfurt (at the same time) produced arms and ammunition, including dum-dum bullets and tear-gas, as well as forged passports and money in various currencies.

H. Meins, an alleged hard-core member of the RAF arrested on June 1, 1972, and awaiting trial for involvement in five murders and 54 cases of attempted murder, died in prison on Nov. 9, 1974, having started a hunger strike on Sept. 14 of that year (as part of a concerted campaign by RAF prisoners awaiting trial). On the following day (Nov. 10) Günter von Drenkmann, president of the West Berlin Supreme Court, was shot dead at his home, with the RAF claiming responsibility for his death "in revenge for the death of H. Meins" (although the victim of this assassination had not been involved in proceedings against the RAF).

The federal Minister of Justice spoke firmly on Nov. 13, 1974, against sympathy campaigns for RAF prisoners in which they were described as political prisoners suffering "isolation torture or destructive imprisonment"; in the name of the federal government he stated that in the FRG no one was persecuted or imprisoned for his political beliefs, that the imprisoned were suspected of serious crimes and that some of them had already been legally sentenced; he added that proceedings were under way against at least 60 accused, of whom 35 were then in detention. On Nov. 29 the federal Ministry of the Interior released 165 pages of documents to show that the RAF was working for the destruction of the social system in the FRG and that with the help of their lawyers the suspects had been able to establish an effective prison-to-prison communications network. Following an official announcement that the main trial of RAF suspects would begin on May 21, 1975, the hunger strike was called off early in February.

Among RAF members sentenced to imprisonment in 1973-74 were the following: Margrit Schiller (in Hamburg on Feb. 9, 1973—two years and three months); Carmen Roll (in Karlsruhe on July 23—four years); Marianne Herzog (in Frankfurt on Dec. 17—two years and three months); Rolf Pohle, a lawyer (in Munich on March 1, 1974—six years and five months); I. Schubert (in June—13 years for armed robbery and membership of a criminal organization; she had in May 1971 been given a six-year sentence—see above—and later hanged herself in her cell in Munich-Stadelheim on Nov. 12, 1977); Bernhard Braun and Brigitte Mohnhaupt (in West Berlin on Aug. 30, 1974—4½ years each); U. Meinhof (in West Berlin on Nov. 29—eight years for attempted murder in connexion with the freeing of A. Baader—see above) and H. Mahler (by the same court)—two years as an accomplice, in addition to the 12 years imposed earlier. (By this time, however, H. Mahler had already changed his mind about the RAF, declaring that it had no mass support and that without such support an armed insurrection was impossible; he joined the newly established Maoist Communist Party of Germany—KPD—and was expelled from the RAF.)

Acts of violence attributed to the RAF in 1974-75 included (i) an unsuccessful attempt made on March 12, 1974, to free three alleged RAF members from prison in Zweibrücken (Saarland); (ii) a bomb explosion on Nov. 20 outside the house of a judge in Hamburg; (iii) an attempt to kill the treasurer of the Christian Democratic Union (Walter Leisler Kiep) near Kronberg (Taunus) on Nov. 30; and (iv) the burning-down of a chalet in Switzerland belonging to Axel Springer (the newspaper magnate) on Jan. 5-6, 1975.

Further prison sentences were imposed in 1975 on RAF members as follows: (i) On Lothar Gend in Bochum on May 21 (15 years, inter alia for shooting and injuring three policemen, having been involved, with Gabriele Kröcher-Tiedemann, in a shooting incident with police) and (ii) on Sigurd Debus (12 years), Karl-Heinz Ludwig (six years), Wolfgang Stahl and Gerd Jürgen Wieland (5½ years each)—in Hamburg on May 30 for four bank raids in which they had stolen DM600,000.

During the trial of A. Baader, G. Ensslin, U. Meinhof and J.-C. Raspe, which opened in Stuttgart on May 21, 1975, U. Meinhof was found hanging in her cell on May 9, 1976 (a verdict of suicide being pronounced by the Stuttgart public prosecutor on June 13). The trial of the three remaining defendants for their part in four murders, 34 attempted murders and the formation of and membership in a criminal organization ended on April 28, 1977, with life sentences for all three of them. During the trial the defendants generally refused to make any concrete declarations on their actions, but A. Baader said in January 1976 that they were "an urban guerrilla group, a small motor to start up the great revolution by armed force".

The defence lawyers argued on Jan. 20, 1976, that the trial should be terminated and the defendants be treated as prisoners of war as they were engaged in partisan warfare which was recognized in international law; defence counsel had repeatedly but unsuccessfully demanded that the accused should be treated as political prisoners because their actions had been inspired by political motives, and not as common criminals. The authorities, however, refused to acknowledge the existence of political prisoners in the FRG.

G. Ensslin said in a written statement on May 4, 1976, that the accused had been organized in the RAF since 1970 and were responsible for attacks on the headquarters of the (US) Central Intelligence Agency in Frankfurt and the US Army in Heidelberg, and also for an attack on the Springer building in Hamburg; she claimed that their actions should be considered within the context of the Vietnam war which, she said, had taken place not only in the Far East but also in West Germany owing to the logistical role of US forces in Europe. Following the death of U. Meinhof the three other defendants made no further appearance in court.

Of RAF members involved in the raid on the office of the Organization of Petroleum Exporting Countries (OPEC) in Vienna in December 1975 (see page 281), Hans-Joachim Klein announced his rejection of terrorism in a letter published in *Der Spiegel* on May 9, 1977, when he stated that the "revolutionary action", of the RAF had been "virtually fascist".

Other prison sentences were imposed on alleged RAF members in 1976 by courts in Hamburg as follows: (i) I. Möller and G. Müller (on March 16)—4½ and 10 years respectively on various charges, including illegal possession of weapons and forging of documents (and complicity in murder in the case of G. Müller, who was a key witness for the prosecution at the trial of A. Baader, G. Ensslin and C.-J. Raspe), and (ii) eight persons (on Sept. 28)—namely Christa Eckes (seven years), Helmut Pohl (five years), Margrit Schiller (four years and eight months), Eberhard Becker (4½ years), Ekkehard Blenck (three years), Ilse Stachowiak and Wolfgang Beer (4½ years' "youth" imprisonment each) and Kay Werner Allnach (two years suspended)—for various offences including membership of a criminal organization, violation of firearms and explosives regulations and forging of documents.

In 1977 Waltraud Boock was sentenced (in Vienna on Feb. 4) to 15 years for aggravated robbery, resisting a state official and contravention of the firearms law. Manfred Grashof and Klaus Jünschke were given life sentences (in Kaiserslautern on June 2) for the murder of a policeman and on other charges, while Wolfgang Grundmann was given four years for unlawful possession of arms and membership of a criminal organization.

Towards the end of 1977 Dierk Hoff (who had given evidence for the prosecution of A. Baader, G. Ensslin, U. Meinhof and J.-C. Raspe) was sentenced (in Frankfurt on Dec. 21, 1977) to four years and eight months for supporting a criminal organization and illegally manufacturing bombs, and Verena Becker was given a life sentence (in Stuttgart on Dec. 28) for the attempted murder of six policemen, membership of a criminal organization and aggravated robbery. V. Becker had earlier been sentenced in December 1974 to six years' "youth" imprisonment for her part in an attack on a British forces yacht club in West Berlin in February 1972 which had caused one death; she had been released in exchange for P. Lorenz in March 1975 (see under separate entry for June 2 Movement).

RAF members also sentenced to imprisonment in 1976-77 were as follows: Peter-Paul Zahl (on March 12, 1976) to 15 years for two cases of attempted murder; Gertraud Will (in Munich on June 15) to two years and 10 months for participating in a criminal organization, using explosives, illegal procurement of arms and aiding and abetting; Irmgard Deschler (on July 12) to five years for preparing an explosives attack, bank robbery, taking a hostage and falsification of documents (this sentence being reduced to 4½ years' "youth" imprisonment on May 12, 1977); Karl-Heinz König (on Aug. 17) to six years for aggravated robbery; Wolfgang Quante (on Nov. 23) to an unlimited term of "youth" imprisonment for membership of a criminal organization (being released on April 4, 1977, having been one of those RAF prisoners whose release was demanded by the attackers of the West German embassy in Stockholm in April 1975); Borvin Wulf and Bernd Geburtig (on March 2, 1977) to 5½ years each for a bomb attack on the house of a former Hamburg Senator of Justice on Oct. 16, 1975, and also for arson, theft, illegal possession of firearms and forgery of documents; Helmut Lülf (in Hamburg on April 28) to four years for membership of a criminal organization, forgery of documents, fraud and aiding and abetting; Dieter Kett (on May 12) to 4½ years on explosives charges (and on May 17 to a further 10 months for insulting the state prosecutor); Robert Jarowoy and Wernfried Reimers (in Frankfurt on June 30) to seven years and three months each on blackmail charges; Rainer and Inge Hochstein (in Hamburg on July 1) to 11 and 10 years respectively for aggravated robbery and membership of a criminal organization; and Uwe Henning (on Oct. 12) to two years and three months for allowing G. Ensslin to use his flat, which served as an RAF hideout and arms store.

Rolf Pohle, another former RAF prisoner exchanged for P. Lorenz, had been arrested in Athens on July 21, 1976, and extradited to the FRG on Oct. 1, 1976; in Munich on March 10, 1978, he was sentenced to three years and three months for extortion (on behalf of the five prisoners exchanged for P. Lorenz, who had been given a total of DM 120,000).

Other RAF members sentenced to imprisonment during 1978 were: Johannes Thimme (in April) to one year and 10 months for membership of a terrorist organization and the construction of explosives; Günter Sonnenberg (in Stuttgart on April 26) to imprisonment for life on two charges of attempted murder on May 3, 1977 (when he had been arrested on the Swiss border with Verena Becker); Kurt Groenewold, a lawyer who had acted as defence counsel for accused RAF members (in Hamburg on July 10) to two years in prison, a fine of DM 75,000 and costs for supporting a criminal organization, in particular by running an information centre of the RAF prisoners to keep terrorist organizations abroad in touch; Klaus Dorff (in Frankfurt on Aug. 2, 1978) to 13 years for two armed attacks on banks in Frankfurt and Dortmund (in which he had stolen DM 225,000); Jürgen Tauras (at the same time) to 7½ years for a bank raid in Hamburg (weapons, ammunition and other equipment having been found in their possession upon their arrest on Feb. 20-21, 1976, in Cologne); Volker Speitel and Hans-Joachim Dellwo (in Stuttgart on Dec. 14, 1978) to respectively two years and two months and two years for supplying a terrorist organization and acting as couriers between lawyers and their imprisoned clients and alleged terrorists outside. Both the last-named had been employed by the law firm of Dr Croissant [see below] and both stated at the trial that they had severed their connexion with the RAF, making full confessions and thus contributing to the prevention of further crimes, in particular by destroying the legend, spread by RAF supporters, that A.

Baader, G. Ensslin and J.-C. Raspe has been "murdered" in prison.

Four RAF members—Brigitte Mohnhaupt, Rolf-Clemens Wagner, Sieglinde Hofmann and Peter Jürgen Boock (the husband of Waltraud Boock)—were taken into custody in Zagreb (Yugoslavia) in May 1978 when they were found to carry stolen Liechtenstein passports. The FRG demanded the extradition of these four persons at the same time as the Yugoslav authorities requested the extradition of six Croatians, one Albanian and one Serb—all émigrés in the FRG whom the Yugoslav government accused of various crimes against the Yugolav state. The West German government refused the Yugoslav request, mainly on grounds of insufficient evidence regarding the Yugoslavs' alleged involvement in crimes. In Yugoslavia the four West Germans were convicted of using false passports and of entering the country illegally but were all released and left the country in November 1978; the Yugoslav government had rejected the FRG's request for their extradition on the ground that the legal requirements for their extradition had not been fulfilled.

In Switzerland, Gabriele Kröcher-Tiedemann was on June 30, 1978, sentenced at Porrentruy to 15 years in prison for attempted murder of two border guards and Christian Möller to 11 years for complicity, both having been arrested at Delémont (north-western Switzerland) in December 1977. Elisabeth von Dyck (wanted inter alia in connexion with the murder of Dr Schleyer and with the attack on the West German embassy in Stockholm) was shot dead by police in Nuremberg on May 6, 1979, allegedly while resisting arrest by drawing a gun.

Dr Klaus Croissant, a lawyer who had acted as defence counsel for various hardcore RAF members, was sentenced in Stuttgart on Feb. 16, 1979, to 30 months' imprisonment for supporting a criminal organization by abusing his status to carry messages between imprisoned terrorists and those still at large; he was also banned from practising as a lawyer for four years. Dr Croissant had been extradited in November 1977 from France where he had sought political asylum in July 1977 after he had been released from investigative custody in West Germany.

Other prison sentences were imposed on RAF members and supporters during 1979 as follows: Christine Kuby (in Hamburg on May 2) to life imprisonment for the attempted murder of two police officers on Jan. 21, 1978 (proclaiming her allegiance to the RAF during her trial); Irmgard Möller and Bernhard Braun, both alleged founder members of the RAF (in Stuttgart-Stammheim on May 31), to life imprisonment and to 12 years respectively for crimes including a bomb attack at the US military headquarters in Heidelberg in May 1972 and an attack on a federal judge (for their earlier sentences, see above); Angelika Speitel, a former employee of Dr Croissant and Siegfried Haag (see under separate entry for Haag-Mayer Group) and described by the prosecution as a particularly active RAF member, (in Düsseldorf on Nov. 30) to two terms of life imprisonment for murder and attempted murder of police officers in September 1978 (being also suspected of involvement in the murders of Drs Schleyer, Ponto and Buback).

Two lawyers who had formerly been employed by Dr Croissant—Arndt Müller and Armin Newerla—were in Stuttgart on Jan. 31, 1980, given prison sentences of four and 3½ years respectively for supporting a terrorist organization and smuggling guns into prison, enabling A. Baader and J.-C. Raspe to kill themselves.

Astrid Proll, one of the founder members of the RAF, was on Feb. 22, 1980, sentenced to five years in prison and a fine of DM 4,500 (the prison sentence being suspended because she had already spent over four years in investigative custody) for armed bank robbery and uttering forged documents. She had been extradited from Britain, where she had gone in 1974 and had married under an assumed name, for which reason she was refused a formal declaration of British nationality; she had repeatedly asserted that she had sincerely changed her attitude towards terrorism.

Gert Schneider and Christof Wackernagel, both RAF members, were in Düsseldorf on Sept. 5, 1980, sentenced to 15 years in prison each for the attempted murder of Dutch policemen in Amsterdam on Nov. 10, 1977. Rolf Clemens Wagner, who had been associated with the RAF since 1975, was sentenced to life imprisonment in Winterthur (Switzerland) on Sept. 26, 1980, for murder committed during a bank raid in November 1979.

During 1981 a number of actions involving the placing or exploding of bombs or the committing of arson were attributed to the RAF. Thus bombs were discovered in two US army helicopters at Erlensee (Hesse) on Feb. 3; the US military information office in Giessen was bombed on March 29; three Molotov cocktails were thrown into a US army labour office in Frankfurt on March 30; arson was attempted at the US international school in Düsseldorf on April 6; a bomb was discovered at the US army administrative office in Wiesbaden on April 16; an explosion took place at the US Andrews Barracks in West Berlin on Aug. 18; an arson attack was made on US barracks in Frankfurt on Aug. 19; seven cars and a motorcycle were set on fire in a US army housing estate in Wiesbaden on Sept. 1; an attack was made on the home of the US consul-general in Frankfurt on Sept. 13; and two bombs were discovered on a railway line leading to the US air force base near Frankfurt on Sept. 16.

Hans-Christian Ströbele, a lawyer, was in West Berlin on Jan. 19, 1981, sentenced to 1½ years in prison suspended for three years for supporting the criminal RAF. Norbert Kröcher was in Düsseldorf on Feb. 10, 1981, sentenced to 11½ years' hard labour for membership of a criminal association and aggravated robberies and extortion (in particular in Sweden), while Manfred Adomeit was given a 6½-year sentence. Petra (Piccolo-) Krause was in Zurich on March 9, 1981, sentenced to 3½ years' hard labour and expulsion from Switzerland for 15 years for her participation in RAF bomb attacks in Berne and Zurich in June 1974.

Karl-Friedrich Grosser was, in Stuttgart on Oct. 12, 1982, sentenced to three years in prison and Jürgen Schneider to 2½ years, for aiding the RAF. Rolf Heissler, who had been released from prison in 1975 in exchange for the release of P. Lorenz (see under June 2 Movement), was on Nov. 10, 1982, sentenced to life imprisonment for killing two Dutch border guards in 1978 and for other offences.

Following the arrest of three leading RAF members—Brigitte Mohnhaupt and Adelheid Schulz (on Nov. 11, 1982) and Christian Klar (on Nov. 16)—the federal Minister of Justice appealed to the "remaining hard core" as well as to the sympathizers and supporters of the RAF on Nov. 19, 1982, to cease their criminal activities and to surrender; he added that only those who made efforts to prevent further possible offences by a terrorist association could expect leniency. An RAF arms cache was uncovered at an unspecified locality on Nov. 12, 1982, and on Nov. 28 it was reported that the security forces had found four more arms caches of the RAF, mainly in the Frankfurt area.

On March 13, 1985, Adelheid Schulz was given three life sentences and R.-C. Wagner two life sentences for the kidnapping and murder of Dr Schleyer, his chauffeur and three bodyguards, with A. Schulz being also convicted of the murder of Dr Ponto. On April 2 Christian Klar and Brigitte Mohnhaupt were each sentenced to five terms of life imprisonment and one of 15 years for the murder of Dr Ponto and that of Dr Siegfried Buback (the chief federal prosecutor), the abduction of Dr Schleyer, the murder of six bodyguards and the attack on Gen. Kroesen in September 1981.

On Dec. 4, 1984, over 30 RAF prisoners in West German prisons started a hunger strike. Although the strike was finally called off in late January 1985, the RAF conducted a bombing campaign against NATO and US military targets, involving about 40 attacks between Dec. 18, 1984 and Jan. 21, 1985.

On Jan. 15, 1985, the RAF and the French Direct Action (AD) announced the establishment of a united urban-based politico-military front. It was believed that the RAF, with some 20 members and up to 400 active supporters, was the dominant of the two groups (although most of its members had been arrested by mid-1984). In a further joint statement issued on Jan. 31, 1985, the RAF and the AD gave their reasons for the killing of the French Gen. René Audran on Jan. 25 (see under entry for Direct Action, page 110).

On Feb. 1, 1985, RAF members murdered (in Munich) Dr Ernst Zimmermann, chief executive of an engineering firm supplying equipment for NATO. The killing was attributed to an RAF "Patrick O'Hara Commando" (named after an Irish Republican Army hunger striker who died in the Maze prison in Belfast in 1982).

The RAF and the AD jointly claimed responsibility for a car bomb attack on Aug. 8, 1985, at a US air force base near Frankfurt airport, killing two US personnel and injuring some 20 people; it appeared that the perpetrators of this attack had first killed a US soldier near Wiesbaden and used his papers to gain access to the base.

The RAF was one of several organizations which claimed responsibility for the explosion of a bomb in a West Berlin discothèque frequented by US servicemen on April 5, 1986, when two persons were killed and some 200 injured, as well as for the murder of Olof Palme, the Swedish Prime Minister, on Feb. 28, 1986.

During 1983-86 further sentences were passed on RAF supporters as follows: Peter Glaser, known as a right-wing extremist, was on March 23, 1983, sentenced to four years and 10 months in prison for his involvement in three murders, aggravated arson at foreigners' hostels and causing explosions. Barbara Augustin, a West German citizen,was sentenced in Switzerland on Sept. 28, 1983, to three years in prison for attempting to smuggle explosives into West Germany for use by the RAF. Monika Kroobs was sentenced in Frankfurt on Dec. 19, 1983, to 1½ years in prison for giving logistical support to the RAF.

Peter-Jürgen Boock was sentenced on May 7, 1984, to four concurrent life terms and one 15-year term for his involvement in the murders of Dr Ponto and Dr Schleyer. At a further trial which ended on Nov. 28, 1986, he was sentenced to life imprisonment for these crimes. Five persons arrested in February 1983 were on March 15, 1985, given prison sentences ranging from five to 14 years for attacks on US military targets and attempted murder of US personnel. (Two of the defendants had been arrested in Poole, Dorset, England, and subsequently extradited to the FRG.)

Gisela Dutzi was sentenced on Aug. 8, 1985, to 8½ years for RAF membership, forging documents and helping to plan attacks on US bases and arms depots. Claudia Wannersdorfer was sentenced in November 1985 to eight years for supporting a terrorist organization and causing a bomb explosion.

Ernst-Volker Staub and Barbara Ernst were, on Feb. 6, 1986, given four-year sentences each for RAF membership, falsifying documents and illegal use of semi-automatic weapons. Manuela Happe was, on March 20, 1986, given a 15-year sentence for RAF membership and two counts of attempted murder.

Ingrid Jacobsmeyer and Christa Ecke were, also on March 20, 1986, sentenced to nine and eight years in prison respectively for illegal possession of arms, falsifying documents and membership of a terrorist organization. Karl-Friedrich Grosser was on Sept. 1, 1986, sentenced to 9½ years in prison for robbery, grievous bodily harm, falsification of identity papers and active support for the RAF. (He had already been given a three-year prison sentence in October 1982—see above.) Helmut Pohl was sentenced to life imprisonment, and Stephan Frey to 4½ years in prison, on Dec. 23, 1986, for membership of a terrorist organization (the RAF), weapons offences and forgery of identity papers (and H. Pohl for participation in a bomb attack on a US air force base in August 1981).

Rolf-Clemens Wagner was sentenced to life imprisonment on March 16, 1987, for participation in the murder of Dr Schleyer.

A judicial panel of West Berlin's Supreme Court on July 2, 1987, refused to readmit H. Mahler (who had been released from prison in 1980) to the legal profession.

Fighting Unit Rolando Olalia

This group, apparently an RAF commando, claimed responsibility for the bombing of a West German development aid agency on Dec. 19, 1986. (Rolando Olalia, murdered on Nov. 13, 1986, was the leader of a left-wing trade union in the Philippines, the May First Movement—KMU.)

Gudrun Ensslin Commando

This Commando claimed responsibility for an attack with (Soviet-made) anti-tank grenades on the car of Gen. Frederick J. Kroesen, US Ground Forces Commander in Europe, who was slightly injured, in Heidelberg on Sept. 15, 1981.

In connexion with this attack Helga Roos, who was arrested on Oct. 19, 1982, was on May 2, 1983, sentenced to four years and nine months in prison for membership of a terrorist organization and for providing logistical support to terrorists.

Haag-Mayer Group

Leadership. Siegfried Haag, Roland Mayer, Günter Sonnenberg (leaders)

This Group was formed in 1976 around the legal practice of Siegfried Haag with the object of directing the activities of a restructured Red Army Faction (RAF) at the end of the first phase of the RAF's operations marked by the suicides of its leading figures (U. Meinhof on May 9, 1976, followed by A. Baader, G. Ensslin and C.-J. Raspe on Oct. 18, 1977). The principal aims of the Group appeared to be the enforcement of the release of imprisoned RAF members and revenge for the deaths of others, rather than the achievement of a political revolution.

The founder members of the Group were thought to include also Sieglinde Gutrun Hofmann, Stefan Wisniewski, Verena Becker, Rolf Heissler (freed from prison in exchange for Peter Lorenz—see under separate entry for June 2 Movement) and Friederike Krabbe—all of whom were, with S. Haag, said to have spent time at a training camp of the Popular Front for the Liberation of Palestine in South Yemen in 1976. According to documents found in S. Haag's possession on his arrest, Waltraud Boock had been one of the most active acquirers of money for the Group.

On Nov. 30, 1976, S. Haag and R. Mayer were arrested at Butzbach (Hesse), where police found in S. Haag's possession not only bank notes stolen in recent bank raids but also detailed plans of attacks to be carried out by at least 11 persons (including G. Sonnenberg, Christian Klar and Knut Folkerts). On Sept. 30, 1977, S. Haag, R. Mayer, Elisabeth von Dyck and Sabine Schmitz were charged with membership of a criminal organization, and S. Haag and E. von Dyck also with complicity in murder by having procured weapons for the attack on the West German embassy in Stockholm (see separate entry for Holger Meins Commando), and on Feb. 23, 1978, S. Haag was charged with murder in connexion with that attack.

On July 11, 1979, S. Haag and R. Mayer were sentenced in Stuttgart-Stammheim to 14 and 12 years in prison respectively for leading a terrorist organization (i.e. their group) and its involvement in the kidnapping of Dr Hanns-Martin Schleyer (see under separate entry for Siegfried Hausner Commando), while Sabine Schmitz was at the same time given a 32-month prison sentence. On Dec. 19, 1979, S. Haag was given a further 15-year sentence for obtaining weapons used in the attack on the West German embassy in Stockholm.

The Hamburg section of the Haag-Mayer Group was held responsible for the killing of Dr Jürgen Ponto (chief executive of the Dresdner Bank) on July 30, 1977, for which the "Red Morning" group had claimed responsibility.

Among other members of the Group, Willy Peter Stoll was fatally shot by police in Düsseldorf on Sept. 6, 1978. He had been an assistant of Dr K. Croissant (the defence lawyer of leading RAF members) and had gone underground in 1975. He was said to have joined the Haag-Mayer Group; to have stolen, together with Knut Folkerts, on July 1, 1977, arms which were used against Dr Hanns-Martin Schleyer; and to have been involved in the murders of Drs Buback, Ponto and Schleyer.

Uwe Folkerts, brother of Knut Folkerts, was (in Stuttgart on Dec. 19, 1978) sentenced to 16 months in prison for supporting the Group.

Holger Meins Commando

Named after one of the first leaders of the Red Army Faction (RAF), who died in prison as a result of a hunger strike on Nov. 9, 1974, this group admitted responsibility for a bomb attack on the West German consulate in Florence on Nov. 16 of that year and for another on a Mercedes car sales agency in Paris on Feb. 8, 1975. On April 24, 1975, six armed members of this Commando seized the West German embassy in Stockholm and took 12 staff members, including the ambassador, as hostages. Swedish police promptly surrounded the building but were warned by the attackers that, if they did not leave the area, one of the hostages would be shot every hour. The police, however, ignored the warning, whereupon the attackers shot the West German military attaché (who died a few hours later). The attackers demanded the release of 26 persons serving terms of imprisonment or in investigative custody on various charges, including membership of the RAF or other alleged terrorist organizations.

A "crisis staff" formed by the West German government decided not to accede to the commando's demands, and the latter thereupon killed the economic attaché at the embassy in Stockholm. However, later on April 24 an accidental explosion set the building on fire and killed one member of the Commando while the five others were captured by the police, with all remaining hostages escaping alive. Of the five Commando members captured, Siegfried Hausner (who had already served a three-year sentence imposed in 1972) was severely injured and died in a prison hospital in Stuttgart-Stammheim on May 4, 1975. The four other Commando members—Karl-Heinz Dellwo, Hanna Elise Krabbe, Bernd Maria Rössner and Lutz Manfred Taufer—were each sentenced in Düsseldorf on July 20, 1977, to serve two life sentences for joint murder in two cases.

The Commando was also one of several groups which claimed responsibility for the murder of Olof Palme, the Swedish Prime Minister, on Feb. 28, 1986.

Ingrid Schubert Commando of the Revolutionary Front of Western Europe

This Commando, named after the convicted RAF member who committed suicide in prison in 1977, claimed responsibility for the murder of Gerold von Braunmühl, a director in the Foreign Ministry, outside Bonn on Oct. 10, 1986, because of his alleged "key role . . . in the imperialist system".

June 2 Movement (*Bewegung 2. Juni*)

This Movement, established in 1973 and named after the date of the death of a student (Benno Ohnesorg), shot by police during a protest demonstration against a visit by the Shah of Iran in West Berlin in 1967, was formed by members of the Red Army Faction (RAF). Among these, Ingrid Siepmann was on Oct. 18, 1974, sentenced to 12 years in prison for six cases of robbery, and Annerose Reiche to seven years for a bank robbery with violence and the attempted freeing of two RAF prisoners, Ingrid Schubert and Irene Görgens (see page 127).

On Feb. 27, 1975, Peter Lorenz, the chairman of the Christian Democratic Union (CDU) in West Berlin, was kidnapped by members of the Movement who announced that he would be tried for "his connexions with the economic system, with the bosses and the fascist powers, as a propagandist of Zionism, of the aggressive policy of the State of Israel in Palestine" and for his "participation in the military coup by Pinochet and his accomplices in Chile". They threatened to kill P. Lorenz unless all their demands were fulfilled—in particular the immediate release of all persons arrested in connexion with demonstrations following the death of Holger Meins and also the release of six RAF members—Verena Becker, Gabriele Kröcher-Tiedemann, Horst Mahler, Rolf Pohle, Ingrid Siepmann and Rolf Heissler; these six to be flown out of the country in the company of Pastor Heinrich Albertz (former Social Democrat Chief Burgomaster of West Berlin at the time of B. Ohnesorg's death).

A government "crisis staff" chaired by the federal Chancellor, Helmut Schmidt, decided to place the life of P. Lorenz above the interests of the state and to accede to the kidnappers' demands. The West Berlin police announced on Feb. 28 that two demonstrators, imprisoned after the death of H. Meins, would be released on March 1. G. Kröcher-Tiedemann and H. Mahler, however, announced on television towards midnight on March 1 that they did not wish to be flown out of the country in exchange for P. Lorenz. H. Mahler subsequently issued a statement in which he declared inter alia: "The strategy of individual terrorism is not the strategy of the working class and as I dissociated myself during my trial (see page 128) from the strategy of the RAF I refuse to be taken out of the country in this way."

The four other prisoners (V. Becker, R. Heissler, R. Pohle and I. Siepmann) and also G. Kröcher-Tiedemann, who had reversed her earlier decision, accompanied by Pastor Albertz, were flown out of the country and eventually reached the People's Democratic Republic of (South) Yemen, where the former prisoners were granted political asylum on March 4. Following the return to Berlin of Pastor Albertz, P. Lorenz was released by the kidnappers late on March 4.

The Movement was also held responsible for the abduction of a Vienna industrialist, Walter Michael Palmers, on Nov. 9-10, 1977, for whose release on Nov. 13 a sum equivalent to almost $2,000,000 was paid as a ransom. Two heavily armed members of the Movement—Juliane Plambeck and Wolfgang Beer—were killed in a car crash on July 25, 1980. (J. Plambeck had been arrested on Sept. 13, 1975, and charged with involvement in the kidnapping of P. Lorenz and the murder of Judge von Drenkmann, but had escaped from investigative custody on July 7, 1976.)

On July 27, 1979, a West Berlin court, in a retrial of six persons tried in June 1976, sentenced to life imprisonment Ilse Jandt and to prison terms of from four to eight years the five other accused, all being found guilty of the murder of a former member of the June 2 Movement who had implicated members of the group in terrorist activities.

For involvement in the abduction of P. Lorenz, Ralf Reinders and Till Meyer were, in West Berlin on Oct. 13, 1980, sentenced to 15 years in prison each; Ronald Fritzsch to 13 years and three months; Gerald Klöpper to 11 years and two months; and Andreas Vogel to 10 years.

Other actions of the June 2 Movement included the explosion of a bomb at the Berlin Kreuzberg town hall on June 12-13, 1980. Of the members of the Movement, Gabriele Rollnik, Angelika Goder and Klaus Viehmann were, in West Berlin on May 15, 1981, sentenced to 15 years in prison each for their part in the kidnapping of P. Lorenz and of W. M. Palmers, and these sentences were confirmed by the Federal Court in Kassel in June 1982. Ingrid Barabass was, in Frankfurt on June 29, 1982, given a four-year prison sentence for membership of the June 2 Movement.

Michael Baumann, a former member of the June 2 Movement, was arrested by British police in London on Feb. 10, 1981, travelled voluntarily to West Berlin on Feb. 12 and was on Oct. 2, 1981, sentenced to five years and two months in prison for involvement in armed bank robberies and bombing attacks on behalf of the June 2 Movement. The same court sentenced Hans Peter Knoll, also a former member of the Movement, to 5½ years' imprisonment for the attempted murder of two policemen in 1971 and arson and other acts of violence in 1972; he had been arrested in Australia on March 1, 1981, and subsequently extradited to West Berlin.

On April 26, 1982, prison sentences were given to Regina Nicolai (4½ years), Karola Magg-Hüttmann and Karin Kamp-Münnichow (three years and nine months each) for supporting terrorist organizations; they had been arrested in France on May 7, 1980, and extradited to the FRG on July 10, 1980, having been found in possession of bank notes from the ransom paid for the release of W. M. Palmers, kidnapped in November 1977.

Mara Cagol Cammando of the Red Army Faction (RAF)

This group (named after Margherita Cagol, the wife of the former head of the Italian Red Brigades) claimed responsibility for killing Prof Karl Heinz Beckurts, a director of the Siemens concern, and his chauffeur near Munich on July 9, 1986. The RAF accused him of supporting the (US) Strategic Defence Initiative (SDI) as well as the use of nuclear energy.

Left-wing Organization opposed to RAF

Revolutionary Cells (*Revolutionäre Zellen*)

This movement, established in 1973 as an offshoot of the RAF, was held responsible for some 70 bomb and arson attacks between 1973 and mid-1978, in particular against industrial property in the Ruhr area. An arsenal belonging to this organization was uncovered in Wiesbaden on Sept. 11, 1978, in connexion with which two women—Leila Bocook (a naturalized Turk) and Sylvia Herzinger—were arrested. On March 23, 1980, members of the organization exploded three bombs at the Federal Labour Court in Kassel and on May 23, 1981, the organization accepted responsibility for arson at US barracks in Frankfurt.

The organization also admitted responsibility for the murder, on May 11, 1981, of Heinz-Herbert Karry (Minister of the Economy and Transport in Hesse) but claimed that its members had intended only to maim him. During 1982 the organization claimed responsibility for a bomb attack on July 2 on the US forces headquarters in Frankfurt and, on July 20, for several bomb attacks on the property of firms building a third runway for Frankfurt airport. (Attacks on US military base had also taken place early in June 1982, and a further bomb exploded on Aug. 11-12 in a Frankfurt residential area housing US military personnel.)

The Revolutionary Cells were further involved in attacks on US and NATO military targets and on company offices between Aug. 15, 1985, and April 2, 1986. The organization also claimed responsibility for a bomb explosion on Oct. 28, 1986, outside the Lufthansa offices in Cologne, carried out on the ground that Lufthansa had been profiting from the expulsion of aliens.

The Revolutionary Cells consist of small groups independent of each other (without authoritarian structure as in the case of the RAF, which they reject) and modelled on the Italian Red Brigades; they have been estimated to have about 200 members. In contrast to the RAF, the Revolutionary Cells intend to mobilize all "victims of the inhuman society" such as squatters, anti-nuclear militants, prisoners and other social outcasts. They have published, about once a year a journal called *Revolutionärer Zorn* (*Revolutionary Rage*).

Ghana

Capital: Accra Pop. 13,590,000

The Republic of Ghana, a member of the Commonwealth, is ruled by a Provisional National Defence Council (PNDC) which came to power on Dec. 31, 1981, overthrowing the existing parliamentary regime, suspending the Constitution and proscribing all political parties. On Jan. 21, 1982, the PNDC appointed a civilian government which included a number of established political figures, although effective power remained in the hands of the PNDC chairman, Flt.-Lt. Jerry Rawlings.

Under the PNDC's programme "people's defence committees" (PDCs) became the basic units of the state structure as "organizing centres for the revolution". Subsequently an Interim National Co-ordinating Committee (INCC) was set up to supervise and co-ordinate the work of the PDCs and also of recently established "workers' defence committees" (WDCs). In July 1982 the INCC was replaced by a 27-member National Defence Committee (NDC), which was, however, dissolved on Dec. 14, 1982, after accusations that it had been infiltrated by "counter-revolutionaries", and its functions were taken over by a standing committee of nine PNDC appointees. In February 1983 it was announced that a Community Defence Committee of between 40 and 100 PNDC appointees would be established, and in April 1983 the NDC was reconstituted.

Under a law promulgated by the PNDC on July 21, 1982, public tribunals of from three to five members were inaugurated on Aug. 26 of that year to deal primarily with cases of profiteering, corruption and the abuse of power, as well as "anti-state" activities involving the creation of disaffection through false information about the government; these tribunals have power to try people in absentia and to pass death sentences.

An attempted coup d'état staged by a sergeant who was a member of the PNDC was crushed on Nov. 23, 1982, and seven soldiers were arrested. On June 19, 1983, another rebel group, acting on orders from two officers, released a number of detainees (including some on trial for the November 1982 attempt) and succeeded in broadcasting statements denouncing Flt.-Lt. Rawlings and the PNDC. However, loyal troops crushed this attempted coup, with 26 people being killed in the fighting.

On Aug. 3, 1983, a total of 15 defendants were sentenced to various terms of imprisonment for their part in the November 1982 attempt; four charged with planning the attempt of June 1983 were sentenced to death (including the two officers); and three others were given prison sentences. On Aug. 4 a group of 16 defendants (some of them already convicted of charges relating to the November 1982 attempt) were sentenced to death for their part in the fighting in June 1983.

According to a statement broadcast from Accra on March 23, 1984, government troops appeared to have defeated several groups of "dissidents" who had "infiltrated the country to create chaos and confusion by attacking vital civil and military installations". Further broadcasts on March 25 referred to four "rebels" captured on March 23 who had in August 1983 been convicted in absentia on charges relating to the June 1983 attempt, and it was added that of these four one had died and the remaining three had been executed by firing squad. On March 26 Accra radio also reported that a further 10 persons had been executed for their involvement in the rebellion and that there was "overwhelming evidence of foreign involvement and international collaboration". On March 29 the Ghanaian government sent a "strong protest" to Côte D'Ivoire accusing it of allowing its territory to be used as a base by the "dissidents" who, the protest alleged, had had the co-operation of "certain elements in Côte d'Ivoire's security forces". On April 5 a special military tribunal sentenced to death eight army officers and a non-commissioned officer for "subversion".

On April 1, 1985, five members of the armed forces and a civilian were condemned to death, having been arrested on Feb. 2 of that year for "plotting to destabilize the country" by assassinating Flt.-Lt. Rawlings (a plan which the alleged conspirators were said to have postponed in January 1985 for fear of causing excessive casualties). On June 21, 1986, seven out of 15 persons condemned to death for planning to overthrow the government were executed by firing squad.

On March 26, 1986, the public tribunal in Accra sentenced two persons to death (one of them in absentia) and a third to 15 years' imprisonment for conspiring to commit crimes and to overthrow the government in 1983. On June 22 the first death sentence (i.e. not that imposed in absentia of the defendant) was commuted to life imprisonment and the prison sentence was shortened to 12 years.

On May 15, 1986, the tribunal sentenced nine persons to death for conspiring to commit an offence and to overthrow the government in 1984-85. According to the prosecution the accused had begun their preparations from a base in Lomé (Togo). Seven of the death sentences were carried out on June 22 after they had been confirmed by the PNDC on June 13. One of those executed was a brother of Maj. Boake Djan, a leader of the Ghanaian Democracy Movement (see below).

Further arrests of persons accused of plotting the overthrow of the government occurred in May-July 1987, in the context of mounting tension in Accra. In a joint statement on July 17, the New Democratic Movement and the Kwame Nkrumah Revolutionary Guards, nine of whose leaders had been arrested since May, declared that they were opposed "as a matter of principle to the use of terrorism as a weapon of political struggle" and denied any connection with a bomb explosion at the New Times Corporation in Accra on July 12.

Association of Recognized Professional Bodies (ARPB)

Leadership. Henry Yarte (nat. sec.)

This legal association claimed on July 28, 1982, that a total of 208 persons had been killed since the PNDC has assumed power, and it called for an end to the curfew imposed on Dec. 31, 1981, the early holding of free elections and return to civilian rule. On June 24, 1983, H. Yarte was arrested in connexion with the printing of "seditious material".

Campaign for Democracy in Ghana

This organization was launched in London in April 1982 by various members of Ghana's banned political parties, who issued a statement claiming that the regime of the Provisional National Defence Council was "an instrument of terror" which had violated human rights and destroyed the freedom of the press. On May 5, 1982, Lagos radio reported that the Campaign had been formed in the Nigerian capital as a forum for all Ghanaians opposed to the existing military regime in Ghana and that it would "employ all legitimate means to ensure that democracy and constitutional order were restored in the country".

Ghanaian Democracy Movement (GDM)

Leadership. John Ashibe Mensah (founder)

Founded. April 1984

This opposition group, established in London by J. A. Mensah (who had been Secretary of Trade until March 1984) was to be open to all Ghanaians who believed in "the restoration of democracy in Ghana", and who were "prepared to fight for it".

In December 1985 it was reported that US customs officials had arrested three Ghanaians—Joseph H. Mensah, John A. Boateng and Kwasi J. Baidoo—on charges of having conspired to buy missiles, anti-aircraft guns and other weapons to arm the GDM. On May 28, 1986, Accra radio reported that J. A. Boateng and K. J. Baidoo had been convicted, and that J. H. Mensah (a former minister in the Busia government of 1969-72) was to be retried as a New York jury had failed to reach a verdict on his first trial.

(On March 18, 1986, police in Rio de Janeiro had announced that 18 persons had been arrested for attempting to smuggle six tonnes of ammunition to rebels in Ghana. In June 1986 nine of these persons were given prison sentences of from four to five years. On Accra radio it was alleged on June 23 that the ammunition had been bought by Godby Osei, who was known to have tried on several occasions to destabilize the PNDC government.)

Kwame Nkrumah Revolutionary Guards (KNRG)

Leadership. Kwesi Pratt (gen. sec.)

K. Pratt was in detention from April 15 to Aug. 7, 1986, having been arrested with a journalist working for the independent weekly *Free Press* (which ceased publication in April 1986 when a spokesman claimed that too many people connected with it had been harassed by the authorities) and also a former secretary-general of the All-Africa Students' Union. He was re-arrested on May 17, 1987. John Ndebugre, the acting general secretary, who was a former Minister of Agriculture, was arrested on July 15.

National Union of Ghana Students (NUGS)

This union, which had originally strongly supported the Rawlings regime, became, in November 1982, the focus for some of the most outspoken opposition, with students demonstrating for the release of political detainees and the transfer of power to a civilian government. Following student attacks on newspaper offices, two universities were officially closed on May 16, 1983, and a third on July 3 of that year. The University of Ghana, Legon, was not reopened until October 1984.

New Democratic Movement (NDM)

Leadership. Kwame Karikari (ch.); Tony Akoto Ampaw (gen. sec.)

T. A. Ampaw was detained on May 17, 1987, and K. Karikari (a former director-general of national broadcasting) on July 15.

Greece

Capital: Athens Pop. 9,930,000

Greece, or the Hellenic Republic, is a parliamentary democracy with a President as head of state who is elected by Parliament for a five-year term and who exercises legislative power jointly with Parliament and executive power jointly with the government headed by a Prime Minister. The unicameral 300-member Parliament is elected for a five-year term by universal adult suffrage under a system of reinforced proportional representation. In parliamentary elections held on June 2, 1985, parties obtained seats as follows: Pan-Hellenic Socialist Movement (Pasok) 161, New Democracy 126, Greek Communist Party (KKE Exterior) 12, KKE Interior (Eurocommunist) 1. Among parties which contested the elections without gaining any seats was the (right-wing) Greek National Political Society (EPEN).

In recent years the internal security of Greece has been disturbed by acts of violence committed by members of several extreme right-wing groups and also of numerous small extreme left-wing organizations. An anti-terrorism law passed by Parliament on April 17, 1978 (by 158 votes to 109), provided inter alia for the mandatory death penalty for terrorist acts resulting in loss of life, life imprisonment for such acts carried out without loss of life and up to 10 years' imprisonment for membership of a terrorist organization. For refusing military service members of the Jehovah's Witnesses sect have been given severe prison sentences.

On Nov. 13, 1984, Parliament unanimously passed a law making torture and other forms of mistreatment of prisoners punishable by imprisonment. (Greece was believed to be the first country to outlaw torture formally.)

Right-wing Organizations

Forbidden Yellow Organization of Air Force Officers

This organization, which had called for the resignation of the chief of the Air Force General Staff, Gen. Nikolaos Kouris, claimed responsibility for two bomb explosions in the centre of Athens on Feb. 6, 1984.

National Front

This organization claimed responsibility for the explosion of a powerful bomb in a bar in Athens on Feb. 3, 1986, when 79 persons were injured, most of them US servicemen from a nearby base. The attack was made in protest against alleged US implication in the Turkish occupation of northern Cyprus.

Left-wing Organizations

Anarchist Action Group

This Group committed arson at the Athens office of *Exormissi*, the Pasok journal, on June 1, 1986, and also at the office of Pasok's regional headquarters and of *Agonistes*, the newspaper of the party's youth movement, on June 23 of that year.

(Anarchist groups were involved in clashes with police in December 1984, May 1985 and on various occasions in 1986. They also took part in violent disturbances in Athens, Salonika and Xanthi on Nov. 17-19, 1985, when police shot dead a demonstrating youth of 15 and damage of about US$5,600,000 was caused in Athens.)

Anti-Military Struggle

This group claimed responsibility for the murder of Georgis Athanasiadis, publisher of the conservative opposition newspaper *Vradyni*, on March 19, 1983. At the funeral of the victim of this action on March 23 about 100,000 supporters of the New Democracy party demonstrated against the socialist (Pasok) government.

Anti-State Struggle

This group claimed responsibility for killing a public prosecutor in Athens on April 1, 1985.

November 12 Group

This Group claimed responsibility for causing four explosions in Athens on Nov. 22-23, 1984, one of them occurring at the office of the conservative newspaper *Messimvrini*.

November 17 Revolutionary Organization

This group claimed responsibility for the assassination of an alleged US intelligence officer in Athens on Dec. 23, 1975, and of a convicted torturer (i.e. a former member of the secret police under the military regime in 1967-74) on Dec. 14, 1976. Following the assassination of a deputy riot police chief and his driver on Jan. 16, 1980, nine members of the group were arrested.

The group also claimed responsibility for several other acts of violence, including (i) the killing of Capt. George Tsantes (the chief of the naval section of the Joint US Military Aid Group to Greece) and his Greek driver in Athens on Nov. 15, 1983 (whereafter the police confirmed that the attacker had used a weapon which had been used in the killing of Dec. 23, 1975); (ii) the murder of a US serviceman on April 3, 1984; (iii) the shooting dead of the publisher of the conservative daily newspaper *Apogermatini* on Feb. 21, 1986 (with the group accusing him of helping the US Central Intelligence Agency to create a climate of uncertainty in Greece); (iv) the killing of three policemen and causing injury to 12 other persons in a police bus on Nov. 26, 1985; and (v) the killing of the chairman of the Khalyvourgiki Steel Company on April 8, 1985.

Revolutionary Group of International Solidarity Christos Kassimis

The Group (named after a Greek shot dead by police in 1977) attempted on March 3, 1985, to bomb the West German embassy in Athens and stated that it was acting in solidarity with the French Direct Action, the West German Red Army Faction and the (Belgian) Fighting Communist Cells (CCC). It also claimed responsibility for two bombs which damaged cars of US servicemen in September 1985, and for bombing a statue of former US President Harry S. Truman in Athens on March 22-23, 1986, in protest against a visit to Greece by the US Secretary of State (George Shultz). (The issue of the restoration of the statue subsequently created friction in relations between the USA and Greece, the Athens City Council voting in April 1986 not to re-erect the monument, while in January 1987 it was reported that the Greek government had reversed this decision.)

Revolutionary Popular Struggle

This group has assumed responsibility for more than 100 minor bombings between 1976 and 1986, in particular for a number of bomb explosions at US military and other targets between March and June 1982, carried out as protests against the US military presence in Greece. After a bomb had exploded outside the Athens City Council office on Oct. 11, 1986, the group stated that it intended "to promote revolutionary change in Greece". Its attacks caused material damage but no casualties.

Grenada

Capital: St George's Pop. 120,000

Grenada is an independent state within the Commonwealth with the British monarch as ceremonial head of state being represented by the Governor-General. It has a bicameral parliament consisting of (i) a House of Representatives (with 15 members) and (ii) a Senate to which seven members are appointed on the advice of the Prime Minister, three on the advice of the leader of the opposition and three on the advice of the Prime Minister after consulting interests which it is considered that members should represent.

The country's 1974 Constitution was suspended in March 1979 when the regime of Sir Eric Gairy was overthrown by the New Jewel Movement (NJM) led by Maurice Bishop, and the country run by a ("new-left") People's Revolutionary Government (PRG) and a Revolutionary Council.

On Dec. 3, 1984, the House of Representatives was reconstituted at a general election which followed the joint US-Caribbean military intervention in Grenada on Oct. 25, 1983, after the death of Bishop at the hands of a rival PRG faction. (In 1983 Bishop sought to improve relations with the USA, a move which led to a power struggle within the PRG and Bishop's execution on Oct. 19, 1983. The US-Caribbean intervention displaced the Revolutionary Military Council and set up an interim council under the Governor, Sir Paul Scoon.)

Several parties which had gone underground or into exile during the PRG rule re-emerged to contest the election in which the New National Party (NNP) won 14 seats and the Grenada United Labour Party (GULP), led by Sir Eric Gairy (who did not himself stand) the remaining one. The successful GULP candidate at first refused to take up his seat, calling the polls "fraudulent". When he did, he was expelled from his party and formed the Grenada Democratic Labour Party.

The New National Party comprises the Grenada National Party (in 1981, a party of similar name—the Grenada National Party for Recovery and Liberation—had been accused of issuing counter-revolutionary pamphlets); the Grenada Democratic Movement, formed in 1983 by right-wing exiles in Barbados and Trinidad; and the National Democratic Movement.

Other parties which unsuccessfully contested the elections were the Maurice Bishop Patriotic Movement (MBPM), formed by three former "moderate" members of the NJM, which won 5 per cent of the votes; the Christian Democratic Labour Party led by Winston Whyte (leader of the former People's Action Group who was arrested in 1979 for plotting against the PRG); and three independent candidates. More radical members of the NJM, most of whose leaders were in prison, ceased to function as a political party and advocated a boycott of the elections.

The strength of the NNP in the House was reduced in 1986 to 12 when the junior Education Minister withdrew from the party and formed the Democratic Labour Congress, and the deputy speaker resigned.

On Dec. 4, 1986, the trial of former government and military officials accused of the murder of Bishop on Oct. 19, 1983, was concluded. Of 18 accused, 14 received death sentences, three received long-term prison sentences, and one was acquitted. The former deputy Prime Minister, Bernard Coard, was among those sentenced to death. An appeal was expected.

Guatemala

Capital: Guatemala City Pop. 7,960,000

The Republic of Guatemala returned to elected civilian government in January 1986 after four years of de facto military rule. The presidential elections of November 1985 were won by Vinicio Cerezo Arévalo of the Christian Democratic Party (PDCG) after a run-off ballot in December, and in the concurrent legislative elections the PDCG gained 51 seats in Congress. The remaining seats were distributed as follows: Union of the National Centre (UCN) 22, Revolutionary Party (PR) and Democratic Party of National Co-operation (PDCN) in coalition 11, National Liberation Movement (MLN) and Democratic Institutional Party (PID) six each, Democratic Socialist Party (PSD) two, and Nationalist Renewal Party (PRN) and Nationalist Authentic Central (CAN) one each. The elections were held under the provisions of a new Constitution promulgated in May 1985 (taking effect in January 1986), which barred members of the opposition guerrilla forces from participating.

The country's four principal left-wing guerrilla organizations have been active since the 1960s in both rural and urban areas, waging an assassination campaign against government officials, judges and members of the armed forces. In February 1982 they established a "unified military command" called the Guatemalan Revolutionary Unity (URNG), which was supported by an umbrella grouping of political parties and popular organizations called the Guatemalan Committee of Patriotic Unity (CGUP). The URNG subsequently boycotted the March 1982 elections, declaring on March 27 that they would continue their operations because the military coup of March 23 had produced merely "a change in the façade of the regime" and that no reforms were possible in Guatemala "without revolutionary changes". They rejected offers of negotiation made in April and June by the military government of Gen. Efraín Ríos Montt, and also an amnesty decreed on May 22 for one month (at the end of which certain areas of the country were to be declared zones of exception and anti-guerrilla operations would intensify, with the assistance of some 25,000 newly recruited and trained paramilitary peasant militias). This last aspect of government policy was extended in 1983 with the designation of "protected villages" and in 1984 by the introduction of a "food for work" programme based in "model villages" in areas termed "poles of development". The army described the villages as "re-education centres for those peasants who have been infiltrated by the country's insurgents", but opponents claimed they were in effect concentration camps. The persistently high level of political killings recorded in Guatemala since the anti-insurgency campaign of the 1960s has continued, even after the restoration of civilian rule in 1986. According to the Mexican-based Guatemalan Commission for Human Rights there were 126 disappearances and 463 extra-judicial killings in the first year of civilian rule; other reports spoke of a crime wave encouraged by the disbandment of police death squads, whose task had been to liquidate those suspected of criminal activity, while killings and disappearances remained widespread in the countryside despite some abatement in the urban areas.

Left-wing Alliances

Guatemalan Committee of Patriotic Unity (*Comité Guatemalteco de Unidad Patriótica,* CGUP)

Leadership. Luis Cardoza y Aragón (head of co-ordinating committee)

This Committee was formed on Feb. 16, 1982 (as announced simultaneously in Panama, Paris and Mexico City on Feb. 19), by the Democratic Front against Repression (FDCR), the 31st January Popular Front (FP-31), several members of the (social democratic) United Revolutionary Front (FUR), and 26 prominent Guatemalan exiles of various political affiliations. These 26 persons signed a founding document and set up an eight-member co-ordinating committee headed by Luis Cardoza y Aragón, a veteran politician who had been a member of the (left-wing) government of President Arbenz Guzmán, overthrown in June 1954; other members of the Committee included Guillermo Toriello Garrido (who had been Foreign Minister under President Arbenz Guzmán), a member of the Committee of Peasant Unity (CUC) and Carlos Gallardo Flores, leader of the Democratic Socialist Party (*Partido Socialista Democrático,* PSD).

The CGUP endorsed the basic programme of the Guatemalan National Revolutionary Unity (URNG—see separate entry), stating that the popular revolutionary war was the only road left open, but that it had no direct links with the guerrillas. The CGUP also denounced the elections to be held on March 7, 1982, as a "farce" on the grounds that "electoral fraud, corruption, persecution and assassination of democratic leaders and of hundreds of party members" had been "the permanent practices of the regime". It declared that the people of Guatemala were carrying on a war aimed at "constructing a new society which responds to its interests and aspirations, confronting the bloodiest dictatorship which Latin America has ever known".

Guatemalan National Revolutionary Unity (*Unidad Revolucionaria Nacional Guatemalteca,* URNG)

Leadership. Raúl Molina Mejía

The formation of this unified military command was announced on Feb. 8, 1982, by the four main guerrilla organizations which had on several earlier occasions (in November 1979, May 1980 and January 1981) declared their intention to unite. They were the Guerrilla Army of the Poor (EGP), the Revolutionary Organization of the People in Arms (ORPA), the Rebel Armed Forces (FAR) and a faction of the (Communist) Guatemalan Labour Party (PGT). It is also known as the Unitary Representation of the Guatemalan Opposition (*Representación Unitaria de la Oposición Guatemalteca,* RUOG). It is close to the Democratic Socialist Party (PSD) and is supported by the Guatemalan Committee of Patriotic Unity (see separate entry).

The URNG announced that it intended to pursue a "popular revolutionary war" as the sole means left to the people "to free themselves from oppression, exploitation, discrimination and dependence on foreign countries". It also denounced "the most odious genocide perpetrated in the whole of the western hemisphere", where, it said, on average 36 persons disappeared or were assassinated every day. The URNG listed as its main objectives (i) an end to repression and a guarantee of life, peace and fundamental human rights for all citizens; (ii) provision for the basic needs of the majority of the people; (iii) equality for the indigenous and the White-descended (*ladinos*) people; (iv) the creation of a new society in which all sectors of the population would be represented in the government; and (v) non-alignment and international co-operation.

By mid-1982 the URNG had an estimated fighting strength of about 6,000, and in addition to its campaign of economic sabotage the command stepped up its action against the military government in 1983 and early 1984. It was reported in February 1985 that the URNG had announced its intention "to accelerate the development of the revolutionary war", and in March 1986 the organization categorically denied press reports that it was prepared to disarm as a gesture of goodwill to the new civilian government.

In January 1987 the URNG renewed its attacks on military targets and the following month proposed a dialogue with the government, but President Cerezo rejected the offer unless the guerrillas agreed to a prior ceasefire.

Left-wing Movements

Democratic Front against Repression (*Frente Democrático contra la Represión,* FDCR)

Leadership. Rafael García

This Front was formed in March 1979 by over 72 parties and organizations, including the (social democratic) United Revolutionary Front (*Frente Unido de la Revolución,* FUR) established in 1977. The objects of the FDCR were defined as the denunciation at national and international level of all repressive actions committed in Guatemala against any popular and democratic sector and the provision of aid to widows and orphans of the victims.

In February 1982 it joined the Guatemalan Committee of Patriotic Unity (CGUP). It has been regarded as having links with the Revolutionary Organization of the People at Arms (ORPA), although it has denied having direct association with any guerrilla movement.

Guatemalan Labour Party (*Partido Guatemalteco del Trabajo,* PGT)

Leadership. Carlos González (sec.-gen.); Mario Sánchez

This party was founded as the Communist Party of Guatemala at an underground congress held in September 1949 (after having previously been known as the Democratic Vanguard of Guatemala formed out of various left-wing groups). It was one of the first and best organized communist parties in Central America. In 1954 the party was outlawed; from then on it worked underground; and from 1961 it conducted armed struggle. At its second congress, held in December 1962, it adopted the name of Guatemalan Labour Party.

In 1969 the party adopted a new programme aimed at "the agrarian anti-imperialist revolution" and "the socialist revolution". However, in 1972-74 all members of the party's central committee were executed or murdered. The party subsequently elected a new leadership and decided in favour of a peaceful road to socialism, but it appeared that this decision was endorsed only by a minority of party members (most of whom were killed or went into exile), whereas a majority of members reverted to armed struggle and participated in the formation of the Rebel Armed Forces (FAR—see separate entry).

By 1980 PGT guerrillas were active in Guatemala City and the south-western departments of Escuintla, Suchitepéquez and Retalhuleu. The PGT is divided into three factions and the guerrilla faction joined the unified military command known as the Guatemalan National Revolutionary Unity (URNG)—see separate entry. In October 1983 PGT members kidnapped a newspaper executive and successfully demanded the publication of a manifesto in North and Central American newspapers in return for his release.

The PGT is officially recognized by the Communist parties of the Soviet bloc countries.

Guerrilla Army of the Poor (*Ejército Guerrillero de los Pobres,* EGP)

Leadership. Rolando Morán (commander)

This movement was formed in 1972 by the survivors of an offshoot of the Rebel Armed Forces (FAR—see separate entry) and greatly extended its activities in 1976, with the result that by the end of that year it controlled certain areas in the country's northern mountains. While the EGP was active mainly among the country's landless Indian peasants in the highland departments of Huehuetenango, El Quiché and Alta Verapaz, some of its members were also involved in incidents in Guatemala City.

When army units opened fire on a peasant demonstration at Panzós (north-east of Guatemala City) on May 29, 1978, President Laugerud García accused both the EGP and Roman Catholic and Protestant clergy of inciting peasants to "invade private estates" and seize land. A group of 27 Indian peasants from the department of El Quiché (north-west of Guatemala City), which had been under virtual military occupation since 1975 because of the activities of the EGP (and also of the Revolutionary Organization of the People in Arms, ORPA), occupied the Spanish embassy in Guatemala City on Jan. 31, 1980, taking the ambassador and other people hostages. When the Guatemalan police, against the express wishes of the ambassador, stormed the building, a petrol bomb was thrown by the peasants and in the ensuing fire 39 people lost their lives, the only survivors being the ambassador and one of the peasants—Yuxa Shona, who was, however, killed by a death squad after being abducted from hospital on Feb. 1.

On Sept. 5, 1980, Elias Barȧhona, press secretary at the Guatemalan Ministry of the Interior, stated at a press conference in Panama that he was a member of the EGP and had infiltrated the government four years earlier.

In June 1981 the guerrillas claimed to have extended their "people's war" to 19 of Guatemala's 22 departments and to be concentrating on the Verapaz oil region near the Mexican border in the north-west. In February 1982 the EGP joined the unified military command known as the Guatemalan National Revolutionary Unity (URNG). In September 1982 four EGP members became the first Guatemalans to be executed judicially under military rule.

The EGP renewed its military action in February 1984, claiming by the end of the year to have carried out 181 operations, killing 686 army troops, and in early 1985 claimed a further 170 army fatalities. In 1985 its armed strength was estimated at about 4,000 with a further 12,000 unarmed members.

The EGP has links with the Committee of Peasant Unity (CUC), the 31st January Popular Front (FP-31) and church-based radical groups.

People's Revolutionary Movement-Ixim (*Movimiento Revolucionario del Pueblo-Ixim,* MRP)

This Marxist-Leninist group was formed in 1982 by dissidents from the Revolutionary Organization of the People at Arms (ORPA) who refused to join the Guatemalan National Revolutionary Unity (URNG) because they felt that it gave too little consideration to Indian demands. ("Ixim" is a Mayan word meaning food.)

Members of the Movement kidnapped the daughter of the President of Honduras (Dr Roberto Suazo Córdova) on Dec. 14, 1982, but released her on Dec. 24 after the Guatemalan government had permitted the publication of an MRP manifesto in local newspapers (this manifesto being also published in newspapers in Mexico and Central America).

Rebel Armed Forces (*Fuerzas Armadas Rebeldes,* FAR)

Leadership. Nicolás Sis (commander); Pablo Monsanto

The FAR was established in December 1962 by the 13th November Revolutionary Movement (*Movimiento Revolucionario Trece de Noviembre,* MR-13) which had arisen out of a rebellion by a group of officers on Nov. 13, 1960, and was led by Luis Turcios Lima (who died in 1966), Marco Antonio Yon Sosa ("El Chino", who was killed in a clash with troops in May 1970) and Luis Trejo Esquivel. The FAR was, on its foundation, joined by part of the Guatemalan Labour Party (PGT), and together they had about 500 members. From 1970 onwards the FAR went into decline but in 1972 it was reorganized with the aim of constituting a mass party, and later it reverted to armed struggle. By 1980 it operated in the northern departments of El Petén and Chimaltenango and also near Lake Izabál (in eastern Guatemala).

Members of the FAR kidnapped the sister of President Efraín Ríos Montt in June 1983 and the sister of President Oscar Mejía Victores in September, but freed both after the publication of a FAR manifesto in various newspapers in October. In January 1984 the group launched an offensive against army positions in El Petén and renewed major military action in early 1985.

In February 1982 the FAR joined the unified military command known as the Guatemalan National Revolutionary Unity (URNG).

Revolutionary Organization of the People in Arms (*Organización Revolucionaria del Pueblo en Armas,* ORPA)

Leadership. Rodrigo "Gaspar" Ilom (commander); Lucrecia Matzar

The ORPA was formed in 1971 by a group of dissidents from the Rebel Armed Forces (FAR), and launched its military campaign in September 1979. It built up its support in rural areas, is anti-racialist and stands for the development of the indigenous people's culture.

ORPA guerrillas, who enjoyed considerable support among the Indian population, were in 1980 active mainly in the western and central departments of San Marcos, Totonicapán, Quezaltenango, Sololá and Escuintla, but also in Guatemala City and areas to the south of it. In September of that year they occupied tourist-frequented areas on the shores of Lake Atitlán (west of Guatemala City), near which the army thereupon established a base from which it launched attacks against the guerrillas. In July 1981 security forces destroyed ORPA bases in the capital. The ORPA guerrillas co-operated closely with those of the Guatemalan Labour Party (PGT), and the organization has links with the Democratic Front against Repression (FDCR).

In February 1982 the ORPA joined the unified military command known as the Guatemalan National Revolutionary Unity (URNG), and by mid-1984 was reckoned to be the most effective of the four main guerrilla groups. It claimed to have inflicted 122 casualties on the army after 10 days of fighting in San Marcos in August 1984.

Tecum Uman Front (*Frente Tecum Uman*)

This Indian guerrilla group was established in 1982, and on Aug. 17, 1982, it ambushed government troops in Chimaltenango department, inflicting 40 casualties.

31st January Popular Front (*Frente Popular 31 de Enero,* FP-31)

This Front, formed in January 1981, took its name from the date of the 1980 attack on the Spanish embassy in Guatemala City by peasants (see under Guerrilla Army of the Poor, EGP).

Its component parties were the Federation of Guatemalan Workers (FTG), the Committee of Peasant Unity (CUC, with about 6,000 members), the Felipe Antonio García Revolutionary Workers' Nuclei (with 1,500 members), the Trinidad Gómez Hernández Settlers' Co-ordinating Body, the Vicente Menchú Revolutionary Christians (named after one of the peasants who died in the embassy siege, with 4,000 members) and the Rubén García Revolutionary Student Front (with 200 members). The FP-31 described its aims as "the removal from power of the military, economic and political forces which sustain the dictatorship and the establishment of a revolutionary, popular and democratic government" by means of guerrilla warfare.

On May 12, 1982, a dozen members of the FP-31 and the Committee of Peasant Unity (CUC), claiming to represent people who had been "persecuted" and whose harvests and farms had been burned, and protesting against killings by the security forces in rural areas, seized the Brazilian embassy in Guatemala City and took some 10 persons, including the ambassador, as hostages. However, after the government had agreed to the occupiers' demand to hold a press conference denouncing the massacres, they were flown to Mexico with some of the hostages who had agreed to guarantee their safety, while the remaining hostages (among them the ambassador) were released unharmed.

In February 1982 the FP-31 joined the Guatemalan Committee of Patriotic Unity (CGUP).

Extreme Right-wing Groups

In retaliation for the killings and other acts of violence perpetrated by left-wing guerrillas, numerous extreme right-wing organizations, some of which were alleged to enjoy government support or to work in close association with the police, have in recent years engaged in attacks on left-wing leaders, including journalists, trade unionists and lawyers. Other particular targets have been teachers and students at the San Carlos University and Catholic priests (especially Jesuits). The loss of life on both sides in the conflict has run into tens of thousands.

Amnesty International alleged on Dec. 11, 1976, that in the past 10 years over 20,000 people, many of them political dissidents, had been killed or had disappeared without trace in Guatemala as a result of action by government or semi-official forces. According to a conservative Guatemalan newspaper (quoted in *The New York Times* on Nov. 28, 1980) there had been, in the first 10 months of 1980, a total of 3,617 violent deaths (including those of 389 university students, 326 school teachers, 311 peasant leaders, 86 university professors and 12 journalists).

In a further Amnesty International report published on Feb. 18, 1981, it was alleged that the murders were being carried out by the police and the army and that secret detentions and summary executions were "part of a clearly defined programme of government" and reflected "a pattern of selective and considered official action" based on denunciations and on decisions made by senior officials of the Ministers of Defence and the Interior in consultation with the Army General Staff. Political killings continued after the military coup of 1982, with a marked increase after the elections of July 1984 and a death toll for the whole of 1984 reaching 4,000. Contrary to many expectations the political violence did not diminish after the return to civilian rule in 1986, and the Americas Watch Committee recorded 277 assassinations in April-June 1986.

Details of some of the known extreme right-wing groups active in Guatemala are given below.

Armed Action Forces (*Fuerzas de Acción Armada,* FADA)

This group was responsible, inter alia, for the murder on Jan. 25, 1979, of Alberto Fuentes Mohr, leader of the Democratic Socialist Party (PSD), a former Foreign Minister (in 1966-70) and supporter of the (centre-left) National Unity Front (FRENU).

Death Squad (*Escuadrón de la Muerte*, EM)

The EM was for many years engaged in killings of alleged left-wing activists or sympathizers and especially leaders of labour and peasant organizations. In 1980 alone it was considered responsible for several hundred such deaths every month. According to a statement made in Panama on Sept. 1, 1980, by Elias Barahona, a member of the Guerrilla Army of the Poor (EGP), the EM was directed by the President, the Prime Minister and a number of generals.

Guatemalan Guerrilla Commandos in Formation (*Comandos Guerrilleros Guatemaltecos en Formación,* CGGF)

This right-wing guerrilla group was formed in 1984 and claimed responsibility for the kidnapping of a student in October of that year.

Secret Anti-Communist Army (*Ejército Secreto Anti-Comunista,* ESA)

Established in 1976, this organization was responsible for the killing of numerous politicians and officials as well as trade unionists and student leaders whose names appeared on regularly published "death lists". The ESA was believed to be linked to the extreme right-wing National Liberation Movement (MLN) led by Mario Sandoval Alarcón, who was Vice-President of Guatemala in 1974-78. The ESA was thought to be involved in the killing of the president of the university students' association on Oct. 20, 1978. It was also thought to be one of the organizations responsible for the murder of Manuel Colom Argueta (the country's leading opposition figure) on March 22, 1979.

In a declaration published in a Guatemalan newspaper in January 1980, Jesuits stated that between January and October 1979 ESA death squads had committed 3,252 murders "with absolute impunity". From Rome it was announced on Feb. 13, 1980, that on Jan. 23 the Jesuit Order had received death threats from the ESA against its 52 priests in Guatemala.

According to a statement made in Panama on Sept. 1, 1980, by a member of the Guerrilla Army of the Poor (EGP), Elias Barahona, the ESA was directed by the President, the Prime Minister and a number of generals.

The White Hand (*La Mano Blanca*)

This group has been active since 1970, when its headquarters were said to be in the police building in Guatemala City. It was, in particular, responsible for the killing, on April 8, 1970, of César Montenegro Paniagua, a (pro-Soviet) communist leader suspected of involvement in the abduction and killing by the Rebel Armed Forces (FAR) of the West German ambassador in Guatemala a week earlier.

The White Hand was reported to be linked to Gen. Carlos Manuel Araña Osorio, who was President of Guatemala in 1970-74 and who was a leading member of the (right-wing) National Liberation Movement (MLN). The White Hand was also believed to be one of the two organizations suspected of involvement in the murder of Manuel Colom Argueta, a leading opposition figure, on March 22, 1979 (the other suspected organization being the Secret Anti-Communist Army, ESA).

A reputed former leader of the White Hand, Brig.-Gen. Manuel Francisco Sosa Avila, who later became Chief of Police, was killed by unidentified assailants in March 1985.

Guinea

Capital: Conakry Pop. 5,400,000

On April 3, 1984, the country's armed forces, consisting of its army, navy, air force, gendarmerie and people's militia, assumed power a week after the death of President Ahmed Sekou Touré, who had held dictatorial power since Oct. 2, 1958, when Guinea achieved its independence. A newly formed *Comité militaire de redressement national* (CMRN) stated that it intended to lay the foundations of "true democracy". Col. Lansana Conté, the chairman of the CMRN, became President of the republic, and a new Cabinet, headed by a Prime Minister and composed mainly of military men, was formed on April 4.

The CMRN released all political prisoners, numbering about 250, promised freedom of the press and declared that former politicians would not face trial except in cases of corruption.

On May 27 the President decreed that the country's name should revert to Republic of Guinea (as it had been called until 1978).

On May 15, 1985, it was announced that 32 former ministers, officers and civil servants associated with the previous regime and detained since April 3, 1984, had been released.

An attempted coup by Lt.-Col. Diarra Traoré (a former Prime Minister and then Minister of National Education) was foiled on July 4, 1985. The President announced on July 7 that in the fighting which took place during the attempt 18 people had died and 229 had been injured, but that Col. Traoré had been arrested and the conspirators would be executed. Those arrested included several members of the Cabinet and of the CMRN, and also former ministers under the Sekou Touré regime. On July 8 it was disclosed that 41 persons had already been detained after an earlier coup attempt in January 1985.

A Court of State Security, assisted by a military tribunal, was established in August 1985 to pass judgment on persons charged with "crimes against the state". The accused were to have legal representation but there was no appeal against the Court's decisions. It was to try an estimated 200 persons arrested in connexion with the attempted coup; they were said to include six out of eight provincial governors and six out of 35 regional prefects. No details of the trials were published but it was reported on Oct. 2, 1985, that 20 persons had been executed on July 8, among them two brothers of the late President Sekou Touré and several of his former ministers and supporters.

(During the 1970s opposition to the Sekou Touré regime had been organized in various groups, most of them based in Paris, but they had remained ineffectual.)

It was announced on May 6, 1987, that 60 people, including nine former Cabinet ministers and 30 military officers, who had been supporters of President Touré, had been sentenced to death following a secret trial.

Guinea-Bissau

Capital: Bissau Pop. 793,000

The Republic of Guinea-Bissau is ruled by a predominantly military Revolutionary Council (composed almost exclusively of Guinean Blacks) which overthrew the government of President Luis de Almeida Cabral, a Cape Verdian *mestiço* (mixed race), on Nov. 14, 1980, and dissolved the institutions of that government. The leaders of the new regime (Maj. João Bernardo Vieira, previously Prime Minister, and Vítor Saúde Maria, previously Foreign Minister) declared after their assumption of power that they intended to pursue the political programmes of the (Marxist) *Partido Africano da Independência da Guiné e do Cabo Verde* (PAIGC), whose principles, they claimed, had been betrayed by President Cabral.

In a Constitution adopted on May 16, 1984, Guinea-Bissau was declared to be "an anti-colonialist and anti-imperialist republic with a policy of national revolutionary democracy", in which the PAIGC would be the leading force in society and state, and the state would direct the economy and control foreign trade.

Eight regional councils elected in March 1984 chose from among their own members a 15-member National People's Assembly which was inaugurated on May 14, 1984. The Assembly subsequently elected the Chairman and the members of a Council of State which would have powers between Assembly sessions. The Chairman of the Council of State is automatically head of state and C.-in-C. of the armed forces.

Early in November 1985 security forces arrested about 50 alleged conspirators, mainly army officers, including Col. Paulo Alexandre Nunes Correia (the First Vice-President). President Vieira claimed on Nov. 15 that the plotters had intended to assassinate him on Nov. 14. In January 1986 several members were expelled from the PAIGC's central committee, among them four persons detained in connexion with the attempted coup. Altogether 63 persons were arrested in the aftermath of the attempt. In a trial by a military tribunal held from June 5 to July 12, 1986, a total of 53 of them were convicted—with the result that 12 were sentenced to death (among them Col. Nunes Correia), seven to 15 years' forced labour and 34 to hard labour for from one to 15 years. Four were acquitted and six had died in detention. On July 19 six of the death sentences were upheld by the ruling Council of State, and they were carried out on July 21; the other death sentences were commuted to 15 years in prison. Those executed included Col. Nunes Correia and also a former Supreme Court judge who was a Portuguese national. Unsuccessful appeals for clemency had been made by, inter alios, President Mario Soares of Portugal.

The government on May 11, 1987, denied reports that 20 army officers had been arrested for conspiring against the President.

Front for the Fight for Guinea-Bissau's National Independence (*Frente da luta pela independência nacional da Guiné "portuguesa"*, FLING)

The FLING was recognized by Senegal in May 1964 as a national liberation movement on an equal footing with the PAIGC, as both claimed to have guerrilla forces active in the then Portuguese Guinea. However, the Foreign Minister of the Republic of Guinea announced on March 17, 1965, that the Council of Ministers of the Organization of African Unity had recognized the PAIGC as the only liberation movement of Portuguese Guinea and had decided to give no further aid to the FLING (which subsequently denied that such a decision had been taken).

Benjamin Pinto Bull, the president of the FLING, claimed on Feb. 13, 1967, that during 1966 the guerrillas of his organization had killed 554 Portuguese soldiers and wounded 319, their own losses being 65 dead, 125 wounded and 17 missing. Claims of rather greater successes were at that time being made by the PAIGC guerrillas, and it was the PAIGC which on Sept. 24, 1975, proclaimed the "Republic of Guinea-Bissau", which within weeks gained widespread international recognition. The FLING thereafter remained in existence as a party in exile (based in Paris and Senegal) opposed to the PAIGC's policy of ultimate union between Guinea-Bissau and the Cape Verde Islands. After the assumption of power by the Revolutionary Council in November 1980 a leading FLING associate inside Guinea-Bissau, Rafael Barbosa (a dissident former PAIGC member said to be supported by right-wing elements in Lisbon), was released from prison but was rearrested shortly afterwards. The new regime thus indicated that it did not identify itself with the aims of the FLING. However, on Jan. 2, 1985, the Council of State decided to release R. Barbosa.

Guyana

Capital: Georgetown Pop. 790,000

The Co-operative Republic of Guyana, a member of the Commonwealth, has under its Constitution, which came into effect on Oct. 6, 1980, a popularly elected executive President and a First Vice-President who is also Prime Minister. There is also a National Assembly to which 53 members are elected for a five-year term by universal adult suffrage, while another 12 members are elected by 10 regional democratic councils from among their own members and by a national congress of local democratic organs.

According to results of general elections held on Dec. 9, 1985, the 53 directly elected seats in the National Assembly were distributed as follows: the (co-operative) People's National Congress (PNC) 42, the (pro-Soviet communist) People's Progressive Party (PPP) 8, the (right-wing) United Force (UF) 2, and the (left-wing) Working People's Alliance (WPA, which had boycotted the 1980 elections) one. It was later reported that the 12 seats reserved for indirect elections were won by the PNC. There was little support for the (centre) Democratic Labour Movement (DLM) formed in 1982 (whose leader Paul Tennassee had been detained temporarily by police after touring Caribbean countries where he was said to have criticized the government of the late Forbes

Burnham), the (centre) People's Democratic Movement (PDM) and the National Democratic Front (NDF) formed in 1985.

The results were called fraudulent by all opposition parties except the UF. The government had rejected demands for international observers, but allegations were supported by Western journalists and diplomats of multiple voting by PNC voters (mainly comprising the African section of the community) and the exclusion from polling booths of PPP supporters (mainly of Asian Indian origin). The role of the army (seen as an instrument of PNC) in transporting ballot boxes was also criticized. Both the PPP and WPA withdrew from the contest during polling day, but later took up their seats.

A statement signed by the Guyana Human Rights Association, Anglican and Roman Catholic bishops and the Guyana Bar Association alleged malpractice in the elections.

In January 1986, an opposition Patriotic Coalition for Democracy (PCD) was formed comprising the PPP, WPA, DLM, NDF and PDM.

A United Republican Party was reported in January 1987 to have been set up by the US-based Guyanese Robert Gangadeen, a former member of the UF.

Conservative Party of Guyana

Leadership. Keshava Keith Moonasar

Six members of this extreme right-wing Toronto-based Conservative Party of Guyana, including the "leader", Keshava Keith Moonasar, were charged in January 1984 in Cleveland, Ohio, with conspiracy in an alleged plot to kill President Burnham, and with contravention of the US weapons laws. The six, five Canadians and one US citizen, pleaded guilty on March 6, 1984.

Guyana Human Rights Association

In a 1986 report, this Association criticized policing practices and described the government's concern for the Amerindian population as "peripheral". The report was dismissed by the government as a "compilation of falsehoods, distortions and scurrilous attacks on the government and people of Guyana".

In 1980, the Association had called for an inquiry into the death of Dr Walter Rodney, a leading member of the WPA who had been considered the founder of the "new left" movement in Commonwealth Caribbean politics. Dr Rodney had died in a car bomb explosion on June 13, 1980.

House of Israel

Leadership. David Hill—also known as Edward Emmanuel Washington ("rabbi")

The leader of this Black supremacist sect, his deputy Rufus Lewis (Prince Jomo) and two sect priests were each sentenced to 15 years' imprisonment on Oct. 30, 1986, for the manslaughter of another sect member in May 1977.

The House of Israel sect had been closely associated with the PNC under the late President Forbes Burnham, and according to critics had regularly helped to break up opposition meetings. Members had been held responsible for acts of violence in 1979 which led to the deaths of the deputy editor and a photographer of *The Catholic Standard* newspaper (which had been critical of the government's human rights record).

Haiti

Capital: Port-au-Prince Pop. 5,272,000

Since Feb. 7, 1986, the Republic of Haiti has been ruled by a National Council of Government (CNG), an interim civilian-military junta under the leadership of General Henri Namphy. The ruling council comprised five members when it assumed power but was later reduced to three, following resignations of its members. There is also a Cabinet including Gen. Namphy, 13 Ministers and 6 Secretaries of State.

The overthrow in February 1986 of former President Jean-Claude Duvalier, who fled to France following two months of spontaneous demonstrations, riots and disturbances, put an end to the 29-year-old Duvalier regime first instituted by Dr François Duvalier ("Papadoc"), which had been one of terror, repression and corruption, and during which supporters of independent political parties were subject to arrest, imprisonment, exile and execution. The main factors leading to the downfall of the Duvalier regime were the failure of the army to repress the revolts, the loss of support from the USA and from the largely Creole middle class and élite, the criticism of the Roman Catholic Church, the dictator's own vacillation in the face of unrest, and the country's appalling economic and social condition.

The new government announced on June 6, 1986, that a constituent assembly would be elected in October 1986 to draft a new Constitution for consideration in a referendum in February 1987 and that presidential and legislative elections were to be held in November 1987 to enable a new government to be sworn in on Feb. 7, 1988. In a decree issued on July 24, 1986, conditions were laid down for the formation of political parties; they included the lifting of restrictions on the activities of the Communist Party (banned for 50 years). A press decree of July 31 guaranteed freedom of expression but also forbade the publication of material deemed to endanger morality or public order and provided for the annual licensing of all journalists by the Ministry of Information.

On Oct. 19, 1986, a total of 101 candidates stood for election to 41 of the 61 seats in the constituent assembly (the remaining 20 to be filled by government appointees). The voters' turnout was less than 5 per cent as groups across the whole political spectrum boycotted the elections either because they favoured an immediate return to civilian government or because they wanted all seats to be open to election.

The provisional ruling council has faced growing popular protest, strikes and demonstrations ever since it took office. By the end of 1986 the country was in a state of chronic political instability and uncertainty. The unrest was fuelled by the fact that the new government included prominent former supporters of J.-C. Duvalier, including one member of the CNG, and by the ruling council's reluctance to prosecute Duvalier aides for violations of human rights under the previous regime. Public anger was aroused further by the discovery that numerous members of the Special Force of National Security Volunteers, known as the Tontons Macoutes, the previously dreaded army of the Duvalier family, had been allowed to escape abroad. In March 1986 in the face of public unrest, four members of the CNG resigned and there were several resignations and dismissals of ministers.

The new Constitution, providing for presidential and legislative elections in November 1987, was approved by referendum in March 1987. On June 22, 1987, the government announced that it would take control of the electoral process away from an independent civilian electoral council established under the Constitution. Following this political, trade union and civic organizations staged a general strike, calling for the removal of the CNG, with up to 24 deaths reported in clashes with the army, and on July 2 the government reversed its decision. The unrest was considered the most serious in the country since the fall of J.-C. Duvalier.

Honduras

Capital: Tegucigalpa Pop. 4,370,000

The Republic of Honduras has an executive President who is elected for a four-year term by universal adult suffrage and who presides over a Cabinet. There is a unicameral National Congress of 134 members, similarly elected for a four-year term.

Since the long presidency of Gen. Tiburcio Carias Andino of the National Party (PN) in 1932-48, Honduran political life has been very unstable and liable to military intervention. In 1986, however, one elected civilian government was directly succeeded by another for the first time since 1929, with José Azcona del Hoyo of the Liberal Party (PLH) as President. Azcona had won only 27 per cent of the vote in the Nov. 24, 1985, presidential elections, but was declared the winner as the leading candidate of the party with the highest total aggregate vote (from three candidates), although the highest single vote was for Rafael Leonardo Callejas of the PN. Former President Roberto Suazo Córdova had precipitated a constitutional crisis in March 1985 in an unsuccessful attempt to ensure the election of his own PLH candidate. In the simultaneous legislative elections the PLH won 67 seats, the PN 63 and the Innovation and Unity Party (PINU) and Christian Democratic Party (PDC) two each.

Unrest in neighbouring countries has not been without effect on the situation in Honduras. Many thousands of refugees from the civil war in El Salvador were by 1982 accommodated in camps just inside Honduras, and there have been reports of military action against these refugees by Honduran troops in co-operation with Salvadorean army units pursuing guerrilla suspects from El Salvador. Still more disruptive has been the presence of Nicaraguan refugees and Nicaraguan "contra" guerrillas in camps in the south of the country, who are also rumoured to have received assistance from the Honduran armed forces.

Among violent actions by indigenous Honduran groups, the most serious appear to have been those committed by militant peasants in support of their demands for accelerating the government's land reform programme, and since 1982 there have been frequent protests over the build-up of US military bases and personnel. A few small armed groups emerged in the late 1970s from radical student groups or as off-shoots of the then outlawed Communist Party (PCH). In 1983 the current Head of the Armed Forces, Gen. Gustavo Adolfo Alvarez Martínez, claimed that 3,000 Hondurans were being trained in guerrilla warfare, mostly in Cuba and the Soviet

Union, and during his term of office (January 1982-March 1984) the armed forces were accused of torturing and killing political prisoners in a "dirty war" against suspected subversives.

On March 21, 1986, the National Congress approved a general amnesty for 31 political prisoners (26 of whom had conducted a hunger strike). The Attorney General announced in May 1986 that both civilian and military personnel accused of political crimes would be allowed to return to Honduras and that legal proceedings against Honduran military officers charged with human rights abuses and other crimes would be halted. On Feb. 2, 1987, he was reported to have announced that a governmental human rights commission had been appointed to reopen investigations into the cases of missing people (about which accusations had been made by a Committee for the Defence of Human Rights and a Committee of Families of Detained-Disappeared Persons).

In September 1986 the president of the Committee for the Defence of Human Rights denounced the existence of a "death list" drawn up by a right-wing faction within the army and also the fact that 58 persons had been killed by death squads so far in 1986.

Left-wing Alliances

Honduran Peasants' National Unity Front (*Frente de Unidad Nacional Campesino Hondureño,* Funacamh)

In 1981 this militant alliance of peasant unions, established in October 1975, embraced six principal peasant unions. The largest of them, with 80,000 members (in 1981), was the National Association of Honduran Peasants (ANACAMH) led by Antonio Julián Méndez, a PINU member of Congress; the second largest, with 20,000 to 30,000 members, was the National Union of Authentic Peasants of Honduras (UNCAH), which was under the influence of the Revolutionary People's Union (URP).

The other main organizations which joined the alliance were the National Front of Independent Peasants of Honduras, the Federation of Farming Co-operatives of the Honduran Land Reform (Fecorah), the National Union of Popular Co-operatives of Honduras (Unacooph), and the National Peasants' Union (UNC).

The Funacamh has co-ordinated a campaign, involving the occupation of land as well as strikes by peasants, with the object of accelerating the execution of the government's land reform programme and of ending abuses.

The leader of the ANACAMH warned landowners on May 1, 1986, not to attempt to defend themselves against peasants' land invasions by employing "death squads".

United National Directorate (*Directorio Nacional Unido,* DNU)

It was reported from Managua (Nicaragua) on April 3, 1983, that the following organizations had joined together to form the DNU: the Cinchonero People's Liberation Movement (MPLC), the Morazanista Front for the Liberation of Honduras (FMLH), Troylan Turcios, the Lorenzo Zelaya Popular Revolutionary Forces (FRP), the Communist Party (PCH), the Central American Revolutionary Workers' Party of Honduras (PRTCH) and the Revolutionary Unity Movement (MUR). (The PCH had gained legal recognition in 1981.) The DNU's stated aim was to form "a single popular army under one command . . . first to struggle for our own liberation" by means of popular war, and "second to play an active part in the event of the regionalization of the Central American crisis".

Left-wing Movements

Cinchonero People's Liberation Movement (*Movimiento Popular de Liberación Cinchonero,* MPLC)

This Movement was established in 1978 as an offshoot of the (pro-Soviet) Communist Party. It took its name from a former national peasant leader, and its political wing is the Revolutionary People's Union (URP—see separate entry). In April 1983 it joined the United National Directorate (DNU), and it reportedly has links with the Farabundo Martí National Liberation Front (FMLN) in El Salvador.

In March 1981 members of the MPLC hijacked a Honduran airliner with 81 passengers and six crew members, diverted it to Managua (Nicaragua)—where 37 of the passengers were released—and successfully demanded the release from detention of 11 Salvadoreans and two Hondurans. After the aircraft had been taken to Panama, the remaining hostages were released by the hijackers who surrendered to the Panamanian authorities (and were later believed to have flown to Cuba).

The MPLC also claimed responsibility for a bomb which exploded in the Constituent Assembly building in Tegucigalpa on Sept. 23, 1981, as part of a protest against imminent joint US-Honduras military manoeuvres.

In September 1982 MPLC members occupied the chamber of commerce building in San Pedro Sula (north-eastern Honduras) and demanded the repeal of anti-terrorist legislation, the expulsion of military advisers from the USA, Argentina, Chile and Israel and the release of 57 political prisoners (including the leaders of the URP), the expulsion of Nicaraguan "contras" and an end to "the repression of the Honduran people". The government, however, denied that there were any military advisers from Argentina, Chile or Israel in Honduras, and the police chief stated that there were no political prisoners in the country—which led opponents of the government to believe that those named had meanwhile been killed.

As a result of negotiations the occupation ended on Sept. 25, 1982, with the release of hostages held and the departure of 12 guerrillas to Panama en route for Cuba (with these guerrillas claiming that they had secured the release of one prisoner). The Movement's action was condemned by a rally of some 30,000 people in San Pedro Sula on Sept. 21.

In August 1983 the MPLC claimed responsibility for bombings in San Pedro Sula, La Ceiba and La

Lima "to express the Honduran people's repudiation of US intervention in Central America".

In November 1986 an MPLC column was reported to have been active in the mountains near the Honduran north coast since the previous month.

Communist Party of Honduras (*Partido Comunista de Honduras,* PCH)

Leadership. Rigoberto Padilla Rush (gen. sec. of central committee)

Established in April 1954, this party has been illegal for most of its life. In 1960 and again in 1965-67 it suffered breakaways of factions opposed to the Party's pro-Soviet line. At its second congress, held in April 1972, the party reaffirmed its loyalty to Marxism-Leninism and "proletarian internationalism" and adopted a new programme and constitution, defining its tasks as "struggle against the domination of US imperialism and the reactionary bourgeoisie and landowners, and for an anti-imperialist, agrarian, popular and democratic revolution". The PCH is officially recognized by the Communist parties of the Soviet-bloc countries.

Although it gained official recognition in 1981 it declared its commitment to armed struggle two years later as a founder member of the United National Directorate (DNU).

Lorenzo Zelaya Popular Revolutionary Forces (*Fuerzas Revolucionarias Populares Lorenzo Zelaya,* FRP)

The FRP originated in the (Maoist) Marxist-Leninist Communist Party (PCML) and in 1983 joined the United National Directorate (DNU). On Sept. 23, 1981, members of this group shot and wounded two US military advisers in Tegucigalpa as part of an "armed struggle against Yankee imperialism". In September 1982 the FPR was reported to have carried out a number of bomb attacks and temporary occupations of buildings in the capital.

Two alleged leading members of the FRP were killed by security forces in San Pedro Sula on March 13, 1987.

Marxist-Leninist Communist Party (*Partido Comunista Marxista-Leninista,* PCML)

The Maoist PCML broke away from the pro-Soviet Communist Party (PCH) in 1971.

Morazanista Front for the Liberation of Honduras (*Frente Morazanista para la Liberación de Honduras,* FMLH)

Established in September 1979, this Front (named after Francisco Morazán, a 19th-century military leader) was reported to have the aim of pursuing a "revolutionary struggle" after Constituent Assembly elections of April 20, 1980. On Aug. 2, 1980, a spokesman for the FMLH stated that its chief objectives were to give land to the peasants, to eliminate the social and economic problems afflicting the masses and to set up a people's government to carry out this programme. In 1983 it joined the United National Directorate (DNU).

National Association of Honduran Peasants (ANACAMH)—see under Honduran Peasants' National Unity Front

National Peasants' Union (*Unión Nacional de Campesinos,* UNC)

Leadership. Marcial Caballero (sec.-gen.)

In early April 1985 over 60 small peasant groups belonging to the UNC occupied an area of some 20,000 hectares of land in protest over what they claimed was the government's failure to implement the agrarian reform law with regard to idle land.

National Union of Authentic Peasants of Honduras (UNCAH)—see under Honduran Peasants' National Unity Front

Peasant Alliance of National Organizations of Honduras (*Alianza Campesina de Organizaciones Nacionales de Honduras,* ALCONH)

This alliance was established on Oct. 10, 1980, as a "revolutionary and belligerent" peasant group under the leadership of Reyes Rodríguez Arévalo, a former leader of the National Association of Honduran Peasants (ANACAMH). Its main aim was to secure peasants' land rights.

Popular Armed Forces (*Fuerzas Armadas Populares,* FAP)

This left-wing guerrilla group emerged in early 1984 when it issued a threat to "exterminate" all US military advisers in Honduras and Salvadorean soldiers trained by US forces at the Puerto Castilla base on the country's northern Caribbean coast.

Revolutionary People's Union (*Unión Revolucionaria del Pueblo,* URP)

Leadership. Tomás Nativi (pres.); Fidel Martínez (sec.-gen.)

The URP was formed in September 1979 by defectors from the Communist Party (PCH) and the Socialist Party (Paso), with the aim of waging armed struggle with the support of peasants and trade unionists. It was active mainly in the country's northern part and was said to be in sympathy with the Popular Revolutionary Bloc (BPR) of El Salvador. On Aug. 15-16, 1980, a group of 15 URP members temporarily occupied the offices of the Organization of American States in Tegucigalpa, and on Oct. 2 of that year the URP announced the start of its "armed struggle".

It was reported in 1981 that Nativi and Martínez had both died in clashes with the Honduran army, but the URP has consistently maintained that both men have been detained as political prisoners.

The URP has links with the Cinchonero People's Liberation Movement (MPLC) and the National Union of Authentic Peasants of Honduras (UNCAH).

Troylan Turcios

This group joined the United National Directorate in April 1983. In February 1987 it claimed responsibility for two acts of violence committed in Tegucigalpa against the presence of "contra" and US troops in Honduras.

Extreme Right-wing Groups

Association for the Progress of Honduras (*Asociación para el Progreso de Honduras,* APROH)

Leadership. Gen. (retd.) Gustavo Adolfo Alvarez Martinez; Miguel Facussé (vice pres.); Oswaldo Ramos (sec.)

APROH was founded in January 1983 by leading army officers and businessmen, ostensibly to promote foreign investment in Honduras, although it has been regarded as a front for right-wing political activities, and it is known to oppose the Sandinista government in Nicaragua and to favour US military intervention in Central America. It was criticized for its links with the strongly anti-Communist Unification Church (the "Moonies"), which gave APROH the sum of $5,000,000 in January 1983 to help it fight subversion. After the arrest of a number of Alvarez's associates in the United States on charges of conspiracy to assassinate President Roberto Suazo Córdova and of smuggling cocaine to finance the plot, APROH was outlawed on Nov. 3, 1984.

Free Honduras (*Honduras Libre*)

After a former president of the United Federation of Honduran Workers (FUTH) had been murdered in San Pedro Sula on May 9, 1986, the Federation issued a series of communiqués claiming that the Free Honduras group had issued a warning to the effect that its two next "executions" would be of leaders of unions affiliated to the Federation. Consequently the group was held responsible when another union president was shot dead on June 30, 1986.

Hungary

Capital: Budapest Pop. 10,710,000

The People's Republic of Hungary, in which de facto power is held by the Politburo of the Central Committee of the Hungarian Socialist Workers' Party, has a Presidential Council (whose Chairman is the head of state), a Council of Ministers under a Prime Minister and a National Assembly elected for a five-year term, with election candidates having to be supporters of the Patriotic People's Front, a mass organization dominated by the party.

Under a law adopted by the National Assembly on Dec. 22, 1983, a choice of candidates was made mandatory for all parliamentary and local council elections, and the membership of the 352-member National Assembly was increased by 35 to accommodate a list of "important public personalities" to be directly elected after nomination by the Patriotic People's Front and without opposition. Following elections held on June 8, 1985, 310 candidates (including 25 independent candidates) who had received the minimum number of votes required were declared duly elected in the first round; 285 candidates who had obtained at least a quarter of the votes were elected as alternate members. The turnout was 93.4 per cent, and the 35-member national list obtained 94 per cent of the votes cast. Of the remaining 42 elective seats, 41 were filled as a result of the second round held on June 22, while the remaining seat had to be contested in a third round.

The regime set up in the wake of the repression of the 1956 rising has become one of the most liberal among the East European communist states as regards economic, social and cultural policy.

A new civil code, which came into effect on March 1, 1978, provided inter alia, in accordance with the Constitution, for the protection of human rights, which were not to be infringed by discrimination on grounds of sex, race, nationality or denomination, by violations of the freedom of conscience, by unlawful restrictions of personal liberty, or by offences against corporal integrity, health, honour or human dignity. The protection of the privacy of mail, or personal and business secrets and of the home were reaffirmed.

However, under a decree reported on Aug. 27, 1985, existing measures against "displaying an attitude harmful to the internal order or security of the Hungarian People's Republic" were extended by lowering the minimum age at which a person might be placed under police surveillance and increasing the maximum period of such surveillance from one to three years.

Dissenting Intellectuals

Some of the dissenting intellectuals were members of the "Budapest School" founded by the Marxist philosopher Georgy Lukacs (who died in 1971) and adopted ideas of the West European "new left", describing the societies of East European countries as "no longer capitalist and not socialist either but controlled by bureaucracies". In January 1973 these intellectuals were officially described as "pseudo-revolutionaries" and "petty-bourgeois romantics" who "objectively" played a "reactionary role". Some of them were subsequently allowed to leave the country. One of them, Ferenc Fehér, announced on Jan. 20, 1977, that some 28 Hungarian intellectuals had sent a letter to the Czechoslovak "Charter 77" group to express solidarity with it and to protest against government reprisals against its members.

The sentences imposed in Prague on Oct. 23, 1979, on six members of VONS led to a protest by 184 Hungarian intellectuals and the sending of two petitions to János Kádár, the First Secretary of the Hungarian Socialist Workers' Party (HSWP)—these documents being signed by 252 persons altogether. A small number subsequently withdrew their signatures under pressure from the authorities who threatened them with dismissal from their posts.

In May 1981 there was in clandestine circulation a dossier compiled by 77 intellectuals in memory of István Bibó (a former Peasant Party politician and historian, who had died in 1979), containing criticism of conditions in Hungary. The dossier was commented upon by two members of the Central Committee of the HSWP, who reported that its joint authors fell into four distinct groups: (i) those whose views were neither of interest nor dangerous; (ii) those who were "traitors" and denied their socialist past; (iii) those who had a scientific and moderate approach; and (iv) those who merely recorded expressions of faith in opposition to the regime. The second of these groups regarded the whole development in Hungary and other "central European" states since 1945 as illegal, as it had been imposed by the Soviets and had never been legitimized by a social contract with the people; this group also stated that in the 1956 rising the people had attempted to restore the multi-party system which had existed until 1948.

Early in September 1981 "a limited group" of the intelligentsia was accused of "ideological confusion" in *Partelet,* the monthly theoretical organ of the Central Committee of the HSWP. While this "ideological confusion", the journal declared, constituted "no political problem, for Hungary's society is mature enough to emerge victorious from this struggle", no opportunity would be given to points of view hostile to the regime.

Peace Group

A Peace Group for Dialogue was formed during 1982 and developed contacts with Western peace activists; it was said to have several hundred members, but after police harassment members of the group decided to dissolve their organization while continuing to work for peace as individuals.

Conscientious Objection

A strong tendency towards pacifism was said to have existed in "basic communities" of mostly young people meeting for private prayer and religious discussion; the Bishop of Pécs was in April 1982 quoted as saying that this movement consisted of over 20,000 followers and some 40 priests. Several priests who had expressed their support for conscientious objection were disciplined (in 1981-82) by the Roman Catholic hierarchy which maintained good relations with the government.

In September 1985 it was reported that several conscientious objectors had been sentenced to imprisonment for terms ranging from 32 to 36 months. In *The Times* (of London) it was alleged on Jan. 27, 1986, that as many as 160 conscientious objectors were currently imprisoned in Hungary.

Exiled Parties

People's Democratic Party

In exile since the Communists came to full power in the late 1940s, this party is affiliated to the Christian Democratic World Union.

Social Democratic Party of Hungary

Leadership. Andor Bolcsfoldi (gen. sec.)

Having been prominent in the pre-war opposition to the Horthy dictatorship, the Hungarian Social Democrats participated in the Communist-dominated government formed in April 1945 after the liberation of Hungary by the Red Army. The left wing of the party merged with the Communists in June 1948, but surviving elements opposed to the merger maintained the party's existence in exile. Following the October 1956 Hungarian uprising, the exiled party's then chairman, Anna Kéthly, was invited to become a member of the coalition government formed by Imre Nagy but was unable to reach Hungary before the suppression of the revolution by Soviet forces in early November. Thereafter the exiled party included many of the 1956 generation of Hungarian refugees.

The Hungarian Social Democratic Party is a consultative member of the Socialist International and also a constituent party of the Socialist Union of Central and Eastern Europe (SUCEE).

Iceland

Capital: Reykjavik

Pop. 240,000

The Republic of Iceland is a multi-party democratic state with a President elected (and re-eligible) for a four-year term by universal adult suffrage. Executive power is held by a Cabinet headed by a Prime Minister, and legislative power by a bicameral 63-member Parliament (*Althing*) similarly elected for a four-year term, consisting of an Upper House constituted by one-third of the whole *Althing*'s members elected at a joint sitting, and the Lower House comprising the remaining two-thirds of its members.

As a result of elections held on April 25, 1987, the seats in the *Althing* were distributed as follows: Independence Party (conservative) 18, Progressive Party 13, Social Democrats 10, People's Alliance (Communist-dominated) 8, Citizen's Party 7, Women's Alliance 6, Independent 1.

Under a law finally passed after the elections of 1983 the voting age had been lowered from 20 to 18 years and the number of seats in the *Althing* increased from 60 to 63.

There has been no evidence of activities of extra-parliamentary opposition groups in Iceland.

India

Capital: New Delhi

Pop. 750,900,000

The Union of India is, under its Constitution with amendments which came into force on Jan. 3, 1977, "a sovereign socialist secular democratic republic" (and a member of the Commonwealth) with a Parliament consisting of the President, the Council of State and the House of the People (*Lok Sabha*), the latter House having 544 members elected by universal adult suffrage for a five-year term (and up to 20 members representing union territories and up to two additional members nominated by the President). The latter is elected for a five-year term by the elected members of Parliament and of the Legislative Assemblies of the states, and in turn appoints a Prime Minister and, on the latter's advice, other ministers, all of whom are responsible to Parliament.

As a result of elections to the *Lok Sabha* on Dec. 24, 27 and 28, 1984, Jan. 28, 1985, and delayed elections held in April, September and December 1985, the seats were distributed as follows: Congress (I) 415, *Telegu Desam* 30, Communist Party of India-Marxist (CPI(M)) 22, All-India *Anna Dravida Munnetra Kazhagam* (AIADMK) 12, Janata (JNP) 11, Akali Dal seven, Assam People's Council (ACP) seven, Communist Party of India (CPI) six, Congress (Socialist) four, Independents four, *Dalit Mazdoor Kisan* Party (DMK-Lok Dal) three, National Conference (Farooq) three, Revolutionary Socialist Party (RSP) three, Bharatiya Janata Party (BJP) two, *Dravida Munnetra Kazhagam* (DMK) two, Forward Bloc two, Kerala Congress (Joseph) two, Moslem League two, Congress (J) one, *Majlis* one, Peasants' and Workers' Party (PWP) one, Plains Tribal Council of Assam (PTCA) one, United Minorities Front one. Two persons were nominated to represent the Anglo-Indian community.

There is in India a profusion of legal political parties both at national and at state level; divisions of existing parties, defections from these parties and formations of new parties have been frequent. Illegal movements are mainly communal, separatist or extreme left-wing organizations.

The internal security situation has been dominated by events in Punjab, where Sikh separatists demand an independent Sikh state of Khalistan. There is also intercommunal violence on a large scale in several parts of the Indian Union.

Right-wing Movement

Hindu Shiv Sena ("Army of Shiva")

This right-wing extremist group emerged in 1986 to organize resistance amongst the minority Hindus against Sikh attacks in Punjab. On March 16, 1986, the town of Batala in Punjab, which has a Hindu majority, was placed under indefinite curfew after members of Hindu Shiv Sena clashed with Sikhs following the death of the group's local branch president.

Left-wing Movements

Dalit Panthers

Leadership. Raja Dhale (founder)

This movement took its name from the word *dalit* (meaning "oppressed") and the (US) Black Panther movement, which it regarded as its model. It was set up in 1972 to defend the interests of the Harijans ("untouchables") who formed 9 per cent of the population of the state of Maharashtra. Its members were involved in clashes with caste Hindus. Later the movement spread from Maharashtra to Gujarat, where upper-caste militants objected to the reservation of government jobs and university places for Harijans and launched early in 1981 an agitation which led to riots in which over 40 people were killed. The Dalit Panthers were also active in encouraging conversions of Harijans to Islam (as a means of escaping from the caste system), and in this connexion at least 23 Dalit Panthers were arrested under the National Security Act in Kanpur (Uttar Pradesh) in August 1981. The government, however, took the line that a ban on conversions would be unconstitutional.

Militant protesters led by Dalit Panthers burnt down a police station on June 13, 1983, after an order to remove a statue erected illegally to commemorate the "untouchable" leader, Dr B. R. Ambedkar, who helped frame India's Constitution. Several people died when police opened fire on the protesters.

Naxalite Movement

Originating from an armed revolutionary campaign launched in 1965, the Naxalite movement took its name from Naxalbari, a town in the Darjeeling district of West Bengal, where a peasant revolt broke out in March 1967 under the local leadership of the (pro-Chinese) Communist Party of India (Marxist) or CPI(M). The movement was started in Siliguri (a town south of Darjeeling), where the CPI(M) committee called for the arming of peasants and the setting-up of rural bases in preparation for armed struggle—the committee being opposed to the policy of the CPI(M) of entering into coalition governments in West Bengal and Kerala, and being itself supported by the Communist Party of China (where the Naxalites were hailed as a "spring thunder over India"). The CPI(M), however, expelled the leaders of the revolt, which was suppressed by the Indian army by August 1967.

On July 2, 1968, supporters of the expelled leaders of the revolt founded a new Revolutionary Communist Party, which was opposed to any participation in parliamentary activities. Naxalites continued their activities during that year, their number being estimated as about 17,000 (including 6,000 in Andhra Pradesh, 5,000 in West Bengal, and 4,000 in Kerala). Kanu Sanyal, the leader of the Naxalbari revolt, continued to call for the formation of village guerrilla units (even if armed with only bows and spears) to create "free zones", but he was arrested on Oct. 31, 1968. Following his release on April 9, 1969, he announced on May 1 that a new "truly revolutionary party", the Communist Party of India (Marxist-Leninist) or CPI(ML) had been formed on April 22, its programme being "to liberate the rural areas through revolutionary armed agrarian revolution, to encircle the cities and finally to liberate the cities and thus to complete the overthrow throughout the country". Early in 1970 Charu Mazumdar, the party's chief theoretician, called on peasants to murder local landowners and thus to become "the sole authority in settling all their local affairs".

The CPI(ML) was officially supported by the Chinese Communist Party, but not by all Indian Maoists. The new party in turn supported tribal rebellion such as that of the Girijan tribesmen in the Srikakulam district (on the border between Andhra Pradesh and Orissa), which had first broken out at the end of 1967 and had continued since then; on Aug. 17, 1969, about 2,000 Naxalites were reported to have been arrested in Srikakulam.

During 1970 Naxalite activities spread in many Indian states. In West Bengal between 10,000 and 20,000 Naxalites, about half of them in the Greater Calcutta area, were reported to have launched a "cultural revolution" on the Chinese model.

At its first congress held secretly in Calcutta on May 15-16, 1970, the CPI(ML) decided to build up a strong "People's Liberation Army" and to create "innumerable points of guerrilla struggle throughout the countryside", to form "red bases through annihilation of class enemies and overthrowing the forces of suppression". However, of the party's leaders many were subsequently killed or arrested.

Charu Mazumdar, then general secretary of the CPI(ML), was expelled from the party on Nov. 7, 1971, for pursuing "a Trotskyite adventurist line", after he had been attacked by Ashim Chatterjee (a Naxalite campaign leader in a West Bengal district). The latter had inter alia demanded that, in accordance with the Chinese Communist Party's policy, the CPI(ML) should actively support the Pakistan regime of President Yahya Khan and should act against the *Mukti Bahini* movement fighting for the independence of East Pakistan (Bangladesh). The expulsion of Charu Mazumdar and his replacement as general secretary of the CPI(ML) by Satya Narain Singh led to divisions of the movement into factions attacking each other and to a general decline in Naxalite activities.

Charu Mazumdar was arrested in Calcutta on July 16, 1972, and died on July 28 of that year. The faction which had followed him was later divided into two groups—(i) one which supported criticism of his policies by the Chinese Communist Party and in particular of his endorsement of individual terrorism and his opposition to participation in other organizations, and (ii) another which continued his policies, supported Marshal Lin Biao's theory that guerrilla warfare was "the only way to utilize and apply the whole strength of the people", and rejected as "revisionism" the Chinese party's criticism of Mazumdar's views. The second group was, however, according to the police in Bihar, almost "wiped out" by mid-1975.

The CPI(ML) led by S. N. Singh, which rejected terrorism, advocated a combination of legal and illegal activities and also participation in mass movements launched by other left-wing parties; it worked for the unification of the extreme left and claimed in August 1974 to have enrolled 90 per cent of the members of the Revolutionary Communist Party in Andhra Pradesh.

At Cochin (Kerala) on Dec. 14-15, 1974, however, dissident members of the CPI(ML) formed the Centre of Indian Communists (as the fourth Communist Party in India). It rejected the "right-wing opportunism" of the Communist Party of India, the "left-wing opportunism" of the Communist Party (Marxist) and the "adventurism" of the CPI(ML); it declared that it would follow the Chinese party's line in ideological struggles while taking local conditions into account in applying it; and it defined its aims as the establishment of a people's government by organizing an armed revolution of the working class and the peasants.

The CPI(ML) was banned on July 4, 1975, under emergency powers, but this ban was revoked on March 22, 1977. Following a series of meetings in April 1977 between S. N. Singh (the party's general secretary) and Charan Singh (the newly appointed Indian Home Affairs Minister) the former gave an assurance that the party had renounced violence and terrorism and wished to participate in democratic processes. Charan Singh thereupon agreed to release all Naxalite detainees irrespective of the nature of their offences or group affiliations.

However, in West Bengal the CPI(ML) faction formerly led by Charu Mazumdar had the greatest following of all the Naxalite groups and rejected all talk of reverting to parliamentary politics. The third CPI(ML) group, led by Ashim Chatterjee and Kanu Sanyal, had before the general elections of March 1977 (won by the Janata Party) issued a statement calling on the people to vote against the Congress (which was defeated in these elections). It was officially stated on May 24, 1977, that some 550 Naxalites detained in West Bengal had been released unconditionally.

In February 1979 Naxalite guerrilla activities were reported to have intensified in West Bengal, Andhra Pradesh, Bihar, Punjab and Kerala and to have spread to Uttar Pradesh, Maharashtra, Tamil Nadu and Assam, with the total strength of the movement being estimated at 15,000. A secret conference of leaders of 13 Naxalite groups held on Jan. 30-Feb. 2, 1981, agreed to abandon terrorist methods and to concentrate on public political agitation. Nevertheless guerrilla activities continued in several states and increased in particular in Kerala and West Bengal.

In Tamil Nadu the leader of an "annihilationist" group named as Kannamani was killed on Dec. 28, 1980, this group being held responsible for several murders and armed robberies; another three of its members were killed by police on Aug. 24, 1981. In Andhra Pradesh a Naxalite faction known as the People's War group was involved in fighting in a village on April 20, 1981, when 13 tribesmen and one policeman were killed. In West Bengal, the pro-Lin Biao faction of the CPI(ML)—led by Nisith Bhattacharya and Azizul Haque—continued to murder policemen, landowners, small businessmen and shopkeepers and to steal arms, while in Bihar the Naxalites were principally involved in an armed struggle between landowners and landless labourers agitating for higher wages.

Home Ministry sources stated on April 13, 1982, that 92 people had been killed in 1981 in 324 violent incidents inspired by Naxalites (compared with 84 killed in 305 incidents in 1980), the states most affected being Andhra Pradesh, West Bengal and Bihar. During the campaign for the May 19 state elections in West Bengal Naxalites carried out attacks on offices of the CPI(M), which nevertheless won the elections at the head of a Left Front. Following these and other attacks on police targets in the state, Nisith Bhattacharya was captured with six of his followers in Bihar on May 27 and two days later the police announced that they had raided the group's hideout in Calcutta and seized three printing presses.

A 164-page document issued in Trivandrum (Kerala) in December 1982 by the "central reorganization committee" of the CPI(ML) gave an analysis of the experiences of the Naxalites over the previous 15 years as a contribution to the process of rebuilding the movement for a "new phase" of activities. Entitled "Towards a New Phase of the Spring Thunder", the document said that despite the "serious mistakes" committed under Charu Mazumdar's leadership the revolutionary programme evolved by him should still form the basis of the movement's political and organizational line. Analysing the causes of the recent setbacks and fragmentation suffered by the Naxalites, it said that the movement's line had deviated to the left in dealing with specific issues, notably in respect of the relationship between armed struggle and other forms of struggle. Whereas in the beginning the armed struggle was seen as being complemented by other forms of action, a gradual shift took place towards a "one-sided emphasis on armed struggle and neglect of other forms of struggle"; this in turn had resulted in a neglect of mass movements, with the result that the Naxalites became "isolated" from the people, making it all the more easy for the state to launch "a massive encirclement and suppression campaign".

The document continued that the movement had failed to produce a concrete political, economic and agrarian programmne to back up its armed struggle and had placed one-sided emphasis on "annihilation of class enemies", with the result that the concept of "political power at the local level" had degenerated into an "abstract, hollow slogan" and the annihilation campaign into "isolated killings". It therefore urged as the theoretical basis for reunification of the movement the upholding of both armed struggle and all other forms of struggle as complementary to it, as well as the upholding of the proletarian revolutionary line of Charu Mazumdar. It also proclaimed support for "Marxism-Leninism-Mao Zedong thought" and opposition to the "Deng-Hua" clique which had "usurped" power in China after Mao's death.

Violent incidents continued to be attributed to Naxalite groups in 1985. In November 1985 it was reported that 58 "extremists" alleged to be Maoist guerrillas belonging to an (unspecified) Naxalite group were killed in a battle with police.

On April 19, 1986, police opened fire on crowds demonstrating in the Gaya district, killing 23 landless labourers and accusing protesters of being Naxalites associated with the leftist organization *Mazdoor Kisan Sangram Samiti* (which was reported on Aug. 17, 1986, to have been banned by the state government). On April 21, 1986, up to 25,000 people were reported to have been detained after a mass demonstration in Patna, the capital of Bihar.

In a move to combat lawlessness in the state, a ban was imposed on Aug. 20, 1986, on all private caste-based armies in Bihar, including those maintained by landlords (*Bhoomihars*) and by ultra-leftist organizations (mainly lower caste and Harijan), the banned armies including *Lal Sena, Lorik Sena, Bhoomi Sena* and *Kunwas Singh Sena*.

On Oct. 7, 1986, a group called the Marxist Co-ordination Committee (of left-wing guerrillas) killed 11 high-caste villagers; later 49 people were arrested. A further 16 people were reported to have been killed by left-wing guerrillas in October, all belonging to the *Rajput* warrior caste. Members from a Maoist Community Centre were reported to have attacked a village on May 29, 1987, beheading 28 villagers and burning 13 others in a revenge attack for the killing of seven guerrillas the previous month.

Separatist Movements

(see also Sikh Movements below)

KASHMIR

Jamaat-i-Tulaba

Leadership. Sheikh Tajamul Islam (pres.)

This student wing of the *Jamaat-i-Islami* (a pro-Pakistan political party) announced on Aug. 5, 1980, that it was planning "an Iran-type revolution for the liberation of Kashmir from illegal occupation and enslavement by India". This was followed by the arrest of 24 Moslem leaders in Jammu and Kashmir. An international youth conference convened by the organization for Aug. 22, 1980, was banned by the government, and Sheikh Tajamul Islam was arrested on that day.

The group was blamed for disrupting a cricket match between India and the West Indies on Oct. 3, 1983.

Kashmir Liberation Army

This previously unknown group kidnapped and shot dead the Indian assistant high commissioner to the United Kingdom, Ravindra Mhatre, in Birmingham on Feb. 3, 1984. The group demanded £1,000,000 ransom and the release of prisoners in India, including the group's president Magbool Boot, sentenced to death for the murder of a policemen in Kashmir in 1976. Boot was executed on Feb. 11, 1984.

Two men convicted of the 1984 kidnapping received life sentences on Feb. 6, 1985. Three others who pleaded guilty to charges connected with the kidnapping received sentences of between two and 20 years, and a sixth man was fined £600.

The court was told that three other Kashmiris, including the person alleged to have shot R. Mhatre, Mohammad Musserat Iqbal, had fled Britain and were thought to be in Pakistan.

The Kashmir Liberation Army also claimed responsibility (as did two other groups) for the planting of a bomb on board an Air-India Boeing 747 (Jumbo jet) killing all 329 people on board. (An inquest later ruled that the origin of the disaster, which happened off the west coast of Ireland on June 23, 1985, remained uncertain.)

MANIPUR

People's Liberation Army (PLA)

The PLA is a Maoist organization operating mainly in Manipur but advocating independence for the whole north-eastern region of India. It draws support from the Meteis, a tribal people of the plain of Manipur, many of whom have rejected Hinduism as a faith identified with New Delhi's cultural domination, and were held responsible for destroying temples and images. Guerrillas of the PLA carried out armed robberies of banks and government offices to obtain funds for the purchase of arms and ammunitions in Thailand and China, and they were believed to have received training from Chinese in Tibet. On Sept. 8, 1980, the state of Manipur was declared a disturbed area.

The PLA continued to be active in 1981, even after its C.-in-C., Biseswar Singh, was captured on July 6. It began to co-operate with the National Socialist Council of Nagaland (see separate entry), carrying out what was reported to be its first combined operation with the latter organization on Feb. 19, 1982, when an army convoy was ambushed on the Kohima-Imphal road and 20 soldiers were killed. On April 13, 1982, nine PLA men were killed in an exchange of fire with security forces near Imphal, the dead including Kunj Behari Singh, who had commanded the PLA since Biseswar Singh's arrest.

The PLA had been declared an illegal organization on Oct. 26, 1981, under the 1967 Unlawful Activities (Prevention) Act.

There have been no reported activities of the PLA in recent years.

NAGALAND

Naga Separatist Movement

Leadership. Angami Zapu Phizo (l.)

The Naga separatist movement has had a history of armed and non-violent resistance to the incorporation of Nagaland in the Union of India, of which that territory became a constituent state in 1972. A Naga National Council (NNC), formed in 1946, agreed upon the achievement of independence by India in 1947 to accept Indian Suzerainty for a period of 10 years, but in 1949 it adopted a policy of non-co-operation with the Indian government. Certain Naga extremists began a campaign of violence in 1952, but Angami Zapu Phizo, president of the NNC, disclaimed any connexion with the disturbances caused by these extremists. However, following the murder of the leader of a faction opposed to A. Z. Phizo in January 1956, the Naga movement was split. A. Z. Phizo dissolved the NNC in May 1956, and formed a "federal Naga government" with its own "parliament". His supporters embarked on an armed rebellion which led to widespread destruction of villages. After the rebels' main forces had been subdued by troops, rebel attacks on loyal villages and other acts of violence continued for many years. A. Z. Phizo left the country, living first in Pakistan and, from June 12, 1960, in London.

Attempts to achieve a negotiated settlement between the government and the rebels met with little success for many years. On Nov. 10-11, 1975, however, agreement was reached in Shillong between the Governor of Nagaland and a delegation of six representatives of the underground Naga movement led by Kevi Yalay Phizo (a minister in the "federal government" and a brother of A. Z. Phizo), whereby (i) the Naga delegation unconditionally accepted the Constitution of India (and thus the status of Nagaland as part of India); (ii) the underground Nagas would deposit their arms at places agreed upon; and (iii) the Naga representatives would have reasonable time to formulate other terms for discussion on a final settlement. A. Z. Phizo, however, repudiated this agreement on Dec. 1, 1975 (while he was in self-imposed exile in London). On May 8, 1976, it was announced that all political prisoners who had accepted the Shillong agreement had been released, among them "Gen." Mowu Angami and 137 of his followers.

On Sept. 9, 1976, it was officially stated that Nagaland was now free from all traces of insurgency and that since March 1975 a total of 1,356 underground Nagas had "come overground" voluntarily.

In June 1977 Morarji Desai, then Indian Prime Minister, had talks with A. Z. Phizo in London, during which he assured the Naga leader that if he accepted the present state of affairs and the agreements made with the Nagas (including the 1975 Shillong agreement), he and the other exiles were welcome to return to Nagaland and he could become Chief Minister of Nagaland if the people wished it. A. Z. Phizo, however, had refused to accept Indian citizenship, and in a statement issued in his name later it was said that the activities of the separatist movement would be intensified.

Raids by Naga guerrillas in January 1979 were not officially attributed to the underground separatist Naga movement. There were, however, still Chinese-trained underground Nagas based in Burma, who were believed to be responsible for an ambush in which seven Indian soldiers were killed on March 27, 1979. On Aug. 8, 1980, a total of 474 Nagas from Burma were officially stated to have taken refuge in the Tuengsang district of Nagaland, and during the later months of 1980 and in 1981 attacks continued to be made by separatists operating in areas near the Burmese border.

By the early 1980s the main rebel forces were divided into two mutually hostile groups: those supporting the exiled leader A. Z. Phizo on the one hand and the adherents of the National Socialist Council of Nagaland (NSCN—see separate entry) on ther other. A third faction, hostile to both main groups, had also emerged under the leadership of "Gen." Mowu Angami. In a night attack on a Burmese village near the Nagaland border on Sept. 27, 1980, pro-Phizo forces killed 75 National Socialists and the following year were reported (in August 1981) to have recently co-operated with the Burmese security forces in an attack on a National Socialist camp.

Recent activities by Nagaland separatists have been attributed to the NSCN.

National Socialist Council of Nagaland (NSCN)

Leadership. Muivah Tangkul; Issak Swu

The NSCN was formed in 1978 by a Maoist breakaway faction of the Naga Separatist Movement led by A. Z. Phizo (see separate entry).

In July 1980 NSCN followers were said to have killed 200 pro-Phizo rebels and to have burnt down 150 villages, to which pro-Phizo forces responded by killing 75 NSCN followers on Sept. 27 and subsequently by co-operating with the Burmese security forces in operations directed against the NSCN.

In February 1982 the NSCN began carrying out combined operations with the People's Liberation Army active in Manipur (see separate entry) but by September 1982 it was reported to be in disarray following the surrender of several of its leading members, notably "Maj." Ithoku Sema. However, further NSCN attacks on security forces and political figures occurred in 1984 and 1985. Those killed included a former Manipur finance minister and a former Manipur chief minister. On Aug. 11, 1985, "Col." Moba Konyak, reportedly second in command, was captured attempting to cross into Burma, and in June 1986 it was reported that amongst high-ranking members arrested were "Capt." Pubi Mao, a regional chairman, and "Cpl." Yarmila, head of the women's wing and secretary to the NSCN leader Muivah Tangkul.

TRIPURA

Tripur Sena

Leadership. Vijoy Rankal (l.)

This separatist and anti-Bengali organization is thought to be an extremist faction of the Tripura Tribal Youth Organization (*Tripura Upajaty Juba Samity*), a legal autonomist organization represented in the Legislative Assembly of the state of Tripura. It was on Oct. 29, 1979, officially reported to be involved in a conspiracy (in collusion with the formerly illegal Mizo National Front in the neighbouring union territory of Mizoram) to establish an independent state of Tripura by force.

In protest against mass immigration of Bengalis, especially from Bangladesh, which had reduced the tribal population of Tripura to a minority of about 30 per cent, a tribal rising broke out in southern and western Tripura on June 6-10, 1980, leading to the murder of up to 2,000 Bengalis. Over 200,000 people who had lost their homes had to be accommodated in government relief camps; and about 40,000 tribal people were said to have fled to the forests to evade arrest. In mid-June posters appeared in many areas ordering all non-tribal people to leave by June 26, failing which they would be exterminated.

In October 1984 seven people were killed in a general strike called and enforced by tribal separatists.

Bands of tribal separatists operating from the Chittagong Hill Tracts area of Bangladesh made frequent raids into border areas of Tripura in late 1980 and throughout 1981, and according to unofficial reports had set up a "revolutionary government-in-exile".

The most recent attacks by tribal separatists have been attributed to the Tripura National Volunteers (see separate entry).

Tripura National Volunteers (TNV)

Since 1985, activities by separatists in Tripura have been attributed largely to the TNV, which was declared illegal on Jan. 22, 1987, under the 1967 Unlawful Activities (Prevention) Act. At the same time, areas in the north-west and south of Tripura were declared "disturbed" following continued attacks on Bengali settlers.

On Jan. 6, 1985, a three-month long amnesty had been offered to activists. However, on April 9, five people were killed after having been kidnapped from the house of a local tribal leader of the Communist Party of India-Marxist. Non-tribal villagers called for a state-wide strike on June 5 to demand greater protection after seven villagers were murdered.

On March 10, 1986, four supporters of the ruling Left Front Coalition were killed in southern Tripura, and following an attack which killed five people on April 4, 1986, the Union government was asked for an increased paramilitary presence in the occupied areas. Over 100 people were estimated to have been killed in the TNV campaign in 1986.

WEST BENGAL

Gurkha National Liberation Front (GNLF)

Leadership. Subhash Ghising (pres.)

This group was formed in the early 1980s to fight for a separate Nepali-speaking state in West Bengal within the Indian Union. The areas claimed are the Nepali-speaking hill districts of Darjeeling, Kurseong, Kalimpong, and parts of the Jalpaiguri and Cooch Behar districts where some 60 per cent of India's 1,500,000 Nepali-speaking citizens live.

In December 1983 Subhash Ghising wrote to King Birendra of Nepal calling for his support, and the letter was recirculated in March 1985 to various heads of state and United Nations officials.

Agitation increased in 1986 after the eviction in March of 10,000 ethnic Nepalese from the north-eastern state of Meghalaya, where natives feared that they were being outnumbered. On July 30, 1986, the army was called out in Darjeeling to quell unrest in tea gardens where tea workers were defecting from pro-communist trade unions to the GNLF. On Aug. 14, S. Ghising announced a suspension of agitation for one month as a token of commitment to the Indian nation.

A meeting convened by the Chief Minister of West Bengal—where the Communist Party of India (Marxist), CPI(M), was the dominant element in the ruling Left Front coalition—unanimously adopted, on Aug. 18, a resolution condemning the GNLF as "anti-state, anti-national, anti-people and divisive". Rajiv Gandhi, the Indian Prime Minister, however, stated during a visit to West Bengal in September that he had found nothing in the statements of the GNLF to imply that it was in any way anti-national or secessionist.

A serious situation arose in October 1986 when GNLF supporters began to burn down the homes of CPI(M) supporters, and the police were given orders to shoot arsonists on sight. On Dec. 17 S. Ghising presented the Union Home Secretary with a memorandum of the GNLF's demands, which included the establishment of a separate state. At a subsequent meeting held on Jan. 25-28, 1987, between a GNLF delegation and the Union Minister of Home Affairs, the GNLF demanded Indian citizenship for all ethnic Nepalese who had arrived in India after the signing of the India-Nepal treaty of peace and friendship in July 1950. Following a further meeting with the Minister on Feb. 3, S. Ghising announced a two-month suspension of the GNLF's agitation. After the GNLF had, on Feb. 7, presented a further memorandum with its demands, R. Ghandi stated that he and the Chief Minister of West Bengal were agreed that there would be no separate Gurkha state in West Bengal.

On April 22, 1987, it was reported that the GNLF had threatened the Union government with the launching of a full-scale armed struggle against the state government of West Bengal. It remained a legal organization, however.

Sikh Movements

All India Sikh Student Federation (AISSF)

Leadership. Harminder Singh Kahlon (sec.)

This militant Sikh youth group of the *Akali Dal* was banned by government decree on March 19, 1984. Members were involved in the mass disturbances in Punjab which led up to the storming of the Golden Temple in Amritsar (see entry for National Council of Khalistan). The secretary, H. S. Kahlon, left the besieged temple where he had taken refuge shortly before the army attack; he was arrested afterwards along with hundreds of other suspected activists. The AISSF stated that it would oppose any rebuilding of the Golden Temple before the army withdrew.

The AISSF was one of three groups (the other two being the Sikh *Dashmesh* Regiment and the Kashmir Liberation Army) to claim responsibility for the planting of a bomb on board an Air India Boeing 747 (Jumbo jet), which crashed off the west coast of Ireland on June 23, 1985, killing all 329 people on board. (An inquest later ruled that the origin of the disaster remained uncertain.)

In March 1986 the group was reported to have demanded an end to the construction of the Sutlej-Yamuna canal which was to carry water from the Ravi-Beas water system in Punjab to Haryana, and on the completion of which the transfer of Chandigarh from Haryana to Punjab was reported to depend (one of the demands of Sikh separatists).

In January 1986 radical Sikhs took over control of the Golden Temple from the moderate committee, and an estimated 20,000 members of the AISSF, led by H. S. Kahlon, and of the militant *Damdami Taksal* Sikh religious school, led by Gurdev Singh, convened a general assembly of baptized Sikhs at the *Akal Takht*. The assembly called for the appointment of Jasbir Singh (the alleged organizer of the International Sikh Federation, who had been charged with sedition in 1984, and a nephew of the militant Sikh leader Sant Bhindranwale killed in the army assault on the temple) as head priest of the *Akal Takht*. The assembly was rejected as "illegal, unjustified and anti-Sikh" by the committee of moderate Sikhs (*Shiromani Gurdwara Prabandhak*). Two AISSF leaders, Manjit Singh and Harminder Singh Sandhu, were appointed to an advisory panel set up by the *Damdami* on Jan. 29, to look after the "religious and political affairs of the Sikhs". On April 29, a sedition case was registered against a five-member "panthic committee" which had formally announced from the temple that day the establishment of a separate Sikh state of Khalistan, with formal recognition to be sought by India and Pakistan.

On April 30, a curfew was declared and 1,300 police entered the Golden Temple to hand back power to the moderate committee. Three hundred people were detained (including 20 Bangladesh nationals and G. Singh, the acting head priest of the *Akal Takht*) and one person died. There followed numerous reprisals by militant Sikhs. On May 22, 20 deaths were reported and between June 1 and 7, a total of 16 people were reported killed.

On June 4, security guards again entered the temple after a temple guard was killed by AISSF activists allegedly led by Burmal Khalsa, the widow of Beant Singh (shot dead immediately following his part in the assassination of Mrs Gandhi).

On April 22, 1986, a faction within the group led by the secretary, H. S. Kahlon, broke away from the main AISSF group, which maintains links with the United *Akali Dal*, and aligned itself with the *Damdami Taksal*.

Dashmesh Regiment

This militant Sikh group emerged in 1984 after the killing of the president of the Amritsar branch of the Bharatiya Janata Party (BJP), and the killing of a Hindu and Congress (I) member, on April 2 and 3 respectively.

It also claimed responsibility for the killing on May 12, 1984, of a Hindu newspaper editor, Ramesh Chandler, which led to reprisals by Hindus and a spate of general violence. On April 6, 1986, six police officers died when four Sikh defendants whom they were escorting into a courtroom for the trial of the murder of R. Chandler attempted to escape; three were successful.

The *Dashmesh* Regiment was one of the groups which claimed responsibility for the planting of a bomb on board an airliner which crashed killing all 329 people on board on June 23, 1985.

Dashmesh, meaning "tenth", refers to the tenth Sikh guru Gobind Singh, who propounded the use of force when necessary.

International Sikh Federation

The alleged leader of this organization, Jasbir Singh, was named in 1984 (by the "co-ordinating mastermind" behind the assassination of Mrs Gandhi, Simranjit Singh) as the man whom S. Singh had met on a number of illicit visits to Pakistan.

J. Singh was subsequently refused entry into Britain, Dubai and Thailand, and he was eventually flown back to India from the Philippines on Dec. 26, 1984, to face charges of sedition, inciting unrest against the Indian government and promoting enmity between religious groups. He was interviewed by the team investigating the assassination of Mrs Gandhi, but it was understood that he denied any involvement in the plot.

In January 1986 J. Singh was called upon, by radical Sikhs who had taken over the Golden Temple from a moderate committee, to become the new head priest of the *Akal Takht*. (The temple was in fact handed back to the moderate committee after intervention by police.)

Khalistan Commando Force

This group identified itself as responsible for the deaths of at least 72 bus passengers in two attacks in early July 1987.

National Council of Khalistan (NCK)

Leadership. Balbir Singh Sandu (l.)

Prior to its formation in 1972, a demand for an independent Sikh state ("Khalistan") had been put forward by Dr Jagjit Singh, then general secretary of the *Akali Dal* (the Sikh political party), who stated that President Yahya Khan of Pakistan had promised his support for the secession of Punjab from India and the establishment of an independent Sikh state. He was expelled from the party on Dec. 29 for his "anti-national" activities. His followers formed the National Council of Khalistan, which from its headquarters in the Golden Temple issued "Khalistan" passports, postage stamps and currency notes.

A youth organization, the *Dal Khalsa*, was founded in 1979 under the leadership of Gajendra Singh, who with four other members of the organization hijacked an Indian airliner on Sept. 29, 1981, forcing the pilot to land at Lahore (Pakistan). The hijackers were overpowered whereupon nearly 100 extremist Sikhs, mainly *Dal Khalsa* members, were arrested in India.

Among critics of the Khalistan movement, Lala Jagat Narain (a newspaper editor) was shot dead on Sept. 9, 1981.

Violence continued in November 1981. Three people were killed on Nov. 29 by a bomb explosion in the temple of the Sikh religious leader, Sant Jarnail Singh Bhindranwale. On April 27, 1982, fighting broke out between Hindus and Sikhs in Amritsar after severed cows' heads had been discovered outside two Hindu temples. Responsibility for the desecration was claimed by the *Dal Khalsa*, which had demanded a ban on smoking in Amritsar (the use of tobacco being forbidden to Sikhs). In all about 600 people were arrested in the disturbances, which spread to other towns and which resulted in both the National Council of Khalistan and the *Dal Khalsa* being banned on May 1, 1982, under the 1967 Unlawful Activities (Prevention) Act.

Further airliner hijacks or attempted hijacks by Sikh extremists in August-September 1982 were accompanied by mounting tension in the Punjab as *Akali Dal* leaders launched a new campaign for an autonomous state of Punjab (similar in status to Kashmir), enlarged to include adjacent Sikh-populated areas, and also in support of various religious demands. Although these demands stopped short of the full independence demanded by the Khalistan movement, secessionists participated in the widespread agitation and demonstrations which developed, to which the authorities responded by arresting thousands of Sikh activists. Talks between the government and Sikh leaders towards the end of 1982 failed to produce any agreement on the Sikhs' political demands, although the Prime Minister on Nov. 25 made concessions to their religious demands by announcing that Amritsar would be declared a holy city and that the sale of tobacco and liquor would be banned within its walls.

In 1983 members of the Council, together with other militant Sikh groups, instigated agitation in the Punjab which led to an army assault on the Sikh central shrine, the Golden Temple, in Amritsar in June 1984 and the assassination of the Prime Minister, Mrs Indira Gandhi, on Oct. 31, 1984.

On April 8, the *Akali Dal* leader Sant Harchand Singh Longowal said that a "sacrifice force" of 100,000 volunteers would be ready to be martyred in a peaceful way for the *Akali* cause. On April 28, 1983, the "beginning of the Sikh War of Independence" was declared by B. S. Sandu after the killing of a police officer outside the Golden Temple, following which 40 activists believed to be hiding inside were ordered to surrender within a week.

On Oct. 6, 1983, President's rule was introduced in Punjab, and by the beginning of June 400 people were estimated to have died, and 2,000 to have been arrested between Oct. 6 and Dec. 16, 1983 alone, in apparently indiscriminate violence and killings in which moderate Sikhs also came under attack from more radical factions. Leadership of the Sikh agitation gradually passed from the moderate Sant Longowal to the Sikh militant leader Sant Bhindranwale, who had taken refuge in the Golden Temple along with his followers.

Tripartite talks began in Delhi on Feb. 14, 1984, to discuss Sikh demands which included a greater degree of religious and political autonomy; the recognition of Chandigarh as the capital of Punjab alone (and not of Punjab and Haryana); a greater share of river water; and the abolition of a sub-clause of Article 25 of the Constitution which was taken to mean that Sikh was a sect of Hinduism. However, talks broke down the next day due to an outbreak of violence, in which 80 people died between Feb. 14 and early March.

On March 4, police and paramilitary forces were given power to arrest suspects and search for arms without a warrant, this being the first time since Indian independence that such powers had been given to security forces. On March 19, President's rule was extended for another six months. In early April there was another outbreak of intense violence, despite an announcement by the government in New Delhi that it would consider amending Article 25, and on April 3 Punjab was declared a "dangerously disturbed area". On April 5 the National Security Act was amended to allow detention for up to six months without trial in Punjab and Chandigarh.

At a mass demonstration at the Golden Temple on April 13 called by Sant Longowal to protest against the "siege" tactics of the security forces, Sant Bhindranwale called on Sikhs to arm themselves with "grenades, bombs, rifles and even submachine-guns".

Tension within the Sikh movement mounted when 160 *Akali* members changed their allegiance from Sant Longowal to Sant Bhindranwale at the end of April. On April 14, a close associate of Sant Bhindranwale, Surinder Singh, was shot dead, and over the next two days, the bodies of three alleged supporters of Sant Longowal were found.

On May 3, security forces entered three Sikh temples at the end of a siege which had begun on April 26 in the central town of Moga, where seven people had died after militant Sikhs inside one of the temples opened fire. Sixteen of the 325 people inside were arrested after the siege. Sant Longowal threatened during the siege to send in a "squad of martyrs" to liberate the temples.

The killing of a Hindu newspaper editor on May 12 led to a spate of intense violence throughout May, with one estimate of an average of three to four deaths a day. (On May 11, Mrs Gandhi had made a conciliatory move towards Sikhs, announcing the release of a number of activists detained since February for burning copies of the Constitution in New Delhi.)

Inside the Golden Temple 11 Sikhs died on June 1 in clashes with security forces outside. Following this incident, and in anticipation of a new wave of agitation announced by Sant Longowal on May 27, in particular a threatened grain embargo, the army was sent into Punjab on the night of June 2. On the same day, Mrs Gandhi appealed to Sikhs to return to negotiations, saying that she was ready to concede most of their demands. On June 3, a state-wide 36-hour curfew was imposed, all road and rail travel was banned, news coverage was barred, and the Pakistan/Punjab border was sealed.

On June 2-3, an estimated 30-40 people died in confrontations throughout Punjab. Sikhs opened fire as the army laid siege to the Golden Temple, starting a fierce gun battle which continued through June 4. Unofficial sources reported that 36 militants died in this fighting, and 200 pilgrims escaped from the temple complex.

During the night of June 5-6, the army began an attack on the Golden Temple (and at the same time on 37 other Sikh shrines throughout Punjab), culminating in the capture of the *Akal Takht* (one of the most sacred parts of the temple which had become the stronghold of those inside, and which the army had been instructed not to damage).

Official figures published in a White Paper stated that 493 "terrorists" and civilians and 92 soldiers were killed in the army assault. Unofficial army figures put the figures at 1,000 and 250 respectively. Amongst those killed was Sant Bhindranwale. Thousands of Sikhs were arrested, including Sant Longowal who had been living in the Golden Temple, but had managed to leave before the assault. On July 27, the Minister of State for Defence reported that 1,421 Sikh soldiers had deserted in protest against the assault, and 35 were subsequently killed, but "other government sources" were reported as putting the figure of deserters at 5,000, with at least 102 killed.

Scattered resistance from groups of militants continued after the assault, and there were further violent incidents throughout Punjab. Sikh leaders refused to allow the temple to be repaired until the military left, but on July 17, a group of *Nihang* (temple guardians) began repair work. On July 21, Punjab was declared "terrorist-affected" and special courts were created to sit in-camera in the affected area.

On June 27, the Golden Temple was reopened to controlled groups of pilgrims. The army completed its withdrawal from the Golden Temple on Sept. 29, 1984. President's rule was extended for a further six months on Oct. 4.

The assassination of Mrs Gandhi by two Sikh members of her bodyguard on Oct. 31, 1984, was followed by an outbreak of violence (described as the worst since Partition in 1947), which left an estimated 2,987 dead (2,416 in Delhi alone) and forced 35,000 Sikhs to take refuge in temples or camps. Three thousand people were arrested for rioting as mobs of Hindu youths attacked male Sikhs. The army was deployed in parts of Uttar Pradesh, Madhya Pradesh, Bihar, West Bengal, Tripura, Himachal Pradesh and Jammu and Kashmir. Most violent incidents occurred in the so-called "Hindi heartland" of the north, where the largest Sikh populations also lived. At the same time, many Sikhs praised Hindu neighbours in Delhi for protecting them.

There followed numerous demonstrations for peace, and by Nov. 13, curfews which had been imposed in Delhi and 20 other places had been largely lifted.

The assassins of Mrs Gandhi were subsequently named as Satwant Singh and Beant Singh. Satwant Singh was critically injured and Beant Singh killed in shooting which broke out in a guard's room where the two men were taken after the attack. (It was alleged they tried to escape.) Kehar Singh, an assistant in the Directorate General of Supply and Distribution and a relative of Beant Singh, was implicated by Satwant Singh and arrested on Nov. 30, 1984. Balbir Singh, a Delhi police sub-inspector, described as having "guided the assassins", was arrested on Dec. 3, after also being implicated by Satwant Singh. On Nov. 30, a former policeman, Simranjit Singh, described as the "co-ordinating mastermind behind the plot", was arrested as he tried to cross into Nepal. Also implicated was Harinder Singh, who had resigned on June 19, 1984, as first secretary at the Indian embassy in Oslo (Norway), and who was alleged to have paid Beant Singh US$100,000 to finance the assassination.

On May 13, 1985, the US Federal Bureau of Information announced that it had discovered a plot to assassinate the Indian Prime Minister, Rajiv Gandhi (Mrs Gandhi's son), on a forthcoming visit. Five Sikhs were arrested and a search was begun for two others, Lal Singh and Ammand Singh. An affidavit filed on May 14 revealed that this group (of no specific name) had intended to cause the "revolutionary overthrow of the government of India".

On Aug. 20, 1985, the moderate Sikh leader Sant Longowal was killed by rival Sikhs after an announcement on July 24 that he had signed an agreement with R. Gandhi for a settlement of the Punjab problem.

On Sept. 30, 1985, President's rule was raised in Punjab, after detention orders against 224 out of 233 Sikhs had been lifted on the previous day. (Simranjit Singh was amongst those not released.)

Three Sikh hijackers were sentenced to death in Pakistan on Jan. 20, 1986, and seven sentenced to life imprisonment (with four acquitted), for the hijack of an Indian airliner to Lahore in September 1981 and for a second hijack of an airliner to Lahore in July 1984. (The death sentences, however, were suspended on Feb. 14, 1986.)

On Jan. 22, 1986, death sentences were passed on three Sikhs who took part in Mrs Gandhi's assassination; Satwant Singh was found guilty of shooting Mrs Gandhi (as was Beant Singh, who had been killed immediately afterwards), whilst Kehar Singh and Balbir Singh were found guilty of conspiring to murder.

Sikh agitation continued through 1986 and the first half of 1987. On May 1, 1986, the Union government extended the ban on the NCK and the *Dal Khalsa*. On July 18, 1986, 2,000 security personnel were involved in an operation to arrest 60 alleged Sikh extremists in the area of Mand (called the capital of Khalistan by some extremists). The following day 11 "hardcore extremists" were arrested, including Sukhinder Singh, responsible for an (unnamed) group which had carried out a number of murders.

In October 1986 R. Gandhi escaped an assassination attempt by three Sikhs in New Delhi.

United Akali Dal

The leader of this militant faction, Joginder Singh, father of the militant Sikh leader Sant Bhindranwale killed in the assault on the Golden Temple, denounced a memorandum for settlement of the Punjab problem signed by the *Akali Dal* leader Sant Longowal and Prime Minister R. Gandhi which had been announced on July 24, 1985. He was also amongst those called to look after the "religious and political affairs of the Sikh" by an advisory panel set up by radical Sikhs who took over the Golden Temple for a period between January and the beginning of May 1986.

Indonesia

Capital: Jakarta Pop. 163,390,000

The Republic of Indonesia is a unitary state with an executive President who governs with the assistance of a Cabinet and who is elected (and is re-eligible every five years) by a 1,000-member People's Consultative Assembly, the highest authority of state. Of the Assembly's members, 500 are from the House of Representatives, the country's legislature, to which 400 are elected for a five-year term by direct universal adult suffrage, and the remaining 100 are appointed. The Assembly's other 500 members comprise representatives of the armed forces (152 seats), delegates of regional assemblies (148), professional group representatives (100) and representatives of parties and political groups (100, appointed in proportion to their elective seats in the House of Representatives).

As a result of elections held on April 23, 1987 (when 91 per cent of the electorate voted), the 400 elective seats in the House of Representatives were distributed as follows: Joint Secretariat of Functional Groups (Golkar) 299, Moslem United Development Party 61, Indonesian Democratic Party 40. This was the fifth election to be held since 1955 (when the first election was held 10 years after independence), and the first time that Golkar succeeded in winning a majority of votes in each of Indonesia's 27 provinces, winning 73 per cent of the total votes cast.

Following the abortive communist-backed coup attempt in 1965 and the subsequent accession to power of Gen. Suharto in place of President Sukarno, effective power passed to a small group of military officers around President Suharto and to the *Kopkamtib* internal security organization, which conducted a country-wide campaign of repression against suspected communists and other left-wing elements. In October 1977 Amnesty International estimated that there were at least 55,000 and probably about 100,000 political prisoners (known as *tapols*), many of them having been held without trial since the 1965 coup attempt (after which—again according to Amnesty International—at least 500,000 persons had been killed and 700,000 arrested).

By December 1979 the government claimed to have released all political detainees except 61 "category A" prisoners described as hard-core communists (who were to be brought to trial the following year). However, in December 1981 the Home Affairs Minister stated that there were 249 "category A" political detainees, while a further 36,648 persons were classified as "category B" (against whom there was no evidence but who were nevertheless considered dangerous) and 1,536,936 as "category C" (released detainees).

An Independence Day amnesty announced on Aug. 17, 1983, provided that 3,198 political prisoners were to be released and a further 14,000 would have their sentences reduced.

Apart from the internal security threat posed by the Indonesian communists, the Suharto regime has come under challenge from Moslem fundamentalist movements, which have gained increasing support within a population which is 90 per cent Moslem, for their aim of transforming the existing secular Republic into an Islamic state. The regime has also continued to be confronted with secessionist movements in outlying regions of the Indonesian polity.

A Social Organizations Bill passed in May 1985 required the adoption of "Pancasila" as the guiding principle of all social, political and religious organizations in Indonesia. The five main tenets of Pancasila are: humanity, nationalism, social justice, democracy and a belief in deity but not the endorsement of any particular religion. The new legislation also provided for the banning or "freezing" of organizations, if they were deemed to be violating the tenets of Pancasila in any way. The Bill was strongly criticized by opposition parties which regarded it as a move towards a one-party state and by Moslem groups who opposed President Suharto's establishment of a secular state by the introduction of Pancasila.

Moslem Fundamentalist Movements

Abode of Islam (*Dar-ul-Islam*)

Leadership. Daud Baruah (l.)

The *Dar-ul-Islam* movement, although banned, was active in Indonesia from the early 1950s onwards as a movement aiming at the violent overthrow of the secular Republic and its replacement by an Islamic state. Revolts organized by it broke out (i) in South Celebes (Sulawesi) in 1951, involving 40,000 to 50,000 rebels, leading to the temporary establishment of an "Islamic Indonesian state" in part of Celebes and lasting until 1956, when it was finally suppressed by government forces, and (ii) in Atjeh province (northern Sumatra) on Sept. 23, 1953, causing many hundreds of casualties before being suppressed a few months later. On April 22, 1977, the police announced the arrest of six former *Dar-ul-Islam* members on a charge of plotting to blow up a power station in West Java.

The *Dar-ul-Islam* movement has its main strength in Atjeh (Aceh), where its Islamic fundamentalism provides the ideological basis for the strong separatist tendencies of the province (see separate entry for Free Aceh Movement). In November 1981 the *Dar-ul-Islam* leader, Daud Baruah, was reported to be under house arrest in Jakarta, but in Atjeh the movement continued to run a parallel administration as the effective government of the province, particularly in matters of law and order. When in late 1981 militant Moslems in Banda Aceh (the main city) launched a series of violent attacks on the local Chinese community, government troops were sent from Jakarta to quell the disturbances only after a delay of several days, apparently because of official wariness about intervening in this traditionally autonomous area.

Holy War Command (*Jihad Komando*)

Leadership. Imran Mohammad Zain

A group of five Moslem extremists said to be members of this Command hijacked an Indonesian airliner on March 28, 1981, and forced it to be flown to Bangkok, demanding that the Indonesian government should release some 80 detainees and also expel all Jews from the country: four of the hijackers were killed on March 30 by Indonesian troops who stormed the airliner at Bangkok airport (with permission from the Thai authorities) and the fifth subsequently died from injuries received, as did the airliner's pilot.

The Indonesian security authorities announced on April 20, 1980, that the organization presumed responsible for the hijacking had been dismantled and its leader arrested, the latter being named as Imran Mohammad Zain and identified as head of the "Indonesian Islamic Revolutionary Council" (apparently the political counterpart of the Holy War Command). In March 1982 a Jakarta court passed a death sentence on Imran Mohammad Zain and it was reported on April 13, 1983, that he had been executed.

Secessionist Movements

Free Aceh Movement

This Movement aspires to independence for Atjeh (Aceh), the north-westernmost province of Sumatra, and is closely orientated to the Islamic fundamentalist ideology of the Abode of Islam (*Dar-ul-Islam*) movement (see separate entry). Arrests of activists charged with plotting to set up such an independent state have been reported periodically. In 1980 the government claimed that the Movement had been suppressed and its leader, Hasan de Tiro, was said to have been killed in October of that year.

Papua Independent Organization (*Organisasi Papua Merdeka*, OPM)

Leadership. Elky Bemei

This movement was founded by educated Papuans who went into exile in 1963, when Irian Jaya (formerly Dutch New Guinea and known as West Irian until 1973) was incorporated into Indonesia. Members of the movement later returned to the territory. The original leaders of the OPM, regarded as pro-Dutch, were later replaced by new leaders who in 1971 formed a "Provisional Revolutionary Government of West Papua New Guinea" which proclaimed the independence of the territory and which had as its president "Brig.-Gen." Seth Rumkorem (a former major in the Indonesian army). In 1976 these insurgents claimed to control a number of "liberated zones" covering 15 per cent of the territory.

The "Provisional Government", with headquarters in the Netherlands, also set up information offices in Dakar (Senegal) and Stockholm, and President Léopold Sédar Senghor of Senegal stated during a visit to Paris in March 1976 that he had allowed that government to set up an office in Dakar because the (Melanesian) Papuans were blacks, differing in race and culture from the Indonesians, and Senegal supported all movements by black people to assert their national identity. The movement, which claimed to control an armed force of 10,000 men, was believed to be responsible for a rebellion in April-May 1977, which was crushed by Indonesian troops after six weeks of fighting.

The government of Papua New Guinea agreed in January 1977 that it would not allow its territory to be used as a base for incursions into Irian Jaya by subversive elements or "dissidents", and early in 1978 Papua New Guinea had, according to the Indonesian Minister of Information, assured Indonesia that all anti-Indonesian movements in Papua New Guinea were banned and that only those members of the OPM who had good intentions (e.g. of seeking work in Papua New Guinea) would be admitted to the country.

In 1977 "Brig.-Gen." Rumkorem was succeeded by Jacob Prai as president of the "Provisional Government", which included 10 persons formerly resident in Irian Jaya but currently holding either Papua New Guinea citizenship or residence permits. At a meeting held in Port Moresby (Papua New Guinea) on April 14-16, 1978, between senior ministers and officials of Papua New Guinea on the one hand and J. Prai and "Brig.-Gen." Rumkorem on the other, the latter were warned that Papua New Guinea would "not at any stage allow itself to be used as a sanctuary for subversive activities against Indonesia". In April 1978 it was reported from Papua New Guinea that over 5,000 guerrillas and civilians, as well as 3,500 Indonesians, had been killed in fighting in Irian Jaya since the beginning of 1976; the Indonesian government, however, described this fighting as a tribal war and consistently referred to OPM guerrillas as "wild gangs".

In June-July 1978 Indonesian military activity increased greatly along Irian Jaya's border with Papua New Guinea, following an ambush by OPM units of an Indonesian helicopter carrying senior military and civilian personnel, seven of whom the OPM seized as hostages. The Indonesian counter-action was informally supported by the Papua New Guinea Defence Forces. These operations caused some 650 refugees to leave Irian Jaya for Papua New Guinea. In September 1978 J. Prai and his "defence minister" (Otto Ondawame) were arrested as "illegal immigrants" in Papua New Guinea and subsequently sentenced to imprisonment; they later obtained sanctuary in Sweden, where they were taken in February 1979 with two other senior OPM members.

Among the reasons for the Papua New Guinea government's firm anti-OPM measures at this time (which included the signing of a border security agreement with Indonesia in 1979) was its discovery that leaders of the movement were seeking to obtain support from Communist bloc countries.

The military commander of Irian Jaya province stated on March 4, 1981, that no military force would be used against OPM rebels, but only persuasion, which had already led to the surrender of hundreds of OPM members and their leaders; that this policy would be pursued until the OPM had been eliminated; but that stern measures would be taken against OPM members refusing to give themselves up.

"Brig.-Gen." Rumkorem, describing himself as "President" of the "Republic of West Papua", reappeared in Rabaul (Papua New Guinea) in September 1982, and was arrested for illegal entry.

In July 1984 the Papua New Guinea government despatched troops into the border area in an attempt to quell OPM activity. In a new border agreement signed on Oct. 29, 1984, the Indonesian government gave a written assurance that reprisals would not be taken against some 10,000 refugees returning from Papua New Guinea to Indonesia. The Papua New Guinea government had insisted that any Indonesian refugees would be repatriated provided that the Indonesian government gave an assurance of their future well-being.

OPM rebels continued to cause security problems for the government of Papua New Guinea during 1985. On Oct. 22, 1985, the Papua New Guinea Prime Minister, Sir Michael Somare, asserted that his government "would not drive out" OPM rebels. In December 1986, five OPM leaders and eight members surrendered to the Papua New Guinea authorities in the Irian Jaya border area. Papua New Guinea asked the United Nations to find a third country which would offer them asylum.

An OPM delegation attended a "world conference of liberation movements" in Libya in March 1986. According to Australian reports the conference ratified the formation of a "revolutionary committee" covering Irian Jaya, Papua New Guinea and the south-west Pacific, and an OPM official said on May 11, 1987, that the movement had turned to Libya for support after failing to win regional backing.

Revolutionary Front for the Independence of East Timor (*Fretilin*)

Leadership. José Gusmão Sha Na Na (l.)

Fretilin superseded a Timorese Social Democratic Association (ASDT) formed after the 1974 revolution in Portugal and advocating full independence for East Timor (then a Portuguese province). As a pro-communist (and anti-Indonesian) revolutionary movement, *Fretilin* was opposed by the other political parties formed in East Timor in 1974 and was soon involved in civil war with them. By Sept. 8, 1975, it claimed to have gained complete control of East Timor; it also announced that it had dropped its original demand for complete independence from Portugal and that it wished to move gradually towards self-government, with the installation of a provisional government early in 1976, the election of a constituent assembly and independence within a few years. The Indonesian government, however, made it clear that it was opposed to a *Fretilin* government.

On Nov. 28, 1975, *Fretilin* declared East Timor independent as the "Democratic Republic of East Timor" and claimed that it had the support of 50 Afro-Asian countries. The pro-Indonesian parties, however, declared on Nov. 29, 1975, that as *Fretilin*'s action had "removed the last remains of Portuguese sovereignty" the territory was now part of Indonesia, and on Dec. 7 Indonesian forces began to occupy East Timor. *Fretilin*'s armed forces were forced to withdraw to remote areas, and the territory was formally incorporated into Indonesia on Aug. 17, 1976. While *Fretilin* continued to offer resistance, the Indonesian government claimed in mid-1978 that about 60,000 *Fretilin* supporters had surrendered in response to an Indonesian amnesty offer of Aug. 16, 1977. Those who surrendered included a former president of *Fretilin* and President of the "Democratic Republic of East Timor", Francisco Xavier do Amaral, who had on Sept. 13, 1977, been replaced by Nicolau dos Reis Lobato (who was killed in battle on Jan. 1, 1979); the former *Fretilin* president was later appointed deputy governor of the new province, now called Loro Sae.

Fretilin nevertheless continued not only to retain some bases inside the territory but also, through its "Government of the Democratic Republic of East Timor" (in exile but enjoying recognition by numerous third-world governments and in particular by those of all the former Portuguese provinces in Africa), to take part in negotiations at the United Nations on the future of East Timor, the occupation of which by Indonesia was condemned by the UN Security Council and the UN General Assembly.

However, in April 1982 an Indonesian military commander in the eastern zone estimated *Fretilin*'s strength at only 130 persons split up into small groups and supported by some 200 sympathizers or sympathizing families; this followed a major Indonesian offensive in July-September 1981 against *Fretilin*'s remaining mountain strongholds, as a result of which some 4,000 inhabitants of the area had been removed to the island of Atauro (off Dili, the capital of East Timor).

In August 1983 the Indonesian government launched another offensive against *Fretilin* which lasted well into 1984. Amnesty International published a report on June 26, 1985, stating that up to 500,000 people in East Timor had been killed or resettled since the Indonesian takeover in 1976. A new government offensive against *Fretilin* was reported to have begun in May 1986.

In March 1986 *Fretilin* and the Timorese Democratic Union (*União Democrática Timorense*, UDT) announced from Lisbon (Portugal) that they would henceforth engage in joint diplomatic and military initiatives to further their demand for self-determination for East Timor. The UDT, formed in 1974, had favoured a gradual approach to self-determination, involving an extended period of association with Portugal, and had no military units in East Timor.

Other Movements

Communist Party of Indonesia (CPI)

Founded in May 1920, the CPI was involved in an unsuccessful rising against Dutch rule (in the Netherlands East Indies) in 1926-27, whereafter it went underground. In the 1930s it took part in the establishment of an anti-fascist front which during World War II opposed the invading Japanese forces. After the proclamation of Indonesia's national independence on Aug. 17, 1945, the CPI took part in the government but in September 1948 this government was overthrown in a right-wing coup, which led to the killing of numerous CPI leaders and to the temporary return of Dutch rule until Dec. 27, 1949, when sovereignty was transferred to the Republic of the United States of Indonesia. The CPI was re-consituted, and in elections in 1955 it became one of the country's four major parties, while in local elections held in 1956 it polled the greatest number of votes.

In subsequent years there was discussion on strategy within the party, whose seventh congress held in 1962 advanced the thesis that "the national interest is above class interest" (to some extent reflecting the strongly nationalist Marxism espoused by President Sukarno). The pro-Chinese faction in the CPI gained in influence, and in 1965 the party led the "30th September Movement" in support of a group of young army officers who staged a coup to prevent a planned right-wing coup. The young officers' attempt was defeated, however, and right-wing generals led by Gen. Suharto installed a military regime; thereafter the CPI and other left-wing forces were vigorously suppressed, with Communists and alleged sympathizers being killed or detained.

The CPI nevertheless claimed to have reconstituted itself in the 1960s and 1970s, with the pro-Moscow wing defining its position in three documents—"The Correct Road of the Indonesian Revolution" (1966), "Pressing Tasks of the Communist Movement in Indonesia" (1969) and "For Democracy, Social Justice and People's Prosperity" (1975)—with the aim of creating a front of national unity and eventually an "anti-imperialist, democratic government as the prelude to advancing to socialism". For its part, the pro-Chinese wing issued a statement on the 60th anniversary of the party in May 1980 declaring its support for an Indonesian application of "Marxism-Leninism-Mao Zedong thought" and also calling for vigilance in confronting "Soviet and Vietnamese hegemonism". The statement was signed by Jusuf Adjitorop, who was identified as "secretary-general of the central committee and member of the political bureau of the CPI central committee".

Whereas the government claimed in December 1979 to have released all but the hard-core elements detained since the 1965 coup attempt, arrests of Communists continued thereafter and the party remained banned. The former strength of the PCI was indicated by the Home Affairs Minister in December 1981, when the total number of Indonesian nationals "involved in the Indonesian Communist Party-affiliated 30th September Movement" was put at 1,580,020. In the same statement the Home Affairs Minister made it clear that over 40,000 ex-detainees who had been adherents of the PCI would have no voting rights in the May 1982 elections.

Four CPI leaders under sentence of death were executed in September 1986. The execution of nine communists convicted of involvement in the "30th September Movement" coup in 1965 was confirmed on Oct. 8, 1986.

Former members of the CPI were barred from voting in the April 1987 elections.

The Petition of 50

On Aug. 17, 1984, a petition entitled "Save Democracy", signed by a group of 50 dissidents, accused President Suharto of attempting to set up a one-party state by institutionalizing the party system. The group, calling itself Petition of 50, included former ministers, senior military men and academics concerned with corruption and what they saw as an abandonment of old nationalist values. A "white paper" signed by 22 members of the Petition of 50 in November 1984 called for an independent investigation into disturbances at Tanjung Priok, near Jakarta, on Sept. 12, 1984, when, according to official figures, 18 died and 53 were injured in anti-government demonstrations.

One of the leading members of the Petition of 50, Gen. Hartano Resko Dharsono, a former secretary-general of the Association of South-East Asian Nations (ASEAN), was charged in June 1985 with subversion against the government. He was convicted and sentenced to 10 (subsequently reduced to seven) years' imprisonment in January 1986.

Iran

Capital: Tehran Pop. 44,210,000

Iran was a monarchy until 1979, when Shah Reza Pahlevi was overthrown by an alliance of liberal, leftist and Shia Islamic fundamentalist opposition activists, the last group being led by Ayatollah Ruhollah Khomeini. A civilian form of government established under a Revolutionary Council headed by Khomeini (and abolished in 1980) became dominated increasingly by fundamentalists, driving most leftist and moderate groups into armed opposition to the regime. Guerrilla activity, largely conducted by the *Mjaheddin e-Khalq* and *Fedayeen e-Khalq* organizations, had been effectively suppressed by the mid-1980s, although armed Kurdish rebel movements continued to be active in the north-west of the country. The *Tudeh* (Communist) party, which had supported the Islamic revolution but later opposed the Khomeini government, was outlawed in 1983, and many of its activists were arrested.

Government authority in the Islamic Republic of Iran is vested in a President (directly elected), Prime Minister and Cabinet, although these are effectively subordinate to the *faqih* or "spiritual leader" (currently Ayatollah Khomeini). In the event of the Supreme Court ruling a President to be incompetent, the *faqih* has the power to dismiss him. The Council of Guardians, a 12-member body composed equally of lawyers and clerics, has the power to veto legislation on the grounds of Islamic law. It must also approve all candidates standing for election to high office. There is a 270-member parliament (*Majlis*), elected by direct universal suffrage. Approximately 90 per cent of the deputies are associated with the ruling Islamic Republican Party, although many have also been endorsed by other movements. The *Majlis* has on occasion strongly criticized the government, and has frequently exercised its right to veto proposed ministerial appointments. A "Council of Experts" nominated Ayatollah Montazeri as Khomeini's successor in 1985, although Montazeri subsequently expressed reservations about the decision.

Since 1980 Iran has been embroiled in the Gulf War with Iraq. After initial Iraqi successes, Iranian forces regained lost territory and invaded Iraq, with the stated purpose of bringing down President Saddam Hussein. By early 1987, they were threatening Basra, Iraq's second city. Iranian casualties have been high, however, in part due to the tactic of using poorly trained, massed infantry in "human wave" assaults against Iraqi defences. Iran has close links with fundamentalist groups in Lebanon, and in 1986 it was revealed that the USA had been covertly supplying arms to the Iranian leadership in an effort to buy the freedom of American hostages held by Islamic factions in Lebanon.

Left-wing Movements

Communist Party of Iran (CPI)

Leadership. Abdullah Mohtadeh (l.)

Founded. September 1983

This Party was formed in opposition to the pro-Soviet *Tudeh* party by a number of Marxist groups, among them the Kurdish Communist Party of Iran (*Komaleh*) which thus became the Kurdish section of the CPI.

The *Komaleh* had been founded in 1969 and had waged guerrilla warfare against government forces since 1979 (in support of its demand for Kurdish autonomy). It co-operated temporarily with the Kurdish Democratic Party of Iran but was soon in open conflict with it and did not, like that party, join the National Council of Resistance for Liberty and Independence (NCR) led by ex-President Bani-Sadr, because the NCR did not aim at social revolution. On Feb. 19, 1982, Djaffar Chafii, a member of the *Komaleh*'s executive bureau, said in Paris that his movement was seeking a social revolution in Iran and that only armed struggle would be able to bring about the overthrow of the existing regime.

People's Fighters (*Fedayeen e-Khalq*)

Leadership. (Ms) Ashraf Deghan (l.)

This militant Marxist guerrilla movement was responsible for numerous acts of violence committed under the Shah's regime with the purpose of hastening its overthrow. It supported the Islamic revolution in its early stages but on March 18, 1979, a spokesman for the movement said that before a constitutional referendum was held the country should be given democratic institutions. The organization took part in the elections to a Constituent Council of Experts on Aug. 3, 1979, but on Aug. 21 of that year Ayatollah Khomeini ordered the closure of its newspaper. Later the *Fedayeen* were involved in clashes with Revolutionary Guards, in particular at Gonbad-e-Qavus on Jan. 9, 1980, when 14 persons were killed and 65 injured.

After the outbreak of war between Iran and Iraq the *Fedayeen* initially strongly supported the Iranian war effort and called for "the defence of the revolution and independence of the country in the face of attacks from the Iraqi fascist regime". However, by mid-1981 elements aligned to the (communist) *Tudeh* party (People's Party—see separate entry) formed the predominant political current within the *Fedayeen*, which accordingly came to echo *Tudeh*'s opposition to the war.

The *Fedayeen* staged a number of simultaneous demonstrations at Iranian missions in Europe on a single day in April 1984. The most serious involved the occupation by *Fedayeen* sympathizers of the Iranian embassy in The Hague (Netherlands), during which the ambassador was clubbed unconscious. In London, embassy staff overpowered a group who had attempted to occupy the building. Prior to their release, they were handcuffed and had notices bearing the legend "terrorist" tied around their necks.

In common with the *Mujaheddin e-Khalq*, they had effectively ceased to pose a serious threat to the Iranian regime by the mid-1980s.

People's Holy Warriors (*Mujaheddin e-Khalq*)

Leadership. Massoud Rajavi (l.)

This left-wing Islamic movement, which attracted support from the educated middle classes and the young, had been active in opposing the Shah's regime for many years. In the initial stages of the Islamic regime it set up, in February 1979, with the *Fedayeen e-Khalq,* a joint committee to co-ordinate and supervise the use of arms confiscated from the Shah's supporters. It took part in the elections of a Constituent Council of Experts on Aug. 3, 1979, when its leader was elected to that Council. He was, however, not allowed to stand as a candidate in the presidential elections of Jan. 25, 1980, on the grounds that he had not endorsed the country's new Constitution.

During the parliamentary elections held in March-May 1979, the *Mujaheddin e-Khalq* lodged complaints against alleged irregularities, and its leader called for the elections to be annulled. In subsequent months members of the organization were involved in clashes with pro-Khomeini groups, in particular the extremist fundamentalist *Hezbollah* (Children of the Party of God). In June 1981 the *Mujaheddin e-Khalq* began to support President Abolhassan Bani-Sadr in his opposition to the rule of the doctrinaire fundamentalist clergy (*Maktabi*), who made use of the *Hezbollah* to disrupt anti-government demonstrations.

After the dismissal of President Bani-Sadr on June 21, 1981, the *Mujaheddin e-Khalq* were exposed to a rigorous government campaign against all opposition. They claimed in particular that a bomb which was exploded in Qom on June 23, killing eight persons and injuring over 50, had been planted by the Islamic authorities to serve as a pretext for the wave of repression against opponents. Following another bomb explosion in Tehran on June 28 (killing 72 leading politicians), for which Ayatollah Khomeini held the *Mujaheddin e-Khalq* responsible, the latter were also accused of having drawn up death lists including the names of the governor of the Evin prison in Tehran and Tehran's revolutionary prosecutor.

Numerous *Mujaheddin e-Khalq* members were subsequently executed, and on July 29, 1981, M. Rajavi arrived in Paris with ex-President Bani-Sadr, and on Oct. 1, he announced that he had formed a provisional government-in-exile (see separate entry for National Council of Resistance for Liberty and Independence). In Iran itself, *Mujaheddin* forces were said to have majority support in the traditionally left-wing strongholds in the northern provinces bordering the Caspian Sea. Moussa Khiabani, described as the most senior *Mujaheddin* leader inside Iran, was killed by Revolutionary Guards in Tehran on Feb. 8, 1982, together with his wife and that of M. Rajavi (then in Paris), and he was succeeded by Ali Zarkesh.

With a membership estimated (in September 1981) at 150,000, the *Mujaheddin e-Khalq* continued to be the most active opposition group within Iran during 1982. Despite a fierce campaign waged against them by the Revolutionary Guards and despite extensive arrests and executions of their members, they carried out repeated attacks and assassinations of government leaders, including Hojatoleslam Mohammed Ali Amininejad, the head of the navy's political-ideological office, who was killed on June 11, 1982; Ayatollah Mohammed Sadduqi, a member of the *Majlis* and a close associate of Ayatollah Khomeini, who was killed in Tehran on July 2; and Ali Mahlojes, a high-ranking member of the ruling IRP, whose assassination was claimed by the *Mujaheddin* on Sept. 2. On Sept. 5, 1982, the *Mujaheddin e-Khalq* claimed to have killed over 100 Revolutionary Guards in Tehran in the past week alone.

Mujaheddin power and influence began to decline from late 1982 onwards as a result of a sustained campaign against the movement by the Revolutionary Guards and armed forces. One of its last major successes was the assassination in October 1982 of Ayatollah Ashrafi Isfahani, one of Khomeini's closest aides, whom the *Mujaheddin* claimed to be responsible for ordering hundreds of executions in western Iranian cities. Sporadic actions continued to be reported during 1983-84, and a number of attacks were staged to coincide with the celebrations to mark the sixth anniversary of the revolution in February 1985. Other bomb attacks on civilian targets which took place that year were condemned by the *Mujaheddin.*

The movement frequently alleged that the regime was engaging in summary executions of suspected sympathizers. In a letter to the United Nations Secretary-General in September 1985, it claimed that over 12,000 such executions had been carried out since June 1981.

The *Mujaheddin e-Khalq* called for a boycott of the presidential elections held in August 1985.

By the beginning of 1986, the *Mujaheddin* appeared no longer to pose any real threat to the regime. In June of that year, Massoud Rajavi and 1,000 followers arrived to take up residence in Baghdad, having left France after their headquarters outside Paris had been raided by the police. Observers commented that France's wish to be rid of the movement resulted from its desire to improve relations with Iran, in part as an effort to secure the release of French hostages currently held by pro-Iranian Shia groups in Lebanon.

On May 13, 1987, however, the *Mujaheddin* claimed to have killed or wounded 200 Revolutionary Guards and destroyed seven Revolutionary Guard bases in an offensive in the Sardasht region of Iranian Kurdistan. Statements by Iranian government sources had previously admitted an increase in operations against "mercenaries and foreign elements".

People's Party (*Tudeh*)

Leadership. Noureddin Kianouri (first sec.); Ali Khavari (provisional l. in exile)

This Communist party had its origins in the Iranian Social Democratic Party (*Adalat*) which had arisen out of a social democratic group founded in 1904. Established in 1920 as the Communist Party of Iran, it was banned in 1931 and forced to continue its work illegally. In 1941 it was reorganized as the *Tudeh* party of Iran, which was itself repressed and officially declared illegal in 1949. In 1965 the party was divided into three factions—respectively of pro-Soviet, Maoist and Castroite orientation—but the first of these remained the official *Tudeh* party. In 1973 it adopted a new programme with the object of uniting all democratic forces by means of "flexibility, initiative and consistency".

From its base in exile in East Germany, the party welcomed the Islamic revolution of 1979 and pledged full support for its "anti-imperialist and democratic" aims. Allowed to operate once again under the new Islamic revolutionary regime, it called in particular for an alliance of all socialist forces which would enjoy the support of the Soviet Union. However, *Tudeh*'s support for the new regime waned as the latter became more committed to clerical fundamentalism; the party also opposed the Iran-Iraq war which broke out in September 1980.

The *Tudeh* party opposed Iran's participation in the Gulf War because (i) it had the effect of strengthening Iraq's relations with conservative Gulf regimes, (ii) it involved the Iranian government in heavy expenditure on arms to the detriment of the masses and (iii) increasing popular discontent with the war could lead to counter-revolution.

In August 1982 the ruling Islamic Republican Party published a strong critique of the policy of *Tudeh* and of the dominant pro-*Tudeh* faction of the *Fedayeen e-Khalq* (People's Fighters—see separate entry), attacking in particular their opposition to the war.

In early 1983, the government moved decisively to crush the *Tudeh* party. Over 1,000 of its leading activists were arrested, including Kianouri and the party's leading theoretician, Eshan Tabari. All party members were ordered to report to Revolutionary Guards' offices. In the first of a series of televised "confessions", Kianouri admitted that he had engaged in acts of "treason and espionage"; other party members "confessed" that they were employed by the Soviet state security service, the KGB. The *Tudeh* central committee denounced the confessions as having been obtained through "physical and psychological torture". The party was formally proscribed on May 4, 1983, when the government declared that "any activity in favour of it will be regarded as illegal and counter-revolutionary". It continued to operate from exile in the Soviet Union and East Germany. According to reports, Iran had acted against *Tudeh* on the basis of information concerning its members supplied by the US Central Intelligence Agency.

In February 1984, 10 members of the party's military section, including Capt. Bahram Afzali, the former Iranian navy commander, were executed after being convicted of treason. The trial of other leaders, including Kianouri and Tabari, was postponed indefinitely shortly before it was due to commence in November 1984. *Tudeh* claimed that this was due to concern that the proceedings would expose crimes committed by the state, while other reports suggested that the decision was taken as a result of Soviet pressure.

Tudeh's founder, Iraj Eskendari, died in East Germany in April 1985 at the age of 77. He had originally gone into exile when the party was declared illegal in 1949, but returned after the revolution in 1979, only to leave again later the same year after disagreements over the extent to which the party should support the Islamic regime.

Union of Communists

This small pro-Chinese formation has actively opposed the Khomeini regime since the revolution, but by mid-1982 the Iranian authorities were claiming to have virtually destroyed it as a significant force. At the end of August 1982 official sources stated that 183 members of the Union had been arrested in Khuzestan and that large arsenals of firearms and explosives had been discovered.

In January 1983 22 Union activists were executed after taking part in an uprising in the town of Amol the previous year.

Unit of Martyr Kalaghi

This previously unknown group claimed responsibility for the bombing of Tehran's main railway station in August 1984, which killed 18 people when it exploded at the height of the morning rush-hour.

The Moderate Opposition

Association for the Defence of Freedom and Sovereignty of the Iranian Nation

This moderate opposition grouping was formed in March 1986 by Dr Mehdi Bazargan, leader of the Freedom Movement. It held its first meeting in May the same year. Its 20-member central committee included five representatives of the Freedom Movement. Seven members of the 1979 provisional government were represented, including Ali Ardalan, Assadollah Mobasheri and Nasser Minachi. The Association stated that it supported the revolution and the Constitution, but was opposed to the continuation of the war. Bazargan and other leading figures in the Association were kidnapped and briefly detained in late May by radical activists who were apparently protesting both at the Association's policies and at the government's willingness to tolerate its existence. Following the incident, Ayatollah Montazeri criticized those who would use violence against non-violent opponents of the regime.

Freedom Movement (*Nelzat-Azadi*)

Leadership. Dr Mehdi Bazargan (l.)

The foremost remaining legal opposition group, the Freedom Movement, consists of moderate politicians grouped around Dr Bazargan, Prime Minister from February to November 1979. At the end of 1982, a letter criticizing the regime's leaders as being "inaccessible" circulated in Tehran. The Movement boycotted the 1984 elections. A further letter, signed by Bazargan and several former Cabinet ministers, was released to coincide with the celebrations marking the sixth anniversary of the revolution in February 1985. The letter attacked the "lack of basic freedoms" in Iran and the current "economic and political crisis" and called for freedom of press, speech and assembly and for an end to the war with Iraq. The Movement's offices were later raided by the (pro-regime) *Hezbollah* party. The following month, Bazargan denounced the war as "disastrous", and suggested (in a letter to the country's Supreme Defence Council) that it might be against the teachings of the Koran. In the wake of this and other statements, he was publicly denounced by Hojatolislam Hashemi Ali Akbar Rafsanjani, parliamentary Speaker and one of the most influential figures in the regime.

Dr Bazargan registered as a presidential candidate prior to the August 1985 elections, but his candidacy was among 27 out of 30 which were rejected by the Council of Guardians.

Iranian National Front (INF)

Leadership. Dr Karim Sanjabi (l.)

The INF was established in December 1977 as a Union of National Front Forces comprising several earlier organizations opposed to the Shah's "dictatorship". At first it advocated a return to constitutional monarchy but in 1978 it called for the abolition of the monarchy and the return from exile of Ayatollah Khomeini. Dr Sanjabi was temporarily Minister of Foreign Affairs in the government of Dr Mehdi Bazargan (appointed by Ayatollah Khomeini in February 1979) but resigned in April 1979 because he was disappointed with the government's lack of power. In the March 1979 referendum on the establishment of an Islamic Republic the INF called for a "yes" vote but it boycotted the August 1979 elections to a Constituent Council of Experts.

On Aug. 21, 1979, Ayatollah Khomeini ordered the closure of the INF's newspaper, and the INF was thereafter in open conflict with the Ayatollah's regime. In July 1981 an INF member, Karim Dastmaltchi, was executed, inter alia for providing "financial support for the counter-revolution" and giving interviews to the foreign press. The INF also called for a boycott of presidential elections held on July 24, 1981 (after the dismissal of President Bani-Sadr), leading to the election as President of Mohammed Ali Radjai (until then Prime Minister).

National Council of Resistance for Liberty and Independence (NCR)

The NCR was set up in 1981 by ex-President Abolhassan Bani-Sadr and Massoud Rajavi, the leader of the *Mujaheddin e-Khalq,* both of whom had reached Paris on July 29, 1981. Bani-Sadr, who had been a close associate of Ayatollah Khomeini, had been elected as first President of the Islamic Republic of Iran on Jan. 25, 1980, but he was later in disagreement with the Ayatollah over the question of the President's powers. After he had refused to sign bills passed by Parliament and had also been criticized for his conduct of the war against Iraq, he was on June 10, 1981, ordered by Ayatollah Khomeini to be dismissed from the post of C.-in-C. of the armed forces (to which he had been appointed on Feb. 19, 1980).

On June 12, 1981, he attacked the rule of the Islamic Republican party as having "worsened the condition of the country day by day", and Parliament thereupon, on June 21, declared him incompetent (by 177 votes to one with one abstention) and on the following day Ayatollah Khomeini formally dismissed him as President, whereupon he disappeared from public life until his arrival in Paris. Bani-Sadr was later named by the NCR as its preferred future President of a "provisional government". On Nov. 6, 1981, it was announced that as a result of negotiations with Dr Saeed Badal, a member of the central committee of the Kurdish Democratic Party of Iran (KDPI), this party had formally joined the NCR.

Bani-Sadr left the NCR in March 1984, reportedly as a result of differences with Rajavi over relations with Iraq, with Rajavi favouring close ties with the Baghdad regime (see entry under *Mujaheddin e-Khalq*). Some opposition groups were also thought to be suspicious of Bani-Sadr's previous association with the regime.

The KDPI was expelled from the NRC in April 1985, reportedly as a consequence of its willingness to negotiate with the government.

National Resistance Movement

Leadership. Dr Shapour Bakhtiar

Dr Bakhtiar had been a supporter of Dr Mossadeq, the (left-wing) Prime Minister of Iran who was overthrown in 1953, and as a leading member of the National Front he was an outspoken critic of the Shah. As the latter's last Prime Minister in January-February 1979, Dr Bakhtiar had a programme of liberalization, including the dissolution of the Shah's secret police and the granting of a greater role to the Moslem religious leaders in drafting legislation. His government was, however, condemned by Ayatollah Khomeini as "a betrayal of our cause" and was eventually brought down by the Ayatollah's followers on Feb. 11, 1979. Dr Bakhtiar subsequently left Iran and settled in France, where he set up his opposition movement.

On May 13, 1979, Ayatollah Khalkhali, then head of Iran's revolutionary courts, declared that Dr Bakhtiar was among those former Prime Ministers on whom sentences of death had been passed under "religious laws". On June 10 and July 12, 1980, the Iranian government announced that a conspiracy by military men to restore Dr Bakhtiar to power had been uncovered and that some 300 persons had been arrested in this connexion. By Sept. 3, 1980, a total of 96 of them, including two generals, had been executed. In Paris Dr Bakhtiar escaped an assassination attempt on July 18, 1980, when three persons were killed and one injured. Ali Tabatabai, a former press attaché at the Iranian embassy in Washington, who was described as a supporter of Dr Bakhtiar and who had been head of a Freedom Foundation (aimed at restoring "a democratic regime" in Iran), was killed in Washington on July 22.

Whilst Dr Bakhtiar had announced the formation of his National Resistance Movement on Aug. 8, 1980, he denied on Sept. 26 that he had formed a government-in-exile in Paris; on Sept. 29 he also denied that he had armed supporters waiting to invade Iran.

In response to an appeal issued on the Movement's radio, thousands of motorists staged a "traffic-jam demonstration" through middle-class districts of Tehran in August 1983, on the anniversary of the proclamation of the monarchist Constitution of 1907. The demonstration passed without incident, but a second one staged in May 1985 resulted in some fighting between participants and Revolutionary Guards.

In September 1984, the Movement claimed responsibility for a bomb attack on a Revolutionary Guards' office in Tehran—this being the first violent incident claimed by the group.

Separatist Movements

Komaleh—see under Communist Party of Iran (CPI)

Kurdish Democratic Party of Iran (KDPI)

Leadership. Dr Abdel Rahman Qasemlu (gen. sec.)

The KDPI was originally formed as an illegal organization after World War II out of an Association for the Resurrection of Kurdistan but was practically liquidated when a Kurdish rebellion in Iran was crushed in 1966-67. Dr Qasemlu—who had been a member of the (communist) *Tudeh* party—was, at a secret KDPI conference held in Baghdad after 1973, elected the party's secretary-general, and he returned from exile to Iran shortly after the February 1979 Islamic revolution.

On Feb. 19, 1979, Kurdish leaders placed their autonomy demands before a government delegation but the new regime took no steps towards accepting these demands. The KDPI thereupon boycotted the March 1979 referendum on the establishment of an Islamic Republic in Iran, largely because the form of the question put to voters, in the KDPI's view, compelled them to vote in favour.

A number of violent incidents led to the outbreak in March 1979 of a Kurdish rebellion in Sanandaj (in the mountainous western part of Iran), involving the loss of between 100 and 200 lives. On March 25 the government announced a detailed autonomy plan for the Kurds, but this plan was not implemented, partly because Turkomans in north-eastern Iran were pressing for similar autonomy, and the Prime Minister (then Dr Mehdi Bazargan) declared on April 4 that autonomy would be granted only on a national basis and not to individual ethnic groups. By this time Kurdish armed groups (*Pesh Merga* or "Forward to Death" fighters) were in control of the principal Kurdish towns in the western mountains.

Fighting also took place between KDPI supporters and Azeri-speaking Shia Moslems in West Azerbaijan (who supported Ayatollah Khomeini) on April 20-26, 1979, when hundreds of people were killed before government troops succeeded in restoring calm. Further fighting occurred towards the end of June 1979, when farmers, with the support of the KDPI (and also of the Kurdish Sunni Moslem Movement led by Shaikh Hosseini) sought to take possession of land from landowners who had been armed by the government and tried to regain possession of land seized by Kurdish peasants after the Islamic revolution. On June 26 the KDPI demanded to know from Ayatollah Khomeini why his regime had armed landowners who had "backed the Shah to the very end" and why the local revolutionary committees had been agitating against the Kurds.

When troops, Revolutionary Guards and police tried to remove the armed Kurds from towns and villages, heavy fighting ensued in July 1979, especially in Marivan (West Azerbaijan), but under an agreement reached on Aug. 5 unarmed Kurds were left in control of Marivan. On Aug. 14 some 2,000 armed Kurds attacked military positions at Paveh (Kermanshah province) and within two days gained control of the town. However, after Ayatollah Khomeini had declared himself C.-in-C. of the armed forces and had taken over direct command, this insurgency was put down with up to 400 people being killed and 29 Kurds being executed by firing squad on Aug. 19-21. At the same time government forces also regained control of Sanandaj.

Meanwhile the KDPI had boycotted the elections to a Constituent Council of Experts on Aug. 3, 1979; although Dr Qasemlu was nevertheless elected to the Council, he did not take his seat because on Aug. 19 a government spokesman announced that the KDPI had been declared illegal with immediate effect on the grounds that it had "instigated bloody incidents" in various Kurdish areas. Ayatollah Khomeini denounced the rebel Kurds as "communist-backed enemies of the revolution" and branded Shaikh Hosseini and Dr Qasemlu as "traitors". The KDPI was also officially accused of receiving aid from abroad (i.e. by implication from the Soviet Union, Iraq, Israel and supporters of the former Shah).

Dr Qasemlu, alleging that the Ayatollah was gradually restoring Iran to "a religious dictatorship of the Middle Ages", appealed, on Aug. 19, 1979, to world leaders to save the Kurdish people from "genocide". In nine major Kurdish towns mass demonstrations took place in support of the Kurdish leaders, many of whom were subsequently arrested. On Aug. 22 Ayatollah Khomeini offered a "pardon" to all Kurds (but not to Dr Qasemlu and Shaikh Hosseini) who "returned to the road of Islam" and surrendered their weapons. He also promised that the equivalent of about $70,000,000 would be made available for the development of the Kurdish region if the rebellion ceased, and he offered a large reward to those who would hand over the Kurdish leaders.

Further clashes nevertheless took place on Aug. 22-26, 1979, in Saqqez (north of Sanandaj), with 300 arrests being made on Aug. 27 and nine military men, accused of siding with the enemy, being executed. A new peace plan submitted by the Kurdish head of the Mahabad municipal council on Aug. 27, 1979, was rejected by Ayatollah Khomeini on the following day, when he sent a special envoy to the Kurdish areas with instructions to "crush" the Kurds and not to negotiate with them. In anticipation of a government offensive (which began on Sept. 3) the KDPI moved its headquarters from Mahabad to Sardesht (near the Iraqi border) and withdrew its armed forces first from Mahabad and later also from Sardesht, and a few days later Iranian troops were in control of most major Kurdish towns.

Dr Qasemlu, however, declared from his hideout (in an interview published in Paris on Sept. 10, 1979) that the rebellion was not ended and that guerrilla war would be pursued. By Oct. 20 Kurdish fighters were reported to have regained control of Mahabad. The government thereupon showed readiness to negotiate with the Kurds, and at a meeting with Dariush Foruhar (then newly appointed Minister of State) on Oct. 16 Shaikh Hosseini handed over an eight-point plan signed by himself, the KDPI, and also the *Komaleh* faction of Marxist-Leninist Kurds. On Dec. 17, the government in turn presented an outline plan for self-government to be applied to all "self-governed regions" of Iran.

However, during December 1979, when the ethnic minorities had largely boycotted the referendum on the country's new Constitution, the government reinforced its military presence in the Kurdish areas. Violent incidents again occurred there (as well as in areas inhabited by Azerbaijanis, Baluchis and Turkomans). The KDPI also announced that it would boycott the presidential elections to be held on Jan. 25, 1980. Dr Qasemlu warned Ayatollah Khomeini on Feb. 3, 1980, that civil war might break out as the armed forces were using heavy weapons against the population, including women and children, and destroying houses.

Early in 1980 the KDPI continued its guerrilla operations, and its followers clashed with Revolutionary Guards, with the result that these guards were in February 1980 withdrawn from Mahabad, Sanandaj and Kamyaran (western Iran) and a measure of regional autonomy was introduced in the Kurdish areas. As Kurdish rebels continued to be active, a new government offensive was launched in April 1980, when more than 1,000 Kurds and 500 government troops were said to have lost their lives. Meanwhile, elections to the Iranian Parliament (held in two rounds on March 4 and May 9) had been cancelled in at least three Kurdish towns because of the presence of "armed gangs". Following the withdrawal of the Kurds a ceasefire was negotiated between President Bani-Sadr of Iran and the KDPI in July 1980 but was over-ruled by Ayatollah Khomeini. In August 1980 government forces were said to have retaken Mahabad (the principal Kurdish city and headquarters of most Kurdish organizations).

After the outbreak of war between Iran and Iraq in September 1980 the KDPI leaders initially declared that they would not hinder the Iranian war effort against Iraq; in fact they intensified their struggle and were reported to be in receipt of substantial aid from the Iraqi government (while the Iranian government supported pro-Iranian Kurds in Iraq). By October 1980 a unified Kurdish council had been formed with other organizations and large-scale Kurdish attacks began against Iranian army units. Government forces responded by launching periodic offensives against Kurdish positions, using helicopter gunships and heavy artillery; extensive casualties were reported to have been sustained by both sides in the frequent engagements. By mid-August 1982 it was estimated that over one-third of the Iranian Army (including several thousand Revolutionary Guards) was fighting in Kurdistan, while the strength of *Pesh Merga* forces was given by Dr Qasemlu (in March 1982) as 12,000 backed by up to 60,000 armed peasants. During this period Kurdish forces increasingly mounted joint operations with guerrillas of the *Mujaheddin e-Khalq*.

The KDPI claimed in August 1982 that the government had started to imprison or resettle hundreds of Kurdish families and that a recent Iranian offensive against Iraq was in fact a manoeuvre to encircle the Kurds; it was also claimed by Kurdish and *Mujaheddin* sources that the army had used incendiary and chemical bombs on Kurdish villages. A further government offensive in October 1982 was reported to have provoked the four main Kurdish tribes (Harkis, Shakkak, Bagzadeh and Simko) into united resistance. A particular cause of tension was said to be the arrival of large numbers of Shia mullahs in the Kurdish region, whose action in offering cash rewards to converts had angered Kurdish Sunni ayatollahs.

In November 1981 it had been announced that the KDPI had joined the National Council of Resistance for Liberty and Independence, which had been set up in France earlier in the year by ex-President Bani-Sadr and other exiled opponents of the Khomeini regime (see separate entry).

In the face of a major government offensive in October 1982, the KDPI agreed with the Marxist *Komaleh* faction "under pressure of events" to co-ordinate their forces. The government claimed further successes in 1983-84, in June of which year the KDPI stated that jet fighters and helicopter gunships had been employed against Kurdish villages near Oroumieh. More heavy fighting followed a government offensive in October 1984. Details of the outcome of the battles were difficult to ascertain, but journalists travelling in the region noted that Kurdish guerrillas remained in control of some rural areas.

In April 1985, the KDPI was expelled from the National Council of Resistance, ostensibly after the *Mujaheddin e-Khalq* had denounced it for demonstrating a willingness to negotiate with the government.

Turkoman Autonomists

In north-eastern Iran the predominantly Sunni Moslem Turkomans called, immediately after the revolution of February 1979, for concessions involving (i) the redistribution of land owned by supporters of the former Shah; (ii) the right to set up their own police force; (iii) the official recognition of their language; and (iv) representation in the local revolutionary committees dominated by Shia Moslems.

Unrest broke out partly after seizure by Turkomans of disputed land, mainly farmed by absentee landlords, and partly over the alleged intransigence of the republican regime in regard to Turkoman demands (including the renaming of Bandar Shah, a town on the Caspian Sea, as Bandar Islam instead of as Bandar Turkoman, as demanded by the Turkomans). In fighting which broke out on March 26, 1979, Turkoman rebels were supported by members of the (left-wing) *Fedayeen e-Khalq*; at least 50 people were killed and over 300 injured before the rebels withdrew in the face of government forces on April 3. The government claimed that this rebellion had been the result of large-scale aid from the Soviet Union, but this was denied by the rebels, who refused to agree to a ceasefire. Army units, said to be assisted by (Moslem) *Mujaheddin e-Khalq* guerrillas, advanced towards the Soviet border while the rebels handed in their weapons at local mosques.

Dr Mehdi Bazargan, then Prime Minister, stated on April 4, 1979, that there would be no settlement between the government and those who demanded regional self-rule or advocated separatism. Through their Turkoman Political and Cultural Society, the Turkomans had earlier inter alia called for a boycott of the referendum of March 30-31 on the new Constitution of Iran.

Unrest occurred again in 1980, when Turkoman *Fedayeen e-Khalq* followers clashed with Revolutionary Guards at Gonbad-e-Qavus on Feb. 9-12 and as many as 32 people were killed, and also at Gorgan (75 miles south-west of Gonbad-e-Qavus), where Revolutionary Guards and troops suppressed a rebellion. Renewed fighting was reported in 1983 after Revolutionary Guards in the area tried to prevent Turkoman women from working on farms and going about unveiled. Several thousand Turkomans fled across the Soviet border.

Monarchist Group

Since the 1979 revolution the Iranian authorities have announced on several occasions that plots against the government had been uncovered, those involved being army officers and other members of the armed forces intent upon restoring the monarchy. The same aim has also motivated the activities of a number of organized groups.

In September 1986, Reza Pahlavi, son of the late Shah, appeared on Iranian state television frequencies to call for the overthrow of the regime. The broadcast was believed to originate from a transmitter inside the country.

Arya

In a telephone call to a news agency in Paris, this pro-monarchist group claimed responsibility for a bomb explosion at Tehran's main railway station in August 1984, which killed 18 people at the height of the morning rush-hour. The attack was denounced by the *Mujaheddin e-Khalq*.

Religious Minorities

The main religious minorities in Iran are the Bahais (numbering 450,000), Christians (200,000), Jews (60,000) and Zoroastrians (20,000). The last three of these groups are officially recognized in the Constitution, whereas the Bahais are not and have been subjected to considerable repression since the 1979 revolution, before which they had held many senior posts under the Shah.

Bahai Community

The Bahai movement was founded in the mid-19th century by Mirza Husain Ali (who called himself Baha'ullah or the Glory of God) in an attempt to save an earlier movement known as Babism. Sayyid Ali Muhammad had, in 1844, proclaimed himself the Bab (Gate) through which Shia Moslems were to communicate with their "Hidden Imam" (which he himself later claimed to be); Babism became a movement trying to overthrow not only the orthodox Moslem religion but also the social order, if necessary by violence. The Bab was subsequently convicted of heresy and was executed in 1850, his movement being suppressed and over 3,000 of its followers being executed in later years.

Baha'ullah, however, developed the Bahai religion as a peaceful movement, whose members would not belong to political parties or secret societies and were required to respect the authority of the state in which they lived; at the same time the Bahais aspired to the establishment of a world government to be achieved gradually by peaceful means. Nevertheless, Baha'ullah was exiled from Iran in 1853 and later settled at Acre (then in Turkish Palestine and later in Israel).

At the establishment of the Islamic Republic in 1979 there were some 450,000 followers of the Bahai religion in Iran, and many of them had held senior posts under the Shah. Ayatollah Khomeini had already declared before his return to Iran that the Bahais were "a political faction" and "unlawful" and that they would "not be accepted". (For orthodox Moslems any person who claimed to be a successor to the Prophet Mohammed, as Baha'ullah had done, was guilty of collective apostasy punishable by death, whereas religions founded before Islam, such as those of the Jews, Christians and Zoroastrians, were recognized in Iran.) In the Islamic Republic the Bahais were considered not only heretical but also unrevolutionary (since they were non-political) and pro-Zionist (since they had their headquarters in Israel).

During 1980 many Bahais were dismissed from their posts, their property was confiscated, their main investment company was closed down and their shrines were desecrated—without their having any redress against action taken against them by Islamic zealots. Bahais arrested included nine members of their spiritual assembly, seized on Aug. 21, 1980, and at least 10 others were subsequently executed for alleged involvement in a planned coup. Seven Bahais were executed on spying charges in Yazy (central Iran) on Sept. 8 and two others assassinated in Nook (Khorassan) on Dec. 17, 1980.

By May 1982 it was reported that about 100 Bahais had been killed since February 1979, of whom some had been executed after being charged with espionage and some for allegedly seeking to establish a dissident movement within the Bahai community.

In October 1982 the Bahai office at the United Nations claimed that 116 Bahais had been killed since the February 1979 revolution. Executions reportedly continued during 1983, and in August of that year all Bahai institutions, including educational and charitable ones, were declared illegal. In the same month, however, the Islamic Revolution Prosecutor-General insisted that no individual had been executed on religious grounds, and that all those killed had been found guilty of espionage or treason. He added that, while the state did not recognize Bahaism as a religion, individuals were free to practise it in private. Over the next few years, the Bahai community abroad reported further instances of maltreatment and killing of their members in Iran.

Iraq

Capital: Baghdad Pop. 15,900,000

The Iraqi monarchy was overthrown in a military coup led by left-wing officers in 1958. A Pan-Arab element in turn staged a successful coup in 1963. In 1968, this regime was overthrown by members of the Arab *Baath* Socialist Party, which has exercised effective authority ever since as the main component of the National Progressive Patriotic Front. According to its 1968 Constitution, the Republic of Iraq is a popular, democratic state, with Islam as the state religion and socialism as the basis of its economy. The "supreme organ of the state" is the *Baath* Party's Revolutionary Command Council (RCC), which is chaired by the party's secretary-general, Saddam Hussein, who is also state President. The President is elected by a two-thirds majority vote of the RCC. Most of the key portfolios in the Cabinet are held by *Baath* Party members. There is a 250-member National Assembly, elected every four years under a system of proportional representation. In the elections in 1984, 73 per cent of seats were won by *Baath* candidates, with the remainder distributed among independents and members of NPPF groups. In practice, the Assembly's powers are limited. All candidates have to express support for the principles of the 1968 revolution. In an effort to reduce support for Kurdish insurgency in the north of the country, there is also a 57-member "Legislative Council" of the Kurdish autonomous region.

Since 1980, Iraq has been at war with Iran. After initial successes, Iraqi forces were pushed back across the border in 1982, and by early 1987 were on the defensive.

Arab Opposition Groups

Al-Dawa Party (The Call)

The *Dawa* party has been the militant organization of the Shia community in Iraq and has been aligned with the Iranian Islamic revolution led by Ayatollah Khomeini (an Islamic Liberation Movement with such ties having first been set up in 1979). At the end of March 1980 the Iraqi government announced that the death sentence would be imposed on persons affiliated to the *Dawa* party. An Iraqi *Mujaheddin* group, presenting itself as being linked to the *Dawa* party, claimed responsibility for a number of acts of violence during 1980, including a grenade attack which slightly wounded Tariq Aziz, a Deputy Prime Minister, on April 1, the shooting of an Iranian embassy employee in Rome on June 4, the killing of an Iraqi diplomat in Abu Dhabi on July 27, and the murder of a leading member of the pro-Iraqi Lebanese regional council of the *Baath* party on July 28.

Ayatollah Bakr al-Sadr, the spiritual leader of the Iraqi Shi'ite community, who had been placed under house arrest on June 1, 1979, was, together with his sister, executed on April 9, 1980. During 1980 the Iraqi government was reported to have deported some 40,000 Shia Moslems to Iran and to have executed 96 others. Iran's support for the militant Shia Moslems in Iraq is said to have taken the form of the training of a group of Iraqi exiles near Damascus (ostensibly to aid Palestinians in Lebanon) and their infiltration into Iraq to commit acts of sabotage. Their reported actions included an attempt to assassinate President Hussein on June 4, 1980.

Unrest in Iraq's southern area inhabited by Shia Moslems continued in the latter part of 1980. On Aug. 27 it was reported from Tehran that the *Dawa* party had stated in a communiqué that Iraqi forces had attacked a village in which units of the party's *Mujaheddin* had sought refuge, that 26 government soldiers had been killed, but that in a retaliatory strike on Aug. 13 some 5,000 government troops had surrounded the village and killed all its inhabitants.

Further deportations of Shia Moslems from Iraq to Iran were reported in 1981-82, while in February 1982 Tehran radio reported that Iraqi *Mujaheddin* had mounted a successful attack on a military convoy of arms in transit from Saudi Arabia to Iraq. Iraqi fears that Shia unrest might affect the capability of its army (in which a majority of other ranks were Shias) were reflected in a new policy adopted from mid-1982 of seeking to accommodate Shia aspirations, notably by the inclusion of five Shias in the Cabinet on June 27, 1982. Nevertheless, the *Dawa* party remained unreconciled to the regime and claimed responsibility for a car bomb explosion at a Baghdad government building on Aug. 1, in which 30 people were killed, and also for a bomb attack on an airline office the following month.

An amnesty offer to all opposition activists made by the Iraqi government in February 1985 was rejected by *Al-Dawa* as "a propaganda ploy of a weak regime at a moment of despair".

Al-Dawa claimed responsibility for the hijacking of an Iraqi airliner on a flight from Baghdad to Amman over Saudi Arabia in December 1986. The hijacking culminated in the aircraft crashing near a remote desert airstrip in Saudi Arabia. Although the hijacking was officially blamed on "Iranian agents", there was speculation that the hijackers had enjoyed the assistance of some of the Iraqi airport security staff.

By the mid-1980s, however, *Al-Dawa* appeared to have declined in strength and to have lost some Iranian support. A leading Iranian official, Ayatollah

Montazeri, was reported to have called for the movement's disbanding. Iranian distaste for the group was thought in part to be a reaction to its insistence on collective leadership and to its communist-style cell structure. One report in early 1987 claimed that it was restricted to 11 small guerrilla bases in the north of Iraq.

Dissident Baathists

Although not organized in a party or group of their own, Baathists opposed to the Iraqi *Baath* Arab Socialist Party have generally been either in sympathy with or directly linked to the *Baath* party of Syria.

On July 28, 1979, it was officially announced in Baghdad that a plot had been uncovered, involving members of the RCC and two Cabinet ministers. Immediately afterwards 28 alleged participants in the plot were tried, and on Aug. 7 a special court passed sentences of death on 22 of them (one of them in absentia) and prison sentences ranging from one to 15 years on 33 others, while the remaining 13 defendants were released. Those condemned to death included not only former Cabinet ministers but also a former secretary-general of the RCC (who was a Shia Moslem) and the commander of one of Iraq's three army corps. The plot was said to have been aided by Syria with the object of removing the dominance of President Hussein's family, promoting union between Syria and Iraq and ending the suppression of dissident members of Iraq's Shia community. The execution of 21 defendants condemned to death was carried out on Aug. 8 in the presence of President Hussein and the remaining members of the RCC.

Following the outbreak of the Iran-Iraq war in September 1980 few detailed reports were allowed to emerge on political developments inside Iraq. It did appear, however, that a major Cabinet reshuffle on June 27, 1982, and a reduction in the size of the RCC the same day were part of a wider purge of Baathist dissidents within the political and military leadership. According to Western reports, President Hussein had come under increasing criticism from such elements not only for his conduct of the war but also for his alleged departure from Baathist "socialist orthodoxy" in his conduct of economic policy.

Tehran radio claimed in April 1986 that a dissident Baathist faction had grown up around Salah Umar Ali al-Tikriti, a former Information Minister and ambassador to the United Nations, until his defection from Iraq in 1982. The radio claimed that the group also included two other former Ministers, Hazim Duwab and Jawad Hashim, and that a fourth member, Dr Tahsin Mualla, former dean of the Baghdad University medical faculty, had recently met with a British Minister of State in the Foreign Office.

Eagles of the Revolution

A spokesman for this hitherto unheard-of group claimed responsibility for the assassination of the manager of the Iraqi Airways office in Nicosia, Cyprus, in November 1985.

Iraqi Communist Party (ICP)

Leadership. Aziz Mohammed (first sec.)

Founded in 1934, the pro-Soviet ICP had a substantial following until 1963, when it was severely repressed and many of its supporters were executed. After coming to power in 1968, the Iraqi *Baath* party took steps to achieve a reconciliation with the ICP, two members of which joined the government in 1972. In 1973 the ICP was admitted to the recently established National Progressive Front. However, from 1975 onwards (i.e. after the collapse of Kurdish resistance to the government) the *Baath* party began to impose restrictions on the ICP. Between 1975 and 1977 a number of ICP members were tried for forming secret cells in the armed forces in contravention of a 1971 law which allowed only *Baath* party members to engage in political activities within the armed forces, the police and the secret service. In May 1979 21 Communists condemned to death on such charges were hanged, while other persons sentenced in this connexion had to serve terms of imprisonment.

In Kuwait it was reported in May and June 1978 that there had been mass arrests of ICP members and of military personnel in Iraq, and that about 1,000 people had been detained and at least another 18 Communists had been executed (in addition to the 21 mentioned above). The Communist press in Iraq had at the same time begun to criticize certain government attitudes and had in particular rejected the Iraqi government's disapproval of the Soviet Union's support for Ethiopia in the latter's campaigns against Somalia and Eritrean secessionists; it also opposed the government's anti-Syrian propaganda and called for "more realistic" autonomy for the Kurds in Iraq (whom a number of Communists were said to have joined in renewed fighting against government forces).

In January 1979 the Communist parties of nine Arab states issued a manifesto denouncing the government of Iraq for its treatment of the ICP. In reply the Iraqi *Baath* party published an anti-communist book alleging that the entire communist movement in the Arab world had been founded by Jews from Palestine. Early in that year Mohammed Aziz, the ICP's first secretary, left Iraq, as did hundreds of other party members, and in mid-March the ICP announced that it had terminated its membership of the National Progressive Front. The two Communist members of the government were subsequently dismissed—a Minister of State on April 25 and the Minister of Transport on May 5, 1979. On July 11 the National Progressive Front accused the ICP of having links with "imperialist and Zionist forces".

On Nov. 12, 1980, the ICP allied itself with six other parties (including the Democratic Party of Kurdistan and the Kurdish Socialist Party) to form a National Democratic and Pan-Arab Front with the aim of overthrowing the Saddam Hussein regime.

During the Iran-Iraq war, which had broken out in September 1980, the ICP sided with Iran and in particular looked to Syria as an ally in its fight against the regime of President Saddam Hussein. It condemned Jordan's support for Iraq, and at a meeting between President Assad of Syria and the ICP's first secretary on Feb. 14, 1982, the two sides agreed that the Iran-Iraq war tended to "divert the Arab states and peoples from their battles against the Zionist enemy and its supporters" and had caused "weakness in the anti-imperialist and anti-Zionist front". However, Iran subsequently distanced itself from the ICP.

Iraqi Mujaheddin

The term "Iraqi *Mujaheddin*" was frequently applied by the official Iranian media to the perpetrators of a large number of guerrilla operations reported by the Iranians. Many of these operations could not be independently confirmed, and observers treated some of the claims with considerable scepticism. Among confirmed attacks which were subsequently "claimed" by the Iraqi *Mujaheddin* were a series of car-bombings in Baghdad in April 1983 and a bomb attack on the Iraqi Airways offices in Nicosia, Cyprus, in July 1984.

Islamic Action Movement of Iraq (*Mouvement de l'action islamique de l'Iraq*)

A group of this name claimed responsibility for exploding a car-bomb outside the Iraqi embassy in Paris on Aug. 11, 1982.

Islamic Action Organization

This group, whose claims were broadcast from Tehran, was identified in some reports with *Al Amal al-Islami* (Islamic *Amal*—see separate entry), another pro-Iranian movement. Attacks claimed in the name of Islamic Action included (i) a lorry-bomb explosion in Baghdad in November 1983; (ii) a bomb attack on the Iraqi Airways office in Nicosia, Cyprus, in July 1984 (also claimed by the Iraqi *Mujaheddin* and the Eagles of the Revolution); and (iii) a grenade attack on an officers' club in Baghdad in January 1985.

Islamic Amal (*Al Amal al-Islami*)

Islamic Amal is a breakaway movement from *Al-Dawa* (see separate entry), and is sometimes identified with the Islamic Action Organization.

It was named as responsible for a "suicide car-bomb" attack on an officers' club in Baghdad in July 1984. The attack, which was reported by the Tehran-based Supreme Assembly for the Islamic Revolution in Iraq, was not independently confirmed. Tehran radio reported in April 1986 that it had carried out a bomb attack on a Baghdad night club, killing two Iraqi officers, and the following month it claimed to have blown up an oil tanker lorry in a suicide car-bomb attack.

Revolutionary Action Organization and **Revolutionary Islamic Organization—Iraqi Branch**

These two previously unknown groups both claimed responsibility for the hijacking of an Iraqi airliner staged in December 1986 (see entry under *Al-Dawa*).

Supreme Council of the Islamic Revolution of Iraq (SAIRI)

The formation of this organization was announced in Tehran (Iran) on Nov. 17, 1982, with the aim of providing a focal point for Iraqi Shia opposition to the prosecution of the war with Iran. Its leader had been banished from Iraq soon after the outbreak of hostilities in view of his dedication to the overthrow of the Iraqi regime and its replacement by an Islamic republic led by a theologian on the Iranian model. The Council's inaugural statement denounced the Iraqi government as a "Zionist regime" and condemned the deportation of Shias from Iraq to Iran; it also alleged that 100,000 people had so far been killed in "an unwanted war".

SAIRI criticized the 1984 general elections as a sham, and described the National Assembly as "merely a propaganda mouthpiece for the Saddam regime". Hojatolislam Seyyed Mohammed Bakr Hakim, the Council's leader since its inception, was replaced by a collective leadership after three years in the post. In November 1986, SAIRI leaders held discussions in Tehran with the Democratic Party of Kurdistan.

Kurdish Movements

Democratic Party of Kurdistan (DPK) (*Al-Hizb ad-Dimuqraati al-Kurid*)

Leadership. Masoud Barzani

Founded in 1946, the DPK was originally led by Mullah Mustapha Barzani who, for over 30 years, led the struggle for autonomy of the Kurds in Iraq. This struggle came to a temporary end in 1975 after the Shah of Iran had ceased to support the Kurds and had concluded a treaty with the government of Iraq. Mullah Barzani died in exile in the United States on March 1, 1979. From 1977 onwards, however, the DPK resumed the armed struggle against Iraqi government forces.

On Jan. 10, 1977, the DPK provisional leadership disclosed that its fighters had seized six technicians, including five Poles, as hostages and had, through one of them whom they released, put forward demands for the return to their homes of all Kurds previously deported from the mountainous northern areas of Iraq, especially the wives, mothers and children of *Pesh Merga* ("Forward to Death") guerrillas (these dependants being held in special camps or prisons); later the DPK also demanded the release of all political prisoners in Iraq. However, on March 29, 1977, the DPK's provisional leadership announced that these and other hostages held by its fighters had been released "on purely humanitarian grounds" following "informal representations" by the governments concerned and by the United Nations; at the same time the DPK appealed for international support for its struggle. According to an unconfirmed report of May 3, 1977, the Iraqi authorities had allowed 40,000 of those interned to return to the north.

The DPK's provisional leadership—headed by M. M. (Sami) Abdulrahman, a former communist who had joined the DPK in 1960—was, in the first half of 1977, accused by the Patriotic Union of Kurdistan (PUK), led by Jalal Talabani, of having links with the (US) Central Intelligence Agency, of receiving funds from Israel and of having bases among Kurds in Turkey. Clashes between the two parties in mid-June

1977 were said to have led to the death of about 400 Talabani supporters and the capture of 400 of his guerrillas, including Ali Askeri, their supreme military commander.

A DPK spokesman said on Aug. 15, 1977, that numerous Kurdish villages had been destroyed in terms of a warning by an RCC member that a 25-mile strip along the Turkish border would be cleared of people. The spokesman also said that 16 Kurds from Halabja (south of Sulaymaniyah) had been condemned to death by a special court and executed. In the first few months of 1979 more Kurds were reported to have been forcibly removed from their homes in northern Iraq. On April 20, 1979, the Turkish and Iraqi governments concluded an agreement designed to crush Kurdish guerrilla activities. Thereupon the Turkish martial law authorities effectively ensured that Kurds in Iraq no longer received supplies from villages in Turkey, while the Iraqi government continued its policy of deporting Kurds from the mountainous northern border area, where *Pesh Mergas* were still carrying on their operations.

In mid-1979 Masoud Barzani (a son of Mullah Barzani) returned to Iraq from Iran (where he had lived since 1975), and in July he was quoted as saying that he and his supporters would intensify their fight in the north "to rescue the Kurdish people from persecution" and "to gain real autonomy for the Kurdish people within a democratic and prosperous Iraq". In August of that year he claimed that there were some 5,000 *Pesh Mergas* fighting in northern Iraq. At the first congress of the newly organized DPK's central committee in November 1979 differences arose between traditionalists led by Idris Barzani (elder brother of Masoud Barzani) and the "intellectual" wing of the party led by M. M. Abdulrahman.

In a message to Ayatollah Khomeini of Iran, Masoud Barzani declared on April 9, 1980, that he fully supported Iran's struggle against the Iraqi *Baath* regime. During the month of April the Iraqi authorities expelled Kurds from Iraq to Iran at the rate of about 2,000 a day. (The Iraqi Kurds, or Faili, had emigrated to Iraq during the first half of the 19th century from Ilan province in Iran.)

By 1981 the DPK had its own radio station, the "Voice of Iraqi Kurdistan", which, on Aug. 12, denounced co-operation between the regimes of Iraq and Turkey against "democratic and national movements" in both countries, and in particular against the DPK and its *Pesh Merga* forces, and also opposed these two governments' joint action against "revolutionary Iran". On Aug. 16, 1981, the DPK received a message of support from the (illegal) Kurdish Socialist Party of Turkey.

At the second congress of the DPK's central committee held between July 21 and Aug. 1, 1981, the party's leadership declared that the DPK was part of the world liberation movement, and it reaffirmed its determination to "intensify efforts to pool all the national, democratic and Islamic forces that oppose Saddam Hussein's fascist regime in the . . . Iraqi National and Patriotic Front" and to "further friendly relations with the glorious revolution of the Iranian peoples under the leadership of Imam Khomeini", with the Arab national liberation movement and with "the progressive regime of the Syrian Arab Republic".

The DPK took part in a conference of 18 Iraqi opposition groups in Tripoli (Libya) in February 1983, which agreed to unite in a "broad national front" to overthrow Saddam Hussein. The conference called for the establishment of a "democratic, popular and unionist" regime which would however grant "genuine autonomy to Iraqi Kurdistan".

During 1984, the DPK claimed successes in the Arbil and Bahdinan areas—the majority of its claims being broadcast on the "Voice of Iraqi Kurdistan" radio. In July of that year, it released five Europeans kidnapped earlier. Sporadic clashes between the Iraqi army and the DPK continued through 1984-85. In November 1986, the DPK reached an agreement with the Patriotic Union of Kurdistan in Tehran, providing for joint action against the Iraqi regime. (The two Kurdish groups had rarely co-operated previously, and on some occasions had fought against each other.) The DPK also discussed possible co-operation with the Supreme Assembly for the Islamic Revolution in Iraq (SAIRI).

With the Iraqi army coming under increasing pressure from Iranian offensives, the DPK extended its area of operations during the mid-1980s, and on some occasions staged joint operations with regular Iranian troops. By early 1986, it was said to have tripled the area under its control in the previous five years. It received arms and supplies from Syria and Libya via Iran, including SAM-7 ground-to-air missiles and artillery. Particularly major successes were reported in May 1986, when the DPK claimed to have captured Mangesh and to be besieging Dihok. The local Iraqi militia was reported to have collapsed in the face of the Kurdish offensive, with many of its members defecting to the DPK.

Idris Barzani, brother of Masoud and a leading DPK commander, died in Tehran in February 1987.

Patriotic Union of Kurdistan (PUK)

Leadership. Jalal Talabani

This group was set up in July 1975 by a merger of a Kurdistan National Party, the Socialist Movement of Kurdistan and an Association of Marxist-Leninists of Kurdistan. It has been engaged in sporadic attacks on government forces, partly from Iranian territory, in support of its demand for complete autonomy for Kurdistan. In a statement issued in Beirut (Lebanon) on Dec. 24, 1977, the PUK announced that the Iraqi government had tortured and executed more than 96 Kurds since September 1977 and was planning to dislocate 1,000,000 Kurds from their lands and to send them to the southern parts of Iraq in a continued drive towards arabizing the Kurdish regions of northern Iraq. Later the PUK was in conflict with the Democratic Party of Kurdistan (DPK—see separate entry), and in October 1978 the PUK claimed in Stockholm that the DPK had executed three PUK members a year earlier.

The PUK signed an agreement with the Iraqi government in January 1984, following elections held in August 1983 to the state-sponsored "Kurdish autonomous region" which included the three governorates of Arbil, Sulaymaniyah and Dihok. The agreement provided for a ceasefire, the extension of the autonomous region southwards to include areas around Kirkuk and Khanuqah, and the creation of a 40,000-strong "Kurdish army", to protect Kurdistan "against foreign enemies".

Despite the agreement, sporadic clashes between the PUK and the government forces continued, partly triggered by army attempts to enforce conscription in PUK-controlled areas. The PUK was particularly critical of the Iraqi-Turkish agreement providing for cross-border operations against "subversive groups", reached in October 1984. After the failure of attempts to patch up the accord, the PUK launched a series of fresh attacks against the army in 1985, and in February of that year rejected the government's amnesty offer. Two Soviet technicians were kidnapped by the PUK in October 1985.

In November 1986, the PUK reached an agreement with the DPK in Tehran to undertake joint action against the Iraqi regime. Speaking on this occasion, Talabani claimed that "Iran wants to unify all Iraqi opposition forces because its aim is self-determination for the Iraqi people". He added that the PUK had "not less than 20,000 fighters" currently controlling large areas of Arbil, Kirkuk, Sulaymaniyah and Salaheddin governorates. In common with the DPK, the PUK was by early 1987 in receipt of considerable weapons supplies via Iran, with whose forces it co-operated in attacks against Iraqi army positions.

Ireland

Capital: Dublin Pop. 3,400,000

The Republic of Ireland is, under its 1937 Constitution, "a sovereign, independent democratic state" with a President, elected for a seven-year term by universal adult suffrage, holding specific constitutional powers and advised by a Council of State. Legislative power is vested in the National Parliament consisting of the President and two Houses—(i) a House of Representatives (*Dáil Eireann*) of 166 members elected for a five-year term by adult suffrage (under a complex system of proportional representation) and (ii) a Senate of 60 members (11 nominated by the Prime Minister, six elected by the universities and 43 chosen by representatives of vocational and administrative bodies). Executive power is held by a government headed by a Prime Minister and responsible to the *Dáil*.

For many years a major security problem has been posed for the Irish government by extremist Republican movements seeking the integration of Northern Ireland in a united Ireland. These movements are dealt with in the section on Northern Ireland under the United Kingdom. For its part, the Dublin government has taken stringent measures of various kinds to suppress the activities of such movements south of the border and has repeatedly declared its belief that the unification of Ireland cannot be achieved by violent means.

Elections to the *Dáil* held on Feb. 17, 1987, resulted in the following distribution of seats: *Fianna Fáil* 81, *Fine Gael* 51, Progressive Democrats 14, Labour Party 12, Workers' Party 4 and independents 4.

According to a report issued on Nov. 4, 1983, by the New Ireland Forum, a body set up by the Irish government in response to an initiative by the (Northern Ireland) Social Democratic and Labour Party, acts of violence committed in the Republic by the Provisional Irish Republican Army (PIRA) and the Irish National Liberation Army (INLA) since 1969 had led to the death of 45 persons as a result of explosions, the murder of eight members of the *Garda* (Republican police) and an increase in robberies from 11 in 1970 to 306 in 1981.

The courts subsequently convicted a number of PIRA militants. After a PIRA post office robbery committed in August 1984, when a police detective was murdered, three men were on March 28, 1985, sentenced to death in Dublin, and of two others one was given a life sentence and the other 10 years in prison; on Feb. 21, 1986, the death sentences were commuted to 40 years' imprisonment without remission. Two other death sentences passed for the murder of a member of the *Garda* on Dec. 3, 1985, were similarly commuted.

On Dec. 7, 1982, the Irish Supreme Court had, for the first time, ordered the extradition to Northern Ireland of a man who claimed to be a member of the PIRA; he was Dominic McGlinchey, wanted for murder in Northern Ireland. The laws of the Republic prohibited extradition for political offences but in this case the Chief Justice declared that McGlinchey's alleged action could not be said to be either a political offence or an offence connected with a political offence. After jumping bail McGlinchey was captured on March 17, 1984, and was on the same day handed over to the Northern Ireland Royal Ulster Constabulary (police). There followed further extraditions of PIRA suspects, e.g. that of Seamus Shannon on July 31, 1984.

Under the Anglo-Irish (Hillsborough) Agreement, which came into force on Nov. 29, 1985, the Irish government inter alia increased *Garda* resources in manpower and support facilities in the border areas.

On Dec. 17, 1986, the Irish government secured the approval of the *Dáil* (and on Jan. 15, 1987, of the Upper House) for a bill providing for Irish ratification of the European Convention on the Suppression of Terrorism, which the government had signed in February 1986. The Convention sought to facilitate the extradition and prosecution of the perpetrators of terrorist acts even though such acts might have been politically motivated (and thus normally excluded from existing extradition arrangements); it had not secured earlier Irish signature because its provisions had been regarded as potentially in conflict with the Irish Constitution, but the interpretation of what constituted a political offence had been modified by the Supreme Court [see above].

The Fitzgerald government justified ratification of the Convention on the grounds of the need to demonstrate Ireland's commitment to the Hillsborough Agreement. It stressed its view, however, that moves to make the system of justice in the North more acceptable to the minority Catholic community did not yet measure up to those envisaged under the agreement, particularly in respect of the use of non-jury, single-judge trials and the use of uncorroborated evidence from "supergrass" informers.

Following the election of a *Fianna Fáil* government in February 1987, the incoming Prime Minister, Charles Haughey, stated that his government would continue to operate the Hillsborough Agreement, but the Justice Minister stated on March 26 that the government would examine the provisions of new extradition legislation contained in the act providing for Irish ratification of the European Convention, before this came into effect in December 1987.

Israel

Capital: Jerusalem (not recognized as such by the United Nations) Pop. 4,233,000

The state of Israel is a parliamentary democracy with a President elected for five years by a simple majority of Parliament, a government under a Prime Minister and a unicameral 120-seat parliament (*Knesset*) elected for four years by universal adult suffrage under a system of proportional representation. There are numerous legal political parties and a few political organizations not recognized by the government.

Elections to the *Knesset*, held on July 23, 1984, and contested by 26 parties (including 12 new groupings), resulted in the following distribution of seats: Labour Alignment 44, *Likud* 41, Zionist Revival Movement (*Tehiya*) 5, National Religious Party 4, Democratic Front for Peace and Equality (*Hadash,* communist-dominated) 4, *Sephardi Tora* Guardians (*Shas*) 4, Change (*Shinui*) 3, Civil Rights Movement 3, Together (*Yahad,* centrist) 3, Progressive List for Peace (PLP) 3, Union of Isreal (*Agudat Israel*) 2, *Morasha* (religious) 2, Israeli Tradition Movement (*Tami*) 1, *Kach* Movement 1, *Ometz* 1.

Before the 1984 elections the Central Elections Committee had (on May 17) prohibited the *Kach* Movement from contesting elections on the grounds that it was anti-democratic, promoted racism and gave public support to terrorist activity, and on May 19 the Committee had barred the PLP from the elections because of its alleged "subversive principles and intentions" and its "identification with enemies of the state". However, on appeal the Supreme Court reversed both decisions on May 27, finding that there were no grounds for the bans.

The *Knesset*, on the other hand, voted on Dec. 25, 1984, to remove from the *Kach*'s leader (Rabbi Meir Kahane, the Movement's sole elected representative) those aspects of parliamentary immunity which allowed him freedom of movement.

On July 31, 1985, the *Knesset* approved (by 66 votes to none) a measure to provide an electoral ban on any party which incited people to racism or which endangered state security.

Israel's overriding security problem has arisen out of the Arab-Israeli conflict and the occupation by Israeli forces of large areas inhabited by Arabs (see main section on Palestinian Movements, pages 266–284).

Inside Israel militant Jewish anti-Arab movements have been active, and there has also been open conflict between secular and ultra-orthodox Jewish religious groups.

Anti-Arab Movements

Bloc of the Faithful (*Gush Emunim*)

Leadership. Rabbi Moshe Levinger

Between 30 and 40 people questioned after the discovery and defusing of bombs planted on Palestinian buses in East Jerusalem on April 27, 1984, were members or supporters of this group committed to furthering Jewish settlement throughout occupied territories. Rabbi Levinger was arrested on May 14, 1984, and later released on bail suspected of having advance knowledge of attacks by members of the "Jewish underground".

In 1983, a number of incidents were reported against Arabs after Rabbi Levinger called for vengeance following the death of an Israeli woman on Feb. 12, 1983.

Jewish Defence League

The League was established in New York in 1968 as an extremist right-wing organization intent upon conducting counter-terrorist operations against militant Palestinians and also advocating the removal from the occupied West Bank and Gaza Strip of the Arab inhabitants unless they swore allegiance to Israel. During a United Nations Security Council debate on the Arab-Israeli conflict in January 1976 an offshoot of the League, calling itself the "Jewish Armed Resistance Strike Unit", claimed responsibility for the planting of several bombs at the UN building in New York in protest against the anti-Zionist stance of the UN majority.

Rabbi Meir Kahane, then leader of the League, unsuccessfully contested the 1977 general elections in Israel under the banner of the *Kach* Movement (but was elected in the 1984 elections—see above). In April 1977 he announced that he would establish a Jewish settlement in Nablus (in the occupied West Bank) but the Israeli authorities subsequently banned him from entering the West Bank. On Aug. 29, 1979, he was sentenced to one year in prison for entering Hebron (on the West Bank) illegally, but nine months of this sentence were suspended.

Early in 1980 groups led by Rabbi Kahane were held responsible for acts of vandalism against the property of Christian churches in Jerusalem. On May 13, 1980, he was detained, together with Baruch Green, a leading member of the *Kach* Movement, under emergency powers following reports that he was setting up an underground army to attack Arabs on the West Bank. Although on Aug. 6, 1980, the Prime Minister (Menahem Begin) lifted the detention order against him (though not that against B. Green), he continued to serve a prison sentence on charges of provoking disturbances until he was released on Dec. 12 of that year. Some of his followers had earlier been involved in a bomb attack on the New York offices of the (Soviet) Aeroflot airline, and in order to enforce his release from prison in Israel four of his organization's members on June 17, 1980, occupied the New York offices of the *Herut* party (M. Begin's wing of the *Likud* front).

The League was strongly opposed to the Israeli withdrawal from Sinai under the 1979 peace treaty with Egypt and participated with other groups such as the *Gush Emunim* (Bloc of the Faithful—see separate entry) extremist settler movement in unsuccessful efforts to prevent the final withdrawal from northern Sinai in April 1982, on the grounds that the area in question had become Israeli territory by right of conquest and settlement.

Members of the *Kach* Movement were among 45 Israelis arrested when they tried to establish a settlement on Temple Mount in East Jerusalem, which is under an Islamic council's jurisdiction, on March 10, 1983.

On Jan. 29, 1984, two members of *Kach* were arrested after the discovery of 268 lbs of explosive charges near the Al-Aksa and Dome of the Rock mosques on Temple Mount.

In November 1984 a leading member of *Kach*, Yehuda Richter, was sentenced to five years' imprisonment on charges including participating in an attack on an Arab bus near Ramallah in March 1984.

Several thousand Jewish and Palestinian demonstrators took part in a protest on Aug. 29, 1984, at a proposed visit by Rabbi Kahane to Umm el Fahm where the Rabbi stated he would set up an emigration office for Palestinians.

He announced on Aug. 20, 1985 that he was resigning as leader of the Jewish Defence League.

"Jewish Underground"

On July 22, 1984, the alleged leader of the so-called "Jewish underground", Menahem Livni, was sentenced along with two others to life imprisonment for murder following attacks carried out on Palestinians. The trial of 25 people, including M. Livni, which opened on May 23, 1984, brought charges against the defendants of membership of a "terrorist organization", participation in attacks on mosques, and attacks in March 1980 on three Palestinians, Karim Khalaf, Bassam Shaka and Ibrahim Tawil, former mayors of Ramallah, Nablus and Bira respectively.

According to the charge sheet, the underground organization had begun to form in 1978. Livni was also said to be the chairman of the Committee for the Renewal of Jewish Settlement in the City of the Patriarchs, a body dedicated to the re-establishment of a Jewish quarter in Hebron.

On March 26, 1987, the Israeli President, following several months of demonstrations, reduced the three life sentences imposed in 1984; only eight of the 24 originally sentenced remained in prison.

Terror against Terror

This militant Jewish group claimed responsibility for grenade attacks on Dec. 30, 1983, which damaged two mosques in Hebron. An anonymous phone caller to the *Jerusalem Post* claimed responsibility on behalf of the group for the attack on a bus near Ramallah on March 4, 1984.

Other Groups

Naturei Carta

Leadership. Rabbi Moshe Hirsch (sec.)

In October 1980 this anti-Zionist Jewish orthodox sect (which claimed to have 5,000 followers in Jerusalem alone) distributed leaflets urging members of the orthodox community to resist state tax collection and even to murder tax collectors. In March 1981 hundreds of members of the sect were involved in street battles with police in Jerusalem. At the same time the sect sent a letter to the United Nations Secretary-General appealing for UN protection of the Jewish holy places in Jerusalem which, the sect claimed, were being subjected to "Zionist oppression".

In a pamphlet published by the sect it was explained that its members refused to accept any monetary benefit—social or religious—offered by the Zionist secular state and that they preferred to use the Yiddish language, not "the spoken secularized Hebrew language of Zionism—a tool of nationalism".

There have been no recent reports of activities by this group, although there have been reports of tension between orthodox and secular Jews (see below).

People against the Ultra-Orthodox

In June 1986 a synagogue in Kiryat Shalom was damaged in an arson attack for which responsibility was claimed by this group, which stated that it would take further steps if damage to bus stops caused by orthodox militants continued. (The bus stops were damaged as a form of protest against advertisements deemed immoral.)

There were further incidents in July and August 1986 as secular protesters daubed swastikas on the main synagogue in Tel Aviv, and orthodox militants disrupted archaeological work at Jewish sacred sites.

Italy

Capital: Rome Pop. 57,130,000

The Italian Republic is, under its 1948 Constitution, "a democratic republic founded on work". It has a bicameral Parliament consisting of a 315-member Senate and a 630-member Chamber of Deputies, the latter being elected for a five-year term by universal adult suffrage; it also has a President elected for seven years at a joint session of both Houses of Parliament and of delegates from 20 regional councils. Any attempts to reconstitute the Fascist Party (which was in power in 1922-43) is prohibited under the Constitution and under a special law passed in 1952. Elections held to the Chamber of Deputies in June 1987 resulted in the following distribution of seats: Christian Democrats 234, Communist Party 177, Socialist Party 94, Italian Social Movement (neo-fascist) 35, Republican Party 21, Social Democratic Party 17, Greens 13, Radical Party 13, Liberal Party 11, Party of Proletarian Democracy 8, others (regional parties) 4.

In recent decades, Italy's society has been exposed to widespread acts of political violence, including murders and kidnappings (although the latter are usually accompanied by demands for ransom and thus by no means all politically motivated). In view of the rising number of acts of terrorism in the 1970s, the government has repeatedly increased the penalties for such acts. Under a decree which came into force on Dec. 15, 1979, mandatory life sentences were introduced for the murder of policemen, members of the judiciary, lawyers and trade union leaders. President Alessandro Pertini (Socialist) declared in a 1981 New Year message that the "terrorist threat" meant that Italy was "at war"; that in his view the terrorism was being organized from abroad; that the bridge constituted by Italy (between Europe on the one hand and Africa and the Middle East on the other) could be destroyed if Italy's democracy was destabilized; and that this constituted a danger to the whole of Europe.

In a report presented by the Italian police on June 22, 1982, it was stated that between 1969 and March 1982 acts of terrorism had led to the death of 364 persons and injury to 1,075, while 1,414 members of armed left-wing groups and 432 of extreme right-wing groups had been imprisoned.

Under a law (the *Legge Cossiga*) enacted in May 1982 the courts were empowered to give lighter sentences to convicted "terrorists" who confessed or gave information to the authorities. The law expired on Jan. 29, 1983, and according to a spokesman for the Ministry of Justice 389 guerrillas from the Red Brigades and the Front Line group had made use of it—78 of them having actively and continuously co-operated with the police, 134 having confessed their crimes and given some information about them, and 177 having formally renounced their group's actions.

On Oct. 4, 1983, the Council of Ministers approved a law reducing the permitted period of preventive detention and placing restrictions on the arrest of suspects, whereby preventive detention was not to be allowed to exceed two-thirds of the maximum proposed sentence, and financial compensation was envisaged for those who could prove that they had been wrongly held. These provisions were, however, not to apply to those held in connexion with terrorism or the Mafia or Camorra.

Under a law which came into force on Aug. 17, 1984, pre-trial detention was reduced to a maximum of six years for serious crimes and of five months for minor crimes (although consecutive detention could be ordered); investigations into serious offences while the suspect was detained were to be completed in two years; 18 months were allowed for the preparation of each of three appeals; and any suspect not questioned within 15 days from the date of his arrest would have to be released.

In a report to Parliament the Italian Prime Minister stated on Aug. 11, 1985, that the main internal security threat to Italy was currently from international terrorism from the Middle East, notably the repercussions of the Iran-Iraq war, extremist Arab threats against US and NATO interests, the activities of Libyan and Iranian exiles abroad, and apparent collaboration between Italian neo-fascists and Moslem extremists. The Prime Minister also said that there remained only a nucleus of the Red Brigades and that this was linked with other European extreme left-wing groups at propaganda level rather than on an operational basis; that some 1,280 members of extreme left- and right-wing groups were in prison in connexion with terrorist offences; but that about 300 supects were still at large.

Figures for 1986 showed that there had been only 30 "incidents of a terrorist nature", the lowest incidence since 1969, and that only one victim and assailant had been killed as compared with over 400 killed in 1969-76. By 1987 Italy had introduced a lenient prison regime for "penitent" convicted terrorists, who were permitted to take social leaves of absence from prison, the government terming this "social rehabilitation".

Right-wing Movements

Armed Revolutionary Nuclei (*Nuclei Armati Rivoluzionari,* NAR)

The NAR is a neo-fascist organization which has been held responsible for major bomb explosions and for the killing of a number of its political opponents. Its actions included an explosion at the Bologna railway station on Aug. 2, 1980, when 85 persons were killed and 194 injured. The Bologna attack was reportedly carried out "in honour of Mario Tutti", a right-wing extremist serving a life sentence for murdering a policeman and also charged with involvement in an explosion on a Rome-Munich express on Aug. 5, 1974. The NAR later denied any involvement in the Bologna station explosion.

On Feb. 22, 1980, NAR members killed a member of the (left-wing) Workers' Autonomy Group. Four suspected NAR members were arrested on Feb. 28 on charges of illegal possession of arms. On March 12 NAR members bombed a Communist Party office in Naples. The group also accepted responsibility for the killing of a policeman on May 28, of a deputy public prosecutor (investigating right-wing attacks) in Rome on June 23, 1980, and of a policeman in Rome on Dec. 6, 1981—one day after police had killed Alessandro Alibrandi, an NAR suspect, in a gun battle north of Rome. The NAR also admitted shooting another policeman in Rome on June 24, 1982. For the killing of the deputy public prosecutor four persons were sentenced to life imprisonment on April 5, 1984.

In connexion with the Bologna station bombing, warrants of arrest were issued on Sept. 11, 1982, against five alleged perpetrators of this attack—Stefano delle Chiaie, a former leader of the neo-Nazi National Vanguard (see separate entry), who had fled to South America in 1976; Maurizio Giorgi; Pier-Luigi Pagliai (who was extradited by Bolivia on Oct. 11, arrived in Rome on Oct. 12 but died on Nov. 5, 1982, from wounds received in a gunfight in Bolivia); Joachim Fiebelkorn (a West German who surrendered to the police in Frankfurt on Sept. 13); and Olivier Danet (a Frenchman detained in France for illicit arms trading with Belgium and linked to various extreme right-wing groups). A sixth suspect, Carmine Palladino, had been murdered in prison on Aug. 4, 1982, by Pier-Luigi Concutelli, who had claimed that Palladino was responsible for the death of Giorgio Vale (a long-sought NAR member shot in a gun battle with police in Rome on May 5, 1982) and who had in April 1981 strangled another prisoner, Ermanno Brezza, a neo-fascist who had turned police informer.

Early in October 1982 police in Milan arrested Roberto Frigato, described as the "killer" of a gang led by Gilberto Cavallini and Pasquale Belsito (both of whom had gone underground), who were accused of being involved in the killing of two *Carabinieri,* various robberies and the Bologna station bomb explosion. Frigato's arrest was made possible through the co-operation with the police of another neo-fascist, and he was also accused of trading in arms and involvement in assassinations and kidnappings in Lombardy and Venetia.

On Feb. 22, 1983, a court in Rome sentenced two NAR members to life imprisonment and two others to terms of 21 years and 15 years and eight months respectively in prison on charges of killing a neo-fascist whom they had mistaken for a police informer. On April 26, 1983, police in Rome arrested Fabrizio Zani, said to be one of the most dangerous right-wing terrorists, with two other persons, all alleged to be members of the NAR, and also uncovered a quantity of weapons, explosives and forged identity documents.

On March 24, 1985, two NAR members were shot dead and four others arrested when they opened fire on police in Piedmont.

On May 2, 1985, a Rome court sentenced 53 NAR adherents to imprisonment for terms ranging from 1½ to 23 years for murders and other crimes committed in 1977-81. On July 30, 1986, five leading NAR members were sentenced to life imprisonment for murders committed in 1981-82, and 21 others were given prison sentences ranging from six months to 25 years. On Nov. 7, 1986, a group of 27 NAR adherents were sentenced in Milan (some of them in absentia) to terms of six months to life in prison for murder, conspiracy and membership of an armed gang.

The trial of 20 people implicated in the 1980 Bologna bombing began on Jan. 19, 1987. The defendants included Gen. Pietro Musumeci, the former deputy chief of the military intelligence service SISMI and Gen. Giuseppe Belmonte, his former assistant; Licio Gelli, the fugitive Grand Master of the banned Propaganda Due (P-2) Masonic Lodge (see separate entry); and Stefano delle Chiaie (see above). P. Musumeci and G. Belmonte were accused of diverting inquiries into the incident to bring suspicion onto the extreme left.

Black Order (*Ordine Nero*)

This group was established in 1974 as a successor to the New Order organization, which was banned in November 1973 (see separate entry). The Black Order claimed responsibility for a bomb explosion at an anti-fascist demonstration in Brescia on May 28, 1974, when eight persons were killed and 95 injured, and also for an explosion on the Rome-Munich express on Aug. 5 of that year, when 12 persons were killed and 48 injured. On this occasion the group accused the Italian government of leading the country towards Marxism and asserted that Nazism would "return to save Italy". On Aug. 12, 1974, it warned the Prime Minister that it had condemned him for "exploitation of the Italian people".

Eight persons (apparently Black Order members) convicted in 1979 of having planted the bomb in Brescia were, on appeal, acquitted on March 2, 1982.

Having planted bombs at several other places, the Black Order claimed responsibility for an explosion at Savona (on the coast west of Genoa) on Nov. 21, 1974 (when one person was killed and eight were wounded), and on Dec. 23 of that year it threatened to place bombs inside churches unless "the Church and the Pope give their immense wealth to the people" and to carry out a "massacre" if "charity institutes refused to accept the sums which the Church will have to give". The group appears to have been dormant since the mid-1970s. Mario Affatigato, a former leader of the group, was extradited from France to Italy on Sept. 7, 1980, being suspected of involvement in the Bologna station explosion of Aug. 2, 1980, attributed to the Armed Revolutionary Nuclei (see separate entry). In a trial which ended on July 20, 1983, the three main defendants (among them Mario Tutti) were acquitted for lack of evidence in the 1974 bombing of the Rome-Munich express. However, on appeal a Bologna court on Dec. 18, 1986, passed life sentences on M. Tutti and Luciano Franci for their involvement in that bombing.

The Black Order had earlier claimed responsibility for planting a bomb on a railway track near Florence on Aug. 9, 1983, which slightly injured two men.

National Vanguard (*Avanguardia Nazionale*)

This neo-fascist group was one of several accused by the Minister of the Interior on Aug. 13, 1974, of trying to create chaos. It had repeatedly accepted responsibility for bomb attacks on offices of left-wing groups before 1974. One of the group's leading members, Pier Luigi Concutelli, was imprisoned after confessing to having murdered, in Rome on July 10, 1976, Judge Vittorio Occorsi, who had been investigating the activities of the New Order (see separate entry); Concutelli was also said to have been associated with extreme right-wing groups in Spain and to have links with the Propaganda Due lodge (see separate entry). For the murder of the judge five right-wing extremists were sentenced to life imprisonment on March 22, 1985.

New Order (*Ordine Nuovo*)

This organization was founded by Tino Rauti, a journalist and former member of the Italian Social Movement (MSI) who was its leader until 1969, when he rejoined the MSI. The organization was banned on Nov. 23, 1973, after 30 of its members (out of an estimated total of 600) had on Nov. 21 been sentenced to prison terms ranging from six months to five years for violating the 1952 *Legge Scelba* (which provided for sentences of three to 10 years for promoting or organizing under any form the reconstitution of the dissolved Fascist Party). At the same time, all property of the New Order was ordered to be confiscated. The movement had earlier claimed responsibility for attacks on the offices of left-wing organizations.

There followed several trials for alleged New Order activities. On Dec. 3, 1975, Sandro Saccucci (an MSI deputy) was sentenced to four years in prison and barred from public office for five years for forming and organizing the New Order; this sentence was, however, suspended pending an appeal, and during the May 1976 election campaign he left the country while he was being sought in connexion with the shooting of a communist after an MSI rally near Rome.

The trial of 119 persons, which had begun on July 16, 1974, on charges of trying to reconstitute the Fascist Party and belonging to the New Order, was repeatedly adjourned.

Propaganda Due (P-2)

Leadership. Licio Gelli (Grand Master)

The existence of this secret Masonic lodge became known in March 1981 when the police recovered a list of 931 alleged members and other documents showing that the lodge had been involved not only in large-scale crimes but also in right-wing terrorist activities in the late 1960s and early 1970s, including a bomb explosion in Milan in 1969. In a report to the government by a Milan magistrate in May 1981 it was stated: "The P-2 lodge is a secret sect which has combined business and politics with the intention of destroying the constitutional order of the country and transforming the parliamentary system into a presidential system."

A special commission appointed in May 1981 reported on June 15, 1981, that the P-2 presented the characteristics of a "secret society" and could therefore be in breach of the Constitution. On June 20 a total of 22 members of the P-2, including a former head of the secret service (SID), were charged with political conspiracy and activities against the state.

The list of alleged P-2 members discovered by the police also contained the names of a number of senior officials and of the editor-in-chief of the Milan *Corriere della Sera*, who were subsequently replaced. Disclosures made during this affair also led to a government crisis and the formation of a largely new administration under the premiership of the leader of the Republican Party (PRI) on June 28, 1981, and to the approval by the government, on July 29, 1981 of a bill outlawing and dissolving all secret societies.

At the request of the Italian authorities Licio Gelli, who had fled to Switzerland, was arrested in Geneva on Sept. 13, 1982, and continued to be held pending his possible extradition to Italy. In March 1983 the High Council of Magistratures declared inter alia that the P-2 had directed its efforts towards political changes and interference in the most sensitive affairs of the state. However, it was also decided officially that mere membership of the P-2 did not constitute an offence.

On Aug. 19, 1983, the Swiss Supreme Court approved L. Gelli's extradition, but he had already (on Aug. 10) disappeared from a high-security prison in Geneva, apparently with the help of a warder, and had fled into France. An international warrant for his arrest was issued on Aug. 20 by an Argentinian federal judge who also ordered the seizure of all his assets in Argentina.

Following further disclosures of alleged involvement in the P-2, Pietro Longo (of the Social Democratic Party, PSDI) resigned on March 24, 1984, from his post as Minister of the Budget.

In a parliamentary report on the P-2 approved by a 40-member commission on July 10, 1984, it was concluded that a list found at L. Gelli's Tuscan villa and containing the names of supposed P-2 members, was authentic except in a few cases.

L. Gelli (then still at large despite a warrant of arrest against him issued in December 1985) was among those whose trial for involvement in the 1980 bomb attack at the Bologna railway station opened on Jan. 19, 1987.

Other Right-wing Groups

A number of small neo-fascist groups claimed responsibility for a bomb explosion on Dec. 23, 1984, on a train in a tunnel between Florence and Bologna in which 15 people were killed and 116 injured.

Left-wing Movements

Armed Proletarian Nuclei (*Nuclei Armati Proletari,* NAP)

The NAP has been responsible for committing numerous acts of violence since its inception in 1974. These included an attack on a subsidiary of the (US) International Telephone and Telegraph Corporation (ITT) in Milan on Oct. 6, 1974—the ITT being alleged to have played a role in the overthrowing of the left-wing Allende government in Chile in 1973.

In April 1975 the NAP was reported to have planned retaliatory action for an attack on communists by right-wing extremists in Rome on April 23. On May 6, 1975, the NAP accepted responsibility for the kidnapping of Dr Giuseppe di Gennaro, a Rome judge, who was, however, released on May 11 after the authorities had agreed to transfer three prisoners to a Piedmont prison (in compliance with one of the demands of the NAP). In June 1975 the police discovered seven NAP cells in Rome, arrested six NAP members and recovered part of a ransom paid in December 1974 for the release of a kidnapped industrialist (Giuseppe Moccia).

By January 1977 the NAP was officially held responsible for 30 political crimes, which included the kidnapping of Guido De Martino (a Socialist leader in Naples) who was released upon payment of the equivalent of about $1,100,000. For this kidnapping 15 people were, in Naples on Jan. 9, 1978, given prison sentences of from eight to 14 years. By October 1977 the NAP was believed to have formed a central command with the Red Brigades (see separate entry), and it later claimed responsibility, together with the Red Brigades, for the murder of a prison guard in Udine on June 6, 1978.

On May 8, 1985, two NAP members were sentenced to life imprisonment and another to 18 years in prison for two murders.

Communist Armed Groups

Nine members of this offshoot of the Red Brigades were sentenced in Rome on Feb. 20, 1986, to terms of one to 10 years in prison for crimes committed in the late 1970s.

Communist Fighting Organization (*Organizzazione Comunista Combatente*)

This group, said to be allied to the Red Brigades, was active in 1980, attacking in particular a politician in Milan on Feb. 10.

On Dec. 23, 1982, a total of 31 of its members were sentenced in Rome to terms of three to 30 years in prison for attempted murder, kidnapping, robberies and other crimes.

Communist Group for Proletarian Internationalism

This group claimed responsibility for bomb explosions in Rome on Oct. 23-24, 1981, the targets including the Chilean embassy, the Guatemalan mission to the Vatican and an Argentine government commercial office. On May 26, 1982, the Group also claimed responsibility for an explosion at the offices of the *International Daily News* in Rome. It further claimed responsibility for bombing the Honduran embassy and the US-Italian cultural exchange bureau in Rome on May 4, 1985.

Communist Power (*Potere Comunista*)

Members of this group set fire to the car of a prison guard in Naples in January 1984, when one person was killed.

Front Line (*Prima Linea,* PL)

Leadership. Sergio Segio (founder); Corrado Alunni (l.)

This organization was established in 1976 and has been responsible for a number of attacks on industrialists and other persons concerned with production. It has co-operated with the Red Brigades (see separate entry).

On Oct. 11, 1978, members of the PL killed Alfredo Paolella, a university professor and forensic expert, whom they considered a "state collaborator"; on Nov. 8 of that year a senior magistrate, his driver and his bodyguard were killed by PL members at Patricia (south of Rome). PL members were also responsible for killing a deputy public prosecutor in Milan on Jan. 29, 1979, a Christian Democrat provincial secretary in Palermo on March 9, two policemen in Genoa on Jan. 25, 1980, a Seveso factory executive on Feb. 5, a suspected informer in Milan on Feb. 7, and a magistrate in Milan on March 19. On Dec. 11, 1979, PL members attacked a business school in Turin (where lecturers were employed by Fiat) in retaliation for the dismissal of "troublemakers" and the temporary halting of recruitment at Fiat's plant in Turin.

Marco Donat Cattin (son of the Christian Democrat Senator Carlo Donat Cattin), who was alleged to be a PL member and against whom a warrant of arrest had been issued in May 1980, fled the country after his father had warned him of his impending arrest. On June 21, 1980, a Milan court sentenced 27 alleged PL members to prison terms for murder and kidnapping; those sentenced included Corrado Alunni (the alleged leader of the Red Brigades) sentenced to 29 years in prison to run concurrently with other sentences imposed on him.

Also in 1980 a group of 21 PL members arrested in Paris on July 7 were extradited to Italy on Oct. 26, and the trial of 108 alleged PL members opened in Turin on Dec. 5, 1980. This trial ended on July 29, 1981, when 94 of the defendants were sentenced, among them Susanna Ronconi (to 14½ years in prison, and most others to 14 years each, while 28 received suspended sentences). On June 25, 1982, an appeals court in Turin upheld the convictions of 91 of the accused but reduced some of their sentences, including that of Susanna Ronconi from 14½ to 13½ years.

Three PL members—Maurice Bignami, Roberto Vitelli and Sergio Segio (the founder of the PL, who was still at large)—were sentenced to life imprisonment in Viterbo on Oct. 24, 1981, for killing two policemen in a bank robbery in 1980. On Feb. 11, 1982, an appeal court in Milan sentenced Corrado Alunni to 29 years and two months in prison and also gave long prison sentences to 29 other defendants. During this trial some of the accused stated that since 1978 there had been links between the PL and the Basque ETA in Spain and that there had been a joint training camp of the two organizations in southern France.

On Aug. 5, 1982, a court in Bergamo sentenced 42 alleged PL members to a total of 467 years in prison. Those sentenced included Sergio Segio and Diego Forestieri, both sentenced in absentia to 24½ and 24 years respectively, Michele Viscardi (12 years and two months) and Marco Donat Cattin (nine years). Sergio Segio, who had been sentenced in absentia in October 1981 (see above) and was sought in connexion with the killing of Judge Emilio Alessandrini in 1979 and of Judge Guido Galli in March 1980, was arrested in Milan on Jan. 18, 1983. Forestieri, who had escaped from prison in October 1981, was recaptured in Milan on Jan. 27, 1983.

On Dec. 4, 1982, a court in Turin sentenced Roberto Rossi, a leading member of the PL, to 13 years and two months in prison and 29 other PL members to between five months' and 13 years' imprisonment.

On April 28, 1983, a court in Florence sentenced 84 PL members to terms of imprisonment ranging from eight years to life for acts of terrorism committed in Tuscany in the late 1970s. (Among those convicted M. Donat Cattin received an eight-year sentence.)

On June 10, 1983, a court in Brescia sentenced another 34 PL members to imprisonment for terms of six months to eight years for membership of a criminal gang.

On Dec. 31, 1983, a court in Turin sentenced nine PL members to imprisonment for life, six to 30 years and nine to between 20 and 30 years for crimes committed in 1976-80. (M. Donat Cattin was again given an eight-year sentence; although he was awarded provisional liberty for having collaborated with the police he was kept in custody to face other charges.)

Further prison sentences of up to 30 years were imposed on PL members during 1984-85. In Novara five PL members were, on Feb. 6, 1986, sentenced to terms of 14 to 26 years in prison for murder and robbery in 1981.

Red Brigades (*Brigate Rosse,* BR)

Leadership. Renato Curcio (l.); Alberto Franceschini (chief ideologue)

Established in 1969, this organization of Marxist-Leninist urban guerrillas, modelled on the *Tupamaros* of Uruguay, was during the first three years of its existence active mainly in Milan, not only in disseminating Marxist-Leninist propaganda but also in attacks on the property of industrialists and other "enemies of the working class". By 1974 its activities had spread to Genoa and Turin and kidnapping operations had begun. Since 1976 the BR have operated in most parts of the country, intimidating, wounding or murdering their victims and seeking the greatest possible publicity for their actions. They have published lists of potential victims among factory directors and managers as well as company security guards, and their numerous kidnappings have led to the payment of considerable sums in ransom to them.

The original declared aim of the Red Brigades was to create a situation in which a fascist coup could be provoked; this would lead to a return of the Communist Party of Italy (CPI) to its "revolutionary" role (which, the BR asserted, the CPI had abandoned by collaboration with the government) and to the consequent outbreak of civil war which would bring the left to power. In a statement issued on March 25, 1979, the BR compared its struggle to those of the (Provisional) Irish Republican Army, the (West German) Red Army Faction (Baader-Meinhof Group) and the Palestine Liberation Organization.

In their Journal No. 4 of December 1981 the BR declared that they intended to progress from being a clandestine organization to the stage of a more centralized party which would proclaim "total class war". In another BR communiqué it was stated that their first target would from then on be "the multinational centre of American imperialism". In a further statement issued on Dec. 19, 1981, the BR called for the creation of a "terrorist international" in which the central position would be held by the BR and the West German Red Army Faction, and which the "European revolutionary forces" of the ETA in Spain and the Irish Republican Army could join once they had abandoned "the stifling perspective of nationalism".

The first Red Brigades' terrorist act was the bombing of a Milan electronics firm's premises in 1970. On June 15, 1972, a group of 21 BR members were tried for kidnapping an engineer on March 3 of that year. A Fiat personnel director kidnapped in Turin on Dec. 14, 1972, was released four days later after he had allegedly supplied the BR with details of Fiat's "espionage system" used against its workers.

On April 18, 1974, BR members abducted Mario Sossi, a senior magistrate in Genoa (who had played an important part in bringing to justice a BR group known as "October 22" responsible for kidnappings in 1972); the BR demanded the release of eight "October 22" members, failing which their victim would be killed; and after a Genoa court had set these men free Sossi was released on May 23. The government, however, did not give in to other demands made by the BR (for passports and safe conducts to Algeria, Cuba, or North Korea for the released eight men), nor was the court order for their release confirmed by the procurator-general or the Supreme Court of Cassation. The BR also claimed responsibility for the murder of two members of the (neo-fascist) Italian Social Movement (MSI) on June 17, 1974.

On Sept. 9, 1974, police arrested Renato Curcio and Alberto Franceschini, who had led the BR since 1972; however, Curcio was liberated from an Alessandria prison on Feb. 18, 1975, by a BR commando including his wife (Margharita Cagol, who was killed in a police raid on June 5, 1975). Curcio was subsequently recaptured in January 1976 and was, on June 23, 1977, sentenced to seven years in prison for wounding a policeman, possessing a firearm and resisting arrest, while four other BR members were given prison sentences ranging from 2½ to five years. During this trial the BR continued their campaign of intimidation by attacking journalists and threatening to take action against jurors and lawyers' families if the trial were proceeded with.

An earlier trial of Curcio and 52 other BR members for belonging to a subversive organization had opened in May 1976 but was postponed after the assassination of Francesco Cocco (a state prosecutor) by the BR in Genoa, and again after the assassination by BR members on April 28, 1977, of Dr Fulvio Croce, head of the Turin lawyers' association. Another BR member, Carlo Picchiura, was sentenced in Padua on June 1, 1977, to 26 years in prison for killing a policeman and was also ordered to pay compensation to the victim's family.

The BR also claimed responsibility for the mortal wounding, on Nov. 16, 1977, of Carlo Casalegno (deputy editor of *La Stampa* of Turin), who died in hospital on Nov. 29; the killing of Angelo Pistolesi, an extreme right-wing activist, in Rome on Dec. 28; and the murder, on Feb. 14, 1978, of Riccardo Palma, a magistrate in Rome.

On March 16, 1978, members of the BR seized Aldo Moro (aged 61), the president of the Christian Democratic Party (DC), who had been Prime Minister between 1963 and 1976. The BR stated that he would be tried by a "people's court" for being "the most loyal executor of directives laid down by imperialist centres"; they also demanded the release of certain detainees as the price of freeing their hostage. The Italian government, however, refused to make any concessions to the BR, and this attitude was widely supported, notably by the three major trade union federations, including the (communist-led) General Confederation of Italian Labour (CGIL).

On April 15, 1978, the BR declared that Aldo Moro had been found guilty and sentenced to death, as his trial by a "people's court" had (they said) exposed "the real and hidden responsibilities in the bloodiest pages of the history of recent years", "the intrigues of those who held power, the conspiracy that covered up murder committed by the state, and the intricate web of personal interests and corruption". On April 20 the BR declared that Aldo Moro would be executed within 48 hours unless an unspecified number of "communist" prisoners was released, and on May 9 Aldo Moro was shot dead by at least two of his kidnappers and his body was found in a car parked in the centre of Rome.

On May 17, 1978, five BR members were arrested, and on June 5 these five—Enrico Triaca, Teodoro Spadaccini, Giovanni Lugnini, Antonio Marini and Gabriella Mariani—as well as a sixth BR member still at large were formally charged with complicity in the murder. Three other suspects were charged on June 6.

When the trial of Renato Curcio and others reopened in Turin on March 9, 1978, one of the defendants, Paolo Ferrari, read out a statement on behalf of the accused, declaring a state of war and threatening further violence against anyone who collaborated with the court. Following the assassination, in Turin on March 10, of a policeman who had taken part in the arrest of Ferrari, the trial was again adjourned until May 20. Meanwhile a senior prison guard, described as a "torturer" of prisoners, was murdered by BR members on April 20, 1978. Nevertheless, on June 23 Curcio was sentenced (in Turin) to 15 years in prison for forming an armed group to subvert the state and for carrying out political kidnappings; Pietro Bassi was given 15 years, Pietro Bertolazzi 14¾ years, Alberto Franceschini 14½ years and 26 others (some of them in absentia) from 2¼ to 13 years, among them Prospero Gallinari, who was sought in connexion with the murder of Aldo Moro and was given a 10-year sentence in absentia. He was later arrested on Sept. 24, 1979.

On June 24, 1978, Massimo Maraschi, another BR member, was sentenced in Alessandria to 24 years in prison for murder, attempted murder and kidnapping, while Pietro Villa, also a BR member, was given five years in Milan for membership of a subversive organization, robbery and sabotage.

Corrado Alunni, the BR leader who was suspected of having masterminded the kidnapping of Aldo Moro, was arrested on Sept. 13, 1978, was a week later sentenced to 12 years and four months in prison for illegal possession of arms and was on Oct. 28 given an additional seven-year sentence for attempted murder and possession of arms. At the same trial in Milan on Oct. 28 Attilio Casaletti was sent to prison for nine years and eight months, Pierluigi Zuffada for 9½ years and three others for terms between two years and four months to three years and four months for BR activities.

Renato Curcio was on Feb. 6, 1979, given a further 12-year prison sentence for attempted murder and possession of arms and a six-year sentence on Nov. 1 for his escape from prison in 1975, while nine other BR members were also sentenced for "terrorist activities" to terms of four months to six years in prison. On Oct. 14, 1979, Curcio received a further 10-year sentence and 13 other BR members were given sentences ranging from eight to 10 years for insulting the judges and inciting BR followers to insurrection during the 1978 trial.

Further acts of violence had been committed by BR members from October 1978 onwards. Girolamo Tartaglione, a senior official at the Ministry of Justice, was shot dead at his home in Rome by BR members on Oct. 10, 1978. During the May 1979 election campaign BR members carried out many attacks, including one on a Christian Democratic Party office in Rome on May 3, when a policeman was killed and two others were injured, while the building was damaged by bombs and the terrorists escaped unharmed. Other policemen killed by BR members included two in Genoa on Nov. 21, 1979, one in Rome on Nov. 27, another in Rome on Dec. 7, three in Milan on Jan. 8, 1980, two (one of them the police chief) in Genoa on Jan. 25, and three in Turin on March 24. BR members also murdered, on Jan. 29, 1980, a Montedison deputy technical director in Mestre, and on Feb. 12 Vittorio Bachelet, deputy president of the High Council of Magistratures and a leading DC member, on the Rome University campus where he taught.

BR members were also responsible for the killing of the head of the anti-terrorist police in Mestre on May 12, 1980; of a Christian Democratic regional councillor in Naples on May 19 (for which four BR members were on July 8, 1980, sentenced to life imprisonment); and of Walter Tobagi, a journalist on the *Corriere della Sera* of Milan, killed on May 28 by a "March 28" column of the BR. Tobagi was co-author of a book on the psychology of terrorism and had, after police had killed four BR suspects on March 28, 1980, written a newspaper article on the "disintegrating myth of the [Genoa] column of the BR".

The Italian police had, in fact, been able to carry out large-scale arrests of BR members (and also of the Front Line organization—see separate entry) during March and April 1980. While Mario Moretti, whom an informer had on Feb. 19, 1980, named as the organizer of the Aldo Moro murder, was still at large, Franco Pinna (described as the BR's military chief) and three other BR members suspected of involvement in that murder, were arrested in France on March 29, 1980.

On Dec. 12, 1980, BR members kidnapped Judge Giovanni D'Urso, who was, however, released by them on Jan. 15, 1981, after the government had, on Dec. 26, acceded to a BR demand to close a maximum security prison on the island of Asinara (off Sardinia) and three newspapers had published BR documents (as also demanded by the BR). A revolt at the Trani prison (in Apulia), where several BR members were detained, was put down by a *carabinieri* unit on Dec. 29. Persons killed by BR members late in 1980 were Renato Briano, a Milan industrialist (on Nov. 12), the director of a Milan steel mill (on Nov. 28) and a prison security chief in Rome (on Dec. 31).

During 1981 BR groups made a number of attacks, inter alia on a transport van of the Italian telephone company on July 29; on an air force barracks near Rome, where they seized a quantity of weapons, on Aug. 19; and on a military convoy in Salerno on Aug. 26, when there followed a clash with police in which one officer was killed and eight other persons were injured, while the attackers escaped with several automatic weapons. On Feb. 9, 1982, four BR members overpowered guards at a barracks and seized a vanload of weapons at Caserta (20 miles north of Naples).

At a trial held in Cagliari (Sardinia) two BR members, who had turned state witnesses, were on Nov. 8, 1981, reported to have said that they had met dissident members of the Palestine Liberation Organization in Mestre (near Venice) and had received a shipment of submachine-guns and hand grenades from them.

Brig.-Gen. James L. Dozier (a US army staff officer and deputy commander of NATO land forces Southern Europe) was abducted in Verona on Dec. 17, 1981, and the BR immediately accepted responsibility for this action. The BR subsequently issued several communiqués, and on Dec. 22 they announced that Gen. Dozier had been found guilty by a "people's court" and would be killed. However, on Jan. 28, 1982, police acting on information received from a suspect freed the general unhurt and arrested the five BR members who were holding him in an apartment in Padua. This police action constituted the first occasion on which Italian police had succeeded in freeing a hostage seized by the BR. The five arrested BR members were said to be members of an Annamaria Ludmann Column which had been active in Venetia. Their names were later given as Antonio Savasta, Cesare Di Lenardo, Giovanni Ciucci, Emilia Libera and Emanuela Frascella. (E. Savasta and E. Libera were, also on Jan. 28, sentenced in absentia to 30 years in prison each for involvement in a gun battle with police in Sardinia in February 1980.)

A court in Verona tried altogether 17 BR members (eight of whom were still at large and were tried in absentia) for involvement in Gen. Dozier's abduction, and on March 25, 1982, the court passed prison sentences totalling over 300 years on the defendants; in particular, C. Di Lenardo was given 27 years and Alberta Biliato 17½ years (both these accused having refused to testify for the state). Antonio Savasta and E. Libera were given 16½ and 14 years respectively after Savasta, who had confessed to having committed 17 murders, had co-operated with the authorities and had given information which had led to the arrest of hundreds of BR suspects.

An under-secretary at the Ministry of Information stated on March 16, 1982, that since the abduction of Gen. Dozier 385 persons had been arrested on terrorism charges—340 from the BR and affiliated organizations and 45 from the extreme right; that 35 arms caches and "safe houses" had been found in the past three months; and that of those captured only 10 per cent had refused to co-operate with the authorities, most of the "terrorists" having realized that they had failed to attain their political aims.

Four of the five abductors of Gen. Dozier were on March 7, 1982, reported to have issued an appeal to their fellow members of the BR to give up the armed struggle which, they claimed, had proved "utterly negative" during the past 10 years. Moreover, Prof Enrico Fenzi, one of the ideologues of the BR, who had in Genoa in 1981 been sentenced to 7½ years in prison for terrorism, declared early in March 1982 that the BR and the idea of armed struggle had failed and that "ten years of bloodstained struggle" had definitively proved that it could "produce no political programme".

Of the eight defendants tried by the Verona court in absentia, Umberto Catabiani, BR leader in Tuscany, was shot dead by police on May 24, 1982; Marcello Capuano (who had been given a 26-year sentence) was captured by police in Rome on May 29,

1982; and Remo Pancelli, also sentenced to 26 years in prison, was arrested near Rome on June 6, 1982. On Jan. 13, 1983, an appeal court in Venice reduced some of the sentences passed by the Verona court, although only insignificant reductions were ordered in the cases of those who had made no confession.

Antonio Savasta, the prominent BR member who had decided to co-operate with the authorities, was on March 10, 1982, reported to have alleged that the Bulgarian secret service had tried to obtain, through a BR infiltrator in the administration, information from Gen. Dozier about NATO and that the Bulgarians had been ready to give aid to the BR. Moreover, he was said to have referred to BR contacts with the Palestine Liberation Organization, which was interested in destabilizing Italy in order to weaken the United States' ability to give aid to Israel.

Persons killed by BR members during 1981 and 1982 included the following: Rafaele Del Cogliano, a Christian Democratic politician and commissioner of the Campania regional government, shot dead in Naples (with his driver) on April 27, 1981; Roberto Peci, seized on June 10 and found dead on Aug. 3, 1981, after his brother Patricio, who had been arrested in 1980, had given the police information on BR activities; Giuseppe Talierco, an industrial manager, killed in Mestre (near Venice) on July 6, 1981; two anti-drug squad policemen assassinated in Rome on June 8, 1982; Antonio Ammaturo, head of the Naples mobile police squad, and his driver, shot on July 17, 1982, by terrorists who issued a statement in which they expressed praise of the activities of the Camorra (the criminal Mafia of Naples); and Ennio Di Rocco, a BR member killed in prison at Trani (near Bari) by other prisoners on July 27, 1982. The last-named had been arrested in Rome on Jan. 4 together with Stefano Petrella, and both were said to have supplied information to the police leading to the arrest of Prof Giovanni Senzani (one of the principal theoreticians of the BR) and to the rescue of Gen. Dozier.

Among persons abducted by BR members was Ciro Cirillo, a Christian Democratic politician from Naples, seized on April 27, 1981, but released on July 24 of that year. He stated in March 1982 that his family and friends had raised 1,500 million lire, or about $1,100,000, paid in ransom to the BR.

The trial of 63 defendants (nine of whom were still at large) for involvement in the abduction and killing of Aldo Moro in 1978 (see above) and in other crimes was held in Rome between April 14, 1982, and Jan. 24, 1983. During the trial Antonio Savasta (one of the defendants who had already been sentenced for involvement in the abduction of Gen. Dozier—see above) made a full confession of all his activities within the BR and stated his conclusion that the BR had failed to realize their aims. On May 3, 1982, he denied that the BR had any links with the Irish Republican Army, the Palestine Liberation Organization, Libya or the Israelis.

Passing judgment, the court imposed life sentences on 32 of the defendants for 17 murders (including that of Moro), 11 attempted murders and four kidnappings during the years 1977-80. Among those imprisoned for life were Mario Moretti, said to have directed the kidnapping of Moro, and Prospero Gallinari, convicted of killing Moro. Two of the accused were given 30-year sentences, and A. Savasta and Emilia Libera each received 16 years, this being the highest sentence given to those who had "repented" of their BR activities, but rather higher sentences were given to those who, while dissociating themselves from the crimes committed by the BR, did not co-operate with the authorities.

On Feb. 26, 1983, a court in Genoa sentenced 10 BR members (among them M. Moretti and P. Gallinari, both already convicted in the Moro murder case) to life imprisonment and four others to prison terms ranging from seven to 18 years for involvement in the murder of five policemen and a trade union official in Genoa in 1978-80. Among seven defendants acquitted at this trial were Patricio Peci and Antonio Savasta, who had served as informers to the Italian security authorities.

On May 9, 1983, four BR members were sentenced in Genoa to prison terms of two to seven years for organizing a terrorist ring in Genoa.

On May 19, 1983, five BR members (two of them being absent) were sentenced to imprisonment ranging from six to 12 years, the latter term being imposed on Francesco Lo Bianco, chief of the BR's "military arm".

At a trial concluded on July 27, 1983, Patricio Peci and Antonio Savasta again received reduced sentences, while, of 61 other members of the Red Brigades and allied groups accused of crimes including 10 murders, 12 were given life sentences (and four were acquitted).

On Aug. 2, 1983, a total of 39 persons were sentenced to imprisonment for terms between 18 months to life for setting up a BR cell in Sardinia.

In a trial of 152 BR adherents which ended in Milan on Nov. 29, 1983, 132 of the accused were sentenced; two of them, convicted of the 1980 murder of Walter Tobagi (see above) were given reduced and suspended sentences for co-operating with the police and were released.

On Feb. 24, 1984, sentences of up to 25 years in prison were passed on 22 BR members for crimes committed in the Genoa area in 1977-81.

Magistrates dealing with crimes attributed to the BR in 1977-82 concluded, on Aug. 13, 1984, a two-year investigation and decided to commit 182 persons for trial, inter alia for 17 important murders. Among these persons were BR members already in prison, such as M. Moretti, Renato Curcio, Prospero Gallinari and Giovanni Senzani, and also Dr Domenico Pittello, accused of treating wounded BR members.

On Nov. 10, 1984, nine BR members were given life sentences and 10 others shorter prison sentences for murdering five policemen and a trade unionist in Genoa in 1978-80 (with only four of the defendants being present).

The BR were held responsible for the murder of another policeman near Rome on Jan. 9, 1985.

On March 14, 1985, a court reviewing the sentences passed in connexion with the kidnapping and murder of Aldo Moro and other murders and crimes confirmed 22 life sentences, including that imposed on M. Moretti, but reduced to 30 years those passed on 10 others who had given information to the police.

Prof Enzo Tarantelli, an adviser to the Christian

Democratic trade union organization, was shot dead by BR members on March 27, 1985.

Barbara Balzerani, who had on Dec. 6, 1984, been sentenced in absentia to life imprisonment for her part in the murder of Aldo Moro and the kidnapping of Brig.-Gen. Dozier, was subsequently arrested and was on July 20, 1985, sentenced in Venice, together with seven other persons, to life imprisonment for the killing of Giuseppe Talierco (see above), while 65 other persons were convicted as accomplices in terrorist acts and received prison sentences and fines.

On Feb. 10, 1986, Lando Conti, a former mayor of Florence, was shot dead by BR members, with the BR giving as grounds for its act L. Conti's friendship with Zionists and his links with the armaments industry and "Western imperialism".

In 1977 the BR were said to consist of cells of between three to five members each, of which only one member was in contact with another cell; several cells constituted a "column" in a city or region. There was also, it was reported, a "strategic directorate". The Red Brigades had an estimated membership in 1980 of about 500 activists, with a further 10,000 supporters.

Thereafter, the active membership of the BR was widely believed to have gone into a significant decline, principally because of the success of the security authorities in penetrating and neutralizing the organization's cells in different parts of the country.

Two apparent offshoots or aliases of the BR are the Fighting Communist Party and the Union of Communist Fighters. The former claimed responsibility for an armed raid on a postal van on Feb. 13, 1987, in which two policemen died, while the latter on March 20, 1987, assassinated Air Force General Licio Giorgeri in Rome. Gen. Giorgeri was Director General of the Department for Aerospace and Missile Procurement within the Ministry of Defence, and comparisons were widely drawn with the assassination of Gen. René Audran by the French Direct Action in January 1986, while the Italian Minister of the Interior stated his belief that the murder of Gen. Giorgeri "was decided outside Italy and carried out by professional killers". Several Italians suspected of involvement were subsequently arrested in France, including (on June 15) Maurizio Locusta, who was said to be the leader of the Union of Communist Fighters. Other arrests of alleged members of the group's "Roman Column" occurred in Italy. France and Italy had signed an anti-terrorist accord in October 1986.

Walter Alasia Column

Leadership. Nicolo Di Maria (l.)

This group broke away from the Red Brigades early in 1980. It was responsible for the abduction of Renzo Sandrucci, an Alfa Romeo executive, on June 10, 1981, near Milan; he was, however, released unharmed on July 23, 1981. On Nov. 25, 1981, a court in Rome sentenced 19 alleged members of the Column to a total of 230 years in prison, among them Nadia Mantovani (the girl friend of Renato Curcio, the Red Brigades' leader), who was given a 17-year sentence.

The police officially claimed on March 1, 1982, that it had broken up the Column after the seizure of four vehicles which the Column had intended to use for an attack on the San Vittore prison (in Milan), where Aurore Betti (the Column's "historic leader") was held; he had been arrested in 1981 and succeeded as leader by Nicolo Di Maria. Early in 1983, however, it appeared that the Column had been reconstituted, as police arrested a number of its alleged members in Milan.

On Dec. 6, 1984, a court in Milan sentenced 19 members of the group to life imprisonment and 89 others to prison terms of up to 30 years for eight murders and 17 attacks in the late 1970s and early 1980s.

Workers' Autonomy (*Autonomia Operaio*)

This organization was established as a successor to Workers' Power (*Potere Operaio*—see separate entry). Prof Antonio Negri (a teacher of political science at Padua University) was, upon his arrest in April 1979, charged with membership of this illegal organization, which was said to have links with the Red Brigades. Franco Piperno (a physics teacher at Cosenza and a founder-member of Workers' Autonomy), was arrested in France in August 1979 and extradited to Italy in October of that year on charges of involvement in the Moro murder and other killings; however, he was released for lack of evidence on June 30, 1980.

The charges against Prof Negri concerning the Moro case were subsequently dropped on April 24, but he was kept in custody on the other charges until July 7, 1983, by which time he had been elected to the Chamber of Deputies as a candidate of the Radical Party. The Chamber, however, decided on Sept. 23, 1983 (by 287 votes to 75, with 227 abstentions) to deprive him of his parliamentary immunity, so that he could be rearrested on charges brought against him and 70 other Workers' Autonomy members in respect of, inter alia, armed insurrection against the state and the formation of an armed band, but meanwhile he had disappeared. On June 12, 1984, he was sentenced in absentia (having fled to France) to 30 years' imprisonment for complicity in the murder of a policeman and in kidnapping and attempted murder of another person as well as for possession of explosives and theft. At the same time Oreste Scalzone, who had also fled the country, was sentenced to 20 years in prison and 58 others were given sentences ranging from five to 20 years. (The chief witness for the prosecution was freed from a life sentence and did not appear in court.)

On Jan. 31, 1986, Prof Negri and seven other members of the teaching staff of Padua University were acquitted of being "the moral leaders" of the Red Brigades and other left-wing groups.

On June 8, 1987, an appeals court acquitted Prof Negri of armed insurrection and kidnapping, but upheld his conviction for organizing armed robbery.

Workers' Brigade for Communism

On July 15, 1981, this group planted at least five bombs in Como, killing a police disposal expert.

Workers' Power (*Potere Operaio*)

Leaders of this movement were involved in the students' unrest which began in 1968. Its members were said to be responsible for an attack on the home of a leader of the Italian Social Movement (MSI), in which two of his sons were burnt to death on April 13, 1973. When Prof Antonio Negri and 24 other left-wing intellectuals were arrested in April 1979, he and several others were known to be members of *Potere Operaio* and were said to have joined the Red Brigades, with Prof Negri becoming one of the latter's leading ideologues. However, charges brought against him in connexion with the murder of Aldo Moro were dropped on April 24, 1980.

Prof Negri was in October 1981 reported to have condemned the murder of a factory director by the Red Brigades as a "barbaric" deed and to have argued that a new political generation had arisen which was engaged in "great struggles for the community, for peace and for a new kind of happiness".

Regional Movements

SOUTH TIROL

Conflict in South Tirol has occurred between extremists from the German-speaking population, who have sought either independence or unification with Austria, and Italian-speakers who wish to maintain Italian rule. The Italian Foreign Minister said that he believed he was the target of a bomb attack on a hotel in Merano on Dec. 31, 1986, and a number of violent incidents occurred in the early months of 1987, although with no fatalities.

Jamaica

Capital: Kingston

Pop. 2,340,000

Jamaica, a member of the Commonwealth with the British monarch as head of state being represented by a Governor-General, has a bicameral Parliament consisting of (i) a 60-member House of Representatives elected for five years by universal adult suffrage and (ii) a 21-member Senate to which 13 senators are appointed by the Governor-General on the advice of the Prime Minister and the remaining eight on the advice of the Leader of the Opposition. The Prime Minister and his Cabinet are responsible to Parliament.

In elections to the House of Representatives held on Dec. 15, 1983, the Jamaica Labour Party (JLP) was unopposed in 54 out of 60 constituencies due to an election boycott by the main opposition People's National Party (PNP) which had accused the government of calling a snap election without completing a revision of the electoral register. The JLP took all 60 seats, defeating minor opposition from the Republican Party, the Christian Conscience and the right-wing Jamaica United Front.

Violence in Jamaica has been notable in the Caribbean context, some if it semi-political in nature and carried out by armed groups receiving patronage from one or other of the major parties.

In 1984, the former Minister of National Security and Justice William Spaulding accused the PNP and the Workers' Party of Jamaica (WPJ) of being involved in the organization of criminal activity and in attempts to "target certain institutions". He alleged that leftist groups were supported by foreign governments, "specifically Cuba".

On Feb. 25, 1985, two prominent members of the WPJ and one former member were shot dead by police in disputed circumstances. The WPJ alleged that the police were detailed to eliminate opponents of the government.

Japan

Capital: Tokyo Pop. 121,047,000

The Empire of Japan is a constitutional monarchy in which the Emperor, as head of state, has no governing power. Executive power is vested in a Cabinet and legislative power in a bicameral Diet consisting of (i) a 252-member House of Councillors and (ii) a 512-member House of Representatives, both Houses being elected by universal adult suffrage of citizens above the age of 20 years; 126 members are elected to the House of Councillors every three years—76 in single-member constituencies and 50 in a national constituency of the whole electorate. The members of the House of Representatives are elected for a four-year term in multi-member constituencies of greatly varying sizes. All organizations wishing to nominate candidates for public office have to be registered as political parties; there are over 10,000 such parties but the vast majority of them are of significance only at local or regional level.

Elections to the House of Representatives held on July 6, 1986, resulted in the following distribution of seats: Liberal-Democratic Party 304, Japan Socialist Party 86, *Komeito* (Clean Government Party) 57, Japan Communist Party 27, Democratic Socialist Party 26, New Liberal Club 6, others 6.

Acts of politically motivated violence have been carried out both by extreme right-wing and by extreme left-wing groups. In March 1977 the police estimated that there were perhaps 40 extreme right-wing formations with a total membership of fewer than 3,000 and advocating an authoritarian government as the best solution to overcome corruption, exploitation and "unequal treaties" with foreign powers. Some of the extreme left-wing groups extended their operations to targets outside Japan, and under a law enacted on May 12, 1978, and entering into force on June 5 of that year the death penalty was extended to hijackers and anyone seizing diplomatic establishments, while the penalty for taking hostages was raised from five years to life imprisonment.

Whereas until 1977 the Japanese government had repeatedly acceded to demands made by hijackers of aircraft (with the then Prime Minister, Takeo Fukuda, stating on Sept. 29, 1975, that human life was "more precious than the earth"), it was reported in June 1978 that the government had mapped out a new policy whereby no further demands by terrorists would be complied with, even if lives had to be sacrificed.

Several left-wing groups were repeatedly involved in violent clashes with each other, and up to 1980 some 80 members of such groups had been killed, and 4,500 wounded, in ideological feuds. In 1985 there was an upsurge in activity by several of the left-wing groups with 85 separate incidents reported by the authorities to have occurred during the course of the year—the highest annual figure for six years and almost double that recorded for 1984. In the 12 months to the end of April 1986 police arrested over 900 "radicals" of whom some 500 were connected to Japan's most prominent left-wing group, *Chukaku-Ha* (Middle Core faction—see separate entry).

Extreme Right-wing Groups

Japan Volunteer Army for National Independence (*Nihon Minzoku Dokuritsu Giyungun*)

This group has since 1983 carried out attacks on premises of *Asahi Shimbun*, a leading liberal daily newspaper, including the shooting of two reporters (one fatally) at an *Asahi* office on May 3, 1987. In a message sent after this last incident the group warned that it had passed "the death penalty on all *Asahi* employees" for their role in the destruction of Japanese culture, and that "all members of the media are equally guilty". The group also warned *Asahi* not to criticize the Unification Church of the Rev. Sun Myung Moon and further claimed responsibility for fires at the US consulate in Kobe in 1981, at the Soviet consulate in Osaka in 1983 and at US military facilities in 1982.

Youth League for the Overthrow of the Yalta and Potsdam Structure

Two members of this group were among four armed men who on March 3, 1977, entered the headquarters of *Keidanren* (the Japanese Federation of Economic Organizations) in Tokyo and temporarily seized about a dozen leaders of the Federation as hostages; at the same time they distributed leaflets denouncing big business for "poisoning Japan's post-war society and its landscape" and also for corruption. However, they surrendered to the police on March 4, all hostages being released unharmed. The other two members of the four-man group had been members of the Shield Society (*Tatenokai*), and extreme right-wing organization which had been disbanded after the suicide of its leader, the well-known writer Yukio Mishima, in November 1970. The leader of the four men, Shusuke Nomura, had earlier served a 12-year sentence for burning down the house of a conservative politician and was quoted as saying that he regarded as political enemies all who had dominated Japan in the last 30 years; that the Liberal-Democratic Party and the Communist Party were "equally guilty"; and that Japan could not be rescued unless all was destroyed.

The League is opposed to the Allied decisions arrived at during the Yalta and Potsdam conferences in 1945 which it regarded as having destroyed Japan's political independence. In January 1987 three members of the League kidnapped the wife of a wealthy property developer, in protest at the escalation of land prices in the Tokyo area.

Extreme Left-wing Groups

The Battle Flag of the Communist League (*Senki Kyosando*)

This left-wing group (also referred to as the War Flag Wing) became the second in Japan to possess the technology to build and launch crude incendiary rockets. In a protest against the official celebration of the 60th anniversary of the accession of Emperor Hirohito and the hosting in Tokyo of the 1986 economic summit meeting of industrialized nations, three such missiles were fired at the US Embassy in Toyko and two at the Imperial Palace on March 25, 1986, and further missiles were launched towards the Prime Minister's official residence and the Transport Ministry on Oct. 14; no injuries or damage resulted.

Fourth (Trotskyist) International—Japanese Section

The Japanese section of the Fourth (Trotskyist) International played a leading role among the radical groups which from 1971 onwards actively opposed the construction and opening of a new international airport at Narita (about 40 miles north-west of Tokyo). Demonstrations by local farmers, left-wing student groups and environmentalists led to several years' delay in the completion of the airport. During disturbances in February-May 1978 four policemen and one civilian died and several hundred persons were injured. On March 26, 1978 (two days before the official opening date), radical groups occupied the air control tower, destroyed vital radar and communications equipment and rendered the airport inoperative; some 14,000 riot police were deployed over the area, 115 persons were arrested and many more were injured. On May 28 police also arrested 50 occupants of a tower-like structure built by opponents of the airport near the proposed main runway and demolished it in a prolonged battle. The government stated on May 28 that the "acts of violence by extremists" had "nothing to do with the anti-airport movement of some local farmers" but were "a serious challenge to democracy". Under new legislation which came into force on May 13, 1978, the Minister of Transport was empowered to remove any structure within two miles of the airport which might be used for sabotage. Although the airport was officially opened on May 20, attacks on its communications and other installations continued upon a sporadic basis, with several bombs exploding in its vicinity in 1984 and 1985. In the first nine months of 1985 a total of 33 "hostile acts" were reported to have been aimed at the airport, compared to 28 during the course of 1984. This increase in the incidence of attacks resulted from the initiation of work on the second phase of the airport's expansion and was co-ordinated by the Anti-Airport Federation, a loose coalition of left-wing groups which was reported to include members of the *Chukaku-Ha* (Middle Core Faction—see separate entry), Japan's most prominent revolutionary movement, which had played a significant role in the original demonstrations against the airport's construction.

On Oct. 20, 1985, over 9,500 riot police using water cannon and tear gas clashed with up to 14,000 demonstrators, some of whom were armed with clubs and petrol bombs, who were attempting to gain access to the airport. In the violence which followed, the most serious since 1978, 241 arrests were made and over 150 people injured.

Hazama Faction of the Revolutionary Workers' Council (*Kakurokyo Hazama*)

In September 1985 this left-wing group became the third within Japan to employ home-made rockets. Four such devices were fired on March 31, 1986, against the Asaka state guest house (allocated to those attending the economic summit meeting of the seven leading industrialized nations in Tokyo on May 4-6), and the Togu Palace, the residence of Crown Prince Akihito. The attacks, which were in protest against the official celebration of the 60th anniversary of the accession of Emperor Hirohito in April and the hosting of the summit, were followed on May 6 by the release of fireworks and smoke bombs in 16 railway stations in Tokyo, causing extensive disruption but no casualties.

Middle-Core Faction (*Chukaku-Ha*)

This Marxist breakaway group from the National Federation of Students' Organizations was created in 1960 to oppose the security treaty concluded between the United States and Japan.

Members of the Faction were repeatedly involved in violent clashes with members of the rival *Kakumaru-Ha* movement (Revolutionary Marxist Faction); in such clashes eight persons were killed in March-June 1975; and on Oct. 30, 1980, *Chukaku-Ha* members were reported to have beaten to death five *Kakumaru-Ha* members as an act of revenge for the murder of a leftist leader four years earlier.

In an explosion at a flat at Yokosuka (south-west of Tokyo) on Sept. 4, 1975, three members of the faction and two other persons were killed. On May 7, 1982, the *Chukaku-Ha* claimed responsibility for several attempts to set fire to Self-Defence Force (i.e. army) facilities and to the Imperial Palace in Tokyo.

By the early 1980s the *Chukaku-Ha* was the most significant of the numerous groups on the far left of the Japanese political spectrum. In September 1984 it conducted an arson attack against the Tokyo headquarters of the ruling Liberal Democratic Party which injured two people and caused over US$3,500,000 worth of damage.

The group has made extensive use of simple missiles, carrying out attacks on government buildings, on Narita airport and (on May 4, 1986) on buildings used in connexion with the Tokyo economic summit of the leading industrial countries.

In opposition to government plans (which took effect in April 1987) to break up and privatize the

Japan National Railways (JNR) public corporation, *Chukaku-Ha* sabotaged JNR installations, causing widespread disruption on two occasions in November 1985 and September 1986. On Sept. 1, 1986, it carried out a series of attacks on officials of a small breakaway union, *Shinkokuro*, which had approved the privatization policy, one official being beaten to death.

Chukaku-Ha was estimated in 1986 to have some 3,000 members, with 250-300 constituting its inner operational "Revolutionary Army". Although considered responsible for some 47 deaths the group maintained a publicly known fortress-like headquarters in a Tokyo suburb.

United Red Army (URA) (*Rengo Sekigun*)

Leadership. Miss Fusako Shigenobu (supreme commander)

The URA was formed in 1969 by a merger of the Red Army Faction (*Sekigunha*), which was an offshoot of the (Trotskyist) Communist League, and the Keihin Joint Struggle Committee against the US-Japan Security Treaty (*Keihin Anpo Kyoto*) to launch an armed campaign for revolution. In February 1972 some of its militants "executed" 14 alleged "deviationists" and for six days resisted police action against them.

In a document issued in May 1977 the URA declared that it would continue to fight for the materialization of a people's republic of Japan by uniting and joining forces with the "oppressed people, comrades and friends in confrontation with Japanese imperialism". During its early operations the URA had stressed the "need to fight again Zionism" and for "the just cause of the Palestinians", but during the hijacking of an airliner to Dacca (Dhaka) in 1977 (see below) the URA affirmed the need of a revolution in Japan, its solidarity with the Japanese people in their struggle against the monarchy and the growing "imperialism", the economic exploitation of South Korea by Japan, the construction of Narita airport and corruption in general. In December 1977 the URA called for the formation of a revolutionary council in Japan in order to prepare for a revolutionary government-in-exile.

Major terrorist operations in which URA members took part have included the following:

(1) The hijacking, on March 30, 1970, of a Japan Air Lines (JAL) airliner and its diversion to North Korea.

(2) A massacre at Lod airport (Tel Aviv) on May 30, 1972, when three URA members opened fire indiscriminately and killed 26 persons and wounded 78 others; of the three gunmen, one committed suicide, one was killed by Israeli police and a third (Kozo Okamoto) was captured. Responsibility for the operation was claimed by the Popular Front for the Liberation of Palestine (PFLP) in Beirut on May 31, stating that the three Japanese had come "to take part with the Palestinian people in the struggle against the power of Zionism and imperialism". Okamoto was sentenced to life imprisonment on July 17, 1972.

(3) The hijacking on July 20, 1973, of a JAL airliner flying from Paris to Amsterdam and its diversion to Benghazi (Libya) where, after the passengers and crew had left it, it was blown up by the hijackers. A statement issued by this group on July 26 described the action as retaliation against the Japanese government for having paid compensation to Israel for the Lod massacre.

(4) An attack on a Shell oil refinery in Singapore on Jan. 31, 1974, when four attackers, claiming to be members of the PFLP and the URA, seized as hostages the five-member crew of a ferry and demanded safe passage out of Singapore. While negotiations proceeded between them and the Singapore authorities five armed men occupied the Japanese embassy in Kuwait on Feb. 6 and held the entire staff as hostages; these armed men demanded from the Japanese government that it should send an aircraft to take the URA members from Singapore to Kuwait. The Japanese government agreed to this demand, and eventually all hostages, both in Singapore and in Kuwait, were released and all the guerrillas were flown to Aden (South Yemen) on Feb. 8.

(5) The occupation of the French embassy in The Hague on Sept. 13, 1974, by three URA members who took 10 persons, including the ambassador, as hostages and demanded the release of Yutaka Furuya, a URA member detained at Orly airport (in France) in late July 1974; after protracted negotiations the hostages were released in exchange for Furuya, and an aircraft carried him and the guerrillas to Damascus on Sept 18.

(6) The seizure of the US consulate and the neighbouring Swedish embassy in Kuala Lumpur (Malaysia) on Aug. 4, 1975, by five URA members who took 52 persons hostage and demanded the release of seven URA prisoners held in Japan. The Japanese government agreed on Aug. 5 to release the seven prisoners, of whom only five agreed to be thus released, and these were flown to Kuala Lumpur on the same day in a Japanese airliner which was, on Aug. 7, flown to Tripoli (Libya) with the five attackers, the five released prisoners and four new hostages (two Malaysian and two Japanese officials, who had replaced 15 of the original hostages, most of whom had been released earlier). In Tripoli the 10 URA members surrendered to the Libyan authorities; and the Malaysian and Japanese officials returned to their countries in the same airliner on Aug. 10.

(7) The hijacking of a JAL airliner on a flight from Paris to Tokyo after taking off from Bombay on Sept. 28, 1977, by a five-member "Hidaka commando" of the URA, who forced it to land in Dacca (Dhaka, Bangladesh) and demanded the release of seven URA prisoners held in Japan and of two common criminals convicted of murder, and also payment of US$6,000,000. The URA prisoners included Junzo Okudaira, who had taken part in the occupation of the French embassy in The Hague in September 1974 and of the US consulate in Kuala Lumpur in August 1975, had been arrested in Jordan, and been extradited to Japan in 1976, together with the body of Toshihiko Hidaka, who was suspected of being involved in the Kuala Lumpur attack and had committed suicide while under arrest abroad. On Sept. 29 the Japanese government agreed to these demands "in principle", but their fulfilment was delayed, particularly in that only six of the named prisoners agreed to be released.

After most of the hostages had been released the airliner left Dacca on Oct. 2 with 29 passengers, the Japanese pilot, two other members of the original crew and four fresh crew members, as well as the five hijackers, the six ex-prisoners and the ransom; after the release of seven passengers in Kuwait and another 10 in Damascus, the airliner (on Oct. 3) reached Algiers, where the remaining 12 passengers and the crew were released and the hijackers and the ex-prisoners were taken to an unknown destination. A Japanese plea for the extradition of the hijackers and the surrender of the ex-prisoners and the ransom was rejected by Algeria on Oct. 5.

(8) The seizure of a bus with a least 15 passengers in Nagasaki on Oct. 15, 1977, by a two-man "suicide commando" of the URA, who threatened to explode 37 bombs throughout Japan unless their demands for ransom and for talks with the Minister of Justice were met; in this case, however, the authorities made no concessions to the attackers; police stormed the bus on the following day and killed one and seized the other terrorist (while several passengers were slightly injured).

No further URA operations were reported after the above. In May 1979 the URA issued statements in which it announced its decision to "solidify internationalism and work out our own salvation with our own efforts" and to "properly eliminate inconsistencies in the establishment of socialism".

In May 1982 Fusako Shigenobu, the movement's leader, was quoted as saying that the URA had abandoned terrorism because it had failed to win international support. She also stated that "under the new situation in the world" it was "important to unify all anti-imperialist forces and to consolidate the movement to build a bigger base". She admitted that URA members were continuing to receive military training in Lebanon but gave no further details. According to the Japanese police, the remnants of the URA had set up their headquarters in a Palestinian refugee camp on the outskirts of Beirut.

In addition to its involvement in the Palestinian cause and its close links with the Popular Front for the Liberation of Palestine (PFLP), the URA also had ties with revolutionary groups in other countries, notably in West Germany and Spain.

On May 20, 1985, Kozo Okamoto was one of 394 prisoners who arrived in Tripoli, Libya, after being released by Israel as part of an exchange deal whereby some 1,150 detainees held by Israel were exchanged for three Israeli soldiers who had been captured in the Lebanon by the Popular Front for the Liberation of Palestine in 1982. The Japanese government, which had earlier requested that Okamoto be excluded from the exchange or be released into Japanese custody, officially notified the government of Israel of its displeasure at his release.

Although the Red Army was not known to have initiated any military operations since 1977, it was believed to have approximately 40 members operating abroad at the time of Okamoto's release, most of whom were in Libya or the Lebanon.

On Sept. 26, 1986, the Tokyo High Court rejected an appeal by 3 URA members, Hiroko Nagata, Hiroshi Sakaguchi, and Yasuhiro Uegaki, against their conviction in 1982 for the murder of 14 fellow members of the URA and 2 policemen in 1971-72. Nagata and Sakaguchi were sentenced to death.

Jordan

Capital: Amman

Pop. 3,510,000

The Hashemite Kingdom of Jordan is a constitutional monarchy which, under its 1952 Constitution, has had a bicameral National Assembly consisting of (i) a 60-member House of Representatives (with 50 Moslem and 10 Christian members) elected for a four-year term in equal numbers (30 each) from the East and the West Bank respectively, and (ii) a 30-member Senate appointed by the King. Owing to the capture of the West Bank by Israel in 1967 no elections to the House of Representatives took place after that of April 1967. Under constitutional amendments passed in November 1974 the Assembly was dissolved after King Hussein had agreed that the Palestine Liberation Organization (PLO) should henceforth have sole responsibility for the West Bank. However, the Assembly was reconvened in extraordinary session in February 1976, when it approved further constitutional amendments postponing new elections indefinitely and empowering the King to recall the existing Assembly when necessary. On Jan. 5, 1984, the King dissolved a National Consultative Council which he had established in 1978, and at the same time he recalled the National Assembly to an emergency session. This session was opened on Jan. 9 and approved constitutional amendments authorizing the holding of separate elections for the East Bank representatives and the appointment of new West Bank members. On Jan. 18 the Assembly appointed seven new representatives from the West Bank, and in elections held on March 12, 1986, when women were allowed to vote for the first time, eight remaining vacant seats in the House of Representatives were filled by East Bank candidates. (The House was thus restored to its full strength of 60 members, as 15 had died since the previous elections.)

Political parties remained banned, but of the 116 candidates contesting the East Bank elections many had political leanings, either towards Baathism or towards Moslem fundamentalism.

Although the life of the King has repeatedly been threatened by militant Palestinians and the Moslem Brotherhood is represented in his country also, Jordan has generally been regarded as one of the most politically stable countries in the Arab world. An attempt to assassinate the King was made on Oct. 6, 1969, by members of an Islamic Liberation Party (*Tahrir*) which had been founded in the 1930s by Shaikh Takieddin Nabhani; it advocated a return to the Caliphate and government based on Koranic law, and was banned in all Arab countries.

There have been no official legal parties in Jordan since the abolition of the semi-official Arab National Union in 1976. At least five groups took advantage of the government's increasing tolerance in 1984, and by 1985 two groups, the Arab Constitutional Party and the Unionist Democratic Party, were close to establishing party structures. In privately circulated documents both groups had expressed support for the PLO and Arab nationalism.

Jordanian subjects and property have been subject to attacks abroad in recent years, with responsibility for various incidents claimed by groups including the Abu Nidal Group, the Arab Revolutionary Brigades and Black September.

Communist Party of Jordan (CPJ)

Leadership. Faïg Warrad (first sec.)

Originally established in 1943 as the National Liberation League, the pro-Soviet CPJ adopted its present name in September 1951. The party was banned in 1957. In July 1967 the party's central committee specified the main lines of its "struggle to eliminate the effects of Israeli aggression" and of "resistance to imperialism". In August 1973 it played a leading role in the formation of a Palestine National Front of the occupied territories. The CPJ has published illegal newspapers from time to time.

In May 1986 members of the politburo were amongst those arrested after three students were killed and 60 wounded in clashes with security forces at Yarmouck University. Following the incidents, King Hussein spoke of the "unholy alliance" between *Al-Fatah*, Jordanian communists and Islamic fundamentalists. (In July 1986 King Hussein had closed all 25 *Al-Fatah* offices in Jordan, stating that the PLO, distinct from the *Fatah* component, was the only legitimate representative of the Palestinians.)

Democratic Front for the Liberation of Palestine (DFLP)

In December 1985 and January 1986 a group of 40 trade unionists believed to be sympathetic to the DFLP were reported to have been arrested after the DFLP allegedly attempted to encourage trade union activity in the West Bank.

Moslem Brotherhood

Members of the Moslem Brotherhood found asylum in Jordan at the time of the movement's suppression by President Nasser of Egypt. It is represented in Amman by a spokesman for its international organization (while its headquarters have remained in Egypt), who stated in an interview (published in *Le Monde* of Paris on Feb. 28, 1980) that nobody in Jordan was perturbed by the movement. Nevertheless, the Moslem Brotherhood has supported the Iranian revolution whereas the Jordanian government has backed Iraq in its war against Iran and has on several occasions extradited Moslem Brotherhood members to Syria (where they were wanted on criminal charges).

In the same interview the Brotherhood spokesman dismissed differences between Sunni and Shia Moslems as "theological quarrels" which were "completely outdated". He also defined the essence of the Moslem Brotherhood as constituting "a protest against the failure of the Arab world", in particular its failure to resolve the Palestinian problem, to resist Western encroachment on Moslem civilization and "to wipe out corruption and chaos".

In December 1985, over 250 Moslem fundamentalists, including members of the Moslem Brotherhood, were reported arrested in Jordan. The timing of the arrests was linked with a rapprochement with Syria where the Brotherhood is one of the more active opposition groups.

Kampuchea

Capital: Phnom Penh Pop. 7,200,000

The People's Republic of Kampuchea (PRK—formerly Cambodia) is a (communist) one-party state ruled by a People's Revolutionary Council set up in January 1979 by members of the central committee of a Kampuchean National United Front for National Salvation (KNUFNS—renamed in 1981 the Kampuchean United Front for National Construction and Defence), whose "Kampuchean Revolutionary Army" had, with strong support from regular forces of the Socialist Republic of Vietnam, overthrown the regime of "Democratic Kampuchea" led by Pol Pot. Elections to a 117-member National Assembly, which was contested by 148 candidates of the KNUFNS, were held on May 1, 1981, and were officially stated to have shown that 99.17 per cent of the 3,417,339 electors had taken part in the vote. In February 1986 the National Assembly voted to prolong its first term for a further five years.

The country's sole legitimate party is the Kampuchean People's Revolutionary Party (KPRP), founded in 1951 (when the Indo-Chinese Communist Party formed in 1930 by Ho Chi Minh was divided into independent communist parties for Kampuchea, Vietnam and Laos). It changed its name to Communist Party of Kampuchea at a secret congress held in Phnom Penh in 1960 and was subsequently divided into supporters of North Vietnam and a Maoist faction led Pol Pot (then known as Saloth Sar). Though the two factions were reunited during the civil war of 1970-75, Pol Pot began in 1973 to purge the pro-Vietnamese faction, most of whose members sought refuge in Vietnam and subsequently held, with defectors from Pol Pot, a "reorganization congress" in January 1979 (after the overthrow of the Pol Pot regime), their party reverting to its original name of KPRP. The fifth congress of the KPRP was held in Phnom Penh in October 1985, at which Heng Samrin, the President of the PRK Council of State, was unanimously re-elected party general secretary.

The various forms of government which Kampuchea has had since it was formally declared independent (as Cambodia) in 1953 can briefly be defined as follows: (i) from 1953 to 1970, a neutralist government under Prince Norodom Sihanouk; (ii) from 1970-75, a right-wing government (of the Khmer Republic) under Lt.-Gen. (later Marshal) Lon Nol; (iii) from 1975 to the end of 1978 a (pro-Chinese) communist government (of Democratic Kampuchea) installed by the Red Khmers (*Khmers Rouges*), with Prince Sihanouk as head of state until April 1976 and thereafter effectively led by Pol Pot as Prime Minister; (iv) since January 1979 a (pro-Soviet) communist government supported by the forces of the Socialist Republic of Vietnam and opposed, since mid-1982, by the Coalition Government of Democratic Kampuchea, comprising the militarily dominant Red Khmers, Son Sann's Khmer People's National Liberation Front and Prince Sihanouk's National Sihanoukist Army.

Coalition Government of Democratic Kampuchea (CGDK)

Leadership. Prince Norodom Sihanouk (pres.), Khieu Samphan (vice.-pres.), Son Sann (prime minister)

An agreement on the formation of this anti-Vietnamese tripartite coalition was concluded, after protracted and complex negotiations, in Kuala Lumpur (Malaysia), on June 22, 1982. Its three main signatories were Prince Norodom Sihanouk (leader of his Sihanoukist forces), Khieu Samphan (Prime Minister of the UN-recognized Democratic Kampuchea—i.e. Red Khmer—"government") and Son Sann (leader of the Khmer People's National Liberation Front, KPNLF).

The formation of the CGDK was strongly criticized by the PRK and by Vietnam, the latter describing it as "a monster created by Chinese expansionism and US imperialism".

Immediately after the signature of the coalition agreement Prince Sihanouk actively appealed for international support. Prior to the meeting of the United Nations General Assembly in September 1982 all three members of the CGDK's "inner cabinet" (Prince Sihanouk, Son Sann and Khieu Samphan) paid visits to other countries to solicit international support for the coalition, with regard both to UN representation and to humanitarian, financial and military aid for the resistance struggle in Kampuchea. The principal CGDK supporters were China and the member nations of the Association of South East Asian Nations (ASEAN, composed of Indonesia, Malaysia, the Philippines, Singapore and Thailand).

Prince Sihanouk addressed the UN General Assembly in New York on Sept. 30, 1982, when he asserted that the CGDK was not a government-in-exile but one which controlled large areas of the country.

During a visit to China by the CGDK leaders in November 1982 discussions were held on the question of Chinese military support, which was subsequently directed mainly to the Red Khmers. A further meeting of the three CGDK leaders with Chinese leaders, including Deng Xiaoping, China's elder statesman, in December 1983 resulted in increased Chinese equipment and ammunition being supplied to the Red Khmers. The three leaders again visited China on July 3-6, 1984, when they met with Zhao Ziyang, the Chinese Prime Minister.

In their armed struggle against the PRK and Vietnamese troops the forces of the three components of the CGDK did not always act in harmony. In March 1984 it was reported that Red Khmer fighters had for the first time co-operated with Sihanoukist forces in an attack. There followed reports of Red Khmer guerrilla attacks on Sihanoukist and KPNLF fighters. At the same time it was reported that the KPNLF and the Sihanoukists had established a new joint radio station and a permanent military committee for co-ordination. However, in the fighting it soon became apparent that their forces had made no significant progress, as by March 1985 all principal bases of the CGDK along the Thai-Kampuchea border were overrun by PRK and Vietnamese forces.

During this period the United States clarified its position on the question of military support for the CGDK. A US official declared in Bangkok (Thailand) on April 7, 1983, that the USA would not give military aid to the CGDK because that would not facilitate the search for a political solution. The USA did, however, give financial aid to the CGDK's two non-communist components for strictly "non-lethal" procurements. A CGDK request for direct military support was refused by the USA in June 1984, and the US Secretary of State (George Shultz) declared on July 14 that the USA would continue to refuse any aid to the Red Khmers, "whose atrocities have outraged the world". On May 15, 1985, the US Senate approved the proposed provision of US$5,000,000 in economic or military assistance to the two non-communist CGDK factions on condition that the ASEAN member countries committed themselves to providing similar aid. On July 10 G. Shultz stated in Malaysia that he saw no need for the USA to supply military aid to the CGDK because such aid was "available from other countries" (i.e. China, which had admitted granting such aid, and the ASEAN countries, some of which had done so covertly). On Jan. 11, 1986, the USA announced that it would grant $3,500,000 in non-lethal aid to the KPNLF and the Sihanoukist forces, to be administered through Thailand. Under a US Foreign Aid Bill signed by the President on Aug. 8, 1985, up to $5,000,000 for non-lethal aid had already been provided (while since 1982 the Central Intelligence Agency was said to have provided the two groups with more than $5,000,000 worth of covert military aid).

Prince Sihanouk was twice reported to have requested to be relieved of his post as president of the CGDK, first at the end of 1982 and again in April 1985, mainly because of differences with the Red Khmers, whom he accused in particular of having failed to support his forces against a Vietnamese offensive in 1985. However, on April 26, 1985, the CGDK office in Beijing (China) announced that he was not retiring.

A meeting of the CGDK cabinet in New York on Oct. 21, 1985, released a statement affirming its readiness to accept an ASEAN formula of indirect "proximity talks" between the various combatants as a means of initiating a peaceful settlement of the Kampuchea issue. The idea of "proximity talks" had been agreed upon in July 1985 at a meeting of the ASEAN Foreign Ministers in Malaysia; under the formulation, the talks would involve the CGDK on the one hand and Vietnam on the other, with the PRK participating only as part of the Vietnamese delegation. Both Vietnam and the PRK rejected the proposals. Of the CGDK leadership, only Prince Sihanouk originally accepted them. Vietnam and the PRK had consistently stated that the internal affairs of Kampuchea had to be settled by the Kampuchean people without external interference and that the "elimination" of the "Pol Pot clique" was the primary precondition for neutral reconciliation within the country. At a meeting of the Indo-Chinese Foreign Ministers in January 1986 the PRK's Premier, Hun Sen, announced that the PRK was prepared to enter into talks with "opposition Khmer individuals and groups". This proposal was rejected by the CGDK on Feb. 11, and prior to this, on Feb. 8, the Coalition had issued a statement reaffirming its readiness to talk directly or indirectly with Vietnam and outlining a four-point plan involving: (i) withdrawal of all foreign forces; (ii) the establishment of a UN control commission; (iii) UN-supervised elections; and (iv) self-determination. On March 9 the CGDK Foreign Ministry broadcast an appeal to Vietnam to consider the four-point plan and begin negotiations. Prince Sihanouk outlined a new CGDK peace plan from Beijing on March 17, 1986. The plan, which was subsequently referred to as the "eight-point proposal", was established as the Coalition's national charter at a meeting of the cabinet held in Beijing on Sept. 6-10, 1986. The proposal envisaged a phased withdrawal of Vietnamese troops from Kampuchea, with a ceasefire during the period of its execution, monitored by a UN observer group. Negotiations would then be held between the PRK government and CGDK, leading to free elections and the possible formation of a quadripartite coalition including members of the Heng Samrin regime, with Prince Sihanouk as President and Son Sann as Prime Minister (as under the CGDK). Kampuchea, under the new administration, would sign a non-aggression treaty with Vietnam and establish firm economic links. The plan was rejected by Vietnam (on March 17) and by the PRK (on March 22).

In October 1986, for the eighth consecutive year, the UN General Assembly adopted resolutions which called for the withdrawal of all foreign forces from Kampuchea and reiterated recognition of the CGDK, which (as Democratic Kampuchea) continued to occupy the Kampuchean seat in the Assembly. Numerous countries have accredited ambassadors to the CGDK, including Bangladesh, North Korea, Egypt, China, Pakistan, Malaysia, Mauritania, Senegal, Sierra Leone, Thailand and Yugoslavia.

"Voice of the Khmer" radio reported on May 14, 1987, that Prince Sihanouk had decided to take a "temporary leave of absence" for one year as CGDK president. He had reportedly announced the decision in Pyongyang (the North Korean capital) on May 7.

Communist Organizations

Communist Party of Kampuchea (CPK)

The CPK originated from the formation of a Cambodian communist organization in 1951, subsequently described as the Kampuchean People's Revolutionary Party (KPRP). In 1952 (prior to full independence) Cambodian communists formed a "government of national resistance" led by Son Ngoc Minh, but following the 1954 Geneva Agreements the armed struggle by communists in Cambodia all but ceased. Some communists formed legal organizations (i.e. the Party of the Masses—*Pracheachon*) to contest elections to the National Assembly in 1955, others infiltrated Prince Norodom Sihanouk's Popular Socialist Community (*Sankum Reastr Niyum*), and still others went underground, some into Cambodia itself and some into North Vietnam.

On Sept. 30, 1960, Cambodian communists held their second congress (alternatively described as the founding congress of the CPK) which resulted in the formation of a "Marxist-Leninist Party in Cambodia" led by Tou Samouth as its general secretary. The party decided to combine revolutionary armed violence with "legal, semi-legal and illegal struggle". Its leadership included Saloth Sar (Pol Pot) and Ieng Sary, both members of a group of young, radical intellectuals who had returned from Paris in the 1950s. The Sino-Soviet controversy led to a conflict within the CPK between supporters of North Vietnam and the Maoists, the latter group probably led by Pol Pot. In July 1962 Tou Samouth disappeared, and Pol Pot was elected CPK general secretary in February 1963. At some time between February and July 1963 the CPK leadership (including Pol Pot, Ieng Sary and Son Sen) went into hiding in the Cambodian countryside and their names were not mentioned in any Cambodian press reports until 1971. However, Pol Pot was thought to have made visits to Hanoi and Beijing in 1965-66. CPK forces (often described as *Khmer Rouge, Khmer Vietminh* or *Khmer Hanoi*) launched a peasant revolt in 1968 in which they were joined by a number of Cambodian communists who had remained as members of Prince Sihanouk's Popular Socialist Community, including Khieu Samphan.

Following the overthrow of Prince Sihanouk's neutralist regime by rightists in 1970 the CPK supported the Prince's Royal Government of National Union of Cambodia (GRUNC) and formed with him the National United Front of Cambodia (FUNC). In 1973 Pol Pot began to purge the CPK of pro-Vietnamese elements, and when in April 1975 GRUNC forces finally gained control of the whole of Cambodia, the dominant political organization in the country was a pro-Chinese, anti-Vietnamese CPK, whose members were drawn entirely from Pol Pot's supporters. However, it was not until September 1977 that it was officially disclosed that the ruling organization in Democratic Kampuchea (as the country had been renamed under its new January 1976 Constitution) was the CPK led by Pol Pot.

In May 1978 the first vice-chairman of the State Presidium, So Phim, reportedly launched a revolt in the south-eastern provinces against the Pol Pot regime and in December the pro-Vietnamese Kampuchean National United Front for National Construction and Defence (KNUFNCD) was formed in the "liberated" eastern zones and began working towards the overthrow of the ruling regime. The KNUFNCD leader, Heng Samrin (a CPK official), took effective control of the country when, with the aid of Vietnamese forces, the Pol Pot government was overthrown in January 1979. A CPK "reorganization" congress was immediately held by the new leadership and it was decided to revert to the name of Kampuchean People's Revolutionary Party (KPRP) to distinguish it from Pol Pot's party. The Pol Pot government had in 1979 transferred its headquarters to the Thai border, where it announced the formation of a Patriotic and Democratic Front of the Great National Union of Kampuchea, the purpose of which was to rally all elements opposed to the Vietnamese-backed KPRP regime. In the light of the creation of this Front, the CPK central committee announced on Dec. 6, 1981, that it had been decided at a party congress on Sept. 3-6, 1981, to dissolve the party "in order to conform with the new strategic line which does not pursue socialism and communism". However, Prince Sihanouk maintained a year later that the CPK still existed, with Pol Pot as general secretary. Following its alleged dissolution the CPK was referred to as the Party of Democratic Kampuchea, or as the Red Khmers (*Khmers Rouges,* or the Army of Democratic Kampuchea—see separate entry for a fuller development of post-1975 Kampuchean developments).

Red Khmers (*Khmers Rouges*)

Leadership. Khieu Samphan (president); Son Sen (vice-president and C.-in-C.)

The Red Khmers (Khmers being the people of Kampuchea and eastern Thailand) were set up in 1967 as the armed wing of the Communist Party of Kampuchea (CPK)—see separate entry—then led by Pol Pot (earlier known as Saloth Sar), which was the pro-Chinese (and anti-Soviet) faction of the original Kampuchean People's Revolutionary Party. In 1968 the Red Khmers began an armed struggle against the government of Prince Norodom Sihanouk, and by the end of that year they were active in 11 out of the country's 19 provinces, allegedly with the support of the *Viet Cong* (the communist armed forces of South Vietnam). When, after his deposition as head of state and the replacement of his government by the (right-wing) Lon Nol regime on March 18, 1970, Prince Norodom Sihanouk proclaimed in Beijing (China) on March 23 that he would form a Government of National Union, a National Liberation Army and a United National Front, three Red Khmer leaders—Khieu Samphan, Hon Youn and Hu Nim—stated on March 26 that they would give unreserved support to the Princes's proclamation.

During the ensuing month the Red Khmers supported the gradual penetration of Kampuchea by *Viet Cong* forces, which led to temporary US intervention in Kampuchea in May-June 1970 and to the proclamation of martial law on May 22.

A Royal Government of National Union, (GRUNC), which had been formed by Prince Norodom Sihanouk in exile in May 5, 1970, with the participation of three Red Khmers, was on Aug. 21, 1970, enlarged by new appointments which gave the Red Khmers a majority in it; in particular Khieu Samphan, until then Minister of Defence, became Deputy Premier.

During the civil war of 1970-75 between Marshal Lon Nol's forces and the supporters of Prince Norodom Sihanouk, the Red Khmers were said to number only about 3,000 (out of a total of 65,000 pro-

Sihanouk troops, of whom 50,000 were North Vietnamese). Following the conclusion of a peace agreement in January 1973 between the United States, North and South Vietnam and the Provisional Revolutionary Government of South Vietnam, Prince Norodom Sihanouk criticized the Red Khmers in October 1973, alleging that they were reducing their military action in order not to provoke the United States to intervene again in Indo-China.

In November 1973 most of the ministries of the Royal Government were transferred from Beijing to Kampuchea, of which Sihanoukists claimed to "control 90 per cent". On April 17, 1975, the civil war ended with the occupation of Phnom-Penh by pro-Sihanouk forces. The Red Khmers thereupon assumed power, with Prince Norodom Sihanouk remaining head of state as "a symbol of national unity" (despite his disagreements with the Red Khmers) until April 1976, when he resigned and was succeeded as head of state by Khieu Samphan, and a new government was formed under Pol Pot, with Ieng Sary as Deputy Premier and Foreign Minister. The CPK thereupon carried out the most radical communist policy programme ever implemented anywhere, involving the forcible removal of the country's urban population to the rural areas and mass execution of alleged reactionaries.

In 1976-77 a number of dissident Red Khmer leaders were alleged to have been involved in a conspiracy, inspired by Vietnam, against Pol Pot and his pro-Chinese policy; the pro-Vietnamese elements were, however, said to have been eliminated in the early months of 1977, many of them by execution. From 1977 onwards Vietnamese forces invaded Kampuchea, and Kampuchean counter-attacks were made into Vietnam in 1978. Vietnamese proposals for a peace settlement were rejected by the Pol Pot regime in Kampuchea which claimed (on April 12, 1978) that Vietnam had since 1975 "conducted subversion and infiltration and interfered in Kampuchea's internal affairs" and also "prepared to stage a coup d'état in order to topple Democratic Kampuchea". In a note of May 15 Kampuchea demanded inter alia that Vietnam should "abandom definitively the strategy aimed at putting Kampuchea under the domination of Vietnam in an 'Indo-China federation'".

In May 1978 So Phim, the first vice-chairman of the State Presidium, reportedly launched a revolt in the south-east aided by other high-level officials (the majority of whom were arrested and executed, as was So Phim).

While conflicting reports appeared in June-August 1978 about further fighting between Vietnamese and Red Khmer forces, Vietnam suggested that Chinese military aid to Kampuchea was responsible for the war, and Hanoi stated on June 21: "On the orders of a foreign country Pol Pot and Ieng Sary have murdered the Kampuchean people."

Eventually the Red Khmer regime of Pol Pot was defeated by the Vietnamese-backed forces of the supporters of the pro-Vietnamese communists, who had formed a Kampuchean National United Front for National Salvation in December 1978, and who assumed power in January 1979, establishing the People's Republic of Kampuchea (PRK).

The new regime was recognized by the members of the Soviet bloc and a number of non-aligned countries but the Red Khmers, although no longer in control of any substantial part of the country and strongly criticized for their violation of human rights while in power, continued to be recognized as the legitimate rulers of Kampuchea by the vast majority of UN member countries on the basis of the principle of non-intervention in the affairs of another state—a principle said to have been violated by Vietnam's action in invading Kampuchea.

Prince Norodom Sihanouk stated in Beijing (where he was living in exile) on Jan. 8, 1979, that he strongly condemned both the Vietnamese invasion and Pol Pot's internal policy; that he nevertheless regarded Pol Pot as the "legal leader of Democratic Kampuchea" and that he had agreed to represent Kampuchea at the United Nations. On Jan. 20, 1979, he revealed that he had refused an invitation from the PRK government to become President of the PRK, but on March 19 he stated that he would no longer represent Pol Pot's government. He had earlier proposed that Kampuchea's fate should be decided at a Geneva conference leading to a ceasefire, and general elections open to all Kampuchean parties.

Inside Kampuchea Red Khmer forces continued to resist the Vietnamese army. According to their radio station (believed to broadcast from southern China), "The Voice of Democratic Kampuchea" (VODK), a national conference attended by 400 leaders on Feb. 1-2, 1979, had adopted a policy of "harassment, hit-and-run and attrition" to be used against the Vietnamese forces; while fighting took place in January-April 1979 there was reported to be widespread hostility against the Red Khmers, who were accused of committing several massacres. On April 5 it was claimed by the Vietnam News Agency that Pol Pot's headquarters at Ta Sanh (about 10 miles from the frontier) had been captured in a four-day battle, in which 1,000 of the defenders had been killed or taken prisoner.

In the fighting during 1979 the Red Khmer forces were generally forced to retreat, often into Thailand. Prince Norodom Sihanouk estimated on Nov. 27, 1979, that 60 per cent of Kampuchea was under Vietnamese control, and the remaining 40 per cent either under Red Khmer or Free Khmer control or a no man's land. Among the numerous refugees who entered Thailand, reaching a total of 130,000 by May 1979, the Red Khmers exercised a certain amount of control and attempted to compel refugees to re-enter Kampuchea and to join the Red Khmer forces.

In Phnom Penh a "people's revolutionary tribunal" on Aug. 19, 1979, sentenced Pol Pot and Ieng Sary to death in absentia on charges concerning a long list of crimes, among them mass killings, displacement of the population (over 2,000,000 from Phnom Penh alone on April 17, 1975), repression and coercion to work, the abolition of all social relationships, religion and culture, ill-treatment of children and the use of terrorism. The PRK Foreign Minister called on China (on Oct. 4) to cease all protection, shelter and support for Pol Pot and Ieng Sary, as required by the 1948 Convention on Genocide.

Ieng Sary, however, declared in an interview (published in *Le Monde* of Paris on June 1, 1979) that the Red Khmer government was prepared to collaborate with Prince Norodom Sihanouk, the Free Khmers and Marshal Lon Nol in order to establish an independent, united and non-aligned Kampuchea; that even the government of the PRK could join the national community if it ceased to collaborate with Vietnam; that the Communist Party (the CPK) was prepared to step aside and to accept "a mixed economy and the existence of a bourgeoisie".

On Sept. 6, 1979, the Red Khmers "ambassador" in Beijing released the draft political programme of a "Patriotic and Democratic Front of the Great National Union of Kampuchea" to be formed by the Red Khmers. The aim of this new organization included the explusion of the Vietnamese from Kampuchea, the overthrow of the PRK government, the establishment of freedom of speech and the press, freedom to choose one's residence and religious freedom, of a National Assembly to be chosen in free elections under UN supervision, and the formation of a government of representatives of all organizations, strata and individuals opposed to the Vietnamese; and an economy based on "individual or family productive activity" with private property being guaranteed and a national currency being re-introduced (the use of money having been abolished under the Pol Pot regime).

A joint congress of the Standing Committee of a "Kampuchean People's Representative Assembly", the Red Khmer government and representatives of the Red Khmer forces and government ministries held in the Cardamom Mountains (west of Phnom Penh) on Dec. 15-17, 1979, adopted the political programme of the Patriotic and Democratic Front (see above) and elected Khieu Samphan as chairman of the Front and as Prime Minister, and he formed a partly reconstructed government (with Pol Pot, the outgoing Prime Minister, being appointed C.-in-C. of the armed forces).

Khieu Samphan and Ieng Sary admitted on Feb. 27 and March 2, 1980, that the Pol Pot regime had committed political errors, and they called for national independence and free elections under UN supervision as the Red Khmers' prime objectives. Huang Hua, then Foreign Minister of the People's Republic of China, declared on March 19, 1980, that China would continue to give "full armed support" to the Red Khmers.

Fighting between Vietnamese and PRK troops on the one hand and Red Khmers (and Free Khmers) on the other continued in the first half of 1980, mainly near the border with Thailand, with the PRK government accusing the Thai government on Feb. 26 of allowing the Red Khmers and Free Khmers to use its territory as a sanctuary. The Red Khmer forces were believed to number between 20,000 and 35,000 men (of whom 15,000 were operating in the western provinces of Battambang, Pursat and Koh Kong, and the rest elsewhere in small guerrilla groups), facing (according to a Red Khmer statement of July 16, 1979) 180,000 Vietnamese and 20,000 PRK troops, as well as some Laotian troops in the northern provinces.

In the second half of 1980 the Red Khmers continued their guerrilla activities in various areas but according to *The New York Times* of Nov. 25, 1980, the Pol Pot forces controlled only enclaves in formerly uninhabited areas and the Vietnamese occupation troops controlled "all of populated Kampuchea". Mutual accusations of border-violations continued to be made by the PRK and Thai governments.

At the United Nations, however, the General Assembly rejected, on Oct. 14, 1980, by 74 votes to 35 with 32 abstentions, a proposal not to recognize the credentials of the Red Khmers' delegation. On Oct. 22 the General Assembly approved, by 97 votes to 23 with 22 abstentions, a call (by members of the Association of South East Asian Nations—ASEAN—viz. Indonesia, Malaysia, the Philippines, Singapore and Thailand) for an international conference in 1981 to bring about the complete withdrawal of Vietnamese forces from Kampuchea and free elections under UN supervision.

In 1981 the UN General Assembly again approved the Red Khmer delegation's credentials (on Sept. 18 by 77 votes to 37 with 17 abstentions). Ieng Sary (the Deputy Premier and Foreign Minister of the Red Khmer's government) said in Jakarta (Indonesia) on Nov. 23, 1980, that his government was willing to let Prince Norodom Sihanouk play a more active role and exercise more power if he accepted that the top priority was the expulsion of the Vietnamese. Ieng Sary also said that his government was ready to associate itself with Son Sann (of the Khmer People's National Liberation Front—see separate entry) on the same condition.

During 1981 the Red Khmers continued their guerrilla warfare but from October onwards they were less successful than before, with the Red Khmers' forces having fallen to about 25,000 and increasing numbers having surrendered—even though they had reportedly received large arms supplies from China through Thailand.

While defectors from the Red Khmers to the PRK were promised employment and full political rights by the government in Phnom Penh, and rewards were offered to those who eliminated their commanders, destroyed their bases or brought back weapons and equipment, or persons who had been kidnapped, others were given prison sentences on various occasions.

In early 1982 the Red Khmers succeeded in retaining a stronghold along the southern part of Kampuchea's border with Thailand, despite massive Vietnamese attacks in the Phnom Malai mountain area. The VODK radio claimed on May 12 that during the current dry season Red Khmer forces had killed or put out of action 21,958 Vietnamese troops, and destroyed 19 Vietnamese tanks, 168 transport vehicles, 50 boats and two aircraft. A Thai officer, on the other hand, estimated that during the current Vietnamese offensive each side had suffered between 100 and 1,000 casualties. On June 27 Red Khmer guerrillas claimed to have killed 20 Soviet advisers and technicians in the Kampong Sila district (as announced by the VODK). (In October 1980 they had claimed to have killed 25 Soviet officials in the same area.)

After protracted negotiations a coalition agreement was signed in Kuala Lumpur (Malaysia) on June 22, 1982, by Khieu Samphan (as Prime Minister of the Red Khmer "government"), Prince Norodom Sihanouk (as leader of the *Moulinaka* movement) and Son Sann (leader of the Khmer People's National Liberation Front, the strongest Free Khmer grouping—see separate entry for Coalition Government of Democratic Kampuchea—CGDK—for Red Khmer involvement in this anti-Vietnamese tripartite organization).

Non-communist Movements

Free Khmers (*Khmers Serei*)

Leadership. (1970) Son Ngoc Thanh (l.); (1979) Van Saren (l.)

The term *Khmers Serei* has been used for a number of different groups of non-communist organizations in Kampuchea. Originally Free Khmers were recruited from among the Kampuchean community in South Vietnam, and these carried out raids (in 1965-67) into Kampuchea then under the neutralist government of Prince Norodom Sihanouk, which the government of South Vietnam accused of allowing (communist) *Viet Cong* forces to operate from bases inside Kampuchean territory. Many Free Khmers were arrested, and their leaders went into exile in Thailand. However, after the overthrow of Prince Norodom Sihanouk in 1970, the arrested Free Khmers were released, and on May 16, 1970, it was announced that the Free Khmers had rallied to the support of the (right-wing) government of Gen. Lon Nol. Son Ngoc Thanh—who had been head of a puppet government of Cambodia under Japanese occupation in World War II and had in 1959 been sentenced to death in absentia for involvement in an anti-government conspiracy—returned from exile in Thailand in 1970, when he was appointed (on March 18) Prime Minister under the Lon Nol regime.

After the overthrow of that regime in 1975, Free Khmers fighting against the Red Khmer government were active in the areas on the border with Thailand, conducting raids into Kampuchea and smuggling wealthy Kampucheans out of the country.

In 1979 the term *Khmers Serei* was applied to several movements (for some of which see separate entries) opposed to both the Vietnamese and the Red Khmers—(i) the Khmer People's National Liberation Armed Forces formed in March 1979 by Gen. Dien Del (a former army officer under the Lon Nol regime), claiming to command over 2,000 men; (ii) the Khmer People's National Liberation Front (KPNLF) led by Son Sann; (iii) the National Liberation Movement of Kampuchea (*Moulinaka*) led by Prince Norodom Sihanouk; (iv) the "Liberation National Government of Kampuchea" formed on Oct. 3, 1979, with Van Saren as "Prime Minister"; and (v) the National Liberation Movement led by In Sakhan. The total strength of these groups was believed to be not more than 6,000 men, who were said to observe an informal truce with the Red Khmers, with many of them being compelled to retreat into Thailand.

Between December 1979 and July 1980 fighting occurred between rival Free Khmer groups, in disagreement partly over their attitude to the Red Khmers and partly over the distribution of food supplied by international relief organizations.

The "Liberation National Government" of Van Saren was reported to be selling such food in Thailand and Kampuchea. There were clashes between Van Saren's followers, the *Moulinaka*, the National Liberation Movement of In Sakhan, and a *Khmer Serei* group led by Mitr Don, who had been a lieutenant of Van Saren. The last-named, however, fled to Thailand in April 1980, after his camp had been destroyed by Red Khmer forces collaborating with breakaway Free Khmer guerrillas.

Khmer Serei forces located in a camp at Non Makmora (the site of which was variously described as being in Thailand, as straddling the border and as being in Kampuchea) were attacked on June 23-24, 1980, by Vietnamese forces and PRK troops who also raided another *Khmer Serei* camp. In Thailand it was claimed that Thai forces had repulsed the Vietnamese on June 24. (The incident was followed by a strong public condemnation of Vietnam's "act of aggression" at a meeting of Foreign Ministers of the Association of South-East Asian Nations—ASEAN—i.e. Indonesia, Malaysia, the Philippines, Singapore and Thailand, who reaffirmed their continued recognition of the "Democratic Kampuchean Government" of the Red Khmers, and also by a US decision to accelerate the delivery of military equipment to Thailand.)

(For Free Khmer participation in the coalition agreement of anti-PRK forces signed in June 1982, see separate entry for Coalition Government of Democratic Kampuchea.)

Khmer People's National Liberation Front (KPNLF)

Leadership. Son Sann (pres.)

The KPNLF was established in France in March 1979 (and was formally established in Kampuchea in October 1979) as a democratic and non-communist movement with the object of uniting all non-communist resistance to the Vietnamese-backed regime in Phnom Penh. Initially it condemned the Red Khmers (see separate entry) and demanded that the Red Khmer leaders should go into exile and that the KPNLF should have a majority in an anti-Vietnamese coalition government. Son Sann, who had been Prime Minister under Prince Norodom Sihanouk in 1967, stated on Sept. 9, 1980, that the Front would fight the Vietnamese separately on condition that the Red Khmers would not attack KPNLF forces or their supply routes. By 1981 the Front claimed to control 9,000 armed men (although other estimates ranged from 3,000 to 6,000) and to have received arms from China. The KPNLF was also equipped with US-made weapons (believed to have come from the Thai army). Press reports in November 1982 alleged that Singapore had provided military assistance to the KPNLF; Phnom Penh radio on Nov. 24, 1982, described two reported shipments of 2,700 and 1,600 AKM47 rifles as a "dangerous and unfriendly act".

During the early part of 1982 the forces of the KPNLF were temporarily dislodged from their strongholds near the Thai border but by June 1982 they were re-establishing themselves in that area.

The heaviest fighting between Vietnamese and People's Republic of Kampuchea (PRK) forces on the one hand and forces supporting the Coalition Government of Democratic Kampuchea (CGDK—see separate entry) on the other since the Vietnamese invasion of Kampuchea in 1979 occurred between December 1982 and April 1983. KPNLF guerrillas launched an offensive in the second half of December 1982, seizing two villages near the Thai border on Dec. 26. In a counter-offensive in January 1983, Vietnamese-PRK forces reoccupied the villages and on Jan. 31 proceeded to attack the KPLNF camp at Nong Chan (also known as Prey Chan), 35 km north-east of Aranyaprathet, forcing some 20,000 refugees who lived there to flee into Thailand.

Further attacks on KPLNF encampments occurred in early 1984; in April heavy fighting took place around Front bases at Sok Sann and Nong Chan. On April 15 combined Vietnamese and PRK forces launched a major offensive against the KPNLF headquarters at Ampil. In the attack about 2,000 troops, supported by tanks and artillery, overran the forward defence lines of the KPNLF encampment, but the KPNLF forces counter-attacked on the following days and held their positions, despite intensive artillery bombardment. Early rains forced the Vietnamese-PRK forces to halt their Ampil offensive on April 24. Son Sann described the successful defence of Ampil by his forces as "a major political victory" that proved the Front to be a "credible force"; he said that he would be seeking more arms and ammunition from China, to equip his forces, which he said numbered 20,000, of whom 7,000 were currently unarmed.

The 1984-85 dry-season offensive against the CGDK forces was the heaviest undertaken by the combined Vietnamese-PRK forces; by March 1985 most of the main CGDK bases along the Thai-Kampuchea border had been overrun. The initial (predominently) Vietnamese thrust occurred on Nov. 18, 1984 when between 1,500 and 2,000 troops attacked the KPNLF camp at Nong Chan. Some 4,000 guerrillas fiercely defended the camp and on Dec. 5 CGDK and Thai officials announced that the camp was entirely under KPNLF control, sections of it having previously fallen to the invading troops. It was not until April 7, 1985, that the KPNLF was driven out of the entire camp by Vietnamese forces. Two more KPNLF camps at Baksei and Sok Sann were overrun on Dec. 9 and 12, and on Dec. 25, some 60,000 civilians fled into Thailand when Vietnamese forces overran the KPNLF's border-camp at Nong Samet (also known as Rithisen). According to Thai officials the Vietnamese capture of Nong Samet took only a few hours and resulted in the death of 55 guerrillas and 63 civilians (a claim disputed by the KPNLF, who stated that only ten of their men had been killed). On Jan. 7, 1985, over 3,500 Vietnamese troops (supported by tanks) breached the Front's defences at Ampil. Heavy fighting ensued, but on Jan. 8, KPNLF forces were ordered to withdraw in order to avoid further casualties. Son Sann had earlier visited the camp to check preparations for the onslaught and see that the civilian population of 23,000 had been evacuated to Thailand.

On Jan. 11, 1985, Son Sann announced that he had ordered his troops to abandon attempts to recapture bases lost to the Vietnamese. He admitted that the Front was not strong enough to fight a conventional war against "the third strongest army in the world". Instead of trying to defend fixed bases, Son Sann said, his forces would adopt guerrilla tactics (in the style of the Red Khmers) and strike at internal PRK targets.

Dissension within the KPNLF became public on Aug. 22, 1985, when Hing Kuthon and Abdul Gaffar Peang Meth were dismissed from its executive committee. By mid-October reports suggested that Gen. Sak Sutsakhan and Gen. Dien Del (described, respectively, as the Front's C.-in-C. and General Chief of Staff) had both sided with the deposed members, criticizing aspects of Son Sann's leadership. A press report on Dec. 20 stated that the rebels, led by Gen. Sak, had formed a Provincial Central Committee for the Salvation of the KPNLF (KPNLF-PCCS). This group announced on Jan. 2, 1986, that it had established an eight-member ruling committee (headed by Gen. Sak) and claimed to be in control of the Front's civilian and military administration. Thai officials allegedly warned Son Sann that a planned visit to a KPNLF camp in early 1986 would be inappropriate, a decision widely regarded as tacit recognition of the KPNLF-PCCS as the Front's leadership. Prince Sihanouk, on the other hand, reportedly urged loyalty to Son Sann. On Feb. 19 Son Sann claimed that he had dismissed Gen. Sak and Gen. Dien from all command positions and had formed an alternative "command committee". By mid-April it appeared that Son Sann had maintained overall charge of the Front, but that military leaders had been given increased autonomy over their operations. However, a report in late August 1986 stated that Son Sann had recently told ASEAN officials of his decision not to take part in the political work of the CGDK whilst the division within the KPNLF was unsolved. A further report in October said that ASEAN had recently turned down a request by Son Sann for weapons to create a new guerrilla unit.

The "Voice of the Khmers" radio station (*Samleng Khmer*—a joint KPNLF-Sihanoukist radio station formed in January 1984) reported on Jan. 20, 1987, that Son San and Gen. Sak had decided to "restore unity" and "re-establish order" within the KPNLF. Prior to this announcement, in November 1986, it was reported that KPNLF forces which were then thought to number some 18,000, with perhaps an extra 5,000 unarmed reserves) were soon to be equipped with anti-aircraft missiles. The report did not reveal which country had agreed to provide the weapons, but China was the main arms supplier to the CGDK.

National Liberation Movement of Kampuchea (*Moulinaka*)

Leadership. Prince Norodom Sihanouk (l.)

This movement was established in August 1979 by Kong Sileah (a supporter of Prince Sihanouk) who brought together small bands of Free Khmers (see separate entry). In 1980 *Moulinaka* units (who by this time were probably under the overall leadership of Prince Sihanouk) were involved in clashes with Free Khmers led by Van Saren. After the death of Kong Sileah on Aug. 16, 1980, *Moulinaka* agreed to co-operate with the Khmer People's National Liberation Front (KPNLF) of Son Sann. Prince Sihanouk held talks with the Chinese Prime Minister, Zhao Ziyang, in Beijing on Jan. 31, 1983, and announced on Feb. 7 that China had agreed to supply *Moulinaka* with more ammunition, but no weapons.

As part of their offensive on rebel bases situated on the Thai border, Vietnamese and PRK troops attacked and captured the *Moulinaka* headquarters at O Smach on April 4, 1983. Thereafter the *Moulinaka* forces established a camp at Tatum (also known as Green Hill) which was later described as the headquarters of the Sihanoukist National Army (ANS).

Duong Khem, a "military commander" of *Moulinaka* and a former Vice-President, said in August 1983 that the movement currently consisted of 1,470 armed men and 3,000 "ready to be armed". *Moulinaka*, he said, remained faithful to Prince Sihanouk and the ANS; relations with the KPNLF and the Red Khmers were described as good. Sihanoukist forces, he said, also enjoyed good relations with the PRK armed forces, many of whom remained deeply faithful to Prince Sihanouk.

Sihanoukist National Army (*Armée nationale sihanoukiste*, ANS)

Leadership. Prince Norodom Sihanouk (l.); Prince Norodom Rannariddh (c.-in-c.)

This non-communist army is the main force of Prince Norodom Sihanouk, the other force being the National Liberation Movement of Kampuchea (*Moulinaka*—see separate entry), whose members appear to have joined the ANS at some time during the 1980s. Both organizations are often referred to by the general term "Sihanoukists". The ANS is also generally regarded as the armed forces of Prince Sihanouk's own political party (National United Front for an Independent National, Peaceful and Co-operative Kampuchea—FUNCINPEC), the formation of which he announced in March 1982 as an apparent successor organization to the Prince's Confederation of Khmer Nationalists. Prince Sihanouk's own forces are part of the tripartite anti-Vietnamese coalition (the Coalition Government of Democratic Kampuchea, CGDK—see separate entry) formed in June 1982, with Sihanouk as its president.

The ANS headquarters at Tatum (also known as Green Hill), situated on an escarpment across the border from the Thai province of Surin, was overrun by Vietnamese troops on March 11, 1985. The camp, which had been defended by 3,000 guerrillas, was the final guerrilla base of the CGDK to fall during the successful 1984-85 dry season offensive launched by Vietnamese and PRK forces in mid-November 1984. A spokesman for Prince Sihanouk described the ANS retreat from Tatum as a "strategic withdrawal" and a son of Prince Sihanouk, Prince Norodom Rannariddh, added that the ANS would henceforth wage guerrilla warfare inside Kampuchea.

In January 1987 the ANS claimed to have over 12,000 fighters, 9,500 of whom were armed. They were said to be largely concentrated in two Kampuchean operation zones.

Kenya

Capital: Nairobi Pop. 19,536,000

The Republic of Kenya, an independent state within the Commonwealth, has an executive President who serves a (renewable) five-year term and is nominated by the Kenya African National Union (KANU), the country's sole legal political party; unless he is the sole candidate he is elected by popular vote. He appoints, and presides over, a Cabinet, and there is also a Vice-President. The unicameral National Assembly consists of 158 members elected for five years by universal adult suffrage and of 12 further members nominated by the President.

In elections to the 158 elective seats of the Assembly held on Sept. 26, 1983, only five members of the outgoing Assembly were returned unopposed, and five Cabinet ministers, 12 assistant ministers and about 40 per cent of the members of the previous Assembly were defeated, while the turn-out was estimated at only about 40 per cent.

The government has repeatedly acted against those whom it has described as "dissidents", in particular against students who in May 1982 issued a statement claiming that Kenya was still legally a multi-party state. President Daniel arap Moi alleged on June 6, 1982, that students had plotted to obtain guns "from outside sources, including certain neighbouring countries", and he also attacked lecturers who, he said, were "teaching subversive literature" aimed at creating disorder in the country.

President Moi announced on Dec. 12, 1983, that Kenya would henceforth refuse to harbour political fugitives from Tanzania and Uganda and would not tolerate movements directed against Kenya's neighbours.

With effect from Jan. 1, 1985, all Kenyan civil servants were required to be KANU members, and the government was to employ only KANU members.

According to Amnesty International in July 1987 a crackdown which began in March 1986 had resulted in the arrest of several hundred political suspects, with reports of torture and prolonged detention without habeas corpus. Many of those arrested were suspected of having links with the *Mwakenya* movement (see below). At least two prisoners were said to have died in custody. In June 1987, however, President Moi stated that there had been no incident of torture and that "we are the freest country in Africa". Several hundred foreigners said to be illegal aliens were expelled in March 1987 after President Moi accused them of causing unrest. Among those arrested were several members of Parliament.

December 12 Movement

This Movement made its appearance with the publication of a pamphlet called *Pambana* (*Struggle*) in February 1982. (Dec. 12 was the date of Kenya's attainment of independence in 1963.) In this pamphlet the Movement criticized "high-level corruption" and foreign influence on Kenya's economy and politics.

Pambana pamphlets were again distributed in Nairobi in 1984, calling for "guerrilla war" in protest against corruption and denial of human rights in Kenya.

According to some reports the December 12 Movement was the forerunner of *Mwakenya* (see separate entry).

Iriria

The *Kenya Times*, the organ of KANU, reported on March 26, 1984, that this foreign-backed political movement was responsible for "violence and banditry" in the Wajir district of north-eastern Kenya where the Ajuran and Degodia tribes had been in armed conflict. The existence of this movement was, however, denied by local leaders.

Kenya People's Redemption Council

This Council was, according to Nairobi University students, an organization of members of the Kenyan air force who attempted to carry out a "1st August Revolution" in 1982 to overthrow the government of President arap Moi—this attempt being foiled by loyal sections of the armed forces. The air force rebels had stated that their aim was to end corruption and mismanagement and to respond to a call by the people "to liberate the country". They announced that the Constitution had been suspended, that a "National Liberation Council" had been set up and that all political prisoners were declared free. They also stated that it was "not the intention of the military to stay in power indefinitely".

The attempt, which was accompanied by widespread looting, was rapidly suppressed, although some rebel members of the air force were not apprehended until September 1982. The air force itself was officially disbanded in order to be replaced by a new one. Nairobi University was closed down and President Moi announced on Oct. 20 that it would be restructured before it was reopened. According to a government statement made early in September, 160 people had died as a result of the attempted coup.

During trials of over 700 air force members by a special court-martial it emerged that the plotters' organization had been infiltrated by an agent of the security services' special branch, and that Maj.-Gen. Peter Kàriuki, who had been commander of the air force at the time of the attempted coup, had been given prior warning of it; on Jan. 18, 1983, he was sentenced to four years in prison for having failed to prevent the attempt. While some of those tried were merely dismissed from the air force, many others were given prison sentences of up to 25 years and 11 former air force members were condemned to death (between Nov. 24, 1982, and March 9, 1983), although no executions were carried out. President Moi announced on Feb. 22, 1983, that of those arrested 412 former servicemen and 61 university students had been pardoned and would be released.

In March 1984 two alleged leaders of the Council, repatriated from Kenya in an exchange of prisoners in November 1983, were sentenced to death. In April 1984 another 10 former members of the Kenyan air force were sentenced to death for treason, and in May a corporal was given a 20-year sentence for mutiny in connexion with the attempted coup. The two sentenced to death in March 1984 were hanged on July 9, 1985, together with nine others sentenced to death by April 1983 and also a private sentenced in April 1984.

A judicial commission of inquiry set up in July 1983 to examine allegations of irregular actions by Charles Njonjo, then Minister of Constitutional Affairs, completed its hearing on Aug. 27, 1984. President Moi stated on Dec. 12, 1984, that the commission's findings had confirmed most of the allegations, which included the contention that C. Njonjo had been linked with the attempted air force coup of August 1982. He had been suspended from his ministerial post on June 29, 1983, had resigned from Parliament on the following day, was suspended from KANU on July 7, 1983, and finally expelled from the party, with 14 other leading members, in September 1984. President Moi stated on Dec. 12, 1984, that as a gesture of conciliation C. Njonjo was to be pardoned. The President also announced that (as part of an amnesty) four political detainees held without trial since 1982 would be released, while another 11 remained in detention.

Movement for Unity and Democracy in Kenya (*Umoja wa Kupigania Demokrasia Kenya*, UKENYA)

Leadership. Yusuf Hassan (ch.)

Founded. Feb. 18, 1987

At the founding of UKENYA in London Y. Hassan said that, unlike the clandestine *Mwakenya* movement, UKENYA was an overt organization; that its establishment was the result of "many years of repression from the hands of the unjust KANU regime of Kenyatta and Moi"; that since February 1986 hundreds of Kenyans had been arrested for calling for democracy; that some had been sentenced to long terms of imprisonment or were detained without trial; that others had been intimidated, harassed and tortured; that others had been deprived of their citizenship; and that many had fled into exile.

UKENYA's political orientation was described by Y. Hassan as being directed against neo-colonialism (i.e. the control of Kenya's industries by foreign companies), against the presence of British and US armed forces in Kenya, and in favour of the creation of a national democratic society and a national independent culture reflecting the diversity of the nationalities of Kenya.

Amnesty International in April 1987 denied Kenyan government allegations that it had funded UKENYA.

Northern Frontier District Liberation Front (NFDLF)

This organization sought independence for Kenya's North-Eastern Province, where the majority of the inhabitants were said to be of Somali origin. It had its headquarters in Mogadishu, the capital of Somalia, whose government had repeatedly reaffirmed that it had no territorial claims against Kenya, but nevertheless supported the NFDLF in the expectation that an independent Northern District state might eventually opt for union with Somalia.

After Kenyan security forces had for years been engaged in clashes with armed Somali *shifta* (bandits), an amnesty announced in Kenya in December 1983 resulted in the return to Kenya of hundreds of NFDLF members who had lived in voluntary exile in Somalia. In September 1984 returning exiles announced that the NFDLF headquarters in Mogadishu had been closed.

Union of Nationalists to Liberate Kenya (or "Belonging to Kenya", *Mwakenya*)

Founded. 1981

This clandestine anti-government movement began in 1984 to recruit members, mainly among university teachers and students, with the alleged objective of creating a communist or socialist party.

When serious student unrest occurred in February-March 1986 the government attributed it to "outside agitators" and temporarily closed two universities in Nairobi. On April 29, 1986, a former chairman of the Nairobi University students' organization was sentenced to five years' imprisonment for possessing a copy of *Mpatanishi* (*The Arbiter*), which was described as a seditious publication, while a university teacher was given a four-year sentence for attending a fund-raising meeting in aid of *Mwakenya*. In the eight weeks to May 16, 1986, prison sentences for sedition, ranging from 10 months to six years, were passed on 17 persons, mostly graduates and lecturers, and some 30 other people were detained between May 6 and 16, among them three senior lecturers at Nairobi University.

On Feb. 4, 1987, it was reported that a KANU district organizer had been sentenced to four years in prison after admitting that he had, on June 15, 1986, taken an unlawful oath binding him to *Mwakenya*, of which he was a member until Jan. 3, 1987. During his trial it was disclosed that other leading KANU members also had links with the *Mwakenya* movement.

During a trial on April 1, 1987, it was alleged that Oginga Odinga, a former Vice-President, had given money to the *Mwakenya* movement. (He had in 1966 founded the Kenya People's Union, which was banned in 1969; he subsequently joined KANU but was expelled from it in May 1982, as he was allegedly "about to launch a socialist opposition party", and he was held under house arrest from November 1982 until October 1983.)

It was reported on April 1987, that Andrew Kimani Ngumba, an MP and a former Assistant Minister, had been expelled from KANU because he had offered to lead *Mwakenya*. Ngumba had fled to Sweden.

Kiribati

Capital: Tarawa Pop. 60,000

Kiribati (previously the Gilbert Islands) became an independent republic within the Commonwealth on July 12, 1979, with an executive President heading a Cabinet, and a 39-member House of Assembly elected by universal adult suffrage for a four-year term (most recently in March 1987).

A dispute over the island of Banaba, whose inhabitants had in 1980 campaigned for the separation of Banaba from Kiribati or for self-government for the Banabans on Banaba, was settled in April 1982 by an agreement providing for compensation to be paid to the Banabans, with the island remaining part of Kiribati.

The first political party the Christian Democratic Party, was formed in September 1985 by opponents of the government's decision to extend fishing rights to the Soviet Union (this agreement being terminated in October 1986).

Democratic People's Republic of Korea

Capital: Pyongyang Pop. 20,380,000

The Democratic People's Republic of Korea (or North Korea) is, under its Constitution adopted on Dec. 27, 1972, "an independent socialist state" in which the working people exercise power through the Supreme People's Assembly, elected by universal adult suffrage, and also through people's assemblies at lower level. The Supreme People's Assembly elects the country's President, who convenes and presides over an Administrative Council (Cabinet). For elections to the Assembly a single official list of candidates is submitted by the Democratic Front for the Reunification of the Fatherland (i.e. of both North and South Korea), which consists of the country's leading party, the Korean Workers' Party (KWP) and also two small parties—the (religious) Chondoist Chongo (officially stated to comprise former Buddhist believers) and the Korean Social Democratic Party (known until January 1981 as the Korean Democratic Party), both formed in 1945. The general secretary of the KWP's Central Committee is also head of state and supreme commander of the armed forces.

In general elections to the Supreme People's Assembly held on Nov. 2, 1986, it was officially claimed that all votes had been cast for the 615 candidates on the sole official list.

Reports of Internal Dissent

A statement by the South Korean Defence Ministry, released on Nov. 17, 1986, suggested that President Kim had been assassinated in a power struggle within the ruling Korean Workers' Party several days earlier. It was claimed that North Korean loudspeakers positioned on the demilitarized zone which divides North from South Korea had broadcast the news, and that further broadcasts made during the night of Nov. 17-18 had suggested that Kim Chong Il had succeeded to the Presidency, whilst others stated that the Defence Minister, Vice-Marshal Oh Jin Wu, had seized power in an army coup. Although Kim Il Sung appeared in public on Nov. 18 to disprove the rumours of his death, the incident was widely interpreted either as an unsuccessful attempt on the life of the President or as further evidence of the discontent amongst elements of the armed forces concerning the succession of Kim Chong Il.

There are an unknown number of political prisoners in North Korea; some South Korean and US intelligence sources have claimed that this figure may be as high as 100,000.

Republic of Korea

Capital: Seoul Pop. 41,210,000

The Republic of Korea (South Korea) has under its Constitution (which was overwhelmingly approved in a referendum on Oct. 22, 1980, and came into effect on Oct. 27) a President elected for a single seven-year term by a 5,000-member electoral college itself elected by universal adult suffrage and a National Assembly (also elected by universal adult suffrage, but for four years). The President is empowered to take emergency measures only in time of armed conflict or a similar emergency, and such measures must be approved by the National Assembly; he can also dissolve the Assembly, with the Cabinet's approval, but not within the first year after the Assembly's election, and not twice for the same reason.

Under an electoral law there are 92 electoral districts, each returning two members, with no party being allowed to nominate more than one candidate in each district; the party winning the largest number of seats obtains a further 61 seats and 31 other seats are distributed, in proportion to the number of seats won, among other parties which win more than five seats. No party can therefore win more than 153 of the 276 seats in the Assembly; constitutional amendments require a two-thirds majority, i.e. approval by at least two parties. Under a Political Parties' Law parties which fail to win a seat or at least 2 per cent of the valid votes cast are dissolved.

As a result of elections held on Feb. 12, 1985, the distribution of seats in the National Assembly was: Democratic Justice Party 148, New Korea Democratic Party (NKDP) 67, Democratic Korea Party 35, Korea National Party 20, others two, independents four.

President Chun Doo Hwan acceded to power in September 1980 in the aftermath of the assassination of President Park Chung Hee in October 1979. Between 1983 and 1985 he pursued a policy of "national reconciliation" which included amnesties for several thousand prisoners, the gradual removal of decrees which banned leading opponents from engaging in political activities and the acceptance of political pluralism within carefully prescribed limits. Increasing militancy, particularly within the student population, however, focused upon the demand for wholesale constitutional reform and resulted in numerous violent clashes and arrests as the authorities sought to contain the growing opposition to Chun's regime.

In April 1986 President Chun agreed to amend the Constitution before the conclusion of his tenure of office (due in 1988) with the proviso that a consensus should be reached between government and opposition as to the nature of the reforms. Negotiations within the National Assembly began in mid-1986 but failed to resolve outstanding differences. In response to growing dissension within the NKDP, Chun announced on April 13, 1987, that no constitutional change would be implemented prior to the Olympic games scheduled to be held in Seoul in mid-1988. Under the continuing pressure of opposition protest, however, this decision was effectively reversed at the end of June 1987 and proposals for major reforms were outlined.

The continuing division of Korea and the existence since 1946 of a communist regime in North Korea have made successive South Korean governments very sensitive to the threat of internal communist subversion. Although an Anti-Communist Law of July 1961 was revoked in December 1980, many of its provisions were incorporated in an amended National Security Law providing inter alia for increased penalities for forming or joining "anti-state organizations" and for a minimum of two years' imprisonment for the circulation of "groundless rumours" by members of such organizations. Meeting or communicating with persons in "non-hostile" communist countries ceased to be an offence, however, this change being intended to facilitate trade with East European countries.

Korean Christian Action Organization

This inter-denominational body has been prominent in a growth of anti-US sentiments among a small but growing minority of the population, arising mainly from a belief that US support for President Chun constitutes an obstacle to the development of democracy in South Korea. In a statement issued on April 15, 1982, the Organization called for the withdrawal of the US ambassador, Richard Walker, who was said to have described student demonstrators as "spoiled brats" (although he claimed to have been misquoted), and also of Gen. John A. Wickham, then commander of the UN forces in Korea (i.e. head of the combined US-South Korean Command). Gen. Wickham, who was regarded as a strong supporter of President Chun, had incurred opposition criticism for releasing regiments under his command for security work at the time of the Kwangju rising in May 1980 (see separate entry for Kwangju Citizens' Committee) and for a controversial suggestion in August 1980 that Koreans were not ready for democracy. (Gen. Wickham was replaced in June 1982.)

The issuing of the April 15 statement resulted in several leaders of the Korean Christian Action Organization being briefly detained, amid a wider sweep by the authorities against suspected dissidents arising from an arson attack on the US cultural centre in the southern port city of Pusan on March 18, 1982. After police investigations in late March in which several thousand people were detained for questioning, a total of 16 people were arrested and formally charged on April 29, including Father Choi Ki Shik, priest at a Roman Catholic centre at Wonju, who was accused of harbouring the principal suspects. Kim Hyong Jang, who was allegedly responsible for planning the operation, was said to have been staying at the Wonju centre since 1980; he was also wanted by the police in connexion with the Kwangju uprising. Two Protestant theology students charged with carrying out the Pusan attack, Moon Bu Shik and Miss Kim Un Suk, had apparently sought refuge afterwards at Wonju, although Father Choi was believed to have advised them in their subsequent decision to surrender to the authorities.

Whereas the government drew public attention to the role of the Christian churches in the Pusan arson case, leaders of both the Protestant and the Catholic communities contended that Father Choi had simply acted within the Christian tradition of providing refuge. Demonstrations held after a mass at Myongdong Cathedral in Seoul on April 26, 1982, were broken up by police, as were demonstrations in Kwangju on May 18. Calls made by Protestant leaders on this latter occasion for the resignation of President Chun were reiterated by the Catholic Council for Justice and Peace on June 4 and at student demonstrations during the same period.

Kim Hyong Jang and Moon Bu Shik were both sentenced to death on Aug. 11, 1982, for planning and implementing the Pusan arson attack, while Miss Kim was sentenced to life imprisonment, Father Choi to three years' imprisonment and the other 12 defendants to terms of between two years and life. During the trial several defendants alleged that evidence had been obtained from them under duress. However, the two death sentences were commuted to life imprisonment in March 1983.

Kwangju Citizens' Committee

Leadership. Mgr Yoon Kong Hie, Roman Catholic Archbishop of Kwangju (ch.)

This Committee, including religious leaders, professors and students, was formed to negotiate with the local martial law commander in Kwangju (the capital of South Cholla, a poor and over-populated province noted for the radicalism of its inhabitants) on the demand made by a mass movement which had erupted in a popular rising on May 19, 1980. This revolt had its origins in a student protest which had begun in March 1980 and had led to the extension of martial law throughout the country on May 17, the banning of all political activities and the arrest of many anti-government politicians.

The demands of the Committee submitted on May 22 were said to include the removal of the head of the Army Security Command, the lifting of martial law, the formation of an interim government led by democratic politicians, the release of all political detainees, freedom of the press, and full compensation for the families of those killed and wounded during the rising in Kwangju. (The Committee stated later that 261 dead bodies had been found, of which 100 had not been identified; according to an official statement of May 31 the casualties were 144 civilians, 27 soldiers and four policemen killed, and those arrested numbered 1,740 of whom 1,010 had been released.)

The negotiations between the Committee and the martial law commander were unsuccessful as the latter rejected all political demands. On May 27 tanks and infantry moved into Kwangju which had until then been occupied by the rebels whose number had risen to about 200,000 or a quarter of the city's population. The rising also spread to many other areas.

On Oct. 25, 1980, five alleged participants in the Kwangju revolt were sentenced to death, and the martial law authorities confirmed that seven other persons had been sentenced to life imprisonment and 163 to prison terms of from five to 20 years. However, under an amnesty of May 2 and another of May 11, 1981, all those connected with the Kwangju revolt were released from prison or had their sentences reduced.

National Liaison Organization for Democratization (NLOD)

The NLOD, which was formed in Seoul on March 17, 1986, is an alliance composed of the Consultative Committee for the Promotion of Democracy (see under New Korea Democratic Party—NKDP), the NKDP itself, the United People's Movement for Democracy and Unification (see separate entry), the National Council of Churches (which represents the country's six main Protestant denominations) and the Korean Catholic Council for Justice and Peace. The movement was established with the objective of hastening the pace of constitutional reform and, to this end, was responsible for the organization of a series of demonstrations.

New Korea Democratic Party (NKDP)

The New Korea Democratic Party, which was formed on Jan. 18, 1985, under the leadership of Le Min U, contained a number of prominent South Korean dissidents who had been banned from participating in political activities in 1980 but who had had their political rights restored in November 1984. The new party also included the Consultative Committee for the Promotion of Democracy (CCPD), a disparate group of opponents of the regime of President Chun Doo Hwan, which had been founded in 1984 under the joint chairmanship of South Korea's two leading dissidents Kim Young Sam and Kim Dae Jung.

Kim Young Sam, the leader of the New Democratic Party (NDP) until its dissolution in 1980, had been expelled from the National Assembly in October 1979 for allegedly engaging in subversive activities. On Nov. 12, 1980, he was one of 811 persons excluded from political activity under a recently passed special law. In May 1981 he was released from house arrest after a year but was rearrested in June 1982 and subjected to periods of detention thereafter.

Kim Dae Jung, who as candidate of the opposition New Democratic Party in the 1971 presidential election had been defeated by President Park Chung Hee, thereafter campaigned against President Park's regime in Japan and in the United States. On Aug. 8, 1973, he was abducted in Tokyo and taken to South Korea, where he was temporarily placed under house arrest.

Kim Dae Jung's kidnapping was also followed by a fusion of student and Christian protest movements against President Park's regime. He was a co-signatory of a declaration read at an ecumenical mass in Seoul's Roman Catholic cathedral on March 1, 1976, calling for the resignation of President Park and the restoration of democracy; on Aug. 28, 1976, he and three other signatories of the declaration were sentenced to eight years in prison (and 14 others to prison terms of between two and five years) for violating an emergency decree of May 1975. On appeal the sentences were reduced on Dec. 29, 1976—Kim Dae Jung's from eight to five years; on Dec. 19, 1977, he was transferred from prison to a hospital, and on Dec. 27, 1978, he and 105 other persons imprisoned under emergency decrees were released under an amnesty.

Although subsequently placed under house arrest, Kim Dae Jung issued, on Nov. 2, 1979 (after the assassination of President Park on Oct. 26), a statement calling for direct elections of a new President and National Assembly. Following the election of President Choi Kyu Hah on Dec. 6, 1979, Kim Dae Jung was released from house arrest on Dec. 8, and his political rights were restored on Feb. 29, 1980. However, under martial law imposed on Oct. 27, 1979, Kim Dae Jung and six others were arrested on May 18, 1980, for "inciting student and labour unrest", and on Sept. 17 of that year he was sentenced to death for plotting rebellion and violating various laws. He admitted that he had been associated with a left-wing movement in 1946, but denied ever having been a communist. He also admitted that he had founded (in the United States in 1973), in collaboration with North Korean sympathizers, a National Congress for the Restoration of Democracy and the Promotion of the Unification of Korea (*Hanmintong*) and for the formation of a similar organization in Japan to oppose "the dictatorial regime of Park Chung Hee" (which had, however, not been founded until after Kim's kidnapping in Japan); but he categorically denied having plotted to overthrow the government, advocated the use of violence or encouraged student demonstrations.

On appeal the death sentence passed on him, and prison sentences given to 16 other defendants, were upheld on Nov. 3, 1980. Although his further appeal against the death sentence was rejected by the Supreme Court on Jan. 23, 1981, the Cabinet later the same day commuted the sentence to life imprisonment, and under an amnesty of March 2, 1982 (which benefited 2,863 persons), his life sentence was reduced to 20 years in prison. On Dec. 16, 1982, he was released from prison and allowed to travel to the United States for medical treatment.

In response to an announcement by Kim Dae Jung that he was considering returning to South Korea "to participate in the people's struggle for the restoration of democratic and human rights", the South Korean authorities stated on Feb. 4, 1985, that he would not be subject to imprisonment upon his return. On Feb. 8, he duly returned and was placed under house arrest.

After the general election of February 1985, the NKDP emerged as the principal party of opposition and in April absorbed the rival Democratic Korea Party. At an NKDP convention held in August Lee Min U was re-elected as party leader and the two Kims were appointed as permanent advisers to the organization. Although Kim Dae Jung was warned by the authorities that, under the terms of his suspended prison sentence, he remained banned from joining or participating in the activities of any political party, he announced on Jan. 8, 1986, that he would accept the position offered. No action was taken against him directly, but his attempts to participate fully within the party were hampered by repeated periods of confinement under house arrest.

On Feb. 12, 1986, the NKDP launched a petition to mobilize support for the introduction of a directly elected presidency rather than the current system of election through an electoral college. This pressure for constitutional reform was increased through the establishment of the National Liaison Organization for Democratization (NLOD—see separate entry), within which the NKDP was a leading constituent element. The NKDP was subject to increasing internal divisions, however, resulting from differences arising from the exact nature of the constitutional reforms demanded, as well as from a growing personal animosity between Lee Min U and the two Kims. On April 8, 1987, the Kims announced that they were leaving the NKDP, and were followed by some 76 NKDP members of the legislature, of whom 67 joined them in the Reunification Democratic Party, which held an inaugural congress on May 1, at which Kim Young Sam was elected president. The remaining 14 NKDP members of the legislature continued under the leadership of Lee Min U who, on April 29, announced that his party had incorporated the People's Democratic Party which had included 12 legislators.

Sammintu

This radical student group was reported to be in favour of the reunification of the Korean peninsula, the liberation of the "masses", the introduction of political pluralism, and an acknowledgment by the authorities of the brutality with which the Kwangju uprising was crushed. In support of this programme 73 members of the group occupied the offices of the US Information Service in Seoul in May 1985. The occupation ended peacefully after US negotiators acknowledged the "extreme brutality" of the suppression of the rising but denied that the US government had been involved in the operation. A total of 32 students, including Ham Un Yong, who was alleged to be the leader of the group, were imprisoned in connexion with the occupation. During the course of 1985 several hundred students were accused of involvement with the group and were arrested for offences ranging from illegal assembly to treason. Those associated with the group were also involved in the occupation in November 1985 of the US Chamber of Commerce in Seoul, the US Cultural Centre in Kwangju and offices belonging to the ruling Democratic Justice Party.

United People's Movement for Democracy and Unification (UPMDM)

The UPMDM, which was established in 1985 and is loosely organized around the leadership of the Rev. Moon Ik Hwan, consists of over 20 civil rights, religious and labour movements. The Rev. Moon was arrested on several occasions during 1985-86 for allegedly engaging in anti-state activities, and on Nov. 12, 1986, the authorities were reported to have forcibly closed the movement's headquarters in Seoul.

Kuwait

Capital: Kuwait Pop. 1,730,000

The Emirate of Kuwait has been ruled by decree since July 3, 1986, when the Amir dissolved the National Assembly elected on Feb. 20, 1985, and requested the Prime Minister to form a new government, declaring that Kuwait was the target of "a fierce foreign conspiracy". The Assembly had been elected by some 57,000 voters only, the franchise being limited to adult male Kuwaiti citizens, excluding members of the armed forces and all those who could not trace their ancestry back to 1920.

Relations between Kuwait and Iran have been tense since the outbreak of the Iran-Iraq war in 1980, since which time Kuwait has given aid to Iraq. In May 1984 Iran was blamed for attacks on Kuwaiti shipping in the Gulf and the Islamic Republic News Agency has reported deportation orders against Iranians in Kuwait.

During 1983-84 the government tightened control over the Shia section of the population, fearing that Iran would try and "export" the Islamic Revolution to the Gulf. Between 20 and 30 per cent of Kuwaiti citizens are thought to be Shias.

Al Dawa

On May 25, 1985, an Iraqi member of this militant Shia Moslem group, seen as having close links with Iran, attempted to assassinate the Amir, Sheikh Jaber al-Ahmad-al-Sabah, in an attack on the Amir's motorcade in which four people were killed. One of the attackers, Ala Muhammed Rida al-Atrash, was sentenced to death by the State Security Court on Nov. 29, 1986, and another man was sentenced to life imprisonment in absentia. According to a report by a top security official in November 1986 a total of 26,898 people were deported in the previous year following the assassination attempt.

On March 27, 1984, 20 people were found guilty of carrying out a number of bomb attacks which took place in December 1983. Five Iraqi Shias, all members of *Al Dawa*, and one Lebanese Maronite were sentenced to death for attacks on the US embassy, the French embassy, the international airport, the Electricity and Water Ministry, the Shvaiba industrial and petrochemical complex, and residential developments used by US nationals.

On Jan. 7, 1987, two persons were sentenced to death for their part in café bombings in Kuwait City which took place on July 11, 1985. Alleged members of the *Al Dawa* group, together with others from the militant Palestinian Abu Nidal Group, were amongst those arrested on July 1, 1986, in connection with the bomb attacks.

Al Jihad al-Islami (Islamic Holy War)

This group originally claimed responsibility for the attacks carried out on May 25, 1985, on the Amir's motorcade and Dec. 12, 1983, on a number of targets described above.

The Forces of the Prophet Mohammed in Kuwait

In June 1987 six Kuwaiti Shias were sentenced to death for their part in the bombing of three of the Emirate's oil installations on Jan. 19, 1987. Responsibility for the attacks was claimed by this previously unknown group, which threatened to kill Kuwaiti leaders, their families, and the "whole of the American regime" if the sentences were carried out. One man was sentenced to life imprisonment, seven received lighter sentences, and two were given suspended sentences for their part in the attacks.

Laos

Capital: Vientiane Pop. 4,120,000

The People's Democratic Republic of Laos was established in December 1975 by the *Neo Lao Hakset* (Lao Patriotic Front, the principal component of which was the *Pathet Lao*), whose chairman became President of the Republic, while the general secretary of the Lao People's Revolutionary Party (LPRP, *Phak Pasason Pativat Lao*—which holds effective political power and is the country's sole legal political organization) became Chairman of the Council of Ministers. (The name of the Lao Patriotic Front was in February 1979 changed to Lao Front for National Reconstruction.) A 264-member National Congress of People's Representatives, elected by local authorities, met in December 1975 and appointed a 45-member Supreme People's Assembly which was inter alia to draft a new Constitution. There have been no general elections since the establishment of the LPRP's regime.

Between 1975 and 1981 refugees estimated at up to one-tenth of the country's population left Laos, with 100,000 of them reaching the United States, over 105,000 remaining in refugee camps in Thailand and some 100,000 believed to have settled illegally in the Lao-speaking provinces of north-eastern Thailand. No precise figures are available for the number of political prisoners (mainly members of former administrations, but also "elements corrupted by the international reactionaries", i.e. the Chinese) or of persons held in "re-education camps".

Following the invasion of Kampuchea by (pro-Soviet) Vietnamese troops in December 1978, relations between Laos and China broke down early in 1979, when Laos effectively suspended its aid agreements with China, alleged that China was concentrating troops on its border with Laos, and admitted (for the first time) that Vietnamese troops (estimated to number 50,000 in 1985) were stationed in Laos. Relations with neighbouring Thailand (which suffered in 1984 as a result of a dispute over the sovereignty of three villages near the Lao-Thai border) have been strained since 1975 by accusations from both countries that the other was harbouring anti-government guerrilla groups.

Resistance to the LPRP's regime and the Soviet and Vietnamese presence in the country by right-wing groups and (pro-Chinese) communists supported by the Red Khmers of Kampuchea took the form of sporadic guerrilla operations which did not appear to constitute a serious threat to the regime, even though one of its principal opponents, Gen. Phoumi Nosavan (who died in November 1985), in August 1982 announced that an anti-communist and anti-Vietnamese "Royal Lao Democratic Government" would shortly be set up inside Lao territory.

Free Lao National Liberation Movement

Leadership. Iang and Sisouk Na Champassak

This organization was reportedly formed in April 1977 by two brothers who were members of an ancient Lao ruling aristocratic family. Sisouk Na Champassak in August 1982 announced himself as spokesman of the "executive directorate" of the National United Front for the Liberation of Laos (a coalition of Lao resistance groups formed in September 1980).

Free People of Laos

The Thai newspaper, the *Bangkok Post*, reported on July 20, 1983, that Lao resistance forces had recently formed this anti-communist league in order to draw world attention to their efforts to drive Vietnamese troops from Laos. Based in southern Laos, many of the organization's members are described as "well educated"; it intended to operate with a resistance coalition, National United Front for the Liberation of Laos.

Hmong Tribesmen

Hmong tribesmen (the name by which the Lao Soung tribe of northern Laos, often called the *Meo*—i.e. barbarian—describe themselves) maintained guerrilla resistance against the LPRP regime from its establishment in 1975. By October 1977, however, the Hmong forces were said to have disintegrated into small bands. On Aug. 30, 1978, it was alleged by Hanoi radio that the creation of a Hmong kingdom in Laos and northern Vietnam had been discussed in Peking between Chinese leaders and Gen. Vang Pao (who had commanded a Hmong force financed by the US Central Intelligence Agency until he had fled to the United States in 1975). In 1980-82 Hmong guerrillas operating in northern Laos were said to be receiving aid from China.

According to a statement made in Peking on Dec. 15, 1981, by Dr Khamsengkeo Sengsthith (a former senior official in the Laotian Ministry of Health who had defected to China), chemical weapons were being used in Laos against Hmong tribesmen by Vietnamese troops.

The Thai newspaper, the *Bangkok Post*, of Dec. 30, 1986, reported that Vietnamese troops based in Laos had on Dec. 26 shot dead 43 Hmong tribesmen as they attempted to cross the Mekong river from Paksone province (Laos) to Nong Khai (Thailand). The Lao government rejected the charge as a "fabrication by certain soldiers in the Thai army".

Lao National Liberation Front

This Front emerged in the late 1970s and was reported to have conducted guerrilla operations in southern Laos in 1980, with fierce fighting in July and various raids in September, November and December being reported by Kampuchean Red Khmer sources. Reports suggest that the Front is organizationally weak, with military units operating independently with little co-ordination.

Royal Lao Democratic Government (RLDG)

Gen. Phoumi Nosavan (the former right-wing Deputy Premier who had fled into exile after an abortive coup attempt in 1965) announced in Bangkok (Thailand) on Aug. 18, 1982, that he had formed an anti-communist and anti-Vietnamese "Royal Lao Democratic Government". However, he died on Nov. 3, 1985.

Lebanon

Capital: Beirut

Pop. 2,670,000

The Republic of Lebanon has an executive President (customarily a Maronite Christian) elected by a 99-member Chamber of Deputies which is itself elected for a four-year term by universal adult suffrage. The President appoints a Cabinet which is customarily headed by a Sunni Moslem Prime Minister. The allocation of top political, administrative and military posts has been subject to the unwritten "National Covenant" of 1943, which also provided that there must be six Christians to every five Moslems in the Chamber; a strict grouping according to party affiliations was therefore not possible. In view of the internal security situation there have been no general elections in Lebanon since 1972, and the life of the Chamber has been repeatedly extended since the expiry of its term in 1976.

The 1943 "National Covenant" according the Lebanese Christians a dominant political role was drawn up on the basis of a 1932 census which had shown the Christians to be in a majority, i.e. 56 per cent of the total population. However, by the mid-1970s it was generally accepted, in the absence of any later official figures, that the Moslems had come to form the majority and therefore had some justification for their demand for fundamental changes in the country's political and economic structure. Of some 20 recognized religious communities, the Christian ones are, in descending order of numerical strength, the Maronites (over 25 per cent of the total population), Greek Orthodox (10 per cent), Greek Catholics, Armenian Orthodox, Armenian Catholics, Protestants, Syrian Catholics, Latin Catholics, Syrian Orthodox and Chaldeans; of the Moslems, the Sunnis form the largest community, followed by the Shias and the small Druse community.

Tensions between Lebanon's various ethnic and religious communities have regularly erupted into open hostility between the various militia groups maintained by the assorted factions. Open civil war, principally between Christian and Moslem groups, broke out in 1975, and has continued at varying degrees of intensity ever since, despite numerous attempts to reach a lasting settlement and the intervention of a (mainly Syrian) "Arab Deterrent Force" in 1976, which itself became embroiled in the fighting. Two of the main causes of the fighting are (i) the resentment felt by the majority Moslem population, particularly the Shia community, at the concentration of political and economic power in Christian hands, and (ii) the presence of large numbers of Palestine Liberation Organization (PLO) guerrillas (see separate entry under Palestinian Movements), who have clashed at different times with both Christian and Shia Moslem militias. Israeli forces invaded Lebanon in 1978 and again on a much larger scale in June 1982, with the stated purpose of expelling the PLO. After laying siege to Beirut, they staged a phased withdrawal over three years, with the last soldiers returning to Israel in June 1985. Israeli forces continue to stage anti-guerrilla operations in the south, however. The Syrian army occupies much of eastern and northern Lebanon, with the tacit acquiescence of the Israelis and the international community in general.

The strongest militias include the Shia Moslem *Amal*, the Christian Phalangist "Lebanese Forces", the Druse Progressive Socialist Party, the Israeli-backed, mainly Christian, South Lebanon Army, the Iranian-backed Moslem fundamentalist *Hezbollah* and the Sunni Moslem *Mourabitoun* (based in Beirut). Much of the depleted regular army is divided along confessional lines. Despite having been expelled by the Israelis in 1982, PLO guerrillas have again built up their strength in the refugee camps in Beirut, Tyre and Sidon.

A number of smaller, shadowy and, in many cases, ephemeral, armed groups also operate in Lebanon, the most notorious being *Al Jihad al-Islami* (Islamic Holy War), which has claimed responsibility for many of the kidnappings of Westerners which have been a feature of Lebanese politics during the 1980s.

Central government authority remains extremely weak, with effective control being exercised by the various political and military factions in their respective heartlands.

Given the often confusing, multi-communal nature of Lebanon, and the absence of any effective central authority, it is not an easy matter to decide which groups qualify as "revolutionary" or "dissident". It has been decided here to limit the criteria to those movements which exhibit, to a greater or lesser degree, armed independence of central government. In practice, these criteria subsume all significant Lebanese political groupings. In many cases, a nominally legal political party has an (again nominally) illegal militia; in these cases, the entry will be found under the militia's name, with cross-referencing where appropriate. For details of purely political movements, see *Political Parties of the World* (second edition, published by Longman in 1984).

In addition to the well-established movements, many more emerge sporadically in response to specific events, and as such are often seen as spin-offs from more permanent organizations, rather than independent movements in their own right. Typical of these are what have been referred to as "telephone groups", so-called because their existence is affirmed by callers to news agencies claiming responsibility for particular incidents.

Christian Groups

Armenian Secret Army for the Liberation of Armenia (ASALA)

ASALA was founded in Beirut on Oct. 22, 1975, but the vast majority of its activities have been concerned with attacks on Turkish interests (see entry under Turkey on page 381).

The Armenian community in Lebanon, estimated to total some 250,000 people, remained neutral during the 1975-76 civil war. The newspaper *Al-Amal*, the organ of the Phalangist Party, alleged on Sept. 12, 1979, that the Armenians were seeking to establish an "autonomous zone" in Bourg Hammoud and Nabaa (in east Beirut). The Armenians, on the other hand, claimed that there was an organized campaign by some parties "to repress their community and to force them to change their policy of neutrality".

In May 1986, ASALA responded to a series of attacks on the Armenian community by threatening to teach those responsible "a hard lesson". Responsibility had been claimed by the Independent Movement for the Liberation of Kidnap Victims (see separate entry), who had threatened to mount "an implacable war" with the aim of driving the Armenians out of west Beirut, on the grounds that they supported hard-liners in the Phalangist Party opposed to political reforms.

The release of an ASALA member from prison in France, where he was serving life imprisonment for an attack at Orly airport in July 1983, was among the demands of the Committee of Solidarity with Arab and Middle Eastern Political Prisoners, which carried out a series of bombings in France in September 1986. The Committee, which was believed to be closely linked to the Lebanese Armed Revolutionary Factions (see separate entries), reportedly received tactical support from ASALA.

Black Brigades

Apparently a hard-line Christian group, the Black Brigades claimed responsibility for a series of car-bomb attacks in Moslem districts of Beirut in July 1986. The bombings were seen by some observers as representing right-wing Phalangist opposition to the implementation of the Syrian-mediated security plan.

Cedar Guardians

Leadership. Col. Etienne Saqr

This far-right group takes its name from the green cedar tree regarded by Christians as the national emblem of Lebanon. It is a member of the Lebanese Front. First active during the 1975-76 civil war, it was involved in mid-1979 in clashes with the Tiger Militia of the National Liberal Party led by ex-President Camille Chamoun (see separate entry). In early 1984, there were rumours that Israeli forces were transporting units of the Cedar Guardians from central to southern Lebanon.

Cells of Revolutionary Liberation—Resistance Against Syrian Imperialism

One of the series of car-bomb attacks against Moslem west Beirut, mounted by hard-line Christian elements opposed to a Syrian-sponsored security plan in July and August 1986, was claimed by this "telephone group".

Christian Revolutionaries of the Cedar Tree

A group of this name claimed responsibility for a car-bomb attack on June 14, 1985, on the home of a leader of the Sunni fundamentalist *Jundullah* organization in Tripoli (see separate entry). A spokesman warned that "no fundamentalist Moslem will be allowed to remain in Lebanon". The cedar tree is regarded as the national emblem of Lebanon by many Christians.

Front for the Liberation of Lebanon from Foreigners (FLLF)

Apparently an anti-Syrian, hard-line Christian body, the FLLF claimed responsibility for planting two car-bombs in west Beirut on Feb. 23, 1982 (as well as for a serious bomb attack in Damascus, Syria, on Nov. 29, 1981, when at least 90 people were killed and over 135 injured, and also for the bombing of the office of the Ministry of Information, including the office of the *Al-Baath* newspaper, in Damascus on Feb. 18, 1982).

In February 1983 the FLLF claimed responsibility for the bombing of the Palestine Research Centre (a PLO-backed institution) in west Beirut, and in August it asserted responsibility for a bomb attack in the Moslem, Syrian-controlled town of Baalbek, in the eastern Bekaa Valley. After a bomb explosion which killed 14 people in a block of flats in a Shia Moslem district of southern Beirut in December 1983, a spokesman for the FLLF announced that its members were the perpetrators of what he termed this "barbecue operation".

Haddad Militia—see South Lebanon Army

Lebanese Forces—see Phalangist Militia

Marada Militia

Leadership. Soleiman Franjié (l.)

The family of Soleiman Franjié, who was President of Lebanon in 1970-76, has traditionally controlled a Christian area centred around Zghorta (northern Lebanon). The ex-President has always retained good relations with the Syrians, and in May 1978 there was an open reconciliation between him and a leading Sunni Moslem, Rashid Karami, who had held numerous posts in Lebanese governments and had been Prime Minister in 1975-76. He thus incurred the enmity of the (extreme right-wing Christian) Phalangists—see separate entry. On June 13, 1978, Phalangist forces, intent upon extending their control to the northern Christian areas, killed the ex-President's eldest son Tony, the latter's wife and his daughter at Ehden (south-east of Tripoli). In ensuing fighting between Phalangists and Franjié's supporters, then organized as the Zghorta Liberation Army (see separate entry), numerous casualties were suffered by both sides.

Followers of Soleiman Franjié, by now organized in the Marada Militia, subsequently fought back against the Phalangists, attacking in particular the family of their leader, Pierre Gemayel. They kidnapped a Phalangist member of Parliament on Feb. 13, 1980, but released him on March 9 after an exchange of prisoners held by the two sides had taken place on March 5. In May 1980 Marada militiamen unsuccessfully attempted to occupy several Phalangist-held villages near Batroun (on the coast, about 25 miles north of Beirut), and over the following two years relations between these two Christian movements remained tense.

Marada militiamen provided artillery support to pro-Syrian Phalangist units loyal to Elie Hobeika during fighting in early 1986 with hard-line Phalangists under Samir Geaga, who were opposed to the recent Syrian-mediated agreement between rival Christian and Moslem groups. Franjié had declared his support for the accord.

National Liberal Party—see Tiger Militia

Phalangist Militia (Lebanese Forces—*Kataëb*)

This militia force is the military arm of the Phalangist Party, which was established in 1936 as a right-wing Maronite Christian formation under the leadership of Pierre Gemayel. In more recent years the Phalangists have been the strongest partner in the Lebanese Front of conservative Christian forces and have been the most active Christian grouping in the country's long-running inter-communal strife. (The Militia is officially entitled the "Lebanese Forces".) A particular object of Phalangist hostility has been the presence in the country of guerrilla forces of the Palestine Liberation Organization (PLO—see separate entry under Palestinian Movements), which was accused of forging an alliance with leftist Moslem groups intent on overthrowing Lebanon's established political and economic structure (under which Christians had enjoyed a traditional ascendancy).

Following serious fighting between the (Christian-officered) Lebanese army and Palestinian guerrillas in April-May 1973, the Phalangists took the lead among Christian groupings in building up unofficial armed militia units to counterbalance the PLO presence. During this period Christian leaders repeatedly condemned the alleged intervention of the Palestinians in internal Lebanese affairs. Pierre Gemayel in particular demanded a national referendum to decide whether the guerrillas should continue to operate from Lebanon and also called on the government to repudiate the Cairo agreement of 1969 under which the Palestinians had been authorized to establish camps in Lebanon and conduct military actions against Israel.

Following further heavy fighting between the two sides in mid-1974, the escalation of hostilities into a virtual civil war began in mid-April 1975 when Phalangist militiamen clashed with Palestinian guerrillas in the Beirut area. According to PLO sources, armed Phalangists on April 13 ambushed a bus returning a group of Palestinians to the Tal Zaatar refugee camp on the outskirts of Beirut as it passed through the suburb of Ain Rumaneh (a Phalangist stronghold in the eastern sector of the capital), killing 27 men, women and children. On the other hand, Phalangist spokesmen claimed that the fighting had started when guerrillas opened fire from a car on a church in Ain Rumaneh in which Pierre Gemayel was attending mass; according to this account, Palestinian reinforcements had quickly arrived in a bus and a shoot-out had occurred between the guerrillas and "the population of the area". Whatever the actual circumstances of this incident, it marked the onset of general hostilities between the Phalangists and other Christian militia groups on the one hand and an alliance of leftist Moslems and their Palestinian allies on the other.

Under the leadership of Bashir Gemayel (the youngest son of Pierre Gemayel), the Phalangist Militia played a major role on the Christian side in the ensuing civil war, which was eventually brought to a precarious ceasefire in late 1976 through the intervention of a predominantly Syrian Arab Deterrent Force (ADF). A feature of the latter stages of the 1975-76 conflict was the support which Syrian forces gave to the Lebanese Christians in their successful counter-offensive against the Moslem-Palestinian side, after the latter had appeared to be gaining the upper hand militarily. This Syrian alignment on the side of the Christians reflected the interest of the Damascus regime in restoring a stable central government in Lebanon under pro-Syrian Christians such as the then President Soleiman Franjié, and with the continued participation of moderate Moslem leaders. For their part, the Phalangists regarded the alliance with the Syrians as a short-term expedient to facilitate the defeat of the Moslem-Palestinian leftists, and remained hostile to Syrian aspirations to hegemony over Lebanon.

Although making common cause with other Christian factions in the struggle against the Moslem-Palestinian leftists, the Phalangist Militia was, for much of the civil war and subsequently, also in conflict with the militia forces by the National Liberal Party (NLP) led by Camille Chamoun (see separate entry for Tiger Militia). Periodic clashes also occurred in the late 1970s between the Phalangists and the Lebanese Armenian community, which had remained neutral during the civil war. Following particularly heavy clashes between the NLP and Phalangists in Beirut in May 1979, the two sides announced the creation of a joint military command, but this agreement failed to prevent the outbreak of further fighting between the two factions. On July 7, 1980, the Phalangists launched an attack on the offices and strongholds of the NLP in east Beirut and defeated the NLP's militia. In October 1980 the Phalangists went on the offensive in Ain Rumaneh (the east Beirut suburb now nominally controlled by the Lebanese army but still containing remnants of the NLP militia), and on Oct. 29

the Phalangists claimed to have purged Ain Rumaneh of NLP groups.

The Phalangists thus established control over much of east Beirut and the Christian enclave north of the capital (except areas held by the militia of ex-President Franjié and by the Armenians), where they took over responsibility for levying taxes and customs duties. They were said to have spent large sums of money on light and medium-sized weapons from France, Britain and West Germany and were also in receipt of arms supplies (including heavy weapons) from the Israelis, as confirmed by Israel for the first time in April 1981. Also in April 1981 the Israelis for the first time intervened directly on the side of the Phalangists when they shot down two Syrian helicopters which were involved in an assault by ADF forces on Phalangist positions in Zahle (20 miles to the east of Beirut).

Following the June 1982 Israeli invasion of Lebanon, Phalangist forces were reported to have co-operated closely with the Israelis in actions to eliminate the military presence of the PLO from Beirut. Immediately after the assassination of President-elect Bashir Gemayel on Sept. 14, 1982, Phalangist Militia units carried out an operation (approved and sponsored by the Israelis) designed to "purge" the Chatila and Sabra refugee camps in west Beirut of PLO guerrillas who had remained in hiding since the general evacuation of Palestinian and ADF forces from the capital during late August. This operation (on Sept. 16-18) in effect became a massacre of civilians, including women and children—the number of dead being variously given as less than 500 and more than 1,200—and was widely condemned by the international community and within Israel itself. An Israeli independent judicial inquiry into the massacre found, in its report published on Feb. 8, 1983, that the killings had been carried out by the Phalangists but that various Israeli political and military leaders bore varying degrees of indirect responsibility for its occurrence, notably in that the Phalangists had been allowed to enter the camps without direct Israeli supervision. Phalangist leaders themselves, on the other hand, have consistently refused to accept any responsibility for the September 1982 Beirut atrocities.

A Lebanese government report published in June 1983 concluded that there was "no evidence that the leadership of the Phalangist Party or the command of the Lebanese Forces were aware in advance of what happened. The investigation did not establish that either of these two commands had issued orders to fighters to support or take part in the operation". From early 1983 onwards, the Phalangists had fluctuating relations with the Israelis. Some Militia leaders resisted the conclusion of the security agreement between Israel and Lebanon, while in February 1983 the Phalangist Party's radio station, the Voice of Lebanon, began to refer to the Israelis as "foreign occupiers".

The Phalangists lost ground to the Druse fighters of the Progressive Socialist Party (PSP—see separate entry) during 1983-84 in the Chouf mountains east of Beirut, despite assistance from Christian sections of the Lebanese army. In early 1985, they were driven out of the Sidon area by a combined alliance of Druse, *Amal* and Palestinian fighters. They also clashed repeatedly with Moslem militias across the "Green Line" dividing Christian east from Moslem west Beirut.

During this period, the Phalangists derived considerable income from the nominally illegal levying of customs duties in ports and harbours under their control, notably "Dock Five" in east Beirut. Various undertakings to hand over control of the ports to the state authorities were never completely carried through.

With Syrian influence in Lebanon increasing after the conclusion of a peace agreement between the rival factions in August 1984, Fady Frem was replaced as Lebanese Forces commander in October by Fouad Abou Nader, a grandson of Pierre Gemayel who had died the same month. Nader was seen as being more pro-Syrian. Later in the year, Nader himself was replaced by Samir Geaga, who in March 1985 led a rebellion against the Phalangist political command, which he accused of being subservient to Syria. Geaga's forces attacked Moslem positions around Sidon in March, but were decisively defeated by Druse, *Amal* and Sunni *Mourabitoun* fighters (see separate entries). In May, Geaga was dismissed and replaced by Elie Hobeika, aged 27, who, despite being the reputed leader of the units which had carried out the Sabra and Chatila massacres, was seen as favouring a degree of Syrian influence in Lebanon. After the conclusion of the Syrian-mediated accord between the Phalangists and Moslem militias at the end of 1985, clashes broke out in Christian areas north and east of Beirut between militiamen loyal to Hobeika and others who favoured Geaga's strongly anti-Syrian line. Although Hobeika's forces received artillery support from the Syrian National Socialist Party and Marada, they were decisively defeated, leaving Geaga effectively in command of the Militia. Hobeika himself fled to Syria, but later returned to Syrian-controlled areas of Lebanon, and in August 1986 staged an unsuccessful assault from west Beirut on Phalangist positions occupied by fighters loyal to Geaga. The fighting took place against a background of car-bomb explosions in east Beirut, believed to be the responsibility of Christian elements opposed to the Phalangist Party's support for Syrian-mediated political and security agreements.

South Lebanon Army (SLA or "Haddad Militia")

Leadership. Col. Antoine Lahad (commander)

This largely Christian Israeli-backed militia was set up by Maj. Saad Haddad, a former Lebanese army officer, ostensibly to defend Christian-inhabited areas of southern Lebanon against Syrian and Palestinian forces.

In February 1978 Maj. Haddad called for the establishment of a "government-in-exile" in the south, which would declare the Syrians to be invaders. These areas were occupied by Israel in March 1978 but were left under Christian militia control after Israel had, in June 1978, withdrawn from southern Lebanon, sectors of which were then occupied by units of the UN Interim Force in Lebanon (UNIFIL) pending the arrival of Lebanese army units. Originally known as the "Haddad Militia", the force achieved quasi-legitimacy as the "South Lebanon Army" during the Israeli occupation of the area in 1982-85. It was subsequently the target of sustained attacks by Moslem and Palestinian fighters.

In a report by Dr Kurt Waldheim (then UN Secretary-General), approved by the UN Security Council on Dec. 8, 1978, it was stated that Israel had (in June 1978) handed over control to "de facto armed groups" (i.e. the Christian militia of Maj. Haddad). By April 1979 Maj. Haddad's forces were in control of an eight-mile-wide strip along the entire border of Lebanon with Israel and prevented the Lebanese army from occupying this area. On April 18 Maj. Haddad declared it "an independent free Lebanese state", called on the Lebanese President (then Elias Sarkis) to resign, declared the Lebanese Parliament to be illegal, and added that no elections would be held in his zone because of the military situation.

Maj. Haddad's declaration was not explicitly supported by Israel, and the Lebanese government accused him of treason and discharged him from the Lebanese army. His declaration was also rejected by France, the United Kingdom, the United States and the Arab states. On April 20, 1979, Maj. Haddad stated that he had set up a military council in his zone to carry out the functions of a government, but he stressed that his forces were still part of the Lebanese Front (an alliance of Lebanon's Christian parties).

From then onwards Maj. Haddad's Militia was involved in several clashes with UNIFIL units. In August 1979 Maj. Haddad accused the United States of supporting the Palestinian guerrillas by seeking to put an end to pre-emptive strikes against them by Israel, and he added that his own forces had been "abandoned by the Christian world" for economic reasons. Close co-operation continued, however, between Maj. Haddad's Militia and Israel, which in April 1980 denied having set up military positions in his proclaimed "independent" state. The UN Security Council repeatedly condemned the actions of the "de facto force". A demand made on March 18, 1981, by the UNIFIL commander (Maj.-Gen. William Callaghan of Ireland) for the ending of Israel's assistance in the Christian-held area was rejected by the head of Israel's northern command.

On Nov. 8, 1981, Maj. Haddad expressed the hope that his "free Lebanon" would "spread and extend to cover all the Lebanese territory", since this was, he claimed, "the wish of every honest Lebanese". Following the June 1982 invasion of Lebanon by Israel, the Israeli Prime Minister announced on June 7 that the extent of "Haddadland" would be enlarged by the area of Beaufort Castle (a crusader fortress which had been a PLO command centre about five kilometres north of Israel's border). In the direct negotiations which opened between Israel and Lebanon at the end of December 1982, the Israeli side demanded that Maj. Haddad's forces should be given a recognized security role in the demilitarized zone sought by Israel in southern Lebanon in return for an undertaking to withdraw its troops.

The report of the office of the military prosecutor into the 1982 massacre of Palestinian civilians at the Sabra and Chatila refugee camps, which was published in 1983, implicitly suggested that the Haddad Militia was involved when it identified the perpetrators as "armed elements not from the Israeli camp . . . perhaps they are from the border element or others who may have suffered under the excesses of the Palestinians".

Maj. Haddad died on Jan. 14, 1984. Ten days previously, aware that he was dying, the Lebanese government had reinstated him with full rights as an army officer. His funeral was attended by Christian and Israeli leaders; the Israeli Prime Minister, Itzhak Shamir, praised him as "a true Lebanese patriot and friend of Israel". Haddad's replacement as commander of the Militia, which was henceforth termed the South Lebanon Army, was Col. Antoine Lahad, a former member of the National Liberal Party and army commander of the northern region until his retirement in 1983. At this time the Lebanese government portrayed the SLA as a legitimate section of the army, although this pretence was gradually abandoned over the ensuing two years, as the SLA came under increasing attack from Moslem fighters of the "Lebanese National Resistance", whose actions were on occasion officially sanctioned by members of the government.

From early 1984 onwards, the Israeli army started to transfer to the SLA control of some of their bases, simultaneously beginning a systematic supply operation. Much attention was directed at this time towards recruiting members of the local Shia Moslem community, in an effort to broaden the Militia's base and present it as a multi-communal force. Although initially successful, large numbers of the Shia members later deserted, many joining *Amal* or *Hezbollah* (see separate entries).

It was revealed in early 1985 that the Israelis were planning that the SLA should patrol the "security zone", a three- to six-mile-wide strip of land to the north of the Israeli border, the function of which was to prevent attacks on Israel by Palestinian guerrillas.

In addition to clashing with *Amal* and *Hezbollah*, some of whose members used suicide car-bombs against SLA positions, the Militia also came into conflict with units of the United Nations Interim Force in Lebanon (UNIFIL), which regarded the SLA as an unauthorized armed organization. UNIFIL positions were from time to time shelled by SLA artillery, and there were several tense confrontations.

During 1986-87, the SLA suffered a series of damaging attacks by *Hezbollah*; a total of 84 SLA men were killed during 1986. Regular Israeli forces frequently had to provide artillery and air support for the SLA during this period.

Tiger Militia

The Tigers represent the military wing of the National Liberal Party (which was led until 1986 by former President Camille Chamoun, who died on Aug. 7, 1987, having passed the NLP leadership on to his son Dany). This Militia constitutes the second strongest group in the (Christian) Lebanese Front after the Phalangists (see separate entry). After the Tiger Militia groups had been attacked and largely defeated by Phalangists, Dany Chamoun accused the Phalangists (on July 8, 1980) of treachery and of attempting forcibly to create a single party for the Christians of Lebanon; he also announced his resignation as leader of the Tiger Militia but stated later that he would move to west Beirut to continue his struggle against the Phalangists, whom he described as "bloodthirsty madmen".

Zghorta Liberation Army

A militia controlled by the Franjié clan, a pro-Syrian Christian family whose home is the northern town of Zghorta. Its leader, Soleiman Franjié, is a former President of Lebanon who has maintained ties with Moslem leaders opposed to the Gemayel regime. In recent years, the Franjié clan militia has been organized as the Marada Militia (see separate entry).

Moslem Groups

Al Jihad al-Islami (Islamic Holy War)

One of the groups most commonly invoked for attacks by Shia fundamentalists on Western interests from 1983 onwards, *Al Jihad al-Islami* is widely believed to be at least in part a cover used by the Mugniyah clan, at least one of whose members was among 17 Shias imprisoned in Kuwait following bomb attacks there in December 1983. In a wider context, other reports suggest that the name is used by a loose network of Shia fundamentalist activists who are also linked to groups such as *Hezbollah* and Islamic *Amal* (see separate entries). Among the spiritual leaders of this network are, in west Beirut, Shaikh Mohammed Hossein Fadlallah, leader of *Hezbollah*, Shaikh Mohammed Haidar and Shaikh Ibrahim Aakid, and in Baalbek Shaikh Abbas Mussavi and Shaikh Sobhi Toufmili. The group receives considerable support from the Islamic regime in Iran, with which it has strong ideological links.

The name was first used by a caller to a Beirut news agency claiming responsibility for the bombing of the US embassy in west Beirut in April 1983. In October of that year, *Al Jihad al-Islami* was one of three groups claiming responsibility for the suicide car-bomb attacks on the headquarters of the US and French contingents of the multinational peacekeeping force in west Beirut. In addition, it also claimed the suicide bombing of Israeli military headquarters in Tyre, in southern Lebanon, after which it issued a statement promising that "we are prepared to send 2,000 of our fighters to die in southern Lebanon in order to expel the Zionist enemy from our country".

In early 1984, *Al Jihad al-Islami* claimed its first kidnapping of a Westerner; over the ensuing three years, it seized a number of Westerners, mostly Americans; on occasion, it offered to release them in return for the freeing by Kuwait of the 17 Shias imprisoned in December 1983. One of the victims, William Buckley, a former US Central Intelligence Agency station head in Beirut, died in captivity in 1985, reportedly as a result of torture. Early in 1986, the group executed a French hostage, Michel Seurat. Various undercover diplomatic initiatives led to the release of some hostages, however, particularly as a result of negotiations conducted by the Archbishop of Canterbury's special envoy, Terry Waite, and to the controversial "arms-for-hostages" deal in which the USA supplied quantities of weapons to Iran in return for the latter exerting influence on the kidnappers. Evidence emerged during early 1987 that some of Waite's missions had been connected with this arrangement. In November 1986, while Waite was visiting Damascus at the same time as the Iranian Foreign Minister, *Al Jihad al-Islami* issued a statement saying that the USA had "embarked on approaches which, if continued, could lead to a solution of the hostage [*sic*] issue". Waite himself, however, disappeared in Beirut in January 1987 while engaging in secret negotiations, and further progress on the release of the hostages seemed to have been frozen by the public revelations of the "arms-for-hostages" arrangement.

There was also some evidence that *Al Jihad al-Islami* was involved in the TWA airliner hijack in 1985, during which a number of US passengers were held captive in support of Shia demands for the freeing of Lebanese prisoners from Israeli detention camps.

After three west Beirut banks had been the subject of bomb attacks in February 1985, a telephone caller claimed responsibility on behalf of *Al Jihad al-Islami*'s "Brigade for Protecting the Poor", saying that the action represented a protest against profiteers.

Amal (Hope)

Leadership. Nabi Berri

Amal was set up in 1979 as the military wing of the political movement of the Shia Moslem community (a traditionally poor and underprivileged section of the population). Largely under the influence of the Islamic revolution in Iran and of the disappearance of the Shia spiritual leader, Imam Moussa Sadr, at the end of a visit to Libya in August 1978, *Amal* began to launch actions against Palestinian and Lebanese leftists supporting Iraq. A large number of Shia Moslems lived in the "independent" Christian enclave in southern Lebanon.

In March 1980, when *Amal* had organized demonstrations against the disappearance of the leader of some 6,000,000 Shia Moslems in Iraq (Ayatollah Mohammed Bakr al Sadr), fighting broke out between *Amal* followers and those of the Arab Liberation Front, said to be backed by the pro-Iraqi faction of the *Baath* Party in Lebanon (see separate entry). Further fighting between *Amal* supporters and pro-Iraqi Lebanese and Palestinians broke out at the end of June 1980 and again in March 1981.

Of the members of a new Cabinet appointed on Oct. 25, 1980, three Shia Ministers of State resigned on Dec. 4, 1980, in response to pressure from *Amal*, which refused to accept them as representatives of the Shia community. However, despite a call by *Amal* to boycott Cabinet meetings, the ministers complied with a request from the Prime Minister to continue in office (in mid-December).

During August 1981 *Amal* forces were involved in clashes with left-wing and Palestinian groups, in particular with the (pro-Soviet) Lebanese Communist Party (LCP—see separate entry) and also the Organization of Communist Action in Lebanon.

By mid-1982 *Amal*'s forces had grown to about 30,000 fighters, which made them the largest (non-Palestinian) fighting force in Lebanon after the

Phalangists (see separate entry). In March 1982 *Amal* proclaimed the Ayatollah Ruhollah Khomeini (the spiritual leader of Iran's Shias) the Imam of all Moslems throughout the world.

Despite having repeatedly clashed with PLO guerrillas in the early 1980s, *Amal* fighters strongly opposed the Israeli invasion of Lebanon in June 1982. Over the ensuing five years, *Amal* members clashed regularly with Israeli soldiers and with the Israeli-backed South Lebanon Army (SLA—see separate entry). *Amal*'s actions were on occasion attributed to the Lebanese National Resistance—see separate entry—a blanket term covering *Amal*, *Hezbollah* and Palestinian factions. *Amal*'s tactics included the use of suicide car-bombs. Considerable numbers of Shia SLA members defected to *Amal* from 1985 onwards. By 1986, however, *Amal* was losing influence in the south to *Hezbollah* (see separate entry), whose members were better paid and which increasingly took the leading role in attacks on the Israelis and the SLA. There was speculation that *Amal* had reached a tacit understanding with the Israelis, prompted by their joint antipathy to the Palestine Liberation Organization (PLO—see separate entry under Palestinian Movements), which had established links with *Hezbollah*. In contrast to *Hezbollah*, *Amal* generally supported the United Nations Interim Force in Lebanon (UNIFIL), although there were a number of confrontations between UNIFIL and *Amal* men. During early 1986, *Amal* also moved against the LCP in southern Lebanon, driving it out of several areas.

In February 1984, *Amal* and Druse forces drove the Lebanese army out of west Beirut, much of which was subsequently brought under *Amal* control. Henceforth, *Amal*, which enjoyed strong political and logistical support from Syria, was one of the principal wielders of political power in Lebanon. Its leaders, notably Nabi Berri, who held a Cabinet post, played a central part in the various discussions aimed at ending the civil strife and achieving meaningful political reforms. For much of the time *Amal* worked closely with the (Druse) Progressive Socialist Party (PSP—see separate entry) and it was a member of several fronts set up to demand political reforms, including the National Salvation and National Unity Fronts.

Amal regularly fought Phalangist units along the Green Line, and in March 1985, in alliance with Druse and Palestinians, drove Phalangists out of positions east of Sidon.

With Syrian encouragement, the *Amal* militia launched a major attack on the Palestinian refugee camps of Bourj al-Brajneh, Sabra and Chatila in May 1985 in an effort to prevent the resurgence of a PLO military presence in the country. After six weeks, during which *Amal* suffered heavy casualties, the siege was called off as a result of mediation by the Syrians and the anti-Arafat Palestine National Salvation Front. Renewed fighting between *Amal* and the PLO broke out in late 1986, leading to a protracted siege of Sabra and Chatila, which was not finally lifted until the beginning of April 1987 when Syrian troops entered the camps. Prior to the entry into Beirut of Syrian peacekeeping troops, *Amal* fighters had clashed heavily with *Mourabitoun* and Druse PSP members, both of whom had become loosely allied with the PLO.

Arab Commando Cells

A note found near the bodies of three kidnap victims, two British and one American, who were shot dead in April 1986, claimed responsibility on behalf of the Arab Commando Cells (a hitherto unknown group). The note said that they had been killed by way of revenge for the US air-raid on Libya earlier the same month. There was some speculation that opportunist kidnappers had "sold" the men to Libyan agents after the raid; the UK Foreign Secretary, Sir Geoffrey Howe, stated later that there was "firm evidence" that the two British victims had been "in Libyan hands" at the time of their deaths.

Arab Red Knights (ARK)

This militia is the armed wing of the Arab Democratic Party (ADP), a Tripoli-based organization of Alawite Moslems closely allied to Syria (whose ruling hierarchy is largely made up of Alawites, who nonetheless are a minority in the mainly Sunni population of Syria). It clashed regularly with the *Tawheed* militia of the Sunni fundamentalist Islamic Unification Movement and with its Palestinian allies. A peace agreement was reached between the ADP and the IUM in September 1984 as a result of Syrian mediation. The agreement provided for the surrender of medium and heavy weapons (to be stored in strongpoints guarded by Lebanese and Syrian troops) and for the entry into Tripoli of a peacekeeping force of Syrian and Lebanese troops and Lebanese policemen, who would stage patrols to monitor the accord. The two militia leaders reportedly undertook to execute any of their members who broke the agreement.

Renewed heavy fighting broke out in December 1986 after *Tawheed* had attacked Syrian checkpoints. An alliance of the ARK, the Syrian National Socialist Party, the *Baath* Party and the Lebanese Communist Party decisively defeated *Tawheed* (see separate entries), some of whose members were subsequently shot in cold blood.

Arab Socialist Union (ASU)

This organization was named as a member of the National Democratic Front announced by the Druse leader Walid Jumblatt in October 1984. In January 1987, the ASU merged with the Nasserite Popular Organization to form a new grouping under the latter name (see separate entry).

An anonymous claim of responsibility on behalf of the "Arab Socialist Unionists" was received after the bombing of the US embassy in west Beirut in April 1983, though it is unlikely that this was the work of the ASU.

Baath Party

A Lebanese wing of the ruling party in Syria, this group maintained a small militia in areas of Lebanon under Syrian influence. It took part in fighting against the Islamic Unification Movement's *Tawheed* militia in Tripoli in December 1986 (see separate entry).

Black Flag

This single-incident group kidnapped three Spanish diplomats in January 1986 in support of a demand that Spain should release two Lebanese Shia prisoners who had been convicted of the attempted assassination of a Libyan diplomat in Spain in 1984. The diplomats were later released unharmed after intervention by *Amal* (see separate entry).

Brigade of the Resistance of the Faithful

Describing itself as an *Amal* splinter group (see separate entry), this Brigade carried out a katyusha rocket attack on the northern Israeli settlement of Kiryat Shimona in January 1986 (at a time when fundamentalist Shia activists were accusing *Amal* of having entered into a secret agreement with Israel).

Druse Independence Revolutionaries

An anonymous telephone caller to a Beirut news agency claimed that a group of this name was responsible for an explosion at *Amal* headquarters in August 1984 which *Amal* sources later said was due to a militiaman playing with a hand grenade in the vicinity of a gas cylinder. The main Druse organization, the Progressive Socialist Party, was at this time closely allied with *Amal* (see separate entries).

Druse Militia—see Progressive Socialist Party

Free Islamic Revolution

A "telephone group" of this name claimed responsibility, along with *Al Jihad al-Islami* and Islamic *Amal* (see separate entries), for the suicide car-bomb attacks on the headquarters of the French and US contingents of the multinational force in Beirut in October 1983.

Group 219-FA

A bomb explosion which damaged the British Bank of the Middle East in west Beirut in late April 1986 was claimed as its work by this previously unknown group. The attack occurred against a background of a series of actions against British interests, in Lebanon and elsewhere, in the wake of the US air-raid on Libya (which had been staged in part by British-based aircraft).

Hezbollah (Party of God)

Leadership. Shaikh Mohammed Hussein Fadlallah (spiritual leader)

Hezbollah's name derives from a Koranic quotation: "Lo, the Party of God, they are victorious". It is the principal fundamentalist Shia group in Lebanon, and as such something of a rival to the more moderate *Amal* (see separate entry). It is seen as subsuming, to a greater or lesser extent, other pro-Iranian Shia groups such as *Al Jihad al-Islami* and Islamic *Amal* (see separate entries), which have claimed responsibility for a number of spectacular attacks on Western interests. One of its leading figures, Shaikh Ibrahim al Amin, has stated that "*Hezbollah* is not an organization but it functions in an organized manner". Some commentators have suggested that *Hezbollah* supporters simply use titles such as *Al Jihad al-Islami* to commit acts, including kidnapping, which are subsequently condemned by *Hezbollah* spiritual leaders, such as Shaikh Fadlallah (the author of a work entitled *Islam and the Logic of Force*). In Islamic theology, such a dualistic approach is known as *taqqiyah*, meaning "to approve of something contradictory to your faith if the need arises".

Israeli air force jets bombed a base allegedly occupied by *Hezbollah* activists at Nabi Chit in the Bekaa Valley in October 1983, in retaliation for a suicide car-bomb attack on Israeli military headquarters in Tyre, responsibility for which was claimed by *Al Jihad al-Islami*. In August 1984, *Hezbollah* supporters were among a group of Shia fundamentalists who set fire to the Saudi consulate in protest at recently introduced restrictions on the issuing of visas to Lebanese wishing to make the *haj* (pilgrimage) to the Moslem holy sites of Mecca and Medina.

From 1984 onwards, *Hezbollah*, together with *Amal* and Palestinian guerrillas, took part in Lebanese National Resistance operations against Israeli forces and the South Lebanon Army (SLA—see separate entry). *Hezbollah*'s more militant, anti-Israeli stance resulted in clashes between it and *Amal*, whom it characterized as prepared to reach understandings with the Israelis. The first such clashes took place in west Beirut in February 1985. In the same month, *Hezbollah* members staged a violent demonstration in Sidon following government-sponsored celebrations to mark the Israeli withdrawal from the city. *Hezbollah* denounced the government, attacked bars and liquor stores and put up posters of Ayatollah Khomeini. Over the next two years, *Hezbollah*'s influence in the south increased at the expense of *Amal*, in part because *Hezbollah* paid their fighters more. The group played a leading role in attacks on the SLA, inflicting several defeats on them and, in one case, completely overrunning an SLA position. By mid-1985, *Hezbollah* had established something of an informal alliance with the Palestine Liberation Organization (PLO—see separate entry under Palestinian Movements), based on their mutual antipathy towards Israel. While *Amal* limited its demands to the total withdrawal of Israeli forces from Lebanon, *Hezbollah*'s rhetoric included exhortations to liberate Jerusalem.

The "Islamic Resistance Front", widely viewed as a cover for *Hezbollah*, claimed responsibility for the kidnapping of two Israeli soldiers in February 1986. One of the soldiers was later killed. During 1986 *Hezbollah* also clashed with UNIFIL peacekeeping forces (which were generally supported by *Amal*). Israeli Air Force jets carried out raids of *Hezbollah*-controlled villages. In the north, *Hezbollah* similarly established links with the Sunni fundamentalist Islamic Unification Movement and its *Tawheed* militia (see separate entry).

A car-bomb attack outside the west Beirut home of Shaikh Fadlallah in March 1985, which killed over 60 people, was reported to be the work of a Lebanese unit which had received supplies and training from the US Central Intelligence Agency (CIA) as part of a covert "counter-terrorism" operation. Reports in Western newspapers stressed that the operation had been dismantled after the bombing, which they claimed had been carried out without the prior knowledge of the CIA.

In its supposed role as effective co-ordinator of Shia fundamentalist anti-Western activity in Lebanon, *Hezbollah* was linked to the numerous kidnappings of Westerners from early 1984 onwards, despite the fact that leading figures such as Fadlallah spoke out against kidnappings, particularly those of teachers, which *Hezbollah* described as a "conspiracy against education". In December 1985, Fadlallah promised that he was "exerting efforts" to secure the release of foreign hostages held in Lebanon. *Hezbollah* was also portrayed by Western sources as being involved in the hijacking of the TWA airliner to Beirut in June 1985, staged to demand the release of Lebanese and Palestinian prisoners held in Israeli detention camps.

At the end of 1985, *Hezbollah* rejected the Syrian-mediated peace agreement reached between the mainstream *Amal* and the (Druse) Progressive Socialist and the Christian Phalangist militias. *Hezbollah* fighters clashed with Syrian troops in the Bekaa Valley in June 1986.

In a political turn-around, however, *Hezbollah* declared its support for the security agreement of June 1986, under which a mixed force of Syrian and Lebanese troops entered west Beirut in August. In conformity with the plan, *Hezbollah* fighters withdrew from the streets, and a statement from the group declared that "it fully approves and supports all steps which may achieve reasonable security for the oppressed Moslems and Christians in the capital".

In January 1987, *Hezbollah* leaders met Terry Waite, the Archbishop of Canterbury's special envoy, in connexion with his effort to secure the release of foreign kidnap victims. Shortly after the meeting, Waite disappeared, and was presumed to have been kidnapped. *Hezbollah* denied that it was holding him, but pointed out that it had warned him not to visit Lebanon on this occasion, and it drew attention to the emerging links between Waite's mission and the US attempts at an "arms-for-hostages" deal with Iran.

Two brothers of a man described in some circles as "head of security" for *Hezbollah* were arrested in West Germany on separate occasions in January 1987. One of the two had been wanted in connexion with the TWA hijack. Two West German businessmen in Beirut were kidnapped the same month.

Independent Movement for the Liberation of Kidnap Victims

This misleadingly named group claimed responsibility for a series of attacks on west Beirut's small Armenian community in May 1986, against whom it threatened to mount an "implacable war" to drive them out of the city, in revenge for their alleged support for hard-line Phalangist policies. In June, it freed two of 11 Armenian hostages whom it said it was holding in support of demands that the Phalangists should release over 2,000 Moslem kidnap victims.

Islamic Amal

Leadership. Hussain Mussavi

Islamic *Amal* was founded by Hussain Mussavi in 1982 after he had been expelled from the command council of *Amal* (see separate entry) after arguments over policy with Nabi Berri and other *Amal* leaders. Although it exists as an independent organization, based currently in the vicinity of Baalbek in the eastern Bekaa Valley, Islamic *Amal* is closely linked to *Hezbollah* (see separate entry), and can be seen as a part of the Shia fundamentalist movement in Lebanon for which *Hezbollah* provides an overall umbrella.

After the bombing of the headquarters of the French and US contingents of the multinational peacekeeping force in October 1983, Hussain Mussavi denied that Islamic *Amal* had been involved, but added that he approved of the action and hoped that his organization would participate in similar operations in the future. Following the bomb attacks, French aircraft staged an unsuccessful raid on Islamic *Amal* positions at Ras al-Ain, in the Bekaa Valley. In retaliation for a suicide bombing of the Israeli military headquarters in Tyre at the same time, Israeli air force jets attacked Islamic *Amal* positions in the Bekaa. Responsibility for the bombing had been claimed by *Al Jihad al-Islami* (see separate entry), another Shia group with close affiliation to *Hezbollah*. In the mid-1980s, Western observers suspected that Islamic *Amal* was to some extent involved in the kidnapping of foreigners, particularly US, French and UK citizens.

Islamic *Amal*'s relations with Syrian forces in eastern Lebanon were at times strained, as Syria was keen to impose some control on the group's activities. In May 1986, there were armed clashes between Syrian troops and Islamic *Amal* members.

Islamic Jihad for the Liberation of Palestine (IJLP)

The previously unknown IJLP claimed responsibility for the kidnapping of four staff members of the private Beirut University in January 1987 (three of the victims being US citizens, the fourth Indian). In response to threatening moves by US naval units in the eastern Mediterranean, the IJLP warned that the four hostages would be executed in the event of any US attack on Beirut. It subsequently demanded the release of 400 prisoners held in detention by Israel in exchange for the release of the hostages. A number of deadlines set by the group passed without incident, however.

Islamic Liberation Organization—Khaled Ibn Walid Forces

Another single-incident group, believed to be connected to *Hezbollah* (see separate entry) and/or the Islamic Unification Movement, it claimed responsibility for the September 1985 kidnapping of four Soviet diplomats in Beirut, threatening to execute them unless the fighting in Tripoli between the IUM's *Tawheed* militia and pro-Syrian forces was stopped. After killing one of the diplomats, the group warned that "we will continue to execute the hostages and will hold the

Soviet Union responsible for restraining its stooges in Lebanon". Despite a ceasefire agreement reached in Tripoli, the kidnappers warned that they would not release the diplomats until they were assured of "Syria's intentions" with regard to Tripoli; they also accused the Soviet Union of "holding Afghanistan hostage". After appeals for their release from *Hezbollah* leaders, the diplomats were eventually freed at the end of October. One report quoted Israeli sources as claiming that the release followed the castration and murder of a relative of an unnamed radical Shia leader by the Soviet state security service, the KGB.

Islamic Resistance Front

A term used to describe attacks on Israelis and Israeli-backed forces in southern Lebanon by Shia guerrillas linked to *Hezbollah* (see separate entry). Responsibility for the kidnapping of two Israeli soldiers, one of whom was soon killed, was claimed on behalf of the Front in February 1986.

Islamic Unification Movement—see Tawheed

Jundullah (Army of God)

This is a fundamentalist Sunni Moslem organization based in Tripoli and allied with the Islamic Unification Movement. The home of one of its leaders was the subject of a car-bomb attack on June 19, 1985, by the hitherto unknown Christian Revolutionaries of the Cedar Tree (see separate entry), who warned that "no fundamentalist Moslem will be allowed to remain in Lebanon".

Lebanese National Resistance

This is not an organization as such but rather a name used by anti-Israeli political leaders and sections of the media to describe operations carried out by such as *Amal*, *Hezbollah* and the Palestine Liberation Organization (PLO) against Israeli forces and the South Lebanon Army. Following the Israeli withdrawal from Sidon in February 1985, President Amin Gemayel praised the "honourable national resistance".

Mourabitoun Militia

Leadership. Ibrahim Koleïlat (l.)

Members of this Sunni Moslem group were reported to have been involved in a clash with guards of Dany Chamoun, then leader of the Tiger Militia of the (Christian) National Liberal Party (NLP)—see separate entry—while he was visiting the Saudi Arabian ambassador in hospital on Dec. 15, 1978. In February 1980 *Mourabitoun* took control of most government buildings in the southern coastal port of Sidon after Syrian troops had withdrawn from them.

Fighting took place in west Beirut in November 1980 between *Mourabitoun* members and followers of the (pro-Syrian) Syrian Nationalist Social Party—also known as the Syrian Popular Party and standing for a Greater Syria, to include also Lebanon.

On April 26, 1981, *Mourabitoun* units attacked the port of Jounieh (north of Beirut), the headquarters of the Phalangist Christian militia, and in this attack military equipment supplied by Libya was used; it was also reported that some 300 Libyans had been attached to the *Mourabitoun* Militia. In June 1981 *Mourabitoun* members were also involved in fighting with Kurdish activists.

During 1984-87, *Mourabitoun*'s influence declined in the face of the rise of Shia groups such as *Amal* and *Hezbollah*, and of the (Druse) Progressive Socialist Party militia (see separate entries). In March 1984, *Mourabitoun* fighters were driven out of positions along the Green Line by Druse units in what was described as a "law and order operation" by the Druse leader, Walid Jumblatt. Further clashes broke out between the two groups in west Beirut in July. They were halted by the intervention of the (mainly Moslem) Sixth Brigade of the Lebanese Army. *Mourabitoun* members took part alongside *Amal* and Druse fighters in attacks on Phalangist positions east of Sidon in March 1985. *Mourabitoun*'s "6th February" Brigade was defeated in battles with *Amal* in west Beirut in June 1986. Prior to the Syrian entry into the city in February 1987, *Amal* was involved in further clashes with *Mourabitoun*, whose fighters on this occasion were allied with the Druse.

Moussa Sadr Brigades

A number of operations were staged by *Amal* sympathizers (see separate entry) invoking the name of the Imam Moussa Sadr, a spiritual leader of Lebanese Shia Moslems who had "disappeared" at the end of a visit to Libya in August 1978, and who was believed by some Shias to be held captive there. Different groups have used other similar names. A group of 12 Shia gunmen, calling themselves the Sons of Moussa Sadr, seized a Kuwaiti aircraft at Beirut airport in February 1982, demanding that it should be flown to Tehran (Iran). The hijackers surrendered to Lebanese army units after freeing all the passengers and crew, and were themselves allowed to go free. (Their leader had led six of the previous eight such operations staged to secure Moussa Sadr's release, and had never been detained.) A further hijack, this time of a Libyan airliner, was staged in June 1983 by two Shias demanding Moussa Sadr's release. The aircraft landed at Cyprus where the hijackers were detained and sentenced to seven years in prison.

The Moussa Sadr Brigades claimed responsibility for the kidnapping of two Libyan diplomats in June and July 1984 in west Beirut. In June 1985 (i.e. during *Amal*'s siege of the Palestinian refugee camps in Beirut) the Imam Moussa Sadr Brigade staged a hijack of a Jordanian aircraft in support of a demand that every Palestinian should leave the camps.

Nasserite Popular Organization

In January 1987 this group (which takes its name from the former Egyptian President Nasser) merged with the Arab Socialist Union (ASU—see separate entry) to form a new organization, also under the name of Nasserite Popular Organization. Celebrations marking the merger were attended by representatives of the Syrian-based Palestine National Salvation Front and an Egyptian opposition delegation.

October 24 Movement

Formerly known as the Popular Resistance Movement, this alliance of Sunni Moslems and Palestinian guerrillas clashed in Tripoli in late 1982 and early 1983 with the pro-Syrian Alawite Moslem Arab Red Knights militia (the armed wing of the Arab Democratic Party—see separate entry), which was supported by Syrian paratroopers. Further communal clashes involving the October 24 Movement took place in Tripoli later in 1983. The name fell into disuse after that time.

Organization for Vengeance for the Martyrs of Sabra and Chatila

Regarded as a "telephone group", this "organization" claimed responsibility for the bombing of the US embassy building in west Beirut in April 1983. Its name refers to the two Palestinian refugee camps whose residents were massacred by Christian gunmen in September 1982.

Organization of the Oppressed of the Earth

This Organization claimed responsibility for attacks on Beirut's dwindling Jewish community during 1985-86. At the end of 1985, it announced that it had killed a Jewish kidnap victim as a protest against the detention by the South Lebanon Army (SLA—see separate entry) of a group of Shia Moslems at Khiam. Early in January a further Jew was killed, ostensibly in retaliation for an SLA raid on a Shia village. In December 1986, the organization claimed responsibility for the murder of three Jews whom it described as "spies" (in a statement which repeated its earlier demands for the release of detained Shias). The following month, it claimed responsibility for the kidnap of four university teachers—three Americans and one Indian; an incident which was also claimed as its work by the Islamic Jihad for the Liberation of Palestine (IJLP—see separate entry).

Popular Liberation Army

A Sunni Moslem militia based in Sidon, the Popular Liberation Army was given responsibility for taking over Palestinian positions around the city as part of a ceasefire agreement between the Palestine Liberation Organization (PLO) and *Amal* in October 1986. The Popular Liberation Army had remained neutral during recent fighting between the two groups. The PLO subsequently recaptured some of the positions.

Popular Resistance Movement—see October 24 Movement

Progressive Socialist Party (PSP)

Leadership. Walid Jumblatt (pres.)

The PSP was founded by Kamal Jumblatt in 1949. Despite its title, it is essentially the political organization of the Moslem Druse community in Lebanon (an ethno-religious group whose heartland is the Chouf Mountain area to the east of Beirut). The Jumblatt clan has for centuries been one of the leading Druse families. After Kamal Jumblatt's assassination in 1977, his son, Walid, took over the leadership of the clan and of the PSP. He maintained close ties with the Syrians, who provided military support to the PSP.

During the civil war of 1975-76, the PSP allied itself with other Moslem groups against the Phalangists (see separate entry). In 1977, it formed the main part of the Lebanese National Movement, and as such was involved in frequent clashes with the Christian militia. Following the withdrawal of the Israeli army from the Chouf mountains, there was heavy fighting in September 1983 between Druse and army units in the hills to the south-east of Beirut. A Druse armoured advance was checked at Souk el-Gharb, largely thanks to the shelling of Druse villages and to military concentrations by US battleships lying offshore. French aircraft also carried out bombing raids in the Chouf, where the Syrian army maintained artillery emplacements. (Both France and the USA had contingents in Lebanon as part of the multinational peacekeeping force introduced in 1982.)

Having succeeded in their aim of preventing (mainly Christian) army units being deployed in the Chouf, and having reduced Phalangist influence in the area, the PSP in October 1983 announced the setting up of a local administration to govern the Chouf "until the return of central government institutions". The move was denounced by a Lebanese government spokesman as "an attempt to partition Lebanon on a canton basis", adding that it formed part of "the long-term strategy of the Syrian government to extend its hegemony over parts of Lebanon".

Henceforward W. Jumblatt was one of the leading figures on the Lebanese political scene, and one of the two main opponents of President Gemayel (the other being the *Amal* leader, Nabi Berri—see separate entry). Jumblatt and the PSP took part in several opposition alliances, including the National Salvation Front (set up in 1983), the National Democratic Front (1984) and the National Unity Front (1985). He joined the Cabinet as Minister of Public Works, Transport and Tourism in April 1984, two months after an *Amal*-PSP offensive had forced the government to resign after the army had been driven out of Moslem west Beirut. Following this success, Druse fighters also drove Phalangists out of positions to the south and south-east of the city, as far down the coast as Damour. In March, the PSP turned against the Sunni *Mourabitoun* militia (see separate entry), driving them out of positions along the Green Line dividing east from west Beirut.

Unlike some other Moslem groups, the PSP maintained contact with Western powers in Lebanon, on occasion providing guards for units of the peacekeeping force and for US diplomats.

In March-April 1985, Druse forces, assisted by *Amal* and local Palestine Liberation Organization (PLO) units, successfully counter-attacked Phalangist fighters loyal to Samir Geaga in battles east of Sidon, during which a number of Christian villages were taken.

The PSP fell out with *Amal* over the latter's siege of the Palestinian refugee camps in Beirut in May-June 1985, however, and it allowed PLO artillery units based in the Druse-controlled areas to shell *Amal* positions around the camps. Although a reconciliation was achieved, relations between the two militias remained tense, and fighting broke out between the PSP and *Amal* in west Beirut in November 1985. During 1986, the PSP became increasingly allied with the PLO and *Mourabitoun* against *Amal* (although Berri and Jumblatt remained in contact), and heavy Druse-*Amal* clashes which broke out in Beirut in early 1987 were halted only by the entry into the city of Syrian troops.

Revenge and Justice Front

This previously unknown group claimed responsibility for the assassination of a French military attaché in east Beirut in September 1986.

Revolutionary Brigade for the Liberation of the Border Strip

A spokesman claiming to represent a group of this name warned in September 1986 that the United Nations Interim Force in Lebanon would be regarded as hostages unless Israeli forces refrained from operating in Lebanon, in accordance with the terms of a UN resolution (No. 425) passed in 1978.

Revolutionary Justice Organization (RJO)

The RJO (which sometimes refers to itself as the Islamic Revolutionary Justice Organization) emerged in 1986 when it claimed to be holding four French television crewmen kidnapped while filming a *Hezbollah* rally in March of that year. In freeing two of them in June, it demanded that the French government should change its policy towards Lebanon. In November 1986, it released two other Frenchmen kidnapped earlier, after which the French government expressed thanks to Syria, Saudi Arabia and Algeria for helping to secure their release. A third television crewman was released in December 1986, following the reported arrest in France of six Arab opponents of President Assad of Syria, apparently as a result of some co-operation between the French and Syrian security services. At the beginning of 1987, the RJO was claiming to be holding two US citizens kidnapped in September and October 1986, in addition to the remaining French television crew member.

Revolutionary Organization of Socialist Moslems (ROSM)

It is not clear whether this group, which has carried out a series of attacks on British interests, is a purely Lebanese organization. Some observers see it as a front for the militant Palestinian Abu Nidal Group (see entry under Palestinian section on page 276). The ROSM has often demanded the release of three men imprisoned in the United Kingdom after being convicted of the attempted assassination of the Israeli ambassador to London, Shlomo Argov, in June 1982 (which provided the immediate trigger for the Israeli invasion of Lebanon). The attack had been claimed by the Abu Nidal Group.

The ROSM first emerged in March 1984, to claim responsibility for the assassination of a British Council official in Greece, which it said was in protest at Britain's attempt "to resume its former colonial role in the world by spreading colonial culture under a new guise" and also at the "continuing detention and persecution of our Moslem fighters" in Britain. The British Council revealed after the shooting that its offices in Beirut and Baghdad (Iraq) had been the subject of bomb attacks the previous week. The killing coincided with the visit by Queen Elizabeth to Jordan (whose diplomats had recently been the subject of attacks by the Abu Nidal Group).

In August 1984 the ROSM claimed responsibility for the kidnapping of a British Reuters journalist in Lebanon; after his release the following month, Reuters expressed its gratitude to President Assad of Syria (the base of the Abu Nidal Group). The ROSM claimed responsibility for the killing of the British deputy high commissioner in India in November 1984, after which it repeated its demand for the release of the three prisoners in the UK, whom it described as ROSM members. Alec Collett, a British journalist who was kidnapped in March 1985, was described by the ROSM as a hostage for the release of its members from Britain. In April 1986, the ROSM released a video-tape of what it claimed was the execution by hanging of A. Collett, which it said was in retaliation for "the joint savage American-British raid on Libya" (a reference to the US air attack on the Libyan cities of Tripoli and Benghazi, which had in part been mounted by aircraft based in Britain). The hanging followed the killing of two British teachers, also apparently in revenge for the raid (see separate entry for Arab Commando Cells).

Sons of Moussa Sadr—see Moussa Sadr Brigades

Sunni Islamic Resistance Movement

A warning to the Syrian army to leave Lebanon was issued in Beirut in the name of this group in December 1986 (at a time when the Sunni fundamentalist Islamic Unification Movement's *Tawheed* militia—see separate entry—was under attack by pro-Syrian forces in Tripoli).

Syrian National Socialist Party (SNSP)

Leadership. Juban Jraysh

The SNSP is a Lebanese organization which believes that Lebanon should be considered as a part of a Greater Syria. (For many centuries prior to the First World War, the area now covered by Lebanon was, theoretically at least, administered from Damascus as part of the Syrian province of the Ottoman Empire.)

The SNSP joined the opposition National Democratic Front established by the Druse leader Walid Jumblatt in October 1984. In early 1986, it provided artillery support to Phalangist elements loyal to their leader, Elie Hobeika, who had signed a Syrian-mediated peace accord with the Druse and with *Amal* (see separate entry), and who was being opposed by units loyal to the hard-line Phalangist Samir Geaga. Later in the year, the SNSP was involved in clashes with the Islamic Unification Movement's *Tawheed* militia around Tripoli, and in December 1986 it took part in the destruction of *Tawheed* as part of a Syrian-backed alliance centred on the Arab Red Knights militia (see separate entry).

In early 1987 there were reports of a split in the SNSP leadership, with one faction continuing to support the recently deposed leader, Isam Mahayri, and the other being grouped around Inaam Rahd.

Tawheed

Tawheed is the armed wing of the Islamic Unification Movement (IUM), which is led by Shaikh Saad Shaban and is a Sunni fundamentalist group which exercised considerable power in Tripoli until it was crushed at the end of 1986. Having initially supported Syrian influence, the IUM came into conflict with the Syrians from 1983 onwards, after which *Tawheed* was frequently involved in clashes with the Arab Red Knights (ARK), the pro-Syrian Alawite militia of the Arab Democratic Party (ADP). This party and the Syrians were opposed to the form of Islamic rule introduced in areas under IUM control by the so-called "Islamic Committee" and "Mosques Committee". The IUM enjoyed the support of pro-Arafat Palestinian guerrillas in the area, who had fought against Syrian-backed Palestine Liberation Organization (PLO) groups on the outskirts of Tripoli in 1983. Having initially taken a neutral position in this conflict, the IUM later intervened on the side of the Arafat loyalists after Tripoli itself had been shelled. In view of their shared fundamentalist stance, the IUM established links with *Hezbollah* during 1985 (see separate entry).

The fighting between *Tawheed* and the ARK was temporarily halted by a Syrian-mediated peace agreement in September 1984 (see separate entry for Arab Red Knights). It broke out again in September 1985, at which time three Soviet diplomats in Beirut were kidnapped by an organization apparently allied to the IUM which was seeking to force Moscow to use its influence to dissuade the Syrians from supporting the ADP (see entry under "Islamic Liberation Organization"). Further clashes, principally involving *Tawheed* and the (Lebanese) Syrian National Socialist Party (SNSP—see separate entry), took place outside Tripoli in June 1986.

Tawheed was decisively defeated in December 1986 after bloody fighting with a Syrian-backed alliance composed of the ARK, the SNSP, the Lebanese Communist Party and the *Baath* Party. The fighting began when *Tawheed* attacked Syrian-manned checkpoints. After its defeat, large numbers of *Tawheed* fighters were massacred by their rivals.

Vengeance Party

This previously unknown group claimed responsibility by telephone for the murder of a kidnapped Dutch Jesuit priest in March 1985.

Left-wing Movements

Committee of Solidarity with Arab and Middle Eastern Political Prisoners (*Comité de solidarité avec les prisonniers politiques arabes et du proche-orient*)

This group, which was believed to be closely linked to the Lebanese Armed Revolutionary Factions (see separate entry), carried out a series of bombing attacks in France in mid-1986 (see entry on the LARF).

Lebanese Armed Revolutionary Factions (Brigades) (*Factions armées révolutionnaires libanaises*, FARL or LARF)

Members of this Maronite Marxist group made an attempt to kill the US chargé d'affaires in Paris (Christian Chapman) in November 1981, when it accused the United States of leading "a fascist, Zionist, reactionary alliance against the Lebanese people", and it later claimed responsibility for killing the US deputy military attaché in Paris (Lt.-Col. Charles Ray) on Jan. 18, 1982.

In February 1984, the group claimed responsibility for the assassination in Rome of the director-general of the Multinational Force and Observers in Sinai. It also claimed responsibility for the kidnapping of a French diplomat in Beirut in March 1985.

The alleged leader of the LARF, Georges Ibrahim Abdallah, was sentenced to life imprisonment in France in February 1987 for complicity in the murder of Lt.-Col. Ray, of an Israeli diplomat in Paris in April 1982, and for the attempted murder of the US consul-general in Strasbourg in March 1984. This trial followed earlier convictions in July 1986 on charges of possession of arms and explosives and false documents and of criminal association, for which he received a four-year prison sentence. His release was one of the demands made by the Committee of Solidarity with Arab and Middle Eastern Political Prisoners during its bombing campaign in Paris in September 1986. Some observers saw the Committee as merely a front for the LARF.

Lebanese Communist Party (*Parti communiste libanais*—LCP)

Leadership. George Hawi (sec.-gen.)

Formed in October 1924, the LCP began its activities by fighting against the French occupation of Lebanon (under a League of Nations mandate) and for national independence, democratic freedoms and social and economic demands of the working people. In 1925 it became affiliated to the Communist International (Comintern). It achieved a measure of legality in 1936 and was recognized by law in 1972. In 1965 it formed part of a National Progressive Front and on the outbreak of civil war in April 1975 it joined the alliance of pro-Palestinian Moslem leftists in the struggle against the Lebanese Christians. During 1981 and 1986, its members were involved in armed clashes with *Amal* (see separate entry).

The objectives of the LCP within the leftist Lebanese National Movement reconstituted in September 1977 have been to safeguard the unity of the people, the territorial integrity of Lebanon and its Arab character, to defend its independence and sovereignty, to liberate southern Lebanon from Israeli occupation, and to strengthen co-operation with Arab countries, in particular with Syria, and with the Soviet Union, other socialist countries and the non-aligned and third-world countries. The final aim of the (pro-Soviet) LCP is to establish a national democratic regime to open the road to transition to socialism. It issues several publications, in particular the daily *An-Nida*.

LCP members in the Tripoli area clashed in October 1983 with militiamen of the anti-Syrian *Tawheed* (see separate entry), the armed wing of the Sunni fundamentalist Islamic Unification Movement (IUM). In October 1984, the LCP was named as a member of the newly formed National Democratic Front, launched by Walid Jumblatt, the Druse leader, to demand political reforms.

In a rare claim of military action against Israeli-backed forces, the LCP asserted responsibility for a suicide bombing of the "Voice of Hope" radio station, 2 km north of the Israeli border. Originally set up by the Haddad Militia, the "Voice of Hope" was currently run by a US missionary organization.

Tension between the LCP and *Amal* in southern Lebanon reached a high point in February 1986, when *Amal* moved to limit the LCP's influence in the area. Several of the Party's central committee members were killed at this time, although *Amal* did not formally claim responsibility.

LCP fighters in December 1986 fought as part of an alliance which included the Syrian National Socialist Party, the Arab Red Knights militia and the *Baath* Party (see separate entries), which effectively destroyed the power of the IUM with the defeat of its *Tawheed* militia.

The LCP is recognized by the Communist parties of the Soviet bloc.

Lesotho

Capital: Maseru — Pop. 1,530,000

The Kingdom of Lesotho is a hereditary monarchy in which, under a decree of Jan. 20, 1986, executive and legislative power is held by the King who will act in accordance with the advice of a six-member Military Council headed by Maj.-Gen. Justin Lekhanya (C.-in-C. of the Lesotho paramilitary force) and of a Council of Ministers consisting mainly of civilians. In this Council, which has no Prime Minister, Maj.-Gen. Lekhanya holds several portfolios including those of Defence and Internal Security. There is no Parliament.

The Military Council came to power by deposing the Prime Minister, Chief Leabua Jonathan, on Jan. 20, 1986. This action followed a raid launched from South Africa on Dec. 20, 1985, when nine persons, including six South African political refugees (of the banned African National Congress), were killed—a raid for which the South African government denied responsibility, which was claimed by the Lesotho Liberation Army [see below]. The South African government declared on the same day that "terrorist elements" were continuing to operate against South Africa from other African countries, and on Jan. 1, 1986, it imposed a de facto blockade on Lesotho.

On Jan. 14 the government of Chief Jonathan arrested opposition party leaders who had returned from a visit to South Africa; they were accused of having plotted with the South African authorities to bring about the downfall of Chief Jonathan; other opposition leaders were arrested later.

Following the assumption of power by the Military Council the South African blockade was lifted. As a result of a meeting in Cape Town on Jan. 21 between a delegation of the Military Council and the South African Foreign Minister it was agreed that "neither side would allow its territory to be used for the planning or execution of acts of violence or terror" and that both sides would take steps to see that this principle was applied. (It was understood that this would mean that South African support for the Lesotho Liberation Army—see below—never officially acknowledged, would now cease.)

Under a decree of March 27, 1986, the King banned all political activity until a new Constitution had been agreed upon. In defiance of this ban the five political parties which had been in opposition to Chief Jonathan's Basotho National Party issued, on May 20, 1986, a joint statement calling on the Military Council to form an all-party government of national reconciliation and to effect a return to elections and civilian rule.

On Nov. 15, 1986, two former ministers under the regime of Chief Jonathan were abducted and killed by unidentified men.

Chief Jonathan died in Pretoria on April 5, 1987.

It was confirmed on June 15, 1987, that Charles Mofeli, the leader of the United Democratic Party, had been detained and the party suspended. On June 2 C. Mofeli had addressed a petition to the King and to Maj.-Gen. Lekhanya, appealing for a lifting of the suspension of political activity and a restoration of parliamentary government.

Basotho Congress Party (BCP)—Dissident Faction

Leadership. Ntsu Mokhehle (l.)

The BCP was originally founded in 1952 (as the National Basutoland Congress) by Ntsu Mokhehle. It gained 25 out of the 60 seats in the first general elections to a National Assembly held in 1965. In elections held in 1970 the BCP claimed to have gained a majority of votes and seats, but the government suspended the Constitution and the BCP refused to co-operate with the regime. In 1973, however, the BCP was split—one section of it accepting seats in an appointed National Assembly and the other remaining, under the leadership of Mokhehle, in opposition and making an unsuccessful attempt to overthrow the government in 1974. On March 10, 1975, prison sentences ranging from four to nine years were imposed on 15 BCP members for high treason. Mokhehle and other leaders of his faction had earlier left the country.

In 1979-80 heavy fighting occurred in parts of Lesotho. Mokhehle stated on Dec. 8, 1979, that guerrilla forces of the BCP, whom he described as the Lesotho Liberation Army (LLA), were active in the country, and on Dec. 14 he claimed that the LLA had 65 Libyan-trained guerrillas and 500-1,000 other men in training in secret mountain camps. Naleli Ntlama, described as political commissar of the LLA, asserted on Nov. 17, 1980, that his organization operated entirely from bases in Lesotho and was not assisted by South Africa but bought its weapons from private gun-runners and smuggled them into the country, or captured them from government forces.

During 1982 the LLA intensified its guerrilla operations.

The BCP, in a statement on Dec. 9, 1982, accused the Prime Minister of Lesotho of having disregarded the national interest by allowing the Communist Party of South Africa to establish "anti-South African military bases on the sovereign territory of the Kingdom of Lesotho".

During 1983-85 the LLA continued its activities, attacking supporters of the ruling Basotho National Party (BNP) and killing members of the Lesotho paramilitary force. A general amnesty for political offenders was announced by the Military Council on Feb. 6, 1986, but it was reported that the LLS had not accepted this and that it had declared that it would oppose the new regime also until the LLA's demands were met, notably those for the restoration of the 1966 Constitution (which had been suspended by Chief Jonathan in 1970), the integration of the LLA in the Lesotho paramilitary force and the holding of elections within six months.

Communist Party of Lesotho (CPL)

Leadership. Jacob Kena (sec.-gen.)

This party was formed in May 1962, mainly by migrant workers employed in the Republic of South Africa. It was the only legal party of its kind in southern Africa until it was banned in February 1970. On Aug. 9, 1983, the office of the CPL was reported to have been raided by security police who confiscated an amount of literature.

The CPL is officially recognized by the Communist parties of the Soviet bloc countries.

Liberia

Capital: Monrovia Pop. 2,190,000

The Republic of Liberia has an executive President elected for four years by universal adult suffrage, a 26-member Senate elected similarly for eight years and a 64-member House of Representatives elected for four years. There is a Cabinet appointed by the President and consisting of civilians, except for the Minister of National Defence (who is a high-ranking officer). There is no Prime Minister.

According to the official results of elections held on Oct. 15, 1985, seats in the House of Representatives were distributed as follows: National Democratic Party of Liberia 51, Liberian Action Party 8, Liberia Unification Party 3, Unity Party 2.

The holding of elections followed five years of rule by a military People's Redemption Council (PRC) headed by C.-in-C. Samuel K. Doe, in power from April 12, 1980, and dissolved on July 21, 1984. A draft Constitution had been approved in a referendum on July 3, 1983. A ban on political activities imposed in 1980 was lifted on July 26, 1984, whereafter a number of political parties were formed. By September 1985 only the above four parties which gained seats in the October 1985 elections had been granted legal status. Two other parties, banned in August 1985 on the ground that they advocated "foreign" (i.e. socialist or communist) policies, were (i) the Liberian People's Party, led by Dr Amos Sawyer and supported by members of the Movement for Justice in Africa (Moja), and (ii) the United People's Party led by Gabriel Bacchus Matthews. Other parties not given legal status were the Convention Democratic Party, the Liberation Party and the National Integration Party.

Numerous attempts to overthrow the existing regime in Liberia have been made since 1980.

Several attempted counter-coups were reported in April-May 1980, following which two further attempts to overthrow the PRC government were made in May and August 1981. In connexion with the May 1981 attempt 13 men were condemned to death by a special court-martial board and executed in June, while the August 1981 plot resulted in the execution of five leading members of the PRC (including its co-chairman and deputy head of state).

The discovery of a further plot was announced by C.-in-C. Doe on Nov. 21, 1983; he named 12 alleged conspirators (most of them army officers) whose ringleader, he alleged, was Brig.-Gen. Thomas Quiwonkpa (who had been Commanding Officer of the armed forces from April 1980 to October 1983). One of the accused said on Dec. 12, 1983, that the aim of the coup had been to establish Brig.-Gen. Quiwonkpa as head of state, to return the country to civilian rule, to try the members of the PRC for "nepotism, tribalism, cuts and delays in government salaries, secret killings and mismanagement of the economy", and to execute three other government officials immediately. While Brig.-Gen. Quiwonkpa was thought to have fled the country, 12 army officers and seven civilians were tried between Jan. 4 and April 5, 1984, with 13 defendants being found quilty of "high treason, murder, mutiny and solicitation to overthrow the government", and sentenced to death. Six others were found not guilty for lack of evidence. The death sentences in 10 of the 13 cases were repealed on April 7 on orders by C.-in-C. Doe, who, on April 12, granted Brig.-Gen. Quiwonkpa unconditional clemency and invited him to return to Liberia.

On Aug. 19, 1984, it was announced that several persons had been arrested in connexion with an alleged plot to overthrow the government. On Aug. 20 C.-in-C. Doe claimed that, among those arrested, Dr Amos Sawyer, the leader of the Liberian People's Party (LPP), had intended to install a socialist government in Liberia (with the aid of foreign countries, including three unnamed African states) after blowing up important public installations, setting fire to the city of Monrovia and carrying out mass arrests. Dr Sawyer was apparently supported by a Revolutionary Action Committee (React). Student protests at the arrest of the alleged plotters were suppressed by troops on Aug. 22; it was later stated officially that 102 persons had been injured, whereas the React movement claimed later that 16 people had been killed as a result of these protests. The university was closed (and not reopened until Nov. 29, 1984). However, on Oct. 6, 1984, it was announced that all those arrested had been released, with C.-in-C. Doe explaining on Oct. 12 that this had been decided for reasons of national unity.

An attempt to assassinate the head of state (Samuel E. Doe) was made on April 1, 1985, by a colonel who was deputy commander of the Executive Mansion Guard. He was captured on April 4 and publicly executed four days later.

Following the elections of Oct. 15, 1985, which had in opposition circles been considered to have been rigged, Brig.-Gen. Quiwonka attempted to stage another coup on Nov. 12. However, it failed, and the Brig-Gen. was reportedly killed on Nov. 15. It was later reported that there had been three days of fighting in which an estimated 1,000 people had been killed. The Minister of Justice stated in early January 1986 that there had been 600 deaths. An undisclosed number of civilians and military personnel were arrested in connexion with the attempt, and on Nov. 19 several organizations, including the Press Union of Liberia as well as teachers' and students' organizations, were banned from holding meetings.

On Sept. 4, 1986, three persons were arrested for having planned a coup for the following day, on which the Foreign Minister stated that the government was in full control and had foiled a planned invasion by "dissidents", some of whom had been involved in the November 1985 attempt. The minister claimed that the rebels were based in neighbouring Côte d'Ivoire and Ghana.

The three legal opposition parties—the Liberian Action Party, the Liberian Unification Party and the Unity Party—announced on March 16, 1986, that they had formed a "grand coalition", and this was joined by the banned United People's Party early in April of that year. These parties called for the resignation of President Doe and thus rejected an appeal for reconciliation made by him at his inauguration in January 1986. Early in August 1986 the leaders of the three legal opposition parties were imprisoned for non-payment of a fine imposed on them by the Supreme Court for defying a court order not to call their alliance a "grand coalition". President Doe was reported to have recommended that they should spend a maximum of 25 years in prison and on their release be banned from political activity for another 25 years. However, on payment of the fines they were released on Aug. 29, 1986.

Liberian Government-in-Exile

Leadership. Bennie D. Warner (founder)

The establishment of this government-in-exile was announced in Côte d'Ivoire on April 28, 1980, by the former Vice-President under President William Tolbert (overthrown and killed on April 12, 1980).

On Aug. 14, 1985, the Liberian head of state accused Bishop Warner of being implicated in an alleged plot to kill Liberian government officials and US citizens in Liberia, these attacks being planned for Aug. 24-25, 1985. However, Bishop Warner, then resident in the United States, denied any involvement.

Libya

Capital: Tripoli Pop. 3,600,000

Formerly an Italian colony, Libya was administered by Britain and France until the attainment of independence as the United Kingdom of Libya in 1951. In 1969 King Idris was overthrown in a bloodless coup by a group of officers led by Col. Moamer al-Gadaffi. As expounded in his *Green Book*, published in the mid-1970s, his regime is committed to achieving social and economic equality and the elimination of class differences.

The Socialist People's Libyan Arab *Jamahiriyah* is a revolutionary "state of the masses", with overall leadership exercised by Col. Gadaffi, who has held no official post since 1979. Legislative power is exercised by the General People's Congress (Parliament), which approves membership to the General People's Committee (which acts as a Cabinet). The Congress's Secretariat acts as the executive branch. A form of "direct democracy" is exercised at local level by "basic people's congresses".

Col. Gadaffi has been an enthusiastic proponent of pan-Arabism, having attempted at one time or another to arrange mergers with Egypt (on three occasions), Syria (twice), Sudan, Tunisia and Chad. A treaty of federation with Morocco, concluded in 1984, was abrogated by Morocco two years later after Col. Gadaffi had denounced as treason a meeting between the Moroccan King and the Israeli Prime Minister. With the exception of South Yemen, Syria and Iran, Libya has had generally stormy relations with Arab countries, particularly with Egypt. Its troops have also been extensively involved in Chad. Col. Gadaffi has provided moral, financial and military support for a number of radical Arab groups. Accusing Libya of responsibility for a number of terrorist incidents, including ones in which US citizens had been killed, the USA carried out an air strike on military targets and alleged "terrorist training sites" in Tripoli and Benghazi in April 1986. A number of bombs hit residential areas, however, and there were a large but uncertain number of civilian casualties.

Libya has repeatedly asserted its right to pursue and execute opposition activists in exile abroad. Col. Gadaffi warned his opponents in December 1982 that "the revolution has destroyed those who opposed it inside the country and now it must pursue the rest abroad". In early 1983, the government declared that exiled opponents who failed to return to Libya would be "liquidated", while in April 1984 a number of basic people's congresses resolved to form "suicide squads" to "chase absconding traitors and stray dogs and liquidate them wherever they may be". Similar declarations have been made subsequently. Libyan exiles have been attacked in several Western European countries as well as Egypt.

Reports of continuing internal opposition to the regime and of attempts to overthrow it (e.g. by an unsuccessful army revolt in Tobruk in mid-August 1980, when several hundred people were reported to have been killed) and reported assassination attempts on Col. Gadaffi have consistently been dismissed by the Libyan regime as being inspired from abroad, especially by Egypt. Opposition to Col. Gadaffi by exiles has been fragmented into groups of Arab nationalists, Islamic fundamentalists and liberals, all of whom have published leaflets and magazines which they have tried to smuggle into Libya through sympathizers in the customs service, armed forces and police. Several such external groups have received support from neighbouring Arab states opposed to the Gadaffi regime.

Libyan diplomats in Europe have also been the subject of a number of attacks, many of which have not been claimed by any group.

Al Borkan (The Volcano)

This group has claimed responsibility for the assassination of the Libyan ambassador in Rome (Italy), in January 1984, and of another Libyan diplomat in the same city in January 1985.

General Students' Organization

This UK-based opposition students' group acts as an umbrella body for the activities of the Libyan National Salvation Front, the Libyan Constitutional Movement and the Libyan National Democratic Movement. It was responsible for organizing a demonstration outside the Libyan People's Bureau in London in April 1984 which culminated in the killing of a British policewoman and the injuring of 11 demonstrators by machine-gun fire from the embassy.

Libyan Committee for the Defence of Democracy and Human Rights

This US-based group periodically issues reports on executions and human rights violations within Libya.

Libyan Constitutional Movement

This exiled opposition group supports the monarchist Constitution of 1951. It forms part of the General Students' Organization in the United Kingdom (see separate entry).

Libyan Liberation Organization

Leadership. Abdel Hamid Bakoush

This Organization was founded by A. H. Bakoush in Egypt in 1982. Bakoush had served as Prime Minister under the monarchy in 1967-68. Detained after the 1969 coup, he had succeeded in escaping to Egypt in 1977. In November 1984, Egyptian security forces foiled an attempt to assassinate Bakoush by a Libyan hit-squad composed of two Maltese and two UK citizens.

Libyan National Association

Leadership. Mustafa Barki (ch.)

This Association was formed in Cairo in December 1980 to encompass the Libyan community in Egypt (said to number about 25,000 people), and to serve the social and humanitarian needs of those who had "escaped from Gadaffi's terror". Egyptian security forces claimed in November 1984 that Mustafa Barki was a target of a Libyan assassination squad which had been arrested in Egypt during the course of an attempt to kill the former Prime Minister, Abdel Hamid Bakoush (see entry on Libyan Liberation Organization).

Libyan National Democratic Movement

A UK-based group affiliated to the General Students' Organization (see separate entry).

Libyan National Salvation Front (*Al-Jabah al-Wataniyah li inqodh Libya*)

Leadership. Dr Mohammed Yusuf al-Magariaf (spokesman)

The creation of this Front was announced in Khartoum (Sudan) on Oct. 7, 1981, its avowed aim being to "liberate Libya and save it from Gadaffi's rule"; to find "the democratic alternative"; and to unite "all nationalist elements inside and outside Libya in an integral programme of action and struggle" in order to replace the existing regime by a constitutional, democratically elected government.

Over the following five years the Front regularly published details of alleged atrocities committed within Libya and of political detainees being held there. It also organized demonstrations and other protests against the Libyan regime in a number of European cities. In Britain it was affiliated to the Libyan General Students' Organization (see separate entry).

In May 1984, a group of guerrillas which the Front claimed as members fought a battle with Libyan security forces in an apartment block in Tripoli. All of the guerrillas were killed, as well as an undisclosed number of Libyan soldiers. The Front also announced that its spokesman Ahmed Ahwash had been killed two days before the battle in a skirmish with Libyan troops on the Tunisian border. The Libyan authorities blamed the action on the outlawed Moslem Brotherhood.

The Front participated in a meeting of eight exiled opposition groups in Cairo in January 1987 (see under "Other Groups").

Moslem Opposition

The Libyan authorities have admitted to the presence within the country of Moslem fundamentalist dissidents, normally referred to officially as members of the outlawed Moslem Brotherhood (see entry for Libyan National Salvation Front). Five alleged Brotherhood members accused of "terrorist activities" were executed in May 1984.

Seven alleged members of the fundamentalist *Hezbollah* (Party of God) in October 1986 made a televised admission to the killing of a member of one of Libya's revolutionary committees. The killing occurred against a background of rising tension between fundamentalists and the authorities, with the revolutionary committees taking a number of measures to control the country's Moslem clerics.

Alleged members of *Hezbollah* and another fundamentalist group, *Jihad* (Holy War), were among nine men executed in public in Tripoli in February 1987. They had been convicted of two murders and several attempted assassinations.

For the *Moussa Sadr* Brigades see entry under Lebanon.

Other Groups

Seven exiled opposition groups, including the Libyan National Salvation Front (see separate entry), agreed to form a joint working group at a meeting in Cairo in January 1987. The Egyptian media named the other six groups as follows: the Libyan National Movement; the Libyan National Struggle Movement; the Libyan National Democratic Front; the Libyan National Organization; the Libyan Struggle Movement; and the Libyan Democratic Party.

Luxembourg

Capital: Luxembourg-Ville Pop. 370,000

The Grand Duchy of Luxembourg is a constitutional hereditary monarchy in which the head of state exercises executive power through a Council of Ministers headed by a Prime Minister and also takes part in the legislative process. There is a unicameral 64-member Chamber of Deputies elected for a five-year term by universal adult suffrage, and also an advisory Council of State of 21 members appointed for life by the sovereign.

As a result of elections to the Chamber of Deputies held on June 17, 1984, seats were distributed as follows: Christian Social Party 25, Socialist Workers' Party 21, Democratic Party 14, Communists 2, *Di Greng Alternativ* (Greens) 2. The elections were unsuccessfully contested by the Communist Revolutionary League and independent socialists.

Although there had been no reports of extra-parliamentary opposition activities, the Chamber of Deputies passed, on July 16, 1982, a Communications Control Bill under which the Prime Minister was, in certain circumstances, empowered to order surveillance by technical means of offences against the security of the state. The Bill, was, however, not approved by the Council of State.

An explosion on Nov. 30, 1985, which destroyed an electricity pylon was the 14th bomb attack in 1985, previous targets having included a gas works, police stations, and a swimming pool. No claims of responsibility were forthcoming for most of these incidents.

Fighting Ecologist Movement (*Mouvement écologiste combattant*)

This group claimed responsibility for an explosion on May 8, 1985, which damaged an electricity pylon.

Madagascar

Capital: Antananarivo Pop. 9,980,000

The Democratic Republic of Madagascar has an executive President elected for seven years by universal adult suffrage. He is also Chairman of a Supreme Revolutionary Council which is "the guardian of the Malagasy Socialist Revolution" and the members of which are, as to two-thirds, nominated by the President and, as to the other third, chosen by the President from a list presented by the National People's Assembly which is elected by universal adult suffrage, normally for five years. The government headed by a Prime Minister appointed by the President is responsible to the National People's Assembly.

In elections to the 137-member National Assembly held on Aug. 28, 1983, when only the seven parties belonging to the National Front for the Defence of the Revolution (*Front national pour la défense de la révolution,* FNRD) were allowed to take part and over 500 candidates were presented, seats were gained (in a 74 per cent poll) as follows: President Didier Ratsiraka's Vanguard of the Malagasy Revolution (Arema) 117, Congress Party for Malagasy Independence (AKFM) 9, Popular Impulse for National Unity (Vonjy) 6, Movement for Proletarian Power (MFM) 3, National Movement for the Independence of Madagascar (Monima) 2. The remaining two parties—the Vondrona Sosialista Monima (DSM) and the Malagasy Christian Democratic Party (Udecma-KMTP)—together obtained less than 1 per cent of the vote and no seats.

Although the organized opposition or semi-opposition parties referred to above have generally pursued their political objectives within the framework of the existing system, the National Movement for the Independence of Madagascar (Monima) has been particularly associated with manifestations of political dissent in recent years. Frequent demonstrations and disturbances by students and unemployed young people discontented with the Ratsiraka regime have often taken the Monima leader, Monja Jaona, as a rallying figure, and Jaona himself has frequently attacked what he describes as the repressive approach of the security authorities to such dissent. Jaona's principal following has been among the Androy population of the South.

Partly in the light of such unrest, Monima was admitted to the National Front in March 1981 and Jaona himself was reported (in August of that year) to have been appointed to the Supreme Revolutionary Council (SRC). However, at a Monima Congress held in Toliary (Tuléar, southern Madagascar) on July 25, 1982, Jaona accused the army and police of carrying out "massacres" in various localities in southern Madagascar, involving inter alia the killing of 50 members of Arema (the President's party).

Jaona later decided to oppose President Ratsiraka in presidential elections, which were held on Nov. 7, 1982, and resulted in the re-election of the President by about 80 per cent of the voters taking part in an 86.6 per cent poll. Jaona thereupon called (on Dec. 14) for a general strike, apparently with the object of obtaining annulment of the elections, which he and many other observers believed had really been won by him. However, on Dec. 15 he was dismissed from the SRC and on the following day was warned not to take part in any political activity; later he was reported to be in detention in a military camp in southern Madagascar. He was released on Aug. 15, 1983, having been allowed to stand as a candidate for Monima in the elections of Aug. 28, 1983, when he was elected as one of Monima's two candidates for Antananarivo.

Meanwhile, allegations of the discovery of an anti-government plot and the subsequent arrest of several priests and military officers were made on Jan. 24, 1982, by Fr Richard Andriamanjato, the leader of the Congress Party for Malagasy Independence (AKFM), who said that mercenaries were involved in this plot. It was later reported that the plotters were believed to have connexions with South African mercenaries. On Sept. 21, 1983, eight defendants accused of involvement in this plot were given suspended prison sentences ranging from three to eight years (while five others were acquitted).

On Oct. 12, 1983, a military tribunal, trying three officers detained since 1977, found them guilty of plotting to overthrow the government and to assassinate President Ratsiraka and sentenced two of them to deportation for life and the third to 10 years' hard labour.

On July 31-Aug. 1, 1985, police and troops with tanks moved against the headquarters of kung fu clubs which were accused of seeking to establish a "state within the state" and planning to seize political power. According to official figures 20 persons were killed, 31 injured and 208 arrested in the ensuing fighting. Those killed included Pierre Mizael Andrianarijaona, grand master of kung fu in Madagascar, who had denounced the "godless" nature of the Ratsiraka regime. (The martial art of kung fu, which had been banned in August 1984, was an unarmed combat discipline. On Dec. 4, 1984, some of its proponents had clashed with unemployed youths who were members of the state-sponsored TTS co-operative groups. In a kung fu attack on the TTS centre on Dec. 4, 1984, 28 persons were officially stated to have been killed, but unofficial estimates put the death toll at 50 at least, and possibly well over 100.)

Serious rioting directed against the Indian minority occurred in parts of Madagascar in February-March 1987.

Malawi

Capital: Lilongwe Pop. 7,060,000

The Republic of Malawi, a member of the Commonwealth, has an executive President appointed for life. He is also the head of the government. The sole legal party is the Malawi Congress Party (MCP) of Dr Hastings Banda, who has led Malawi since independence in 1964 and was made Life President in 1971. In a general election held on May 27-28, 1987, over 200 candidates of the MCP contested the 111 elective seats in the National Assembly and President Banda directly appointed a further 10 members.

There has, in recent years, been little evidence of political dissent inside Malawi, partly as a result of stringent internal security measures. The opposition movements in exile described below have never appeared to constitute a serious threat to the regime, and the opposition of members of the Jehovah's Witnesses sect has apparently been forcibly subdued.

Congress for the Second Republic

Leadership. M. W. Kanyama Chiume (l.)

M. W. K. Chiume was dismissed as Minister of External Affairs on Sept. 7, 1964 (i.e. shortly after Malawi had become independent in July of that year), being accused of having been "under the steering hand" of China. He subsequently set up the Congress for the Second Republic. Dr Banda alleged on Oct. 10, 1965, that the People's Republic of China was supporting Chiume with funds and guns and was training infiltrators (against whom military operations were conducted in Malawi in April-November 1965).

Thereafter, nothing was heard of any activities by Chiume or his followers until May 1, 1976, when Dr Banda (who had become President of the Republic of

Malawi in 1966) announced the arrest of a "group of agents" who had, he said, been sent by Chiume and had confessed that their mission had been to assassinate him (the President).

Malawi Freedom Movement (Mafremo)

Leadership. Orton Chirwa (l.); Mackenzie Chirwa (sec.-gen.); Edward Nyapanka (c. in c. of armed wing)

Orton Chirwa was dismissed on Sept. 7, 1964 (i.e. shortly after Malawi had become independent in July of that year), as Minister of Justice and Attorney General—Dr Hastings Banda (then Prime Minister) having accused him and other ministers of wanting "to introduce bribery and corruption into ministerial posts". Chirwa had previously criticized Dr Banda's foreign policy as "fascist and dictatorial". He left the country for Tanganyika (now Tanzania) on Oct. 30, 1964, and was later admitted to Britain as a political refugee.

In 1977 he founded Mafremo in Dar es Salaam with the aim of restoring "democracy, justice and liberty" in Malawi. In the second half of 1981 he attempted, as reported in *The Guardian* (London) on Jan. 19, 1982, to strengthen Mafremo and to forge some kind of unity with the Congress of the Second Republic (also based in Dar es Salaam) and the Socialist League of Malawi (based in Maputo, Mozambique). On Jan. 6, 1982, it was officially announced in Lilongwe that he and his wife and son had been arrested in Central province: it was later said that he had been connected with the murder of a chief (a supporter of Dr Banda) in 1964.

On May 5, 1983, both O. Chirwa and his wife were sentenced to death for treason, the formal charge being that they had conspired to overthrow the lawfully constituted government of Malawi by force or other unlawful means. (This sentence was passed by a Malawi Traditional Court presided over by a Malawian chief; before this court the accused had no right to engage counsel.)

An appeal against the sentence by the two defendants was rejected by the National Traditional Court in Blantyre. In February 1984 the two death sentences were commuted to life imprisonment on orders of President Banda (following appeals for clemency by the UN Commission on Human Rights, the European Communities' Council of Foreign Ministers and many individuals). The defendants' son, Fumbani Chirwa, held without trial since December 1981, was released in February 1984.

On Jan. 10, 1987, guerrillas of the Movement attacked a police station and killed three policemen. Announcing this attack, Maputo radio (in Mozambique) stated on Jan. 13 that E. Nyapanka had declared that his Movement had decided to begin an armed struggle to create conditions for the establishment of a democratic and popular government in Malawi.

Save Malawi Committee (Samaco)

Founded. May 1983

In a statement issued in Lusaka (Zambia) on May 31, 1983, this Committee declared that it was "not another political party but just a committee to unite all forces against the Malawi government, to stir Malawians into passive resistance and civil disobedience to prevent John Tembo (then Governor of the Reserve Bank of Malawi) from succeeding President Banda [as was widely believed that he would], and to save the nation from anarchy". Samaco also claimed that its "fundamental overriding preoccupation" was "to mount a massive campaign at home and abroad" aimed at "democratizing the country, stopping the unnecessary flow of blood" and disseminating factual information about Malawi.

A meeting organized by Samaco and held in Lusaka on June 11-12, 1983, was attended by representatives of the Congress for the Second Republic, the Malawi Freedom Movement and the Socialist League of Malawi. However, they reached no decision on early unification of their movements.

Socialist League of Malawi (Lesoma)

Leadership. Dr Attai Mpakati (founder)

This organization was established in Maputo (Mozambique) and has claimed to have the support of Cuba and the Soviet Union. In 1979 Dr Mpakati was reported to have received a parcel bomb which blew his hands off, and in March 1979 President Banda of Malawi had "claimed credit" for this assassination attempt. In 1980 Lesoma was said to have formed a People's Liberation Army of Malawi, but there have been no reports of activities of such a force.

On April 1, 1983, it was announced in Zimbabwe that Dr Mpakati had been found shot dead in Harare on March 28. Lesoma officials in Dar es Salaam alleged that he had been assassinated by Dr Banda's agents, but the Malawi high commission in Harare denied on April 3 that it was implicated in this murder.

In March 1984 Lesoma was joined by members of the Zimbabwe branch of the Congress for the Second Republic of Malawi (CSRM) who dissolved this branch because of dissatisfaction with the CSRM leader, M. W. Kanyama Chiume.

In a statement issued in Bulawayo (Zimbabwe) on Feb. 3, 1987, James Mbena (an executive member of Lesoma) called for the imposition of economic sanctions against Malawi which, he claimed, President Banda had "reduced to the status of a South African bantustan". He also accused Dr Banda of giving military support to South Africa by providing military bases to the "South African-sponsored MNR bandits" in Mozambique.

Religious Sect

Jehovah's Witnesses

The sect of Jehovah's Witnesses (the Watchtower Bible and Tract Society, whose members are opposed to military service) was outlawed as a subversive organization by the government of Malawi in October 1967.

On Sept. 17, 1972, President Banda declared at a congress of the Malawi Congress Party (MCP) in Zomba that members of the sect were "Devil's Witnesses" who neither believed in the government nor wanted to pay tax. The congress thereupon adopted a resolution under which members of the sect would be deprived of their livelihood and expelled from their villages unless they joined the MCP. There followed violent action by members of the MCP's youth section and the paramilitary Young Pioneers against sect members failing to produce MCP membership cards, resulting in the flight of some 20,000 of them to Zambia.

Malaysia

Capital: Kuala Lumpur Pop. 15,560,000

The Federation of Malaysia, consisting of Peninsular Malaysia, Sabah and Sarawak, is an independent member of the Commonwealth and a parliamentary monarchy, whose Supreme Head of State is elected for five years, from among themselves, by the nine rulers of the Malay states. Malaysia's parliament consists of (i) a 68-member senate—26 of its members being elected (for six years) by the 13 state Legislative Assemblies and 42 appointed by the head of State, and (ii) a 177-member House of Representatives elected (for five years) by universal adult suffrage. The country's Cabinet, headed by a Prime Minister, is appointed by the head of state and responsible to parliament.

In federal general elections held on August 3, 1986, parties obtained seats in the House of Representatives (*Dewan Rakyat*) as follows: National Front 148, Democratic Action Party 24, Pan Islamic Malayan Party one, Independents four. The National Front embraces 14 political organizations (the leading party being the United Malays National Organization—UMNO) representing all the main ethnic communities. Its most recent recruit has been the United Sabah National Organization which joined the UMNO on Nov. 29, 1986.

The government's policy of promoting ethnic Malay economic interests is expressed in the National Economic Policy (introduced in 1970 after anti-Chinese riots), which features reverse discrimination in favour of the economically backward but numerically larger "bumiputras" (indigenous peoples, especially Malays). Such policies have been criticized by non-Malay groups amid continuing underlying inter-communal tensions. The 1986 election campaign was drawn along racial lines with opposition parties to the National Front becoming firmly equated with the Malay Chinese who comprise one-third of Malaysia's population.

Under Essential (Security Cases) Regulations promulgated by the government on Oct. 4, 1975, all acts affecting security were to be tried by a single judge (sitting without a jury); appeals would be limited to cases involving severe penalties; there would be no recourse to the Privy Council; the judge was bound to impose the maximum penalty; and suspects could be arrested without warrant and be kept in preventive custody for 75 days. The Minister of Justice confirmed later that the regulations abolished the principle of the onus of proof of culpability lying with the prosecution, and that guilt was presumed until innocence was proved.

According to an Amnesty International report of Aug. 29, 1979, over 1,000 persons were then being held without trial, 53 of them for over eight years. On July 30, 1981, the government announced the release of 21 such detainees, among them four politicians arrested on Nov. 4, 1976, in connexion with alleged communist subversion, a former deputy minister and member of the UMNO, the chairman of the (opposition) Malaysian People's Socialist Party, and four members of the (opposition) Democratic Action Party re-elected to the federal House of Representatives in 1978 (notwithstanding their detention). On Feb. 4, 1982, it was officially announced that the total number of releases had reached 168, leaving 444 persons still held without trial—although further arrests were made under internal security provisions later that month.

Under a Societies (Amendment) Bill passed by the federal House of Representatives on April 9, 1981, all clubs, societies and associations were required to register as either political or non-political bodies, and the Registrar of Societies was empowered to take action against any society registered as non-political which was deemed to have involved itself in political affairs, without any appeal being possible except to the Minister of Home Affairs.

The Minister of Information announced on July 4, 1983, that from May 1, 1984, the national news agency, Bernama, would be the sole distributor of all news and that foreign news agencies would no longer be able to deal directly with local newspapers, radio or television. During 1986 the government expelled four foreign journalists and banned sales of *Time* and *The Asian Wall Street Journal* temporarily.

Amendments to the Official Secrets Act 1972 approved in December 1986 provided among other things for a minimum one-year prison term for violations of the Act.

Communist Movements

Communist Party of Malaya (CPM)

Leadership. Chin Peng (sec.-gen.)

Established in 1930, the CPM was banned on July 23, 1948, after being engaged in an armed insurrection in the Federation of Malaya, which became an independent state within the Commonwealth on Aug. 31, 1957. The insurrection was not finally suppressed (with the help of British, Australian and New Zealand forces) until July 31, 1960, when a 12-year state of emergency was ended. According to official statements the insurrection had resulted in the death of 11,048 persons—6,710 communist guerrillas, 1,865 soldiers and police and 2,473 civilians—in addition to which 510 civilians were listed as missing. Chin Peng settled in Beijing (China) in 1961.

The CPM, which initially had some 15,000 fighters in the field, was largely composed of ethnic Chinese (who form about 35 per cent of Malaysia's population), and followed the policy of the Communist Party of China, by which it was supported. From 1966 onwards a Malayan National Liberation Army (MNLA), organized by the CPM, carried on guerrilla activities near Malaysia's border with Thailand, and it had its own radio station, the "Voice of the Malayan Revolution".

Agreement on Thai-Malaysian co-operation against the MNLA was first reached in July 1968 and was confirmed in a military co-operation agreement signed on March 7, 1970. Protracted fighting between guerrillas and Malaysian troops (supported by Thai forces) continued until June 1971, when the Malaysian government announced the formation of a National Action Committee to cope with "the serious and growing communist threat" and to induce the people of the rural areas to side with the government and not to allow themselves to be recruited by the MNLA.

In 1971, however, China began to improve its relations with Malaysia and gave progressively less publicity to MNLA operations. When the two governments decided, on May 31, 1974, to establish diplomatic relations with each other, China undertook to "respect Malaysia's independence and sovereignty" and to enjoin those Chinese in Malaysia who retained their Chinese nationality of their own will "to abide by the laws of the government of Malaysia".

MNLA guerrilla activities continued in 1975, but by 1980 communist guerrillas in Malaysia were said to have been reduced to about 3,000 split into three factions (CPM, CPMM-L and CPM-RF), with 12 army brigades being deployed in the border area. In November 1980 Musa bin Ahmad (described as chairman of the CPM), who had resided in Beijing for 25 years, defected to the Malaysian authorities, and on Jan. 6, 1981, he alleged in a broadcast that China still intended to turn Malaysia into one of its satellites.

The "Voice of the Malayan Revolution" radio station ceased broadcasting on July 1, 1981, but was on July 4 of that year replaced by the "Voice of Malayan Democracy", which announced on June 20, 1982, that the MNLA had been renamed the Malayan People's Army (*Tentara Rakyat Malaya*). According to a statement by the Malaysian Deputy Inspector-General of Police on Oct. 28, 1981, there were only about 230 insurgents still operating in the jungles of Pahang, Perak and Kelantan.

In a new party constitution adopted on April 29, 1980, the CPM was described as "a proletarian party guided by Marxism-Leninism-Mao Zedong thought", whose revolution could "never attain victory by taking the road of parliamentary democracy, armed uprising in the cities or urban guerrilla war" but only by "using the countryside to encircle the cities and seize political power by armed force".

The Chinese Foreign Minister said on Feb. 28, 1984, during an official visit to Malaysia, that China would not end its "moral support" for the CPM.

The *Bangkok World* reported on Feb. 12, 1985, that Malaysia and Thailand had recently launched their "biggest-ever military drive" against CPM guerrillas. Malaysian authorities estimated at this time that there were about 260 active "communist terrorists" in peninsular Malaysia, about 100 in Sarawak and about 2,000 in southern Thailand.

Communist Party of Malaysia (MCP)

Leadership. Ah Leng (gen. sec.)

The MCP was formed in 1983 by the merger of the Communist Party of Malaya—Revolutionary Faction and the Communist Party of Malaya—Marxist-Leninist (CPMM-L), which broke away from the Communist Party of Malaya (CPM) in 1970 and 1974 respectively. Both groups rejected the Maoist theory of using the countryside to encircle the cities as unworkable in Malaysia (where the rural population is predominantly Malay, whereas the CPM membership is mainly Chinese), and advocated rallying support among the Chinese population in the towns and the use of urban guerrilla warfare. Fighting occurred between CPM and CPMM-L forces in southern Thailand in 1982.

The MCP, unlike the CPM, recognizes the existence of Malaysia and the independence of Singapore, and seeks to win the support of both the Malay peasantry and the urban Chinese. It is pro-Chinese.

Malayan People's Army—see under Communist Party of Malaya (CPM)

Moslem Fundamentalist Groups

Abim

This Moslem fundamentalist group came into conflict with the government in 1980-81. Some Moslem fundamentalists were reported to have harassed non-Moslems, in particular Indians and Chinese.

Crypto

Nine leaders of this grouping, which was described by the authorities as a "deviant Islamic cult", were arrested under the Internal Security Act on March 27, 1982, after evidence had come to light of its extremist political teachings.

Dakwah (Missionary) Moslem Movement

This Movement, said to have grown significantly in 1978-80, was involved in violent clashes with police in South Johore in August 1980, when about eight persons were killed and 23 injured and a curfew was imposed in Batu Pahat. The *Dakwah* advocated inter alia the destruction of symbols of modern or Western life, such as television sets, and the exclusion of women from higher education (such education of women being regarded as contrary to the Koran). Militant Moslems were also responsible for the destruction of temples of the 700,000-strong Hindu community.

Maldives

Capital: Malé Pop. 180,000

The Republic of Maldives, a full member of the Commonwealth since 1985, has an executive President elected for a five-year term by universal adult suffrage, a Cabinet presided over by the President and a People's Council *(Majlis)*. There are no political parties and no organized dissident groups, although the government of President Maumoon Abdul Gayoom (in power since November 1978) has found it necessary to take action against certain members of the former regime of President Ibrahim Nasir.

Mali

Capital: Bamako Pop. 8,210,000

Since 1968 the Republic of Mali has been ruled by a Military Committee of National Liberation (MCNL) with an executive President (Brig.-Gen. Moussa Traoré), who is head of state and government, as well as secretary-general of the *Union démocratique du peuple malien* (UPDM), the country's sole legal political party. An 82-member National Assembly is elected for a three-year term by universal adult suffrage on a list of the UDPM.

According to the official results of elections held on June 9, 1985, President Moussa Traoré was re-elected by 99.94 per cent of the votes cast in a 99.74 per cent turnout, and for the 82 candidates for the National Assembly a similar majority was recorded, with 35 of the candidates not having sat in the previous Assembly.

The President has repeatedly promised a return to civilian government, but this has been confined to the appointment of civilians to the Cabinet. Opposition to the regime has come from certain officers of the armed forces, students and trade unionists as well as Malians in exile. Attempted coups were foiled by the regime in October 1978 and in December 1980.

Malta

Capital: Valletta Pop. 380,000

The Republic of Malta is an independent member of the Commonwealth and has a President elected for a five-year term by a House of Representatives which normally has 65 members elected, usually for five years, by universal adult suffrage. The President appoints a Prime Minister and, on the latter's advice, the other ministers. In general elections held on May 10, 1987, the Nationalist Party (NP) obtained 50.91 per cent of the votes and 34 seats, while the Labour Party gained 48.87 per cent of the votes and 33 seats. The seats of the NP included two "bonus" seats awarded under a previously adopted constitutional amendment designed to prevent a party which failed to win a majority of votes from gaining a majority of seats (as was the case with the Labour Party in December 1981). Parties not represented in Parliament are the Communist Party and the Progressive Constitutional Party.

The conflict between the two major parties has deeply divided society in Malta. For more than a year after the 1981 elections the (Christian democratic) Nationalist Party pursued a boycott of Parliament on the ground that the result was due to "gerrymandering"; it has also accused the Labour Party of using dictatorial measures.

From June 1982 to March 1983 the Nationalist Party conducted a civil disobedience campaign. The conflict was intensified in June 1983, when a bill was passed providing for the expropriation of certain Church property in order to finance the government's free education policy. Following a raid by police and troops on the Nationalist Party's headquarters on Nov. 26, 1983, the Prime Minister stated that arms and radio transmitting equipment had been found. In a further raid—on a warehouse on Nov. 28—a cache of submachine-guns, rifles and hand grenades was said to have been discovered. However, the dispute over the introduction of free education in Church schools was finally settled by an agreement reached on April 27, 1985, by representatives of the Maltese government, the Roman Catholic Archbishop of Malta and the Vatican Secretary of Public Affairs, to the effect that there would be a gradual introduction of such free education over a three-year period. This agreement was reached only after there had been 20 bombing incidents between Sept. 25 and Dec. 31, 1984, not only at Nationalist Party premises but also at diplomatic missions.

An assembly of foreign policy specialists held in Milan on Nov. 23-25, 1986, by the International Security Council (a private organization) found inter alia that there had been in Malta "an alarming deterioration in the standards of human and civil rights"; that there had been "cases of unchecked mob violence against critics of the government, including trade unions, independent newspapers, the Catholic Church, the courts and opposition parties"; that radio and television (a government monopoly) had been "used systematically as a partisan instrument", and that the independence of the judiciary had "fundamentally been compromised".

No extra-parliamentary opposition groups have, however, been reported to exist in Malta.

Mauritania

Capital: Nouakchott Pop. 1,890,000

The Republic of Mauritania (a member of the Arab League) is ruled by a Military Committee of National Salvation (CMSN) of 27 members, headed by a chairman who is President of the Republic. There is also a civilian Council of Ministers headed by a Prime Minister, but there is neither a parliament nor a legal political party.

On Dec. 19, 1980, the CMSN published a draft Constitution providing inter alia that Mauritania should be "an Islamic, parliamentary, indivisible and democratic republic" with a President elected for a (non-renewable) six-year term and a National Assembly which would be elected for a four-year term. Political parties were to be permitted (although not the Mauritanian People's Party, which had been the country's sole legal party until July 1978). However, by 1987 this Constitution was not yet endorsed.

Former President Ould Daddah, overthrown in July 1978 and resident in France since October 1979, was on Nov. 21, 1980, reported to have been sentenced in absentia to hard labour for life on charges of high treason, violating the Constitution and damaging Mauritania's economic interests. Over the following two years other leading members of former regimes were prominent in various opposition groups (mostly operating in exile) and at least two attempts were made to overthrow the government—in March 1981 and February 1982. As a result of the latter attempt 10-year prison sentences were passed on Col. Mustapha Ould Mohamed Salek (who overthrew President Ould Daddah in 1978 and effectively led the Mauritanian regime until mid-1979) and on two former ministers.

Under an amnesty of Dec. 21, 1984 (announced by President Moaouia Ould Sidi Mohamed Taya, who had assumed power in a bloodless coup on Dec. 12), ex-President Ould Daddah and Col. Ould Mohamed Salek were released, after over 160 political prisoners had already been set free by mid-December. In addition cases were terminated against 133 other persons who were to be prosecuted for their political views.

African Liberation Forces of Mauritania (*Forces de libération africaine de Mauritanie*, FLAM)

This organization opposed alleged discrimination exercised against the black population, mainly in southern Mauritania. In June 1986 leading members of the black community signed a "Manifesto of the Oppressed Black Mauritanians". A group of 20 leading public figures, most of them supporters of the FLAM, were on Sept. 29-30 sentenced to imprisonment for up to five years for holding unauthorized public meetings and distributing tracts denouncing Mauritanian "apartheid" and "increasing Arabization of Mauritanian society". The trial was followed by outbreaks of violence and arson in Nouakchott and the port city of Nouadhibou, which led to the arrest of several hundred people during October.

Free Man Movement

This Movement aims at representing the interests of the (mixed-race) Haratines who have complained of forced Arabization and of discrimination based on colour. The Haratines are the descendants of freed black slaves who adopted Moorish (Arab-Berber) customs and the local Hassaniya Arabic dialect, continued to perform menial work and are still in many cases regarded as the property of their Arab-Berber employers. Many Haratines are workers on land owned by absentee landlords, and the official abolition of slavery on July 5, 1980, was widely regarded as a first step towards land reform.

Early in 1980 the clandestine Free Man Movement distributed tracts denouncing the ruling armed forces as having a "shady racist side" and alleging that the Haratines were "oppressed because of the colour of their skin". A number of the Movement's leaders were arrested and tried at Rosso (near the border with Senegal).

(A representative of the UN Commission on Human Rights reported on Aug. 27, 1984, that slavery had been virtually abolished in Mauritania.)

Mauritanian Democratic Union (*Union démocratique mauritanienne,* UDM)

The UDM was established in Senegal and inter alia called for a joining of forces between black Africans (making up about one-third of Mauritania's population) and the (mixed-race) Haratines (almost equal in number to the black Africans) to confront the country's dominant Arab-Berbers.

Movement of Nasserite Unionists (*Mouvement des unionistes nassérites,* MUN)

Leadership. Khoury Ould H'miti (l.)

The MUN was a clandestine organization, and Khoury Ould H'miti was an Arab nationalist and secretary-general of the sole trade union in Mauritania, the *Union des travailleurs de Mauritanie* (UTM). The MUN was named in connexion with alleged Libyan destabilization plans which the Mauritanian government newspaper *Chaab* sought to prove through the publication of documents on April 26, 1984. Khoury Ould H'miti was among a number of people arrested in March 1984 following disturbances at certain schools which were allegedly prompted by a Libyan-inspired secret organization. The UTM publically distanced itself from H'miti after his arrest.

Ahmed Baba Miske, a former permanent representative of Mauritania at the United Nations, was arrested on April 24, 1984, and placed under house arrest for his alleged part in the disturbances. He had been arrested on a previous occasion after it was claimed that Libya had planned a coup in Mauritania in December 1980. Shortly before this approximately 100 students had been arrested and three Libyan diplomats expelled, accused of fomenting a pupils' strike against Iraqi teachers in some northern Mauritanian towns.

Both Ould H'miti and Baba Miske were released under the amnesty of Dec. 21, 1984.

Organization of Mauritanian Nationalists (*Organisation des nationalistes mauritaniens,* ONAM)

Leadership. Khatri Ould Die (l.)

The ONAM was formed in Paris on May 28, 1984, was led by a group of army officers, former ministers, diplomats and officials, and had its headquarters in Dakar, Senegal. It opposed the regime of President Taya, whose leaders, it claimed, had leanings towards the Algerian-Polisario camp, which would never solve the country's problems. The ONAM was said to be supported by Morocco, Libya, Iraq and Saudi Arabia, and it favoured Moroccan control over Western Sahara.

K. Ould Die, himself a former army officer and the founder of the ONAM, was arrested in Dakar on Nov. 8, 1984, on the occasion of a visit to Senegal by the then Mauritanian Minister of the Interior, and was deported to Italy.

Walfougi Front

The formation of the Armed Front for the Self-determination of the Black African Population of the Southern Mauritanian Regions of Walo, Fouta and Guidimalia (or Walfougi Front) was announced in March 1979 in a letter to foreign ambassadors accredited in Dakar. In leaflets distributed in early 1979, black Africans criticized the military government and Mauritania's membership of the Arab League, and a number of blacks were arrested in this connexion.

The black community has also opposed the imposition of Arabic as the main national language and called for the continued use of French and the numerous tribal languages. The blacks have also called for an even distribution of posts in the administration between the country's ethnic communities and supported the cession of the southern half of Western Sahara to the Saharan Arab Democratic Republic (of the Polisario Front).

Mauritius

Capital: Port Louis Pop. 970,000

Mauritius is an independent state within the Commonwealth, with the British monarch as head of state being represented by a Governor-General. It has a Cabinet headed by a Prime Minister and a Legislative Assembly with 62 elective seats and up to eight additional seats filled by the Supreme Court from those unsuccessful candidates with the greatest number of votes.

As a result of elections held on Aug. 21, 1983, the 62 elective seats in the Legislative Assembly were distributed as follows: An alliance of the Mauritian Socialist Movement and the Labour Party 37, Mauritian Militant Movement 19, Mauritian Social Democratic Party 4, Organization of the People of Rodrigues 2. About 85 per cent of the electorate of 540,000 were estimated to have taken part in the elections.

Internal unrest in Mauritius has arisen mainly in connexion with labour disputes, and there appears to be no organized extra-parliamentary opposition.

Mexico

Capital: Mexico City Pop. 78,800,000

The United Mexican States are a federal republic consisting of 31 states and a federal district (around the capital), with an executive President who is elected by universal adult suffrage for a six-year term and who heads a Cabinet. There is a bicameral National Congress consisting of (i) a Federal Chamber of Deputies of 400 members elected by universal adult suffrage for three years, 300 of them directly elected by a majority vote and the other 100 by proportional representation, and (ii) a 64-member Senate (comprising two senators for each state and for the federal district) also elected by universal adult suffrage for three years. Each state has a governor elected for six years and a Chamber of Deputies elected for three years.

In elections to the Federal Chamber of Deputies held on July 7, 1985, the ruling Institutional Revolutionary Party (PRI), which had been in power since 1929, gained 292 of the 300 seats filled by majority vote. Of the remaining seats, 6 went to the right-wing opposition National Action Party (PAN) and 2 to the Authentic Party of the Mexican Republic (PARM). Of the 100 seats filled by proportional representation the PAN won 32, the United Socialist Party of Mexico (PSUM) 12, the Popular Socialist Party (PPS) 11, the Socialist Workers' Party (PST) 12, the Mexican Democratic Party (PDM) 12, the PARM seven, the Mexican Workers' Party (PMT) six, and the Revolutionary Workers' Party (PRT) six.

At the beginning of 1987, five groups on the highly fractured political left—the PSUM, the PRT, the Revolutionary Patriotic Party (PRP), the Revolutionary Movement of the People (MRP) and the Communist Union of the Left (UCI)—announced an agreement in principle to form a single party by June 1987.

The most serious disturbances for over 50 years occurred in Mexico City in the summer and autumn of 1968 when a strike by some 150,000 students developed into a full-scale revolt against the "establishment" of the ruling PRI by left-wing (but mainly middle-class) students, which was suppressed by the armed forces with substantial loss of life and hundreds of arrests. Various left-wing guerrilla groups, some of them tracing their origins back to the 1968 events, remained active in subsequent years, in particular in Guerrero state (said to be the poorest of the country's 31 states). Guerrilla activities of left and right declined considerably in the 1980s, although in 1984 right-wing death squads were suspected of having assassinated an investigative reporter and an (amnestied) former leader of the People of the Poor.

During 1985 and 1986, there were violent internal disturbances protesting against alleged electoral fraud by the PRI in state governorship and municipal elections. Demonstrations and strikes were organized by the PAN and other opposition parties. The claims of fraud have been backed by independent and international observers. Large-scale violent demonstrations took place in Nueva León and Sonora, following the state governorship elections there, in July 1985, which the PRI officially won. There were simultaneous riots in ten states in December 1985 and January 1986 opposing the inauguration of PRI mayors. Ten people were killed and scores injured. In July 1986 in Chihuahua the PAN, the Roman Catholic Church, small businesses and the independent left embarked on a campaign of civil disobedience following the PRI's claims of victory in gubernatorial elections.

In August 1985, there were rallies against the government's economic policies. In particular, demands were made for a moratorium on repayment of the foreign debt.

In January 1987 some 340,000 students at Mexico City's National Autonomous University (UNAM) went on strike in protest against the proposed academic reforms which would have included tougher entry requirements. The strike ended when the authorities yielded to student demands.

Left-wing Movements

Coalition of Workers, Peasants and Students of the Isthmus (*Coalición Obrera, Campesina y Estudantil del Istmo,* COCEI)

This leftist grouping was organized in the Tehuantepic isthmus in the late 1970s. It won the municipal elections in Juchitán, Oaxaca, in March 1981, but the council was suspended by the PRI-controlled state legislative in August 1983. The COCEI occupied the town hall until in December a police and military operation resulted in the arrest of the group's leaders and the installation of a PRI-dominated council which was stated to have been elected in November.

National Workers' and Peasants' Popular Assembly

This coalition of more than 100 small groups called a national strike on June 5, 1984, to protest against the government's economic austerity programme; the strike received very limited support.

Poor People's Party (*Partido de los Pobres,* PLP)

This group, founded in the late 1960s, was responsible for killing 10 soldiers near Acapulco on June 25, 1972, and for the kidnapping of a senator of the ruling Institutional Revolutionary Party and four aides on May 30, 1974 (all five being, however, freed by army action on Sept. 7, 1974). The party's leader, Lucio Cabañas ("El Professor"), was killed on Dec. 2, 1974, after a five-month operation by the armed forces in Guerrero state, during which at least 800 peasants were reported to have been killed.

The then deputy leader of the movement, Francisco Fierro Loza, accepted a government amnesty and emerged from hiding in 1984. On July 7 he was assassinated by unidentified gunmen. The movement resumed its guerrilla activities with the kidnapping in May 1985 of the leader of the PSUM, who was released after payment of a substantial ransom.

Right-wing Group

Apostolic Anti-Communist Alliance (AAA)

This group, using a name similar to that used by a group accused of hundreds of political murders and disappearances in Argentina during the mid-1970s, claimed responsibility for the killing in Mexico City on Nov. 6, 1986, of Ivan Menéndez, editor of the Spanish-language version of *Le Monde Diplomatique*.

Mongolia

Capital: Ulan Bator Pop. 1,890,000

The Mongolian People's Republic is "a sovereign democratic state of working people" in which "supreme state power" is vested in the People's Great *Hural* (Assembly), elected for a five-year term by universal adult suffrage, and in which effective political power is held by the (communist) Mongolian People's Revolutionary Party (MPRP), the First Secretary of whose Central Committee is head of state and chairman of the Assembly's Presidium. The post of First Secretary has been held since December 1984 by Jambyn Batmönh. There is also a Council of Ministers as the country's highest executive power.

In elections held in June 1986 the Assembly's 370 seats were filled by the sole list of officially nominated candidates. There has been no evidence of organized political opposition.

Morocco

Capital: Rabat Pop. 23,400,000

The Kingdom of Morocco is "a sovereign Moslem state" and "a constitutional democratic and social (hereditary) monarchy", with the King appointing, and presiding over, the Cabinet. There is a unicameral Chamber of Representatives, the 306 members of which are elected for a six-year term—206 of them by direct universal adult suffrage and 100 by an electoral college consisting of local councillors and representatives of professional and employees' organizations.

As a result of elections held on Sept. 14, and Oct. 2, 1984, seats in the Chamber of Representatives were distributed as follows: *Union constitutionnelle* 83, *Rassemblement national des indépendants* 61, *Mouvement populaire* 47, *Istiqlal* 41, *Union socialiste des forces populaires* (USFP) 36, *Parti national démocratique* 24, *Union marocaine du travail* five, *Confédération démocratique du travail* three, *Union générale des travailleurs marocains* two, *Parti du progrès et du socialisme* (PPS, communist) two, *Organisation de l'action démocratique et populaire* one, *Parti du centre social* one.

Although all political parties supported the Moroccan government in its annexation of Western Sahara in 1975 and 1979, members of left-wing parties were on a number of occasions detained or tried. In September 1981 three leaders of the USFP were sentenced to a year in prison after issuing a statement criticizing some aspects of an Organization of African Unity resolution on a referendum to be held in Western Sahara, but on Feb. 26, 1982, the King granted them a pardon and they were released. However, *Al Bayane*, the newspaper of the PPS, reported that 19 members of this party were being held in prisons at that time.

A challenge to the government arose in January 1984 when riots broke out in major cities after the official announcement of measures to reduce subsidies on the prices of basic foodstuffs. In subsequent clashes with police some 60 rioters (according to diplomatic sources) were killed, and in February the USFP newspaper reported that 558 persons had been sentenced to prison terms after the riots. The King revoked the official measures on Jan. 22 and blamed the disturbances on Marxist-Leninists, supporters of the Ayatollah Khomeini of Iran and the Israeli secret service.

Further trials arising out of the January riots followed in subsequent months. On March 19, 1984, a total of 91 people were sentenced for law and order violations to terms of imprisonment ranging from three months to two years. On May 26 prison sentences of between one and 15 years were imposed on 39 persons. On June 24 two men were reported to have received life sentences.

A statement issued by the *Comité d'action pour la libération des prisonniers d'opinion au Maroc* (CALPOM) in early April 1985 said a large number of students had been arrested in January 1985 during disturbances in universities and again in March 1985 during peaceful demonstrations to mark the anniversary of the rioting in Casablanca in 1965. On April 25, 1985, nine students sentenced to prison terms of four to five years commenced a hunger strike in support of demands for improved conditions. Three youths had died during a hunger strike undertaken by 34 young people in prisons in Marrakech and Rabat in July and August 1984. They were protesting against restrictions placed on prison visits and against the prohibition on studying and taking examinations in prison. (The hunger strike was reported to have ended on Sept. 4, 1984, after the prisoners received verbal assurances that their grievances would be remedied.)

During 1986 concern for the treatment of political prisoners was expressed by Amnesty International and by three opposition parties—*Istiqlal*, the PPS and the USFP—which denounced the practice of torture at the time, and demanded guarantees of family visits to prisoners as well as calling for 60 people imprisoned after the food riots in January to be granted the status of political prisoners.

External attempts to destabilize the government were highlighted by two events in the mid-1980s. After a trial for treason of Moslem fundamentalists on Sept. 3, 1985, government spokesmen alleged that Algeria was financing and training opposition elements through Polisario guerrillas (see entry below), and that, furthermore, Algeria was arranging meetings between leftists and fundamentalist politicians.

Left-wing Movements

Forward Movement (*Ilal Amam*)

This Movement emerged in 1974, when a large number of persons were arrested between March and September for distributing "seditious literature" and forming three extreme left-wing groups—*Ilal Amam*, the 23rd March Group and *Al-Moutakalinine* ("Rally")—which were to be merged in a Marxist-Leninist front with a "Red Army". Their declared objective was to set up a "people's democratic republic" to be headed by Abraham Serfaty, an anti-Zionist Jewish engineer who had been a member of the Moroccan Communist Party (banned in 1952) and of the Party of Liberation and Socialism (which existed in 1968-69) and who was said to have Maoist views. On Feb. 15, 1977, a total of 176 of the arrested persons were sentenced to terms of imprisonment, 44 of them for life, among them A. Serfaty. On Feb. 23, 1980, three students were given prison sentences for attempting to reconstitute *Ilal Amam* and for disturbing the public order.

On Feb. 13, 1986, *Ilal Amam* members were among a group of 26 people sentenced to between three and 20 years' imprisonment for posing a threat to Morocco's internal security and giving intelligence information to Polisario guerrillas fighting Morocco for control of the Western Sahara (see separate entry). According to Reuters reports of Dec. 25, 1986, they went on a hunger strike in December 1986 to demand a transfer of all of the group to one prison from the various prisons where they were being detained.

National Union of Moroccan Students (*Union nationale des étudiants du Maroc,* UNEM)

This student organization was officially banned in January 1973 after it had for years agitated for educational reforms and for certain rights such as co-determination and dispensation from military services (rights which were granted in April 1972) and had also organized protest demonstrations against the detention in Casablanca of a group of students and teachers on charges of having established "Marxist cells" and thus endangered internal security. Despite the ban the UNEM remained active, and its leaders were on several occasions detained for demonstrating and distributing anti-government leaflets. In 1976 three of them were said to have died in prison.

The ban on the UNEM was lifted in November 1978 but the union's members continued to protest against the authorities allegedly preventing them from conducting normal activities among students. In 1980 they also agitated for the release of political prisoners, and a strike call by the UNEM in February 1981 was reported to have been followed by a majority of Morocco's 12,000 university students, mainly in protest against delays in implementing university reforms decreed in 1975. At that time the majority of the members of the UNEM's executive committee were affiliated to the (left-wing) *Union socialiste des forces populaires* (USFP) and the remainder to the (communist) *Parti du progrès et du socialisme* (PPS).

Moslem Fundamentalists

On Sept. 3, 1985, a trial of alleged Moslem fundamentalists including Abdelkarim Mouti, the leader of the *Islamic Youth Movement* (see below), ended with 14 people being sentenced to death for treason. Nine of them had been tried in absentia, including A. Mouti. Three of the accused admitted in court that they had been plotting to overthrow the monarchy and establish an Islamic state and that they were trained in Algerian guerrilla camps run by the Polisario Front which was fighting Morocco for control of the Western Sahara.

On Oct. 24, 1985, a group of 30 Moslem fundamentalists were sentenced to between one year and life in prison on charges of subversion, 15 of them being sentenced in absentia. On the same day 31 Moslem fundamentalists were convicted of charges of subversion. Of these, 20 received life imprisonment sentences and 11 between one and 30 years' imprisonment.

Islamic Youth Movement

Leadership. Abdelkarim Mouti

On June 21, 1984, the trial opened of 71 Moslem fundamentalists accused inter alia of membership of this Movement, conspiracy to overthrow King Hassan, incitement to revolt and distribution of subversive literature. On July 31, 1984, a total of 13 were sentenced to death, seven of them in absentia. The rest of the group received sentences of between five years' and life imprisonment.

Religious Minority

Bahais

In early April 1984 the International Federation of Human Rights, the Paris-based human rights organization, reported that 16 members of the Bahai community in Morocco had been convicted on charges relating to public order and attacks on the Moslem faith, and at the end of secret trials in Casablanca in December 1983 and February 1984 had been sentenced to prison terms ranging from between three to five years.

Six Bahai women sentenced at that time had their convictions annulled at an appeal court in Casablanca on Aug. 13, 1984. The court also reduced sentences passed between December 1983 and February 1984 on 10 Bahai men.

Western Sahara

Popular Front for the Liberation of Saguia el Hamra and Rio de Oro, or Polisario Front (*Frente Polisario*)

Leadership. Mohamed Abdelazziz (sec.-gen.)

This Front was established in May 1973 as a national liberation movement in the (then Spanish) Western Sahara. After the governments of Morocco and Mauritania had, under an agreement concluded in Madrid with Spain in November 1975, divided the Western Sahara between themselves, the Front decided to take up its armed struggle against both these governments as from November 1975, with the support of the government of Algeria. In February 1976 the Front proclaimed a Saharan Arab Democratic Republic (SADR).

Following the overthrow of the Mauritanian government of President Mokhtar Ould Daddah in July 1978, the Front declared a ceasefire in its military operations against Mauritania, and this decision was followed by a peace agreement between the Front and the new government in Mauritania on Aug. 5, 1979, and the withdrawal of Mauritanian forces from the Western Sahara. The territory vacated by Mauritania was, however, formally annexed by Morocco on Aug. 11-12, 1979.

Heavy fighting between the Polisario Front and Moroccan forces took place in the second half of 1979 and in 1980, with both sides making conflicting claims of successes. While the Front repeatedly asserted that it controlled large areas of the Western Sahara, Morocco retained full control over what it called the "useful triangle" near Bou Craa, the centre of the phosphate mines (although these were closed between 1977 and July 1982). By 1981 Morocco had built a wall of fortifications across the desert to protect the most important localities, but its defence expenditure had risen to about one quarter of its annual budget. It was increasingly supplied with sophisticated arms by the United States and was also reported to receive financial support from Saudi Arabia. On the other hand, it has been claimed in Morocco that the Polisario Front has been supported not only by Algeria and Libya but also by the Soviet Union, which was said to have supplied the Front with tanks, heavy artillery and ground-to-ground missiles in 1982. Libyan support was, however, withdrawn after a treaty of federation with Morocco in September 1984.

The Polisario Front was based in three large camps near Tindouf, in southern Algeria, where some 120,000 Saharan refugees were housed. With some international assistance, the Front provided them with basic education and health care. Many of the young male refugees were active as Polisario Front guerrillas; in early 1986, Abdelazziz claimed that the Front fielded a total of 20,000 fighters.

Efforts to find a peaceful solution to the conflict, made by the Organization of African Unity (OAU), have been unsuccessful. The SADR was admitted to the OAU in February 1982, at the instigation of the OAU's secretary-general and on the ground that 26 of the 50 OAU member states had recognized the SADR. However, under the OAU's Charter, a quorum of two-thirds of its members was required for any decision on whether the SADR was an independent sovereign state entitled to OAU membership (which was denied by Morocco and other member states supporting the latter); during 1982 it emerged that no such quorum was obtainable and that the OAU was divided into a majority "radical" section (which favoured admission of the SADR) and a minority "moderate" section (which opposed it).

A Polisario Front congress held in October 1982 elected the Front's secretary-general, M. Abdelazziz, as President of the SADR, which also had a "Cabinet" headed by a "Prime Minister".

A further congress, attended by 1,400 delegates, was held "in liberated territories" in December 1985, when all seven members of the executive committee were re-elected, with Abdelazziz again being named as secretary-general of the Front and also President of the SADR. A 13-member SADR government included Mohamed Lamine as Prime Minister, Mansour Oumar as Minister of Foreign Affairs, and Ibrahim Ghali, one of the Front's leading guerrilla commanders, as Defence Minister. A 27-member Polisario Front "political bureau" was also chosen.

Over 50 countries which had by then recognized the SADR as "a sovereign and independent state" included not only the majority of the OAU member states, but also Cuba and Iran, and those member states of the Arab League which were opposed to the Egyptian-Israeli reconciliation.

In an effort to facilitate a diplomatic solution, the Polisario Front decided not to take up its seats at the 19th OAU Assembly of Heads of State and Government, held in June 1983, at which a resolution was passed calling on both sides to negotiate a ceasefire prior to the holding of a referendum. The following month, King Hassan warned that, regardless of the result of any such plebiscite, he would not feel obliged "to hand over the Sahara on a silver platter to a rabble of mercenaries". At the 20th OAU summit in November 1984, Morocco announced its withdrawal from the organization after SADR delegates had taken up their seats. Despite this decision, the OAU continued to exert efforts towards achieving a diplomatic settlement.

Subsequent diplomatic activity focused on the United Nations, whose Decolonization Committee passed a resolution calling for direct negotiations in

November 1985. Proximity talks arranged by the UN secretary-general, Javier Pérez de Cuéllar, were held in April 1986, involving Moroccan and Polisario Front representatives, UN officials and observers from Algeria and Mauritania. The talks foundered, however, on Morocco's refusal to agree to direct negotiations. In October the same year, the UN General Assembly agreed by 98 votes to nil (with 44 abstentions and 16 countries absent, including Morocco) that the Western Sahara issue was "a question of decolonization which remains to be completed on the basis of the exercise by the people of the Western Sahara of their inalienable right to self-determination and independence".

From 1983 onwards, the military situation became increasingly stalemated, largely due to the maintenance and extension of Morocco's defensive wall, which by 1986 enclosed 200,000 sq km of the territory's total 260,000 sq km area. Polisario Front attacks were largely restricted to harassing operations against the wall, although it occasionally demonstrated its ability to stage larger-scale offensives. From 1985 onwards, the Front also attacked foreign vessels (mainly fishing boats) and light aircraft which it deemed were infringing its territorial waters or airspace. In 1985, the sinking of one Spanish vessel, and a subsequent attack on a naval patrol craft which went to assist it, led to the closure of the Polisario Front's mission in Madrid, which had been opened the previous year.

By mid-1987, a total of 68 countries had recognized the SADR, including most notably Mauritania and India, as well as several Latin American states.

Mozambique

Capital: Maputo Pop. 13,960,000

The People's Republic of Mozambique is, under its 1975 Constitution, "a sovereign, independent and democratic state" in which "power belongs to the workers and peasants united and led by Frelimo"—the Front for the Liberation of Mozambique—which is "the leading force of the state and society" (and sole legal party). The president of Frelimo is also head of state and of the Council of Ministers. The state's nominal supreme organ is the indirectly elected People's Assembly.

On Feb. 28, 1979, the People's Assembly passed a law providing for the imposition of the death penalty for certain crimes against the security of the people and the state and for those whose reintegration into society appeared impossible. Revolutionary military courts were set up under a law of March 30, 1979. The main threat to the government has come from the Mozambican National Resistance (RNM or Renamo—see below).

An Amnesty International report of Aug. 31, 1985, alleged that the government of Mozambique made arbitrary use of the death penalty for political and non-violent offences. The report noted that in the previous 4½ years 70 persons had been executed for offences including politically motivated kidnapping, agitation against the state and crimes against humanity in the conflict between the government and RNM and that in 1983 several prisoners had been summarily executed without trial.

African National Union of Rombezia (*União Nacional Africana da Rombezia*, UNAR)

The UNAR was said to have been set up in the 1960s, allegedly by the Portuguese secret police. In 1985 it was reported to have been reorganized as a secessionist movement with the aim of creating a sovereign state in Mozambique north of the Zambezi river. It is thought to be backed by Portuguese ex-colonists from Mozambique, numbers of whom have settled in South Africa.

Mozambican National Resistance (*Resistência Nacional Moçambicana,* RNM)

Leadership. Afonso Dlakama (pres.); João da Silva Ataide (spokesman in Lisbon)

This organization was set up mainly by Mozambicans who had fled to Rhodesia (now Zimbabwe) to escape the Frelimo regime, and with the alleged help of the Smith regime in Rhodesia. From 1976 onwards, RNM guerrillas were active in Mozambique, at first near the Rhodesian border, but by 1979 they had penetrated further into Manica and northern Sofala provinces. During that year 36 persons were sentenced to death by Mozambican revolutionary military courts for treason and sabotage (attributed not only to RNM guerrillas but also to Rhodesian agents, the government alleging in September 1979 that rebel activity inside Mozambique was due to a combination of Rhodesian officers, mercenaries and traitors).

According to Mozambican official statements made on several occasions during 1981, the RNM was then supported not only by former members of the Rhodesian secret service but also by the South African Defence Force, which was alleged to have supplied both arms and military instructors to the RNM guerrillas. However, both South Africa and the RNM categorically denied that such aid had been given.

By June 1982 the RNM claimed that the area of its activities covered more than half of Mozambique's 10 provinces, and that the "rapid advance towards our ultimate goal of shaking the parasite Frelimo yoke imposed on the nation could not have been achieved without the widespread and spontaneous support of the population". The RNM also gave a warning that it would treat as enemies any Portuguese military personnel sent to Mozambique as advisers at the request of the government of Mozambique. The group's claims were, however, challenged by Western observers, according to whom the RNM guerrillas operated only in rural areas inhabited by less than a quarter of the country's population, and they had only about 3,000 trained fighters (with more than that number still being trained).

In September 1982 Mozambican officials claimed that RNM forces were operating from bases in Malawi. On the other hand RNM activities were obviously inflicting great damage on the economy of Malawi, and following a visit to Malawi by the Foreign Minister of Mozambique on Oct. 17, 1982, it appeared that facilities for the RNM in Malawi had been closed down.

On March 17, 1983, the RNM's radio station—*Voz da Africa Livre* ("Voice of Free Africa", said to be broadcasting from South Africa)—announced that the first assembly of military and political cadres of the RNM had been held in Geneva; it was also claimed that a government-in-exile had been set up with a six-member cabinet.

In June-August 1983 the RNM conducted an offensive in the provinces of Nampula and Zambezia. On Aug. 21 it captured a group of 24 Soviet technicians and four members of the local militia at a tantalum mine in central Zambezia, where two Soviet technicians and two militiamen were killed. On the other hand the Mozambican army claimed on Sept. 28 to have destroyed the RNM's largest provincial base at Tomé in Inhambane province.

Following the signing in March 1984 of the Nkomati Accord between Mozambique and South Africa—by which each side agreed not to serve as a base for acts of violence or aggression against the other—the RNM claimed in April of that year that it had stockpiled enough equipment and weapons to enable its war to be maintained for a further two years. It also claimed that all 10 provinces of Mozambique were now affected by guerrilla activities (including the north-eastern province of Cabo Delgado, where a new front had been established).

Between April and September 1984 the RNM attacked inter alia a train, a convoy of lorries and a hydroelectric scheme. The Mozambican authorities, however, claimed on July 3 that since January 1984 a total of 93 rebel bases had been seized, 1,200 guerrillas had been killed and 340 captured, while an estimated 10,000 civilians seized by the rebels had been freed.

Between May and September 1984 tripartite discussions were held by the governments of Mozambique and of South Africa with the RNM, which stated that it had handed to the leader of the Mozambican delegation a list of its demands, calling in particular for an end to the one-party state in Mozambique, the dissolution of the People's Assembly, the creation of a government of "national reconciliation" and RNM leadership of the government and of the armed forces if Samora Machel was to remain President.

Although the South African Foreign Minister (who had been chairman at the tripartite meetings) announced on Oct. 3, 1984, that the government of Mozambique and the RNM had agreed in principle to end the conflict and to work for peace, and that an eventual ceasefire would be monitored by South Africa, the RNM declared that it would continue fighting until a date and conditions for a truce were set, and that it would not accept the presence of South African troops in Mozambique; on Nov. 2 it announced that it was withdrawing from the tripartite talks.

On Oct. 3 the RNM had already declared that it would launch a guerrilla offensive involving the deployment of some 21,000 fighters in all provinces. By mid-November it claimed to have surrounded Maputo. It appeared to concentrate its attacks not only on the country's transport system but also on civilians and foreigners (the latter including seven East German technicians seized in December); Mozambique's trade with Malawi and Zimbabwe was disrupted; and power supplies to Beira and Maputo were interrupted in December 1984 and January 1985 respectively.

On Dec. 25, 1984, President Machel claimed that the RNM was continuing to receive supplies and equipment from South Africa and to gain access to Mozambique from South Africa. The South African Foreign Minister, however, denied early in February 1985 that any such assistance was provided by a South African government department, and on March 16 he revealed the discovery of a counterfeiting ring in Johannesburg which had manufactured false notes to purchase goods from Mozambique for resale in order to finance arms and supplies for the RNM, which was also said to receive support from certain "international bankers, financiers and businessmen". The South African government also stated that it had taken disciplinary action against members of the South African Defence Force for proven or potential connexions with the RNM.

In March 1985 the South African government announced that it would no longer attempt to bring about a peace settlement between the government of Mozambique and the RNM but would seek to co-operate with that government "to eliminate the [RNM] threat", and on April 24 the South African Foreign Minister announced that the two governments had agreed to establish "a joint operational centre" on the border between the two countries as from May 1, 1985.

The RNM, on the other hand, claimed in April 1985 to have achieved "air supremacy" by the acquisition of (Soviet-built) SAM-7 ground-to-air missiles. On Aug. 13 RNM action damaged the oil pipeline from Beira to Mutare (formerly Umtali) in Zimbabwe, which was guarded by some 1,500 Zimbabwean troops. (From early July 1985 Zimbabwean forces estimated at between 7,000 and 10,000 men were deployed in joint operations with the Mozambican army against the RNM.)

On Aug. 28, 1985, a combined Mozambican-Zimbabwean force captured the RNM headquarters (known as Casa Banana) in Sofala province, whereupon President Machel presented the South African Foreign Minister (on Aug. 28, 1985) with evidence that the group was still receiving assistance from South Africa, and this was conceded by the Minister on Sept. 19, but with the added claim that Mozambique was also violating the Nkomati Accord by continuing to support the banned African National Congress (ANC) in its campaign against the South African government.

Early in 1986 the RNM intensified its activities inter alia by destroying a sugar refinery, cutting the railway line from Swaziland to Maputo, attacking a train near Maputo and sabotaging power lines from South Africa to Maputo. The group also recaptured a number of towns and the Casa Banana base, and advanced in many areas where government troops lacked training and arms and were reduced to purely defensive operations.

In July 1986 the Mozambican armed forces Chief of Staff accused the government of Malawi of continuing to harbour RNM rebels, and on Sept. 11 President Machel threatened (i) to close the border with Malawi unless President Banda ceased his support for the RNM and (ii) to install missiles along the border. President Banda, however, continued to maintain that the RNM did not operate from Malawian territory. John Tembo, a senior aide of President Banda, headed a deputation to Maputo on Sept. 17, when he announced that his country would no longer allow the group to maintain bases there and proposed the creation of a joint security commission. The RNM nevertheless intensified its campaign, and early in November its spokesman in Lisbon said that it was his movement's intention to put pressure on Zimbabwe to remove its troops from Mozambique.

The RNM's activities also caused a mass exodus of Mozambicans to South Africa which, on Aug. 1, 1986, put into operation an electrified fence along part of the border. Late in September a representative of the Mozambican armed forces declared that South African troops were fighting alongside RNM guerrillas. Following the death of President Machel in an air crash on Oct. 19, the Mozambican media continued to broadcast reports of a build-up of South African armoury as support for the RNM. The South African government, however, reaffirmed that it would abide by the Nkomati Accord provided the principles enunciated in it were adhered to.

In early October 1986 it was reported in Zimbabwe that thousands of RNM supporters were leaving Malawi as a result of an expulsion order by President Banda. On the other hand a Mozambican administrator was on Dec. 16 quoted as saying that members of Malawi's armed forces were participating in RNM raids into Mozambique.

The proposed joint security commission agreed upon by Malawi and Mozambique subsequently held meetings which led to the signing, on Dec. 18, 1986, of an accord on mutual co-operation and of a protocol covering defence, state security and public order. On Dec. 19 the government of Malawi sent to Maputo a group of 57 persons (mostly Portuguese) whom the RNM had released from captivity; they were said to have been sent to Mozambique against their will, apparently in order to provide the Mozambican government with information about the RNM. According to Mozambican sources some 200,000 Mozambicans fled to Malawi between mid-October and late November 1986 as a result of the continuing guerrilla war, and a considerable number fled to Zimbabwe.

On Jan. 15, 1987, President Joaquim Alberto Chissano, the successor of the late President Machel, and Robert Mugabe, the Prime Minister of Zimbabwe, issued a joint statement in Harare, reaffirming that their military operations would be increased until the RNM was wiped out. It was reported at the same time that already one-third of Zimbabwe's national army was engaged in Mozambique.

In a statement issued in Lisbon and reported on Feb. 7, 1987, the RNM declared that it was ready to hold talks with the government of President Chissano, provided all foreign troops were withdrawn from Mozambique and an atmosphere of conciliation was established, permitting the holding of elections.

Britain began to assist in training Mozambican officers in January 1986 at a base in Zimbabwe.

According to a report by a correspondent in Maputo of *The Times* of London, published on March 14, 1987, over 10 years of warfare have had a devastating effect on the country. About 1,000,000 peasant farmers were said to have been made homeless and vast tracts of the country's most fertile lands to have been laid waste; roads and railways to have been sabotaged, causing a food transport crisis threatening some 2,000,000 people with famine; and more than 1,000 health posts and schools to have been destroyed and hundreds of their staff murdered, maimed or mutilated (the RNM having specifically focused its attacks on agents and facilities of the state). Important economic installations were said to have been shut down or destroyed, and the country's exports to have been reduced from £163,500,000 ($260,000,000) in 1980 to £50,300,000 ($80,000,000) in 1986.

It was reported in March 1987 that RNM president A. Dlakama had in the previous year sought to "africanize" the movement, by removing elements associated with the colonial period, including Evo Fernandes, the former secretary-general, who was a (white) Portuguese citizen of Goan descent.

The RNM leadership is predominantly Ndau-speaking and this factor has given it some support in parts of Central Mozambique, while inhibiting support in the south. As of March 1987 the RNM was said to enjoy freedom of operation (if not continuous control) in 10-15 per cent of the country, notably areas of Zambezia, Tete, and Sofala. Some sections of the RNM, however, were considered essentially bandit organizations with no political objectives.

Namibia

Capital: Windhoek Pop. 1,550,000

The territory of Namibia (South West Africa), a former League of Nations mandate administered as an integral part of South Africa, was in October 1966 declared to be under United Nations responsibility; in fact, however, it continued to be under the control of the Republic of South Africa. The latter appointed, on July 6, 1977, an Administrator-General for a transitional period which was to lead to the territory's independence. The South African government took further steps, without United Nations consent, (i) by holding elections (by universal adult suffrage) in December 1978 to a 50-member Constituent Assembly which was, in May 1979, converted into a National Assembly with legislative powers (and with the addition of 15 nominated members); (ii) by creating, on July 1, 1980, a 12-member Council of Ministers with executive powers in internal matters (subject to the veto of the Administrator-General, and with the South African government retaining responsibility for constitutional matters, foreign affairs and overall security), while with effect from Aug. 1, 1980, the Council of Ministers also controlled a defence force, the "South West African Territorial Forces", and from Sept. 1, 1980, the police (except the security police); and (iii) by holding elections for Administrative Assemblies in eight of the territory's ethnic areas in November 1980. The elections for the National and the Administrative Assemblies were contested by a number of political parties, among which the (multi-racial) Democratic Turnhalle Alliance (DTA) held an absolute majority in the National Assembly. All elections were boycotted by the South West Africa People's Organization (SWAPO), the territory's liberation movement.

However, on Jan. 18, 1983, the National Assembly was dissolved after the Council of Ministers had resigned following the failure of the president of the DTA (Peter Kalangula) to convert the Alliance into a unitary party, as well as serious disputes between the DTA and the Administrator-General. The latter thereupon took over the government of the territory until an independence plan could be agreed.

On Nov. 12, 1983, the DTA and six other political parties formed a Multi-Party Conference (MPC), and on Feb. 24, 1984, the leaders of the DTA and five other member parties of the MPC reached agreement on common aims in pursuit of independence for Namibia under MPC leadership and published a Windhoek Declaration of Basic Principles in which they committed themselves to the implementation of UN Security Council Resolution 435 (1978) as "the only concrete plan on independence" (see page 245).

On June 17, 1985, a Transitional Government of National Unity was given powers of limited self-government by the South African State President (P. W. Botha). Its Council of Ministers was composed of members of the MPC, while the South African government retained responsibility for foreign affairs and defence and the Administrator-General held limited powers of veto and the South African State President held overall powers of veto over legislation.

South West Africa People's Organization (SWAPO)

Leadership. Sam Nujoma (pres.); Hermann Toivo ja Toivo (sec.-gen.); Daniel Tjongarero (nat. ch.)

SWAPO was founded in June 1960 by Hermann Toivo ja Toivo (who later received a 20-year prison sentence in 1968 for offences under the South African "Terrorism Act" of 1967). In its early years SWAPO sent petitions to the United Nations in order to gain that organization's support. These petitions asked the United Nations to terminate immediately the League of Nations mandate, to entrust the temporary administration of the territory to a UN commission composed of African states, to arrange for free general elections to enable South West Africa to accede to (i) self-government immediately through the establishment of a democratic African government based on the principle of one man, one vote, and (ii) independence not later than 1963. The UN General Assembly and various UN committees passed successive resolutions condemning South Africa's policies in the territory.

SWAPO's guerrilla operations, supported from the outset by the liberation committee of the Organization of African Unity (OAU) as a means of furthering the eventual independence of South West Africa, began in September 1965.

At the United Nations the Security Council called, on March 20, 1969, for South Africa's immediate withdrawal from Namibia, the voting being 13 to none, with Britain and France abstaining. At a meeting with a special representative of the UN Secretary-General early in October 1972 Sam Nujoma reiterated SWAPO's demand for South Africa's "immediate and total withdrawal" from South West Africa. SWAPO also insisted on the territory's independence as a unitary state. It therefore opposed South African measures whereby Ovamboland became the first self-governing territory of South West Africa on May 1, 1972, and SWAPO also boycotted elections held to elective seats in an Ovamboland Legislative Council on Aug. 2-3, 1973.

Before the UN Council for Namibia (created in May 1967), Nujoma declared in May 1973 that the people of Namibia rejected further diplomatic contacts (which had failed to lead to any agreement on eventual independence for Namibia) and that an "intensification of armed liberation struggle" was "the only language" which the South Africans understood. On Dec. 11, 1973, the UN General Assembly passed a resolution, by 107 votes to two (Portugal and South Africa) and with 17 abstentions, recognizing SWAPO as the "authentic representative of the Namibian people".

SWAPO again boycotted elections in Ovamboland, held on Jan. 13-17, 1975, to fill 42 elective seats in an enlarged Legislative Council. The result of the election, in which 55 per cent of the voters were officially stated to have taken part, was interpreted by the South African authorities as a "rejection of SWAPO".

SWAPO also boycotted a constitutional conference called by the South African administration and held at the Turnhalle in Windhoek beginning on Sept. 1, 1975. On that date SWAPO released its own proposals for a Namibian constitution, under which Namibia was to become a republic with a president elected by the people and a Cabinet chosen from a single-chamber legislature. On Dec. 2, 1975, the government of the neighbouring Republic of Botswana recognized SWAPO as the only legitimate representative of the people of Namibia.

After SWAPO had rejected the constitutional proposals made at the Turnhalle negotiations, the information and publicity secretary of SWAPO's internal wing (Daniel Tjongarero) said on Aug. 30, 1976, that SWAPO insisted on the holding of elections on the basis of one man, one vote for political parties rather than ethnic groups, and only after withdrawal of South Africa's "occupying forces". He also declared that the United Nations had entrusted SWAPO with "the sole responsibility for liberating the country" but did not regard SWAPO as the only political force in Namibia; he added that SWAPO envisaged no direct takeover of the territory, which should be handed over to the United Nations for a transitional period, during which other political groups would also play a major role.

The UN General Assembly decided on Dec. 20, 1976, to grant SWAPO observer status and to invite it to participate in the Assembly's sessions and in the work of all international conferences convened under the Assembly's auspices. In October-November 1976 and April 1977 SWAPO was strengthened by the accession of six political groups until then considered to be moderate, viz. four Nama breakaway groups, the Namibian African People's Democratic Organization (NAPDO) and a Herero royalist association.

By 1977 the armed wing of SWAPO was known as the People's Liberation Army of Namibia (PLAN), its supreme commander being named as Dimo Hamamba. At that time the guerrillas engaged not only in the laying of land mines but also in the abduction of young Ovambos from mission schools who were taken to Angola for training. Even before the South African-sponsored constitutional (Turnhalle) conference had decided (in March 1977) to set up an interim government, SWAPO had declared that it had no alternative but to fight on the battlefield "however long it might take" and that only an international conference would eventually bring the war to an end. Of SWAPO's aims, Nujoma said on Feb. 4, 1977: "We are an African party which believes in neutrality and non-alignment." He admitted that SWAPO was receiving "large donations from Soviet Russia" but added that this did not mean that SWAPO automatically followed Soviet foreign and international policy.

On June 17, 1977, Nujoma declared his support for the efforts of five Western member states of the UN Security Council (Britain, France, Canada, the Federal Republic of Germany and the United States) to find a peaceful way of bringing Namibia to independence; he also said that, although he did not accept a South African-appointed Administrator-General for the territory, he would accept one appointed by the UN Council for Namibia; that SWAPO would take part in free elections as long as all South African troops were first withdrawn; and that SWAPO would accept the presence of a UN peacekeeping force during the interim period before independence.

Following the assumption of office by the territory's first (South African) Administrator-General on Sept. 1, 1977, SWAPO and other opposition groups were allowed to hold political meetings, and the emergency regulations in force in the three northern "homelands"(Ovambo, Kavango, and East Caprivi) were repealed. SWAPO, however, declined to have any discussions with the Administrator-General (whom it regarded as illegal) on SWAPO participation in general elections, and at the end of September 1977 SWAPO's central committee decided to reject "bogus elections under the armed forces with a view to installing a puppet neo-colonial Turnhalle regime" and to continue and intensify the armed struggle.

In early 1978 the external and internal branches of SWAPO issued conflicting statements about SWAPO's aims. Nujoma declared on Feb. 26 inter alia that "majority rule" was "out", stating: "We are not fighting for majority rule. We are fighting to seize power in Namibia for the benefit of the Namibian people. We are revolutionaries, we are not counter-revolutionaries." The publicity secretary for SWAPO's internal branch, however, said on Feb. 28 that SWAPO wished "to establish in Namibia a democratic secular government founded on the will and the participation of all the Namibian people"; that it was prepared to test its strength in "free and fair elections"; and that it would accept the same restrictions on the movements of its active forces in northern Namibia as those applying to the South African troops, and also the presence of a "token force" of 1,500 such troops in Namibia up to the elections. The South African government in principle accepted the Western powers' proposals on April 25, 1978.

During February-March 1978 there were serious clashes between SWAPO and Democratic Turnhalle

Alliance (DTA) supporters, leading inter alia to the death of an Ovambo minister and to that of Chief Clemens Kapuuo (president of the DTA). Among persons detained under a new internal security proclamation in April 1978 were nine of the 13 members of the executive committee of SWAPO's internal wing.

On May 4, 1978, the South African Minister of Defence (then P. W. Botha) announced that in a "limited operation" against SWAPO forces South African troops had invaded Angola, and according to Angolan sources they had reached Cassinga (a town 115 miles north of the Namibian border) and hundreds of persons, mainly Namibian refugees, had been killed. SWAPO announced in New York on May 8 that in view of the "grave situation" created by the South African invasion of Angola SWAPO would take no further part in negotiations with the five Western powers. Nevertheless SWAPO endorsed the five-power agreement (providing for Namibia's independence to be achieved by Dec. 31, 1978) on July 12, and the UN Security Council endorsed the plan on July 22. On the other hand, the question of the Port of Walvis Bay (over which the South African government had assumed control the previous year, on the ground that it had been part of the Cape Province until 1922) remained unresolved, with the South African government making it clear that it would break off all discussions if the UN Security Council insisted that Walvis Bay should be reintegrated in Namibia (as demanded by SWAPO and also the five Western powers). After the UN Security Council had passed, on July 27, 1978, two resolutions—the second of which (adopted unanimously) declared that Walvis Bay must be reintegrated within Namibia—the South African government decided on July 31 to withhold its final approval of the UN plan for transition to independence, based on the Western powers' proposals and containing no reference to the Walvis Bay question.

New proposals made by the UN Secretary-General on the basis of a report by the UN Commissioner for Namibia (who had visited the territory in August 1978) were approved by SWAPO on Sept. 4, 1978, but rejected by the South African government on Sept. 20, when it was announced that elections would be held (without UN supervision) to a Constituent Assembly on Nov. 20-24, 1978; any participation in these elections was immediately rejected by SWAPO on Sept. 22.

The UN Commissioner's report provided for the early achievement of independence by Namibia through free and fair elections to be held under UN supervision and control by a UN Transition Assistance Group (UNTAG). This plan was incorporated in UN Security Council Resolution 435 (1978) adopted on Sept. 24, 1978, by 12 votes to none (with Czechoslovakia and the Soviet Union abstaining and China not participating in the vote). The resolution also welcomed SWAPO's acceptance of the plan. The South African government, however, in addition to rejecting this plan, had earlier in September rejected a SWAPO proposal for a separate ceasefire agreement, emphasizing that it would not enter into any agreement with SWAPO.

After further negotiations the South African government agreed on Oct. 19 that the proposed elections—then rescheduled for Dec. 4-8, 1978—were to be followed by UN-supervised elections at a later date. SWAPO strongly opposed this compromise and called for a UN Security Council meeting to improve "comprehensive mandatory economic sanctions" on South Africa, but no such resolution was in fact passed.

The South African-organized elections, in which 80.2 per cent of the electorate was officially stated to have taken part, gave the DTA an overwhelming overall majority (of 41 out of 50 seats) in the Constituent Assembly. At a closed session the Assembly agreed, on Dec. 21, 1978, in principle to the holding of UN-supervised elections in 1979—but only provided several conditions were met.

The then vice-chairman of SWAPO's internal wing, Daniel Tjongarero, said on Jan. 4, 1979, that SWAPO would take part in the proposed UN-supervised elections provided no changes were made in the UN Secretary-General's independence plan. The central committee of SWAPO's external wing, however, made no such statement but reiterated on Jan. 9 that it would continue its armed struggle as the only means of achieving genuine liberation for Namibia.

Renewed SWAPO attacks on South African military camps in Ovamboland in February 1979 induced R. F. Botha, the South African Foreign Minister, to point out to the UN Secretary-General that "the whole delicate edifice of agreement" on a Namibian settlement was "in danger of collapse". He said that SWAPO was seeking to block the settlement, especially by making "outrageous demands"—including the establishment (by SWAPO) of five armed bases inside South West Africa, the complete withdrawal of South African troops and the refusal to place SWAPO forces under UN monitoring.

In the absence of any final agreement on the modalities of achieving a transition to independence, the South West African Constituent Assembly decided on May 2, 1979, to set itself up as a National Assembly (with the addition of up to 15 nominated members) with wide-ranging legislative powers. S. Nujoma thereupon declared in Luanda on May 15 that this step had virtually destroyed efforts to solve the Namibian problem through negotiation. In the meantime South African forces had carried out more raids on targets in Angola and Zambia, claiming on March 11 to have destroyed more than 12 SWAPO bases.

Following the destruction of SWAPO's offices in Windhoek, Tjongarero dissolved the organization's national executive branch within Namibia (of which he had been the leader) in June 1979, but in August of that year SWAPO's central committee decided in Angola that he had acted unconstitutionally and declared his action null and void, and he was relieved of his position in September 1979. On July 22, 1980, the central committee expelled three of its members and six other officials (all from the Caprivi Strip) for alleged counter-revolutionary and secessionist activities aimed at dismembering Namibia's national territory by accepting separate independence for the Caprivi Strip. Those expelled included Mishake Albert Muyongo (acting vice-president of SWAPO), who announced in Lusaka (Zambia) on Aug. 6 that he would reassert the separate existence of the Caprivi African National Union (CANU, which had been one of SWAPO's constituent parties); however, the Zambian government did not allow CANU to be established in Zambia, and it was officially alleged in Windhoek that numerous Caprivians were being detained in Zambia.

The Chief of the South African Defence Force (SADF) declared on Dec. 2, 1982, that South Africa was "capable of maintaining the situation for a long time to come or until a lasting solution is arrived at". SWAPO, on the other hand, asserted that its guerrillas were operating in most of the northern half of Namibia, where they had launched "more than 800 attacks against military targets".

In talks on the issue of Namibia's independence, held in Cape Town between Javier Pérez de Cuéllar, the UN Secretary-General, and P. W. Botha, then Prime Minister of South Africa, on Aug. 22-24, 1983, it emerged that the main obstacle to agreement on the implementation of the UN plan for Namibia's transition to independence was South Africa's insistence on the withdrawal of the Cuban troops from Angola (this demand being supported by the United States) as a precondition for any progress towards Namibia's independence.

Figures issued in September 1983 by the South West African Territorial Force showed that since 1966 over 10,000 lives had been lost in the fighting between South African forces and SWAPO, including 7,894 lives of SWAPO guerrillas; in the first nine months of 1983 a total of 90 civilians and 663 SWAPO fighters were said to have been killed.

In December 1983 the SADF launched a major offensive against SWAPO bases, attacking targets more than 150 miles inside Angola, whose troops were engaged in mounting counter-attacks. The Chief of the SADF said late in December that SWAPO guerrillas were beginning to join forces with Cuban and Angolan troops against South African forces. Early in January 1984 the SADF claimed to have destroyed 11 Soviet-made T-54 tanks and to have killed 324 Cubans, Angolans and SWAPO members. However, on Jan. 8, 1984, the South Africans began to withdraw from the main battle zones after 21 of their soldiers had been killed.

The South African Foreign Minister had, on Dec. 15, 1983, offered, in a letter to the UN Secretary-General, an experimental one-month disengagement of South African troops in Angola on condition that the Angolan government would give an assurance that its own forces and those of SWAPO and the Cuban troops would "not exploit the situation by making attacks on Namibia". This offer was rejected by Angola and by SWAPO, while the UN Security Council passed, on Dec. 20, with only the United States abstaining, a resolution stating that South Africa should "unconditionally withdraw" all its occupation forces from Angola.

Following talks between Angolan, US and South African delegations the South African Prime Minister (P. W. Botha) announced on Jan. 31, 1984, that a process of disengaging South African forces from Angola was to begin immediately and that the experimental one-month truce was to start on Feb. 1. The UN Security Council, however, passed, on Jan. 6, another resolution (with the United Kingdom and the United States abstaining), again demanding the SADF's immediate and unconditional withdrawal, failing which the Security Council would consider "measures in accordance with the appropriate provisions of the UN Charter".

Under a Lusaka accord reached on Feb. 16, 1984 (after mediation by Chester Crocker, US Assistant Secretary of State for African Affairs), it was agreed to extend the ceasefire beyond 30 days should all parties so wish; for this purpose a joint monitoring commission (JMC) was set up. S. Nujoma declared in New York on Feb. 23 that his forces would observe the ceasefire, but he also reasserted SWAPO's right to continue to fight for Namibia's independence. In effect a timetable agreed for the South African withdrawal was not adhered to, as clashes took place between SWAPO fighters and members of the JMC, while South Africa claimed that SWAPO guerrillas were violating the Lusaka accord. After the South African withdrawal was repeatedly delayed it came to a halt at Ngiva (some 30 miles north of the Namibian border) by mid-October 1984.

On March 1, 1984, Hermann Toivo ja Toivo, the founder of SWAPO, was released from prison in South Africa, having served 16 years of his 20-year sentence. (The release of political prisoners was a required element of the UN Security Council Resolution 435.) At a SWAPO annual committee meeting in Luanda in August 1984 he was elected to the newly created post of SWAPO secretary-general. Also released were, on May 25, 1984, a group of 54 (out of an estimated 114) unofficial prisoners of war held in an internment camp in Namibia since May 1978, when they had been captured in southern Angola.

On May 11-13, 1984, SWAPO took part, together with delegations from South Africa and the Namibian Multi-Party Conference, in a conference on the independence of Namibia held in Lusaka, with President Kaunda of Zambia and Prof Willie van Niekerk, the South African Administrator-General of Namibia, as joint chairmen, but this conference failed to reach agreement. At a meeting held in Cape Verde on July 25, 1984, between S. Nujoma and Prof van Niekerk, the former rejected a South African government offer of a ceasefire and insisted that any ceasefire agreement should be linked to the implementation of the UN Security Council Resolution 435.

After compulsory military service in the South West African Territorial Force had been introduced in November 1984, an emergency zone was declared on March 11, 1985, over wide areas in northern Namibia where, according to the Commissioner of the South West African police, "the security forces could no longer guarantee the safety of the public".

The formation of a Namibian Transitional Government of National Unity on June 17, 1985, was opposed by SWAPO, with a SWAPO representative stating that his organization would not participate in any government which had not been elected by the Namibian people and which was not internationally recognized, and that SWAPO's military wing would continue its guerrilla war against the South African occupying forces.

In June 1985 the Chief of the SADF cited three cases of increased SWAPO activity in northern Namibia, in response to which the SADF had carried out "hot pursuit" operations inside Angola, in which 61 SWAPO insurgents had been killed. Another follow-up operation was carried out by South and South West African forces in mid-September 1985, when S. Nujoma claimed that in the past seven months of 1985 his forces had destroyed 11 South African bases in northern Namibia, had killed over 400 soldiers, and had carried out over 3,000 acts of sabotage. A South African statement released on Oct. 18 was to the effect that 538 SWAPO "terrorists" had been killed since the beginning of 1985. The strength of SWAPO guerrillas was then estimated at some 8,000, of whom about 65 per cent were possibly engaged in anti-UNITA operations with the Angolan forces.

The South African State President (P. W. Botha) stated in the South African Parliament on March 4, 1986, that the implementation of the UN Security Council Resolution 435 was to commence on Aug. 1, 1986, on condition that by then "a firm and satisfactory agreement" had been reached on the withdrawal of Cubans from Angola. However, military operations were continued later during 1986, with the SADF launching, on Nov. 13, a "pre-emptive" raid on a SWAPO base in Cunene province (southern Angola) and claiming to have killed 39 SWAPO insurgents (against the loss of two South Africans).

During the first six months of 1987 a total of 515 SWAPO guerrillas were killed (as announced by the South African military headquarters in Windhoek on July 2).

Nauru

Capital: Domaneab Pop. 7,500

The Republic of Nauru, an independent state with special status within the Commonwealth, has a unicameral Parliament of 18 members elected for up to three years by universal adult suffrage and a President elected by Parliament for its duration from among its members. There is a five-member Cabinet consisting of members of Parliament. President Hammer DeRoburt rules with the support of a majority of members of Parliament.

An opposition Democratic Party of Nauru was formed in late 1986.

Nepal

Capital: Katmandu Pop. 16,630,000

The Kingdom of Nepal is, under its 1962 Constitution, a "constitutional monarchical Hindu state". Political parties have been banned since Jan. 5, 1961; the "basic units of democracy" are elected village and provincial councils (*panchayats*); under amendments to the Constitution approved in a referendum (which rejected the restoration of political parties) on April 2, 1980, 112 members of the country's National Assembly (*Rashtriya Panchayat*) are elected by direct adult suffrage and another 28 members are nominated by the King; and the Prime Minister is appointed by the King on the recommendation of the National Assembly to which the Council of Ministers (Cabinet) is responsible.

In elections to 108 of the 112 elective seats in the National Assembly, begun on May 12, 1986, only 39 of the sitting members were re-elected and the other 69 were newly elected members. The turnout was reported to have been about 60 per cent of the country's 8,700,000 voters.

A general amnesty, announced by the King on April 13, 1980, for all who were accused of political offences, was thought to affect between 200 and 300 people, half of them in prison in Nepal and the remainder in exile, mainly in India, where many opponents of King Birendra have lived since the latter's father, King Mahendra, abolished parliamentary democracy in December 1960. In 1983, opposition groups claimed that 168 political prisoners were still in prison. Following the appointment of a new Prime Minister who pledged to release all political prisoners, it was announced on Aug. 30, 1983, that 52 had been released to date.

In 1985 the capital (Katmandu) and other places were rocked by a series of bomb attacks, responsibility for which was claimed by various opposition organizations.

There have been reports of incidents where individuals, including newspaper editors, have been detained for criticizing the government.

Communist Party of Nepal (CPN)

The CPN, founded in Calcutta (India) in 1948, operated openly in Nepal from 1950 to 1952, when it was banned for alleged complicity in an attempted left-wing coup. In 1953 it nevertheless obtained more than half the votes in Katmandu municipal elections, gaining five out of 18 seats. Legalized in 1956, it gained only 7.5 per cent of the votes in 1959 parliamentary elections.

After the banning of all political parties in 1961, the CPN was divided, and by 1962 there were (i) a pro-Soviet section led by Keshar Jung Raimajhi, and (ii) a pro-Chinese section led by Pushpa Lal (who had been the leader of the original CPN). The Raimajhi section has continued to agitate, with the Nepali Congress and other opposition parties, for the legalization of political parties. Later this section was divided into three factions, all of which were prepared to take part in *Panchayat* elections and to co-operate with the Nepali Congress. In November 1978 K. J. Raimajhi signed a declaration issued by four banned parties and calling for the establishment of a constitutional monarchy.

The Pushpa Lal section of the CPN was later divided into four factions, two of which abandoned their former pro-Chinese line, adopted an independent attitude and were prepared to co-operate with the Nepali Congress. In 1984 these two factions joined with two of the pro-Soviet groups in forming a Leftist Unity Front.

Two further sections were (i) the Fourth Congress Group, which broke with the Chinese Communist Party and claimed that no communist state existed anywhere, and (ii) the *Mashal* (Torch) Group, which broke away from the Fourth Congress Group and retained a pro-Chinese attitude. Both rejected all co-operation with the Nepali Congress.

In the elections to the National Assembly on May 12, 1986, Padma Ratna Tuladhar, reportedly a leading figure in the Communist Party, won a seat in Katmandu.

Communist Party of Nepal—Marxist-Leninist (CPNM-L)

This independent Maoist Party, an offshoot of the Naxalite movement in India, launched a campaign against landowners in eastern Nepal in the early 1970s, when its two leaders were sentenced to death. Later it was divided into three factions. Its primary aim has been the overthrow of the monarchy, and it has rejected co-operation with the Nepali Congress, which it regards as an instrument of the Indian government and of capitalism.

Janwadi Morcha (Democratic Front)
Samyukta Mukti Bahini (United Liberation Torch-bearers)

Both these organizations claimed responsibility for a series of bomb explosions in Katmandu on June 20, 1985, in which six people died, including one member of the National Assembly, Damber Jang Gurung. One man reported to have been carrying a bomb died when the device exploded in Pokhara on June 19, and a woman also alleged to be carrying a bomb was killed in the town of Birganj. Other bombs were found or exploded near the Indian border.

On July 8, 1985, the government announced that 1,400 people had been arrested in connexion with these incidents. On June 1, 1987, four people were sentenced to death and 23 to terms of between five years and life imprisonment for the bombings. Two of those sentenced to death—former members of parliament Ram Raja Prasad Singh and his brother Laxman Prasad Singh—were still at large in India.

Nepali Congress Party (NCP)

Leadership. Krishna Prasad Bhattarai (acting pres.)

The NCP was founded in Calcutta (India) in 1946 under the leadership of Bisheshwar Prasad Koirala (who had been active in the Indian Congress Party and its struggle for Indian independence). In 1947 the left wing of the NCP broke away to form a Nepali National Congress. In March 1950 the NCP absorbed the Nepali Democratic Congress founded by Mahendra Bikram Shan (a member of the Nepali royal family). On Sept. 29, 1950, it was announced in Katmandu that NCP supporters had plotted to assassinate the Prime Minister, and in November-December 1950 NCP followers were involved in a revolt against the government which induced the latter to introduce constitutional reforms. The NCP thereupon took part in the formation of an interim government on Feb. 12, 1951. Following a Cabinet crisis a new government was formed on Nov. 16, 1951, with Matrika Prasad Koirala (then president of the NCP and a brother of B. P. Koirala) as Prime Minister.

In July-August 1952 M. P. Koirala and his supporters left or were expelled from the NCP and formed a National Democratic Party. In January 1955 the NCP launched a civil disobedience campaign, inter alia with the aim of enforcing the holding of a general election.

In the country's first elections, held in February-April 1959, the NCP gained 74 of the 109 seats in the lower house of parliament, and B. P. Koirala thereupon formed a government which was sworn in on May 27, 1959. However, on Dec. 15, 1960, King

Mahendra abolished parliamentary government, dissolved all political parties and arrested most of their leaders, including B. P. Koirala, who remained imprisoned until Oct. 30, 1968, when he was released after the NCP had on May 15, 1968, offered the King its "loyal co-operation". On the following day NCP leaders living in exile in India were pardoned.

The state of emergency imposed by the King had been ended in April 1963 with the introduction of the *panchayat* system of indirect representation, under which political parties remained banned. Ramraja Prasad Singh, a leading member of the NCP who had been elected to the National *Panchayat* early in 1971, was arrested on July 19 of that year and was given a 2½-year prison sentence for alleged anti-state activities, having declared his opposition to the *panchayat* system; however, the King pardoned him on Aug. 25, 1971, and directed that he should be allowed to take his seat in the Assembly from which the Speaker had barred him.

B. P. Koirala, who was then living in exile in India, had threatened King Mahendra with armed struggle against his regime, but to King Birendra (who succeeded to the throne at the death of his father, King Mahendra, on Jan. 31, 1972) he offered co-operation in building "a progressive democratic and prosperous Nepal".

On Dec. 16, 1975, some 50 political prisoners were reported to have been released, among them several former NPC members. B. P. Koirala returned to Katmandu from India on Dec. 30, 1976, but was arrested, with several other NPC followers accompanying him, for "anti-national activities". He had, while in India, stated (on May 26, 1975) that he wanted to carry on "peaceful agitation" for the establishment of democratic institutions in Nepal, and had claimed that the NPC was leading "a big democratic movement" inside Nepal which was attempting to counter "pro-Chinese communist influence" in that country. On Feb. 23, 1978, a special tribunal cleared B. P. Koirala of three charges of treason and sedition, and on March 3 he was acquitted of other charges. He was received by the King on Oct. 30 and said afterwards that in his view a policy of national conciliation would lead to unity and was desirable. An earlier call made by him to party workers to cease all political activities was, however, received with dismay by the central working committee of the NCP, which declared on Oct. 30, 1978, that the party's fight for the restoration of civil and human liberties had been "utterly belied by the betrayal of B. P. Koirala".

Following the outbreak of student unrest in April 1979 B. P. Koirala was placed under house arrest and three other NCP leaders—Ganesh Man Singh (deputy leader of the NCP), Krishna Prasad Bhattarai (acting president of the NCP and former Speaker of parliament) and Gokal Prasad (former editor of a government-controlled newspaper)—were taken into custody on April 27, 1979. However, after the Indian government had reportedly advised the King to come to an understanding with the NCP leaders, the above three and 61 other political leaders were released on May 9, 1979. B. P. Koirala said after his release that the King should not delude himself that he could keep the throne by sheer armed force, and he later welcomed the King's decision to hold a constitutional referendum. However, in this referendum held in May 1980, the policies of the NCP for a restoration of party pluralism were rejected (by 2,443,452 votes to 2,007,452, with about 372,000 spoilt or invalid ballot papers). The first direct parliamentary elections held on May 9, 1981, were boycotted by B. P. Koirala, who died in Katmandu on July 21, 1982. In December 1982 the NCP held its first open conference since 1959 in the capital.

On Dec. 30, 1983, K. P. Bhattarai was one of a large number of opposition politicians temporarily detained in order to prevent a "national reconciliation day" scheduled for Dec. 31, to demand the restoration of political parties.

At an NCP national convention attended by 1,200 party workers and delegates held on March 13-15, 1985, the government was criticized for inflation, alleged food shortages and an incorrect land-ownership policy. However, in his opening speech, K. P. Bhattarai stressed his support for the monarchy, describing it as an essential political institution.

Up to 350 supporters of the NCP were reported to have been detained on the first day of a campaign of civil disobedience launched on May 23, 1986, including K. P. Bhattarai, and the NCP general secretary, Girija Prasad Koirala. Two weeks later, it was claimed that 6,000 had been detained, including at least 16 newspaper editors and journalists. In early June it was confirmed that two editors had been charged with sedition.

The NCP stated in 1986 that members would perhaps take part in elections to the National Assembly held on May 12, on condition that political prisoners were released and candidates were not obliged to be members of one of the six *panchayat* class organizations. However, these demands were not met, and no members took part. Later the party announced that it would take part in local *panchayat* elections held on March 21 and 24, 1987, after having been officially declared winner of the mayoral elections in Katmandu. However, its results were disappointing and it claimed that there had been ballot-rigging and booth-capturing.

In a manifesto issued in January 1956 the NCP defined its aim as the achievement of socialism by peaceful and democratic methods and of a government which would be a constitutional monarchy on the British model, with a Cabinet responsible to the people's representatives and a unicameral legislature elected by universal adult suffrage, a foreign policy based on neutrality and coexistence, industrialization and state planning of the national economy.

Netherlands

Capital: Amsterdam
Seat of Government: The Hague Pop. 14,480,000

The Kingdom of the Netherlands (comprising the Netherlands in Europe, the Netherlands Antilles and Aruba) is a constitutional and hereditary monarchy. The Netherlands in Europe has a bicameral Parliament consisting of (i) a 75-member First Chamber elected by the country's 11 provincial councils and (ii) a 150-member Second Chamber elected by direct universal suffrage and by proportional representation. Executive power rests with the Crown and a Council of Ministers whose members may not be members of Parliament.

As a result of elections held on May 21, 1986, seats in the Second Chamber were distributed as follows: Christian Democratic Appeal 54, Labour Party 52, Party of Freedom and Democracy 27, Democrats-66 nine, State Reform Party three, Radical Political Party two and Pacifist Socialist Party, Reformed Political Association and Reformational Political Federation one each. Parties which gained no seats included the Communist Party of the Netherlands, the (neo-fascist) Centre Party, the Socialist Party, the Evangelical People's Party and the Greens.

Free South Moluccan Organization

This Organization was set up by South Moluccans, of whom some 15,000 had been brought to the Netherlands in 1951 after the Indonesian government had, in 1951, incorporated into the unitary Indonesian Republic the state of Negara Indonesia Timur (East Indonesia—one of 16 states making up the Republic of Indonesia), which included a Republic of the South Moluccas (Republik Maluku Selatan, RMS) proclaimed in April 1950. After South Moluccans who had remained in Indonesia had continued their resistance to the Indonesian government, the "President" of the RMS was arrested in 1963 and executed in 1966, whereafter he was succeeded as "President" of the RMS by Dr Jan Alvares Manusama. The latter was resident in the Netherlands, where certain South Moluccans pursued their aim of restoring the RMS and, to further their aim, resorted to acts of violence—which were, however, not approved by Dr Manusama.

Following a number of serious incidents in 1974-75, from early 1976 onwards a joint Dutch-Moluccan commission met periodically to discuss relations between the Dutch and South Moluccan communities.

Nevertheless, armed South Moluccans undertook further violent action in 1977. On May 23 two groups attacked a train and a school in the northern Netherlands and took 54 passengers and some 100 school children and teachers as hostages against demands for the release of South Moluccans in prison. Although all the school children and some of the train passengers were subsequently released, the Dutch government eventually decided to use force and on June 11 troops stormed the train and the school; this action resulted in the death of two hostages and six South Moluccans, among them one who was said to have undergone guerrilla training in South Yemen. On Sept. 22, 1977, eight of those who had been involved in the two actions were sentenced to terms of imprisonment of between one and nine years.

In a declaration presented in Parliament on Jan. 26, 1978, the Netherlands government stated that "for juridical, historic and political reasons" it could not "recognize or support an autonomous South Moluccan republic". The Deputy Prime Minister and Minister of Justice said at the same time that the government would nevertheless continue to respect the South Moluccans' right to their traditions, religion and language and would carry on its efforts to integrate the community (estimated at about 36,000), if the Moluccans so wished.

In July 1980 Eddie Aponno, said to be the organization's leader, advised Moluccans in the Netherlands to return to Indonesia, adding that they had been "following dreams for too long" and that their president-in-exile (i.e. Dr Manusama) had deceived them.

Left-wing Groups

Action Group against Nuclear War

This Group claimed responsibility for three bomb attacks on military air bases on Nov. 14-15, 1985.

Northern Terror Front

A group of this name claimed responsibility for a fire-bomb attack on a police station in Groningen on Feb. 3, 1985.

Red Aid (*Rood Hulp*)

This group was set up to aid extremist movements in other countries such as the Armenian Secret Army for the Liberation of Armenia, the Irish Republican Army, the Basque separatist ETA and the Red Army Faction in the Federal Republic of Germany.

It was one of several groups which claimed responsibility for the assassination of the British ambassador at The Hague on March 22, 1979.

Red Resistance Front

In May 1980 the Dutch police produced documents to show that this Front was linked with the Basque separatist ETA.

New Zealand

Capital: Wellington Pop. 3,250,000

The Dominion of New Zealand, a member of the Commonwealth, is a parliamentary democracy with the British monarch as head of state represented by a Governor-General. It has a unicameral 95-member House of Representatives elected for a three-year term by universal adult suffrage in 88 single-member constituencies and four Maori constituencies. It has a Cabinet headed by a Prime Minister and appointed by the Governor-General.

As a result of elections held on July 14, 1984, seats in the House of Representatives were distributed as follows: Labour Party 56, National Party 37, Social Credit Political League two. The Labour Party won all four "special seats" reserved for Maoris. Among parties which gained no seats were the New Zealand Party (which obtained 12 per cent of the votes cast), the (ecologist) Value Party and the New Zealand Women's Political Party.

The Social Credit Political League changed its name to the New Zealand Democratic Party with effect from July 1, 1985, and the New Zealand Party decided on March 26, 1986, to merge with the National Party.

Among Maoris there are several protest movements focusing on issues of land rights and racial discrimination. These include a Waitangi Action Committee based in Auckland; a Maori "self-government" party *(Manu Motuhake)*, which was founded in 1979 and unsuccessfully contested the general election of 1981; and the Maori Unity Movement *(Kotahitanga)*, founded in 1983 with Mrs Eva Rickards as president, and comprising urban-based militant Maoris and traditional tribal organizations.

Nicaragua

Capital: Managua Pop. 3,272,000

The Republic of Nicaragua is governed by a unicameral legislature and an executive President, Daniel Ortega Saavedra, who was inaugurated in January 1985. D. Ortega had previously been Co-ordinator of the Junta of National Reconstruction, which had constituted the government since the revolution of 1979. In the general elections of November 1984 the Sandinista National Liberation Front (FSLN—a political party which had grown out of the movement which overthrew the Somoza regime) gained 61 seats in the National Assembly, while the Democratic Conservative Party (PCD) won 14, the Independent Liberal Party (PLI) nine, the Popular Social Christian Party (PPSC) six and the Communist Party (PCN), the Socialist Party (PSN) and the Marxist-Leninist Popular Action Movement (MAP-ML) two each.

The main political opposition group operating inside Nicaragua, the Democratic Co-ordinating Board (CD), boycotted the elections because of what it claimed was the FSLN's "unwillingness to cede power". The CD had been formed in 1981 and comprised the Social Christian Party (PSCN), the PCD, the Social Democratic Party (PSD), the Constitutionalist Liberal Movement (MLC), the Higher Council for Private Enterprise (Cosep), the Confederation for Trade Union Unification (CUS) and the Nicaraguan Workers' Central, but the PCD did not join in the boycott. In late October 1984 the government attempted to institute a national dialogue with representatives from all sectors of public life, but CD leaders withdrew when their demand for the postponement of elections was rejected, and the attempt was abandoned a month later when the government failed to obtain unanimous support for a joint resolution condemning US aggression against Nicaragua.

A new Constitution was promulgated on Jan. 9, 1987, which stipulated a democratic form of government and political pluralism, involving all political organizations except those advocating a return to *Somocismo* (the practices of the Somoza regime). At the same time President Ortega announced the formal reintroduction of the state of emergency, which was originally declared in March 1982, partially lifted in 1984 and renewed in October 1985 with certain modifications. In the last two months of 1985 and in early 1986 the government detained a number of opponents on suspicion of aiding "contras" (i.e. the counter-revolutionary guerrillas) and in particular imposed restrictions on opposition news media and a number of leading Church officials.

Since 1981 several former supporters of the Sandinista revolution have left the country and joined guerrilla groups based in Honduras to the north and Costa Rica to the south. These contra forces, which also contain some officials from the Somoza era and a number of Miskito Indians from the country's Caribbean coast, have made several attempts to unite, but they have failed to agree on whether or not to include Somozists and on their approach to US aid. Nicaragua's relations with its immediate neighbours have been severely strained by strong allegations that the contras have received active support fom the Honduran armed forces and passive assistance from the Costa Rican authorities.

Anti-Sandinista Alliances

The main contra groups to develop were the Nicaraguan Democratic Force (FDN) on the Honduran border and the Democratic Revolutionary Alliance (ARDE) on the Costa Rican border. There have been a number of US-sponsored attempts to unite these two groups which have been only partially successful because they strained the tensions already existing in ARDE.

The Nicaraguan Unity for Reconciliation (*Unidad Nicaragüense para la Reconciliación,* UNIR) was formed on Sept. 5, 1984, by the FDN, the Miskito guerrilla group Misura and the component members of the ARDE except the Sandinista Revolutionary Force (FRS), causing a split in the ARDE leadership between Edén Pastora Gómez (of the FRS) and Alfonso Robelo Callejas. Despite its declaration that the two groups would "fight together until the liberation of the country, oppressed by the totalitarian Marxist-Leninist regime and occupied by foreign [i.e. Cuban] forces", to establish "a temporary government of national reconciliation with a priority mission to begin the democratic process", the UNIR did not succeed in uniting the contras and was replaced by the Nicaraguan Opposition Union (UNO).

Nicaraguan Opposition Union (*Unión Nicaragüense de la Oposición*, UNO)

Leadership. Pedro Joaquín Chamorro Barrios

The UNO was formed on June 12, 1985, at a meeting in San Salvador (El Salvador), to supersede the UNIR, as "an umbrella group for all democratic forces seeking a new government in Nicaragua". It incorporated the FDN, the ARDE (although as in the case of the UNIR Robelo joined it but Pastora did not) and Misura, and in September 1985 the new Miskito guerrilla group KISAN became a member. The leaders were Arturo Cruz of the CD, Adolfo Calero Portocarrero and Robelo, but in January 1987 Robelo and the ARDE withdrew on the ground that all US aid had gone to the FDN and none to the ARDE. In the same month Cruz resigned from the leadership over what he called "differences in the perception of what the Nicaraguan democratic opposition's real plans should be", and specifically its failure to adopt a "pluralist" political line. In February Calero resigned and was replaced by Pedro Joaquín Chamorro Barrios of the CD, a former editor of the opposition newspaper *La Prensa*, who had left the country to join the contras in February 1985.

Southern Opposition Bloc (*Bloque Opositora del Sur*, BOS)

Leadership. José Dávila Membereno, Alfredo César Aguirre

The BOS was formed on Aug. 2, 1985, by the ARDE (but without Robelo) and a number of other Costa Rican-based groups, including Nicaraguan Rescue and Conciliation, and its fighting strength was estimated in early 1987 at 2,300. It issued a statement giving the four conditions it required for unity with UNO: (i) agreement on a common political objective; (ii) guarantee of equal rights for each member within any new alliance; (iii) "a change of attitude" on the part of those said to be discriminating against BOS members in giving aid (i.e. the United States, which gave far more aid to the northern contras); and (iv) effective unification of all contra activities. The BOS and UNO drafted a "unity document" on March 15, 1986, but none of the three UNO leaders would sign it and Pastora disputed the idea that the UNO might play a part in the direction of ARDE forces.

Anti-Sandinista Movements

Democratic Revolutionary Alliance (*Alianza Revolucionaria Democrática*, ARDE)

Leadership. Alfonso Robelo Callejas (political commander); Fernando Chamorro Rapaccioli (military commander); Adolfo "Popo" Chamorro

This organization was formed in San José (Costa Rica) in December 1982 by representatives of four groups: (i) the Sandinista Revolutionary Front (FRS) led by Edén Pastora Gómez, who had on July 7, 1981, resigned as Deputy Minister of Defence and head of the Sandinista people's militia; (ii) the Nicaraguan Democratic Movement (MDN) led by Alfonso Robelo Callejas; (iii) the Misurasata Indian group led by Brooklyn Rivera; and (iv) the Nicaraguan Democratic Union (UDN) with its armed wing, the Nicaraguan Armed Revolutionary Forces (FARN). It was subsequently joined by the Christian Democratic Solidarity Front (FSDC, a right-wing exiled faction of the Nicaraguan Social Christian Party, PSCN, led by José Dávila Membereno) in September 1983, by the Nicaraguan Workers' Federation (FTC, a small union body based in Costa Rica) and the Christian Workers' Solidarity (STC). Pastora stated that the group's aim was not to overthrow Sandinism but to "rechannel the revolution" and prevent Somozists regaining power, and the Alliance declared its intention "to make deep social, political and economic changes in Nicaragua", but without what it termed the "totalitarianism" of the FSLN.

The ARDE launched its first military offensive in April 1983 in the south of the country, apparently operating from bases in Costa Rica. Two months later Robelo travelled to Washington to seek US financial assistance, and it was reported that the US Central Intelligence Agency (CIA) had begun channelling aid to the ARDE in June, although Pastora denied it. Disagreement between the two leaders resulted in Pastora's resignation as the ARDE military commander in October 1983, after which he led the FRS as a separate group, although it co-ordinated its activities with those of the ARDE. After further disputes with Robelo and other ARDE leaders Pastora finally left in May 1986 and was granted political asylum by the Costa Rican authorities.

The ARDE's main military efforts against the Nicaraguan government have been an airborne rocket attack on Sept. 8, 1983, on Managua airport, the mining of the Atlantic port of El Bluff on Feb. 24, 1984, the temporary capture of the town of San Juan del Sur in April 1984, and a seaborne attack on Bluefields on May 16, 1985. A government offensive was launched on May 23, 1985, which within two months forced the ARDE south of the San Juan river (which forms part of the border with Costa Rica). In 1985 the ARDE's fighting strength was estimated at around 3,000.

There have been a number of joint offensives with the Nicaraguan Democratic Force (FDN), but repeated US-sponsored efforts to unite the ARDE and the FDN have split ARDE.

Jeane Kirkpatrick Task Force

This contra guerrilla group, named after the then (right-wing) US ambassador to the United Nations, was formed in October 1984.

National Liberation Army (*Ejército de Liberación Nacional*, ELN)

Leadership. Pedro Ortega ("Juan Carlos") (l.)

This Somozist group was formed in 1979 in Honduras by former National Guards under President Somoza. Late in 1980 it claimed to have access to 4,000-6,000 armed men inside Nicaragua and several hundred elsewhere. It has also claimed to favour elections, free enterprise and respect for human rights, and to have influence with the autonomist Misurasata organization (see separate entry) on Nicaragua's east coast. The ELN has operated independently of the Nicaraguan Democratic Force (FDN).

Nicaraguan Anti-Communist Movement (*Movimiento Anticomunista Nicaragüense*)

This right-wing guerrilla group emerged in August 1985 when it kidnapped (and later released) a group of US Christian activists and journalists travelling on the Coco river (on the Costa Rican border).

Nicaraguan Democratic Force (*Fuerza Democrática Nicaragüense*, FDN)

Leadership. Adolfo Calero Portocarrero (c.-in-c.); Enrique Bermúdez (military commander); Edgar Chamorro Coronel; Indalecio Rodríguez

The formation of the FDN as a political-military organization was announced on Nov. 27, 1981, by a clandestine radio station claiming to be inside Nicaragua and declaring that its aim was to "liberate our people from Marxist totalitarianism". The FDN's component groups were the "September 15 Legion", the Misurasata Indian movement (see separate entry) and the Nicaraguan Democratic Union/Nicaraguan Revolutionary Armed forces (UDN/FARN), which later left to join the Democratic Revolutionary Alliance (ARDE). The FDN has operated from bases in Honduras and Miami and planned to establish a "liberated" zone inside Nicaragua.

In October 1982 the FDN appointed an eight-man directorate including Edgar Chamorro Coronel, Alfonso Callejas and an ex-Somocist colonel, Enrique Bermúdez. On Feb. 9, 1983, the FDN was joined by Adolfo Calero, the leader of the Democratic Conservative Party (PCD), who declared that armed struggle was "the only road left open".

The first major armed encounter between Nicaraguan troops and FDN units took place in the Atlantic Zone on March 18, 1982, and according to officials 11 FDN members and three soldiers were killed. In November 1982 the government declared the north of the country a military emergency zone and in early 1983 the FDN attempted to establish a bridgehead in Nicaragua, but by March had been forced to withdraw. The FDN also began a campaign of economic sabotage, the most serious incidents being the firing of oil storage facilities at the port of Corinto on Oct. 10, 1983, and the mining of the same port in March 1984, which was apparently organized by the US Central Intelligence Agency (CIA). Further offensives were launched in December 1983 (acting in co-operation with the ARDE), April 1984 and February 1985, but were checked by the army, and after a major army offensive beginning in December 1985 it was reported in March 1986 that three-quarters of the 2,000 FDN members fighting in Nicaragua had been forced to retreat back to Honduras. In December 1986 Nicaraguan troops crossed the Honduran border in forays against contra bases, in response to which President Azcona of Honduras called on US aid to airlift Honduran troops to the border region.

Official US aid to the FDN began in 1982 as part of the US administration's arms interdiction campaign (i.e. of the alleged supply of arms by the Nicaraguan government to the left-wing Salvadorean guerrillas), and the sums subsequently approved by Congress were $24,000,000 in November 1983, $28,000,000 in October 1984, $27,000,000 in June 1985 (as humanitarian aid, with a prohibition on the channelling of this aid via the CIA) and $100,000,000 in August 1986.

Early in 1985 reports emerged of human rights abuses by FDN members against Sandinista officials and foreign aid workers, and in 1986 it was reported that FDN members had embezzled US aid and been involved in the trafficking of Colombian cocaine.

Nicaraguan Democratic Movement (*Movimiento Democrático Nicaragüense*, MDN)

Leadership. Alfonso Robelo Callejas (l.); Fabio Gadea Mantilla

The MDN was formed as an anti-goverment political movement in April 1978 by a group of businessmen, and joined the first post-revolutionary government in July 1979. After one of its rallies was banned in November 1980 it withdrew from the Council of State (the current legislative body), and in November 1981 it refused to co-operate with other parties seeking a dialogue with the government. In June 1982 Robelo left the country when his property was confiscated for his subversive activities, and the MDN was a founder member of the Democratic Revolutionary Alliance (ARDE) in December 1982.

Nicaraguan Democratic Union/Nicaraguan Armed Revolutionary Forces (*Unión Democrática Nicaragüense/Fuerzas Armadas Revolucionarias Nicaragüenses*, UDN/FARN)

Leadership. Fernando Chamorro Rapaciolli (l.)

The UDN was formed by conservative businessmen; its leader had actively opposed the Somoza regime and had recognized the FSLN, at the time of the overthrow of that regime, as leader of the revolutionary process, but he had since come to criticize it for its undemocratic procedure. He claimed late in 1980 that the UDN/FARN was fighting not for a return to a right-wing dictatorship but for democracy and that it would therefore not accept into its ranks former National Guards who wished to revert to the old ways.

The group carried out a number of attacks in 1980, by the end of which it claimed to have 2,000 members. Late in March 1981 it claimed that a 600-man "freedom force" was waiting in Honduras and would soon be joined by "thousands of supporters" from Guatemala and Miami (Florida) to carry out an invasion which would cause a popular insurrection to "liberate" Nicaragua with the help of the governments of El Salvador, Guatemala and Honduras.

In November 1981 the UDN/FARN joined the Nicaraguan Democratic Force (FDN) and later left it to join the Democratic Revolutionary Alliance (ARDE) in September 1982.

Nicaraguan Democratic Union Assembly (*Asamblea Nicaragüense de Unidad Democrática*, Anude)

Leadership. José Dávila Membereno

This opposition group was formed in Costa Rica in September 1982. Its founders included José Dávila, a leader of the exiled section of the Social Christian Party, which joined the Democratic Revolutionary Alliance (ARDE) in September 1983. Dávila was quoted as saying that the Anude had offices in Costa Rica, Venezuela and Europe and maintained links with the military forces in Honduras; that one of its aims was to foster the creation of a united opposition front; and that in his view only violence would remove the Sandinistas. While the Anude was said to represent right-wing elements who had opposed the Somoza regime, it appeared at the same time to maintain links with Somozist groups.

Nicaraguan International Rescue from Communism (*Salvación Internacional de Nicaragua del Comunismo*, SINC)

Five members of this right-wing group hijacked a Costa Rican aircraft with 22 persons on board at San José airport on Oct. 29, 1981. The hijackers demanded the release of seven members of SINC who had been imprisoned in December 1980 after attacks on the left-wing Radio Noticias del Continente transmitter (the transmissions of which were suspended by the Costa Rican government on Feb. 20, 1981). The government eventually agreed to the release of the seven prisoners, one of whom was, however, reported to choose to remain in prison. The other six, and the five hijackers, were flown to El Salvador, where they were arrested. In November 1981 it was announced that they were all to be returned to Costa Rica, where the hijackers were to face trial.

Nicaraguan National Rescue and Conciliation (*Rescate y Conciliación Nacional de Nicaragua*)

Leadership. Alfredo César Aguirre

This group was formed in October 1983 as the Recovery of the Original Nicaraguan Revolution, and in August 1985 it joined the Southern Opposition Bloc (BOS).

Third Way Movement (*Movimiento Tercera Via*, M-3V)

Leadership. Abelardo Taboada, Luis Riva, Eduardo Sánchez, Sebastián González

This contra group was formed in San José (Costa Rica) in October 1983 to "provide an option which would fill the void between the northern forces and the southern". In late 1984 its fighting strength was estimated at 300.

Left-wing Party

Workers' Front (*Frente Obrero*, FO)

The armed members of the extreme left-wing FO—which was founded in 1974 and affiliated to the (pro-Chinese) Communist Party—had before 1979 formed the People's Anti-Somozist Militias (Milpas). The Sandinista government, however, claimed that the FO and Milpas were threatening production and provoking unrest in some areas by inciting workers to strike and take over land.

By October 1979 some 70 FO members were reported to be under arrest; on Jan. 25, 1980, the government closed down the daily *El Pueblo*, the mouthpiece of the FO; and on April 10, 1980, a member of the junta declared that neither the FO nor the Communist Party would be allowed to participate in the Council of State.

Autonomist Movements

Misura

This group was formed in July 1982 by a breakaway Misurasata faction (see separate entry) led by

Steadman Fagoth Müller, and was originally known as Guerrilla Miskito. In August 1984 it joined the Nicaraguan Unity for Reconciliation (UNIR) and in August 1985 it joined the Nicaraguan Opposition (UNO) and the Nicaraguan Indigenous Communities Union (KISAN). Immediately prior to the formation of the KISAN Fagoth Müller had been charged with kidnapping 12 members of the group and of betraying the group, and had been expelled.

Misurasata

This group was originally formed as the official channel of communication between the government and the English-speaking Black community and the Miskito, Sumo and Rama Indians in the east coast province of Zelaya (the Mosquito coast). Its opposition to the government developed when the leader Steadman Fagoth Müller was arrested (with about 70 others) in February 1981 and accused of having been a security agent for President Somoza, while two of the others were charged with fomenting a separatist plot. (There had been an autonomist tradition on the Mosquito coast since the 18th century when the British had established a protectorate known as the Miskito Kingdom, which also embraced part of present-day Honduras; however, the Miskito King was deposed in 1894, when most of the area was incorporated in Nicaragua.)

The arrest of the Misurasata leaders was followed by protest demonstrations which led to clashes in which four soldiers and four Miskito Indians were killed on Feb. 21, 1981; the government thereupon released all those arrested except the three charged as stated above but the unrest continued. S. Fagoth Müller, having been released provisionally, fled to Honduras on May 11, 1981, and on May 21 it was reported that many other Miskito Indians had left Nicaragua to join the 100,000 already living in the Honduran Mosquito region.

In July 1982 there was a split in Misurasata when a faction led by Steadman Fagoth Müller broke away to form Guerrilla Miskito (since renamed Misura—see separate entry), while the main organization headed by Brooklyn Rivera left the Nicaraguan Democratic Force (FDN) and joined the Democratic Revolutionary Alliance (ARDE). There was a further split in 1984 when, after two years of guerrilla campaign, Rivera entered into negotiations with the government, dividing the group between his supporters and a pro-ARDE (and anti-negotiation) faction led by Joaquín Suazo Jessy, Guillermo Espinoza and Rafael Zelaya. The negotiations were unsuccessful and Rivera was expelled from the group in mid-1985, when Misurasata joined the Nicaraguan Indigenous Communities Union (KISAN). Misurasata was by 1987 considered largely inactive.

Nicaraguan Indigenous Communities Union (KISAN)

Leadership. Diego Wykliffe

This guerrilla group was established at a meeting of Indians in southern Honduras on Aug. 31-Sept. 3, 1985, designed to unite Misurasata and Misura (see separate entries); the former leaders of these two organizations, Brooklyn Rivera and Steadman Fagoth Müller, were excluded from the meetings. The KISAN joined the Nicaraguan Opposition Union (UNO) in September 1985.

In March and April 1986 there was a large-scale migration of Miskitos from northern Nicaragua across the border into Honduras; the government initially gave the figure of 2,500 and claimed that all of these had been abducted by the KISAN, but the figure was later revised to 9,000. At the same time a split developed between those willing to negotiate with the government through Misatán (formed on the government's initiative in July 1984 to improve relations with the Indian community) and those committed to a military overthrow of the Sandinista government.

Niger

Capital: Niamey Pop. 6,110,000

The Republic of Niger is ruled by a Supreme Military Council which, on assuming power in April 1974, suspended the Constitution and dissolved the National Assembly and the *Parti progressiste nigérien*, until then the country's sole legal political organization. The President of the Supreme Military Council, Lt.-Col. Seyni Kountché, heads a (largely civilian) Council of Ministers, to which a Prime Minister was first appointed on Jan. 24, 1983.

An apparent attempt to overthrow President Kountché, made on Oct. 5-6, 1983, in his absence at a Franco-African summit meeting in France, was foiled by the armed forces led by the Deputy Army Chief of Staff. The instigators of the attempt escaped abroad. They were said to include several officers who had held high government offices. The President announced on May 16, 1984, that a commission of inquiry into the attempt had completed its work but he did not disclose its findings.

Popular Front for the Liberation of Niger (*Front populaire de libération du Niger*, FPLN)

Leadership. Abdoulaye Diori, Kamed Moussa

A. Diori was the son of ex-President Hamani Diori, who had been deposed in April 1974 and kept in detention until April 1980, whereafter he was held under house arrest until he was eventually released under an amnesty declared on April 14, 1984. K. Moussa, a former senior official at the Defence Ministry, had gone into exile in 1981.

According to official reports the Front was responsible for an armed attack by 14 Libyan-trained Tuareg tribesmen on an oasis town on May 29-30, 1985, with the object of seizing arms and ammunition for use in further planned raids; this attack was, however, repelled by government troops.

Sawaba Party

Leadership. Djibo Bakary (l.)

The Sawaba Party was set up as the Niger section of the (federalist) *Parti du regroupement africain* (PRA) founded in July 1958, when it represented the ruling parties in Dahomey (later called Benin), Niger and Senegal. Djibo Bakary, the leader of the Sawaba Party and then Prime Minister, advocated a vote for independence in the 1958 referendum (in which the Constitution of the Fifth French Republic was approved), but in general elections held on Dec. 14, 1958, the Sawaba Party was defeated by an alliance dominated by the *Rassemblement démocratique africain* (RDA). The results in the six seats which the Sawaba Party won (out of a total of 60) were later annulled, and in subsequent elections these seats went to the RDA alliance, whose leader, Hamani Diori, was elected Prime Minister in December 1958.

The Sawaba Party was officially dissolved in December 1959. Djibo Bakary lived in Guinea until 1974, when he was allowed (by the new military regime) to return to Niger on condition of not engaging in political activities. On Aug. 2, 1975, it was announced that he had been arrested, with two other men, for "attempting to divide the people and to set up an ideological clique with the object of seizing power". He was not released from detention until April 14, 1980, but was thereafter kept under house arrest. He was finally released under an amnesty declared on April 14, 1984.

Nigeria

Capital: Lagos (new capital, Abuja, under construction) Pop. 95,200,000

The Federal Republic of Nigeria, an independent state within the Commonwealth, consists of 19 federative states and a federal capital territory and is ruled by a 28-member Armed Forces Ruling Council formed on Aug. 28, 1985, and headed by Maj.-Gen. Ibrahim Babangida, President of the Republic and C.-in-C. of the Armed Forces. The country's National Council of Ministers consists of both officers and civilians. There is also a National Council of State. President Babangida announced on Jan. 13, 1986, that there would be a return to civilian rule on Oct. 1, 1990.

On Dec. 20, 1985, the Minister of Defence announced that a plot to overthrow the government had been discovered while it was in its planning stage, and that a number of officers from each of the armed forces had been arrested. (Their number was later given as "some 300".)

A special military tribunal, which sat from Jan. 23 to Feb. 25, 1986, found that the plot had been hatched as early as September 1985, and that Maj.-Gen. Mamman Vatsa (Minister for the Federal Capital territory and a member of the Armed Forces Ruling Council) and 12 other defendants were guilty of conspiring to overthrow the government. All 13 were sentenced to death; a further defendant was dismissed from the army, and two others were given life sentences. Ten of the death sentences were carried out on March 5, among them that on Maj.-Gen. Vatsa; three of the death sentences were commuted to life imprisonment, and the two life sentences to five and 10 years' imprisonment respectively.

Clashes between Christians and Moslems occurred widely in 1986 and the early months of 1987. About 20 people died, and many mosques and churches were desecrated, in religious riots centred on Kaduna state in March 1987, following which President Babangida announced a ban on religious preaching at institutions of higher learning and that anyone disturbing other people's freedom of religion "will be regarded as an enemy of the nation and will be dealt with as such." Religious tensions have been compounded by regional disparities, the Moslem population being concentrated in the relatively backward north of the country.

Yen Izala

This sect of dissident Moslem fundamentalists was led by Alhaji Mohammadu Marwa (alias Maitatsine), who originally came from Northern Cameroon and who preached a revolutionary version of Islam which rejected the prophet Mohammed as a Moslem leader; the sect opposed all official authority and demanded absolute loyalty to Mohammadu Marwa as its leader. Believed to have some 3,000 members, the sect was responsible for serious riots in Kano (northern Nigeria) between Dec. 18 and 31, 1980, which were forcibly suppressed by the Nigerian army. According to an official inquiry, a total of 4,177 persons lost their lives in the riots; these included the leader and numerous other members of the sect and also large numbers of civilians killed as "infidels" by members of the sect and of other civilians killed by police or army action. Further serious disturbances occurred in 1981-82, and the sect was banned on Nov. 18, 1982.

A commission of inquiry into the disturbances stated in a report released on Sept. 21, 1983, inter alia that over 500 people might have died in the riots, that over 1,000 people had lost property worth over 3,000,000 naira, and that people from Cameroon, Chad and Niger had taken part in the disturbances. The government accepted a recommendation of the commission for the reorganization of the system of Koranic education so as to fit it into the needs of Nigeria's development processes. Further unrest occurred in 1985.

Norway

Capital: Oslo Pop. 4,150,000

The Kingdom of Norway is a constitutional hereditary monarchy in which the monarch exercises authority through a Council of State (Cabinet) headed by a Prime Minister and responsible to Parliament (the *Storting*) of 157 members elected for a four-year term by universal adult suffrage. The *Storting* divides itself by election into an Upper House (*Lagting*) of 39 members and a Lower House (*Odelsting*) of the remaining 116 members, these two Houses having to consider separately any questions relating to legislation; in the event of disagreement a bill can be approved only by a two-thirds majority of the *Storting* as a whole.

As a result of elections held on Sept. 8-9, 1985, seats in the *Storting* were distributed as follows: Labour Party 71, Conservatives 50, Christian People's Party 16, Centre Party 12, Left Socialists six, Progressive Party two. Parties which gained no seats were the Liberal Party (with 3.1 per cent of the valid votes cast), the Red Electoral Alliance, the Liberal People's Party and the Communist Party.

Extreme right-wing groups, which were in 1980 reported to have links with similar groups in other countries, are the National Union (*Nasional Samling*, NS) and the Norwegian Front (*Norsk Front*, NF)

There have also existed in Norway neo-Nazi groups, including the National People's Party, the Norwegian-German Army, the Norwegian National Popular Party, and Vigilante.

Oman

Capital: Muscat Pop. 2,000,000

The Sultanate of Oman is ruled by decree, with the advice of an appointed Cabinet and a 55-member State Consultative Assembly consisting of members of the government and appointed citizens' representatives. There are no recognized political parties.

In the 1970s the main threat to Oman's internal security came from the Popular Front for the Liberation of Oman operating principally in Dhofar province on Oman's western border with South Yemen. There have been no reports of disturbances in recent years involving the PFLO, however.

Popular Front for the Liberation of Oman (PFLO)

The PFLO had its origins in a Popular Front for the Liberation of the Occupied Arabian Gulf formed with the object of overthrowing the Sultan of Oman and also other "conservative" regimes in the Gulf Area. At its second congress, held in Aden in 1968, this organization's leadership was taken over by Marxist-Leninists. In February 1972 it merged with a National Democratic Front for the Liberation of the Occupied Arabian Gulf to form the Popular Front for the Liberation of Oman and the Arabian Gulf (PFLOAG). In its activities it had the support of the People's Democratic Republic of Yemen (South Yemen), from whose territory it conducted most of its operations, and also of China (until 1973) and later of the Soviet Union.

After a meeting between PFLOAG spokesmen and delegates of the Communist parties of Iraq and the Soviet Union in Aden in March 1974, the organization changed its name to "Popular Front for the Liberation of Oman", thus indicating that it was to be a national liberation movement fighting against British and Iranian "occupation armies" in Oman, and not a revolutionary organization trying to overthrow governments in the Gulf area. Efforts to achieve a ceasefire between Oman and the PFLO made by an Arab League conciliation commission, set up in March 1974, remained ineffective.

An agreement on the normalization of relations between Oman and South Yemen came into effect on Nov. 15, 1982, and appeared to bring a formal end to 15 years of hostility between the two states. In a gesture towards former rebels who had taken refuge in South Yemen, the Omani government on Jan. 3, 1983, proclaimed a further amnesty for "all Omani citizens who are still in South Yemen", offering them a four-month "period of grace" to return to Oman, where "all measures" would be taken to receive and settle them.

On March 18, 1984, a delegation for the PFLO visited Syria for talks with the ruling *Baath* party and expressed support for Syrian policies: according to the official Syrian News Agency, the talks focused on "imperialist-Zionist-reactionary conspiracies to which the Arab nation is being exposed".

Pakistan

Capital: Islamabad Pop. 96,180,000

The Islamic Republic of Pakistan is ruled by an executive President (Gen. Zia ul-Haq, who took power in a military coup in 1977). It has a bicameral legislature consisting of (i) a National Assembly to which 217 members were directly elected on a non-party basis by universal adult suffrage on Feb. 25, 1985, and to which 20 women members were subsequently nominated by the provincial assemblies, and (ii) a Senate of 87 members chosen by the National and the provincial assemblies.

The legislature was to operate within the provisions of a series of constitutional amendments passed on March 2, 1985, which restored substantial sections of the 1973 Constitution, but which redefined the powers of the President and the Prime Minister in favour of the President and named Gen. Zia as national President for a five-year term. A bill adopting these amendments was passed by the National Assembly after prolonged debate on Oct. 16, 1985, once agreement had been reached on an indemnity clause covering the activities of the armed forces during the period of military rule. Martial law was finally lifted with effect from Jan. 1, 1986, although the President retained the right to reimpose it whenever he considered it necessary, and the government maintained a modified form of press censorship.

The National Assembly passed the Political Parties Bill on Dec. 9, 1985, allowing political parties, which had been officially dissolved in 1979, to operate legally after registration with the Electoral Commission. Under this new law a party could be banned, or its registration subsequently revoked, if it spoke or acted against "the ideology, integrity and sovereignty of Pakistan", against morality or the maintenance of public order, or against the integrity and independence of the armed forces, or if it failed to expel any member who "defames or brings into ridicule the judiciary or the armed forces". The first party to apply for registration was the pro-Zia faction of the Moslem League, which was led by Mohammed Junejo, the Prime Minister, and held 170 of the 217 directly elected seats in the National Assembly. The issue of registration caused division within the opposition Movement for the Restoration of Democracy (MRD), with some parties arguing that registration would be tantamount to recognizing the legality of military rule.

Gen. Zia had himself opposed the legalization of political parties as being contrary to his islamicization policy, which had been introduced in 1980 and endorsed in a national referendum held on Dec. 19, 1984. The referendum, which recorded a turnout of about 62 per cent and a "yes" vote of 97.71 per cent, also gave Gen. Zia a personal five-year mandate. The islamicization policy had alienated non-Sunni Moslem groups but was welcomed—to varying degrees—by the more right-wing parties. Under the policy 10 of the elected seats in the Assembly were reserved for non-Moslems, and a further 20 indirectly elected seats were allotted to women.

In the month before the lifting of martial law there was increased activity on the part of the military courts established by Gen. Zia, and over 200 prison sentences in excess of three years were imposed on detainees. The courts had operated in secret on the basis that defendants should prove their innocence, and martial law regulations of Sept. 27, 1982, made retroactive to 1977, introduced the death penalty for armed robbery, sabotage and subversion. At the end of December 1985 Gen. Zia announced that all sentences passed by military courts should stand, but in the next six months the cases of all political detainees held without trial or conviction or beyond the term of their original sentence were reviewed and those concerned were released unless the provincial authorities could justify their continued detention.

Party Alliance

Movement for the Restoration of Democracy (MRD)

This Movement was formed on Feb. 5, 1981, as an alliance originally of seven political parties—the Pakistan People's Party (PPP), the Solidarity Party (*Tehrik-i-Istiqlal*), the National Democratic Party, the Pakistan Republican Party, the *Jamiat-i-Ulema-i-Pakistan*, a faction of the Moslem League led by Khwaja Khairuddin, and the Kashmir Moslem Conference—whose leaders signed a declaration calling for the immediate lifting of martial law, President Zia's resignation, fair and free elections to the National and Provincial Assemblies within three months and restoration of the 1973 Constitution. On Feb. 6, 1981, the declaration was also signed by leaders of the National Liberation Front and the Labourers' and Farmers' Party.

Following student unrest and the arrest during February 1981 of numerous opposition leaders the action committee of the Movement for the Restoration of Democracy met in Lahore on Feb. 23-24 and issued a call for a civil disobedience movement to remove the government, beginning with a day of protest on March 2 and culminating in a general strike on March 23. The *Jamiat-i-Ulema-i-Pakistan*, however, was not represented at the Lahore meeting and subsequently withdrew from the alliance. Seven of those who took part in the meeting were afterwards arrested, among them Begum Bhutto (the widow of Zulfiqar Ali Bhutto, the former Prime Minister hanged in 1979 for "conspiracy to murder"). The planned day of protest, however, received only limited support, partly as a result of the arrests of political leaders in the wake of the hijacking of a Pakistani aircraft by members of the militant movement *Al Zulfiqar* (see separate entry).

The MRD launched a civil disobedience campaign on Aug. 14, 1983, in protest against the continuation of martial law. The campaign was intended to be nationwide, but it gained substantial support only in Sind province, and President Zia rejected the MRD demand for collective discussions between the government and the political parties (then officially disbanded) and ordered troops into Sind. In the resultant violence over 5,000 opposition leaders (mostly from the PPP) were arrested, and the death toll by the end of September was said by the authorities to be about 60 and by the MRD to be over 150. Nearly all those detained were released by the end of January 1984.

The MRD called for a boycott of the December 1984 referendum and also of the February 1985 elections, and up to 2,000 leading members were detained for several weeks. On Aug. 3, 1986, the MRD challenged the government to hold elections by the end of the year, and on Sept. 14 it defied a government prohibition on political rallies, sparking off another wave of unrest in which some 2,000 were detained and up to 40 died. As in 1983 the main action occurred in Sind, causing resentment among Sindhi members of the alliance over the lack of support from other provinces. The MRD attempted to stage another civil disobedience campaign later in September, but there was only a limited response and the government refused the Movement's demand for talks.

The MRD had been joined in 1983 by the Pakistan National Party (PNP) and the National Liberation Front (NLF), and in January 1984 by People's Solidarity (*Awami Tehrik*), but the lifting of martial law and the relative failure of the August 1986 protest fostered provincial separatism and caused a rift in the Movement in 1986. In February of that year the leaders met but failed to agree on a unified political platform, and many of them objected to the high profile assumed by Benazir Bhutto of the PPP, including Khwaja Khairuddin, who resigned as secretary-general in July. Also in July a new coalition was formed by left-wing members of the MRD called the Awami National Party (ANP), which refused to join the August protest, as did *Tehrik-i-Istiqlal,* which broke away from the MRD on Oct. 12, 1986.

Left-wing Movements

Al Zulfiqar

Leadership. Murtaza Bhutto (l.)

This movement, named "Sword" (*Zulfiqar*, the first name of Z. A. Bhutto, the former Prime Minister who was hanged in April 1979), was established in February 1981 by the late Z. A. Bhutto's elder son, Murtaza Bhutto. The latter had in 1978 sought support for his father, then under arrest and being tried for "conspiracy to murder". After his father's execution, M. Bhutto finally settled in Kabul (Afghanistan), where he established the headquarters of a Pakistan Liberation Army (PLA), an organization dedicated to the overthrow of President Zia. The PLA was divided into a political wing led by Raja Anwar, a former adviser on student affairs to the Pakistan People's Party (PPP), and a military wing composed largely of students and trained by dissident Pakistan army officers, which began operations in December 1979 and which during 1980 claimed responsibility for numerous acts of terrorism and sabotage.

In December 1980 12 members of the military wing arrested inside Pakistan were tried by a military court in Peshawar for subversion, sabotage and attempting to wage war against Pakistan, with 12 others, among them Murtaza Bhutto, being tried in absentia. In February 1981 Raja Anwar was found to be a government agent and was sentenced to death at a secret trial in Afghanistan. M. Bhutto agreed, at the request of his mother (Begum Nusrat Bhutto), to dissolve the PLA but after visiting Libya for talks with Col. Gadaffi, the Libyan leader, he reorganized the PLA as *Al Zulfiqar*.

Al Zulfiqar claimed responsibility for the murder in Lahore on Sept. 25, 1981, of Chaudhri Zahur Elahi, a leader of the Moslem League and a former member of President Zia's Cabinet, and for the injuring in the same attack of Mushtaq Hussain, the presiding judge at Z. A. Bhutto's trial in 1977-78. The Interior Minister said on Jan. 14, 1982, that 481 suspects were in custody out of 1,000 originally sent for guerrilla training in Afghanistan. An alleged member of *Al Zulfiqar* was in May 1983 hanged for the murder of C. Z. Elahi, and in August 1984 a total of 98 alleged members were tried by a military court on a number of charges including hijacking and assassination. Of these 98, two had already been hanged for the murder of a policeman in 1982 and 42 were tried in absentia, including the brothers Murtaza and Shahnawaz Bhutto. (The latter died under mysterious circumstances in France in July 1985.)

Awami National Party (ANP)

Leadership. Khan Abdul Wali Khan (pres.)

The ANP was formed on July 29, 1986, by four regional left-wing parties within the Movement for the Restoration of Democracy (MRD): the National Democratic Party (DNP), the Labourers' and Farmers' Party, People's Solidarity (*Awami Tehrik*) and the Pakistan National Party (PNP). (See separate entries.) The ANP stated on Aug. 18, 1986, that it was not ready to join the MRD's civil protest.

The ANP supported the Soviet-backed government in Afghanistan, called for the removal of "all vestiges of imperialist domination" in Pakistan and opposed all US influence. The party recognized five nationalities within the country: Punjabi, Pathan, Baluchi, Sindhi and Saraiki, and the leader of *Awami Tehrik*, Rasool Baksh Paleejo, said that "the class struggle will take a back seat in favour of working for the rights of small nationalities".

The party's senior vice-president, Fazil Rahu, who had been detained without trial from August 1983 until June 1986, was killed on Jan. 17, 1987; police claimed that the murder was part of a long-standing family feud, but the ANP maintained that the national intelligence service had been responsible.

Communist Party of Pakistan (CPP)

Leadership. Ali Nazish (gen. sec.)

Originally a section of the Communist Party of India, the CPP became an independent organization in 1948. Ten officers and three civilians, including Sajjad Zaheer, then the party's general secretary, and another member of its executive, were sentenced to prison terms in 1953 on charges of conspiring to seize power and set up a communist government under military domination. After four Communists had been elected to the parliament of East Pakistan, the CPP was banned in 1954, and it has remained illegal since then. In the late 1970s the CPP moved from a pro-Chinese to a pro-Soviet attitude.

In a press statement issued in Karachi on March 1, 1982, the party's central committee denounced the "Zia ul-Haq military dictatorship"; appealed to "the progressive and democratic forces of the world to raise their voice in militant solidarity with the just struggle of the people of Pakistan" to save "the lives of the political workers in torture chambers" and to secure the "release of thousands of detainees"; and declared that it was "only through the united struggle of the patriotic and democratic forces" that the country could get rid of the military junta and "have a democratic government".

On Dec. 10, 1986, it was reported that Jam Saqi, a former leader of the CPP who had been tried on charges of sedition in December 1981, had been released from prison in Karachi.

Jamiat-i-Ulema-i-Pakistan (JUP)

Leadership. Maulana Shah Ahmad Noorani (pres.); Maulana Abdus Sattar Niazi (sec.-gen.)

Established in 1968 by left-wing mullahs, this progressive fundamentalist party gained seven seats in the 1970 National Assembly elections (in the North-West Frontier Province and Baluchistan). In 1977 it became one of the original members of the Pakistan National Alliance (see separate entry) opposed to the then ruling Pakistan People's Party led by Z. A. Bhutto, but broke away from it in July 1978. It was one of the three major parties which registered with the Election Commission by Sept. 20, 1979, as required under an amended Political Parties Act announced by President Zia on Aug. 30, 1979. Originally a member of the Movement for the Restoration of Democracy (see separate entry) founded in February 1981, it withdrew from this Movement in the following months.

Maulana Noorani and other JUP leaders met Gen. Zia for talks in October 1983 and reiterated JUP demands for the release of all political prisoners, the restoration of the 1973 Constitution and press freedom, and the party boycotted the December 1984 referendum and the February 1985 elections.

Labourers' and Farmers' Party (*Mazdoor Kissan*)

Leadership. Fatheyab Ali Khan

This Punjab-based party, which drew its support from rural areas, was a signatory of the declaration issued on Feb. 6, 1981, at the establishment of the Movement for the Restoration of Democracy (see separate entry), in whose subsequent campaign for a return to parliamentary government it played a full part.

National Democratic Party (NDP)

Leadership. Khan Abdul Wali Khan (pres.); Begum Nasim Wali Khan (vice-pres.)

The NDP was formed in 1976 as a successor to the banned National Awami Party (NAP), which represented peasant and worker interests and had taken a pro-Chinese line. The banning of the NAP was due to its alleged involvement in terrorist activities in favour of the secession of Baluchistan and the North-West Frontier Province. Having been a member of the Pakistan National Alliance formed in January 1977, in February 1981 the NDP joined with other parties to form the Movement for the Restoration of Democracy (see separate entry) and has been active since in campaigning for early elections. In April 1984 the founder of the NDP, Khan Abdul Ghaffar Khan (father of Khan Abdul Wali Khan, then aged 92), returned to Afghanistan after two years in Pakistan, saying that he had lost hope that he would ever be able to lead the Pathans to regain their honour and dignity.

National Liberation Front (NLF)

Leadership. Miraj Mohammed Khan (pres.)

The NLF joined the Movement for the Restoration of Democracy (see separate entry) in 1983. Its president was detained during the August 1983 disturbances, and allegedly tortured. He was released on June 16, 1985.

Pakistan National Party (PNP)

Leadership. Mir Ghaus Ali Bakhsh Bizenjo (ch.); Syed Qaswar Gardezi (sec.-gen.)

This Baluchistan-based party broke away from the National Democratic Party (see separate entry) on June 1, 1979. Its chairman had been a leading member of the National Awami Party and had been Governor of Baluchistan under Z. A. Bhutto's regime in 1972-73. The PNP refused to register with the Election Commission by Sept. 30, 1979, as required by an amended Political Parties Act announced by President Zia on Aug. 30, 1979.

The PNP stands for increased decentralization, with complete autonomy for Pakistan's four provinces and the federal government retaining responsibility only for defence, foreign affairs and communications.

The PNP joined the civil disobedience campaign staged by the Movement for the Restoration of Democracy (MRD—see separate entry) in August 1983, and was subsequently seen as a member of the MRD. In July 1986 it was a founder member of the Awami National Party (ANP—see separate entry).

Pakistan People's Party (PPP)

Leadership. Begum Nusrat Bhutto, Benazir Bhutto (co-ch.)

At its foundation on Dec. 1, 1967, the PPP described its policy as one of Islamic socialism, democracy and independence in foreign affairs. It was established by Zulfiqar Ali Bhutto, who had been Minister of Foreign Affairs in 1963-66 and had earlier held other ministerial appointments since 1958. Although he served under President Ayub Khan, he disagreed with the President over the terms of the 1966 Tashkent Declaration which ended the 1965-68 war between India and Pakistan and which Z. A. Bhutto regarded as a surrender to India. After leaving the government in June 1966 he denounced the President's rule as "a dictatorship under the label of democracy" and, having failed to persuade the existing opposition parties to accept his programme, decided to form his own party. As a result of his propaganda campaign, which was accompanied by student unrest, he was arrested on Nov. 13, 1968, under emergency regulations, together with other persons, including seven members of the PPP and five of the left-wing National Awami Party.

Bhutto was released on Feb. 14, 1969 (with over 200 other political detainees), and the state of emergency was ended as from Feb. 17. He did not, however, take part in talks between a Democratic Action Committee (formed by eight other opposition parties) and the government of President Ayub Khan. The East Pakistan section of the PPP was dissolved on March 3, 1969, because Z. A. Bhutto had failed to support East Pakistan's demand for full autonomy, but on March 10 he entered into a political alliance with the pro-Chinese wing of the National Awami Party led by Maulana Abdul Hamid Khan Bhashani, who had wide support in East Pakistan.

Following the breakdown of law and order throughout Pakistan, the resignation of President Ayub Khan on March 25, 1969, and the proclamation of martial law by Gen. Yahya Khan on the same day, the Constitution was abrogated, the National and Provincial Assemblies were dissolved, the activities of political parties were restricted by a ban on public meetings, and Gen. Yahya Khan assumed the office of President on March 31, 1969. Full-scale political activity was resumed on Jan. 1, 1970, but under a regulation which laid down inter alia that "no political party shall propagate opinions or act in a manner prejudicial to the ideology, integrity or security of Pakistan"; persons carrying arms would not be permitted to participate in political processions or public meetings; and no person should obstruct or disturb any meeting or procession of a political nature. In the first general elections held in Pakistan on the basis of "one man, one vote" on Dec. 7, 1970, the PPP gained 81 out of the 291 contested seats of the National Assembly (all but one of them in Punjab and Sind provinces) and became the strongest party in West Pakistan.

Following the secession of East Pakistan (as Bangladesh) in December 1971, Z. A. Bhutto succeeded Gen. Yahya Khan as President of (West) Pakistan and, in a Cabinet of civilians formed on Dec. 24, took responsibility for Foreign Affairs, Defence, the Interior and Interprovincial Co-ordination, with most other portfolios being held by PPP members. While martial law was maintained, the PPP government introduced numerous reforms in the social, educational and economic fields and also a new interim Constitution (approved by the National Assembly on April 17, 1972), under which Z. A. Bhutto was sworn in as President on April 21—martial law having ended on the previous day when declared illegal by the Supreme Court. In October 1972 the PPP reached agreement with the other political parties on a new Constitution providing for a federal and parliamentary form of government, and such a Constitution was adopted by the National Assembly on April 10, 1973 (with all-party support). Under this Constitution Z. A. Bhutto relinquished the office of President on Aug. 13, having been elected Prime Minister by the National Assembly on the previous day. In the

Senate, newly elected in July, the PPP held 35 of its 45 seats.

During 1975, however, the PPP was weakened by the defection of a number of its leading members; among them, Ghulam Mustafa Khar, former Governor and Chief Minister of the Punjab, resigned from the PPP on Sept. 24, accusing Z. A. Bhutto of imposing a dictatorship on the country. Altogether two members of the National Assembly and 15 of the Punjab Assembly resigned from the PPP in September 1975. Others who resigned from the PPP were Mohammad Haneef Ramay (former Chief Minister of Punjab) on Oct. 15, and Rasul Bakhsh Talpur (former Governor of Sind) on Oct. 17; like G. M. Khar they had been founder members of the PPP. Nevertheless, in the general elections held on March 7, 1977, the PPP gained 155 of the 200 general seats in the National Assembly. G. M. Khar later rejoined the PPP and was, in June 1977, appointed political adviser to Z. A. Bhutto, then Prime Minister.

The rule of Z. A. Bhutto came to an end in July 1977 when, after his conflict with the Pakistan National Alliance (PNA), his government was overthrown by a bloodless coup by the army under the leadership of its Chief of Staff, Gen. Mohammed Zia ul-Haq. Under the military regime a number of Z. A. Bhutto's political opponents were released from prison, among them J. A. Rahim (released on July 23).

The PPP's central committee then decided on Aug. 3, 1977, to participate in the general elections which were planned for Oct. 18, 1977 (but in fact never took place). Also during August 1977, several leading PPP members withdrew their support from Z. A. Bhutto, among them Mir Taj Mohammad Khan Jamali (former Minister of Health), who announced on Aug. 13 that he was forming an independent group which would contest the elections in Baluchistan in co-operation with the PNA, and also Rana Mohammad Hanif Khan (former Minister of Local Government) and Syed Nasir Ali Rizvi (deputy general secretary of the PPP), who resigned from the PPP on Aug. 17.

On Sept. 3, 1977, Z. A. Bhutto was arrested on a charge of conspiracy to murder: he was found guilty and sentenced to death, with four other men, on March 18, 1978. Gen. Zia stated on Sept. 6 that Z. A. Bhutto was "an evil genius" who had been "running this country on more or less Gestapo lines, misusing funds, blackmailing people, detaining them illegally and even perhaps ordering people to be killed". On Sept. 17 ten other leading members of the PPP were arrested, among them four members of Z. A. Bhutto's last Cabinet. The arrest of Z. A. Bhutto was followed by demonstrations in his favour, in particular in Punjab and Sind. On Oct. 1, Gen. Zia postponed the proposed elections indefinitely mainly on the grounds that the election campaign had resulted in "a state of confrontation . . . between the political parties". Foreign observers, however, took the view that the real reason for the postponement was Gen. Zia's fear that the PPP would win the elections.

Despite mass arrests of PPP supporters, including the intermittent detention, or house arrest, of Z. A. Bhutto's wife and daughter, pro-PPP demonstrations continued during the next few months, and the death sentence imposed on Z. A. Bhutto was followed by numerous protest demonstrations. The military authorities arrested a number of PPP supporters, among them three former ministers and four former members of the National Assembly who were on April 6, 1978, officially stated to have plotted to blow up the Lahore High Court (where Z. A. Bhutto had been tried) and other public buildings.

Despite widespread international criticism, especially by other Islamic governments, of the death sentence imposed on Z. A. Bhutto, an appeal by him against his conviction and sentence was dismissed by the Supreme Court on Feb. 6, 1979 (with four of the seven judges rejecting his appeal and three upholding it). On March 24 the court implicitly recommended that the death sentence should not be carried out; nevertheless, and despite numerous international appeals for clemency, President Zia refused to commute the sentence and Z. A. Bhutto was hanged on April 4, 1979.

Following Z. A. Bhutto's execution, the government temporarily adopted a conciliatory attitude to the PPP, releasing some of its leaders from detention and lifting the censorship on its newspaper, *Musawat*. However, Miss Benazir Bhutto (Z. A. Bhutto's daughter) and Lt.-Gen. Tikka Khan immediately launched an anti-government campaign, and pictures and tape recordings of speeches of Z. A. Bhutto were sold freely. Leadership of the PPP thereafter passed to Z. A. Bhutto's widow, Begum Nusrat Bhutto.

On July 25, 1979, the four men condemned to death with Z. A. Bhutto were also hanged. (Miss Bhutto alleged—as revealed on July 12—that her father had not been hanged but had died by accident in a struggle with officers who had offered that his life would be spared if he signed two documents admitting that he was responsible for the loss of East Pakistan in 1971 and that he had invited Gen. Zia to take power in 1977—documents which he had refused to sign. These allegations were dismissed by a government spokesman on Aug. 20.)

In elections to municipal and district councils held in Punjab, Sind, the North-West Frontier Province (NWFP) and Baluchistan between Sept. 20 and 27, 1979, candidates were forbidden to identify themselves with political parties, but those supported by the PPP were reported to have won between 60 and 80 per cent of the seats in Punjab and the NWFP, and to have been returned unopposed to many seats in Sind. In Rawalpindi, 31 of the 50 seats were won by PPP-supported candidates, most of whom had been imprisoned or flogged under President Zia's regime.

The PPP was one of Pakistan's four major parties (the others being the Pakistan National Alliance, the National Democratic Party and the Pakistan National Party) which refused to register by Sept. 30, 1979, under an amended Political Parties Act announced by President Zia on Aug. 30, 1979. On Oct. 16, 1979, the President finally announced that the proposed general elections had been postponed indefinitely, and all political parties were dissolved. The announcement was followed by the arrest of numerous political leaders (officially stated on Oct. 21 to number 372) and the banning of the PPP newspapers *Musawat* and *Sadaqat*.

A petition by members of the PPP seeking a declaration that elections to the National and Provincial Assemblies would be held under laws in force before 1977, power would be transferred to elected representatives of the people, and fundamental rights would be restored and military courts abolished was dismissed by the Supreme Court on April, 27, 1981. Meanwhile, Begum Bhutto and her daughter were detained in mid-March 1981, the former being released from prison and placed under house arrest in Larkana in July, as was the latter in December 1981. Gen. Tikka Khan, the PPP secretary-general who had been arrested in February 1981, was among eight politicians released to mark Independence Day on Aug. 14, 1981. Later that year the government initiated legal proceedings against the Bhutto family for the recovery of approximately 5,000,000 rupees which had allegedly been misappropriated by Z. A. Bhutto for personal and PPP use during his period of office.

In November 1982 Begum Bhutto left Pakistan for Europe to seek medical treatment, and Miss Bhutto was released from house arrest in January 1984 to go to London. She returned to Pakistan on July 18, 1985, to bury her brother Shahnawaz (an alleged member of the *Al Zulfiqar* militant movement established in February 1981 by another brother, Murtaz) and was placed under house arrest on Aug. 29 for defying a govenment order restricting her movements. She was released and returned to England on Nov. 4, but went back to Pakistan on April 10, 1986, and the following month was elected co-chairman of the party along with her mother. Within the party she replaced some long-standing officials by much younger members, and in particular she removed Ghulam Mustafa Jatoi as president of the Sind branch of the PPP (who then left the party in August to form the National People's Party).

The PPP information secretary, Sheikh Rafiq Ahmed, stated in 1986 that the party would not seek registration under the new political parties law as that would legitimize military rule, and that the party would prefer to "strengthen the MRD and put the present civil regime to the test, to see whether it accepts the democratic norm, the right to organize a political party and the rights of assembly, expression and free speech".

(*Al Zulfiqar* operated independently of the PPP, which disclaimed any connexion with guerrilla activities.)

People's Solidarity (*Awami Tehrik*)

Leadership. Rasool Baksh Paleejo (pres.); Imtiaz Alam (gen. sec.)

Awami Tehrik is a Maoist Sind-based party advocating radical social change and opposed to the landowning interests of the Pakistan People's Party (PPP). Rasool Baksh Paleejo had been arrested in 1979 and sentenced to 12 months' imprisonment for making a speech against the military government, but was not released until June 1986. *Awami Tehrik* joined the Movement for the Restoration of Democracy on Jan. 26, 1984, and was a founder member of the Awami National Party (ANP) in July 1986 (see separate entries).

Right-wing Movements

Jamaat-i-Islami

Leadership. Mian Tufail Mohammad (pres.); Qazi Hussain Ahmad (sec.-gen.)

Dating from 1941, this extreme right-wing and ultra-orthodox Islamic party advocates the establishment of an Islamic state in Pakistan. Following the military takeover of July 1977 it supported the police under President Zia's regime in their repression of anti-Bhutto demonstrators. Expelled from the Pakistan National Alliance (PNA) in 1979 (when it accepted representation in President Zia's government), the *Jamaat-i-Islami* was one of three major parties which registered with the Election Commission by Sept. 30, 1979, as required under an amended Political Parties Act announced a month earlier.

Following President Zia's decision of Oct. 16, 1979, to postpone elections and to ban party political activity, *Jamaat-i-Islami* pressed for early elections and the ending of martial law while continuing to give broad support to the regime's objectives. In April 1982 a party spokesman said that co-operation with the Zia regime hitherto had been based on the expectation that democracy would eventually be restored. (For the activities of the party's militant student organization, see separate entry for *Jamiat-i-Talaba*.)

On Feb. 21, 1986, party leaders called for an Islamic revolution and the creation of an Islamic state.

Jamiat-i-Talaba (JIT)

Leadership. Shabbir Ahmed

The JIT is the youth wing of the *Jamaat-i-Islami*. It is a rigidly orthodox right-wing Islamic fundamentalist organization strongly opposed to the emancipation of women and to liberal and Western influences in education. It stands for Islamic emphasis in the teaching of economics, history and other subjects. The organization is based on elitist principles, full members being known as "the pure ones".

Gen. Zia's announcement on Feb. 5, 1984, of a ban on all student organizations in Islamabad and all provinces except Baluchistan sparked off two months of student protest, and three JIT leaders were sentenced to 15 lashes and one year's imprisonment after disrupting a meeting addressed by the President on March 12 in Peshawar.

Jamiat-i-Ulema-i-Islam

Leadership. Maulana Fazlur Rahman (pres.); Maulana Mufti Mahmud (l.)

This fundamentalist party advocates a Constitution in accordance with Islamic teachings. Formerly allied with the National Awami Party (which was banned in 1975), the *Jamiat-i-Ulema-i-Islam* was a founder member in January 1977 of the Pakistan National Alliance formed to contest the March 1977 general elections against the then ruling Pakistan People's Party led by Z. A. Bhutto, its leader becoming president of the Alliance. Following the military takeover of July 1977, the party accepted representation in President Zia's government in 1979 but continued to press for an early end to martial law and the holding of democratic elections.

In response to a ruling by a court in India to allow the opening of a Hindu temple on the site of a Moslem mosque in Uttar Pradesh, the party staged a protest in the town of Jacobabad on March 2, 1986, in the course of which nine Hindu temples were sacked.

Solidarity Party (*Tehrik-i-Istiqlal*)

Leadership. Air Marshal Asghar Khan (pres.); Ashaf Vardag (acting pres.); Musheer Ahmad Pesh Imam (sec.-gen.)

Founded in 1968, on a platform of maintaining both Islamic and democratic values, the *Tehrik-i-Istiqlal* was one of the three major parties which registered with the Election Commission by Sept. 30, 1979, as required under the amended Political Parties Act announced by President Zia on Aug. 30, 1979. Previously it had been a constituent party of the Pakistan National Alliance formed in January 1977 but had withdrawn in November of that year.

Although the *Tehrik-i-Istiqlal* was banned, like all other parties, in October 1979, its central working committee met in Lahore on April 5-6, 1980, and demanded the immediate ending of martial law, elections to the National and Provincial Assemblies and the release of political prisoners. Air Marshal Asghar Khan was released from house arrest on April 18, 1980, but was again placed under house arrest on May 29 after making speeches denouncing the martial law regime. (He was finally released from house arrest in early October 1984.) On Aug. 8, 1980, Ashaf Vardag called for a *jihad* (holy war) against the government and said that the only way to end the martial law regime was by co-operation between all parties opposed to it, including the Pakistan People's Party.

At a meeting in Lahore on April 5-6, 1980, the central committee of the *Tehrik-i-Istiqlal* demanded the immediate ending of martial law, elections to the National and Provincial Assemblies and the release of political prisoners.

In February 1981 the *Tehrik-i-Istiqlal* joined with eight other parties in the Movement for the Restoration of Democracy (MRD—see separate entry) to campaign for an end to martial law and a return to parliamentary democracy. Following President Zia's creation at the end of 1981 of an appointed Federal Advisory Council to act as a bridge between the martial law administration and a future Islamic democratic government, Mian Manzoor Ahmed Watoo (a leading member of the party) said that the formation of the Council was "a bogus stunt devoid of all meaning and content" and that only an elected assembly could have a mandate for constitutional change.

Unlike other members of the MRD the party favoured registration under the new political parties law of December 1985; it refused to join the August 1986 protest and formally seceded from the MRD on Oct. 12, 1986.

Other Parties

Moslem League

Leadership. Khwaja Khairuddin (sec.-gen.)

This party, earlier referred to as the "Conventionist" Moslem League, was one of three groups into which the original Moslem League (which claimed independence for Pakistan in 1947) was divided in 1962. It continued to hold a dominant position under the regime of President Ayub Khan, who joined it in May 1963 and became its leader. However, in the 1970 elections, the League gained only two seats (in Punjab) out of the 291 contested seats of the National Assembly. Following the July 1977 military takeover, the Moslem League took a restrained line in calling for a return to parliamentary government and in July 1978 accepted representation in President Zia's government.

The pro-Zia faction of the League, led by Mohammed Khan Junejo, Prime Minister since March 1985, was legally registered as a political party on Feb. 9, 1986. The dissident faction had broken with the main group in 1979, and in 1981 had joined the Movement for the Restoration of Democracy (MRD—see separate entry). Its leader, Khwaja Khairuddin, publicly criticized the government of Z. A. Bhutto and had thereupon been expelled from Pakistan, being regarded as a citizen of Bangladesh, where he had his origin, although he had opposed the creation of Bangladesh.

National People's Party (NPP)

Leadership. Ghulam Mustafa Jatoi (ch.)

The NPP was founded on Aug. 30, 1986, by Ghulam Mustafa Jatoi, who had left the Pakistan People's Party (PPP) after disagreement with its leader, Benazir Bhutto. The NPP aimed to be a centrist party, willing to negotiate with the government. Shortly before the formation of the NPP G. M. Jatoi had travelled to London to meet another former PPP member, Ghulam Mustafa Khar, who returned to Pakistan on Aug. 30.

Separatist Movements

SIND

The civil unrest of August 1983 and August 1986 was strongest in Sind province, and the relative failure of these two protests aroused resentment among Sindhi opposition politicians against their colleagues in the Punjab in particular. New nationalist groups emerged in the province, including *Awami Tehrik* (People's Solidarity—see separate entry), the Sind-Baluchistan Patriotic Front, *Jai Sind* and the left-wing *Sind Hari* peasant committees. Moreover, in 1985 and 1986 severe violence broke out between ethnic groups, principally in Karachi, when it involved conflict between the Pathan community and the Mohajirs (Urdu-speaking and of Indian origin—the word Mohajir meaning refugee and referring to those Indians who fled to Pakistan at the time of partition in

1947). The problem was particularly acute in Karachi because within its population of about 7,000,000 in 1986 the Sindhis (comprising some 15 per cent) and the Mohajirs (45 per cent) felt under increasing threat from the Pathans (about 20 per cent), whose influx had increased since the Soviet intervention in Afghanistan in 1979, and the Punjabis (15 per cent), whose influence had grown under the Zia regime. Members of the Pathan community were also extensively involved in the trafficking of illegal arms and drugs.

Mohajir Quomi (People's) Movement (MQM)

Leadership. Altaf Hussain

The MQM was formed to represent the interests of Mohajirs on the premise that along with the Sindhis they had been exploited by the Pathans and Punjabis and subject to discrimination in employment and education. In January 1987 the MQM called a strike in protest against the murder of a Mohajir man and his two daughters, provoking clashes with the police in Karachi and Hyderabad.

Sind-Baluchistan Patriotic Front (SBPF)

Leadership. Mumtaz Ali Bhutto

The SBPF was founded in 1986 by Mumtaz Ali Bhutto, a former member of the Pakistan People's Party, who declared: "The young Sindhis want independence. They want nothing more to do with the Punjab." In December 1986 the Front was criticized by the Prime Minister, Mohammed Junejo, for openly propagating "parochial ideologies".

"PATHANISTAN"

A claim to separate nationhood for the Pathans was first made in 1946 by political leaders of the then Indian North-West Frontier Province (NWFP) who strongly objected to a British proposal to group the NWFP with the Punjab. Among these leaders, Nawebzade Allah Nawez Khan, Speaker of the NWFP Legislative Assembly, declared on Dec. 16, 1946: "We frontier Pathans are a nation of 3,000,000, with our distinicitve culture, civilization, language, literature, names and nomenclature, legal codes, customs and calendar, history and traditions, aptitudes and ambitions." However, the tribal assemblies of the leading tribes in the NWFP assured the British Governor that they were part of Pakistan, and a referendum in July 1947 resulted in an overwhelming majority in favour of union with Pakistan (and not with India).

The government of Afghanistan had earlier asked the British government to give the inhabitants of the NWFP (and also of Baluchistan) an opportunity to decide whether they would join Afghanistan or India, or whether they aspired to complete independence. On the other hand, Mohammed Ali Jinnah, the leader of the Moslem League, was strongly opposed to the idea of an independent Pathan state (and also to union with Afghanistan). The July 1947 referendum was, therefore, confined to the question of Pathan union either with Pakistan or with India, and it was boycotted by the autonomist Redshirt movement led by Khan Abdul Ghaffar Khan. The latter and also the Fakir of Ipi, a tribal leader in Waziristan in the NWFP, subsequently campaigned for autonomy, some of their followers being arrested in mid-1948; Khan Abdul Ghaffar Khan was sentenced to three years in prison on June 16 and the Redshirt organization was banned on Sept. 16, 1948. Following elections held in the NWFP in November-December 1951, in which the Moslem League gained an overwhelming majority, the provincial Minister of Education observed that the result had "buried the myth of Pathanistan for all time".

During later years the government of Afghanistan pursued its claims to the Pathan-inhabited parts of the NWFP on the grounds that Pathanistan had "historically always been part of Afghanistan"; it also demanded, with Soviet support, that the principle of self-determination should be applied to the issue.

In 1985 and 1986 there were a number of incidents in the NWFP in which attacks were carried out by those described as saboteurs and agents of the Afghan government, chiefly against Afghan refugees living in Pakistan.

In December 1985 the Pakistan government launched a military campaign against a number of tribal chiefs in the province, who were believed to derive their financial backing from arms and drug trafficking and to receive assistance from Afghanistan. After several weeks of fighting, which included the destruction of 400 homes by government troops, a pact was concluded on March 3, 1986, under which the government gave assurances of respect for the tribesmen's customs and autonomy and the tribal leader, Malik Wali Khan Kokkihel, pledged his loyalty to the government.

SHIA MOSLEMS

Shia Moslems constitute more than a quarter of Pakistan's population and have frequently been in conflict with the central government on various issues. A Shia convention meeting in Islamabad in defiance of a government order issued on July 4, 1980, condemned *zakat*—a 2½ per cent tax on wealth, i.e. on all savings and deposit accounts of more than Rs1,000 (over $100), securities, annuities and life insurance policies, levied under Islamic law on June 20, 1980—as contrary to Shia teachings. The convention led to a demonstration and a clash with police in which at least one man was killed and 13 were injured. On July 6 President Zia agreed to amend the tax laws, and on Sept. 15 it was announced that, although tax already paid would not be refunded, Shias would be allowed to claim exemption by means of a sworn affidavit before a magistrate.

Since the introduction of the islamicization policy there have been frequent outbreaks of sectarian violence between Shias and Sunnis. In one such outbreak in February-April 1983 at least 12 people died in clashes over the ownership of a religious site in a suburb of Karachi, and on Sept. 16, 1986, Sunni objection to the route of a traditional Shia procession in Lahore sparked off riots there and in other towns which left nine dead. There was also an ethnic aspect to this rivalry as the Shias were mostly of Afghan origin, and there was resentment against the large numbers of Afghan refugees.

AHMADIS

The Ahmadis, followers of the 19th-century prophet Mirza Ghulam Ahmed (and also known as Qaidanis after his birthplace), came into conflict with the government over its islamicization policy as the government has refused to recognize them as true Moslems. (Of some 10,000,000 adherents worldwide, up to 4,000,000 live in Pakistan, with a further 10,000 in exile in the United Kingdom, including the leader, Hazrat Mirza Tahir Ahmed.) A government decree of April 26, 1984, forbade Ahmadis to call themselves Moslems, to perform Moslem religious rites (such as the call to prayer) or to call their places of worship mosques, and disenfranchised them unless they agreed to register with the electoral authorities as non-Moslems. The government has also tried to exclude Ahmadis from senior administration posts, and in the case of 10 leading Ahmadis murdered between April 1983 and mid-1985 no steps were taken to apprehend those responsible.

Palestinian Movements

After World War I Palestine—which had been part of the Ottoman Empire (one of the central powers defeated in the war)—became a British mandate under League of Nations auspices. However, in the Balfour Declaration published in November 1917 the British government had stated that it viewed "with favour the establishment in Palestine of a national home for the Jewish people, . . . it being clearly understood that nothing shall be done which may prejudice the civil and religious rights of existing non-Jewish communities". In the Middle East this declaration was strongly opposed by the Arabs, in particular those in Palestine.

In September 1921 the British government promulgated a Constitution providing for the setting-up of a Palestinian state, but this instrument was never implemented because the Arabs were unwilling to accept the concessions made in it to Zionism. In 1929 there occurred the first large-scale clashes between Jews and Arabs in Jerusalem. Following increased Jewish immigration from Europe (after the advent to power of Hitler in Germany in 1933) an Arab High Committee was formed in 1936 to unite Palestinian Arabs in opposition to the Jews, and there followed a three-year civil war between them. A British report (of the Peel Commission) published in July 1937 recommended the partition of Palestine, but this was rejected by the Arabs. In the same year the British government outlawed the Arab High Committee and arrested or exiled its leading members. A new British proposal, reducing the size of the proposed Jewish state from that envisaged by the Peel Commission, was rejected by both Zionists and Arabs in 1938.

In a White Paper published in May 1939 the British government declared that there would be no partition; that it was not British policy that Palestine should become either a Jewish or an Arab state; that an independent Palestinian state should be set up within 10 years; that meanwhile Jews and Arabs should be asked to take an increasing share in the country's administration; and that Jewish immigration into Palestine should be limited to 75,000 persons during the next five years, after which there was to be no further immigration without Arab consent. By 1939 the Jewish population in Palestine had risen to 445,457 or 30 per cent of the country's total. The progress of the war in Eastern Europe and mass liquidation of Jews by the Nazis brought about massive illegal immigration into Palestine by Jews from many parts of Europe.

By the end of World War II the Jewish Agency was ready to ensure the provisional government of a Jewish state through the Jewish National Council representing local Jews; on the other hand, the League of Arab States formed in March 1945 proclaimed its intention of defending the Arab cause in Palestine. Amid a serious deterioration of the security situation, various new partition proposals failed to move the Arab side from its demand for a unitary Palestinian state based on majority rule; accordingly, the British government decided in February 1947 to refer the Palestine question to the United Nations (as the successor to the League of Nations for the purposes of the mandate). On the basis of recommendations by a UN special committee, the UN General Assembly on Nov. 29, 1947, took its historic decision in favour of partition (and thus in favour of the creation of a Jewish state) by 33 votes to 13 with 10 countries abstaining and one being absent.

The UN decision was opposed by the Arabs, who declared their determination to resist it by force. Nevertheless, the military forces of the Jews moved to establish full control over the area of the proposed Jewish state, which was officially proclaimed as Israel on May 14, 1948, a few hours before the termination of the British mandate at midnight. Simultaneously, the unco-ordinated armies of Egypt, Transjordan, Syria, Lebanon and Iraq (backed by Saudi Arabian units) invaded the new state with the declared objective of establishing the independence of Palestine for its lawful inhabitants on the basis of majority rule. However, initial Arab advances were quickly stemmed by Israeli forces, who in a successful counter-attack not only secured virtually all of the territory allotted to the Jews under the UN partition plan but also took control of substantial additional areas. Under separate armistices signed in early 1949 between Israel on the one hand and Egypt, Transjordan, Syria and Lebanon on the other (but not Iraq), the Jewish state was left in control of three-quarters of the territory of Palestine. Of what remained in Arab hands, the southern coastal strip around the town of Gaza came under Egyptian administration, while the central area of Palestine west of the Jordan river (including the Old 'City of Jerusalem) was incorporated into the Hashemite Kingdom of Jordan (as Transjordan was renamed in June 1949).

During the 1948-49 hostilities, between 700,000 and 900,000 Arabs either fled or were expelled from Jewish-held territory, leaving the State of Israel with a substantial Jewish majority. Most of the refugees were housed in refugee camps in the West Bank and Gaza Strip, which thus became the centres of a burgeoning Palestinian Arab nationalism having as its fundamental aim the recovery of the homeland which the Jews were seen as having expropriated. Palestinian *fedayeen* (lit. "martyrs") groups responsible for many guerrilla movements, which in 1964 came together in the loose framework of the newly formed Palestine Liberation Organization (PLO). During this period the broader tensions arising from unremitting Arab hostility to the Jewish state had erupted into a second fullscale conflict, fought between Israel and Egypt in late 1956.

In the third Arab-Israeli war (of June 1967) Israel extended its control of territory to the whole of the area of Palestine by capturing the Gaza Strip from Egypt and the West Bank (including east Jerusalem) from Jordan, while at the same time also taking the Golan Heights from Syria and overrunning the Egyptian Sinai peninsula. The hostilities resulted in a further exodus of Arab refugees, principally to Jordan and Lebanon, but the bulk of the Palestinian inhabitants of the West Bank and Gaza stayed put under Israeli military administration. The Palestinian guerrilla movements, operating at this stage mainly from Jordan and Syria, were thus deprived of their natural bases within the confines of Palestine and found it even more difficult to penetrate to targets in Israel proper, especially after King Hussein had expelled the guerrillas from Jordan in 1970-71. Thereafter, Lebanon became the main centre of Palestinian military activities against Israel, while militant PLO factions increasingly resorted to terrorist attacks on Israeli targets outside the Middle East theatre of conflict.

The outcome of the 1967 war set a new tone for the Arab-Israeli conflict, which for some years thereafter revolved less around the fundamental Palestinian Arab challenge to the legitimacy of Israel and more around the quest of Egypt, Syria and Jordan for the recovery of their lost territories. The crucial outcome of the fourth Arab-Israeli war (of October 1973) was that Egypt re-established control of the eastern side of the Suez Canal (this being the first territory wrested from Israel by military force since its creation in 1948) and was thus psychologically enabled to move towards a rapprochement with the Jewish state. This process got under way with President Sadat's historic visit to Jerusalem in November 1977, which was followed by the conclusion of the Camp David framework agreements in September 1978 and ultimately by the signature of a full peace treaty between Egypt and Israel in March 1979. For the Egyptians the importance of the peace treaty was that Israeli-controlled Sinai would be restored to Egyptian control by April 1982. For the Palestinians, on the other hand, the whole Camp David peace process represented a betrayal of the Arab cause (a view widely shared in the Arab world), particularly because it did not provide for the genuine self-determination of the Palestinian people in their own land.

The PLO and all Arab states except Egypt therefore refused to participate in the US-sponsored negotiations with Israel on the granting of some form of "autonomy" to the Palestinian inhabitants of the West Bank and the Gaza Strip, as envisaged under one of the Camp David agreements. For this and other reasons these negotiations had made virtually no progress by early 1983 (nearly four years after their commencement), during which period Palestinian opposition to the process was strengthened by the oft-repeated claim of the Begin government that Israel possessed an historic right to sovereignty over the whole of the biblical "Land of Israel" *(Eretz Israel)*—i.e. including the West Bank, Gaza and the Golan Heights. In pursuance of this aspiration, the Israelis not only greatly expanded Jewish settlement of the occupied territories (especially the West Bank) but also passed new legislation in July 1981 strengthening the status of Jerusalem as the "indivisible" capital of Israel (as first proclaimed immediately after the June 1967 war); moreover, in late December 1981 Israel effectively annexed the Golan Heights.

Meanwhile, the Palestinian guerrilla organizations had become increasingly embroiled in the internal hostilities which broke out in Lebanon in 1975, and thereafter their virtually autonomous activities in Lebanon were viewed with increasing concern by Israel. During the late 1970s numerous military interventions were carried out by the Israelis to counter the threat to Israel's northern border area posed by the PLO presence in southern Lebanon; at the same time Israel gave active support to the Lebanese Christians in their continuing struggle with the Palestinian-backed Lebanese Moslem factions. Eventually, some six weeks after completing their withdrawal from Sinai, the Israelis launched a fullscale invasion of Lebanon in June 1982 with the declared objective of eliminating the military presence of the PLO from that country. After a two-month Israeli siege of Palestinian positions in west Beirut, an agreement was eventually reached under which PLO units withdrew from the Lebanese capital by early September, together with Syrian troops of the Arab Deterrent Force stationed in Lebanon since late 1976. But although the PLO had suffered heavy losses during the Israeli campaign, it subsequently became clear that the various Palestinian guerrilla movements remained operational notwithstanding the dispersal of many activists to a number of Arab countries. Moreover, on the political and diplomatic front the PLO continued to play a prominent role in Arab opposition to any Middle East peace settlement which did not provide for the establishment of a sovereign Palestinian state.

As at June 30, 1986, the number of Palestine refugees registered with the United Nations Relief and Works Agency for Palestine Refugees in the Near East (UNWRA) totalled 2,145,794. They were distributed as follows:

	In camps	**Not in camps**
Jordan	204,221	618,403
Gaza Strip	240,046	195,432
West Bank	92,445	272,870
Syria	72,486	178,467
Lebanon	140,037	131,387
Totals	749,235	1,396,559

Of these refugees a total of 349,224 were pupils at UNWRA schools.

In addition there were an estimated several hundred thousand "displaced persons" in the area.

A series of negotiations between Yassir Arafat, the PLO leader, and King Hussein of Jordan during 1983-85 laid the basis for a possible peace settlement along the lines of a federation between Jordan and an independent Palestinian state on the West Bank. The initiative was strongly opposed by Israel and by radical PLO factions, and effectively collapsed in early 1986. After several years of factional conflict, the PLO was reunified in early 1987, leading to the possibility that it would play a more commanding role in discussions over the Palestinian people's future.

Umbrella Organization

Palestine Liberation Organization (PLO) (*Munazamat Tahrir Falastin*)

Leadership. Mohammed Abed Arouf (Yassir) Arafat—code-named Abu Ammar (ch. of executive committee); Mohammed Affani—code-named Abu Mutasem (chief of staff)

An Iraqi proposal for the creation of a "Palestinian entity" was adopted at a meeting of the Council of the Arab League in Cairo on Sept. 16-19, 1963. At an Arab League summit meeting held in Cairo on Jan. 13-16, 1964, it was decided, on an initiative sponsored by President Nasser of Egypt, to set up the PLO under the leadership of Ahmed Shukairy (previously spokesman of Palestinian affairs at the United Nations). The inaugural session of what later became known as the Palestine National Council (PNC)—the Palestinian "parliament-in-exile"—was held in the then Jordanian part of Jerusalem in May-June 1964 and decided (on May 28) to form the PLO as "the only legitimate spokesman for all matters concerning the Palestinian people". The PLO was to be financed by the Arab League and to recruit military units among Palestinian refugees to constitute a Palestine Liberation Army (PLA) which was to be "the vanguard for the liberation of the usurped parts of Palestine" taken by Israel in 1948 (but not of the parts of Palestine then controlled by Egypt and Jordan).

The Jerusalem meeting also adopted (on June 2, 1964) the Palestine National Charter (or Covenant) as the basic statement of Palestinian aims, this document being regarded by the Israelis as enshrining the PLO's objective of destroying the Jewish state. As amended in 1968 and reaffirmed subsequently, the 33-article Charter states inter alia that "Palestine is the homeland of the Palestinian Arab people . . . [and] is an indivisible part of the Arab homeland" *(Art.1)*; that "Palestine, within the boundaries it had during the British mandate, is an indivisible territorial unit" *(Art.2)*; that "the Palestinian Arab people possess the legal right to their homeland and have the right to determine their destiny after achieving the liberation of their country in accordance with their wishes and entirely of their own accord and will" *(Art. 3)*; that "the Palestinians are those Arab nationals who, until 1947, normally resided in Palestine regardless of whether they were evicted from it or have stayed there" and also all those born after that date of a Palestinian father "whether inside Palestine or outside it" *(Art. 5)*; that "the Jews who had normally resided in Palestine until the beginning of the Zionist invasion will be considered Palestinians" *(Art. 6)*.

The Charter also declares that "armed struggle is the only way to liberate Palestine" *(Art. 9)*; that "the liberation of Palestine, from an Arab viewpoint, is a national duty", involving the repelling of "Zionist and imperialist aggression against the Arab homeland" as well as "the elimination of Zionism in Palestine" *(Art. 15)*; that "the liberation of Palestine, from a spiritual point of view, will provide the Holy Land with an atmosphere of safety and tranquillity, which in turn will safeguard the country's religious sanctuaries and guarantee freedom of worship and of visit to all, without discrimination of race, colour, language or religion" *(Art. 16)*; that "the partition of Palestine in 1947 and the establishment of the state of Israel are entirely illegal, regardless of the passage of time, because they were contrary to the will of the Palestinian people and to their natural right in their homeland, and inconsistent with the principles embodied in the Charter of the United Nations, particularly the right to self-determination" *(Art. 19)*; that "the Balfour declaration, the mandate for Palestine and everything which has been based on them are deemed null and void" on the grounds that "claims of historical or religious ties of Jews with Palestine are incompatible with the facts of history and the true conception of what constitutes statehood" *(Art. 20)*; that "the Palestinian Arab people . . . reject all solutions which are substitutes for the total liberation of Palestine and reject all proposals aiming at the liquidation of the Palestinian problem or its internationalization" *(Art. 21)*; that "Zionism is a political movement originally associated with international imperialism and antagonistic to all action for liberation and to progressive movements in the world [and] is racist and fanatic in its nature, aggressive, expansionist and colonial in its aims and fascist in its methods" *(Art. 22)*; and that "the Palestine Liberation Organization . . . is responsible for the Palestinian Arab people's movement in its struggle—to retrieve its homeland, liberate and return to it and exercise the right of self-determination in it—in all military, political and financial fields and also for whatever may be required by the Palestine case on the Inter-Arab and international levels" *(Art. 26)*.

From the outset King Hussein of Jordan refused to allow the PLA to train forces in Jordan or the PLO to levy taxes from Palestinian refugees in his country. By 1966 the PLA had a detachment in Syria and in December of that year Shukairy concluded an agreement on co-operation between the PLA and Yassir Arafat's *Al-Fatah*, the main Palestinian guerrilla organization. When the Six-Day War broke out in June 1967, Shukairy placed the PLA under the "national command" of Egypt and Syria (but not Jordan); however, the PLA units were scattered by Israeli forces on the first day of the war, with the result that the PLO and PLA took no effective part in the hostilities and were largely discredited in Arab eyes. At the end of 1967 Shukairy was replaced as leader of the PLO by Yehia Hammouda.

At a meeting in Cairo in February 1969 the PNC unanimously adopted a plan of action stating inter alia that peace would be possible only "in a democratic free Palestinian state where all Palestinians, Christians, Moslems and Jews will be equal and free from Zionist racism" and that it would oppose all attempts to impose "peaceful settlements" contrary to the rights of the Palestinian people. The meeting expressed particular opposition to the terms of Resolution 242 unanimously adopted by the UN Security Council on Nov. 22, 1967, because it made no reference to the rights of the Palestinian people.

(Resolution 242 had emphasized "the inadmissibility of the acquisition of territory by war" and had affirmed that the requisites for a just and lasting peace in the Middle East included "withdrawal of Israeli armed forces from territories occupied in the recent conflict" [i.e. the June 1967 war] as well as "termination of all claims or states of belligerency and respect for an acknowledgment of the sovereignty, territorial integrity and political independence of every state in the area and their right to live in peace within secure and recognized boundaries free from threats or acts of force". It referred only indirectly to the Palestinians, in affirming the necessity "for achieving a just settlement of the refugee problem".)

Having become de facto leader of the PLO in February 1969 by virtue of *Al-Fatah*'s dominance, Arafat proceeded to form a Palestine Armed Struggle Command (PASC), which by the end of that year had been joined by all Palestinian guerrilla organizations including the Syrian-backed *Al-Saiqa*. Following the expulsion of Palestinian guerrillas from Jordan in late 1970 and early 1971—see under separate entry below for the Movement for the National Liberation of Palestine *(Al-Fatah)*—the main centre of PLO military activities became Lebanon, particularly the hilly Arqoub region around Mount Hermon in the southeast adjoining the Israeli-occupied Golan Heights (and extending into Syrian territory), where *Al-Fatah* and *Al-Saiqa* guerrillas had first established a presence in 1969. Palestinian guerrilla operations against northern Israeli settlements, mounted from that area and other parts of southern Lebanon, provoked direct Israeli cross-border retaliatory raids, giving rise in turn to increasing concern on the part of the Lebanese government.

As early as November 1969 the Lebanese authorities had, through Egyptian mediation, entered into the "Cairo agreement" with Palestinian guerrilla leaders with the aim of regulating their military activities on Lebanese territory. Regular clashes nevertheless continued to occur between guerrillas and the Lebanese armed forces seeking to apply the agreement. A direct Israeli commando raid on Beirut on April 10, 1973, in which three top-ranking guerrilla leaders were assassinated, served to fan Lebanese resentment at the Palestinian presence. Although a further agreement was reached by the two sides in May of that year underlying tensions remained acute and were a major cause of the eventual outbreak of fullscale civil war in Lebanon in 1975.

From the early 1970s the PLO issued numerous statements condemning individual guerrilla actions outside Palestine, particularly airliner hijackings, asserting that they harmed the Palestinian cause and that those responsible (notably militants of the Popular Front for the Liberation of Palestine—PFLP) would be tried before Palestinian tribunals. On the other hand, the PLO has not condemned raids on Israeli territory (even where they resulted in civilian casualties) or attempts to kill "reactionary" Arab leaders.

A summit meeting of Arab heads of state held in Algiers on Nov. 26-28, 1973, recognized the PLO as the sole legitimate representative of all Palestinians, the only dissenter being King Hussein of Jordan, who would not agree to the PLO representing Palestinians in Jordan. However, at a further meeting of Arab heads of state held in Rabat (Morocco) on Oct. 26-29, 1974, the Arab leaders affirmed "the right of the Palestinian people to establish an independent authority under the leadership of the PLO as the sole legitimate representative of the Palestinian people in all liberated Palestinian territory" and undertook to "support this authority upon its establishment in all respects and degrees".

The UN General Assembly decided on Oct. 14, 1974, to invite the PLO to take part in a debate on the Palestine question, and Arafat accordingly addressed the Assembly as the first speaker in this debate on Nov. 13, when he appealed for international support for the PLO. He said inter alia that he had come "bearing an olive branch and a freedom fighter's gun"; that in "the Palestine of tomorrow" Jerusalem would "resume its historic role of a peaceful 'high place' for all religions"; that the PLO included in its perspective "all Jews who at present live in Palestine and who choose to live here with us in peace and without discrimination"; and that he appealed to every Jew individually to "turn away from the illusory promises made by the Zionist ideology and the Israeli leaders" who had "nothing to offer to Jews but blood, wars and distress". He asserted that the Palestinian revolution was not animated by racial or religious motives and that its target had never been the Jew as an individual but "racialist Zionism and open aggression", adding: "We make a distinction between Judaism and Zionism; while maintaining our opposition to the colonialist Zionist movement we respect the Jewish faith."

The permanent representative of Israel at the United Nations declared in reply that Israel would "not allow the establishment of the authority of the PLO in any part of Palestine" and that the PLO would "not be imposed on the Palestinian Arabs" and "not be tolerated by the Jews of Israel". He claimed that it was not true that the Palestinians had been deprived of a national state or had been uprooted, saying: "Jordan is Palestine, geographically, ethnically and historically, and without the Palestinians, who constitute the majority of its population, Jordan would be a state without people." He declared that Israel was determined "to pursue the murderers of the PLO and to destroy their bases".

At the end of the debate the UN General Assembly adopted, on Nov. 22, 1974—against the votes of Israel, the United States and some other states—two resolutions (i) recognizing the PLO as the representative of the Palestinian people, who were "a principal party" in the establishment of a just and durable peace in the Middle East and who had the right to regain "their rights by all means in accordance with the purposes and principles of the UN Charter", and (ii) granting the PLO permanent observer status at the UN General Assembly and at international conferences sponsored by the United Nations.

The PLO thereafter obtained recognition as the representative of the Palestinian people from a number of international organizations. It became a full member of the movement of non-aligned countries in August 1975 and a member of that movement's Co-ordinating Bureau in August 1976. In February 1975 the Council of Ministers of the Organization of African Unity (OAU) decided during a meeting in Addis Ababa to grant "token aid" to the PLO and recommended that Arafat should address the next OAU summit (which he did in July 1975). In August 1976 the PLO became, as the representative of Palestine, a full member of the Arab League. It also became a member of the Organization of the Islamic Conference. In addition, the PLO has been authorized to set up representative offices in many of the world's capitals, some of these missions being accorded full diplomatic status by the host government.

In the civil war in Lebanon in 1975-76 the militant PLO guerrilla factions sided with the left-wing Moslem groups against the right-wing Maronite Christian militias. In May 1976 an attempt by Syria to impose a ceasefire was strongly opposed by most Palestinian leaders and the Lebanese National Movement (of left-wing Moslems), whereas *Al-Saiqa* and some PLO units supported Syria and fought against forces of the Movement. On June 4, 1976, Palestinian and left-wing Lebanese forces formed a "joint general command" (although *Al-Saiqa* did not participate) and succeeded in preventing the Syrian army from gaining control of key positions north of the Damascus-Beirut highway. In view of the continuing warfare in Lebanon Arafat called on all Arab heads of state to halt a "new massacre against the Palestinian revolution", and on July 7, 1976, he announced that the headquarters of the PLA (the PLO's armed wing) were being moved from Damascus to Beirut in order to detach them from close Syrian control. The civil war was brought to a ceasefire by the occupation of Beirut and other towns in late 1976 by an Arab Deterrent Force (ADF), nominally of mixed Arab composition but in fact overwhelmingly (and later exclusively) made up of Syrian troops; nevertheless, no lasting solution had been achieved of Lebanon's deep-seated internal divisions, and particularly of the antagonisms arising from the substantial Palestinian presence in that country.

While the Lebanese conflict was at its height the PLO achieved a significant political success when PLO-backed National Bloc candidates achieved a substantial victory in municipal elections held in the Israeli-occupied West Bank on April 12, 1976. The success of the National Bloc lists—consisting of pro-PLO and *Rakah* (New Communist) candidates, other Arab nationalists and pro-Syrian Baathists—was accompanied by an escalation of serious unrest among the Palestinian inhabitants of the West Bank, setting the pattern of frequent anti-Israeli and pro-PLO demonstrations which by the late 1970s were taking a steady toll of lives on both sides. Since the April 1976 victory of the National Bloc the Israeli authorities have allowed no further elections to take place in the West Bank.

At a conference of heads of state and government of African and Arab states held in Cairo in March 1977, King Hussein of Jordan and Arafat, who had not met since the September 1970 action by Jordan against Palestinian guerrillas, were publicly reconciled with each other. Thereafter, Arafat and the majority PLO wing pursued a policy of close co-operation with Jordan on the Palestinian question.

At a meeting of the PNC held in Cairo on March 12-20, 1977, the delegates were divided into a majority "moderate" group consisting of *Al-Fatah, Al-Saiqa* and the Popular Democratic Front for the Liberation of Palestine (which later dropped the word "Popular" from its title) on the one hand, and on the other the "rejection front" led by the PFLP and also including the PFLP-General Command, the Arab Liberation Front (ALF) and the Popular Struggle Front (PSF). The "moderates" were said to favour the establishment of a Palestinian state in any part of Palestine which could be "liberated", the PLO's participation in Middle East peace talks and the creation of the Palestinian government-in-exile, while the "rejectionists" (backed by Iraq and Libya) opposed any negotiations involving Israel and any "partial" settlement implicitly accepting the existence of a Jewish state and also called for continued armed struggle until the whole of Palestinian territory had been liberated.

At the Cairo session the PNC adopted a new programme and decided to unify all Palestinian combat forces under a supreme military council commanded by the chairman of the PLO's executive committee (i.e. Yassir Arafat), to be financed by the Palestine National Fund. The PNC had, at this session, received a message of support from "the mayors of all West Bank municipalities".

The US State Department declared (for the first time) on Sept. 2, 1977, that Palestinian participation in a settlement of the Palestine question was necessary to ensure the successful outcome of an international peace conference. Arafat welcomed this statement on Sept. 13 as a positive step confirming that the Palestinian cause was "the essence of the conflict in the Middle East" and also confirming "the correctness of the stand adopted by the PLO". A PLO spokesman said in Beirut at the same time that the PLO would continue to reject Resolution 242 of the UN Security Council because it referred to the Palestinians as a refugee problem and not as "a national people with rights to an independent state". The US statement was, however, rejected as inadequate by Zouheir Mohsen (then the *Al-Saiqa* leader) and by Dr Georges Habash of the PFLP on Sept. 14.

Israel consistently refused any negotiations with the PLO then and subsequently. On Sept. 1, 1977, the *Knesset* (Israel's Parliament) resolved by 92 votes to four with six abstentions that Israel would "not negotiate with representatives of the PLO". Israel also rejected the inclusion of any reference to the PLO or any Palestinian entity in a programme for an international peace conference.

Following the visit to Jerusalem by President Sadat of Egypt on Nov. 19-21, 1977, the PLO and the Syrian government issued a joint statement on Nov. 23, condemning the visit and calling for the convening of a pan-Arab people's conference to dissuade Egypt from its course of rapprochement with Israel. At a meeting held in Tripoli (Libya) on Dec. 2-5, 1977, by the PLO and five Arab States (Algeria, Iraq, Libya, Syria and South Yemen), the factions of the PLO asked for the establishment of an "Arab resistance and confrontation front" and reaffirmed their rejection of UN Security Council resolutions 242 and 338 (the latter having been adopted on Oct. 22, 1973, at the end of the fourth Arab-Israeli war) and of any international conference based on them; they also called for the establishment of an independent Palestine state "without reconciliation, recognition or negotiation with the enemy". The meeting eventually adopted, without Iraq's concurrence, a "Tripoli declaration" which stated that the four states and the PLO would form the nucleus of a pan-Arab front for resistance and confrontation which would be open to other Arab countries; that they would "freeze" their diplomatic relations with Egypt and boycott Egyptian companies and persons conducting business with Israel, and also meetings of the Arab League held in Egypt. The PLO also joined the permanent secretariat of an Arab People's Conference (in Tripoli, Libya) comprising representatives of Algeria, Iraq, Libya, Syria, South Yemen, the Lebanese National Movement and Egyptian opposition groups. Early in February 1978 it was stated in Algiers that the PLO and Syria had secretly agreed to re-open the PLO bases in Syria which had been closed during the civil war in Lebanon in 1976.

The Camp David agreements signed by Israel and Egypt in September 1978 were strongly condemned by Arafat on Sept. 19 as "a dirty deal which the Egyptian people will reject and which does not decide our destiny". He accused President Sadat of Egypt of having "traded Arab Jerusalem for the Sinai desert", and he warned President Carter of the USA and "US interests in the Middle East" that they would "pay" for the Camp David decisions. On the West Bank, 19 of the 29 municipalities called (on Oct. 1) for the establishment of an independent Palestinian state under the leadership of the PLO.

An Arab summit conference held in Baghdad on Nov. 2-8, 1978, rejected the Camp David agreement and agreed inter alia that "all the Arab countries" should "give all forms of support and aid and facilities to the Palestinian resistance's struggle in all its forms through the PLO as the sole legitimate representative of the Palestinian people within and outside the occupied Arab territories for the sake of their liberation and the recovery of their legitimate national rights".

At a meeting between King Hussein and Arafat on March 17, 1979, the King agreed to the opening of a PLO political office in Amman but he was reported to be still opposed to the re-establishment of Palestinian camps in Jordan. At a further Baghdad Arab summit conference on March 27-31, 1979 (after the signature in Washington of the peace treaty between Egypt and Israel on March 26), the PLO sided with Iraq, Libya and Syria in taking a hard line against Egypt, which became subject to an Arab diplomatic and economic boycott which included suspension of Egypt's membership of the Arab League. In February 1979 Arafat asked OPEC member countries to "exert economic pressure on the United States in order to bring about changes in US policies towards the Middle East". Thereafter the PLO and other Arab League members refused to participate in the US-sponsored negotiations between Egypt and Israel on the granting of "autonomy" to the West Bank and Gaza Palestinians, as envisaged under the Camp David agreement.

Meanwhile, the Israelis had been taking an increasingly vigorous line against the PLO guerrilla presence in southern Lebanon, while at the same time consolidating a buffer zone under the control of Maj. Saad Haddad's anti-PLO Lebanese Christian forces immediately to the north of the border. The Israelis were concerned not only to prevent direct Palestinian attacks on northern Israel, but also to forestall any penetration further south of the Syrian ADF forces. In March 1978 a major Palestinian raid on Israel was immediately followed by an Israeli invasion of southern Lebanon with the aim of clearing the area of PLO bases. This led directly to the deployment of a UN peace-keeping force (UNIFIL) in two border areas; but this force proved largely powerless to control the situation after Israeli troops withdrew in June 1978, especially since the more radical PLO factions insisted on continuing the military campaign.

Early in 1979 the PLO resumed its attacks on Israeli positions from Lebanon and these again led to counter-action by the Israelis, their Prime Minister (Menahem Begin) declaring in April of that year that pre-emptive strikes would be used by Israeli forces at any time and in any place rather than in retaliation for specific actions; this policy was formally agreed to by the Israeli Cabinet on July 1. The PLO and the Lebanese National Movement had earlier, on June 6, agreed to withdraw from southern Lebanon to "deprive Israel of any possible pretext for continuing its attacks on civilian targets". The PLO subsequently closed down its headquarters in Tyre and withdrew also from Nabatiyeh (north-east of Tyre), and on Oct. 4, 1979, the PLO announced a unilateral ceasefire in Lebanon, entailing the cessation of PLO guerrilla action against Israel from Lebanese territory, but not elsewhere. (The PFLP dissociated itself from this decision on Oct. 5.) In June 1980 Arafat announced that he had ordered the closure of all guerrilla offices in Sidon and their withdrawal to refugee camps.

A further escalation of tensions occurred in April 1981 when Israeli planes for the first time intervened directly in support of Lebanese Christian Phalangists then under attack by the Syrians, who responded by deploying surface-to-air missiles in the Bekaa Valley in eastern Lebanon. During the subsequent Israeli-Syrian crisis major Israeli air strikes were mounted on PLO positions throughout Lebanon, including a heavy raid on west Beirut on July 17 (the first since December 1974) in which, according to Israeli sources, the headquarters of two Palestinian organizations were destroyed. Palestinian guerrillas, by now regrouped in southern Lebanon, responded by launching heavy rocket attacks on northern Israeli settlements in the second half of July 1981. Through US mediation a ceasefire came into effect on July 24, 1981, inaugurating a period of several months of relative stability in the border area; nevertheless, Arafat's insistence that the ceasefire applied only to cross-border hostilities (on which ground he reserved the right to continue military operations within Israel and also against the Haddad enclave) and the rejection of the ceasefire by some PLO militants ensured that tensions remained acute.

From November 1981 Israeli spokesmen frequently accused the PLO of violating the ceasefire by moving supplies and reinforcements into the border area and by harassing Christian positions in the Haddad enclave. A resumption of Israeli air strikes on PLO positions in April 1982 was followed by a steady build-up of tension during May and further PLO rocket attacks on northern Israel. After the attempted assassination of the Israeli ambassador in London on June 3, Israeli forces on June 6 launched a fullscale invasion of Lebanon code-named "Peace for Galilee" with the declared objective of destroying the military capability of the PLO in that country and creating the conditions for a restoration of effective central government authority.

In their rapid advance up Lebanon's western coastal roads Israeli forces cut off and eventually overran Palestinian bases in Tyre, Sidon, Saadiyat and Damour. Meanwhile, a second Israeli force crossed the central sector of the border and quickly captured the PLO's mountain fortress of Beaufort Castle (which was handed over to Maj. Haddad's forces) as well as Nabatiyeh further north. A third Israeli advance from the Golan Heights in the east rapidly penetrated the PLO-held Arqoub region on the slopes of Mount Hermon. By mid-June Israeli forces had completely encircled the Lebanese capital, in the western area of which large numbers of PLO fighters as well as substantial contingents of Syrian ADF troops found themselves trapped.

There followed two months of intensive negotiations in which US and other mediators eventually established the basis for an evacuation of the PLO and Syrian forces trapped in Beirut (which was the scene of further heavy fighting during this period as Israeli forces closed in on Palestinian refugee camps harbouring PLO guerrillas). The evacuation plan (which did not have the status of a legal agreement in view of Israel's refusal to sign any formal pact to which the PLO was a party) applied only to the Palestinian and Syrian forces in Beirut and not to those elsewhere in Lebanon. As carried out from Aug. 21, the withdrawal took place in daylight, partly by sea and partly overland by way of the Beirut-Damascus highway (the land route being used in particular by the Syrian ADF forces and the Palestine Liberation Army); Palestinians evacuated by sea (mainly to a staging-post in Cyprus) were transferred later to various Arab countries which had agreed to receive them. Those evacuated were permitted to take with them light weapons only and the whole process was supervised by a newly deployed international peace-keeping force of US, French and Italian soldiers, assisted by the regular Lebanese army.

The evacuation was completed on Sept. 1, 1982 (some three days ahead of schedule), by which time the official Lebanese total of evacuees (including regular Syrian troops and several hundred Palestinian women and children) was 14,656 whereas the Israeli count put the corresponding total at 14,847. The Lebanese count gave the number of regular Syrian evacuees as 2,700, whereas the Israelis put the figure at 3,500; both accounts agreed that over half of all those leaving Beirut went to Syria. Other Arab destinations of Palestinian guerrillas were Tunisia, South Yemen, Algeria, Jordan, Sudan, North Yemen and Iraq. Arafat himself left Beirut on Aug. 30 bound for Greece, where he was welcomed by the Greek Prime Minister Andreas Papandreou.

On leaving the Lebanese capital the PLO leader vowed that the Palestinian struggle would be continued "so that we can win the war"; on arriving in Greece he denied that the Palestinian withdrawal from Beirut represented a defeat, adding that he was proud to have been instrumental in preventing a full Israeli assault on the Lebanese capital. Arafat's decision to go to Greece from Beirut was said by a PLO spokesman on Sept. 1 to signify his disappointment over the lack of general Arab support for the Palestinians during the recent Lebanon crisis. Following the withdrawal from Beirut, the main PLO headquarters became Damascus (the Syrian capital).

The PLO suffered heavy losses as a result of the Israeli invasion of Lebanon, in terms of military infrastructure, arms and personnel; by mid-August 1982 the Israelis had captured some 6,000 Palestinian guerrillas (and had killed at least 1,000 others), who were placed in special internment camps and denied prisoner-of-war status because as "terrorists" they did not conduct their operations "in accordance with the rules of war". Nevertheless, the PLO retained a substantial military presence in northern and eastern Lebanon, and many guerrillas evacuated from Beirut to Syria in August 1982 were later reported to have moved back across the Lebanese border. By late 1982 the Israeli authorities estimated that there were 7,000 PLO guerrillas in Lebanon and insisted that they must be withdrawn as a necessary pre-condition for an eventual Israeli withdrawal jointly with Syrian troops.

Suspecting that some 2,000 heavily armed PLO fighters remained in hiding in Palestinian refugee camps in Beirut, the Israelis in mid-September 1982 sponsored an operation by Lebanese Christian

Phalangist militiamen designed to clear guerrillas from the Chatila and Sabra camps in west Beirut; however, this operation on Sept. 16-18 turned into a wholesale massacre of civilian occupants including women and children—the total number of deaths being later estimated at between 700 and 800. The atrocities provoked almost universal international condemnation as well as a major political crisis in Israel itself, while for his part Arafat claimed that not only Israel but also the United States bore responsibility in that President Reagan had guaranteed the security of Palestinian civilians in Beirut under the August 1982 evacuation agreement.

As regards the Israeli role, an official Israeli inquiry under Chief Justice Itzhak Kahan found in a report published on Feb. 8, 1983, that the actual massacre had been perpetrated by Phalangist militiamen but that certain Israeli political and military leaders bore varying degrees of indirect responsibility. Particular censure was directed against Defence Minister Ariel Sharon for having allowed the Phalangists to enter the camps without direct Israeli supervision.

On the broad diplomatic front, President Reagan's new Middle East peace plan of Sept. 1, 1982—envisaging in particular the granting of self-government to the West Bank and Gaza Strip Palestinians in some sort of federation with Jordan—led to divisions within the PLO, although the precise alignment of the various factions remained unclear. Whereas the "rejectionist" wing condemned the Reagan plan as running counter to the PLO's commitment to a fully independent Palestinian state, the moderate wing appeared unwilling to reject it outright and Arafat himself entered into exploratory talks on the federation concept with King Hussein of Jordan in late 1982.

Shortly after the appearance of the new Reagan proposals Arafat subscribed on behalf of the PLO to a new Middle East peace plan issued on Sept. 9 by a summit conference of the Arab League in Fez (Morocco) and envisaging inter alia the establishment of an independent Palestinian state coupled with the issuing of "peace guarantees" by the UN Security Council to "all countries in the region". However, this apparent willingness to give implicit recognition to Israel found no favour with the militant Palestinian factions, which condemned "all forms of recognition, negotiation and making peace with the expansionist Zionist state".

At a session held in Algiers on Feb. 14-23, 1983, the Palestine National Council adopted a resolution recording its refusal to consider the Reagan peace plan as a "sound basis for a just and lasting solution to the Palestinian problem and the Arab-Israeli conflict". However, at the instigation of Arafat (who was re-elected chairman of the PLO executive committee at the Algiers meeting) the PNC resolution appeared to stop short of a total rejection of the US plan.

At this stage, the PLO's executive committee was composed of three representatives from *Al-Fatah*, two from the Popular Front for the Liberation of Palestine (PFLP), one each from *Al-Saiqa*, the Popular Front for the Liberation of Palestine-General Command (PFLP-GC) and the Democratic Front for the Liberation of Palestine (DFLP), together with six independents.

Talks were held between King Hussein of Jordan and Yassir Arafat in April 1983 in an effort to make progress towards a Jordanian-Palestinian federation, on the general basis of a compromise between the Fez and Reagan plans. Although unsuccessful, they served to lay the foundations for further discussions.

Further developments were disrupted by an internal rebellion within *Al-Fatah*, which, while initially concerned with policy disagreements, rapidly swelled to include denunciations by radicals from *Al-Fatah* and other PLO groups of Arafat and the established *Fatah* leadership, and of their international lifestyle based on attempts to find a "diplomatic" solution to the Palestinian question. The situation was complicated by the support offered to the anti-Arafat factions by Syria, and, to a lesser extent, Libya and Iran. Open fighting between the rival factions erupted in mid-1983, leading to the withdrawal of the Arafat loyalists from northern Lebanon. Gradually contacts were resumed, but serious differences remained, and it was not until the 18th Palestine National Council in early 1987 that a degree of unity was re-established.

The rebellion was triggered by the promotion by Arafat in May 1983 of two officers who had been criticized for cowardice and imcompetence during the Israeli invasion of Lebanon the previous year. The promotion was denounced by three *Fatah* commanders, Col. Saed (Abu) Musa, Col. Khaled Al (Abu) Amlah and Nimr (Abu) Saleh. Although Arafat took steps to remove the source of grievance, the rebellion soon progressed to wider issues, focusing on the *Fatah* leadership's alleged corruption and lack of commitment to the armed struggle. Mediation efforts by Syria, the DFLP, the PFLP and *Al-Saiqa* failed as Arafat refused to consider some of the more far-reaching demands put forward by the rebels, who subsequently became organized as the Fatah Revolutionary Council. Open fighting broke out between Arafat loyalists and rebel supporters in the Bekaa Valley and outside Damascus in June, when the PFLP-GC backed the rebels, together with some more minor PLO factions.

With the Libyan and Syrian governments offering increasingly open support to the rebels, some of whom were beginning to demand Arafat's resignation, the Syrians on June 24, 1983, expelled Arafat and Khalil al Wazir, a senior *Fatah* leader, from the country. The Syrian leadership subsequently described Arafat as "a defeatist on the path of the wilderness", while the PLO leader spoke of "a Syrian Libyan aggression against the Palestinian revolution". Arafat retained considerable support among residents of refugee camps in Lebanon, Jordan and Syria, and among Palestinians on the West Bank. The Jordanian government, whose relations with Syria had been strained for some time, described Arafat's expulsion as "an attempt to destroy the independence of the legitimate Palestinian institutions".

Various reform proposals put forward by the *Fatah* central committee in July were rejected by the rebels, and, with fighting between the factions intensifying, the Arafat loyalists withdrew in September to the refugee camps of Baddawi and Nahr el-Bahred; outside the northern Lebanese town of Tripoli. During the ensuing siege of the camps by *Fatah* rebels and members of the PFLP-GC, the Syrian government repeatedly denied allegations that its forces were providing tank and artillery support to the rebels. Observers treated such denials with some scepticism, however. On the rebel side, the leader of the anti-Arafat factions appeared increasingly to be Ahmed Jabril, commander of the PFLP-GC and a former Syrian army officer, rather than the *Fatah* commanders who had initiated the split. Strenuous mediation efforts by, among others, the Soviet Union, Saudi Arabia and the Gulf Co-operation Council, the Lebanese leader Rashid Karami (a resident of Tripoli), and the Indian government acting on behalf of the Non-Aligned Movement, failed to produce a settlement, and at the end of December 1983 the *Fatah* loyalists were evacuated from Lebanon by sea in ships flying the United Nations flag. Arafat himself travelled to Cairo for talks with President Mubarak—an action that drew strong criticism from within the PLO, in particular from *Fatah* loyalists. In January 1984 Abu Musa and Abu Amlah were expelled from *Al-Fatah*, which announced that they would be put on trial for treason.

Outside *Al-Fatah*, the other main PLO groups had divided into two broad alliances: the strongly anti-Arafat National Alliance, which included the *Fatah* Revolutionary Council, *Al-Saiqa*, the PFLP-GC and the Palestine Popular Struggle Front—PPSF, (all Damascus-based groups), and the more moderate Democratic Alliance, which sought to play a mediating role and which included the PFLP, DFLP, Palestine Communist Party and the Palestine Liberation Front.

The first serious moves towards resolving the dispute after the Tripoli fighting followed in June 1984, when representatives of *Al-Fatah* held talks in Aden (South Yemen) with the Democratic Alliance, which in turn met National Alliance leaders in Damascus. Contacts continued during 1984, but serious obstacles to a settlement remained, including the question of the forthcoming 17th session of the Palestine National Council, which the National Alliance insisted should not take place until the internal disputes had been resolved. There were also sharp differences over the question of relations with Egypt: the *Fatah* leadership favoured a resumption of ties with Cairo, with the proviso that this would not imply acceptance of the Camp David accords, while the other two alliances insisted that no such links could be contemplated until the Egyptian government had abrogated the agreement. Observers noted that at this time the PFLP was hardening its position, while the DFLP appeared to be showing greater willingness to compromise with *Al-Fatah*. A "merger agreement" between the DFLP and the PFLP, announced in late 1983, had had no practical effect.

Despite a boycott by both the National and the Democratic Alliances, the 17th PNC session was held in Amman in November 1984, amid allegations that the meeting was inquorate and the the *Fatah* leadership had "co-opted" onto the Council a number of their supporters in order to achieve a semblance of quoracy. The PNC Speaker, Khaled al Fahoun, who was among those boycotting the session, claimed that he had received sufficient notifications of non-attendance from PNC members to prove that the meeting would be inquorate. (Fahoun had earlier been appointed chairman of a "joint body for national salvation" set up by the National Alliance.)

The Council session was attended by representatives from Morocco, Egypt, Algeria and Syrian opposition groups, and was addressed by King Hussein, who proposed launching a joint initiative on the basis of "territory for peace" and of UN Security Resolution 242. The Council voted to study his proposals. In a keynote address, Arafat talked of the need to "rectify" the relationship with Syria. He also tendered his resignation, but this was not accepted. The Executive Committee appointed at the end of proceedings included five places left vacant for representatives of the "independent Palestinian factions" (i.e. those which had boycotted the session.)

Following this session, Arafat and Hussein reached agreement in February 1985 to work towards a peace settlement based on a confederation of Jordan with an independent Palestinian state on the West Bank. Jordanian officials claimed that the PLO had implicitly accepted resolution 242 as a basis for settlement in agreeing to call for the complete withdrawal by Israel from the occupied territories in accordance with UN resolutions. Arafat and other *Fatah* leaders refused to confirm this publicly, however. The agreement was denounced by radical PLO factions, and in March 1985 the four member groups of the National Alliance, together with the PFLP, announced the formation of the Palestine National Salvation Front (PNSF), which would aim to achieve the abrogation of the Hussein-Arafat accord and to consolidate a "strategic alliance" with Syria. The Front received diplomatic support and encouragement from the Syrian, Libyan and Iranian governments.

During the remainder of 1985, there ensued sustained diplomatic efforts to find a framework for negotiations that could lead to the establishment of a Palestinian entity on the West Bank. In particular, these efforts focused on the question of Palestinian representation at any possible peace conference. The principal parties involved in these discussions were the Arafat wing of the PLO, Egypt, Jordan, the USA and Israel. To some extent, the USA effectively played a mediating role between Israel and Jordan, which in turn acted as intermediary between the USA and the PLO. The negotiations foundered on, among other things, the difficulty of finding Palestinian representatives who would be acceptable both to the PLO and to Israel, which refused to countenance any dealing with PLO members. Within the PLO, Arafat's room for manoeuvre was restricted; some observers suggested that he personally might have been willing to acknowledge Israel's right to exist, but felt constrained not to do so in view of the damage such an unprecedented move would cause to what remained of Palestinian unity. In spite of declarations of optimism from all sides, little real progress had been made by the end of the year.

In Lebanon, the *Amal* militia in May 1985 launched an offensive against PLO guerrillas (who were largely *Fatah* loyalists) in the refugee camps of Sabra, Chatila and Bourj el-Brajneh. Aimed at removing the independent Palestinian military presence in Beirut, the attack was supported by the Syrian government. To some extent, it served to reunite pro- and anti-Arafat forces in Lebanon against a common enemy. Artillery units of PNSF groups based in the Druse- controlled hills to the east of Beirut shelled *Amal* positions, while

Dr Georges Habash, leader of the PFLP, left Damascus, accusing Syria of bearing responsibility for the fighting, during which large numbers of civilians were killed by *Amal*'s bombardment of the camps. Other PNSF leaders expressed their displeasure at the attack, and the ceasefire which ended the fighting in June was reached largely through PNSF mediation. During 1985-86, the PLO in Lebanon benefited from the support of the Druse Progressive Socialist Party, and, in particular, the fundamentalist Shia group, *Hezbollah,* which was growing in influence at the expense of *Amal*, whom it accused of entering into secret agreements with Israel. *Amal* again laid siege to the Beirut camps at the end of 1986, ostensibly in retaliation for the PLO's refusal to abandon positions captured from the militia in fighting outside Sidon, in the south. Conditions in the camp grew increasingly appalling as the siege persisted, with many civilians dying for want of medical supplies and attention. Denounced by Palestinian leaders of virtually every persuasion, the siege was lifted only as a result of the entry of Syrian troops into Beirut in April 1987.

All the main PLO factions with bases in Lebanon came under attack from the Israeli air force during 1983-87, often in retaliation for guerrilla attacks against Israel. In a striking departure from such small-scale raids, Israeli aircraft in October 1985 bombed PLO headquarters in Tunis, ostensibly in revenge for the recent killings of three Israelis on a yacht in Cyprus. The raid was widely condemned, also by Western states; even the US government offered a qualified criticism. The PLO's international standing was, however, damaged by the Cyprus yacht killings and the subsequent hijacking of the *Achille Lauro* cruise liner (see entry under Palestine Liberation Front) and guerrilla attacks on Rome and Vienna airports (see Abu Nidal Group). The mainstream PLO leadership condemned all three actions. In an effort to clarify this position, Arafat stated during a visit to Cairo in November 1985 that he condemned acts of terrorism wherever committed, as well as all operations outside the occupied territories. Confusion arose as to whether the "Cairo declaration", as it became known, included Israel itself in those territories.

King Hussein announced the abrogation of the Jordanian-Palestinian accord in February 1986, accusing the PLO of unreliability. In particular, he criticized its failure to accept the UN Resolution 242, and claimed that he had secured US agreement that the PLO would participate in an international peace conference if such acceptance was forthcoming. While criticizing the decision, the loyalist PLO attempted to keep open the possibility of co-operation, issuing a statement "reaffirming the PLO's commitment to the Jordanian-Palestinian process of peace". The Jordanian government, however, moved swiftly to reduce *Fatah* influence in the country, closing all 25 of the movement's offices and expelling *Fatah* officials. It also sponsored a rival *Fatah* grouping under Col. Atallah Atallah (Abu Zaim), head of the PLO's military intelligence at the time of the Israeli invasion of Lebanon, and subsequently criticized as corrupt and ineffective by Abu Musa and the *Fatah* rebels. Atallah claimed widespread support among Palestinians in Jordan, but there was little evidence of this, and he and his followers were expelled from *Al-Fatah*.

During late 1985 and early 1986, much of the PLO's administrative headquarters was transferred from Tunis to Baghdad (Iraq) and North Yemen, reportedly as a result of tension with the Tunisian government.

Contacts between the Arafat loyalists and other PLO groups multiplied during 1986, although serious differences remained, notably over *Al-Fatah*'s refusal to abrogate the Hussein-Arafat accord. In October 1986, a joint meeting in Cairo of the DFLP, PCP, ALF, PLF and *Al-Fatah* agreed to "promote national unity" with a view to the convening of the 18th PNC session. There were also contacts between *Al-Fatah* and the PFLP.

In late March 1987 six hard-line PLO groups met in Tripoli, Libya, at the invitation of Col. Gadaffi and under the chairmanship of Khaled al Fahoun. The six comprised the PFLP, the DFLP, the PFLP-GC, the PPSF, and PLF (Yacoub faction—see PLF entry) and the *Fatah* Revolutionary Council (the *Fatah* "rebels"). At the close of their talks, they issued a statement calling for the abrogation of the Hussein-Arafat accord, for the complete freezing of relations with Egypt and for the continued rejection of UN Security Council Resolution 242.

The 18th PNC session was eventually held in Algiers in April 1987, and marked the effective reunification of the PLO under Arafat's leadership. Prior to the opening of the session there was intense dialogue between eight leading PLO organizations, including the Abu Nidal Group. These meetings resulted in an agreement to abrogate the Hussein-Arafat accord and to concentrate military operations inside the "occupied territory". They also covered political and organizational reforms within the PLO, and cleared the way for the attendance at the session of all the major PLO groups, with the notable exception of the PFLP-GC, the *Fatah* Revolutionary Council (i.e. the *Fatah* rebels), *Al-Saiqa* and the Abu Nidal Group. President Assad of Syria was reported to have failed to respond to an invitation to attend the session.

Resolutions passed at the conference included rejections of Resolution 242, of the Reagan and Camp David plans and of "the interplay of roles" (a reference to Jordanian-Palestinian joint negotiating teams). The session supported the convening of an international conference "with full powers" to be attended by "the permanent members of the UN Security Council and the parties to the conflict in the region, including the PLO on an equal footing with the other parties". It stressed the need to "defend the camps" in Lebanon and "emphasized the importance of pursuing the alliance with the heroic Lebanese national movement under Brother Walid Jumblatt (the Druse leader) and the other national and Islamic (i.e. *Hezbollah*) leaders and forces "with whom the PLO had co-operated in Lebanon". It declared its support for Iraq in the war with Iran. A generally conciliatory resolution on Jordan emphasized "the special and distinctive relationship" between Jordanians and Palestinians, but stressed that the PLO should be regarded as the "sole, legitimate representative" of the Palestinians on the West Bank. A resolution which criticized Egypt (albeit in somewhat obscure, diplomatic terms) provoked an Egyptian response involving the closing of all PLO offices and institutions in the country.

In protest at the PLO's willingness to enter into peace discussions within the international conference framework, *Hezbollah* subsequently severed its alliance with Palestinian guerrillas in Lebanon.

Main PLO Factions

Abu Nidal Group (Revolutionary Council of *Fatah*)

Leadership. Sabri Khalil al-Banna—code-named Abu Nidal (l.)

This militant faction, which broke away from *Al-Fatah* in 1973 was founded by Banna, a *Fatah* member who had been appointed PLO delegate to Iraq in 1970. His first independent action—the seizure by five guerrillas of the Saudi embassy in Paris—was carried out under the title of *Al-Iqab* (see separate entry). The Group was subsequently based in Iraq and was supported by that country's government, although in the late 1970s it appeared to come under the influence of Syria.

The Group was held responsible for the killing of the secretary-general of the Afro-Asian People's Organization (a former Egyptian minister) in Nicosia (Cyprus) on Feb. 18, 1975—an assassination which was strongly condemned by the PLO's executive committee. There followed a gun battle between Egyptian commandos sent to Cyprus and Cypriot forces (the latter being supported by Palestinians, according to Egypt), and the Egyptian government decided on Feb. 27 to revoke all special privileges granted to Palestinians in Egypt (estimated at between 39,000 and 50,000).

The Abu Nidal Group has also been held responsible for a series of attacks on, and assassinations of, "moderate" PLO representatives—such internecine conflict also involving Iraqi diplomats abroad, several of whom were attacked in various capitals in the mid-1970s in what the Iraqi regime regarded as retaliatory action by the PLO leadership. Because of his association with attacks on "moderate" Palestinian leaders, Abu Nidal was in 1974 condemned to death by the PLO. The Group has stated that it regards Arafat and other PLO leaders as "traitors" who are prepared to deal with "Zionists". Up to July 23, 1982, the Group was responsible for killing nine PLO officials. Two self-confessed followers of Abu Nidal murdered the PLO representative in Paris on Aug. 3, 1978—although responsibility was also claimed by the "Rejectionist Front of Stateless Palestinians". Abu Nidal was also believed to be behind the Black June militant Palestinian movement which appeared in late 1976.

After some years of apparent inactivity, the Abu Nidal Group re-emerged in the early 1980s and was believed to have carried out—through a grouping identifying itself as *Al-Asifa*—an attempt on the life of the Israeli Ambassador in London on June 3, 1982. Although this attack was subsequently portrayed as the work of the Lebanese-based Revolutionary Organization of Socialist Moslems (ROSM), many commentators suggested that the ROSM (which took part in subsequent attacks on British interests—see entry under Lebanon) was merely a front for the Abu Nidal Group.

In August 1982, the Group claimed responsibility for the bombing of a Jewish restaurant in Paris. In April the following year, it carried out the assassination of Dr Issam Ali Sartawi, a leading Palestinian moderate who had advocated mutual recognition by the PLO and Israel.

Abu Nidal was reportedly expelled from Baghdad to Damascus in November 1983, but returned to Baghdad in June the following year for treatment for a heart complaint, at which time it was reported that his readmission to Iraq was on condition that he curtailed the activities of the Group. In November 1984, he was widely but erroneously reported to have died of a heart attack. Some reports suggested that his Group was responsible for the hijacking of an Egyptian airliner in November 1985, claimed by "Egypt's Revolution" (see Egypt section).

At the end of December 1985 guerrillas apparently attached to the Revolutionary Council of *Fatah* carried out particularly brutal attacks at Rome and Vienna airports, resulting in the deaths of many civilians as well as most of the guerrillas. Commentators noted that both Italy and Austria had maintained generally good relations with the PLO. Abu Nidal himself admitted responsibility for the attack, which he described as "absolutely legitimate" in an interview in January 1986. A warrant for his arrest was subsequently issued by the Rome public prosecutor. The guerrillas who staged the Rome attack carried statements which read: "As you have violated our land, our honour and our people, so we in turn shall violate all that is yours, including your children. Our tears shed shall be transformed into your shed blood." The statement was signed by the Palestinian Martyrs. Speculation that Libya provided a base for the Abu Nidal Group and afforded it material support led to the imposition of US sanctions. After initially applauding the operation, the Libyan authorities joined in the almost universal condemnation which the attack received from the PLO and the Arab world in general. In an interview after the attack, the PFLP-GC commander, Ahmed Jabril, claimed that the Abu Nidal Group received considerable support from Iran, adding that Abu Nidal himself spent much of his time there. Jabril also claimed that the Group received assistance "from revolutionary organizations" around the world and from some conservative Arab states.

The group's "Che Guevara Brigade" asserted responsibility for the assassination of Zafer al Masri, the recently appointed Mayor of Nablus on the Israeli-occupied West Bank, in March 1986.

According to PLO sources, representatives of the Revolutionary Council of *Fatah* attended discussions held between a number of mainstream PLO groups prior to the 18th session of the PNC in April 1987. The representatives reportedly endorsed an agreement to restrict operations to Israeli-controlled territories. The sources added that Abu Nidal himself had contemplated attending the session, but had decided against this. In May 1987, it was reported that Abu Nidal Group supporters in southern Lebanon were co-operating with local *Fatah* units.

It was further reported in early June 1987 that Syria had closed the group's offices and forced many of its followers to leave the country.

Arab Liberation Front (ALF)

Leadership. Abdel Rahim Ahmad (l.)

The ALF was established in April 1969 by the Baathist government of Iraq as the sole Palestinian guerrilla group to be permitted in that country (as a counterweight to the Syrian-backed *Al-Saiqa*). With its headquarters being in Lebanon (where it was backed by the pro-Iraqi faction of the Lebanese *Baath* party), the ALF was in 1978 and 1980 involved in raids against targets in Israel and in the latter year also in clashes with (Shi'ite Moslem) *Amal* forces and with Israeli troops. The ALF's then leader, Dr Abdel Wahab Kayyale, was assassinated in Beirut in December 1981.

The pro-Iraqi ALF is a member of the "rejection front" within the PLO. Militant offshoots of the Front have been involved in terrorist actions in Western Europe, notably the attack on Orly airport (Paris) in January 1975.

The ALF stayed out of the internecine PLO disputes which arose following the rebellion within *Al-Fatah*. In October 1986, it took part in the Cairo meetings of five leading PLO groups which agreed to "promote national unity" prior to convening the PNC session. It also played an active part in the crucial reconciliation discussions which preceded the session.

Democratic Front for the Liberation of Palestine (DFLP)

Leadership. Nayef Hawatmeh (sec.-gen.)

The Popular Democratic Front for the Liberation of Palestine (as the DFLP was originally known) seceded from the Popular Front for the Liberation of Palestine (PFLP—see separate entry) in February 1969 on the grounds that the PFLP had developed bourgeois tendencies. Hawatmeh, a Christian Arab, is a Marxist who has close links with the Soviet bloc countries. In accordance with its policy of carrying out increased passive and active resistance to Israeli rule in the occupied territories, it has mounted raids into these territories from Lebanese and Jordanian territory, in particular in 1974. In that year Hawatmeh stated (on May 16) that a PDFLP action (which resulted in the death of 20 Israeli children and injury to over 70 others at Maalot, northern Israel) had been a deliberate attempt to sabotage a United States peace mission in the Middle East. This action was followed by massive Israeli attacks on Palestinian camps in Lebanon, causing large numbers of casualties.

In 1978 the PDFLP was reported to be among those guerrilla groups which had set up cells in the West Bank territory, and in 1979 it claimed responsibility for another attack on Maalot. At the same time, it sought to develop relations with left-wing Israeli groups prepared to recognize the claim of the Palestinians to basic political rights. Since the early 1980s the designation "Popular" has been dropped from the Front's official title.

The DFLP is a Marxist-Leninist movement standing for the establishment of a binational state of Palestine for both Jews and Arabs. As a member of the PLO it formed, with *Al-Fatah* and *Al-Saiqa*, the majority "moderate" wing of that organization during the 1970s, in part because of close personal relations between Hawatmeh and the PLO leader, Yassir Arafat. However, the setbacks suffered by the Palestinian movement in Lebanon during 1982 and Arafat's policy of rapprochement with Jordan contributed to the DFLP's gravitation into the "rejectionist" camp led by the PFLP. In late 1982 and early 1983 the DFLP associated itself in particular with condemnations by the militant PLO factions of the new US peace plan announced by President Reagan on Sept. 1, 1982, envisaging the creation of a self-governing Palestinian entity in the West Bank and Gaza Strip which would be linked to Jordan.

Despite this stance, the DFLP played a leading role in efforts to restore the unity of the PLO in the wake of the split within *Al-Fatah* in mid-1983. In June of that year, it merged with the PFLP, "to enhance the unity of the PLO". The merger had no practical effects, however, and the two groups continued to function as separate entities. The DFLP subsequently joined the "moderate" Democratic Alliance, which continued to play a mediating role between the *Fatah* loyalists and the hard-line factions grouped in the National Alliance. It played a major part in discussions leading to the convening of the 18th PNC in April 1987.

The DFLP claimed responsibility for two guerrilla attacks staged in Jerusalem in February and April 1984, which resulted in a number of civilian deaths.

Al-Fatah (*Tahir al-Hatani al Falastani*—Movement for the National Liberation of Palestine)

Leadership. Mohammed Abed Arouf (Yassir) Arafat—code-named Abu Ammar (l.); Salah Khalaf—code-named Abu Iyad (deputy l.)

Al-Fatah (which is a reversed acronym of the full Arabic title of the organization as given above) was formed in the late 1950s by Palestinian students, including Yassir Arafat, at foreign universities. The Arabic word *Fatah* can be translated as "victory". Having its origins in the Moslem Brotherhood (of which Arafat himself became a member while studying engineering at Cairo University), *Al-Fatah* was intended from the outset to be a Palestinian national movement not tied to or influenced by any Arab government.

Arafat had his first base in the Gaza Strip, where he decided to maintain a Palestinian force outside President Nasser's direct control (Gaza then being under Egyptian administration). After Algeria had achieved its independence in 1962 *Al-Fatah* established training camps in that country (and also in Kuwait), but with limited success. In 1964 *Al-Fatah* was allowed to establish itself in Syria, which supplied it with training facilities and enabled it to form storm troops known as *Kuwat al-Asifa* which, operating from Jordan, carried out its first raids into Israel in January 1965. According to Israeli sources there were 31 *Al-Fatah* raids during 1965—27 from Jordan and four from Lebanon. The first Israeli reprisal took place on May 27 of that year against *Al-Fatah* staging camps in Jordan.

Following the access to power of an extreme left-wing government in Syria in 1966, *Al-Fatah* came under Syrian control, and it published its own newspaper (*Saut al-Asifa* or *Voice of the Storm*) in Damascus. From the end of 1966 its incursions into Israel increased greatly and led to Israeli reprisals against

Syria. when the June 1967 Arab-Israeli war broke out, *Al-Fatah*'s fighting strength was about 500 men, but most of its forces trained in Algeria arrived too late to take part in the fighting. After the war Arafat and the Syrian Chief of Staff worked out plans for subversive warfare inside Israel, but by November 1967 most of *Al-Fatah*'s forces on the Israeli-occupied West Bank had been killed, captured or repulsed.

In response to *Al-Fatah* incursions from Jordan, Israeli forces attempted in March 1968 to attack an *Al-Fatah* base at Karameh (in Jordan) but succeeded only partly in the face of fierce resistance by Palestinian guerrillas backed by Jordanian forces. *Al-Fatah* thereupon moved its headquarters from Damascus to Amman, where it greatly expanded its strength, accepting also former members of the Moslem Brotherhood (as a result of which it was regarded with suspicion by President Nasser of Egypt and the Baathist government in Syria).

Arafat had earlier begun moves to unify the diverse Palestinian guerrilla organizations. At a meeting convened by him in Cairo on Jan. 20, 1968, in which the Palestine Liberation Organization (PLO) did not take part, the organizations represented agreed that their objective was to regain by force of arms the whole of Palestine. At a meeting of the Palestine National Council (PNC)—the Palestinian "parliament-in-exile"—held in Cairo on Feb. 1-5, 1969, and attended by representatives of most of the guerrilla organizations and of the PLO, *Al-Fatah* gained virtual control of the PLO by obtaining four seats on its 11-member executive committee, of which Arafat himself was elected chairman. In 1969 President Nasser allowed *Al-Fatah* to use a Cairo radio station for broadcasts by the "Voice of *Fatah*" *(Saut al-Fatah)*.

Of *Al-Fatah*'s guerrilla members *(fedayeen)*, then numbering between 20,000 and 25,000, some 10,000 were located in bases and staging camps in Jordan, over which King Hussein gradually lost control. In November 1968 Arafat had been the principal negotiator of an agreement with King Hussein, under which Palestinian guerrillas in Jordan had to carry identity cards, conform to certain rules in their operations against Israel and not wear uniforms or carry arms in the towns—but they retained their weapons and were free to make their own decisions. This agreement was followed by increased *Al-Fatah* guerrilla activities which led to Israeli attacks on Iraq and Jordan.

The Israelis estimated that there were in 1969 some 7,500 trained Palestinian guerrilla fighters along their borders with Jordan, Syria and Lebanon. However, the guerrillas did not succeed in their objective of causing the Arab population in the occupied territories to rise against Israeli rule, nor had the Arab states any intention of allowing the *fedayeen* to build up strong conventional forces on their territory which would have attracted Israeli reprisals and constituted an internal danger to themselves.

During 1969 *Al-Fatah* (and also the Syrian-backed *Al-Saiqa*) established a strong base in southern Lebanon, where the Lebanese army had difficulty in containing them within the few square miles which they were originally allocated. Their raids into Israel led to Israeli reprisal action against Lebanese territory. After armed clashes between Lebanese army units and Palestinian guerrillas, a ceasefire was signed in Cairo on Nov. 2, 1969, when the "Cairo agreement" was concluded, under which a Higher Committee for Lebanese Affairs was set up by both Lebanese and guerrillas (who had found no mass support in Lebanon). The guerrillas, however, continued their military operations until early in 1970, when a 10,000-strong Christian militia in southern Lebanon gained the upper hand over them. Israeli forces made a strong attack against guerrillas in Lebanon on May 12, 1970.

In Jordan a conflict arose in 1970 between the Palestinian guerrillas and the government, which on Feb. 10 issued decrees forbidding the carrying of weapons in public in Amman and other towns and villages, the storage of arms and ammunition and activities of political parties. When the Palestinians defied these decrees, the King suspended them and serious hostilities developed between the guerrillas and the Jordanian armed forces, interspersed with periods of ceasefire. King Hussein announced on Aug. 29 (after he had talks with President Nasser) that he was accepting a US peace initiative, and he warned the Palestinian guerrillas that his army was exercising its absolute right to military movement throughout the country. This announcement was followed by further fighting between Palestinians and Jordanian forces in and around Amman (the Jordanian capital) and the hijacking of several airliners by the Popular Front for the Liberation of Palestine (PFLP), which also had a guerrilla presence in Jordan. On Sept. 16 King Hussein placed Jordan under military rule, whereupon the guerrillas appointed Arafat as "general commander of all the armed forces of the revolution". They also declared a general strike and demanded the establishment of a national government in Jordan.

After Arafat had rejected an order by the Jordanian military governor that the guerrillas should surrender their weapons and also an ultimatum ordering them to leave Amman, the Jordanian army began to eject them forcibly in the course of what the Palestinians came to call the "Black September" of 1970. This operation was completed within 10 days, after the guerrillas had failed to obtain any support from other Arab states (although Syrian forces gave them limited support in northern Jordan until they were finally expelled from Jordan by Sept. 23). The fighting was ended by an agreement concluded in Cairo on Sept. 27, 1970, by King Hussein, Arafat and Arab heads of state and providing that both Jordanian troops and guerrillas would be withdrawn from population centres; that Jordan would return to civilian rule; and that a ceasefire would be supervised by an Arab truce commission. On Oct. 13, 1970, the Cairo agreement was enlarged by a further agreement signed in Amman by King Hussein and Arafat, stipulating that the guerrillas' camps should be sited along the Israeli border and not around Jordan's main population centres (as had been demanded by Arafat), with the King abandoning his demand for control of the guerrillas' militia. Jordan returned to civilian government on Oct. 16.

The Jordanian government led by Wasfi Tell, which took office on Oct. 28, 1970, was, however, intent upon a complete removal of the Palestinian guerrillas from Jordan. On Dec. 10 Wasfi Tell and Arafat signed an agreement providing that the militias of both the Palestinians and of Jordan should hand in their weapons, and by January 1971 the Jordanian army had cleared the Palestinians from all areas adjoining Israel. The result of these developments was that many Palestinian guerrillas took refuge in Syria, where President Hafez Assad assumed presidential powers on Feb. 22 and promised support for their armed struggle against Israel.

In April 1971 the guerrillas once again tried to fight back against the Jordanian army, and *Al-Fatah* subsequently openly called for the overthrow of King Hussein, whereupon Wasfi Tell accused it on June 2 of plotting to set up a breakaway state in Jordan. On July 13 the Jordanian army moved in force against the Palestinians, and on the next day Arafat declared war on the Jordanian government. The latter thereupon declared, on July 16, all previous agreements to be null and void. Many guerrillas crossed into Israel and gave themselves up, and by July 20 Jordan was cleared of hostile Palestinians.

Arab heads of state meeting in Tripoli (Libya) on July 30, 1971, condemned King Hussein but took no action against him, except that Libya and Syria broke off diplomatic relations with Jordan. During the whole of 1971 about 9,000 Palestinian guerrillas escaped from Jordan, mainly to Syria, where the government kept them under tight control, with the result that many moved to Lebanon, whose army confined them to a restricted area in the south-eastern Arqoub region on the slopes of Mount Hermon, which became known as "Fatahland". By 1972 there were some 4,000 guerrillas in this area, from which they conducted raids into Israel which were usually followed by Israeli counter-action.

Mgr Hilarion Capucci, the Greek Catholic Archbishop of Jerusalem, was on Dec. 9, 1974, sentenced to 12 years' imprisonment by an Israeli court for smuggling arms and explosives into Israel on behalf of *Al-Fatah*. His release was repeatedly called for by Palestinian guerrillas carrying out hijacking and other operations, and he was eventually released in November 1977 upon a request by the Vatican.

The first attack on Israel from the sea was launched by eight *Al-Fatah* guerrillas on Tel Aviv on March 5-6, 1975, when altogether 18 persons were killed and one of the guerrillas was captured alive. Another group of 11 *Al-Fatah* members, wishing to demonstrate that there would be no peace settlement without the Palestinians, invaded Israel from the sea on March 11, 1978, and killed 34 Israelis and a US citizen and injured over 70 Israelis before nine of them were killed and the two others captured. According to Israeli officials the raid had been organized by Khalil al-Wazir (Abu Jihad), the head of *Al-Fatah*'s military wing, whom they considered also responsible for the (Black September) massacre at the 1972 Olympic Games in Munich.

The Israeli Prime Minister (Menahem Begin) said on March 13, 1978, that "dozens of training courses" had been conducted for *Al-Fatah* and other PLO members in the Soviet Union and other East European countries, and he called on West European governments to close PLO offices in their countries. On March 14-15, 1978, Israel launched a major military intervention in Lebanon designed to ensure that Palestinian guerrillas would no longer strike at Israel; however, no lasting solution was achieved to Israel's security problem. (For subsequent developments leading to the Israeli invasion of Lebanon in June 1982, see under Palestine Liberation Organization above.)

Since Yassir Arafat became leader of the PLO in 1969, *Al-Fatah* has been the leading "moderate" Palestinian faction, and by virtue of its status as by far the largest guerrilla movement has generally been able to exercise a controlling influence over the PLO's policy line. Describing itself as an "Arab nationalist organization", *Al-Fatah* encompasses a broad political spectrum within its membership and has accordingly sought to transcend dissension with Palestinian ranks over ideological orientation. The movement has informed the United Nations that its objectives are (i) to liberate the whole of Palestine from "foreign occupation and aggression" and (ii) to form an independent, democratic, sovereign Palestinian state where all legitimate and legal inhabitants would share equal rights, irrespective of religion or language (but with Jews being limited to those living in Palestine since before 1917 and their offspring).

The *Al-Fatah* leadership has consistently condemned Palestinian military operations directed against civilians, particularly those mounted outside the Middle East theatre and involving innocent neutrals. It has also endeavoured, in the interests of good relations with all Arab states, not to get involved in the internal political disputes of Arab League members. For example, whereas the radical Palestinian factions fought on the Moslem leftist side throughout the 1975-76 civil war in Lebanon, *Al-Fatah* guerrillas refrained from active involvement in the conflict in its early stages, and Arafat himself sought to play a mediatory role; not until the Syrians became heavily involved from mid-1976 on the side of the Lebanese Christians did *Al-Fatah* guerrillas enter the hostilities, and then principally in defence of Palestinian refugee camps.

Following the trauma of the PLO's enforced evacuation from Beirut in August 1982, support for *Al-Fatah*'s policy line within the PLO appeared to diminish. Two factions previously belonging to the "moderate" PLO wing, *Al-Saiqa* and the Democratic Front for the Liberation of Palestine, increasingly associated themselves with the "rejectionist" camp led by the PFLP, particularly in opposition to President Reagan's new peace plan of Sept. 1, 1982, envisaging the creation of a self-governing Palestinian political entity linked to Jordan—an option which Arafat himself was ready to explore with King Hussein. Nevertheless, Arafat and *Al-Fatah* retained their dominance of the PLO at the session of the Palestine National Council held in Algiers in February 1983, when the "rejectionists" failed to commit the PLO to total opposition to the Reagan plan.

From mid-1983 onwards, *Al-Fatah* was split between the "rebel" *Fatah* Revolutionary Council and those remaining loyal to the Arafat leadership. The split had implications for the whole of the PLO, and as such is covered in detail under the PLO umbrella heading.

Among guerrilla actions staged by loyalist *Fatah* members during 1983-86 was the hijacking of an

Israeli civilian bus in early 1984, which culminated in two of the guerrillas responsible being killed following capture, and a grenade attack on Israeli soldiers at the Wailing Wall in east Jerusalem in October 1986. *Fatah* members also staged unsuccessful seaborne attacks on Israel, and sporadically fired katyusha rockets into northern Israel from the border areas of Lebanon.

In a prisoner exchange carried out in November 1983, a total of 4,500 Lebanese and Palestinians were released from detention in Israel in return for the freeing of six Israeli soldiers held by *Al-Fatah* in Lebanon.

Fatah Revolutionary Council ("Fatah rebels")

Leadership. Col. Saed (Abu) Musa; Col. Khaled al (Abu) Amlah

The *Fatah* Revolutionary Council arose out of the rebellion against the authority of Yassir Arafat launched by Abu Musa, Abu Amlah (both former Jordanian army officers who had defected during the Jordanian-PLO fighting) and Nimr al (Abu) Saleh in Lebanon in May 1983. Full details of this rebellion and the subsequent divisions within the PLO are covered under the main PLO heading. A member of the hard-line National Alliance and Palestine National Salvation Front, the Damascus-based *Fatah* Revolutionary Council was essentially composed of *Fatah* guerrillas in areas of eastern and northern Lebanon under Syrian control. It took no part in the reconciliation meetings of the main PLO groups held in late 1986, and it also stayed away from the 18th session of the PNC in April 1987. Abu Musa and Abu Amlah were expelled from *Al-Fatah* in January 1985. Within Lebanon, however, divisions between the "loyalists" and "rebels" were blurred by the *Amal* assaults on the Beirut refugee camps in May-June 1985, during which the (pro-Arafat) guerrillas in the camps received artillery support from *Fatah* Revolutionary Council positions in the hills around the city.

Palestine Liberation Army (PLA)

Leadership. Tariq al-Khodra (chief of staff)

The Damascus-based PLA comprises the regular armed forces of the PLO and as such is theoretically a constituent part of the umbrella organization, rather than an independent guerrilla movement in its own right. In practice, it is currently under strong Syrian influence. In September 1983, Tariq al-Khodra announced that he no longer recognized the authority of Arafat as PLO chairman.

Palestine Liberation Front (PLF)

Leadership. Talat Yacoub (l.); Mahmoud Abul Abbas (rival faction l.)

Formed by Yacoub in 1977 as a breakaway group from the Popular Front for the Liberation of Palestine—General Command (see separate entry), the PLF has received backing from Iraq and Syria. In August 1978 over 180 people died in a bomb explosion which destroyed the PLF's headquarters in Beirut. Four of its members raided Nahariya in northern Israel on April 22, 1979—allegedly to emphasize the Front's rejection of the March 1979 Egyptian-Israeli peace treaty. Israeli forces thereupon attacked Palestinian positions in Lebanon for four days, during which about 60 people were killed, including 27 Palestinians.

The movement subsequently split into three wings, at least two of which were still in existence in 1987. One faction remained loyal to Yacoub in Damascus; a second, pro-Arafat, wing under Mahmoud Abbas (a member of the PLO executive committee) moved to Tunis after the Yacoub faction had declared itself against Arafat and joined the Democratic Alliance in early 1984; a third, minor faction, under Abdel Fatah Ghanem, was reportedly based in Libya.

In September 1985, the Arabic service of Radio Monte Carlo reported that "the PLF" had held its seventh congress in Tunis, and had passed a resolution opposing the Hussein-Arafat accord. The radio also reported a news conference in which Abbas, whom it described as "the new secretary-general of the PLF", promised that the group would "continue the struggle, using all means and methods, for PLO unity and legitimate leadership".

It was fighters belonging to this wing of the PLF who staged the hijacking of the Italian cruise liner *Achille Lauro* in October 1985, during which a US passenger was killed. The hijackers surrendered to the Egyptian authorities after negotiations with, among others, Mahmoud Abbas, whose Tunis-based organization eventually admitted responsibility for the action, which had been strongly condemned by the mainstream PLO as well as by the hard-line Syrian-based factions. (The Yacoub wing was a member of the Democratic Alliance.) The hijackers were subsequently tried and convicted by Italian courts, after an aircraft carrying them from Egypt to Tunis (where they were supposedly to have been tried by the PLO) was intercepted by US fighters and forced to land at a NATO base in Italy. Abbas, who was also on the aircraft, was allowed to go free—a controversial decision which the Italian government was later forced to rescind. After the trial of the hijackers, who had reportedly implicated Abbas in the planning of the operation, an Italian magistrate issued an arrest warrant for Abbas himself.

In an effort to resolve the factional division within the PLF, the 18th PNC session decided that Yacoub "should continue in his work as secretary-general" and that a "unifying conference" would be held to resolve the differences between the two main wings.

Palestine Popular Struggle Front (PPSF)

Leadership. Samir Ghosheh

This Iraqi-backed group was originally formed in Jordan in 1968 by members of the Popular Liberation Forces (the commando wing of the Palestine Liberation Army). Closely identified with *Al-Fatah* in the early 1970s, the small PSF later became part of the "rejection front" within the PLO.

As such, the PPSF participated in the hard-line National Alliance and Palestine National Salvation Front, set up in 1984-85 in the light of the internal PLO divisions following the rebellion within *Al-*

Fatah. It took part in the reconciliation discussions preceding the 18th session of the PNC, however, and by mid-1987 had effectively resumed its place in the PLO mainstream.

Popular Front for the Liberation of Palestine (PFLP)
(*Al-Jabha Al-Shabiyya li Tahrir Falastin*)

Leadership. Dr Georges Habash (l.)

After the 1948 war Dr Habash (a Christian Arab) moved from Palestine to Lebanon, where in 1959 he founded an Arab Nationalist Movement (ANM)—*Haraka al-Quamiyyin al-Arab* or *Haraka*—as a pro-Nasserite organization with Marxist leanings. After the 1967 war Dr Habash moved to Jordan and formed the PFLP as the guerrilla organization of the ANM, with headquarters in Amman. Whereas *Al-Fatah* is a broad-based nationalist movement, the PFLP is a Marxist-Leninist organization which considers itself to be conducting "a class struggle against Zionism and imperialism" and to be "an important cadre of organic rapport between the Palestinians and international revolutions".

From its training camps in Jordan the PFLP began in 1968 to commit acts of violence against targets in Israel and the occupied territories and also against Israeli airliners, in reprisal for which Israel destroyed 13 Arab airliners in Beirut on Dec. 28, 1969. During this early phase probably the best known PFLP activist was Leila Khaled, who was responsible for the hijackings of a US airliner to Syria in August 1969 (by the "Che Guevara commando unit" of the PFLP) and of an Israeli airliner over England in September 1970 (which resulted in her arrest).

Dr Habash was quoted at this time as saying that the PFLP was justified in killing civilians travelling to Israel on the following grounds: "We have no control over the land that was stolen from us and called Israel . . . ; whoever goes to Israel should ask for our permission. . . . Our struggle has barely begun, the worst is yet to come. And it is right for Europe and America to be warned now that there will be no peace until there is justice for Palestine. . . . We will never agree to a peaceful settlement. If the Arab countries think they can gang up and make peace over our heads, they are mistaken. All we have to do is to assert our power in one country and the rest will lose their resolve. . . ."

The PFLP's policy of mounting terrorist attacks on Israeli targets anywhere in the world came under strong criticism from the PLO mainstream led by Yassir Arafat, it being repeatedly stated by the PLO leadership that those responsible for such actions would be brought to trial before Palestinian tribunals. At a congress in Tripoli (Lebanon) in March 1972 the PFLP announced that it had ceased hijacking operations because the practice tended to create a "revolutionary élite" at the expense of enabling the masses to participate in the liberation of Palestine. Nevertheless, the PFLP and its various offshoots continued to be identified with extremist Palestinian terrorist operations.

In furtherance of its aims, the PFLP established close links with revolutionary groups in other countries, notably the Japanese Red Army and the West German Red Army Faction. Both of these organizations were represented at a conference of Palestinian and other groups convened by Dr Habash in northern Lebanon in May 1972, when it was reportedly agreed that each of the movements would participate in terrorist attacks on behalf of any of the others. The first fruit of this agreement was the attack carried out by three young Japanese at Lod airport in Israel on May 30, 1972, in which many civilians and two of the attackers were killed (see entry for United Red Army under Japan).

Together with the Japanese Red Army, the PFLP was responsible for an attack on a Shell refinery and ferry in Singapore on Jan. 31, 1974, by four terrorists who were, however, seized and held in Singapore until Feb. 7, when they were handed over to Japanese Foreign Ministry officials. The latter took them to Kuwait, where a group of PFLP and Japanese Red Army members had seized the Japanese embassy on Feb. 6 and were holding its staff as hostages until their colleagues from Singapore were released. The PLO condemned these operations of the PFLP on Feb. 8 and expressed regret that they had taken place.

During 1973 PFLP members had been involved in arms smuggling operations by the left-wing Turkish People's Liberation Army; the PFLP also claimed responsibility for an attempt on the life of Joseph Edward Sieff (later Lord Sieff), a prominent Zionist and businessman in London, in December 1973. For these and other operations Dr Habash came to be regarded as an "arch-killer" by the Israelis, who made an abortive attempt to capture him in August 1973 by intercepting an Iraqi airliner over Lebanon in the mistaken belief that the PFLP leader was on board.

The PFLP had also, in 1970, recruited the international revolutionary "Carlos Martínez" (Ilich Ramírez Sánchez), a Venezuelan who was subsequently held responsible for numerous acts of terrorism in various countries. These included the temporary seizure—carried out by a self-styled "Arm of the Arab Revolution"—of several ministerial representatives of the Organization of Petroleum Exporting Countries (OPEC) in Vienna in December 1975.

On June 27, 1976, a "Haifa section" of the PFLP (including two West Germans) hijacked an Air France airbus (with 247 passengers and a crew of 12) and diverted it to Entebbe (Uganda). A PFLP spokesman in Beirut, however, denied on June 28 that his organization was in any way involved. The hijackers demanded the release of prisoners held not only in Israel but also in West Germany (i.e. members of the Red Army Faction), Switzerland, France and Kenya (i.e. PFLP members arrested there in January 1976 for planning to attack an Israeli airliner). The hijack operation was ended by the intervention of some 200 airborne Israeli commandos on July 3-4, though not without casualties.

Following their expulsion from Jordan in 1970-71 (along with other Palestinian guerrilla units), PFLP adherents became increasingly active in Lebanon not only in organizing anti-Israeli operations but also in supporting leftist Lebanese Moslem groups in their developing internal conflict with the dominant Maronite Christians. On May 1, 1973, PFLP guerrillas kidnapped two Lebanese army corporals and held them hostage against the release of PFLP members arrested earlier for attempting to plant bombs. This incident led to intense fighting between Palestinians and Lebanese troops and the declaration of a state of siege in Lebanon from May 7 to 23, 1973, and contributed to the steady escalation of Palestinian-Lebanese tensions which were one of the underlying causes of the civil war of 1975-76.

Within the broad Palestinian liberation movement the PFLP has been the leading opponent of any "partial" solution to the Palestinian question (i.e. any settlement which falls short of the establishment of a state based on majority rule in the whole of Palestine). In September 1974 the PFLP representative withdrew from the PLO executive committee, accusing the PLO leadership of having secret contacts with the US Secretary of State (then Dr Henry Kissinger) and preparing for a peace settlement which would guarantee the existence of Israel and increase US influence in the Middle East. Although the PFLP remained a member of the PLO as such through its continued participation in the Palestine National Council, it was thereafter the leading faction within the "rejection front" of militant Palestinian groups who opposed any compromise on the basic aims of the PLO as enshrined in the Palestine National Charter.

The PFLP leaders attempted to mediate between the rival *Fatah* factions in the wake of the rebellion within that organization in mid-1983. In June of that year, it announced a merger with the Democratic Front for the Liberation of Palestine (DFLP) "in an effort to enhance the unity of the PLO". The merger had no practical consequences, however, and while the PFLP joined with the DFLP and two other groups to form the moderate "Democratic Alliance", it subsequently adopted a harder line, and in March 1985 became part of the newly formed "rejectionist" Palestine National Salvation Front (PNSF), based in Damascus. Two months later, however, Habash denounced Syria as being responsible for *Amal*'s offensive against the Beirut refugee camps. While the PFLP continued to criticize the *Fatah* leadership, the siege was to some extent a turning point, and direct contact between the two groups resumed in late 1986. The PFLP resumed its role in the mainstream PLO when its representatives, led by Habash, took part in the 18th PNC session in April 1987, on which occasion Habash told journalists that the PNSF had effectively ceased to exist.

The PFLP, together with the Abu Nidal Group, claimed responsibility for the assassination of Zafer al-Masri, the recently appointed Mayor of Nablus in the Israeli-occupied West Bank, in March 1986. Demonstrators at his funeral chanted slogans denouncing the PFLP, along with President Assad and King Hussein.

Popular Front for the Liberation of Palestine—General Command (PFLP-GC)

Leadership. Ahmed Jabril (l.)

Established in 1968 by dissident members of the Popular Front for the Liberation of Palestine (PFLP), this guerrilla group was subsequently responsible for a series of terrorist acts. These included the blowing-up of a Swiss airliner in February 1970 (when 47 persons were killed), an attack on an Israeli school bus in May 1970 (when 12 children and several adults died) and the killing of 18 Israelis (among them 12 children and five women) at Kiryat Shemona in northern Israel in April 1974.

The PFLP-GC was held responsible for the kidnapping in Beirut on June 29, 1975, of a US colonel, who was released after the US embassy had paid for 10 tons of food and clothing to be distributed among the poor affected by the fighting in Beirut. It also claimed responsibility for an explosion in Jerusalem on July 4, 1975, when 13 people (including four Arabs) were killed and over 70 injured.

In 1977 a pro-Iraqi faction led by Abul Abbas broke away from the (pro-Syrian) PFLP-GC and formed the Palestine Liberation Front. On March 16, 1979, Salem Ahmad Hassan, a self-confessed "soldier" of the PFLP-GC, was sentenced to life imprisonment in London for killing Col. Abdul Razzak al-Nayef (a former Iraqi Prime Minister) on July 9, 1978—the defendant having called him "a traitor" who deserved to die. The PFLP-GC was also reported to have a strong group in Uppsala (Sweden), where some of its members were charged with illegal activities in 1980. Other PFLP-GC members had been killed in a bomb explosion near Tel Aviv on May 23, 1979.

As part of the "rejection front" within the PLO, the PFLP-GC stands for the destruction of Israel and the "liberation" of the whole of Palestine. Together with other militant Palestinian factions, it has therefore strongly opposed all moves towards a "partial" settlement of the Palestinian question. As evidence of this, the group publicly applauded the assassination by the Abu Nidal Group of the moderate PLO adviser, Dr Issam Ali Sartawi, in April 1983.

Soon after the emergence of the split within *Al-Fatah* later the same year, the PFLP-GC sided openly with the rebels and took an active part in the fighting around the Tripoli refugee camps in the second half of 1983. During the battles, Jabril appeared to be acting as effective leader and spokesman of the anti-Arafat factions. This stance provoked some dissent within the PFLP-GC; a group of officers announced in August 1983 that they had formed a "provisional command" opposed to Jabril, and in September armed clashes broke out in the Baddawi camp between the two factions.

The PFLP-GC joined the National Alliance and the Palestine National Salvation Front—PNSF (Syrian-based anti-Arafat groups) and remained firmly opposed to any reconciliation with the mainstream PLO leadership. Jabril was expelled from the PLO at the *Fatah*-dominated 17th session of the PNC held in Jordan in November 1984. The group remained outside the mainstream, even after the reconciliation of all the leading groups at the 18th PNC session in April 1987, which was boycotted by the PFLP-GC.

In May 1985, the PFLP-GC exchanged three Israeli soldiers held since 1982 for 1,155 guerrillas held by Israel (not all of whom were PFLP-GC members; one of those released was Kozo Okamoto, who had led the Japanese United Red Army group which had carried out the massacre at Lod Airport in 1972).

Al-Saiqa (*The Storm*)

Leadership. Issam al-Qadi (l.)

Formed in 1968 by the Syrian Baathist goverment

as a counter-balance to *Al-Fatah*, *Al-Saiqa* was recruited from among Palestinian Baathists in refugee camps and was led by regular Syrian army officers. The movement was originally the military wing of the Vanguards of the Popular War for the Liberation of Palestine. Operations carried out by *Al-Saiqa* have included the action taken on Sept. 23, 1973, by two of its members calling themselves "Eagles of the Palestine Revolution", who had entered Austria from Czechoslovakia and seized two Jews (who had just arrived from the Soviet Union) and an Austrian customs officer; they demanded, in return for the release of these hostages, the closure of an Austrian transit camp for Jews from the Soviet Union wishing to reach Israel. The Austrian Federal Chancellor (Dr Bruno Kreisky) acceded to their demand and was thereupon intensely criticized by Israel, whose Prime Minister (then Golda Meir) called his decision "the greatest encouragement to terrorism throughout the world".

In 1978 *Al-Saiqa* was among the Palestinian groups which set up resistance cells on the Israeli-occupied West Bank, and it also had bases in Lebanon, where it became a major arm of Syrian intervention in the 1975-76 civil war and was temporarily in conflict with other Palestinian groups in that country, notably *Al-Fatah*. On Dec. 23, 1981 four self-confessed members of the "Eagles of the Palestine Revolution" were sentenced to death in Ankara (Turkey) for an attack on the Egyptian embassy in that city in July 1979, when an embassy official and two Turkish policemen lost their lives.

Within the PLO *Al-Saiqa* was during the 1970s generally regarded as part of the "moderate" wing led by *Al-Fatah*; however, following the events in Lebanon during mid-1982 *Al-Saiqa* increasingly associated itself with the "rejectionist" factions led by the Popular Front for the Liberation of Palestine (PFLP) in opposition to any compromise on basic Palestinian demands.

In the wake of the rebellion within *Al-Fatah*, *Al-Saiqa* leaders initially attempted to act as mediators, but subsequently the organization allied itself with the hard-line factions, joining the National Alliance and the Palestine National Salvation Front. Under Syrian influence, it remained hostile to Arafat even after the majority of the hard-line factions had re-established contacts with the mainstream PLO leadership.

Other Palestinian Groups

Apart from the main PLO factions described above, the 1970s and '80s witnessed the proliferation of a complex array of other Palestinian groups and sub-factions—many of them formed as splinter groups of the larger movements. Often identifying themselves in connexion with specific actions, such groups have been denounced by the official PLO leadership when they mounted attacks on civilian targets (especially those outside Palestine). On the other hand, the Israeli authorities have always maintained that the tactical purpose of such groups is to divert responsibility from the PLO itself.

Arab Armed Struggle Organization *(Organisation de la lutte armée arabe)*

This group claimed responsibility for a bomb explosion on a Marseilles-Paris express train on Dec. 31, 1983, when two persons were killed and 20 were injured.

Arab Guerrilla Cells

This hitherto-unknown group claimed responsibility for the Rome and Vienna airports attacks in December 1985, which they claimed declared "the birth of a revolutionary and suicide group". The attacks were widely thought to be the work of the Abu Nidal Group.

Arab Revolutionary Brigades *(Brigades révolutionnaires arabes)*

A group of this name claimed responsibility for killing the second secretary at the Israeli embassy in Paris on April 3, 1982, and for killing the ambassador of the United Arab Emirates, also in Paris, on Feb. 8, 1984.

Black September Group

Leadership. Abu Daoud

This Group, which took its name from the month in which *Al-Fatah*'s forces were defeated by Jordanian troops in 1970, broke away from *Al-Fatah* because it disagreed with the latter's emphasis on the need for political action as a "national liberation movement". The Black September Group belonged to the minority grouping of "avenging" Palestinians, members of which committed individual acts of violence.

It was held responsible for the killing of Wasfi Tell (the Jordanian Prime Minister) in Cairo on Nov. 28, 1971 (in revenge for the killing of its former leader, Abu Ali Iyad, in July 1971). However, Abu Daoud, the group's leader, was said to have stated later that *Al-Fatah* had been responsible for the assassination of Wasfi Tell, which, he said, had been organized by Abu Yussef (Mohammed Yussef Najjar), then a member of the PLO's political department and chairman of the Higher Committee for Palestinian Affairs in Lebanon (who was killed by Israelis raiding Beirut on April 10, 1973).

Other acts of violence attributed to the Black September Group included the hijacking of a Sabena airliner at Lod (Israel) in May 1972; the murder of 11 Israeli athletes at the Olympic Games in Munich on Sept. 5, 1972; the seizure of the Israeli embassy in Bangkok (Thailand) in March 1973; and the murder in Khartoum (Sudan) of the US ambassador and the Belgian chargé d'affaires at the Saudi Arabian embassy on March 1, 1973.

In August 1973 two members of the Group made an attack at Athens airport, killing five people and injuring 55 others; they were sentenced to death in Athens, as confirmed by the Greek Supreme Court on March 9, 1974. Their sentences were, however, commuted to imprisonment after three members of the (Pakistani) Moslem International Guerrillas had on Feb. 2 seized a Greek cargo ship in Karachi and had held the ship's first officer and chief engineer hostage pending the release of the two Black September members. However, after the latter's death sentences had been commuted, the Pakistanis released their hostages and were themselves flown to Libya.

Abu Daoud was among the 1,000 political prisoners released by King Hussein of Jordan under an amnesty in September 1973, most of these prisoners having been held since the 1970-71 Jordanian action against Palestinian guerrillas. His release had been demanded by the *Al-Iqab* guerrillas who seized the Saudi embassy in Paris earlier the same month. *Al-Iqab* was later identified as a cover for the Abu Nidal Group. On March 24, 1973, Abu Daoud was reported to have stated that the Black September organization was actually part of *Al-Fatah* and that its operations in Amman and in Munich had been planned by Salah Khalef, the second-ranking leader of *Al-Fatah*; that Black September received its orders from the *Al-Fatah* leadership; but that he was not certain that Yassir Arafat himself was in control of these orders.

On Jan. 7, 1977, Abu Daoud was arrested in Paris, where he had arrived as a member of a PLO delegation attending the funeral of Mahmoud Saleh, a PLO representative in Paris who had been killed on Jan. 3. However, a French court released Abu Daoud on Jan. 11 after the West German authorities had not immediately made their request for his extradition on charges of his involvement in the attack on the Israeli athletes in Munich in 1972 and as Israel was considered to have no right to ask for his extradition. Abu Daoud said after his arrival in Algiers that he was "a revolutionary Palestinian" but "not a terrorist" and he added that he was innocent of the charges raised against him in West Germany.

Soon after the outbreak of fighting between pro- and anti-Arafat forces in Lebanon in mid-1983, guerrillas described as belonging to Black September and its September Martyrs Group joined in on the side of the *Fatah* rebels from positions in the Bekaa Valley and along the Beirut-Damascus highway.

Black September claimed responsibility for the assassination in June 1985 of Fahd Qawasmeh, a PLO executive committee member and *Fatah* loyalist, who was also a former Mayor of Hebron (on the West Bank), and who had close links with the Jordanian regime.

Force 17

Force 17 is a shadowy organization believed to be the "commando" wing of *Al-Fatah*. Israeli officials held it responsible for the Larnaca (Cyprus) yacht harbour killings of three Israeli tourists in October 1985. Force 17 was said to have transferred its headquarters from Tunis to Amman in January 1986, though it was unclear if it remained in Jordan following Hussein's breach with Arafat the following month.

Al-Iqab (Punishment)

Five members of this group seized the Saudi Arabian embassy in Paris on Sept. 5, 1973, in an attempt to enforce the release of Abu Daoud, the Black September leader then held in prison in Jordan. The five men were subsequently allowed to take five Saudi Arabian diplomats to Kuwait in an aircraft placed at their disposal, but in Kuwait they surrendered to the authorities and their hostages were released. (Abu Daoud was released under a Jordanian amnesty in the same month.) It was subsequently revealed that this was the first operation to be mounted independently by guerrillas working under instructions from Sabri Khalil al-Banna (Abu Nidal—see separate entry for Abu Nidal Group).

Islamic Jihad for the Liberation of Paletine—see entry under Lebanon

Islamic Revolutionary Vanguard

A group of this name claimed responsibility for the attempted assassination of Zaki al-Hallou, an official of the Popular Front for the Liberation of Palestine, in Greece in 1983.

Palestine Revenge Organization

This previously unknown group claimed responsibility for the assassination of Munza Abu Ghazalah, head of *Al-Fatah*'s naval wing, in Athens in October 1986.

Palestinian Arab Revolutionary Committee

This minor faction, based in eastern Lebanon, is described as Libyan-backed. A position occupied by the group came under attack by Israeli aircraft in September 1985.

Palestinian Communist Party (PCP)

Leadership. Bashir al-Barghuti (gen.sec.)

The PCP was established in Beirut in February 1982 to include Communists of the Israeli-occupied West Bank and the Gaza Strip, Palestinian members of the Jordanian Communist Party living outside Jordan, and the members of the Palestinian Communist Organization in Lebanon.

The immediate objective of the PCP is to fight for the withdrawal of Israel from all territories seized in 1967, the creation of an independent Palestine and the return of the Palestinian refugees to their homeland, in conformity with UN decisions. It supports Soviet initiatives on the Middle East conflict and the convocation of an international conference to establish peace in the Middle East.

In early 1984, after the *Fatah* split had increased factional divisions within the PLO, it joined the "moderate" Democratic Alliance and took part in the reconciliation meetings held in Cairo in October 1986. PCP representatives also attended the 18th session of the PNC in Algiers in April 1987, the first occasion on which it was accepted as an official member-group by the PNC.

Panama

Capital: Panama City

Pop. 2,180,000

The Republic of Panama has a 67-member unicameral Legislative Assembly, elected for a 5-year term by universal and compulsory adult suffrage. Under the Constitution an executive President is elected for a 5-year term by a simple majority of the popular vote, failing which the Assembly appoints the President by a simple majority. The President has a Cabinet and is assisted by 2 Vice-Presidents elected by popular vote. Effective power, however, lies with the Panamanian Defence Forces under the command of Gen. Manuel Antonio Noriega Morena. In October 1985, he forced the resignation of President Dr Nicolás Ardito Barletta, whose regime had faced continual internal protests over economic austerity measures, and replaced him with Eric Arturo del Valle, leader of the Republican Party.

In elections of May 6, 1984, the National Democratic Union (UNADE) a coalition of centrist and right-wing parties, won 40 seats in the Legislative Assembly. The Democratic Opposition Alliance (ADO), an electoral alliance mainly comprising four conservative opposition parties, won 27, claiming that the elections had been fraudulent. The Democratic Revolutionary Party (PRD) is the major party in the UNADE and is dominant in the Cabinet. The Labour Party (Pala) provides the second highest number of Cabinet ministers. The National Liberal Party (PLN) and the Republican Party (PR) are two further parties within the UNADE.

The three main components of the ADO are the Christian Democratic Party (PDC), the Liberal Republican and Nationalist Movement (Molirena) and the Authentic Panamenist Party (PPA).

Legal status was withdrawn in mid-November 1984 from seven parties which in the May elections had not won the percentage of votes required by the electoral law for their continued existence—the Panamenist Party (PP) and the Popular Front (Frampo), both members of the UNADE, as well as the Panamanian People's Party (PPP), the Popular Action Party (Papo), the National People's Party (PNP), the Socialist Worker's Party (PST), and the United People's Front (Frepu).

In October 1979, an alleged right-wing plot was uncovered and attributed to the Panamanian National Front. In October 1984, and again in May 1985, there were demonstrations called by the ADO against alleged fraud in the May 1984 elections. Throughout 1985 and 1986, there was increasing social and labour unrest. Widespread demonstrations, strikes and stoppages, organized by the National Council of Organized Workers (CONATO), which represented 19 national unions and some 50 per cent of the nation's workers, protested against the government's continued austerity economic policies, including labour reforms. There were general strikes in July 1985 and March 1986. There have been protests also against alleged violence and intimidation by the Defence Forces, following the abduction and beating of Carlos Ivan Zúñiga, the opposition Popular Action Party's leader, and the murder on Oct. 10, 1985, of Hugo Spadafóra, one of the army's leading critics.

Following two days of anti-government demonstrations and a call by the opposition parties for continued civil disobedience, a national state of emergency was declared on June 11, 1987. Under the government's decree eight articles of the Constitution were suspended, including its guarantees of freedom of expression and assembly, freedom from undue search and seizure, freedom of movement, the inviolability of correspondence and telephone calls, and the right to be informed of the reason for arrest and to consult a lawyer.

Revolutionary Committees of Panama

An unsigned communiqué dated March 27, 1986, and published in the Panama City newspaper *La Prensa* on April 10, 1986, contained a warning that these Committees would "attack US positions in the country" if the United States stepped up its campaign of "blackmail" in Panama and its "attacks on Libya and Nicaragua". Gen. Noriega Morena, the commander of the Panamanian Defence Forces, thereupon declared that the Committees' objective of attacking the Panama Canal was "a tactical excuse to create a climate of uncertainty in the country to justify the application of the doctrine of national security". In the view of *La Prensa* this might lead to the eventual declaration of a state of emergency (which was in fact declared on June 11, 1987).

Papua New Guinea

Capital: Port Moresby

Pop. 3,330,000

Papua New Guinea is an independent state within the Commonwealth, with the British monarch as head of state being represented by a Governor-General. Legislative power is exercised by the House of Assembly of 109 members elected by universal adult suffrage. Executive power is held by a Cabinet headed by a Prime Minister.

Elections held in June 1987 resulted in a victory for the ruling Pangu Pati party.

Following a rapid increase in crimes of violence a temporary state of emergency was proclaimed in Port Moresby on June 17, 1985, when wide powers of search and arrest were given to troops and reservists and marches were prohibited.

Inter-tribal Fighting

Hostility between various tribes of Papua New Guinea has led to serious clashes from time to time.

In further fighting in the Highlands in December 1985 ten tribesmen were killed, and in early 1986 police quelled disturbances caused by some 3,000 tribesmen in the Prime Minister's constituency in the Western Highlands province.

Paraguay

Capital: Asunción

Pop. 3,680,000

The Republic of Paraguay is, under its 1967 Constitution, a "representative democracy" with an executive President elected (and re-eligible) for a five-year term by universal adult suffrage. Since coming to power in a military coup in 1954, President (Gen.) Alfredo Stroessner has been elected for seven successive terms as the candidate of the National Republican Association—Colorado Party, which has been the country's dominant party since 1940. Legislative power is held by a bicameral Congress consisting of a Senate of at least 30 members and a Chamber of Deputies of at least 60 members, both elected for five-year terms by direct adult suffrage. However, the party which gains a majority in parliamentary elections obtains two-thirds of the seats in both Houses of Congress, the remainder of the seats being divided among the minority parties in proportion to their electoral strength.

In elections held on Feb. 6, 1983, some 90 per cent of the votes were, according to official results, cast in favour of President Stroessner and his National Republican Association—Colorado Party, while the remaining votes went to the Radical Liberal Party and Liberal Party (in a 90 per cent poll), all other parties having called for abstention. Unregistered parties include the Christian Democratic Party (PDC), the Authentic Liberal Radical Party (PLRA) and the Popular Colorado Movement (Mopoco)—see entries below—all of which participated in the formation in 1978 of the National Agreement (AN) as a broad alliance of opposition parties, together with the (registered) Febrerista Revolutionary Party (PRF).

Under legislation introduced in 1981, parties were prohibited from urging voters to return blank ballot papers or to abstain as a form of protest; in order to be registered, a party was required to have 10,000 members distributed among at least one-third of the country's electoral districts; the Communist Party and any party with "similar aims" remained banned; and other prohibited parties were those with international links and those which preached "racial, religious or class struggle" or "hatred among Paraguayans".

On April 8, 1987, the state of siege in force since 1947 was allowed to lapse after President Stroessner declared that he no longer needed extraordinary security powers to maintain peace.

While externally the regime's record on human rights has been severely censured by international bodies such as the Inter-American Human Rights Commission, within Paraguay it has encountered increasing opposition from the growing independent trade union and student movements, from a large, broad-based social movement led by hospital workers at the capital's public *Hospital de Clinicas,* as well as from certain elements within the Roman Catholic Church. The growing list of opposition organizations also includes many women's groups, shanty-town organizations and human rights groups, while the media continue to play a key role in voicing the new movement's demands.

Authentic Radical Liberal Party (*Partido Liberal Radical Auténtico*, PLRA)

Leadership. Dr Domingo Laíno (l.); Dr Juan Manuel Benítez Florentín (pres.); Miguel Abdón Saguier (gen. sec.)

This centre-left party broke away from the Unified Liberal Party (PLU) in 1978, its founding members including Dr Laíno (the leader of the Radical Liberal Party, PLR, from Jan. 25, 1974, until 1977—see separate entry), Carlos Alberto González and Miguel Abdón Saguier. The PLRA has been refused legal status despite the fact that it is probably the largest of the liberal factions and is the leading member of National Accord (AN, formed in 1978—see separate entry). The PLRA has maintained a policy of boycotting elections held by the Stroessner regime and calls for democratization, the lifting of the state of siege and respect for human rights.

In June 1978, Dr Domingo Laíno visited the United States where he testified on the human rights situation in Paraguay before the General Assembly of the Organization of American States and recommended that sanctions should be taken against his country. After his return to Asunción he was arrested on July 7 and was charged with subversion and association with left-wing extremists, but was released on Aug. 9, 1978. He was again temporarily arrested in 1979 and in September-October 1980. In March 1981 he was among several AN leaders who visited Brazil to hold talks with Brazilian opposition groups and with exiled leaders of the Popular Colorado Movement (Mopoco—see separate entry). On Dec. 17, 1982, he was deported from Paraguay for what were termed "subversive activities".

From May 1984 to 1987 many PLRA supporters were detained in separate incidents. Dr Laíno made several unsuccessful attempts to return to Paraguay. Abdón Saguier was arrested on Sept. 9, 1985, after assuming sole responsibility for the calling of an unauthorized political meeting raided by the police in Itapuá. On Sept. 13, 1986, Abdón Saguier was again arrested and detained on charges of sedition and inciting violence after he had publicly declared that the people had the right to rebel against tyranny. He was finally released on Feb. 12, 1987.

Dr Laíno was eventually permitted to return to Paraguay on April 25, 1987, after over four years in exile in Buenos Aires (Argentina). In a televised statement broadcast the same day, he stressed the need for non-violent action and dialogue, in order to avoid future confrontation between Paraguayans. In an interview published in the newspaper *Ultima Hora* on May 2, he stated that Paraguayans now had "optimum conditions" to develop a policy through the national dialogue which had been promoted by the Catholic Church.

The PLRA has a trade union affiliate, the Authentic Radical Liberal Workers' Movement (*Movimiento Obrero Liberal Radical Auténtico,* MOLRA) and a youth wing, the *Juventud Liberal Radical Auténtico*.

Christian Democratic Party (*Partido Demócrata Cristiano,* PDC)

Leadership. Luis Alfonso Resck (l. in exile); Alfredo Rojas León (pres.)

Established in May 1960, this party has consistently opposed the Stroessner regime. It boycotted the presidential elections of 1968 (when it demanded the lifting of the state of siege, the release of political prisoners and the return of exiles to Paraguay). In the longer term it seeks the "transformation of the existing political structure into a true democracy" and economic development on the basis of private ownership and free enterprise. In February 1971 the Electoral Commission refused to grant it the status of a political party, and therefore it could not take part in elections. However, it continued to advocate the boycott of elections and, in 1978, joined the National Accord (*Acuerdo Nacional*, AN—see separate entry). In 1981 it denounced the legislation amending the electoral law (see above).

In March 1981 L. A. Resck was among several AN leaders who were detained at the airport and who had their documents confiscated after returning to Paraguay from Brazil where they had contacted members of the Brazilian opposition and exiled members of the Popular Colorado Movement (Mopoco—see separate entry). On June 24, 1981, L. A. Resck was arrested and deported to Argentina three days later after having publicly endorsed a statement made by the Venezuelan Senate (on May 4) condemning the Stroessner regime.

The PDC was among the AN constituent parties to organize an unprecedented mass opposition rally, on June 21, 1987, attended by some 30,000 people.

The party is organized in districts and regions and has separate sections for youth, labour, farmers and women; it has a national committee appointed by its highest authority, the national convention.

The PDC is affiliated to the Christian Democratic International and the Christian Democratic Organization of America.

Inter-Trade Union Movement of Paraguayan Workers (*Movimiento Intersindical de Trabajadores de Paraguay,* MIT-P)

The MIT-P (or MIT) was established on May 1, 1985, to unite trade union opposition to the regime and as an alternative to the government-controlled Paraguayan Confederation of Workers (*Confedera-*

ción Paraguaya de Trabajadores, CPT) described by the International Confederation of Free Trade Unions (ICFTU) in April 1986 as the "government-controlled completely discredited official labour federation". The MIT brought together the country's main independent unions which had developed significantly during the 1980s. Throughout 1985-86 the MIT, composed of 4,000 members in seven unions, demanded improved working conditions and an increase in the minimum wage, announcing, in mid-1985, a "battle-path for democracy" which included publishing a monthly newsletter, obtaining radio time and improving worker support networks. It staged a demonstration on May 1, 1986, which was broken up by the police with several hundred arrests.

In July 1985 the International Labour Organization transferred its recognition from the official CPT to the MIT.

National Accord (*Acuerdo Nacional,* AN)

Leadership. Waldino Ramón Llovera (pres.)

The AN, formed in 1978, is an opposition coalition not recognized as a political party and consisting of the Febrerista Revolutionary Party (*Partido Revolucionario Febrerista*, PRF) and several parties which are themselved not recognized—the Christian Democratic Party (PDC), the Popular Colorado Movement (Mopoco) and the Authentic Radical Liberal Party (PLRA)—see separate entries. The AN has called for the boycott of elections called by the Stroessner regime.

In June 1980, the then president of the AN, Carlos Caballero Gatti (who was also president of the PRF), organized a meeting in Paris of all European committees for solidarity with Paraguay, which called for intensified steps to enable about 1,000,000 Paraguayan exiles to return to their country. On June 11, 1980, the government prohibited a planned meeting of the Socialist International in Asunción and accused Caballero Gatti of "connivance with international communism".

In its programme for "National Convergence" launched on Aug. 14, 1984, the AN called for the lifting of the state of siege, the release of all political prisoners, the defence of human rights, the abolition of repressive laws, the establishment of a new electoral law and a law on political parties, freedom of expression and the ending of government control over the media, the defence of national sovereignty, an independent judiciary and a fairer distribution of wealth. It has been represented at the very few political rallies to have been permitted in recent years, including one on May 14, 1985, attended by some 5,000 people. The failure of an attempt by the Roman Catholic Church to arrange conciliation talks between the opposition and the government of Gen. Stroessner was followed, on Feb. 14, 1986, by a demonstration organized by the AN in Asunción and attended by an estimated 15,000 supporters. Llovera, the president of the AN, had stated on Feb. 7, 1986, that the Church-sponsored talks were the last resort for a peaceful solution between the opposition and the government.

On June 21, 1987, the AN organized an unprecedented rally attended by 30,000 people in Coronel Oviedo, Caaguazú, to win support for a proposal for the creation of a national democratic front "to struggle for freedom and abolish the shameful dictatorship". Addressing the participants, the PLRA leader, Dr Domingo Laíno, stated that "after 33 years of violating and oppressing the great and noble Paraguayan nation" the dictatorship was now more weak and isolated than ever.

The AN is informally supported by an international alliance of political exiles, the Paraguayan Accord in Exile (APE—see separate entry).

National Republican Association—Colorado Party in Exile (*Asociación Nacional Republicana—Partido Colorado en el Exilio, ANR-PC en el Exilio*)

This movement was formed in exile in 1973 by a minority faction of the Popular Colorado Movement (Mopoco—see separate entry), but claims to have a following in Paraguay among the membership of the mainstream Colorado Party.

Paraguayan Accord in Exile (*Acuerdo Paraguayo en el Exilio*, APE)

Leadership. Arturo Acosta Mena (gen. sec.)

The APE was formed in 1978 at a meeting in Amsterdam (Netherlands) as a coalition of exiled members of Paraguayan opposition groupings in Latin America, North America and Europe. Although there is no formal organization link, its broad front strategy and its policies are in agreement with the line pursued inside Paraguay by the National Accord, also formed in 1978 (see separate entry).

Paraguayan Communist Party (Creydt faction) (*Partido Comunista Paraguayo,* PCP)

Leadership. Oscar Creydt (l.)

This party, which like the PCP (Maidana faction—see separate entry), claims to be the historic representative of the Paraguayan communist movement, was formed after the abortive guerrilla warfare of the early 1960s. When the communist guerrillas were finally defeated in 1965 the then general secretary of the sole Paraguayan Communist Party, Oscar Creydt, was expelled by the pro-Soviet majority faction; he took about 50 members with him and founded an alternative party aligned with Beijing (China). The PCP combines Marxist-Leninist theory with an intense patriotism; it advocates revolutionary change and looks in particular to the peasantry to take up arms against the regime.

According to the chief of Paraguay's investigative police on March 15, 1982, the PCP, which he claimed had obtained funds from China, had been "totally disrupted" following the recent arrest of 31 alleged members. The prisoners, who were displayed to the Paraguayan press by the police authorities, were mostly peasant activists but there was no substantial evidence of their involvement with the party. Antonio González Arce, one of those arrested, claimed that although this faction of the PCP had relations with the

People's Republic of China it remained independent. He was released early in 1986.

Paraguayan Communist Party (Maidana faction) (*Partido Comunista Paraguayo*, PCP)

A small group of communists existed in Paraguay in the early 1920s but the party was not formally constituted until Feb. 19, 1929. The PCP held its first congress in 1934, when it had about 500 active members. It opposed the Chaco War against Bolivia and consequently its leaders, including Obdulio Barthe and Oscar Creydt, were imprisoned. The party supported the Febrerista coup of 1936 and was legalized by the Franco government, only to be outlawed again after 15 days, together with all other political parties. In June 1946 it was again legalized; exiled members returned and the party claimed 10,000 members. After a change of regime in January 1947 it was banned yet again and its leaders were imprisoned. It took part in an abortive rebellion of August 1947, following which many communists were arrested.

The exiled PCP leadership subsequently concentrated on organizing in urban areas. It was involved in the general strike of August 1958, when three prominent members, Julio Rojas, Dr Maidana (then the party's first secretary) and Alfredo Alcorta (the head of the party's foreign department), were arrested; they were to spend the following 19 years in prison. The defeat of the strike led the party to adopt a military strategy in 1959. Small guerrilla columns operated in Paraguay from 1960, but suffered infiltration and severe losses until their final defeat in 1965.

Discontent over the direction of the guerrilla campaign by the general secretary, Oscar Creydt, led to the formation of the *Partido Comunista Leninista Paraguayo* in 1963, under the leadership of O. Barthe. In 1965 this group became the *Comité para la Defensa y Reorganización del PCP*; it received the recognition of the Soviet Communist Party and in 1967 announced the reconstitution of the party and the expulsion of Creydt, whose supporters, also claiming the name PCP, followed a pro-Chinese line—see separate entry for PCP (Creydt faction).

The "Soviet line" PCP continued to operate clandestinely in Paraguay and in 1971 it approved a Marxist-Leninist programme. It has advocated a democratic broad front strategy combined with international pressure on the Stroessner regime to produce improvements in human rights and the removal of repressive legislation.

In November 1975 some party organizations were discovered by the police and by mid-January 1976 about 70 people had been arrested; it was reported that several—including the general secretary, Miguel Angel Soler, and two central committee members had died under torture. Dr Maidana was reported to have been released from prison on Feb. 3, 1977, and he subsequently became the party's general secretary; however, he and Emilio Roa, a member of the PCP's central committee, were later reported to have been kidnapped in Buenos Aires on Aug. 27, 1980 (allegedly in a joint Argentinian-Paraguayan police operation) and they have since disappeared without trace. It was reported that they were handed over to Paraguay but the authorities have never confirmed this.

Paraguayan Confederation of Workers in Exile (*Confederación Paraguaya de Trabajadores en el Exilio*, CPT-E)

This organization represents trade unionists exiled following a general strike in 1958 (the last to be held in Paraguay). It supports the development of the independent unions within Paraguay and is in sympathy with the policies of the National Accord formed in 1978 (see separate entry).

Paraguayan Peasant Movement (*Movimiento Campesino Paraguayo*, MCP)

This umbrella group, which includes the Permanent Assembly of Landless Peasants, the Commission of Relatives of the Disappeared and Murdered Persons, the Peasant Women's Co-ordinating Committee and the Peasant Youth Commission, was reportedly active in 1985-86. Sindulfo Coronel, an active campaigner for peasant rights in the organization, was arrested, along with his nephew, Hilarion Coronel, at the end of February 1986.

Peasant Agrarian Leagues (*Ligas Agrarias Campesinas*)

This land rights movement, founded in the early 1960s, attracted considerable support among landless peasants, and organized production and distribution co-operatives serving about 20,000 peasants by 1969. Claiming that the Leagues were communist-inspired, the regime launched a wave of repression in rural areas in the mid-1970s; leaders of the movement were killed, arrested or forced into exile. After some years of clandestine activity, the Leagues re-emerged in 1980 as a result of increasing land conflicts in the eastern region between, on the one hand, Paraguayan peasants, and, on the other, Brazilian settlers and others with legal title to farmlands.

Permanent Assembly of Social Organization

Leadership. Dr Carlos Filizzola

The Permanent Assembly of Social Organization was in 1986 the most highly mobilized opposition organization in Paraguay and its leader, Dr Filizzola (the president of the National Association of Doctors, Nurses and Students at the Hospital de Clínicas in Asunción), was reportedly the most popular and militant union leader in the country. Throughout 1986 medical workers at the Hospital de Clínicas, Asunción's main teaching hospital and the only health care centre that services the poor, became the focal point of resistance to the regime, supported by a vast new social movement representing key sectors of the population. Police violently broke up a number of work stoppages and peaceful demonstrations staged by employees at the hospital to protest against low wages and the lack of medical resources. On May 13, 1986, Paraguayan police began a blockade of the University Hospital that lasted more than 72 hours, in an apparent attempt to prevent staff members from holding meetings after opposition political rallies were banned on Independence Day, May 14. Doctors at the hospital had been on strike for higher pay for three weeks while hospital staff were also demanding the release of Dr Filizzola who had been arrested at the beginning of the month.

Dr Filizzola was arrested on two subsequent occasions during 1986, the second being on Nov. 29, several days after he had harshly criticized opposition political parties, during a debate at the headquarters of the Febrerista Revolutionary Party (*Partido Revolucionario Febrerista*—PRF—the only legalized party within the opposition grouping National Accord—AN—see separate entry), for their "lethargy" which, he said, had effectively kept the regime in power. He said that they had "no concrete proposals and no base among the grass roots", and did "not really respond to the needs of the poor". He went on to warn his audience that, if the emerging social movement did not find a valid expression of its demands in the existing political parties, "we will build a party or movement which is truly concerned about the rights and struggles of our people". Dr Filizzola was finally released on Dec. 24, 1986, following an anti-government demonstration by over 1,000 doctors, nurses and medical students on Dec. 1.

Popular and Democratic Broad Front (*Frente Amplio Democrático y Popular*, Fadepo)

This co-ordinating committee was created in the early 1980s to bring together representatives of the various exiled democratic groups to work out a common strategy for opposing the Stroessner regime.

Popular Colorado Movement (*Movimiento Popular Colorado*, Mopoco)

Leadership. Epifanio Méndez Fleitas (l.); Waldino Ramón Llovera (pres.)

The Mopoco was formed in 1959 as a result of a split in the Colorado Party between pro-military supporters and civilian opponents of Stroessner. Established as a democratic nationalist party, it is opposed to military intervention in politics and is broadly in favour of state involvement in the economy.

In 1973 a division emerged within the movement, the majority of members favouring co-ordinated action with other opposition forces, while a minority, seeking to emphasize the link with mainstream coloradismo, renamed itself the National Republican Association—Colorado Party in Exile (*ANR-PC en el Exilio*—see separate entry). The majority faction went on to join the National Accord formed in 1978 (AN—see separate entry).

A leader of the Mopoco, Dr Augustín Goiburú, was officially held responsible for an alleged plot to kill President Stroessner and to abduct ministers and other office-holders of the regime, this plot having been discovered by police after the arrest and interrogation of students in Asunción on Nov. 29, 1974. The plot was said to be supported by the (Argentinian) People's Revolutionary Army (ERP) and to be planned for January 1975. The police announcement was followed by numerous arrests (totalling over 1,000 as stated by the Minister of the Interior in early March 1975) while many Mopoco supporters fled the country. Dr Goiburú was seized by Argentinian security forces in Parana and reportedly handed over to the Paraguayan authorities in February 1977, since when he has disappeared. Other members of the movement were kidnapped while in Brazil.

In December 1983 a number of prominent members of the Mopoco, including its former president, Miguel Angel González Casabianca, were permitted to return to Paraguay after more than 20 years in exile; however, they have since been subjected to continual surveillance. In March 1984 the leading daily newspaper, *ABC Color*, published an interview with González Casabianca, leading to the arrest of its editor and publisher and the closure of the paper as a "focus for subversion".

At its conference on April 6-7, 1985, in the Argentinian border town of Posadas, the Mopoco rejected violence but reiterated that it would continue to struggle to end the "long record of evil actions and crimes of the dictatorship".

On June 21, 1987, the Mopoco was among the AN constituent parties to organize an unprecedented mass opposition rally attended by some 30,000 people in Coronel Oviedo.

The Mopoco has never been accorded legal status.

Peru

Capital: Lima

Pop. 19,700,000

The Republic of Peru has an executive President elected for a five-year term by universal adult suffrage who governs with the assistance of an appointed Council of Ministers and two Vice-Presidents. There is a bicameral Congress consisting of a 60-member Senate and a 180-member Chamber of Deputies elected similarly and at the same time as the President.

As a result of general elections held on April 14, 1985, the centre-left American Popular Revolutionary Alliance (APRA) secured a majority in both congressional chambers, the seats in the Chamber of Deputies being distributed as follows: APRA 107, United Left (IU) 48, Democratic Convergence (formed in 1984 as an electoral coalition between the right-wing Christian Popular Party and a splinter group of APRA, the *Movimiento de Bases Hayistas*) 12, the centre-right Popular Action (AP) 10, the National Left one and Independents two.

In presidential elections held on the same day, Alan García Pérez won 45.74 per cent of the votes cast and was inaugurated in July after the withdrawal of the second-placed candidate had obviated the need for a further ballot. An estimated 70 per cent of the electorate voted, with 1,087,976 of 7,557,182 votes blank or invalid.

The activites of left-wing terrorists, notably the Maoist *Sendero Luminoso* (Shining Path) movement, have dominated the Peruvian political scene since 1980. An estimated 9,530 people died between 1980 and 1987, including 3,676 civilians and 5,495 guerrillas, and states of emergency have been in almost continual operation in many parts of the country (notably Ayacucho) since 1983. In July 1984 the armed forces were given nationwide responsibility for counter-insurgency activities, but at the same time they were blamed for numerous atrocities and "disappearances". In July 1986 the first case of officers convicted of violating human rights resulted in the imprisonment of 11 officers for the murder in 1983 of 34 peasants. In February 1987 Amnesty International alleged that the extent of massacres carried out by armed forces in June 1986 following mutinies by prisoners in three prisons had been subject to a cover-up by the government.

Popular Revolutionary Commandos (*Comandos Revolucionarios del Pueblo*, CRP)

This group, formed in 1985, seized a radio station on July 18, 1985, denounced the "unjust social order" in Peru, and announced that it would adopt a "vigilant attitude" towards the APRA government.

Shining Path (*Sendero Luminoso*, SL)

Leadership. Dr Manuel Abimael Guzmán Renose ("Comrade Gonzalo") (l.)

The SL took its name from the title of one of its first pamphlets, *The Shining Path of Juan Carlos Mariategui*. Juan, or José, Carlos Mariategui, 1894-1930, had been the founder of the Peruvian Socialist Party which was formed on Oct. 7, 1928, and later became the Peruvian Communist Party; he had advocated a return to the peasant communes of the Inca empire.

In a 32-page pamphlet published in July 1982, the SL called itself a new type of Marxist-Leninist-Maoist party with the aim of waging "a people's war" from the countryside in order to carry it eventually into the cities. It had broken off relations with China in 1979 and called the Chinese Communist leaders "traitors". Its policy was rejected by all other (legal) left-wing groups in Peru.

President Belaúnde Terry stated on Dec. 26, 1982, that the SL was "a gang of murderers" and not a political party. He appealed to SL members to surrender unconditionally within 48-72 hours to save further loss of life. However, on Dec. 29 the President was reported to have ordered that, since the time limit for a surrender had expired, terrorists were to be attacked immediately and killed (although those who wished to surrender could still do so).

By Jan. 18, 1983, the President had placed eight provinces under military control and troop reinforcements had been sent to the areas concerned. Late in January about 32 SL fighters were said to have been killed in clashes with police and anti-SL peasants.

Further heavy clashes in the Ayacucho area occurred during April 1983. Thereafter the government took further steps to quell a virtual SL insurrection, but appeared to be making little progress against guerrillas operating in favourable terrain.

Following a mutiny of prisoners at three Lima prisons, El Frontón, Lurigancho and Santa Barbara, on June 18-20, 1986, some 270 prisoners were reported to have died in the resulting military assault, including virtually all the SL prisoners held at Lurigancho. At two of the prisons, the military used rocket-firing helicopters, anti-tank missiles and submachine guns to break down the defences of the prisons. After a criticism of military excesses, President García stated on June 27, 1986, that over 100 SL prisoners had been executed only after they had surrendered, and that of 124 prisoners killed at Lurigancho, 20 at most had died in the fighting. The President promised that those responsible would be brought to trial, and it was later announced that 15 officers and 80 soldiers had been detained. However, in a report, published in February 1987 by Amnesty International, the Peruvian government was accused of a massive cover-up; the report alleged in addition that 30-60 survivors of the El Frontón mutiny and army assault had been taken to a naval base where they had been tortured and had subsequently "disappeared".

At the end of June 1986 the SL threatened to kill 10 APRA members for every guerrilla killed in the mutinies. On June 29, dynamite attacks were reported on government offices and banks in Lima. In October 1986 it was reported that 28 police officers had been killed since the mutiny.

Towards the end of 1986, SL activities again appeared to intensify, with targets now including Peruvian and foreign businessmen and representatives. Mortar attacks were reported on the presidential palace, and in January 1987 an attack on the Indian embassy was carried out whilst President García was on a tour of India. On Jan. 6, 1987, the regional leader and two helpers of a government unemployment scheme were reported to have been murdered by a gang of 50 guerrillas.

In February 1987 a total of 793 students were arrested and 90 subsequently charged with terrorism after a raid by 4,000 police on three Lima universities.

Until 1987, however, government efforts to stem the activities of the SL had had little effect, apart from in regions such as Puno, where government land reforms had resulted in a loss of following of the movement.

In connexion with municipal elections held in 1983, and also with the congressional and presidential elections of 1985, the SL called for abstention, while it increased the number of its bomb attacks.

A new offensive announced in June 1984 marked an intensification of the SL's campaign, with the continuation of the strategy of attacking representatives of central authority, including village mayors, being executed after mock trials and peasants suspected of collaborating with security forces being killed. By late 1984 the group was active in the main coca-growing area of the north-eastern Upper Huallaga river valley (where security forces claimed that the SL was giving protection to illegal cocaine traders in return for arms and supplies).

On Sept. 27, 1985, SL members killed 14 peasants in a town north of Ayacucho in retaliation for the formation of a government-backed defence patrol. In October 1985, a bombing campaign was carried out to celebrate the 57th anniversary of the Peruvian Communist Party, and in December 1985, 49 explosions were let off in Lima to celebrate the birthday of the group's founder, Dr Manuel Abimael Guzmán Renose.

On Feb. 7, 1986, a nationwide state of emergency was proclaimed, and a four-hour curfew imposed in Lima and the neighbouring port of Callao on Feb. 9.

Early in 1986 the SL was held responsible for bomb attacks on foreign embassies, the assassination of several leading APRA members and the killing, on May 4, 1986, of Rear Adml. Carlos Ponce de León Canossa, a member of the navy's general staff and the highest ranking member of the military to have been killed by the SL. (After the killing, 448 people were reported to have been arrested.)

In 1986 the group was also reported active in the northern departments bordering Ecuador and the southern departments bordering Bolivia; Puno, situated in the south and traditionally one of the country's poorest areas, reportedly experienced more attacks between April and June 1986 than anywhere except Lima. From 1986 onwards SL activities increasingly focused on urban areas, with some 9,000 troops already in operation in the rural Andean region.

During the first quarter of 1987 there occurred, in Lima alone, 29 bombings, 12 murders and two electricity blackouts due to guerrilla sabotage attributed to the SL.

Among prominent SL members Emilio Antonia Díaz Martínez (held responsible for planning a prison mutiny in 1984) died in the 1986 prison mutinies; Claudio Bellido (third in command) was killed in October 1986; Laura Zambrano Padilla was given a 10-year prison sentence in November 1986 for involvement in an attack on a police station in 1983; and Walter Palacio Gutiérrez (SL military chief) was captured in July 1987. A reward of US$80,000 was offered by the police in May 1987 for information leading to the arrest of Dr M. A. Guzmán Renose (the SL leader).

A document signed by the SL central committee and dated August 1986, entitled *To Develop the Popular War Serving World Revolution*, expressed satisfaction with the armed campaign and claimed that the SL had carried out some 30,000 actions since 1980. In May 1987, a document sent to the media stated that the group had signed a pact with the Spanish Communist Party promising mutual support.

Estimates of the number of SL activists have varied between 2,000 and 3,000.

Tupac Amarú Revolutionary Movement (*Movimiento Revolucionario Tupac Amarú,* MRTA)

Leadership. Marco Turkowsky (l.)

This pro-Cuban group, which has no obvious links with the *Sendero Luminoso* (see separate entry), supports an "anti-imperialist stance" and became active in September 1984 with a series of bomb attacks. Its name derives from an eighteenth-century Peruvian who rebelled against Spanish rule.

The targets of MRTA bomb attacks in Lima in 1984 included a naval hospital on Sept. 7, the residence of the then Transport and Communications Minister on Sept. 14, and the US embassy and a US-owned department store on Sept. 28.

On Sept. 29. 1984, staff at two US press agencies were forced at gun-point by MRTA members to transmit a message against "Yankee imperialism", and on Nov. 27, following the detention of nine MRTA members, two journalists were kidnapped in order that the MRTA could broadcast a protest against the detainees' alleged torture.

On March 19, 1985, a bomb attack was carried out on the residence of the then Labour Minister; on May 16, there was an attack on the residence of the US ambassador; and on June 8, two car bombs exploded outside the presidential palace during a visit to Peru by President Alfonsín of Argentina. All the incidents were attributed to the MRTA.

In September 1985 the MRTA reportedly made it known that it was prepared to suspend its activities to allow the government to introduce measures to assist the Peruvian people. The truce would continue so long as there were no new acts of oppression, but it insisted on applying "exemplary punishment" against those whom it considered to have violated human rights. However, on Aug. 7, 1986, the MRTA announced an end to the truce, stating that promises made by the government had turned into measures that did not represent the people's interests.

On June 23, 1986, MRTA members occupied the offices of an Italian news agency, forcing the manager to issue condemnations of recent "killings of political prisoners". In September 1986, a total of 288 people were arrested following the planting of bombs in Lima which killed two people; guerrillas left MRTA leaflets calling for the overthrow of the government. In December 1986 the group was blamed for eight bomb attacks in Lima only hours after President García had called for a united effort to develop society. The MRTA was also blamed for attacks on offices of the APRA in Lima in February 1987.

Philippines

Capital: Quezon City (Manila) Pop. 54,380,000

Under the terms of a new Constitution, approved by a plebescite on Feb. 2, 1987, the Republic of the Philippines is ruled by a President who is elected for a single six-year term by universal adult suffrage of all citizens above the age of 15 years. Legislative power is held by a bicameral National Assembly consisting of a 250-member House of Representatives and a 24-member Senate. The first elections under the new Constitution were held on May 11, and resulted in victory for the supporters of President Corazon Aquino, who obtained some 70 per cent of the votes and 22 seats in the Senate.

The corrupt and authoritarian regime of the previous President, Ferdinand Marcos, had faced growing opposition following the assassination of Benigno Aquino, the regime's foremost liberal opponent, who was shot dead at Manila airport in August 1983 upon returning from a three-year period of self-imposed exile in the USA. Although those members of the military who were suspected of involvement in the crime were acquitted, it was widely believed that Marcos had sanctioned Aquino's death. In the face of mounting domestic and foreign pressure Marcos held a presidential election in February 1986 and was opposed by Corazon Aquino, the widow of the murdered man. Although Marcos claimed victory it was generally accepted that Aquino had polled the greater number of votes. He agreed to step down (after an assurance of safe passage to the USA) following the defection of his Defence Minister, Juan Ponce Enrile, and the Chief of Staff of the armed forces, General Fidel Ramos, both of whom retained their positions under C. Aquino who was sworn in as President on Feb. 25.

On March 25 President Aquino proclaimed an iterim "Freedom Constitution" (which replaced the 1973 Constitution formulated by Marcos), and in October an appointed constituent assembly finalized the draft Constitution which guaranteed a wide range of liberal freedoms and imposed specific checks upon the power of the executive, and its approval amounted to the *de facto* election of Aquino as President.

Following the release of all political prisoners held under the Marcos regime, in March 1986, the new government entered into negotiations with the country's two principal guerrilla organizations: the (Moslem autonomist or secessionist) Moro National Liberation Front and the (Maoist) New People's Army (NPA). A temporary ceasefire was achieved with the NPA in late 1986, but fighting resumed in early 1987 following the failure of talks to produce a long-term settlement.

The new government had also to contend, during 1986 and 1987, with several coup attempts by politicians or elements of the armed forces which sought to re-establish the Marcos regime.

Communist Party of the Philippines—Marxist-Leninist (CPP-ML)

Leadership. José Maria Sison (ch.)

The CPP-ML was established on Dec. 26, 1968, on the "firm ideological foundation of Marxism-Leninism—Mao Zedong Thought" after breaking away from the (pro-Soviet) Communist Party of the Philippines (*Partido Komunista ng Pilipinas*, PKP) founded in 1930. While the PKP obtained legal recognition in October 1974, the CPP-ML was engaged in underground activities through its armed wing, the New People's Army (NPA); it also set up a National Democratic Front as an alliance of various left-wing movements, led by Antonio Zumel and active at least since 1972.

The party's original close relations with the Chinese Communist Party were suspended in 1975 when China established diplomatic relations with the Philippine government of President Marcos.

Although the CPP-ML remained a prohibited organization after the fall of President Marcos, J. M. Sison, who had been held under arrest since Nov. 8, 1977 (see below under New People's Army), was released on March 5, 1986, under the new government's policy of releasing political prisoners.

In May 1986 J. M. Sison announced the formation of a People's Party (*Partido ng Bayan*) which held its first major congress on Aug. 30-31, when it outlined a radical left-wing programme calling inter alia for the dismantling of US military bases in the Philippines. Although the congress was attended by Bernabé Buscayno, the NPA organizer, and several leading figures in the new party were alleged to be members of the CPP-ML and the NPA, J. M. Sison denied that the Party was a legal front for the CPP-ML.

Cordillera People's Liberation Army (CPLA)

This Army was formed from an NPA guerrilla unit operating in the Cordillera region of the country's main island of Luzon. The group, which had been active since at least 1980, was led by Father Conrado Balweg, a Roman Catholic priest who had been disowned by the Church in June 1983 because of his involvement in the guerrilla movement.

Fr Balweg seceded from the NPA and announced the formation of the CPLA on April 29, 1986, because of the NPA's reluctance to begin peace talks with the new government of President Aquino. A ceasefire was signed between the CPLA and the government on Sept. 13 and, following further talks, an agreement was concluded on Dec. 15, whereby the organization became a participant in the newly created Cordillera Regional Development Council, which had been established by the new government to consider the issue of regional autonomy for Cordillera.

Moro National Liberation Front (MNLF)

The MNLF was established in 1968 as a militant Moslem organization in rebellion against the central government with the particular objective of achieving independence or autonomy for the Moslem population of the Philippines within a defined geographical area.

Islam had been introduced into parts of the Philippines in the 14th century, mainly by Malays and by the Dayaks of Borneo, and it might have spread to the whole of the archipelago if the latter had not been colonized by Spain in the 16th century, when the Philippine Moslems were called Moros (after the Moslem Moors in Spain) and were ruthlessly suppressed. According to the 1970 census there were then 2,100,000 Moslems (out of a total Philippine population of 38,000,000) concentrated in the four southern provinces of Cotabato, Lanao del Norte, Lanao del Sur and Sulu. They were generally an underprivileged minority, inadequately schooled and poorly represented in public offices; only 29.1 per cent of them regarded themselves as Filipinos, and 21.2 per cent favoured secession from the Philippines.

In 1971 the *Manila Times* estimated that 800,000 Moslems were refugees evicted from their land by Christians. Up to September 1971 over 1,800 people were said to have been killed in clashes between Christians and Moslems within 18 months.

During this period of massacres and attrocities committed by extremists among Christians and Moslems, the MNLF emerged as a unified Moslem movement. The conflict was exacerbated by army intervention, and in particular by the massacre of 40 unarmed Moslems by army units at Tacub (Lanao del Norte) in 1971. This incident led to accusations of "genocide" made against the Philippine government in the Moslem world, with Libya taking the lead in a movement to defend the Moslem cause in the Philippines. The first armed units of the MNLF were said to have been trained in Sabah (Malaysia), whose Chief Minister (Tun Datu Haji Mustapha) was a native of Sulu, with Libya giving material aid. There were said to be between 15,000 and 20,000 Philippine Moslems as refugees in Sabah.

After it had been claimed by the Philippine government on Dec. 18, 1972, that a peaceful settlement had been reached between Moslem rebels and the armed forces, a meeting took place on Jan. 3, 1973, between President Marcos and some 300 Moslem leaders, after which the President ordered the cessation of military operations (except in self-defence) to enable dissident Moslems to take advantage of a selective amnesty and economic benefits under an offer due to expire on Feb. 26, 1973.

On an official Libyan initiative, the fourth conference of Foreign Ministers of the Organization of the Islamic Conference meeting in Benghazi (Libya) on March 24-27, 1973, decided inter alia to appeal to the Philippine government (i) to end immediately the reported repression and mass extermination of Moslems in the southern Philippines and (ii) to take prompt measures to provide protection and security for the Moslem minority and to resettle the thousands of refugees in their homes. The conference also appointed a five-nation delegation consisting of the Foreign Ministers of Afghanistan, Libya, Saudi Arabia, Senegal and Somalia to discuss the issue with the government in Manila (which agreed to allow the delegation access to all areas of the Philippines to investigate allegations of persecution of the Moslem minority).

After the delegation had visited refugee camps and the scenes of recent incidents in the Philippines, President Marcos announced on Aug. 18, 1973, the creation of new administrative divisions in Mindanao (the southern-most of the main islands of the Philippines and the principal area of Moslem population) and the establishment of a council to help displaced people. Other government measures to end hostilities between Christians and Moslems included provisions for the teaching of Arabic to Moslem children, the codification of Moslem laws and the establishment of a Moslem bank and a number of cultural institutions. Fighting nevertheless continued during late 1973 and early 1974.

At the fifth conference of Foreign Ministers of the Organization of the Islamic Conference, held in Kuala Lumpur on June 21-25, 1974, it was disclosed that Islamic oil producers had contributed aid to Moslems in the Philippines and that the Libyan government in particular had been supplying funds to the Moslem rebels. In a resolution adopted on June 25 the ministers called on President Marcos to halt all operations against the Moslem rebellion and to negotiate a political solution with representatives of the MNLF, i.e. to go beyond the "socio-economic measures proposed by the Philippine government" and to achieve "a just solution within the framework of the national sovereignty and territorial integrity of the Philippines".

In January 1975 talks were held in Jeddah (Saudi Arabia) between a delegation led by Nur Misuari of the MNLF and representatives of the Philippine government, with the executive secretary of the Organization of the Islamic Conference presiding. However, on Feb. 3, 1975, President Marcos described the negotiations as fruitless and declared that his government would never agree to the MNLF's demand for an autonomous state of Mindanao.

Although President Marcos had stated on March 18, 1973, that the Moslem rebellion had been "practically crushed", this claim was contradicted by later announcements. In April 1973 it was officially stated that in Mindanao 276,487 persons had been evacuated before advancing rebels, and at the end of that month the President himself said that "nearly a million people" had abandoned their homes in Mindanao. A conditional amnesty offer made earlier in the year was abandoned in mid-April for lack of response by the rebels. The government's forces were strengthened by various measures, including the setting-up of armed "self-defence units" by civilians and the introduction of military service for up to 12 months.

During 1974-75 fighting continued, especially in Cotabayo province, in Lanao del Sur, near Zamboanga City and on Jolo Island. On June 24, 1974, the President announced a broad amnesty for Moslems who were prepared to give up fighting, and also the appointment of a number of Moslems to national and municipal government posts, some of the appointees being former rebel leaders. On Nov. 1 he ordered troops to cease hostilities for two months in Lanao del Sur and Lanao del Norte. On Nov. 3 he offered an amnesty to "ideological subversives", including also persons who might have "committed illegal acts to promote political beliefs or enhance views about the social order, the economic system or the form of government"; those surrendering were required to give up their weapons and pledge their loyalty to the government. On Feb. 10, 1975, he announced that he had ordered a ceasefire throughout the southern provinces of the Philippines. (By Sept. 16, 1974, about 1,000 Moslems were said to have surrendered in Mindanao.)

The MNLF subsequently boycotted talks between the government and about 140 leaders of 27 different Moslem groups, which opened in Zamboanga City on April 17, 1975. The MNLF had stated on March 31 that the rejection of its demand for an autonomous Moslem state had closed the door to further negotiations; it regarded the Moslem leaders involved in the new talks as being "already in the service of the Marcos government". In a statement issued on April 19, the Moslem participants in the talks rejected partition of the Philippines as a solution to the rebellion and presented a list of demands for reforms designed to bring about peace.

On April 21 President Marcos agreed to integrate former rebels in the armed forces, and he announced the establishment of two regional offices in Mindanao and Sulu under Moslems who would take over government administration in those areas, and also the allocation of US$7,000,000 for development projects in Mindanao. (The Islamic Development Fund of the United Arab Emirates allotted, in April 1975, US$350,000,000 for development projects in Mindanao.) Some 500 rebels leaders met government representatives for further talks in Marawi City on May 11, 1975.

While numerous clashes between rebels and government forces continued between February and August 1975, the government on Sept. 6 ordered a halt to operations against rebels in the south in order to negotiate the surrender of further insurgent leaders. On Nov. 10 another MNLF leader and 1,000 MNLF rebels were officially stated to have surrendered, the total of those who had surrendered since April 1985 being given as 9,000 (out of an estimated total of 16,000 MNLF forces). President Marcos stated on Jan. 22, 1976, that in 39 months of fighting 2,000 government troops had been killed and 4,000 injured. After more fighting had taken place near Zamboanga City and in Lanao del Sur, nearly 30,000 inhabitants were said to have fled from their homes by the end of March 1976.

During 1976 the MNLF denied involvement in the hijacking of two aircraft by Moslem rebels—(i) on April 7, when three men claiming to be MNLF members seized a Philippine Airlines DC-8 and eventually diverted it to Benghazi on April 8, and (ii) on May 21, when six men claiming to be MNLF supporters forced an airliner to land at Zamboanga City where, however, it was stormed by troops on May 23, with the result that the airliner was destroyed and 16 people, including three of the hijackers, were killed and 19 injured. The remaining three hijackers were condemned to death on Nov. 4, 1976.

Although further major guerrilla attacks occurred in June-October 1976, the acting chief of staff of the Philippines armed forces claimed on Oct. 28 that the situation was "under control". During that period 35 Japanese and at least four other foreigners were kidnapped by guerrillas who demanded ransom to pay for food and supplies.

Talks between the Philippine government and the MNLF—arranged in November 1976 by Mrs Imelda Marcos (the President's wife) with Col. Gadaffi (the Libyan leader)—took place in Tripoli in December 1976 and led, under the auspices of the Organization of the Islamic Conference, to an agreement in principle, reached on Dec. 30, on the granting of a degree of autonomy to 13 provinces in Mindanao, the Sulu archipelago and Palawan Island and to the establishment of a ceasefire, to be effected gradually between Dec. 24, 1976 and Jan. 20, 1977. President Marcos announced on Jan. 4 that a referendum would be held in 13 provinces to determine which of them wished to be part of an autonomous Moslem region within the Philippines—but the holding of such a referendum was rejected by the MNLF. After diplomatic relations had been established between Libya and the Philippines early in January, talks were resumed in Tripoli on Feb. 7, 1977, but were suspended on March 3 as no agreement was reached on which of the provinces were to be included in the proposed autonomous region. The Moslems were said to have demanded that it should incorporate three predominantly Christian provinces (Palawan, South Cotabato and Davao del Sur) because of potential oil reserves off Palawan and the rich agricultural land of the two other provinces, and also the formation of their own army and the right to their own flag.

After talks between Col. Gadaffi on the one hand and Imelda Marcos, Juan Ponce Enrile (the Philippine Defence Secretary) and Estelito Mendoza (Philippine Solicitor General) on the other had begun on March 10, 1977, and a three-stage peace plan proposed by the Libyan leader had been accepted, President Marcos proclaimed, on March 26, an autonomous region of 13 southern provinces (including the three predominantly Christian ones mentioned above) and announced the creation of an administration to govern the area provisionally and to supervise the referendum which was to decide on administrative arrangements for autonomy, to be followed by the election of a regional assembly. (On April 12 the President also announced that Nur Misuari, the MNLF leader, could return from exile in Libya to take part in the organization of a provisional government.)

The referendum, held on April 17, 1977, was on April 23 officially stated to have resulted in 97.93 per cent of the total votes cast in the 13 southern provinces (in a poll of about 75 per cent of the registered voters) having been in favour of rejecting autonomy for the region under MNLF rule. The MNLF had boycotted the referendum on the ground that no such consultation had been provided for in the first Tripoli agreement (of December 1976).

New talks which were begun in Manila on April 24, 1977, broke down on May 1 with each side accusing the other of trying to discard the first Tripoli agreement. Gen. Carlos P. Romulo (the Philippine Foreign Secretary) said on May 6 that the major obstacles which had resulted in the impasse were the MNLF's demands for complete control of the region, for the establishment of a separate army of 15,000 men and for the regional (i.e. not national) auditing of finance, as well as the question of MNLF representation in the Cabinet and in the Supreme Court.

A provisional regional government formed by President Marcos (under the provisions of a law of February 1977 dividing the Philippines into 12 partly autonomous regions) met in Zamboanga City on May 10, the MNLF having refused to take up the 15 seats (out of a total of 29) offered to it by the President.

At the eighth conference of Islamic Foreign Ministers (in Tripoli) on May 16, 1977, the MNLF was "as an exception" granted observer status at the Organization. In its final communiqué issued on May 22, the conference expressed concern at the Philippine government's policy towards the Moslems and charged its five-nation committee with pursuing "its mission of mediation between the MNLF, which is the legitimate representative of the Moslem people in the southern Philippines, and the Philippine government". The conference also proposed the creation of a fund, to be financed by all Moslem nations, to assist Philippine Moslems.

Nur Misuari (the MNLF president) was at the same time quoted as saying that the MNLF had decided to revert to its original demand for total independence for the southern Philippines, a demand which (he said) it had abandoned "in a spirit of reconciliation" after the fifth conference of the Islamic Foreign Ministers in 1974. He added that the MNLF was prepared to resume fighting with the 50,000 men at its disposal; that it received no aid from Cuba, China or the Soviet Union but only from Moslem countries (whereas, he claimed, the Philippine government was aided mainly by the United States and Israel); and that the MNLF was "a Moslem nationalist movement trying to free a Moslem country from the Philippine colonial yoke".

The ceasefire of December 1976 held for most of the year 1977, although both sides accused each other of violations, the MNLF being alleged to have violated the ceasefire 300 times and the army 703 times, killing over 600 people. More incidents occurred later in 1977, with government forces launching on Sept. 20 a three-front initiative north of Zamboanga City, on Basilan and on Jolo. Two high-ranking army officers were killed on Oct. 10 and 13 respectively, and on Oct. 21 the MNLF claimed that the army had massacred 400 civilians in retaliation, but this was officially denied. On Nov. 7, 1977, President Marcos announced that since 1973 from 30,000 to 50,000 civilians had lost their lives and 500,000 had been rendered homeless as a result of this conflict. In February 1978 the Defence Ministry stated that during 1977 over 800 people had been killed in various clashes, and in April 1978 the Ministry reported that over 2,000 people had been killed or injured in January-March 1978 in violations of the ceasefire.

During 1980 MNLF guerrillas continued to be involved in a number of raids and ambushes of government troops, while the government claimed that several MNLF leaders had surrendered with their followers. These leaders were said to include Amelil Malaquiok (Commander Rony), who surrendered in March and was on April 1 appointed chairman of the standing committee of the executive council of Mindanao's autonomous region No. 12, and Jamil Lucman, who surrendered on Sept. 2 and was also appointed a government official. After the lifting of martial law on Jan. 17, 1981, restrictions still remained in force in several southern provinces where clashes continued to occur between MNLF forces and government troops. However, on Feb. 23, 1982, it was officially claimed that since 1973 a total of 46,000 Moslems had "turned their backs" on the rebellion.

The government continued its attempts to undercut the appeal of the MNLF through the granting of limited concessions towards local autonomy. The MNLF, however, steadfastly refused to participate in the political process on the grounds that the government had failed to implement in full the terms of the Tripoli Agreement and continued to demand the creation of an independent Moslem state. Sporadic clashes with government troops continued, but by the end of 1982 it was widely believed that the MNLF was demoralized and incapable of prosecuting the guerrilla war with its past effectiveness.

The movement's military capability was retarded by increasingly severe internal divisions resulting from ideological and personal differences which were aggravated by the efforts of the Islamic Conference Organization to prevail upon the movement's leadership to accept a form of autonomy for the southern provinces rather than to continue to press for independence. By late 1982 three distinct groupings had emerged—(i) the main MNLF faction led by Nur Misuari and supported initially by Libya and more recently by Iran; (ii) the Moslem Islamic Liberation Front (MILF) led by Hashim Salamat and supported by Egypt; (iii) the smaller Bangsa Moro National Liberation Front (BMNLF) led by Dimas Pundato and supported by Saudi Arabia. In addition to clashes with troops there were several instances of hostages being seized by unidentified Moslem insurgents.

During her election campaign Mrs Aquino pledged to "respect and substantiate" the Moslem aspirations for autonomy and it was acknowledged that her brother-in-law, Agapito Aquino, had met Nur Misuari for talks in Madrid on Jan. 13, 1986. Following her election President Aquino urged insurgents of all persuasions to cease fighting and begin negotiations with the new government. All factions of the MNLF had observed an unofficial ceasefire since the fall of the Marcos regime, and on March 13 the MILF and BNMLF responded to the President's offer by sending delegates to Manila to begin peace negotiations. The talks failed to produce a settlement, however, and were abandoned in April.

Following talks in Jeddah between Agapito Aquino and Nur Misuari in mid-August the latter returned to the Philippines where he attended an MNLF congress in Jolo on Sept. 3-5, and was reported to have spoken in favour of accepting a peace settlement on the basis of legislative and judicial autonomy for the country's 5,000,000 Moslems, rather than continuing the struggle for complete independence which the Aquino government had consistently maintained was unacceptable. On Sept. 5, President Aquino flew to Jolo for a meeting with Nur Misuari.

Further talks were held in Jeddah which resulted in the signing of an agreement on Jan. 4, 1987, whereby

Nur Misuari agreed to modify his demand for complete independence in favour of the acceptance of "full autonomy", the precise definition of which was to be the subject of further negotiation. On Jan. 13, however, the MILF launched a series of co-ordinated military attacks throughout western Mindanao in protest at its "exclusion" from the negotiations. There followed several days of intensive fighting as MILF forces clashed with units from the army and the MNLF resulting in at least 30 deaths. A truce was negotiated on Jan. 17, and it was agreed that all three guerrilla factions should attend talks in Manila on Feb. 9, but the MILF delegation failed to keep this appointment.

A second session of talks was held in Zamboanga City on Feb. 20 (although once again the MILF chose not to participate) at which the MNLF presented to the government representatives its definition of "full autonomy" which was believed to include the establishment of an autonomous legislature, judiciary and defence force for the Moslem area. A further session of talks was held on March 12 at which the MNLF's chief negotiator, Habid Hashim, threatened to resume the war if a settlement was not reached without further delay. On the same day the MILF announced that it would not recognize any agreement arrived at without its participation in the talks and that it would only return to the negotiating table if future talks were held under the auspices of the Islamic Conference.

On April 6, at least ten Moslem guerrillas were killed in a clash with government troops who were alleged to have launched an attack on their base in the Bukidnon region of Mindanao. A further round of talks, which had been scheduled for that day, was suspended by the MNLF in a protest over the incident. Habid Hashim declared that the negotiations would be resumed only if the government withdrew all units from the Bukidnon region. On May 6, 1987, however, it was announced that the two sides had agreed to form a joint commission to draft an autonomy package to be presented to a new congress to be held in July 1987.

New People's Army (NPA)

As the military wing of the Communist Party of the Philippines—Marxist-Leninist (CPP-ML—see separate entry) which broke away from the (pro-Soviet) Communist Party of the Philippines (PKP) in 1968, the NPA thereafter intensified guerrilla warfare against government forces, whereas the *Hukbalahap* (originally oganized by the PKP as an anti-Japanese army during World War II) was subdued by government forces in the 1970s. The NPA was first set up by about 60 fighters in northern Luzon (the largest and most northerly of the main Philippine islands) led by José Maria Sison (who became chairman of the CPP-ML).

In a report of Sept. 6, 1971, a Senate committee stated that the armed strength of the NPA was only 350 men and posed "no real military threat". However, on July 9, 1972, President Marcos ordered a full-scale military offensive against the NPA in the Palanan area, about 200 miles north of Manila. Fighting between Communists and army units continued in both northern and southern Luzon, and a number of bomb explosions in Manila during August 1972 were attributed to communist agents. The President thereupon declared on Sept. 4, 1972, that his military commanders had warned him that, unless the national forces (including 618,000 men in the army) were appreciably strengthened, the communist movement could overwhelm them within two years; that the Communists were "eroding the will to resist of local authorities by political assassinations"; and that out of fear many people were contributing funds to the Communists' "invisible government".

Further bomb explosions occurred in the Manila area on Sept. 12 and 19, 1972. After the President had, on Sept. 21, signed a decree proclaiming martial law, he was on Sept. 24 reported as asserting that the NPA had 10,000 "active guerrillas" and 100,000 sympathizers and was fighting on both major islands of the Philippines (Luzon and Mindanao).

According to an armed forces report of Jan. 12, 1974, the Communists in the Philippines were then divided into three forces—the NPA, the traditional (pro-Soviet) Communist Party (which was recognized as a legal party in October 1974) and a remnant of the *Hukbalahap*; of these the NPA was regarded as the strongest and most active, having expanded its operations from the Cayagan river valley (northern Luzon) to the Visayan Islands, Mindanao, Panay and Negros. However, at the end of 1974 large numbers of Communists were said to have surrendered as a result of a conciliation campaign by President Marcos, notably 1,700 communist insurgents during November, over 1,400 NPA members in early December and 1,200 PKP members at the end of December.

On Aug. 27, 1976, President Marcos and military leaders presented 25 captured rebel leaders, among them Bernabé Buscayno, the leader of the NPA, and Victor Corpuz, the NPA's guerrilla training chief, both of whom were sentenced to death on Nov. 8, 1977. José Maria Sison, the founder of the NPA, was captured on Nov. 8, 1977, in La Union province (125 miles north of Manila). It was stated at the same time that a more militant element had taken over the leadership of the NPA and wished to form a united front against the government with the help of the "Christian left".

In April 1978 the NPA began to instruct its unarmed supporters to seize weapons from government forces and to hand them over to NPA units, and in the following year it was reported to be extending its operations northwards from central Luzon and also to Samar (where, according to church sources, the NPA was tacitly supported by about two-thirds of the population) and to other adjacent islands. The NPA had also, in 1979, infiltrated the area of the Kalinga tribe, which it supported in opposing a hydro-electric project on the Chico River (a tributary to the Cagayan) in northern Luzon.

During 1981 the NPA extended its activities to further areas in various parts of the country, claiming to have 10,000 armed men, including 2,500 hardcore regulars; they were not known to receive any assistance from outside, and captured or bought their arms from police or army units. In the same year the government forces resorted to applying the "strategic hamlets" concept (first used by the British in Malaya in the 1950s and later by the United States in Vietnam), which involved the uprooting of families from their homes and lands and the relocation of about 250,000 people (mainly in the three Davao provinces in Mindanao); although the Defence Minister ordered the reversal of this policy in March 1982, there was no evidence that the hamlets had been dismantled. While the strategic hamlets exposed and immobilized some guerrilla forces by depriving them of their mass base, they also increased anti-government sentiments among the people.

By May 1982 it was apparent that the NPA had not only extended the area of its activities but had also intensified its "liquidation campaign", in which nearly 150 local councillors had been murdered.

The sphere and scale of NPA operations increased steadily during 1983 and 1984 as the movement sought to exploit the government's weakness in the aftermath of the assassination of Benigno Aquino. Despite numerous local offensives undertaken by the army, the NPA was believed to be increasing in overall size and was reported to have opened many new fronts of activity, particularly in Mindanao where a loose alliance between NPA and Moro National Liberation Front (MNLF—see separate entry) units was believed to be in operation. The NPA's urban activities also increased with "Sparrow Units" (small groups of urban guerrillas) having reportedly accounted for the deaths of 22 police in Davao by mid-1984. On May 24 such a unit was believed to have been responsible for the assassination of Brig.-Gen. Tomas Karingal, the police chief of northern Manila.

The government's concern over the growing incidence and effectiveness of the NPA's attacks, particularly in the south of the country, led to the announcement of new counter-insurgency measures on Aug. 8, 1984. These included greater efforts to expose communist "infiltration" of religious organizations, and the upgrading of the Philippine Constabulary and the Integrated National Police (PC-INP) in an attempt to improve discipline and to reduce corruption and thus to increase its efficiency as an anti-insurgency force. Figures released by the government showed that between 1981 and mid-1984 some 2,300 soldiers and 2,602 civilians had been killed and over US$16,000,000 worth of damage inflicted by military actions conducted by the NPA.

On Jan. 9, 1985, the Defence Minister, Juan Ponce Enrile, stated that the NPA "constituted the most formidable threat to our national security today and will continue to do so". Since 1981, he suggested, the movement had grown by 23 per cent per annum, and during 1984 had been active in over 80 per cent of the country's 73 provinces resulting in the deaths of over 900 soldiers and 1,000 civilians. Although some 1,000 guerrillas had been killed in the course of the year, he estimated that the front line strength of the movement remained above 20,000 fighters.

The NPA chose to boycott the presidential election campaign in early 1986 on the grounds that Corazon Aquino was a representative of "the landowners and the capitalists", but the movement did not interfere with the elections as it had done in previous campaigns. Similarly the movement remained aloof from C. Aquino's popularist campaign to remove Marcos from office (following the disputed election results) which it characterized as "a conflict within the ruling class". On Feb. 26, the day after C. Aquino was sworn in as President, NPA representatives confirmed that the guerrilla war would be continued despite C. Aquino's campaign pledge to seek a six-month ceasefire with the communist insurgents.

The NPA's distrust of, and contempt for, President Aquino (based upon her class background and her retention of key figures from the previous regime such as J. P. Enrile and Gen. Fidel Ramos) was somewhat diminished by her genuine effort to dissociate her government from that of Marcos. In addition to dismantling much of the coercive apparatus of the former regime, the President initiated the wholesale release of political prisoners. On March 5, the wishes of Enrile and Ramos were over-ruled and four remaining prisoners were released despite warnings from the military leaders that their liberation would encourage the communist insurgents and further demoralize the army. The four were José Maria Sison, the chairman of the central committee of the CPP-ML, who had been imprisoned at a military base in Manila since 1977; Bernabé Buscayno (alias Commander Dante), the commander-in-chief of the NPA; Alexander Birondo, the leader of an NPA special operations unit; and Ruben Alegre, a member of Birondo's special unit which was alleged to have been responsible for the assassination of Brig.-Gen. Karingal (see above).

The central committee of the CCP-ML on March 14 rejected a government amnesty for those guerrillas who surrendered their weapons, on the grounds that the struggle would be continued until a peace agreement was negotiated and that meaningful negotiations could only occur if the government severed its remaining connexions with the former regime. Ten days later, however, separate statements were issued by the NPA and the National Democratic Front (NDF, organized by the CCP-ML) which recognized the reforms undertaken by the Aquino regime and which agreed to consider entering ceasefire talks without preconditions.

According to government figures released on June 4, a total of 375 NPA fighters had been killed in clashes with the security forces since the election of Corazon Aquino, and 358 government soldiers and 261 civilians had died in insurgent-related violence in the same period. Although President Aquino expressed the hope that an unofficial truce would be recognized whilst the talks were in progress, sporadic clashes continued, and in a single week in late June a total of 23 soldiers were killed in two NPA ambushes in Quezon province and Ilocos Norte.

Secret ceasefire talks between the government and the NPA were begun in late June 1986 but were impeded by procedural disagreements and also by actions attributed to elements of the army, including the arrest of Rodolfo Salas, the overall commander of the NPA on Sept. 29, 1986 (whereafter he was charged with rebellion on Oct. 2), and the murder of a prominent trade unionist and leading member of the newly-formed People's Party *(Partido ng Bayan)* on Nov. 12. These events were followed by the killing by an NPA "Sparrow Unit" on Nov. 19 of a prominent supporter of J. P. Enrile and the removal of the latter from his post as Minister of Defence in the aftermath of an attempted anti-government coup.

However, a 60-day truce between the government and the NPA was agreed on Nov. 27, and under an agreement which came into force on Dec. 10 a National Ceasefire Committee was established.

Further talks held from January 1987 onwards failed to resolve outstanding issues. The ceasefire was no longer observed after Feb. 8, whereafter fighting was resumed, with over 50 people reported killed in the first three days.

In a televised statement on Feb. 28 President Aquino unveiled a new scheme designed to encourage guerrillas to surrender their weapons in return for an unconditional amnesty together with a financial reward and the promise of training for future employment. The programme, which it was estimated would cost over US$50,000,000, was to last for six months and was to include the establishment of national rehabilitation centres throughout the country. Although condemned by the NPA's leadership as a "desperate bribe" on the part of the government, early reports suggested that some fighters had taken advantage of the terms offered in the package. The announcement of the programme was followed by an attempt by the government to enter into negotiations with regional and local commanders of NPA units in an effort to exploit the divisions alleged to exist within the movement as to the attitude which should be adopted towards the new government. An offer by the NPA's central leadership to resume negotiations at a national level on condition that "the roots of the conflict" were placed upon the agenda, was rejected by the government on March 5 on the grounds that the local negotiations were making satisfactory progress.

By the end of February 1987 over 180 people were reported to have been killed in the renewed fighting, with clashes between the two sides averaging eight per day, the same as for the 1986 average but three fewer than for 1985.

Poland

Capital: Warsaw

Pop. 37,200,000

The Polish People's Republic is, under its Constitution as amended in February 1976, "a socialist state" in which the role of "the leading political force in the building of socialism" is vested in the Polish United Workers' Party (PUWP). The PUWP dominates a Patriotic Movement of National Rebirth (PRON) formed in 1982 to replace an earlier National Unity Front (NUF), of which the other members were the United Peasants' Party, the Democratic Party, the "social organizations of the working people" and "the patriotic associations of all citizens" (including the Roman Catholic *Znak* and *Pax* groups). Under an amendment to the Constitution adopted in 1976 the Polish state was to "strengthen friendship and co-operation with the Soviet Union and other socialist states".

The PRON was, under amendments to the Constitution approved by the Diet (*Sejm*) on July 8, 1983, to be "a platform for uniting the patriotic forces of the nation for the benefit of the Polish People's Republic and for the co-operation of political parties, organizations, social associations and citizens in matters of the functioning of the socialist state and the comprehensive development of the country irrespective of their outlook". The 1983 constitutional amendments also enabled the Chairman of the Council of State (head of state, elected by the *Sejm*) to declare, in the event of an internal threat to the state, a state of emergency without the approval of the *Sejm* or the Council of State.

While supreme power is exercised by the Politburo of the central committee of the PUWP, the authority of the Republic is vested in the *Sejm* elected by universal adult suffrage, normally for a four-year term. Elections were held on Oct. 13, 1985, under new regulations providing for a choice between two candidates in 74 districts for 410 of the 460 seats, with the remaining 50 seats being filled from a "national list" of public figures nominated by the PRON. According to official results the turnout was 78.86 per cent in the districts and 78.64 per cent for the national list, with the turnout being lower in some areas traditionally of strong support for Solidarity (the free trade union movement—see below).

For the first time in any country of the Soviet bloc there emerged in Poland during 1980-81 a workers' movement which succeeded in creating a strong independent trade union federation. This new "Solidarity" movement replaced the existing official trade union organization controlled by the state (which was dissolved on Jan. 1, 1981) and confronted the government with demands of an increasingly political nature, which were eventually seen as a threat to the regime. It was also supported by the Roman Catholic Church, of which the vast majority of the population are practising members and which took part in some of the negotiations between the Solidarity leaders on the one hand and representatives of the government and the PUWP on the other.

Martial law was eventually ended on July 22, 1983. An amnesty declared on the previous day covered, in addition to other offenders, 295 persons accused of political offences, but not over 60 others, mostly former officials of Solidarity and of the Social Self-Defence Committee (KOR). However, on Sept. 29, 1983, the Minister of Justice stated that 2,565 political prisoners had benefited from the amnesty while 83 arrested under martial law were still being held. Another 648 political offenders had, according to official information, by the end of October 1983 surrendered themselves under the amnesty in return for a pardon. On Nov. 24, 1983, the amnesty was extended until the end of the year, and on Jan. 4, 1984, a government spokesman announced that another 411 activists had surrendered, bringing the total to 1,120 since July 1983; on Feb. 7, 1984, the spokesman stated that there were 54 political prisoners left in custody and another 180 in detention awaiting trial.

In October 1983 the National Barristers' Council (of some 3,500 members) called for the freeing of political prisoners, the introduction of a special status for political offenders still in prison, the reinstatement of those dismissed from their posts for political reasons, the abolition of the death penalty and a review of the conditions under which political prisoners were held.

The authorities, however, continued to introduce new restrictive measures. Under a bill passed in December 1983 they were empowered to refuse a passport to persons suspected of endangering state security. A press law passed on Jan. 26, 1984, provided for stricter control of the contents of newspapers.

On May 10, 1985, the *Sejm* adopted amendments to the penal code which inter alia provided for heavier sentences for political offences such as attending an illegal meeting.

Legislation passed by the *Sejm* in July 1985 provided for greater government control over university staffing. By the end of November 1985 more than 70 senior university officials, including the rectors of the universities of Gdansk, Poznan and Wroclaw and of the Warsaw Polytechnic, were dismissed as being politically unacceptable, whereupon several others resigned in protest.

Under an act of July 17, 1986, on "special procedures towards perpetrators of some offences" more than 100 offenders against the state and public order were released, and the Minister of the Interior announced on Sept. 1, 1986, that he had ordered the release of a further 225 such offenders, but that those accused of espionage, terrorist activities or treason would remain in detention and that a nationwide security operation had been launched to disband any remaining "conspiratorial groups and structures" (while no legal action would be taken against over 3,000 people interviewed by the security services).

Under an amnesty of January 1987 all 225 detainees recognized as political prisoners by the authorities were released, as their prison terms were replaced by heavy fines.

Solidarity (*Solidarnosc*)

Leadership. Lech Walesa (ch.)

The Solidarity movement arose out of the formation, early in 1980, of various independent workers' committees, strike committees and finally trade unions. An important event at the beginning of these developments was the holding of a service of commemoration in the Gdansk shipyard on Dec. 18, 1979, for workers killed by troops during demonstrations and strikes in 1970 (against major price increases) in Gdansk, Gdynia and Szczecin; the service, called by students and dissident groups, was attended by some 4,000 persons, although many dissidents—including members of the Social Self-Defence Committee (KOR—see separate entry)—were arrested before and during the service. Some 25 workers at the Elektromontaz plant were dismissed for taking part in the service, and the staff of this plant thereupon formed, on Jan. 25, 1980, a five-member "workers committee" which included Lech Walesa (who had been one of the organizers of the 1970 demonstrations and had since lost his job) to campaign for the reinstatement of the 25 workers.

Strikes which began during July 1980 as wage disputes soon assumed overtly political dimensions as the strikers called for the legalization of independent trade unions, the lifting of censorship in the Polish press, the release of imprisoned dissidents, the strengthening of the position of the Roman Catholic Church and changes in government priorities in social welfare. In August the strikers began to form inter-factory strike committees to negotiate directly with the authorities on demands covering, in addition to those on pay and working conditions, the disbandment of the official trade unions, the erection of a monument to the workers killed in 1970 and publication of all the workers' demands in the mass media.

By Aug. 23, 1980, the government began to negotiate with the inter-factory committees, and on Aug. 30 an agreement was reached in Gdansk between an inter-factory committee, led by L. Walesa, and a government delegation, with the committee explicitly acknowledging the undisputed "leading force" represented by the Polish United Workers' Party (PUWP), while the government, in addition to consenting to a new wage agreement, expressed readiness to recognize legitimate new unions which could be based on the strike committees, to introduce within three months a bill moderating the censorship laws and to permit the broadcasting of Roman Catholic church services on Sundays. A similar agreement was signed in Szczecin, and by Sept. 1 both regions were largely back to normal working. However, industrial unrest continued to spread elsewhere, in particular among coal miners in Silesia, with whose inter-factory committee agreement was reached on Sept. 3.

Solidarity was formally established at a conference held on Sept. 18, 1980, in Gdansk by some 250 delegates of unofficial trade unions formed in may areas during September 1980. On Sept. 24 Solidarity applied for the registration of its statutes by the Warsaw district court, but the court objected to Solidarity's statement that the holding of a major trade union post was incompatible with political office. Describing this statement as a breach of human and political rights, the court insisted that Solidarity should incorporate in its statute a specific recognition of the PUWP as the only "leading political force"—as had earlier been agreed by the Gdansk inter-factory committee at the end of August. Solidarity responded that its acceptance of the Polish Constitution was itself a guarantee of recognition of the role of the PUWP. When the presiding judge eventually announced the recognition of Solidarity, he added a statement amending several of the union's statutes, including those relating to the right to strike, and inserted among the statutes the disputed clause of recognition of the PUWP. Solidarity accepted the registration but not the amendments and applied to the Supreme Court for their annulment.

On Oct. 27, 1980, Solidarity presented new demands to the Prime Minister (Jozef Pinkowski), with an ultimatum threatening a national strike unless negotiations were begun immediately—on the reversal of the Warsaw district court's decision, the granting of greater access of Solidarity to the media, the right to a trade union newspaper, the implementation of all agreed but outstanding wage increases and the cessation of alleged harassment by local bodies. Following a further threat of a general strike the Supreme Court pronounced in favour of Solidarity on Nov. 10; as proposed by the latter, the recognition of the PUWP was incorporated in the annexe to the statutes.

It was announced on Nov. 17, 1980, that further disputes in Gdansk had been settled at a meeting between Solidarity and Stanislaw Kania (who had succeeded Edward Gierek as First Secretary of the PUWP on Sept. 6, 1980), and on Nov. 24 it was announced that Solidarity had been allotted a weekly hour-long broadcast on Warsaw radio.

The national co-ordinating commission of Solidarity announced on Dec. 10, 1980, that it had formed a "committee for the defence of those prosecuted for their convictions" to campaign for the release of political prisoners, which it described as "vital for the restoration of an atmosphere of confidence between the authorities and society". However, during early January 1981 Solidarity failed to reach agreement with the government over its demand for a five-day working week. On Jan. 7 Solidarity militants declared every Saturday work-free and threatened strike action if any worker were penalized for taking any Saturday off. Following further strike threats "preliminary agreement" was reached on Jan. 30 on three issues—the free Saturday, access to the media and the registration of Rural Solidarity (see separate entry).

Under the final agreement reached on Jan. 31, 1981, between the government and Solidarity the latter accepted (i) the norm of a 40-hour week and an eight-hour working day as a target; (ii) 38 work-free Saturdays during 1981; (iii) an interim government proposal for what amounted to a 42-hour working week (for which details were worked out on Feb. 18) and (iv) the publication of a nationally distributed weekly newspaper of Solidarity (in addition to its three existing weeklies) and time to be allowed for Solidarity programmes on radio and television. However, these new agreements did not lead to immediate industrial peace.

Following his appointment as Prime Minister, Gen. Wojciech Jaruzelski called, on Feb. 12, 1981, on Solidarity members to resist agitators proposing "false anarchistic paths contrary to socialism" and stressed the government's determination to "bar the way" to those who were striving "to achieve counter-revolution".

In a "resolution concerning the aims and methods of the union", dated Feb. 12, 1981, Solidarity accused the government inter alia of having held up progress on the proposed laws on the trade unions and on the revision of censorship, and of having arrested activists in alleged violation of the Gdansk agreement. The resolution, however, also condemned "local and regional strikes pursuing disparate aims without the consent of the national co-ordinating commission, often against its advice" and "sometimes provoked by advocates of confrontation among those in authority as a means of disrupting our unity", which "would mean the destruction of our movement and would herald a period of uncontrolled social conflict".

On Feb. 13, 1981, the national co-ordinating commission of Solidarity indicated its willingness to comply with a request by Gen. Jaruzelski for "three months of honest work, 90 days of calm, to put some order into the economy". An official Solidarity spokesman said on Feb. 16 that Solidarity would support the new government as long as it was offered a genuine partnership; he also denied PUWP allegations that Solidarity was attempting to supplant the party as the country's leading political force.

At a meeting of the national co-ordinating commission of Solidarity in Bydgoszcz on March 23-24, 1981, L. Walesa was strongly criticized for his "autocratic" handling of the negotiations with the government over the occupation (on March 16) of the United Peasant Party's headquarters in Bydgoszcz by members of Rural Solidarity. The meeting decided (i) to declare a four-hour national strike on March 27; (ii) to seek immediate new negotiations with the government; and (iii) to call an indefinite general strike starting on March 31 unless such negotiations proved successful. S. Kania called this decision "a call for self-annihilation" and accused Solidarity of turning a local incident into a "national catastrophe". Talks between the government and Solidarity on March 25 ended inconclusively after the Minister of Justice had failed to present a report on the Bydgoszcz incident as demanded by Solidarity, and the four-hour warning strike was observed by some 13,000,000 workers on March 27, 1981, bringing virtually the whole country's industry and communications to a standstill.

In the Soviet Union, the German Democratic Republic, Czechoslovakia and Hungary the latest strike action was strongly condemned as serving counter-revolutionary forces, and Tass (the official Soviet news agency) stated on March 29, 1981, that there was now "an open struggle" between Solidarity and the Polish state. However, on March 30 it was announced that agreement had been reached between Solidarity and the government on the handling of the Bydgoszcz incident. Under this agreement the government undertook (i) to withdraw police units from Bydgoszcz, (ii) to set up a special commission to examine the farmers' case for union recognition and (iii) to pay in full all workers who had taken part in the strike of March 27, while Solidarity undertook (i) to suspend the strike alert for March 31, (ii) to halt any other occupations or activities creating tensions and (iii) to set up mechanisms for the solution of local disputes without resorting to national strike action.

L. Walesa described the March 30 agreement as "a 70 to 80 per cent success", and thanked the Pope for his assistance (by having written to Cardinal Wyszinski, the Polish Primate, on the subject and having appealed for a peaceful settlement of the dispute). Although the national co-ordinating commission of Solidarity again severely criticized L. Walesa on March 31 for not having insisted on the formal registration of Rural Solidarity. L. Walesa firmly declared on April 11 that he would not resign as chairman of Solidarity as long as the possibility of "adventurism and irresponsibility" continued in the organization. The commission had earlier (on March 31) decided by 25 votes to four with six abstentions to call off the planned general strike.

On April 14, Solidarity issued a draft policy statement in which it argued that either rationing should be introduced for most goods or the "price mechanism" should be brought into play to reduce excess spending power (but with lower-income groups receiving additional assistance), and that luxury goods should be more heavily taxed and a progressive system of income tax should be introduced. It also declared its readiness to withhold all wage claims until the end of 1981, and described its aim as the achievement of social egalitarianism and its basic task as being to defend the working people and to ensure that the state also adhered to this principle. Moreover, the statement called for the observance of civil liberties such as "the right to profess one's own views, freedom of speech and the printed word, the right to honest information and to assemblies and free associations" and for the limitation of censorship measures. It attributed Poland's crisis to bureaucracy and the lack of democratic processes under previous administrations but claimed that "the severe economic crisis, the outbreak of social protest [in 1980] and the establishment of Solidarity [had] paved the way for reform and renewal". Proposals for such reform included "more autonomy for individual concerns, which should have more freedom to determine manning levels", and "an active policy of job creation by the state", which should form a fund for the aid of the unemployed and the retraining of displaced workers. It emphasized that Solidarity was "the main guarantee of the renewal process" but at the same time "must be determined and ready to make sacrifices".

The emergence of Solidarity in Poland was strongly opposed in the Soviet Union. The journal *Literaturnaya Gazeta* declared on May 13, 1981, that Solidarity had achieved nothing positive but had links with the "totalitarian, terrorist organization KOR" (the Social Self-Defence Committee) and was "a social movement following aims which have nothing to do with trade unionism but which are by their objective content political aims". The Central Committee of the Communist Party of the Soviet Union (CPSU), on June 7, accused the PUWP leadership of failure to control the "anti-socialist forces" in Poland and of allowing the latter to take control of the party's "horizontal structures" reform movement. (This movement within the PUWP consisted of various groups such as the Movement for Horizontal Consultations created in Gdansk in November 1980 to link like-minded party organizations in a "horizontal", i.e. not vertical or hierarchical, structure.) In a statement by the CPSU Central Committee, published on June 9, 1981, and dealing with the "profound crisis" in Poland which had "spread across the country's entire political and economic life", the need was stressed "to oppose in a determined manner any attempts by the enemies of socialism to take advantage of the difficulties". However, it was conceded that the PUWP had been "falling back step by step under the pressure of internal counter-revolution supported by imperialist foreign centres of subversion" and that "the enemies of socialist Poland" had been "gaining control of one position after another", with counter-revolution "using Solidarity's extremist faction as a strike force" and with "a wave of anti-communism and anti-Sovietism" developing.

The Central Committee of the PUWP approved on June 11, 1981, a resolution stating that politically motivated strikes were inadmissible and that partnership with Solidarity was acceptable only as long as the relationship was "based on socialist principles". During the ninth congress of the PUWP on July 14-20, 1981, the party's then First Sectretary, S. Kania, declared inter alia that the PUWP saw positive elements in Solidarity and was ready to work with it, although there was concern over that element in Solidarity which attempted to turn it into a political party, "an opposition party in respect of the socialist state"; he claimed that this destructive element was being encouraged by KOR and "other opponents of socialism".

Increases in food prices by an average 100 per cent on July 22, 1981, were followed by violent protest demonstrations and strikes which the Central Committee of the PUWP described, on Aug. 12, as "a great danger to peace". On the same day Solidarity leaders called for a two-month voluntary suspension of all strikes and demonstrations—but this call was not followed by all regional sections of the organization. The national co-ordinating commission of Solidarity also suggested that members should volunteer to work on eight (normally work-free) Saturdays to aid the failing economy. At this time there was a succession of Warsaw Pact military manoeuvres near Poland's border and in the Baltic Sea and on Sept. 1 S. Kania and Gen. Jaruzelski (then Prime Minister) had a meeting with four Soviet generals.

Internal unrest nevertheless continued. On Aug. 17, 1981, Solidarity called a two-day occupation and strike affecting most printing presses in protest against its inability to use the state-controlled media in answering criticism by the government and the PUWP. The action virtually stopped all distribution of newspapers, and L. Walesa had some difficulty in preventing the organization's militant branches in Lodz, Wroclaw, Cracow and Lublin from continuing the action, which was formally ended on Aug. 20. Further Solidarity demands, for such things as uncensored coverage of the forthcoming congress of the movement, were rejected by S. Kania on Aug. 26.

L. Walesa had declared at a rally in Gdansk on Aug. 14, 1981 (the first anniversary of the outbreak of the shipyard strike): "We do not want to overthrow the power of the state. Let the government govern the country, and we will govern ourselves in the factories." In a televised statement on Sept. 1 he said, however, that the authorities were "losing social acceptance" and that the situation was forcing Solidarity "to assume responsibility for the fate of the country".

Evidence of further disagreement emerged on Sept. 2-3, 1981, when the national co-ordinating commission of Solidarity accused the government of retreating from the implementation of the agreements of August 1980 on censorship and the media. The Central Committee of the PUWP, approving a draft of the self-management bill, rejected Solidarity's demands for more extensive powers regarding the appointment of managers. On Sept. 4, S. Kania affirmed that the authorities were willing to declare a state of emergency.

Solidarity held its first national congress in two stages in Gdansk on Sept. 5-10 and Sept. 20-Oct. 7, 1981 (by which time it was said to have nearly 10,000,000 members). It re-elected L. Walesa as its chairman and approved a large number of resolutions. It was, however, still in dispute with the government on (i) self-management in commercial enterprises, including procedures for appointing and dismissing managers; (ii) censorship and Solidarity's disputed claim to free and uncensored access to the mass media; (iii) government proposals for economic reform; (iv) the reduction of the meat ration from 3.7 to 3.0 kg per month; and (v) proposed food and tobacco price rises.

At the opening of the congress the minister in charge of trade union affairs (Stanislaw Ciosek) stated that the state structures were initiating and assimilating socialist renewal and stressed the need for Solidarity to co-operate with the government but within "the political framework for the existence of any kind of organization" based on respect for (i) the principle of social ownership of the means of production; (ii) the constitutional role of the PUWP as the leading force in Polish society; (iii) the inviolability of Poland's international alliance; and (iv) Solidarity's undertaking not to play the role of a political party.

In the national co-ordination commission's report to the congress, presented on Sept. 6, it was stated that Solidarity had so far taken no direct action on economic matters but that the proven inefficiency of the government now necessitated a more active economic strategy for the movement; that the authorities' monopoly of broadcasting systems encroached upon the rights of society as a whole; that Solidarity was the object of virulent, hostile and often slanderous propaganda; that Solidarity's access to the mass media was one of the basic conditions for stability and social calm in Poland; and that union consultation on the creation of self-management systems in enterprise was a political prerequiste for the achievement of Solidarity's other major. aims.

On Sept. 8, 1981, the congress issued a call to the *Sejm* to hold a national referendum before creating the proposed self-management law, failing which Solidarity would conduct its own referendum and even, if necessary, ignore the law after its approval by the *Sejm*. Also on Sept. 8 the congress approved a "message to the working people of Eastern Europe" stating inter alia (according to *Trybuna Ludu*, the organ of the PUWP): "We assure you that, despite the lies disseminated in your countries, we are a genuine, 10,000,000-strong representative organ of workers, created as a result of workers' strikes. . . . We support those of you who have decided to take the difficult path of struggle for a free trade union movement. . . . We believe that soon your representatives and ours will be able to meet and exchange experiences as trade unionists."

Finally the first stage of the congress issued, on Sept. 10, a programmatic declaration which contained the following paragraphs (according to the Polish press): "Solidarity's supreme goal is the creation of dignified living conditions in a Poland which is economically and politically sovereign. It is intended to create a life free from poverty, exploitation, fear and lies in a society organized on the principles of democracy and the rule of law. Today the nation expects: first, an improvement in food supplies, through the establishment of a control over their production, distribution and pricing, in co-operation with Rural Solidarity; secondly, an economic reform, through the creation of authentic workers' self-management, the elimination of the party's right to make senior appointments, and the introduction of effective economic mechanisms; thirdly, truth, through public control of the mass media and the removal of lies from Polish schools and culture; fourthly, democracy, through the holding of free elections to the *Sejm* and people's councils [i.e. organs of local government in the provinces—voivodships—on which issue the congress passed a separate resolution on Sept. 10]; fifthly, justice, through the ensurance of the equality of all before the law, the release of those imprisoned for their beliefs and the defence of those repressed for publishing or union activities; sixthly, saving the threatened health of the nation by protecting the natural environment, increasing health spending and guaranteeing the rights of handicapped people in society; and seventhly, coal for the population and for industry, through guarantees of appropriate living and working conditions."

The congress's first stage (ending on Sept. 19, 1981) gave rise to strong criticism from sections of the PUWP, whose Warsaw branch executive stated on Sept. 11 that Solidarity was developing into a political and social movement aiming at a counter-revolutionary change of the system. Some PUWP members urged the banning of Solidarity, thus engendering a further polarization of positions. A Solidarity bulletin claimed on Sept. 15 that the deputies to the *Sejm* had been undemocratically elected (as they had been presented mainly on uncontested lists), and J. Kuron, the KOR chairman, said on Sept. 16 that until free elections could be held power should be taken over by a "committee of national salvation" composed of the PUWP, other parties, the Church and the trade unions; he added that the PUWP as a whole was "completely and utterly paralysed" and that "sooner or later a situation will be reached in which nothing can be done with this government".

The Politburo of the PUWP stated on the same day (Sept. 16, 1981) that the party would use all means to prevent a political takeover, but on Sept. 23 Stefan Olszowski, a hard-line member of the politburo, said that a broad-based national front could be formed, including Solidarity and church representatives as well as those of political parties. On Sept. 25 the *Sejm* unanimously approved new laws on state enterprises and on workers' self-management, laying down inter alia that factory directors could not be appointed or dismissed without approval by both the management and the workers' councils (except in certain cases of key or strategic importance). The approval of these laws by the government was severely criticized at the second part of the Solidarity congress, but L. Walesa repudiated those Solidarity members who "would like to overthrow everything, the *Sejm* included", and added that "within five years they would have replaced the system with greater totalitarianism than the present system".

On Oct. 7, 1981, the Solidarity congress approved overwhelmingly an eight-chapter programme in which it described itself "not only as the force able to protest but also as the force which desires to build a Poland which will be just for everybody" and as "the only guarantor for society" which would, however, have to act gradually to maximize its public support. Rejecting the government's programme for economic stabilization because it failed to mobilize several important reserves in the economy and did not enjoy public confidence, Solidarity insisted on the abolition of centralized management of the economy and on its separation from political authority.

The second stage of the congress also decided (on Sept. 28) that Solidarity should have a centralized union structure (in accordance with a proposal by L. Walesa), with a 107-member national commission comprising 69 regionally elected members (each representing 140,000 members) and the heads of the 38 regional chapters; the national commission itself would elect a 19-member presidium headed by the overall chairman of the organization.

On Oct. 16, 1981, S. Kania accused right-wing groups within Solidarity of deliberately obstructing every step taken by the government to alleviate the crisis and of being the chief impediment to the implementation of the agreements of August 1980; he called on Solidarity to ban all strikes and to work on all Saturdays throughout the winter. Solidarity, however, rejected the first of these demands on Oct. 20 as contrary to its rights under international law. The Solidarity presidium had on Sept. 19 called for the suspension of "all unjustified strikes and those called before all possible means of agreement had been exhausted" but added on Sept. 20 that it could not agree to any negotiations on the content of the August 1980 accords and that it would not refrain from "any statutory permitted actions aimed at giving full effect to the social contracts concluded with the government and ratified by the *Sejm*".

Despite an appeal by Solidarity to its members on Oct. 22, 1981, to avoid any further protest actions, strikes broke out in several areas, and on Oct. 23 the national co-ordinating commission called for a one-hour national strike on Oct. 28 in protest against alleged harassment of Solidarity officials by the authorities; it also threatened further selective "active strikes" unless by the end of October steps had been taken to improve the meat supply situation and to set up the proposed "social council for the national economy". The one-hour strike called for Oct. 28 was generally observed throughout the country.

On Oct. 30 the national co-ordinating commission called on Solidarity members to end all unco-ordinated local strikes—but some of these strikes nevertheless continued for a few days longer. On Nov. 3 the national co-ordinating commission called on workers to take control of their workplaces if necessary rather than to stop all production by striking. A meeting of the national co-ordinating commission held on Nov. 4, 1981, called for (i) for formulation of draft regulations for a revision of the procedures governing elections to the *Sejm* and the people's councils; (ii) the foundation of a social council to implement them; and (iii) the implementation of true self-management in factories.

By this time the Polish economic crisis had reached unprecedented proportions. On Nov. 12 it was officially stated that during the first 10 months of 1981 labour productivity had fallen by 14 per cent, the level of industrial production by 10 per cent, that of coal production by 20 per cent, that of construction by 21 per cent and that of exports by 15 per cent, while wages had increased by 25 per cent. At the same time L. Walesa appealed to workers in Western countries to exert pressure on their respective governments for the speeding-up of emergency aid to Poland because, he said, the political and economic reforms in Poland were in danger of collapse owing to "dangerous social tensions and spontaneous outbursts of popular anger". L. Walesa did not have whole-hearted support from some sections of Solidarity, however—as evidenced when Andrzei Gwiazda and 14 other members of the Gdansk regional executive resigned on Nov. 23 in protest against what they called his "excessively moderate" attitude towards the government.

On Nov. 28, 1981, the PUWP Central Committee approved a call made by Gen. Jaruzelski (who had succeeded S. Kania as First Secretary of the PUWP on Oct. 18) for the development of an emergency powers law which would give the government full powers for safeguarding the population and the economy. On Nov. 30 the Council of Ministers approved a series of bills to expedite the realization of the reforms due to be implemented in January 1982, but Solidarity rejected these measures as inadequately prepared and creating a "socially dangerous situation".

At a meeting of the Solidarity presidium and regional heads in Radom on Dec. 3, 1981, L. Walesa was reported to have said that "confrontation" was inevitable and that Solidarity was aware that it was dismantling the system. J. Kuron was said to have stated that "total negation of the so-called government provisional pre-reform system and the state of emergency should become the field of confrontation" and also to have called for the preparation of "action to overpower the authorities". Militant Solidarity members were said to have called for the creation of a "so-called worker militia" armed with helmets and batons, its first task being the "liberation" of the radio and the television headquarters, and for the immediate establishment of a "social council for the national economy" to act as a "provisional national government".

On Dec. 4, 1981, the Solidarity presidium issued a statement in which it laid down conditions for achieving a national accord, including (i) the cessation of anti-union repression, (ii) the passage of a law on trade unions in a version approved by Solidarity, (iii) the holding of democratic elections to local and provincial councils and (iv) the establishment of a "social council for the national economy". Following a meeting with Archbishop Glemp, L. Walesa stated at a Solidarity presidium meeting on Dec. 10 that he had written evidence of a campaign by the authorities to provoke confrontation but that Solidarity would "not retreat any more" and would respond with strike action if the *Sejm* accepted either the trade union law or the emergency powers law.

Early in December 1981 the Polish authorities claimed to have conclusive evidence that Solidarity leaders were planning a deliberate confrontation with the government with the ultimate aim of overthrowing it. Earlier, the army had been strengthened by the extension of national service by two months on Oct. 16, and Gen. Florian Siwicki, the army Chief of Staff, became a candidate member of the PUWP Politburo on Oct. 28.

At a meeting of Solidarity's national co-ordinating commission in Gdansk on Dec. 11-12, 1981, it was proposed to conduct a national referendum on Jan. 15, 1982, with the particular aim of obtaining a vote of no confidence in the government. During the following night the armed forces detained virtually the whole Solidarity leadership (including L. Walesa) and on Dec. 13 the Council of State (exercising collectively the functions of the head of state) announced the introduction of a state of martial law and the creation of a Military Council of Salvation.

This Council and the Council of Ministers subsequently issued a number of decrees which in effect (i) banned all trade union and most other organized non-governmental activities; (ii) abolished the right to strike; (iii) provided for the internment of up to 6,000 persons in specially erected internment camps; (iv) declared a large part of the economy to be under military discipline; (v) made work compulsory for most men; (vi) set up "summary trial" courts for dealing with infringements of martial law; (vii) closed down all except the official news media and most communications links, as well as closing the national frontiers and airspace; and (viii) reformed the higher education system. Among other measures taken by the authorities was an increase by about 300 per cent in retail prices of fuel and most staple foods with effect from Feb. 1, 1982.

In announcing the imposition of martial law (a "state of war"), Gen. Jaruzelski said that "a group of people presenting a threat to the safety of the state", including Solidarity activists and also activists of illegal anti-state organizations, had been interned. Although Solidarity was not officially banned, all gatherings were prohibited, all publications were subjected to prior censorship and the right of workers to organize and carry out "strikes of any nature whatsoever and demonstrations" was suspended.

Solidarity was reported to have set up, immediately after the declaration of martial law, a provisional executive to direct operations in the absence of its interned leaders and to produce a bulletin. However, strikes by Solidarity members in Gdansk ended on Dec. 15, 1981, and a rally in Warsaw on Dec. 17 was put down by troops with water cannon, one person being killed. There were also reports of several clashes between striking workers and troops, with seven miners being shot dead by troops near Katowice on Dec. 17. On Dec. 29, however, Poland was officially reported to be free of strikes.

During the first few weeks of martial law the Roman Catholic Church continued to press for the resumption of three-party negotiations between Solidarity, the government and the Church. Gen. Jaruzelski said on Dec. 25, 1981, that the independent trade unions would continue to play a role in Poland's affairs.

At the end of January 1982 the total of martial law detainees was offically given as 4,177 held in 24 different camps. This figure included a number of former office-bearers in the PUWP and the government who were held for alleged abuse of power while in office. Several Solidarity activists were sentenced to terms of imprisonment for from three to nine years for organizing strikes after Dec. 13, 1981, L. Walesa, who had also been detained, was formally interned on Jan. 26, 1982; in a letter (published in *Le Monde* of Paris on Feb. 1) he claimed that there was a campaign for his "gradual elimination" from the political arena.

A "Solidarity resistance committee" describing itself as the acting leadership of the union stated early in February 1982 that the organization's members would not attempt to negotiate independently with the authorities, as trade union unity was essential at this time. Thereafter there were frequent reports of Solidarity supporters being arrested for illegal trade union activities and the only two Solidarity presidium members still at large (Zbigniew Bujak and Wladyslaw Frasyniuk) called repeatedly for continued public resistance. On April 12, 1982, an unofficial Solidarity radio transmitter began weekly broadcasts in Warsaw, demanding a resumption of dialogue between the government, the Church and the trade unions, the restoration of Solidarity and the release of martial law detainees. A resurgence of disturbances in May 1982, particularly in Warsaw and Cracow, coincided with an appeal by underground Solidarity leaders for protest actions on May 13 to mark the fifth month of martial law.

The Polish television network announced on July 11, 1982, that "Radio Solidarity" had been dissolved after the discovery and confiscation on July 8 of a set of broadcasting equipment and the arrest of a number of people. However, "Radio Solidarity" broadcast again on July 13, when it announced a two-month break in transmissions (the station's organizer, Zbigniew Romaszewski, having gone underground). A further "Radio Solidarity" transmitter was seized on Aug. 30.

It was reported on July 13, 1982, that underground Solidarity bulletins had called for the temporary suspension of strikes and protest actions in order to facilitate the rapid resumption of dialogue with the authorities; however, the PUWP daily organ *Trybuna Ludu* replied on July 15 that there could be "no agreement with the enemies of socialism, with the anti-socialist underground, and with those who still have not set aside the strike weapons, who distribute hostile publications and who encourage young people to demonstrate".

Social tensions worsened again at the beginning of August 1982, following the failure of the authorities to respond positively to the offer of negotiations with Solidarity, and on Aug. 1 a new appeal for mass resistance was launched by Zbigniew Bujak, who delivered a tape-recorded message to some 15,000 people attending a ceremony in a Warsaw cemetery to commemorate the Polish uprising of 1944. Z. Bujak's message coincided with a new leaflet campaign by

Solidarity's acting leadership for the restoration of the union's rights, the release of all remaining detainees and the ending of martial law. *Trybuna Ludu* dismissed the new appeals on Aug. 3 as "dreams", but added that such unrealistic expectations could still endanger social calm, and on Aug. 12 the ("hard-line") army newspaper *Zolnierz Wolnosci* demanded a new crackdown on the opponents of the regime.

A major rally involving some 10,000 people was held on Aug. 13, 1982, outside the PUWP headquarters in Gdansk, but was dispersed by police using tear gas and water cannon; other rallies were reported on the same day in Warsaw, Wroclaw and Cracow. Heavy contingents of police and militia then moved into Gdansk in preparation for the second anniversary (on Aug. 16) of the forming of the Gdansk inter-factory strike committee (which had led to the ultimate foundation of Solidarity), but no incidents were reported there, although a demonstration of some 2,000 people took place on the same day in Warsaw.

Leaflets distributed by Solidarity in late August 1982 called for a nationwide protest, including strikes, to mark the second anniversary of the Gdansk agreement. Although the extent to which this call was followed remained unclear because of the severance of telephone links in many parts of the country, it became clear that major protests had taken place in several cities, notably Lubin, where five people were killed in several days of clashes with government riot squads (the *Zomos*).

On Oct. 8, 1982, the *Sejm* approved two laws on trade unions which effectively dissolved all existing unions and created the framework for new and more closely controlled unions to replace them. The new legislation was intended primarily to dismantle Solidarity, whose underground leadership nevertheless affirmed that the union would continue in existence and called a one-day protest strike for Nov. 10, to be followed by a general strike in early 1983. However, the Nov. 10 action attracted only limited support, and amid a general easing of social tensions L. Walesa was released from internment on Nov. 12. During his detention the Solidarity chairman had been kept completely isolated from the public in remote locations but had reportedly refused to make any accommodation with the authorities. His wife had reported in March 1982 that he had refused an offer to be allowed to emigrate permanently from Poland.

On the basis of plans outlined by Gen. Jaruzelski on Dec. 12, martial law was suspended on Dec. 31, 1982—the government thereby relinquishing its powers inter alia to intern people without trial, to impose curfews and to ban public meetings. The government nevertheless retained the right to reimpose martial law at any time, while certain martial law provisions were institutionalized within the penal code, notably specifications that workers or students who stirred up unrest could be dismissed and also that military courts would continue to try those accused of major economic or social crimes. At the same time, seven members of the Solidarity presidium were excluded from a general release of political detainees, as were some 1,500 others who (according to a government statement on Jan. 4, 1983) had been convicted or were awaiting trial for political crimes.

On Jan. 3, 1983, the first of the new trade unions created under the October 1982 legislation came into being, it being officially stated that 2,500 such unions had been legally registered and that a further 4,000 applications were pending. Under the new regulations each new union could represent only one workplace or factory and strikes of a "political" character were banned. The acting Solidarity leadership had consistently condemned the new union regulations and had refused to enter into any discussions with the government during their formulation.

L. Walesa himself, having returned to his home in Gdansk, came under various forms of pressure from the authorities in late 1982 and early 1983, including official inquiries into alleged irregularities in Solidarity's finances under his chairmanship and also in his own tax returns. On Dec. 16 he was prevented from delivering a speech at a rally in Gdansk to commemorate the 1970 food price demonstrations, having intended (according to a text pre-released to Western correspondents) to assert that the spirit of Solidarity remained alive and that "given time and different methods" the movement would achieve ultimate victory.

Despite the formal abolition of Solidarity it continued to operate at underground level through a Provisional Co-ordinating Committee (TKK) which issued, on Jan. 27, 1983, a programme describing the state of martial law as "a totalitarian dictatorship" and calling on the public to boycott the newly formed trade unions and to prepare for a general strike. In April it was reported that an illegal "inter-factory workers' committee" had been formed by Zbigniew Bujak (the only member, apart from L. Walesa, of the Presidium of Solidarity still at large). However, the calls by the TKK and this committee met with little response. The authorities arrested, between January and September 1983, hundreds of "conspirators". A call was made by the TKK on Aug. 3, 1983, for public demonstrations by Solidarity supporters on Aug. 31, for a boycott of public transport and for a reduction in their rate of work—but the government banned all meetings and marches until Sept. 15, 1983.

Having been awarded the 1983 Nobel Prize for Peace, L. Walesa did not attend the award ceremony in Oslo on Dec. 10 of that year (for fear of not being allowed to return to Poland). In his acceptance speech, read for him by a Solidarity member living in the West, he called for renewed dialogue between the state authorities and the people, emphasized the importance for Europe of stability in Poland and added that Poland ought to be helped and deserved help. (On Dec. 5 he had said that Western sanctions imposed on Poland after the declaration of martial law should be lifted. He had had a secret meeting with the TKK on Nov. 19-20, 1983, and he subsequently publicly opposed food price rises planned by the government, criticized the government's handling of the economy, insisted on the need to restore Solidarity and called for urgent reforms, while encouraging former Solidarity members to participate in workers' councils and the co-operative movement.)

After demonstrations in support of Solidarity had late in 1983 led to disturbances and confrontation with police, L. Walesa stated on Feb. 24, 1984, that no further demonstrations of strikes would be called.

After an amnesty had come into effect on July 23, 1984, the Minister of Justice stated on Aug. 24 that 630 out of 652 political prisoners serving sentences or awaiting trial had been released. The remaining 22 prisoners included Bogdan Lis and Piotr Mierzejewski (both of the Provisional Co-ordinating Committee, TKK) and 11 copper miners from Lubin sentenced on Nov. 29, 1983, for causing an illegal strike and an explosion.

L. Walesa and the TKK issued, on July 24, a joint statement calling for the restoration of free trade union activity and of civil rights. The TKK members, however, refused to emerge from clandestinity and insisted that they would continue operating towards constructing an independent trade union movement. At subsequent meetings of Solidarity leaders and other dissidents L. Walesa stressed that Solidarity wished to reach an accommodation with the government, and a former Solidarity adviser stated on Aug. 10 that the movement was ready to work within the trade union law provided the government was prepared to accept "social and trade union pluralism".

A clandestine TKK meeting held in Gdansk on Feb. 13, 1985, was also broken up by police, who arrested several leading Solidarity members. Three of them—Bogdan Lis, Adam Michnik and Wladyslaw Frasyniuk—were on June 14 sentenced to 3½, three and 2½ years in prison respectively for fomenting unrest and illegal protests. L. Walesa, who had also been present at the meeting, called (on March 3) for further strikes against price rises, and on March 9 he was ordered not to leave Gdansk without permission—this being the first restriction to be placed on him since his release from detention in November 1982. In August 1985, however, he called on Solidarity to abandon strikes and anti-government demonstrations.

On Sept. 30, 1986, Solidarity leaders announced that they were ready to work within the system to improve the country's political and economic conditions, and that they would take measures to end Solidarity's underground activities and to "ease the transition to legal and open undertakings"; that the TKK was to be disbanded and L. Walesa would remain titular head of Solidarity; but that a Temporary Council of Solidarity (TRS) was being formed (without Walesa) by seven members (including Z. Bujak, W. Frasyniuk and Bogdan Lis). The authorities, however, declared the TRS to be against the law.

During a visit to Poland Pope John Paul II, giving his blessing to Solidarity, stated on June 11, 1987, that it was legitimate for Poles to fight peacefully for human rights.

Rural Solidarity (Independent Self-Governing Trade Union for Private Farmers)

Leadership. Jan Kulaj (ch.)

Rural Solidarity was established in December 1980 as the (uncollectivized) Polish peasants' counterpart to the independent Solidarity trade union organization of industrial workers which had emerged earlier in the year. After an application for its registration had been deferred by the Warsaw district court on Dec. 30, 1980, farmers embarked on protest action involving the occupation of local government offices and agricultural strikes in various areas and the setting-up of a national strike committee in Rzeszow (south-eastern Poland) on Jan. 12, 1981. Stanislaw Kania, then First Secretary of the PUWP, had said at a meeting of the United Peasants' Party (UPP) on Jan. 11 that there was "no room in the Polish countryside for a political opposition of an anti-socialist character".

A preliminary agreement reached on Jan. 30, 1981, between the government and the national co-ordinating commission of Solidarity covered also the registration of Rural Solidarity. The Supreme Court, on the other hand, ruled on Feb. 10, 1981, that there was no legal basis for recognizing the organization as a trade union but that it could be registered as an association. The farmers thereupon threatened to withhold their produce from the market unless 60 specific demands were met, mainly on the level of state investment in agriculture. On Feb. 19 (after the appointment of Gen. Wojciech Jaruzelski as First Secretary of the PUWP), Rural Solidarity was granted (i) the right to private ownership of land (to be formalized in new provisions to be inserted in the Constitution), (ii) equality of treatment of private and state farms and (iii) increased government investment in agriculture. The organization's basic structure and policy were established at a meeting of 490 delegates in Poznan on March 8-9, 1981.

In an incident in Bydgoszcz, where police broke up the occupation of provincial council offices on March 19-20, 1981, by protesting farmers, the latter's leader, Jan Rulewski, was seriously injured; the incident led to two-hour protest strikes by Solidarity members in Szczecin, Torun, Grudziadz and Bydgoszcz on March 20, when Lech Walesa, the Solidarity chairman, expressed his personal opposition to a general strike (for which he was severely criticized at a meeting of Solidarity's national co-ordinating committee in Bydgoszcz on March 23).

On April 17, 1981, it was announced that the government had reached a 10-point agreement with the private farmers and had undertaken (i) to create by May 10 the legal basis for registration of Rural Solidarity, (ii) to incorporate the farmers' rights in the new trade union law and (iii) to adopt no disciplinary measures against those occupying party offices. The farmers in turn agreed to call off all protest actions. The Warsaw district court finally registered Rural Solidarity as an "Independent Self-Governing Trade Union for Private Farmers" on May 12. J. Kulaj claimed that it represented some 2,500,000 of Poland's 3,500,000 private farmers (who worked on about 70 per cent of all agricultural land and produced 80 per cent of the country's agricultural output). The *Sejm* had on May 6 almost unanimously approved the proposed amendments to the trade union bill.

On Aug. 17, 1981, Rural Solidarity was, under an agreement with the Ministry of Agriculture, awarded a share in the rural development fund, but on Aug. 28, Rural Solidarity called on its members to withhold tax contributions in protest against the government's alleged failure to approve the agreement and its alleged intention of renegotiating it so as to include the official Polish Union of Agricultural Circles and Organizations (PZKiOR).

Under the martial law regime proclaimed on Dec. 13, 1981, Rural Solidarity was suspended (along with the urban free trade union movement) and its leader, J. Kulaj, interned. After the latter had undertaken to avoid resistance to the government and to co-operate with the UPP, he was released from detention in late April 1982.

Under legislation adopted by the *Sejm* on Oct. 8, 1982, creating the framework for new and more closely controlled workers' organizations, Rural Solidarity was effectively replaced by new organizations which lacked the essential character of trade unions. The government argued that trade unions of private landowners existed in no country in the world and that landowners' associations with the character of agricultural chambers were a more normal form of organization for private farmers. Events since the registration of Rural Solidarity, it maintained, had shown that a complete reform of the system for the representation of farmers was required, since "the ambitions and the selfish interests of the leading groups became predominant, and a significant role was played by the influences, and not infrequently the pressures, exerted by external centres alien to the interests of the countryside".

The legislation specified that the names of the national, provincial and parish organizations grouped within the PZKiOR would be changed in order to incorporate the word "Farmers", thus emphasizing that the PZKiOR represented farmers (both state and private) as well as other rural groups. It was stated that the new organizations were regarded as the appropriate forum of activity for members of Rural Solidarity. As in the case of its industrial counterpart, however, the Rural Solidarity organization appeared to have continued widespread popular support notwithstanding its effective dissolution.

Other Groupings

Citizens' Committees against Violence (KOPP)

These Committees were established in November 1984 in various cities to monitor police activities in the wake of the murder of Fr Popieluszko (see below under Church-State Relations). Shortly afterwards they were officially warned to disband or face prosecution, and Western correspondents were told that they would risk prosecution or suspension of reporting rights if they attended press conferences given by the Committees.

Confederation for an Independent Poland (KPN)

Leadership. Robert Leszek Moczulski (ch.)

This organization, which the Polish authorities regarded as an anti-Soviet movement, was to have announced on Feb. 27, 1980, that it intended to nominate candidates for the election to the *Sejm* to be held on March 23, 1980, for which all official candidates were nominated by the National Unity Front dominated by the PUWP. However, its planned meeting was banned by the authorities and two of its leaders were arrested. On Dec. 17, 1980, the KPN announced the temporary suspension of its activities in view of the country's "dangerous situation".

On March 6, 1981, four leading KPN members—R. L. Moczulski, Romuald Szeremitiewow, Tadeusz Stanski and Tadeusz Jandziszak—were formally charged with seeking the violent overthrow of Poland's constitutional system. During the trial R. L. Moczulski was reported to have told the court on July 3 that he rejected the legitimacy of the Yalta agreement (by which the Allies had laid down the post-war boundaries in Europe) and of the Polish People's Republic, and that he supported the concept of a "Greater Poland" (including eastern territories which had become part of the Soviet Union in 1945). Following the imposition of martial law on Dec. 13, 1981, the four were all convicted on Oct. 8, 1982, and sentenced to prison terms of seven years (R. L. Moczulski), five years (R. Szeremitiewow and T. Stanski) and two years' suspended (T. Jandziszak).

At the first congress of the free trade union movement Solidarity (held in September-October 1981) the KPN had advocated the extensive reprivatization of agriculture and commerce. The military newspaper *Zolnierz Wolnosci* had accused the KPN on Nov. 25, 1981, of setting up a paramilitary wing.

On March 9, 1985, seven KPN members, among them R. L. Moczulski, were arrested after a meeting. Following the detention of other activists in August 1985, a government spokesman said that 231 persons were currently under detention for "politically motivated offences", that 44 of them had been sentenced and that 187 were awaiting trial (whereas in 1984 there had been only about 25 detainees). On April 22, 1986, Moczulski and four other prominent KPN members were sentenced to imprisonment for terms of two to 2½ years for plotting to overthrow the communist system, but they were all released under an act of July 17, 1986, laying down "special procedures towards perpetrators of some offences".

Direct Action (*Akcja Bezposrednia*)

This hitherto unknown group claimed responsibility for an explosion in front of party headquarters in Gdynia on Feb. 28, 1987, and in pamphlets accused the leaders of Solidarity of "leading the good life with money from abroad" instead of "fighting the regime". According to dissident circles the explosion was likely to have been a "provocation" carried out by the security services.

Independent Artists' and Writers' Groups

An independent artists' union (ZPAP) was suspended on April 21, 1983, after refusing to retract a series of statements in support of Solidarity and calling for an amnesty.

An independent writers' union was disbanded by the authorities on Aug. 21, 1983, because of its alleged "anti-socialist tendencies"; an appeal against its dissolution was rejected by a Warsaw court on Sept. 10, 1983.

Social Self-Defence Committee (SSDC or KOR)

Leadership. Jacek Kuron (ch.)

KOR was established on Oct. 3, 1977, and replaced an earlier Workers' Defence Committee (WDC), which had been formed on Sept. 23, 1976, and had, without being officially recognized, given financial aid to the families of workers who had been dismissed or imprisoned after strikes and demonstrations against rises in food prices announced on June 24, 1976, but withdrawn on the following day. Early in 1977 the WDC began to challenge the official attitude to the question of human rights. Although Edward Gierek (then First Secretary of PUWP) had stated that no action would be taken against the WDC, several of its members were in January 1977 fined for "illegal collection of funds".

In May 1977 WDC supporters accused the civic militia of having killed a student in Cracow on May 7 after he had collected signatures for a petition calling for a commission of inquiry into the prosecution of workers on charges arising out of riotous demonstrations. (Students in Cracow subsequently formed a new solidarity committee to replace the existing official student organization.) Also in May 1977 five WDC members were detained without trial for three months; after writing a letter to the prosecutor-general appealing for their release, Prof Edward Lipinski, the doyen of Poland's economists and a WDC member, was expelled from the PUWP. The five WDC members were, however, released on July 23, 1977; the charges against one of them were withdrawn; and five workers imprisoned in connexion with riots were released.

When the majority of the WDC members decided to replace the organization by KOR, the latter's objects were listed as the collection of information regarding political, racial or religious repression as well as any violation of human or civic rights and also the provision of moral and legal aid to victims of arbitrary bureaucratic measures. The 23 founder members of KOR included Prof Lipinski, Jerzy Andrzejewski and (Mrs) Halina Mikolajska. On Oct. 20, 1977, a new independent monthly called *Glos* (*Voice*) published a "Declaration of the Democratic Movement" signed by 110 persons, including five members of KOR. Claiming that the existing decay of authority was caused by the fact that citizens were deprived of their rights and the state of its sovereignty, the declaration stated that there was "a large social base to undertake a social struggle for democracy and independence in a lasting way and on a broad scale". The declaration called for freedom of belief, speech, assembly and work, and for the application of the UN covenants on human rights, which would require basic legal changes in Poland, including the liberalization of education, trade unions and science and the creation of a consumers' movement.

Adam Michnik, a leading member of KOR, declared in October 1977 that the "Democratic Movement" was not an opposition in the traditional sense and did not want power but action in defence of civic and human rights and for the extension of democratic freedom. He also took the line that in terms of the 1975 Final Act of the Helsinki Conference on Security and Co-operation in Europe (CSCE) respect for human rights was no longer "the internal affair of each country" but was an international problem. In August 1978 KOR entered into a co-operation agreement with the Charter 77 movement in Czechoslovakia.

During the strikes for higher wages in July 1980 J. Kuron, writing in KOR's journal *Robotnik* ("The Worker"), advised strikers on how to conduct wage negotiations but warned them against carrying disputes on to the streets, as this had caused armed confrontations in 1970 and 1976. Nevertheless, workers in a number of enterprises campaigned not only for the right to elect independent delegates to the official trade unions but also for the right of their unofficial "workers' committees" to form inter-factory organizations which would negotiate directly with the authorities on such issues as a complete revision of the trade union system in Poland. During August 1980 shipyard workers in Gdansk and Szczecin, after striking and occupying the shipyards, achieved considerable concessions in this respect (see separate entry for Solidarity). Negotiations between a Gdansk strike committee led by Lech Walesa and a government commission led by Mieczyslaw Jagielski (a Deputy Premier) led to the conclusion of a wage agreement and government recognition of legitimate new unions as well as other government concessions, while the strike committee explicity acknowledged that the PUWP remained the undisputed "leading force" in the country. A similar agreement was reached in Szczecin, and after parliamentary approval of these agreements work was back to normal in both regions by Sept. 1, 1980. KOR on the other hand, warned workers (in *Robotnik* on Oct. 19, 1980) that the actions of certain elements among them appeared likely to provoke Soviet armed intervention in Poland.

By February 1981 KOR was increasingly attacked in the press (not only in Poland but more especially in that of the Soviet Union, the German Democratic Republic and Czechoslovakia) for alleged subversive propaganda links with right-wing groups in London and elsewhere with the aim of undermining the stability of Polish society through its extremists' involvement with Solidarity. J. Kuron and A. Michnik were strongly attacked during a debate in the PUWP Central Committee in February 1981, and on March 5 J. Kuron was arrested and formally charged with "publicly defaming the Polish nation, the Polish People's Republic, the state system and its highest organ". However, he was released after undertaking to present himself to the authorities twice a week. A. Michnik was arrested on March 12, and on June 24 *Pravda* (the organ of the Central Committee of the Communist Party of the Soviet Union) claimed to have documentary evidence that he had been in contact with Western spies working in Eastern Europe, according to two women who had in March 1979 defected from West to East Germany.

At the end of the second part of the first congress held by Solidarity, Prof Edward Lipinski announced on Sept. 28, 1981, that KOR considered its work as completed and had therefore decided to dissolve itself, the struggle for an independent Poland having now been taken over by "the strong arm of Solidarity". He died on July 13, 1986.

Church-State Relations

A bishops' conference held in Warsaw on Sept. 20-21, 1983, expressed concern at the frequent removal of crosses which had been erected in schools and factories during the Solidarity period; this concern led to attacks on the Church in several official publications. At a PUWP central committee meeting on Oct. 14-15, a member of the politburo declared that "militant clericalism and instigatory pronouncements" by clergymen would not be tolerated. Official measures were taken against certain priests accused of fomenting opposition to the state, among them Fr Jerzy Popieluszko, who was, in July 1984, charged with abuse of religious freedom and with concealing arms and ammunition—these charges being suspended under the amnesty of July 21. However, on Oct. 19 he was kidnapped, and on Oct. 30 his dead body was found. Three members of the security forces and an official of the Ministry of the Interior were, on Feb. 7, 1985, sentenced to terms of imprisonment for from 14 to 25 years for their involvement in Fr Popieluszko's murder, and these sentences were confirmed by the Supreme Court on April 12. As a result of this murder Solidarity supporters announced that human rights monitoring committees would be set up in the main cities to check the implementation of the human rights provisions of the Helsinki Final Act.

Archbishop Jozef Glemp (created a cardinal on Feb. 2, 1983) had in December 1984 banned a priest from preaching in Warsaw churches because his anti-communist sermons were "alien to the spirit of the Gospel". In February 1985 the cardinal restated the need for priests to keep out of politics. In June 1985 two priests were tried for leading an illegal strike and breaking into a school building; the final result of the trial (after an appeal) consisted of suspended prison sentences and heavy fines imposed on the defendants.

Exiled Movements

Since the establishment of Communist rule after World War II a number of Poland's former political parties have continued to exist in exile, as does a "Polish government in exile" established in London following the German conquest of Poland in 1939.

Communist Party of Poland

Leadership. Kazimierz Mijal (gen. sec.)

Founded. 1966

This party was founded in Albania by K. Mijal who had been (i) an associate of President Boleslaw Bierut in Poland in the 1950s and (ii) a member of the pro-Soviet faction of the PUWP, of which he had been a central committee member, and a Minister of State and Minister for Communal Energy until his removal from the Council of Ministers in 1957, allegedly because of his "Stalinist" views. In 1966 he defected to Albania from where he made regular broadcasts on the Polish service of Radio Tirana. On Nov. 18, 1984, he was reported to have been arrested in Poland, charged with re-entering the country with forged papers and with distributing illegal documents.

The party has denounced the PUWP as "counter-revolutionary", "social democratic" and "a party of the bourgeoisie" and has described the Chinese Communist Party as "the vanguard of the world revolution".

Polish Christian Labour Party

Leadership. Konrad Sieniewicz (gen. sec.)

This party was formed in 1937 as a merger of two formations with roots in 19th-century Polish politics (the National Workers' Party and the Christian Democratic Party). It formed part of the London-based government in exile during World War II, following which it was forced to suspend its activities in Poland in July 1946. The exiled party, now based in Rome, is affiliated to the Christian Democratic World Union.

Polish Socialist Party

Leadership. Stanislaw Wasik (ch.); Tadeusz Prokopowicz (gen. sec.)

This historic Polish party formed part of the London-based government in exile during World War II, after which it continued as an exiled party in rejection of the forcible merger with the Communist Party instituted in Poland in December 1948. The exiled party is a member of the Socialist International and a constituent party of the Socialist Union of Central and Eastern Europe (SUCEE).

Portugal

Capital: Lisbon Pop. 10,230,000

The Republic of Portugal is, under its 1976 Constitution reflecting the aims of the 1974 revolution, "a democratic state based . . . on pluralism . . . with the objective of ensuring the transition to socialism". It has a President elected by universal adult suffrage for a five-year term; an Assembly of the Republic of 250 members elected by universal adult suffrage for a four-year term; and a government under a Prime Minister appointed by the President. In elections held on July 19, 1987, the Social Democratic Party gained an outright majority in the Assembly.

Under a law passed on June 16, 1978, and promulgated on Sept. 19 of that year prison sentences of two to eight years were provided for leaders of organizations promoting fascism and violence against democratic institutions or national unity and sentences of one to two years for members of such organizations.

On July 27, 1984, the Assembly of the Republic passed the general provisions of an Internal Security and Civil Protection Bill which allowed that under certain circumstances homes could be searched without a warrant, private mail could be opened, public meetings could be suspended and measures could be taken against civil servants who refused to help with police inquiries.

In recent years the principal extra-parliamentary opposition to the government has come from small extreme left-wing groups.

Anti-capitalist and Anti-militarist Organization

This organization exploded a bomb at a Radio Free Europe relay station at Gloria de Ribatejo on May 7, 1985 (one day before a visit to Portugal by President Reagan of the United States).

Autonomous Revolutionary Groups (*Grupos Autónomos Revolucionarios*, GAR)

On April 10, 1985, this group planted a bomb at a government housing office in Oporto, and on Aug. 31, 1985, it bombed the South African embassy in Lisbon.

Autonomous Revolutionary Workers' Commandos

This group was responsible for killing a public sector official in Setúbal on Nov. 24, 1984.

People's Forces of 25 April (*Forças Populares de 25 Abril,* FP-25)

Established on April 30, 1980, this extreme left-wing group took its name from the date of the 1974 revolution which overthrew the Caetano regime. Members of the group have been involved in bank raids, bombings and extortion. It was responsible for the murder on May 12, 1980, of Clariano Baia, a Lisbon businessman who had refused to pay a "revolutionary tax" equivalent to about £12,000, and for the shooting of Diamantino Monteiro Pereira, another Lisbon businessman, on Dec. 6, 1982, for dismissing hundreds of workers from his factory.

The Minister of the Interior said on Feb. 13, 1982, that a 24-hour strike called by the trade unions for the previous day had been used as a cover for "a communist-inspired plan to subvert the democratic state of law"; three persons arrested in this connexion and found in possession of arms and of a pre-recorded tape containing a "proclamation to the nation" were found to be members of the FP-25.

Early in 1984 FP-25 members were involved in numerous acts of violence, including two murders, a bank raid, the planting of over 100 small bombs and a series of bomb attacks. In operations against the FP-25 on June 18-20, 1984, police arrested 42 persons, among them Lt.-Col. Otelo Saraiva de Carvalho (who had played a leading part in the 1974 revolution).

On Oct. 26, 1984, five alleged members of the FP-25, including Lt.-Col. Saraiva de Carvalho, were charged with founding, promoting and directing a "terrorist" organization (a crime punishable by imprisonment for up to 20 years under Art. 288 of the penal code). Numerous other detainees were accused of FP-25 membership. Further arrests relating to FP-25 activities were made on Aug. 20, 1984, and Feb. 21, 1985.

Meanwhile FP-25 members still at large made further bomb attacks, their targets including British, French and West German business premises and an industrialist who was murdered on March 23, 1985.

The trial of 74 suspected FP-25 members, due to begin on July 22, 1985, was postponed after one of the prosecution's key witnesses had been shot by an FP-25 member on July 19 (he died of his wounds in August). The FP-25 also claimed responsibility for killing the director-general of the prison service in Lisbon on Feb. 15, 1986, and for a car bomb explosion at the US embassy on Feb. 18.

Saraiva de Carvalho was on May 20, 1987, found guilty of organizing a terrorist group and sentenced to 15 years' imprisonment; in total 47 of the co-defendants were convicted, and 16 acquitted.

Qatar

Capital: Doha Pop. 310,000

The state of Qatar has a Council of Ministers appointed by and presided over by the head of state (the Amir) and assisted by a 30-member Advisory Council appointed for a three-year term. There is no parliament and there are no official political parties.

Although at least 70 per cent of the population are immigrants (including many from the Indian sub-continent) and there is a Shi'ite minority, there have been few signs of internal political tension. However, immigrants thought to hold "suspect" political views are deported.

Romania

Capital: Bucharest Pop. 23,020,000

In the Socialist Republic of Romania the Communist Party has the leading role, as reaffirmed in the 1965 Constitution. There is a Grand National Assembly elected for a five-year term by all citizens above the age of 18 years and from one or more candidates in single-member constituencies. Authority is exercised in part through the Front of Socialist Democracy and Unity, a popular front organization, the National Council of which acts as a consultative body to the Council of Ministers (the government). For the national minorities there are also two consultative National Councils, one Hungarian and the other German.

Ultimate power is in the hands of a 15-member Permanent Bureau of the Executive Political Committee of the Central Committee of the Romanian Communist Party. The Bureau is presided over by President Ceausescu, who is also head of state and General Secretary of the Party.

Government is strongly centralized, and there is no evidence of the existence of organized groups of dissenters (except for an attempt to set up an independent trade union). Civil rights are limited and emigration is strictly controlled, with the result that there have been a number of cases of illegal emigration and of defections.

Under a decree which came into force on April 28, 1983, private owners of typewriters were required to register them with the police, and persons with a criminal record or presenting "a danger to public order or state security" were forbidden to own typewriters. (Private ownership of copying equipment was already forbidden.) The decree was believed to be intended to stop the production of clandestine material critical of the regime.

A number of dissident intellectuals left the country legally as emigrants. Those who attempted to cross the border illegally risked severe punishment if caught in the attempt, or if returned to Romania, e.g. by the Yugoslav authorities, or they ran the risk of being murdered abroad (as did Paul Goma—see below), apparently by Romanian security agents. (On July 21, 1982, two French citizens were sentenced in West Germany to 11 years and 4½ years in prison respectively for attempting to murder a Romanian exile working for Radio Free Europe.)

Those who expressed their dissent inside Romania committed a punishable offence. Among them Radu Filipescu, who had distributed leaflets calling for the replacement of President Ceausescu, was sentenced, in September 1983, to 10 years' imprisonment for attempting to change the socialist system and endangering state security.

Human Rights Activists

Following the publication of the "Charter 77" manifesto in Czechoslovakia there appeared in Paris, on Feb. 9, 1977, the text of a letter signed by eight Romanian intellectuals who declared their solidarity with the manifesto and with the peoples of Eastern Europe who, they claimed, were under "foreign occupation". The signatories stated in particular: "The Romanian occupation of Romania is even more painful and more efficient than a foreign occupation. We all live under the same boot, the same violation of elementary rights, the same lies. Poverty, economic chaos, demagogy, insecurity and terror reign everywhere." This letter subsequently received support from 128 other Romanians.

The eight signatories of the letter declared, in another letter addressed to the 35 governments which had signed the Helsinki Final Act of 1975 and released in Belgrade on Feb. 15, 1977, that Romania's committment to respect for human rights and freedom of movement and of information, as laid down in the Constitution and the international conventions signed by the Romanian goverment, were "nothing but empty words".

President Ceausescu thereupon, in a speech on Feb. 17, 1977, attacked the "traitors who denigrate their country to please their masters and to pocket large amounts of money" and claimed that there was "intensified activity by certain neo-fascist circles" abroad and that Western countries were even supporting "outcasts and traitors by granting them funds and facilities...to agitate against the Helsinki resolutions, détente, peace and co-operation in Europe".

Among the authors of the two letters, Paul Goma (a writer) was on March 16, 1977, quoted as saying that there were in Romania four mental hospitals where opponents of the regime were detained, and this allegation was said to have been confirmed by Dr Ion Viana, a psychiatrist who had drawn attention to such "misue of psychiatry" in October 1976.

Goma was arrested early in April, expelled from the Writers' Union on April 22, but allowed to leave the country five months later. At a press conference in Paris on Nov. 24, 1977, he made a strong attack on the Romanian regime, asserting inter alia that labour camps had been reopened; that psychiatric internment methods had been reactivated; that thousands of people had been forcibly displaced, among them 4,000 miners; that he himself had been ill-treated during his imprisonment in April-May 1977; and that Elena Ceausescu (the President's wife and a member of the Permanent Bureau of the Communist Party's Central Committee) had ordered the destruction of a church in Bucharest and the withdrawal from libraries of all books about and pictures of churches. Goma was one of three Romanian émigrés to whom parcel bombs were addressed from Madrid in February 1981.

A leading figure among those who expressed concern at the situation of ethnic minorities in Romania was Carol Kiraly, a Romanian of Hungarian extraction and a former high-ranking official of the Romanian Communist Party, who repeatedly made allegations of repression of minority groups. In an open letter sent to the party leadership in December 1977 (and published in the West in January 1978) he alleged that Hungarians in Romania (who according to official statistics numbered 1,700,000) were subject to discrimination and that this form of oppression "in violation of Romania's Constitution" included the closure of Hungarian universities and schools (such as the closure of the Hungarian section of the University of Cluj in Transylvania in 1977), the suppression of the Hungarian language and the appointment of Romanians to nearly all key positions in towns with Hungarian majorities. He stated that there was "a wide gap" between the government's theory and its practice regarding its policies on ethnic groups and that "forced assimilation" was being applied to all minority groups in the country (principally Hungarians, Germans and Serbs).

Following talks with government ministers and officials, Kiraly was obliged to abandon his campaign and agreed, on Feb. 11, 1978, to move to the remote Transylvanian town of Caransebes, but he was reported to have refused to renounce his appeal and to declare that his letter was a fake or a fabrication of the (US) Central Intelligence Agency and Radio Free Europe. In March 1978 he was removed from his post as vice-president of the Hungarian National Council but he remained a member of the Communist Party. The Romanian government branded him as a traitor and denied all allegations of repression of minorities. At meetings of the Hungarian and German National Councils in Bucharest on March 13-14, 1978, the presidents of these two Councils emphasized that there was "full equality of rights of all citizens in the country without distinction as to nationality".

While C. Kiraly had claimed that his letter had the support of some 16 prominent Romanians, it was reported on April 24, 1978, that three leading members of the Hungarian community had sent separate appeals to the Romanian leadership protesting against the government's alleged discriminatory policies towards the minority groups and demanding a number of improvements. In particular Prof. Lajos Takacs (who was an alternate member of the Communist Party's Central Committee and a former chancellor of the University of Cluj, and who was re-elected vice-president of the Hungarian National Council on March 13, 1978) made 18 demands for improvements, which included (i) the allocation of increased powers to the Hungarian National Council in order to enable it to select and delegate the representatives of the group to local and central bodies, (ii) the creation in the Romanian Parliament of a permanent commission responsible for matters concerned with the minorities, and (iii) the drawing-up of a new statute for the various nationalities in the country. He also asked for the Hungarian language to be used on a much wider scale, complaining that almost half of the Hungarian pupils in secondary and vocational schools were being educated in the Romanian language only. These demands do not appear to have elicited any public reaction by the government.

Free Trade Union of Romanian Workers

Leadership. Ion Cana; Gheorghe Brasoveanu; Nicolae Dascalu

Following its establishment, this union published a manifesto in which it called for the legalization of unofficial trade unions and for the implementation of the right to free assocation.

In April 1979 the union, in an open letter to President Ceausescu, protested against the frequent arrests of its members. These included I. Cana and G. Brasoveanu (an economist), said to be confined in psychiatric institutions in March 1979, and N. Dascalu, who succeeded them as chairman of the union and who was in June 1979 sentenced to 18 months in prison for allegedly passing state secrets to Amnesty Internaional. In addition Fr Gheorghe Calciu-Dumitreus was imprisoned in June 1979 for alleged involvement with the union (as reported on June 13, 1980).

(The official Romanian trade unions admitted in November 1980 that they had not always adequately represented the interests of the workers. In a paper published by the central council of the unions on Nov.

16 it was stated inter alia that, although the unions enjoyed the right of co-determination in all economic affairs and organizations, this right had not always been observed, to the disadvantage of the workers.)

Exiled Party

Social Democratic Party

Leadership. Eugenie Boeuve Voinea (Paris rep.)

Originally founded in 1893, the Romanian Social Democratic Party was split when the left wing broke away in 1921 to form the Communist Party. Following the Social Democratic-Communist merger of October 1947, opposition Social Democrats were progressively outlawed, but those who escaped from the country maintained the party's existence in exile.

The Romanian Social Democratic Party is a consultative member of the Socialist International and a constituent party of the Socialist Union of Central and Eastern Europe (SUCEE).

Rwanda

Capital: Kigali Pop. 6,070,000

The Rwandese Republic is, under its Constitution approved in a referendum on Dec. 17, 1978, "a democratic, social and sovereign and republic based on government of the people, by the people and for the people". It has an executive President, elected for a five-year term by the people and re-eligible, and a (legislative) National Development Council (NDC). The latter body has 70 seats filled by direct elections by universal adult suffrage from a list of candidates who are members of the *Mouvement révolutionnaire national pour le développement,* the country's sole legal political organization (founded in 1975).

After elections to the NDC held in December 1983 it was recorded that 17 former members had lost their seats and 23 new ones had been elected.

The government of President Juvénal Habyarimana (in power since 1973) surmounted a challenge to its authority in May 1980 when a number of prominent officials were arrested for allegedly plotting against the security of the state. These included Maj. Théonaste Lizinde, described as former chief of security and presidential adviser on foreign affairs. Of those arrested, 25 persons were sentenced on Nov. 25, 1981, by a state security court—the "principal instigators" of the attempted coup, Maj. Lizinde and Alphonse Kazenga, receiving the death sentence and the 23 others terms of imprisonment ranging from two to 23 years. Nevertheless, no organized opposition movements have appeared in Rwanda to date.

St Christopher and Nevis
(often abbreviated to **St Kitts and Nevis**)

Capital: Basseterre (on St Kitts) Pop. 50,000

St Kitts and Nevis, consisting of the Caribbean islands of St Kitts and Nevis, became an independent state with a federal Constitution within the Commonwealth on Sept. 19, 1983, with the British monarch as head of state represented by a Governor-General. It has a unicameral National Assembly consisting of 11 members elected for five years by universal suffrage (eight representing St Kitts and three Nevis) and a number of senators not exceeding two-thirds of the elected members, with two-thirds appointed by the Governor-General and one-third on the advice of the Leader of the Opposition. The Prime Minister and the Cabinet are responsible to the Assembly.

In Nevis Island there are a Nevis Island Assembly and a Nevis Island Administration. The Assembly has the power to provide for the separation of Nevis from the Federation. Nevis has a Deputy Governor-General appointed by the Governor-General.

In elections held on June 21, 1984, the ruling conservative coalition government comprising the People's Action Movement (PAM) and the Nevis Reformation Party (NRP) were returned to power; the PAM won eight seats, the NRP won all three Nevis seats (in two it was challenged by the newly formed People's Democratic Party), and the opposition Labour Party took the remaining two St Kitts seats. (The Labour Party had boycotted the independence celebrations in 1983, condemning the special provisions made for Nevis.) The elections were a setback for the NRP which no longer held the balance of power in the enlarged Assembly.

There have been no reports of internal opposition outside existing legal parties.

St Lucia

Capital: Castries

Pop. 134,000

St Lucia, one of the Windward Islands, is an independent state within the Commonwealth with the British monarch as head of state being represented by a Governor-General. It has a bicameral Parliament consisting of (i) a 17-member House of Assembly elected for five years by universal adult suffrage and (ii) an 11-member Senate appointed by the Governor-General (six senators on the advice of the Prime Minister, three on the advice of the Leader of the Opposition and two by consultation with religious, economic and social bodies). The Prime Minister and the Cabinet are responsible to Parliament.

In a general election held on April 6, 1987, the ruling conservative United Workers' Party (UWP) won nine seats in the House of Assembly, the opposition St Lucia Labour Party (SLP) eight, and the left-wing Progressive Labour Party (PLP) none. Parliament was dissolved immediately after its official opening on April 14 and a second general election called for April 30, which brought, however, no changes in the distribution of seats. The PLP contested only four seats in the second election to avoid splitting the anti-government vote in marginal constituencies.

In July 1983, the Prime Minister, John Compton, alleged that the PLP had recruited 26 St Lucians to go to Libya for training in terrorist techniques (14 did not leave for Libya, however, because their passports were impounded), and that the party had received US$40,000 out of US$1,000,000 which he claimed had been allocated by Libya for political activities in the Caribbean.

St Vincent and the Grenadines

Capital: Kingston

Pop. 127,883

St Vincent and the Grenadines are an independent state with the status of a "special member" of the Commonwealth, with the British monarch as its head of state being represented by a Governor-General. It has a House of Assembly consisting of 13 members (with provision for an increase to 15 members under a constitutional amendment approved in June 1986), elected by universal adult suffrage and six senators appointed by the Governor-General. There is a Cabinet collectively responsible to the House of Assembly.

In elections to the House of Assembly held on July 24, 1984, the (centrist) New Democratic Party (NDP) won nine seats, defeating the ruling St Vincent Labour Party (SVLP) which won the remaining four. Other parties which contested the elections were (i) the (new left) United People's Movement, (ii) the Movement for National Unity, founded in 1982 and (iii) the Progressive Democratic Party. In a by-election held on Feb. 14, 1985, the NDP won a further seat from the SVLP.

Rastafarians

The Rastafarian sect is traditionally non-political (see also under Dominica, page 81) but members gave active support to the coup which brought to power the former left-wing government of Grenada, led by Maurice Bishop, in March 1979. On Dec. 7, 1979 (two days after a general election), members of this sect were said to be involved in a rising on Union Island (in the Grenadines), where rebels occupied strategic positions for eight hours in protest at the return of the former St Vincent Labour Party government, which they accused of neglecting the interests of the Grenadines' inhabitants. The alleged leader of the rising, Lennox Charles (or Rasta Bomba), was in mid-1980 sentenced to eight years in prison for robbery and causing an explosion. There have been no reports of Rastafarian activity under the NDP government.

São Tomé and Príncipe

Capital: São Tomé Pop. 110,000

The Democratic Republic of São Tomé and Príncipe is an "independent, unitary and democratic state" in which "the leading force" is the Movement for the Liberation of São Tomé and Príncipe (*Movimento de libertação de São Tomé e Príncipe,* MLSTP). The President of the Republic, who is secretary-general of the MSTLP (Manuel Pinto da Costa, in office since 1976), is elected for a five-year term by a 40-member National People's Assembly which consists of members of the MSTLP and is elected by directly elected People's District Assemblies.

Following the appearance of pamphlets distributed by separatists calling for the independence of Príncipe because food supplies were being withheld from that island by the authorities in São Tomé, disturbances occurred on Dec. 26-27, 1981, when several people were injured. The government attributed the unrest to "internal reactionary forces" and "enemies of the revolution".

Democratic Opposition Coalition of São Tomé and Príncipe

The formation of this coalition was announced in Lisbon (Portugal) on March 19, 1986, by two exiled opposition parties, the National Resistance Front of São Tomé and Príncipe (FRNSTP) and the Independent Democratic Union of São Tomé and Príncipe. Leaders of the coalition stated that to achieve their aim of democratic government in São Tomé and Príncipe "recourse to armed struggle" was acceptable. The coalition received a setback when Carlos da Graça resigned on May 11, 1986, as leader of FRNSTP. He said that his resignation was prompted by the government's new policies of liberalizing the economy and improving relations with neighbouring countries and by his own wish to play a constructive role in that process. He said that he would, however, remain in exile until all foreign troops, which in 1986 comprised approximately 1,000 Angolan and Cuban troops, were removed from his country.

On April 30, 1986, 76 men arrived at Walvis Bay, Namibia, from São Tomé and Príncipe, claiming to be members of the FRNSTP seeking military aid from South Africa and training by the Angolan rebel movement UNITA. C. da Graça said on May 11 that the men had been expelled from the FRNSTP for organizing a military training camp in Gabon.

Saudi Arabia

Capitals: Riyadh (royal capital)
Jeddah (administrative capital)

Pop. 11,540,000

The Kingdom of Saudi Arabia is under the direct rule of the King, who is also the Prime Minister and who presides over a Council of Ministers. There is no parliament nor are there any legal political parties.

Opposition to the regime has come mainly from some Shias and Moslem fundamentalists inside the country and from other (mainly left-wing) groups based outside Saudi Arabia. Sporadic disturbances during the annual *haj* (pilgrimage to Mecca) have involved fundamentalist Iranian pilgrims. There has been little organized opposition to the regime over the past few years.

Committee for the Defence of the Rights of Man in Saudi Arabia (*Comité de défense des droits de l'homme en Arabie Saoudite*)

This Committee was set up in Paris 1972 by representatives of clandestine parties in Saudi Arabia—including the (Arab nationalist) Party of Labour, the *Baath* Party of Saudi Arabia, the Communist Party of Saudi Arabia (see separate entry), the (Shia) Organization of the Islamic Revolution and the (Sunni) *El-Salaf el-Saleh*. A spokesman for the Committee announced in Paris in January 1983 that during the past few months some 150 persons, most of them favouring the establishment of a constitutional and democratic regime, had been arrested in Saudi Arabia without any charges being laid against them.

There have been no reports of activities of the above parties.

Communist Party of Saudi Arabia

Leadership. Ahmad Musa (gen. sec.)

Established in 1954 as the National Reform Front, this (very small, pro-Soviet) party was renamed Saudi National Liberation Front in 1958 and took its present name in 1975. It has operated from South Yemen and has defined its aim as the establishment of "a broad fatherland front including all national and opposition forces in Saudi Arabia and abroad in order to overthrow the King's regime and to liquidate the influence of US imperialism and the international monopolies which control our national resources". The party has never been legal in Saudi Arabia.

Moslem Revolutionary Movement in the Arabian Peninsula

Established in 1974, this Movement of only a few hundred members was built up by its leader and found support in Egypt and some of the Gulf states. It was aimed at obtaining universal Moslem recognition of Mohammed al-Qatani as the expected "Mahdi" or prophet (as prophesied by certain Mahdist sects). On Nov. 20, 1979, some 200 armed members of the organization took over the Grand Mosque in Mecca with the object of forcing the congregation (of some 50,000 Moslems) to recognize their "Mahdi". The government announced on Nov. 25 that the Ulema (the supreme body of Islamic jurisdiction) had decided to lift the Koranic ban on the use of weapons in the mosque, and about 2,200 troops thereupon entered the mosque, taking until Dec. 3 to overcome all resistance by the intruders. The Movement had, on Nov. 27, declared that it was responsible for the action at the mosque and that it was directed against the Saudi Arabian royal family, whom it denounced as "corrupt".

On Jan. 9, 1980, a total of 63 of the intruders were executed by being beheaded on instructions of Saudi religious courts; 19 other death sentences were commuted to terms of imprisonment and 22 women and children were sent to corrective institutions. Of the insurgents, 102 were said to have died during or after the occupation of the mosque, while troop casualties were officially given as 127 dead and 451 injured, and civilian casualties as 26 dead and 109 injured. The "Mahdi" was reported to have been killed in the fighting. Those beheaded included not only Saudi Arabians but also Egyptians, Yemenis and Kuwaitis. In some other Islamic states, including Iran, responsibility for the Mecca attack was attributed to the United States and to Zionism; accordingly, anti-American demonstrations and riots took place in several such countries.

From the writings of the organization's leader it appeared that it condemned all current rulers of Islamic states as not upholding the religion of Islam which laid down that obedience was owed "only to those who lead by God's book" and not to those who had made religion into a way of satisfying their materialistic interests.

Popular Front for the Liberation of the Arabian Peninsula

In a statement referred to in a broadcast from Tripoli (Libya) on Nov. 18, 1982, this Front condemned the "despotic" rulers of Saudi Arabia as being responsible for "the sell-out of the Palestinian cause" and the use of American aircraft "to defile the Arabian peninsula's sky"; it called for these rulers to be brought to trial and for the establishment of an Islamic administration "to preserve the sanctity of God's House" in Arabia.

Shia Moslem Fundamentalists

Saudi Arabia's Shia minority, concentrated in the oases of Qatif and Hasa in the Eastern province, form an underprivileged section of the population and constitute about one-third of the workforce in the country's oil production. Its younger generation has been greatly influenced by the Islamic revolution in Iran. Pro-Iranian demonstrations in the Eastern province in November-December 1979 (also described as an "uprising") were put down by troops, and there was further loss of life when troops intervened to disperse a Shia demonstration in Qatif in February 1980 to celebrate the first anniversary of the Iranian revolution. The government, however, responded to the unrest by devoting increased resources to material improvements in Qatif.

The Lebanese-based militant Shia movement *Al Jihad al-Islami* (Islamic Holy War—see entry under Lebanon) claimed responsibility for the assassination of a Saudi engineer in a café in Madrid (Spain) in September 1984, and for two bomb explosions in the Saudi town of Salamiyah in May 1985. There were unconfirmed reports of other bombings in Saudi cities over the ensuing two months.

Union of the People of the Arabian Peninsula

Leadership. Nasser al-Said (l.)

This left-wing underground organization expressed sympathy with the action taken against the Grand Mosque in Mecca on Nov. 27, 1979, by the Moslem Revolutionary Movement in the Arabian Peninsula (see separate entry) and called it "a spontaneous response to social injustice under the rule of the monarchy". The organization's leader also alleged that over 7,000 sympathizers with the action in Mecca had been arrested throughout the country.

Al-Said later disappeared during a stay in Beirut (Lebanon) in 1981, when he was allegedly under the protection of the Democratic Front for the Liberation of Palestine. It was rumoured that he had been abducted and imprisoned in Saudi Arabia.

Senegal

Capital: Dakar Pop. 6,440,000

The Republic of Senegal has an executive President elected by universal adult suffrage for a five-year term, and re-eligible, who chooses and presides over a Cabinet responsible to a 120-member National Assembly elected at the same time as the President. (For creation of Confederation of Senegambia see under The Gambia, page 122.)

Under constitutional amendments made in 1976, 1978 and 1981, a total of 14 political parties (including several extreme left-wing groups) were registered (although no party was allowed to be identified with a race, a religion, a sect, an ethnic group, a sex, a language or a region). Until 1978 the country had in effect been a one-party state. In elections to the National Assembly held on Feb. 27, 1983, and contested by eight parties, the ruling Socialist Party of Senegal (*Parti socialiste du Sénégal*) obtained 111 seats, the Democratic Party (*Parti démocratique sénégalais,* PDS) eight and the National Democratic Rally (*Rassemblement national démocratique,* RND) one (in a 56 per cent poll). Parties which contested the elections without gaining any seats were the *Ligue démocratique—Mouvement pour le parti du travail* (LD-MPT), the *Mouvement démocratique et populaire* (MDP), the *Parti africain de l'indépendance* (PAI), the *Parti de l'indépendance et du travail* (PIT) and the *Parti populaire sénégalais* (PPS). Six other legal parties which took no part in the elections were the *Ligue communiste des travailleurs* (LCT), the *Mouvement républicain sénégalais* (MRS), the *Mouvement révolutionnaire pour la démocratie nouvelle-And-Jëf* (MRDN-AJ), the *Organisation socialiste des travailleurs* (OST), the *Parti africain pour l'indépendance des masses* (PAIM), and the *Union démocratique du peuple* (UDP).

An *Alliance démocratique sénégalaise* (ADS) was formed in July 1985 by five left-wing opposition parties—the Democratic Party, the LD-MPT, the MRDN-AJ, the OST and the UDP. However, in September 1985 ADS activities were reported to have been banned.

A *Parti pour la libération du peuple* (PLP) was formed in 1983, and an *Union démocratique sénégalaise* (UDS) was recognized in 1985.

With most shades of opposition to the government of President Abdou Diouf being channelled through legal opposition parties, extra-parliamentary dissidence has in recent years been confined to small groups variously espousing leftist, Islamic fundamentalist and separatist objectives.

Movement of the Democratic Forces of the Casamance (*Mouvement des forces démocratiques de la Casamance,* MFDC)

In pamphlets distributed in Dakar on Dec. 26, 1982, this Movement called for the complete independence of the region of the lower Casamance (situated to the south of The Gambia). On the same day several hundred pro-independence demonstrators attempted to replace Senegalese flags on official buildings at Ziguinchor (the regional capital) with their own. They were prevented from doing so by police, who arrested three leading demonstrators (among them the Rev. Augustin Diamankoun Senghor) and some 50 others, who were taken to Dakar for trial before the State Security Court. A mass demonstration in favour of maintaining the unity of the state of Senegal, held at Ziguinchor on Dec. 29 by the ruling Socialist Party, was supported also by the (opposition) Democratic Party.

Of the persons arrested in December 1982, and another nine arrested in May 1983, the State Security Court subsequently passed prison sentences ranging from two to five years on 32 defendants. This verdict was followed by a protest demonstration at Ziguinchor on Dec. 18, 1983, leading to street battles with police, the deaths of at least 25 people (including 19 demonstrators) and the arrest of 265. In a subsequent trial, which ended on Jan. 4, 1986, Cherifo Bassene was sentenced to hard labour for life for sedition, having favoured independence for the Casamance; 31 other defendants were sent to prison for between two and 15 years; all the accused had pleaded not guilty and claimed that confessions made earlier had been extracted by torture.

The MFDC was said to have widespread support in the Casamance, where many of its inhabitants wanted better representation in the central government and some favoured close ties with The Gambia.

Rally for National Salvation (*Rassemblement pour le salut national,* RSN)

Leadership. Sidi Lamine Niasse (liaison officer)

The RSN declared in a statement published on July 28, 1981, that it took its inspiration for action from the principles of Islam. Sidi Lamine Niasse's brother, Ahmed Khalifa Niasse, also known as "the ayatollah of Kaolack" (a town to the south-east of Dakar), had earlier called for the establishment of an Islamic state in Senegal, but had left the country in 1979 to go to France, and to Libya in February 1980. In October 1980 the government of The Gambia accused Libya of financing the recruitment of Gambian nationals for military training in Libya by A. K. Niasse; the latter later went to Niger, from which country he was extradited to Senegal in January 1982. He was, however, released from detention late in March 1982, after he had called on his followers in Libya to return to Senegal and to refrain from all subversive activities. He claimed on April 3 that his call had been obeyed by some 15 of his supporters; but on May 24, 1982, he was rearrested after expressing his opposition to a visit to Senegal by the French (Socialist) President, François Mitterrand. An application for registration of the RSN as a political party was reported to have remained unsuccessful because of its Islamic fundamentalist character and its leader's close relations with Libya.

Revolutionary Movement for New Democracy (*Mouvement révolutionnaire pour la démocratie nouvelle,* MRDN)

In tracts distributed by this extreme left-wing Movement in May 1982, during a visit to Senegal by President Mitterrand of France, the latter was accused of directing "neo-colonialism under the colours of social democracy"; the ministers in President Mitterrand's Cabinet were condemned as "revisionists".

Roots of the Nation (*Rénu Rewni*)

On April 2, 1975, the State Security Court passed sentences of between three months and five years in prison on 13 persons accused of attempting to set up an illegal left-wing opposition party under the above name, and of distributing *Xaré Bi*, an unauthorized cyclo-styled newspaper. Another group of nine persons were given shorter prison sentences on Oct. 20, 1975, for belonging to an illegal party named as "Let Us Struggle Together" (*Andjet*), said to be identical with the *Rénu Rewni*.

Seychelles

Capital: Victoria (on Mahé)

Pop. 70,000

The Republic of Seychelles, a member of the Commonwealth, has an executive President elected by universal adult suffrage at the same time as a National Assembly (to which 23 members are elected on a list presented by the Seychelles People's Progressive Front, the country's sole legal political organization, and another two members are appointed to represent small islands without fixed population). The President is head of the Cabinet and also holds portfolios; there are seven other ministers.

On June 17, 1984, President France Albert René was re-elected, as the sole candidate, by 92.6 per cent of the vote (of an electorate of 35,000).

Since the overthrow of President James Mancham in June 1977, the left-wing government of President René has survived two major coup attempts involving foreign mercenaries. On Nov. 16, 1979, it was announced that a plot "sponsored from abroad with the co-operation of mercenaries" standing ready in Durban (South Africa) had been uncovered and that a number of persons had been arrested; several French nationals said to have been involved in the plot were recalled by the French government and others were deported. A further attempt to overthrow the Seychelles government was made on Nov. 25, 1981, by a group of mercenaries led by Col. Michael Hoare (who had been a leader of mercenaries in the Congo in 1964-65) and consisting mainly of South Africans. The coup was foiled by the Seychelles Defence Force, and seven of the mercenaries were arrested in Seychelles while 45 of them returned to South Africa in an Indian airliner which they had commandeered.

On July 6-7, 1982, a court presided over by the Chief Justice of Seychelles sentenced four of the mercenaries to death and two others to 20 and 10 years in prison respectively on a charge of treason and illegal import of firearms. In Pietermaritzburg (South Africa) the Natal Supreme Court sentenced, on July 29, 1982, a total of 42 of the mercenaries, among them Col. Hoare, to effective prison terms ranging from six months to 10 years on charges arising from the hijacking of the Indian airliner. During the trial the South African government admitted that members of the South African Defence Force had been involved in the attempt but stated that neither the government nor the State Security Council had been aware of it. Of the 42 persons sentenced in South Africa, all but Col. Hoare were released in May 1984, and Col. Hoare himself on May 6, 1985 (under an amnesty). The six mercenaries sentenced in Seychelles were pardoned by President René on July 22, 1984, and were deported to South Africa on the following day.

Gérard Horeau, a former head of the Seychelles immigration service, who had played a prominent part in the November 1981 attempt and had also been implicated in an alleged plot of October 1982 (and whose extradition from Britain, applied for by the Seychelles government, had been refused by the British government), was shot dead in London on Nov. 29, 1985, by an unknown assailant.

Movement for Resistance (*Mouvement pour la résistance*)

Following student protest demonstrations held on Oct. 11-12, 1979, against government plans to introduce compulsory national service for young people above the age of 15 years, the Movement for Resistance distributed leaflets calling for the resignation of the government, the withdrawal of Tanzanian troops (which had been present in Seychelles since 1977, when the regime of President James Mancham was overthrown) and the holding of elections under international control.

Paul Chow, a spokesman for the Movement, claimed in London on Nov. 28, 1981, that it consisted of people who had been "forced into exile by the illegal and oppressive regime of France Albert René" and intended to achieve "the restoration of democracy in Seychelles"; he also said that the Movement's first choice as President of Seychelles would be ex-President Mancham, but denied that the latter was involved in the South African-backed attempt to overthrow the Seychelles government in November 1981. On the other hand, Chow claimed on Nov. 29, 1981, that some 100 Seychelles exiles had backed the attempted coup with finance and other help.

On Dec. 2, 1983, the South African Minister of Law and Order announced that five persons had been detained by the South African police in connexion with an attempt to recruit mercenaries for a further coup instigated by the Movement, but they were all released a few days later.

Seychelles Democratic Party

Leadership. David Joubert (l.)

Founded. September 1985

D. Joubert, based in London, had been a minister in the government of J. Mancham, who had been the leader of the original Seychelles Democratic Party but had earlier in 1985 announced that he was no longer actively involved in politics.

Seychelles Liberation Committee

This Committee was established in 1979 by exiles in Paris with the aim of seeking the overthrow of President France Albert René and the abolition of the one-party system.

Seychelles National Movement (SNM)

Leadership. Gabriel Horeau (interim pres.)

Founded. November 1984

This Movement, based in London, has claimed to have some 100 members in the United Kingdom and 250 in Australia. It was to be a broadly based opposition party (while the Movement for Resistance—see separate entry—was expected to concentrate on clandestine work within the Seychelles).

Seychelles Popular Anti-Marxist Front (SPAMF)

It was reported by Johannesburg radio on Dec. 3, 1981, that the SPAMF had disclosed that it had had prior knowledge of the abortive coup led by Col. Michael Hoare the previous month, but had decided not to participate because it regarded the plan as unworkable and foolhardy. However, a SPAMF spokesman also revealed that his group had sought the backing of the South African government for a large-scale coup attempt of its own, but had been turned down because the South African authorities stated that they could not afford to be involved in such adventures.

Sierra Leone

Capital: Freetown Pop. 3,600,000

The Republic of Sierra Leone is an independent state within the Commonwealth. Under a 1978 Constitution approved in a referendum in June of that year it is a one-party state, with the All-People's Congress (APC) as the country's sole legal party. It has an elected executive President serving a seven-year term, a First and a Second Vice-President and a Cabinet appointed and presided over by the President. There is a House of Assembly of 105 elective constituency seats, 12 seats held by elected paramount chiefs and up to seven seats filled by persons appointed by the President.

The existence of plots to overthrow the government was officially implied in announcements made (i) in September 1981 concerning the discovery of a large cache of arms and ammunition in Freetown, and (ii) in February 1982 of the compulsory retirement of five army officers after a shooting incident near the President's residence in late January.

The foiling of another plot was announced by government sources on March 23, 1987. It involved an attempt to raid a military arsenal, and it led to the arrest of 27 junior army officers and an assistant police superintendent, who was reported to have implicated a number of leading figures in the attempted coup, among them Francis M. Minah, then First Vice-President and Minister of Justice, who was thereupon dismissed and placed in detention.

On Dec. 30, 1986, President Momoh had ordered the release from prison of nine persons serving life sentences for plotting against the government in 1974.

Since the introduction of the one-party Constitution in 1978 several opposition groups have been established outside Sierra Leone.

National Alliance Party

This left-wing group was set up by exiles in the United States.

Sierra Leone Alliance Movement (SLAM)

Leadership. Ambrose Ganda

This Movement, based in Britain and led by Ambrose Ganda (a barrister), has published a newsletter, copies of which were said to circulate within Sierra Leone. It has advocated "national recovery" for Sierra Leone in terms similar to those previously propagated by *The Tablet*, an independent biweekly newspaper which had criticized alleged official corruption and mismanagement and whose printing machinery was destroyed by gangs in Freetown on Sept. 1, 1981, whereafter its editor had left the country in order to recommence publication in the United States.

Sierra Leone Democratic Party (SLDP)

Leadership. Edison Milton Gorvie (interim ch.)

Founded. July 30, 1984

This Party was formed in London under the leadership of a committee which declared itself to be opposed to the one-party administration in Sierra Leone. It proclaimed its aim as being the return of Sierra Leone to "democracy, justice and freedom", and it claimed to have support within the country itself.

In 1986 members of the SLDP were said to have been involved in a plan to invade Sierra Leone with the help of dissident exiles and British mercenaries. President Momoh stated on March 12, 1986, that a cargo vessel seized in Brest (France) on Feb. 21 had been found to carry jeeps, rubber boats, communications equipment and military uniforms on behalf of the SLDP (according to the vessel's captain). The plan was reported to involve the transport of arms from Yugoslavia to a West African state near Sierra Leone; in this state two SLDP leaders (E. M. Gorvie and ex-Capt. Abdul Kamara) were to be picked up in order to carry out a landing and a coup in Freetown and to kill President Momoh and install E. M. Gorvie as Prime Minister. The latter was, however, reported to be estranged from SLDP activists and to have denied any involvement in the above plan.

Sierra Leone Freedom Council

The Council was founded by former members of the Sierra Leone People's Party (SLPP), which had been the country's opposition party before the establishment of a one-party system in 1978 (whereupon all SLPP members of the House of Assembly had joined the ruling All-People's Congress).

Singapore

Capital: Singapore Pop. 2,560,000

The Republic of Singapore, an independent member of the Commonwealth, has a unicameral parliament of 79 members elected by universal adult suffrage for four years. Parliament elects a President of the Republic (for a four-year term) who appoints the Cabinet which is headed by a Prime Minister and responsible to parliament. In elections held on Dec. 22, 1984, the ruling People's Action Party (PAP) won 77 of the 79 seats in parliament, with one further seat each being won by the Workers' Party and the Singapore Democratic Party. Parties which unsuccessfully contested the elections were the United People's Front (UPF), the Singapore United Front (SUF), the *Barisan Sosialis* (Socialist Front), the Singapore Justice Party (SJP), the Singapore Malay National Organization (SMNO or *Pekemas*-PKMS) and the Islamic Movement (IM).

On July 27, 1984, Parliament passed a constitutional amendment which provided for the creation of three "non-constituency seats" in the legislature for opposition members in the event of no opposition candidates being returned at a general election. The non-constituency MPs, however, are not entitled to vote on constitutional amendments, the budget and important financial bills. In January 1985 the Workers' Party refused the offer of a non-constituency seat to supplement the two opposition candidates returned at the 1984 election.

The leader of the PAP, Lee Kuan Yew, has been Prime Minister since 1959. During the 1976 parliamentary election campaign the opposition parties began to allege that the government had become authoritarian and repressive in character and that Singapore had become a "police state", but the ruling party stressed in its campaign that the government had given Singapore the highest living standard in Asia after Japan and that the Internal Security Act had normally been used only against subversive elements known to be connected with communist organizations.

The government stated in December 1986 that only 35 persons were detained under the Internal Security Act. Poo Soo Kai and Dr Lim Hock Siew, two co-founders of the *Barisan Sosialis* who had been detained since Feb. 2, 1963, for "pro-communist agitation" (except during the period from December 1973 to January 1976) were released from detention on Aug. 26, 1982, and Sept. 6, 1982, respectively, on condition that they refrain from political activity.

On the other hand 16 alleged Marxist activists, including a number of Catholic social workers, were arrested on May 21, 1987, and detained under the Internal Security Act.

Communist Party of Malaya (CPM)

Originally established in 1930, the CPM was proscribed in July 1948 but pursued an armed insurrection in the Federation of Malaya until 1960, whereafter it conducted sporadic underground activities both in Malaysia (see separate entry under that country) and in Singapore (which seceded from the Malaysian Federation in 1965).

Five alleged members of the CPM were arrested in Singapore early in August 1975, when police seized a quantity of weapons. On Oct. 3, 1975, the government announced the arrest of six members of a Mao Zedong Thought League, said to have been formed in 1970 by an underground group of CPM followers and to be in contact with the Malayan National Liberation Front (MNLF—see separate entry).

On May 27, 1976, it was officially announced that the police had uncovered a communist attempt to launch a new phase of "subversion and terrorism" in Singapore and that since January 1976 a total of 56 people had been arrested under the Internal Security Act, of whom 23 had been released after interrogation, 10 had been handed over to the Malaysian authorities, and 17 continued to be detained. The communist movement's branches abroad were said to have been established to recruit students from Singapore and Malaysia, and those detained were alleged to have links with an organization in Kuala Lumpur (Malaysia), with training camps in Johore (Malaysia) and with guerrilla groups in southern Thailand.

On Sept. 6, 1976, the government announced that it had broken up an underground communist cell and arrested four alleged members of the Malayan Communist Youth League (affiliated to the CPM). In 1978 the CPM was reported still to be operating underground in Singapore, but there have been no more recent reports of CPM activities in Singapore. The CPM has advocated the dissolution of the Malaysian Federation and the union of Singapore with Malaya.

Malayan National Liberation Front (MNLF)

Following the assassination in June 1974 of the Malaysian police chief, it was officially announced on June 21, 1974, that 30 suspected saboteurs and members of the MNLF (described as a branch of the Communist Party of Malaya, CPM—see separate entry) had been arrested. The MNLF advocated the reintegration of Singapore in Malaysia (which would be communist and pro-Chinese).

Tan Chay Wa, a district committee member of the MNLF, was arrested in Malaysia on June 2, 1979, and charged with possessing a semi-automatic pistol and seven rounds of ammunition. After pleading guilty, he was sentenced to death in Johore Baru on Jan. 14, 1981, and hanged on Jan. 18, 1983.

People's Liberation Organization of Singapore (PLOS)

Leadership. Zainul Abiddin bin Mohammed Shah (l.)

It was officially announced on Jan. 10, 1982, that 10 members of this "Moslem extremist" organization had been arrested for attempting to overthrow the government by force of arms (with the alleged support in men and funds of foreign powers) and that they would be detained under the Internal Security Act providing for internment without trial for an indefinite period. The movement's leader was said to be a member of the Workers' Party of Singapore (which had won its first parliamentary seat in a by-election on Oct. 31, 1981).

A further group of 10 PLOS members were arrested on Oct. 10, 1982, on the same charges.

Solomon Islands

Capital: Honiara (Guadalcanal) Pop. 270,000

The Solomon Islands are an independent state within the Commonwealth, with the British monarch as head of state being represented by a Governor-General. Legislative power is vested in a unicameral 38-member National Parliament elected by universal adult suffrage for up to four years. There is a Cabinet composed of a Prime Minister and 14 other ministers and responsible to Parliament.

As a result of general elections held on Oct. 24, 1984, the distribution of seats in the National Parliament was as follows: United Party 13, People's Alliance Party 12, *Solomons Ano Sagufenua* four, National Democratic Party one, independents seven (vacant one).

Kwaio Fadanga

This traditionalist group, formed in East Kwaio (Malaita province), was led by custom chiefs who, in 1983, declared the area's "independence". Their activities prevented voting in the East Kwaio constituency in the general elections of Oct. 24, 1984. The United Party Prime Minister elected on Nov. 19, 1984, declared inter alia that he would open negotiations with the East Kwaio secessionist movement.

Somalia

Capital: Mogadishu Pop. 4,650,000

The Somali Democratic Republic (a member of the Arab League) is ruled by the leadership of the Somali Revolutionary Socialist Party (SRSP), whose secretary-general, Gen. Mohammed Siyad Barre, is head of state and directs the government with the assistance of an appointed Council of Ministers. A People's Assembly of 171 members is elected by citizens above the age of 18 years for a five-year term on a list of the SRSP. Official results of elections to the Assembly held on Dec. 31, 1984, showed that 99.86 per cent of the electorate had voted for the list.

Under the country's 1979 Constitution the President was elected by the Assembly for a six-year term, but under a constitutional amendment passed by the Assembly on Dec. 1, 1984, presidential election was to be by universal suffrage for a seven-year term.

By 1980 Somalia faced serious internal difficulties as a result of its defeat in hostilities conducted since 1977 over Somali claims to territory under Ethiopian control, this defeat being in part due to substantial Soviet and

Cuban support for Ethiopia. On Oct. 21 of that year a state of emergency was declared in order "to deal with hostile elements in the country and attacks from Ethiopia". A series of bomb explosions in Mogadishu in January 1981 was followed by the arrest of suspected Soviet sympathizers. The general state of emergency was eventually lifted on March 1, 1982—although it was reimposed in the "battle zones" on the Ethiopian border on Aug. 15.

A general amnesty was announced on Feb. 21, 1981, for any Somali who had committed an offence against the state before Feb. 14, 1981, and who returned to the country within three months. The number of political detainees in Somalia was, in April 1981, thought to be between 5,000 and 10,000. On Oct. 20, 1981, it was announced that an amnesty involving the release of over 5,000 prisoners did not cover those convicted of crimes against the sovereignty, security and unity of the state. Earlier, on May 8, 1981, four persons had been condemned to death for grave crimes against the state alleged to have been committed on behalf of "foreign powers".

Democratic Front for the Salvation of Somalia (DFSS)

Leadership. Dr Hassan Haji Ali Mireh (ch.).

The DFSS was set up at a conference held from Sept. 19 to Oct. 5, 1981, by representatives of the Somali Salvation Front (SSF—see separate entry), the Democratic Front for the Liberation of Somalia (led by Ahmed Abderahman Aydeed) and the Somali Workers' Party (led by Hussain Said Jama). Its formation was announced by Radio Kulmis, broadcasting from Ethiopia and describing itself as "the mobile station of the DFSS", having previously called itself "the voice of the SSF". On Oct. 27, 1981, the DFSS claimed in a further broadcast that it had achieved "major victories" on the battlefield against President Siyad Barre's regime and that hundreds of soldiers had been deserting him and joining the DFSS forces; the broadcast also called on Western nations to cease their aid to President Siyad Barre and to adopt a neutral attitude to Somalia.

On Nov. 1, 1981, five Somali officials were reported to have sought political asylum in Libya and to have decided to join the DFSS. On Nov. 25, 1981, it was reported that five members of the President's regime (including a former Minister of Information and two former members of the SRSP's central committee) had announced in Beirut (Lebanon) that they had decided to join the DFSS.

At its foundation the DFSS announced its policies as including the destruction of Siyad Barre's regime; the establishment of a democratic system under a new constitution; the holding of free elections for a people's parliament; the removal of all US air, naval and ground bases from Somalia; the pursuit of a non-aligned, neutral policy and good-neighbourly relations with East African countries, in particular in the Horn of Africa; support for the Arab people in their opposition to the 1979 peace treaty between Egypt and Israel; and support for the Palestine Liberation Organization and all liberation movements fighting against apartheid.

In October 1982 it was announced that the DFSS had formed a joint military committee with the Somali National Movement (see separate entry) as well as another committee which would seek to establish the basis for an eventual unification of the two movements.

Clashes between the DFSS and government forces continued at varying intensity during 1982-87, many of them in the border area and some reportedly also involving Ethiopian forces.

The movement's first congress took place in February and March 1983, and re-elected Col. Ahmed Abdullahi Yusuf as chairman. Shortly afterwards the DFSS denied that, despite claims by the Somali Defence Ministry, over 500 DFSS members had surrended as a result of an amnesty in February 1983.

At a second congress, held in November 1983, changes took place in the DFSS leadership, whereby Hussain Said Jama and Ahmed Abderahman Aydeed were removed from their posts. At the same time former members of their respective parties (the Somali Workers' Party and the Democratic Front for the Liberation of Somalia) were expelled from the DFSS.

A number of leading DFSS members opposed to Col. Yusuf's leadership reportedly accepted the offer of a government amnesty in January 1984. According to government spokesmen, some 200 former DFSS guerrillas returned to Somalia from exile in Ethiopia in May 1984. Libyan support for the DFSS was suspended as part of an agreement to re-establish diplomatic relations between Libya and Somalia concluded in April 1985. (Relations with Libya had been severed by Somalia in August 1981, in part as a protest against alleged Libyan support for the Somali Salvation Front.)

In October 1985, Col. Yusuf and several of his supporters were detained by the Ethiopian authorities following a shooting incident. Yusuf had apparently advocated a reduction in Ethiopian influence over the DFSS and the conclusion of merger agreements with other dissident Somali organizations. At a congress held in March 1986 the DFSS leadership was entrusted to Dr Hassan Haji Ali Mireh.

The DFSS claimed responsibility for the hijacking in November 1985 of a Somali Airways aircraft to Addis Ababa (the Ethiopian capital). The hijackers were given political asylum after unsuccessfully demanding the release of political prisoners in Somalia, including a number convicted of carrying out bombings in Hargeisa in 1984.

Somali Islamic Youth Union

Members of this group accounted for many of the 300 Islamic activists arrested by security forces in the Burao area in April 1986 on charges of "anti-government" activity. The majority had been released by early 1987.

Somali National Movement (SNM)

Leadership. Ahmad Muhammad Silyanyo (pres.)

The SNM was founded in London in April 1981 by Somali exiles in Europe and the United States, most of them Issaqs from northern Somalia opposed to President Siyad Barre's government which was strongly based on southerners. At its foundation the SNM declared its aim to be to organize "internal resistance" with a view to overthrowing the Siyad Barre regime "by any means, including force of arms" and to restore Somalia's "former neutrality". The Movement subscribes to a moderate form of Islamic nationalism and to the concept of the mixed economy.

The SNM began guerrilla operations inside Somalia during 1982 and in early January 1983 mounted a successful attack on a prison at Mandera (south of the port of Berbera), freeing over 700 prisoners, including several political detainees.

It was reported from Ethiopia on April 15, 1982, that at a meeting held between March 29 and April 8 delegates from the SNM and the Democratic Front for the Salvation of Somalia (DFSS—see separate entry) had decided in principle to implement the unification of the two movements into "one organization with a clear national democratic programme". It was subsequently announced in October 1982 that the DFSS and the SNM had established a joint military committee to facilitate operations against government forces as well as a separate committee charged with elaborating the basis for an eventual union of the two movements.

A call for immediate unification with the DFSS was issued at the SNM's third congress in July 1983. The congress also elected a 36-member central committee and an 11-member executive committee under the chairmanship of Yusuf Ali Shaykh Madar. He was, however, replaced by Ahmad Muhammad Silyanyo at the movement's fourth congress in November 1984.

Guerrilla activities by the SNM during the period 1983-86 included attacks on government forces in the Hargeisa area in June and November 1984. In March 1986, the opposition Radio Halgan announced that the SNM was stepping up its campaign in northern Somalia. On Jan. 24, 1987, SNM guerrillas kidnapped and briefly held 10 members of the French agency *Médecins sans frontières* who were working in refugee camps close to the Ethiopian border; they were all released on Feb. 6.

Ethiopian and Somali troops clashed near the border in Somalia's north-western Todghere province in Febraury 1987, in an area where SNM guerrillas had carried out a number of operations recently. The SNM subsequently claimed that its fighters were responsible for the clashes. According to an Ethiopian. tank officer captured by the Somalis, the SNM had provided guides and interpreters for Ethiopian units operating in Somali territory.

Somali Patriotic Liberation Front (SPLF)

Leadership. Hussein Said Jama

The SPLF was formed as a breakaway group from the Democratic Front for the Salvation of Somalia (DFSS—see separate entry) following the expulsion of Said Jama from the DFSS executive committee in November 1983. Said Jama was formerly leader of the Somali Workers' Party, one of the founding groups of the DFSS. The SPLF was largely composed of former moderate DFSS members.

Somali Salvation Front (SSF)

Leadership. Col. Ahmed Abdullahi Yusuf (l.)

Founded in February 1979, the SSF superseded a Somali Democratic Action Front established in 1976 with Osman Nur Ali (a former minister in President Siyad Barre's first Cabinet formed in 1969) as secretary-general and based in Rome. While President Siyad Barre is of the Marrehan tribe (part of the Darod confederacy of southern Somalia), the SSF was based mainly on the rival Mijertein tribe (of the same confederacy), which had been dominant in Somalia's government until Gen. Siyad Barre came to power in 1969.

The SSF was based mainly in Ethiopia but also had representatives in Kenya and South Yemen. In 1980 it claimed to have its headquarters at Warder, near which a Somali army unit was defeated (as announced on Aug. 6, 1980). It also claimed to have inflicted heavy casualties on Somali troops, in particular on Feb. 8 (52 soldiers killed) and on July 2-3, 1980 (72 soldiers killed). It was supplied with weapons by Libya and conducted further hit-and-run operations against the Somali army from March 1981 onwards, claiming to have 10,000 active members. In October 1981 the SSF became a founder member of the broader-based Democratic Front for the Salvation of Somalia (see separate entry).

At a news conference in Washington (reported by Radio Kulmis, Addis Ababa (Ethiopia), on Jan. 30, 1981), the SSF leaders set out their aims as being (i) "to liquidate the fascist rule" in Mogadishu; (ii) to form a provisional government in which all Somalis would "participate equally and by right"; (iii) to draw up a constitution within 12 months; (iv) to form a democratic government and to hold free and independent elections; (v) to be non-aligned in foreign affairs; and (vi) to support liberation fronts against colonialism and apartheid as practised in Africa and elsewhere.

Somali Workers' Party—see Democratic Front for the Salvation of Somalia

United Somali Students Union

A number of secondary school students were sentenced to death in May 1986 after being convicted of membership of this organization. Several were subsequently reported to have died as a result of torture.

South Africa

Capitals: Pretoria (administrative)
Cape Town (legislative)
Bloemfontein (judicial)

Pop. 32,390,000 (including that of all black homelands, whether "independent" or not)

The Republic of South Africa is an independent state with a Parliament with three separate chambers for white, coloured (mixed race) and Indian representatives, an executive President chosen by an electoral college of 50 whites, 25 coloureds and 13 Indians drawn from the three chambers, a Cabinet which might include coloureds and Indians, and standing committees of the three chambers to promote consensus. The (white) House of Assembly has 166 members directly elected in single-member constituencies, eight members elected by the 166 directly elected members on the basis of proportional representation, and four members appointed by the President. The (coloured) House of Representatives has 80 directly elected members, three indirectly elected and two appointed members. The (Indian) House of Delegates has 40 directly elected, three indirectly elected and two nominated members.

As a result of elections to the (white) House of Assembly held on May 6, 1987, the directly elected seats in that House were distributed as follows: National Party (NP) 123, Conservative Party (CP) 22, Progressive Federal Party (PFP) 19, New Republic Party one, independents one. Indirectly elected members were: NP six, CP one, PFP one, and nominated members were NP four. The elections were also contested by the *Herstigte Nasionale Party*, which failed to obtain any seats (having held one until then).

Elections to the elective seats in the (coloured) House of Representatives, held on Aug. 22, 1983, resulted in the following distribution of these seats: Labour Party 76, People's Congress Party one, independents two, vacant one. The turnout was 30.9 per cent of registered coloured voters. (It was estimated that, despite a legal obligation to register, only about 40 per cent of the eligible coloured population had in fact registered.)

Elections to the elective seats in the (Indian) House of Delegates, held on Aug. 28, 1983, resulted as follows: National People's Party 18, Solidarity 17, Progressive Independent Party one, independents four. About 18 per cent of eligible Indians had not registered as voters.

Africans (blacks) have parliamentary representation only in their designated "homelands" and not at national level.

In recent years conditions in South Africa have been increasingly dominated by the issue of apartheid or "separate development" for the country's different race groups. Under the growing influence of militancy among non-whites in pursuit of obtaining eventual full political rights for blacks, coloureds and Indians, the government has, on the one hand, gradually introduced a relaxation, or even revocation, of certain apartheid laws (to the extent that it has repeatedly claimed that apartheid was "dead") and on the other hand introduced more and more stringent internal security measures.

The non-white militancy has taken various forms. Acts of violence, for most of which responsibility has been acknowledged by the banned African National Congress (ANC), have been repeatedly ascribed by the government to outside agitation by "communists" supported by certain foreign countries. Other forms of militancy, carried out despite official prohibition, have included mass demonstrations (sometimes connected with funerals of victims of violent incidents), stay-aways from work, lengthy boycotts (of schools by black and coloured children, of bus and train services and of businesses owned by non-blacks), rent boycotts (especially in Soweto and other black townships), and strikes (a number of which have been settled by agreements with black trade unions, especially in the mining industry).

The school boycotts were, however, practically ended after more than two years on Jan. 7, 1987, when most pupils returned to school.

Various internal security measures taken by the government involved the proclamation of a state of emergency in defined areas and culminated in the imposition of a national state of emergency on June 12, 1986, on the grounds that "the ordinary laws of the land" were "inadequate to enable the government to ensure the security of the public and to maintain public order" and that plans had been made "by radical and revolutionary elements . . . which pose a real danger for all population groups in the country". The new regulations reaffirmed previous measures exempting the state and its agents from civil or criminal proceedings in courts of law regarding action taken in the performance of their duties under the emergency regulations. They also contained new severe restrictions on reporting or expression of opposition to the government (especially in the press, on radio and on television). Within the first week after the proclamation of the new regulations between 2,000 and 4,000 arrests were made of leaders of anti-apartheid organizations. (Various statements had earlier been made about detentions. The Minister of Law and Order had said on April 26, 1986, that 18,569 persons were detained, including 3,681 juveniles, and 7,097 arrested since July 1985. He added that in the same period 371 had been killed and 1,194 injured by police, while 416 had been killed and 740 injured by other people.) On Sept. 19, 1986, the Minister stated that since September 1984 a total of 1,776 civilians and 56 members of the police and security forces had been killed in unrest, and that about 50 per cent of the civilians killed or wounded had been "victims of their own people". He added that currently "more than 70 per cent of unrest-related deaths" were "the murders of innocent black civilians by blacks". He also said that during 1986 there had been 17 land-mine, 55 hand-grenade and 47 limpet-mine attacks, that 80 terrorists had been arrested and 45 killed, and that large quantities of arms and ammunition had been confiscated.

Since 1960 the South African government has built up the strongest military force of any country in Africa in preparation for an anticipated low-intensity guerrilla war of long duration, and also for any major onslaught. South African defence measures have included the erection of defensive fences along the country's northern border and the extension of compulsory military service by white men to two years full-time followed by a total of 720 days over a 12-year period in the "Citizen Force"; thereafter white males are liable to service in commando units (for some categories of men for up to 1,000 days over a 20-year period).

The unrest has had far-reaching consequences for the South African economy, which has in addition been exposed to an overseas campaign for disinvestment in South Africa and the withdrawal from their South African activities of a number of foreign (mainly US) firms. On Aug. 27, 1985, the governor of the South African Reserve Bank stated inter alia that the outflow of capital from the country was due to the "distorted perception" in the international community of "the nature, extent and possible consequences of the current unrest". At the same time certain sections of the South African business community began to press for political reforms, and some even held talks with the ANC in order to "establish common ground" for an eventual ANC participation in government.

Anti-Apartheid Movements

African National Congress (ANC)

Addresses. P.O. Box 31791, Lusaka, Zambia; P.O. Box 30, Penton Street, London N1 9PR, United Kingdom

Leadership. Nelson Mandela (pres. in prison); Oliver Tambo (acting pres.); Alfred Nzo (sec.-gen.)

The ANC was founded on Jan. 8, 1912, as the South African Native National Congress at a conference held in Bloemfontein by representatives of the African peoples of Southern Africa (i.e. then the Union of South Africa, the Rhodesias, Basutoland, Bechuanaland and Swaziland). The principal object of the conference was to unite all the African people as a unified nation, overcoming tribal and ethnic divisions and opposing British colonialism and the British and Boer (Afrikaner) domination in the Union of South Africa established in 1910. Before World War I the organization worked mainly through petitions to the authorities but later it began to organize black labourers brought into the towns with the development of industry. It changed its name to African National Congress in 1925.

Following the advent of the (white) nationalist government in South Africa in 1948, the ANC sought co-operation with the South African Indian Congress (SAIC—see separate entry), the (white) Congress of Democrats and the Coloured People's Organization—with members of the Communist Party of South Africa being prominent among the leaders of these organizations.

After the introduction in the House of Assembly on Feb. 20, 1950, of a Population Registration Bill providing for the classification of South Africa's population in race groups, the ANC's council of action decided on March 4, 1950, to cease all co-operation with the government. A civil disobedience campaign against "unjust laws"—a campaign involving deliberate violation of the apartheid laws—was organized jointly by the ANC, the SAIC and the Coloured People's Organization. The campaign began on June 26, 1952, and lasted to the end of that year; it led to the arrest of some 8,500 people for disobeying apartheid laws.

The ANC repeatedly condemned the use of violence as "damaging the cause of the Africans themselves" (especially after riots in Port Elizabeth had led to the deaths of at least 12 people on Oct. 18, 1952). On April 20, 1953, the ANC, the SAIC and their joint "franchise action committee" reaffirmed their belief in "non-violent struggle against the injustice of white supremacy and apartheid" and for "the fundamental human rights of freedom of speech, association and movement" and called on the non-whites "to make the policy of apartheid unworkable in every sphere of life".

A milestone in the history of the ANC was reached at a Congress of the People, which ended at Kliptown (Johannesburg) on June 26, 1955, with the adoption of a Freedom Charter, which was conceived by Prof Z. K. Matthews, a leading ANC member, and which in effect became the political platform of the ANC. The Charter opened with the following sentence: "We, the people of South Africa, declare for all our country and the world to know: that South Africa belongs to all who live in it, black and white, and that no government can justly claim authority unless it is based on the will of all the people." The Charter included the following demands: (i) "every man and woman shall have the right to vote for and to stand as candidates for all bodies which make laws"; (ii) "the national wealth of the country, the heritage of all South Africans, shall be restored to the people"; (iii) "the mineral wealth beneath the soil, the banks, and monopoly industry shall be transferred to the ownership of the people as a whole"; (iv) "restriction of land ownership on a racial basis shall be ended and all the land redivided among those who work it, to banish famine and land hunger".

In the Transvaal the ANC executive subsequently declared that the ANC aimed at replacing the government of the few by a government of people's democracy in which the power of the state would be exercised by the working people of all colours, together with all other democratic classes who would work for the changes set out in the Freedom Charter.

The absence from the Freedom Charter of any reference to African liberation and to Pan-Africanism eventually led to the breakaway of the Africanists from the ANC, who had already objected to the ANC's decision to co-operate with non-African and pro-communist organizations and who in 1959 formed the Pan-Africanist Congress (PAC—see separate entry).

The ANC also opposed the Bantu Education Act (which came into force on April 1, 1955, and which placed the education of all Africans under the control of one government department) and called on all African parents to withdraw their children from school indefinitely—a call which was, however, not followed.

In December 1956 a total of 156 prominent anti-apartheid activists were arrested—among them three ANC leaders (ex-Chief Albert Luthuli, president-general since 1952; Oliver Tambo, then general secretary; and Walter Sisulu, a former secretary)—on charges of high treason or of contravening the 1950 Suppression of Communism Act, in particular by campaigning against government legislation, convening the Congress of the People, adopting the Freedom Charter and advocating in it the establishment of a communist state. However, the case against ex-Chief Luthuli and the majority of those arrested was withdrawn or quashed, and the remaining 28 defendants were found "not guilty" on March 29, 1961, after the court had found that the ANC did not have a policy of violence.

An All-African People's Conference held in December 1958 adopted a resolution proposed by the ANC, calling for the imposition of an economic boycott against South Africa, and this call was taken up by the sixth world congress of the International Confederation of Free Trade Unions (ICFTU) and by trade unions in a number of countries. The ANC received further international recognition when the 1960 Nobel Peace Prize was awarded to ex-Chief Albert Luthuli for his persistent opposition to racial violence. Ex-Chief Luthuli had been dismissed from his post as tribal chief in September 1952 after he had rejected a government demand that he should relinquish the presidency of the ANC. In a speech made on April 28, 1959, he had declared: "We of the ANC have no desire to dominate others by virtue of our numerical superiority. We are working for a corporate multiracial society. We are prepared to extend the hand of friendship to white South Africans who are our brothers and sisters." On May 22, 1959, he was banned from attending meetings for five years and confined to a district in Natal. In 1960 he was fined for publicly burning his pass, and later he was sentenced to imprisonment. On May 23, 1964, he was confined to his home for another five years on the ground that he had engaged in "activities furthering the cause of communism". He died in July 1967.

However, the ANC abandoned its non-violent policy in 1961 as a result of the shooting at Sharpeville (near Vereeniging, Transvaal) on March 21, 1960, when police killed 69 blacks (among them women and children) and wounded 180 during a protest demonstration against the pass laws called by the PAC. After the Sharpeville shooting both the ANC and the PAC were declared unlawful organizations on April 5, 1960. The ANC, however, refused to disband and went underground, while several hundred of its members went abroad and ANC offices were established in various African capitals and also in Moscow.

Early in June 1961 the ANC leadership decided that it would be unrealistic and wrong to continue preaching peace and non-violence at a time when the government met the ANC's demands with force. On Dec. 16, 1961, the ANC published the manifesto of *Umkhonto we Sizwe* ("Spear of the Nation") in which it declared: "We shall not submit and we have no choice but to hit back by all means in our power in defence of our people, our future and our freedom." *Umkhonto*, described as "the nucleus of an army of national liberation" and founded already in November 1960, was to conduct acts of sabotage as "properly controlled violence" without loss of life (i.e. with the consent of the ANC). In fact, however, *Umkhonto* began immediately to send volunteers abroad to be trained in guerrilla warfare.

Umkhonto began its campaign by exploding bombs at public buildings, blowing up power pylons, cutting telephone lines, attempting to derail trains and committing widespread arson (500,000 tons of sugar cane being destroyed by fire in Natal during 1962). A Sabotage Act enacted on June 27, 1962, laid down a minimum penalty of five years' imprisonment and the death penalty as a maximum for acts of sabotage; it also provided for new restrictions on suspects without any right of appeal to a court. *Umkhonto* was offically banned on May 10, 1963.

In July 1963 the police discovered the "high command" of *Umkhonto we Sizwe* in Rivonia (Johannesburg), and this led to the trial of eight alleged *Umkhonto* leaders, who were on June 12, 1964, sentenced to life imprisonment. They included Nelson Mandela, who had been one of the principal organizers of the ANC. During the trial the prosecution produced documents to show that the defendants had planned, with assistance from "friendly governments", to stage an invasion from the sea and to set up in a neighbouring country a political authority which would conduct guerrilla warfare in South Africa and would eventually become a provisional revolutionary government.

Between 1964 and 1972 there followed several further trials of alleged *Umkhonto* members who were given long-term prison sentences for "terrorist activities" and/or receiving military training abroad. In a trial which ended on March 16, 1964, three Africans were sentenced to death for murder; they were executed on Nov. 6, 1964.

During 1976 several whites were sentenced to imprisonment for furthering the aims of the ANC. Among them was Breyten Breytenbach, who was given a nine-year prison sentence on Nov. 26 after admitting that he had (with others) formed a white ANC wing (latter called *Okhela*) aimed at the overthrow of the South African government.

By 1976 the leadership of *Umkhonto* was named as consisting of Joe Modise (leader), Chris Hani (political commissioner) and Joe Slovo (chief of staff, based in Mozambique). J. Slovo was also a leading member of the South African Communist Party (SACP—see separate entry).

In 1977 the Southern African authorities announced a number of successful counter-insurgency operations. J. T. Kruger, then Minister of Justice and the Police, said on Jan. 25 that 65 Africans trained abroad had been arrested and that a quantity of weapons had been seized; he also said that the ANC had instructed detainees to commit suicide rather than "betray the cause" under interrogation. On Aug. 27 the South African police claimed (i) to have foiled a massive terrorist plan by the ANC and the SACP to invade South Africa and (ii) to have "wiped out" several "terrorist" bases near Durban as well as several more near Johannesburg.

During a trial of Africans for recruiting people for military training abroad or themselves undergoing such training, a state witness alleged on Aug. 18, 1977, that in the early 1960s a total of 55,000 black South Africans had undergone guerrilla training in the "army" of the ANC.

Among trials of ANC supporters which took place in 1977-78 was that of Solomon Mahlangu, who was condemned to death for murder and other crimes on March 2, 1978, and who was executed on April 6, 1979.

According to the chief of the South African security police, quoted on June 2, 1978, there were at that time an estimated 4,000 black South Africans undergoing military training in Angola, Mozambique, Tanzania and Libya. The South African Terrorism Research Centre stated a year later that in the 31 months up to June 1979 there had been 91 violent incidents involving 110 bombs, hand grenades or firebombs, and in the previous three years eight persons had been killed and 142 wounded in urban terrorist incidents.

ANC members who fled to the neighbouring states of Botswana, Lesotho or Swaziland (to escape the South African security police) could not legally be politically active in those countries whose governments did not allow the establishment of guerrilla bases (whereas those of Angola, Mozambique and Zambia tacitly allowed such bases, even if officially describing them as refugee camps).

There was an escalation of ANC guerrilla activities in 1979 and early 1980, including several attacks on police stations (notably in Soweto in May and November 1979, at Soekmekaar in the northern Transvaal on Jan. 3, 1980, and in a white suburb of Johannesburg on April 4, 1980) and the temporary seizure of a bank and 25 hostages at Silverton, near Pretoria, on Jan. 25, 1980, as well as an attack on the SASOL I fuel plant complex (for distilling petrol from coal) at Sasolburg, Transvaal, on June 1 (when the damage caused was estimated at about £3,000,000). According to Tambo (the ANC's acting president) attacks made on SASOL II had been "unsuccessful". All three ANC guerrillas involved in the Silverton incident were killed by police, while two of the hostages also lost their lives. On Nov. 20, 1980, three ANC members were condemned to death for murder and robbery as participants in the Soekmekaar attack, and on Nov. 26 six others were given prison sentences ranging from 10 to 20 years for high treason on charges arising out of the Silverton attack. The State President, however, commuted the three death sentences to life imprisonment on June 2, 1982.

In a treason trial of ANC members concluded on Nov. 15, 1979, one of the accused, James Mange, was sentenced to death and 11 others received prison sentences ranging from 13 to 15 years; on appeal the death sentence against Mange was overruled on Sept. 11, 1980, and he was instead given a 20-year prison sentence.

In February 1980 the South African Defence Force took over from the police responsibility for the security of northern Natal, where a major guerrilla arms cache was discovered early in February. An even larger cache was later found near Springs (Transvaal), as announced on March 3.

On Jan. 30, 1981, the Chief of the South African Defence Force announced that a South African commando had attacked and destroyed "the planning and control headquarters" of the ANC at Matola (a suburb of Maputo, Mozambique) where, he said, "numerous terrorists" had been killed and a large quantity of weapons, sabotage equipment and documents had been seized. On April 2, 1981, the police announced the discovery of further arms caches near Johannesburg, intended for use by ANC infiltrators from Mozambique via Swaziland. Further death sentences were passed on ANC members in 1981 and 1982—(i) on three men on Aug. 19, 1981, for involvement in the Sasolburg action (see above) and (ii) on three others on Aug. 6, 1982, for attacks on police stations in 1979 and 1981.

The head of the South African security police claimed on Aug. 18, 1982, that in the past 18 months over 35 insurgents had been arrested or "otherwise neutralized" and that the number of guerrilla attacks had risen from 19 in 1980 to 55 in 1981. During 1981 there had been a rocket attack on the Voortrekkerhoogte military complex near Pretoria on Aug. 12 and another on a police station near Pretoria on Dec. 26, leading to the discovery of an arms cache near Hammanskraal (now in Bophuthatswana). ANC attacks launched in 1982 included one on a fuel depot and transformers at a coal mine near Paulpietersburg (Transvaal) in May 1981.

A number of leading ANC members were assassinated outside South Africa. These included Joe Gqabi, a senior member of the ANC executive, killed in Harare (Zimbabwe) on July 31, 1981; Petrus Nyaose, a senior ANC member, and his wife, killed by a car bomb in Swaziland on June 4, 1982; and Dr Ruth First, research director of the Centre for African Studies at the University in Maputo (Mozambique), the wife of Joe Slovo and also a member of the South African Communist Party, killed by a letter bomb on Aug. 17, 1982.

On Dec. 9, 1982, South African commandos raided the homes of alleged ANC members in Maseru (Lesotho) in an action in which 42 people were killed—30 of them being reported to have been South

African refugees and the others civilians. The Chief of the South African Defence Force said on the same day that, while some women and children had been killed in "cross-fire", the 12 targets of the raid had been the planning and control headquarters for ANC guerrilla activities against South Africa, and that a number of trained "terrorists" had during the past month arrived in Maseru with orders to assassinate leaders of the Ciskei and Transkei black homelands. The Maseru raid was unanimously condemned by the UN General Assembly on Dec. 14 and by the UN Security Council on the following day. King Moshoeshoe II of Lesotho said before the Security Council that his government had dealt firmly with those few ANC "freedom fighters" whom it had found to be armed but that it would continue to refuse to hand them over to the South African authorities.

The ANC inter alia accepted responsibility for a car bomb attack on the South African air force headquarters in Pretoria on May 20, 1983, when 19 persons were killed and about 200 injured. In retaliation the South African air force raided alleged ANC targets in Matola (Maputo, Mozambique) on May 23, and claimed afterwards that 41 ANC members, 17 Mozambican soldiers and six civilians had been killed (but this was denied by the Mozambican authorities). The ANC office in Lusaka (Zambia) denied on May 23 that the ANC had any military bases in Mozambique. The Foreign Minister of Mozambique declared on May 24 that his government would continue to support the ANC but was not in any way connected with ANC attacks inside South Africa.

Following a series of explosions on Oct. 10, 1983, at Warmbaths (60 miles north of Pretoria), where petrol storage tanks, railway wagons and a petrol tanker were damaged, South African forces destroyed an alleged ANC office in Maputo on Oct. 17.

On March 21, 1984, O. Tambo admitted that a clause in the Nkomati Accord of March 15, in which Mozambique and South Africa agreed not to allow their territories to be used for attacks against each other, created a "temporary problem" for the ANC, as it denied the ANC transit facilities through Mozambique. However, he declared that these difficulties would be overcome and that (as claimed previously) all ANC actions had been "planned and staged in South Africa".

President Botha offered on several occasions to release the imprisoned ANC leader Nelson Mandela, provided he renounced the use of force as a means for change in South Africa. To such an offer made on Jan. 31, 1985, Mandela replied in a statement made public on Feb. 10 that the ANC had turned to violence "only when other forms of resistance were no longer open to us". Earlier he had called on the government to legalize the ANC and negotiate with it as a political party.

In a survey among urban blacks carried out in late 1981 it was found that some 76 per cent of these people regarded Mandela as the most popular leader. Since then the ANC's colours (black, green and gold) have continued to be displayed on numerous occasions.

At an ANC meeting held in Kabwe (Zambia) on June 16-23, 1985, it was decided by the 250 delegates to adopt a policy of assassination of black policemen, councillors and others considered to be collaborators of the South African regime, and also of certain white politicians. (The ANC thus abandoned its previous policy of attacking only inanimate targets.) The meeting also elected a new 30-member national executive committee, including (for the first time) five non-blacks, among them Joe Slovo, a leading member (and subsequently general secretary) of the South African Communist Party.

In an interview which was published in the *Cape Times* (without official permission) on Nov. 4, 1985, O. Tambo stated inter alia that the ANC had "taken the earliest opportunity to dispel the notion that we were fighting to drive the whites out to somewhere, and we made it clear that they belong to South Africa". In the event of a future majority-ruled South Africa, he said, the ANC's policy would be to nationalize some strategic industries. He reaffirmed that the ANC would continue to use violence against military pesonnel and police. He added that negotiations could take place once the South African government had released N. Mandela. He also advocated South Africa's eventual return to the Commonwealth (which South Africa had left in 1961).

From September 1985 onwards the ANC held meetings in Zambia with various businessmen from South Africa to discuss in particular the economic policies which an ANC-led government would implement in South Africa, but these meetings did not lead to any agreements. At the same time the ANC endeavoured to enhance its standing with Western nations, especially the United States, through visits to their capitals by O. Tambo.

At a press conference held in Lusaka and publicized in South Africa with official permission on Jan. 9, 1986, O. Tambo announced an escalation of the ANC's political and military campaign against the South African government and urged its armed wing "to attack, advance and give the enemy no quarter". He also said that the ANC intended to organize support by means of "mass units", i.e. military groups among the local population, and that the ANC hoped to establish its own "democratic councils" elected by universal suffrage to replace the virtually destroyed community council system of the government.

On May 19, 1986, the South African Defence Force raided alleged ANC offices in Botswana, Zambia and Zimbabwe (one person being killed in Botswana and two in Zambia). Robert Mugabe, the Prime Minister of Zimbabwe, said later on the same day that his country would not be deterred from providing political, material and moral aid to the ANC, and O. Tambo declared on May 20 that the ANC had no camps or training facilities in Zambia.

In addition to a series of prison sentences imposed on ANC members for violent crimes, a number of death sentences were carried out in 1985-86. Those executed included Malesela Benjamin Moloise, hanged on Oct. 18, 1985, for murdering a policeman, and three other ANC members, hanged on Sept. 9, 1986, one of them for involvement in a major bomb attack in Durban in December 1985 and the two others for murdering a political activist in May 1984.

In a New Year message broadcast from Addis Ababa (Ethiopia) on Jan. 15, 1987, O. Tambo listed as ANC successes the creation of "mass democratic organizations" including street committees, the Council of South African Trade Unions (COSATU), the United Democratic Front, the National Education Crisis Committee (NECC) and their affiliates. In his message he appealed inter alia to "the young lions of our revolutionary struggle" (i.e. the "comrades"—see separate entry for South African Youth Congress) to act as "a disciplined revolutionary force" towards "united mass action as distinct from militant but uncoordinated action by different groups at different times and places".

On Jan. 19, 1987, it was reported that the ANC was planning to create people's militia units in areas under its control after the Pretoria government's structures were destroyed, in order to defend the people's committees already formed by residents in these areas.

In a message to the white people of South Africa, broadcast from Addis Ababa on Jan. 20, O. Tambo called on the ANC to address itself to the question of the role to be played "by our white companions in the struggle to root out apartheid", and he urged the black population "to work consciously to mobilize our white compatriots to join the democratic forces and to make them realize that their future is threatened by the continuation of apartheid and not by the struggle for a democratic non-racial South Africa".

On Jan. 22 the ANC called on the whites within the South African Defence Force (SADF) who wanted to be "on the side of liberation" to do everything possible from within to wreck the SADF.

Initiatives taken at the United Nations by the ANC to counter "the grave threat to peaceful relations between ethnic groups" constituted by apartheid in South Africa met with growing response among the international community from 1952 onwards. The ANC was also instrumental in the setting-up of a liberation committee by the Organization of African Unity (OAU) created in 1963, and the ANC was subsequently recognized by the OAU as a national liberation movement qualifying for the receipt of official OAU support.

Regular publications issued by the ANC include the *ANC Weekly News Briefing* (London) and *Sechaba* (monthly official journal).

Azanian People's Liberation Army—see under Pan-Africanist Congress of Azania (PAC)

Azanian People's Organization (Azapo)

Azapo was set up in September 1979 as a new black consciousness movement (in succession to the banned Black People's Convention, BPC—see separate entry) and had African as well as coloured and Indian members (Azania being the African nationalists' name for South Africa). At its inaugural conference it adopted the slogan "One Azania, one people" (formerly used by the BPC).

Azapo also declared itself opposed to all institutions created by the government and to the principle of ethnically based institutions, and advocated the setting up of a single parliamentary state as well as of a common education system for all races. Many Azapo office bearers were subsequently placed in detention.

Black People's Convention (BPC)

Leadership. Sipho Buthelezi (sec.-gen.)

The BPC held its first national congress at Hammanskraal (near Pretoria) on Dec. 16, 1972, when it limited its membership to non-whites (Africans, coloureds and Indians) and declared in its constitution that it intended to "unite and liberate blacks from psychological and physical oppression". It also aimed to "preach and popularize the philosophy of black consciousness and black solidarity, create and maintain an egalitarian society and unite South African blacks in a political organization which will articulate their aspirations and seek their freedom". When two men closely associated with the BPC were placed under banning orders, Sipho Buthelezi (the BPC secretary-general) declared that blacks were used to "these intimidatory actions" through restrictions "by job reservation, influx control, house permits, lack of freehold rights, poor wages, disease, poverty and squalor". By October 1973 three leading BPC members were banned under the 1950 Suppression of Communism Act, which meant that they could no longer be politically active, and by November 1974 some 20 BPC members were being detained under the "Terrorism" Act.

Widespread riots began in Soweto (the country's largest concentration of Africans) near Johannesburg on June 16, 1976, the immediate cause being protest demonstrations by school children against the use of the Afrikaans language as a medium of instruction. The riots led to the death of 176 persons (all but two of them being blacks), injury to 1,228 persons (among them 22 policemen), the arrest of 1,298 persons and material damage estimated at up to £35,000,000. Hlaku Kenneth Rachidi, the national president of the BPC, declared on June 27, 1976, that "a new era of political consciousness" had dawned for black people in South Africa; but he said that the disturbances had become "a generalized expression of revulsion by the black community against their political powerlessness and dehumanization under the apartheid system"; and he appealed for consultation between white and black leaders to find ways and means of getting out of the situation of confrontation in which the country was placed.

After unrest among blacks had continued in Soweto and elsewhere until August 1976, causing the death of another 84 persons, numerous members of the BPC and of the South African Students' Organization (SASO—see separate entry) were arrested.

In December 1976 the BPC strongly attacked the Black United Front formed on Nov. 29 by three black "homelands" leaders, including Chief Gatsha Buthelezi (Chief Minister of KwaZulu); the BPC declared that it would have nothing to do with these homelands leaders and that if the latter wished to become leaders in the "liberation struggle" they would have to "show their credentials by getting out of the oppressive Bantustan [i.e. black homelands] scheme".

Rachidi was arrested on Oct. 19, 1977, when the BPC was (together with 17 other organizations, including its welfare arm, the Black Community Programme) declared unlawful. Rachidi was released from detention on Oct. 27, 1978, but on Dec. 18 of that year he was placed under a five-year banning order. Similar orders were imposed on several other BPC members. Nevertheless the black consciousness movement retained its influence among younger black people who were opposed to the African National Congress on the grounds that it was under the influence of white leaders of the South African Communist Party (see separate entries) and that its strategy meant that after inadequate training its youngest recruits were being sent on "suicide missions" in its sabotage campaign.

Detainees' Parents Support Committee

At the end of 1986 this Committee estimated that in the course of that year more than 25,000 people had been detained, almost all of them under the emergency regulations.

Natal Indian Congress (NIC)

Leadership. George Sewpersadh (pres.); M. D. Naidoo (vice-pres.)

The original NIC was, after World War II, superseded by the South African Indian Congress (see separate entry). It was later reactivated and co-operated with the Transvaal Indian Congress (see separate entry), with which it issued, after the August 1983 election to the coloured) House of Representatives and the (Indian) House of Delegates, a joint statement approving the "massive stayaway by our people" as expressing their unity in rejecting apartheid.

National Education Crisis Committee (NECC)

In 1986 this Committee decided to draft a new syllabus for alternative "people's schools" which would promote anti-racism and anti-sexism and the use of the English language for the children's own purposes. (The government, however, responded to this initiative by laying down new details of its own school syllabus.)

National Forum

A conference of the committee of this militant black organization held on June 11-12, 1983, attended by delegates of some 200 organizations, adopted unanimously a manifesto stating inter alia: "Our struggle for national liberation is directed against the system of racial capitalism, which holds the people of Azania [the African nationalists' name for South Africa] in bondage for the benefit of the small majority of white capitalists and their allies, the white workers and the reactionary sections of the black middle class." The organization accordingly regarded the United Democratic Front (see separate entry) as too moderate and rejected its multiracial approach.

Pan-Africanist Congress of Azania (PAC)

Leadership. Johnson Mlambo (ch.)

The establishment of the PAC in April 1959 was strongly influenced by the emergence of the pan-African idea as an intellectual and political movement among Afro-Americans and Africans who regarded Africa and peoples of African descent as homogenous and who advocated the political unity of Africa, or at least close collaboration among African states in one form or another. Their object has been to modernize Africa on the basis of equality of rights and the principle of "Africa for the Africans".

A first pan-African conference was convened in London in 1900 by Henry Sylvester Williams. Among Afro-Americans a split subsequently developed between Marcus Garvey, who called for the goal of "Africa for the Africans" to be achieved by people of African descent through their personal endeavour, and Dr W. E. B. duBois, who believed that co-operation with white liberals was essential in the African's struggle to achieve equality, and who organized four pan-African congresses after World War I. Garvey's attacks on duBois as a "white man's nigger" and "traitor to the race" were later reflected in the South African PAC's attacks on the multiracial African National Congress (ANC—see separate entry).

At the fifth pan-African congress, held in Manchester in 1945, a strong influence was exerted by George Padmore, a pro-Marxist West Indian, while others who attended the congress included Peter Abrahams of South Africa, Kwame Nkrumah of the Gold Coast (later Ghana) and Jomo Kenyatta of Kenya. The congress issued the slogan "Colonial and subject peoples of the world unite" and laid the basis for an African nationalist liberation movement fighting against racialism, colonialism and imperialism and aiming to bring about decolonization.

The pan-African movement, however, did not become a reality until Ghana achieved independence in 1957 and two conferences were held in Accra in 1958—(i) a Conference of Independent African States (in April), at which Dr Nkrumah emphasized the responsibility of these states "to hasten the total liberation of Africa, the last stronghold of colonialism", and (ii) an All-African People's Conference (in December), to work out a strategy of "African non-violent revolution" and to set up a permanent secretariat in Accra. These conferences were attended by delegates from African as well as Arab states, and pan-Africanism was then given a strong multiracial colour.

The PAC founded in South Africa succeeded an Africanist movement formed earlier by Anton Lembede, who was one of the founders of an African National Congress Youth League (ANCYL) in 1944. The ANCYL had embraced various tendencies, among them an African nationalist group (including A. P. Mda and Oliver Tambo), who stood for "African political assertion" but wanted to avoid "extremist and inward-looking nationalism", and an Africanist group (including Anton Lembede, Peter Raboroko and Walter Sisulu). After Lembede's death in 1948 A. P. Mda became president of the ANCYL, taking the line that "African nationalism only hates white oppression and white domination, and not the white people themselves".

The founding conference of the PAC of South Africa (in April 1959) was attended by nearly 300 Africans who had been expelled from the ANC, or had left it in protest against its policy of alliance with left-wing whites and Indian organizations. The PAC stood for "a government of the Africans for the Africans", an African being "everybody who owes his only loyalty to Africa and who is prepared to accept the democratic rule of an African majority"; it guaranteed "no minority rights" because minorities thought "in terms of individuals—not groups"; and whites and upper-class Indians were excluded from those deemed to owe their first loyalty to Africa. The PAC rejected multiracial co-operation on the ground that it was a way of "safeguarding white interests", and it regarded South Africa as an integral part of Africa and as incapable of solving its problems in isolation. The PAC also rejected both communism and liberalism. The conference elected Robert M. Sobukwe as first PAC president and Potlako K. Leballo as national secretary. Sobukwe defined the PAC's aims as "the overthrow of white domination and the maintenance of the right of self-determination for the African people", the attainment of these objects by 1963 and the ultimate establishment of a United States of Africa.

On Feb. 14, 1960, the PAC announced that on March 21 of that year it would launch a non-violent campaign against the pass laws (first introduced in the 19th century and later consolidated, with the effect that from 1952 Africans were required to produce on demand a reference book which normally included a residence permit, an employer's certificate, a tax receipt and a curfew pass). The campaign began peacefully in most towns but led to a confrontation between some 20,000 Africans and the police at Sharpeville (north of Vereeniging, Transvaal), where the police opened fire, killing 69 Africans and wounding 180. A state of emergency was declared on March 30 (and remained in force until Aug. 31, 1960); over 1,900 persons of different races were arrested; and under a bill passed by Parliament on April 5 both the PAC and the ANC were banned. In protest against numerous arrests at Langa (Cape Town) some 30,000 Africans led by Philip Kgosana went on strike and marched towards police headquarters in Cape Town on March 30, but turned back peacefully after the police had promised Kgosana an interview with the Minister of Justice. However, when Kgosana presented himself for the interview he was arrested, and during the next few days the police forcibly ended the strike. Among 19 PAC members sentenced to imprisonment on May 4, 1960, for inciting Africans to support the PAC's campaign was Sobukwe, who was given a three-year sentence.

Having been banned, the PAC activated its underground organization known as *Poqo* ("Alone, for Africans only"), which was responsibile for numerous acts of violence in 1961-63, involving the killing of at least three tribal chiefs and an unsuccessful attempt on the life of Chief Kaiser Matanzima of the Transkei. P. K. Leballo, acting president of the PAC since the imprisonment of Sobukwe, stated in Maseru (Basutoland—now Lesotho) on March 25, 1963, that *Poqo* had been a slogan since 1950 and more especially since 1960; that the PAC had more than 150,000 members; and that its "revolutionary council" was discussing the timing and manner of action for a rising to be launched in South Africa in 1963.

Poqo was organized in a system of cells of 10 members each with one leader, and no women or non-Africans were admitted as members (while the PAC also excluded communists from membership); *Poqo* members were enjoined to infiltrate all spheres of life and to further the aims of *Poqo* in any organization of which they were members; they were to await instructions from the national committee before acting to "achieve freedom in 1963 for the African people" by overthrowing the government and murdering all whites and African chiefs and headmen who supported the government.

A number of serious attacks by *Poqo* members during 1962 were later described as having been premature, i.e. carried out without the national committee's instructions. These attacks involved the killing of whites at Paarl (where six Africans were killed by police retaliating against the *Poqo* attack on Nov. 22), at Queenstown, in the Transkei and elsewhere. Six *Poqo* members who murdered a chief on Oct. 29, 1962, were sentenced to death at Umtata (Transkei) on Oct. 29, 1962.

Poqo's intentions were, however, thwarted when the Lesotho police searched the PAC offices in Maseru (from which Leballo had fled) early in April 1963 and found a list of between 15,000 and 20,000 names of alleged *Poqo* members, and also detained 13 PAC members. In South Africa police arrested 15 PAC "ringleaders" and Leballo's secretary who was carrying letters with instructions to PAC cell leaders to rise against the whites within two weeks. Sobukwe, whose prison term was due to expire, was affected by a General Law Amendment Act (which came into force on May 2, 1963) providing that any person serving a prison sentence for sabotage or similar crimes could be detained, after expiry of the sentence, for an indefinite period (and that any suspect could be detained for 90 days, renewable for a further 90 days "as required", without any court having powers to order that person's release).

On June 20, 1963, the Minister of Justice (then B. J. Vorster) gave the number of suspected *Poqo* members arrested during the previous 12 months as 3,246, and on June 13, 1964, it was officially announced that 162 *Poqo* members had been charged and convicted of various crimes, and that the "mopping-up" of *Poqo* had been completed. Trials of alleged PAC or *Poqo* members led to death sentences imposed in Cape Town for murder on one African on Oct. 20, 1966, on nine Africans on Dec. 14, 1966, on four others on Jan. 31, 1976 (all these murders having been committed in 1962) and on two Africans on April 19 and June 17, 1967, respectively.

In 1964 the PAC had adopted the name of PAC of Azania—Azania being an African name for South Africa. (In his book *Black Mischief* Evelyn Waugh used Azania as the name of an ancient East African Kingdom.)

Leballo, who left Basutoland on Aug. 21, 1965, continued to be acting president of the PAC, with headquarters in Dar es Salaam (Tanzania). Sobukwe was released from detention on May 13, 1969, but was thereafter restricted to the municipal area of Kimberley, and he died on Feb. 26, 1978. Shortly afterwards a PAC meeting attended by some 100 members at Arusha (Tanzania) elected Leballo as president in succession to Sobukwe.

In Swaziland the authorities arrested, in April 1978,

some 50 PAC officials at Manzini, among them Joe Mkwanazi, the chief official who had sought refuge in Swaziland in 1963; those arrested were said to have been involved in the training of guerrillas and in tribal faction fighting.

Changes in the PAC leadership took place in 1979, when Lancelot Dube (described as the commander of the PAC's Azanian People's Liberation Army) was killed in a car accident in January, and Leballo resigned the PAC presidency on May 2. He was succeeded by a three-member presidential council consisting of David Sibeko (previously PAC representative at the United Nations), Vusumzi Make and Elias Ntloedibe. However, on June 12, 1979, Sibeko was killed and Make wounded in an attack for which six PAC members were, on June 15, 1981, sentenced by the Tanzanian High Court to 15 years in prison for manslaughter—the court having rejected the government prosecutor's argument that there had been a conspiracy against Sibeko by elements within the ANC's military wing.

By 1982 it appeared that the influence of the PAC among South African blacks was far inferior to that of the ANC or the various organizations of the black consciousness movement.

On Feb. 15, 1985, four PAC members were released from prison after accepting the condition to renounce the use of violence as a means of effecting change.

In a statement issued on July 16, 1985, J. Mlambo reaffirmed the PAC's policy based on the idea that the armed struggle against apartheid had to be carried out by Africans alone; at the same time he declared that the PAC was ready to meet representatives of the ANC and to form a united front with all forces confronting the apartheid regime.

Port Elizabeth Black Civic Organization (PEBCO)

This Organization was established in 1979. Its chairman and three members of his executive were detained by the security police on Jan. 11, 1980, after they had opposed the removal of blacks from a township at Walmer, Port Elizabeth, to a new site 12 miles away.

In protest against the rising cost of living in the townships in its area, the PEBCO organized a stay-away for March 16-18, 1985, which led to riots and clashes with police, in which 12 people were killed. This was followed by a further incident near Uitenhage on March 21, when police opened fire on a procession of mourners; the death toll was later given as 20.

The PEBCO is a member of the United Democratic Front (see separate entry).

South African Communist Party (SACP)

Leadership. Joe Slovo (gen. sec.)

A Communist Party of South Africa (CPSA) was established in Cape Town on July 30, 1921, by a merger of several Marxist groups, including the International Socialist League created in 1915 after the South African Labour Party had abandoned its internationalist stand and had from then on increasingly represented the interests of white workers. A 1924 CPSA congress decided not to return to the Labour Party but to concentrate on the interests of African workers. In the period following World War II some of the party's leading members held office in the African National Congress (ANC—see separate entry), the South African Indian Congress (SAIC—see separate entry), and a number of trade unions (mainly of non-white workers), and four leading members were elected (as "Native Representatives") to the House of Assembly and the Cape Provincial Council respectively.

However, the party decided to dissolve itself on June 20, 1950, on which date the House of Assembly passed the third reading of a Suppression of Communism Bill, which came into force on July 17, 1950. The Act, which effectively banned the CPSA, was amended by a further act which came into force on July 23, 1951, but with retroactive effect from July 17, 1950, which inter alia provided for the "naming" as a communist any person who had professed communism before July 17, 1950, for the unseating of communist members of Parliament or Provincial Councils, and for making private (as well as public) advocacy of communism a punishable offence.

The CPSA was reconstituted as the South African Communist Party (SACP), led by a central committee based in London. At a congress held in 1962 it adopted a programme, "The Road to South African Freedom", which defined as the party's foremost task the building and strengthening of a united front of national liberation. The party was strengthened by the arrival in Britain of several leading communists who had fled South Africa or had, in 1963, been allowed to leave that country on exit permits (excluding any legal return to South Africa).

The Communist Party co-operated closely with the ANC, although it regarded the latter's Freedom Charter of 1955 as merely a short-term programme and only the beginning of the party's programme of establishing a Marxist state. A number of communists served on the ANC's national executive (notably Albert Nzula and Moses Kotane, both former CPSA secretaries, and J. B. Marks, a former member of the CPSA central committee). The party supported the sabotage campaign of the ANC but (according to the testimony of Ahmed Mohammed Kathrada, a prominent party member and one of the defendants in the Rivonia trial, speaking on April 20, 1964) it did not consider guerrilla warfare to be feasible and did not regard sabotage as a substitute for "mass action", without which no freedom could be obtained.

Former leaders of the CPSA sentenced in 1965-66 included Advocate Abram Fischer who had at times acted as chairman of the party's central committee. He was on May 9, 1966, sentenced to life imprisonment on charges of conspiracy with the ANC and its armed wing, *Umkhonto we Sizwe*, to commit sabotage, and to 24 years in prison on six counts of Communist Party membership. He denied, however, that he had been involved in the creation of *Umkhonto we Sizwe*, which, he claimed, had never reported to the party's central committee nor received orders from it. (He died on May 8, 1975.)

During a trial of four Indians in Pretoria (who were on Nov. 1, 1972, given five-year prison sentences) the judge found that Ahmed Timol, an alleged co-conspirator and leader of the "main unit" of the Communist Party of South Africa, had stayed in England in 1966-70 in contact with known communists; he further found that Timol had after his return been charged with organizing groups of communist supporters and had on his arrest been found in possession of Communist Party and ANC pamphlets and of copies of secret correspondence with the party's central committee in London. (Before being brought to trial Timol committed suicide by jumping from the 10th floor of the Johannesburg police headquarters.)

The South African governmant has repeatedly denounced the South African Communist Party as its principal enemy intent upon organizing a "total onslaught" on the Pretoria regime. At the same time it has expressed confidence in its ability to deal with any communist threat. J. T. Kruger, the Minister of Justice and the Police, assessing the prospects of communism in South Africa, said on Sept. 8, 1976, that communist activities in South Africa would continue for some years but that he wished to tell the party's leaders in London that as long as their party lived South Africa would continue to beat it.

The party's quarterly journal, *African Communist*, is published in London. The party's leadership has co-operated closely with that of the Communist Party of the Soviet Union. After a meeting in Moscow between a delegation led by Dr Yusuf Dadoo (then SACP chairman) and Soviet party officials, it was announced on Nov. 18, 1975, that the Soviet side had reaffirmed its "firm support for the just efforts" of the South African party.

South African Indian Congress (SAIC)

The SAIC was preceded by a Natal Indian Congress which was founded in 1894 to fight discrimination against Indians in South Africa, and which conducted a campaigh of non-violence *(satyagraha)* under the leadership of Mahatma Gandhi (who lived in South Africa in 1893-1914 and later practised *satyagraha* in India). A passive resistance campaign was also conducted in the Transvaal in 1906 against the pass laws which forced Indians to carry certificates of registration at all times; Indians who refused to register were sent to prison (among them Mahatma Gandhi), and many Indians were deported to India.

The SAIC became active after World War II. On May 28, 1950, its then president, Dr G. M. Naicker, issued a statement describing as "a serious challenge to world peace" the South African government's policy of apartheid, as expressed inter alia in the Population Registration Bill introduced in the House of Assembly on Feb. 20, 1950; he appealed to the United Nations to outlaw the South African government "from the family of democratic nations". (At the United Nations the government of India was the prime mover of initiatives against South Africa's apartheid policies.)

The SAIC has co-operated with the African National Congress (in the Congress Alliance)—see separate entry—while stressing that it adhered to methods of non-violence or passive resistance. At the abortive 1959-61 treason trial I. A. Cachalia (a former executive member of the SAIC) said that it was the duty of resisters not to fight back against violence used by police and that for the SAIC to abandon extra-parliamentary and occasionally unlawful methods would simply mean the abandonment of its struggle.

South African Students' Organization (SASO)

SASO was set up in 1968 as the student section of the black consciousness movement, of which the Black People's Convention (BPC—see separate entry) became the overall political organization. A SASO conference held at Hammanskraal (near Pretoria) on July 5, 1972, expressed the Organization's total rejection of the South African government's policies of separate development and its opposition to the black homelands' leaders whom SASO's leaders regarded as having allowed themselves to become involved in the government system. SASO also refused to enter into any dialogue with white students (including the "liberal" National Union of South African Students, NUSAS). The conference accordingly deposed SASO's current leader, Temba Sono, who had recommended co-operation with homelands and other apartheid organizations in order to convert them to SASO's thinking.

The emergence of SASO brought with it an entirely new development in that members of the coloured population groups combined with Africans, identifying themselves as blacks, and no longer as a separate group standing somewhere between whites and blacks—as had been the view of most coloured people and that of practically all whites. In the view of SASO's coloured members, they and Africans were equally disenfranchised and discriminated against and should join together in the struggle for their rights.

In 1973 the authorities held SASO responsible for student riots, especially at the University of the Western Cape (for coloureds) in Bellville (near Cape Town), at the (African) University of Fort Hare and at the Bethesda Teacher Training College (near Pietersburg, Transvaal). On March 2, 1973, it was announced that banning orders had been issued against six SASO leaders (two of them being placed under 12-hour house arrest). On July 26, 1973, Henry Isaacs (a student at the University of the Western Cape and the newly elected president of SASO) was restricted to the magisterial district of Pietermaritzburg (Natal) after students at his university had demanded to be taught by black lecturers "with whom we can communicate meaningfully and share our aspirations as members of an oppressed community". There were then 70 white and only 12 non-white teachers at that university.

Abraham Tiro, a SASO leader expelled for his political activities at the (black) university at Turfloop (Transvaal) in 1972, was killed by a parcel bomb sent to him near Gaborone (Botswana) on Feb. 1, 1974. Nine Africans, most of them members of SASO, were sentenced in Pretoria on Dec. 21, 1976, to imprisonment for five or six years for organizing illegal rallies to express support for the assumption of power by Frelimo (the Mozambique Liberation Front) in September 1974 and for "conspiratorial agreement" aimed at "a total change in South Africa".

The cause of SASO received worldwide publicity through the death in police custody in Pretoria on

Sept. 12, 1977, of Steven Biko, who had been the founder of SASO, its president in 1968-69, and later honorary president of the BPC and also an executive member of the Black Community Programme (set up to implement the self-help ideas of the black consciousness movement). He had first been restricted to King William's Town in 1973, had later been in detention until Nov. 30, 1976, and was finally arrested on Aug. 19, 1977, and he was the 20th political detainee to die in custody in South Africa within 18 months. According to the findings of an inquest concluded on Dec. 2, 1977, he died of intensive brain injuries but "the available evidence" did "not prove that death was brought about by an act or omission involving an offence by any persons, i.e. any particular person . . . or persons . . .". No prosecution followed these findings at the inquest.

SASO was one of the 18 organizations banned on Oct. 19, 1977. Barney Pityana, its then secretary-general, was arrested at the same time; on his release from detention on Aug. 10, 1978, he was placed under a banning order, but later he and his family escaped via Lesotho to Britain, where they were granted refugee status in October 1978.

South African Youth Congress (Sayco)

Leadership. Peter Mokaba (first pres.)

This Congress was formed in March 1987 with the object of creating a national federation which would co-ordinate the activities of the numerous township youth groups also known as the "comrades". It claimed a membership of 500,000 and has adopted the slogan "Victory or Death—Victory is certain" and the colours of the African National Congress (ANC—see separate entry): black, green and gold. It was expected to wield considerable influence within the United Democratic Front (UDF—see separate entry). P. Mokaba had earlier been convicted of undergoing guerrilla training but had been released on appeal after a year in prison.)

Causes supported by the Sayco have included a rent boycott and a railway strike in Soweto.

In battles between black vigilantes and "comrades" at a squatters' camp at Cross Roads near Cape Town on May 18-20 and June 9-11, 1986, the "comrades" were defeated, and the authorities razed many of the shanties in the area to the ground, making some 60,000 people homeless.

In a statement made by the Minister of Law and Order on Feb. 12, 1986, reference was made to the part played by young black and coloured people, ranging in age from below 12 to below 15 years, some of whom had been members of "people's courts" (which had sentenced people to death) or had been involved in the killing of alleged police informers or collaborators with the government by the "necklace" (i.e. the placing of a tyre round the victim's neck and setting it on fire).

Spear of the Nation (*Umkhonto we Sizwe*)—see under African National Congress (ANC)

Transvaal Indian Congress (TIC)

A Transvaal British Indian Association was first founded in 1902 by Mahatma Gandhi (see also under South African Indian Congress). In the 1940s the TIC was taken over by its radical members who participated in a 1952 defiance campaign against "unjust laws". The TIC was a signatory of the 1955 Freedom Charter (see under African National Congress, ANC) but after the bannings which followed the Sharpeville shootings of 1960 (see under Pan-Africanist Congress) its leaders were banned or went into exile. The TIC was, however, reactivated on April 30, 1983, when it reaffirmed its commitment to the Freedom Charter and to the Congress Alliance in which the ANC was the senior partner.

United Democratic Front (UDF)

Leadership. Popo Molefe (sec.-gen.)

The UDF was formed in Johannesburg on May 21, 1983, by 32 organizations, which included the Transvaal Indian Congress (see separate entry), the Council of Unions of South Africa, the South African Allied Workers' Union, the Soweto Civic Association and the National Union of South African Students (NUSAS). It was formally launched on Aug. 20, 1983, to oppose the 1982 constitutional proposals which excluded blacks from representation in parliament. It undertook to propagate the aims of the 1955 Freedom Charter (see entry for African National Congress, ANC). It claimed to have the support of the South African Council of Churches and of the Azanian People's Organization (Azapo, see separate entry) but it was opposed to the National Forum (see separate entry).

The UDF called for a boycott of the August 1983 elections to the coloured and Indian chambers of parliament, whereupon the Minister of Law and Order stated on Aug. 20 that the government would not tolerate any disruption of the elections and that the UDF was a cover for the banned ANC and South African Communist Party (see separate entry). The UDF, however, denied on Oct. 10 that it was connected with the ANC and affirmed that it was committed to achieving an end to apartheid by peaceful means.

The UDF leadership originally consisted of three presidents—Archie Gumede, Oscar Mpetha and Albertina Sisulu (the wife of Walter Sisulu, a leading ANC member sentenced to life imprisonment in 1964)—and among persons declared patrons of the UDF was the imprisoned ANC president, Nelson Mandela. At its first national conference, held in Krugersdorp on April 6-7, 1985, the UDF elected a 16-member executive council.

By that time some 40 UDF members were in detention, and a number of them were charged with treason, but these charges were subsequently withdrawn. In July 1985 the UDF stated that 11 of its members had so far been "murdered", a further 27 were missing and 20 others were intended targets of alleged government-assisted assassination squads. In protest the UDF, together with other organizations, launched a boycott of all shops in the eastern Cape except those owned by blacks.

On Oct. 9, 1986, the UDF was officially declared an "affected organization" under an act of 1974 forbidding organizations to raise or receive funds from abroad. (The UDF was said to have received such funds equivalent to at least US$1,000,000, mainly from Scandinavia.)

On Jan. 27, 1987, the UDF reaffirmed its commitment to non-violent opposition, even though there was "a daily shrinking of the legal terrain in which the democratic movement could still operate".

Western Cape Suicide Squads

This group was responsibile for grenade attacks made on June 12, 1985, on the homes of coloured members of Parliament. Although the African National Congress (ANC) disowned this group, a South African commando made what was described as a retaliatory attack on 10 alleged ANC centres of activity in Gaborone (Botswana) on June 14, when 12 persons were killed and six injured.

White "Backlash" Movements

Afrikaner Resistance Movement (*Afrikaanse Weerstandsbeweging,* AWB)

Leadership. Eugene Terre'Blanche (l.)

This Movement was established with the avowed object of maintaining white supremacy in South Africa by all possible means. To this end the AWB has called for the abolition of all political parties, for the right to vote to be restricted to white Christians approved as eligible by a special court (thus excluding Jews) and for a government controlled by an AWB Higher Council *(Opperraad)*. The AWB was organized on paramilitary lines, and had a swastika-like emblem as well as a blackshirt youth movement.

The AWB has been responsible for a number of threats and acts of violence against persons advocating racial desegregation, and on June 29, 1978, a group of 10 of its members were fined for assaulting a university professor. On Dec. 11, 1982, it was officially announced that the AWB's leader had been arrested with eight other members of the Movement, after the police had uncovered illegal arms caches in different parts of the country, mainly weapons and explosives hidden in metal countainers.

After AWB members had disrupted meetings of the ruling National Party in April 1983, the Prime Minister ordered an investigation into its activities. Under standing orders of the Commissioner of Police members of the police force were forbidden to become members of the AWB.

The Movement's leader has campaigned for the restoration of the independent Boer republics of the Transvaal, the Orange Free State and Northern Natal. He has emphasized that the Afrikaner people were entitled to land in these areas; he has denied that his Movement was based on racism, has rejected the 1983 Constitution and the concept of power-sharing, and has been reported to favour the disenfranchisement of Jews in South Africa.

White Commando *(Wit Kommando)*

Established in May 1980, this group is officially regarded as a white "underground terror movement" opposed to the policies of the government of P. W. Botha, which it regards as "a Marxist set-up" likely to convert South Africa from a well-developed country to "a state of chaos"; its members declared themselves ready to "take up arms to force whites not to serve blacks". The movement claimed responsibility for a number of bomb attacks, e.g. against the offices of an adviser to the Prime Minister and of a non-racialist white councillor in Durban. Its declared policy was "to warn first, and later to eliminate, if necessary, all persons, institutions and organizations promoting racial integration and black rule in South Africa".

After a number of members of the Commando had been arrested, South Africa's Director of Security was on March 8, 1981, quoted as saying that they were "part of an international right-wing network", some of them being of Italian origin and linked with European extremists. The Commando is said to have about 500 members; although it has an Afrikaans name, it also admits non-Afrikaners to membership.

White Liberation Movement (*Blanke Bevrydingsbeweging*)

This ultra-right Movement formed in 1987 has called for the eviction of all non-whites from the Republic of South Africa. On June 16, 1987, the government banned the display of the Movement's posters, which it considered "undesirable".

Spain

Capital: Madrid Pop. 38,600,000

The Kingdom of Spain is, under its 1978 Constitution, a "democratic state" and a "parliamentary monarchy" which guarantees the right to autonomy of all "nationalities and regions" of Spain. The country has a Cabinet headed by a Prime Minister and responsible to a bicameral Parliament consisting of a Congress of Deputies of 350 members elected by direct adult suffrage and a 208-member Senate also elected by adult universal suffrage, both for four-year terms. As a result of elections held on June 22, 1986, parties were represented in the Congress of Deputies as follows: Socialists 184, Popular Coalition 105, Democratic and Social Centre 19, Convergence and Union (Catalonia) 18, United Left (mainly communist) 7, Basque Nationalist Party 6, United People *(Herri Batasuna)* 5, Basque Left 2, Aragonese Regional Party 1, Canaries Independent Grouping 1, Galician Coalition 1, Valencian Union 1.

The granting of autonomy to various regions of Spain has met the aspirations of most autonomist regional parties except in the Basque region (consisting of the provinces of Avala, Guipúzcoa and Vizcaya, but not including Navarra, claimed as "Basque" by many Basque nationalists), where violent resistance to the Spanish regime has been carried out by the pro-independence Basque Nation and Liberty (*Euzkadi ta Azkatasuna*—ETA) and its supporters in several other groups. Internal security has also been disturbed by operations of right-wing organizations, involving also some high-ranking officers who had served under the Franco regime and intent upon restoring a traditional authoritarian regime, as well as by extreme left-wing (both anarchist and communist) groups. According to police sources, political violence claimed 60 lives in 1985.

An anti-terrorist law published on Aug. 26, 1975, laid down the death penalty for terrorist acts causing (i) the death of a member of the police or the armed forces or a state official and (ii) the death or mutilation of a kidnap victim.

In June 1978 the government banned the wearing of paramilitary uniforms, and in November of that year it decreed that the national flag could not be used by political organizations as their own symbol. On Oct. 29, 1980, the Congress of Deputies passed (by 298 votes to two with eight abstentions) a bill providing inter alia for the suspension of certain fundamental rights in the case of persons suspected of terrorist acts or complicity in or defence of such acts.

On Nov. 24, 1983, the Congress of Deputies approved new anti-terrorist measures for the Basque region, empowering judges to ban political associations, to close down media organs supporting terrorism, and to order the detention of suspects without trial for up to 2½ years, and enabling the police to search homes, tap telephones and arrest suspects without a warrant. It was also made possible to reduce or even lift convictions in the cases of prisoners who turned informers.

A commission of five European experts under the chairmanship of Sir Clive Rose (a retired British diplomat), appointed by the Basque government in June 1985 to study policy options in the region, issued its report on April 4, 1986. It recommended inter alia (i) that negotiations with ETA should never be discounted; (ii) that ETA terrorism cases should be tried in ordinary law courts, rather than in the specially created court in Madrid; (iii) that steps should be taken to accommodate Basque nationalism within the European Communities with some form of representation while abiding by the terms of the 1979 Statute of Guernica (which had inter alia provided for the creation of the Basque parliament and police force); (iv) that the Basque police force should gradually assume all security duties in the region, including the struggle against ETA terrorism; and (v) that measures should be taken to stimulate the region's economy. The commission also condemned the practice of paying ransoms to free ETA kidnap victims.

The first of these proposals was opposed by all regional political parties except the *Herri Batasuna* (ETA's political wing). The Basque Premier said on April 11 that any agreement would have to involve the central government in order to be effective; on Aug. 14 he said that the Basque government and the Basque Nationalist Party (PNV) had unsuccessfully tried to arrange direct contact for informal talks between ETA and the central government, although the PNV still opposed all political negotiation.

Extreme Right-wing Movements

Almond Trees (*Almendros*)

This name was adopted by a group of officers of the armed forces and civilians who were believed to have planned a right-wing coup for the spring of 1981, communicating with each other through code words in certain publications, including *El Alcázar*, the Civil War veterans' newspaper. Members of the group were among those arrested after an attempted coup of Feb. 23, 1981, by Lt.-Col. Antonio Tejero Molinas, allegedly supported by certain high-ranking military officers, such as Gen. Armada Comyn (Deputy Chief of Staff of the army) and Lt.-Gen. Milans del Bosch y Ussia (Captain-General of the Valencia military region).

Some of the military leaders associated with the February 1981 coup attempt were also implicated in a further right-wing plot to seize power on the eve of the general elections of Oct. 28, 1982. On Oct. 3, 1982, the Spanish Defence Ministry announced that on the previous day three artillery officers had been detained in connexion with an operation planned against the security of the state, namely Col. Jesús Crespo Cuspinera, his brother Lt.-Col. José Crespo Cuspinera and Col. Luis Muñoz Gutiérrez.

In addition some of the officers who had been sentenced for their involvement in the February 1981 coup attempt—namely Lt.-Gen. Milans del Bosch, Lt.-Col. Tejero, Gen. Luis Torres Rojas and Maj. Ricardo Pardo Zancada—were held incommunicado from Oct. 2. The latest plot had been uncovered after Col. Muñoz had visited Lt. Gen. Milans del Bosch in prison in Madrid, while Lt.-Col. Tejero was known to be a close friend of the Crespo brothers.

Documents taken from the home of Col. Muñoz and Col. Jesús Crespo showed that the officers had planned a coup (on the model of the Greek military takeover of 1967) under the codenames "Operation Cervantes" and "Operation Mars".

Meanwhile, Lt.-Col. Tejero had formed a new right-wing political party called Spanish Solidarity (SE), though he had been sentenced in June 1982 to 30 years' imprisonment for his role in the February 1981 coup attempt (this conviction being temporarily in abeyance because he was appealing against it). The new party was seen as having been intended to serve as the political "front" for the October 1982 coup attempt; in the Oct. 28 elections it received only 28,451 votes.

As a result of an appeal by the officers against the sentences passed on them in June 1982 and of a counter-appeal by the state, the Supreme Court in Madrid decided on April 28, 1983, to increase several of the prison sentences imposed—notably that against Gen. Armada Comyn (whom the court regarded as a co-leader of the attempted coup) from six to 30 years; that against a divisional chief of staff from three to 10 years; and those against Gen. Torres Rojas and Maj. Pardo Zancada from six to 12 years. The court also confirmed the 30-year sentences imposed upon Gen. Milans del Bosch and Lt.-Col. Tejero.

Three other army officers were, on April 15, 1984, sentenced to 12 years and one day each in prison for conspiracy to rebellion in connexion with the coup planned for Oct. 27, 1981.

Anti-communist Apostolic Alliance (*Alianza Apostolica Anticomunista*, AAA)

Members of this organization have been responsible for both threats and acts of violence not only against left-wing activists but also against members of the government. In December 1976 the AAA issued a warning that "the night of the long knives" would arrive if the President of the Council of State—who had been kidnapped on Dec. 11 by members of the First of October Anti-fascist Resistance Group (GRAPO)—were not released. On Jan. 24-25, 1977, AAA members attacked a meeting of left-wing labour lawyers in Madrid, spraying it with machine-gun fire, killing five people and wounding four. Of several persons arrested in connexion with this attack, some were said to belong to the New Force (see separate entry).

On Feb. 24, 1977, the AAA issued a death threat against the Prime Minister (then Adolfo Suárez González), condemning him as a "traitor". After AAA members had planted a bomb which destroyed the office of a satirical newspaper in Barcelona, killing one and injuring 15 persons (one of whom died later), 12 AAA members were arrested in various cities early in October 1977.

On Sept. 28, 1978, the AAA announced, together with the Anti-terrorist Organization against the ETA and the Warriors of Christ the King (see separate entries) that they had set up a "committee for private justice" to execute the Prime Minister, the Ministers of the Interior and Defence and other "agents of freemasonry, separatism and Marxism". The AAA also claimed responsibility for sending a letter bomb to the Madrid office of the independent daily *El País*, on Oct. 30, 1978, injuring three persons, one of whom died on Nov. 1.

During 1980 the AAA was responsible for causing a bomb explosion in Bilbao on July 23, killing a woman and two children, and for the killing of a club owner at Ondárroa (near Bilbao) on Aug. 31.

Anti-terrorist Liberation Group (*Grupo Antiterrorista de Liberación,* GAL)

This group, which operated from 1983 onwards, mainly against ETA militants in France, was believed to be organized by French underworld figures including members of the former Secret Army Organization (OAS) which had opposed the French withdrawal from Algeria. By September 26, 1985, GAL members had killed 18 persons.

Earlier, a French court had on April 18, 1985, sentenced two GAL members to five years in prison for arms offences, and on Dec. 12, 1985, a Spanish court sentenced two GAL members to 30 years in prison for murdering a French citizen in Hendaye in 1984. On Jan. 14, 1986, the police in Barcelona announced the arrest of several GAL members who had killed a French citizen in Biarritz in December 1984. In another attack near Bayonne (France) on Feb. 16, 1985, GAL members killed two French citizens in error.

In Portugal, the police had announced on Aug. 27, 1985, that they had detained three Portuguese GAL members connected with attacks on bars in France on Feb. 8 and 13, 1985. Another Portuguese GAL member was arrested by French police on Feb. 13.

Anti-terrorist Organization against the ETA (ATE)

Early in 1976 this Organization was involved in attacks on property of alleged supporters of the separatist Basque Nation and Liberty (ETA) and on bookshops selling "left-wing propaganda". On Sept. 28, 1978, it joined in the formation of a "committee for private justice" with the Anti-communist Apostolic Alliance (AAA) and the Warriors of Christ the King (see separate entries).

Armed Spanish Groups (*Grupos Armados Españoles*, GAE)

Members of this movement, strongly opposed to the Basque separatists, were involved in clashes with Basques in which two of its members were killed by ETA members at Baracaldo (near Bilbao) on Jan. 5 and 23, 1980. GAE members killed a Basque nationalist near San Sebastian on Jan. 16, 1980, and also placed a bomb in a bar at Baracaldo on Jan. 20, which killed four and injured 19 persons; another GAE member was killed by ETA supporters in Baracaldo on Jan. 23, 1980.

Jauzibia

Four members of this anti-terrorist group were detained in connexion with the murder of a Spanish Basque exile working in France on March 1, 1984.

Spanish Basque Battalion (*Batallón Vasco Español*, BVE)

During 1980 alone the BVE was responsible for 16 political killings (out of a total of 126 for the whole of

Spain). Those killed by BVE members included two members of the Basque separatist ETA (killed in Madrid and San Sebastian respectively on Feb. 2, 1980); two persons killed on Nov. 23 in a bar in Hendaye (France), where 10 others were injured, in an action against Basque separatists; a leading ETA member killed on Dec. 30, 1980, by a car bomb planted by the BVE in Biarritz (France); and two Basque nationalists and a Communist shot dead in Tolosa on June 24, 1981. On March 21, 1981, French police arrested a member of a BVE commando which had attacked three Basque exiles in St Jean-de-Luz (France).

On June 25, 1985, two BVE members were sentenced to a total of 231 years in prison for murdering seven ETA members.

Spanish Solidarity (SE)—see under Almond Trees

Warriors of Christ the King (*Guerrilleros del Cristo Rey*)

Leadership. Mariano Sánchez Covisa (l.)

In January 1970 this organization declared that its enemies were "the adversaries of the Church and of Spain, principally the progressives, the heretical and subversive Christian movements". In 1975 it embarked on reprisals against members of the Basque separatist ETA and their families, and its activities carried out in early 1976 were said to have led to a temporary decrease in separatist operations. In February 1977 the organization's leader was thought to have co-operated with Italian right-wing extremists, one of whom had been sentenced by an Italian court (in absentia) to 23 years in prison for attempting to attack a train. On Sept. 28 the organization joined the Anti-communist Apostolic Alliance (AAA) and the Anti-terrorist Organization against ETA in forming a "committee for patriotic justice" with the object of "executing" leading figures of the regime.

Extreme Left-wing Movements

Armed Libertarian Groups (*Grupos Armados Libertarios*, GAL)

The GAL are believed to stand to the left of the anarchist National Labour Confederation (CNT) and to have arisen out of splits in a *Front d'Alliberament de Catalunya* (FAC). The movement was held responsible for many acts of violence, including bank robberies in 1980-81 to provide liquid funds to finance its activities.

Armed Revolutionary Struggle (*Loita Armada Revolucionaria*, LAR)

This group claimed responsibility for four explosions at the port of Vigo on Oct. 1, 1980, when some 30 Citroën cars ready for export were destroyed.

Autonomous Anarchist Groups (GAS)

In December 1979, five GAS members were arrested in connexion with preparations for causing explosions at flats housing some 300 military families in Barcelona.

First of October Anti-fascist Resistance Group (*Grupo de Resistencia Anti-fascista Primero de Octubre*, GRAPO)

GRAPO took its name from Oct. 1, 1975, the date of Gen. Franco's last political appearance, on which occasion it killed four policemen. It was set up as the armed wing of the (Maoist) Reconstituted Spanish Communist Party (*Partido Comunista Español Reconstituido*, PCE-R) founded in Galicia in 1963 as an offshoot of an Organization of Spanish Marxist-Leninists (OMLE). The PCE-R never had any mass support and was in some quarters regarded as manipulated and infiltrated by right-wing fascist elements.

On July 18, 1976, GRAPO members carried out bomb attacks in several towns, and between July 28 and Oct. 25 of that year 45 GRAPO members were arrested. On Dec. 11, 1976, a GRAPO commando kidnapped the President of the Council of State and demanded the release of 15 political prisoners and their transfer to Algeria; on Jan. 24, 1977, GRAPO members also kidnapped the President of the Supreme Council of Military Justice (in retaliation for the killing of a student during a demonstration on Jan. 23); and on Jan. 28 GRAPO members killed two policemen and a civil guard in Madrid. However, the two senior officials kidnapped by GRAPO were freed in a police operation on Feb. 11, 1977.

On May 17, 1977, GRAPO bombed the US cultural centre in Madrid. After further acts of violence by the Group, including the murder of two civil guards in Barcelona on June 5 and bomb attacks on French embassy and cultural premises in Madrid on July 11-12, police arrested six GRAPO members on Aug. 6, 1977, in Madrid, three others on Sept. 23 and a further 18 in Barcelona, Benidorm and Madrid early in October 1977. On March 22, 1978, however, GRAPO members killed the director-general of the Spanish prison service in Madrid in revenge for the death, at the hands of prison guards, of an imprisoned anarchist.

GRAPO also claimed responsibility for killing a policeman in Barcelona on Aug. 28, 1978, and a brigadier-general in Madrid on March 5, 1979; it was believed responsible for a bank raid in Barcelona on March 7, 1979, when a policeman was killed, and for killing another policeman in Seville on April 6, 1978. The alleged GRAPO leader, Juan Carlos Delgado de Codex, was shot dead by police in Madrid on April 20, 1978.

GRAPO was also held responsible for a bomb explosion in Madrid on May 26, 1979, when nine persons (said to be right-wing militants) were killed and 61 injured; for the killing of four policemen and civil guards in Seville, León and Madrid in May-July 1979; and for a bomb explosion on July 5 at the Madrid branch of the Banque Nationale de Paris in retaliation for the killing by Paris police on June 28-29 of two members of the PCE-R. Between July and October 1979 police arrested numerous GRAPO suspects, among them two (on July 26) who confessed to involvement in the Madrid bomb explosion on May 26, the killing of the brigadier-general on March 5, and that of several policemen. J. M. Sánchez Casas, who was said to have succeeded J. C. Delgado de Codex as GRAPO leader, was arrested on Oct. 15, 1979.

Various trials of GRAPO members resulted in prison sentences being imposed as follows: 37 years for one GRAPO member, 25 years for another, and from 13 months to 10 years for five others on May 4, 1979—the charges against them including the murder of a police captain on Sept. 27, 1977; 10 years each for five GRAPO members convicted on May 21, 1979, of kidnapping (in December 1976 and January 1977) the two senior officials, mentioned above, with two others being given six-year terms; 25 years each for two men and a woman, sentenced on Jan. 2, 1980, for killing a GRAPO member whom they suspected of giving information to the police; from 17 months to 19 years for eight GRAPO members (on Jan. 8, 1980) for kidnapping a radio technician to broadcast a GRAPO message in July 1977; 10 years (also imposed on Jan. 8, 1980) for six GRAPO members for attacks and robberies in Seville in January 1978; 18, 11, seven and two years respectively for four persons (on March 14, 1980) for crimes including robbery with violence in 1977; two years for each of two GRAPO members (on March 21, 1980) for bomb attacks on the office of the *Diario-16* magazine in Madrid in June 1977; 74 years (on June 4, 1980) for a GRAPO member who had killed a civil guard and injured three others in January 1977; 30 years each for two GRAPO members (on July 16, 1980), one of them being J. M. Sánchez Casas, and 18 years for a woman for shooting a civil guard in Barcelona in February 1979; an additional 33 years for J. M. Sánchez Casas (on Nov. 18, 1980) for murdering the brigadier-general on March 5, 1979, with two others receiving 30 years and a woman 20 years for complicity in this crime; 47 years (on Dec. 1, 1980) for a GRAPO member convicted of robbery with violence; 24 years each for two GRAPO members (on Feb. 20, 1981) for murdering a policeman in 1979; and 15 years each for five men and three years each for two women (on March 9, 1981) for planning to murder a general in 1979, with one of the defendants being given an additional 31 years for three other attempted murders.

Meanwhile, GRAPO had continued its campaign of violence during the early 1980s. On July 22 of that year a civil guard was killed and 30 others were injured by a bomb placed under a civil guard bus by GRAPO members in Logroño province (northern Spain). On Sept. 2 GRAPO members killed a general in Barcelona and mortally wounded another, apparently in retaliation for the killing of a leading GRAPO member by police in Madrid on Aug. 29, 1980. On Nov. 23 an air force colonel was killed by GRAPO in Saragossa, and on Dec. 12 the secretary-general of the National Youth Front (a more extreme splinter group of the right-wing New Force) was killed by GRAPO members in Madrid. For killing a (reputedly liberal) general (and also a policeman) in Madrid on May 4, 1981, four GRAPO members were, on June 17, 1983, sentenced to imprisonment for from 25 to 50 years. Four suspected GRAPO members were shot by civil guards in Catalonia on June 17, 1981.

Among GRAPO members tried in 1981, J. M. Sánchez Casas and Alfonso Rodríguez García were on July 9 each given 270-years sentences and fines of 150,000,000 pesetas (US$1,500,000) for the Madrid bomb explosion of May 26, 1977; on Aug. 2, J. M. Sánchez Casas was given a further 26 years for robbery with murder, together with another man given the same sentence and a woman sentenced to 15 years.

One of GRAPO's earlier leaders, Enrique Cedán Calixto, who had escaped from prison in 1979, was killed in a shootout with police in Barcelona on Sept. 5, 1981. Another GRAPO member serving a long sentence for robbery and planting explosives died in a Madrid hospital on June 19, 1981, after starting a hunger-strike on March 14 in protest against prison conditions.

During 1977-79 GRAPO had an active local group known as *Comando Barcelona*, which was responsible (according to the police) for a series of bank robberies, attacks on premises of firms and organizations, and also for murders between February and May 1979.

Juan Martín Luna, alleged to have been GRAPO's leader, sentenced to 37 years in prison in 1978, escaped from prison in 1980 but was killed by police on Dec. 5, 1982.

From November 1982 to January 1983 GRAPO observed a conditional truce, the condition being a total amnesty for political prisoners and the introduction of "full political and trade union liberties".

By January 1985 nearly 20 GRAPO members were being held in detention in seven Spanish cities.

Iberian Federation of Anarchist Groups (FIGA)

Leadership. Alejandro Mata Camacho (l.)

This small group broke away from the (anarchist trade union) National Confederation of Labour (*Confederación Nacional de Trabajo,* CNT) in 1978. Its leader was, in Madrid on March 11, 1983, sentenced to 33 years' imprisonment for five armed robberies at banks and savings banks and for possession of arms.

Organization of Spanish Marxist-Leninists (OMLE)—
see under First of October Anti-fascist Resistance Group (GRAPO)

Reconstituted Spanish Communist party (PCE-R)—
see under First of October Anti-fascist Resistance Group (GRAPO)

Red Guerrillas (*Guerrilleros Rojos*)

This group claimed responsibility on June 27, 1977, for a series of attacks on the cars of French tourists north of Barcelona, these attacks being accompanied by demands for the release of a militant Basque arrested in France on June 2, 1977, on suspicion of involvement in the kidnapping and murder in May-June

1977 of an industrialist and former Mayor of Bilbao by the *Bereziak* wing of the ETA; the Basque in question was freed by a court in Aix-en-Provence on Sept. 6, 1977, subject to certain restrictions, but he later failed to report to police as required under the terms which had been specified by the court in his release order.

Revolutionary Anti-fascist and Patriotic Front (*Frente Revolucionaria Antifascista Patriotica*, FRAP)

Members of this organization, formed in 1973 by various Maoist groups, were responsible for killing a number of policemen and civil guards in 1973-77. According to a Spanish police statement on May 19, 1973, FRAP had in a programme drawn up by a congress in Italy in April 1973 called for the "overthrow of the present regime by means of revolutionary struggle", the establishment of a "popular democratic and federal republic" and the creation of "an army in the service of the people".

On Sept. 12, 1975, a military court in Madrid sentenced three FRAP members to death for murdering a policeman on July 14, 1975, and two other FRAP members to 30 and 25 years in prison respectively. On Sept. 18 the court passed death sentences on five further FRAP members (three men and two women) and a 20-year prison sentence on another FRAP member for killing a civil guard on Aug. 16 of that year. The death sentences of the two women and that of one of the men sentenced on Sept. 12 were subsequently commuted to 30 years' imprisonment, and the two women were later released under an amnesty of May 1977.

On Sept. 23, 1975, the Public Order Court in Madrid sentenced five FRAP members (including a woman tried in absentia) to from 11 to 18 years in prison for illegal assocation connected with the killing of a policeman in Madrid on May 1, 1973. On May 9, 1977, a Barcelona industrialist was killed as he tried to dismantle a time bomb strapped to his chest by FRAP members who had demanded a ransom of 500,000,000 pesetas; four persons detained in connexion with this incident were released under an amnesty of November 1977.

Struggle (*Gatazka*)

This group, which was opposed to national service, accepted responsibility for planting a mine in the Basque port of Fuenterrabía, which was struck by a Spanish naval patrol boat on May 14, 1984, killing a sailor.

Union of Anti-fascist Youth (*Unión de Juventudes Antifascistas*)

In May 1981 a member of this organization was sentenced to 15 months in prison for supplying the First of October Anti-fascist Resistance Group (GRAPO) with information which GRAPO had used to commit acts of violence.

Separatist Movements

BASQUES

Autonomous Anti-capitalist Commando (*Comando Autónomo Anticapitalista*)

This group has been described as an extreme left-wing offshoot of the Basque Nation and Liberty movement (ETA, see below).

On Sept. 29, 1979, the police in San Sebastian announced the detention of four members of this group suspected of being involved in an attack on a municipal office and a bank robbery earlier that month. The police also discovered arms, explosives and other equipment assembled by the group. Members of this group killed a civil guard and a fisherman near San Sebastian on April 6 and a bar owner in Azpeitia (south-west of San Sebastian) on Dec. 7, 1980.

On Sept. 24, 1985, a member of this group was sentenced in Madrid to 53 years in prison for having murdered a Socialist senator in February 1984.

Basque Nation and Liberty (*Euzkadi ta Azkatasuna*, ETA)

Leadership. José Antonio Urrutikoetxea Bengoetxea (commander)

Basques in Spain have since the late 19th century campaigned for either autonomy within the Spanish state or complete independence for the Basque areas, defined by them as the provinces of Vizcaya, Guipúzcoa, Alava and Navarra; some of them have also campaigned for the inclusion of certain areas of France partly inhabited by Basques, namely Labourd, Basse-Navarre and Soule (all bordering on the Spanish province of Navarra and forming part of the French department of Basses-Pyrénées). Until 1936 the Basques enjoyed a measure of autonomy under the Spanish Republican government, and during the 1936-39 Civil War the Basque provinces held out for a long time as a Republican enclave within Nationalist-controlled territory. After the Civil War militant Basque nationalism was quiescent, until ETA was formed in 1959 as a breakaway group from the Basque Nationalist Party (*Partido Nacionalista Vasco*, PNV), which remained a legal autonomist party opposed to the use of violence.

In 1960 the Spanish government issued a decree authorizing military courts to try cases of "military rebellion", an offence which included the dissemination of false or tendentious news intended to cause internal disorders, international conflict or loss of prestige to the Spanish state and its institutions, and also the holding of illegal meetings and the fomenting of strikes; penalties included death or life imprisonment for sabotage, causing explosions, arson, kidnapping, armed assault and armed robbery. The decree was later suspended but was reimposed on Aug. 15, 1968, after the head of the political police in Guipúzcoa province had been assassinated on Aug. 2 and a partial state of emergency declared in the province on Aug. 5.

In the ensuing years numerous alleged ETA activists were sentenced to long terms of imprisonment, among them several priests. In particular, a court-martial in Burgos, on Dec. 28, 1970, condemned to death six defendants and sentenced nine others to long prison terms totalling over 700 years. After the Holy See and the bishops of three Basque dioceses had pleaded for clemency, Generalissimo Franco, then head of state, commuted the death sentences to 30 years' imprisonment.

In other trials held in July and August 1971 the Burgos military court passed prison sentences for various acts of violence on 12 Basque separatists.

In 1971 ETA was reported to have split into two factions: (i) a non-Marxist "military" section, which had attempted to form, with other groups outside ETA, a Basque National Front (*Frente Nacional Vasco*, FNV); and (ii) a Marxist section, trying to set up a mass movement among the Basque working class. The second faction was said to consist of two parts—one known as *Sayoak*, intent upon spreading the Basque struggle to the whole of Spain, and another, *Borriak*, wishing to confine its activities to Spanish and French Basque country. Reference was also made at this time to the existence of a pro-Chinese faction of ETA, named as *Kommunistak*.

In January 1972 ETA described its objective as being "the reunification of the Basque country north and south of the Pyrenees and the defence of the interests of the working class until it effectively assumes the political, cultural and economic control of Euzkadi" (the Basque country).

During 1972 ETA continued its "armed struggle" which included the temporary abduction of a prominent industrialist who was released after he had agreed to ETA demands relating to the reinstatement of dismissed striking workers and pay increases. In 1973 ETA intensified its activities, carrying out further abductions, using machine guns and planting bombs. One of its bombs killed Adml. Luis Carrero Blanco, the Spanish Prime Minister, on Dec. 23, 1973. The year 1974 was marked by numerous trials of ETA suspects on many different charges such as abductions, the use of explosives and bank robberies.

On Dec. 11, 1974, some 200,000 workers in the Basque region held a one-day strike called for by ETA in support of a demand for an amnesty for political prisoners and of a hunger strike by some 150 imprisoned Basques. After several policemen had been killed by ETA supporters early in 1975, the government declared a state of emergency in Guipúzcoa and Vizcaya, where 152 ETA supporters were subsequently detained, among them six priests alleged to be ETA militants.

On May 1, 1975, it was announced that ETA, the Socialist Party for the National Liberation of the Catalan Lands (SNAP) and the Union of the People of Galicia (UPG) were joining forces and had appealed to all "democratic and revolutionary forces" to support them.

Among ETA members tried in 1975 were three sentenced to death, but two of the death sentences were subsequently commuted to 30 years' in prison.

After the death of Generalissimo Franco on Nov. 20, 1975, ETA continued its campaign of violence. In revenge for the killing by civil guards of a Basque demonstrator on Sept. 8, ETA shot dead, on Oct. 4, the president of the Provincial Council of Guipúzcoa.

It was announced at a press conference held in France late in September 1976 that the political-military wing of ETA (ETA-pm) had been formed as a new "nationalist and revolutionary party" which would continue to campaign for the aims of the existing ETA—i.e. the creation of a united and independent Basque state comprising both the Spanish and the French Basque provinces—but would be non-violent and aim at "strengthening the autonomous organs of the Basque people" within the framework of "bourgeois democracy" in Spain. In April 1977 ETA-pm set up the Basque Revolutionary Party (*Euskal Iraultzako Alderdia*, EIA), which was legalized in March 1978.

On March 23, 1977, ETA offered to observe a ceasefire until June 15 of that year (the date of general elections) on condition that the government agreed to all Basque demands, including the recognition of Basque as an official language, the independence of the Basque provinces, an amnesty for all political prisoners and exiles, and the dissolution of the "repressive" security forces. The government, for its part, decided on March 20 to offer a choice of voluntary exile to Basque political prisoners, and on May 22 five of them, who had been sentenced to death at the 1970 Burgos trial, were flown to Norway, with the sixth following on June 6, together with another ETA member sentenced to death in Burgos on Aug. 29, 1975. Further ETA members awaiting trial—some of them (including Ignacio Pérez Beotegui) in connexion with the assassination of Adml. Carrero Blanco in December 1973—were flown to Denmark, Austria or Norway on June 9, and some others were released.

However, other ETA groups, in particular the military wing (ETA-m) and *Bereziak* ("Storm Troops", which had split off from ETA-pm), carried on with acts of violence which were directed mainly against members of the police force.

On Oct. 2, 1977, the Bilbao newspaper *Egin* published a declaration by ETA-pm announcing that the armed struggle would be relegated to a secondary position and that priority would be given to political action, with the practice of extorting "revolutionary taxes" (which had been publicly denounced by the Basque National Party on Sept. 16) being abandoned.

ETA-m continued its violent activities beyond the end of 1977. However, following an appeal by all major political parties to ETA to renounce violence as a political instrument, ETA-m stated on Jan. 13, 1978, that it would abandon its terrorist activities provided the government fulfilled conditions involving the granting of a total amnesty, the unconditional legalization of all political parties and the removal of all state security forces from the Basque provinces. (The government had already decided, on Oct. 17, 1977, on an amnesty for most political offences committed before June 15, 1977; this applied inter alia to nine suspects detained after a bomb attack in Madrid on Sept. 13, 1974, and to all suspects held in connexion with the assassination of Adml. Carrero Blanco, who were formally amnestied on Jan. 20, 1978.

As the government made no further concessions, ETA-m committed further serious acts of violence in 1978-79. ETA-pm, on the other hand, conducted, notwithstanding its earlier renunciation of violence, in

June-July 1979 a bombing campaign designed to disrupt the tourist industry and in support of demands for the replacement of the National Police by ordinary warders at a maximum security prison in Old Castile holding some 100 Basques and for the transfer of these prisoners to prisons in the Basque region. On July 3 ETA-pm members seriously wounded a deputy of the Union of the Democratic Centre (UCD) in an attempt to kidnap him, and on July 29 ETA-pm caused the death of five persons and injury to 113 others by explosions at railway stations and the international airport of Madrid; however, on Aug. 2 ETA-pm announced that it was ending its campaign because it did not wish to fight against the Spanish people.

ETA-m meanwhile continued its attacks and inter alia killed the army chief of manpower with two colonels and a chauffeur in Madrid on May 25, 1979, two army officers in Bilbao on Sept. 19 and the military governor of Guipúzcoa in San Sebastian on Sept. 23. Early in November, however, ETA-m offered a ceasefire provided the government was willing to negotiate and conceded immediately (i) the legalization of all Basque political parties and (ii) an amnesty for all ETA activists. During 1979 five ETA-m members were sentenced to varying terms of imprisonment.

During the campaign leading to a referendum which was held on Oct. 25, 1979, and led to approval of a regional autonomy statute for Alava, Guipúzcoa and Vizcaya (by 90.3 per cent of the votes cast in a 58.9 per cent poll), ETA-m staged no major acts of violence from Oct. 4 onwards; nevertheless, it opposed the proposed statute as a barrier to full self-determination for the Basque nation, while the *Herri Batasuna* party called for abstention from voting. ETA-pm, on the other hand, called for a "yes" vote, regarding the proposed statute as a short-term solution which might ultimately lead to independence.

In November 1979, a group styling itself ETA *Autónomo* broke away from ETA-m.

After the election of the first regional parliament of the Basque region on March 9, 1980, when the *Herri Batasuna* party gained 11 seats (out of the total of 60) and 16.3 per cent of the votes cast, the party declared that it would not take its seats until some 200 imprisoned ETA members has been amnestied. However, the party nominated as its spokesman in parliament Iñaki Pikabea Burunza, an ETA-m member then on trial for terrorism (see below).

ETA-pm, on the other hand, claimed responsibility for launching an anti-tank grenade at the Prime Minister's residence near Madrid on Feb. 21, 1980, when it announced that it would use its weapons unless the government (i) ordered that an immediate referendum should be held in Navarra on the question of joining the Basque region (this possibility having been provided for in the statute for the Basque region), (ii) returned all Basque prisoners to Basque prisons, (iii) lifted the extra security measures taken in the region and (iv) ordered the immediate formation of an autonomous police force as provided for in the statute.

Of the total of 126 people killed in political violence during 1980, 85 were, according to the police, killed by ETA-m and 33 by other extremists, while eight ETA suspects were killed by the police; ETA-m was said to have raised the equivalent of over £100,000,000 by extortion and robberies in 1980.

During 1981 ETA followers continued to be involved in the killing of policemen, civil guards and retired military officers, as well as in other acts of violence. In particular ETA-m on Jan. 29 kidnapped the chief nuclear engineer at the Lemóniz power station construction site (near Bilbao), demanding in return for his release the commencement within a week of the demolition of the power station. After Iberduero, the company building the station, had refused to negotiate with ETA-m (although it was ready to halt construction work temporarily and to accept the Basque government's eventual decision on carrying on with the project) and some 10,000 people had demonstrated in Bilbao for the engineer's release, he was found murdered on Feb. 6, 1981.

The murder was condemned by the Premier of the Basque government and by all parties except the *Herri Batasuna*; trade unions called a 24-hour strike in protest against ETA terrorism for Feb. 9. The Basque parliament resolved on Feb. 12, 1981 (with only the Basque Left and the *Herri Batasuna* abstaining), that work at Lemóniz should be resumed. ETA-pm had also condemned the murder (on Feb. 11) and had accused ETA-m of leading the region into civil war.

However, on Feb. 28, 1981 (i.e. after an attempted right-wing coup in Madrid involving civil guard and army officers on Feb. 23), ETA-pm announced an indefinite and unconditional ceasefire and urged ETA-m to follow suit. ETA-pm released the honorary consuls of Austria, El Salvador and Uruguay whom it had kidnapped on Feb. 19-20, 1981. At the same time it demanded (i) the broadcasting in full on radio and television of an Amnesty International report on alleged police brutality in Spain and its publication in national and Basque newspapers; (ii) the similar broadcasting and publication of a report by the Basque parliament of alleged violations of human rights by the police and civil guards; and (iii) the showing on television of photographs of a Basque who had died in custody on Feb. 13. Few of the media complied with these demands (most coverage being given to the attempted right-wing coup).

ETA-m, on the other hand, pursued its policy of provoking a right-wing coup or backlash which would lead to a popular rising in the Basque region, and committed further murders.

The Spanish Commissioner of Police said on April 30, 1981, that ETA-m activities were being directed by seven of the organization's leaders who were habitually resident in France. Early in May 1981 the police uncovered a plan drawn up jointly by ETA-m, ETA-pm and ETA *Autónomo* to free some 80 ETA prisoners from the Carabanchel prison in Madrid. Among ETA members tried during 1981 was Iñaki Pikabea Burunza, an ETA-m member and spokesman of the *Herri Batasuna* party in the Basque regional parliament, who was on June 30 given a 33½-year sentence for murdering an Irún municipal councillor on Dec. 16, 1977, and for other offences, with three further defendants being sentenced to a total of 78 years in prison.

In February 1982 ETA-pm ended the ceasefire

which it had announced on Feb. 28, 1981 (see above), but this decision was not approved by a minority which called itself ETA-pm (VII Assembly) and which announced on Sept. 29, 1982, its dissolution as a terrorist organization. ETA-pm was also referred to as ETA-pm (VIII Assembly).

ETA-m, however, as the most militant of the ETA factions, from January 1982 onwards carried out further attacks on military and civilian targets, including an attack on the Banco de Vizcaya in Bilbao on Feb. 5, 1983 (in protest against the Spanish banks' decision to refuse to pay "revolutionary taxes" to ETA).

During 1984 ETA-m and ETA-pm (VIII Assembly) were engaged in bomb attacks and assassinations, while the Anti-terrorist Liberation Group (GAL, see separate entry) promised to kill one Basque activist for every ETA victim. In the first seven months of 1984 ETA was responsible for 19 killings and the GAL for nine.

During the same year some ETA members sought "social integration" as offered by the Spanish government to ETA members not wanted by the police or the judicial authorities. Those who sought such integration and announced their abandonment of the armed struggle included two leaders of ETA-pm (VII Assembly)—José Miguel Goiburú Mendizábal and José Angel Aramendi Albizú.

On Aug. 23, 1984, the government announced that it was willing to enter into direct negotiations with ETA when and where it wished and without intermediaries but that it would not make any political concessions and would grant no amnesty to those guilty of crimes. ETA, however, dismissed the offer and reiterated its earlier demand for acceptance of the KAS Alternative of 1978 (see entry for Patriotic Socialist Coalition) as its minimum requirement.

Among the violent actions taken by ETA-m late in 1984 and early in 1985 was the killing, on March 7, 1985, of the commander of the autonomous Basque police force.

On March 13, 1985, the Basque regional government issued a declaration calling on all Basques to "overcome the fear of fear" and to stand up to violence, and on the following day the Basque parliament unanimously adopted a motion urging all Basques to oppose violence resolutely and formally calling on ETA to surrender its arms and to accept the democratic system.

In June 1985 the Spanish government offered new peace terms to ETA-m's military chief, Domingo Iturbe Abásolo. ETA attacks, however, were continued during the following months, when the director-general of defence policy was killed on July 29, 1985, and another high-ranking officer (Vice-Adml. Cristóbal Colón de Carvajal) on Feb. 6, 1986.

From March 1986 onwards there was a renewed series of ETA-m bombings and assassinations, including the "execution" on Sept. 10 of a former ETA-m woman member who had returned to Spain from abroad under the government's June 1985 peace terms. (According to a statement made by the Interior Ministry in September 1986, a total of 107 ETA members had returned to Spain under an amnesty in the past three years.) On Oct. 25, 1986, ETA-m also assassinated the military governor of Guipúzcoa.

During its long campaign ETA has had numerous supporters in various countries, in particular in France, where ETA was banned on Oct. 8, 1972. The French Minister of the Interior stated in November 1972 that his government would not allow refugee activities "tending to aim a blow at the integrity of the national territory", that "Spanish refugees must not take part in any demonstrations which disturb public order", and that French territory must not be used as a base for activities across the border. The French government did not then comply with Spanish demands for the extradition of Basque (or other) "terrorists", and the French Prime Minister declared on June 8, 1981, that France was "a country of asylum". However, on July 29, 1981, the French government agreed to intensify border controls and to "give full support to the Spanish authorities in their fight against terrorism".

On Feb. 22, 1983, the French authorities arrested the alleged ETA-pm leader, Pedro Aztorkitza Ikazzuriaga, and other ETA-m leaders were also arrested in France during August 1983. In a change of French policy, six suspected ETA members were, on Jan. 10, 1984, deported from metropolitan France, being later sent to Venezuela. On March 28, 1984, it was announced that ETA refugees would no longer obtain residence permits for living in the French Basque region. (Of some 600-700 Spanish Basques then living in France about 200-300 were estimated to be active ETA members.)

On June 14, 1984, the French government undertook to deport ETA suspects (but not to extradite them to Spain). Those deported from France in 1984 included Eugenio Etxebeste Arizguren, regarded as ETA's political chief (expelled on Aug. 3); he was succeeded as ETA leader by José Antonio Urrutikotxea Bengoetxea.

On Jan. 30, 1985, the French police dismantled a major ETA-m base at Anglet (near Bayonne) and arrested eight persons, among them ETA-m's "chief of staff". On Feb. 22, 1985, two ETA detainees were deported from France to Cape Verde, one of them being Tomás Linara Echeverría, presumed to be an ETA-m leader.

The formation of the Chirac government in France in March 1986 resulted in increased French co-operation in the fight against ETA-m violence. Domingo Iturbe Abásolo (Txomin), ETA-m's military chief, was arrested near Biarritz on April 27 and was deported to Gabon on July 13; in October it emerged that he and other ETA-m members were living in Algeria, where he was killed in a car accident on Feb. 27, 1987. Between July and November 1986 the French government extradited a number of ETA suspects to Spain, especially after the French police had, in a raid on a factory in Hendaye, found weapons and plans for ETA attacks on targets in Madrid and Barcelona. The Spanish police alleged that the factory had been used as a front for laundering money obtained by ETA through robberies, kidnapping and extortions; captured documents showed that some 90 Basque companies were paying "revolutionary taxes" demanded by ETA, contributing to ETA's annual budget of some 250,000,000 pesetas.

The Belgian government extradited two ETA suspects to Spain on July 14, 1984. In retaliation ETA-pm carried out a bomb attack on the Palace of Justice in Antwerp on Aug. 5.

ETA members were also active in Costa Rica, where Gregorio Jiménez Morales was arrested in September 1983, when he was said to be implicated, with 11 other ETA supporters, in a plot to kill Alfonso Robelo, alleged to be a leader of the Democratic Revolutionary Alliance (ARDE, a Nicaraguan guerrilla group), at the instigation of the Sandinista government in Nicaragua. On Sept. 30 the residence of the British ambassador in Costa Rica was attacked by ETA members demanding the release of G. Jiménez Morales.

Patriotic Socialist Coalition (*Koordinadora Abertzale Sozialista*, KAS)

The KAS was set up in 1975 by the ETA-pm and Basque radical parties. In 1976 it formulated a KAS Alternative as a series of conditions for a truce in ETA's struggle, and this was adopted by the ETA-m in 1978. It contained demands for a full amnesty for all political prisoners, the legalization of all Basque parties, the withdrawal of the state security forces from the region, the elevation of Basque (Euzkera) as the official language of the region, the entry into force of the autonomy statute in the four historic regions of Euzkadi (i.e. including Navarra), the right to create an independent Basque state, and the recognition of national links between "South and North Euzkadi" (i.e. the Spanish and French Basque regions).

Spanish Prisoners' Trade Union (COPEL)

Leadership. Daniel Pont (l.)

This illegal organization was alleged to have co-operated with ETA in kidnapping operations, robberies and mutinies in prisons during 1977-80. Its presumed leader and 10 other members were arrested in February 1980, when they were found to be in possession of weapons which were to be smuggled into prisons, and to have planned more robberies and prison mutinies.

CANARY ISLANDS

Movement for the Self-Determination and Independence of the Canary Archipelago (*Movimiento para la Autodeterminación y Independencia del Archipiélago Canario*, MPAIAC)

Leadership. Antonio Cubillo

This organization was first established in 1961 as an autonomist movement of the Canaries. It had its headquarters in Algiers, while some of its followers were involved in acts of violence in the Canary Islands. In 1971 the Movement claimed that following the declaration of a state of emergency by the Spanish authorities on Dec. 14, 1970, over 200 persons had been arrested, among them 29 MPAIAC activists—but the Spanish government later denied this. On Sept. 28, 1976, Antonio Cubillo appealed to the Spanish government to "avoid recourse to violence" and to recognize the MPAIAC as the legitimate representative of the people of the islands and to commence negotiations in an African country on a timetable for the decolonization of the Canaries under the auspices of the Organization of African Unity (OAU). In the absence of any response to his appeal, Cubillo ordered the Movement on Nov. 1, 1976, to begin a campaign of "armed propaganda".

After the Spanish authorities had announced on Feb. 26, 1977, that about 20 MPAIAC militants had been arrested and that the Movement was virtually dismantled, Cubillo ordered an armed struggle to begin. On March 25 a teenage militant was shot dead by a soldier while he was allegedly trying to steal arms from a military depot. In revenge the MPAIAC caused a bomb explosion at Las Palmas airport; this led to the diversion of two Jumbo jets to Tenerife where they collided on the runway, causing the death of 582 people.

Cubillo thereupon suspended his Movement's armed activities until April 11, 1977, when his campaign designed to disrupt tourism was resumed, involving some 80 bomb attacks during 1977. On Oct. 12 of that year police defused two bombs wrapped in separatist flags and planted near a place where the Spanish King was due to stand during a ceremony. During demonstrations called on Tenerife in support of a general strike called by the MPAIAC, a student was killed by civil guards on Dec. 12, 1977. On Feb. 24, 1978, a policeman was wounded while defusing a bomb planted by the MPAIAC in Tenerife; he died on March 8. On April 5 an MPAIAC bomb exploded at the civil guard headquarters in Las Palmas (without causing any casualties).

An attempt to assassinate Cubillo in Algiers was attributed by him (on April 10, 1978) to the "Spanish secret service and police" with the co-operation (he alleged) of the Spanish Socialist Workers' Party (PSOE), which had come out strongly in favour of continued Spanish sovereignty over the Canary Islands. On May 7 the Algerian state security court passed sentences of death on two Spaniards (on one of them in absentia) for involvement in the assassination attempt, and a 20-year prison sentence on an accomplice. One of those sentenced to death claimed that he had been sent to Algeria by the (Maoist) Revolutionary Anti-fascist and Patriotic Front (FRAP), which had described Cubillo as an agent of the (US) Central Intelligence Agency (CIA). The Spanish government denied any involvement in the assassination attempt.

Sentences passed on MPAIAC members included prison terms of four years and two months and one year and two months respectively imposed on April 2, 1979, on two members for an attack on a bank in Tenerife on Dec. 27, 1977, and a 5½-year term for another member on May 22, 1980.

In a programme published in Algiers on Jan. 2, 1973, the MPAIAC listed as its objects (i) the creation of an independent Canary Islands Republic, to be called the Guanch Republic (after the islands' original inhabitants, regarded as being exploited and repressed by Spain); (ii) limited autonomy for each of the seven main islands; (iii) election of a national assembly by universal suffrage; and (iv) restoration of the Guanch language. The programme also advocated respect for private property, workers' participation and control of foreign interests in the islands. The Spanish government was called upon to open negotiations on the constitutional proposals contained in the programme. In 1977 the MPAIAC stated that it wanted to make the Canaries Archipelago a socialist African independent republic which would be a member of the OAU.

The liberation committee of the OAU had recognized the MPAIAC as a liberation movement in July 1968, and in February 1978 the OAU Council of Ministers supported the committee's recommendation for material and financial aid to be given to the Movement (with only Morocco and Mauritania voting against this decision). The Spanish government thereupon made great efforts to dissuade African governments from giving such aid. A Spanish parliamentary delegation which had visited nine West African countries reported on May 7, 1978, that only Senegal, The Gambia and Liberia had expressed clear support for continued Spanish sovereignty over the Canary Islands. However, at a further meeting of the OAU Council of Ministers in July 1978, the earlier recommendation was no longer pursued.

The MPAIAC's aims were implicitly rejected at a Council of Europe conference of members of local authorities and regional bodies which declared on Oct. 18, 1979, that the Canary Islands (as also the Azores and Madeira) were "peripheral regions of Europe" in the economic development of which European countries should participate.

The MPAIAC has used a "Voice of the Free Canaries" radio transmitter in Algeria, with the Spanish government having repeatedly protested to the Algerian government against its protection of this transmitter.

CATALONIA

Free Land (*Terra Lliure*)

This Catalan nationalist group, which demanded equal rights for the Spanish and Catalan languages in Catalonia, claimed responsibility for blowing up an electrical installation (which was to be used by a nuclear plant in Tarragona province) on Aug. 18, 1980. On May 21, 1981, the group claimed responsibility for seizing and injuring a signatory of a "Manifesto of the 2,300" issued by Spanish-speaking intellectuals in Catalonia, complaining of discrimination against them because they did not speak or write Catalan.

Early in October 1986 the group claimed responsibility for two bomb explosions in Barcelona in protest against the city's (successful) bid to host the 1992 Olympic Games.

In November 1986 it was disclosed that several of the group's founder members had left it, among them Joan Carles Monteagudo, who was thought to be responsible for collaborating with the ETA-m.

Milicia Catalana

This right-wing anti-separatist group emerged in mid-1986 when it bombed two bookshops in Catalonia and proclaimed its policy of maintaining the unity of Spain. On Aug. 14, 1986, the group caused forest fires near the Montserrat monastery, a symbol of Catalan nationalism.

CEUTA AND MELILLA

Ceuta Liberation Movement (*Movimiento de Liberación Sebta*, MLS)

The MLS stands for the integration of Ceuta into the Kingdom of Morocco.

It was alleged in the daily *Faro de Ceuta* on May 20, 1982, that 200 Moroccan residents of the Spanish enclave of Ceuta had signed a complaint to the Spanish authorities about three members of the Moroccan community in Ceuta whom they identified as Moroccan secret policemen and whom they accused of involvement in activities in connexion with the MLS, including kidnapping and the distribution of clandestine leaflets. The first of the signatories of the complaint had his car set on fire on May 23 and thereupon asked the police for protection.

Moroccan Patriotic Front

This organization stands for the restoration of Moroccan sovereignty over the cities of Ceuta and Melilla. Members were responsible for several bomb attacks in the Spanish enclaves of Ceuta and Melilla (on Morocco's Mediterranean coast) in late 1978 and early 1979 in protest against Spain's insistence on these cities' status as part of the Kingdom of Spain.

Terra Omnium

Leadership. Aomar Mohamedi Dudu

This group was formed in mid-1985 to represent the political and cultural rights of the Moslems in Melilla, numbering an estimated 27,000 out of a total population of some 72,000. (According to government figures, 2,827 of the Moslems in Melilla then enjoyed Spanish nationality, and unofficially it was claimed that only another 6,500 had "basic papers" which did not entitle them to buy houses in Melilla or to travel to mainland Spain.)

A. M. Dudu, expelled from the Spanish Socialist Party (PSOE), stated that *Terra Omnium* was to become a full-scale political party (the Party of Moslem Democrats). The Spanish Minister of the Interior stated that virtually all Moslems who applied for residence permits under a new Organic Law on the Rights and Liberties of Foreigners, which was to come into force on July 24, 1985, would obtain Spanish citizenship within 10 years if all conditions were fulfilled; those whose papers were not in order by March 1, 1986, would face expulsion. A. M. Dudu thereupon stated that the government's undertakings were insufficient, called for a moratorium on the law's application to Ceuta and Melilla, and threatened a protest march on Madrid.

GALICIA

Armed Galician League (*Liga Armada Gallega*, LAG)

This separatist group claimed responsibility for killing a civil guard in Santiago de Compostela on Aug. 28, 1978.

Guerrilla Army of Free Galicia (*Ejército Guerrillero de la Galicia Libre* or *Ejército Guerrilleiro do Pobo Galego Ceibe*, EGPGC)

This group claimed (by telephone) responsibility for planting seven explosive devices in various towns of Galicia early in February 1987, shortly before the trial of three alleged members of the organization in La Coruña for attempted armed robbery and illicit possession of arms on May 29, 1986.

Sri Lanka

Capital: Colombo

Pop. 15,837,000

The Democratic Socialist Republic of Sri Lanka (formerly Ceylon) is an independent state within the Commonwealth with a multi-party system and parliamentary democracy. It has an executive President elected for a six-year term by universal adult suffrage, who is head of state and President of the government and appoints (or dismisses) the Prime Minister and members of the Cabinet. The President is also empowered to dissolve Parliament (a 168-member Assembly similarly elected for a six-year term under a system of modified proportional representation).

Under a constitutional amendment approved in a referendum on Dec. 22, 1982, the current term of the Assembly, due to expire in August 1983, was extended for another six years. Since then the distribution of seats in the Assembly has been as follows: United National Party 143, Tamil United Liberation Front (TULF) 15, Sri Lanka Freedom Party six, Ceylon Workers' Congress one, Communist Party one (vacant two). The TULF members forfeited their seats on Oct. 23, 1983, after refusing to take a required oath forswearing separatist aspirations.

In recent years extra-parliamentary dissidence in Sri Lanka has been mainly related to the grievances and demands of the minority Tamil community, against a background of frequent outbreaks of serious inter-communal tension between the Tamils and the Sinhalese majority (the latter comprising some 70 per cent of the population). A state of emergency declared in May 1983 has been routinely extended in an attempt to contend with a mounting security threat posed by Tamil guerrillas fighting for a separate Tamil state—Eelam—in the north and east of the island. Negotiations between representatives of the government and the Tamil community (often with the help of Indian mediation) had apparently made no real progress, until mid-1987, and the Sri Lankan government had on May 26 launched a large-scale offensive against positions in the north-east around Jaffna held by the Liberation Tigers of Tamil Eelam (LTTE, the strongest and most militant of the many Tamil separatist groups—see separate entry). However, an Indian-Sri Lankan agreement on proposals for "peace and normality" was concluded in July. The Indian Prime Minister, Rajiv Gandhi, arriving in Sri Lanka on July 29, 1987, signed this agreement with President Jayawardene, and it was apparently generally accepted by Tamil groups (including, after some hesitation, the LTTE).

Tamil Movements

Communist Party of Tamil Eelam

This party was formed in 1984 and operates the Voice of Tamil Eelam radio station which broadcasts regular pro-Tamil reports.

Eelam National Democratic Liberation Front (ENDLF)

This Front was formed on May 17, 1987, out of the merger of breakaway factions of the Eelam People's Revolutionary Liberation Front (EPRLF—see separate entry) and the People's Liberation Organization of Tamil Eelam (PLOTE—see separate entry). At a press conference held on May 17 a spokesman for the ENDLF said that the Front would work towards building a base for forming an "Eelam People's National Democratic Republic" and a "Tamil national army".

Eelam National Liberation Front (ENLF)

This alliance of four Madras-based Tamil militant organizations was formed on April 11, 1985, and was made up of the Liberation Tigers of Tamil Eelam (LTTE), the Eelam People's Revolutionary Liberation Front (EPRLF), the Tamil Eelam Liberation Organization (TELO) and the Eelam Revolutionary Organization of Students (EROS—for this and other ENLF members see separate entries). In a joint press release the members announced that the alliance had been formed to "co-ordinate their efforts in the armed struggle for national independence". The "unity move" had further been prompted by "the escalation of state violence and genocide". The ENLF arose out of a previous merger between the TELO, the EPRLF and the EROS which had been announced on April 18, 1984.

On June 20, 1985, the ENLF and the People's Liberation Organization of Tamil Eelam (PLOTE, the only significant Tamil separatist group not in the coalition—see separate entry) confirmed an earlier announcement made by the Sri Lankan Minister of National Security, that the two sides had agreed to a three-month ceasefire. Representatives of the ENLF members attended talks in July and August 1985 in Bhutan, along with representatives of the Sri Lankan government and officials from the Tamil United Liberation Front (TULF, a moderate political party now based in Madras, India). The talks were eventually abandoned in mid-August by the ENLF members in response to recent alleged Tamil deaths at the hands of the security forces and armed Sinhalese.

Internal dissension within the ENLF broke out in late April 1986 with fighting between the LTTE and TELO forces. On Aug. 30, 1986, it was reported that the LTTE had recently left the ENLF, having stopped attending meetings earlier that year. On Dec. 13, the LTTE launched a full scale offensive throughout the Tamil-dominated areas against EPRLF members. More fighting between LTTE and EPRLF guerrillas in the Batticaloa district in the east of the island on Feb. 16-17, 1987, resulted in 57 deaths.

On March 28, 1987, it was reported that the ENLF had been "virtually wound up" and that its Madras office had been closed down. In an operation launched by the LTTE against TELO, EPRLF and PLOTE forces the government estimated that 98 people had been killed by April 4.

Eelam People's Revolutionary Liberation Front (EPRLF)

Leadership. K. Pathmanabha (also known as Ranjith)

This Tamil separatist organization, based in Madras (India), reportedly adheres to a more coherently Marxist ideology than the other major separatist groups. The EPRLF was one of four militant Tamil groups which came together in April 1985 to form the Eelam National Liberation Front (ENLF—see separate entry). Douglas Anand, described as the "military leader" of the EPRLF, and nine other members were arrested in November 1986 in the south Indian state of Tamil Nadu in connexion with the shooting of an Indian social worker. K. Pathmanabha was one of 23 people charged (mostly in their absence) in a Sri Lankan court on March 23, 1987, with conspiring to overthrow the government by "use of violence and armed revolution" between August 1983 and April 1986. The majority of those charged were ultra-leftist Sinhalese intellectuals. Breakaway factions of the EPRLF and of the People's Liberation Organization of Tamil Eelam (PLOTE, see separate entry) formed in Madras on May 17, 1987, the Eelam National Democratic Liberation Front (see separate entry).

Eelam Revolutionary Organization of Students (EROS)

Leadership. Vellupillai Balakumar

This Tamil separatist group is closely associated with the largest and most powerful separatist organization, the Liberation Tigers of Tamil Eelam (LTTE—see separate entry). The EROS was one of four Tamil separatist groups that formed an alliance (the Eelam National Liberation Front, ENLF—see separate entry) on April 11, 1985.

Members of this group were implicated in numerous bomb attacks carried out between October 1984 and April 1987. Its targets included economic installations, in particular those of multinational concerns.

On May 2, 1987, the group received aid worth US$800,000 from the government of the (Indian) state of Tamil Nadu, and in June 1987 it was reported to be receiving training from the Palestine Liberation Organization.

Liberation Tigers of Tamil Eelam (LTTE)

Leadership. Velupillai Prabakharan

The LTTE (also known as the "Tamil Tigers" or the "Liberation Tigers") is currently the strongest and most effective of the Tamil separatist organizations operating in Sri Lanka, with an estimated 3,000 fighters. Formed in 1972 by Velupillai Prabakharan, it has as a primary objective the establishment of a separate Tamil state—Eelam—in the Northern and Eastern provinces (Tamils being the majority in the former province and, due to a progressive settlement policy by Sinhalese farmers, a minority in the latter). In common with the other major Tamil groups the LTTE is based in the southern Indian state of Tamil Nadu and professes a socialist ideology. However, at least two of the other leading Tamil organizations (the People's Liberation Organization of Tamil Eelam—PLOTE, and the Tamil Eelam Liberation Organization, TELO—see separate entries) were formed by leading LTTE figures who left the group over ideological differences.

During the 1970s the LTTE carried out a number of guerrilla operations which included the killing of police offices and the destruction of a Sri Lankan airliner. Parliament passed, on May 19, 1978, a bill banning the organization and empowering the President to proscribe any group advocating the use of violence and directly or indirectly connected with any unlawful activity. The LTTE continued to carry out sporadic assassinations and other minor acts of guerrilla warfare in the early 1980s.

On July 23, 1983, Tamil guerrillas (who were not specifically described as LTTE members) killed 13 soldiers in Jaffna district and, in apparent retaliation for this act, large-scale communal violence broke out in Sri Lanka in late July. Much of the violence, in which almost 400 people were killed, took the form of attacks by the majority Sinhalese community on the Tamil minority.

During inconclusive "amity talks" held on an Indian initiative between January and December 1984 and involving the (legal) Tamil United Liberation Front (TULF), the LTTE launched, in August of that year, a full-scale "armed revolutionary struggle" against the government on the ground that the democratic process has been "fully exhausted".

On April 11, 1985, the LTTE joined with three other Tamil separatist groups to form an Eelam National Liberation Front (ENLF, see separate entry). By May 1985 the LTTE was in control of Jaffna town (in northern Sri Lanka) and much of the Jaffna peninsula. Following continued armed actions by the LTTE, security forces carried out large-scale military operations on May 17-23, 1986, and on May 25 the government claimed that it had regained control of the whole Jaffna peninsula.

However, the LTTE guerrillas continued to be active in the ensuing months, and on Oct. 27 the LTTE announced that from Jan. 1, 1987, the Jaffna peninsula would be administered by a "Tamil Eelam secretariat", as opposed to the current controlling government agent. It was also reported that the LTTE controlled much of the peninsula's infrastructure.

On Jan. 2, 1987, a Tamil radio station stated that the LTTE had recently formed a new political party named Liberation Tigers of Tamil Eelam People's Front which, led by Velupillai Prabakharan, would function under the LTTE.

Fighting between LTTE guerrillas and government security forces continued in the first half of 1987, causing hundreds of casualties. (The Indian government claimed that in the largest government offensive, begun on May 26, between 500 and 600 people, mainly civilians had been killed in "carpet bombing" by the Sri Lankan air force.)

On April 7, 1987, the government of the (Indian) state of Tamil Nadu announced that it had granted the LTTE aid worth US$2,400,000

Organization for the Protection of Eelam Tamils from Genocide

Leadership. S. C. Chandrahasan

The leader of this organization (based in the southern Indian state of Tamil Nadu) was deported from India in August 1985 along with an official spokesman for the Liberation Tigers of Tamil Eelam (LTTE—see separate entry). According to Tamil sources their deportation reflected the Indian government's displeasure with the Tamil militants over their failure to respond to a recent invitation for discussion in New Delhi.

People's Liberation Organization of Tamil Eelam (PLOTE)

Leadership. Uma Maheswara

The PLOTE was formed in 1979 by Uma Maheswara, a former member of the Liberation Tigers of Tamil Eelam (LTTE—see separate entry), who had left the LTTE on account of ideological differences. In common with other Tamil secessionist groups the PLOTE sought a separate, socialist Tamil homeland (Eelam) in the northern and eastern provinces of Sri Lanka. The PLOTE was the most significant separatist organization outside the Eelam National Liberation Front (ENLF—see separate entry) alliance of four Tamil groups formed in April 1985. On Sept. 20, 1984, the organization's public relations officer was quoted as stating that unlike the ENLF members the PLOTE advocated mass insurrection as opposed to guerrillas tactics, and that it sought alliances with any communist country, except China.

In common with the members of the ENLF, the PLOTE agreed to a three-month ceasefire in mid-June 1985, prior to government-Tamil talks in Bhutan in July and August 1985 attended by a PLOTE representative. The talks were eventually abandoned in August after the death of a large number of Tamil civilians at the hands of the security forces on Aug. 16-17, in the vicinity of Vavuniya and Trincomalee in the eastern part of the island.

A PLOTE spokesman announced on Oct. 29, 1986, that PLOTE forces had recently suspended operations following a series of attacks upon them by LTTE guerrillas operating in the northern provinces.

Breakaway factions of the PLOTE and of the Eelam People's Revolutionary Liberation Front (EPRLF, see separate entry) formed in Madras (India) on May 17, 1987, the Eelam National Democratic Liberation Front (ENDLF, see separate entry).

Tamil Eelam Liberation Organization (TELO)

Leadership. A. Selvam (gen. sec.)

This Tamil separatist organization was formed by Sri Sabaratnam, who had left the Liberation Tigers of Tamil Eelam (LTTE—see separate entry) over ideological differences. The group has been described as a major force within the separatist movement and as the second largest such group after the LTTE.

The TELO joined with three other Tamil groups on April 11, 1985, to form a co-ordinating alliance of Tamil guerrillas, the Eelam National Liberation Front (see separate entry).

Fighting between TELO and LTTE guerrillas between April 29 and May 6, 1986, resulted in the destruction of 22 TELO camps and the death of over 100 members, including Sri Sabaratnam (see ENLF section for more detailed analysis of internal separatist fighting). In southern India, Tamil Nadu police arrested 108 TELO members, mainly in Madras, between Dec. 23 and 27, 1986. The arrests were part of a general disarming operation aimed at Tamil militants during November and December.

Tamil People's Protection Party

This Batticaloa-based group was described as a "newly formed terrorist group" by Colombo radio on Aug. 29, 1986; the report stated that the security forces had recently captured a member of the organization.

Left-wing Sinhalese Movement

People's Liberation Front (*Janatha Vimukthi Peramuna,* JVP)

Leadership. Rohana Wijeweere (ch.)

This Sinhalese Maoist movement was founded in 1967 by a group led by Rohana Wijeweere. Although it supported the United Front coalition in the 1970 elections, Wijeweere and over 4,000 of the JVP's members were arrested by the United Front government in March 1971. In consequence it launched a revolt in April, which was quickly crushed; a state of emergency was imposed, the JVP was banned and Wijeweere was eventually sentenced to life imprisonment in 1974. The JVP was legalized in 1977, however, and on his release later in the same year Wijeweere repudiated the use of violent methods. In the 1983 presidential elections Wijeweere took third place and 4.19 per cent of the vote. The JVP was again banned after communal riots (mainly in Jaffna and Colombo) in 1983.

Following its proscription and in the light of the escalating violence between Tamil guerrillas and the armed forces in the Northern and Eastern provinces, the JVP is thought to have concentrated on propaganda work in the southern Sinhalese heartlands and universities and on building up supplies of arms. JVP supporters were amongst 3,000 Sinhalese detained in early February 1987 in order to prevent reprisals against Tamils following the recent killings of 43 Sinhalese villagers by the Liberation Tigers of Tamil Eelam (LTTE—see separate entry). On April 15 a JVP unit raided an army camp near Kandy, seizing a number of automatic weapons. Late in May police arrested some 140 JVP members; at the same time six of the country's universities situated in predominantly Sinhalese areas were closed following allegations that student leaders were forming links with the JVP; and 18 trade unions with alleged JVP affiliations were proscribed. The government claimed that JVP guerrillas had, on June 7, launched simultaneous raids on military targets.

The JVP's avowed aim was "to protect the nation against an impending Indian invasion".

Moslem Movement

Hezbollah (Party of God)

The Iranian news agency broadcasting from the Indian capital (New Delhi) on May 2, 1985, announced that this new Moslem political movement had recently become active in the north and east of Sri Lanka. *Hezbollah* had met for the first time in Colombo on April 28. Moslems are thought to account for some 8 per cent of the Sri Lankan population.

Sudan

Capital: Khartoum

Pop. 21,500,000

The Republic of Sudan is ruled by a Supreme Council whose five members, representing three political parties, act collectively as head of state. Elections were held in April 1986 to a Constituent Assembly at the end of a one-year period of transitional military rule which followed the overthrow of the former President Jaafar al-Nemery. Only 260 deputies were elected out of a total of 301 provided for in the Assembly, civil war in the south having caused the postponement of polling in 41 out of 68 southern constituencies. Attempts by the new civilian government to enter into peace negotiations with the dominant southern rebel movement were suspended indefinitely in August 1986.

Opposition to President Nemery's rule, which had been threatened by a number of coup attempts since 1971, intensified in the southern provinces from June 1983, when in defiance of a 1972 Addis Ababa agreement—which in unifying the south had brought an end to nine years of civil war—President Nemery redivided the south into the three separate regions of Bahr el Ghazal, Upper Nile and Equatoria which had existed prior to 1972. The situation was further aggravated in September 1983 when the Sudanese penal system was modified to incorporate the principles of Islamic law, an action which was strongly opposed by the non-Arab, non-Moslem population of the southern provinces.

President Nemery was deposed on April 6, 1985, by the armed forces acting in conjunction with an alliance of civilian professional organizations and trade unions which had staged strikes and demonstrations directed against the regime in the days prior to the coup. Those political parties which had been banned under the previous one-party system subsequently rallied to the new government, initially composed of a Transitional Military Council (TMC), and a Council of Ministers composed of military and civilian members. The principal southern rebel movement refused to participate in the new administration and the guerrilla war intensified. The Chairman of the TMC, Gen. Abdel Rahman Swar el-Dahab, formally ceded power to the newly-elected civilian government on May 6, 1986, and on the same day Dr Sadiq el-Mahdi, a long-standing opponent of President Nemery and leader of the Umma (People's) Party—the majority party in the Assembly—was elected Prime Minister by the Assembly itself.

Relations with Libya, broken off in 1981, were restored after the coup. The Libyan regime had actively supported opposition to President Nemery, but ceased its support for the southern rebels following the rapprochement with the new government. Ethiopia continued to provide logistical support and refuge to the rebels.

A 1982 "Charter of Integration" between Egypt and Sudan was suspended in October 1985, and the new Sudanese rulers proceeded with attempts to obtain the extradition from Egypt of President Nemery who had sought asylum there. Relations subsequently improved, and a "Brotherhood Charter" covering areas of mutual co-operation was signed by the two countries' Prime Ministers in February 1987.

Anya-Nya II

Leadership. Maj. Gordon Kong (military commander); David Dogok Puoch (sec.)

Formed in 1975 by southern secessionists from the Dinka and Nuer tribes, this movement first emerged as an armed guerrilla group in 1982. The name was adopted from the original Anya-Nya (meaning "snake poison") guerrilla arm of the South Sudan Liberation Movement which was active in the 1963-72 civil war between the northern and southern regions. In early 1983 it began attacking police stations and military patrols, reportedly receiving assistance and instruction from some sympathetic southern army officers.

In July 1983 a group of 15 Anya-Nya guerrillas captured five foreign aid workers who were released after clashes between guerrillas and the armed forces. It emerged that Anya-Nya II was the armed wing of the Southern Sudan Liberation Front, whose leaders had been active in the earlier secessionist campaign, namely Aquot Attem, a former defence secretary for the original Anya-Nya; Lt.-Col. William Chuol, who deserted from the regular army in May 1983 with a battalion from the garrison at Nasir; and Samuel Gaitut, a former Anya-Nya military commander in Upper Nile province and a former minister in the national government.

The growth of the movement during 1983 was attributed to (i) the redivision of the southern region into three separate regions in June 1983; and (ii) increasing dissatisfaction within the armed forces towards the policy of rotating troops between northern and southern garrisons (manifested in an attempted mutiny of southern troops stationed at Bor, who in February 1983 resisted being replaced by northern troops). This dissent resulted in a large number of defections to the emerging southern rebel movements, who thus experienced an influx of men and arms.

In 1983-84 a power struggle developed within the ranks of the leadership, weakening the movement and resulting in the emergence of the Sudan People's Liberation Movement (SPLM) as the dominant faction (see separate entry). Reports in October 1983 of a unification of the two groups proved premature; leaders of the groups met in March 1984, after which it appeared that the SPLM under Col. John Garang had assumed the direction of the southern rebellion. Leadership quarrels, continued, however, resulting in armed clashes between the factions, in the course of which Samuel Gaitut was killed in April 1984.

The movement was further split by differences in aims and ideology; the Anya-Nya II "old guard" leadership had as their primary aim the achievement of secession for the south, while Col. Garang's SPLM aspired to being a national liberation movement seeking to overthrow the Nemery regime and install a unified national government. Following the death of Gaitut, Lt.-Col. Chuol fought against and killed Aquot Attem to assume the leadership of the movement.

By September 1984 the Nemery government had made contact with Anya-Nya II with the intention of exploiting rivalries among the southern rebels; henceforth Anya-Nya II and a number of southern tribes known to be hostile to the largely Dinka guerrillas of the Sudan People's Liberation Army (the armed wing of the SPLM) were supplied with arms with which to attack SPLA positions. The Transitional Military Council, which assumed power after the overthrow of President Nemery, and likewise its civilian successor government pursued this policy of fomenting inter-tribal warfare in an attempt to wear down and eliminate the southern rebellion.

Lt.-Col. Chuol was killed in a clash with the SPLA in August 1985, after which Maj. Gordon Kong, who had been active in the original Anya-Nya movement, and was briefly prominent in the military command of the SPLA, assumed the leadership, and concentrated on attacking SPLA positions. The movement was therefore by mid-1985 effectively acting as a militia force on behalf of the government.

In September 1985 Anya-Nya II accused the SPLA of destroying agricultural projects in areas around El Damazin; in the following month fierce fighting occurred between the SPLA and Anya-Nya II on two fronts in Upper Nile and Bahr el Ghazal, Anya-Nya II justifying its attacks by accusing the SPLA of having "raped women, killed citizens and robbed them of their properties", and describing the SPLA as a "tool in foreign hands".

By September 1986 the movement was concentrating its attacks on SPLA positions near oilfields in Upper Nile province, where the government was anxious to regain control.

In a restructuring of the leadership in February 1986, a six-member provisional politburo was formed, with David Dogok Puoch named as secretary of the movement, and Maj. Kong as head of a 13-member military command. Officers were appointed to oversee those areas where Anya-Nya II was particularly active, in north-eastern and north-western Upper Nile, and the area around Bentiu.

National Socialist Alliance

This pro-Nemery party, the leadership of which was obscure, was formed in Khartoum in mid-December 1985, eight months after the coup which deposed the former President. The transitional military government declared it to be illegal, and about 18 alleged members were arrested.

Sudan People's Liberation Movement (SPLM)

Leadership. Col. John Garang

The SPLM, whose armed wing, the Sudan People's Liberation Army (SPLA), was also led by Col. Garang, emerged as part of the Anya-Nya II southern secessionist movement in November 1983, when the

SPLA were held responsible for the kidnapping of 11 foreign workers at French and US economic development projects in the south near Bentiu. President Nemery accused Libya and Ethiopia of assisting the SPLA, whose demands at this time were (i) the reversal of the September 1983 decision to impose Islamic (*sharia*) law throughout Sudan; (ii) and end to French economic assistance to Sudan; and (iii) an end to work on the Jonglei canal irrigation project in the Kongor region and on the oil pipeline construction project, which would transport oil from the south to Port Sudan.

Col. Garang, a former commander of the government garrison at Bor, had left active service in the late 1970s to study in the USA, where he obtained a doctorate, and subsequently taught at the University of Khartoum. He defected to the Anya-Nya II movement with a group of armed supporters from the regular army after being sent by President Nemery to quell an attempted mutiny at the Bor garrison in February 1983, an incident which culminated in a full-scale battle between government troops and rebels in May 1983, and resulted in the defection of many regular southern troops to Anya-Nya II (see separate entry).

Attempts at forming a united front by the southern rebel movements were unsuccessful, but Col. Garang emerged in early 1984 as the principal opponent to the government in the south. Continuing internecine quarrels among the southern factions hampered the activities of the SPLA and prevented its expansion into a wider area of southern Sudan (see below for main areas of military activity).

In February 1984 the SPLA killed three expatriate employees of the US company Chevron in an attack on the company's base near Bentiu, claiming that aircraft belonging to Chevron were being used by the army to monitor guerrilla activity. In the same month the SPLA took six foreign hostages from a base of the French consortium, the Compagnie de Construction Internationale (CCI), at Sobat; the CCI was responsible for the Jonglei canal project. While two of the hostages, a pregnant woman and small child, were released in the following month, the remaining four were held for 11 months, during which they spent the time in camps in Ethiopia; they were handed over to representatives of the Ethiopian government on their release. The SPLA also claimed at this time to have attacked a Nile river boat, killing about 1,000 people and taking over 200 prisoners. During the latter part of 1984 the taking of foreign hostages became a less frequent tactic, although attacks on government installations and on the regular armed forces increased.

By March 1984 Col. Garang was proclaiming the SPLA to be a national liberation movement—thus provoking a definitive ideological split between the SPLA and the Anya-Nya II leadership. The SPLA's main grievances were (i) that the Nemery government had abrogated the 1972 Addis Ababa agreement which had unified the southern regions; (ii) that Islamic law had been imposed on the non-Moslem south; and (iii) that the natural resources of southern Sudan (timber, grain, water and minerals) had been "stolen" by the central government. For this reason the SPLA also opposed a plan to refine oil drilled in the south at Kosti in central Sudan. The movement's aim was the overthrow of the Nemery regime and the installation of a "people's democratic and socialist government". Joseph Adohu, a prominent southerner and former secretary of the now-defunct Council for the Unity of Southern Sudan, whose leaders had been arrested by President Nemery, was named in March 1984 as one of the leaders of the SPLM, along with Col. Garang. The military committee which ran the SPLA under Col. Garang consisted of Lt.-Col. Korbino Kuanyin, Lt.-Col. William Nyuan and Maj. Gordon Kong, all of whom had been members of the first Anya-Nya movement during the civil war. A statement from Joseph Adohu in April 1984 ruled out the possibility of negotiation with the Nemery regime, and denied government allegations that the SPLM/SPLA was Marxist-Leninist in doctrine.

The main areas of SPLA activity were confined to the central part of Bahr el Ghazal and eastern Upper Nile close to the Ethiopian border, with sanctuaries across the border in Ethiopia. The movement failed during this period to consolidate its control throughout the southern region, large areas of Equatoria remaining outside the rebellion (this region being traditionally hostile to the Dinka people, from whom the SPLA derived much of its support). The SPLA succeeded in taking control only of the Boma plateau area in eastern Equatoria in April 1984.

Following the overthrow of President Nemery in April 1985, Col. Garang called upon the new military leaders to cede power within one week to a civilian government. This demand was not met, and following the failure of several attempts to arrange a meeting between Col. Garang and the new military leaders, the SPLA announced that it would not participate in the new administration. The transitional government continued to seek a military rather than a negotiated settlement to the southern problem, and increased the number of troops in the area, while giving logistical support to Anya-Nya II and other ethnic groups traditionally hostile to the SPLA in order to promote intertribal fighting in the south. The SPLA ceased to be supported by the Libyan government after the April 1985 coup, but the Ethiopian government continued to assist it in response to the Sudanese government's support for the secessionist movements in Tigre and Eritrea (see separate entries under Ethiopia).

The SPLA denied government reports that it had helped to stage an attempted army mutiny in Khartoum in September 1985, which the TMC described as the prelude to an attempted coup. The leader of the Sudanese National Party, Philip Ghaboush (whose party later won eight seats in the Constituent Assembly), was accused of collusion in the attempted mutiny with the SPLA. Col. Garang maintained that the mutiny was the action of government troops attempting to resist transfer to southern garrisons.

In October 1985 Col. Garang declared his movement to have as its basic ideology "Sudanism and nationalism", and stated that he was committed to national unity based on cultural diversity and consensus.

During 1985 the SPLA laid siege to Bor and several other southern towns, and by September had succeeded in virtually cutting transport links to Malakal, the capital of Upper Nile province. At this time Col. Garang announced his readiness to negotiate with the transitional government, subject to a number of conditions, namely (i) the dissolution of the TMC and of the Cabinet; (ii) the lifting of the state of emergency which had been imposed after the April 1985 coup; (iii) the repeal of *sharia* laws; and (iv) the abrogation of accords with Egypt and Libya. The SPLM leader also called for the holding of a national conference to discuss the southern issue.

Negotiations with the SPLM did not begin until March 1986 when, in the first of a series of meetings, the National Alliance for Salvation (NAS), the alliance of professional organizations which had been instrumental in organizing the strikes which had contributed to the downfall of President Nemery, met SPLM representatives at Koka in Ethiopia. The "Koka Dam declaration" of March 1986 specified the conditions under which the SPLM would participate in a national conference.

The SPLM refused to recognize the election of April 1986, and intensified its guerrilla activities in the south in order to disrupt the process, afterwards declaring the Constituent Assembly to be unrepresentative, as polling had been postponed in a large proportion of southern constituencies. The movement's aim was now to make further inroads into Equatoria and to cut off the provincial capital, Juba.

Col. Garang met the Prime Minister, Dr Sadiq el-Mahdi, in Ethiopia in July 1986, after which it was announced at separate press conferences that contacts were to be maintained.

SPLA attacks succeeded in forcing the closure of the airport at Juba for part of the month of July 1986, when thousands of citizens were reported to be fleeing the city, and a number of foreign nationals were evacuated.

The government announced in August 1986 that all contacts with the SPLA had been suspended in response to the shooting down, on Aug. 16, of a civilian aircraft soon after take-off from Malakal, which had caused the death of all 60 people on board. The attack on the aircraft came soon after a warning issued by the SPLA to the effect that it would shoot down aircraft in the vicinity of Malakal. In the latter part of 1986 guerrilla action severely hampered the distribution of food and other emergency aid to areas of southern Sudan which were affected by famine. In April 1987 the SPLA rejected a government offer of a cease-fire pending the resumption of peace negotiations, and demanded that the state of emergency, in force since the coup of April 1985, should be lifted in conjunction with the implementation of any cease-fire.

Suriname

Capital: Paramaribo Pop. 393,748

The republic of Suriname has since February 1980 been ruled by a National Military Council (NMC, renamed the Supreme Council), led by Lt.-Col. Desi Bouterse who successively dismissed the country's President, suspended the Constitution (on Aug. 15, 1980) and stated that the country would follow a "clear socialist course". The NMC succeeded in foiling several attempted coups—in March 1981, March 1982 and October-December 1982, when the NMC declared a state of martial law on Dec. 8, dismissing the mainly civilian government set up in March 1982, destroyed various opposition media headquarters in Paramaribo and also the head office of the *Moederbond* trade union, and appointed a new interim government of seven military and five civilian officials on Dec. 12. In ensuing disturbances some 40 persons were said to have been killed, 17 of them in summary executions. (For alleged attempted coup of November 1983 see below under Movement for the Liberation of Suriname.)

On Jan. 1, 1985, a National Assembly, comprising 14 military officers, 11 trade union leaders and six representatives of the private sector, was appointed to prepare the drafting of a new Constitution. On Aug. 2 the Assembly approved a bill which inter alia confirmed the position of Lt.-Col. Bouterse as head of the government and specified that the government organs were the Council of Ministers (Cabinet) and above it the NMC (later referred to as the Supreme Council).

In November 1985 the existing ban on political parties was lifted to allow for public political meetings, and in 1987 the parties which announced that they would contest elections included the Party for the Development of Suriname, the Suriname National Party, the Progressive Reformed Party, the Indonesian Peasants' Party, the Progressive Workers' and Farm Labourers' Union, the Surinamese Peasants' Party, and the New Democratic Party (led by Lt.-Col. Bouterse).

Brunswijk Rebel Group (or Surinamese Liberation Army)

Leadership. Ronnie Brunswijk

This guerrilla group began its campaign to overthrow the leadership of Lt.-Col. Bouterse with an attack on three military posts on July 21, 1986, and by late November 1986 it controlled most of the eastern and some southern areas of Suriname.

The rebel forces, thought to number between 100 and 300, were composed largely of *boschneger* (Bush negroes), the descendants of escaped slaves who lived an autonomous existence in rain forests, together with some foreign mercenaries. Discontent amongst the 50,000 *boschneger* arose from plans drawn up after independence in 1975 for them to be moved into towns, and from a belief that Lt.-Col. Bouterse's regime favoured a small minority clique of mostly Creole officers. Its leader, R. Brunswijk, a *boschneger,* was a former army sergeant recruited to protect Lt.-Col. Bouterse and dismissed in 1985. In May 1986 he travelled to the Netherlands, where he had talks with leaders of the Movement for the Liberation of Suriname (see separate entry) from which his group received financial and logistical support.

In response to the attack of July 21, the government despatched the "élite" Echo company, but its commander was captured and himself joined the rebels. In August, Lt.-Col. Bouterse described the situation as "very, very serious", and claimed furthermore that the attacks were part of an international conspiracy.

In September 1986 the rebels shot down a helicopter used to transport troops to the rebel areas. On Sept. 11 the army announced that it had destroyed the rebel headquarters in the Marowijne area, but a further army offensive in mid-October closer to Paramaribo failed. In October, a guerrilla attack on a state-run palm oil plantation about 50 km from the town of Albina caused an estimated US$17,000,000 worth of damage. In the same month, airline services to the interior of the country were suspended after guerrillas shot down two aircraft, and on Nov. 5, all international flights into Suriname (apart from those of the state-owned Suriname Airways) were suspended. Also on Nov. 5, rebels set fire to the offices of the state-owned palm oil company.

By Nov. 8, the eastern province of Marowijne, with the exception of army posts in Moengo (the second-largest city in Suriname and centre of the bauxite mining region) and Albina, were under guerrilla control, and rebel activities were spreading south of the capital. On Nov. 14, some 1,500 residents of Albina were reported to have been evacuated.

On Nov. 20 rebels gained control of Moengo, but on Dec. 1 the military announced that the area had been cleared of rebels in an operation which began on Nov. 28 and in which dozens of guerrillas and one soldier were killed.

On Dec. 1, a state of emergency was reimposed throughout the south and east of the country. By Dec. 16, the government claimed to have regained control of the areas of economic importance, although the bauxite mines remained shut. Damage to the economy was estimated at US$53,000,000.

The number of refugees reported to have crossed into French Guiana by the end of 1986 was estimated to be 4,500. At the same time, French Guiana was accused by the Surinamese government of not opposing the transportation of arms to the rebels through its territory.

On Jan. 16, 1987, two soldiers were killed in an attack on an army convoy, following which seven guerrillas were reported to have died in a "mopping-up" operation. At the end of January, the Suralco aluminium refinery stopped production after rebels destroyed two power pylons.

On April 7, 1987, R. Brunswijk was reported to have met with Dr Henk Chin a Sen (the leader of the Movement for the Liberation of Suriname) in Suriname and to have declared a new independent state called "Free Suriname" in rebel-held territory. On July 10, a spokesman for the group, Eddie Jozefzoon, rejected a government amnesty offer as a "trick and a smoke screen".

Movement for the Liberation of Suriname

This Movement was formed in the Netherlands in January 1983 by Dr Henk Chin a Sen (who had been Prime Minister of Suriname from March to December 1980 and its President thereafter until February 1982). On Feb. 6 the Movement's founder defined its aim as being the removal from power of Lt.-Col. Bouterse "by peaceful means, particularly by political, diplomatic and economic pressure".

Later in 1983 the military authorities claimed to have discovered a plot scheduled for Nov. 25, 1983, and organized by the Movement. They alleged that the Movement intended to invade Suriname from French Guiana with a band of mercenaries recruited by Surinamese exiles in the Netherlands, but the Movement accused the government of inventing the plot.

In 1984 the authorities alleged that the Movement was behind a further invasion plan scheduled for April 1.

In May 1986 the Movement held talks with R. Brunswijk, to whose Brunswijk Rebel Group (see separate entry) the Movement supplied arms and logistics, and in November 1986 Dr Chin a Sen met with R. Brunswijk in Suriname to draw up a strategy for the takeover of the capital and the formation of a political platform. Dr Chin a Sen was, however, reported to have stated that he himself had no political ambitions.

On Dec. 4, Dr Chin a Sen claimed in the Netherlands that government troops in the east of Suriname had carried out mass killings of civilians. The claims were supported by *boschneger* refugees and by the US Secretary of State, George Shultz.

In a visit to the US State Department in April 1987 Dr Chin a Sen suggested that there were two possible courses of action open for rebels in Suriname: either, with a minimum amount of assistance from the USA and Brazil, they would be able to overthrow the regime within a few days, or they would continue to undermine the political and economic base of the country.

Swaziland

Capital: Mbabane Pop. 650,000

The Kingdom of Swaziland is ruled by a Paramount Chief (Ngwenyama) or King, who exercises authority through a Cabinet headed by a Prime Minister. There is a bicameral Parliament with purely advisory functions, consisting of (i) a House of Assembly of 40 members elected from among their own ranks by an electoral college of 80 members who are themselves elected by *tinkhundla* or tribal assemblies, and another 10 members appointed by the monarch, and (ii) a Senate consisting of 10 members elected by the House of Assembly and a further 10 members nominated by the monarch. All political parties were banned under a Constitution proclaimed on Oct. 13, 1978. A new Parliament was elected under the above procedure in October 1983.

While there is no evidence of the existence of indigenous revolutionary movements, a problem has been created for the Swaziland authorities by the presence of numerous members of the (banned South African) African National Congress (ANC). The South African Defence Force has conducted a number of raids against alleged ANC bases in Swaziland. On March 30, 1984, it was disclosed that in a non-aggression pact signed in February 1982 the governments of South Africa and Swaziland had inter alia undertaken to combat terrorism and to prevent any activity within their boundaries which might threaten the integrity of either side. From April 1984 onwards, clashes became frequent between ANC members and the Swaziland authorities, and in 1984 alone some 100 ANC supporters were deported from Swaziland.

Sweden

Capital: Stockholm Pop. 8,350,000

The Kingdom of Sweden is a parliamentary democracy in which the monarch has purely ceremonial functions as head of state. There is a Cabinet headed by a Prime Minister and responsible to a unicameral Parliament *(Riksdag)* of 349 members elected for a three-year term by universal adult suffrage. As a result of elections held on Sept. 15, 1985, seats in the *Riksdag* were distributed as follows: Social Democratic Labour Party 159, Moderate Party 76, Centre Party 44, Liberal Party 51, Communist Left Party 19. (The seats gained by the Centre Party included one allotted to the Christian Democratic League.)

Extremist political activities in Sweden have been largely confined to neo-Nazi groups opposed to the presence of alien communities, members of which (e.g. Iranians and Yugoslavs) have in some cases themselves committed acts of violence directed against the regimes of their countries of origin.

For the assassination of Sweden's Prime Minister, the Social Democrat Olof Palme, on Feb. 28, 1986, responsibility was claimed by several non-Swedish extremist groups, among them the West German Red Army Faction and a European Nationalist Union. However, the assassin had managed to escape, and no person has so far been convicted of having committed this crime.

Extreme Right-wing Groups

There is in Sweden a large minority of alien residents, making up about 12 per cent of the total population, or some 1,000,000 persons, including about 400,000 from Finland and other large groups from Turkey, Yugoslavia and Greece. The presence of these foreigners has led to growing hostility by young Swedes and by at least five extreme right-wing groups calling for the repatriation of these aliens. Although these groups have remained small, several have been reported to have links with neo-fascist groups in other countries; a group mentioned in this context has been the *Nordiska Rikspartiet*.

New Nazi Party

In March 1979 members of this party were responsible for plastering the wall of a comprehensive school at Olofström (a town in southern Sweden with a large immigrant population) with posters demanding the maintenance of racial purity in Sweden. The posters described Hitler as a hero and contained a warning of a coming second "crystal night" (i.e. a pogrom).

Switzerland

Capital: Berne

Pop. 6,370,000

The Swiss Confederation is a republic in which power is held by the electorate which consists of all adult citizens. These elect the Federal Assembly as well as cantonal and local councils and have powers to vote on constitutional amendments and other matters, including international treaties, in a referendum if requested by a fixed minimum of voters. The bicameral Federal Assembly consists of (i) a Council of States composed of two members for each of 20 cantons and one for each of six half-cantons, and (ii) a 200-member National Council elected for a four-year term in proportion to the population of the cantons (each canton or half-canton being represented by at least one member). The President of the Confederation, who is also President of the Federal Council (government), is elected, together with a Vice-President, for a one-year term by the two Houses of Parliament, which also elect the members of the government.

In elections to the National Council held on Oct. 23, 1983, parties gained seats as follows: Radical Democratic Party 54, Social Democratic Party 47, Christian Democratic People's Party 42, Swiss People's Party 23, Independents' Party 8, Liberal Party 8, National Action 5, Progressive Organizations of Switzerland/Autonomous Socialist Party 4, Evangelical People's Party 3, Greens, 3, Party of Labour (communist) 1, with one independent and one independent ecologist.

Switzerland has been the scene of numerous acts of violence committed by political extremists from outside the country, notably Palestinians, Armenians and members and supporters of the West German Red Army Faction. Internally, unrest was caused in the city of Zurich during 1980-81 by groups of young people resorting to violence in the expression of their discontent with the affluent society of Switzerland, but apart from individual leaders no specific organization was held responsible for the violent incidents which occurred. In Lausanne, however, a group calling itself "Red Lausanne" staged an unauthorized demonstration of some 400 people on Oct. 4, 1980, leading to clashes with the police force, three members of which were injured. The group was said to have no proper structure and no clear motives other than dissatisfaction with having to live in a regimented world.

Jura Movements

The canton of Jura was established with effect from Jan. 1, 1979, in the north-western part of the canton of Berne as a canton inhabited overwhelmingly by French-speaking Swiss. The leaders of the newly-established cantonal government continued to press for the incorporation into their canton of certain areas in the canton of Berne inhabited by French-speaking people. Among the latter, however, there exists a strong movement in favour of remaining inside the canton of Berne.

Béliers ("Rams")

The *Béliers* are the youth movement of the *Rassemblement jurassien,* an alliance of various political parties in power in the canton of Jura. Members of this movement have repeatedly been involved in clashes with anti-separatist (though French-speaking) Swiss who have opted for their areas to remain within the canton of Berne. Five members of the *Béliers* staged a brief demonstration on Sept. 10, 1982, in the hall of Schönbrunn Palace in Vienna, where the 1815 Treaty of Vienna had been signed, settling inter alia the fate of the Swiss Jura by allotting it to the canton of Berne.

A "second revolutionary faction" of the *Béliers* claimed responsibility for a bomb attack on a court building at Moutier (north of Berne) on Sept. 3, 1985, but members of the movement itself denied any connexion with this attack.

Jurassic Liberation Army

This pro-separatist movement claimed on Sept. 26, 1982, that it was responsible for stealing two ballot boxes at the village of Vellerat while local elections were in progress. Although inhabited by French-speaking people, Vellerat had remained inside the canton of Berne after the establishment of the canton of Jura. The villagers of Vellerat had, on Aug. 14, 1982, declared themselves independent of the canton of Berne.

Sangliers ("Wild Boars")

The *Sangliers* are the youth movement of the *Force démocratique,* the pro-Berne organization in the southern part of Jura. Members of this movement have on a number of occasions been involved in clashes with (pro-separatist) *Béliers* (see separate entry).

Other Movements

Autonomous Cells *(Cellules autonomes)*

During February and March 1985 this group carried out bomb attacks on various targets, including offices of the (communist) Swiss Party of Labour, a police station and a military lorry.

New Social order (*Nouvel order social,* NOS)

This movement was, in 1980, reported to have links with other, mainly neo-Nazi, organizations in various countries of Europe and elsewhere.

Syria

Capital: Damascus

Pop. 10,270,000

The Syrian Arab Republic is, under its 1973 Constitution, a "socialist popular democracy" with an executive President, who is secretary-general of the *Baath* Arab Socialist Party and also president of the National Progressive Front (NPF) embracing the country's five legal parties—the *Baath,* the (Nasserite) Socialist Unionist Movement, the (also Nasserite) Arab Socialist Union, the (anti-Egyptian) Arab Socialist Party and the Syrian Communist Party. There is a legislative People's Council, in which all parties and also independents are represented. The government, the *Baath* party and the armed forces are dominated by members of the minority Alawite sect of the Shia Moslem community (constituting only about 12 per cent of the country's population, whereas some 70 per cent are Sunni Moslems).

Sunni Moslems have strongly opposed the 1973 Constitution and have demanded that it should recognize Islam as the state religion, but an amendment to the Constitution adopted in February of that year stated merely that the President must be a Moslem. Serious disturbances occurred at the time, and in a referendum held in March 1973 to approve the Constitution many Sunni Moslems abstained or voted against its adoption.

The principal opposition to the regime of President Hafez al-Assad (as leader of the Syrian *Baath* party) has come from Moslem extremists within the Sunni community, their strongest organization being the Moslem Brotherhood; violent actions against his regime have also been carried out by dissident Baathists supported by the *Baath* party of Iraq. On the international scene, Syria has been implicated in the activities of some of the more militant Palestinian groups.

Moslem Fundamentalists

Moslem Brotherhood

Leadership. Shaikh Bayanouni (spiritual l. and sec.-gen.); Issam al-Attar (l. based in Aachen, West Germany)

Deriving from this historic movement originally founded in Egypt (see pages 84-85), the Syrian offshoot of the Moslem Brotherhood has in recent years been engaged in a bloody struggle for supremacy with the regime of President Assad. Although most of its members are Sunni Moslems, the Moslem Brotherhood of Syria shares many objectives with the Shia revolutionaries who came to power in Iran in February 1979. In Syria the Brotherhood not only propagates Islamic fundamentalist tenets but also demands free elections, a more liberal economy and an end to Alawite dominance. According to Shaikh Bayanouni, the Islamic state which it wishes to establish in Damascus will not take away the religious rights of Christians and other non-Moslems and will create "a political movement which will satisfy all the people"; however, full rights will be accorded only to those whose ideologies do not contradict that of Islam.

The Moslem Brotherhood is well organized not only in Syria, where it is said to have cells in the armed forces and publishes an underground journal called *Al-Nazeer* ("The Herald"), but also in many other countries, including Austria, West Germany, the United Kingdom and the United States, where there are Syrian émigrés and where funds are collected on its behalf. According to the Syrian government, the Moslem Brotherhood is supplied and encouraged by the country's enemies, including Israel, the United States, Jordan, Iraq, the Phalangists in Lebanon and also Egypt.

Acts of violence committed by its members in Syria in their struggle against the regime of President Assad began to escalate in 1978, when "extremist Moslems" were offically held responsible for the death of a

Soviet adviser to the Syrian air force in February and for a number of assassinations during March of that year. In an attack on an artillery school at Aleppo on June 16, 1979, a total of 63 army cadets (believed to have been Alawites) were killed, and the government held the Moslem Brotherhood responsible.

The Minister of the Interior stated on June 22, 1979, that the United States and Israel had "reactivated" the Brotherhood "in an attempt to weaken Syria's opposition to Egypt's peace treaty with Israel"; he also accused the Brotherhood of having instigated earlier attacks on prominent Alawites and Baathists, and he promised that the government would "liquidate" the movement. On June 24 it was announced that a group of 14 men had been sentenced to death (12 of them in absentia) for their part in the Aleppo killings. Among another 200 Brotherhood members arrested after these killings, 18 were sentenced to death for murder and other acts of violence, 15 of them were hanged on June 28 and the three others had their sentences commuted to life imprisonment.

Early in August 1979 Husni Mahmoud Abou, the leader of the Aleppo faction of the Moslem Brotherhood, was arrested (together with his deputy); early in September he appeared on television, saying that his organization had planned a wave of assassinations and bombings aimed at causing civil war in Syria; and on Dec. 26, 1979, he and four other Brotherhood members were executed in Damascus for alleged participation in the Aleppo killings.

Among the acts of violence attributed to the Moslem Brotherhood was the killing of an Alawite religious leader on Aug. 30, 1979, which led to fighting between Alawites and Sunnites in Latakia, where 12 persons were killed, and to bombings and assassinations in Damascus. During September 1979 Abdul Satar al-Zaim, a leading member of the Brotherhood, was killed in a gun battle some 40 miles north-east of Damascus. Further clashes involving Moslem Brotherhood members took place in Aleppo in November and December 1979.

Early in February 1980 it was reported that since the beginning of that year Moslem Brotherhood activists had assassinated at least 12 Soviet military advisers. Late in February the Syrian security forces launched an offensive against the Brotherhood, which led to the outbreak of a general insurgency on March 8 in Aleppo and other northern cities. Violence and unrest spread in northern Syria, as a result of which the government withdrew heavy armoured brigades from the Syrian-Israeli front to use them against the Moslem extremists, of whom about 100 were said to have been killed (against some 80 government or party officials). Further clashes occurred during May and June, when the authorities claimed that Capt. Ibrahim Youssef, the presumed leader of the insurgency in Aleppo in June 1979, had been killed on June 2.

Following an attempted assassination of President Assad on June 26, 1980, the People's Council approved, on July 7, a law instituting the death penalty for membership of the Moslem Brotherhood, with the proviso that those who left it within a month would be pardoned. This amnesty was later extended to Aug. 27, when the government claimed that several hundred Brotherhood members had surrendered to the authorities; violent clashes nevertheless continued during July and August in northern Syria, with several hundred Brotherhood or other opposition activists being killed, summarily executed or arrested. According to a government statement the military leader of the Brotherhood, Hisham Jumbaz, was killed at Homs on Aug. 16 (with five other Brotherhood members). Of those who had surrendered, some 200 Brotherhood members were (as claimed in the Western press early in September) massacred by security forces at a camp east of Aleppo on Aug. 14, 1980.

On June 1, 1981, Moslem Brotherhood gunmen were reported to have killed 15 soldiers, three intelligence service members and four boys in Aleppo after the army was said to have killed 50 people in the previous week. Later in 1981 the Syrian authorities continued their "suppression campaign" against internal opponents and in particular the Moslem Brotherhood, with arrests inside Syria and assassinations outside it (including that of the wife of Issam al-Attar, reported on Sept. 27). Widespread unrest was reported on Oct. 8, 1981, from Aleppo, Homs and Hama, a senior Syrian officer being killed by a Moslem Brotherhood follower on Oct. 6. On Nov. 29 a bomb said to have been planted by the Moslem Brotherhood in Damascus killed 64 people and injured 135 others.

Battles between Moslem Brotherhood and army units continued in Aleppo and Hama (which was cut off from the rest of Syria for five days in mid-December), with Communists being said to be in league with the Moslem Brotherhood. By January 1982 some 35,000 Syrians were said to have disappeared as a result of continued fighting, and on Jan. 18 it was reported that several hundred army officers had been arrested on charges of carrying out hostile activities against the Syrian regime and plotting a coup, apparently in association with the Moslem Brotherhood. On Jan. 25, 1982, it was reported that after the Moslem Brotherhood had warned Soviet experts to leave Syria about 100 Soviet military experts had repatriated their families.

In early February 1982 an armed insurrection by Brotherhood activists broke out in the northern city of Hama, apparently after a newly appointed military governor had employed forceful methods in trying to curb the movement. Clashes between Brotherhood members and security forces seeking illegal arms in Hama led to a declaration of rebellion from two of the city's mosques on Feb. 3, the inhabitants being told that they had been "liberated" from the Assad regime. A communiqué issued on Feb. 10 by a group called "the command of the Islamic revolution in Syria" stated that the rebels had raided the arsenal of the local headquarters of the *Baath* party and occupied the police station and the governor's office; it also claimed that many units of regular Syrian forces had defected to fight alongside the rebels.

The Syrian security forces responded by encircling Hama with tanks and heavy artillery and mounting a prolonged bombardment of the city in which much of it was destroyed. The government made repeated claims about Feb. 12 that Hama had been brought under control, but it was not until late February that the rebels appeared to have been overcome. In reducing the insurgency the Syrian security forces inflicted large numbers of casualties, the number of dead being estimated by Western sources as running into many thousands, most of them civilians.

In a speech on March 7, 1982, President Assad attributed the insurgency to the Moslem Brotherhood, claiming that it had "transformed mosques and houses of God into warehouses to stockpile ammunition" and used them as barricades from which rebels had "opened fire and killed citizens". He also claimed that the Brotherhood had the backing of Israel (suggesting that the uprising had been timed to divert Syrian attention from the Israeli annexation of the Golan Heights in December 1981) and that it had been armed by the United States and Iraq.

The *Baath* party's eighth congress, held in January 1985, discussed the "measures taken to liquidate" the Brotherhood, resolving to "show no leniency in applying the principle of the sovereignty of law and order and preventing any encroachment on it". In the same month, however, the Interior Ministry announced that certain leading members of the Brotherhood's "Vanguard Organization" were to be allowed to return home from exile in Europe under the terms of a presidential pardon. The pardon had apparently been offered after Vanguard members had expressed "new convictions", which were "radically different" from their previously held beliefs, during recent contacts with Syrian government officials in Europe.

In February 1985, two Brotherhood members who had been deported from West Germany hijacked the aircraft which was to carry them to Damascus, and forced it to land in Austria, where they later pleaded guilty to charges of air piracy and received sentences of five years in prison.

Other Movements

Arab Communist Organization

On July 29, 1975, the Supreme State Security Court in Damascus sentenced 14 members of this Organization for a series of acts of sabotage, including the bombing of Egyptian, Jordanian and US diplomatic or information offices. The court imposed sentences of death on four Palestinians and three Syrians (two of the latter death sentences being commuted to life imprisonment), of life imprisonment on two Palestinians and a Syrian and of 15 years' hard labour on two Palestinians and two Syrians.

Baathist Dissidents

Syria became the main power base of the *Baath* Arab socialist movement in 1963, and the *Baath* party of Syria, as the left wing of the movement, was thereafter separated from the right-wing "historic" *Baath* party of Iraq under the leadership of the movement's founder, Michel Aflaq.

Early in April 1975 about 200 members of the Syrian party, who were understood to be supporters of the Iraqi party, were arrested on charges of plotting against the government. The sixth congress of the Syrian party, held on April 9, 1975, denounced the Iraqi party as "a rightist clique" in alleged collusion with Iran and a traitor to "the cause of the Arab nation". The assassination of a member of the *Baath* party's pan-Arab command in Syria (who was of Iraqi origin) on July 10, 1976, was officially attributed to Iraqi Baathists.

A former secretary-general of the Syrian *Baath* party until 1964. Hammoud el-Shufi, resigned as Syria's permanent representative at the United Nations on Dec. 27, 1979, declaring that he hoped to participate in the formation of a new opposition front in exile "to defend the democratic aspirations of the Syrian people". He accused the Syrian regime of having mounted an "impossible degree of repression" in 1979 and of having imprisoned "former Presidents, Prime Ministers and army officers by the hundreds"; he also denounced "the real monopoly of political power and economic wealth" of the Alawite minority.

A group calling itself "the Vanguard of the Arab Revolution" claimed on Feb. 8-9, 1981, to have been involved in heavy fighting with Syrian army units in Aleppo where it attempted to storm a prison in order to release Salah Jadid, a former Syrian chief of staff and senior *Baath* party member; the group also claimed to have "executed" a Syrian secret agent in Kuwait "in revenge for the execution of Salah al-Bitar". (The latter had been co-founder of the *Baath* party, had been Prime Minister of Syria between 1963 and 1966 and had later lived in exile after his right-wing *Baath* faction had been finally ousted by the left wing, which has since then remained in power in Syria. Known to be seeking to set up an opposition front Bitar was assassinated in Paris on July 21, 1980, in the course of an "assassination campaign" against external opposition members, as expressly confirmed by President Assad on July 24, 1980.)

Another Baathist dissident group, known as the "National Salvation Command", claimed responsibility for bomb explosions at the Prime Minister's offices in Damascus on Aug. 17, 1981, and at the *Baath* party's headquarters (also in Damascus) on Sept. 12; the latter explosion resulted in the death of the three members of a "Martyr Kamal Jumblatt group" who had caused the explosion, and also of about 43 persons working at the party headquarters. (Kamal Jumblatt, a Druse who had been the leader of the Progressive Socialist Party of Lebanon, had been assassinated in March 1977.)

In March 1982 exiled Baathist dissidents participated in the formation of the National Alliance for the Liberation of Syria (see separate entry) together with the Moslem Brotherhood and other political and religious opposition groups.

Islamic Front in Syria—see under National Alliance for the Liberation of Syria

National Alliance for the Liberation of Syria

Leadership. Hammoud el-Shufi (spokesman)

This Alliance was formed in March 1982 by about 20 political and religious groups with the aim of consolidating opposition to the Assad regime from within Syria and abroad. The announcement of its formation was made in New York on April 3 by Hammoud el-

Shufi, who said that it included the Moslem Brotherhood and the closely related Islamic Front in Syria, as well as dissident members of the ruling *Baath* party, such as himself (see entry for Baathist Dissidents).

The aims of the Alliance as set out in its charter included the forcible overthrow of the Assad government and its replacement by a constitutional, elective system in which freedom of faith, expression and association would be guaranteed. Islam would be the country's religion and the *Sharia* (Islamic law) would be the basis of legislation, but the rights of non-Moslems would be protected. On matters of external policy the Alliance would support "the liberation of Palestine from the Zionist occupation", work for Arab unity and abide by the principles of the non-aligned movement.

National Salvation Command—see under Baathist Dissidents

Party of Communist Action

In March and April 1982 several members of this independent illegal communist formation were arrested in Syria, including one of the Party's founders, Fateh Jamous, who had been wanted by the authorities since 1976. Several of the Party members arrested were later found dead. A further 30 alleged Party members were arrested in August 1984.

17 October Movement for the Liberation of Syria

According to a claim broadcast by the Lebanese Phalangist "Voice of Lebanon" radio, this hitherto-unknown organization was responsible for two car bomb attacks in the northern town of Tartus on April 15, 1986, which reportedly killed 27 people. It was not known whether these attacks were linked to a wave of bomb explosions on Syrian buses and trains the following day.

Syrian Liberation Front

Representatives of this alliance of Moslem and communist exiled opponents of President Assad attended the 17th session of the PLO's Palestine National Council held in Jordan in November 1984.

Vanguard of the Arab Revolution—see under Baathist Dissidents

Taiwan

Capital: Taipei

Pop. 20,000,000

Taiwan, officially the Republic of China, has a President elected (and re-eligible) by the National Assembly for a six-year term. The National Assembly, the vast majority of whose members are life members elected in mainland China in 1948, has limited powers. The country's highest administrative organ is the Executive *Yuan*, whose Council (the Cabinet) is responsible to the Legislative *Yuan* composed of elected members. The Legislative *Yuan* is controlled by the Nationalist Party (Kuomintang) and the great majority of its members are mainland Chinese who have held their seats since 1948 (although some Taiwanese have since been elected to fill vacancies in it). In addition to the ruling Kuomintang, there are two minor legal parties—the China Democratic Socialist Party and the Young China Party.

The Kuomintang's approach to internal security questions has been largely conditioned by Taiwan's position vis-à-vis the People's Republic of China, where the Communists are regarded as having usurped the Nationalists' rightful authority over the whole of China in 1948. Mainly to guard against the threat of internal communist subversion, fundamental constitutional liberties have remained suspended under a state of siege which is to stay in force as long as "the Communist rebellion" continues on the mainland; thus public meetings, strikes, demonstrations, petitions and the "spreading of rumours" are forbidden. Although executions on political charges, which had been numerous in the 1950s and 1960s, became less frequent in the 1970s, several hundred people were still detained for political reasons in the early 1980s, including alleged "communist agents" as well as "rebels" of the Formosan Independence Movement.

In the late 1970s the government adopted a more liberal internal policy, notably by holding elections to regional assemblies in which large numbers of independent candidates were returned. Nevertheless, the growth of opposition activities gave the authorities cause for considerable concern, and elections to the National Assembly and the Legislative *Yuan* scheduled for December 1978 were postponed until December 1980 (when the successful independent candidates included the wives of two recently imprisoned dissident leaders). During this period resentment of the political domination of Taiwan by immigrants from the mainland (who formed only 13 per cent of the population) led to demands both for the democratization of the regime and for acceptance that Taiwan was now a state independent of and separate from mainland China. The demand for Taiwanese independence has received strong support from the Presbyterian Church (with about 200,000 members), while in the absence of legal party opposition, pro-democratization opponents of the Kuomintang regime have grouped themselves around a number of anti-government magazines, notably the monthly review *Formosa* (see entry for Formosa Group below).

Although these loosely organized opposition groups were effectively contained by the authorities, in 1986 the first non-government-sponsored opposition party was established within Taiwan. Although its formation contravened the country's martial law regulations no action was taken against its founders and the party (the Democratic Progress Party—see separate entry) won several seats in legislative elections on Dec. 6, 1986. Martial law was lifted on July 15, 1987 (but replaced by a strict National Security Law incorporating serious limitations on political activity).

Communist Party of China (CPC)

With regard to Taiwan, the object of the CPC ruling in Beijing (China) has always been the incorporation of the island in the People's Republic of China (whereas the object of Taiwan's ruling party, the Kuomintang, has been its own return as the government of mainland China). Alleged agents of the CPC were arrested in Taiwan and sentenced to death or imprisonment on various occasions (pro-communist activities being a capital offence under Taiwan's Constitution), although the party does not appear to have any substantial underground organization on the island. On the other hand, a number of prominent persons have over the years defected from Taiwan to the People's Republic.

In August 1970 a military court in Taipei sentenced two brothers—Quintin and Rizal Yuyitung—respectively to two and three years' "re-education" in prison for "spreading communist propaganda" during 20 years while they were publisher and chief editor respectively of the Manila-based *Chinese Commercial News* (by publishing reports of the New China News Agency and pictures of Mao Zedong). Although born in the Philippines, they had been deported to Taiwan on May 5, 1970.

On Dec. 13, 1970, it was confirmed that a deputy director of the Broadcasting Corporation of China (i.e. Taiwan) had been arrested and had confessed to having been one of Communist China's principal agents in Taiwan for 20 years; on Dec. 10, 1971, he was sentenced to life imprisonment, while a leader-writer for the *China Daily News*, arrested with him, was given a five-year prison sentence, also for "communist propaganda".

Further trials of alleged communist agents in the late 1970s included that of Wu Chun-fa, who was sentenced to death in April 1979 and executed the following month, while 13 of his suspected associates received prison sentences ranging from two years to life.

Miss Lee Ya-ping, a US resident and publisher of the California-based *International Daily News*, a Chinese-language daily newspaper, was arrested in Taiwan on Sept. 17, 1985, and charged with sedition on the grounds that she had "forwarded Chinese Communist conspiracies" against Taiwan in her newspaper. She was sentenced to two years under "protective control" on Oct. 3.

Democratic Coalition Movement—see Formosa Group

Democratic Progress Party (DPP)

The DPP was formed on Sept. 28, 1986, by some 130 members of the *Tangwai* (a loose coalition of opponents of the Kuomintang regime), who called for an immediate end to martial law in Taiwan and for the establishment of direct trade, tourist and postal links with the Chinese mainland. The new party's foundation, which was designed to provide greater cohesion for opposition candidates intending to contest seats in elections for the Legislative *Yuan* and the National Assembly, was a clear breach of the country's martial law regulations which prohibited the existence of political parties other than the Kuomintang and its two small allied parties. The *Tangwai* had been unofficially tolerated because its members had campaigned as independents rather than as participants within an overtly organized grouping. Despite this, however, the authorities failed to initiate any punitive action against the founders of the DPP, and on Oct. 7 President Chiang announced his intention to lift martial law in the near future. The Kuomintang's central standing committee approved the move with regard to the main island of Taiwan and the Pescadores (a group of small islands in the Taiwan Strait) but maintained the necessity of retaining martial law on the islands of Quemoy and Matsu as a defence against a possible attack from the Chinese mainland. The committee also stressed that the dismantling process should be gradual and that new political parties should be permitted to operate only if they were explicitly anti-communist and did not advocate Taiwanese independence from mainland China, over which the Kuomintang continues to claim legal jurisdiction despite the success of the "Communist rebels".

On Nov. 10, a DPP national convention in Taipei, attended by 165 delegates representing 2,500 members, ratified the party's constitution and elected a 31-member central executive committee and an 11-member standing committee. Chiang Peng-chien, a leading member of the *Tangwai*, was elected to a one-year term as chairman of the new party. The convention was followed by a rally of 10,000 DPP supporters which passed off without police interference. Although the Taiwanese Interior Minister denounced both the convention and the rally as illegal, no further action was taken against those involved. DPP members participated in the elections on Dec. 6, and won 12 and 11 seats respectively in the Legislative *Yuan* and the National Assembly; the Kuomintang won 73 and 84 seats, whilst independent candidates secured the remaining two and five seats which were open for election.

On Nov. 30, 1986, Hsu Hsin-liang, one of Taiwan's most prominent dissidents and a founder of the Formosa Group (see separate entry), attempted to return to the country in order to offer his support to the DPP in the elections, but, having been in exile in the USA since his proscription by the authorities in 1979, he was denied access to the country. Several thousand demonstrators, however, who had marched to Taipei's airport to greet his return, clashed with riot-police in the worst incident of unrest since 1979.

Formosa Group

Leadership. Huang Hsin-chieh (publisher); Shih Ming-teh (general manager)

A monthly magazine called *Formosa* (this being the original Portuguese name for Taiwan) was founded in August 1979 by a number of opposition leaders (including democrats, socialists, feminists and supporters of Taiwanese independence) who had earlier in the year joined forces in a "Democratic Coalition Movement". Quickly reaching a circulation of over 100,000, *Formosa* pressed for a representative parliament, a free press, an amnesty for political prisoners and the ending of martial law; it also publicized the grievances of factory workers, farmers and fishermen. Its general manager, Shih Ming-teh, had been arrested in 1962 for his political activites inside the student movement and had served 15 years in prison before being released in 1977.

The magazine opened offices in all major cities of Taiwan and the authorities regarded these offices as "cells" for recruiting activities with a view to obtaining political power; it was also claimed by the government that members of the *Formosa* group had communist connexions. An application by the group to hold a mass rally of native-born Taiwanese in Kaohsiung (Taiwan's second largest city and its southern port) in December 1979 was refused by the authorities, but the rally was nevertheless held on Dec. 10 and led to riots in which 182 civil and military police were injured. The authorities thereupon arrested members of the staff of *Formosa* and banned the magazine: by the end of January 1980 a total of 65 persons said to have been involved in riots were under arrest.

Eight of those arrested following the Kaohsiung disturbances were brought to trial before a Taipei military tribunal in March 1980, the state prosecutor demanding the death sentence for all of them. They were sentenced on April 18—Shih Ming-teh to life imprisonment, Huang Hsin-chieh (the publisher of *Formosa* and also a member of the Legislative *Yuan*) to 14 years and six others (including two members of the Taiwan Provincial Assembly) to 12 years each. The defendants (who claimed that their purported "confessions" had been extracted under duress) denied that they had attempted to overthrow the government (a charge on which they were convicted) and that they wished to promote independence for the Taiwanese.

A total of 31 alleged participants in the riots were on June 2, 1980, given prison sentences ranging from 10 months to six years, and on June 5 the executive secretary of the Taiwan Presbyterian Church was sentenced to seven years in prison for having sheltered Shih Ming-teh before his arrest in Taipei on Jan. 8, 1980, while 10 other Church members were given prison sentences ranging from two to seven years.

The suppression of the magazine and the imprisonment of those connected with its production effectively destroyed what little organization the movement possessed, and no activity by the Formosa Group has been reported in recent years. In mid-1984, however, the Taiwanese authorities released six of those who had been imprisoned in connexion with the riots of December 1979, including the executive secretary of the Taiwan Presbyterian Church. On Jan. 20, 1987, the Defence Ministry announced the release of a further 26 people who had been imprisoned for politically motivated crimes, some of whom had been involved in the Kaohsiung riots.

19 May Green Movement Headquarters

This group was established in 1986 as a radical offshoot of the Democratic Progress Party (see separate entry), and derived its name from the date of the 1949 proclamation of martial law. During 1986 and 1987 it organized demonstrations to demand the ending of martial law and the introduction of political pluralism.

Taiwan Democratic Party (TDP)

The TDP was formed in Japan by Hsu Chao-hung who had fled there following his release from prison in Taiwan in 1975 after serving a four-year sentence for engaging in subversive activities. Hsu later returned to Taiwan and on Sept. 16, 1985, was sentenced to a further term of six years' imprisonment after being found guilty of attempting to overthrow the government by illegal means.

Taiwan Independence Movement

This Movement, mainly based abroad and regarded as subversive by the Taiwan government, stands for an independent Taiwan ruled by Taiwanese (and not by the Kuomintang regime dominated by Chinese who came from the mainland in 1948). It advocates self-determination for the people of Taiwan and repudiates "all forms of dictatorship—Chinese Communist or Nationalist".

It was responsible for bomb explosions at the US Information Service office at Tainan in 1970 and at the Bank of America in 1971, and also for an incident in October 1976 in which Hsieh Tung-min (then Governor of Taiwan and since 1978 vice-President) had his left hand blown off by a letter bomb. Although the Movement was effectively suppressed in Taiwan, it was reported in 1978 to be supported by many Taiwanese in Japan (where it had some 10,000 members) and in the United States.

The American section of the Movement—United Formosans for Independence—was believed to be responsible for bomb explosions in 1979 at offices of China Airlines and the Washington office of the Coordination Council for North American Affairs (the Taiwan government's semi-official representative in the United States). It does not appear to have been active in recent years, however.

United Formosans for Independence—see Taiwan Independence Movement

Tanzania

Capital: Dar es Salaam (to be replaced by Dodoma) Pop. 21,730,000

The United Republic of Tanzania, a member of the Commonwealth, has an executive President who is elected for a four-year term by universal adult suffrage and is re-eligible, and who is head of state and of the government. There is a Vice-President who is the head of the Executive of the islands of Zanzibar and Pemba. The Cabinet is headed by a Prime Minister, and the separate Executive in Zanzibar deals with internal Zanzibari affairs under the control of a Revolutionary Council of Zanzibar. Legislative power is vested in a National Assembly, partly elected in mainland Tanzania for a five-year term by universal adult suffrage and partly appointed by the President. All candidates must be approved by the country's sole legal political organization, the Revolutionary Party (*Chama Cha Mapinduzi*—CCM), but voters may have a choice between two or more candidates in any one constituency.

In elections held on Oct. 27, 1985, a total of 328 candidates approved by the CCM contested (i) the 156 elective seats in the House of Assembly (101 for the mainland and 55 for Zanzibar and Pemba) and (ii) 50 seats in the Zanzibar House of Representatives.

On Dec. 28, 1985, the High Court in Dar es Salaam sentenced Hatty Maghee and eight junior army officers to life imprisonment for attempting to assassinate the President, to remove him from office and to overthrow the government. H. Maghee, a former airline pilot, was said to be the leader of this conspiracy, the discovery of which had first been announced on Jan. 21, 1983.

An amnesty announced on Nov. 5, 1985, did not apply to political prisoners (nor to those under sentence of death or serving life sentences).

Tanzanian Revolutionary Youth Movement (or Tanzanian Democratic Youth Movement)

Leadership. Moussa Membar (founder)

Five members of this Movement, demanding the resignation of President Nyerere, hijacked a Tanzanian airliner on an internal flight on Feb. 26, 1982, and diverted it to Stansted (Essex, England), where the five men surrendered on Feb. 28 after intervention by Oscar Kambona, a former Tanzanian minister who had lived in exile in London since 1967 (but who disclaimed any prior knowledge of the hijack or of the hijackers' Movement). The five men were, in London on Sept. 17, 1982, sentenced to imprisonment for terms ranging from three to eight years (under a 1971 Hijacking Act). Moussa Membar, described by the judge as the group's leader, said during the trial that the Movement had been set up by himself in 1979 with the object of returning Tanzania to democracy, and that it had 3,000 members and also many sympathizers among Tanzanian officials. The government had not demanded the extradition of the five men during the proceedings in London.

Thailand

Capital: Bangkok Pop. 52,654,000

The Kingdom of Thailand is a constitutional monarchy with a bicameral Parliament consisting of (i) a 261-member Senate appointed by the King on the recommendation of the Prime Minister and (ii) a 347-member House of Representatives elected by universal adult suffrage, and with a Cabinet headed by a Prime Minister appointed by both Houses of Parliament meeting jointly. The country has been under military rule since October 1976, with the principal cabinet posts being held by former officers of the armed forces.

Elections to the House of Representatives held on July 27, 1986, when a reported 61 per cent of the electorate took part in voting, resulted in seats being distributed as follows: Democrat Party 100,

Thai Nation Party (*Chart Thai*) 63, Social Action Party 51, United Democratic Party 38, *Prachakorn Thai* 24, United Thai Party (*Ruam Thai*) 19, *Rassadorn* Party 18, Community Action Party 15, Progressive Party 9, Mass Party (*Muanchon*) 3, National Democracy Party (*Chart Prachitippatai*) 3, other parties 4.

The current Prime Minister, Gen. Prem. Tinsulanond, has survived two abortive coup attempts (in April 1981 and September 1985), both led by one of the so-called "young Turk" army officers, Col. Manoon Rupkachorn.

A 1952 act banning communist activities under pain of imprisonment for from 10 years to life was reinforced on Oct. 17, 1976, by an order defining "communist activities" as "any activities aimed at undermining national security, religion, the monarchy, and the democratic form of government with the King as head of state", nationalizing private property without fair compensation or setting up a social system under which all property was held to be common property. The order also empowered the Prime Minister inter alia to declare any area communist-infested and to prohibit people from entering or living in such an area; measures could also be taken to prevent food and other commodities from reaching communist organizations.

Left-wing Movements

Asia 88

This communist group was reported to have been set up in May 1982 and to be supported by Lao Communists.

Committee for the Co-ordination of Patriotic and Democracy-loving Forces (CCPDF)

Leadership. Udom Sisuwan (ch.); Bunyen Wothong (vice-ch.); Thirayat Bunmi (gen. sec.)

The CCPDF was formed in 1977 by the Communist Party of Thailand (CPT) (which then had a guerrilla force estimated at up to 14,000, as well as 15,000 members of village militia groups) and former members of the Socialist Party and the United Socialist Front (see separate entries). Its members included two former socialist members of the House of Representatives, a former leader of the Nationalist Students' Centre of Thailand, a trade union leader and a peasant leader. After the invasion of Kampuchea by Vietnam in December 1978, and the resultant fall of the Pol Pot regime in Kampuchea, with China diverting its aid from the Thai Communists to the (Pol Pot) Red Khmer guerrillas, fighting broke out in April 1979 between a pro-Chinese and a pro-Vietnamese faction of the CCPDF, with members of the latter seeking refuge in Laos in June 1979 with the object of setting up a rival communist party.

Communist Party of Malaya (CPM)

Activists of this Maoist party, mainly Chinese from Malaya who had entered southern Thailand, were by 1970 said to consist of about 400 guerrillas in Thailand's southern provinces (notably Pattani, Yala and Narathiwat) and 1,200 on the border with Malaysia. In these areas they were able to win the support of the Moslem community (constituting about 40 per cent of the population in four provinces). By the end of 1975 there were said to be about 3,500 communist guerrillas in the above-named provinces, some 1,000 of them being Moslem separatists. Military operations against the guerrillas resulted inter alia in the occupation by troops of a camp for some 400 guerrillas on Oct. 1, 1975; guerrillas, on the other hand, destroyed, in May 1976, a camp for training village defence volunteers, killing 15 persons, and also attacked a police camp. On July 15, 1976, guerrillas raided Trang, a provincial capital some 80 miles from the Malaysian frontier.

On Nov. 10, 1976, a Thai-Malaysian general border committee decided in Pulau (Penang, Malaysia) to organize joint operations against the Malaysian guerrillas in Thailand's extreme south, and on Jan. 14, 1977, some 2,000 Malaysian troops entered Thailand for joint operations with the Thai army in Songkhla province; most guerrillas were, however, said to have evaded contact with the joint force whose operation was concluded on Feb. 6 with the withdrawal of the Malaysian troops.

Under a revised border agreement signed in Bangkok on March 4, 1977, details were laid down for further joint Thai-Malaysian operations against the guerrillas. In a second such operation (in the Sadao district of Songkhla province) from March 14 to April 20, 1977, eight permanent guerrilla camps were officially stated to have been destroyed (one of them capable of accommodating up to 400 people). Further joint operations began (i) on July 4 in the Betong salient (projecting into the Malaysian state of Perak), a guerrilla stronghold since 1961, and (ii) on July 7 further east, after which it was announced on July 13 that the headquarters of the CPM had been captured. Although the Betong salient operation was ended on Aug. 10 guerrillas continued to be active in that area. Renewed joint Thai-Malaysian operations against the guerrillas were conducted in April-May 1978 and in February 1979. During 1978 the number of Malaysian communist guerrillas operating in southern Thailand was estimated at 2,500.

Thailand and Malaysia signed a further agreement in June 1983, providing for the establishment of a regional border commission to co-ordinate joint counter-insurgency measures along their shared border. According to official Thai estimates in late December 1983, some 1,200 CPM guerrillas were active in the border area. Prior to this announcement an estimated 700 Malaysian communist guerrillas had surrendered on Nov. 7; CPM members were also amongst 361 communist insurgents who surrendered in the southern Thai province of Yala on Aug. 13, 1985.

Lt.-Gen. Wanchai Chitchamnong, the Fourth Army region commander, stated on May 8, 1986, that CPM guerrillas constituted "the only major insurgency" in the Thai-Malaysian border area. He said that this was despite the fact that the Thai Army had been in contact with CPM guerrillas for over two years in an attempt to persuade them to end their armed struggle. Lt.-Gen. Wanchai further referred to the establishment of a Thai forward command post in Pattani to deal specifically with CPM guerrillas.

Communist Party of Thailand (CPT)

Leadership. Thong Chaemsri (gen. sec.)

Originating as the Thai section of the Chinese Communist Party in 1942, the CPT became fully constituted in 1952, when it was banned. This pro-Chinese organization pledged itself to fighting a people's war in the rural areas of Thailand, and began guerrilla activities in 1965 in the north-east of the country (bordering Laos), spreading to the northern provinces and being supported by Hmong tribesmen. In 1969 the CPT established a military wing, the Thai People's Liberation Armed Forces, and the following year it was estimated that between 1,000 and 1,600 CPT guerrillas were operating in the north and some 1,500 in the north-east; they achieved a number of successes—killing 17 policemen and officials (whereafter the construction of a strategic road near the Burmese border was abandoned in July 1970) and also the governor of Chiang Rai province on Sept. 20, 1970. While in March 1970 there had been no evidence that they were receiving significant supplies of arms from China or North Vietnam, their arms supplies greatly increased in 1971 when they began to use mortars, and their strength in the north-eastern provinces alone was said to have risen to between 4,000 and 5,000 men. These guerrillas also made raids on US air bases (used by aircraft bombing North Vietnam) between July 1968 and January 1970, in January 1972 and in June-October 1972.

On Sept. 17, 1974, the CPT claimed for the first time to have established "liberated zones" or "bases" but did not give details of their whereabouts. In October-November 1974 the CPT guerrillas claimed to have killed over 40 soldiers in the north-eastern provinces and to have destroyed four military posts, but the military authorities stated on Dec. 21, 1974, that 215 of the guerrillas had surrendered. It was, however, officially admitted in February 1975 that government forces' losses exceeded those of the guerrillas. In March 1975 martial law was imposed for one year in 28 provinces bordering Laos and Kampuchea, and this was extended for another year on March 9, 1976 (and re-imposed on April 12, 1976, in four provinces where it had been lifted in December 1975).

On Aug. 5, 1975, the guerrillas' strength was variously estimated at between 5,500 and 8,000 men. On April 30, 1976, an army spokesman stated that in the past year about 500 members of the armed forces and the civil service had been killed by guerrillas in all areas. The CPT's radio station, broadcasting as the "Voice of the People of Thailand" (VOPT), it was believed from Yunnan in southern China, claimed on June 27, 1976, that in 1975 the CPT guerrillas had shot down or damaged 18 helicopters. Bangkok radio had, however, announced earlier that a fighter-bomber shot down on June 11, 1976, was the first Thai aircraft thus lost in peace-time. In heavy fighting between June 14 and July 4, 1976, government losses were given as 28 soldiers killed and 85 seriously wounded, and guerrilla losses as over 150 dead. On July 7, 1976, guerrillas made their first raid in the central plains area, overrunning an army outpost in Nakhon Ratchasima province (150 miles north-east of Bangkok).

After the coup of Oct. 6, 1976 (when the military National Administrative Reform Council assumed power) communist guerrilla activity increased greatly; in December 1976 there were said to be 2,000 guerrillas in the north, 3,500 in the north-east, 400 in the central provinces and 2,000 in the south—all having been strengthened by former members of moderate left-wing parties. The VOPT claimed on Oct. 16, 1977, that in the year since the 1976 coup the guerrillas had carried out 717 attacks (compared with 450 in the previous year); had killed 1,475 government troops and had shot down five aircraft.

On June 14, 1976, the Thai Defence Minister estimated the total of communist guerrillas at between 8,000 and 9,000. In an earlier government document of September 1976 it had been asserted that since 1966 over 1,100 guerrillas had received political and military training in Vietnam, Laos or China. By 1978 it was believed that some 1,500 Thai guerrillas were operating at least 15 bases inside Kampuchea with the active support of the Kampuchean army (of the Pol Pot regime). Thai insurgents co-operating with the Kampuchean army were said to have been responsible, between June and October 1978, for 42 per cent of all guerrilla incidents in Thailand and for more than half the civilian casualties.

However, as a result of the growing conflict between Vietnam on the one hand and China and Kampuchea on the other, aid to the CPT guerrillas in Thailand from all these outside sources was greatly reduced during the latter part of 1978. The CPT at first attempted to maintain a neutral position between China and Vietnam, with the party's leadership (many of whose members were ethnic Chinese) taking a pro-Chinese line, whereas many of the Socialists who had joined the guerrillas in 1976-77 adopted a pro-Vietnamese attitude. Some 1,000 pro-Chinese Thai Communists were on June 21, 1979, reported to have been expelled from Laos since March, while several hundred pro-Vietnamese CPT members sought refuge in Laos where they subsequently set up the *Phak Mai* (New Party—see separate entry). These developments weakened the Thai guerrillas, of whom 500 were on July 10, 1979, reported to have surrendered in the past three months.

The VOPT adopted, in a broadcast on June 7, 1979, a pro-Chinese attitude, accusing Vietnam of preparing to invade Thailand and calling on the entire Thai people, including all insurgents, to unite against Vietnamese "aggression". Further such broadcasts, calling for the formation of "a broad national united front" against the "Vietnamese regional hegemonists and their masters, the Soviet social imperialists", continued until July 10, 1979, when they were suspended without any reason being given. The Thai government rejected the call for a united front on July 11 as an attempt to bring about a conflict between Thailand and Vietnam made solely to serve the ends of the CPT.

According to a report by the Bangkok correspondent of *Le Monde*, published on Feb. 23, 1980, the pro-Chinese CPT had condemned the policies of the Pol Pot regime in Kampuchea (which it had previously supported) and had implied that in the conflict with Vietnam (which had invaded Kampuchea in December 1978) Kampuchea had been the aggressor. On July 25, 1980, it was reported that many pro-Soviet Thai Communists (previously trained in Laos) had returned to Thailand. Altogether about one-half of the students and intellectuals who had joined the guerrillas since 1976 returned to Bangkok in 1979-81 as a result of disillusionment with the Chinese-dominated CPT. Udom Thonguai, a leading member of the CPT, surrendered in Bangkok on Dec. 22, 1980.

Despite these divisions and setbacks, guerrilla activities continued in various areas of Thailand. Heavy fighting took place in 1979 in Chiang Rai province (northern Thailand) where over 1,000 troops supported by artillery and aircraft launched an offensive on July 4, in which, it was claimed on Aug. 3, at least 100 guerrillas were killed or wounded, against 200 soldiers killed and 103 wounded; 35 other soldiers were, however, killed in a guerrilla attack on Aug. 25.

The CPT itself claimed in January 1980 that its forces had fought 518 battles with Thai security forces in 1979, especially in north and north-east Thailand and also south of the Isthmus of Kra. By September 1980 CPT guerrillas were said to be operating in 50 of the country's 71 provinces and to number between 8,000 and 15,000. Government forces' losses were given as 544 killed in 1979 (the lowest figure for four years) and 512 in 1980, whereas insurgents' losses in 1980 were stated to be 310 killed and 115 captured (with 1,372 having surrendered), including large-scale surrenders in Uthai Thani province, about 120 miles north of Bangkok, announced on Oct. 4.

The main areas of fighting were (i) in 1980 the southern provinces, where government forces were in August said to have gained full control of the Banthat mountain range and where joint Thai-Malaysian operations were conducted in the Songkhla border province against Malayan communist guerrillas, and (ii) in February-May 1981 the highlands of Phetchabun (about 200 miles north of Bangkok).

On Dec. 22, 1980, government forces had been reported to have seized the north-eastern headquarters of the CPT and its satellite camps. The VOPT resumed its broadcasts from southern China to CPT groups in south and south-eastern Thailand on Dec. 31, 1980. On Jan. 13, 1982, Gen. Saiyud Kerdpo, Supreme Commander of the Armed Forces, gave the total strength of communist insurgents in Thailand as about 7,000 men.

The commander of the Fourth (southern) Army Region affirmed on April 18, 1982, that he would continue his campaign to destroy the CPT in that region, where he estimated the guerrillas to number 3,000 (and where government casualties in the previous two months had amounted to at least 40 killed and 200 wounded); he added that he would later move the forces to the extreme south "to neutralize Islamic separatist groups and Thai-based elements of the Communist Party of Malaya".

The fourth congress of the CPT was held between March and May 1982, when an interim general secretary, Udom Sisuwan, was appointed; in September he surrendered to the authorities, reportedly revealing that the CPT leadership was in a state of disunity. Internal dissension within the CPT was caused partly by a reduction in Chinese support, itself a result of a growing Sino-Thai common approach to the Kampuchea issue. It was reported that an enlarged central committee (comprising 25 full and 10 alternate members) had, following the congress, a slender majority in favour of a more flexible approach to replace the former Maoist emphasis on rural guerrilla struggle. However, the eight-man politburo (which included Thong Chaemsri who was eventually to emerge as general secretary), who were the effective holders of political power within the CPT, was thought to be composed of traditional Maoists.

According to government sources quoted in November 1981 and March 1982, the CPT's main base for guerrilla warfare, established in Nan province (in northern Thailand near the border with Laos) in 1952, had been moved to Tak province (near the Burmese border).

Squadron Leader Prasong Sonsiri, secretary-general of the National Security Council, confirmed on Sept. 10, 1982, earlier estimates that the CPT's fighting strength was at about 7,000.

The Thai army commander, Gen. Arthit Kamlang-ek, claimed on Jan. 23, 1983, that the communist insurgency in north-eastern Thailand had been virtually brought to an end. He was speaking at a ceremony in which nearly 500 CPT guerrillas plus several hundred dependants and sympathizers in Mukdahan province formally defected to the government—this being the second such mass defection in the area within two months. Thai military officials claimed that the latest surrenders had reduced the number of CPT insurgents in the north-east to about 250 and represented a major success for the government's new approach of using political persuasion rather than military force.

In early October 1983, Gen. Arthit made a call for increased political organization in rural and urban areas to combat CPT recruitment. Similarly, Lt.-Gen. Chaovalit Yongchaiyut, then Deputy Army Chief of Staff, issued a statement in late October criticizing the lack of political progress made to match the military successes against the CPT. He issued a warning that a failure to apply Prime Ministerial guideline 66/2523 (which had been issued in 1980 and emphasized the importance of political as well as military responses to end the CPT insurgency) would "lead the masses and fronts—even more than before—to go back to the CPT".

Surachai Sae Dan, a CPT leader arrested in June 1981 allegedly while he was attempting to negotiate a ceasefire with authorities in southern Thailand, was on Oct. 21, 1983, sentenced by a military court in Bangkok to 23 years' imprisonment for sedition.

In an operation on July 3, 1984, members of the Internal Security Operations Command and Special Branch police arrested 16 suspected Communists in various parts of Bangkok. Among those arrested was Phirun Chartvanitkun (a former student leader who had been elected to full membership of the CPT Central Committee at its fourth congress in 1982), his wife and fellow central committee member Chonthira Kladyu, and two other central committee members,

Prasong Arunsantirole and Manote Methangkun. A number of targeted Communists, including CPT politburo member Prasit Tapientong, escaped arrest. All of those arrested were held under the Anti-Communist Activities Act, which allowed detention without trial for up to 480 days. The *Far Eastern Economic Review* of Aug. 23, 1984, reported that six CPT defectors (who had given themselves up under an amnesty offered by the authorities in 1980) had been arrested by police in the north-eastern province of Sakhon Nakhon on July 20. By mid-August over 30 suspected Communists or communist sympathizers were reported to have been arrested, including a professor from Kasetsart University, Dr Preecha Piempongsarn, and the editor of the Thai-language newspaper *Matuphum*, Chatcharin Chaiwat. The anti-communist activities during July and August 1984 caused concern in some sections of Thai society where people feared that the amnesty policy had been abandoned in favour of a new campaign against dissenters.

Martial Law was lifted in 29 provinces on May 23, 1984, and in 13 southern provinces on Oct. 11, because of the reduced threat from communist insurgents (the lifting of the regulations did not, however, apply to all the districts in the provinces). On Aug. 18 five soldiers were killed when CPT guerrillas attacked an army patrol in Surat Thani province in southern Thailand. On Aug. 23 a further nine soldiers were killed in the same area in similar circumstances. Lt.-Gen. Chaovalit, in a speech made in October 1984, claimed that the CPT "will never again be able to pose an armed threat to the country". He went on to claim that in northern Thailand there were only 50-80 communist insurgents left, with a similar number in the north-east, whereas in the south there were between 1,200 and 1,500 armed insurgents with a command centre in Chumphon province. In an assessment in April 1985 Lt.-Gen. Chaovalit estimated that the armed strength of the CPT had been further reduced to about 500, "most of whom were operating more like criminals rather than revolutionaries". This theme was reiterated by Gen. Arthit while speaking on Aug. 13 at a ceremony held in the southern province of Yala to accept the surrender of 361 communist insurgents; he said that the "CPT and other terrorist movements in the southern border provinces no longer exist", and that "we now have only small groups of criminal bandits who operate under the cloak of terrorist movements". Thai authorities revealed in August 1985 that Chaovalit Thapkua, a former CPT central committee member, had defected in April after being released from house arrest by the CPT.

Lt.-Gen. Chaovalit again stressed the continuing relevance of guideline 66/2523 during an annual review of anti-communist strategy held on Oct. 30, 1985. He warned his audience that disunity between civil and military officials, and between political parties, could conceivably result in victory for the CPT; that the CPT had transferred its activities from the jungle and from reliance on rural armed support; and that it had been attempting to infiltrate political parties, student bodies and religious and charitable foundations in urban areas. The *Far Eastern Economic Review* on Jan. 9, 1986, reported that the only significant concentrations of CPT guerrillas were in (i) the southern provinces (between 260 and 350) and (ii) in the north-east and in particular Nakhon Phanom province (between 85 and 115).

Green Star Movement

It is not clear if the Green Star Movement (also known as the Yellow Star Movement) is a fully independent organization or whether it is linked to the Thai People's Revolutionary Movement or to *Phak Mai*/CPT splinter groups operating in north-east Thailand (see separate entries).

Thai intelligence sources reported in June 1985 that this new movement, led by "Comrade" S. Narong, was recruiting members for arms training in Sayaboury province (Laos). A report produced by a Thai newspaper in March 1987, said to be based on a Communist Party of Thailand document, claimed that the Green Star Movement had between 200-300 armed personnel and was currently recruiting members in north-east Thailand to act as "a supporting base for foreign elements which will arrive for the liberation of Thailand". The report described it as "noteworthy" that some of the movement's members looked like Lao or Vietnamese soldiers and did not speak fluent Thai.

New Party (*Phak Mai*)

Leadership. Thoetphum Chaidi, Bunyen Wothong (leaders)

This pro-Vietnamese Communist Party was formed in 1978 by Thai Communists who had sought refuge in Laos after the split of the Communist Party of Thailand (see separate entry). The Party's two leaders were respectively a former trade union leader and a former Socialist (and vice-chairman of the Committee for the Co-ordination of Patriotic and Democracy-loving Forces, CCPDF—see separate entry).

Confused and often contradictory reports on the *Phak Mai*'s activities suggest that it was divided into a number of factions during 1979, several of which were in 1981 united by the Lao government into the Thai People's Revolutionary Movement (see separate entry), which has subsequently been referred to as the *Phak Mai*.

The first division within the *Phak Mai* occurred in November 1979, and a year later Thoetphum Chaidi had reportedly left Laos and returned to Thailand. Guerrillas of one of the party's factions on Jan. 27, 1981, were said to have taken control of areas in and around the southern Thai province of Nakhon Phanom. On Feb. 27, 1981, it was claimed that the *Phak Mai*'s headquarters ("office 75") were at Wattai airport in Vientiane (Laos); by early 1982 its base had reportedly been shifted to a Lao town bordering north-eastern Thailand. Between June and August 1982 various reports suggested that; (i) as many as three pro-Vietnamese factions deriving from the CPT's 1978 split were operating in Laos; (ii) Bunyen Wothong was leading a movement based in Pakse province (Laos) variously described as "Asia 88", *Isan Ekkarat* and Independent North East Party; and (iii) Thai guerrilla groups led by (the *Phak Mai*-associated) Muangthong and Sumit Niamsa ("Comrade Yut") were active in north-east Thailand.

Socialist Party

Leadership. Col. Somkid Srisangkhom (l.); Khaisaeng Suksai (deputy l.)

Until October 1976 the Socialist Party was a legal party which, in January 1975 elections, had obtained 15 out of the 269 seats in the House of Representatives (but only two in the April 1976 elections). Composed largely of students and intellectuals, the party advocated land reform, the setting-up of co-operatives, state control of key services and industries, and the withdrawal of all US forces from Thailand. Following the assumption of power by the National Administrative Reform Council on Oct. 6-7, 1976, when all political parties were dissolved, numerous Socialists were arrested and some party leaders fled the country. Four of these, among them Khaisaeng Suksai, declared in Laos on Oct. 14, 1976, that, while the party had previously used only constitutional and parliamentary methods, this was no longer possible and that, since the "enemies of the people" had "first resorted to violent means to suppress and persecute the people", the Socialists were determined to wage an armed struggle until victory was achieved and were prepared to join with any "patrotic and democratic parties and mass organizations". This declaration was broadcast by the "Voice of the People of Thailand" (VOPT) radio station of the Communist Party of Thailand (CPT) on Oct. 21, 1976. Socialists subsequently joined the guerrilla forces of the CPT and also the Committee for the Co-ordination of Patriotic and Democracy-loving Forces (see separate entry).

The Socialist Party subsequently became the (legal) Social Democratic Party (led by Col. Somkid Srisangkhom and, as General Secretary, Klaew Norpati); in general elections to the House of Representatives held in April 1983 the party gained two seats.

Thai People's Revolutionary Movement

This movement (which is also referred to as the *Phak Mai* or New Party—see separate entry) was reportedly established in July 1981 by the Lao government by the bringing together of "several groupings of Thai people". According to Thai sources the movement's leadership consists of a Presidium chaired by Saly Vongkhamsao (a vice-chairman of the Lao Council of Ministers and chairman of the State Planning Committee), a Vietnamese and a Soviet board of advisers, a seven-member political executive committee and a 13-member military executive committee, whose members include Bunyen Wothong (a founder member and former leader of the *Phak Mai*). It receives financial backing from the Soviet Union and Cuba and its leadership is thought to perceive Thailand as a neo-colony dominated by monopoly capitalists and feudalists who have undermined the country's independence and failed to establish democratic ideals. Its main guerrilla headquarters are reported to be in a former US Central Intelligence Agency base in Sayaboury province (Laos); however, operations (consisting mainly of mobilization and propaganda work in the 17 provinces of north-eastern Thailand) are divided into four zones—(i) the Sayaboury zone led by Muangthong and responsible for activities in Nan, Uttaradit, Phitsanutok and Loei; (ii) the Khammouane zone led by Sakda and responsible for activities in Nakhon Phanom, Mukdahan, Nong Khai, Udon Thani and Sakhon Nakhon; (iii) the Savannakhet zone led by Chaidaen and responsible for Ubon Ratchathani, Yasothon, Roi Et and Mahasarakham; and (iv) the Champassak zone led by Thanong and Sa-Ngop with unknown operational areas.

The *Far Eastern Economic Review* reported on Nov. 8, 1984, that Thai intelligence sources had recently discovered that a guerrilla training course for the movement's members, conducted by Soviet and Vietnamese instructors, had taken place in Laos between April 24 and May 31.

United Socialist Front (USF)

Leadership. Klaew Norpati (l.)

Until October 1976 the USF was a legal political party which in elections to the House of Representatives gained 10 seats in June 1975 but only one in April 1976. Support for the USF came mainly from the impoverished north-eastern provinces, and its aims were similar to those of the Socialist Party, with which it had an electoral agreement after the coup of Oct. 6, 1976, and on Feb. 10, 1977, a statement (similar to that of the Socialist Party of Oct. 14, 1976) issued in the name of the USF declared its readiness to wage an armed struggle against the military regime.

Former USF members subsequently took part in the formation of the Committee for the Co-ordination of Patriotic and Democracy-loving Forces (CCPDF—see separate entry). However, certain former USF members formed, together with former members of the Socialist Party, a Social Democratic Party of which Klaew Norpati became the leader and which was the only left-wing party to take part in the elections of April 22, 1979, to the 301-member House of Representatives provided for under a new Constitution which was approved on Dec. 18, 1978.

Right-wing Organizations

Nawapon

Leadership. Dr Watama Keovimal (l.)

This extreme right-wing Buddhist nationalist movement was in March 1976 reported to claim 500,000 members, to be supported by wealthy businessmen and politicians and to have links with the National Security Council and Thai military intelligence. During the election campaign of February–April 1976 members of *Nawapon* were involved in violent action against left-wing parties and moderate politicians. On Oct. 6, 1976, thousands of members took part in an attack on left-wing students at Thammasat University (Bangkok), which led to the arrest of some 3,000 students and the death of about 40 of them and to the proclamation of martial law, the annulment of the 1974 Constitution and the assumption of power by a National Administrative Reform Council consisting of high-ranking offices of the armed forces.

Red Bulls (*Gaurs*)

Leadership. Maj.-Gen. Sudsai Hasdin (l.)

This extreme right-wing organization, mainly of technical college students, was involved in numerous acts of violence against members of the left-wing National Student's Centre during the election campaign of February–April 1976, and in particular in a bomb attack on Feb. 14 on the headquarters of the New Force Party (a left-wing party formed in 1974 by a group of intellectuals opposed to the military regime). On Aug. 21, 1976, hand grenades thrown into the buildings of the Thammasat University by Red *Gaurs* killed two and wounded 36 persons. Red *Gaurs* were also involved in the storming of the university of Oct. 6, 1976, which led to the assumption of power by the National Administrative Reform Council. On March 11, 1981, the organization's leader, who was also the leader of the extreme right-wing Mass Line Party, was appointed as minister attached to the office of the Prime Minister, Gen. Prem Tinsulanond.

Secessionist Movements

Mujahadin Pattani Movement

According to a spokesman for the Fourth Army this movement is a coalition of three Moslem secessionist movements (PULO, the Pattani National Liberation Front—BNPP, and the *Barisan Nasional Pembebasan Pattani*) and the *Barisan Revolusi Nasional*, formed in September 1985 in an attempt to "revive the situation in the south in their favour".

National Revolutionary Front (*Barisan Revolusi Nasional*, BRN)

Formed in 1961, this Front is thought to be led by Abdul Karim Hassam. It seeks an independent and socialist state in the southern Thai provinces of Pattani, Narathiwat, Yala and Satun. It was one of three movements based in southern Thailand which formed the Mujahadin Pattani Movement in September 1985 (see separate entry).

Pattani Islamic Nationalities' Revolutionary Party (*Phak Patiwat Phaochon Islam Pattani*, PPPIP)

Many of this organization's members were formerly aligned to the National Revolutionary Front (see separate entry). In common with other southern-based Moslem groups it seeks secession for a number of Thai provinces bordering Malaysia.

Pattani National Liberation Front

This organization is led by Badri Hamdan and was first formed in 1947. Its membership consists of a number of Malaysians. In Malaysia both the Kelantan state government and the *Parti Islam* have in the past proffered their support to the Front.

Pattani United Liberation Organization (PULO)

Leadership. Tunku Bira Kotanila; Sama-eh Thanam

Established in 1960, this Moslem secessionist movement conducted operations in the far south of Thailand, where Moslems constituted up to 40 per cent of the population in three provinces (Pattani, Yala and Narathiwat). On Dec. 4, 1975, a bomb was thrown at a Moslem demonstration at Pattani, killing 11 and wounding 44 people; as the perpetrators of this attack were not arrested, PULO sent threatening letters to leading members of the government and to Thai embassies abroad. After serious unrest had continued in the three provinces the government agreed on Jan. 24, 1976, to take action against alleged murderers; anti-government demonstrations nevertheless continued to be mounted until March 4 of that year.

On Oct. 9-10, 1977, four PULO members were arrested and confessed to being members of a PULO sabotage unit and to causing an explosion near the King and Queen at Tambon Sateng (Yala province) on Sept. 22, when 47 people were injured. The four were sentenced to prison terms of up to 60 years in late September 1982. During 1980 PULO terrorist activities, including arson, bombing and kidnapping, increased markedly; on June 7 PULO activists were reported to have killed five Buddhists in Mayo district; on June 30 PULO claimed responsibility for bomb explosions in Bangkok which injured 40 persons; and on July 19 PULO announced the start of a campaign against Thai embassies abroad. In a letter published on the same day in the *Bangkok Post* PULO accused the Thai armed forces of committing "genocide and massacres" against Moslems in Pattani and threatened further acts of violence, including the hijacking of aircraft. At the same time PULO was reported to have united with two other Moslem secessionist groups. On June 6, 1981, over 50 persons were injured in three explosions caused in Bangkok by PULO members.

PULO has demanded complete independence for those southern provinces of Thailand (inhabited by Moslems of Malay stock) which had been independent until they were conquered and annexed by Thailand (then Siam) in the 19th century. In 1980 PULO was estimated to have in the region of 3,000 members.

The commander of the general border office of the army's Joint Operations Centre announced on Jan. 27, 1985, that foreign-trained PULO forces had entered southern Thailand on Nov. 1, 1984, from Kelantan state (Malaysia) and had divided into groups of 10, 13 and 17 to carry out operations in Pattani, Yala and Narathiwat provinces respectively. No armed operations by the PULO forces had been reported as at Jan. 27, 1985, but there were reports of PULO members engaging in "political activities" in Yala province and Muang district.

Reports in May 1986 stated that PULO had in September 1985 united with two other Moslem secessionist movements to form the *Mujahadin Pattani* Movement (see separate entry).

Sabillillah Movement

This Moslem secessionist group has demanded independence for Thailand's southern provinces with a substantial Moslem population. After a bomb had exploded at Bangkok airport on June 24, 1977, literature signed by members of the Movement was found in a suitcase containing a further bomb, which was defused.

Thai Moslem People's Liberation Armed Forces

This organization was formed in August 1977 as an armed wing of the Communist Party of Thailand (CPT) and as a separate organization from the Pattani United Liberation Organization (PULO)—for both of which see separate entries.

Togo

Capital: Lomé

Pop. 2,960,000

The Togolese Republic is ruled by an executive President who is head of state and of the government (which has no Prime Minister). The President is elected by universal adult suffrage for a seven-year term on the proposal of the *Rassemblement du peuple togolais* (RPT), the country's sole legal political organization. There is a National Assembly similarly elected from a list proposed by the RPT.

In elections held on March 23, 1985, a total of 216 candidates contested seats for the 77 deputies in the National Assembly, with 22 alternate deputies being elected at the same time. All citizens who were above the age of 25 years and were members of the RPT were eligible to stand.

In 1970, and again in 1977, it was officially announced that the authorities had foiled coup plots by followers of the former Togolese President Sylvanus Olympio, who was overthrown and killed on Jan. 13, 1963, and for whose death President Gnassingbe Eyadema (who came to power in January 1967) personally accepted responsibility. The alleged leader of the first attempt (made in August 1970), Noë Kutuklui, was on Dec. 1, 1970, sentenced in absentia to 20 years' detention. The 1977 plot was said to have involved a number of mercenaries and eventually resulted in the conviction of 15 alleged ringleaders in August 1979, when 10 were sentenced to death (eight in absentia). The two defendants sentenced to death who were present in court, a Maj. Sanvi and Emmanuel de Souza, were subsequently pardoned by the President, who also rehabilitated other members of the de Souza family who had been deprived of their nationality.

An amnesty granted on July 1, 1985, led to the release of three of those sentenced in August 1979.

The treatment of prisoners in Togo has been criticized in reports by a government commission of inquiry, four representatives of the Association of African Jurists, two French lawyers and Amnesty International (with the last-named concluding after a visit to Togo in October 1985 inter alia that torture of prisoners was "common practice"). The contents of the Amnesty International report were, however, rejected by the Togolese government.

Togolese Movement for Democracy (*Mouvement togolais pour la démocratie*, MTD)

Leadership. Gilchrist Olympio (l.); Paulin Lossou (sec.-gen.)

This movement, based in Paris, claimed on Jan. 15, 1980, that (contrary to an announcement by President Gnassingbe Eyadema to the effect that there were only 11 political prisoners in Togo) several hundred political prisoners were "languishing in Togo's prisons" because they had shown opposition to the regime.

In 1983 the MTD asserted that an alleged plot by mercenaries to assassinate President Eyadema had been "fabricated" by the Lomé government.

An alleged member of the MTD, Ati Randolph, and also Prof. Yema Gu-Kono were arrested in September 1985 and were, on July 30, 1986, given five-year prison sentences for distributing literature hostile to the President.

In the latter half of 1985 President Eyadema blamed the MTD for a number of bomb attacks in Lomé, where two persons were killed and damage was caused to prominent buildings. On Sept. 24 he announced that 15 persons had been arrested for involvement in the attacks and for inciting the armed forces to rebel and overthrow the government. Later in 1985 the Togolese authorities accused the government of Ghana of harbouring MTD members. However, an amnesty granted on Jan. 13, 1986, covered, among others, 14 of the persons arrested for subversion in 1985.

A further attempt to overthrow the government was carried out on Sept. 23-24, 1986, by some 60 attackers, of whom 21 were captured by security forces. Following continued fighting the President requested French military aid (under a 1963 defence agreement), which was supplied between Sept. 26 and Oct. 5 and was reinforced by Zaïrean troops. The Togolese government stated on Sept. 29 that the attacks were part of a plan to instal in power Gilchrist Olympio (a son of the late President Sylvanus Olympio, killed in 1963) and Capt. Francisco Lawson, a former army officer and leading member of the exiled opposition. For their involvement in the attempt, the state security court in Lomé sentenced, on Dec. 19, 1986, (i) 13 persons to death (three of them in absentia, including Gilchrist Olympio) and (ii) 14 others to life imprisonment. Those convicted included three Ghanaians, two Malians and a Burkinabe national.

Trinidad and Tobago

Capital: Port of Spain Pop. 1,149,000

The Republic of Trinidad and Tobago, a member of the Commonwealth, has a President elected for a five-year term by an electoral college constituted by the members of the country's bicameral Parliament which consists of (i) a 36-member House of Representatives elected for five years by universal adult suffrage and (ii) a 31-member Senate appointed by the President (16 senators on the advice of the Prime Minister, six on the advice of the Leader of the Opposition and nine at his own discretion). The Prime Minister and his Cabinet are collectively responsible to Parliament.

In elections to the House of Representatives held on Nov. 9, 1981, the People's National Movement (PNM) was returned for a sixth consecutive term of office by gaining 26 seats; the United Labour Front (ULF) gained eight seats; and the Democratic Action Congress (DAC) gained the two seats allotted to the island of Tobago.

In a general election to the House of Representatives held on Dec. 15, 1986, the umbrella opposition National Alliance for Reconstruction (NAR) decisively defeated the People's National Movement, which had ruled for 30 years. The NAR, formed in 1984 by the three-party Trinidad and Tobago National Alliance and the Organization for National Reconstruction, won 33 seats, the PNM three. Other parties which unsuccessfully contested the elections were the Joint Action Committee and the People's Popular Movement.

In January 1987, the new government acknowledged the right of the island of Tobago to full internal self-government under the terms of an act passed in 1980.

In 1983, 30 people were reported to have been arrested in connection with a coup plot by a Black Moslem group allegedly with the support of a Middle Eastern government (which was not specified). There have been no recent reports of internal political opposition outside existing legal parties.

Tunisia

Capital: Tunis Pop. 7,260,000

The Republic of Tunisia has an executive President and a National Assembly, both elected for five-year terms by universal adult suffrage. The ruling Destour Socialist Party (PSD), called the Neo-Destour Party until 1964, was for many years the country's sole legal party, until it decided in April 1981 in favour of a pluralist system. The first multi-party elections since independence in 1956 were subsequently held on Nov. 1, 1981, and were contested by three opposition parties as well as by a National Front alliance of the PSD and *Union générale des travailleurs tunisiens* (UGTT) trade union federation. The National Front won all of the seats in the Assembly and the three opposition parties all failed to attain the minimum 5 per cent share of the vote which the government had earlier specified as a requirement for eventual legal recognition. The (pro-Soviet) Tunisian Communist

Party had been restored to full legality in July 1981 (after being banned since 1963) without conditions being attached as to performance in the elections. Subsequently the two other parties contesting the 1981 elections—the *Mouvement des démocrates socialistes* (MDS) and the internal faction of the *Mouvement de l'unitè populaire* (MUP)—were granted legal status on Nov. 19, 1983. Elections to the 125 seats in the National Assembly on Nov. 2, 1986, were boycotted by the five legalized opposition parties because of concern over alleged electoral malpractices.

A serious challenge to the government was posed by a one-day strike called by the UGTT on Jan. 26, 1978, which led to civil disorder and the arrest of union leaders. When the UGTT announced a new strike campaign on July 29, 1985, approximately 100 union activists, including the president of the UGTT, were arrested and the union's headquarters were closed down for two months in October 1985.

A government announcement of the doubling of foodstuff prices led to riots in major towns in January 1984. An estimated 100 people were killed and about 1,000 arrested. The measures were withdrawn on Jan. 6, 1984, and the government blamed "hostile elements" for inciting the riots to destabilize the regime.

The Tunisian government has not granted legal status to Moslem fundamentalist groups. On Dec. 17, 1985, the Prime Minister said the authorities would continue to fight "extremism, fanaticism and ideological extravagance", adding that "there will not, in my opinion, be any Khomeinism in Tunisia", making reference to the Ayatollah Ruholla Khomeini, the leader of the Islamic Republic of Iran. Following the arrest in France in August 1986 of six Tunisian passport holders, said by Tunisian offical sources to be linked to the pro-Iranian *Hezbollah* movement in Lebanon, Tunisia severed its diplomatic relations with Iran on March 26, 1987, accusing the Iranian embassy of being instrumental in the recruitment of Islamic militants to carry out destabilization acts. A pro-Iranian network of Islamic militants was said to have been discovered in Tunisia at the time.

Arab National Rally (*Rassemblement national arabe*, RNA)

Leadership. Bechir Essid

The formation of the RNA was announced on May 15, 1981, by Bechir Essid, a Tunis barrister, who stated that the party sought the "development and expansion of the Arabic-Moslem personality of the Tunisian people" and would campaign for "the total unity of the Arabic countries". It was noted by Western press sources that the new party appeared to be differentiating itself from the main Moslem fundamentalist current in Tunisia and that the phraseology of its programme echoed precepts subscribed to by the Libyan regime. The RNA did not contest the November 1981 general elections and has not been legally recognized (fundamentalist movements being ineligible for registration as parties).

Bechir Essid was found guilty of a number of anti-government activities on March 22, 1984, and sentenced to two years' imprisonment. On June 22, 1985, he was further sentenced to one year's imprisonment for "propaganda inciting murder and pillage" and "attacking the dignity" of the President and government during the food price riots of 1984.

Islamic Liberation Party (ILP)

According to the weekly magazine *Maghreb*, a Tunisian branch of the Islamic Liberation Party (ILP) was established in January 1983. The ILP had been founded in Jordan in 1948, and sections existed in other Arab countries. It is a Moslem fundamentalist organization.

On Aug. 25, 1983, 30 members of the ILP were sentenced by a military tribunal on charges of belonging to an illegal organization. They were 19 officers and 11 civilians, who claimed that their aims had been peaceful. They were sentenced to between two and eight years' hard labour or imprisonment.

On March 16, 1985, a total of 36 ILP members charged with subversive activities were sentenced to between six and 18 months' imprisonment.

Islamic Progressive Movement (*Mouvement islamique progressiste*, MIP)

This small Moslem fundamentalist group stands to the left of the more substantial Islamic Trend Movement (see separate entry).

Islamic Trend Movement (*Mouvement de la tendance islamique*, MTI)

Leadership. Rachid Ghanouchi (pres.); Abdel Fatah Mourou (sec.-gen.)

After the establishment of the Islamic Republic of Iran in February 1979, the Moslem fundamentalist (or "integralist") movement greatly increased its following in many Arab countries, including Tunisia, in particular among students. Before the creation of the MTI in 1981, Abdel Fatah Mourou was, together with Hasen Ghodbani, among the leaders of the Khwanyia Movement, whose publication, *Al Moujtamaa*, was banned for three months early in December 1979, when legal proceedings were instituted against its editor and director.

Violent incidents at a number of colleges and schools during February 1981 were officially attributed to activists of the newly formed MTI, but early in May 1981 the MTI leaders rejected such allegations, claiming that the authorities were mounting a campaign against the MTI to deny it legal existence.

On July 11–18, 1981, large-scale arrests took place of Moslem fundamentalists, among them the MTI's president and secretary-general. Following protests against these arrests by the MTI and other opposition groups, the Minister of the Interior stated on July 30 that they were the result of an attempt by Islamic fundamentalists at M'Saken (100 miles south of Tunis) to replace by their own nominee a government-appointed imam (Moslem priest). Referring also to other incidents, the Minister claimed that the group had "contacts with foreign quarters with expansionist aims". On Sept. 4, 1981, a total of 99 Islamic fundamentalists were sentenced (many of them in absentia) to prison terms ranging from one to 11 years, the heaviest sentences being imposed on the MTI's president (11 years) and its secretary-general (10 years). On appeal the president's sentence was, on Oct. 3, 1981, reduced to 10 years.

On Sept. 14, 1981, it was reported that, following demonstrations in support of Ayatollah Khomeini, the Iranian leader, 140 persons had been detained, among them leaders of the MTI. The Movement boycotted general elections held on Nov. 1, 1981, mainly because it objected to the provision that no party gaining less than 5 per cent of the votes would be entitled to offical recognition.

A group of 36 MTI members charged with sedition and attempting to reconstruct the MTI (after the imprisonment of many of its leaders in 1981) were on July 27, 1983, given prison sentences for from two to 10 years. However, on Aug. 1, 1984, pardons were granted to 17 MTI members, among them the MTI president and its secretary-general.

Following Tunisia's severance of diplomatic relations with Iran in March 1987, on the grounds that the Iranian embassy had fomented Moslem agitation in Tunisia, some 250 MTI members were arrested, among them the MTI president. These arrests led to student protests and clashes between police and demonstrators, of whom 20 of the latter were given prison sentences ranging from four to six years in June 1987. Thereafter some 150 other MTI members were arrested.

The MTI has unsuccessfully demanded that all restaurants should be closed for Ramadan, and it has been strongly opposed to tourism and the establishment of Western-type boutiques. Calling the Tunisian President a "despot", the Movement issued, in October 1981, a statement calling for the "resuscitation of the Islamic personality of Tunisia so that it can recover its role as a great home of Islamic civilization in Africa and put an end to the situation of dependency, alienation and decay".

Popular Revolutionary Movement (*Mouvement populaire révolutionnaire*, MPR)

On Nov. 12, 1982, the Tunisian security services announced that about 10 "terrorists" belonging to this organization had been arrested as they were "preparing criminal acts against certain institutions in the capital and its suburbs".

On July 23, 1983, a group of 12 members of the MPR were sentenced to prison terms ranging from two to 10 years for membership of an illegal organization and for planning to attack the United States embassy and the Saudi cultural centre as part of an attempt to destabilize the regime. All the accused denied the charges and claimed that they had been tortured while awaiting trial.

Popular Unity Movement (*Mouvement de l'unité populaire*, MUP)

Leadership. Ahmed Ben Salah (sec.-gen. of external faction)

The MUP was formed in 1973 by followers of the former Economy and Finance Minister, Ahmed Ben Salah, who had originally been a leading theorist of the ruling PSD but had been dismissed and sentenced to 10 years' imprisonment in 1970. After escaping from prison in 1973, Ben Salah later reappeared in exile and as leader of the newly formed MUP campaigned against the Bourguiba regime, with some support within the country.

After the MUP had refused to seek participation in the November 1979 elections, a split developed within the party in early 1981 when President Bourguiba on Feb. 13 granted an amnesty to all MUP members still subject to restrictions or exile, with the specific exception of Ben Salah himself. The amnesty decision was taken after a meeting between the President and MUP activists opposed to the leadership of Ben Salah, this group having the previous month been suspended from MUP membership for entering into contracts with the Interior Ministry for the party's legalization without reference to the official party leadership.

Subsequently, both factions of the party made official applications for legal registration, each claiming to be the authentic MUP. Moreover, the internal MUP faction participated in the November 1981 general elections, whereas the Ben Salah faction continued the party's established policy of boycotting such polls. The internal MUP obtained only 0.8 per cent of the vote in the election and thus failed to attain the 5 per cent share which the government had earlier specified as a minimum requirement for eventual legal registration. (The internal faction, led by Mohammed Balhadj Amour, was granted legal party status on Nov. 19, 1983.)

Progressive Socialist Rally (*Rassemblement socialiste progressiste*, RSP)

On Aug. 15, 1984, *Al Mawquif*, the RSP newspaper, was suspended by the authorities for six months after publication of an article deemed to be offensive to the Islamic religion, but the suspension order was revoked the following day at the instigation of the Prime Minister.

Two members of the RSP were arrested for their part in a demonstration on April 17, 1986, outside the United States embassy after the US air raid on Tripoli and Benghazi in Libya on April 15, 1986. They were given prison sentences of four months each.

In May 1987, a group of 14 members of the RSP were sentenced to six months in prison on charges of belonging to an illegal association. The leader of the RSP was among those detained. They were, however, released by the end of May 1987.

Revolutionary Movement for the Liberation of Tunisia (*Mouvement révolutionnaire pour la libération de la Tunisie*, MRLT)

On March 21, 1985, seven members of the MRLT were sentenced to between five and seven years' hard labour for sabotage attacks which were carried out from Libya.

Tunisian Armed Resistance (*Résistance armée tunisienne*, RAT)

According to the Tunisian authorities, this organization was established among Tunisians working in Libya, where they had been given military training. On Jan. 28, 1981, the movement claimed responsibility for an attack launched on the previous day by some 50 armed men from Algerian territory against the Tunisian town of Gafsa, this attack being intended as "the starting point of a movement whose final aim is the liberation of our people from the dictatorship of the *Parti socialiste destourien* and from neo-colonialist domination". The Tunisian government regarded the attack as having been planned and organized in Libya (while the Algerian government disclaimed any involvement in it), and it was repulsed with heavy losses and numerous insurgents were arrested.

Of those involved in the attack, 15 were on March 27, 1981, condemned to death (two of them in absentia) and 24 were given prison sentences ranging from six months to 20 years (five in absentia). The 13 men hanged on April 17 included Ezzedine Sharif (the alleged organizer of the attack, who had previously served a prison sentence for involvement in the December 1962 assassination plot against President Bourguiba) and Ahmed Mergheni (the military commander of the attack).

The Tunisians involved in the attack were (according to *The Sunday Times* of Feb. 17, 1980) part of a "force of 7,000 volunteer soldiers and terrorists currently training in 20 Libyan camps" and recruited from Egypt, Tunisia, Algeria, Morocco, Mali, Niger, Chad, Guinea, Senegal and the Côte d'Ivoire, and also from South Yemen, Pakistan, the Philippines and North Korea, and including some members of the Irish Republican Army (IRA). These men, described by Col. Gadaffi, the Libyan leader, as "the liberators of the Third World", were said to be receiving training from "several thousand Soviet, Cuban and East German instructors", with planning for guerrilla operations being carried out by a "Bureau for Exporting the Revolution" (*Maktab Tasdir Athaoura*) supervised by Col. Gadaffi.

Turkey

Capital: Ankara

Pop. 51,429,000

Under its Constitution, overwhelmingly approved in a referendum held on Nov. 7, 1982, Turkey is a democratic, secular and social state in which legislative power belongs to the Grand National Assembly (parliament) and in which the President and the Council of Ministers exercise executive power.

As a result of general elections held on Nov. 6, 1983, and of subsequent by-elections, realignments, dissolution of parties and defections of individual deputies, the 400 seats in the Grand National Assembly were, by May 11, 1987, distributed as follows: Motherland Party 255, Socialist Democratic Populist Party 63, True Path Party 40, Democratic Left Party 23, independents 17, vacant two.

Turkey was under martial law from Sept. 12, 1980, onwards, and all political parties were dissolved in October 1981. However, under a presidential decree of April 23, 1983, the ban on political activity was lifted, with certain restrictions remaining in force; in particular some 100 former party leaders were barred from political activity for 10 years. In the elections of November 1983, when voting was compulsory and all persons aged 21 years or over were entitled to vote, those who had failed to vote in the 1982 constitutional referendum were excluded. Moreover, 12 parties were effectively barred from taking part in the elections because the National Security Council exercised its constitutional powers to veto the choice of their candidates.

The military regime, headed by Gen. Kenan Evren as President of the Republic, endeavoured to dismantle the existing militant organizations of the extreme left and also brought to trial many right-wingers who had been involved in violent attacks on the left carried out before the military takeover in 1980. The National Security Council, which had then assumed power, was formally dissolved on Dec. 6, 1983, but Gen. Evren remained President of the Republic under transitional provisions of the 1982 Constitution.

By early 1981 some 30,000 persons were in detention for suspected terrorist activities, the majority of them being members of some 40 different left-wing groups. On Aug. 14, 1981, the Prime Minister declared that since the military takeover there had been 459 victims of political violence as against 3,710 in the preceding 21 months. By the end of December 1981 it was officially stated that most terrorist groups in Turkey had been dismantled; that about 45,000 persons had been arrested since Sept. 12, 1980, with about 30,000 of them having been charged with offences, for which 85 death sentences had been passed, of which 11 had been carried out. It was also claimed that no less than 662 organizations were operating against Turkey from abroad; 286 of them were described as extreme left-wing, 17 as separatist and 280 as religious extremist. The National Security Council stated on Jan. 1, 1982, that 7,662 alleged terrorists were still at large, some of them in Europe, and it announced shortly afterwards that since September 1980 a total of 794,661 rifles or pistols and 5,271,000 rounds of ammunition had been seized.

The Turkish news agency Akajans reported on Feb. 12, 1982, that there were 24,377 persons (including 13 former politicians and 64 trade union leaders) under arrest and another 7,034 in detention (for up to 45 days), all officially for "terrorist activities" or for "attempting to overthrow the democratic order by revolutionary struggle under cover of Marxism-Leninism".

On Jan. 13, 1983, it was reported that there were then 9,817 persons awaiting trial for martial law offences, including some 3,000 for whom the death penalty had been demanded; that another 6,942 persons were under investigation for alleged offences; and that 27,818 persons had already been sentenced by martial law courts, of whom 98 had received death sentences, 24 of which had been carried out.

On May 7, 1985, the Grand National Assembly adopted a bill providing for leniency for members of illegal organizations who turned state's evidence; a presidential veto on the bill was overruled by the Assembly on June 5.

On March 11, 1986, the Assembly passed legislation restricting the use of the death penalty and reducing prison terms by more than half. (None of the death sentences passed had been carried out since 1984.)

By March 19, 1987, martial law had been lifted everywhere except in four Kurdish-speaking provinces, but a state of emergency (administered by the civilian provincial governor) persisted in four other Kurdish-speaking provinces and in Istanbul.

Left-wing Movements

Communist Party of Turkey (CPT)

Leadership. Haydar Kutlu (gen. sec.)

Communists took part in the Turkish national movement in 1918-22, during which the CPT was founded on Sept. 10, 1920. The party was banned in 1923, and under Articles 141 and 142 of the Turkish penal code of 1926 (modelled on that of Fascist Italy) communist propaganda and activities were prohibited; moreover, any initiatives designed to overthrow the Constitution by force or to set up an association with the object of establishing the domination of one social class by another were made liable to long terms of imprisonment or even the death penalty. The CPT, however, continued its underground activities and, since World War II, has had its headquarters in East Berlin.

Following the military takeover in September 1980, hundreds of alleged party members were arrested, and in September 1981 it was stated in the Turkish press that the party had divided Turkey into six sections and had called for the establishment of a Kurdish state in eastern Anatolia and of an "independent socialist state" without military bases in Cyprus. It was also said to have called for the repeal of Articles 141 and 142 of the penal code to enable it to assume power legally, failing which it would set up a national democratic front as an umbrella organization of all "antifascist" elements.

On Aug. 15, 1982, three party leaders were given long prison sentences for their activities, and on May 25, 1983, nine party members were, in Istanbul, sentenced to death and eight others to life imprisonment for attempting the armed overthrow of the state; another 40 were given prison terms of up to 24 years.

On March 29, 1985, a military court in Ankara sentenced 234 CPT members to imprisonment for from 32 months to 17 years and five months. A sentence of six years and five months in prison was imposed in Izmir on Nov. 13, 1986, on Servet Ziya Corakli, a writer, for his membership of the CPT.

Early in 1987 the CPT was, according to the police in Istanbul, "trying hard" to recruit sympathizers from among university students.

Confederation of Revolutionary Trade Unions of Turkey (DISK)

Leadership. Abdullah Bastürk (ch.); Fehmi Isiklar (sec.-gen.)

DISK was established in 1967 as a legal trade union organization. Those of its members who had been found guilty of acts of violence before 1974 were amnestied in that year. The organization was involved in numerous strikes and also in a May Day demonstration in Istanbul (where it was banned) in 1978, when troops opened fire and killed about 90 persons, and in another one in 1979 in Izmir (where it was permitted). In September 1980 (when its membership had reached 400,000) DISK's activities were suspended.

At the end of a five-year trial a military court in Istanbul sentenced 264 senior DISK members to prison terms of up to 10 years on Dec. 23, 1986 (under an article of the penal code forbidding "organizing to establish the supremacy of one social class over another"). Cetyn Vygour, former leader of the miners' union (affiliated to the DISK), was given a 15-year prison term after being convicted of having links with the banned Revolutionary Left (*Dev-Sol*—see separate entry). The court also ordered that the DISK and 28 of its 31 affiliated trade unions should be disbanded. (More than 2,000 DISK members were reported to have fled Turkey to avoid prosecution.)

Illumination Group

This left-wing group was, according to the police in Istanbul, active in early 1987 in order to recruit sympathizers from among university students.

Marxist-Leninist Armed Propaganda Unit

This grouping, said to be the "hit squad" of the Turkish People's Liberation Party (see separate entry), was held responsible for numerous assassinations, including those of several US servicemen in Turkey, carried out in 1979-80. On Jan. 2, 1980, members of the Unit killed Abraham Elazar, manager of the Israeli airline El Al in Istanbul. On Sept. 17, 1980, Zeki Yumurtaci, a leader of the Unit awaiting trial on murder charges, was killed in a shooting incident.

Four members of the Unit, said to have been involved in the killing of 29 persons (also including US servicemen) in May and November 1979, were killed by police in May 1981.

On Sept. 30, 1984, a court in Istanbul sentenced 22 members of the Unit to death and 45 to life imprisonment for committing 87 murders, including those of the US servicemen in 1979.

Revolutionary Communist Union of Turkey

A member of this group was sentenced to death in September 1985, and 17 others were given prison sentences of up to 24 years. A further four members were sentenced to death in Adana in May 1986.

Revolutionary Left (*Dev-Sol*)

The *Dev-Sol* was the first extreme left-wing group to pledge itself to public opposition to the military regime set up on Sept. 12, 1980. Members of *Dev-Sol* sentenced to imprisonment in 1971-73 had been amnestied in 1974.

In 1980 *Dev-Sol* members were responsible for the assassination of Gun Sazak (deputy chairman of the National Action Party) on May 22; of Dr Nihat Erim (Prime Minister in 1971-72) on July 19; of an intelligence agent in Istanbul on July 30; of two policemen in Ankara on Sept. 1; and of a senior policeman in Istanbul on Sept. 17. *Dev-Sol* was also held responsible for the murder of a deputy chief of security in Istanbul on Feb. 6, 1981.

On May 1, 1981, it was reported that Mustafa Isik, a *Dev-Sol* member suspected of having killed two security agents, had been shot dead by police. On Nov. 16, 1981, six *Dev-Sol* members were condemned to death for the assassination of Dr Erim in July 1980 and of the Istanbul police chief early in 1981. On March 15, 1982, five *Dev-Sol* members were sentenced to death in Izmir for four political murders and "conspiracy to establish a proletarian dictatorship", while three other defendants were given life sentences and 43 prison sentences of from two to 15 years.

On Feb. 17, 1984, in Istanbul, seven alleged *Dev-Sol* members were sentenced to death and 46 to imprisonment for from three to 20 years.

According to government sources *Dev-Sol* had, before the military takeover of Sept. 12, 1980, agreed on co-operation with the Popular Front for the Liberation of Palestine (PFLP) led by Dr Georges Habash, whereby the PFLP would supply *Dev-Sol* with weapons and training and enable it to open an office in Beirut. Since March 1980 the PFLP was said to have supplied *Dev-Sol* with 1,000 pistols, 300 Kalashnikov machine-pistols, 500 hand grenades and 10 small grenade-throwers.

According to the police in Istanbul, *Dev-Sol* was early in 1987 again trying to recruit sympathizers from among university students.

Revolutionary People's Union

In a trial of members of this Union (said to be part of the Turkish Communist Party—Marxist-Leninist—see separate entry) which ended in Adana in April 1984, over 80 death sentences were passed, as well as 16 life sentences and 133 prison sentences of up to 27 years. In a further trial which ended in Adana on April 28 another seven Union members were given death sentences for forming an armed organization to establish a Marxist dictatorship, while two defendants were given life sentences and another 17 prison sentences of up to 12 years each.

Revolutionary Way (*Dev-Yol*)

Leadership. (Mrs) Gulten Çayan (based in Paris)

Before the military takeover of September 1980 this organization had held a dominant position in several small towns and had engaged in numerous acts of violence, in particular against political opponents. Under the military regime large numbers of the organization's members were arrested and tried.

By the end of 1981 *Dev-Yol*'s headquarters were believed to have been set up in Paris, the organization's six-member committee being headed by Gulten Çayan, whose husband, Mahir Çayan, had been the most influential leader of the Association of Revolutionary Youth (*Dev-Genc*) and a founder-member of the Turkish People's Liberation Army (TPLA—see separate entry). In 1971 he had been tried for conspiring to overthrow the state and for involvement in other crimes, including the murder of the Israeli consul-general in Istanbul in May 1971; during the trial he had escaped from prison in November of that year but had himself been killed, with other TPLA members, on March 30, 1972.

An attempt to revive the *Dev-Yol* group in Turkey in 1982 appears to have failed, as many hundreds of alleged *Dev-Yol* supporters were arrested and tried on various charges, including an attempt to create a left-wing "liberated zone" at Fatsa on the Black Sea coast.

Trials of *Dev-Yol* members concluded in 1984-86 resulted in convictions as follows:

On Jan. 24, 1984, eight men were sentenced to death, three to life imprisonment and 150 to prison terms of up to 24 years at Giresun (Erzincan province). In Izmir on May 21, 1984, 13 men were sentenced to death, 14 to life imprisonment and another 80 to prison terms of up to 26 years.

On Jan. 29, 1985, six men sentenced to death had their sentences commuted to life imprisonment, while 22 were sentenced to imprisonment for from three to 14 years. On March 14, 1985, three further death sentences were passed, and on April 16 five other men were also sentenced to death for terrorist activity before the 1980 coup, and 10 to life imprisonment, while 75 were given prison terms ranging from five to 20 years. On May 15 one defendant was sentenced to death in Erzincan, while 12 others received life sentences and 132 prison terms of from five to 20 years. On May 21 two others were given death sentences and 68 prison sentences ranging from one to 14 years. On Nov. 11 a court in Erzurum sentenced 11 *Dev-Yol* members to death and 362 to terms of imprisonment.

In June 1986 three members received death sentences in Erzincan for trying to overthrow the state, while two were given life sentences and 42 terms of imprisonment for up to 16 years. Over the same period a military court in Adana sentenced 19 members to death, 13 to life imprisonment and 156 to imprisonment for up to 24 years.

On Feb. 16, 1987, two alleged *Dev-Yol* members were sentenced to death in Erzurum, one to life imprisonment and 46 others to imprisonment for between two and nine years.

Turkish Communist Party—Marxist-Leninist (AKKO)

This Maoist party, formed in 1973, attempted to set up a Turkish Revolutionary Peasants' Liberation Army. On Jan. 30, 1980, a total of 98 members of the party were arrested and charged with murder, and by September 1981 there were 178 alleged party members being tried for armed insurrection. The AKKO's principal founder, Ibrahim Kaypakkaya, died in custody following the military takeover of September 1980.

In 1984 over 80 of its members were sentenced to death and 168 to terms of imprisonment.

Turkish Peace Association (TPA)

Leadership. Mahmut Dikerdem (pres.)

Established in 1977, this Association was officially dissolved shortly after the military takeover of Sept. 12, 1980. On Feb. 26, 1982, 42 of its leading members were arrested, among them Mahmut Dikerdem (a former ambassador).

However, by March 10, 1986, all detained leaders of the TPA were released. Nevertheless 12 of its members were on April 28, 1987, sentenced to varying terms of imprisonment, with Mahmut Dikerdem being given four years and two months, for being members of an illegal oganization seeking to overthrow the state.

The Association was officially regarded as the Turkish section of the World Peace Council founded in Warsaw in 1950 and based in Helsinki.

Turkish People's Liberation Army (TPLA)

The TPLA, formed in 1970, was responsible for a number of terrorist actions in 1971 for which its then leader, Deniz Gezmis, and 17 other TPLA members were sentenced to death on Oct. 9, 1971, with five others also being condemned to death on Dec. 27, 1981. The execution of Gezmis and two others was carried out on May 6, 1972, and there followed further acts of violence by TPLA members during that year.

On June 6, 1984, an Ankara court passed two death sentences, one sentence of life imprisonment and 18 others of up to 15 years in prison on TPLA members for seeking to establish a Marxist-Leninist social order.

Turkish People's Liberation Party Front (TPLF)

During 1980-81 numerous members of this organization were arrested and tried for various offences.

Trials concluded in 1984-86 were as follows: (i) on Sept. 28, 1984, four TPLF members were sentenced to death, five were given life sentences and 16 were given prison terms of up to 16 years for murder, armed robbery and attempting to overthrow the state; (ii) on Nov. 8, 1984, an Istanbul court sentenced 10 members to death on similar charges, as well as 25 to life imprisonment and 71 to prison terms of up to 23 years; (iii) on March 26, 1985, three TPLF members were sentenced to death in Izmir; and (iv) on Aug. 5, 1986, three members were sentenced to death (also in Izmir) for acts of violence carried out before the 1980 coup.

Turkish Revolutionary Peasants' Liberation Army—

see under Turkish Communist Party—Marxist-Leninist (AKKO)

Turkish Teachers' Union (*Tob-Der*)

Leadership. Gultekin Gazioglu (pres.)

On Dec. 26, 1972, prison sentences of up to eight years and 10 months were imposed on 59 members of the Turkish Teachers' Union for having founded a "secret organization" and carried out communist propaganda and illegal activities. After the military takeover of Sept. 12, 1980, *Tob-Der* was closed down and its property confiscated. Its president left for West Germany soon afterwards and was subsequently deprived of his Turkish nationality. On Dec. 25, 1981, a total of 50 former officials of the union were sentenced to imprisonment for from one to nine years on charges of attempting to overthrow the state.

Turkish Workers' Party

This party broke away from the Communist Party of Turkey (CPT—see separate entry) in 1975. Its dissolution was ordered by the constitutional court in 1980 on the ground that its demand that Kurdish children should be educated in their own language contravened the Constitution.

On Jan. 28, 1984, a military court in Istanbul sentenced 14 former leaders of this banned party to between eight and 12 years in prison for attempting to form an organization aimed at creating a Marxist-Leninist state, while another 88 defendants were each given five years' imprisonment.

Turkish Workers' and Peasants' Liberation Army (*Tikko*)

On May 28, 1984, a court in Ankara sentenced 27 alleged members of this organization to death, another eight to life imprisonment and a further 129 to prison terms ranging from three to 29 years for trying to set up a Marxist dictatorship. On June 10 of that year a court in Istanbul passed two life sentences and 50 shorter prison sentences on members accused of violent offences committed before the 1980 coup. On June 14, 1984, a court in Diyarbakir sentenced 10 alleged *Tikko* members to death, two to life imprisonment and nearly 100 to prison terms of up to 24 years.

Worker-Peasant Party of Turkey (*Türkiye Isçi Köylü Partisi,* TIKP)

Leadership. Dogu Perinçek (ch.)

This Maoist formation was established in January 1978 and was originally legal although not represented in parliament. Immediately after the September 1980 military takeover Dogu Perinçek and 24 other members were arrested, as were 42 other leading members in November 1980—all being charged with trying to establish an illegal organization aimed at "overthrowing the basic social order".

After the Turkish military government had threatened to deprive all political refugees of their Turkish nationality, Mustapha Kemal Çamkiran, a leading TIKP member who had fled to West Germany, returned to Turkey in March 1981 and was thereupon detained at a military prison until February 1985, when he was released.

On May 24, 1983, death sentences were imposed in Diyarbakar on 35 leading TIKP members for attempting to establish a separate Kurdish state, while 28 others were given life sentences and 331 were sent to prison for from three to 36 years.

At the end of February 1985 D. Perinçek and four other TIKP members were conditionally released from detention.

The TIKP is opposed to "imperialism and [Soviet] social-imperialism". In its constitution it has described itself as "the revolutionary political party of the working class of Turkey with the ultimate aim of the realization of the classless society".

Right-wing Movements

Various movements of the extreme right were engaged in violent action against the left in the period before the September 1980 military takeover. Thereafter such movements generally backed the Evren regime in its offensive against the extreme left but were themselves frequently the subject of trials brought by the authorities for illegal activities mainly carried out in the period before September 1980.

Grey Wolves ("Idealists")

Leadership. Col. Alparslan Türkes (l.)

This organization is the militant youth wing of the extreme right-wing National Action Party (also led by Col. Türkes—see separate entry). Assassinations attributed to Grey Wolves members included that of Abdi Ipekçi (editor of the influential daily *Milliyet* and friend of Bülent Ecevit, the former leader of the Republican People's Party), who was murdered on Feb. 1, 1979. The person convicted of this crime was Mehmet Ali Agca, who was condemned to death in absentia in April 1980 after escaping from prison in November 1979 and fleeing the country.

The sentence was confirmed by the Turkish Consultative Assembly on March 4, 1982, but meanwhile Agca had shot and wounded the Pope in Rome on May 13, 1981, and had been sentenced to life imprisonment by an Italian court on July 22, 1981. A Turkish request for his extradition was refused by Italy.

On March 29, 1986, a Rome court sentenced Agca to one year in prison and two months' solitary confinement for illegally importing the weapon used in the attack on the Pope; during his trial Agca alleged that the Grey Wolves had been implicated in preparations for the attack.

Trials of Grey Wolves members had earlier taken place in June 1984, when one defendant was sentenced to death in Izmir; in October 1984, when one was sentenced to death and another to life imprisonment, while 20 others received prison sentences of from five to 36 years; on Dec. 12, 1984 (at Eskisehir), when one member was sentenced to death and 14 others received prison sentences ranging from eight to 29 years; and in March 1985, when two members were sentenced to death; and in December 1985, when seven were sentenced to death and 86 to imprisonment for up to 36 years.

National Action Party (NAP) (*Milliyetçi Hareket Partisi*)

Leadership. Col. Alparslan Türkes (ch.)

Established in 1948, this right-wing party claimed a membership of over 300,000 prior to the September 1980 military takeover. Formerly known as the Republican Peasant Nation Party, it had taken part in various coalition governments and in the 1977 elections obtained 16 of the 450 Assembly seats.

In its campaign against political extremism of both the left and the right, the Evren regime has taken action against many hundreds of NAP members for alleged political violence, including the murder of left-wing opponents. By August 1981 nearly 600 party activists were on trial.

On May 11, 1984, two NAP members were sentenced to death in Izmir for murders and robberies committed before the 1980 coup; another defendant was given a life sentence; and a further 20 received prison sentences of up to 36 years.

On July 15, 1986, a military court in Ankara sentenced three NAP members to death, six others to life imprisonment, seven to 36 years and 27 members to 25 years each in prison for murder, bombing and robberies committed in the late 1970s.

Col. Türkes was sentenced by a military court in Ankara on April 7, 1987, to just over 11 years in prison, while five other defendants were sentenced to death, nine to life imprisonment and 221 to imprisonment for up to 36 years. Col. Türkes was not to serve any more time in prison as he had earned remission after being detained for 4½ years, but he was sentenced to 11 years' enforced residence in Ankara.

The NAP was strongly anti-communist and nationalist, standing for the defence of freedom and of the interests of the peasantry. It promoted the formation of various militant right-wing organizations outside its own party framework, such as the Grey Wolves (see separate entry).

Moslem Fundamentalists

On Jan. 8, 1987, President Kenan Evren warned the nation that "concessions to Moslem fundamentalists would be just as dangerous to Turkey as communism", and he called on the country's politicians to unite against them.

The principal Moslem fundamentalist organizations which have been active in Turkey are listed below.

Alevi Moslem Sect

After the Sunni and the (Shia) Alevi Moslem sects in Turkey had for several centuries lived in relative peace with each other, a polarization had begun in 1970, with the Sunnis favouring conservative policies and the generally under-privileged Alevis left-wing ones. In December 1978 fighting broke out between members of the two sects at Kharamanmaras (south-eastern Turkey) and 111 persons were killed and over 900 buildings destroyed. Some 800 persons were subsequently tried, 330 of them for "armed insurrection and murder"; on Aug. 8, 1980, 22 of the defendants were condemned to death, and over 360 other persons received prison sentences of varying lengths. However, only 13 of the 22 death sentences were upheld by the supreme military court on July 11, 1983, while five out of 14 persons serving life sentences were acquitted.

A further riot at Çorum (northern Anatolia) led to the imposition of a curfew on May 28, 1980, when 22 persons, most of them members of the Alevi sect, were believed to have been killed and mainly Alevi-owned shops and houses had been destroyed. In January 1982 it was reported that a group of left-wing Armenians, led by Garbis Altinoglu, had been involved in the killings at Kharamanmaras in December 1978.

Moslem Brotherhood Union

The principal Islamic fundamentalist party, opposed to the institutionalization of the secular state in Turkey under the 1928 Constitution, has been the National Salvation Party (see separate entry). Islamic fundamentalism has, however, also been propagated by the relatively small Turkish section of the Moslem Brotherhood (deriving from the movement originally formed in Egypt—see page 84).

Like other Islamic fundamentalist movements, the Turkish Moslem Brotherhood seeks the establishment of a state based on the rule of Koranic law.

National Salvation Party (NSP) (*Milli Selamet Partisi*)

Leadership. Prof. Necmettin Erbakan (ch.)

Founded in October 1972 as the continuation of the proscribed National Order Party, the NSP became the principal political expression of Islamic fundamentalism in Turkey. Having become, with 48 seats, the third strongest parliamentary party in 1973, it entered a coalition government (led by the Republican People's Party) in January 1974—the first Islamic party to share power since the secularization of the state in 1928. After further governmental participation from March 1975 (this time in coalition with the Justice Party), it gained votes in the June 1977 general elections but saw its representation in the 450-member Assembly halved to 24 seats. It went into opposition in December 1977.

Following the military takeover of September 1980, the NSP came into conflict with the Evren regime and was, together with all other registered parties, officially dissolved in October 1981. The party leader, Prof. Erbakan, had earlier been brought to trial in April 1981 (together with 33 other NSP members) on charges of attempting to create an Islamic state in Turkey. He was eventually sentenced to four years' imprisonment on Feb. 24, 1983, for "anti-laicism".

Nationalist View Organization (NVO)

Leadership. Cemalettin Kaplan

This organization is based in West Germany under the leadership of C. Kaplan, a former mufti who considers himself to be the Khomeini of Turkey. According to official Turkish sources reported on Feb. 5, 1987, its militants were trained in Iran and supplied with funds and weapons (one Kalashnikov and 120 rounds of ammunition per man) by the Khomeini regime in Iran. Their object was said to be to destroy the secular regime in Turkey and to replace it with a regime based on the religion of Islam, under which a Union of Islamic Societies and Congregations could establish itself in the country. The militants were said to be infiltrating Turkey's eastern provinces.

On Feb. 6, 1987, it was reported that three members of the organization had been arrested after entering Turkey illegally and that their interrogation had revealed that the NVO was carrying out fundamentalist activities in Istanbul and Konya.

Armenian Movements

During World War I the government of the Ottoman Empire decided in August 1915 to "solve the Armenian question once and for all" by exterminating the (Christian) Armenians. The action which followed and which was later described by Armenians as "systematic genocide" resulted in the death of some 1,400,000 people and the flight of the survivors from Turkey, half of them to the Russian part of Armenia and the remainder to Middle East countries, Europe and North America. In mid-1981 the total number of Armenians was estimated at 6,000,000, of whom some 2,800,000 lived in the Armenian Soviet Socialist Republic, about 200,000 in Lebanon, about the same number in France and some 500,000 in the United States.

While many of these Armenians became assimilated to the peoples of the countries to which they had moved, others maintained their own culture and associations and their adherence to the Armenian Catholic Church. It was only in the third generation since the events of 1915 that a demand was raised by Armenians for the establishment of a united and independent Armenia (which some of them wanted to be socialist). In France a Committee for the Defence of the Armenian Cause (*Comité de dèfense de la cause arménienne,* CDCA) was set up in 1965, and it has published a journal, *La Cause Arménienne*. In Lebanon Armenians first began to commit acts of violence directly related to their cause in the 1970s.

The organizations subsequently formed to conduct "warfare" against the Turkish authorities (and also those who were deemed to co-operate with them) represented, however, only a minority of the Armenians as a whole; many Armenian organizations repeatedly condemned those of their fellow countrymen engaged in acts of violence. The Turkish government, on the other hand, has not given in to the demands made by militant Armenians and consistently refuses to accept any responsibility for the 1915 events.

The principal Armenian groups responsible for violent activities are listed below.

Armenian Liberation Movement (*Mouvement libération arménienne*)

This organization was set up by Armenians in France to support the Armenian Secret Army for the Liberation of Armenia (ASALA—see separate entry). However, in a statement issued on Nov. 17, 1981, it condemned the militant Armenian grouping known as the Orly Organization (see separate entry), calling it "one of the biggest anti-Armenian provocations".

Armenian National Liberation Movement

In a radio programme identified as the "Voice of the Armenians of Lebanon" broadcast by the "Voice of the Arab Revolution" on April 10, 1982, it was declared that this Movement believed "in the necessity of armed resistance against the enemy—the Turkish government". It was claimed that the Movement had reactivated the Armenian armed struggle which had been "buried for 63 years"; that it had "achieved international status along with other revolutionary organizations and struggling peoples"; that it had "forced the Turkish government to recognize our cause"; and that since 1979 the Armenian people in the diaspora had revised their ideas as a result of the Lebanese civil war, the Iranian revolution and the organization of progressive Armenian youth in Europe and the United States.

The same broadcast asserted that the Movement had entered its second phase, consisting of "heavy attacks against imperialists, Zionists and reactionaries, continuous strikes against our main enemy, direct communication with the Armenian masses and the peoples of the world, and firm relations with revolutionary organizations and joint operations together with the Kurdish Workers' Party"—based on "the natural unity of the Armenian and Kurdish peoples".

Armenian Revolutionary Army

On July 27, 1983, six members of this group attacked the Turkish embassy in Lisbon killing two persons, but the attackers blew themselves up as police moved in. The group also claimed responsibility for a car bomb exploded outside the Turkish embassy in Vienna, on June 20, 1984, when one person was killed and two were injured.

Three members of the group stormed the Turkish embassy in Ottawa (Canada) on March 12, 1985, and killed a Canadian security guard and held 12 persons hostage for more than four hours before surrendering to the police. On Oct. 1, 1986, the three attackers were sentenced to life imprisonment.

Armenian Secret Army for the Liberation of Armenia (ASALA)

Established in 1975, this organization, based in Beirut and consisting of Lebanese of Armenian descent, has directed several hundred violent operations, mainly against Turkish institutions abroad but also against the airlines and other agencies of countries whose governments were considered to be favourably inclined towards the Turkish government (i.e. notably against targets in Switzerland, Britain, France, Italy and the United States).

Although the ASALA's declared objective is the "liberation" and unification of Armenia, a spokesman for the organization has been quoted as saying that the Soviet part of Armenia, i.e. the Armenian Soviet Socialist Republic, is "liberated" and constitutes no problem. The ASALA regards itself as part of the worldwide revolutionary movement and thus at peace with the Soviet Union; it is strongly anti-American, has described the Turkish state as having a "fascist regime" and seeks to co-operate with the left-wing Kurdish movement. It regards the Armenian question as a product of "imperialist conflicts" and therefore attacks imperialism wherever it may be (like the Popular Front for the Liberation of Palestine but unlike the Justice Commandos for the Armenian Genocide—see separate entry).

The ASALA claimed responsibility for the killing of the Turkish ambassador in Vienna on Oct. 22, 1975, and of that in Paris (with his chauffeur) on Oct. 24, as well as that of the Turkish press attaché in Paris on Dec. 22, 1979. It made similar claims for the bombing of the Turkish Airlines office in Rome on March 3, 1980 (when two passers-by were killed); for the shooting of four persons at the Turkish consulate in Lyons (France) on Aug. 5; for the wounding of the Turkish press attaché in Paris on Sept. 26; and for explosions at the Alitalia office in Madrid on Oct. 5, the Turkish airlines office in London on Oct. 12, the Swissair office in Madrid on Nov. 2, and the Turkish consulate-general in Strasbourg on Nov. 10, 1980.

The following year it was responsible for an attack on a Turkish economic and financial counsellor near Paris on Jan. 13, 1981; for the murder of two Turkish diplomats in Paris on March 4; for an attack on a Turkish diplomat in Denmark on April 2; and for an attack on the Turkish Airlines office in Copenhagen on Sept. 15, 1981. Four ASALA members surrendered to the French police in Paris on Sept. 25, 1981, after they had temporarily seized 50 hostages at the Turkish consulate and had demanded the release of Armenian political prisoners in Turkey, as well as of five Turkish and five Kurdish revolutionaries. The Turkish government maintained that there were no such prisoners in Turkey.

After Mardiros Jamkodjian, an ASALA member, had been sentenced in Geneva on Dec. 19, 1981, to 15 years in prison following his admission that he had killed a Turkish consular employee in Geneva in June 1980, the ASALA threatened action against "all Swiss government and civil institutions and all representatives of the Swiss government" unless the sentence was reconsidered within a week. However, the ASALA's position changed after Max Kilndjian, another Armenian (who had on Dec. 23, 1981, been given a two-year sentence in France for complicity in an attempt to murder the Turkish ambassador in Switzerland on Feb. 6, 1980) had been released on Jan. 29, 1982. (Responsibility for the February 1980 attack had been claimed by the Justice Commandos for the Armenian Genocide.) The ASALA declared on the same day that the French government had complied with its demands (including the granting of political status to the four men arrested in connexion with the action at the Turkish consulate in Paris on Sept. 24-25, 1981) and that further operations against French interests would therefore be halted.

The ASALA's operational capability was reported to have been weakened as a result of the Israeli invasion of Lebanon in mid-1982; nevertheless, attacks attributed to its members continued to occur in France and elsewhere in late 1982 and early 1983.

In 1983 the ASALA claimed responsibility for an attack on the Turkish embassy in Brussels on July 14 and for an attack on Orly airport (near Paris) on July 15, when eight persons received fatal injuries and 55 others were also injured while waiting for a flight to Israel. (For the latter attack three Armenians were, on March 3, 1985, sentenced respectively to life imprisonment and 15 and 10 years in prison.) On July 16 the ASALA warned the French government of continued bloodshed unless all Armenian suspects were released within two days (which demand was not met). The ASALA further claimed responsibility for three bomb attacks on French targets in Tehran (Iran) on July 23-24, and other ASALA attacks were carried out on the French embassy in Tehran on Aug. 7 and 10 and Sept. 7, 1983. From March 27, 1984, the ASALA carried out further attacks, in particular on French targets in Iran.

On June 13, 1986, three ASALA members convicted of conspiring to kill a Turkish diplomat were sentenced in Ottawa to between two and nine years in prison. During the trial of Monte Melkonian, a leading ASALA member (sentenced to six years in prison in Paris on Dec. 12, 1986), it was disclosed that documents found in his possession had implicated the ASALA in attacks on Armenian targets in Europe in the name of fictitious Turkish organizations (the intention being to stir up anti-Turkish feeling).

ASALA Revolutionary Movement (ARM)

This Movement was formed in 1983 as a more moderate group than the Armenian Secret Army for the Liberation of Armenia (ASALA—see separate entry). It criticized inter alia the policy of attacking uninvolved civilian targets, but the ASALA dismissed the new Movement as an alleged tool of the Turkish government and the (US) Central Intelligence Agency (CIA).

Greek-Bulgarian-Armenian Front

This group claimed responsibility for a car bomb explosion outside the Turkish consulate in Melbourne (Australia) on Nov. 23, 1986, when one person was killed.

Justice Commandos for the Armenian Genocide

Like the Armenian Secret Army for the Liberation of Armenia (ASALA—see separate entry), this organization, established in 1975 and based in Beirut, has claimed responsibility for the deaths of Turkish diplomats in various countries and for a number of other acts of violence in 1977 and again in 1980-82. Pierre Gulumian, a member of the group, was killed while assembling a bomb near Paris on July 30, 1982, and another unexploded bomb planted by the group was found on Aug. 9. The Commandos also claimed responsibility for the death of the Turkish ambassador to Yugoslavia, shot on March 9, 1983, for which a court in Belgrade sentenced two Armenians (on March 4, 1984) to 20 years in prison.

In 1979 the organization had declared that its revolutionary activity would "not cease until the Turkish state as heir to the Ottoman Empire has condemned the Armenian genocide and has entered into negotiations with representatives of the Armenian people with a view to facilitating the restoration of the occupied territories to their rightful owner, the Armenian people" (as envisaged in the 1923 Treaty of Lausanne).

Levan Ekmegian Suicide Commando

This Commando claimed responsibility for an attack on the Istanbul bazaar on June 16, 1983, when three persons (including one of the attackers) were killed and 27 were injured. The Secret Army for the Liberation of Armenia (ASALA—see separate entry), however, claimed on June 20 that 25 persons, including 17 soldiers, had died in the attack.

Pierre Gulumian Commando

On Sept. 7, 1982, a military court passed the death sentence (which was carried out on Jan. 29, 1983) on an alleged member of this Commando who had on Aug. 7 carried out an attack on the international airport near Ankara which caused the deaths of nine persons and injuries to 82 others. The Commando was also responsible for two bomb attacks on Turkish targets in Paris on May 23, 1983.

Organization of 9th June

This organization was formed in June 1981 in order to exert pressure on the Swiss authorities to release Mardiros Jamkodjian, arrested for the murder of a Turkish consular employee in Geneva on June 9, 1981 (see also under Armenian Secret Army for the Liberation of Armenia). The Organization claimed responsibility for a number of explosions of Swiss targets during 1981.

Organization of 3rd October

This secret group took its name from the day in 1980 on which two members of the Armenian Secret Army for the Liberation of Armenia (ASALA—see separate entry) were injured at a Geneva hotel while they were preparing a bomb; both were arrested and were subsequently given suspended prison sentences and expelled from Switzerland early in 1981. Following the arrest of the above two Armenians, the group engaged in numerous acts of violence designed to bring about their release.

Later the group also claimed responsibility for explosions at the Paris office of Alitalia on Oct. 20, 1981, and at the Olympic travel office in Paris on Aug. 22 (the group objecting to the activities of these offices in promoting emigration of Armenian families from the countries of the Middle East to the United States).

Orly Organization

This group took its name from Orly airport (Paris), where the French authorities on Nov. 11, 1981, arrested a member of the Armenian Secret Army for the Liberation of Armenia (ASALA—see separate entry), who was, however, later released by a French court for lack of incriminating evidence against him. The group claimed responsibility for several attacks on French targets in 1981-82, and in 1983 for a bomb attack at a trade fair in Marseilles (France) on Sept. 30, killing one person and injuring 25.

Although the ASALA denied any connexion with this group, there was a widespread belief that the ASALA had directed the group's activities.

Suisse XV

This group of Armenian activists claimed responsibility for attacks on targets in Switzerland in January 1982. These actions were accompanied by calls for the release of Mardiros Jamkodjian, sentenced on Dec. 19, 1981, to 15 years' hard labour for murdering a Turkish consular employee in Geneva on June 9, 1981 (see under Armenian Secret Army for the Liberation of Armenia).

Yeghin Kechichian (or Yaya Kashakan) Suicide Squad

Leadership. Wasken Sakaseslian—alias Agop Agopian (l.)

This group of four men, formed within the Armenian Secret Army for the Liberation of Armenia (ASALA—see separate entry), attacked the Turkish consulate-general in Paris on Sept. 24, 1981, killed a guard and took 51 persons as hostages pending the fulfilment of a demand for the release of alleged Armenian political prisoners in Turkey. The Turkish authorities, however, stated that there were only two Armenian political prisoners (both clergymen) in Turkey and refused to negotiate with the attackers. On Sept. 25 the French police stormed the building concerned, setting all the hostages free and arresting the four attackers, who were sentenced to seven years' imprisonment on Jan. 31, 1984. One of them committed suicide in prison on Sept. 24, 1985, and the three others were deported to Lebanon on Aug. 5, 1986.

Kurdish Movements

In 1960 the Kurdish minority in Turkey was said to number about 4,000,000 people with their own language and customs, resident mainly in south-eastern Turkey. Of the total of some 8,500,000 Kurds, about 2,500,000 were then resident in western Iran, 1,500,000 in Iraq and 400,000 in Syria (for Kurdish movements in Iran, Iraq and Syria, see under those countries). In the Treaty of Sèvres concluded in 1920 between the Western allies and the Sultan of Turkey, provision was made for an autonomous Kurdistan, but this treaty was superseded by the 1923 Treaty of Lausanne, which practically determined Turkey's present boundaries but contained no mention of special rights for the Kurds.

Except for a brief attempt in Iran in 1945-46, there has never been an independent Kurdistan, and the Turkish government has never recognized the existence of a Kurdish minority in Turkey. A Kurdish nationalist movement first arose before World War I, and anti-Turkish revolts by Kurds were suppressed in 1908, 1925 and 1930-33. In later years unspecified Kurdish separatist organizations were referred to by the Turkish authorities on several occasions.

At a trial which ended in Diyarbakir on Dec. 1, 1983, three defendants were sentenced to death for high treason and politically motivated murder; 10 others were given life sentences on charges including seeking to set up a separate left-wing Kurdish state; and 56 were sent to prison for up to 24 years. In another trial which ended in Diyarbakir on April 19, 1984, a group of 29 Kurds were sentenced to death (19 of these sentences being commuted to life imprisonment) for attempting to set up a separate (Kurdish) state within Turkey; another two received life sentences, six were sent to prison for 24 years each, and another 149 for up to 20 years. On the same day another 19 Kurds were sentenced to death in Diyarbakir, while a further 170 were given varying prison terms. At Adana two more Kurds were sentenced to death on May 4, 1984, with 23 receiving life sentences and 12 being sentenced to imprisonment for between 10 and 24 years.

On Jan. 10, 1985, a court in Diyarbakir sentenced three Kurds to death, while another 14 death sentences were immediately commuted to imprisonment for from 15 to 24 years; one Kurd was given a life sentence, 26 were sent to prison for from 10 to 24 years, and 27 for up to five years.

On July 17, 1985, 10 Kurdish separatists were sentenced to death in Diyarbakir and 38 others to prison terms of up to 24 years.

The principal Kurdish nationalist movements active in Turkey are listed below.

Kurdish Militant Organization

This organization, said to have links with the banned Kurdish Workers' Party (see separate entry), was reported to be conducting guerrilla warfare in 1983.

Kurdish Workers' Party (KWP or **Apocular)**

Leadership. Nemesi Kilic (sec.-gen.)

Established in 1974, this party was given the name of Apocular after Abdullah Ocalan, a leading Kurdish nationalist who founded the party and some years later fled to Syria and was in December 1981 reported to be in Lebanon. According to a Turkish military prosecutor, the party had been set up as the Ankara Democratic Patriotic Association of Higher Education and had rapidly established regional organizations in eastern and southern Anatolia. It also took part in local elections, gaining second place in mayoral elections in Diyarbakir in 1977.

After September 1980 many hundreds of Apocular members were arrested. They included Kemal Pir, who had been second-in-command to Ocalan, and who, after escaping from prison in September, was arrested near Siverek (southern Turkey) on Dec. 4, 1980; he was said to have been involved in 11 murders in Urfa province. The party was then held responsible for 200 murders as well as hold-ups and kidnappings in eastern Turkey. It had also claimed to have taken part in causing an explosion at the Turkish consulate-general in Strasbourg (France) on Nov. 10, 1980—for which the Armenian ASALA organization (see separate entry) had also claimed responsibility.

In August 1984 militant KWP members attacked two villages, released a large number of Kurdish inmates from a prison and shot down an army helicopter. Clashes with government forces took place in November, when over 800 suspected separatists were officially stated to have been arrested. The Minister of the Interior confirmed on Oct. 17 that Turkish troops had, with Iraqi consent, recently entered Iraqi territory in pursuit of Kurdish separatists.

On May 25, 1985, the Minister of the Interior admitted that security forces were waging a limited guerrilla war against Kurdish separatists. While government figures indicated that 84 soldiers, 125 guerrillas and 125 civilians had been killed in clashes since 1984, a representative of the KWP claimed in March 1986 that some 1,500 Turkish soldiers had been killed in the warfare.

The killing of 12 government soldiers in an ambush by KWP members on Aug. 12, 1986, was followed by an attack, on Aug. 15, by Turkish Air Force bombers on three alleged guerrilla hideouts in northern Iraq, when some 200 people were officially stated to have been killed. In retaliation for the killing of 14 civilians on Feb. 23, 1987, the Turkish Air Force carried out a further cross-border operation on March 4, when about 100 Kurds were said to have been killed. Following the killing of a further nine civilians in a separatist attack, the Turkish security forces carried out a major operation along the border with Syria during March 1987.

Major trials of KWP members were held: (i) in Diyarbakir on Feb. 19, 1985, when death sentences were passed on 22 KWP militants, life sentences on 24 others and prison sentences ranging from three to 36 years on 276 others: (ii) in Diyarbakir on Feb. 21, 1986, when 23 KWP members were sentenced to death, six to life imprisonment and 151 to terms of imprisonment of up to 24 years; (iii) in Adana (ending on Aug. 6, 1986), where 25 defendants were sentenced to death, 25 others to life imprisonment and 230 to prison terms of up to 24 years each; and (iv) at Elazig in December 1986, when six alleged KWP members were sentenced to death and 66 to prison terms for from four months to life.

Liberty Party (*Komala-Azadi*)

A group of this name, said to have links with the Kurdish Workers' Party (see separate entry), was also reported in 1983 to be engaged in guerrilla warfare.

Socialist Party of Turkish Kurdistan

Leadership. Kemal Burkay (l.)

After the military takeover of Sept. 12, 1980, the leader and four other members of the central committee of this party, which had already been a clandestine organization, were reported to have fled abroad, presumably to East Germany. The detention of 31 other members of the party was announced in mid-December 1980. In order to avoid dissolution on charges of separatism, the party had earlier, according to security officials, operated under the name of Socialist Party of Iraqi Kurdistan.

The party is said to seek the establishment of an independent Kurdistan based on Marxist-Leninist principles in its political and social organization.

Pacifist Sect

Jehovah's Witnesses

On Dec. 12, 1984, five members of this pacifist sect were sentenced in Ankara to six years in prison and 18 others to terms of four years and two months for distributing propaganda against the nation and its army.

Uganda

Capital: Kampala

Pop. 15,480,000

The Republic of Uganda, a member of the Commonwealth, has an Executive President, who is both head of state and Minister of Defence, and a Cabinet under a Prime Minister. The President (Yoweri Museveni) is the leader of the National Resistance Movement (NRM), whose armed wing, the National Resistance Army (NRA) assumed power on Jan. 26, 1986, after a protracted civil war.

Most of the posts in the government are held by members of the NRM, but among the ministers there are also former members of the following parties: the Conservative Party (CP), the Democratic Party (DP), the Federal Democratic Movement of Uganda (Fedemu), the Uganda Freedom Movement (UFM), the Uganda National Rescue Front (UNRF) and the Uganda People's Congress (UPC).

There is also a National Resistance Council (NRC), established on Jan. 26, 1986, to act as a legislative body pending the holding of elections.

Party politics has been banned but political parties have kept their offices open with skeleton staffs.

The NRA, which exercised unchallenged control of southern Uganda, was by July 1987 thought to have some 30,000 fighters and to be increasing its strength by recruiting new members from among the Baganda tribal grouping. In northern Uganda, however, government forces controlled only the major towns while guerrilla warfare continued to be fought, mainly by the remnants of the Uganda National Liberation Army and the Ugandan Democratic People's Movement (see below).

The Museveni government has repeatedly accused the government of the Sudan of aiding the Ugandan rebels. These accusations have been rejected by the Sudanese government, with the result that the Ugandan Minister of Foreign Affairs stated on Feb. 10, 1987, that either the Sudanese were committed to aiding the rebels, or they were indifferent to, or incapable of containing the activities of the Ugandan rebels within their own territory.

On June 8, 1987, President Museveni was nevertheless quoted as claiming that the war against the rebels in the north was "finished" and that what remained were largely "security duties, not defence duties". On July 31 he said that, under a partial amnesty offered in May to all rebels except those wanted for acts of genocide, murder, kidnapping and rape, more than 1,000 rebels had surrendered. He added that his troops had seized over 4,000 guns but that the government was still faced with several thousand rebels in the northern and eastern provinces.

Guerrilla Movements

Force Obote Back Again (FOBA)

Early in June 1986 this group was reported to be planning attacks on government establishments.

Ugandan exiles in London claimed on Sept. 7, 1986, that ex-President Obote (who was in exile in Zambia where he was held under armed guard) had given his blessing to FOBA, which was then estimated to have some 20,000 fighters. On Sept. 12 FOBA forces were reported to have taken control of an area of 4,900 square kilometres in northern Uganda.

President Museveni said on April 7, 1987, that an attempt by FOBA elements operating out of Kenya to destabilize the Samia area had been contained and that they had been prevented from setting up a base in the Ruwenzori mountains.

Uganda National Liberation Army (UNLA)

Leadership. Lt.-Gen. Bazilio Okello

The UNLA had originally been Uganda's Army under the regime of President Obote, following whose overthrow in July 1985 it was greatly weakened, partly by defections. Of all the armed factions which had existed in Uganda before January 1986 the UNLA remnant was the only one to remain hostile to the government of the NRM. It was reported to co-operate with forces loyal to ex-President Idi Amin (who had been overthrown in April 1979). Members of the UNLA were active in areas bordering the Sudan, where they terrorized the local population. Evidence of massacres committed by UNLA members were produced in February 1986.

President Museveni claimed on Nov. 20, 1986, that the NRA had, since August 1986, killed 1,000 UNLA members. Fighting nevertheless continued almost daily in the following months. In a battle fought on Jan. 18, 1987, more than 6,000 government troops were reported to have killed 350 rebels at Corner Kilak (between Lira and Kitgum in northern Uganda). Documents found at Corner Kilak reportedly showed that the rebels had hoped to install Prince Ronald Mutebi (the heir to the former kingdom of Buganda—see also entry for Baganda Royalist Movement) as head of state.

While UNLA guerrillas continued to dominate the northern Ugandan countryside, with widespread support from the local Acholi people, the NRA generally retained control of the major towns, except that on Feb. 15, 1987, some 5,000 rebels temporarily occupied Gulu.

Uganda National Unity Movement

Leadership. Al-Haj Suleman Ssalongo (ch.)

The chairman of this Movement, who was also the commander of its Uganda National Army, was on June 28, 1987, quoted as saying that his Movement had decided to fight against the NRA because President Museveni had involved Libyans, Cubans and North Koreans in solving Uganda's problems and hundreds of Libyans (he alleged) had, in eastern Uganda, killed Ugandans opposed to the government.

Uganda People's Army (UPA)

This group, consisting of former members of ex-President Obote's party, the Uganda People's Congress, was in June 1987 reported to be engaged in terrorist activities in eastern Uganda, particularly the assassination of chairmen of the government's village councils, and to have obtained some support from the local population.

At the same time a spokesman for the UPA claimed that it had also carried out operations in east-ern Uganda.

Ugandan Democratic People's Movement (UDPM)

Leadership. John Okello (chief co-ordinator)

The objective of the UDPM, founded in May 1986, was defined by J. Okello on Oct. 6, 1986 in London, where he said that its forces were not fighting to reinstate any of the previous Presidents of Uganda, but to restore democracy to the country; he added that they would fight until the government was brought down, unless President Museveni accepted a round-table conference of all groups and fighting forces based in Uganda and outside.

A representative of the UDPM had stated in Juba (Sudan) in late September that the Movement had several thousand fighters, most of them former members of the Uganda National Liberation Army (UNLA), that it hoped to gain the support of the latter's leader (Gen. Bazilio Okello), and that it was in touch with ex-President Obote. He also said that UDPM fighters were active in northern and in south-western Uganda, but he denied that it was receiving aid and logistical support from the Sudan (with fewer than 50 of his men being in Juba at that time).

On Aug. 20, 1987, the UDPM was joined by (i) the People's Democratic Movement led by Otema Allimadi (who had been Prime Minister under President Obote), (ii) the United National Front led by Col. William Omaria Lo Arapai (who had fought to reinstate President Obote in 1979), and (iii) a dissident faction of the Federal Democratic Movement (Fedemu) led by Samuel Luwero.

Other Dissident Groups

Baganda Royalist Movement

On Sept. 2, 1986, it was reported that 25 alleged plotters had been arrested on Aug. 24 for planning to overthrow the government and set up an independent monarchist state for the Baganda tribe.

However, Prince Roland Mutebi (the son of Sir Edward Mutesa, the first President of Uganda, and heir to the royal family of Buganda) was on Jan. 24, 1987, reported to have applied to all Ugandans to co-operate fully with President Museveni and the NRM-NRA to ensure the country's hard-won peace, stability and tranquillity.

Bahais

On Jan. 7, 1987, a group of 12 members of the Bahai faith were arrested at the Bahai temple in Kampala on suspicion of plotting to overthrow the government.

Uganda Freedom Movement (UFM)

Although the UFM was one of the parties represented in the Museveni government, it appeared during 1987 that its leadership was divided. Francis Bwengye (described as deputy chairman and secretary-general of the UFM) was on March 22 reported to have stated that the NRA was responsible for the murder of Dr Andrew Lukatome Kayiira (chairman of the UFM and Minister for Energy) which occurred on March 6, 1987 (whereas four persons charged with his murder on March 26 included three former UFM guerrillas). On April 7 Bwengye announced that the UFM had decided to fight against the NRM. However, Paulo Kalule Kagodo, the new UFM chairman, strongly dissociated his Movement from Bwengye's announcement on April 24, emphasizing that in 1986 the UFM had handed over its army and its whole arsenal to the NRM, whose aims it continued to support.

On May 14, 1987, Bwengye alleged in London that rebel forces had captured an estimated 2,000 soldiers in northern Uganda and that over 20,000 Ugandans were being held in concentration camps for alleged anti-government activities.

Uganda Human Rights Activists (UHRA)

Leadership. Lance Sera K. Muwanga (sec.-gen.)

This organization was founded in Sweden in 1982 and established in Uganda in August 1985. In October 1986 its secretary-general accused the government of "gross human rights violations", alleging that many innocent people were being tortured and killed in northern Uganda on the pretext that they were fighting against the government. President Museveni rejected the accusation as baseless, and early in March 1987 the organization's secretary-general was arrested.

(An Amnesty International delegation, which had visited Uganda in early May 1987, concluded that there had been a "massive qualitative improvement" in the human rights situation in Uganda as the mass killings by the Army and the practice of torture had ended.)

Uganda People's Front

This Front was formed by Ugandan exiles in Kenya on May 10, 1987, with the object of overthrowing the Museveni government.

Union of Soviet Socialist Republics (USSR)

Capital: Moscow Pop. 278,620,000

The USSR (Soviet Union) is, under its 1977 Constitution, "a socialist state of the whole people" in which "the Communist Party of the Soviet Union (CPSU) is the leading and guiding force of Soviet security and the nucleus of its political system, of all state and public organizations". The USSR comprises 15 Union Republics, by far the largest of which is the Russian Soviet Federative Socialist Republic (RSFSR). There are also Autonomous Republics (16 within the RSFSR and four in three other Union Republics) and Autonomous Regions (five within the RSFSR and three in three other Union Republics). There are Supreme Soviets (parliaments) for the USSR and for each of the Union Republics, the Autonomous Republics and the Autonomous Regions. There is a USSR Council of Ministers headed by a Chairman (Prime Minister) and there are Councils of Ministers in each Union Republic.

There are no officially recognized opposition organizations, but a number of groups have been established from time to time to campaign for the observance of civil rights. The principal documents cited by such groups are the 1948 Universal Declaration of Human Rights (on the adoption of which the Soviet Union had abstained from voting), the 1967 International Covenants on Economic, Social and Cultural Rights and on Civil and Political Rights (the ratification of which by the Soviet Union was announced on Sept. 26, 1973), and also the Final Act of the 1975 Helsinki Conference on Security and Co-operation in Europe (CSCE), of which the Soviet Union was a signatory.

The Soviet Union has always emphasized that the rights specified in the above-mentioned covenants could be restricted in the interests of internal security, public order, public health or morals, and the rights and freedoms of others; it has not ratified an additional protocol to the Covenant on Civil and Political Rights empowering a Human Rights Committee to consider communications from citizens of a signatory state complaining of violations of the covenant.

The task of ensuring internal security is carried out by the State Security Committee (*Komitet Gosudarstvennoye Bezhopasnosty*, KGB), the secret police first set up after the 1917 October Revolution and successively known as the Cheka, the GPU, the NKVD (Public Security Department), the MVD (a tribunal with powers to deal with political offenders, abolished in 1953) and therafter the KGB.

The civil rights groups formed in the Soviet Union have included independent trade unions; organizations propagating autonomy for national minorities and the prevention of their Russification; groups campaigning for freedom of religious worship; and other groups, in particular among Jews, calling for freedom to emigrate. A number of intellectuals have proposed various forms of changes in the country's political and social system and freedom of expression for writers and artists. An important role in activities of these "dissidents" has been played by privately produced typescripts circulated as unauthorized publications known as *samizdat.*

Penalties to which dissenters are exposed range from expulsion from official bodies (such as the Writers' Union of the CPSU), dismissal from employment and restriction to a certain locality ("internal exile") to imprisonment in penal institutions, including labour camps of varying degrees of severity, and to internment in psychiatric hospitals—or a combination of these forms of punishment. A number of dissidents have been deprived of their nationality, allowed to emigrate or even expelled from the USSR. On the other hand, 140 political prisoners were released and pardoned on Feb. 20, 1987.

Although the cause of dissenters in the Soviet Union has received considerable attention in the West, it has also been pointed out that it has not elicited widespread response in the USSR. In a survey on *Dissent in the USSR—Politics, Ideology and People*, published in 1975 by the Johns Hopkins University Press, Walter O'Connor came to the following conclusion: "Dissent and dissenters may be a natural product of over 50 years of Soviet history, but just as natural is their failure to strike a responsive chord among the masses. The interest in freedom and the rule of law is not broad enough, is not sufficiently a 'mass' interest, to make its accommodation critical."

The individual dissidents who have received widespread attention in the West have, however, not established any dissident movements in the Soviet Union.

The most prominent among these dissidents have been Alexander Solzhenitsyn (expelled from the Soviet Union on Feb. 13, 1974); Dr Andrei D. Sakharov (released from internal exile in December 1986); Vladimir Bukovsky (exchanged on Dec. 18, 1976, for Luis Corvalán Lepe, secretary-general of the Chilean Communist Party); Anatoly Kuznetsov (a novelist who reached Britain on July 24, 1969); Dr Zhores A. Medvedev (a biologist who left the Soviet Union in 1973); and his brother, Dr Roy A. Medvedev (threatened with arrest in January 1983 unless he discontinued his "anti-state activities"). The activities of these and other individual dissidents in the Soviet Union have been described in the forerunner of this book, *Political Dissent—An International Guide to Dissident, Extra-Parliamentary, Guerrilla and Illegal Political Movements* (Longman/Gale, 1983). Some of their works are listed in the select bibliography to this book—see pages 427–428.

Civil Rights Movements

A Public Group to assist the Fulfilment of the Helsinki Accord in the Soviet Union ("Helsinki Group"), founded on May 13, 1976, was dissolved in 1982 (as announced on Sept. 8 of that year). Most of its members had been imprisoned, exiled or sent into internal exile. These included Maj.-Gen. (rtd.) Pyotr Grigorenko (who left for the United States in November 1977), Dr Yury Orlov (who was allowed to emigrate to the United States and arrived there on Oct. 5, 1986), Yelena Bonner Sakharova (who was released from internal exile together with her husband, Dr Andrei Sakharov, on Dec. 23, 1986) and Anatoly Shcharansky (who was released to the West on Feb. 11, 1987).

Other civil rights movements which were active between 1969 and 1981 were similarly dissolved or made unable to continue their activities as their members were imprisoned or sent into internal exile, or had left the country.

However, they were survived by the publication the *Chronicle of Current Events*, which appeared regularly—at first every two months—from April 30, 1968, onwards in *samizdat*, i.e. as self-published literature issued in typescript of not more than 10 copies (which was not subject to censorship). The principal function of the *Chronicle* was to record developments in the civil rights movement and in particular trials and other official action affecting dissenters. Those found guilty of producing or distributing copies of the *Chronicle* were liable to severe penalties, and mere possession of a copy was also a punishable offence.

On May 13, 1983, Aleksei Smirnov, an editor of the *Chronicle of Current Events*, was sentenced to six years' hard labour and four years' internal exile for "anti-Soviet agitation and propaganda", and on Sept. 8, 1984, Yuri Shikhanovich, another editor of the *Chronicle*, was sentenced to five years' imprisonment and five years' internal exile for "anti-Soviet activities".

Free Trade Union

Free Interprofessional Association of Soviet Workers (SMOT)

The creation of this Association was disclosed on Oct. 29, 1978, by eight persons who claimed that it had 100 members. However, the authorities soon took action against SMOT members, among them Lev Volokhonsky (a founder member), sentenced on June 12, 1979, to two years in a labour camp for "spreading anti-Soviet slander"; Anatoly Pozdniakov, arrested on Sept. 10, 1979, tried on Oct. 30 and transferred to a psychiatric hospital; Vladimir Borisov, arrested in August 1979, sent to a psychiatric hospital and expelled from the Soviet Union on June 22, 1980; Mark Morozov, arrested on Nov. 2, 1978, and subsequently exiled to Vorkuta (northern Urals) for five years (for spreading "anti-Soviet fabrications"), and on Jan. 13, 1981, sentenced to eight years' hard labour (for spreading "anti-Soviet propaganda"); Mikhail Sokolov, sentenced on April 1, 1980, to three years in a labour camp for "hooliganism" (after allegedly making derogatory remarks about President Brezhnev); and Vselovod Kuyakin (who had also been involved in an unsuccessful attempt to form Free Trade Union of Soviet Workers in 1977-79), arrested on April 22, 1981, and sentenced on Dec. 27 of that year to one year in a labour camp and five years' internal exile for "anti-Soviet agitation and propaganda".

Mrs Albina Yakoreva, a SMOT organizer expelled from the Soviet Union, stated in Vienna on Aug. 8, 1982, that SMOT had increased significantly during the last year, that it had 300 active members and 1,500 sympathizers and that 21 new branches had been set up during 1982 alone.

On May 24, 1983, Lev Volokhonsky was sentenced again, this time to five years in prison and four years' internal exile, for anti-Soviet agitation.

Nationalist Movements

THE BALTIC REPUBLICS

The incorporation into the Soviet Union of the Baltic republics of Estonia, Latvia and Lithuania in 1940 has not been officially recognized by most Western nations, and the former independent governments of these three states are still represented by legations in London. As the three countries had formerly been part of the Tsarist empire, the Soviet government regarded their post-World War I independence as an aberration from historical legality.

On the occasion of the 40th anniversary of the 1939 Soviet-German non-aggression pact—which led to the Soviet annexation of the three Baltics Republics—45 Estonian, Latvian and Lithuanian citizens published an appeal to the United Nations, the Soviet Union and the two (East and West) German governments to revoke that pact on the grounds that secret protocols attached to it had enabled the Soviet Union to occupy the three Baltic republics in the following year. The signatories also called for the withdrawal of "foreign" (i.e. Soviet) troops from these republics. Of the signatories Prof. Juri Kukk (an Estonian chemistry lecturer deprived of his post in September 1979 after applying for permission to emigrate to Sweden) was on Jan. 8, 1981, sentenced to two years in a labour camp, together with Mart Niklus, who was given 10 years in a special-regime labour camp and five years' internal exile for "defaming the Soviet system" and "anti-Soviet propaganda". Another signatory, Enn Tarto, was sentenced on April 19, 1984, to 10 years in prison, inter alia for maintaining "criminal links" with an Estonian exile group in Stockholm.

In October 1981 a group of 37 Estonians, Latvians and Lithuanians signed a "Baltic declaration" calling for the inclusion of the three republics in a North European nuclear-weapons-free zone. Three of the signatories were later given heavy prison sentences—Ints Calitis, reported on Sept. 24, 1983, to have been sentenced to six years' imprisonment for "anti-government activities and direct calls for the overthrow of the system established in Latvia"; Gunnars Astra, sentenced on Dec. 14, 1983, to seven years' hard labour and five years' internal exile; and Mrs Lagle

Parek, sentenced on Dec. 16 to six years' hard labour and three years' internal exile.

Opposition to the incorporation in the Soviet Union of the three Baltic republics has been expressed on a number of occasions, especially by students in Estonia and by Roman Catholics in Lithuania. In addition to those mentioned above several other nationalists have been given similar sentences since 1983 for "anti-government activities" or "anti-Soviet agitation".

CRIMEAN TARTARS

During World War II the Soviet government forcibly deported (in May 1944) over 200,000 Tartars from the Crimea, where they had lived for centuries, to Uzbekistan and Kazakhstan, on the grounds that they had collaborated with the Germans; the Crimean Tartar Republic was abolished and all vestiges of its existence were destroyed. According to the Tartars' own estimate, 110,000 of them, or over 26 per cent, died of thirst or suffocation during the three to four months long journey to Central Asia (whereas the Soviet authorities put the death toll at "only" 22 per cent).

Following the denunciation of Stalin's mass deportations by Nikita Khrushchev in 1956, the Tartars began a campaign for their rehabilitation and their return to the Crimea. As a result two decrees of the USSR Supreme Soviet were signed on Sept. 5, 1967, by President Podgorny, stating that (i) the fact that "a certain section" of the Tartar population had collaborated with the Germans should not be used to blame the entire Tartar people, especially as a new generation had entered the work and political life of the people, and (ii) the Tartars were free to live anywhere in the Soviet Union and to return to the Crimea if they so wished.

However, of 6,000 Tartars who thereupon travelled to the Crimea only a few were allowed to settle there, with the result that the Tartars launched a new agitation. This led to clashes with police and troops near Tashkent (Uzbekistan) on April 21, 1968, and to the arrest, on May 16-18, of some 800 Tartars who had come to Moscow to ask for an official inquiry into the above clashes. Trials which followed included those of Gomer Bayev (a Tartar engineer), sentenced to two years in prison at Simferopol (Crimea) on April 29, 1969; Prof. Rollan Kadiyev (a physicist), Izzet Khairov (also a physicist), Reshat Bairamov and Ridvan Gafarov (both electrical engineers), each given four years in a labour camp in Tashkent on Aug. 5, 1969; and six others sentenced to a year in prison on the same occasion.

In the following years, however, up to October 1978 some 16,600 Tartar families were allowed to return to the Crimea, but 700 others were considered to be illegally resident in the Crimea and were reported to have been arrested, with their houses being demolished. Some of the Tartars were involved in demonstrations against the eviction, and at least two committed suicide. Some 200 who tried in Moscow on March 15, 1979, to submit to the USSR Supreme Soviet a petition calling for the unhampered return of their people to the Crimea were arrested and forcibly taken back to Tashkent.

Of the activists among the Crimean Tartars, Mustafa Dzhemilev (Abduldzhemil) was sentenced in Omsk on April 15, 1976, to 2½ years in a strict-regime labour camp for "spreading anti-state propaganda", this sentence being confirmed by the Supreme Court of the RSFSR on May 25, 1976. On March 6, 1979, he was sentenced to four years' internal exile for having disregarded conditions imposed upon him after his release on Dec. 22, 1977. In February 1979 he renounced his Soviet citizenship and applied for permission to emigrate.

A cousin of his, Rechat Dzhemilev, who was a spokesman for the Crimean Tartars, was in July 1979 sentenced to three years' imprisonment for "spreading slanderous fabrications", and another Tartar, Mamedi Chobanov, was in July 12, 1979, sentenced to three years in a labour camp for "anti-Soviet propaganda".

In February 1984 Mustafa Dzhemilev was sentenced to a further three years' hard labour for "anti-Soviet slander".

UKRAINIAN NATIONALISTS

Activities by Ukrainian nationalists directed mainly against the Russification of the Ukraine have led to trials of such activists on various charges on a number of occasions.

In the spring of 1966 trials took place in Kiev, Lvov, Ivano-Frankoist, and Tarnopol of 30 Ukrainian intellectuals, of whom 20 were sentenced to imprisonment for up to six years. According to a report on these trials, drawn up by Vyacheslav Chornovil (a journalist and then an official of the Young Communist League) and submitted to the first secretary of the Ukrainian Communist Party, the only offence proved against them was that they had discussed ways of defending Ukrainian culture against forcible Russification and had possessed books on this question, some of them dating back to before the 1917 October Revolution.

Chornovil also maintained that Article 62 of the Ukrainian criminal code, under which the accused had been sentenced, completely negated the freedom guaranteed to citizens by the Constitution of the USSR, with the result that it seemed possible to classify as "slanderous fabrications" all statements which did not coincide with official directives.

Chornovil was consequently tried in Lvov in November 1967 for "anti-Soviet activities" and sentenced to three years in prison, which were later reduced to 18 months. In February 1973 he was, also in Lvov, sentenced to seven years in a strict-regime labour camp and five years' internal exile for "anti-Soviet agitation and propaganda" and on suspicion of involvement in the publication of *The Ukrainian Herald*, an underground journal.

Levko Lukyanenko (a lawyer) was sentenced at Gorodnya (Ukraine) on July 20, 1978, to 10 years in a special-regime labour camp and five years' internal exile for "anti-Soviet agitation". He had been arrested at Chernigov on Dec. 12, 1977, having previously been condemned to death in 1961 for treason and for trying to set up a "Marxist" group propagating self-determination for the Ukraine, this sentence having been commuted to 15 years in a severe-regime labour camp.

Yuri Badzyo (a Ukrainian historian) was sentenced on Dec. 25, 1979, to seven years in a labour camp and five years' internal exile for "slandering the Soviet Union"; he had written a book on Russo-Ukrainian relations, accusing the Soviet leadership of attempting to eliminate non-Russian cultures within the Soviet Union's post-war boundaries.

Ukrainian Liberation Front

Members of this Front claimed responsibility for a bomb attack on the Luxembourg offices of Aeroflot (the Soviet national airline) on Nov. 11, 1980. (In Paris a Ukrainian group set fire to two cars belonging to the Soviet embassy on Nov. 24, 1981.)

Ukrainian Reactionary Forces

A group referred to by this name claimed responsibility for the killing of a Soviet diplomat near the Soviet embassy in New Delhi (India) on March 21, 1985.

Religious Opposition

In a decree issued after the 1917 October Revolution and probably formulated by Lenin, it was laid down that it was illegal "to restrain or limit freedom of conscience" and that every citizen was entitled to "profess any religion or none at all". The Constitution of 1918 recognized the right of all citizens to conduct religious and anti-religious propaganda. However, in the late 1920s pressure on the Churches increased and a 1929 law restraining religious associations was sporadically enforced. During the 1941-45 war, on the other hand, Stalin made concessions to the Churches in order to gain their support.

Under the administration of Nikita Khrushchev a determined campaign was conducted against all religious groups in 1960-64. In terms of a 1961 decree the administration of places of worship was transferred from the local clergy to parish councils consisting of laymen (which might be dissolved and the churches closed if the membership fell below 20). As a result some 10,000 churches were reported to have been closed between 1961 and 1964 and the number of theological seminaries reduced from eight in 1959 to three in 1964.

Thereafter it was officially admitted that the anti-religious campaign had been counter-productive, and measures against religious minorities were less stringent than before. They included the outlawing of whole denominations; the enforced merging with other denominations; the enforced closure of legally existing places of worship; state control of all places of worship through registration regulations; the legal provision that no religious association (parish) was a person at law; arbitrary distinctions in recognizing central representative bodies; restrictions on local and national church congresses; libelling in the press without the right of reply; the suppression of old religious customs; and discrimination against believers at places of work and in housing, education and public life.

The 1929 law was amended by a decree of June 23, 1975 (published in November 1975), with the result of abolishing the state's obligation to provide alternative premises for church buildings confiscated by the state and also the concession allowing parents to give religious instruction to their children (these provisions of the 1929 law having already been disregarded in practice).

According to an official Soviet source quoted in March 1977, there were then some 1,200 groups of religious dissenters "with anti-Soviet tendencies" existing illegally and refusing to register with the authorities.

On the other hand, a delegation of 226 US church leaders who visited the Soviet Union in June 1984 and met (registered) religious communities of various denominations found, according to one member of the delegation, that there were "vital religious communities wherever they went", that new churches had been opened, that the number of seminary students in Moscow, Leningrad and Odessa had been doubled, and that a monastery had been re-opened in Moscow.

ORTHODOX CHURCH

According to a report published on Dec. 17, 1970, by the (British) Minority Rights Group (a research and information unit), the Orthodox Church in the Soviet Union had the allegiance of some 30,000,000 people. Trials of dissenting Orthodox Christians have frequently been reported, notably in connexion with the appearance of unauthorized publications, and the authorities have also taken action against members of Orthodox seminars. Against this background, organizations in defence of freedom of religion have been formed by members of the Orthodox Church on various occasions.

Christian Committee for the Defence of Believers' Rights

Founding members of this organization of adherents to the unofficial Orthodox Church included (i) Lev Regelson, who was on Sept. 24, 1980, convicted of producing and distributing, in 1974-79, material slandering the USSR and of "maintaining criminal contacts with Western journalists" and given a suspended sentence of five years after confessing his "guilt" and expressing repentance; and (ii) Viktor Kapitanchuk, who was similarly given a five-year suspended sentence on Oct. 9, 1980 (see also below).

Committee for the Defence of Believers in the Soviet Union

This Committee was established in December 1976 by three members of the Russian Orthodox Church—the Rev. Gleb Yakunin, Varsonofy Haibulin (a former priest) and Viktor Kapitanchuk—in order to "co-operate with public and state organizations" in dealing with grievances of believers in the USSR, on the basis of their belief that the freedom of religion guaranteed by the Constitution was widely disregarded. Fr Yakunin was arrested on Nov. 1, 1979, and on Aug. 28, 1980, he was sentenced in Moscow to five years in a labour camp, to be followed by five years' internal exile, for "anti-Soviet agitation". Kapitanchuk was arrested on March 12, 1980; he was also involved in the founding of the Christian Committee for the Defence of Believers' Rights (see separate entry) and was on Oct. 9, 1980, given a five-years suspended sentence after pleading guilty to "anti-Soviet agitation and propaganda".

ROMAN CATHOLIC CHURCH

The Roman Catholic Church was estimated, in the 1970s, to have about 3,000,000 members in the Soviet Union, most of them in Lithuania, where they constituted about 85 per cent of the population.

The trial of two Lithuanian Catholic priests—Fr Juozas Zdebskis and Fr P. Bubnis, each of whom was sentenced on Nov. 11, 1971, to one year's detention under a 1966 decree making it illegal to give formal religious instruction to minors—led to mass protests and the signing by 17,054 Lithuanian Catholics in December 1971 and January 1972 of a petition sent to Leonid Brezhnev (then General Secretary of the CPSU) and also Dr Kurt Waldheim (then UN Secretary-General) asking the government of the USSR "to secure for us freedom of conscience which is guaranteed by the Constitution of the USSR but which up to the present does not exist in practice". In the petition it was pointed out inter alia that two bishops had been exiled for an unspecified period without trial; that Catholics were often dismissed from their employment solely because of their religion; that believers were not allowed to restore burned-out churches even at their own expense; and that private religious education was forbidden, while atheism was "compulsorily inculcated".

The funeral, on May 18, 1972, of a Catholic worker who had burned himself to death in Kaunas on May 14, was followed by demonstration calling for "freedom for Lithuania" and leading to clashes with police and subsequent prison sentence for a number of rioters.

The Ukrainian Catholic Church was forcibly incorporated in the Orthodox Church in 1946 but continued to lead a clandestine existence. Of its leading clerics, Joseph Slipyj-Kobernickyj-Dyckowsky, Archbishop of Lvov and Metropolitan of Halyc, was deported to Siberia in 1945 but released to the Vatican in 1963. In 1963 he was recognized by the Holy See as the Major Archbishop of the Ukrainian Rite Catholic Church, and he was created a Cardinal in 1965. Before the Roman Catholic Bishops' Synod in Rome he stated in 1974 that any priest who secretly read mass in the Soviet Union was "being sentenced to three years' hard labour in Siberia". (In fact the Ukrainian Archbishop Basil Welytschovsky had been given such a sentence on March 27, 1970.)

In a letter to the Synod by the Association for the Patriarchal System in the Ukrainian Catholic Church and published on Oct. 21, 1974, it was alleged that the clergy and laity of this Church were exposed to "terrible persecution" by the Communist regime in the Soviet Union, and the Congregation for the Eastern Churches and the Roman Curia were accused of abandoning their "Church-in-exile" in order to improve relations with Moscow. However, on March 27, 1980, the Pope nominated Mgr Myroslav Ivan Lubachivsky as head of the Ukrainian Catholic Church in succession to Cardinal Slipyj.

As detailed below, Roman Catholics in the Soviet Union have formed a number of organizations to defend freedom of religion and of worship, although without constituting any serious political challenge to the Communist regime.

Association for the Patriarchal System in the Ukrainian Catholic Church

This Association was formed to oppose the officially recognized Roman Catholic Church in the Ukraine.

Catholic Committee for the Defence of Believers

This Committee was established in November 1978 by Fr Alfonsas Svarinskas and four other Lithuanian Roman Catholic priests. It decided to co-operate closely with the (Orthodox) Committee for the Defence of Believers in the Soviet Union (see separate entry). The Committee was to protest in particular against the closure of monasteries and of religious publishing and printing houses and the refusal to allow the Roman Catholic community to express itself on radio and television. Fr Svarinskas claimed that of 628 churches in Lithuania 95 per cent were without a priest; that there were only 711 priests as against 1,500 before World War II; and that the number of young people admitted to the Kaunas seminary was half that of the priests who died.

After being accused of calling on believers "to struggle against the Soviet system" Fr Svarinskas was, on May 6, 1983, sentenced to seven years' imprisonment and three years" internal exile. Another founder of the Committee, Fr Sigitas Tamkevicius, was, on Dec. 2, 1983, sentenced to six years in a labour camp and four years' internal exile for "anti-state agitation and propaganda". On Feb. 3, 1984, an exile group in Sweden was reported to have claimed that 130,000 Lithuanians had signed a petition against these two sentences.

OTHER CHRISTIAN GROUPS

Council of Churches of the Evangelical Christians and Baptists (*Initsiatniki*)

This organization broke away from the officially tolerated All-Union Council of Evangelical Christians-Baptists (representing more than 500,000 Baptists in the Soviet Union) as it rejected the Soviet authorities' right to oversee religious affairs. It was therefore totally outlawed and its members were prosecuted for "distributing religious propaganda and perverting the minds of children". Between 1961 and 1964 over 200 dissident Baptists were sentenced to imprisonment for up to 10 years, and although most of them were released after the dismissal of N. Khrushchev in 1964 more Baptists were arrested in 1966-67. Letters sent in May and June by five wives of imprisoned Baptists to President Podgorny and U Thant (then UN Secretary-General) were accompanied by a list of 202 Baptist prisoners, of whom 169 had been sentenced in 1967.

In October 1974 it was reported that a clandestine bible printing works had been uncovered in Riga (Latvia), with 15,000 copies of the New Testament and 16 tons of paper being seized. (Some 220,000 copies of the New Testament were said to have been distributed from Riga in 1973, against only 10,000 bibles having been printed for the whole of the Soviet Union by official permission of the Soviet authorities in that year.)

Pastor Georgi P. Vins, a leading member of the outlawed Council, was on Jan. 31, 1975, sentenced to five years in prison and another five years in exile for unauthorized religious activity. As a result of negotiations between the Carter administration in the United States and the Soviet authorities, Pastor Vins was, on April 27, 1979, exchanged in New York, together with four other imprisoned Soviet citizens, against two Soviet citizens sentenced in the United States for espionage. Further arrests of Baptists were reported later in 1980 on various charges, including alleged violation of the laws on the separation of church and state.

According to German Baptist sources there were in early 1983 an estimated 2,000 unregistered Baptist congregations with some 100,000 adherents in the Soviet Union, over 100 lay preachers and a number of illegal printing presses. Over 50 Baptists were believed to be in prison.

Committee for the Right to Free Emigration (Pentecostalists)

This Committee was established in Moscow by a group of Pentecostalists, as announced by them on June 29, 1979. It had been reported on Feb. 24, 1977, that the unofficial Pentecostalist Pastor Nikolai Goretai of a village in the north-western Caucasus had stated that applications for permission to emigrate to any country where they might be "able to practise their religion freely" had been made to the USSR Supreme Soviet by 90 persons in his village and by 525 in other Pentecostal communities in the USSR, but the Emigration Office had refused the applications. On March 24, 1977, he claimed that there were 484 Pentecostalists at Nakhodka (near Vladivostok) and more than 500 elsewhere who wished to emigrate.

It was later estimated that during the year 1979 some 30,000 Pentecostalists had applied for exit visas; however, the Soviet authorities announced in February 1980 that no such visas would be issued.

After attempting for 17 years to obtain permission to emigrate, seven Pentecostalists entered the US embassy in Moscow on June 27, 1978, and were allowed to remain there until between April and July 1983 when they were given exit visas allowing them to emigrate to Israel with their families.

On Nov. 25, 1980, Pastor Goretai was reported to have been sentenced to seven years in a labour camp and five years' internal exile for "anti-Soviet agitation and propaganda". (He had already served a five-year sentence in a labour camp and five years in internal exile imposed in 1961.)

In 1981-82 sentences were passed on a number of Pentecostalists in the Ukraine. They included five who were said to have applied for permission to emigrate and to have renounced their Soviet citizenship, and who were on Aug. 5, 1981, reported to have been convicted of anti-Soviet slander in Dnepropetrovsk, four of them being sentenced to five years in a labour camp and five years' internal exile, and the fifth to three years in prison and three years in exile. Among others Pavel Achtyorev was on Feb. 4, 1982, sentenced to seven years in a labour camp and five years in exile for printing "slanderous" publications.

In June 1983 Vasily Baratz, a leading member of the Committee, was sentenced to five years' hard labour for anti-Soviet activities. On the other hand some 70 Pentecostalists who had started a hunger strike in a Far East village in September 1983 to protest against their alleged persecution were told in December 1983 that they would be allowed to emigrate to West Germany.

Free Adventists

The spiritual leader of this group of Seventh-Day Adventists, Vladimir Shelkov (83), was on March 23, 1979, sentenced in Tashkent to five years in a strict-regime labour camp and to confiscation of his house for allegedly spreading false information designed to discredit the Soviet system (after he had previously served 23 years in prisons or banishment) and he died on Jan. 27, 1980. Four other members of the group were sentenced to from two years suspended to five years in a strict-regime labour camp. During 1981 a number of Seventh-Day Adventists were sentenced to from two to five years' detention in a labour camp, inter alia for circulating illegal leaflets, a five-year sentence being imposed on Rostislav Galetsky, a senior minister of the sect, accused of transmitting "slanderous material" to the Western press and of contravening the Soviet laws on the formation of religious sects (as reported on April 5).

Jehovah's Witnesses (Watchtower Society)

This sect, whose members are conscientious objectors to military service, is banned in the Soviet Union. From time to time (e.g. on April 18, 1975) it was reported that members had been sentenced to imprisonment for practising their religion.

JEWISH COMMUNITY

Against the Jewish religion a sustained campaign was officially pursued in the Soviet Union between 1948 and 1953, although after Stalin's death in the latter year a more liberal policy was adopted. In 1961, however, Khrushchev's Government launched an attack on Jewish culture and religious observances. According to official Soviet figures the number of Synagogues fell from 450 in 1956 to 96 in 1963. Dr Nahum Goldmann, then president of the World Jewish Congress, stated on Feb. 17, 1964, that there was only one rabbinical seminary with four students in the USSR; that there were no rabbis under 70 years old; that only one (limited) edition of the Jewish prayer book had been printed in the past 40 years; and that no Hebrew bibles were available. The baking of *matzoh* (unleavened bread for Passover) was forbidden between 1961 and 1965.

In 1965, however, the authorities again adopted a more liberal attitude. The admission of 30 students to the rabbinical seminary was permitted; the printing of 10,000 copies of the Jewish prayer book was allowed; and the number of Yiddish books published was increased. The Soviet press recalled that Lenin had demanded "a tireless struggle" against anti-semitism, and a number of Soviet Jews were allowed to emigrate in 1965-66.

In an article in *Izvestia* (the daily organ of the USSR Supreme Soviet) it was stated early in January 1977 that "militant anti-communists" were "advocating the departure of Jews from our united multinational society" and "the creation of a ramified network of circles to study Hebrew in order to 'bring closer spiritually' the young people to 'God's chosen country' and its state religion [i.e. to Israel]". Zionists, the article continued, planned to establish "direct and permanent contacts between Jewish religious communities in the USSR and Zionist centres abroad" and while anti-semitism was "banned in the Soviet Union by law" Zionists would never "be allowed to propagate racialism in the Soviet Union unpunished".

Official action was accordingly taken against Zionist activities and the private tuition of Hebrew, but the number of Jews permitted to leave the country (which had risen to over 34,500 in 1973 and had been reduced thereafter to 13,222 in 1975, 14,261 in 1976 and 16,737 in 1977) was allowed to rise again (to 28,864 in 1978 and 51,320 in 1979). Thereafter it fell drastically to 21,471 in 1980, 9,400 in 1981, about 1,700 in 1982, 1,300 in 1983, 896 in 1984, 1,140 in 1985 and 943 in 1986. However, it rose again in 1987, when 1,424 Jews left the Soviet Union during the first four months of the year.

According to the British All-party Parliamentary Committee for the Release of Soviet Jewry, a total of 383,000 Jews were, at the end of 1985, still awaiting visas allowing them to leave the Soviet Union after relatives abroad had issued invitations to join them; as far as was known, 11,000 (refuseniks) had been refused a visa, of whom 8,200 had been waiting between five and 10 years and 1,200 for over 10 years. (Soviet officials maintained that only 4,000 Jews had been refused exit visas.)

Other Internal Opposition Groups

Group for Establishing Trust between the USSR and the USA

The formation of this Group was announced in Moscow on June 4, 1982, by a group of 11 intellectuals, whose spokesman, Sergei Batovrin, explained that the Group sought "the participation of the Soviet and the American public, on equal terms, in the dialogue between politicians" on questions of disarmament; he also claimed that the official Soviet "Peace Committee" served only to echo the Communist Party's policy. All the 11 intellectuals involved were subsequently subjected to restrictions, Batovrin being arrested on Aug. 6 (for evading military service) and subsequently confined in a psychiatric hospital until Sept. 7. (It appeared that the official intention was to keep the members of the Group away from an officially-approved "Peace March 1982" mainly organized by women's disarmament movements from Scandinavian countries for the second half of July 1982.)

According to Batovrin, who left the Soviet Union on May 19, 1983, the Group at that time had 16 members and 900 sympathizers in 12 different cities. In August 1983 a woman said to have links with the Group was sentenced to five years in prison and three years' internal exile for anti-Soviet agitation. After attending a Group meeting in Moscow on Aug. 9, 1984, some 50 members were detained by police.

Makhno's Anarchist Group

Named after a Ukrainian guerrilla leader who had fought against both the White Army and the Bolsheviks in the years after 1917, this Group claimed responsibility for sending letter bombs (none of which exploded) to Soviet offices in London, including the Soviet embassy, during January 1983.

Pamyat (Memory)

Leadership. D. Vasiliev

This organization was set up in 1980 as a society for the protection of historic churches and monuments and was not officially registered. By 1986 it had begun to organize marches and demonstrations at which it proclaimed its anti-semitism and anti-Zionism, and in particular its opposition to allowing Jewish emigrants to return to the Soviet Union and to alleged Jewish influence on public life in the Soviet Union. It has also attacked so-called "enemies of the people", calling for the execution of dismissed officials (hitherto allowed to retire on pension). It is widely believed to be gaining influence among officials opposed to the reforms implemented by Mikhail Gorbachev (the General Secretary of the Communist Party of the Soviet Union) under his *glasnost* (openness) policy of allowing greater freedom of expression. A march organized by the movement in Moscow in May 1987 was joined by some 400 people, and Pamyat representatives subsequently met with the Moscow Communist Party chief.

External Organizations

Peasants' Party of Latvia

This exiled formation is affiliated to the Christian Democratic World Union.

People's Labour Union (*Narodno Trudovoi Soyuz*, NTS)

The NTS was founded as an anti-Soviet organization by Russian émigrés in Belgrade in 1930. It began to infiltrate agents into the Soviet Union in 1937. During World War II it collaborated with the Germans in occupied Soviet territory but it later aroused the suspicions of the German authorities who arrested many of its members. In the 1950s, when it was based in

Frankfurt (West Germany), it resumed its infiltration of agents and propaganda into the Soviet Union. The Soviet authorities have repeatedly claimed to have seized NTS publications found in the possession of dissidents (such as Vladimir Bukovsky and Alexander Ginsburg) and also of foreign "tourists". The NTS was also said to have recruited persons of Russian extraction to visit the Soviet Union in order to obtain copies of books and other documents for publication outside the Soviet Union.

Social Democratic Party of Latvia

Leadership. Bruno Kalnins (ch.)

This party in exile is a member of the Socialist Union of Eastern Europe (SUCEE) and a consultative member of the Socialist International. Inside the Soviet Republic of Latvia, Dr Fricis Menders (84), a former leader of the party, was on Nov. 1, 1969, sentenced to five years in a labour camp for "defaming the Soviet state" after he had reportedly supplied a manuscript to a US historian who was collecting material for a study of the 1917-18 revolutionary period in Latvia. Dr Menders had been deported to Siberia by the Tsarist authorities in 1906 and had later been sentenced to 10 years in a labour camp in 1948. On June 11, 1981, Juris Burmeistar, said to be the party's underground leader, was reported to have been sentenced to 15 years in a labour camp for "treason", together with D. A. Limanis, who was given a 10-year sentence.

Social Democratic Party of Lithuania

Leadership. J. Skorubskas (ch.)

This party in exile is a member of the Socialist Union of Central and Eastern Europe (SUCEE) and a consultative member of the Socialist International.

Socialist Party of Estonia

Leadership. Johannes Mihkelson (ch.)

This party in exile is a member of the Socialist Union of Central and Eastern Europe (SUCEE) and a consultative member of the Socialist International.

Union of Christian Democrats of Lithuania

This exiled formation is a member of the Christian Democratic World Union.

World Congress of Free Ukrainians

Dr Valentyn Moroz (a Ukrainian nationalist who reached the United States in the exchange of April 27, 1979, against two Soviet citizens convicted of spying) regarded the above Congress as most representative of the 3,000,000 Ukrainians in emigration (of whom 2,000,000 were in the United States), and he called, on May 18, 1979, for observer status to be granted to the Congress by the United Nations.

United Arab Emirates

Capital: Abu Dhabi Pop. 1,622,464

The United Arab Emirates (UAE) are a federated state of seven sheikhdoms without parliament or political parties.

The highest federal authority is the Supreme Council of Rulers comprising the seven hereditary rulers of the sheikhdoms. Decisions of the Supreme Council require the approval of at least five members, including the rulers of Abu Dhabi and Dubai.

Isolated incidents against UAE representatives abroad have been reported. The Arab Revolutionary Brigades claimed responsibility for an attack on the UAE vice-consul in Rome on Oct. 26, 1984.

On July 13, 1985, Dubai police announced that they had arrested 45 "Iranian infiltrators".

Joint Opposition Front

At a meeting held in London in November 1980, agreement was reached by various opposition leaders on the formation of a united political opposition front and the establishment, as its military arm, of a movement for the liberation of the UAE. In its manifesto the meeting called for the overthrow of the existing regime, the establishment of a democratic and popular regime, the control of national wealth and its use in the interests of the country's citizens, and the use of all forms of struggle to recover the three Gulf islands seized by Iran at the end of November 1971 (i.e. Abu Musa and the Greater and Lesser Tunbs).

There have been no reports of activities by this group in recent years.

United Kingdom

Capital: London

Pop. 56,620,000

The United Kingdom of Great Britain and Northern Ireland is a hereditary constitutional monarchy in which the monarch, as head of state, has numerous specific responsibilities. The supreme legislative authority is Parliament consisting of (i) a House of Commons of 650 members elected for not more than five years by universal adult suffrage (and in single-member constituencies) and (ii) a House of Lords with more than 1,000 peers or peeresses having a seat for life (a majority by virtue of heredity). The government is headed by a Prime Minister who is leader of the party which commands a majority in the House of Commons. There is no written Constitution.

As a result of general elections held on June 11, 1987, seats in the House of Commons were distributed as follows: Conservatives 375, Labour 229, Alliance 22 (i.e. Liberal Party 17, Social Democratic Party five), Official Unionist Party (Northern Ireland) nine, Democratic Unionist Party (Northern Ireland) three, *Plaid Cymru* (Welsh Nationalists) three, Scottish National Party three, Social Democratic and Labour Party (Northern Ireland) three, *Sinn Féin* (Northern Ireland) one, Ulster Popular Unity Party (Northern Ireland) one, Speaker one.

Parties which unsuccessfully contested the elections included the Green Party, the Workers' Party (NI), the Communist Party, the Red Front, the Orkney and Shetland Movement, the Workers' Revolutionary Party, the Alliance Party of Northern Ireland, the National Front Flag Group, the Protestant Reformation Party and the Socialist Party of Great Britain.

A Prevention of Terrorism (Temporary Provisions) Act, replacing a 1976 act of the same name, was enacted on March 22, 1984. It was limited to five years' duration and subject to annual renewal by Parliament. It provided inter alia that the Secretary of State for Northern Ireland might proscribe in Great Britain specified organizations which appeared to be concerned with terrorism occurring in the United Kingdom and connected with Northern Ireland. It also gave police the power to arrest without warrant any person suspected of involvement in the commission, preparation or instigation of acts of terrorism relating to Northern Irish or international affairs or any person subject to an exclusion order; such persons could be detained for a maximum of seven days.

A committee appointed to review the 1976 Act had pointed out, in its report published on Feb. 9, 1983, that there was a major trend towards terrorism beyond the context of Northern Ireland, indicative of increasing internationalization, expressed in the growth of international links of terrorist groups associated with Northern Ireland and in an increase in terrorist incidents in Great Britain unconnected with Northern Ireland.

Extreme Right-wing Movements

The National Front, despite divisions and defections, has remained the major extreme right-wing party in Britain. A British National Party led by John Tyndall was formed in April 1982 and contested 53 constituencies in the general election of the following year.

The following extreme right-wing movements have been active in recent years.

British Movement (BM)

Formed in 1968 by Colin Jordan (who left it in 1976) and with Michael McLaughlin as chairman, the BM was by 1980 organized in some 25 branches; it claimed a membership of 4,000 and had a small women's division and two journals—*British Patriot* ("the Voice of White Britain") and *British Tidings* ("Bulletin of the British Movement"). An anti-semitic and anti-immigration movement, it encouraged military training and had its own Leader Guard providing uniforms and special training.

On Jan. 20, 1981, a BM member (Rod Roberts) was sentenced to seven years in prison for arson, possession of arms and ammunition and an offence against the Race Relations Act, while six other persons were also convicted. Marches planned by the BM in Plymouth and Peterborough were prevented by bans imposed respectively on July 18 and Aug. 25, 1981. The BM was also reported as having provided mercenary units for foreign wars (e.g. in Angola). One of the largest extreme right-wing movements in Britain (after the National Front), it was wound up by McLaughlin in 1983-84.

National Action Party

Formed in the early 1980s by Kevin Randall, Eddy Morrison (who was expelled in 1986) and others, the party espouses national socialist views on race, nationalism, the "Jewish Conspiracy" etc., and lays considerable emphasis on physical opposition to the left.

National Socialist Action Party

Leadership. Tony Malski

This group, with a national socialist ideology, was formed around 1982, and advocates the formation of paramilitary groups. In mid-1986 a member in

Dundee, Scotland, was convicted of sending fascist propaganda and a concealed razor blade to an anti-apartheid activist.

Extreme Left-wing Groups

In addition to the left-wing parties mentioned in the introduction above which contested the 1987 general election, and the Socialist Workers' Party, which works to organize "rank and file" movements within trade unions but does not reject the use of force, the following groups have existed in recent years.

Communist Party of Britain—Marxist-Leninist (CPB-ML)

Founded by Reg Birch, the CPB-ML became the largest Maoist party in Britain and was partially recognized by the Chinese. In 1979, however, it adopted a pro-Albanian attitude. It does not discount the use of armed guerrilla warfare on behalf of the "oppressed working class". In its publication *The Worker* it has violently attacked the concept of "social democracy" and the Labour Party.

Revolutionary Communist League of Britain (RCLB)

This Maoist group was formed in 1978 by the merger of a Communist Federation of Britain Marxist-Leninist, founded in 1969, and a Communist Unity Association of Britain, Marxist-Leninist.

Revolutionary Communist Party (RCP)

Address. BM RCP, London WC1N 3XX

Leadership. Frank Richards (ch.)

The RCP contested the 1983 general election but not that of 1987. In August 1985 the party's chairman explained that the RCP supported the Irish Republican Army as the military wing of a national liberation movement "leading the fight against British rule in Ireland"; that British rule was "the central barrier to social progress in Ireland"; and that the RCP would continue to give unconditional support to the Republican movement as long as it remained "the leading force in the struggle against British imperialism and the biggest threat to the stability of the United Kingdom".

Revolutionary Communist Party of Britain (Marxist-Leninist)

This pro-Albanian party is hostile to all other communist parties, in particular to both Soviet and Chinese "revisionism". Its publication is the *Workers' Weekly*.

Revolutionary Workers' Party

This party, founded in 1962, is Trotskyist, of the Posadist school, and has published the newspaper *Red Flag*.

Spartacist League

This Trotskyist League was formed in 1976 by members of the US party of the same name (see separate entry). It is affiliated to the International Spartacist Tendency.

Nationalist Groups

ENGLAND

An Gof 1980 Movement

Members of this Cornish nationalist group bombed the magistrate's court at St Austell (Cornwall) on Dec. 8, 1980.

English People's Liberation Army

A group of this name claimed responsibility for sending a parcel bomb (which was defused before it could explode) to the London headquarters of the Campaign for Nuclear Disarmament on March 23, 1983.

SCOTLAND

Army of Gael (*Armach Nan Gaidheal*)

This militant Scottish nationalist group claimed responsibility for starting a fire on Nov. 24, 1982, at an Edinburgh hall where the Prime Minister (Mrs Margaret Thatcher) was due to address Scottish Conservatives two days later. The person who made this claim in a telephone call to a Glasgow newspaper stated that his group would "avenge the savage destruction of Scotland and the crippling of our steel industry" and would "by fire, flames and force of arms . . . smash English rule and free the Scottish nation".

Gaelic Language Defence League (*Ceartas* or Justice)

In a statement issued in March 1981 this organization expressed regret at the defeat of a private member's bill, introduced in the House of Commons by Donald Stewart of the Scottish National Party and designed to give the Gaelic language legal status for the first time. The statement added that the League, having tried "all legal means" to enhance the status of the language, would recommend five steps to be carried out until the authorities agreed to formal bilingualism and a Gaelic radio and television service in Scotland. These steps included the destruction of English road signs and of selected radio and television transmitters.

Demands for legal status for Gaelic have been opposed on the grounds that very few Scots now speak the language.

Scottish National Liberation Army (SNLA)

The SNLA, which was believed to have only a few active members, claimed responsibility, on Nov. 23, 1982, for 10 incendiary bombs during the previous eight months, including one sent to the Queen and another to the then Secretary of State for Defence (John Nott) in July. It was also thought to have made unspecified attacks in protest against proposed steelworks closures in Scotland. In addition it was said to have sent a letter bomb to the Lord Provost of Glasgow in February 1983 and another to the Prime Minister at 10 Downing Street, London, in March of that year.

The SNLA also claimed responsibility for exploding a bomb on Dec. 10, 1983, at the Royal Artillery barracks in Woolwich, injuring five persons.

Scottish Socialist Republican League

Six members of this League were on Oct. 14, 1980, sentenced to imprisonment for from six to 16 years on various bombing charges.

Siol Nan Gaidheal

This paramilitary group of Scottish nationalists was, on two occasions, prohibited by the police from wearing claymores (traditional Scottish Highlanders' swords) and dirks (daggers) at parades in Glasgow in March 1980 and in Aberdeen in November of that year. The Scottish National Party was said to have threatened to expel the group from its ranks because of its alleged militaristic behaviour.

WALES

Cadwyr Cymru

Members of this group were responsible for a firebomb attack on the Conservative party office at Shotton (Clwyd) on March 28, 1980.

College for the Welsh People's Movement (*Mudiad Coeg I'r Cymry*)

On Jan. 21, 1981, this Movement claimed responsibility for forcing doors and damaging a computer at the University College of Wales in Aberystwyth in protest against alleged injustice to Welsh students, constituted by the College authorities' refusal to increase Welsh language education.

Mudiad Amddiffyn Cymru (MAC)

Members of the MAC were responsible for a firebomb attack on the Conservative Party office in Cardiff on March 28, 1980.

Remembrancer (*Cofiwr*)

Members of this Welsh historical movement were responsible for several cases of arson at holiday cottages in Wales in 1980 (see also under Welsh Language Society).

Sons of Glyndwr

A group of this name was responsible for a number of attacks on holiday houses in North Wales during 1982 and on one in West Wales on Feb. 17, 1983 (see also under Welsh Language Society).

Welsh Language Society (*Cymdeithas yr laith Cymraeg*)

Leadership. Wayne Williams (ch.)

Established in 1962, this Society was originally concerned almost exclusively with the defence and expansion of the use of the Welsh language. From its beginnings it campaigned for a separate Welsh television channel and for increased use of the Welsh language in radio broadcasts. However, gradually some members of the society began to use violence, inter alia by destroying cottages owned as second homes by English people, and by removing English-language road signs.

At a conference held in September 1980 the Society decided (i) to continue its campaign for refusing to renew television licences until the precise terms of a Broadcasting Bill then under consideration were known; (ii) to co-operate with groups opposing proposals to bury radioactive waste in rural areas; and (iii) to persuade estate agents not to sell empty houses to second-home buyers.

Between December 1979 and the end of 1982 there were more than 60 arson incidents against second homes in Wales owned by non-residents of Wales. Although the Society condemned such attacks, it sympathized with the motives of those who committed them, on the grounds that the sale of such houses resulted in inflated prices which put housing beyond the means of most Welsh people.

On June 25, 1981, the chairman of the Society was sentenced to nine months in prison for his part in a conspiracy to damage television relay stations in Avon, Somerset and Sussex during 1980 (as part of a campaign for a Welsh television channel) after he had admitted the Society's liability for causing damage worth £43,000.

Welsh Socialist Republican Movement

Eight members of this Movement appeared in black berets and IRA-style uniforms in a procession at Abergele in July 1981 to mark the 12th anniversary of the death of two Welsh nationalists blown up by their own bomb on the eve of the investiture of the Prince of Wales in 1969. A further rally in memory of these two men was held by the Movement in Caernarvon on March 13, 1982, at which support was expressed for the "Troops Out" movement calling for the withdrawal of British forces from Northern Ireland; this rally was also attended (for the first time) by deputations from the Provisional *Sinn Féin* (the political wing of the Provisional Irish Republican Army—see separate entry) and the Irish Republican Socialist Party.

Workers' Army of the Welsh Republic (WAWR)

This group claimed responsibility for a number of bomb attacks in October 1981 during a tour of Wales by the Prince and Princess of Wales and also for one behind government offices in Swansea on Nov. 16, 1982.

Northern Ireland

Capital: Belfast Pop. 1,550,000

Northern Ireland is a province of the United Kingdom of Great Britain and Northern Ireland. Its population is traditionally deeply divided between (i) a Protestant majority (constituting some 60 per cent of the total population), politically represented mainly by various Unionist parties standing for the maintenance of Northern Ireland's status as part of the United Kingdom, and (ii) a Roman Catholic minority standing for eventual union of Northern Ireland with the Republic of Ireland and politically represented mainly by the Social Democratic and Labour Party (SDLP) and, increasingly in recent years, by the Provisional *Sinn Féin* (the political arm of the Provisional Irish Republican Army—PIRA). An attempt to bridge the sectarian divide in the province has been made by the constitution of the Alliance Party, which has, however, received only limited support.

All efforts made since the introduction of direct British rule in 1972 to set up a workable democratic government in Northern Ireland based on the principle of power-sharing between the two communities have failed, largely because of Unionist opposition to any power-sharing with Republican parties in Northern Ireland.

In elections to a Northern Ireland Assembly held on Oct. 20, 1982, parties gained seats as follows: Official Unionist Party (OUP) 26, Democratic Unionist Party 21, Social Democratic and Labour Party (SDLP) 14, Alliance Party 10, Provisional *Sinn Féin* five, Independent Unionist one, Ulster Popular Unionist Party one.

However, the Assembly failed to function as the SDLP and Provisional *Sinn Féin* members refused to take their seats and the Alliance Party as well as the OUP temporarily withdrew from it. The Assembly was finally dissolved on June 19, 1986. The continuation of direct rule has been approved by the British Parliament from time to time.

Political violence in Northern Ireland, which flared up in August 1969 with clashes between Protestants and Catholics, has induced the British government sharply to increase its military presence in the province. Enormous damage has been caused to Northern Ireland's infrastructure by arson and bombings.

UK emergency legislation passed in the context of the Northern Ireland civil unrest has included the following measures: (i) The Northern Ireland (Emergency Provisions) Act 1978, renewed every six months by the UK Parliament; (ii) the Prevention of Terrorism (Temporary Provisions) Act 1984, renewable annually up to its maximum life of five years; and (iii) the Northern Ireland (Emergency Provisions) Act 1987, enacted on May 15, 1987, and subject to annual renewal up to its maximum life of five years.

Statistics on terrorist activities in Northern Ireland have been issued annually by the Secretary of State for Northern Ireland. They have, inter alia, shown the following particulars for the year 1986 (with the 1985 figures in parentheses): shooting incidents 285 (196), explosions 172 (148), armed robberies 724 (450), amount stolen £1,207,152 (£655,690), malicious fires 906 (748), deaths 61 (54)—comprising 37 (25) civilians and 24 (29) members of the forces; persons convicted on charges of terrorist offences 584 (648)—including 26 (38) convicted of charges of murder.

The promotion of cross-border co-operation between the British and Irish governments in security and related matters was one of the provisions of the Hillsborough Agreement approved by the Irish and British parliaments on Nov. 21 and 27, 1985, respectively.

Under a revised UK-US extradition treaty, ratified by the US Senate on July 17,1986, a number of alleged Irish Republican Army terrorists were extradited to the United Kingdom for trial.

Approval of the European Convention on the Suppression of Terrorism (which had been ratified by the United Kingdom on Oct. 25, 1978) was the subject of a bill approved by the *Dáil* (the lower house of parliament of the Republic of Ireland) on Dec. 17, 1986, and by the Irish Senate on Jan. 15, 1987. The principal object of the convention was to facilitate the extradition and prosecution of perpetrators of terrorist acts even though such acts might be politically motivated and therefore be excluded from earlier extradition arrangements. However, under the bill the implementation of the new extradition procedure was deferred until December 1987.

Loyalist Movements

Protestant Action Force

This small group emerged in Armagh City in mid-1982 and has been responsible for killing a *Sinn Féin* election worker in October of that year and for other attacks on Catholics in March 1983. The group's name had earlier been used as a cover by the Ulster Volunteer Force (see separate entry).

The Third Force

Plans for the establishment of this Force were revealed by the Rev. Ian Paisley, the leader of the Democratic Unionist Party, at a rally at Newtownards (Co. Down) on Nov. 23, 1981. Dr Paisley had earlier said on Nov. 16 that, in view of official plans to set up an Anglo-Irish Inter-Governmental Council and of the British government's refusal to establish a third security force (in addition to the Army and the police), Ulster Unionists would make the province of Northern Ireland ungovernable and would demonstrate that such a third force was already in existence. The Newtownards rally was attended by Unionist supporters in paramilitary uniform, but estimates of numbers involved in the parade of the "Third Force" varied between 5,000 and 15,000.

James Prior, then Secretary of State for Northern Ireland, had made it clear on Nov. 18, 1981, that private armies had no place in society and that the law did not recognize any distinction between one private army and another, and he added on Nov. 24 that the government would not allow private armies to take over the work of the police and would "not adopt methods which abandon the rule of law or which are intended to punish the innocent".

Ulster Defence Association (UDA)

The UDA has been regarded as the strongest of various extreme Protestant paramilitary organizations set up in response to the violent activities of the Provisional Irish Republican Army (PIRA). Thomas Herron, then secretary of the UDA, claimed on Oct. 16, 1972, that it had some 50,000 members trained in all aspects of guerrilla warfare. After the PIRA had established "no-go" areas (where the writ of the Northern Ireland government did not run) in parts of Londonderry, the UDA established its own "no-go" areas in different parts of Northern Ireland in May–June 1972 in protest against the continued existence of the PIRA "no-go" areas; this UDA action led to clashes between UDA members and the Army.

After two UDA leaders had had talks on June 13, 1972, with William Whitelaw, then Secretary of State for Northern Ireland, the UDA agreed to postpone the establishment of further "no-go" areas but stated that if no action had been taken within 14 days to remove the PIRA areas it would put up permanent barricades all over the province. After another meeting with Whitelaw, the UDA declared on June 28 that it would carry out its plan and that some of its barricades would be permanent until the PIRA barricades in Londonderry were taken down. The Army tried in Belfast on July 3, 1972, to prevent the UDA from setting up barricades, but in order to avoid a confrontation the Army agreed that soldiers should set up the road-blocks and that the UDA should be allowed to patrol the streets behind them.

Although the Army had cleared the PIRA's Londonderry areas in a swift operation on July 31, 1972, UDA members continued their activities in Belfast, where clashes between the Army and UDA units occurred on Sept. 7-8, 1972, leading to the death of two UDA members, and again on Oct. 12-13 and Oct. 16; thereafter Herron threatened that the UDA would possibly go over to an offensive against the Army. However, the threat was not carried out and Herron himself was assassinated in September 1973 (it was thought by a member of a rival Protestant group). The UDA itself was held responsible for numerous assassinations, mainly (but not exclusively) of Roman Catholics.

Trials of a number of UDA supporters or members took place in England and Scotland, where the UDA was in 1974 thought to have some 1,000 members. On Dec. 4, 1974, three defendants connected with the Conservative Party were sentenced in Winchester to imprisonment for from five to 10 years for involvement in an attempt to import guns and explosives from Canada for the UDA.

On June 26, 1979, a total of 11 UDA members convicted in Dumfries and Paisley of conspiring to further their organization's aims by unlawfully acquiring guns and ammunition were sentenced in Glasgow to terms ranging from seven to 16 years in prison; they included the supreme commander in Scotland and the Dumfries and Paisley area commanders of the UDA.

Whilst remaining a paramilitary organization, the UDA has, through its leaders, expressed its willingness to consider, in a New Ulster Study Group and (in 1981) in an Ulster Loyalist Democratic Party, other constitutional options, principally that of establishing an independent state of Northern Ireland.

Ulster Freedom Fighters (UFF)

This organization has been said to operate under the aegis of the Ulster Defence Assocation (UDA—see separate entry), although the latter has on occasion disowned it. In 1973 members of the UFF claimed responsibility for killing two young Catholics, and also for several bombings, in the Belfast area. Late in June 1973 the UFF accepted responsibility for the murder of a Catholic ex-senator and former election agent for the leader of the Social Democratic and Labour Party (SDLP).

The UFF was officially banned in Northern Ireland on Nov. 12, 1973, but nevertheless continued to be involved in assassinations both in the Republic and in Northern Ireland. In particular, the UFF accepted responsibility for killing the (Protestant) *Fine Gael* Senator Billy Fox at Clones (Co. Mohaghan) on March 11, 1974, for which five alleged members of the Provisional IRA were sentenced in Dublin on June 7 of that year to penal servitude for life.

The UFF also claimed responsibility for numerous other murders, mainly of Catholics, in Belfast, between Sept. 16 and Nov. 28, 1974, and in late 1981 and early 1982 for several murders which, the UFF alleged, were in response to the Provisional IRA's campaign during the hunger strike of its prisoners which had cost 64 lives.

Later the UFF claimed responsibility for an attack on March 14, 1984, on Gerry Adams (the Provisional *Sinn Féin* leader and member of the UK House of Commons) and three other *Sinn Féin* members, all of whom were injured. For this attack three men were on March 22, 1985, sentenced to imprisonment for between 12 and 18 years.

Ulster United Loyalist Front

Founded. Aug. 7, 1985

This Front was formed by some 650 Unionists, including members of the Official Unionist Party (OUP), the Democratic Unionist Party (DUP) and the paramilitary Ulster Defence Association (UDA). The Front was determined to resist by all possible means the implementation of the Hillsborough Agreement, which it regarded as paving the way towards the eventual incorporation of Northern Ireland into the Republic of Ireland.

Ulster Volunteer Force (UVF)

The UVF was formed in 1912 as a paramilitary organization to prevent the establishment of a Home Rule government in Ireland; it was recruited from among Protestants and was armed with rifles and ammunition smuggled in from the continent of Europe; and it was at the time supported by the Conservatives in Britain opposed to the granting of home rule to Ireland. In the 1960s it was revived to take part in the Protestant struggle against the Irish Republican Army (IRA).

Following the killing of a young Catholic by a UVF member (who considered his victim to be a member of the IRA), the UVF was banned in 1966 as the Northern Ireland government wished to prevent the escalation of sectarian warfare. It was re-legalized on May 15, 1974, but was again proscribed in November 1975, after it had been involved in various acts of violence.

A number of alleged UVF members were later sentenced to imprisonment in Scotland. They included one given a seven-year sentence in Dumfries on Nov. 26, 1974, for illegal possession of arms, and nine others sentenced in Glasgow on June 22, 1979, to terms ranging from 12 to 18 years for conspiring to further the aims of their organization (which was not banned in the United Kingdom) between 1975 and February 1979.

In a trial which ended on April 11, 1983, 14 loyalists, including 13 UVF members, were sentenced to life imprisonment after being convicted of over 60 terrorist offences, mainly on the evidence of a self-confessed UVF commander who had been granted immunity from prosecution after turning crown witness.

On the other hand, a UVF member who had in August 1982 given evidence against 29 men charged with 59 terrorist offences had later retracted his evidence and was himself sentenced on June 13, 1983, to 10 years in prison for armed robbery.

In March 1984 a number of UVF members were arrested in Northern Ireland on allegations of planning to extort money from a chain of grocery retailers by threatening to poison food on sale in its shops.

Three suspects arrested in Glasgow on Oct. 21-23, 1985, were on March 13, 1986, sentenced to eight years in prison for conspiring to further the aims of the banned UVF by acquiring weapons and explosives.

Republican Movements

Catholic Reaction Force

This group, using automatic weapons—one of which had previously been used in operations by the Irish National Liberation Army (INLA—see separate entry) killed three men and injured seven in an attack on Nov. 20, 1983, on a Pentecostal gospel hall in Co. Armagh. The group described the attack as "token retaliation" for recent sectarian violence against Catholics in Armagh.

Irish National Liberation Army (INLA)

The INLA, with headquarters in Dublin, was set up as the military wing of an Irish Republican Socialist Party (IRSP), which had broken away from the Official Irish Republican Army in December 1974. The IRSP has been a legal political party in the Republic of Ireland with the aim of "ending British rule in Ireland" and establishing "a united democratic socialist republic".

In 1975 the INLA began to conduct armed warfare in order to bring about a British military withdrawal from Northern Ireland which was to be united with the Republic on the basis of "socialist principles". The INLA claimed responsibility inter alia for the murder of Airey Neave, former Conservative spokesman for Northern Ireland affairs in the British House of Commons, in London in March 1979, and of a former police reservist and a police constable in Northern Ireland in July 1979.

On July 2, 1979, the British government decided to proscribe the INLA, both in Northern Ireland under the Northern Ireland (Emergency Provisions) Act and in the United Kingdom under the Prevention of Terrorism (Temporary Provisions) Act. The INLA, however, continued its bombing campaign and in particular made two bomb attacks on a school of infantry on Salisbury Plain on March 7, 1980. Of INLA members convicted of various offences and held in the Maze prison (Belfast), three (among them one described as the "officer commanding" INLA prisoners), died there between May and August as a result of a hunger strike in support of a demand for "special status" for these prisoners; the INLA, however, ended its use of hunger strikes on Sept. 6, 1980.

In 1982 the INLA claimed responsibility (i) for the killing on June 4 in Dublin of a former director of operations of the Official IRA, who was said to have killed the founder of the IRSP (Seamus Costello) in Dublin in 1977; (ii) for an attack on a Protestant Belfast city councillor on Sept. 1; and (iii) for a bomb explosion which killed a British soldier and two children in Belfast on Sept. 15; and (iv) for several other bomb explosions in Belfast in October.

Three INLA members arrested in Paris on Aug. 28, 1982, were found in possession of arms and explosives and of a list of potential British targets; the French police also believed that they were in touch with the Basque separatist ETA organization in Spain.

In the most serious attack against the British forces by the INLA, 11 soldiers and six civilians were killed by a bomb at a public house at Ballykelly (Co.

Londonderry) on Dec. 6, 1982. For involvement in this attack four INLA members were, on June 12, 1986, sentenced to life imprisonment, while a fifth defendant was given a 10-year sentence.

On Jan. 5, 1983, the government of the Republic of Ireland declared the INLA to be a proscribed organization.

A member of the INLA's army council, in an interview with a US radio station in mid-January 1983, defended his organization's activities and stated that the INLA would maintain its attacks on police and troops because they represented "the physical oppression of the British presence" and that it would in future "carry out operations against any element within the British Establishment depending on logistics and intelligence available". He also declared that the INLA differed from the Irish Republican Army (IRA) in that it was a revolutionary socialist organization and that, while the IRA was quite likely to lay down its arms when the British withdrew from Ireland, the INLA believed that the resolution of the national question was "just the first stage in the process for establishing a 32-county socialist state". He also envisaged that "at some point in the future the most conscious revolutionary element within the IRA would enter into a broad front with the INLA".

On Nov. 25, 1986, an INLA member was sentenced to life imprisonment for involvement in an attempt to bomb the Chelsea army barracks in London in November 1985.

In a number of trials of alleged Republican terrorists courts ruled that the evidence supplied by a co-defendant who had turned crown witness (a "supergrass") was not admissible, with the result that the accused were acquitted for lack of reliable evidence. This was the case in the trial of 24 INLA members who were freed on appeal on Dec. 24, 1986, since the validity of the evidence of Harry Kirkpatrick (a former INLA member) had been questioned; he had himself been sentenced on June 3, 1983, to terms of life imprisonment on each of five murder charges and given a nominal total of 922 years' imprisonment.

By the end of 1986, however, it became apparent that the INLA was divided into four factions. In a feud between these factions 11 persons were killed in Northern Ireland and the Republic of Ireland between December 1986 and March 1987. It was believed that three of the factions wanted the INLA to be disbanded, whereas the fourth faction, led by Gerard Steenson, refused to disband. Those killed included, on Feb. 1, Mary McGlinchey (the wife of Dominic McGlinchey, the PIRA member serving a 10-year prison sentence in the Republic of Ireland) and Steenson himself, shot dead on March 15.

People's Liberation Army (PLA)

In December 1986 this group was reported to have been established in Northern Ireland. It had claimed responsibility for killing an officer of the Royal Ulster Constabulary (RUC, the Northern Ireland police) in Belfast on Nov. 10 and for an attack outside a police station, also in Belfast, on Nov. 29.

The PLA has also been referred to as the Irish People's Liberation Organization.

Provisional Irish Republican Army (PIRA or **"Provos")**

The Provisional IRA broke away from the Irish Republican Army (IRA) in 1969 as a direct-action organization intent upon launching a guerrilla campaign and making Northern Ireland ungovernable by forcing the British government to withdraw its armed forces and to relinquish all responsibility for the province. At political level the PIRA has operated through the Provisional *Sinn Féin*, which has remained a legal party both in the Republic and in Northern Ireland, whereas the PIRA was declared a proscribed organization under the Prevention of Terrorism (Temporary Provisions) Bill enacted in the United Kingdom on Nov. 29, 1974. (The Official IRA suspended its military activities in 1972 and was disbanded thereafter. By 1977 it was superseded by *Sinn Féin*—The Workers' Party, which in 1982 dropped the prefix *Sinn Féin*.)

The PIRA is organized on military lines. It has a women's section known as *Cumann Na mBan*, which has been involved in gathering information, planting fire-bombs and providing shelter in "safe houses". The youth wing of the PIRA is known as *Fianna Na h'Eireann*, whose members assist the PIRA in gathering intelligence, acting as look-outs and transporting weapons.

The PIRA began its campaign in Northern Ireland in 1969 by sniping at British soldiers and bombing property; by September 1971 the PIRA was using rocket launchers, and in April 1973 letter bombs appeared, to be followed by parcel bombs sent to senior civil servants. In August 1971 the Northern Ireland authorities introduced internment without trial of suspects, which remained in force for four years despite a civil disobedience campaign called by the Roman Catholic opposition parties in Northern Ireland. Action by British troops against the PIRA led to the death of 13 persons in Londonderry from army gunfire on Jan. 30, 1972, and in a reprisal action for this so-called "bloody Sunday" the British embassy in Dublin was attacked by PIRA members.

By that time a state of confrontation had been reached between the PIRA on the one hand and, on the other, the British Army, the Ulster Defence Regiment (UDR) and the Royal Ulster Constabulary (the Northern Ireland police), while members of paramilitary Protestant organizations (of which the Ulster Defence Association—see separate entry—was the strongest) were responsible for numerous killings (mainly, but not exclusively, of Catholics).

Following a meeting between Protestant churchmen and leaders of the PIRA and the Provisional *Sinn Féin* at Feakle, Co. Clare (in the Republic of Ireland), on Dec. 10, 1974, the PIRA observed a temporary ceasefire from Dec. 22, 1974, to Jan. 16, 1975. Although renewed from Feb. 10, 1975, the ceasefire gradually broke down in the course of 1976. Later PIRA activities in Northern Ireland included several fire-bomb attacks, mainly in Belfast, during August and September 1977, when property worth several million pounds was destroyed. On Jan. 1, 1978, the PIRA admitted that it had been responsible for organizing 46 bombing and shooting incidents since the beginning of the year. On Feb. 17, 1978, a total of 12 people were killed and 30 were injured in a PIRA fire-bomb attack on a restaurant in Co. Down. A new series of fire-bomb attacks was carried out between October 1978 and March 1979.

By that time it was clear that the PIRA was receiving weapons from abroad, including US-made M-60 machine-guns (firing up to 550 rounds a minute) which were first used in January 1978. In the most serious action carried out by the PIRA in Northern Ireland during 1979 a total of 18 British soldiers were killed by two bombs at Warrenpoint (Co. Down) on Aug. 27.

In the course of a further spate of sectarian killings in Northern Ireland, the PIRA declared on Jan. 21, 1981, that by shooting dead (on that day) a former Speaker of the Northern Ireland House of Commons and his son, also a former member of that House, it had made "a deliberate attempt on the symbols of hated Unionism" in "direct reprisal for a whole series of loyalist assassinations and murder attempts on nationalist people and nationalist activities".

The killing of the Rev. Robert Bradford, an Official Unionist member of the British House of Commons, on Nov. 14, 1981, was described by the PIRA as an "execution" carried out in the course of its campaign against the British presence in Northern Ireland.

In connexion with PIRA activities in the Republic of Ireland, Seamus Twomey, then chief of staff of the PIRA, was in October 1973 sentenced to three years in prison for membership of the proscribed PIRA and for receiving money taken in an armed robbery; he escaped from prison in Dublin shortly afterwards, spent several years in Northern Ireland and was rearrested in Dublin on Dec. 3, 1977. On June 12, 1978, he was given a five-year prison sentence for his escape and a concurrent three-year sentence for PIRA membership.

The most conspicuous operation carried out by PIRA members in the Republic was the killing on Aug. 27, 1979, of Earl Mountbatten of Burma (a cousin of Queen Elizabeth II and uncle of the Duke of Edinburgh) by a bomb placed on his fishing boat. The two alleged perpetrators of this crime were sentenced to life imprisonment in Dublin on Nov. 23, 1979.

In England the PIRA carried out a bombing campaign between March 8, 1973, and May 1976. Of those involved in causing explosions in London on March 8, 1973, eight were sentenced to life imprisonment in Winchester on Nov. 15 of that year, while a ninth defendant was sentenced to 10 years in prison; those given life sentences included Dolours Price, her sister Marion, Hugh Feeney and Gerald Kelly, all of whom were later, with other PIRA prisoners, involved in hunger strikes in support of their demand to be granted special status as "political prisoners". PIRA actions carried out in England in 1974 included a bomb attack on a public house in Guildford (Surrey) on Oct. 5, in which five people were killed; another such attack in Woolwich (London) on Nov. 7, when two persons were killed and 34 injured; and a third one on a public house in Birmingham on Nov. 21, in which 21 persons lost their lives and 120 were injured.

In connexion with the Guildford and Woolwich attacks, life sentences were imposed on Oct. 22, 1975, on four men and a young woman. Numerous other bomb explosions took place in December 1974 and January 1975, and two bomb factories were discovered—one in Southampton in December 1974 and another in Hammersmith (London) on Feb. 27, 1975. For involvement in this PIRA campaign a number of suspected PIRA members were during February and March 1975 sentenced to imprisonment for terms of up to 20 years. A bomb explosion at the Hilton Hotel in London on Sept. 5, 1975, killed two and injured 63 people and was attributed to the PIRA. Prominent persons killed by the PIRA included Ross McWhirter, the publisher who had called for the establishment of a reward fund for information leading to the arrest of bombers and who was shot dead on Nov. 27, 1975. Further bomb explosions took place in February-March 1976 after the death of Frank Stagg, a PIRA member who had been on hunger strike while serving a 10-year sentence for planning to attack targets in Coventry. A number of other alleged bombers were sentenced to imprisonment between May 1976 and January 1977.

Following the suspension of its bombing campaign between May 1976 and January 1977, the PIRA declared in Dublin on Feb. 1 that its "campaign against military and economic targets" would be "maintained" through the coming year both in the six counties (i.e. Northern Ireland) and on the British mainland; "confident of victory", it forecast "a future phase of war which will be more intense than anything experienced to date".

Following a number of sporadic explosions, the PIRA bombing campaign in England was resumed on Dec. 17, 1978, with bombings in London and five other cities and an attack on an oil storage tank at Canvey Island (Essex) on Jan. 17, 1979. Later the PIRA claimed responsibility for shooting, during February and March 1980, three British soldiers in West Germany, one of whom later died of his wounds.

The PIRA was responsible for further bomb attacks in London in December 1980 and January 1981. Another bomb explosion was caused by the PIRA at the Sullom Voe oil terminal (Shetlands), which the Queen was opening on May 9, 1981 (when, however, no injuries were caused). Further PIRA bomb attacks, carried out in London during October and November 1981, resulted in the death of two civilians and a bomb disposal expert and in injury to other persons, among them Lt.-Gen. Sir Steuart Pringle (Commander-General of the Royal Marines).

After two major bomb attacks carried out in London on July 20, 1982, resulting in the death of 11 soldiers, the PIRA declared that it had carried them out "in accordance with the right of self-defence under Article 51 of the United Nations Charter".

By 1980 it was evident that public support for the PIRA among the Roman Catholic section of Northern Ireland's population was increasing notably, mainly at the expense of the traditional Catholic parties (the largest of which is the Social Democratic and Labour Party). In the Republic, however, the growth of public support for the PIRA was not quite so marked. At funerals of PIRA casualties of the struggle the organization was able to rally thousands of sympathizers.

A number of convicted prisoners from among the many hundreds (of PIRA members and other Republicans), held mainly in the H Blocks of the Maze prison near Belfast, conducted a hunger strike between Oct. 27, 1980, and Oct. 3, 1981, with the object of obtaining special treatment and ultimately the status of political prisoners—a demand which the British government steadfastly refused to grant. This hunger strike, resulting in the death of many involved in it, appeared to further the cause of the PIRA, as evidenced by several election results.

In a by-election held on April 9, 1981, in Fermanagh and South Tyrone, to a seat in the British House of Commons, Robert Sands, a PIRA hunger striker (serving a 14-year term for arms offences and standing as an Anti-H Block/Armagh, Political Prisoner), won the seat against an Official Unionist (Harry West) by gaining 30,492 votes (a majority of 1,446 votes). However, Sands died in prison on May 5. In a further by-election held on Aug. 20, 1981, the seat was taken by Owen Carron, a member of the Provisional *Sinn Féin*, as the candidate of the same committee which had nominated Sands (the majority being increased to 2,230 votes).

For the general elections held in the Republic on June 11, 1981, the National H Block/Armagh Committee nominated nine prisoners (four of them on hunger strike) and two of these candidates, both being PIRA members, were elected—Paddy Agnew and Kieran Doherty, the latter dying on Aug. 2, the 73rd day of his hunger strike.

Lennie Murphy, reported to be the leader of the loyalist Ulster Volunteer Force (see separate entry), was shot in Belfast on Nov. 16, 1982, and died later, with the PIRA claiming that he had been "executed for the murder of 20 innocent Nationalists" and for planning to set up a new loyalist "terror team" in Belfast.

Cross-border co-operation in security matters was illustrated by the case of Dominic McGlinchey, a prominent PIRA member, who was wanted in Northern Ireland for the murder of a woman in March 1977 but had fled to the Republic. On Dec. 7, 1982, the Irish Supreme Court ordered his extradition to Northern Ireland (this being the first case in which the Republic had ordered the return to the North of a person wanted for terrorist offences). McGlinchey had claimed immunity from extradition on the ground that his action had been carried out under instructions from the PIRA, but the Chief Justice decided that his offence could not be considered political. After he had jumped bail he was captured in Co. Clare on March 17, 1984, and extradited to Northern Ireland on the following day. On Dec. 24, 1984, he was sentenced to life imprisonment for the 1977 murder, but his conviction was quashed by the Northern Ireland Appeal Court on Oct. 9, 1985. He was, however, not released but extradited to the Republic to face other specific arms charges on which he was, in Dublin on March 11, 1986, sentenced to 10 years in prison. (He was suspected of having been a leading member of the Irish National Liberation Army—see separate entry—since 1984.)

On Jan. 16, 1983, a county court judge, William Doyle. was killed by PIRA members.

On Sept. 23, 1983, a group of 38 convicted Republican prisoners escaped from the Maze prison in Belfast; 19 of them were recaptured within two days, and several others later—three of them in Amsterdam on Jan. 16, 1986, and another in Dublin on Feb. 14, all being eventually extradited to Northern Ireland.

On Dec. 17, 1983, a PIRA bomb exploded outside Harrods department store in London killing two police officers and three shoppers and injuring 81 other persons, among them 13 policemen.

A bomb planted by the PIRA at the Grand Hotel in Brighton and exploded on Oct. 12, 1984, killed five persons (but not the Prime Minister, Margaret Thatcher, nor other members of the government staying at the hotel for a Conservative Party conference) and injured over 30 other persons. Of the PIRA members involved in this attack, Patrick Magee was, on June 23, 1986, sentenced to a minimum of 35 years in prison on seven charges including the murder of five persons (and on a charge of conspiracy to plant bombs at English seaside resorts in 1985); four other PIRA members were sentenced to life imprisonment and a sixth to eight years in prison.

On Feb. 28, 1985, PIRA members killed nine RUC officers in an attack on a police station at Newry (Co. Down).

On Aug. 5, 1986, the PIRA announced that anyone involved in administration, maintenance or building work at army and police installations in Northern Ireland would be considered a legitimate target for assassination.

The PIRA also claimed responsibility for a bomb explosion at the British Army of the Rhine (BOAR) headquarters at Rheindahlen (West Germany) on March 23, 1987, when over 30 persons were injured. The bomb was of a type used previously by the PIRA in Northern Ireland. (Responsibility for this explosion was, however, also claimed by a National Democratic Front for the Liberation of Germany.)

On April 25, 1987, Lord Justice Gibson (a Northern Ireland judge) and his wife were killed by the PIRA at Killen (Co. Down).

Among supporters of the PIRA in other countries, an organization known as the Northern Irish Aid Committee (NORAID) based in the United States (where it was officially declared to be an agent of the PIRA) has been accused by the British authorities of shipping weapons to both the PIRA and the Irish National Liberation Army (INLA—see separate entry). On July 22, 1983, a court in New York sentenced Gabriel Megahey (an Irish citizen described as the head of the PIRA in the United States) to seven years in prison for conspiring with three others to purchase and smuggle arms, including surface-to-air missiles, to Ireland for use by Republican terrorists. Of the three other defendants, two were sentenced to three years and the third to two years in prison.

On July 28, 1984, Martin Galvin, national publicity director of NORAID, was banned from entering the United Kingdom, but he nevertheless appeared at the *Sinn Féin* rally in Belfast on Aug. 12, when he managed to evade arrest. On Aug. 21 he appeared in Dublin, where his presence was officially described as unwelcome. He again entered Northern Ireland in August 1985, while some 100 NORAID members were present there from Aug. 4 to 13 and took part in a march through Belfast on Aug. 11.

The PIRA has repeatedly received moral support from Col. Moamer al-Gadaffi, the Libyan leader, who, in an interview broadcast on Irish television on

Oct. 28, 1986, called on "all Irish youth in the North and South to participate in the struggle for the liberation of Ulster". On May 14, 1987, it was claimed in London that Libya had in 1986 supplied the PIRA with quantities of explosives in retaliation for the use of British bases by US aircraft in air-raids on Libya.

United States of America

Capital: Washington, D.C. Pop. 239,280,000

The United States of America, consisting of 50 member states with a measure of internal self-government, has an executive President elected for a four-year term by a college of representatives elected directly in each state, and re-eligible once only; he is both head of state and head of the executive, whose other members he nominates. Legislative power is held by Congress consisting of a 100-member Senate and a 435-member House of Representatives. In each state two senators are elected by direct adult suffrage for a six-year term, with one-third of the Senate's membership being renewed every two years. Members of the House of Representatives are similarly elected for a two-year term. There is a traditional two-party system, but the constitutional separation of executive and legislative functions precludes party government in the accepted sense (as the President's party may be faced with a majority of the other party in Congress).

As a result of elections held on Nov. 4, 1986, seats were distributed as follows: (i) in the Senate—Republicans 55, Democrats 45; (ii) in the House of Representatives—Democrats 258, Republicans 177. Parties which contested the 1984 presidential elections, in which the Republican candidate Ronald Reagan was re-elected, included the (right-wing) American Party, the (social-democratic) Citizens Party, the (pro-Soviet) Communist Party USA, the Libertarian Party, the Populist Party, and three Trotskyist parties—the Socialist Workers' Party, the Workers' League and the Workers' World Party.

Political organizations outside the legal parties which have taken part in elections have included (i) extreme right-wing organizations, among which the Ku Klux Klan has continued to be involved in violent action in pursuance of its white supremacy policy, while others have acted towards similar objectives; (ii) extreme left-wing organizations; and (iii) national liberation movements, among which the Armed Forces of Puerto Rican National Liberation (see below under Puerto Rico) have been responsible for numerous acts of violence in recent years.

Within black America there has been in recent years a strong tendency towards self-help as many blacks have come to regard white racism as persistent and endemic and as having been little modified by civil rights legislation. While *de jure* segregation had been abolished, *de facto* segregation continued in many cities where new ghettoes had been created in areas deserted by whites.

Several of the major underground movements of the 1960s and 1970s have since faded away, notably the Black Power movement which had among its leaders Stokeley Carmichael and Floyd McKissick and which had included the Black Panther Party led by Eldridge Cleaver; on the extreme right the Minutemen of 1959-67; and on the extreme left the Weather Underground of 1969-81.

Extreme Right-wing Movements

The Covenant, the Sword and the Arm of the Lord

This group, described as the political and paramilitary arm of the Church of Zarepath-Horeb and as part of an anti-Semitic Christian Identity Movement, had a paramilitary training camp in the Ozark Mountains in Arkansas, which was taken control of by state and federal law officers on April 22, 1985. On Sept. 4 of that year one of the group's leaders was sentenced to 20 years in prison on various charges, including arson attacks on a church for homosexuals and a Jewish centre in Indiana; six other members were given shorter prison terms.

Ku Klux Klan

The first Ku Klux Klan was founded in Tennessee in 1865 and rapidly developed into a political organization with the aim of restoring white supremacy in the South (lost in the civil war) by terrorizing the newly emancipated and enfranchised Negroes; it was banned by special legislation under President Grant in 1871.

A second Ku Klux Klan emerged in Georgia in

1915 as an anti-Negro, anti-Jewish, anti-Catholic, anti-foreign and anti-labour organization, whose members attacked not only the organization's political opponents but also bootleggers, gamblers and wifebeaters. In 1920-24, it grew into a nation-wide movement with between 4,000,000 and 5,000,000 members and politically dominated the southern states and also Indiana, Colorado and Oregon. After 1926 its influence declined, and in 1939 it was discredited by the discovery of its links with the pro-Nazi German-American *Bund*. In 1944 it was disbanded when the government attempted to collect unpaid taxes of $685,000 owed by Ku Klux Klan business enterprises. Thereafter the Ku Klux Klan was revived in Atlanta (Georgia) by Dr Samuel Green.

A sub-committee of the House of Representatives committee on un-American activities found, after a public investigation into the Ku Klux Klan conducted between Oct. 19, 1965, and Feb. 24, 1966, that, as its members had intimidated and done physical violence "to young and old, male and female", its activities should be curbed.

During the 1964-66 civil rights campaign numerous Ku Klux Klan members were involved in acts of violence (including arson and murder) directed against blacks and white civil-rights workers. The first time an all-white Mississippi jury convicted Ku Klux Klan members of murdering civil rights workers was on Oct. 20, 1967, but the prison sentences imposed on the four defendants ranged only from three to seven years.

Although numerically declining, the Ku Klux Klan has remained active in recent years, mainly in the southern states. Members of the Klan were involved in an attempted invasion of the island of Dominica in early 1981 (purely for gain—see also under National Socialist (Nazi) Party of America), and in this connexion Stephen Donal Black (national "Grand Wizard" of the Klan) and one of his lieutenants were sentenced to three years in prison in New Orleans on July 23, 1981, for plotting to overthrow the government in Dominica.

By 1986 the Ku Klux Klan consisted of three main divisions. The first of these, the Invisible Empire, had about 4,000 members in the late 1970s, and according to the US Justice Department it was the most violence-prone Klan in America. However, its "Imperial Wizard", James W. Farrands (a Yankee, i.e. an inhabitant of New England, and a Catholic), denied in late 1986 that his members were terrorists and stressed that they were "a respectable political movement". He said that the Klan supported the aims of some blacks to create a new Africa in the southern states, and that there was "a lot to be said for apartheid". He also said that his movement believed in protectionism, the sterilization of single-parent women after their second child, and the prohibition of abortion.

The second division, the United Klans of America Inc. with about 2,500 members was, according to Farrands, the biggest of the three divisions but consisted mainly of middle-aged men who had joined it in the 1960s. The third division, the Knights of the Ku Klux Klan, was said to be based in Florida.

In recent years Klan members (and other white supremacists) have been prevented, if necessary by National Guardsmen and state troopers, from disputing civil rights demonstrations. In a number of civil actions juries have ordered the payment of substantional damages to the families of blacks lynched in earlier years (e.g. against the United Klans of America Inc. and six past or present members, ordered in February 1987 to pay $7,000,000).

According to Klanwatch, a civil rights organization based in Montgomery, Alabama, the Ku Klux Klan was by 1986 "much a spent force" as most of its dangerous members had joined neo-Nazi groups.

National Socialist German Workers' Party—Foreign Branch (NSDAP-AO)

The existence of this neo-Nazi organization in the United States was referred to by the Bavarian Ministry of the Interior in connexion with the case of Helmut Oxner, an alleged member of the organization, who killed three foreigners and injured two other persons in Nuremberg on June 24, 1982, and who committed suicide before police could arrest him. He had earlier been charged with offensive and threatening behaviour.

National Socialist (Nazi) Party of America

This small party has taken over from the National Socialist German Workers' Party (the NSDAP created and led by Adolf Hitler) not only its insignia (such as the swastika) but also its racialist and nationalist tenets and its hierarchical structure. In 1981 six members of the party were tried for plotting terrorist bombing attacks at Greensboro (North Carolina) between July and November 1980. In April 1981 two members of the party were said to be involved in an attempt to invade the island of Dominica (see also under Ku Klux Klan).

The Order (*Brüder Schweigen* or Silent Brotherhood)

This group, founded in September 1983, had according to investigations by law enforcement agencies, intended to wage war against the US government (which it described as a "Zionist Occupation Government" or ZOG), had incited whites to kill blacks, Jews and public officers, and had called for the use of counterfeiting and robbery to finance its activities. Many members of the group were or had been members of an "Aryan Nation" group (or Church of Jesus Christ Christian), an official of which had established a computer link-up for extremist groups, known as the Aryan Liberty Network. Among those killed by the group were a Jew (shot in Denver on June 18, 1984) and a suspected police informer. However, the group's founder, Robert Jay Mathews, died during a police siege near Seattle on Dec. 8, 1984, and on Feb. 6-7, 1985, a federal judge in Seattle sentenced 10 of the group's members to terms of imprisonment ranging from 40 to 100 years for racketeering and other offences, the maximum sentences being imposed for the two killings of 1984; another 13 defendants were sentenced to 20 years each. It was believed that of an estimated $4,000,000 stolen by The Order significant sums had been channelled to leaders of the Ku Klux Klan and to neo-Nazi groups.

Black Separatist Movement

Nation of Islam

Leadership. The Rev. Louis Farrakhan

The leader of this Black Muslim group has advocated the creation of a black nation state within the United States. On Sept. 15, 1985, he expressed anti-Semitic views and declared that the black people of America and of the western hemisphere were "the chosen people".

On May 1-2, 1985, he had stated that he had turned down an offer of weapons from Col. Moamer al-Gaddaffi the Libyan leader, but that he had accepted a $5,000,000 interest-free loan to assist a company of his to market products aimed at the black market. (Col. Gadaffi had on March 2 inter alia urged US blacks to struggle to establish an independent state.)

Extreme Left-wing Movements

Revolutionary Communist Party (RCP)

This independent Maoist party was founded in 1967 as the Bay Area Revolutionary Union in California and took its present name in 1975. Originally pro-Chinese, it denounced the Chinese leadership as revisionist after the arrest of the "gang of four" in 1976. It has staged demonstrations against Deng Xiaoping (during the latter's visit to Washington in 1979) and against Soviet representatives at the United Nations. It advocates a boycott of elections, which it regards as meaningless, and has called for revolutionary war and armed seizure of power by the working class. In 1984 it formed, with other small Maoist groups, a Revolutionary Internationalist Movement.

Revolutionary Fighting Group

This, until then unknown, group claimed responsibility for a bomb explosion on Staten Island, New York, on Jan. 29, 1982, when extensive damage was caused to a building housing an office of the Federal Bureau of Investigation (FBI).

Spartacist League

This League was formed in 1964 after its members had been expelled from the (Trotskyist) Socialist Workers' Party. After being expelled from the Fourth International, International Committee, the League founded, in 1966, the International Spartacist Tendency as an independent Trotskyist organization.

It was later listed by the California Attorney General as operating in California in 1979; it was said to have several hundred members and to have, in addition, a Spartacus Youth League. The group denied, however, that it advocated the use of violence, as claimed by the Attorney General.

Puerto Rico

Capital: San Juan Pop. 3,500,000

The Commonwealth of Puerto Rico is, under its 1952 Constitution, "a free state associated with the United States", in which executive power is vested in a Governor who is elected by universal adult suffrage of resident citizens and who presides over an Executive. There is an elected bicameral legislature consisting of a 27-member Senate and a 51-member House of Representatives.

As a result of elections held on Nov. 6, 1984, seats in the House of Representatives were distributed as follows: Popular Democratic Party 33, New Progressive Party (PNP) 17, Puerto Rican Independence Party 1. Parties not represented in parliament are two others advocating complete independence for Puerto Rico—the (pro-Soviet) Puerto Rican Communist Party and the Puerto Rican Socialist Party.

The PNP has advocated the transformation of Puerto Rico into a state within the United States of America, although in a plebiscite held on July 23, 1967, a majority of Puerto Rico's voters (60.5 per cent of those who took part in the vote) had favoured the retention of the existing commonwealth system, whereas 38.9 per cent had voted for statehood to be given to Puerto Rico and less than 1 per cent had voted for independence (in a 68.5 per cent poll).

The Independence Issue

Political violence in Puerto Rico has come mainly from left-wing groups advocating complete independence for the island on the ground that the existing constitutional system relegates Puerto Rico, in their view, to the status of a US colony. These groups, and the pro-independence parties, have therefore made efforts to set in motion, under United Nations auspices, a "decolonization" process for Puerto Rico.

Acts of violence by pro-independence groups have not been confined to the island; many have been carried out in the United States, which contains a considerable minority population of Puerto Rican origin. According to the Federal Bureau of Investigation

(FBI) there were in 1982 a total of 51 recorded acts of terrorism (against 42 in 1981 and 29 in 1980), of which 25 were ascribed to Puerto Rican independence organizations, 10 of these acts to the Armed Forces of National Liberation (FALN), resulting in three deaths and 19 injuries.

Armed Forces of National Liberation (*Fuerzas Armadas de Liberación Nacional Puertorriqueña*, FALN)

Leadership. Carlos Alberto Torres (l.)

This organization has been involved in acts of violence in various parts of the United States since 1972. By early 1979 it had claimed responsibility for over 100 bombing incidents. On July 3, 1978, two Puerto Rican nationalists attacked and occupied the Chilean consulate in San Juan in support of their demand for the release of Puerto Rican nationalists sentenced in the 1950s, but they surrendered on July 4 without their demand being met.

On April 11, 1979, a FALN member was sentenced to 10 years in prison in New York for unlawful possession of bombs and weapons. In 1980 FALN members attacked both Democratic and Republican party offices during the presidential election campaign. On Aug. 4, 1980, two FALN members were sentenced in Chicago to 30 years in prison each on conspiracy and illegal possession of arms charges. Early in March 1981 the FALN was reported to have issued bomb threats against army recruiting stations. The FALN also claimed responsibility for four bomb explosions in New York's Wall Street area on Feb. 28, 1982.

Five alleged FALN members arrested by the police refused to give evidence before a New York Federal Grand Jury on Sept. 28, 1982, on the grounds that they did not wish "to collaborate with a tool of coercion aimed at all advocates of Puerto Rican independence". Four further explosions in New York on Dec. 31, 1982, in which three policemen were injured, were also caused by the FALN, according to a telephone caller later identified as Luis Rosado.

On Aug. 5, 1985, a federal district court in Chicago convicted four persons (three of whom did not deny their FALN membership) of conspiracy and violations of weapons and explosives regulations.

It appeared, however, that the effectiveness of the FALN had been largely undermined by activity of the Federal Bureau of Investigation (FBI).

The FALN has had links with the Puerto Rican Socialist Party (supported by Cuba) and a Puerto Rican Solidarity Committee.

Armed Liberation Commandos (*Comandos Armados de Liberación*, CAL)

This pro-independence guerrilla group was reported to have been active in August 1981.

Armed Pro-Independence Movement (*Movimiento Independentista Armado,* MIRA)

This guerrilla group was also reported as having been active in August 1981.

Armed Revolutionary Movement

Two members of this small pro-independence group were shot dead by police on July 25, 1978, when they were, according to the police, planning to sabotage a television transmitter. It was later established that two policemen, claiming to act on an order from the commander of the police intelligence division, had shot the two men after they had been arrested and disarmed. The two policemen were on May 21, 1985, sentenced to terms of imprisonment of 20 and 30 years respectively, while the police commander was given a 30-year sentence.

Full Group of Reflection on Puerto Rico

Leadership. Sarah Sosa (l.)

This Roman Catholic organization, based in San Juan, was in August 1981 reported to have called for the ending of Puerto Rico's status as a "US colony" and for "full transfer of power to the people".

Organization of Volunteers for the Puerto Rican Revolution (*Organización de Voluntarios para la Revolución Puertorriqueña*, OVRP)

This small group was responsible for isolated acts of violence in 1979-80, including an attack on communications installations on July 14, 1980 (causing $800,000 worth of damage).

Puerto Rican Armed Resistance Movement (*Movimiento de Resistencia Armada Puertorriqueña*, MRAP)

This group, an offshoot of the Armed Forces of the National Liberation (FALN—see separate entry), has claimed responsibility for numerous bomb attacks, including several on the Panam terminal at Kennedy Airport, New York, on May 16-17, 1981, in which a young airport employee was killed. In a communiqué the group threatened to commit further acts of violence against Argentine, Guatemalan, Honduran and US offices.

Puerto Rican Popular Army (*Ejército Popular Boricua*, EPB, or *Los Macheteros*)

This clandestine group first claimed responsibility for attacks on 10 aircraft of the US Air Force in January 1981. An explosion, followed by a fire and a second blast at an electric power station at San Juan on Nov. 27, 1981, was also, according to an accompanying telephone call, the work of the *Macheteros* group.

The *Macheteros* also claimed responsibility for an armed robbery of $7,000,000 from a depot in West Hartford (Connecticut) on Sept. 12, 1983. In this connexion 14 persons were arrested in Puerto Rico and the United States on Aug. 30, 1985, but the principal figure in the robbery (Victor Manuel Gerena) was believed to have been granted asylum in Cuba.

Uruguay

Capital: Montevideo Pop. 3,010,000

The "Eastern Republic of Uruguay" has an executive President and a National Congress consisting of a 99-member Chamber of Deputies and a 30-member Senate, all elected by universal adult suffrage for five-year terms. The President appoints, and presides over, a Cabinet.

In elections to the Chamber of Deputies held on Nov. 25, 1984, seats were gained as follows: Colorado Party 41, Blanco Party 35, Broad Front (*Frente Amplio*) 21, Civic Union two.

The country had been effectively under military rule since February 1973, with all political parties being proscribed. On March 1, 1985, legal status was restored to all previously banned organizations including the Communist Party (PCU), which contested the elections as part of the Broad Front.
which contested the elections as part of the Broad Front.

The National Liberation Movement (*Movimiento de Liberación Nacional*, or *Tupamaros*, MLN-T), which had been founded in 1962 and had since then been the country's principal revolutionary movement, held its first legal convention in Montevideo on Dec. 20-22, 1985, when it ratified an announcement of Sept. 4 to the effect that it would abandon the armed struggle and become a legal political party, and that it would merge with the (socialist) March 26 Movement (*Movimiento 26 de Marzo*); the convention also decided that the MLN-T should join the Broad Front.

Following the legalization of the country's trade union confederations (together with that of political parties on March 1, 1985) there has been an increase in industrial action over workers' various grievances, but no new revolutionary movements have emerged.

Vanuatu

Capital: Port Vila Pop. 140,000

The Republic of Vanuatu (formerly the British and French condominium of the New Hebrides) is an independent state within the Commonwealth. Its President is elected for a five-year term by an electoral college consisting of parliament and the presidents of the country's regional councils. The unicameral parliament is elected by universal adult suffrage for a four-year term. Executive power is vested in the Prime Minister (elected by parliament from among its members) and a Council of Ministers appointed by him.

In parliamentary elections held on Nov. 2, 1983, the Party of Our Land (*Vanuaaku Pati*) obtained 24 seats, the Union of Moderate Parties 12, and the *Na-Griamel, Frend Melanesia* and *Namake Auti* parties one seat each. The Vanuatu Independence Alliance Party lost the one seat which it had held since 1979.

Secessionist Movements

On May 28, 1980 (i.e. two months before Vanuatu was due to attain independence), some 800 supporters of the secessionist *Na-Griamel* movement (which had for many years campaigned for the independence of the island of Santo) captured the British district commissioner and some of his officials and police, occupied the police station and cut off all communications with Port Vila. On June 1 Jimmy Stevens, the leader of *Na-Griamel*, announced the formation of a six-member "Provisional Government of the independent state of Vemerana" with himself as "Prime Minister". The action was said to be supported by some French settlers and by US businessmen seeking the establishment of an independent tax-haven country. Some 1,400 people were evacuated from Santo by June 4, and the New Hebrides government imposed a blockade on Santo. Unsuccessful attempts at secession were made on other islands, notably Aoba, Malekula (Molicollo) and Tanna, during June 1980.

On July 24, 1980, a joint Anglo-French force of 200 men established itself in Santo Town without meeting opposition. Some 150 troops from Papua New Guinea, with Australian support, replaced the Anglo-French forces on Aug. 19. The secessionists were subsequently arrested, among them Jimmy Stevens who was on Nov. 12 sentenced to 14½ years' imprisonment. Some 700 other persons were also tried, and most of them were convicted in connexion with secessionist activities. A list of prohibited immigrants published by the New Hebrides government in October 1980 contained the names of 110 French nationals said to have promoted the secession of Santo.

The methods used to suppress the secession were strongly criticized in a document issued late in 1980 by the Vanuatu Council of Churches, which referred to numerous reports of police brutality in carrying out "massive arrests" and the "detention for long periods of mostly innocent people"; the document called for an immediate end to the "un-Christian tactics" of the government and an inquiry into the assassination of an opposition deputy, Alexis Yolou. It was reported at this stage that most of the 13 opposition members of parliament were either living in exile or in prison.

In January 1981 the government announced that 583 persons had been convicted in connexion with the secessionist activities of 1980, and another 256 were convicted in March 1981 in connexion with events on Tanna.

However, on April 9, 1981, the government announced that it would not initiate any further prosecutions against persons involved in the rebellion, but would "forgive and forget" it. In December 1981 all those convicted were released, except Stevens and his "chief of police", Timothy Wells. Stevens escaped from prison on Sept. 12, 1982, but was recaptured on the following day; on Oct 26, he was sentenced to an additional 25 months in prison.

Venezuela

Capital: Caracas

Pop. 17,320,000

The Federal Republic of Venezuela, consisting of 20 autonomous states, a federal district, two federal territories and 72 federal dependencies, has an executive President elected by universal adult suffrage for a five-year term and presiding over a Cabinet appointed by him. There is a bicameral Congress consisting of (i) a Senate to which two senators from each of the 20 states and from the federal district are elected for a five-year term by universal adult suffrage (while additional senators are selected to represent minorities and all former Presidents of the Republic are life members of the Senate) and (ii) a Chamber of Deputies with currently 196 members similarly elected (at least two members for each state and one for each federal territory). The President is not elegible for two consecutive terms.

As a result of elections held on Dec. 4, 1983, seats in the Chamber of Deputies were distributed as follows: Democratic Action Party (AD) 109, Christian Social Party (COPEI) 60, Movement towards Socialism (MAS) 10, Democratic Republican Union (URD) eight, Opina three, Movement of the Revolutionary Left (MIR) two, Communist Party of Venezuela (PCV) two, Movement of National Integration (MIN) one, New Alternative one. Smaller left-wing parties which unsuccessfully contested the elections obtained less than 10 per cent of the votes between them.

In the 1960s, a major offensive against the Venezuelan government by well-organized left-wing guerrillas failed for various reasons, including a significant improvement in the economy. The remaining left-wing guerrilla groups have been small and of limited effect in recent years.

Red Flag (*Bandera Roja*)

This small Marxist-Leninist group broke away from the Armed Forces of National Liberation (FALN—the main guerrilla group active in the 1960s and 1970s) and was engaged in various guerrilla operations until 1978. Its leaders, the brothers Carlos and Argenis Betancourt, were both arrested in 1977 but the group remained active.

Gabriel Puerte Aponte, the group's leader, was arrested in 1982 along with other members, but clashes with army and police units continued through that year, with responsibility for one incident claimed by the Américo Silva Front (*Frente Américo Silva*), said to be the armed wing of the underground Red Flag organization.

In June 1983 the authorities claimed to have broken up the movement with the discovery of a guerrilla cell in Ciúdad Guayana, 600 km south of Caracus. Among 24 people arrested was the Chilean citizen Juan Pablo Miranda Herrena, reported to be the leader of the movement.

Responsibility for two bomb attacks reported on Sept. 16, 1984, at Radio Apolo (in Turmero) and at the Caracas office of the newspaper *El Aragueño* was claimed by the Maracay regional people's committee of the *Bandera Roja*.

On Feb. 17, 1987, four alleged guerrillas arrested in Caracas were said to be members of the organization.

Vietnam

Capital: Hanoi Pop. 60,000,000

The Socialist Republic of Vietnam (proclaimed after North-Vietnam-backed communist insurgents had effectively reunified the country by overthrowing the government of South Vietnam in1975) is, under its 1980 Constitution, "a state of proletarian dictatorship" in which the Communist Party of Vietnam (CPV) is the "only force leading the state and society". It has a Council of State (the collective presidency of the Republic) elected for a five-year term by the National Assembly from among its members. The National Assembly itself is elected, also for five years, by adult suffrage. A Council of Ministers, headed by a Chairman, and also elected by the National Assembly, is responsible to that Assembly. In elections to the National Assembly held on April 19, 1987, the Assembly's 496 members were elected from a list of 829 candidates approved by the Vietnam Fatherland Front (consisting of the CPV as well as of the Democratic Party, the Socialist Party, trade unions and mass organizations).

According to a defector quoted on Feb. 2, 1980, there were then some 700,000 political prisoners in Vietnam, among them many former South Vietnamese political figures held in re-education camps. In an interview in June 1982 the Vietnamese Foreign Minister, Nguyen Co Thach, stated that the number of detainees then held in re-education camps was 16,000.

Since 1975 an increasing number of Vietnamese have left their country as refugees, largely as a result of political and racial persecution, food shortages and the removal of much of the urban population of South Vietnam to "new economic zones" in which living conditions were, according to refugees, "appalling". Late in1980 the government was reported as regarding at least 750,000 Vietnamese as "unwanted", and by 1982 the total of those who had fled Vietnam was said to exceed 500,000. In 1985 the number of refugees leaving Vietnam by sea ("boat people") was some 25,000 compared with an average of 10,000 per month during 1979-81. In part this was the result of Vietnam's agreement to participate in a UN-sponsored Orderly Departure Programme, whereby the government allowed a number of legal departures.

Secular Opposition Groups

Front of the People and the Army for National Salvation

At a trial in Hue, which ended on March 6, 1980, a former Vietnamese soldier was sentenced to death, two others were given life sentences and unspecified numbers of defendants were sent to prison for from eight to 20 years for founding this organization, conducting propaganda and persuading people to flee the country.

Militia Front for the National Renaissance in Vietnam

On Aug. 9, 1986, Ngo Van Truong (also known as Ngo Quang Toan), a member of this Front, was sentenced to death, having been found guilty of forming "an extremely dangerous counter-revolutionary organization". A former soldier in the South Vietnamese army, he had been arrested in January 1984 in Ho Chi Minh City whilst boarding a train for the central city of Hue, carrying some 400 anti-government leaflets.

Other members of the organization (all described as former officials in the South Vietnamese government) were sentenced to prison terms ranging from three years to life.

National Front for the Liberation of the Central Highlands

The formation of this Front was reported from Thailand on July 21, 1981. It was said to have its own provincial government (the "Dega") inside Vietnam; to be composed of Rhade tribes from Dac Lac province and of other Vietnamese, Kampuchean and Lao hill tribes; and to be aided by China by way of groups opposed to the Vietnam government operating from the territories of Kampuchea and Laos.

National Restoration Movement

According to a US intelligence assessment released on April 30, 1980, this anti-communist Movement existed throughout South Vietnam but was weak in numbers and without effective leadership.

National Salvation Committee

Leadership. Truong Nhu Tang (l.)

The formation of this Committee was announced in Paris in January 1981 by Truong Nhu Tang with the object of bringing together all elements opposed to the Vietnamese government, including supporters of the former Saigon regime; he added in his announcement that the Chinese government, with which he had had discussions in September 1980, had promised him unconditional aid. Also present at these discussions had been Hoang Van Hoan, a former member of the Political Bureau of the Communist Party of Vietnam who had defected to China in 1979 and had in absentia been sentenced to death for high treason by the Vietnamese Supreme Court in June 1980.

Truong Nhu Tang had been Minister of Justice in the South Vietnamese Provisional Revolutionary (i.e. communist) government from 1969 to the reunification of Vietnam in 1976, had fled from Vietnam in September 1979 and had reached France in March 1980. At a press conference in Paris on June 9, 1980, he said inter alia that he wished to fight against both "American intervention and the despotism of a corrupt government"; that the (communist) National Liberation Front, which he had joined, had intended to build "an independent, democratic, peaceful, neutral and prosperous South Vietnam" before unifying the country step by step; and that the North Vietnamese leaders had "rushed" the unification and had "instead of a policy of reconciliation and national accord conducted a policy of vengeance and repression".

Truong Nhu Tang declared that the (pro-Soviet) Vietnamese leadership was faced with four basic dilemmas—(i) ideologically, it was pursuing "a Marxist-Leninist brand of working-class communism" (although Vietnamese communism was a peasant movement) and had carried out a massive purge of peasant elements in the party, describing them as "Maoists"; (ii) economically, it claimed to be able to "build an advanced socialist society without passing through the capitalist stage" in the absence of any industrial basis; (iii) politically, it had committed "serious strategic and tactical errors"; and (iv) socially, the "party state" was producing "a class of corrupt bureaucrats that broadens the gulf between the party and the people". He admitted that there was no resistance inside Vietnam worthy of the name and that the population of the south, although disillusioned, confined themselves to passive opposition; he nevertheless expressed the hope that he would be able to contribute to the development of a resistance movement which would accept "friendly aid free from political conditions" from the United States and China.

National Salvation Front

Members of this Front, said to have been set up in 1975 as an underground organization by officers and officials of the former South Vietnamese regime and by Chinese "reactionary capitalists", were tried in 1979 for conducting propaganda, plotting murders of government officials, hoarding weapons and forcing many Chinese to emigrate. Two persons, including the alleged chairman of the Front, were sentenced to death and 18 others to prison terms of from two to 20 years in Ho Chi Minh City (Saigon) on July 13. Another member of the Front was sentenced to death and 10 other defendants to prison terms of from 12 to 20 years at Cam Ranh on Nov. 28 (inter alia for organizing armed groups and enticing people to escape abroad).

National United Front for the Liberation of Vietnam

This anti-communist organization claims to have a membership of 10,000, of whom 500 are organizing guerrilla activities in Vietnam. Its leader, Hoang Co Minh, was formerly a vice-admiral in the navy of South Vietnam. Since late February 1984 Vietnam Resistance Radio (VRR) has broadcast from the organization's "base camp number 15". The VRR announced on March 8, 1984, that the Vietnam National Resistance Front (see separate entry) had been disbanded and had merged into the National United Front for the Liberation of Vietnam.

Overseas Volunteer Forces for the Restoration of Vietnam

Founded in Australia in 1980 by overseas Vietnamese dedicated to the overthrow of communist rule in Vietnam, this organization claims to have 1,000 fighters at its disposal. The Vietnamese government announced in July 1982 that Vo Dai Ton, a former official in the South Vietnamese government, had recently confessed to being the organization's leader. It was alleged that he claimed to have infiltrated central Vietnam in an attempt to organize various resistance groups; he admitted Chinese, Thai and US support.

United Front for the Struggle of the Oppressed Races (*Front unifié de lutte des races opprimées,* FULRO)

This Front was set up as the political organization of the tribal people of the central highlands of Vietnam (whom the French collectively termed Montagnards) and has demanded autonomy for the 12 northern provinces of southern Vietnam. The Montagnards had repeatedly risen in revolt against the government of South Vietnam, notably in September 1964, when they hoisted a red flag with three yellow stars as the symbol of their autonomist movement, and in September 1965 when they temporarily seized several towns. In March 1975 FULRO forces led a communist attack on South Vietnamese forces—the Provisional Revolutionary Government (PRG) of South Vietnam having promised the Montagnards local autonomy. By the end of the Vietnamese war on April 30, 1975, most new officials appointed in the central highlands by the PRG were said to have been drawn from FULRO. However, early in 1976 FULRO groups were offering armed resistance to the communist regime, and some groups of FULRO members were reportedly engaged in guerrilla activities in 1979. An official government broadcast in September 1982 claimed that FULRO was in a state of disintegration, many of its leading members (including its first vice-president) having defected or surrendered. However, an unofficial report in February 1983 alleged that eight Vietnamese soldiers had recently been killed in attacks by FULRO forces and guerrillas of the National Front for the Liberation of the Central Highlands (see separate entry).

United Front of Patriotic Forces for the Liberation of Vietnam

At a trial in December 1984 of 21 leading members of this organization (which Vietnamese authorities claim was the largest and best organized of its kind), five were sentenced to death (only three were subsequently executed in early 1985, two having their sentences commuted to life imprisonment) after being found guilty of spying and of conducting a campaign of sabotage in the southern Mekong delta since 1981, aimed specifically at foreign personnel (i.e. French and Soviet citizens). During the trial the prosecution alleged that the United Front had received financial support from China and training and intelligence assistance from Thailand; a defendant reportedly confessed that he had been in contact with officials from the US embassy in Thailand. The organization was also accused of attempting to (i) recruit overseas Vietnamese; (ii) release and arm Vietnamese prisoners; and (iii) introduce large amounts of counterfeit currency into Vietnam to destabilize the economy.

United Organization of Free Vietnamese in Europe

This Organization has claimed to represent 16 Vietnamese émigré groups. A spokesman for the organization declared in January 1981 that it would never recognize Truong Nhu Tang (the founder of the National Salvation Committee—see separate entry) as its leader.

Vietnam National Resistance Front

In a broadcast on Vietnamese Resistance Radio on March 8, 1984, Nguyen The Minh, chairman of the Front's central leadership council, announced that the Front had officially disbanded and merged with the National United Front for the Liberation of Vietnam (see separate entry) on Dec. 1, 1983. During the broadcast the Front was described as having been founded in Saigon (Ho Chi Minh City) in July 1975, and again in April 1982.

Religious Opposition

Cao Dai Sect

Two followers of this sect, based mainly in southern Vietnam, were sentenced to death on Aug. 17, 1983, for plotting a coup near Ho Chi Minh City (Saigon) with the backing of China and other countries.

Roman Catholic Resistance

Numerous Roman Catholic priests, officially regarded as enemies of the state, were detained for "re-education" and some of them were tried and sentenced in courts.

On Jan. 4, 1983, it was reported that in a US State Department report it was claimed that Roman Catholics in central Vietnam had been forcibly relocated and required to work in government construction projects, that the Church's teaching role had been restricted, and that many churches and all but one seminary in southern Vietnam had been closed. On March 12, 1983, Cardinal Trinh Van Can, Archbishop of Hanoi, had been placed under house arrest and 130 priests sent to re-education camps.

On July 7, 1983, the Jesuit Regional Superior (Fr Nguyen Cong Doan) was sentenced to 12 years in prison, and four other Jesuits and two laymen also received prison sentences, while a former South Vietnamese Army officer was given a life sentence, for inciting rebellion in collaboration with the United States and other foreign powers. On Aug. 2, 1984, it was reported that out of 2,500 Vietnamese Catholic priests, over 200 were being held in prison or in a re-education camp, among them Archbishop Philippe Nguyen Kim Dien of Heu, arrested for criticizing the government supported Solidarity Committee of Patriotic Vietnamese Catholics (established in November 1983).

United Buddhist Church

The acting president of this Church, Thich Thieu Minh, whose group at the An Quang pagoda in Saigon had opposed the South Vietnamese regime—without supporting the (communist) National Liberation Front seeking to overthrow it—had been imprisoned by President Nguyen Van Thieu's government in 1969. Following the communist victory in 1975, he was arrested in April 1978 and was on Oct. 25 of that year reported to have died in a re-education camp. Seven members of the An Quang pagoda, arrested in April 1977, were tried in Ho Chi Minh City (Saigon) on Dec. 8-9, 1978 for "agitating against the military service law and other social duties, discouraging Buddhist believers from joining revolutionary organizations and discriminating against participants in patriotic organizations". Three of the accused were given seven, three and two years' prison sentences respectively, and among the others the vice-chairman of the Institute for the Propagation of the *Dharma* (the United Buddhist Church's organization dealing with secular affairs) was given a two-year suspended sentence. The Paris office of the United Buddhist Church stated on Jan. 17, 1979, that 37 monks were known to be in prison in Vietnam.

A spokesman for the Church said in Paris in November 1981 that its leaders had been under pressure to join a new Buddhist Church of Vietnam established on Nov. 7, 1981, at a Conference for the Reunification of Vietnamese Buddhism. (The new Church committed itself to work for national unity within the framework of the Vietnam Fatherland Front.) On Feb. 25, 1982, both the vice-chairman and the secretary-general of the Institute for the Propagation of the *Dharma* were again arrested.

Reports in late March and early April 1984 referred to the arrest of 12 Buddhist nuns and monks associated with the An Quang pagoda.

Western Samoa

Capital: Apia (Upolu)

Pop. 159,000

Western Samoa is an independent member of the Commonwealth. Under its Constitution adopted in 1960 the head of state is elected for a five-year term by the Legislative Assembly. (However, the current head of state is holding this office for life.) Executive power is vested in a Prime Minister who must be supported by a majority in the Legislative Assembly and who appoints other ministers. Of the 47 members of the Legislative Assembly, 45 are Samoans chosen through *matai* suffrage (with the right to vote being restricted to the elected heads of extended family units) and two other members are elected through universal adult suffrage by persons (mainly naturalized citizens) registered on a separate roll.

In elections to the Legislative Assembly held on Feb. 22, 1985, a total of 31 seats were won by members or declared supporters of the Human Rights Protection Party (HRPP), and 16 by the recently-formed Christian Democratic Party (CDP), Defections from the HRPP provoked a government change in January 1986, the new Prime Minister being supported by 15 CDP members and 12 formerly of the HRPP.

There have been no reports of extra-parliamentary opposition in Western Samoa.

Yemen Arab Republic

Capital: Sana'a

Pop. 6,850,000

Under a provisional Constitution of 1974 the Yemen Arab Republic (North Yemen) is "an Arab, Islamic and independent state". It has an executive President elected by a provisional Constituent People's Assembly of 159 members (such an Assembly having first been formed in February 1978 to draft an electoral law and to prepare "free elections"). The President appoints a Cabinet headed by a Prime Minister. On July 17, 1978, the Assembly elected a new President, whom it re-elected (without opposition) on May 22, 1983, for a second five-year term. In addition two further bodies were set up—(i) a 15-member Consultative Council in May 1979, and (ii) a 52-member Committee for National Consultation in May 1980 with the object of preparing for a General People's Congress of 700 elected and 300 appointed members. Such a Congress first met in August-September 1982. It was to meet every two years and be re-elected every four years, while the Constituent Assembly continued to meet. The country has no political parties.

There have been many incidents involving political violence, and two of the Republic's Presidents have been assassinated—the pro-Saudi Lt.-Col. Ibrahim al-Hamadi in October 1977 and his successor, Lt.-Col. Hussein al-Ghashmi, in June 1978.

Under a decree of Feb. 7, 1979, all political prisoners detained in the past five years were pardoned, and 494 were subsequently released. On March 15, 1979, a general amnesty was granted to all opponents of the regime who declared their loyalty and surrendered their arms. Under a further decree of Aug. 20, 1979, the President pardoned a number of political prisoners, including those sentenced to death, who were released.

Relations with the South Yemeni government have continued to improve, with frequent ministerial and other meetings taking place to discuss possible unification of the two countries. The first session of a "Yemen Council", composed of the two Presidents of the respective countries, took place in December 1981, and regular contacts continued, although problems ensued following the South Yemeni civil war and the flight into North Yemen of supporters of the deposed President Mohammed of South Yemen.

Islamic Front

Leadership. Shaikh Abdullah Bin Hussein al-Ahamr

This Front was described as a pressure group consisting of conservative tribes in remote mountain regions supported and financed by Saudi Arabia to oppose North Yemen's proposed merger with South Yemen. Its leader was a member of the country's Consultative Council and also the head of the Hashed tribal confederation (centred around Sada'a, in the northern part of the country). In July 1977 he led an unsuccessful insurrection aimed at the establishment of a strict Moslem regime in North Yemen.

Party of Popular Yemenite Unity (PPYU)

According to a statement by Dr Abdul Karim Ali al-Iryani, the Prime Minister of the Yemen Arab Republic, reported early in May 1982, the PPYU was "a 100 per cent Marxist-Leninist organization" and constituted the strongest and most active of the opposition forces in his country; he said that its headquarters were in Aden, and that it had received weapons via South Yemen and had guerrillas crossing the frontier from that country. He also claimed that the PPYU was not distinct from the Yemen Socialist Party (YSP), the sole legal party of South Yemen, and that three of the PPYU's leaders, whom he named as Yehya el-Chami, Mohammed Kassem el-Thawr and Jarallah Omar, were members of the YSP's political bureau.

Yemen People's Democratic Republic

Capital: Aden Pop. 2,290,000

The Yemen People's Democratic Republic (South Yemen) is a one-party state in which the Yemen Socialist Party (YSP) is the sole legal party, whose Central Committee nominates the President (head of state) and a Council and Ministers presided over by a Chairman (Prime Minister). A Supreme People's Council (SPC) consisting of 71 YSP members and 40 independents is elected by popular vote for a four-year term. In elections held on Oct. 28-30, 1986, the turnout was officially stated to have been 89 per cent. At its first meeting on Nov. 6, 1986, the newly elected SPC elected a 15-member Presidium with President Haider Abu Bakr al Attas as Chairman, thereby confirming him as head of state for five years.

Although firmly tied to the Soviet Union by a treaty of friendship and co-operation concluded in October 1979 (which was said to entitle the USSR to station up to 25,000 troops in South Yemen) and the only Arab country to express support for the Soviet intervention in Afghanistan in December 1979, South Yemen has since then made efforts to expand its relations with other countries, including North Yemen and Saudi Arabia.

Six months of tension between rival factions in the government and party hierarchy culminated in open civil war in January 1986. The then President Ali Nasser Mohammed attempted to have his opponents killed in a pre-emptive strike, but several of them survived; there ensued 10 days of heavy fighting, involving party militiamen, all three branches of the armed forces and tribal warriors. Evidence emerged after the fighting of massacres by both sides, but particularly by supporters of President Mohammed. The fighting precipitated the evacuation of foreign nationals, mostly in Soviet or British naval vessels. By the end of January, President Mohammed had fled the country, reportedly for neighbouring North Yemen, and the rebel forces were victorious. Haider Abu Bakr al Attas took over as President, and Ali Salim al-Bid became secretary-general of the YSP. One of President Mohammed's principal opponents, Abdel Fattah Ismail, a former secretary-general of the YSP and Chairman of the Council of Ministers, was reported to have been killed during the fighting.

Approximately 12,000 people followed President Mohammed into exile, and by early 1987 he was reported to have assembled a force of several thousand armed supporters along the border inside North Yemen. The new government offered amnesties to the exiles to persuade them to return, and there were several discussions on the subject with North Yemeni officials. In November-December 1986 there was some evidence of armed opposition by supporters of ex-President Mohammed inside the country. The total number of lives lost in the civil war was given as 4,200 by the President of the Supreme Court on Dec. 4.

National Grouping of Patriotic Forces of South Yemen

Leadership. Abdul Qawee Mackawee (sec.-gen.)

This Grouping was established in March 1980 in Baghdad, the Iraqi capital.

A. Q. Mackawee had been the leader of the Front for the Liberation of Occupied South Yemen (FLOSY), one of the two movements fighting for the establishment of an independent South Yemen (the other being the National Liberation Front, which later became the ruling YSP); he had also briefly been Chief Minister of Aden in 1965. Following the establishment of the Democratic People's Republic under the control of the National Liberation Front in November 1967, A. Q. Mackawee left the country and in August 1972 established in North Yemen a

United National Front of South Yemen, which comprised most of the leading opponents of the Aden regime. However, this movement was banned by the government of North Yemen on Dec. 2, 1972, after an agreement had been concluded in Tripoli (Libya) on Nov. 28 of that year on the proposed establishment of a united Yemeni Republic to be based on Islamic socialism.

At a conference held in Cairo on Feb. 10, 1981, A. Q. Mackawee described his organization's case as one which should be supported by all members of the Islamic Arab nation, who should resist the advance of international communism (as in Afghanistan). He said that more than half of South Yemen's people had fled the country "in search of security, peace and a decent living", and he declared that South Yemen was not only a Soviet colony but "a springboard for communism" which threatened the security, safety and stability of all the Arab and Moslem countries.

The Grouping has declared its objectives as being to bring together all "progressive national and patriotic forces" opposed to what it calls "the puppet fascist regime" in South Yemen. It has undertaken to fight against "all forms of foreign presence in South Yemen", to liberate the country from "the authority of the secessionists and their overlords" and to unify the two Yemens.

National Liberation Army

Several men claiming to be members of this group were among 13 South Yemenis sentenced in Aden on April 7, 1982 (12 of them to death and the other to 15 years in prison) for "plotting" to sabotage South Yemen's economic and oil installations after being allegedly trained by the (US) Central Intelligence Agency (CIA) in Saudi Arabia and having brought explosives into the country. Of the death sentences two were on April 12 commuted to 15 years' imprisonment, whereas the other 10 were carried out on April 22, 1982.

South Yemen Liberation Front

This Front was established in Cairo (Egypt) in July 1980. It has defined its aims as being "to put an end to Marxist influence in South Yemen, using all legal means and methods, to put an end to subservience to anti-Arab and anti-Islamic forces and to establish a national democratic regime which democratically represents the people through honest, free elections". (A Yemeni National Unity Front had earlier been set up in Cairo by Mohammed Ali Haithem, who had been Prime Minister of South Yemen in 1969-71 and who escaped an assassination attempt in Cairo in October 1975. The Egyptian capital has become a haven for South Yemeni exiles.)

Yugoslavia

Capital: Belgrade Pop. 23,120,000

The Socialist Federal Republic of Yugoslavia, in which effective power is exercised by the League of Communists of Yugoslavia (LCY), is composed of six socialist republics (Bosnia and Herzegovina, Croatia, Macedonia, Montenegro, Serbia and Slovenia) and two autonomous provinces (Kosovo—known as Kosovo-Metohija until 1968—and Vojvodina), both being parts of Serbia. Under the 1974 Constitution there is, at federal level, a Federal Assembly elected for a four-year term and consisting of (i) a Federal Chamber composed of delegates of self-managing organizations and communities and of socio-political organizations and (ii) a Chamber of Republics and Provinces consisting of delegates of the elected Republican and Provincial Assemblies. All election candidates are subject to screening by the Socialist Alliance of the Working People of Yugoslavia, an overall political organization under the leadership of the LCY. All elections take place under the delegate system laid down in the 1974 Constitution.

The principal (illegal) political groups in opposition to the existing regime in Yugoslavia are as follows: (i) Albanian nationalists, partly supported by the government of the Socialist People's Republic of Albania; (ii) Croatian nationalists, supported largely by Croatian émigré organizations, including remnants of the *Ustashi* (Fascist) regime of Croatia during World War II; (iii) Serbian nationalists, including royalists and supporters of the *Chetnik* movement of World War II; (iv) Cominformists, i.e. pro-Soviet Communists opposed to the 1948 break between Yugoslavia and the Soviet Union and (v) Socialists, either democratic or tending towards the West European "New Left".

For the internal defence of the state the Yugoslav government has developed two systems: (i) the "General People's Defence" constituted by the regular Army (the country's only truly centralized institution) and territorial units capable of mobilization at short notice, with their own weapons and their own command and embracing practically all men and women capable of bearing arms; and (ii) "Social Self-Protection" aimed at "countering any negative manifestations in political and economic life, in ideology and culture, and also the machinations of foreign information services, diversionary and terrorist attempts, hostile propaganda, corruption and attacks on social and general property", its fundamental function being—as stated in January 1976 by Lazar Kolichevski (then a member of Yugoslavia's collective Presidency)—"to unmask and to prevent hostile activities against our society and the workers".

Albanian Nationalists

Of the more than 1,600,000 Albanians of Yugoslav nationality, about two-thirds live in the autonomous province of Kosovo, where they constitute about 77 per cent of the population, while the remainder live in parts of Macedonia and of Montenegro. The standard of living of Albanians in Yugoslavia has remained among the lowest of any population sector in that country, the average per capita income in Kosovo province being only about one-third of that of the Federative Republic of Serbia.

In August-September 1966 it was officially disclosed that in dealing with Albanians accused of secessionist activities the security police in what was then the Kosovo-Metohija (or Kosmet) autonomous region had been guilty of irregularities involving the murder and torture of a number of Albanians, and as a result of these disclosures changes were made in the structure of the LCY. In particular, Alexander Rankovic, who had been organizational secretary of the LCY's Executive Committee, was expelled from that body on July 1 and from the LCY on Oct. 4, 1966.

During discussions on constitutional changes in 1968, a minority of the Albanians in Kosovo called for the formation of an Albanian republic based on the Kosmet region as a full constituent member of the Federal Republic of Yugoslavia, while some were said to have called for Kosovo's incorporation into Albania. In student demonstrations in favour of an Albanian republic held in Pristina (the capital of Kosovo) in November 1968, and also in Tetovo (north-west Macedonia) on Dec. 23, 1968, rioters caused damage to property, and the organizers of the Tetovo disturbances were on June 25, 1969, given prison sentences ranging from 18 months to seven years.

Following demonstrations in Pristina in late December 1974 by students and others, calling for a greater Albania incorporating inside Albania not only Kosovo but also other Yugoslav areas inhabited by Moslems of Albanian origin, five persons were on Jan. 14, 1975, sentenced to imprisonment for from three to nine years for "attempting to overthrow the constitutional order and attacking the territorial integrity of Yugoslavia".

On Feb. 7, 1976, a group of 19 men were reported to have been given up to 15 years in prison for "conspiring against the government and supporting the secession of Kosovo from Yugoslavia". They were said to have tried to recruit followers among the Albanians in Yugoslavia and to have called for the violent overthrow of the government. On Feb. 27 that year another 12 men were given prison sentences of from 18 months to nine years for anti-Tito activities in December 1974. A further two students were sentenced on March 13 to 12 and six years' hard labour respectively for being members of the Kosovo "nationalist liberation movement".

Following a campaign in the Albanian press during 1979, when Yugoslavia was accused of allowing widespread exploitation of the Kosovo Albanians by other Yugoslav nationalities, disturbances took place in Pristina early in 1980, leading to a number of arrests and to prison sentences ranging from three to eight years being imposed on eight persons on June 9, 1980, and from three to six years imposed on July 7 on three Albanians from Macedonia.

On March 11-12, 1981, some 2,000 (out of a total of 50,000) students at the University of Pristina caused disturbances, and these were resumed on March 25-26 and again on April 1-2, having spread to miners and other workers. As a result, a state of emergency was declared in Kosovo on April 3. It was officially claimed on April 6 that the (Cominformist) Communist Party of Yugoslavia (see below) had been involved in the disturbances, and that the Albanian nationalists had close links with both pro-fascist and Cominformist organizations in Stuttgart (West Germany), Brussels, the United States and elsewhere. Stane Dolanc, a member of the Presidium of the LCY, admitted on the same day that the demonstrators had demanded full republican status for Kosovo, but he declared: "A republic of Kosovo is not possible within the framework of Yugoslavia—neither in terms of our Constitution nor in terms of what was achieved in the national liberation war, especially in view of the fact that the establishment of a republic of Kosovo in Yugoslavia would in essence mean the downfall of Yugoslavia."

Lazar Mojsov (then President of the LCY Presidium) claimed at a meeting of the LCY's Central Committee on May 7, 1981, that the riots in Pristina had been initiated by a clandestine "Albanian Marxist-Leninist Communist Party in Yugoslavia", the aim of which, he said, was the overthrow of the constitutional order in Yugoslavia and the proclamation of an Albanian republic; he maintained that this organization was directed by a "foreign agents' centre", which (he strongly suggested) was close to the government of Albania.

Gen. Franjo Herljevic (Federal Secretary for Internal Affairs) claimed in an interview published on May 13, 1981, to have "concrete evidence" of the pursuit of pan-Albanian goals in Yugoslavia by official representatives of the Albanian government, and of the existence of a clandestine "Red Front" closely linked with the ruling Albanian Party of Labour and with the Albanian intelligence services. A formal Yugoslav protest against "gross interference" by Albania in Yugoslav internal affairs was rejected by the Albanian government on May 15.

Further disturbances took place at the University of Pristina between May 12 and May 19, 1981. Teachers who had supported the students' action and also LCY members and journalists involved in the disturbances were warned that they would be suspended or otherwise disciplined. Gen. Herljevic, reporting to the Federal Assembly on June 8, 1981, stated that during

April and May "nationalists and irredentists" had organized 16 mass demonstrations in 11 communes, causing extensive damage to public and private property; that 506 persons had already been convicted of offences connected with the disorders; that 154 persons were accused of belonging to clandestine organizations or of similar offences; and that eight demonstrators and one policeman had been killed and 257 persons injured, including 33 members of the security forces.

In his capacity as Yugoslav Interior Minister, Stane Dolanc stated in a radio interview broadcast on Sept. 29, 1982, that some 700 people had been arrested in Kosovo since March 1982 for activities against the state, and that 320 had been tried for political offences; 55 illegal groups belonging to four different organizations had been uncovered, he said, and over 1,300 people punished. However, the situation in the province remained tense, and despite the improvements brought about mainly by the presence of heavy security reinforcements and the general absence of street violence, there was evidence of continuing and open resistance; for example, 126 attacks on militiamen had been recorded in the province so far in 1982, and, he said, the arrested conspirators had increasingly openly questioned the territorial integrity of Yugoslavia by expressing their support for Enver Hoxha (then First Secretary of the Albanian Party of Labour).

Yugoslavia's 1981 census had shown that 77.5 per cent of the Kosovo population were of Albanian origin, compared with 73.8 per cent in 1971, while 13.2 per cent were Serbs and 1.7 per cent Montenegrins, compared with 18.4 per cent and 2.5 per cent respectively in 1971; the increasing predominance of the Kosovo Albanians was partly due to their high birth rate (thought to be the highest in Europe), but partly also to the emigration of the Kosovo Serbs and Montenegrins, who were in some areas reportedly harassed by Albanian activists.

The traditional tensions between the Kosovo Serbs and Albanians have been heightened in recent years by the severe economic difficulties experienced by the province. Although the federal government had made major investments in Kosovo, the Albanians claimed that these were largely prestige projects or that they otherwise created little local employment.

In the early 1980s the Albanian press maintained a continuing attack on the Yugoslav authorities over a series of arrests and convictions of Albanians in Kosovo, which were variously described as "mass verdicts", as "mounting terror" and as "a real inquisition" which "violated national feelings". Yugoslavia for its part presented a formal note to the Albanian embassy in Belgrade on Dec. 7, 1981, alleging Albanian interference in its internal affairs (although the embassy refused to accept the document). Milos Minic, then a member of the Presidium of the LCY representing Serbia, accused the Albanian secret services, in a speech delivered at Pristina University on Feb. 19, 1982, of direct involvement in the Kosovo disturbances.

During 1981-82 a number of attacks were made on Yugoslav institutions in Brussels and West Germany, where several Yugoslav representatives were killed; in some cases Kosovo Albanians were thought to have been responsible. Strains were accordingly generated in Yugoslavia's relations with Belgium, and on Aug. 26, 1981, the Yugoslav ambassador in Brussels was withdrawn in protest at Belgium's alleged failure to ensure adequate protection for Yugoslav citizens.

Late in 1982 bombs exploded in Pristina on several occasions. Two policemen were shot dead in western Kosovo on April 2, 1983; for this murder an Albanian was condemned to death on Aug. 11, 1983. Altogether over 100 Albanians were sentenced to varying terms of imprisonment between late 1982 and September 1983.

On April 25, 1984, it was reported that an Albanian sentenced to death (for murder) on July 30, 1982, had been executed. On May 24 a Belgrade court sentenced six Albanians to imprisonment for terms ranging from four to 13 years for "hostile activities". Other trials of alleged Albanian nationalists took place in 1984-85.

On Aug. 19, 1985, a total of 71 persons were sentenced to imprisonment for up to 20 years for involvement in the theft of 13.5 tonnes of silver from a lead refinery in Kosovo between 1978 and 1984, the proceeds having allegedly been used to finance nationalist activities.

In order to stem the growing tide of emigration of Serbs and Montenegrins from Kosovo, the federal and provincial governments approved, in June 1986, new measures for Kosovo, including compulsory bilingual education, stringent penalties for Serbs and Montenegrins trying to sell their houses to ethnic Albanians, and employment and housing incentives to encourage the return of those who had recently left Kosovo. (A Federal Assembly commission had reported on April 9, 1986, that Serbs and Montenegrins in Kosovo were the victims of physical violence, threats and harassment, and that there had been serious lapses in the work of the security services to protect them.)

In Albania Ramiz Alia (the head of state), reporting on the activities of the central committee of the ruling Albanian Party of Labour on Nov. 3, 1986, explicitly rejected Yugoslav allegations that Albania had laid claim to Yugoslav territory and had interfered in Yugoslavia's internal affairs (although Albania remained opposed to Yugoslav "revisionism").

Movement for Liberation

In November 1985 it was reported that the police had uncovered this secret Movement which allegedly sought the creation of an ethnically pure Kosovo. Its members were said to include officers of the People's Army and informants within Kosovo's security forces.

Croatian Nationalists

Ustashi Movement

The *Ustashi* movement has its origins in the independent state of Croatia set up by Hitler and Mussolini in 1941, and its aim is to restore an independent, anti-communist state in Croatia. Since World War II supporters of this movement have been responsible for numerous murders, bomb attacks and other acts of terrorism in various parts of the world.

According to documents of the Australian Security Intelligence Organization (ASIO) produced in the

Australian Senate on March 27, 1972, there existed in Australia, from 1956 onwards, three Croatian terrorist organizations aiming at the overthrow of the Yugoslav Government—(i) the Croatian Revolutionary Brotherhood (HRB), (ii) the United Croatians of West Germany, and (iii) the Croatian Revolutionary Organization—all of which were set up within the Croatian Liberation Movement and the Croatian National Resistance and were supported by two youth organizations, the Croatian Youth and the World League of Croatian Youth.

In Australia members of the *Ustashi* organization were held responsible for two bomb attacks against Yugoslav property in Sydney on Sept. 16, 1972, and according to the Australian police Croatian dissidents had set up a military training camp.

In the Federal Republic of Germany an attack on the Yugoslav trade mission in Bad Godesberg was made on Nov. 29, 1962, by some 25 members of a Croatian "Brotherhood of the Cross" (which was said to have about 200 members and which was banned in Germany on March 12, 1963, as a right-wing extremist organization which had decided on a policy of violence in protest against the existing regime in Yugoslavia). The 25 Croats involved in the attack were on June 25, 1964, given prison sentences, their leader being sentenced to 15 years' hard labour for manslaughter and other offences.

In Sweden two *Ustashi* members temporarily occupied the Yugoslav consulate in Gothenburg on Feb. 10, 1971, and threatened to kill the staff unless the Yugoslav authorities released Miljenko Hrkac (detained in Belgrade in connexion with a bomb attack on a cinema in which one person was killed and 77 were injured). However, on Feb. 11 the two Croats surrendered to the Swedish police and on March 19 they were each sentenced to 3½ years' imprisonment in Gothenburg. (Miljenko Hrkac was on Dec. 26, 1975, condemned to death in Belgrade for terrorist acts, including the above bomb attack.)

On April 7, 1971, the Yugoslav ambassador to Sweden was fatally wounded by *Ustashi* members, and five Croats involved in this act were on July 14, 1971, sentenced to imprisonment ranging from two years to life.

On Sept. 15, 1972, three *Ustashi* members hijacked a Swedish airliner and forced it to land at Malmö airport. They demanded that in return for the release of the aircraft the Swedish government should hand over to them the seven Croats imprisoned in Sweden as stated above. The Swedish government acceded to this demand, but only six of the seven imprisoned Croats agreed to be handed over to the hijackers. The airliner was flown to Madrid, where the hijackers surrendered to the police. The Spanish authorities thereupon detained all nine Croats but refused to extradite them to Yugoslavia, as had been requested by the latter.

Croatian nationalists sentenced in Yugoslavia during 1972 included four student leaders given sentences of from one to four years on Oct. 5; seven students sentenced on Oct. 6 to from six months to two years for attempting to overthrow the social order and elected representative bodies; Zlatko Tomicic (former chairman of an independent Writers' Union and former editor of the banned literary review *Hrvatski Knizevsni List*), sentenced on Oct. 5 to three years' strict imprisonment for extensive subversive activity and collaboration with Croatian political émigrés (this sentence being increased to five years by the Supreme Court of Croatia late in March 1973); four Croats given prison sentences ranging from two to five years on Oct. 10 for "hostile propaganda against the people and the state"; and seven others to from one to 6½ years in strict imprisonment on Nov. 27 for having formed a "terrorist group" and being in contact with *Ustashi* organizations in the Federal Republic of Germany and in Austria.

On June 7, 1973 two *Ustashi* members were sentenced at Tuzla (Bosnia) to 12 and 10 years in prison respectively for involvement in an *Ustashi* attempt to cause disturbances in order to secure the separation of Croatia from Yugoslavia.

A group of 15 Croatian nationalists, arrested in Zadar in June 1974, were on Feb. 17, 1975, given prison sentences of from 1½ to 13 years for subversive activities, in particular for having formed, four years earlier, an organization which was to become the basis of a Croatian Liberation Army, and which planned to acquire arms and ammunition, to commit sabotage and to assassinate political leaders, among them Dr Vladimir Bakaric (then the Croatian member of Yugoslavia's collective Presidency). Some of the defendants were also accused of having established links with the *Ustashi* organization abroad and of having adopted a "code of racial purity" banning marriages of Croats with other nationalities. The ultimate aim of the group was said to be the creation of a "great Croatian state" including also Bosnia-Herzegovina and parts of Serbia and Montenegro. The defendants denied that the organization referred to in the indictment existed but affirmed that armed struggle was the only means of attaining "Croatian liberation".

On April 1983 Jandra Fracin was sentenced to death for having caused explosions in various parts of Croatia, for which he had, it was alleged, been paid by the *Ustashi*.

Croatian Fighting Unit

A group of 22 men alleged to be members of this *Ustashi* organization were sentenced, in trials held in April-May 1985, to imprisonment for up to 20 years for planting explosives, carrying out a series of bombings in Croatia and along the Dalmatian coast in 1981-84, and engaging in hostile propaganda. The group was said to have maintained contacts with right-wing Croatian émigrés in West Germany.

Croatian Liberation Fighters

This underground movement, supporting the creation of a free and independent Croatia, has been responsible for acts of terrorism in the United States, in particular for bomb attacks on a Yugoslav bank in New York on March 17, 1980, and on the house of the Yugoslav chargé d'affaires in Washington, D.C., on June 1, 1980.

Croatian National Resistance (*Hrvatski Narodni Odbor*, HNO)

This group appears to have been active mainly in

the Federal Republic of Germany, where it was banned on June 9, 1976. Its chairman was on June 25, 1964, given a 3½-year prison sentence for his involvement in an attack on the Yugoslav trade mission in Bad Godesberg on Nov. 29, 1962 (when a doorman was killed). On May 25, 1978, he was again arrested and, with others, accused of various crimes against the Yugoslav state, which applied unsuccessfully to the Federal Republic for his extradition to Yugoslavia.

On June 9, 1976, the HNO and also *Drina*, another extreme right-wing Croatian organization, were banned by the German federal government because by their constant calls for violent action against Yugoslav institutions and representatives they endangered the internal security of the Federal Republic of Germany.

Croatian Revolutionary Brotherhood (HRB)

A group of 19 members of this organization, trained in Australia and Austria, entered Yugoslavia (apparently from Austria) in July 1972 but were liquidated by the Yugoslav security forces, who killed 15 of the infiltrators (who in turn had killed 15 members of these forces). Three of the remaining attackers were sentenced to death in Sarajevo in December 1972 and executed on March 17, 1973, and a fourth had his death sentence commuted to imprisonment for 20 years. All the Croats executed, and six of those killed by the security forces, had Australian citizenship.

The HRB was banned in the Federal Republic of Germany in 1968.

Other Alleged Croatian Nationalists' Offences

Between 1981 and 1984 several Roman Catholic clergymen were sentenced to terms of imprisonment for alleged political offences, officially linked with Croatian nationalism.

In September 1985 four youths were sentenced to prison terms of up to four years and four months for "hostile propaganda and planning terrorist actions" after being found guilty of proclaiming "the re-establishment of an independent Croatia". Also in September two Catholic priests were each sentenced to 30 days in prison as a result of allegations that they had made remarks denying the existence of Yugoslavia and referring to part of Montenegro as belonging to "the state of Croatia". On April 8, 1986, another Catholic priest was sentenced in Banja Luka (Bosnia-Herzegovina) to four years in prison for "inciting religious and [Croat] national hatred".

Serbian Nationalists

A number of Serbian nationalists, in particular former *Chetniks* (i.e. followers of the late Gen. Draja Mihailovic, who had during World War II been opposed by the partisans led by Josip Broz Tito), were dealt with by the courts in 1972-75.

Two Serbian nationalists accused of having, by producing and distributing tracts and books in 1970-71, tried to undermine "the unity and fraternity of the people of Yugoslavia" and to bring about "a change of the constitutional order by force" were on June 27, 1972, sentenced to imprisonment for one year and for 14 months respectively, while two others were given suspended sentences.

Dr Djura Djurovic, who had been an aide of Gen. Mihailovic and had been released in 1962 after serving 17 years in prison, was on Oct. 23, 1975, sentenced to five years in prison for anti-Tito articles of his published abroad five years earlier. He was, however, released under the amnesty proclaimed on Nov. 24, 1977.

In February 1976 a group of 17 alleged Serbian nationalists were sentenced at Bosansko Grahovo (central Yugoslavia) to varying terms of imprisonment, some of them for having connexions with the *Chetnik* movement in Western Europe. On June 28, 1976, three Bosnian Serbs were sentenced at Bihac (Bosnia) to 15, nine and seven years in prison respectively for having been in contact with *Chetnik* supporters abroad and for engaging in anti-Yugoslav propaganda.

In Western Europe the *Chetniks* were organized in the *Ravnagora* movement, one of whose leaders (Borivoje Blagojevic) was assassinated in Brussels on March 8, 1975. Other Serbian nationalists murdered in Brussels included the editor of *Vascrc Spoije*, a Serbian royalist anti-Tito newspaper, on May 13, 1975, and two other alleged Serbian royalists, found killed on Aug. 11, 1976.

On the other hand, two members of a "secret Serbian nationalist organization" were held responsible for the murder, on March 29, 1976, of the Yugoslav vice-consul in Lyons (France) whom they claimed to have "executed" as "a traitor for his crimes against the Serbian people in emigration".

On Sept. 3, 1985, six persons were sent to prison for terms ranging from eight months to 3½ years for spreading Serbian nationalist *Chetnik* propaganda.

Cominformists

Pro-Soviet Communists who opposed the 1948 break between Yugoslavia on the one hand and the Soviet Union and the Cominform (the successor to the Communist International) on the other have frequently attracted the attentions of the Yugoslav authorities. According to Ivo Pervan, Croatian Under-Secretary of the Interior (speaking in November 1975), so-called Cominformists had formed nine secret organizations working in Yugoslavia, committing acts of terrorism and being supported by subversive groups in various countries (notably Australia, Canada, France, the Federal Republic of Germany, Sweden and the Soviet Union). At the end of November 1975 the Croatian security services officially disclosed that they had dossiers on some 2,900 Cominformists, and that there was a network of 29 members intent upon setting up a new Yugoslav Communist Party.

The Communist Party of Yugoslavia was subsequently reported to have been established at a secret conference held in Bar (on the Adriatic coast) during 1974. The party's programme (as published on Feb. 24, 1976, in the *Daily Telegraph* of London) contained a condemnation of President Tito for having "betrayed" the original Communist Party of Yugoslavia and having, by a coup d'état, opened the way to "counter-revolutionary terror" and established "a regime of personal dictatorship" under which "more than 200,000 Communists" had been "expelled and arrested".

The programme declared that the new party was "an inseparable organic part of the international communist movement" and proposed, for a transitional regime leading to "genuine people's democracy", (i) the formation of a United National Front of all socialist and democratic parties and groups opposed to Tito; (ii) the formation of a provisional government of all parties; (iii) the disbandment of the secret police and the counter-intelligence organizations in the Army and militia and the abolition of all concentration camps and political prisons; (iv) the abolition of the Presidency of the Republic, dismissal of Marshal Tito from all ruling functions, prohibition of his political activity, and confiscation of the property which he had obtained illegally; (v) the nationalization of the principal means of production; (vi) a new electoral law giving every adult the right to vote, irrespective of his political views, and elections for a constitutional assembly within 12 months; and (vii) Yugoslavia's withdrawal from agreements made with Western governments.

Also during 1974, a total of 32 alleged Cominformists were sentenced, in trials which ended in Pec (Kosovo) on Sept. 18 and in Titograd (Montenegro) on Sept. 20, to prison terms ranging from one to 14 years. One of the principal defendants at the Pec trial, Komnen Jovovic (given 14 years), was released under the amnesty proclaimed on Nov. 24, 1977.

Numerous other alleged Cominformists tried in 1975-78 included several leading figures of this movement, notably Dusan Brkic, a former Deputy Premier of Croatia expelled from the Communist Party of Croatia in 1950, who was given an eight-year sentence by a Belgrade district court on March 12, 1976.

Vlado Dapcevic, a former colonel and an alleged prominent Cominformist, was condemned to death in Belgrade on July 5, 1976, this sentence being immediately commuted to 20 years in prison. In 1948 he had already been sentenced to 20 years, but had been amnestied in 1956 and had thereupon left the country. On Aug. 9, 1975, he disappeared in Bucharest and was thereafter taken to Belgrade, apparently against his will. At his 1976 trial he was charged with high treason for articles written in 1956-75 calling for the overthrow of the Tito government; with participation in the creation of the new Communist Party of Yugoslavia in Bar in 1974 (see above); and also with accepting funds from Albania in return for allegedly advocating the surrender of parts of Kosovo and Macedonia to Albania.

Mileta Perovic, a former colonel and former Yugoslav consul in Paris, was on April 13, 1978, sentenced to 20 years in prison for "several grave crimes against the party and the state" committed in 1956-77. In 1949 he had already been sentenced to 18 years in prison but he had been pardoned in 1956 and had left the country in 1958. In Kiev (USSR) he had headed a group of pro-Moscow Yugoslavs and attempted, with ex-Col. Dapcevic, to set up the (pro-Moscow) Communist Party of Yugoslavia; at the secret congress establishing this party in Bar in 1974, he was, "on his own instructions", elected its secretary-general. The USSR later expelled him and some of his associates, and in 1975 he went to France, from where he was expelled after attempting to set up the party's headquarters in Paris.

Other Dissidents

Committee for the Defence of Freedom of Thought and Expression

In January 1986 this group of intellectuals sent a letter to the Federal Assembly and to the Assembly of the Serbian Republic calling for an investigation into what they called the abuse of psychiatry for political purposes, for which they claimed to have evidence relating to 40 such cases.

Democratic Socialists

Leading figures among those who advocated democratic socialism for Yugoslavia have been the veteran Communist Milovan Djilas and the (Russian-born) writer Mihajlo Mihajlov. However, neither of them has created an organized movement. In his book *The New Class* written in 1955-56 Djilas concluded inter alia that communism tended to develop into a tyranny of expert political managers. On Sept. 5, 1957, his book was banned in Yugoslavia and on Oct. 5 he was sentenced to seven years in prison. On April 7, 1962, he was sentenced to another five years in prison in connexion with his book *Conversations with Stalin*. He was released from prison under an amnesty of Dec. 31, 1966. Thereafter he refrained from further political activities.

Criticism of the Yugoslav regime from a socialist point of view was also expressed from 1968 onwards by a number of academics associated with the journal *Praxis*, the organ of the Croatian Philosophical Society, which ceased publication in February 1975, after eight teachers at the University of Belgrade, associated with *Praxis*, had been suspended indefinitely for "intriguing with others on how to seize power".

Between 1981 and 1984 the authorities tolerated a degree of freedom of expression, but on April 12, 1984, the president of the Socialist Alliance of the Working People of Yugoslavia criticized those who, he said, were openly supporting a multi-party system.

On April 20 the police detained 28 persons (among them Milovan Djilas) meeting at a Belgrade flat; although suspected of planning hostile activity, with two of them being charged with disseminating hostile propaganda, all of them were released. One of those released, Radomir Radovic, was found dead a few days later; according to a post mortem (announced on May 10) he had taken a drug overdose. A group of 19 prominent intellectuals alleged on May 8 that five of those detained had been subjected to psychological and physical ill-treatment in order to extract confessions.

One of the above 28, Dr Vojislav Seselj, was arrested in Sarajevo on May 15, 1984, for alleged "counter-revolutionary activities, anarcho-liberalism and nationalism" and for "attempting to overthrow the power of the working class". These charges were based on a manuscript (found in his flat) in which he had criticized the Tito regime, but which had never been published or disseminated. He was subsequently sentenced to eight years in prison on the lesser charge of "hostile propaganda"; on appeal his sentence was reduced to four years; in August 1985 the sentence was further reduced to two years and two months by the Yugoslav Federal Court; and he was finally released on March 15, 1986.

Six other intellectuals who had taken part in meetings of a debating circle known as the "Free University" were charged with anti-state activities. Only three of them were sentenced (on Feb. 4, 1985) to terms of two, 1½ and one year in prison respectively but were then released pending an appeal. On Aug. 7, 1985, it was reported that the appeal court had reduced the sentences of the first two to 1½ years and to eight months respectively and had acquitted the third defendant.

The above trials of intellectuals were widely regarded as the most serious political trials in Yugoslavia since the death of President Tito on May 4, 1980.

On March 21, 1986, a court in Tuzla (Bosnia) sentenced two men to 5½ and five years respectively for "maliciously and falsely presenting social conditions in the country" and "denigrating the person and achievements of Comrade Tito and the highest League of Communists and state leaders".

In an Amnesty International report on May 28, 1985, it was claimed that over 500 persons per year had been found guilty of political offences and had been given prison sentences of up to 15 years merely for expressing their views.

Moslem Fundamentalism

During 1981-84 the popularity of Moslem fundamentalist ideas was reported to be growing in Bosnia-Herzegovina, where about 43 per cent of the population were Moslems. On Aug. 20, 1983, a group of 11 Moslems were sentenced to terms ranging from five to 15 years in prison for alleged counter-revolutionary activities inspired by Moslem nationalists and for attempting to create an Islamic state in Bosnia-Herzegovina. The defendants, however, denied the charges and declared that they had merely been seeking greater freedom of expression.

On April 8, 1986, a district court in Bosnia-Herzegovina passed a three-year prison sentence on Halil Mehtic, a Moslem religious leader, for "provoking national hatred, discord and intolerance" by urging Moslems not to associate with Serbs and Croats and by making defamatory remarks about communism.

Exiled Parties

Croatian Peasants' Party

Leadership. Juraj Krnjevic

The leader of this exiled formation has been officially described in Yugoslavis as a "war criminal", in line with the government's approach to all manifestations of Croatian nationalism (see separate section above). In August 1977 a Dr Nikola Novakovic was reported to have been sentenced in Sarajevo to 12 years in prison for "counter-revolutionary and nationalist activities" by taking up contact with this party.

Slovene People's Party

This exiled formation is affiliated to the Christian Democratic World Union.

Yugoslav Socialist Party

Leadership. Marko Milunovic

This formation of exiled democratic socialists opposed to what they regard as the illegal assumption of sole power by the Yugoslav Communists after World War II is a consultative member of the Socialist International and a constituent party of the Socialist Union of Central and Eastern Europe (SUCEE).

Zaïre

Capital: Kinshasa Pop. 30,360,000

The Republic of Zaïre is a "united, democratic and social state" with an executive President elected for a seven-year term (and eligible for re-election); he is head of state, head of the National Executive Council (Cabinet) and leader of the Popular Revolutionary Movement (*Mouvement populaire de la révolution*, MPR), the country's sole legal political organization, whose political bureau he appoints. There is a National Legislative Council of 268 members elected by universal adult suffrage for a five-year term on a list of the MPR.

In April 1980 President Mobutu Sese Seko signed ordinances replacing the existing National Documentation Centre by a National Intelligence Service (SNI) with responsibility for external security and by a National Research and Investigations Centre (CNRI) with responsibility for internal security.

On Aug. 28, 1986, a new Civil Guard was set up with responsibility for public order and security; it is directly answerable to the head of state.

Internal Opposition

Internal opposition to President Mobutu found expression in a parliamentary report completed by a five-member committee in October 1980 and revealing substantial foreign currency deals by the Mobutu family and outside interests. The five members of the committee were all arrested on Dec. 31, 1980, and on Jan. 2, 1981, a total of 13 people's commissioners (i.e. members of the National Legislative Council) were deprived of their parliamentary immunity because they had, as officially stated, "carefully prepared a 50-page pamphlet . . . denigrating established institutions, harming the head of state's reputation, creating confusion in people's minds and inciting them to revolt". The lifting of the 13 members' immunity was opposed by 17 members of the Legislative Council, while 22 others abstained from voting.

On July 1, 1982, the 13 men (and 25 other defendants) were each sentenced by the State Security Court to 15 years' imprisonment for having been implicated in an attempt to create a second political party in Zaïre. Although they were released under an amnesty declared on May 19, 1983, six of them were (as reported in November 1983) rearrested and sent into internal exile.

The amnesty, which covered political prisoners and dissidents in exile, was thought to affect over 100 people.

On March 28, 1984, two bombs exploded in Kinshasa, killing two persons and causing damage to the radio and post office headquarters. Several exiled opposition groups claimed responsibility.

The major exiled opposition groups denied any involvement in an action by rebels who temporarily occupied the town of Moba (in Shaba province, on the shores of Lake Tanganyika) on Nov. 13-15, 1984, when it was officially claimed that about 12 civilians and over 100 rebels had been killed in fighting between government troops and the rebels. The government alleged that the rebels had launched their incursion from Tanzania, but the Tanzanian authorities denied on Nov. 23 that Tanzania was harbouring armed opposition groups. According to Amnesty International the re-occupation of Moba by government troops had been followed by torture and many summary executions of prisoners. President Mobutu himself admitted in November 1986 that there had been "bad behaviour" by his troops.

Moba was again attacked on June 16-17, 1985, by rebels who, however, were routed after five hours of fighting which had resulted in heavy casualties among the rebels and the death of two soldiers.

External Opposition

A number of organizations hostile to the regime of President Mobutu have been founded by Zaïreans in exile, mainly in Brussels.

Congo National Movement—Lumumba (*Mouvement national du Congo—Lumumba*, MNC-Lumumba)

Leadership. Paul-Roger Mokede (pres.); François-Emery Lumumba-Tolenga (sec.-gen.)

This Movement was named after Patrice Lumumba, the first (and left-wing) Prime Minister of the independent Republic of the Congo (proclaimed on June 30, 1960), who was murdered in February 1961. After giving a press conference in Brussels during the second invasion of Shaba province by forces of the Congolese National Liberation Front, in May 1978, Paul-Roger Mokede was expelled from Brussels to Paris. President Mobutu had previously protested to the Belgian government against its toleration of active Zaïrean opposition groups in Belgium.

The Movement described the Kinshasa bombings of March 28, 1984 (see above), as retaliation for the killing of some 200 militants by Zaïrean forces in Kivu province in November 1983.

On April 1, 1984, the Movement's secretary-general was reported to have been expelled from Brussels to Paris.

In September 1985 the Movement agreed with the Congolese Social Democratic Party (whose first secretary, Allah Fior Muyinda, was based in Switzerland) to form a joint working commission with the object of bringing together other groups opposed to the Mobutu regime.

Congolese Front for the Restoration of Democracy (*Front congolais pour le rétablissement de la démocratie*)

This Front was established in Brussels in October 1982 as an alliance of a number of rival opposition groups by Nguza Karl I Bond, who had had a long diplomatic and political career during which he was State Commissioner for Foreign Affairs in 1972-74 and 1974-77, a member of the political bureau of the ruling MPR in 1972-77 and its director in 1974-77, Vice-President of the National Executive Council (Cabinet) and State Commissioner for Foreign Affairs and International Co-operation from February 1976 to August 1977.

He was arrested on Aug. 13, 1977, and on Sept. 13 he was condemned to death for undermining Zaïre's external security (by failing to reveal his knowledge of the impending rebel action in Shaba by the Congolese National Liberation Front), a charge to which he pleaded not guilty. The death sentence was on Sept. 15 commuted to life imprisonment, and on July 14, 1978, he was released under an amnesty declared by President Mobutu. On March 6, 1979, he was reappointed State Commissioner for Foreign Affairs and International Co-operation, and on Aug. 27, 1980, he was given the post of First State Commissioner (Prime Minister). His resignation from this post was announced on April 17, 1981, when he was in Belgium, where he stated that his return to Zaïre would mean his return to prison.

Nguza subsequently strongly attacked President

Mobutu's regime, stating on June 25, 1981, that he was "pro-Western" and shared the West's valid concern for "keeping Zaïre out of communist hands" but that the "human rights violations, the economic misery" in Zaïre and "the President's pilfering of state coffers" were equally important. Before a US House of Representatives' sub-committee on Africa he stated on Sept. 15, 1981, that the West should abandon its "blind and uncritical support" for President Mobutu and that the situation in Kinshasa was ripe for uprisings.

Of the groups which had joined the Front, the People's Revolutionary Party led by Laurent Kabila (see separate entry) left the Front in September 1983 over disagreements with its leadership.

Nguza himself returned to Kinshasa on June 27, 1985, after announcing his desire for reconciliation with President Mobutu, and in July 1986 he was appointed Zaïre's ambassador to the United States.

Congolese Progressive Students (ECP)—see under Council for the Liberation of the Congo-Kinshasa

Congolese Socialist Party (PSC)—see under Council for the Liberation of the Congo-Kinshasa

Council for the Liberation of the Congo-Kinshasa (*Conseil pour la libération du Congo-Kinshasa*, CLC)

Leadership. Mungul Diaka (pres.); Mbeka Makosso (sec.-gen.)

The CLC was established in Brussels in November 1978 as a merger of various exile groups in opposition to the Mobutu regime—(i) the Congolese National Liberation Front (FNLC), (ii) the National Movement for Union and Reconciliation in Zaïre (MNUR), (iii) the People's Revolutionary Party (PRP), (iv) the Congolese Socialist Party (*Parti socialiste congolais*, PSC) and (v) the Congolese Progressive Students (*Etudiants congolais progressistes*, ECP).

Mungul Diaka had a varied career under President Mobutu. Having been appointed Minister of Education in October 1967, he was dismissed on July 5, 1968, for alleged "grave shortcomings incompatible with the revolutionary objectives of the new regime"; on Feb. 11, 1972, he was sentenced to 10 years in prison for plotting against President Mobutu, but he was later reprieved, and in March 1979 he was appointed State Commissioner for Higher Education and Scientific Research. He held this post until January 1980, when he stated to have fled to Brazzaville (Congo) after a judicial inquiry had begun into alleged fraud and maladministration. In December 1980 some 30 distributors of CLC pamphlets were reported to have been arrested in Kinshasa, while Mungul Diaka stated that three Zaïrean parliamentarians were being interrogated on suspicion of having helped him to flee Zaïre.

The declared aim of the CLC has been the restoration of democracy and fundamental human rights in Zaïre.

However, after the declaration of the amnesty of May 28, 1983, Mbeka Makosso announced that he intended to return to Zaïre.

National Movement for Union and Reconciliation in Zaïre (*Mouvement national pour l'union et la réconciliation au Zaïre*, MNUR)

Leadership. Mbeka Makosso (founder)

This Movement was set up in Brussels by Mbeka Makosso (formerly Joseph Mbeka), who had been Minister of the Economy under President Mobutu from November 1969 to February 1972 and later ambassador in Washington and Tehran. It subsequently joined the Council for the Liberation of the Congo-Kinshasa (CLC) on its formation in November 1978 (see separate entry).

People's Revolutionary Party (*Parti de la révolution populaire*, PRP)

Leadership. Laurent Kabila (l.)

The PRP is a remnant of the *Comité national de libération* which in 1964 conducted insurrectional activities under the leadership of Pierre Mulele. Since 1967 the PRP has claimed to hold guerrilla strongholds in the Fizi Baraka area (on the western shore of Lake Tanganyika). It was responsible for the kidnapping of four students from the United States in Tanzania on May 19, 1975, and for their release in July 1975 upon payment of ransom by the students' parents. In November 1978 the PRP joined the Council for the Liberation of the Congo-Kinshasa (see separate entry).

Zaïre Committee

This human rights group based in Belgium claimed on Feb. 29, 1984, that 27 political prisoners had been hanged in a prison near Kinshasa in late 1983, and that between June and December 1983 another 55 prisoners had died in the same prison.

Zambia

Capital: Lusaka Pop. 6,670,000

The Republic of Zambia, a member of the Commonwealth, has an executive President elected by universal adult suffrage for a five-year term (and eligible for re-election). He appoints a Prime Minister and a secretary-general of the United National Independence Party (UNIP), of which he is the president and which is the country's sole legal political party. He also appoints the Cabinet, which is subordinate to UNIP's central committee. There is a National Assembly to which 125 members (chosen from candidates approved by UNIP local committees) are elected at the same time as the President and 10 additional members are nominated by the President.

During the year 1980 two attempts to overthrow President Kenneth Kaunda's regime were reported to have been foiled. The first of these, reported on Feb. 22, related to an alleged attempt to assassinate the President in January 1980 by nine army officers who were captured, interrogated and hanged. The second attempt, which was confirmed by President Kaunda on Oct. 27, was made on Oct. 16 when Zambian security forces put to flight some 200 men, mainly Katangese gendarmes (who had been involved in secessionist activities in Zaïre) said to be in the pay of Zambian dissidents supported by South Africa. In connexion with this attempt, seven men were on Jan. 20, 1983, condemned to death for treason (among them Valentine Musakanya, a former governor of the Bank of Zambia, and four Zaïreans) and an eighth defendant was given a 10-year prison sentence, all of them having pleaded "not guilty". On April 2, 1985, the convictions of Musakanya and of one of the Zaïreans were overturned by five appeal judges in the Lusaka High Court, while the 10-year prison sentence (passed on a former officer of the Zambian Air Force) was quashed. The court found that the evidence given against these three men had been obtained under duress and was therefore inadmissible. The five other death sentences were, however, upheld.

Zimbabwe

Capital: Harare (formerly Salisbury) Pop. 8,500,000

The Republic of Zimbabwe, an independent state within the Commonwealth, has a President chosen by the Legislature and required to act on the advice of the Prime Minister and the Executive Council (Cabinet). The Legislature consists of (i) a House of Assembly of 100 members, 80 of whom are elected by universal adult suffrage on a common roll and 20 on a roll of Whites, Coloureds and Asians; and (ii) a Senate of 40 members, 10 of whom are chosen by the White members of the House of Assembly, 14 by Black members of the House, 10 by a Council of Chiefs and six by the President on the advice of the Prime Minister.

In elections to the 20 non-Black seats in the House of Assembly held on June 27, 1985, the Conservative Alliance of Zimbabwe (CAZ—previously known successively as the Rhodesian Front and the Republican Front) obtained 15 seats (one CAZ member defecting to join the ruling party in June 1986), the Independent Zimbabwe Group gained four seats, and the remaining seat went to an independent (who was Minister of State in the Office of the Prime Minister). In elections held on July 1-14, 1985, to the 80 common roll (Black) seats the Zimbabwe African National Union (ZANU) gained 64 seats, the Zimbabwe African People's Union (ZAPU) 15 seats, and the ZANU (Sithole) Party one.

Serious internal unrest has persisted in Zimbabwe mainly as a result of a conflict between ZANU (led by Robert Mugabe, the Prime Minister) and ZAPU (led by Joshua Nkomo), the former being supported mainly by the majority Shona population group and the latter by the minority Ndebele people of Matabeleland (south-western Zimbabwe). Dissidents of ZAPU's Zimbabwe People's Revolutionary Army (ZIPRA, which had in 1980 been merged into Zimbabwe's National Army) have continued to be involved in armed clashes with government troops. Regulations under a 1965 Emergency Powers Act have been renewed by parliament at half-yearly intervals every January and July.

Following the discovery of large quantities of arms in Matabeleland which, according to the government, had been hidden in caches by guerrillas loyal to Joshua Nkomo in preparation for a military coup, the President of the Republic issued on Feb. 16, 1982, a proclamation declaring that 11 companies owned by Nkomo and other leading ZAPU members were illegal organizations and that they had been seized by the state; he explained that in the light of the arms finds they were "likely to endanger, disturb or interfere with defence, public safety or public order". The Prime Minister announced on Feb. 17 that he had relieved Nkomo and three other ZAPU members of their responsibilities in the government. Senior military advisers to Nkomo, as well as former ZIPRA members said to have undergone secret military training in Matabeleland, were arrested during March 1982.

The situation was aggravated by deserters from the National Army, estimated by mid-June 1982 as numbering some 2,000 many of whom had turned to banditry and had been attacking and killing Whites.

Several sessions of talks between Mugabe and Nkomo failed to achieve a peaceful solution of the conflict, which was, early in 1983, greatly exacerbated by the intervention of the fifth brigade of Zimbabwe's Army which had been trained by North Korean instructors and was said to be totally committed to the Prime Minister. According to Nkomo and numerous observers, this unit was guilty of terrorizing the Ndebele people and of committing atrocities.

On Aug. 17, 1983, Nkomo alleged in the House of Assembly that 3,000 or more people had been killed and thousands maimed by security forces in the campaign against dissidents. A large number of people fled from Matabeleland to the neighbouring country of Botswana, where by September 1983 an estimated 3,000 refugees were held in a settlement at Dukwe.

At the first congress held by ZAPU since Zimbabwe became independent in 1980, Nkomo said on Oct. 13, 1984, that ZANU was concerned solely with remaining in power and that in less than five years the promise of independence had turned into "a reality of suspicion, terror and failure", and he blamed the government for having "driven former guerrilla independence fighters into banditry".

On Nov. 9, 1984, a group of five rebels murdered (at Beitbridge) Senator Moven Ndlovu, a member of ZANU's central committee. This action was followed by riots in which over 180 people were injured and the local ZAPU office was burned down; some 80 persons detained included several ZAPU officials but Nkomo denied that his organization was responsible for the murder. In response to the murder the Prime Minister dismissed two ZAPU members from his government, one of them being Cephas Msipa (ZAPU secretary-general), who announced on Nov. 29 that he was resigning from ZAPU but not joining ZANU. (The five alleged killers of Senator Ndlovu were acquitted on Aug. 15, 1986, when the court found that they had been tortured before confessing to the murder.)

On the other hand, the High Court in Harare had on July 20, 1986, sentenced to death four soldiers accused of murdering a lieutenant and three civilians in February 1983.

In a report issued by the (New York) Lawyers' Committee for Human Rights on May 21, 1986, it was claimed that the Zimbabwe authorities had, over the past three years, committed a wide range of human rights violations against their political opponents and other people.

The Zimbabwe police stated in January 1987 that dissident activity had decreased in 1986, for which year it gave the following figures: 1,073 sightings of guerrillas (50 per cent less than in 1985); 15 captured (85 in 1985); 16 civilians killed by dissidents (156 in 1985). These figures were disputed by the Catholic Commission for Justice and Peace in Harare, which claimed that since June 1986 guerrilla unrest and military activity in Matabeleland had increased.

In Johannesburg (South Africa) it was reported on Aug. 20, 1986, that the Rev. Ndabaningi Sithole, the leader of the (legal) ZANU (Sithole) party, had signed an agreement in Washington with the Mozambican National Resistance Movement, which was fighting a guerrilla campaign against the Mozambican government, whose troops had been reinforced by troops from Zimbabwe.

International Revolutionary Groupings

In addition to direct links between revolutionary movements in different countries, some international revolutionary groupings have been established, but their effectiveness has remained uncertain. They include the groupings described below.

International Revolutionary Movement (*Movimiento Revolucionario Internacional*, MRI)

In mid-1985 it was reported that this movement, based in Europe, had held meetings in Lima (Peru),

Bogotá (Colombia) and Panama to plan the formation of an armed front for the "liberation" of Latin America and that it was offering political support and economic aid to revolutionary movements in the region.

Nationalist European Union (*National-Europäische Union*)

Police in West Berlin announced on Sept. 9, 1984, that 13 persons had been arrested in connexion with an attempt to set up an organization under the above name as a successor to the banned Action Front of National Socialists/National/Activists (ANS/NA).

This group was one of several which claimed responsibility for the assassination of Olof Palme, the Swedish Prime Minister, on Feb. 28, 1986.

Pan-Arab Command

The formation of this Command was announced on March 2, 1985, by Col. Moamer al-Gadaffi, the Libyan leader, who declared that its object would be "to assume responsibility for the command of "the revolutionary forces in the Arab homeland". It was subsequently reported in Libya that the Command had been joined by a number of (small-scale) radical Arab movements, including the Palestinian Communist Party, the (Sunni) Lebanese *Mourabitoun*, the Tunisian Free Unions' Movement, the Sudanese Democratic Unionist Party, the Iraqi *Mujaheddin* and several Iraqi Kurdish groups, including the Kurdish Democratic Party and the Democratic Party of Kurdistan.

At the Command's inaugural meeting held in Tripoli on March 29-31, 1985, Col. Gadaffi was elected as leader of the Command and it was decided to adopt "revolutionary violence and armed struggle" as a means of achieving the aims of the component movements. The meeting also resolved that a danger to one movement would be regarded as a danger to all and that a United Pan-Arab Force should be formed, to be composed of 10 per cent of each movement's force.

At a further meeting, held on Feb. 2-4, 1986, a call was made on Arab states to boycott US products and to withdraw assets from US banks; it was also resolved to establish "a revolutionary striking force and martyr [i.e. suicide] units" which would launch attacks against "US interests" in response to any US attack on an Arab country. In Tripoli it was claimed that this meeting had been attended by, among others, representatives of the ruling Syrian *Baath* Party, the *Fatah* Revolutionary Council, the Popular Front for the Liberation of Palestine—General Command and the Palestinian Popular Struggle Front, as well as representatives from Lebanon, Jordan, Oman, "Yemen", Bahrain, Iraq and the "Arabian Peninsula".

World Union of National Socialists

This international body was formed in 1966 on an initiative by the British and US Nazi movements. It claimed responsibility for a bomb explosion at a Jewish film festival held at a Paris cinema on March 29, 1985, resulting in 18 casualties.

SELECT BIBLIOGRAPHY

General

Adams, James, *The Financing of Terror*. New English Library, London, 1986.

Alexander, Yonah, Carlton, David, and Wilkinson, Paul, *Terrorism: Theory and Practice*. Westview Press, Boulder, Colorado, 1979.

Alexander, Yonah, and Ebinger, Charles K., *Politics, Terrorism and Energy*. Praeger, New York, 1982.

Amnesty International Annual Reports. Amnesty International Publications, London.

Clutterbuck, Richard C., *Guerrillas and Terrorists*. Ohio Univ. Press, 1982.

Day, Alan J., *Peace Movements of the World*. Longman, Harlow, 1986.

Day, Alan J., and Degenhardt, Henry W., *Political Parties of the World* (2nd ed.). Longman, Harlow, 1984.

Dobson, Christopher, and Payne, Robert, *The Weapons of Terror*. Macmillan, London, 1979.

Evans, Alona E., and Murphy, John F., *The Legal Aspects of International Terrorism*. Lexington Books, Lexington, Mass., 1979.

Fanon, Frantz, *Black Skin, White Masks*. Grove Press, New York, 1962.

Fanon, Frantz, *The Wretched of the Earth*. Grove Press, New York, 1965 and 1968.

Greenshaw, Martha, *Terrorism, Legitimacy and Power*. Wesleyan Univ. Press, Middletown, Conn., 1983.

Haycock, David, *Regular Armies and Insurgencies*. Croom Helm, London, 1979.

Hayes, David, *Terrorism and Freedom Fighters*. Wayland, Hove, 1980.

Hobday, Charles, *Communist and Marxist Parties of the World*. Longman, Harlow, 1986.

Humana, Charles, *World Human Rights Guide*. Pan Books, London, 1987.

Janke, Peter (ed.), *Guerrilla and Terrorist Organizations. A World Directory and Bibliography*. Harvester Press, for Institute for the Study of Conflict, London, 1983.

Laqueur, Walter, *The Age of Terrorism*. Weidenfeld & Nicolson, London/Little, Brown, New York, 1986.

Livingstone, Neil C., *The War against Terrorism*. Lexington Books, Lexington, Mass., 1982.

Lodge, Juliette, *Terrorism: The Challenge to the State*. Martin Robertson, Oxford, 1981.

Mickolous, Edward F., *The Literature of Terrorism*. Greenwood Press, Westport, Conn., 1980.

O'Neill, Bard E., Heaton, William R., and Alberts, Donald J., (eds.) *Insurgency in the Modern World*. Westview Press, Boulder, Colorado, 1980.

Smith, Bradley F., *The Shadow Warriors*. André Deutsch, London, 1983.

Sterling, Claire, *The Terror Network*. Weidenfeld & Nicolson, London, 1981.

Sterling, Claire, *The Time of the Assassins*. Angus & Robertson, London, 1984.

Eastern Europe and the USSR

Bukovsky, Vladimir, *To Build a Castle: My Life as a Dissenter*. Deutsch, London, 1978.

Djilas, Milovan, *The New Class*. Holt, Rinehart & Winston, New York, 1974.

Djilas, Milovan, *The Unperfect Society. Beyond the New Class*. Allen & Unwin, London, 1972.

Grigorenko, Petro G., *Memoirs*, Harvill Press, London, 1983.

Kopelev, Lev, *No Jail for Thought*. Secker & Warburg, London, 1975.

Labedz, Leopold (ed.), *Solzhenitsyn – a Documentary Record*. Allen Lane, London, 1970; Penguin, Harmondsworth, 1972.

Medvedev, Roy A., *Let History Judge*. Knopf, New York, 1971; Macmillan, London, 1972.

Medvedev, Roy A., et al., *Détente and Socialist Democracy*. Spokesman Books, Nottingham, 1978.

Medvedev, Roy A., *On Stalin and Stalinism*. Oxford Univ. Press, 1979.

Medvedev, Roy A., *Political Essays*. Spokesman Books, Nottingham, 1976–78.

Medvedev, Roy A., *Samizdat Register: Voices of the Socialist Opposition in the Soviet Union* (2 vols.). Merlin Press, London, 1977–78.

Medvedev, Zhores A., *The Medvedev Papers*. Macmillan, London, 1971.

Medvedev, Zhores A., *The Rise and Fall of D. T. Lysenko*. Columbia Univ. Press, New York, 1969.

Medvedev, Zhores A. and Roy A., *A Question of Madness*. Macmillan, London, 1971.

Mihajlov, Mihajlo, *Underground Notes*. Routledge, London, 1977.

Myant, Martin, *Poland: A Crisis for Socialism*. Lawrence & Wishart, London, 1982.

Plyushch, Leonid, *History's Carnival*. Collins/Harvill, London, 1979.

Religion in Communist Lands. Keston College, Heathfield Road, Keston, Kent BR2 6BA.

Sakharov, Andrei D., *Alarm and Hope*. Collins/Harvill, London, 1979.

Sakharov, Andrei D., *My Country and the World*. Collins/Harvill, London, 1975.

Sakharov, Andrei D. (ed. Salisbury, Harrison E.), *Sakharov Speaks*. Harvill, London, 1974.

Solzhenitsyn, Alexander (ed. Klimoff, Alexis), *Alexander Solzhenitsyn Speaks to the West*. Bodley Head, London, 1978.

Solzhenitsyn, Alexander, *Cancer Ward*. Bodley Head, London, 1970.

Solzhenitsyn, Alexander, *Détente: Prospects for Democracy and Dictatorship*. Transaction Books, USA, 1980.

Solzhenitsyn, Alexander, *Gulag Archipelago* (3 vols.). Harvill and Fontana, London, 1974–78.

Solzhenitsyn, Alexander, *Mortal Danger*. Bodley Head, London, 1980.

Solzhenitsyn, Alexander, *Nobel Prize Lecture*. Stenvalley Press, 1973.

Solzhenitsyn, Alexander, *One Day in the Life of Ivan Denisovich*. Bodley Head, London, 1971; Panther, 1978.

Solzhenitsyn, Alexander, *Warning to the Western World*. BBC and Bodley Head, London, 1976.

Solzhenitsyn, Alexander, et al., *From Under the Rubble*. Harvill, London, 1975.

Voinovich, Vladimir, *The Ivankiad*. Cape, London, 1978; Penguin, Harmondsworth, 1980.

Asia and the Far East

Banerjee, Sumanta, *In the Wake of Naxalbari. A History of the Naxalite Movement in India*. Verry, Lawrence Inc., USA, 1980.

Bhutto, Z., *My Execution*. South Asia Books, Columbia, Mo., USA, 1980.

Clutterbuck, Richard, *Conflict and Violence in Singapore and Malaysia, 1945–1983*. Graham Brash, Singapore, 1985.

Goyal, Des Raj, *Rashtriya Swayamsevak Sangh*. South Asia Books, Columbia, Mo., USA, 1979.

Shakir, Moin, *Politics of Minorities*. South Asia Books, Columbia, Mo., USA, 1980.

Singh, Mohinder, *The Akali Movement*. South Asia Books, Columbia, Mo., USA, 1978.

The Middle East and the Arab World

Becker, Jillian, *The PLO: The Rise and Fall of the Palestine Liberation Organisation.* Weidenfeld & Nicolson, London, 1984.

Cobban, Helena, *The Palestine Liberation Organisation: People, Power and Politics.* Cambridge Univ. Press, 1984.

Dobson, Christopher, and Payne, Ronald, *Terror! The West Fights Back.* Papermac, London, 1982.

Israeli, Raphael, *The PLO in Lebanon: Selected Documents.* Weidenfeld & Nicolson, London, 1983.

Iyad, Abu (with Eric Rouleau), *My Home, My Land: A Narrative of the Palestinian Struggle.* Times Books, New York, 1981.

Kostiner, Joseph, *The Struggle for South Yemen.* St Martin's Press, New York, 1984.

Laffin, John, *The PLO Connection.* Corgi Books, London, 1982.

Pipes, Daniel, *In the Path of God: Islam and Political Power.* Basic Books, New York, 1983.

Wright, Robin, *Sacred Rage: The Crusade of Militant Islam.* Linden Press, New York, 1985.

Yodfat, Aryeh, and Arnon-Ohanna, Yuval, *PLO Strategy and Tactics.* Croom Helm, London, 1981.

Africa

Davidson, Basil, *The People's Cause: A History of Guerrillas in Africa.* Longman, Harlow, 1981.

Fanon, Frantz, *Towards the African Revolution: Political Essays.* Monthly Review Press, New York, 1967.

Friedland, Elaine Alice, *A Comparative Study of the Development of Revolutionary Nationalist Movements in Southern Africa—FRELIMO (Mozambique) and the African National Congress of South Africa.* Diss., City University of New York, 1980.

Hodges, Tony, *Western Sahara: The Roots of a Desert War.* Croom Helm, London, 1984.

Roux, Edward, *Time Longer than Rope: a History of the Black Man's Struggle for Freedom in South Africa.* Univ. of Wisconsin Press, Madison, 1964.

Latin America

Debray, Régis, *Revolution in the Revolution?* Monthly Review Press, London and New York, 1967.

Dahlin, Therrin C., et al., *The Catholic Left in Latin America. A Comprehensive Bibliography.* G. K. Hall, Boston, Mass., 1981.

Dunkerley, James, *Rebellion in the Veins: Political Struggle in Bolivia, 1952–1982.* Verso Editions, London, 1984.

Dunkerley, James, *The Long War: Dictatorship and Revolution in El Salvador.* Junction Books, London, 1982.

Fauriol, Georges, (ed.) *Latin American Insurgencies.* Georgetown Univ. Center for Strategic and International Studies, 1985.

Lafeber, Walter, *Inevitable Revolutions: The United States in Central America.* Norton, New York, 1983.

Marighella, Carlos, *For the Liberation of Brazil.* Penguin, Harmondsworth, 1972.

Ó Maoláin, Ciarán, *Latin American Political Movements.* Longman, Harlow, 1985.

Schooley, Helen, *Conflict in Central America.* Longman, Harlow, 1987.
Torres, Camilo (ed. John Gerassi), *Revolutionary Priest.* London, 1971; Random House, New York, 1971.

Western Europe

Adams, Gerry, *Falls Memories.* Brandon Book Publishers, Dingle, Co. Kerry, 1982.
Alexander, Yonah, and Myers, Kenneth A., *Terrorism in Europe.* St Martin's Press, New York, 1982.
Arthur, Paul, *Government and Politics of Northern Ireland.* Longman, Harlow, 1980.
Aust, Stefan, *The Baader-Meinhof Group.* Bodley Head, London, 1986.
Becker, Jillian, *Hitler's Children.* Michael Joseph, London, 1977; Panther Books, London, 1978.
Bishop, Patrick, and Mallie, Eamonn, *The Provisional IRA.* Heinemann, London, 1986.
Clutterbuck, Richard L., *Britain in Agony: Growth of Political Violence.* Faber, London, 1978; Penguin, Harmondsworth, 1980.
Coogan, Tim Pat, *The I.R.A.* Pall Mall Press, London, 1970; Fontana Books, London, 1980.
Kelley, Kevin, *The Longest War: Northern Ireland and the IRA.* Zed Books, London, 1982.
Pisano, Vittorfranco S., *The Red Brigades: A Challenge to Italian Democracy.* Institute for the Study of Conflict, London, No. 120, July 1980.
Tomlinson, John, *Left, Right—The March of Political Extremism in Britain.* Calder, London, and Riverrun, New York, 1981.
Townshend, Charles, *Political Violence in Ireland.* Clarendon Press, Oxford, 1983.

North America

Bayes, Jane H., *Minority Politics and Ideologies in the United States.* Chandler & Sharp, Novato, Calif., 1982.
Goldstein, Robert J., *Political Repression in Modern America. From Eighteen-Seventy to the Present.* Schenkman, Cambridge, Mass., 1981.
Lader, Lawrence, *Power on the Left: American Radical Movements since 1946.* Norton, New York, 1979.
Linedecker, Clifford L., *The Swastika and the Eagle: Neo-Nazism in America Today.* A. & W. Pubs., New York, 1983.
Viguerie, Richard A., *The New Right: We're Ready to Lead.* Caroline House, Aurora, Ill., 1981.

Index

INDEX

Page numbers for the main entries for countries are printed in **bold** figures.

A

Aakid, Shaikh Ibrahim, 214
Abadia Ray, Adelaida, 63
Abbas, Abul, 282
Abbas, Mahmoud Abul, 280
ABC Color (Paraguay), 290
Abdallah, Ahmed, 64ff.
Abdallah, Georges Ibrahim, 109ff.; 221
Abdallah, Mouzaoir, 64ff.
Abdelazziz, Mohamed, 239
Abdón Saguier, Miguel, 287
Abdul Gaffar Peang Meth, 199
Abduldzhemil (USSR), 389
Abdullahi, Abdi-Nasir Sheikh, 104
Abdulrahman, M. M. (Sami), 173
Abeliuk Manasevich, René, 50; 54
Abesu Ondo, Eugenio, 97
Abim (Malaysia), 231
Abode of Islam (Indonesia), 160
Aboriginal rights movement (Canada), 39
Abou, Husni Mahmoud, 359
Abu Nidal Group (Palestinian), 88; 192; 207; 220; 275ff.; 282ff.
Accord in Exile (Paraguay), 288
Aceh separatists (Indonesia), 160-61
Acholi people (Uganda), 385
Achtyorev, Pavel, 392
Acosta Mena, Arturo, 288
Action directe (Belgium), 22
Action directe (France), 109; 131; 137; 186
Action Front of National Socialists/National Action (ANS/NA) (West Germany), 125; 426
Action Group against Nuclear War (Netherlands), 250
Ad Mapu (Chile), 50; 54
Adams, Gerry, 399
Adjitorop, Jusuf, 163
Adomeit, Manfred, 130
Afamando, Pedro, 10
Affani, Mohammed, 268
Affatigato, Mario, 180
Afghan Islamic and National Revolutionary Council, 4
Afghan Islamic and Nationalist Revolutionary Council, 2
Afghan Islamic Association, 2; 3
Afghan Islamic Coalition, 2
Afghan Nasr Organization, 2
Afghan National Liberation Front, 2ff.
Afghanistan, **1**; 218; 261; 265; 294; 414
Aflaq, Michel, 360
African Liberation Forces of Mauritania, 234
African National Congress (ANC), 26; 222; 242; 326ff.; 356
African National Union of Rombezia (Mozambique), 240
African Party for the Independence of Cape Verde (PAICV), 46
Afrikaner Resistance Movement (South Africa), 337
Afzali, Capt. Bahram, 166
Agca, Mehmet Ali, 379
Agnew, Paddy, 403
Agricultural Workers' Union (El Salvador), 95
Agudat Israel, 176
Aguiñada Carranza, Mario, 94
Agyp, Osman, 101
Ah Leng, 231
Ahamr, Shaikh Abdullah Bin Hussein al-, 413
Ahenakew, David, 39
Ahidjo, Ahmadou, 37
Ahmad, Abdel Rahim, 277
Ahmad, Musa bin, 231
Ahmad, Qazi Hussain, 263
Ahmadis (Pakistan), 266
Ahmed, Hazrat Mirza Tahir Ahmed, 266
Ahmed, Mirza Ghulam, 266
Ahmed, Shabbir, 263
Ahmed, Sheikh Rafiq, 263
Ahomadegbe, Justin, 24
Ahwash, Ahmed, 226
Ai Chau Hseu, 36
Ai Mong, Maj., 35
Aït Ahmed, Hocine, 6ff.
Ajuran people (Kenya), 201
Akali Dal (India), 151; 157ff.
Al-Ahram (Egypt), 86ff.
Al Amal al-Islami (Iraq), 173
Al-Asifa (Palestinian), 276
Al Bayane (Morocco), 237
Al Borkan (Libya), 225
Al Dawa (Kuwait), 207
Al-Dawa Party (Iraq), 171; 173
Al-Fatah (Palestinian), 192; 269ff.; 277; 283
Al-Iqab (Palestinian), 284
Al Jihad (Egypt), 85ff.
Al Jihad al-Islami (Lebanon), 79; 109; 207; 214; 216; 318
Al Mawquif (Tunisia), 374
Al Moujitamaa (Tunisia), 373
Al-Moutakalinine (Morocco), 238
Al-Saiqa (Palestinian), 269; 270; 273; 282; 283
Al Takfir Wal Hijira (Egypt), 85
Al Zulfiqar (Pakistan), 259ff.
Alam, Imtiaz, 263
Alawite Moslems (Lebanon), 215
Alawite Moslems (Syria), 358
Albania, **4**; 310; 396; 415; 420
Albanian nationalists (Yugoslavia), 415; 416
Albanian Party of Labour, 416; 417
Albertz, Heinrich, 133
Alcorta, Alfredo, 289
Alegre, Ruben, 298
Alende, Oscar, 17
Alessandrini, Emilio, 182
Alevi Moslem Sect (Turkey), 380
Alfarista Radical Front (Ecuador), 82
Alfaro, Eloy, 83
Alfaro Vive, Carajo! (Ecuador), 59; 83
Alfonsi, Prosper, 111
Alfonsín Foulkes, Raúl, 13
Algeria, **6**; 89; 108ff.; 220; 239; 271; 272; 274; 375
Ali, Mirza Husain (Baha'ullah), 170
Ali, Osman Nur, 325
Ali Khan, Fatheyab, 260
Ali Mireh, Hassan Haji, 324
Alia, Ramiz, 417
Alianza Anticomunista Argentina (AAA), 17
Alianza Chilena Anticomunista (Acha), 50; 53; 54

Alianza Democrática (AD) (Chile), 46; 50
Alianza Nacional Popular (ANAPO) (Colombia), 59
Allianza Revolucionaria Democratica (ARDE), 252
All-Africa Students' Union (Ghana), 136
All India Sikh Student Federation, 156ff.
All-People's Congress (APC) (Sierra Leone), 321
All-Union Council of Evangelical Christians-Baptists (USSR), 391
Allamand Zavala, Andrés, 53
Allende Gossens, Salvador, 45ff.
Alley, Lt.-Col. Alphonse, 24
Alliance (UK), 395
Alliance Party (Fiji), 106
Alliance Party (Northern Ireland), 395; 398
Allimadi, Otema, 386
Allnach, Kay Werner, 129
Almeyda Medina, Clodomiro, 48ff.
Almond Trees (Spain), 338
Alpha-66 Group (Cuba), 69
Altamirano, Carlos, 49
Altinoglu, Garbis, 380
Alunni, Corrado, 181ff.
Alvarez Córdova, Enrique, 90ff.
Alvarez Martínez, Gen. Gustavo Adolfo, 146; 149
Amal (Lebanon), 213ff.; 274ff.
Amaral, Francisco Xavier do, 162
Ambedkar, B. R., 152
America Battalion (Colombia), 59; 83
American Party (USA), 404
American Popular Revolutionary Alliance (APRA) (Peru), 291
Americas Watch Committee, 58; 59; 142
Américo Silva Front (Venezuela), 409
Amin, Idi, 385
Amin, Shaikh Ibrahim al Amin, 216
Amininejad, Hojatoleslam Mohammed Ali, 165
Amlah, Col. Khaled Al ("Abu Amlah"), 273ff.
"Ammar, Abu", 268ff.
Ammaturo, Antonio, 185
Amnesty International, 28; 29; 58-59; 64; 83; 99; 121; 141; 160; 162; 200ff.; 230; 238; 291; 344; 371; 386; 421; 422
Amour, Mohammed Balhadj, 374
Ampaw, Tony Akoto, 136
An Gof 1980 Movement (UK), 396
Anarchist Action Group (Greece), 136
ANC; *see* African National Congress
Ancestors' Blood (French Polynesia), 118
Àndjet (Senegal), 319
Andriamanjato, Richard, 228
Andrianarijaona, Pierre Mizael, 228
Andrzejewsji, Jerzy, 309
Angami, "Gen." Mowu, 155
Anglican Church (Guyana), 145
Anglo-Irish (Hillsborough) Agreement, 175
Anglo-Irish Inter-Governmental Council, 399
Angola, **8**; 245ff.; 316; 329; 395
Ankara Democratic Patriotic Association of Higher Education (Turkey), 384
Annamaria Ludmann Column (Italy), 184
Anti-Airport Federation (Japan), 189
Anti-Capitalist and Anti-Militarist Organization (Portugal), 310
Anti-Communist Political Front (El Salvador), 96
Anti-Marxist Group (Chile), 54
Anti-Military Struggle (Greece), 137
Anti-Slavery Society (UK), 21
Anti-State Struggle (Greece), 137
Anti-Terrorist Liberation Group (GAL) (Spain), 339
Antigua and Barbuda, **12**
Antigua Caribbean Liberation Movement, 12
Antigua Labour Party, 12
Antonio lo Muscio Commando (France), 110
Antonio Marín, Pedro ("Tiro Fijo"), 61
Anwar, Raja, 259
Anya-Nya II (Sudan), 352
Aouegui, Antoine, 115
Apithy, Sourou Migan, 24
Apogermatini (Greece), 137
Apostolic Anti-Communist Alliance (Mexico), 236
Apponno, Eddie, 250
April 1 Bubi Nationalist Group (Equatorial Guinea), 98
April 5 Group (China), 56
April 5 People's Detachment (Chile), 54
April 5 Tribune (China), 56
April 19 Movement (Colombia), 59
Aquino, Agapito, 296
Aquino, Benigno, 293; 298
Aquino, Corazon, 293ff.
Arab Armed Struggle Organization (Palestinian), 283
Arab Commando Cells (Lebanon), 215
Arab Communist Organization (Syria), 360
Arab Constitutional Party (Jordan), 192
Arab Democratic Party (Lebanon), 215
"Arab Deterrent Force" (Lebanon), 209ff.; 270
Arab Guerrilla Cells (Palestinian), 283
Arab High Committee (Palestinian), 266
Arab Human Rights Organization, 19
Arab League, 235; 239; 258; 268ff.
Arab Liberation Front (Lebanon), 214
Arab Liberation Front (Palestinian), 270; 277
Arab National Rally (Tunisia), 373
Arab National Union (Jordan), 192
Arab Nationalist Movement (Palestinian), 281
Arab People's Conference (Palestinian), 271
Arab Red Knights (Lebanon), 215
Arab Revolutionary Brigades (Jordan), 192
Arab Revolutionary Brigades (Palestinian), 283
Arab Revolutionary Brigades (UAE), 394
Arab Socialist Nasserite Party (Egypt), 87
Arab Socialist Union (Lebanon), 215; 87
Arafat, Yassir, 268ff.
Arakan Independence Organization (Burma), 31; 33
Arakan Liberation Army (Burma), 31
Arakan Liberation Party (Burma), 33; 34
Arakan National Liberation Party (Burma), 33
Aramburú, Lt.-Gen. Pedro Eugenio, 14
Aramendi Albizú, José Angel, 345
Araña Osorio, Gen. Carlos Manuel, 142
Arbenz Guzmán, Jacobo, 139
Ardalan, Ali, 166
Ardito Barletta, Nicolás, 285
Argentina, **13**; 147; 181; 407
Argentine Anti-communist Alliance, 16ff.
Argentine Nationalist Commando, 17
Argov, Shlomo, 220
Arias Sánchez, Oscar, 66
"Arm of the Arab Revolution" (Palestinian), 281
Armach Nan Gaidheal (UK), 396
Armed Action Forces (Guatemala), 142
Armed Forces of National Liberation (Puerto Rico), 406
Armed Forces of National Liberation (Venezuela), 409
Armed Forces of National Resistance (FARN) (El Salvador), 89; 91; 193
Armed Forces of Puerto Rican National Liberation, 404
Armed Liberation Commandos (Puerto Rico), 407
Armed Liberation Group (Guadeloupe), 115
Armed Liberation Group of Martinique, 117
Armed Pro-Independence Movement (Puerto Rico), 407
Armed Proletarian Nuclei (Italy), 181
Armed Revolutionary Movement (Puerto Rico), 407
Armed Revolutionary Nuclei (Italy), 179
Armée nationale sihanoukiste, ANS (Kampuchea), 200
Armenian Catholic Church (Lebanon), 209ff.
Armenian Catholic Church (Turkey), 380
Armenian Liberation Movement (Turkey), 381
Armenian National Liberation Movement (Turkey), 381
Armenian nationalists (Austria), 18
Armenian nationalists (France), 107
Armenian nationalists (Turkey), 380
Armenian Orthodox Church (Lebanon), 209ff.
Armenian Revolutionary Army (Turkey), 381
Armenian Secret Army for the Liberation of Armenia (ASALA) (Lebanon), 109; 210; 250

Armenian Secret Army for the Liberation of Armenia (ASALA) (Turkey), 381ff.
Army of Gael, 396
Arocena, Eduardo, 69
Arrostito, Norma, 15
Arthit Kamlangek, Gen., 367
Arturo Jarrín, Ricardo, 83
Arya (Iran), 170
Aryan Liberty Network (USA), 405
"Aryan Nation" (USA), 405
ASALA Revolutionary Movement (Turkey), 382
Ashgar Khan, Air Marshal, 264
Asia 88 (Thailand), 365; 368
Asian Wall Street Journal, 230
Askeri, Ali, 174
Assad, Hafez al-, 220; 275; 279; 282; 358ff.
Assam People's Council (India), 151
Assembly of First Nations (Canada), 39
Association for a French Republican Corsica, 114
Association for the Defence of Freedom and Sovereignty of the Iranian Nation, 166
Association for the Patriarchal System in the Ukrainian Catholic Church (USSR), 391
Association for the Progress of Honduras, 149
Association for the Resurrection of Kurdistan (Iran), 168
Association for the Study of Scientific and Democratic Socialism (China), 57
Association of Aid for Victims of Terrorism in Corsica, 114
Association of Comorian Trainees and Students, 65
Association of Corsican Patriots (APC), 111ff.
Association of Marxist-Leninists of Kurdistan (Iraq), 174
Association of Revolutionary Youth (Turkey), 377
Association of South-East Asian Nations (ASEAN), 163; 193ff.
Astaforoff, Marey, 40
Astra, Gunnars, 388
Ataide, João da Silva, 240
Atallah, Col. Atallah ("Abu Zaim"), 275
Athanasiadis, Georgis, 137
Atjeh separatists (Indonesia), 160-61
Atonement and Holy Flight from Sin (Egypt), 85
Atrash, Ala Muhammed Rida al-, 207
Attar, Islam al-, 358
Attas, Abu Bakr al, 414
Attasut (Greenland), 79
Aubron, Joëlle, 110
Aubuisson, Roberto D', 96
Audran, Gen. René, 110; 131; 186
Augustin, Barbara, 131
Australia, **17**; 120; 231; 320; 408; 418; 419
Australia Party, 18
Australian Democratic Labor Party, 18
Australian Democratic Party, 18
Australian Labor Party, 18
Australian League of Rights, 18
Australian National Front, 18
Australian Security Intelligence Organization (ASIO), 417
Austria, **18**; 276; 283; 418; 419
Austrian Freedom Party, 18
Austrian People's Party, 18
Austrian Socialist Party, 18
Authentic Liberal Radical Party (PLRA) (Paraguay), 286ff.
Authentic Panamenist Party (PPA), 285
Authentic Party of the Mexican Republic (PARM), 235
Authentic Peronist Party (Argentina), 14ff.
Authentic Radical Liberal Workers' Movement (Paraguay), 287
Autonomia Operaio (Italy), 186
Autonomous Revolutionary Groups (Portugal), 311
Autonomous Revolutionary Workers' Commandos (Portugal), 311
Avanguardia Nazionale (Italy), 180
Avila, Capt. Eduardo, 96
Awami League (Bangladesh), 20
Awami National Party (Pakistan), 259ff.
Awami Tehrik (Pakistan), 259ff.
Ayub Khan, Field Marshal Mohammed, 261ff.
Azanian People's Organization (South Africa), 331
Azcona del Hoyo, José, 146; 253
Azerbaijanis (Iran), 169
Aziz, Tariq, 171
Aztorkitza Ikazzuriaga, Pedro, 345

B

Baader, Andreas, 127ff.
Baader-Meinhof Group or Gang (West Germany), 127ff.
Baath Party (Iraq), 171; 358
Baath Party (Lebanon), 214; 215; 277
Baath Party of Saudi Arabia, 317
Baath Party (Syria), 172; 258; 426
Baathism (Jordan), 192
Baathist dissidents (Iraq), 172
Baathist dissidents (Syria), 360
Babangida, Ibrahim, Maj.-Gen., 256
Babism (Iran), 170
Bachelet, Vittorio, 184
"Back to Liège" (Belgium), 22
Badal, Saeed, 167
Badzyo, Yuri, 390
Baganda Royalist Movement (Uganda), 386
Bagaza, Col. Jean-Baptiste, 37
Bagzadeh (Iran), 169
Bahais (Egypt), 88
Bahais (Iran), 170
Bahais (Morocco), 239
Bahais (Uganda), 386
Bahamas, **19**
"Baha'ullah", 170
Bahrain, **19**; 426
Baia, Clariano, 311
Baidoo, Kwasi J., 135
Bairamov, Reshat, 389
Baires, Aquiles, 96
Bakaric, Vladimir, 418
Bakary, Djibo, 256
Bakhtiar, Shapour, 109; 167
Bakoush, Abdel Hamid, 225ff.
Bakunin-Gdansk-Paris-Guatemala-Salvador Group (France), 108
Balaam Facho (Chad), 44
Balaguer, Joaquín, 81
Balfour Declaration, 266
Baltic declaration, 388
Baltic Republics (USSR), 388
Baluchis (Iran), 169
Baluchistan, 261; 265
Balweg, Conrado, 293
Balzerani, Barbara, 186
Bamana, Younoussa, 118
Banaba (Kiribati), 202
Banda, Hastings, 228ff.
Bandera Roja (Venezuela), 62; 409
Bangladesh, **20**; 31; 152; 194
Bangladesh Communist Party, 20
Bangladesh Moslem League, 20
Bangladesh National Party, 20
Bangsa Moro National Liberation Front (BMNLF) (Philippines), 296
Bangui, Gen. Sylvestre, 42ff.
Bani-Sadr, Abolhassan, 164ff.
Banna, Sabri Khalil al- ("Abu Nidal"), 276; 284
Banna, Shaikh Hassan Al-, 84
Bar Association (Guyana), 145
Barabass, Ingrid, 133
Barahona, Elias, 140; 142
Baratz, Vasily, 392
Barbados, **21**
Barbados Labour Party, 21
Barbie, Klaus, 25
Barbier, Marcel, 22
Barbosa, Rafael, 144
Barco Vargas, Virgilio, 58
Barghuti, Bashir al-, 284

Barisan Sosialis (Singapore), 322
Barki, Mustafa, 226
Barrueto, Victor, 50
Barsimantov, Yacov, 109
Barthe, Obdulio, 289
Baruah, Daud, 160
Baruch Green (Israel), 177
Barzani, Idris, 174
Barzani, Mustapha, 173ff.
Basantes Borja, Fausto, 83
Basha, Hassan Abu, 86
Basotho Congress Party—Dissident Faction (Lesotho), 223
Basotho National Party (Lesotho), 222ff.
Basque Nation and Liberty (France), 110
Basque separatists (Spain), 109; 110; 182; 250; 342ff.; 400
Bassene, Cherifo, 319
Bassi, Pietro, 183
Bastürk, Abdullah, 376
Batallón América (Colombia), 59; 83
Bateman, Cayón, 60
Batmönh, Jambyn, 237
Batovrin, Sergei, 393
Battalion 861 (Burma), 35
Battek, Rudolf, 77
Battle Flag of the Communist League (Japan), 189
Baumann, Michael, 133
Bavadra, Timoci, 106
Bavaria Party (West Germany), 125
Bay Area Revolutionary Union (USA), 406
Bayev, Gomer, 389
Bazaglio Recino, Rogelio, 92
Bazargan, Mehdi, 166ff.
Becker, Eberhard, 129
Becker, Verena, 129; 132
Beckurts, Karl Heinz, 133
Bednarova, Otta, 77
Bee Htoo, Gen., 34
Beer, Wolfgang, 129; 133
Begin, Menahem, 177; 267; 271; 279
Behrend, Uwe, 126
Belaúnde Terry, Fernando, 291
Belgium, **22**; 68; 417; 422; 423; 68
Belize, **23**
Belize Popular Party, 23
Belliso, Claudio, 292
Belmonte, Gen. Giuseppe, 179
"Belonging to Kenya", 202
Belsito, Pasquale, 179
Bemei, Elky, 161
Ben Bella, Ahmed, 6ff.
Ben Salah, Ahmed, 374
Benda, Václav, 73; 77
Benin, **24**
Benin People's Revolutionary Party, 24
Benítez Florentín, Juan Manuel, 287
Berhane Meskel Reda Wolde, 105
"Berlin Appeal", 124
Bermúdez, Col. Emilio Gil, 59
Bermúdez, Enrique, 253
Bernard, Henry, 116
Bernard, Vilem, 78
Berri, Nabi, 214ff.
Bertolazzi, Pietro, 183
Berufsverbot (West Germany), 125
Besse, Georges, 110
Besse, Helyette, 110
Betancourt, Argenis, 409
Betancourt, Carlos, 409
Betancur Cuartas, Belisario, 59ff.
Betti, Aurore, 186
Bharatiya Janata Party (BJP) (India), 151
Bhashani, Maulana Abdul Hamid Khan, 261
Bhashani (Bangladesh), 20
Bhattacharya, Nisith, 153
Bhattarai, Krishna Prasad, 248
Bhindranwale, Sant Janail Singh, 157ff.
Bhoomi Sena (India), 154
Bhutan, **25**; 349
Bhutto, Begum Nusrat, 259ff.
Bhutto, Benazir, 259ff.
Bhutto, Mumtaz Ali, 265
Bhutto, Murtaza, 259ff.
Bhutto, Shahnawaz, 260
Bhutto, Zulfiqar Ali, 259
Bianco, Francesco Lo, 185
Bibó, István, 150
Bid, Ali Salim al-, 414
Bidart, Philippe, 111
Bidegaín, Óscar, 14
Bierut, Boleslaw, 310
Bignami, Maurice, 182
Biliato, Alberta, 184
Birch, Reg, 396
Birendra, King of Nepal, 156, 248ff.
Birondo, Alexander, 298
Bishop, Maurice, 137; 316
Bitar, Salah al-, 360
Bitterman, Chester Allen, 60
Biya, Paul, 37
Bizenjo, Mir Ghaus Ali Bakhsh, 261
Black, Stephen Donal, 405
Black Brigades (Lebanon), 210
Black Flag (Lebanon), 216
Black Order (Italy), 179
Black Panther Party (USA), 404
Black Power movement (USA), 404
Black separatists (USA), 406
Black September (Jordan), 192
Black September, 278; 279
Black September Group (Palestinian), 283ff.
Black War (France), 108
Blagojevic, Borivoje, 419
Blanco Party (Uruguay), 408
Blenck, Ekkehard, 129
Bloc of the Faithful (Israel), 176ff.
Bloque Opositora del Sur (BOS) (Nicaragua), 252
Bo Mya, Gen., 33, 35
Bo Thet Tun, 30
Boateng, John A., 135
Bocock, Leila, 134
Bojarsky, Franz Joachim, 126
Bokassa, Jean-Bédel, 41
Bokoko Itogi, Bwelalele, 98
Bolcsfoldi, Andor, 150
Bolívar, Simon, 59
Bolivia, **25**; 289
Bolivian Socialist Falange (FSB), 25
Bonafini, Hebe de, 13
Bonapartists (Corsica), 111
Bongo, Omar, 121
Boni Liberation Front (French Guiana), 115
Bonner Sakharova, Yelena, 388
Boock, Peter Jürgen, 130; 131
Boock, Waltraud, 129ff.
Boot, Magbool, 154
Bophuthatswana, **26**
Bophuthatswana Democratic Party, 26
Borgonovo Pohl, Mauricio, 92
Borisov, Vladimir, 388
Born, Jorge, 15
Born, Juan, 15
Bosch, Orlando, 69
"Boschneger" (Suriname), 355
Bossay, Luis, 52
Botha, P. W., 243ff.; 330
Botha, Roelef F. "Pik", 11, 245
Botswana, **26**; 244; 329; 425
Botswana Democratic Party, 26
Botswana Independence Party, 26
Botswana National Front, 26

Botswana People's Party, 26
Botswana Progressive Union, 26
Bourguiba, Habib, 374ff.
Bouterse, Lt.-Col. Desi, 354
Bozanga, Simon Narcisse, 43
Bozize, François, 41ff.
Bradford, Robert, 402
Brang Seng, 33
Brasoveanu, Ghorghe, 313
Braun, Bernhard, 128ff.
Braunmühl, Gerold von, 133
Brazil, **27**; 287; 355
Brazilian Communist Party, 27
Brazilian Labour Party, 27
Brazilian Socialist Party, 27
Brezhnev, Leonid, 388; 391
Brezza, Ermanno, 179
Briano, Renato, 184
Brigade for Protecting the Poor (Lebanon), 214
Brigade of the Resistance of the Faithful (Lebanon), 216
Brigate Rosse (BR) (Italy), 109; 178ff.
Briones, Carlos, 49
British Movement (UK), 395
British National Party (UK), 395
British Patriot (UK), 395
British Tidings (UK), 395
Brkic, Dusan, 420
Broad Front (Uruguay), 408
Broad Left Front (Ecuador), 82
Brotherhood of the Cross (Yugoslavia), 418
Brüdwer Schweigen (USA), 405
Brunei, **27**
Brunei National Democratic Party, 27
Brunei National United Party, 28
Brunswijk Rebel Group (Suriname), 355
Brüsewitz, Oskar, 123
Buback, Siegfried, 127; 131
Bubnis, P., 391
Buckley, William, 214
"Budapest School" (Hungary), 149
Bujak, Zbigniew, 305; 306
Bukovsky, Vladimir, 47; 387; 394
Bulgaria, **28**
Bulgarian Agrarian People's Union, 28
Bulgarian Communist Party, 28
Bulgarian National Committee in exile, 29
Bulgarian Turks, 29
Bull, Benjamin Pinto, 144
Bunyen Wothong, 365; 368ff.
Burdin, Abubakar Ahmed, 65
Bureau for Exporting the Revolution (Libya), 375
Burj, Omar Mohamed al-, 100
Burkay, Kemal, 384
Burkina, **29**
Burkinabe Confederation of Trade Unions, 30
Burma, **30**; 57; 155
Burma Socialist Programme Party (BSPP, Lanzin Party), 30ff.
Burmeistar, Juris, 394
Burmese Communist Party, 30ff.
Burmese Communist Party ("White Flag"), 31
Burnham, Forbes, 144
Burundi, **37**
Buscayno, Bernabé ("Commander Dante"), 293, 298
Busse, Friedhelm, 126
Buthelezi, Chief Gatsha, 331
Buthelezi, Sipho, 331
Bwengye, Francis, 386

C

Caballero, Marcial, 148
Caballero Gatti, Carlos, 288
Cabañas, Lucio ("El Professor"), 236
Cabinda separatists (Angola), 12
Cabral, Luis de Almeida, 143
Cáceres Monié, Gen. Jorge, 17
Cadwyr Cymru (UK), 397
Cagol, Margherita, 133; 183
"Cairo Agreement", 269; 278
"Cairo declaration", 274
Calciu-Dumitreus, Gheorghe, 313
Caledonian Front (New Caledonia), 119
Caledonian Union (New Caledonia), 118ff.
Calero Portocarrero, Adolfo, 252ff.
Calitis, Ints, 388
Call, The (Iraq), 171
Callaghan, Maj.-Gen. William, 213
Callejas, Rafael Leonardo, 146
Calvo, Jairo de Jésus, 63
Calvo, Oscar William, 62ff.
Cameroon, **37**; 257
Cameroon People's Democratic Movement, 37
Cameroonian Organization Fighting for Democracy, 38
Camilleri, Michel, 110
Çamkiran, Mustapha Kemal, 379
Camorra (Italy), 178
Campaign for Democracy in Ghana, 135
Campaign for Nuclear Disarmament (UK), 76; 396
Cámpora, Héctor José, 14, 16
Camus (Guadeloupe), 115
Cana, Ion, 313
Canada, **39**; 68; 244; 419
Canary Islands, **346**
Cao Dai Sect (Vietnam), 412
Cape Verde, **40**; 144
Caprivi African National Union (CANU) (Namibia), 245ff.
Capuano, Marcello, 184
Capucci, Hilarion, Mgr., 279
Caraballo, Francisco, 63
Carbone Bacigalupo, Emilio, 25
Cardoza y Aragón, Luis, 139
Carlos Duran, Juan, 25
Carmichael, Stokeley, 404
Carrero Blanco, Adml. Luis, 343
Carron, Owen, 403
Carter, James E. (Jimmy), 271
Casalegno, Carlo, 183
Casaletti, Attilio, 183
Casamance separatists (Senegal), 319
Castillo, Fabio, 94
Castillo Velasco, Jaime, 46
Castro, Henry, 59; 62
Castro, Jaime, 61
Castro Ruz, Fidel, 40; 67; 127
Catabiani, Umberto, 184
Catholic Commission for Justice and Peace, 425
Catholic Committee for the Defence of Believers (USSR), 391
Catholic Council for Justice and Peace (South Korea), 204ff.
Catholic Reaction Force (Northern Ireland), 400
Catholic Standard (Guyana), 145
Cavallini, Gilberto, 179
Çayan, Gulten, 377
Çayan, Mahir, 377
Cayetano Carpio, Salvador, 92
Ceausescu, Elena, 313
Ceausescu, Nicolae, 312
Cedán Callixto, Enrique, 341
Cedar Guardians (Lebanon), 210
Cells of Revolutionary Liberation—Resistance Against Syrian Imperialism (Lebanon), 210
Central African Democratic Union, 41
Central African Movement for National Liberation, 41
Central African People's Rally, 42
Central African Republic, **41**
Central African Revolutionary Party, 42
Central African Socialist Party, 42
Central American Revolutionary Workers' Party of Honduras, 147
Central Intelligence Agency (USA), 11; 60; 67; 128; 137; 173; 194; 208; 214; 217; 253; 313; 346; 369; 382; 415
Centre Democrats (Denmark), 79

Centre of Indian Communists, 153
Centre Party (Finland), 106
Centre Party (Netherlands), 250
Centre Party (Norway), 257
Cerda, Eduardo, 50
Cerezo Arévalo, Vinicio, 138ff.
Cerny, Albert, 77
Cerruti, María del Rosario de, 13
Césaire, Aimé, 115
César Aquirre, Alfredo, 252ff.
Ceuta Liberaton Movement (Spain), 347
Ceylon; *see* Sri Lanka
Chacón, Juan, 91
Chad, 42; **44**; 225; 257; 375
Chafii, Djaffar, 164
Chakma tribespeople (Bangladesh), 21
Chaldeans (Lebanon), 209ff.
Chama Cha Mapinduzi (Tanzania), 364
Chami, Yehya el-, 414
Chamorro, Adolfo "Popo", 252
Chamorro Barrios, Pedro Joaquín, 252
Chamorro Coronel, Edgar, 253
Chamorro Rapaciolli, Fernando, 252, 254
Chamoun, Camille, 210ff.
Chamoun, Dany, 213; 218
Champassak, Iang Na, 208
Champassak, Sisouk Na, 208
Chandler, Ramesh, 157
Change (Israel), 176
Chaovalit Thapkua, 368
Chaovalit Yongchaiyut, Lt.-Gen., 367ff.
Chapman, Christian, 221
Charles, Eugenia, 80
Charles, Lennox ("Rasta Bomba"), 316
Charles Martel Club (France), 108
Charlotte, Raymond, 115
Charry Rincón, Fermín, 61
Chart Prachitippatai (Thailand), 365
Chart Thai (Thailand), 365
Charter 77 (Czechoslovakia), 73ff.; 124; 150; 309; 312
Chatcharin Chaiwat, 368
Chatterjee, Ashim, 152
"Che Guevara Brigade" (Palestinian), 276
"Che Guevera commando unit" (Palestinian), 281
Cheikh, Mustapha Said, 64
Chetniks (Yugoslavia), 415; 419
Chiaie, Stefano delle, 179
Chiang Ching-kuo, 57
Chiang Kai-shek, 57, 362
Chiang Peng-chien, 362
Children of the Party of God (Iran), 165
Chile, **45**; 147
Chilean Anti Communist Alliance (Acha), 50ff.
Chilean Communist Party (PCCh), 50; 54; 387
Chilean Human Rights Commission, 46
Chilean Socialist Bloc, 47ff.
Chilean Socialist Party, 50; 52
Chin a Sen, Henk, 355
Chin Peng, 231
China, 31; 35; **55**; 154; 193ff.; 208; 228; 231; 245; 258; 288; 291; 293; 296; 361ff.; 365; 366ff.; 396; 406; 410ff.
China Daily News (Taiwan), 362
China Democratic Socialist Party (Taiwan), 361
"China Spring", 57
Chinchonero People's Liberation Movement (Honduras), 147
Chinese Commercial News (Taiwan), 362
Chinese Democratic Movement, 57
Ching, Charlie, 118
Chirwa, Fumbani, 229
Chirwa, Orton, 229
Chissano, Joaquim Alberto, 242
Chittagong Autonomists (Bangladesh), 21
Chittagong Hill Tracts (Bangladesh), 156
Chitunda, Jeremiah, 10
Chiume, M. W. Kanyama, 228ff.
Choi Ki Shik, 204
Choi Kyu Hah, 205
Chondoist Chongo (Korea), 203
Chonthira Kladyu, 367
Chornovil, Vyacheslav, 389
Chow, Paul, 320
Christian Bavarian People's Party—Movement of Bavarian Patriots (West Germany), 125
Christian Committee for the Defence of Believers' Rights (USSR), 390
Christian Conscience (Jamaica), 187
Christian Democratic Appeal (Netherlands), 250
Christian Democratic International, 47; 287
Christian Democratic Labour Party (Grenada), 138
Christian Democratic Organization of America, 47; 287
Christian Democratic Party (Argentina), 13
Christian Democratic Party (Bolivia), 25
Christian Democratic Party (Brazil), 27
Christian Democratic Party (Chile), 45ff.
Christian Democratic Party (El Salvador), 88
Christian Democratic Party (Guatemala), 138
Christian Democratic Party (Honduras), 146
Christian Democratic Party (Kiribati), 202
Christian Democratic Party (Panama), 285
Christian Democratic Party (Paraguay), 286ff.
Christian Democratic Party (Western Samoa), 413
Christian Democratic Solidarity Front (Nicaragua), 252
Christian Democratic Union (West Germany), 125; 133
Christian Democratic World Union, 77; 150; 310; 394; 421
Christian Democratic Youth (Chile), 47
Christian Democrats (Italy), 178
Christian Identity Movement (USA), 404
Christian Labour Party (Poland), 310
Christian Left (Chile), 47ff.
Christian People's Party (Belgium), 22
Christian People's Party (Denmark), 79
Christian People's Party (Norway), 257
Christian Popular Party (Peru), 291
Christian Revolutionaries of the Cedar Tree (Lebanon), 210
Christian Social Party (Belgium), 22
Christian Social Party (Luxembourg), 227
Christian Social Party (COPEI) (Venezuela), 409
Christian Social Popular Movement (El Salvador), 90; 94
Christian Social Union (West Germany), 125
Christian Workers' Solidarity (STC) (Nicaragua), 252
Chronicle of Current Events (USSR), 388
Chukaku-Ha (Japan), 188ff.
Chun Doo Hwan, 204ff.
Chung-kuo Kuomin-tang (China), 57
Church of Jesus Christ Christian (USA), 405
Church of Zarepath-Horeb (USA), 404
CIA; *see* Central Intelligence Agency
Cienfuegos, Fermán, 89; 91
Cinchonero People's Liberation Movement (Honduras), 147
Ciosek, Stanislaw, 303
Cipriani, Georges, 110
Cirillo, Ciro, 185
Cirwa, Mackenzie, 229
Ciskei, **58**
Citizens' Committee against Violence (KOPP) (Poland), 308
"Citizens for America", 11
Citizens of Voting Age (West Germany), 125
Citizen's Party (Iceland), 151
Citizens Party (USA), 404
Ciucci, Giovanni, 184
Civic Action Service (France), 108
Civic Front (Chile), 49
Civic Union (Uruguay), 408
Civil Rights Movement (Israel), 176
Civil Rights Movements (USSR), 388
Clara Elizabeth Ramírez Front (El Salvador), 92
Clark Amendment (Angola), 11
Clean Government Party (Japan), 188
Cleaver, Eldridge, 404
Coalition Government of Democratic Kampuchea (CGDK), 193

Coalition of Workers, Peasants and Students of the Isthmus (Mexico), 236
Coard, Bernard, 138
Cocco, Francesco, 183
Cogliano, Rafaele Del, 185
College for the Welsh People's Movement (UK), 397
Collett, Alec, 220
Colom Argueta, Manuel, 142
Colombia, **58**; 425
Colombian Confederation of Workers (CTC), 59
Colombian Revolutionary Armed Forces (FARC), 60ff.
Colón de Carvajal, Vice-Adml. Cristobal, 345
Colorada Party (Uruguay), 408
Cominformists (Yugoslavia), 415ff.
Commandos in France against the Maghrebian Invasion, 108
Commission for Human Rights (Guatemala), 139
Commission of Relatives of the Disappeared and Murdered Persons (Paraguay), 289
Committee against Genocide of Blacks by Substitution (Guadeloupe), 115
Committee for Human Rights (East Germany), 123
Committee for the Defence of the Armenian Cause (France), 380
Committee for the Defence of Believers in the Soviet Union, 390
Committee for the Defence of Freedom of Thought and Expression (Yugoslavia), 420
Committee for the Defence of Human Rights (Honduras), 147
Committee for the Defence of Human Rights in Bahrain, 19
Committee for the Defence of Liberties in Czechoslovakia, 77
Committee for the Defence of Persons Unjustly Persecuted (VONS) (Czechoslovakia), 76
Committee for the Defence of the Rights of Man in Saudi Arabia, 317
Committee for the Renewal of Jewish Settlement in the City of the Patriarchs, 177
Committee for the Restoration of Democracy in Burma, 32
Committee for the Right to Free Emigration (Pentecostalists) (USSR), 392
Committee of Families of Detained-Disappeared Persons (Honduras), 147
Committee of Peasant Unity (CUC) (Guatemala), 139
Committee of Solidarity with Arab and Middle Eastern Political Prisoners (CSPPA), 108; 210; 227
Committee to Liquidate or Neutralize Computers (France), 109
Communal Leap Party (Cyprus), 70
Communal Liberation Party (TKP) (Cyprus), 70
Communist Armed Groups (Italy), 181
Communist Fighting Organization (Italy), 181
Communist Group for Proletarian Internationalism (Italy), 181
Communist International (Comintern) (Lebanon), 221
Communist International (Yugoslavia), 419
Communist League (Japan), 190
Communist Party of Arakan (Burma), 33
Communist Party of Argentina, 15; 17
Communist Party of Australia, 18
Communist Party of Australia (Marxist-Leninist), 18
Communist Party of Bangladesh, 20
Communist Party of Belgium, 22
Communist Party of Benin, 24
Communist Party of Brazil, 27
Communist Party of Britain—Marxist-Leninist (UK), 396
Communist Party of Bulgaria, 28
Communist Party of Burma—"Red Flag" Party, 33
Communist Party of Burma—"White Flag" Party, 30ff.
Communist Party of Canada, 39
Communist Party of Canada (Marxist-Leninist), 39
Communist Party of Chile, PCCh, 46ff.; 387
Communist Party of China, 55; 152; 231; 293; 310
Communist Party of China (Taiwan), 362
Communist Party of Colombia, 61; 62
Communist Party of Corsica, 112
Communist Party of Cuba, 67
Communist Party of Czechoslovakia, 71
Communist Party of Ecuador, 83
Communist Party of Egypt, 87
Communist Party of El Salvador, 89
Communist Party of Finland, 106
Communist Party of France, 107
Communist Party of Germany, 125
Communist Party of Guadeloupe, 115
Communist Party of Haiti, 146
Communist Party of Honduras, 146; 148
Communist Party of India (CPI), 151
Communist Party of India-Marxist (CPI(M)), 151ff.
Communist Party of Indonesia, 162
Communist Party of Iran, 164
Communist Party of Iraq, 172
Communist Party of Italy, 178ff.
Communist Party of Japan, 188
Communist Party of Jordan, 192; 284
Communist Party of Kampuchea, 193ff.
Communist Party of Lebanon, 221
Communist Party of Lesotho, 223
Communist Party of Luxembourg, 227
Communist Party of Malaya (CPM) (Malaysia), 231
Communist Party of Malaya (CPM) (Singapore), 322
Communist Party of Malaya (CPM) (Thailand), 365
Communist Party of Malaysia (MCP), 231
Communist Party of Malta, 233
Communist Party of Morocco, 238
Communist Party of Nepal (CPN), 248
Communist Party of Nepal—Marxist-Leninist (CPNM-L), 248
Communist Party of Netherlands, 250
Communist Party of Nicaragua, 251, 254
Communist Party of Norway, 257
Communist Party of Pakistan (CPP), 260
Communist Party of Palestine, 426
Communist Party of Paraguay, 286; 288-89
Communist Party of the Philippines, 293
Communist Party of the Philippines—Marxist-Leninist, 293
Communist Party of Poland, 310
Communist Party of Puerto Rico, 406
Communist Party of Romania, 312ff.
Communist Party of Saudi Arabia, 317
Communist Party of South Africa, 223; 329; 334ff.
Communist Party of the Soviet Union (CPSU), 289; 302; 335; 387
Communist Party of Spain, 292
Communist Party of Syria, 358
Communist Party of Thailand, 365ff.
Communist Party of Turkey, 376
Communist Party (UK), 395
Communist Party (USA), 404
Communist Party of Uruguay (PCU), 408
Communist Party of Venezuela (PCV), 409
Communist Party of Yugoslavia, 416; 419
Communist Power (Italy), 181
Communist Revolutionary League (Luxembourg), 227
Communist Union of the Left (UCI) (Mexico), 236
Community Action Party (Thailand), 365
Comorian Union for Progress, 64
Comoros, **64**; 118
Compton, John, 315
Concentration of Popular Forces (Ecuador), 82
Concutelli, Pier-Luigi, 179ff.
Confederation for an Independent Poland (KPN), 308
Confederation for Trade Union Unification (Nicaragua), 251
Confederation of Nationalist Committees (Corsica), 112
Confederation of Revolutionary Trade Unions of Turkey (DISK), 376
Conference on Security and Co-operation in Europe (CSCE), 74; 309; 387
Congo, 12; 43; **65**
Congo National Movement - Lumumba (Zaïre), 422
Congolese Front for the Restoration of Democracy (Zaïre), 422
Congolese National Liberation Front (Zaïre), 422
Congolese Party of Labour (Congo), 65
Congolese Progressive Students (Zaïre), 423
Congolese Social Democratic Party (Zaïre), 422
Congolese Socialist Party (Zaïre), 423
Congress (I) (India), 151; 248
Congress (J) (India), 151

Congress (Socialist) (India), 151
Congress for the Second Republic (Malawi), 228
Congress Party for Malagasy Independence (AKFM) 227ff.
Conscientious objection (Finland), 106
Conscientious objection (East Germany), 124
Conscientious objection (Hungary), 150
Consejo Indio Sud-americano, CISA, 50
Conservative Action (West Germany), 125
Conservative Alliance of Zimbabwe (CAZ), 424
Conservative Party (Ecuador), 82
Conservative Party of Guyana, 145
Conservative Party (Uganda), 385
Conservative Party (UK), 395, 399
Conservative People's Party (Denmark), 79
Conservatives (Colombia), 58
Conservatives (National Coalition Party) (Finland), 106
Conservatives (Norway), 257
Constitutionalist Liberal Movement (MLC) (Nicaragua), 251
Consultative Committee for the Promotion of Democracy (South Korea), 205
Conté, Col. Lansana, 143
Conti, Lando, 186
Contreras, Marcelo, 50
Convention Democratic Party (Liberia), 223
Co-ordinating Board of Opposition forces (Equatorial Guinea), 98
Coptic Church (Egypt), 85; 88
Corakli, Servet Ziya, 376
Cordillera People's Liberation Army (Philippines), 293
Cordillera Regional Development Council (Philippines), 293
Cornish nationalists (UK), 396
Coronel, Hilarion, 289
Coronel, Sindulfo, 289
Corpuz, Victor, 297
Correa, Germàn, 53
Correa, Pedro, 48; 52
Corse du Sud (Corsica), 112
Corsica, **111**
Corsican Guerrillas and Partisans, 112
Corsican Movement for Self-Determination, 112
Corsican National Liberation Army, 112
Corsican National Liberation Front (FLNC), 111ff.
Corvalán Lepe, Luis, 47; 387
Costa Rica, **66**; 68; 252ff.
Costa Rican People's Army, 66
Costello, Seamus, 400
Côte d'Ivoire, 24; **66**; 135; 224; 375
Coulibaly, Hamilton, 30
Council of Churches (Vanuatu), 409
Council of Churches of the Evangelical Christians and Baptists (USSR), 391
Council of South African Trade Unions, 331
Covenant, Sword and the Arm of the Lord (USA), 404
Crespo Cuspinera, Col. Jésus, 338
Crespo Cuspinera, Lt.-Col. José, 338
Creydt, Oscar, 288ff.
Crimean Tartars (USSR), 388
Crisis Committee (New Caledonia), 120
Croatian Fighting Unit (Yugoslavia), 418
Croatian Liberation Army (Yugoslavia), 418
Croatian Liberation Fighters (Yugoslavia), 418
Croatian Liberation Movement (Yugoslavia), 418
Croatian National Resistance (Yugoslavia), 418
Croatian Peasants' Party (Yugoslavia), 421
Croation Revolutionary Brotherhood (Yugoslavia), 418; 419
Croatian Revolutionary Organization (Yugoslavia), 418
Croatian Youth (Yugoslavia), 418
Crocker, Chester, 11; 246
Croissant, Klaus, 130ff.
Cross, James Richard, 40
Cruz, Arturo, 252
Crypto (Malaysia), 231
Cuba, 10; 11; 40; 52; 60; **67**; 89; 100; 105; 117; 146; 147; 187; 229; 239; 246; 292; 296; 316; 323; 369; 375; 386; 407
Cuban Nationalist Movement, 69
Cubans United, 69
Cubelas, Rolando, 68
Cuevas Hormazábal, Jaime Anselmo, 50
Cumann Na mBan (Northern Ireland), 401
Curcio, Renato, 182ff.
Customs and Economic Union of Central Africa (UDEAC), 98
Cymdeithas yr laith Cymraeg (UK), 397
Cyprus, **70**; 376
Cyprus Democracy Party, 70
Czech Writers' Union, 72
Czechoslovak Communist Party, 71
Czechoslovak Musicians' Union, 77
Czechoslovak People's Party, 70; 77
Czechoslovak Social Democratic Party, 78
Czechoslovak Socialist Party, 70
Czechoslovakia, **70**; 245; 301; 309

D

Dacko, David, 41ff.
Daddah, Mokhtar Ould, 239
Daddah, Ould, 234
Dadoo, Yusuf, 335
Dahab, Gen. Abdel Rahman Swar el-, 351
Dahabi, Mohammed el-, 85
Dahomey Liberation and Rehabilitation Front (Benin), 24
Dahomeyan Communist Party (Benin), 24
Dakwah (Missionary) Moslem Movement (Malaysia), 232
Dal Khalsa (India), 157ff.
Dalit Mazdoor Kisan Party (DMK-Lok Dal) (India), 151
Dalit Panthers (India), 152
Damdami Taksal (India), 157
Danet, Olivier, 179
Danish National Socialist Alliance, 79
Daoud, Abu, 283ff.
Dapcevic, ex-Col., 420
Dapcevic, Vlado, 420
Dar-ul-Islam (Indonesia), 160
Dascalu, Nicolae, 313
Dashmesh Regiment (India), 157
Dastmaltchi, Karim, 167
Dávila Membereno, José, 252ff.
Death squads (Bolivia), 25
Death squads (Colombia), 58; 59
Death squads (El Salvador), 96
Death squads (Guatemala), 142
Death to Kidnappers (Colombia), 59
Debizer, Pierre, 108
Debus, Sigurd, 128
December 12 Movement (Kenya), 201
Declercq, Pierre, 118
Decolonization Committee (Morocco), 239
Défense légitime (France), 108
Deferre, Gaston, 113
"Dega" (Vietnam), 410
Deghan, Ashraf, 164
Degodia people (Kenya), 201
Delgado, Javier, 63
Delgado de Codex, Juan Carlos, 340
Dellwo, Hans-Joachim, 129
Dellwo, Karl-Heinz, 132
"Demand of Chile", 52
Democrat Party (Thailand), 364
Democratic Action (AD) (El Salvador), 88
Democratic Action Congress (Trinidad and Tobago), 372
Democratic Action Party (Malaysia), 230
Democratic Action Party (Venezuela), 94; 409
Democratic Alliance (Chile), 46ff.
Democratic Alliance (Palestinian), 274; 277; 282; 284
Democratic Alternative (Finland), 106
Democratic Co-ordinating Board (Nicaragua), 251
Democratic Coalition Movement (Taiwan), 363
Democratic Conservative Party (Nicaragua), 251
Democratic Convergence (Peru), 291
Democratic Front (Comoros), 64
Democratic Front against Repression (Guatemala), 139

Democratic Front for Peace and Equality (Israel), 176
Democratic Front for the Liberation of Palestine, 273ff.; 318
Democratic Front for the Liberation of Somalia, 324
Democratic Front for the Salvation of Somalia (DFSS), 324
Democratic Institutional Party (PID) (Guatemala), 138
Democratic International, 11
Democratic Justice Party (Korea), 204
Democratic Korea Party, 204
Democratic Labour Congress (Grenada), 138
Democratic Labour Movement (DLM) (Guyana), 144
Democratic Labour Party (Barbados), 21
Democratic Labour Party (Brazil), 27
Democratic Left (Ecuador), 82
Democratic Left Party (Turkey), 375
Democratic Movement (Poland), 309
Democratic Movement for Independence (Canada), 39
Democratic Opposition Alliance (ADO) (Panama), 285
Democratic Opposition Coalition of São Tomé and Príncipe, 316
Democratic Party (Poland), 299
Democratic Party (Senegal), 318
Democratic Party (USA), 404; 407
Democratic Party (Vietnam), 410
Democratic Party of Côte d'Iviore (PDCI), 66
Democratic Party of Cyprus (DIKO), 70
Democratic Party of Ecuador, 82
Democratic Party of Kurdistan, 426
Democratic Party of Kurdistan (Iraq), 172ff.
Democratic Party of Luxembourg, 227
Democratic Party of Mexico (PDM), 235
Democratic Party of Nauru, 247
Democratic People's Party (Cyprus), 70
Democratic Popular Movement (Ecuador), 82
Democratic Progress Party (Taiwan), 362
Democratic Rally (DISY) (Cyprus), 70
Democratic Reform Party (Equatorial Guinea), 98
Democratic Republican Union (URD) (Venezuela), 409
Democratic Revolutionary Alliance (Nicaragua), 252
Democratic Revolutionary Party (PRD) (Panama), 285
Democratic Salvadorean Front, 90
Democratic Socialist Federation (Chile), 49ff.
Democratic Socialist Party (PSD) (Guatemala), 138; 142
Democratic Socialist Party (Japan), 188
Democratic Socialists (Yugoslavia), 420
Democratic Turnhalle Alliance (DTA) (Namibia), 243ff.
Democratic Unionist Party (Northern Ireland), 395ff.
Democratic Vanguard of Guatemala, 140
Democrats-66 (Netherlands), 250
Denard, Col. Bob, 24
Deng Xiaoping, 55ff.; 193; 406
Denmark, **79**
DeRoburt, Hammer, 247
Desai, Morarji, 155
Deschler, Irmgard, 129
Destour Socialist Party (Tunisia), 372ff.
Dev-Genc (Turkey), 377
Dev-Sol (Turkey), 377
Dev-Yol (Turkey), 377
Dhale, Raja, 152
Dharsono, Gen. Hartano Resko, 163
Diaka, Mungul, 423
Díaz Martínez, Amilio Antonio, 292
Die, Khatri Ould, 234
Dien Del, Gen., 198ff.
Dienstbier, Jirí, 73ff.
Dikerdem, Mahmut, 378
Dinka people (Sudan), 352
Diori, Abdoulaye, 256
Dios Carmona, Juan de, 53
Diouf, Abdou, 318
Direct Action (Belgium), 22
Direct Action (Canada), 39
Direct Action (France), 109; 131; 137; 186
Direct Action (Poland), 308
"Dirty war" (Argentina), 13
"Dirty war" (Honduras), 147
Djibouti, **80**
Djilas, Milovan, 420
Djurovic, Djura, 419
Dlakama, Afonso, 240ff.
Dobner, Antonin, 76
Doe, Samuel K., 223ff.
Doherty, Kieran, 403
Dolanc, Stane, 416; 417
Dominica, **80**; 405
Dominica Defence Force (DDF), 80
Dominica Freedom Party, 80
Dominica Labour Party, 80
Dominica Liberation Movement Alliance, 80
Dominican Left Front, 81
Dominican Liberation Party, 81
Dominican Popular Movement, 82
Dominican Republic, 59; **81**
Dominican Revolutionary Party, 81
Donat Cattin, Carlo, 181
Donat Cattin, Marco, 181ff.
Dorff, Klaus, 129
Doukhobors (Canada), 40
Doyle, William, 403
Dozier, Brig.-Gen. James L., 184
Dravida Munnetra Kazhagam (DMK) (India), 151
Drenkmann, Günter von, 127
Druse (Lebanon), 209ff.
Druse Independence Revolutionaries (Lebanon), 216
Duarte, José Napoleón, 88ff.
Dubcek, Alexander, 71
duBois, W. E. B., 332
Dudu, Aomar Mohamedi, 347
Dunn, Archibald Gardner, 92
Duong Khem, 200
Durán, Juan Carlos, 25
Duray, Miklos, 78
D'Urso, Giovanni, 184
Dutschke, Rudi, 127
Dutzi, Gisela, 131
Duvalier, François ("Papadoc"), 145
Duvalier, Jean-Claude, 145ff.
Duwab, Hazim, 172
Dyck, Elisabeth von, 132
Dzhemilev, Mustafa (Abduldzhemil), 389

E

"Eagles of the Palestine Revolution", 283
Eagles of the Revolution (Iraq), 172
East Kwaio secessionist movement (Solomon Islands), 323
Eastern Anti-Guerrilla Bloc (El Salvador), 96
Ecevit, Bülent, 379
Echeverría, Enrique, 83
Eckes, Christa, 129; 131
Ecologist Party (Belgium), 22
Ecuador, 59; 60; 61; 68; **82**
Ecuadorean Communist Party, 83
Ecuadorean Roldosista Party, 82
Ecube, Alejo, 98
Eduardo, Sánchez, 254
Eelam National Democratic Liberation Front (Sri Lanka), 348
Eelam Revolutionary Organization of Students (Sri Lanka), 349
Egypt, **84**; 105; 194; 225; 266ff.; 296; 324; 375; 415
Egyptian Communist Party, 87
Egyptian Communist Workers' Party, 87
Egyptian Liberation Organization, 87
Egypt's Revolution, 87; 276
El Auténtico (Argentina), 14
El Combatiente (Colombia), 63
El Pueblo (Nicarauga), 254
El-Salaf el-Saleh (Saudi Arabia), 317
El Salvador, 61; **88**; 146; 253
Elahi, Chaudri Zahur, 260
Elazar, Abraham, 376
Elisabeth van Dyck Commando (France), 110

Eloy Alfaro Popular Armed Forces (Ecuador), 83
Enbata Movement (France), 110ff.
Enders, Thomas O., 91
Endijimongou, Patrice, 43
English People's Liberation Army (UK), 396
Enrile, Juan Ponce, 293ff.
Enríquez, Miguel, 48
Ensslin, Gudrun, 127ff.
Eppelmann, Rainer, 124
Equatorial Guinea, **97**
Erbakan, Necmettin, 380
Erikson, Bert, 22
Erim, Nihat, 377
Eritrean Liberation Front—Popular Liberation Forces (Ethiopia), 100ff.
Eritrean Liberation Front—Revolutionary Council (Ethiopia), 101
Eritrean People's Liberation Front (EPLF) (Ethiopia), 101ff.
Eritrean Relief Association (Ethiopia), 103
Eritrean Unified National Council (EUNC) (Ethiopia), 103
Ernst, Barbara, 131
Ershad, Hossain Mohammed, 20
Eskendari, Iraj, 166
Eskimo people; *see* Inuit people
Espinoza, Guillermo, 255
Essid, Bechir, 373
Estonia (USSR), 388
Estrella Roja (Red Star) (Argentina), 16
ETA; *see* Euzkadi ta Azkatasuna
Ethiopia, **99**; 323ff; 351ff.
Ethiopian Democratic Union, 105
Ethiopian People's Democratic Union, 105
Ethiopian People's Revolutionary Party (EPRP), 105
Etxebeste Arizguren, Eugenion, 345
European Convention on Human Rights, 119
European Convention on the Suppression of Terrorism, 175; 398
European Nationalist Union, 356
European Workers' Party, 108
Euzkadi ta Azkatasuna, ETA (Basque separatists), 109, 110, 182, 250; 342ff.; 400
Evangelical People's Party (Netherlands), 250
Evren, Gen. Kenan, 375; 380
Exploration (China), 57
Eyademe, Gnassingbe, 371

F

Facussé, Miguel, 149
Fadlallah, Shaikh Mohammed Hossein, 214ff.
Fagoth Müller, Steadman, 254-55
Fahoun, Khaled al, 274ff.
Faili (Iraqi Kurds), 174
Fakuda, Takeo, 188
Fang people (Equatorial Guinea), 98
Farabundo Martí Front for National Liberation (FMLN) (El Salvador), 62; 89ff.; 147
Farabundo Martí Popular Liberation Forces (FPC) (El Salvador), 89; 92
Faraq, Mohammed Abdel-Salam, 85ff.
Faroe Islands, **79**
Farouk, former King of Egypt, 84
Farrakhan, Louis, 406
Farrands, James M., 405
Fascist Party (Italy), 178; 180
"Fatah rebels" (Palestinian), 280
Fatah Revolutionary Council (Palestinian), 273ff.; 280; 426
Fatherland Front (Bulgaria), 28
Fayad, Alvaro, 60
Febrerista Revolutionary Party (Paraquay), 288; 290
Febres Cordero, León, 82ff.
February 28 Popular Leagues (LP-28) (El Salvador), 89ff.
Fedayeen-e-Khalq (Iran), 163ff.
Federal Bureau of Investigation (FBI) (USA), 159; 406
Federal Democratic Movement of Uganda (Fedemu), 385; 386
Federation for a New Caledonia (FNSC), 118
Federation of Guatemalan Workers (FTG), 141
Federation of Saskatchewan Indians (Canada), 39
Feeney, Hugh, 402
Fehér, Ferenc, 150
Fenzi, Enrico, 184
Fernandes, Evo, 242
Fernando Póo Liberation Front (Equatorial Guinea), 98
Ferrari, Paolo, 183
"Fiancés of Death" (Bolivia), 25
Fianna Fáil (Ireland), 175
Fianna Na h'Eireann (Northern Ireland), 401
Fiebelkorn, Joachim, 179
Fierro Loza, Francisco, 236
Fighting Communist Cells (Belgium), 137; 22
Fighting Communist Party (Italy), 186
Fighting Ecologist Movement (Luxembourg), 227
Fighting Unit Rolando Olalia (West Germany), 131
Fiji, **106**
Filipescu, Radu, 312
Filizzola, Carlos, 289ff.
Fine Gael (Ireland), 175
Fine Gael (Northern Ireland), 399
Finland, **106**
Finnish Christian Union, 106
Finnish People's Democratic League, 106
Firmenich, Mario Eduardo, 14ff.
First, Ruth, 329
First of October Anti-Fascist Resistance Group (GRAPO) (Spain), 339; 340
Fischer, Advocate Abram, 334
Flemish Bloc (Belgium), 22
Flemish Militant Order (Belgium), 22
Folkerts, Knut, 132
Folkerts, Uwe, 132
Fontaine, Jean, 117
Forbidden Yellow Organization of Air Force Officers (Greece), 136
Force 17 (Palestinian), 284
Force Obote Back Again (Uganda), 385
Forces armées populaires (FAP) (Chad), 44
Forces of the Prophet Mohammed in Kuwait, 207
Forestieri, Diego, 182
Formosa Group (Taiwan), 362
Formosan Independence Movement (Taiwan), 361
Foruhar, Dariush, 168
Forward Bloc (India), 151
Forward Movement (Morocco), 238
Forward Party (Greenland), 79
"Forward to Death" (Iran), 168
"Forward to Death" (Iraq), 173ff.
Fourth Congress Group (Nepal), 248
Fourth International—Japanese Section, 189
Fox, Billy, 399
Fracin, Jandra, 418
France, 24; 30; 42; 64; 91; 97; **107**; 167; 186; 213; 219; 244; 272; 319; 342ff.; 371; 373; 381ff.; 411; 419
Franceschini, Alberto, 182ff.
Franci, Luciano, 180
Franco Bahamonde, Generalissimo, 341; 343
François, Thédore, 116
Franjié, Soleiman, 210ff.
Franjié, Tony, 211
Frascella, Emanuela, 184
Frasyniuk, Wladyslaw, 305, 307
Free Aceh Movement (Indonesia), 161
Free Adventists (USSR), 392
Free Costa Rica, 66
Free Democratic Party (West Germany), 125
Free German Labour Party, 125
Free German Workers' Party, 125
Free Homeland (Colombia), 61; 62
Free Homeland Montoneros (Ecuador), 83
Free Honduras, 149
Free Interprofessional Association of Soviet Workers (SMOT), 388
Free Islamic Revolution, 216
Free Khmers (Kampuchea), 196ff.

Free Land (Spain), 347
Free Lao National Liberation Movement, 208
Free Man Movement (Mauritania), 234
Free National Movement (Bahamas), 19
Free People of Laos, 208
Free Press (Ghana), 135
Free South Moluccan Organization (Netherlands), 250
Free Trade Union of Romanian Workers, 313
"Free University" (Yugoslavia), 421
Freedom Foundation (Iran), 167
Freedom Movement (Iran), 166
Frei Montalva, Eduardo, 45ff.
Frelimo—Front for the Liberation of Mozambique, 240ff.; 335
Frem, Fady, 212
French Guiana, 114; **116**; 355
French Polynesia, **117**
Frend Melanesia (Vanuatu), 408
Frente Obrero (Nicaragua), 254
Fresno, Juan Francisco, 51; 54
Frias Alape, Jacobo, 61
Frigato, Roberto, 179
Fritzsch, Ronald, 133
"Front 219 AF" (Lebanon), 79; 216
Front calédonien (New Caledonia), 119
Front de la jeunesse (Belgium), 22
Front de libération du Québec (Canada), 40
Front de libération national du Tchad (Frolinat), 44
Front de libération nationale Kanak et Socialiste (FLNKS) (New Caledonia), 118ff.
Front for the Liberation of Lebanon from Foreigners, 210
Front for the Liberation of the Enclave of Cabinda (Angola), 12
Front for the Liberation of Occupied South Yemen (FLOSY), 414
Front indépendantiste (FI) (New Caledonia), 118; 120
Front Line (Italy), 178ff.
Front militant départmentaliste (Martinique), 117
Front national (FN) (France), 110
Front national uni des Komores, FNUK, 65
Front of the People and the Army for National Salvation (Vietnam), 410
Front of Socialist Democracy and Unity (Romania), 312
Front of Socialist Forces (Algeria), 6, 7
Front uni de libération Kanake (FULK) (New Caledonia), 120
Fuentes Mohr, Alberto, 142
Fuerza Democrática Nicaragùense (FDN), 253
Full Group of Reflection on Puerto Rico, 407
Furuya, Yutaka, 190

G

Gabon, 24; **121**;
Gabonese Democratic Party, 121
Gadaffi, Col. Moamer al-, 29; 225; 260, 275; 295; 375; 403; 406; 426
Gadea Mantilla, Fabio, 253
Gaelic Language Defence League (UK), 396
Gafarov, Ridvan, 389
Gaffar Khan, Khan Abdul, 265
Gailani, Sayed Ahmed, 2ff.
Gairy, Sir Eric, 137ff.
Galetsky, Rostislav, 392
Galicia (Spain), 347
Gallardo Flores, Carlos, 139
Galli, Guido, 182
Gallinari, Prospero, 183ff.
Galvin, Martin, 403
Gambia, **122**; 319
Gambian People's Party, 122
Gambian Socialist Revolutionary Party, 122
Ganda, Ambrose, 321
Gandhi, Indira, 157ff.
Gandhi, Mahatma, 335
Gandhi, Rajiv, 156ff.
"Gang of Four" (China), 55; 406
Gangadeen, Robert, 145
Garang, Col. John, 352ff.
Garbidjian, Varadjian, 109
Garces, Adriana, 63
García, Carlos Mario, 63
García, Col. José Guillermo, 89
García, Rafael, 139
García Pérez, Alan, 291ff.
Gardezi, Syed Qaswar, 261
Garretón, Oscar, 50
Gaw Lin Da, Col., 35
Gayoom, Maumoon, Abdul, 232
Gaza Strip, 177; 267
Gazioglu, Gultekin, 378
Gazmuri (Chile), 50
Geaga, Samir, 211ff.; 219; 221
Geburtig, Bernd, 129
Gelli, Licio, 179ff.
Gemayel, Amin, 218
Gemayel, Bashir, 211ff.
Gemayel, Pierre, 211ff.
Gend, Lothar, 128
General Confederation of Italian Labour (CGIL), 183
General Confederation of Labour (CGT) (Argentina), 14; 16
General Students' Organization (Libya), 225
Gennaro, Guiseppe di, 181
Georges, Pingon, 122
Gerena, Victor Manuel, 407
German Action Groups, 125
German Centre Party, 125
German Democratic Republic (East Germany), **123**, 165; 301; 309; 375; 384; 388
Germany, Federal Republic of (West Germany), 18; **124**; 156; 191; 217; 244; 388; 394; 402; 403; 416
Gezmis, Deniz, 378
Ghaffar Khan, Khan Abdul, 261
Ghali, Ibrahim, 239
Ghana, **134**; 224; 371
Ghanaian Democracy Movement, 135
Ghanem, Abdul Fatah, 280
Ghanouchi, Rachid, 373
Ghashmi, Lt.-Col. Hussein al-, 413
Ghazalah, Munza Abu, 284
Ghising, Subhash, 156
Ghjustizia Paolina (Corsica), 112
Ghodbani, Hasen, 373
Ghosheh, Samir, 280
Gibson, Sir Maurice (Lord Justice), 403
Gierek, Edward, 301; 309
Gilbert Islands; *see* Kiribati
Gimma, Abu Bakr, 103
Ginsburg, Alexander, 394
Giorgeri, Air Force General Licio, 186
Giorgi, Maurizio, 179
Giorgis Tekle Mikael, 103
Girijan tribespeople (India), 152
Giscard d'Estaing, Valéry, 112
Glaser, Peter, 131
Glasnost (USSR), 393
Glemp, Cardinal Jozef, 304
Glos (Poland), 309
Goder, Angelika, 133
Goiburú, Augustin, 290
Goiburú Mendizábal, José Miguel, 345
Golan Heights, 267ff.; 360
Goldmann, Nahum, 392
Goma, Paul, 313
González, Carlos, 140
González, Juan Luis, 52
González, Leonel, 89ff.
González, Sebastián, 254
González, Valentín, 63
González Alberto, Carlos, 287
González Arce, Antonio, 288
González Casabianca, Miguel Angel, 290
Gorbachev, Mikhail, 76; 123; 393
Gordon, Aníbal, 17

Gordon, Marcelo, 17
Goretai, Nikolai, 392
Görgens, Irene, 127; 133
Gorvie, Edison Milton, 321
Goshu Wolde, Lt.-Col., 99
Goumba, Abel, 41ff.
Government-in-exile (GRAE) (Angola), 9ff.
Government-in-exile (Gabon), 121
Government-in-exile (Liberia), 224
Government-in-exile (Palestinian), 270
Government-in-exile (Poland), 310
Graça, Carlos da, 316
Graiver, David, 15
Grashof, Manfred, 129
Greece, 29; **136**; 272
Greek-Bulgarian-Armenian Front (Turkey), 382
Greek Catholics (Lebanon), 209ff.
Greek Communist Party (KKE Exterior), 136
Greek National Political Society (EPEN), 136
Greek Orthodox Church (Lebanon), 209ff.
Green, Samuel, 405
Green Alternative (Austria), 18
Green Book (Libya), 225
Green Jackets (Denmark), 79
Green Party (UK), 395
Green Star Movement (Thailand), 368
Greenland, **79**
Greenpeace (Belgium), 23
Greens (Finland), 106
Greens (Italy), 178
Greens (Luxembourg), 227
Greens (Netherlands), 250
Greens (Canada), 39
Greens (West Germany), 76; 120; 125
Gregorio, Joséde, 46
Grenada, **137**; 316
Grenada Democratic Labour Party, 138
Grenada Democratic Movement, 138
Grenada National Party, 138
Grenada United Labour Party (GULP), 138
Grey Wolves ("Idealists") (Turkey), 379
Grigorenko, Maj.-Gen. (rtd) Pyotr, 388
Groenewold, Kurt, 129
Gröning, Joachim, 126
Gros-Loius, Chief Max, 39
Grosser, Karl-Friedrich, 130; 131
Group 219-FA (Lebanon), 79; 216
Group for Establishing Trust between the USSR and the USA, 393
Grundmann, Wolfgang, 129
Gruntorad, Jiri, 76
Grupo Antimarxista, GRAPA (Chile), 54
Gu-Kono, Yema, 371
Guadalupe Martínez, Ana, 92
Guadeloupe, **115**
Guanch people (Canary Islands), 346
Guardado, Facundo, 95
Guatemala, **138**; 407
Guatemalan Committee of Patriotic Unity (CGUP), 138, 139
Guatemalan Guerrilla Commandos in Formation, 142
Guatemalan Labour Party (PGT), 139ff.
Guatemalan National Revolutionary Unity (URNG), 138ff.
Gudrun Ensslin Commando (West Germany), 132
Guenther, Rolf, 124
Guéret, François, 42
Guerre noire (France), 108
Guerrilla Army of the Poor (EGP) (Guatemala), 139; 140
Guerrilla Miskito (Nicaragua), 255
Guevera, Che, 127
Guiana National Liberation Front (French Guiana), 115
Guinea, **143**; 375
Guinea-Bissau, **143**
Guinean Liberal Party, 98
Gulf Co-operation Council, 274
Gulf war, 164ff.; 172; 178; 207
Gullo, Carlos Dante, 15
Gulumian, Pierre, 382
Gurkha National Liberation Front (India), 156
Gurung, Damber Jang, 248
Gush Emunim (Israel), 176ff.
Gutierrez Menoyo, Eloy, 69
Guyana, **144**
Guzmán Renose, Manuel Abimael ("Comrade Gonzalo"), 291ff.
Gwiazda, Andrzei, 304

H

Haag, Siegfried, 130; 132
Haag-Mayer Group (West Germany), 132
Habash, Georges, 87; 271; 275; 377
Habré, Hissène, 44
Habyarimana, Juvénal, 314
Hadash (Israel), 176
Haddad, Maj. Saad, 212ff.; 271ff.
Haddad Militia (Lebanon), 212ff.
Haibulin, Varsonofy, 390
Haidar, Shaikh Mohammed, 214
"Haifa section" (Palestinian), 281
Haile Selassie (Ras Tafari), 80; 99ff.
Haithem, Mohammed Ali, 415
Haiti, **145**
Hajek, Jiri, 73
Hakim, Hojatolislam Seyyed Mohammed Bakr, 173
Hallou, Zaki al-, 284
Ham Un Yong, 206
Hamadi, Lt.-Col. Ibrahim al-, 413
Hamamba, Dimo, 244
Hamdan, Badri, 370
Hammouda, Yehia, 269
Hanif Khan, Rana Mohammad, 262
Hanmintong (Korea), 205
Happart, J., 22
Happe, Manuela, 131
Haque, Azizul, 153
Haratines (Mauritania), 234
Harijans ("untouchables") (India), 152
Harkat-i-Inkalab-i-Islami (Afghanistan), 2; 4
Harkis (Iran), 169
Hashim, Habid, 297
Hashim, Jawad, 172
Hasina, Sheikh, 20
Hassam, Abdul Karim, 370
Hassan, Salem Ahmad, 282
Hassan, Yusuf, 201
Hassan II, King of Morocco, 238
Haughey, Charles, 176
Hausner, Siegfried, 128; 132
Havel, Václav, 73
Hawatmeh, Nayef, 277
Hawi, George, 221
Hazama Faction of the Revolutionary Workers' Council (Japan), 189
Hébert, Mathieu, 40
Heissler, Rolf, 130ff.
Hejdanek, Ladislav, 73; 77
Hekmatyar, Gulbuddin, 2ff.
Helsinki Final Act, 74; 77; 124; 309; 310; 312; 387
"Helsinki Group" (USSR), 388
Heng Samrin, 193ff.
Henning, Uwe, 129
Herero Royalist Association (Namibia), 244
Herljevic, Gen. Franjo, 416
Herrera Rebollo, Carlos, 92
Herron, Thomas, 399
Herstigte Nasionale Party (South Africa), 326
Herut party (Israel), 177
Herzinger, Sylvia, 134
Herzog, Marianne, 128
Hess, Rudolf, 125ff.
Hezbollah (Lebanon), 213ff.; 275; 276; 373
Hezbollah (Libya), 226

Hezbollah (Sri Lanka), 351
Hezbollah party (Iran), 166
Hezbollahi (Children of the Party of God) (Iran), 165
Hidaka, Toshihiko, 190
"Hidaka commando" (Japan), 190
Higher Committee for Palestinian Affairs in Lebanon, 278; 283
Hill, David, 145
Hill, Jaime, 92
Hindu Shiv Sena ("Army of Shiva") (India), 152
Hirohito, Emperor of Japan, 189
Hirsch, Rabbi Mosche, 177
Hizb-i-Islami (Afghanistan), 2; 3
H'miti, Khoury Ould, 234
Hmong people (Laos), 208
Hmong people (Thailand), 366
Ho Chi Minh, 127; 193
Hoang Co Minh, 411
Hoare, Col. Michael, 320
Hobeika, Elie, 211ff., 221
Hochstein, Inge, 129
Hochstein, Rainer, 129
Hodeiby, Hassan el-, 84
Hoff, Dierk, 129
Hoffmann, Karel, 72
Hoffmann, Karl-Heinz, 125ff.
Hoffmann Defence Sports Group (West Germany), 125
Hofmann, Sieglinde Gutrun, 130, 132
Holger Meins Commando (West Germany), 132
Holy War (Egypt), 85ff.
Holy War (Libya), 226
Holy War Command (Indonesia), 161
Home Rule Party (Faroe Islands), 79
Homeland and Truth (Costa Rica), 66
Hon Youn, 195
Honduran Peasants' National Unity Front, 147
Honduras, **146**; 252ff.; 407
Hong Kong, **56**
Horeau, Gabriel, 320
Horeau, Gérard, 320
Hosseini, Shaikh, 168
Houphouët-Boigny, Félix, 66
House of Israel (Guyana), 145
Howe, Sir Geoffrey, 76; 215
Hoxha, Enver, 417
Hpang Hpa, 35
Hrkac, Miljenko, 418
Hsieh Tung-min, 363
Hsing Chung Hui (China), 57
Hsu Chao-hung, 363
Htoon Yi, Col., 35
Hu Hsin-liang, 363
Hu Nim, 195
Hu Yaobang, 56ff.
Huang Hsin-chieh, 363
Huang Hua, 197
Hubel, Klaus, 126
Huerta, Daniel (Chile), 51
Human Rights Alliance (China), 57
Human Rights Association (Guyana), 145
Human Rights Protection Party (Western Samoa), 413
Hun Sen, 194
Hungarian minority (Czechoslovakia), 78
Hungarian minority (Romania), 313
Hungarian Socialist Workers' Party, 149ff.
Hungary, **149**; 301
Hunter, Fred, 23
Huron Indians (Canada), 39
Hurtado, Hernando, 63
Husák, Gustáv, 71
Hussain, Altaf, 265
Hussain, Mushtaq, 260
Hussein, King of Jordan, 191ff.; 267ff.; 282
Hussein, Saddam, 171ff.
Hutu tribespeople (Burundi), 37

I

Iberian Federation of Anarchist Groups (Spain), 341
Iceland, 151
Idris, ex-King of Libya, 225
Idriss Miskine Group (Chad), 44
Ieng Sary, 195ff.
Ikhwani (Egypt), 84
Ilal Amam (Morocco), 238
Illia, Arturo Umberto, 14
Illumination Group (Turkey), 376
Ilom, Rodrigo "Gaspar", 141
Imam, Musheer Ahmad Pesh, 264
Independence Party (Iceland), 151
Independent Artists' and Writers' Groups (Poland), 308
Independent Democratic Movement (Chile), 53
Independent Democratic Union of Cape Verde (UCID), 41
Independent Democratic Union of São Tomé and Príncipe, 316
Independent Grouping of Reflection and Action (Central African Republic), 42
Independent Labor Party (Australia), 18
Independent Liberal Party (PLI) (Nicaragua), 251
Independent Movement for the Liberation of Kidnap Victims (Lebanon), 217
Independent North East Party (Thailand), 368
Independent Zimbabwe Group, 424
India, **151**; 248; 261; 265
Indian minority (Madagascar), 228
Indo-Chinese Communist Party, 193
Indonesia, **160**; 250
Indonesian Democratic Party, 160
"Indonesian Islamic Revolutionary Council", 161
Ingrid Schubert Commando of the Revolutionary Front of Western Europe (West Germany), 132
Innovation and Unity Party (PINU) (Honduras), 146
Institutional Revolutionary Party (PRI) (Mexico), 235
Inter-American Human Rights Commission, 60; 67; 287
Inter-Trade Union Movement of Paraguayan Workers, 287
International Committee of the Red Cross, 11
International Daily News (Taiwan), 362
International Federation of Human Rights, 6ff.; 77; 239
International Jazz Federation (IJF) (Czechoslovakia), 77
International Revolutionary Movement (Zimbabwe), 425
International Sikh Federation (India), 157
International Spartacist Tendency, 39; 396; 406
Interpol (France), 110
Intransigent Party (Argentina), 13; 17
Inuit Ataqatigiit, Eskimo Movement (Greenland), 79
Inuit people (Canada), 39
Invisible Empire (USA), 405
Iparretarak (France), 111
Ipekçi, Abdi, 379
Iqbal, Mohammad Musserat, 154
Iran, 19; **163**; 171; 178; 192; 207; 214; 218; 225; 239; 275; 276; 296; 317ff.; 358; 373; 380; 394
Iranian National Front (INF), 167
Iraq, 89; 100; 105; 168; **171**; 192; 234; 258; 266.; 272; 275; 276ff.; 280; 360; 426
Iraqi Communist Party (ICP), 172
Iraqi Mujaheddin, 171; 173
Ireland, Northern, 175; 395; **398**
Ireland, Republic of, **175**; 400; 401
Irian Jaya (Indonesia), 161
Iriria (Kenya), 201
Irish National Liberation Army (INLA), 175; 400; 403
Irish People's Liberation Organization, 401
Irish Republican Army (IRA), 81; 114; 175ff., 182; 250; 375, 396-401
Irish Republican Socialist Party, 397; 400
Iryani, Abdul Karim Ali al-, 414
Isaías Barquet, Nahim, 83
Isan Ekkarat (Thailand), 368
Isfahani, Ayatollah Ashrafi, 165
Isik, Mustafa, 377
Isiklar, Fehmi, 376

Islam, Sheikh Tajamul, 154
Islambouli, Lt. Khalid Hassan Sharfiq, 86
Islamic Action Movement of Iraq, 173
Islamic Action Organization (Iraq), 173
Islamic Alliance for the Liberation of Afghanistan, 2ff.
Islamic Amal (Iraq), 173
Islamic Amal (Lebanon), 214ff.
Islamic Front (North Yemen), 413
Islamic Front for the Liberation of Bahrain, 19
Islamic Groupings (Egypt), 86
Islamic Guidance Society (Egypt), 86
Islamic Holy War (Kuwait), 207
Islamic Holy War (Saudi Arabia), 318
Islamic Jihad for the Liberation of Palestine (IJLP), 217
Islamic Liberal Party (Egypt), 86
Islamic Liberation Organization—Khaled Ibn Walid Forces (Lebanon), 217
Islamic Liberation Party (Jordan), 192
Islamic Liberation Party (Tunisia), 373
Islamic Movement (Singapore), 322
Islamic Party (Afghanistan), 2ff.
Islamic Progressive Movement (Tunisia), 373
Islamic Republican Party (Iran), 166
Islamic Resistance Front (Lebanon), 216, 218
Islamic Revolutionary Vanguard (Palestinian), 284
Islamic Trend Movement (Tunisia), 373ff.
Islamic Unification Movement (Lebanon), 221
Islamic Unity of the Mujaheddin of Afghanistan, 1ff.
Islamic Youth Movement (Morocco), 238
Ismail, Abdel Fattah, 414
Ismail, Gen. Mohammed Nabawi, 87
Israel, 30; 59; 85; 147; 168; **176**; 185; 191; 191; 192; 212; 266ff.; 296; 324; 360; 377; 382
Israeli Tradition Movement, 176
Issaias Afewerki, 100; 102
Istiqlal (Morocco), 237
Isunza, Jaime, 53
Italian Social Movement (MSI), 178; 180; 183
Italy, 18; **178**; 272; 276; 379; 381
Iturbe Abásolo, Domingo ("Txomin"), 345
Ivory Coast; *see* Côte d'Iviore
"Iyad, Abu Ali"; *see* Khalaf, Salah

J

Jabril, Ahmed, 274; 276; 282
Jacobsmeyer, Ingrid, 131
Jadid, Salah, 360
Jagielski, Mieczyslaw, 309
Jai Sind (Pakistan), 264
Jam, Abd al-Whab Mahmud, 101
Jama, Hussein Said, 325
Jamaat-i-Islami Afghanistan, 2; 3
Jamaat-i-Islami (Bangladesh), 20
Jamaat-i-Islami (Pakistan), 154; 263
Jamaat-i-Tulaba (India), 154
Jamaica, **187**
Jamaica Labour Party (JLP), 187
Jamaica United Front, 187
Jamali, Mir Taj Mohammad Khan, 262
Jamiat-i-Talaba (JIT) (Pakistan), 263
Jamiat-i-Ulema-i-Islami (Pakistan), 263
Jamiat-i-Ulema-i-Pakistan, 259ff.
Jamkodjian, Mardiros, 381ff.
Jamous, Fateh, 361
"Jan Patocka Alternative University" (Czechoslovakia), 75
Janata Party (India), 151
Jandt, Ilse, 133
Jandziszak, Tadeusz, 308
Janwadi Morcha (Democratic Front) (Nepal), 248
Jaona, Monja, 227
Japan, **188**
Japan Communist Party, 188
Japan Socialist Party, 188
Japan Volunteer Army for National Independence, 188
Jaramillo Lyon, Armando, 50; 53
Jarowoy, Robert, 129
Jaruzelski, Gen. Wojciech, 301ff.
Jatiya Party (Bangladesh), 20
Jatiya Samajtantrik Dal (Bangladesh), 20
Jatiya Samajtantrik Dal-Rob (Bangladesh), 20
Jatoi, Ghulam Mustafa, 263, 264
Jawara, Sir Dawda, 122
Jayawardene, Junius R., 348
Jazz Section (Czechoslovakia), 77
Jeane Kirkpatrick Task Force (Nicaragua), 253
Jehovah's Witnesses (Czechoslovakia), 78
Jehovah's Witnesses (Finland), 107
Jehovah's Witnesses (Greece), 136
Jehovah's Witnesses (Malawi), 229
Jehovah's Witnesses (Turkey), 384
Jehovah's Witnesses (USSR), 392
Jeune Afrique (France), 108
Jewish Armed Resistance Strike Unit (Israel), 177
Jewish Community (USSR), 392
Jewish Defence League (Israel), 176
Jewish underground (Israel), 176ff.
"Jihad, Abu"; *see* Wazir, Khalil al-
Jihad (Libya), 226
Jihad (Pakistan), 264
Jihad Komando (Indonesia), 161
Jiménez, Damian, 82
Jiménez Morales, Gregorio, 346
Jinnah, Mohammad Ali, 265
John, Patrick R., 80
John Paul II, His Holiness Pope, 301; 379
Joint Action Committee (Trinidad and Tobago), 372
Joint National Council for the Revolution (Angola), 10
Joint Opposition Front (UAE), 394
Joint Secretariat of Functional Groups (Golkar) (Indonesia), 160
Jonathan, Chief Leabua, 222
Jones Ivina, Francisco, 98
Jordan, **191**; 267; 373; 426
Jordan, Colin, 395
Joubert, David, 320
Jovovic, Komnen, 420
Jraysh, Juban, 220
Jumblatt, Kamal, 219; 360
Jumblatt, Walid, 215; 218ff.; 275
Jundullah (Army of God) (Lebanon), 218
June 2 Movement (West Germany), 133
Junejo, Mohammed, 258ff.
Jünschke, Klaus, 128ff.
Jura movements (Switzerland), 357
Justice Commandos for the Armenian Genocide (Turkey), 382
Justicialist Liberation Front (Frejuli) (Argentina), 14; 16
Justicialist National (Peronist) Movement (Argentina), 13
Justicialist Party (Argentina), 17

K

Ka La La Ta (Burma), 32
Kabila, Laurent, 423
Kach Movement (Israel), 176ff.
Kachin Independence Army (Burma), 33
Kachin Independence Organization (Burma), 33ff.
Kádár, János, 150
Kadiyev, Rollan, 389
Kagodo, Paulo Kalule, 386
Kahan, Itzhak, 273
Kahane, Rabbi Meir, 176
Kahlon, Harminder Singh, 156ff.
Kakumaru-Ha (Japan), 189
Kakurokyo Hazama (Japan), 189
Kalangula, Peter, 243
Kalnins, Bruno, 394
Kamara, Abdul, 321
Kambona, Oscar, 364
Kamp-Münnichow, Karin, 133
Kampuchea, **193**; 366ff.; 410

Kampuchean National United Front for National Salvation (KNUFNS), 193
Kampuchean People's Revolutionary Party (KPRP), 193
Kampuchean Revolutionary Army, 193
Kanak Liberation Party (Palika) (New Caledonia), 118
Kania, Stanislaw, 301ff.
Kania, Wolf, 77
Kannamani (India), 153
Kapitanchuk, Viktor, 390
Kaplan, Cemalettin, 380
Kapuuo, Chief Clemens, 245
Karami, Rashid, 210; 274
Karen National Liberation Army (KNLA) (Burma), 33
Karen National Union (Burma), 31ff.
Karenni National Progressive Party (KNPP) (Burma), 34ff.
Karenni People's Liberation Organization (Burma), 34
Karenni Revolutionary Army (Burma), 34
Karikari, Kwame, 136
Karim, Farid Abdel, 87
Karingal, Brig.-Gen. Tomas, 298
Káriuki, Maj.-Gen. Peter, 201
Karry, Heinz-Herbert, 134
Kashmir Liberation Army (India), 154
Kashmir Moslem Conference (Pakistan), 259
Kataëb (Lebanon), 211
Kathrada, Ahmed Mohammed, 334
Kaunda, Kenneth, 246; 424
Kaw Lin Da, 36
Kawthoolei Moslem Liberation Force (Burma), 34
Kayah New Land Revolutionary Council (Burma), 36
Kayan New Land Council (Burma), 32; 34
Kayiira, Andrew Lukatome, 386
Kaypakkaya, Ibrahim, 378
Kayyale, Abdel Wahab, 277
Kazakhstan (USSR), 389
Kazenga, Alphonse, 314
Keihin Anpo Kyoto (Japan), 190
Keihin Joint Struggle Committee against the US-Japan Security Treaty, 190
Kelly, Gerald, 402
Kelly, Guillermo Patricio, 17
Kemal, Saïd Ali, 64
Kena, Jacob, 223
Kennedy, John F., 67
Kenya, **200**; 325; 386
Kenya African National Union (KANU), 200ff.
Kenya People's Redemption Council, 201
Kenya People's Union, 202
Kerala Congress (Joseph) (India), 151
Ketema Yifru, 99
Kéthly, Anna, 150
Kett, Dieter, 129
KGB (State Security Committee) (USSR), 166; 387
Khaing Mo Lin, 31
Khaing Ye Khaing, Maj., 31
Khairov, Izzet, 389
Khairuddin, Khwaja, 259ff.
Khaisaeng Suksai, 369
Khalaf, Karim, 177
Khalaf, Salah ("Abu Iyad"), 277, 283, 284
Khaled, Leila, 281
Khales, Maulavi Mohammad Yunus, 2ff.
"Khalistan" (India), 157ff.
Khalistan Commando Force (India), 157
Khalkhali, Ayatollah, 167
Khalsa, Burmal, 157
Khar, Ghulam Mustafa, 262ff.
Khavari, Ali, 165
Khiabani, Moussa, 165
Khieu Samphan, 193ff.
Khin Maung Gyi, 32
Khmer Hanoi (Kampuchea), 195
Khmer People's National Liberation Front (KPNLF) (Kampuchea), 193ff.
Khmer Republic (Kampuchea), 193
Khmer Vietminh (Kampuchea), 195
Khmers Rouges (Kampuchea), 193ff., 208; 365
Khmers Serei (Kampuchea), 198
Khodra, Tariq al-, 280
Khomeini, Ayatollah Ruhollah, 163ff.; 215ff.; 237; 373ff.
Khrus Sangai, 35
Khrushchev, Nikita, 77; 389ff.
Khun Phan, Brig.-Gen. L., 33
Khwanyia Movement (Tunisia), 373
Ki-Zerbo, Joseph, 30
Kianouri, Noureddin, 165
Kiep, Walter Leisler, 128
Kilic, Nemesi, 384
Kilndjian, Max, 382
Kim Chong Il, 203
Kim Dae Jung, 205ff.
Kim Hyong Jang, 204
Kim Il Sung, 203
Kim Un Suk, 204
Kim Young Sam, 205ff.
Kiraly, Carol, 313
Kiribati, **202**
Kirkpatrick, Harry, 401
Kisan (Nicaragua), 252ff.
Kissinger, Henry 282
KKE Interior (Eurocommunist) (Greece), 136
Klaew Norpati, 369
Klanwatch (USA), 405
Klar, Christian, 131; 132
Klein, Hans-Joachim, 129
Klöpper, Gerald, 133
Knights of the Ku Klux Klan (USA), 405
Knoll, Hans Peter, 133
Ko, Ibrahima, 30
Kohnert, Walter-Franz, 126
Koirala, Bishewar Prasad, 248ff.
Koirala, Girija Prasad, 249
Koirala, Matrika Prasad, 248
Koleïlat, Ibrahim, 218
Kolingba, Gen. André, 41
Komala-Azadi (Turkey), 384
Komeito (Japan), 188
Kong, Maj. Gordon, 352ff.
Kong Sileah, 199
König, Karl-Heinz, 129
Konyak, "Col." Moba, 155
Kopkamtib (Indonesia), 160
Korea, Democratic People's Republic of (North Korea), 194; **203**; 375; 386; 425
Korea, Republic of (South Korea), 33; 190; **203**
Korea National Party, 204
Korean Christian Action Organization, 204
Korean Democratic Party, 203
Korean Social Democratic Party, 203
Korean Workers' Party (KWP), 203
Kosovo (Yugoslavia), 416
Kountché, Lt.-Col. Seyni, 255
Kouril, Vladimir, 77
Kouris, Gen. Nikolaos, 136
Krabbe, Friederike, 132
Krabbe, Hanna Elise, 132
Krause, Petra (Piccolo), 130
Kreisky, Bruno, 283
Krnjevic, Juraj, 421
Kröcher-Tiedemann, Gabriele, 128
Kröcker, Norbert, 130
Kroesen, Gen. Frederick J., 131; 132
Kroobs, Monika, 131
Ku Klux Klan (USA), 81; 404
Kubisova, Marta, 73; 77
Kuby, Christine, 130
Kühnen, Michael, 125
Kukk, Juri, 388
Kulaj, Jan, 307ff.
Kung fu clubs (Madagascar), 228

Kunwas Singh Sena (India, 154
Kuomintang (China), 57
Kuomintang (Taiwan), 56; 361ff.
Kuomintang Third Army (Burma), 36
"Kurdish autonomous region" (Iraq), 174
Kurdish Communist Party of Iran (Komaleh), 164
Kurdish Democratic Party (Turkey), 426
Kurdish Democratic Party of Iran (KDPI), 168
Kurdish Militant Organization (Turkey), 383
Kurdish Socialist Party (Iraq), 172ff.
Kurdish Socialist Party of Turkey, 174
Kurdish Sunni Moslem Movement (Iran), 168
Kurdish Workers' Party (KWP or Apocular) (Turkey), 381; 384
Kurdistan National Party (Iraq), 174
Kuron, Jacek, 303; 304; 309
Kutlu, Haydar, 376
Kutuklui, Noë, 371
Kuwait, 103; 190; **206**; 214; 284
Kuwat al-Asifa (Palestinian), 277
Kuyakin, Vselovod, 388
Kuznetsov, Anatoly, 387
Kwaio Fadanga (Solomon Islands), 323
Kwame Nkrumah Revolutionary Guards (Ghana), 135
Kwangju Citizens' Committee (South Korea), 204
Kyaw Win, 32

L

Labillois, Wallace, 39
Labor Party (Australia), 18
Labour Alignment (Israel), 176
Labour Party of Belgium, 22
Labour Party of Dominica, 80
Labour Party (Ireland), 175
Labour Party (Northern Ireland), 395
Labour Party (Malta), 233
Labour Party (Mauritius), 235
Labour Party (Netherlands), 250
Labour Party (New Zealand), 251
Labour Party (Norway), 257
Labour Party (Pala) (Panama), 285
Labour Party (St Kitts and Nevis), 315
Labour Party (St Lucia), 315
Labour Party (UK), 395
Labourers' and Farmers' Party (Pakistan), 259ff.
La Cause Arménienne (France), 380
Lafay, Jean-Paul, 114
Lagos, Ricardo, 50
Lahad, Col. Antoine, 212ff.
Laíno, Domingo, 287ff.
Lal, Pushpa, 248
Lal Sena (India), 154
Lala, Rodolphe Idi, 41ff.
Lamine, Mohamed, 239
Lammers, Eric, 22
"Lamoraille"; *see* Aouegui, Antoine
Langlois, Yves, 40
Lao Front for National Reconstruction, 107
Lao National Liberation Front, 208
Lao Patriotic Front, 207
Lao People's Revolutionary Party (LPRP), 207
La Opinion (Argentina), 15
Laos, 31; 193; 197; **207**; 365ff.; 410
Laporte, Pierre, 40
Lara Velado, Roberto, 94
Larma, Manabendra, 21
Latin Catholics (Lebanon), 209ff.
Latinus, Paul, 22
Latvia (USSR), 388
Laugerud García, Gen. Kjell Eugenio, 140
Laurin, Camille, 39
Lavanderos, Jorge, 53, 54
"La Violencia" (Colombia), 58; 61
Lawson, Capt. Francisco, 372
Le Min U, 205
Le Pen, Jean-Marie, 110
League of Communists of Yugoslavia (LCY), 415
League of Nations, 243
Leballo, Potlako K., 333
Lebanese Armed Revolutionary Faction (FARL), 109ff.; 221
Lebanese Communist Party, 221
Lebanese Forces, 211ff.
Lebanese Front, 210; 213
Lebanese National Movement, 221; 271
Lebanese National Resistance, 213; 218
Lebanon, 15; 126; 164; 171; 191; **209**; 266ff.; 318; 324; 384; 426
Lebret, Yves, 65
Lecante, Albert, 114
Lee Kuan Yew, 322
Lee Ya-ping, 362
Left Front Coalition (India), 156
Left Radical Movement (France), 107
Left Radicals (Corsica), 111
Left Socialists (Norway), 257
Left Socialists (Denmark), 79
Leftist Revolutionary Nationalist Movement (MNRI) (Bolivia), 25
Leftist Unity Front (Nepal), 248
Lehrman, Lewis, 11
Leigh, Gen. Gustavo, 51
Leka, Mbret Shquiparvet (King Leka I of the Albanians), 5
Lekhanya, Maj.-Gen. Justin, 222
Lenardo, Cesare di, 184
Léon Echaiz, René, 53
Leonard, Maj. Nadjita Yombal, 44
Lesotho, **222**; 329
Lesotho Liberation Army, 222ff.
Lesotho Paramilitary Force, 223
"Let Us Struggle Together" (Senegal), 319
Letelier, Orlando, 46; 69
Levan Ekmegian Suicide Commando (Turkey), 382
Levin, Shlomo, 126
Levinger, Rabbi Moshe, 176
Lewis, Rufus, 145
Li Wen-han, Gen., 36; 57
Libera, Emilia, 184ff.
Liberal-Democratic Party (Japan), 188
Liberal Front Party (PFL) (Brazil), 27
Liberal German Workers' Party, 126
Liberal Movement (Chile), 51
Liberal Party (Australia), 18
Liberal Party (Brazil), 27
Liberal Party (Canada), 39
Liberal Party (Honduras), 146
Liberal Party (Italy), 178
Liberal Party (Norway), 257
Liberal Party (Paraguay), 286
Liberal Party (UK), 395
Liberal People's Party (Finland), 106
Liberal People's Party (Norway), 257
Liberal Reformist Party (Belgium), 22
Liberal Republican and Nationalist Movement (Molirena) (Panama), 285
Liberals (Colombia), 58
Liberation Front for Equatorial Guinea (Frelige), 98
Libération Kanake Socialiste (New Caledonia), 119; 120
Liberation Leagues (El Salvador), 93
"Liberation National Government of Kampuchea", 198
Liberation Party (Liberia), 223
Liberation Tigers of Tamil Eelam (Sri Lanka), 349
Liberia, **223**
Liberia Unification Party, 223ff.
Liberian Action Party, 223ff.
Liberian People's Party, 223ff.
Libertarian Party (USA), 404
Liberty Party (Turkey), 384
Libya, 42; 44; 66; 81; 89; 103; 162; 174; 178; 185; 190; 215; 218; 223; **225**; 239; 260; 276; 294ff.; 315; 317; 319; 324ff.; 351; 374, 375; 386; 403; 404
Libyan Committee for the Defence of Democracy and Human Rights, 225

Libyan Constitutional Movement, 225
Libyan Democratic Party, 226
Libyan Liberation Organization, 225
Libyan National Association, 226
Libyan National Democratic Front, 226
Libyan National Democratic Movement, 225
Libyan National Movement, 226
Libyan National Organization, 226
Libyan National Salvation Front, 225ff.
Libyan National Struggle Movement, 226
Libyan Struggle Movement, 226
Likud (Israel), 176
Lim Hock Siew, 322
Limanis, D.A., 394
Lin Biao, Marshal, 153; 55
Linara Echeverría, Tomás, 345
Lipinski, Edward, 309
Lis, Bogdan, 307
Lis, Ladislav, 76
Lithuania (USSR), 388; 391
Litomisky, Jan,77
Liu Qing, 56
Liu Xinwu, 56
Livni, Menahem, 177
Lizinde, Maj. Théonaste, 314
Llovera, Waldino Ramón, 288; 290
Lobato, Nicolau dos Reis, 162
Locusta, Maurizio, 186
Lon Nol, Marshal, 193ff.
London, Artur, 77
Longo, Pietro, 181
Longowal, Sant Harchand Singh, 158
López Portillo, José, 90
López Rega, José, 17
Lorenz, Peter, 129ff.
Lorenzo Zelaya Popular Revolutionary Forces (Honduras), 147; 148
Lorik Sena (India), 154
Los Macheteros (Puerto Rico), 407
Lossou, Paulin, 371
Loyalist movements (Northern Ireland), 398
Lubachivsky, Myrosalv Ivan, 391
Lubota, Francisco Xauter, 12
Ludwig, Karl-Heinz, 128
Luengo, Luis Fernando, 52; 54
Lugnini, Giovanni, 183
Lukacs, Georgy, 149
Lukyanenko, Levko, 389
Lülf, Helmut, 129
Lumumba, Patrice, 422
Lumumba-Tolenga, François-Emery, 422
Luna, Juan Martin, 341
Lusaka accord, 11
Lutheran Church (East Germany), 124
Luwero, Samuel, 386
Luxembourg, **227**
Luxemburg, Rosa, 127

M

M-10 (France), 110
M-19 (Colombia), 59ff., 83
McGlinchey, Dominic, 175; 401; 403
McGlinchey, Mary, 401
McGuire, Marian, 81
Machel, Samora, 241ff.
Machoro, Eloi, 120
Mackawee, Abdul Qawee, 414
McKissick, Floyd, 404
Mackuandji Bondjale Oko, Teodoro, 98
McLaughlin, Michael, 395
McWhirter, Ross, 402
Madagascar, 64; **227**
Madres de la Plaza de Mayo (Argentina), 13
Mafia (Italy), 178
Maga, Hubert, 24
Magaña, Alvaro, 88
Magariaf, Mohammed Yusuf al-, 226
Magee, Patrick, 403
Magg-Hüttmann, Karola, 133
Maghee, Hatty, 364
Mahayri, Isam, 221
Mahdi, Sadiq el-, 351; 354
Mahendra, former King of Nepal, 248ff.
Mahler, Horst, 127
Mahlojes, Ali, 165
Mahmud, Maulana Mufti, 263
Mahn Ba Zan, 35
Mahn Ngwe Aung, 34
Mai, Tetua, 118
Maidana, Dr., 289
Maidou, Henri, 42ff.
Maira, Luis, 47
"Maitatsine" (Nigeria), 257
Majlis (India), 151
Makhno's Anarchist Group (USSR), 393
Makosso, Mbeka, 423
Malagasy Christian Democratic Party (Udecma-KMTP), 227
Malan, Gen. Magnus, 11
Malaquiok, Amelil ("Commander Rony"), 296
Malawi, **228**; 241ff.
Malawi Congress Party (MCP), 228
Malawi Freedom Movement (Mafremo), 229
Malayan National Liberation Army (MNLA), 231
Malayan National Liberation Front (MNLF) (Singapore), 322
Malayan People's Army, 231
Malaysia, 28; 190; 194; **230**; 294; 322; 365; 370
Maldives, **232**
Mali, **232**; 375
Malski, Tony, 395
Malta, **233**
Mancham, James, 320
"Manifesto of the Oppressed Black Mauritanians", 234
Manote Methangkun, 368
Manuel Rodríguez Patriotic Front (FPMR) (Chile), 47ff.
Manusama, Jan Alvares, 250
Mao, "Capt." Pubi, 155
Mao Zedong, 55ff.; 127, 153
Mao Zedong Thought League (Singapore), 322
Maohi Republic Provisional Government (Mayotte), 118
Maoist Communist Party of Germany (KPD), 128
Mapindouzi militia (Comoros), 64
Mara Cagol Commando of the Red Army Faction (West Germany), 133
Marada Militia (Lebanon), 210
Maraschi, Massimo, 183
March 26 Movement (Uruguay), 408
March 28 column (Italy), 184
Marcos, Ferdinand, 293ff.
Marcos, Imelda, 295
Marcuse, Herbert, 127
Mardoqueo Cruz Urban Guerrillas (El Salvador), 93
Maria, Nicolo Di, 186
Maria, Vítor Saudé, 143
Mariani, Gabriella, 183
Mariategui, Juan (or José) Carlos, 291
Marie-Jeanne, Alfred, 117
Marini, Antonio, 183
Marino Ospina, Iván, 60
Markov, Georgi, 28
Maronites (Lebanon), 209ff.
Marrehan tribespeople (Somalia), 325
Marroquín, Francisco, 94
Martí, Farabundo, 89
Martin, Max, 116
"Martinez, Carlos"; *see* Ramírez Sánchez, Illich
Martínez, Fidel, 148
Martinique, **116**
Martinique Independence Movement, 117
Martino, Guido de, 181

Martyr Kamal Jumblatt group (Syria), 360
Marulanda Vélez, Manuel (alias "Tiro Fijo"), 61
Marwa, Alhaji Mohammadu (alias "Maitatsine"), 257
Marx, Arnd Heinz, 125
Marxist Co-ordination Committee (India), 154
Marxist-Leninist Armed Propaganda Unit (Turkey), 376
Marxist-Leninist Communist Party (Honduras), 148
Marxist-Leninist Party in Cambodia, 195
Marxist-Leninist Party of Germany, 125
Marxist-Lennist Popular Action Movement (Nicaragua), 251
Mashal (Torch) Group (Nepal), 248
Masri, Zafer al-, 276; 282
Mass Line Party (Thailand), 370
Mass Party (Thailand), 365
Massera, Adml. Eduardo Emilio, 13
Massie, Jacques, 108
Mata Camacho, Alejandro, 341
Mathews, Robert Jay, 405
Matos, Maj. Huber, 68
Matthei, Gen. Fernando, 47
Matthews, Gabriel Bacchus, 223
Mattini, Luis, 16
Matuphum (Thailand), 368
Matzar, Lucrecia, 141
Maung Hun, 32
Maung Sein Nyunt, 32
Maurice Bishop Patriotic Movement (MBPM) (Grenada), 138
Mauritania, 194; **233**; 239
Mauritanian Democratic Union, 234
Mauritanian People's Party, 233
Mauritian Socialist Movement, 235
Mauritius, **235**
Mauro Araujo, Américo, 95
"Mavinga Declaration" (Angola), 10
Maximiliano Hernàndez Martinez Anti-Communist Alliance (El Salvador), 91; 96
May First Movement (KMU) (Philippines), 131
Mayer, Roland, 132
Mayotte, 64; **118**
Mazdoor Kisan Sangram Samiti (India), 154
Mazumdar, Charu, 152
Mba-Adessole, Paul, 121
Mba Oñana Nchama, Lt.-Col. Fructuoso, 97
Mba Ondo, Marcos, 97
Mbadinga, Max Anicet Koumba, 121
Mbaikoua, Alphonse, 41ff.
Mbena, James, 229
M'Bida, André-Marie, 38
Médecins sans frontières (France), 325
Medvedev, Roy A., 387
Medvedev, Zhores A., 387
Megahey, Gabriel, 403
Mehtic, Halil, 421
Meinhof, Ulrike, 127ff.
Meins, Holger, 127ff.
Meir, Golda, 283
Mejía Victores, Oscar, 141
Melida Montes, Ana, 92
Melkonian, Monte, 382
Membar, Moussa, 364
Mena, José Ricardo, 95
Menders, Fricis, 394
Méndez, Antonio Julián, 147
Méndez, Col. Vicente, 69
Méndez Fleitas, Epifianio, 290
Mendoza, Estelito, 295
Mendoza, Humberto, 93
Menéndez, Ivan, 236
Mengistu Haile Mariam, Lt.-Col., 100ff.
Ménignon, Nathalie, 109
Mensah, John Ashibe, 135
Mensah, Joseph H., 135
Mergheni, Ahmed, 375
Merino Castro, Adml. José Toribio, 52
Messimvrini (Greece), 137
Metei people (India), 154
Metro Clandestine Committee of Resisters (Guadeloupe), 115
Mexico, 59; 91; **235**
Meyer, Till, 133
Mhatre, Ravindra, 154
Michnik, Adam, 307; 309
Micianova, Jana, 78
Middle Core faction (Japan), 188ff.
Mierzejewski, Piotr, 307
Mihailovic, Gen. Draja, 419
Mihajlov, Mihajlo, 420
Mihkelson, Johannes, 394
Mijal, Kazimoerz, 310
Mijertein tribespeople (Somalia), 325
Mikolajska, Halina, 309
Milans del Bosch y Ussia, Lt.-Gen., 338ff.
Milic, Milos, 417
Milicias Rodriguistas (Chile), 51
Militancia (Argentina), 17
Militant Departmentalist Front (Martinique), 117
Militant Movement (Mauritius), 235
Militia Front for the National Resistance in Vietnam, 410
Millamán, Rosamel, 50
Milunovic, Marko, 421
Minachi, Nasser, 166
Minah, Francis M., 321
Minchell, Luis, 52
Minutemen (USA), 404
Miranda Herrena, Juan Pablo, 409
Mishima, Yukio, 188
Miske, Ahmed Baba, 234
Miskito Indians (Nicaragua), 252ff.
Misuari, Nur, 294
Misura (Nicaragua), 252ff.
Misurasata (Nicaragua), 252ff.
Mitr Don, 198
Mitterrand, François, 109ff.; 319
Mizo National Front (India), 155
Mlynar, Zdenek, 75
Mobasheri, Assadollah, 166
Mobutu Sese Seko, Marshal, 9; 11; 421
Moccia, Giuseppe, 181
Moczulski, Robert Leszek, 308
Mofeli, Charles, 222
Moh Heng, 36
Mohajir Quomi (People's) Movement (MQM), 265
Mohammad, Abdallah Idris, 101
Mohammad, Mian Tufail, 263
Mohammadi, Maulavi Mohammed Nabi, 2ff.
Mohammed, Ali Nasser, 413; 414
Mohammed, Aziz, 172
Mohammed Khan, Miraj, 261
Mohammed Shah, Zainul Abiddin, 323
Mohnhaupt, Brigitte, 128ff.
Mohsen, Zoutheir, 271
Mohtadeh, Abdullah, 164
Moi, Daniel Arap, 200ff.
Mojsov, Lazar, 416
Mokede, Paul-Roger, 422
Mokhehle, Ntsu, 223
Molina, Arturo Armando, 92
Molina, Jorge, 52
Molina Mejía, Raúl, 139
Möller, Christian, 130
Möller, Irmgard, 128ff.
Moloise, Malesela Benjamin, 330
Momoh, Maj.-Gen. Joseph Saidu, 321
Mon National Liberation Army (Burma), 35
Monarchist Group (Iran), 170
Monge Alvarez, Luis Alberto, 66
Mongolia, **237**
Monsanto, Pablo, 140
Montazeri, Ayatollah, 164ff.
Monteagudo, Joan Carles, 347
Montenegro Paniagua, César, 142

Montes, Jorge, 47
Montoneros (Argentina), 14
Montoneros 17 de Octobre (Argentina), 14
Montoneros Patria Libre, MLP (Ecuador), 83
Moon, Rev. Sun Myung, 188
Moon Bu Shik, 204
Moon Ik Hwan, Rev., 206
Moonasar, Keshava Keith, 145
"Moonies" (Honduras), 149
Mor Roig, Arturo, 16
Mora, Marcial, 50
Morán, Rolando, 140
Morasha (Israel), 176
Morazán, Francisco, 148
Morazanista Front for the Liberation of Honduras, 147; 148
Moretti, Mario, 184ff.
Moro, Aldo, 183ff.
Moro National Liberation Front (MILF) (Philippines), 294ff.
Morocco, 24; 108; 225; 234; **237**; 274; 375
Moroz, Valentyn, 394
Morozov, Mark, 388
Morrison, Eddy, 395
Moshoeshoe, King of Lesotho, 330
Moslem Brotherhood (Egypt), 84ff.
Moslem Brotherhood (Jordan), 192
Moslem Brotherhood (Libya), 226
Moslem Brotherhood (Palestinian), 277; 278
Moslem Brotherhood (Syria), 358ff.
Moslem Brotherhood Union (Turkey), 380
Moslem fundamentalists (Egypt), 84ff.
Moslem fundamentalists (Indonesia), 160
Moslem fundamentalists (Israel), 178
Moslem fundamentalists (Jordan), 192
Moslem fundamentalists (Libya), 226
Moslem fundamentalists (Malaysia), 231
Moslem fundamentalists (Morocco), 238
Moslem fundamentalists (Pakistan), 263
Moslem fundamentalists (Saudi Arabia), 317; 318
Moslem fundamentalists (Senegal), 318
Moslem fundamentalists (Syria), 358ff.
Moslem fundamentalists (Tunisia), 373ff.
Moslem fundamentalists (Turkey), 379ff.
Moslem fundamentalists (Yugoslavia), 421
Moslem International Guerrillas (Pakistan), 283
Moslem Islamic Liberation Front (Philippines), 296
Moslem League (India), 151
Moslem League (Pakistan), 258ff.
Moslem minority (Melilla), 347
Moslem minority (Sri Lanka), 351
Moslem Mujahid movement (Burma), 31
Moslem Revolutionary Movement in the Arabian Peninsula (Saudi Arabia), 317
Moslem United Development Party (Indonesia), 160
Mossadeq, Mohammed, 167
Motherland Party (Turkey), 375
Mothers of the Plaza de Mayo (Argentina), 13
Moto Nsa, Severo, 99
Moulinaka (Kampuchea), 197ff.
Moumié, Félix, 38
Mounien, Rosan, 116
Mountbatten of Burma, Adml. of the Fleet, 1st Earl, 402
Mourabitoun (Lebanon), 218; 426
Mourou, Abdel Fatah, 373
Moussa, Kamed, 256
Moussa Sadr Brigades (Lebanon), 218
Mouti, Abdelkarim, 238
Moutoudou, Albert, 38
Mouvement corse pour l'autodétermination (Corsica), 112
Mouvement de la tendance islamique (Tunisia), 373ff.
Mouvement de l'unité populaire (Tunisia), 373; 374
Mouvement islamique progressiste (Tunisia), 373
Mouvement populaire (Morocco), 237
Mouvement populaire révolutionnaire (Tunisia), 374
Movement against the Cancer of Marxism (Chile), 55
Movement for Democracy and Independence (Central African Republic) 42
Movement for Democracy in Algeria, 6ff.
Movement for Independence of Réunion, 117
Movement for Justice in Africa (Moja) (Gambia), 122
Movement for Justice in Africa (Moja) (Liberia), 223
Movement for Liberation (Yugoslavia), 417
Movement for Liberty and Future of Equatorial Guinea (Molifuge), 98
Movement for National Renewal (Morena) (Gabon), 121
Movement for National Unity (St Vincent and the Grenadines), 316
Movement for Order and Peace (New Caledonia), 120
Movement for Proletarian Power (Madagascar), 227
Movement for Resistance (Seychelles), 320
Movement for the Islamic Revolution (Afghanistan), 2ff.
Movement for the Liberation of the Central African People, 42
Movement for the Liberation of São Tomé and Príncipe, 316
Movement for the Restoration of Democracy (Pakistan), 258ff.
Movement for the Unification of National Liberation Forces of Guadeloupe, 116
Movement for United Popular Action (MAPU) (Chile), 53
Movement for Unity and Democracy in Kenya, 201
Movement of Nasserite Unionists (Mauritania), 234
Movement of National Integration (MIN) (Venezuela), 409
Movement of the Democratic Forces of the Casamance (Senegal), 319
Movement of the Revolutionary Left (Chile), 16-17; 48ff.
Movement of the Revolutionary Left (MIR) (Bolivia), 25
Movement of the Revolutionary Left (MIR) (Venezuela), 409
Movement towards Socialism (MAS) (Venezuela), 409
Movimiento 19 de Abril, M-19 (Colombia), 59ff., 83
Movimiento Tercera Via, M3V (Nicaragua), 254
Mozambican National Resistance (MNR or Renamo), 240ff.; 425
Mozambique, 11; 12; 229; **240**; 330
Mpakati, Attai, 229
Mpatanishi (The Arbiter) (Kenya), 202
Msipa, Cephas, 425
Mualla, Tahsin, 172
Muanchon (Thailand), 365
Muangthong (Thailand), 368; 369
Mubarak, Hosni, 274; 88
Mudarasi, Hojatoleslam Hadi al-, 20
Mudiad Amddiffyn Cymru (UK), 397
Mudiad Coeg I'r Cymry (UK), 397
Mugabe, Robert, 242; 330; 424
Mughrabi, Ali Mustafa al-, 85
Muhajid, Farid, 87
Muhammad, Sayyid Ali, 170
Mujahadin Pattani Movement (Thailand), 370
Mujaheddin (Afghanistan), 1ff.
Mujaheddin (Iraq), 171; 173; 426
Mujaheddin-e-Khalq (Iran), 163ff.
Mujjaddedi, Imam Seghbatullah, 2ff.
Mukti Bahini (East Pakistan/Bangladesh), 152
Mulele, Pierre, 423
Müller, Arndt, 130
Müller, Gerhard, 128ff.
Multi-Party Alliance (Chile), 46ff.
Multi-Party Conference (MPC) (Namibia), 243ff.
Muñoz Guttiérrez, Col. Louis, 338
Murphy, Lennie, 403
Musa, Ahmad, 317
Musa, Col. Saed ("Abu Musa"), 273ff.
Musakanya, Valentine, 424
Musawat (Pakistan), 262
Museveni, Yoweri, 385ff.
Mussavi, Hussain, 217
Mussavi, Shaikh Abbas, 214
Mustapha, Shukri Ahmed, 85
Mustapha, Tun Datu haji, 294
Musumeci, Gen. Pietro, 179
"Mutasem, Abu", 168
Mutebi, Prince Ronald, 385; 386
Mutesa, Sir Edward, 386
Muwanga, Lance Sera K., 386

Muyinda, Allah Fior, 422
Muyongo, Mishake Albert, 245
Mwakenya (Kenya), 201ff.

N

Na-Griamel (Vanuatu), 408
Nabhani, Shaikh Takieddin, 192
Naccache, Anis, 109
Nader, Fouad Abou, 212
Naga National Council (India), 154
Naga Separatist Movement (India), 154
Nagaland (India), 154
Nagata, Hiroko, 191
Nai Nol Lar, 35
Nai Tala Mon, 35
Naing Lu Hta, 34
Naisseline, Nidoish, 120
Najib, Dr, 1ff.
Najjar, Mohammed Yussef, 283
Namake Auti (Vanuatu), 408
Nambele, Raphaël, 42ff.
Namibia, 11; **243**
Namibian African People's Democratic Organization, 244
Namphy, Gen. Henri, 145
Narain, Lala Jagat, 157
Narodno Trudovoi Soyuz (USSR), 393ff.
Narong, "Comrade" S., 368
Nasional Samling (Norway) 257
Nasir, Ibrahim, 232
Nasser, Ahmed Muhammad, 101ff.
Nasser, Gamal Abdel, 84ff.; 193; 218; 268; 277ff.
Nasserite Popular Organization (Lebanon), 218
Nation of Islam (USA), 406
National Accord (AN) (Paraguay), 287ff.
National accord for peaceful evolution towards complete and genuine democracy (Chile), 46; 51; 54
National Action Party (PAN) (Mexico), 235
National Action Party (Turkey), 379
National Action Party (UK), 395
National Alliance (Palestinian), 274; 280; 282
National Alliance for the Liberation of Syria, 360
National Alliance Party (Sierra Leone), 321
National Assembly of Civil Society (Chile), 52
National Association of Salvadorean Teachers (ANDES), 95
National Awami Party (Bangladesh), 20
National Barristers' Council (Poland), 300
National Bloc (West Bank), 270
National Bloc of Working People (Czechoslovakia), 78
National Commission on the Disappearance of Persons (CONADEP) (Argentina), 13; 17
National Committee of Public Salvation (Comoros), 64
National Conciliation Party (PCN) (El Salvador), 88
National Conference (Farooq) (India), 151
National Convention Party (Gambia), 122
National Council of Churches (South Korea), 205
National Council of Khalistan (India), 157ff.
National Council of Organized Workers (Conato) (Panama), 285
National Council of Resistance for Liberty and Independence (Iran), 167
National Democracy Party (Thailand), 365
National Democratic Accord (ANDE) (Chile), 47ff.
National Democratic Action (ADN) (Bolivia), 25
National Democratic and Pan-Arab Front (Iraq), 172ff.
National Democratic Front (Burma), 31ff.
National Democratic Front (Guyana), 145
National Democratic Front (Lebanon), 215
National Democratic Front (Philippines), 293; 298
National Democratic Front for the Liberation of Germany, 403
National Democratic Movement (Grenada), 138
National Democratic Organization, Orden (El Salvador), 95; 96
National Democratic Party (Antigua and Barbuda), 12
National Democratic Party (Austria), 18
National Democratic Party (Chile), 48, 52
National Democratic Party (Egypt), 84
National Democratic Party of Germany (NPD), 126
National Democratic Party of Liberia, 223
National Democratic Party (Nepal), 248
National Democratic Party (Pakistan), 259ff.
National Democratic Party (Solomon Islands), 323
National Democratic Rally (Senegal), 318
National Democratic Union (UNADE) (Panama), 285
National Democratic United Front (Burma), 33ff.
National Falange (Chile), 45
National Front (Corsica), 112
National Front (Czechoslovakia), 70
National Front (France), 107
National Front (Greece), 136
National Front (Malaysia), 230
National Front (Panama), 285
National Front (Tunisia), 372ff.
National Front (UK), 18; 395
National Front Flag Group (UK), 395
National Front for the Defence of the Revolution (Madagascar), 227
National Front for the Liberation of Angola (FNLA), 9ff.
National Front for the Liberation of the Central Highlands (Vietnam), 410
National Front for the Liberation of the Congo (Zaïre), 423
National Front of Corsica, 112
National Front of Independent Peasants of Honduras, 147
National Grouping of Patriotic Forces of South Yemen, 414
National Guerrilla Co-ordinating Board (Colombia), 61, 62
National Indian Brotherhood (Canada), 39
National Integration Party (Liberia), 223
National Islamic Front of Afghanistan, 2ff.
National Left (Peru), 291
National Liberal Party (Lebanon), 210ff.
National Liberal Party (Panama), 285
National Liberation Army (Bolivia), 16
National Liberation Army (Colombia), 59ff.
National Liberation Army (Guadeloupe), 116
National Liberation Army (Nicaragua), 253
National Liberation Army (South Yemen), 415
National Liberation Front (FLN) (Algeria), 6; 8; 120
National Liberation Front of Bahrain, 20
National Liberation Front (Burma), 35
National Liberation Front (Pakistan), 259ff.
National Liberation Front (Vietnam), 411; 412
National Liberation Front (South Yemen), 87
National Liberation League (Jordan), 192
National Liberation Movement (Guatemala), 138; 142
National Liberation Movement (Kampuchea), 198ff.
National Liberation Movement (Uruguay), 17; 408
National Liberation Party (Costa Rica), 94
National Liberation Party—Anti-Communist Secret Army (El Salvador), 96
National Movement for the Establishment of Democracy in Djibuti, 80
National Movement for the Independence of Madagascar (Monima), 227
National Liberation Party (Gambia), 122
National Movement for Union and Reconciliation in Zaïre, 423
National Party (Australia), 18
National Party (Chile), 48ff.
National Party (Honduras), 146
National Party (New Zealand), 251
National Peasants' Union (UNC) (Honduras), 147ff.
National People's Party (Norway), 257
National People's Party (Pakistan), 264
National People's Party (Panama), 285
National Popular Alliance (Colombia), 59
National Progressive Front (Lebanon), 221
National Progressive Patriotic Front (Iraq), 171
National Progressive Unionist Party (Egypt), 87
National Reconstruction Front (Ecuador), 83
National Religious Party (Israel), 176
National Renewal Party (Chile), 53
National Republican Alliance (Arena) (El Salvador), 88
National Republican Association - Colorado Party (Paraguay), 286

National Republican Association - Colorado Party in Exile (Paraguay), 288ff.
National Resistance Army (Uganda), 385
National Resistance Front of São Tomé and Príncipe, 316
National Resistance Movement (Iran), 167
National Resistance Movement (Uganda), 385
National Restoration Movement (Vietnam), 410
National Revolutionary Front (Thailand), 370
National Revolutionary Movement (MNR) (El Salvador), 90, 94
National Revolutionary Movement—Historic Faction (MNR-H) (Bolivia), 25
National Salvation Command (Syria), 360
National Salvation Committee (Vietnam), 410
National Salvation Front (Vietnam), 411
National Salvation Movement (Dominican Republic), 82
National Salvation Party (Turkey), 380
National Socialist Action Party (UK), 395
National Socialist Council of Nagaland (India), 155
National Socialist German Workers' Party - Foreign Branch (USA), 405
National Socialist (Nazi) Party of America, 405
National Union (Norway), 257
National Union for the Total Independence of Angola (UNITA), 8ff.
National Union Movement (Chile), 53
National Union of Cameroon Students, 38
National Union of Ghana Students, 136
National Union of Moroccan Students, 238
National United Front for an Independent National, Peaceful and Co-operative Kampuchea, 200
National United Front for the Liberation of Laos, 208
National United Front for the Liberation of Vietnam, 411ff.
National United Front of Cambodia (FUNC), 195
National Unity Front (FRENU) (Guatemala), 142
National Unity Front (Poland), 299; 308
National Unity Party (Cyprus), 70
National Vanguard (Italy), 180
National Workers' Command (Chile), 53
National Workers' Front (Chile), 53
Nationale Front (Austria), 18
Nationalist Authentic Central (CAN) (Guatemala), 138
Nationalist Democratic Union, UDN (El Salvador), 95
Nationalist Democratic Union (El Salvador), 94
Nationalist European Union, 426
Nationalist movements (USSR), 388
Nationalist Party of China, 57
Nationalist Party (Malta), 233
Nationalist Party (Taiwan), 361ff.
Nationalist Renewal Party (PRN) (Guatemala), 138
Nationalist View Organization (Turkey), 380
Nativi, Tomás, 148
Naturei Carta (Israel), 177
Nauru, **247**
Navarra, Wilfredo, 69
Nawapoon (Thailand), 369
Nawez Khan, Nawebzade Allah, 265
Naxalite movement (India), 152, 248
Nayef, Col. Abdul Razzak al-, 282
Nazario Sargen, Andrés, 69
Nazish, Ali, 260
N'dalla, Claude-Ernest, 65
Ndebele people (Zimbabwe), 424
Ndebugre, John, 136
Ndlovu, Moven, 425
Ndongmo, Albert, 38
Ne Win, Gen., 30ff.
Neave, Airey, 400
Negri, Antonio, 186
Neguib, Mohammad, 84
Nelzat-Azadi (Iran), 166
Nemery, Jaafar al-, 351ff.
Neo Lao Hakset, 207
Neo-Nazi movements (Austria), 18
Neo-Nazi movements (Denmark), 79
Neo-Nazi movements (West Germany), 125
Neo-Nazi movements (Norway), 257
Neo-Nazi movements (Sweden), 356
Neo-Nazi movements (USA), 426
Neo-Nazi movements (UK), 426
Nepal, **247**
Nepali Congress Party (NCP), 248ff.
Netherlands, **250**; 288; 355
Neue Aktion Rechte (Austria), 18
Neves, Tancredo, 27
Nevis Reformation Party, 315
New Alternative (Venezuela), 409
New Birth Party (Cyprus), 70
New Caledonia, **118**
New Dawn Party (Cyprus), 70
New Death Squad (El Salvador), 96
New Democracy (Greece), 136
New Democratic Movement (Ghana), 135, 136
New Democratic Party (St Vincent and the Grenadines), 316
New Democratic Party (Canada), 39
New Force Party (Thailand), 370
New Ireland Forum, 175
New Jewel Movement (Grenada), 137
New Korea Democratic Party (South Korea), 204ff.
New Liberal Club (Japan), 188
New Liberalism (Colombia), 58
New Mon State Party (Burma), 34ff.
New National Party (Grenada), 138
New Order (Italy), 179ff.
New Party (Thailand), 368
New People's Army (NPA) (Philippines), 293ff.
New People's Revolutionary Front (Colombia), 62
New Progressive Party (Puerto Rico), 406
New Turkish Unity Party, 70
New Ulster Study Group (Northern Ireland), 399
New Wafd (Egypt), 85
New Zealand, 120; 231; **251**
New Zealand Party, 251
Newerla, Armin, 130
Ngo Quang Toan, 410
Ngo Van Truong, 410
Ngouabi, Marien, 65
Ngumba, Andrew Kimani, 202
Nguyen Co Thach, 410
Nguyen Cong Doan, 412
Nguyen Kim Dien, Philippe, 412
Nguyen The Minh, 412
Nguyen Van Thieu, 412
Nguza Karl I Bond, 422
Niasse, Ahmed Khalifa, 319
Niasse, Sidi Lamine, 319
Niazi, Maulana Abdus Sattar, 260
Nicaragua, 66; 90; **251**
Nicaraguan Anti-Communist Movement, 253
Nicaraguan Democratic Force (FDN), 253
Nicaraguan Democratic Movement (MDN), 252; 253
Nicaraguan Democratic Union/Nicaraguan Armed Revolutionary Forces, 254
Nicaraguan Democratic Union Assembly, 254
Nicaraguan Indigenous Communities Union (KISAN), 255
Nicaraguan International Rescue from Communism, 254
Nicaraguan National Rescue and Conciliation, 252; 254
Nicaraguan Opposition Union (UNO), 252
Nicaraguan Unity for Reconciliation, 252
Nicaraguan Workers' Central, 251
Nicaraguan Workers' Federation (FTC), 252
Nicaraguense de Unidad Democrática, Anude, 254
Nicolai, Regina, 133
"Nidal, Abu"; *see* Banna, Sabri Khalil al-
Niger, **255**; 257; 375
Nigeria, **256**
Nihon Minzoku Dokuritsu Giyungun (Japan), 188
Niklus, Mart, 388
19 May Green Movement Headquarters (Taiwan), 363
Njonjo, Charles, 201
Nkomati Accord, 241ff.; 330

Nkomo, Joshua, 424
Nomura, Shusuke, 188
Non-Aligned Movement, 270; 274
Non-conformist Youth of Colombia, 62
Nong Chan, 199
Noorani, Maulana Shah Ahmad, 260
Noriega Morena, Gen. Manuel Antonio, 285
Norodom Rannariddh, Prince, 200
Norodom Sihanouk, Prince, 193ff.
Norsk Front (Norway), 257
North Atlantic Assembly, 23
North Atlantic Treaty Organization (NATO), 1; 22; 23; 110; 131; 178
"North Borneo Liberation Army" (Brunei), 28
North Queensland Party (Australia), 18
North West Frontier Province (Pakistan), 261; 265
Northern Frontier District Liberation Front (Kenya), 202
Northern Ireland; *see* Ireland, Northern
Northern Irish Aid Committee (NORAID), 403
Northern Terror Front (Netherlands), 250
Norway, **257**
Norwegian Front, 257
Norwegian National Popular Party, 257
Nott, John, 396
Novakovic, Nikola, 421
November 12 Group (Greece), 137
November 17 Revolutionary Organization (Greece), 137
Novo Sampol, Guillermo, 69
Novo Sampol, Ignacio, 69
Nsomo Okomo, Martin, 98
Ntlama, Naleli, 223
Nuclear Disarmament Party (Australia), 18
Nuclear-Free Australia Party, 18
Nuer people (Sudan), 352
Nujoma, Sam, 243ff.
Nunes Correia, Col. Paulo Alexandre, 144
Núñez Muñoz, Ricardo, 49; 50
Nya Maung Mae, 34
Nyapanka, E., 229
Nyerere, Julius K., 364
Nyobé, Ruben Um, 38

O

Obiang Nguema Mbasago, Lt.-Col. Teodoro, 97ff.
Obote, Milton Apollo, 385
Obregón Cano, Ricardo, 14
Ocalan, Abdullah, 384
Occorsi, Vittorio, 180
Ochagavia Fernando (Chile), 48
October 17 Montoneros (Argentina), 14
"October 22" group (Italy), 182
October 24 Movement (Lebanon), 219
Odinga, Oginga, 202
Official Unionist Party (Northern Ireland), 395; 398; 400
Oh Jin Wu, Vice-Marshal, 203
Ohnesorg, Benno, 127; 133
Okamoto, Kozo, 190ff.; 282
Okello, Lt.-Gen. Bazilio, 385ff.
Okello, John, 386
Okito, Jean Tandalet Ozi, 42
Okudaira, Junzo, 190
Olalia, Rolando, 131
Olszowski, Stefan, 303
Olympio, Gilchrist, 371ff.
Olympio, Sylvanus, 371ff.
Oman, **257**; 426
Omar, Jarallah, 414
Omega 7 (Cuba), 69
Ometz (Israel), 176
Ommat Liberation Front (Burma), 34
Ondawame, Otto, 161
Ondo Mena, Damian, 97
Opango, Col. Joachim Yhombi, 65
Opina (Venezuela), 409
Oqueli, Héctor, 94
Orcue, Fr Alvaro, 59
Order, The (USA), 405
Orderly Departure Programme (Vietnam), 410
Ordine Nero (Italy), 179
Ordine Nuovo (Italy), 180
Organisasi Papua Merdeka, OPM (Indonesia), 161ff.
Organization for Liberation from Communism (El Salvador), 97
Organization for National Reconstruction (Antigua and Barbuda), 12
Organization for Vengeance for the Martyrs of Sabra and Chatila (Lebanon), 219
Organization of 3rd October (Turkey), 383
Organization of 9th June (Turkey), 382
Organization of African Unity (OAU), 10; 103; 144; 237; 239; 243; 270; 331; 346ff.
Organization of American States (OAS), 67; 93; 148; 287
Organization of Communist Action (Lebanon), 214
Organization of Mauritanian Nationalists (ONAM), 234
Organization of Petroleum Exporting Countries (OPEC), 129; 281
Organization of the Islamic Revolution (Saudi Arabia), 317
Organization of the Oppressed of the Earth (Lebanon), 219
Organization of the People of Rodrigues (Mauritius), 235
Organization of Volunteers for the Puerto Rican Revolution, 407
Oriach, Frédéric, 110
Orkney and Shetland Movement (UK), 395
Orlov, Yury, 388
Orly Organization (Turkey), 381; 383
Oromo Liberation Front (OLF) (Ethiopia), 104
Orsoni, Alain, 112
Orsoni, Guy, 112ff.
Ortega, Eugenio, 45ff.
Ortega Saavedra, Daniel, 251ff.
Orthodox Church (Ethiopia), 99
Orthodox Church (USSR), 390
Ouandié, Ernest, 38
Oubangian Liberation Front (Central African Republic), 42
Oubangian Patriotic Front (Central African Republic), 41
Oubangian Patriotic Front—Party of Labour (Central African Republic), 42ff.
Oueddei, Goukouni, 44
Ouedraogo, Maj.-Gen. Baptiste, 29
Oukanga, Francis-Albert, 42
Oumar, Acheikh Ibn, 44
Oumar, Mansour, 239
Outlet (Antigua and Barbuda), 12
Overseas Volunteer Forces for the Restoration of Vietnam, 411
Oxner, Helmut, 405
Oyono, Daniel, 99
Oyono, Luis Nguema, 99
Özal, Turgut, 70

P

P-2 lodge (Italy), 180
Pa-O National Army (Burma), 35
Pa-O National Organization (Burma), 34; 35
Pabón Pabón, Rosemberg, 59ff.
Pacem in Terris (Czechoslovakia), 78
Pachmann, Ludek, 125
Pacifist Socialist Party (Netherlands), 250
Padilla Rush, Rigoberto, 148
Paez Indians (Colombia), 63
Pagliai, Pier-Luigi, 179
Pahlavi, Mohammed Reza, 163; 173
Pahlavi, Reza Cyrus, 170
Paisley, Rev. Ian, 399
Pakistan, 105; 152; 194; **258**; 375
Pakistan Liberation Army, 259
Pakistan National Alliance, 259; 261; 262
Pakistan People's Party, 259ff.
Pakistan Republican Party, 259
Palach, Jan, 72
Palaung State Liberation Army (Burma), 35
Palaung State Liberation Organization (Burma), 34ff.

Paleejo, Rasool Baksh, 260
Palestine Armed Struggle Command, 269
Palestine Liberation Army, 269; 280
Palestine Liberation Front (PLF), 280
Palestine Liberation Organization (PLO), 15; 22; 61; 88; 89; 182; 184ff.; 191; 209ff.; 219; 267ff.; 324; 361
Palestine National Council (PNC), 268ff.; 361
Palestine National Front, 192
Palestine National Salvation Front (PNSF), 215; 219; 280, 282
Palestine Popular Struggle Front-PPSF, 270; 274; 280; 426
Palestine Research Centre, 210
Palestine Revenge Organization, 284
Palestinian Arab Revolutionary Committee, 284
Palestinian Communist Organization, 284
Palestinian Communist Party, 284; 426
Palestinian Fedayeen, 267
Palestinian Martyrs, 276
Palestinian militants (France), 107; 112
Palestinian Movements, **266**
Palladino, Carmine, 179
Palme, Olof, 131; 132; 356; 426
Palmers, Walter Michael, 133
Palous, Martin, 73
Palous, Radim, 75
Pambana (Struggle) (Kenya), 201
Pamyat (Memory) (USSR), 393
Pan-Africanist Congress of Azania (South Africa), 332
Pan-Arab Command, 426
Pan-Hellenic Socialist Movement (Pasok) (Greece), 136
Pan Islamic Malayan Party, 230
Panama, 61; **285**; 425
"Pancasila" (Indonesia), 160
Pancelli, Remo, 185
Pangu Pati party (Papua New Guinea), 286
Paolella, Alfredo, 181
Paoli, Pasquali, 112
Papandreou, Andreas, 272
Papua Independent Organization (Indonesia), 161ff.
Papua New Guinea, 120; **286**; 408
Paraguay, **286**
Paraguayan Communist Party (Maidana faction), 289
Paraguayan Communist Party (Creydt faction), 288
Paraguayan Confederation of Workers, 287
Paraguayan Confederation of Workers in Exile, 289
Paraguayan Peasant Movement, 289
Pardo, Rafael, 63
Pardo Zancada, Maj. Ricardo, 338ff.
Parek, Lagle, 388
Park Chung Hee, 204ff.
Parti congolais de travail (Congo), 65
Parti du progress et du socialisme (Morrocco), 237
Parti québécois (Canada), 39
Parti socialiste congolais (Zaïre), 423
Partisans of Justice and Freedom, PDL (Lebanon), 109
Party for Freedom and Progress (Belgium), 22
Party of Communist Action (Syria), 361
Party of Democratic Kampuchea, 195
Party of Freedom and Democracy (Netherlands), 250
Party of God (Lebanon), 216ff.
Party of God (Libya), 226
Party of Labour (West Germany), 126
Party of Labour (Saudi Arabia), 317
Party of Liberation and Socialism (Morocco), 238
Party of our Land (Vanuatu), 408
Party of Popular Yemenite Unity (North Yemen), 414
Party of Proletarian Democracy (Italy), 178
Party of the Brazilian Democratic Movement (PMDB), 27
Party of the Masses (Kampuchea), 195
Party Ra'ayet (Brunei), 28
Pascal Allende, Andrés, 48
Pasha, Nokrashy, 84
Pastora Gómez, Edén, 252ff.
Patasse, Ange, 42
"Pathanistan" (Pakistan), 265
Pathet Lao (Laos), 207
Patocka, Jan, 73
Patria Libre (Colombia), 61; 62
Patria y Verdad (Costa Rica), 66
Patrick O'Hara Commando (West Germany), 131
Patriotic Armed Group of the Congo, 65
Patriotic Coalition for Democracy (PCD) (Guyana), 145
Patriotic League for Development (Burkina Faso), 30
Patriotic Movement of National Rebirth (PRON) (Poland), 299
Patriotic People's Front (Finland), 107
Patriotic People's Front (Hungary), 149
Patriotic Union (Colombia), 58
Patriotic Union of Kurdistan (Iraq), 173ff.
Patriots for Germany (West Germany), 125
Pattani Islamic Nationalities Revolutionary Party (Thailand), 370
Pattani National Liberation Front (Thailand), 370
Pattani United Liberation Organization (Thailand), 370
Pax (Poland), 299
Paz Estenssoro, Víctor, 25
"Peace Committee" (USSR), 393
Peace Conquerors (Belgium), 23
Peace Group for Dialogue (Hungary), 150
Peasant Agrarian Leagues (Paraguay), 289
Peasant Party (Hungary), 150
Peasant Women's Co-ordinating Committee (Paraguay), 289
Peasant Youth Commission (Paraguay), 289
Peasants' and Workers' Party (India), 151
Peasants' Party of Latvia (USSR), 393
Peci, Patricio, 185
Peci, Roberto, 185
Pedro León Abroleda Brigade (Colombia), 62
Pedro Pablo Castillo Front (El Salvador), 92
Pehoua, François, 42
Peiper Vengeance Group (France), 108
Pensioners' Party (Finland), 106
Pentecostalists (Czechoslovakia), 78
People against the Ultra-Orthodox (Israel), 178
People's Action Group (Grenada), 138
People's Action Movement (St Kitts and Nevis), 315
People's Action Party (PAP) (Singapore), 322
People's Alliance (Iceland), 151
People's Alliance Party (Solomon Islands), 323
People's Anti-Somozist Militias (Milpas) (Nicaragua), 254
People's Democracy (Ecuador), 82
People's Democratic Movement (Guyana), 145
People's Democratic Movement (Uganda), 386
People's Democratic Organization for Independence and Socialism (Gambia), 122
People's Democratic Party (Hungary), 150
People's Democratic Party (South Korea), 206
People's Democratic Party (St Kitts and Nevis), 315
People's Fighters (Iran), 164ff.
People's Forces of 25 April (Portugal), 311
People's Holy Warriors (Iran), 164ff.
People's Labour Union (USSR), 393ff.
People's Liberation Army (Colombia), 62ff.
People's Liberation Army (India), 154
People's Liberation Army (Northern Ireland), 401
People's Liberation Army of Malawi, 229
People's Liberation Army of Namibia (PLAN), 244
People's Liberation Movement (El Salvador), 94
People's Liberation Organization of Singapore (PLOS), 323
People's Liberation Organization of Tamil Eelam (Sri Lanka), 350
People's Movement (Egypt), 88
People's National Congress (Guyana), 144
People's National Movement (Trinidad and Tobago), 372
People's National Party (Jamaica), 187
People's Party of Brunei, 28
People's Party (Faroe Islands), 79
People's Party (Iran), 165
People's Party (Panama), 285
People's Party (Philippines), 293; 298
People's Patriotic Party (Burma), 35
People's Popular Movement (Trinidad and Tobago), 372
People's Pressure Movement (Barbados), 21
People's Progressive Party (Guyana), 144

People's Revolutionary Armed Forces (El Salvador), 92
People's Revolutionary Army (Argentina), 48; 290
People's Revolutionary Army (El Salvador), 89ff.
People's Revolutionary Movement-Ixim (Guatemala), 140
People's Revolutionary Party (MPRP) (Mongolia), 237
People's Revolutionary Party (Zaïre), 423
People's Socialist Movement of Germany—Party of Labour, 126
People's Socialist Union (Chile), 51ff.
People's Solidarity (Pakistan), 259ff.
People's Union (Belgium), 22
People's United Party (Belize), 23
People's War group (India), 153
People United (Costa Rica), 66
Perdue, Michael E., 81
Pereira, Diamantino Monteiro, 311
Pérez, Luis Julián, 82
Pérez Alvarado, Humberto, 69
Pérez Beotegui, Ignacio, 343
Pérez de Cuéllar, Javier, 240; 246
Perinçek, Dogu, 379
Permanent Assembly of Landless Peasants (Paraguay), 289
Permanent Assembly of Social Organizations (Paraguay), 289ff.
Perón, Isabel Martínez de, 17
Perón, Gen. Juan Domingo, 14ff.
Peronist Montonero Movement (Argentina), 14ff.
Peronist Revolutionary Movement (Argentina), 15
Perovic, Mileta, 420
Pertini, Alessandro, 178
Peru, 25; 68; **290**; 425
Peruvian Communist Party, 291ff.
Peruvian Socialist Party, 291
Pervan, Ivo, 419
Pesh Merga (Iran), 168ff.
Pesh Merga (Iraq), 173ff.
Petition of 50 (Indonesia), 163
Petrella, Stefano, 185
Peyrefitte, Alain, 110
Phak Mai (Thailand), 368
Phak Pasason Pativat Lao, 207
Phalangists (Lebanon), 211ff.; 273; 358
Philippines, **293**; 375
Phirun Chartvanitkun, 367
Phizo, Angami Zapu, 154
Phizo, Kevi Yalay, 155
Phoumi Nosavan, 208
Picchiura, Carlo, 183
Pidjot, Roch, 118
Pierre Gulumian Commando (Turkey), 382
Pikabea Burunza, Iñaki, 344
Pilgrim, John, 64
Pinkowski, Jozef, 301
Pinna, Franco, 184
Pinochet Ugarte, Gen. Augusto, 45ff.
Pinto da Costa, Manuel, 316
Piperno, Franco, 186
Pir, Kemal, 384
Pistolesi, Angelo, 183
Pittello, Domenico, 185
Piza, Benjamín, 66
Pizarro Léon Gómez, Carlos, 59ff.
Plaid Cymru (UK), 395
Plains Tribal Council of Assam (India), 151
Plambeck, Juliane, 133
Poder Popular Local (El Salvador), 90
Podgorny, Nikolai, 389; 391
Pognon, Gratien, 24
Pohl, Helmut, 129; 131
Pohle, Rolf, 128ff.
Pol Pot, 193ff.; 365; 366
Poland, **299**
Polisario Front (Western Sahara), 235; 239
Polish United Workers' Party (PUWP), 299ff.
Pomare parti (French Polynesia), 118
Ponce de León Canossa, Rear Adml. Carlos, 292
Ponto, Jürgen, 127; 132
Poo Soo Kai, 322
Poor People's Party (Mexico), 236
Popieluszko, Jerzy, 308; 310
Popular Action (AP) (Peru), 291
Popular Action Party (Papo) (Panama), 285
Popular Alliance (Costa Rica), 66
Popular and Democratic Broad Front (Paraguay), 290
Popular Armed Forces (Honduras), 148
Popular Caledonian Rally for the Republic (New Caledonia), 118
Popular Colorada Movement (Mopoco) (Paraguay), 286ff.
Popular Democratic Front for the Liberation of Palestine, 270
Popular Democratic Movement (MDP) (Chile), 46ff.
Popular Democratic Party (Puerto Rico), 406
Popular Front for the Liberation of the Arabian Peninsula (Saudi Arabia), 317
Popular Front for the Liberation of Niger, 256
Popular Front for the Liberation of the Occupied Arabian Gulf (Oman), 258
Popular Front for the Liberation of Oman, 257ff.
Popular Front for the Liberation of Palestine, 87; 132; 190ff.; 269; 281; 377; 381
Popular Front for the Liberation of Palestine—General Command, 270; 273ff.; 282; 426
Popular Front for the Liberation of Saguia el Hamra and Rio de Oro (Morocco), 239
Popular Impulse for National Unity (Vanjy) (Madagascar), 227
Popular Liberation Army (El Salvador), 93
Popular Liberation Army (Lebanon), 219
Popular Liberation Front (Ethiopia), 100
Popular Movement for Independent Guadeloupe, 116
Popular Movement for Liberation of Angola Party of Labour (MPLA-PT), 8
Popular Resistance Armed Forces (Chile), 48; 53
Popular Revolutionary Bloc (BPR) (El Salvador), 89ff.; 148
Popular Revolutionary Commandos (Peru), 291
Popular Revolutionary Movement (Tunisia), 374
Popular Revolutionary Movement (Zaïre), 421
Popular Roldosista Party for People, Change and Democracy (Ecuador), 82
Popular Social Christian Party (Nicaragua), 251
Popular Socialist Community (Kampuchea), 195
Popular Socialist Party (Mexico), 235
Popular Struggles Committees (Dominican Republic), 81; 82
Popular Union for the Liberation of Guadeloupe, 116
Popular Unity (Chile), 46ff.
Popular Unity Movement (Tunisia), 374
Popular Vanguard Party (Costa Rica), 66
Populist Party (USA), 404
Portugal, 10; 240; 244; **310**
Pospichal, Petr, 76
Potolot, Joseph, 43
Pozdniakov, Anatoly, 388
Prachakorn Thai (Thailand), 365
Pracheachon (Kampuchea), 195
"Prague Spring", 71
Prai, J., 161
Prasad, Gokal, 349
Prasit Tapientong, 368
Prasong Arunsantirole, 368
Prasong Sonsiri, Squadron Leader, 367
Pratt, Kwesi, 135
Praxis (Yugoslavia), 420
Preecha Piempongsarn, 368
Prem Tinsulanond, Gen., 365; 370
Prensa, La (Nicaragua), 252
Prensa, La (Panama), 285
Preparatory Committee for Free Trade Unions (Czechoslovakia), 77
Presbyterian Church (Taiwan), 362ff.
Prey Chan, 199
Price, Dolours, 402
Price, Marion, 402
Pringle, Lt.-Gen. Sir Steuart, 402
Prior, James, 399
Progessive Party of Martinique, 115; 116

Progress and Fishing Industry Party (Faroe Islands), 79
Progress Party (Australia), 18
Progress Party (Denmark), 79
Progress Party (Equatorial Guinea), 98ff.
Progressive Constitutional Party (Malta), 233
Progressive Democrats (Ireland), 175
Progressive Federal Party (South Africa), 326
Progressive Labour Movement (Antigua and Barbuda), 12
Progressive Labour Party (St Lucia), 315
Progressive Liberal Party (Bahamas), 19
Progressive List for Peace (PLP) (Israel), 176
Progressive Party (Belize), 23
Progressive Party (Iceland), 151
Progressive Party (Norway), 257
Progressive Party (Thailand), 365
Progressive Party of the Working People (AKEL) (Cyprus), 70
Progressive People's Party (Gambia), 122
Progressive Socialist Party (PSP) (Lebanon), 219; 275; 360
Progressive Socialist Rally (Tunisia), 374
Project for National Development (Chile), 52ff.
Prokopowicz, Tadeusz, 310
Proll, Astrid, 130
Propaganda Due (P-2) (Italy), 180
"Protected villages" (Guatemala), 138
Protestant Action Force (Northern Ireland), 398
Protestant Church (Ethiopia), 99; 106
Protestant Church (East Germany), 123
Protestant Church (Guatemala), 140
Protestant Church (South Korea), 204
Protestant Church (Lebanon), 209ff.
Protestant Reformation Party (UK), 395
Provisional Co-ordinating Committee (TKK) (Poland), 306ff.
Provisional Government of the independent state of Vemerana (Vanuatu), 408
Provisional Irish Republican Army (PIRA or "Provos"); *see* Irish Republican Army
Provisional Sinn Féin (Northern Ireland); *see* Sinn Féin
Puerte Aponte, Gabriel, 409
Puerto Rican Armed Resistance Movement, 407
Puerto Rican Communist Party, 406
Puerto Rican Independence Party, 406
Puerto Rican Socialist Party, 406; 407
Puerto Rican Solidarity Committee, 407
Puerto Rico, **406**
Puerto Rico Popular Army, 407
Pundato, Dimas, 296
Punjab (India), 157ff.
Puoch, David Dogok, 352
Pupu Here Aia party (French Polynesia), 117
Pupu tiama Maohi (French Polynesia), 118

Q

Qadi, Issam al-, 282
Qasemlu, Abdel Rahman, 168ff.
Qatani, Mohammed al-, 317
Qatar, **312**
Qawasmeh, Fahd, 284
Quante, Wofgang, 129
Quebec Liberation Front (Canada), 40
Quieto, Roberto, 14
Quintin Lame, Manuel, 63
Quintin Lame Commando (Colombia), 59ff.; 83
Quiwonkpa, Brig.-Gen. Thomas, 224

R

Rabuka, Lt.-Col. Sitiveni, 106
Rachidi, Hlaku Kenneth, 331
Radical Civic Union (Argentina), 13
Radical Liberal Party (Denmark), 79
Radical Liberal Party (Ecuador), 82
Radical Liberal Party (Paraguay), 286
Radical Party (Chile), 49ff.
Radical Party (Italy), 178
Radical Political Party (Netherlands), 250
Radical Revolutionary Youth (Argentina), 17
Radio Free Europe (Portugal), 311
Radio Free Europe (Romania), 312; 313
Radio Halgan (Somalia), 325
Radio Kulmis (Somalia), 324; 325
Radio Solidarity (Poland), 305
Radio Venceremos (El Salvador), 89
Radjai, Mohammed Ali, 167
Radovic, Radomir, 420
Rafsanjani, Hojatolislam Hashemi Ali Akbar, 166
Rahd, Inaam, 221
Rahman, Maulana Fazlur, 263
Rahman, Sheikh Omar Abdel, 86; 88
Rahu, Fazil, 260
Raimajhi, Keshar Jung, 248
Rajavi, Massoud, 164ff.
"Rally" (Morocco), 238
Rally for National Salvation (Senegal), 319
Rally for the Republic (RPR) (French Polynesia), 117
Ramay, Mohammad Haneef, 262
Ramírez Sánchez, Ilich ("Carlos Martínez"), 114; 281
Ramos, Gen. Fidel, 293; 298
Ramos, Oswaldo, 149
Randall, Kevin, 395
Randolph, Ati, 371
Ranjith (Sri Lanka), 349
Rankal, Vijoy, 155
Rankovic, Alexander, 416
Rannariddh, Prince Norodom: *see* Norodom Rannariddh, Prince
Rapai, Col. William Omaria Lo, 386
Raquel Mercado, José, 59
Rasoul Sayaf, Ghulam Abdur, 2ff.
Raspe, Jan-Carl, 127ff.
Rassadorn Party (Thailand), 365
Rassemblement National Arabe (Tunisia), 373
Rassemblement pour le progrès (RPP) (Djibouti), 80
Rassemblement socialiste progressiste (Tunisia), 374
Rastafarians (Dominica), 81
Rastafarians (St Vincent and the Grenadines), 316
Ratsiraka, Didier, 227
Rauch, George von, 127
Rauti, Tino, 180
Rawlings, Flt.-Lt. Jerry, 134
Ray, Lt.-Col. Charles, 109; 221
Reagan, Ronald, 11; 89; 273; 279; 311; 404
Real Union of Bubi People of Eri (Equatorial Guinea), 98
Rebel (Corsica), 112
Rebel Armed Forces (FAR) (Guatemala), 139ff.
Recovery of the Original Nicaraguan Revolution, 254
Red Aid (Netherlands), 250
Red Army (Japan), 281
Red Army Faction (West Germany), 110; 127ff.; 137; 182; 250; 281; 356; 357
Red Brigades (Italy), 109; 178ff.; 182
Red Bulls (Thailand), 370
Red Electoral Alliance (Norway), 257
Red Flag (UK), 396
Red Flag (Venezuela), 409
Red Front (UK), 395
Red Front (Yugoslavia), 416
Red Gaurs (Thailand), 370
Red Guerrillas (Spain), 341
Red Hand (France), 38
Red Khmers (Kampuchea), 193ff.; 208; 365
Red Morning Group (West Germany), 132
Red Pa-O (Burma), 36
Red Resistance Front (Netherlands), 250
Redshirt Movement (Pakistan), 265
Reformational Political Federation (Netherlands), 250
Reformed Political Association (Netherlands), 250
Regelson, Lev, 390
Reiche, Annerose, 133
Reimers, Wernfried, 129

Reinders, Ralf, 133
Reinette, Luc, 115ff.
"Rejectionist Front of Stateless Palestinians", 87; 276; 277
Remembrancer (UK), 397
Ren Wanding, 57
Renaissance Party (Cyprus), 70
René, France Albert, 320
Renewal Action Party (PAR) (El Salvador), 88
Rengo Sekigun (Japan), 190
Rénu Rewni (Senegal), 319
Republic of the South Moluccas (Netherlands), 250
Republican movements (Northern Ireland), 400
Republican Party (Chile), 50ff.
Republican Party (Faroe Islands), 79
Republican Party (Italy), 178
Republican Party (Jamaica), 187
Republican Party (Panama), 285
Republican Party (USA), 404; 407
Republican Peasant Nation Party (Turkey), 379
Republican Progress Party (Central African Republic), 43
Republican Turkish Party (Cyprus), 70
Resck, Luis Alfonso, 287
Restrepo Valencia, Camilo, 59
Reunificiation Democratic Party (South Korea), 206
Réunion, **117**
Réunion Communists, 117
Revenge and Justice Front (Lebanon), 220
Révolution Québecoise (Canada), 40
Revolutionary Action Committee (React) (Liberia), 224
Revolutionary Action Organization (Iraq), 173
Revolutionary Angolan Government-in-Exile (GRAE), 9ff.
Revolutionary Armed Forces (Argentina), 14; 16
"Revolutionary Army" Group (Denmark), 79
Revolutionary Brigade for the Liberation of the Border Strip (Lebanon), 220
Revolutionary Caribbean Alliance (Guadeloupe), 116
Revolutionary Cells (West Germany), 134
Revolutionary Co-ordinating Board (Argentina), 16
Revolutionary Co-ordinating Board of the Masses (El Salvador), 95
Revolutionary Committees of Panama, 285
Revolutionary Communist League of Britain (UK), 396
Revolutionary Communist Party (Argentina), 15; 17
Revolutionary Communist Party of Britain (Marxist-Leninist), 396
Revolutionary Communist Party (India), 152
Revolutionary Communist Party (UK), 396
Revolutionary Communist Party (USA), 406
Revolutionary Communist Union of Turkey, 377
Revolutionary Council of Fatah (Palestinian), 276
Revolutionary Democratic Front (FDR) (El Salvador), 89ff.
Revolutionary Fighting Group (USA), 406
Revolutionary Front for the Independence of East Timor (Fretilin), 162
Revolutionary Front of Proletarian Action (Belgium), 23
Revolutionary Group of International Solidarity Christos Kassimis (Greece), 137
Revolutionary Islamic Organization—Iraqi Branch, 173
Revolutionary Justice Organization (Lebanon), 220
Revolutionary Left (Turkey), 377
Revolutionary Marxist Faction (Japan), 189
Revolutionary Movement for New Democracy (Senegal), 319
Revolutionary Movement for the Liberation of Tunisia, 374
Revolutionary Movement of Salvadorean Students, 95
Revolutionary Movement of the People (MRP) (Mexico), 236
Revolutionary National Party (Burma), 35
Revolutionary Organization of the People in Arms (ORPA) (Guatemala), 139;141
Revolutionary Organization of Socialist Moslems (Lebanon), 220; 276
Revolutionary Party (Guatemala), 138
Revolutionary Party (Tanzania), 364
Revolutionary Party of Central American Workers (El Salvador), 93
Revolutionary Patriotic Party (PRP) (Mexico), 236
Revolutionary People's Army (Ethiopia), 105
Revolutionary People's Union (URP) (Honduras), 147; 148
Revolutionary People's Union (Turkey), 377
Revolutionary Popular Struggle (Greece), 137
Revolutionary Rage (West Germany), 134
Revolutionary Socialist Party (RSP) (India), 151
Revolutionary Trade Union Movement (Czechoslovakia), 72;77
Revolutionary Unity Movement (MUR) (Honduras), 147
Revolutionary University Students (UR-19) (El Salvador), 95
Revolutionary Way (Turkey), 377
Revolutionary Workers' Party (PRT) (Mexico), 235
Revolutionary Workers' Party (UK), 396
Revolutionary Workers' Party—People's Revolutionary Movement (El Salvador), 93
Reyes, Echanelía, 61
Reyes, Tomás, 46
Rhade tribespeople (Vietnam), 410
Ricardo Franco Front (Colombia), 61ff.
Richards, Frank, 396
Richter, Yehuda, 177
Ridder, Dorothea, 127
Ríos Montt, Gen. Efraín, 138ff.
Riva, Luis, 254
Rivera, Brooklyn, 252ff.
Rizvi, Syed Nasir Ali, 262
Roa, Emilio, 289
Robelo Callejas, Alfonso, 252ff.
Roberts, Rod, 395
Robleh Awale, Aden, 80
Robotnik (Poland), 309
Roca, Roberto, 89; 93
Rocco, Ennio Di, 185
Rodney, Walter, 145
Rodríguez, Dimas, 92; 94
Rodríguez, Indalecio, 253
Rodríguez, Manuel, 53
Rodríguez Arévalo, Reyes, 148
Rodríguez Bautista, Nicolas, 62
Rodríguez García, Alfonso, 341
Rodríquez Militia (Chile), 51
Rohingya Patriotic Front (Burma), 34
Rojas, Ernesto, 63
Rojas, Julio, 289
Rojas León, Alfredo, 287
Rojas Pinilla, Gen. Gustavo, 59
Roll, Carmen, 128
Rollnik, Gabriele, 133
Roman Catholic Church (Burundi), 37
Roman Catholic Church (Chile), 45; 54
Roman Catholic Church (Czechoslovakia), 78
Roman Catholic Church (East Germany), 123
Roman Catholic Church (Guatemala), 140
Roman Catholic Church (Guyana), 145
Roman Catholic Church (Haiti), 145
Roman Catholic Church (Hungary), 150
Roman Catholic Church (South Korea), 204ff.
Roman Catholic Church (Malta), 233
Roman Catholic Church (Mexico), 236
Roman Catholic Church (Paraguay), 287ff.
Roman Catholic Church (Poland), 299ff.; 310
Roman Catholic Church (USSR), 389, 391
Roman Catholic Church (Yugoslavia), 419
Roman Catholic Resistance (Vietnam), 412
Romania, **312**
Romaszewski, Zbigniew, 305
Romero, Carlos Humberto, 89ff.
Romero y Galdames, Oscar Arnulfo, 95ff.
Romulo, Gen. Carlos P., 295
Ronconi, Susanna, 182
Rood Hulp (Netherlands), 250
Roos, Helga, 132
Roots of the Nation (Senegal), 319
Rosado, Luis, 407
Rose, Sir Clive, 338
Rose, Paul, 40
Ross Díaz, Alvin, 69
Rossi, Roberto, 182

Rössner, Bernd Maria, 132
Rouillan, Jean-Marc, 109ff.
Royal Lao Democratic Government, 208
Rubén Ndongo, Manuel, 98
Rubén García Revolutionary Student Front (Guatemala), 147
Rucci, José Ignaci, 16
Ruhland, Karl-Heinz, 127
Rulewski, Jan, 307
Rumkorem, "Brig.-Gen." Seth, 161
Rural Party (Finland), 106
Rural Solidarity (Poland), 301; 302; 307ff.
Rwanda, **314**

S

Saadi, Vicente Leónidas, 17
Sabah, Sheikh Jaber al-Ahmad-al, Amir of Kuwait, 207
Sabata, Jaroslav, 73
Sábato, Ernesto, 17
Sabatova, Anna, 73; 76
Sabbe, Osman Saleh, 100ff.
Sabillillah Movement (Thailand), 371
Saccucci, Sandro, 180
Sadaqat (Pakistan), 262
Sadat, Mohamed Anwar el, 85ff.; 267, 271
Sadduqi, Ayatollah Mohammed, 165
Sadr, Ayatollah Bakr al-, 171
Sadr, Imam Moussa, 214
Sadr, Ayatollah Mohammed Bakr al-, 214
Sáenz de Phillips, Carmen, 48
Safrano, Max, 116
Saharan Arab Democratic Republic (SADR), 235; 239
Sai Lek, Col., 35
Said, Nasser al-, 318
St Kitts and Nevis, **314**
St Lucia, **315**
St Pierre and Miquelon, **117**
St Vincent and the Grenadines, **315**
St. Vincent Labour Party (SVLP), 316
Saiyud Kerdpo, Gen., 367
Sak Sutsakhan, 199
Sakaguchi, Hiroshi, 191
Sakaseslian, Wasken ("Agop Agopian"), 383
Sakda (Thailand), 369
Sakhan Nakhon, 368
Sakharov, Andrei, 387; 388
Sakharova, Yelena Bonner; *see* Bonner Sakharova, Yelena
Salama, Sheikh Hafez, 86
Salamat, Hashim, 296
Salamuni, Ismail, 86
Salas, Rodolfo, 298
Saleh, Mahmoud, 284
Saleh, Nimr al (Abu Saleh), 273; 280
Salek, Col. Mustapha Ould Mohamed, 234
Sallah, Koto, 122
Sallustro, Oberdán, 16
Saloth Sar, 193
Salvador Cayetano Caspio Worker's Revolutionary Movement (El Salvador), 93
Salvadorean Authentic Institutional Party (PAISA), 88
Salvadorean Christian Peasant's Federation/Agricultural Workers' Union, 95
Salvadorean Communist Party (PCS), 92ff.
Salvadorean Suicide Commandos, 93
Saly Vongkhamsao, 369
Sama-eh Thanam, 370
Samayoa, Salvador, 92
Samizdat (USSR), 387; 388
Sammintu (South Korea), 206
Samudio Molina, Gen. Rafael, 61
Samyukta Mukti Bahini (Nepal), 248
Sánchez, Gen. Juan Carlos, 16
Sánchez Casas, J. M., 341
Sánchez Covisa, Mariano, 340
Sanderson, Chief Solomon, 39
Sandhu, Harminder Singh, 157
Sandinista National Liberation Front (FSLN) (Nicaragua), 251ff.
Sandinista Revolutionary Force (Nicaragua) 252
Sandoval Alarcón, Mario, 142
Sandrucci, Renzo, 186
Sands, Robert, 403
Sandu, Balbir Singh, 157ff.
Sanford, Francis, 117
Sanjabi, Karim, 167
Sankara, Capt. Thomas, 29
Sankum Reastr Niyum (Kampuchea), 195
Santos, Eduardo dos, 8ff.
Santos Millao, José, 50
Santucho, Roberto Mario, 16
Sanvi, Maj., 371
Sanyal, Kanu, 152; 153
Sanyang, Kukli Samba, 122
Sao Hso Noom, 36
São Tomé and Príncipe, **316**
Saqi, Jam, 260
Saqr, Col. Etienne, 210
Saraiva de Caravalho, Lt.-Col. Otelo, 311
Sarkis, Elias, 213
Sarney, José, 27
Sarran, Claude, 119
Sartawi, Issam Ali, 276
Sassou-Nguesso, Col. Denis, 65
Saudi Arabia, 100; 103; 216; 220; 234; 239; 266; 274; 294; 296; **317**; 374; 415
Saut al-Asifa (Palestinian), 277
Savasta, Antonio, 184ff.
Save Malawi Committee (Samaco), 229
Savimbi, Jonas, 9ff.
Savrda, Jaromir, 76
Saw Maw Reh, 34
Saw Maw Reh Bya Reh, 34
Saw Tun Qo, 33
Sawaba Party (Niger), 256
Sawyer, Amos, 223ff.
Sayaf, Ghulam Abdur Rajoul, 2ff.
Sazak, Gun, 377
Scalzone, Oreste, 186
Schafik Handal, Jorge, 89; 96
Schelm, Petra, 127
Schiller, Margrit, 128ff.
Schleicher, Régis, 110
Schleyer, Hanns-Martin, 127ff.
Schmidt, Helmut, 133
Schmitz, Sabine, 132
Schneider, Gert, 130
Schneider, Jürgen, 130
Schubert, Ingrid, 127ff.
Schulz, Adelheid, 130
Scoon, Sir Paul, 138
Scotland, 396; 399; 400
Scottish National Liberation Army (UK), 396
Scottish National Party (UK), 395
Scottish Socialist Republican League, 397
Sebe, Maj.-Gen. Charles, 58
Sebe, Maj.-Gen. Kwane, 58
Sebe, Lennox, 58
Secka, Cheyassin Papa, 122
Second International, 28
Secret Anti-Communist Army (Guatemala), 142
Secret Army Organization (OAS) (France), 339
Secret Builler-Roussarie Army (France), 108
Section squarely against Le Pen (France), 110
Segio, Sergio, 181ff.
Sekaninova-Carterova, Gertruda, 77
Sekou Touré, Ahmed, 143
Sema, "Maj." Ithoko, 155
Sendero Luminoso (Bolivia), 25
Sendero Luminoso (Peru), 61; 62; 291ff.
Senegal, 24; 122; 144; 194; 234; 294; **318**; 375
Senegambia, 122

Senghor, Augustin Diamankoun, 319
Senghor, Léopold Sédar, 161
Sengsthith, Khamsengkeo, 208
Senki Kyosando (Japan), 189
Senzani, Giovanni, 185
Sephardi Tora Guardians (Israel), 176
September 4 Commando (Chile), 52
September 11 Commando (Chile), 55
September 15 Legion (Nicaragua), 253
September Martyrs Group (Palestinian), 284
Serbian minority (Romania), 313
Serbian nationalists (Yugoslavia), 415; 419
Serfaty, Abraham, 238
Service d'action civique, SAC (France), 108
Seselj, Vojislav, 420
Seurat, Michel, 214
Seventh-Day Adventists (USSR), 392
17 October Movement for the Liberation of Syria, 361
Seychelles, 65; **319**
Seychelles Democratic Party, 320
Seychelles Liberation Committee, 320
Seychelles National Movement (SNM), 320
Seychelles Popular Anti-Marxist Front (SPAMF), 320
Sha Na Na, José Gusmão, 162
Shaban, Shaikh Saad, 221
Shahjahan Siraj (Bangladesh), 20
Shaka, Bassam, 177
Shakkak (Iran), 169
Shamir, Itzhak, 213
Shan, Mahendra Bikram, 248
Shan State Army (Burma), 35
Shan State Independence Army (Burma), 35
Shan State Nationalities Liberation Organization (Burma), 32; 36
Shan State Progress Party (Burma), 34-35
Shan United Army (Burma), 35-36
Shan United Revolutionary Army (Burma), 35-36
Shannon, Seamus, 175
Shanti Bahini (Bangladesh), 21
Sharif, Ezzedine, 375
Sharon, Ariel, 273
Sharpe, Mario, 54
Shcharansky, Anatoly, 388
Shelkov, Vladimir, 392
Shenouda III, Pope, 88
Shield Society (Japan), 188
Shigenobu, Fusako, 190ff.
Shih Ming-teh, 363
Shi'ite Moslems (Bahrain), 19
Shi'ite Moslems (Iraq), 171
Shi'ite Moslems (Jordan), 192
Shi'ite Moslems (Kuwait), 207
Shi'ite Moslems (Lebanon), 209ff.
Shi'ite Moslems (Pakistan), 265
Shi'ite Moslems (Saudi Arabia), 318
Shikhanovich, Yuri, 388
Shining Path (Bolivia), 25
Shining Path (Peru), 61; 62; 291ff.
Shinui (Israel), 176
Shiromani Gurdwara Prabandhak (India), 157
Shona, Yuxa, 140
Shona people (Zimbabwe), 424
Shufi, Hammoud al-, 360
Shukairy, Ahmed, 268ff.
Shultz, George, 137; 194; 355
Shwe Aye, 34
Sieff, Joseph Edward (Lord Sieff), 281
Sieniewicz, Konrad, 310
Siepmann, Ingrid, 133
Sierra Leone, 194; **321**
Sierra Leone Alliance Movement, 321
Sierra Leone Democratic Party, 321
Sierra Leone Freedom Council, 321
Sierra Leone People's Party (SLPP), 321
Sihanouk, Prince Norodom: *see* Norodom Sihanouk, Prince
Sihanoukist National Army (Kampuchea), 200
Siitoin, Pekka, 107
Silent Brotherhood (USA), 405
Siles Zuazo, Hernán, 25
Silva Cimma, Enrique, 49ff.
Silva Henríquez, Raúl, 54
Silva Ulloa, Ramón, 52; 53
Silyanyo, Ahmad Muhammad, 324
Simard, Francis, 40
Siméoni, Edmond, 111
Simko (Iran), 169
Sinai Peninsula, 177; 267
Sind-Baluchistan Patriotic Front (SBPF) (Pakistan), 265
Sind Hari Peasant Committees (Pakistan), 264
Sind separatists (Pakistan), 264
Singapore, 190; 231; **322**
Singapore Democratic Party, 322
Singapore Justice Party (Singapore), 322
Singapore Malay National Organization (SMNO or Pekemas—PKMS), 322
Singapore United Front, 322
Singh, Ammand, 159
Singh, Balbir, 159
Singh, Beant, 157ff.
Singh, Biseswar, 154
Singh, Charan, 153
Singh, Gajendra, 157
Singh, Ganesh Man, 249
Singh, Gobind, 157
Singh, Gurdev, 157
Singh, Harinder, 159
Singh, Jagjit, 157
Singh, Jasbir, 157
Singh, Joginder, 159
Singh, Kehar, 159
Singh, Kunj Behari, 154
Singh, Lal, 159
Singh, Laxman Prasad, 248
Singh, Manjit, 157
Singh, Ram Raja Prasad, 248ff.
Singh, Satwant, 159
Singh, Satya Narain, 152
Singh, Simranjit, 157ff.
Sinn Féin (Northern Ireland), 395, 397ff.
Siol Nan Gaidheal (UK), 397
Sis, Nicolás, 140
Sison, José Maria, 293ff.
Sisulu, Walter, 328; 332
Sithole, Ndabaningi, 425
Siumut (Greenland), 79
Siwicki, Gen. Florian, 305
Siyad Barre, Gen. Mohammed, 323ff.
Slansky, Rudolf, 77
Slipyj-Kobernickyj-Dyckowsky, Joseph, 390
Slovak Freedom Party, 70
Slovak Reconstruction Party, 70
Slovene People's Party (Yugoslavia), 421
Slovo, Joe, 329; 334
Slum Dwellers Union (El Salvador), 95
Smirnov, Aleksei, 388
So Phim, 195ff.
Soares, Mario, 144
Sobukwe, Robert M., 333
Social Action Party (Thailand), 365
Social Christian Action Movement (Dominican Republic), 82
Social Christian Movement (Chile), 53
Social Christian Party (Ecuador), 82
Social Christian Party (Nicaragua), 251ff.
Social Christian Reformist Party (Dominican Republic), 81
Social Christian Unity Party (Costa Rica), 66
Social Credit Party (Canada), 39
Social Credit Political League (New Zealand), 251
Social Democratic and Labour Party (SDLP) (Northern Ireland), 175; 398; 399
Social Democratic Party of Brazil, 27
Social Democratic Party of Bulgaria, 28

Social Democratic Party of Chile, 51ff.
Social Democratic Party of Cyprus, 70
Social Democratic Party of Denmark, 79
Social Democratic Party of the Faroe Islands, 79
Social Democratic Party of Finland, 106
Social Democratic Party of West Germany, 125
Social Democratic Party of Hungary, 150
Social Democratic Party of Iceland, 151
Social Democratic Party (Adalat) (Iran), 165
Social Democratic Party of Italy, 178, 181
Social Democratic Party of Latvia (USSR), 394
Social Democratic Party of Lithuania (USSR), 394
Social Democratic Party of Mauritius, 235
Social Democratic Party (Nicaragua), 251
Social Democratic Party (Portugal), 311
Social Democratic Party (Romania), 314
Social Democratic Party (Thailand), 369
Social Democratic Party (UK), 395
Social Self-Defence Committee (KOR) (Poland), 300ff., 309
Socialist and Revolutionary Labour Party (Gambia), 122
Socialist Alliance of the Working People of Yugoslavia (SAWPY), 420
Socialist Arab Nasserist Party (Egypt), 87
Socialist Convergence (Chile), 50
Socialist Democratic Populist Party (Turkey), 375
Socialist Front (Singapore), 322
Socialist International, 29; 91ff.; 150; 288; 310ff.; 394; 421
Socialist Kanak Liberation (New Caledonia), 120
Socialist Labour/Liberal Socialist Alliance (Egypt), 84
Socialist League of Malawi (Lesoma), 229
Socialist Movement of Kurdistan (Iraq), 174
Socialist Party of Australia, 18
Socialist Party of Belgium (Walloon), 22
Socialist Party of Belgium (Flemish), 22
Socialist Party of Chile, 48ff.
Socialist Party of Corsica, 111
Socialist Party of Cyprus (EDEK), 70
Socialist Party of Ecuador, 82
Socialist Party of Estonia (USSR), 394
Socialist Party of France, 30; 43; 107
Socialist Party of French Guiana, 114
Socialist Party of Great Britain (UK), 395
Socialist Party of Honduras (Paso), 148
Socialist Party of Italy, 178
Socialist Party of Nicaragua, 251
Socialist Party of Poland, 310
Socialist Party of Senegal, 318
Socialist Party of Thailand, 369
Socialist Party of Turkish Kurdistan, 384
Socialist Party of Vietnam, 410
Socialist Party-One (PS-1) (Bolivia), 25
Socialist People's Party (Denmark), 79
Socialist Union of Central and Eastern Europe (SUCEE), 29; 78; 150; 394; 421
Socialist Unity Party (SED) (East Germany), 123
Socialist Workers' Party (Australia), 18
Socialist Workers' Party (Belgium), 22
Socialist Workers' Party (Chile), 47
Socialist Workers' Party (Mexico), 235
Socialist Workers' Party (Panama), 285
Socialist Workers' Party (UK), 396
Socialist Workers' Party (USA), 404; 406
Socialists (Yugoslavia), 415
Society of Repudiation and Renunciation (Egypt), 87
Soilih, Ali, 64ff.
Sokolov, Mikhail, 388
Sole Bloc of Guinean Democratic Forces, 99
Soler, Miguel Angel, 289
Solidarité et participation (Belgium), 22
Solidarity (Poland), 300ff.
Solidarity Committee of Patriotic Vietnamese Catholics, 412
Solidarity Party (Pakistan), 259; 264
Solomon Islands, 120; **323**
Solomons Ano Sagufenua (Solomon Islands), 323
Solzhenitsyn, Alexander, 387
Somali Abo Liberation Front, SALF, 105
Somali Democratic Action Front, 325
Somali Islamic Youth Union, 324
Somali National Movement (SNM), 324
Somali Patriotic Liberation Front (SPLF), 325
Somali Revolutionary Socialist Party (SRSP), 323
Somali Salvation Front (SSF), 324ff.
Somali Workers' Party, 324
Somalia, 39; 104ff.; 202; 294; **323**
Somare, Sir Michael, 162
Somkid Srisangkhom, Col., 369
Somoza Debayle, Anastasio, 16; 251ff.
Son Ngoc Minh, 195
Son Ngoc Thanh, 198
Son Sann, 193ff.
Son Sen, 195ff.
Sonnenberg, Günter, 129
Sons of Freedom (Canada), 40
Sons of Glyndwr (UK), 397
Sons of Moussa Sadr (Lebanon), 218
Sosa, Sarah, 407
Sosa Avila, Gen. Manuel Franco, 142
Sossi, Mario, 182
South Africa, 10; 11; 26; 222ff.; 240ff.; 243ff.; 316; 320; **326**; 356; 424; 425
South African Indian Congress, 335
South African Students' Organization, 335
South African Youth Congress, 336
South American Indian Council, 50
South Lebanon Army (SLA), 212ff.
South Sudan Liberation Movement, 352
South Tirol (Italy), 187
South Tirol liberation group (Austria), 18
South West Africa People's Organization (SWAPO) (Namibia), 11; 243ff.
South Yemen; *see* Yemen, People's Democratic Republic of
South Yemen Liberation Front, 415
Southern Opposition Bloc (Nicaragua), 252
Souza, Emmanuel de, 371
Spadaccini, Teodoro, 183
Spadafóra, Hugo, 285
Spain, 68; 97; 191; **239**
"Sparrow Units" (Philippines), 298
Spartacist League (UK), 396
Spartacist League (USA), 406
Spartacus Canada, 39
Spartacus Youth League (USA), 406
Spaulding, William, 187
Special Force of National Security Volunteers (Haiti), 146
Speitel, Angelika, 130
Speitel, Volker, 129
Springer, Axel, 128
Sri Lanka, **348**
Srp, Karl, 77
Ssalingo, Al-Haj Suleman, 386
Stachowiak, Ilse, 129
Stagg, Frank, 402
Stahl, Wolfgang, 128
Stalin, Joseph, 390; 392
Stange Oelckers, Gen. Rodolfo, 52
Stanski, Tadeusz, 308
Starek, Jiri, 73
State Reform Party (Netherlands), 250
Staub, Ernst-Volker, 131
Steenson, Gerard, 401
Stella, Yves, 112
Stern, Jan, 73
Stevens, Jimmy, 408ff.
Stewart, Donald, 396
Stoll, Willy Peter, 132
Stone, Richard, 91
"Stop the Foreigners" (Austria), 18
"Strategic hamlets" (Philippines), 297
Ströbele, Hans-Christian, 130
Stroessner (Gen.) Alfredo, 286ff.

Stuardo, Julio, 52
Student Revolutionary Movement (Colombia), 63
Suárez González, Adolfo, 339
Suazo Córdova, Roberto, 140; 146ff.
Suazo Jessy, Joaquín, 255
Subercaseaux, Julio, 52
Sudan, 100ff.; 225; 272; **351**; 385; 386
Sudan People's Liberation Movement, 352ff.
Sudanese Democratic Unionist Party, 426
Sudsai Hasdin, Maj.-Gen., 370
Suharto, Gen., 160ff.
Suisse XV (Turkey), 383
Sukarno, Ahmed, 160ff.
Sule, Anselmo, 49
Sumit Niamsa ("Comrade Yut"), 368
Sun Myung Moon, 188
Sun Yat-sen, 57
Sunni Islamic Resistance Movement (Lebanon), 220
Sunni Moslems (Lebanon), 209ff.
"Supergrasses" (West Germany), 125
"Supergrasses" (Ireland), 176
Supreme Council of the Islamic Revolution of Iraq (SAIRI), 173
Supreme Council of Peronist Montoneros (Argentina), 14; 15
Supreme Revolutionary Council (Afghanistan), 2; 3
Surachai Sae Dan, 367
Suriname, 115; **354**
Svarinskas, Alfonsas, 391
Swaziland, 242; 329; **356**
Sweden, 419; **356**
Swedish People's Party, 106
Switzerland, **357**; 381ff.; 422
Swu, Issak, 155
Sylvestre, Louis, 23
Syria, 15; 100; 103; 109; 172; 192; 209ff.; 225; 258; 266ff.; **358**; 384
Syrian Catholics (Lebanon), 209ff.
Syrian Liberation Front, 361
Syrian National Socialist Party (SNSP) (Lebanon), 220
Syrian Orthodox Church (Lebanon), 209ff.
Szeremitiewow, Romuald, 308

T

Ta Mana Te Nunaa (French Polynesia), 118
Tabakov, Stefan, 28
Tabatabai, Ali, 167
Tablet, The (Sierra Leone), 321
Taboada, Abelardo, 254
Tahrir (Jordan), 192
Taiwan, 33; 56ff.; **361**
Taiwan Democratic Party, 363
Taiwan Independence Movement, 363
Takacs, Lajos, 313
Talabani, Jalal, 173ff.
Talierco, Giuseppe, 185ff.
Talpur, Rasul Bakhsh, 262
Tambo, Oliver, 327ff.
Tami (Israel), 176
Tamil Eelam Liberation Organization (Sri Lanka), 350
"Tamil Tigers" (Sri Lanka), 349
Tamlevicius, Sigitas, 391
Tan Chay Wa, 323
Tangkul, Muivah, 155
Tangwai (Taiwan), 362
Tanzania, 65; 329; **364**; 422; 423
Tanzanian Democratic Youth Movement, 364
Tanzanian Revolutionary Youth Movement, 364
Tarantelli, Enzo, 185
Tartaglione, Girolamo, 183
Tarto, Enn, 388
Tatenoaki (Japan), 188
Taufer, Lutz Manfred, 132
Tauras, Jürgen, 129
Tavini huiratiraa (French Polynesia), 118
Tawheed (Lebanon), 221
Tawil, Ibrahim, 177
Taya, Moaouia Ould Sidi Mohamed, 234
Te Eaa Pi (French Polynesia), 117
Te Taata Tahiti Tiama party (French Polynesia), 118
Te Toto Tupana (French Polynesia), 118
Téariki, John, 117
Tecum Uman Front (Guatemala), 141
Teferi Benti, Brig.-Gen., 101
Tehiya (Israel), 176
Tehrik-i-Istiqlal (Pakistan), 259; 264
Teitelboim, Volodia, 49
Tejero Molinas, Lt.-Col. Antonio, 338ff.
Telegu Desam (India), 151
Tell, Wasfi, 278; 279; 283
Telmessani, Omar, 84
Tembo, John, 229; 242
Tennassee, Paul, 144
Terra Omnium (Spain), 347
Terre'Blanche, Eugene, 337
Terror against Terror (Israel), 177
"Terrorist international" (Italy), 182
Thai Moslem People's Liberation Armed Forces, 371
Thai Nation Party, 365
Thai People's Liberation Armed Forces, 366
Thai People's Revolutionary Movement, 369
Thai Revolutionary Council, 36
Thailand, 31ff. 57; 154; 194; 194ff.; 207; 231; 322; **364**; 410ff.
Thakin Ba Thien Tin, 31ff.
Thakin Chit, 31
Thakin Than Tun, 31
Thakin Zin, 31
Thatcher, Margaret, 396; 403
Thawr, Mohammed Kassem el-, 414
Thieh Thieu Minh, 412
Thimme, Johannes, 129
Thirayat Bunmi, 365
Third Force (Northern Ireland), 399
Third International, 47
Third Way Movement (Nicaragua), 254
13th November Revolutionary Movement (Guatemala), 140
30th September Movement (Indonesia), 163
31st January Popular Front (Guatemala), 139ff.
Thoetpum Chaidi, 368
Thong Chaemsri, 366ff.
Tibet, 154
Tiger Militia (Lebanon), 210ff.
Tigre People's Liberation Front (TPLF) (Ethiopia), 104ff.
Tikka Khan, Lt.-Gen., 262ff.
Tikriti, Salah Umar Ali al-, 172
Time (Malaysia), 230
Timerman, Jacobo, 15
Timorese Democratic Union, 162
Timorese Social Democratic Association (ASDT),162
Tin U, Gen., 30
Tin Yee (also known as Ne Win), 31
Tiro, Hasan de, 161
Tito, Marshal Josip Broz, 420; 421
Tjibaou, Jean-Marie, 119, 120
Tjongarero, Daniel, 243ff.
Tob-Der (Turkey), 378
Tobagi, Walter, 184ff.
Today (China), 56
Together (Israel), 176
Togo, 135; **371**
Togolese Movement for Democracy, 371
Toivo ja Toivo, Hermann, 243
Tolbert, William, 122; 224
Toledo Plata, C., 60
Tomasek, Frantisek, 78
Tomicic, Zlatko, 418
Tomin, Julius, 75
Tominova, Zdena, 73
Tontons Macoutes (Haiti), 146
Toriello Garrido, Guillermo, 139
Torres, Carlos Alberto, 407
Torres Restrepo, Camilo, 62

Torres Rojas, Gen. Luis, 338ff.
Tou Samouth, 195
Toufmili, Shaikh Sobhi, 214
Touré, Soumane, 30
Trade Union Co-ordinating Committee (El Salvador), 95
Transitional Government of National Unity (GUNT) (Chad), 44
Transitional Government of National Unity (Namibia), 243ff.
Transjordan, 266ff.
Traoré, Lt.-Col. Diarra, 143
Traoré, Brig.-Gen. Moussa, 232
Trejo Esquivel, Luis, 141
Triaca, Enrico, 183
Trinh Van Can, 412
Trinidad and Tobago, **372**
Tripur Sena (India), 155
Tripura (India), 155
Tripura National Volunteers (India), 156
Tripura Tribal Youth Organization (India), 155
Troops of Revolutionaries and Resistance Fighters (Djibouti), 80
"Troops Out" movement (Northern Ireland), 397
Trotskyist League (Canada), 39
Trotter, Desmond, 81
Troylan Turcios (Honduras), 149
True Path Party (Turkey), 375
Truong Nhu Tang, 410ff.
Tsantes, Capt. George, 137
Tudeh (Communist) Party (Iran), 164ff.
Tuladhur, Padma Ratna, 248
Tunisia, 108; 225; 272; 275; **372**
Tunisian Armed Resistance, 375
Tunisian Communist Party, 372-73
Tunisian Free Unions' Movement, 426
Tunku Bira Kotanila, 370
Tupac Amarú Revolutionary Movement (Peru), 59; 83; 292
Tupaj Katari Revolutionary Liberation Movement (Bolivia), 25
Tupamaros (Uruguay), 16; 408
Turbay Ayala, Julio César, 59ff.
Turcios, Troylan, 147
Turcios Lima, Luis, 141
Türkes, Col. Alparslan, 379
Turkey, 29; 70; 173ff.; 283; **375**
Turkish Communist Party—Marxist-Leninist (AKKO), 378
Turkish minority (Bulgaria), 29
Turkish Peace Association, 378
Turkish People's Liberation Army, 281; 378
Turkish People's Liberation Party Front, 378
"Turkish Republic of Northern Cyprus", 70
Turkish Revolutionary Peasants' Liberation Army, 378
Turkish Teachers' Union, 378
Turkish Workers' and Peasants' Liberation Army (Tikko), 378
Turkish Workers' Party, 378
Turkoman Political and Cultural Society (Iran), 168
Turkowsky, Marco, 292
Tutsi tribespeople (Burundi), 37
Tutti, Mario, 179ff.
23rd March Group (Morocco), 238
Twomey, Seamus, 402
"Txomin"; see Iturbe Abásolo, Domingo

U

U Nu, 30, 32
U Ribellu (Corsica), 112
U Sao Hso Lane, 36
U Thant, 391
Udom Sisuwan, 365, 367
Udom Thonguai, 367
Uegaki, Yasuhiro, 191
Uganda, **385**
Uganda Freedom Movement, 385; 386
Uganda Human Rights Activists, 386
Uganda National Army, 386
Uganda National Liberation Army, 385ff.
Uganda National Rescue Front, 385
Uganda National Unity Movement, 386
Uganda People's Army, 386
Uganda People's Congress, 385
Uganda People's Front, 386
Ugandan Democratic People's Movement, 385; 386
Uhl, Petr, 77
Uighurs (China), 57
Ukeiwé, Dick, 120
Ukrainian Catholic Church (USSR), 391
Ukrainian Herald (USSR), 389
Ukrainian Liberation Front (USSR), 390
Ukrainian nationalists (USSR), 389ff.
Ukrainian Reactionary Forces (USSR), 390
Ulster Defence Association (Northern Ireland), 399; 400
Ulster Defence Regiment (Northern Ireland), 401
Ulster Freedom Fighters (Northern Ireland), 399
Ulster Loyalist Democratic Party (Northern Ireland), 399
Ulster Popular Unionist Party (Northern Ireland), 398
Ulster Popular Unity Party (Northern Ireland), 395
Ulster United Loyalist Front (Northern Ireland), 400
Ulster Volunteer Force (Northern Ireland), 400
Umkhonto we Sizwe (South Africa), 328
Umoja wa Kupigania Kemokrasia Kenya (UKENYA), 201
Ungo, Guillermo Manuel, 90ff.
Unification Church (Honduras), 149
Unification Church (Japan), 188
Unified Nasserite Organization—Cairo, 70
Unified Popular Action Front (FAPU) (El Salvador), 89ff.
Unified Popular Action Movement (Chile), 49ff.
Union calédonienne (New Caledonia), 120
Unión Cívica Radical (UCR) (Argentina), 13; 17
Unión Democrática Nicaragüense/Fuerzas Armadas Revolucionarias Nicaragüenses (UDN/FARN), 254
Union for a Democratic Republic of the Comoros, 64
Union for French Democracy—Rally for the Republic, 107
Union of Agricultural Circles and Organizations (PZKiOR) (Poland), 307
Union of Cameroonian Peoples, 38
Union of Christian Democrats of Lithuania (USSR), 394
Union of Communist Fighters (Italy), 186
Union of Communists (Iran), 166
Union of Israel, 176
Union of Moderate Parties (Vanuatu), 408
Union of National Front Forces (Iran), 167
Union of Nationalists to Liberate Kenya, 202
Union of Soviet Socialist Republics (USSR), 12; 52; 71; 87; 89; 100; 102; 103; 105; 107; 117; 123; 146; 166; 168; 168; 172; 196ff.; 202; 208; 218; 222; 229; 239; 245; 258; 265; 274; 296; 301; 302; 308; 309; 323; 369; 375; 381; **387**; 406; 414; 415; 419
Union of the Corsican People (UPC), 111ff.
Union of the Democratic Centre (Argentina), 13
Union of the National Centre (UCN) (Guatemala), 138
Union of the People of the Arabian Peninsula (Saudi Arabia), 318
Union Party (Faroe Islands), 79
Union progressiste mélanesienne (New Caledonia), 120
Union socialiste des forces populaires (Morocco), 237ff.
Unionist Democratic Party (Jordan), 192
Unit of Martyr Kalaghi (Iran), 166
UNITA; *see* National Union for the Total Independence of Angola
Unitary Representation of the Guatemalan Opposition, 139
United Akali Dal (India), 157; 159
United Arab Emirates (UAE), 103; 394
United Buddhist Church (Vietnam), 412
United Croatians of West Germany (Yugoslavia), 418
United Democratic Front (South Africa), 336
United Democratic Party (Belize), 23
United Democratic Party (Lesotho), 222
United Democratic Party (Thailand), 365
United Dominica Labour Party, 80
United Federation of Honduran Workers (FUTH), 149
United Force (UF) (Guyana), 144
United Formosans for Independence (Taiwan), 363
United Front for the Struggle of the Oppressed Races (Vietnam), 411
United Front of Patriotic Forces for the Liberation of Vietnam, 411
United Kingdom, 213, 217, 220; 231; 244; 266; 320; 334; 381; **395**

United Klans of America Inc. (USA), 405
United Labour Front (Trinidad and Tobago), 372
United Left (IU) (Peru), 291
United Left Coalition (Chile), 53ff.
United Liberation Torch-Bearers (Nepal), 248
United Malays National Organization—UMNO (Malaysia), 230
United Minorities Front (India), 151
United National Democratic Party (Antigua), 12
United National Directorate (DNU) (Honduras), 147ff.
United National Front of the Comoros, 65
United National Front (Uganda), 386
United National Front of South Yemen, 415
United National Front (Yugoslavia), 420
United National Independence Party (Zambia), 424
United Nations, 28; 73; 162; 173; 177; 193ff.; 196; 239; 243ff.; 266ff.; 335; 388; 394; 402; 406; 410
United Nations: Commission on Human Rights, 229; 234
United Nations: Council for Namibia, 244
United Nations: General Assembly, 28; 162; 193ff.; 240, 244; 266ff.; 269; 330
United Nations: High Commissioner for Refugees, 104
United Nations: Interim Force in Lebanon (UNIFIL), 212ff.; 271
United Nations: International Labour Organization, 288
United Nations: Relief and Works Agency for Palestine Refugees in the Near East (UNRWA), 268
United Nations: Secretary-General, 77; 240; 391
United Nations: Security Council, 11; 24; 162; 213, 243ff.; 269ff.; 330
United Nations: Transition Assistance Group (UNTAG), 245
United Nations: Universal Declaration of Human Rights, 74; 387
United Organization of Free Vietnamese in Europe, 412
United Pan-Arab Force, 426
United Party (Solomon Islands), 323
United Peasants' Party (Poland), 299; 307
United People's Front (FPU) (Bolivia), 25
United People's Front (Frepu) (Panama), 285
United People's Front (Singapore), 322
United People's Movement (Antigua), 12
United People's Movement for Democracy and Unification (South Korea), 296
United People's Movement (St Vincent and the Grenadines), 316
United People's Party (Liberia), 223ff.
United Popular Action Movement (Chile), 50ff.
United Red Army (URA) (Japan), 190
United Republican Party (Guyana), 145
United Revolutionary Front (FUR) (Guatemala), 139
United Sabah National Organization (Malaysia), 230
United Socialist Front (Thailand), 369
United Socialist Party of Mexico (PSUM), 235
United Somali Students Union, 325
United States, 11; 33; 36; 59; 67; 68; 88; 89; 103, 138, 178, 181, 190; 147; 164; 185; 189, 194ff.; 204ff.; 207; 213ff., 219ff.; 224ff.; 239; 244 246; 251ff.; 267; 285, 293; 311; 317; 321; 324; 355; 360; 362; 363; 374; 381; 383; 394; **404**; 406, 407, 408; 411; 416; 418; 423; 426
United Thai Party, 365
United Workers' Party (St Lucia), 315
Unity Party (Greenland), 79
Unity Party (Liberia), 223ff.
University Revolutionary Front, FUR-30 (El Salvador), 95; 96
Ureta, Gastón, 51
Uribe Escabor, Diego, 62
Urrutikoetxea Bengoetxea, José Antonio, 342
Uruguay, **408**
Ustashi Movement (Yugoslavia), 417
Uzbekistan (USSR), 389

V

Valdés, Julio de Peña, 82
Valdés Subercaseaux, Gabriel, 45ff.
Valladares, Armando Fernando, 68
Valle, Eric Arturo del, 285
Valle, Gen. Juan José, 14
Vallières, Pierre, 40
Value Party (New Zealand), 251
Van der Stoel, Max, 75
van Niekerk, Willie, 246
Van Saren, 198
Vang Pao, Gen., 208
Vanguard Nationalist Revolutionary Movement (Bolivia), 25
Vanguard of the Arab Revolution (Syria), 360
Vanguard of the Malagasy Revolution (Arema) (Madagascar), 227
Vanguard Organization (Syria), 360
Vanguards of the Popular War for the Liberation of Palestine, 283
Vanuaaku Pati (Vanuatu), 408
Vanuatu, 120; **408**
Vanuatu Independence Alliance Party, 408
Vardag, Ashaf, 264
Vargas Pazzos, Gen. Frank, 83
Vasiliev, D., 393
Vásquez Castaño, Fabio, 62
Vatican, 78; 279
Vatsa, Mamman, Maj.-Gen., 256
Velandia Hurtado, Col. Hernando Darío, 59
Venezuela, 61; 68; 254; 287; **409**
Vengeance Party (Lebanon), 221
Venstre Liberals (Denmark), 79
Verdugo, Osvaldo, 52
Viana, Ion, 313
Vicente Menchú Revolutionary Christians (Guatemala), 147
Videla, Gen. Jorge Rafael, 13
Vides Casanova, Gen. Carlos Eugenio, 96
Viehmann, Klaus, 133
Vieira, Maj. João Bernardo, 143
Viet Cong (Kampuchea), 195; 198
Vietnam, 193ff.; 208; 366; 369; **410**
Vietnam Fatherland Front, 410; 412
Vietnam National Resistance Front, 412
Vietnam Resistance Radio (VRR), 411; 412
Vigilante (Norway), 257
Villa, Pietro, 183
Villacorta, Jorge, 94
Villalobos, Joaquín, 89; 92
Vins, Georgi P., 392
Viscardi, Michele, 182
Vitelli, Roberto, 182
Vlaamse Blok (Belgium), 22
Vlaamse Militanten Orde (Belgium), 22
Vo Dai Ton, 411
Vodavonic, Hernán, 52
Vogel, Andreas, 133
Voice (Poland), 309
"Voice of Democratic Kampuchea" (VODK), 196
"Voice of Fatah" (Palestinian), 278
"Voice of Free Africa (Mozambique), 241
"Voice of the Free Canaries" (Spain), 347
"Voice of Hope" (Lebanon), 222
"Voice of Iraqi Kurdistan", 174
"Voice of Lebanon", 212; 361
"Voice of Malayan Democracy", 231
"Voice of the Broad Masses of Eritrea" (Ethiopia), 102
"Voice of the Eritrean Revolution" (Ethiopia), 101
"Voice of the Malayan Revolution", 231
"Voice of the People of Burma" (VOPB), 31
"Voice of the People of Thailand", 366; 369
"Voice of the Storm" (Palestinian), 277
"Voice of White Britain" (UK), 395
Voinea, Eugenie Boeuve, 314
Volcano (Libya), 225
Volksunie (Belgium), 22
Volokhonsky, Lev, 388
Voltaic Progressive Front (Burkina Faso), 30
Vradyni (Greece), 137
Vygour, Cetyn, 376

W

Wa National Organization (WNO) (Burma), 34
Wa National Organization Army (WNO/WNA) (Burma), 36

Wackernagel, Christof, 130
Wagner, Rolf-Clemens, 130ff.
Waite, Terry, 214; 217
Waldheim, Kurt, 77; 213; 391
Wales, 397
Walesa, Lech, 300ff.
Walfougi Front (Mauritania), 235
Wali Khan, Begum Nasim, 260
Wali Khan, Khan Abdul, 260ff.
Wali Khan, Kokkihel Malik, 265
Walker, Richard, 204
Wallis and Futuna Islands, **121**
Walloon Party (Belgium), 22
Walter Alasia Column (Italy), 186
Wanchai Chitchamnong, Lt.-Gen., 365
Wannersdorfer, Claudia, 131
War Flag Wing (Japan), 189
Warner, Bennie D., 224
Warrad, Faig, 192
Warsaw Pact, 71
Washington, Edward Emmanuel ("Rabbi Washington"), 145
Wasik, Stanislaw, 310
Watama Keovimal, 369
Watoo, Mian Manzoor Ahmed, 264
Wazir, Khalil al ("Abu Jihad"), 273; 279
Weather Underground (USA), 404
Wei Jingsheng, 56
Weil, Ekkehard, 18
Weisbecker, Thomas, 127
Wells, Timothy, 409
Welsh Language Society (UK), 397
Welsh Socialist Republican Movement (UK), 397
Welytschovsky, Basil, 391
Were Di (Belgium), 22
West Bank, 177; 191; 192; 267
West Bengal, 156
Western Cape Suicide Squads (South Africa), 337
Western European Union, 110
Western Sahara, 234ff.; 237ff.
Western Samoa, **413**
Western Somali Liberation Front (WSLF), 104
Westland New Post (Belgium), 22
White Commando (South Africa), 337
White Hand (Guatemala), 142
White Liberation Movement (South Africa), 337
White Warriors' Union (El Salvador), 97
Whitelaw, William, 399
Whyte, Winston, 138
Wickham, Gen. John A., 204
Wieland, Gerd Jürgen, 128
Will, Gertraud, 129
Williams, Henry Sylvester, 332
Williams, Wayne, 397
Windhoek Declaration of Basic Principles (Namibia), 243
Wisniewski, Stefan, 132
Wolf, Jirí, 77
Women's Alliance (Iceland), 151
Women's Political Party (New Zealand), 251
"Worker, The" (Poland), 309
Worker (UK), 396
Worker-Peasant Party of Turkey, 379
Worker and Peasant United Popular Action Movement (Chile), 50
Workers' Army of the Welsh Republic (UK), 397
Workers' Autonomy (Italy), 179; 186
Workers' Brigade for Communism (Italy), 186
Workers' Defence Committee (Poland), 309
Workers' Front (Nicaragua), 254
Workers' League (USA), 404
Workers' Party of Barbados, 21
Workers' Party of Brazil, 27
Workers' Party of Ethiopia, 99
Workers' Party (Ireland), 175
Workers' Party (Northern Ireland), 395
Workers' Party of Jamaica (WPJ), 187
Workers' Party of Mexico, 235
Workers' Party of Singapore, 322
Workers' Power (Italy), 186ff.
Workers' Revolutionary Organization (El Salvador), 92
Workers' Revolutionary Party (Argentina), 16
Workers' Revolutionary Party (Colombia), 62ff.
Workers' Revolutionary Party (UK), 395
Workers' Self-Defence Movement (Colombia), 63
Workers' Students' and Peasants' Movement (Columbia), 62
Workers' World Party (USA), 404
Working People's Alliance (Guyana), 144
World Anti-Communist League, 33
World Assembly for Peace and Life, against Nuclear War (Czechoslovakia), 76
World Congress of Free Ukrainians (USSR), 394
World Jewish Congress (USSR), 392
World League of Croatian Youth (Yugoslavia), 418
World Peace Council, 378
World Union of National Socialists, 426
Woungly-Massaga, M., 38
Writers' Union (Romania), 313
Writers' Union (USSR), 387
Writers' Union (Yugoslavia), 418
Wu Chun-fa, 362
Wulf, Borvin, 129
Wykliffe, Diego, 255
Wyszinski, Cardinal, 301

X

Xaré Bi (Senegal), 319
Xinjiang dissidents (China), 57

Y

Yacoub, Talat, 280
Yaguer, Raúl Clemente, 15
Yahad (Israel), 176
Yahya Khan, Gen. A. M., 152; 157; 261
Yakoreva, Albina, 388
Yakunin, Rev. Gleb, 390
Yarmila, "Cpl.", 155
Yarte, Henry, 135
Yaya Kashakan Suicide Squad (Turkey), 383
Yeghin Kechichian Suicide Squad (Turkey), 383
Yellow Star Movement (Thailand), 368
Yemen, People's Democratic Republic of (South Yemen), 2; 103; 132ff., 190; 225; 258; 271-74; 325; 375; **413**; 414; 426
Yemen Arab Republic (North Yemen), 272; **413**; 426
Yemen Socialist Party (YSP), 414
Yemeni National Unity Front, 415
Yéweiné, Yéweiné, 120
Yolou, Alexis, 409
Yon Sosa, Marco Antonio (alias "El Chino"), 141
Yoon Kong Hie, 204
Young China Party (Taiwan), 361
Young National Democrats (West Germany), 126
Young Pioneers (Malawi), 230
Youth Front (Belgium), 22
Youth League for the Overthrow of the Yalta and Potsdam Structure (Japan), 188
Yugoslav Socialist Party, 421
Yugoslavia, 130; 194; 382; **415**
Yumurtaci, Zeki, 376
Yussef, Abu, 283
Yusuf, Col. Ahmed Abdullahi, 324
Yuyitung, Quintin, 362
Yuyitung, Rizal, 362

Z

Zaheer, Sajad, 260
Zahir Shah, former King Mohammad of Afghanistan, 1ff.
Zahl, Peter-Paul, 129

Zaid, Mohammad, 34
Zaim, Abdul Satar al-, 359
"Zaim, Abu", 275
Zain, Imran Mohammad, 161
Zaïre, 9ff.; 371; **421**; 424
Zaïre Committee, 423
Zaldívar Larraín, Andrés, 46
Zambia, 9ff.; 245ff.; 329; 385; **424**
Zamora, Rubén, 94
Zani, Fabrizio, 179
Zarkesh, Ali, 165
Zau Mei, Brig.-Gen., 33
Zdebskis, Juozas, 391
Zelaya, Rafael, 255
Zepeda, Hugo, 52
Zghorta Liberation Army (Lebanon), 211; 214
Zhao Ziyang, 56ff.; 193; 199
Zhivkov, Todor, 29
Zia, Begum, 20
Zia ul-Haq, Gen. Mohammad, 258ff.
Zimbabwe, 26; 229; 240ff.; **424**
Zimbabwe African National Union (ZANU), 424
Zimbabwe African National Union (ZANU-Sithole), 424
Zimbabwe African People's Union (ZAPU), 424
Zimbabwe People's Revolutionary Army (ZIPRA), 424
Zimmermann, Ernst, 131
Zinsou, Emile Derlin, 24
Zionist Revival Movement (Israel), 176
Znak (Poland), 299
Zuffada, Pierluigi, 183
Zumel, Antonio, 293
Zúñiga, Carlos Ivan, 285